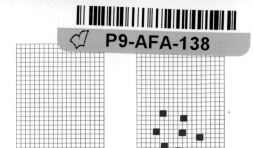

Psychiatric Disorders in Children and Adolescents

Barry D. Garfinkel, M.D., F.R.C.P.(C.)
Director of the Division of Child and Adolescent Psychiatry
Associate Professor of Psychiatry
Department of Psychiatry
University of Minnesota Medical School
Minneapolis, Minnesota

Gabrielle A. Carlson, M.D.
Director of Child Psychiatry
Professor of Psychiatry
Department of Psychiatry
SUNY at Stony Brook
Stony Brook, New York

Elizabeth B. Weller, M.D.
Director, Division of Child Psychiatry
Professor of Psychiatry and Pediatrics
Department of Psychiatry
Ohio State University College of Medicine
Columbus, Ohio

1990
W.B. SAUNDERS COMPANY
Harcourt, Brace, Jovanovich Inc.

Philadelphia □ *London* □ *Toronto*
Montreal □ *Sydney* □ *Tokyo*

W. B. SAUNDERS COMPANY
Harcourt Brace Jovanovich, Inc.

The Curtis Center
Independence Square West
Philadelphia, PA 19106

Library of Congress Cataloging-in-Publication Data

Psychiatric disorders in children and adolescents / [edited by]
Barry D. Garfinkel, Gabrielle A. Carlson, Elizabeth B. Weller.

p. cm.

1. Child psychopathology.   2. Adolescent
   psychopathology.   3. Child psychiatry.   4. Adolescent
   psychiatry.   I. Garfinkel, Barry D.   II. Carlson,
   Gabrielle A.   III. Weller, Elizabeth B., 1949–   .
   [DNLM: 1. Mental Disorders—in adolescence.   2. Mental
   Disorders—in infancy & childhood. WS 350 P974]

RJ499.P728 1990   618.92'89—dc20   90–10683

ISBN 0–7216–2612–2

Editor: Martin Wonsiewicz
Designer: Terri Siegel
Production Manager: Peter Faber
Manuscript Editor: Jeanne Carper
Illustration Coordinator: Brett MacNaughton
Indexer: Kathleen Garcia

Psychiatric Disorders in Children and Adolescents   ISBN 0–7216–2612–2

Last digit is the print number: 9   8   7   6   5   4   3   2   1

Contributors

L. Eugene Arnold, M.Ed., M.D.
Professor and Vice Chairman, Department of Psychiatry, Ohio State University College of Medicine. Attending Physician, Ohio State University Hospitals, Columbus, Ohio.
Learning Disorders; Tics and Other Stereotyped Movements

Gerald J. August, Ph.D.
Assistant Professor of Psychiatry, University of Minnesota Medical School, Minneapolis, Minnesota.
Functional Neuropsychological Assessment in Child Psychiatry

Lorian Baker, Ph.D.
Research Professor, Department of Child Psychiatry, University of California, Los Angeles, Neuropsychiatric Institute, Los Angeles, California.
Specific Communication Disorders

Gail A. Bernstein, M.D.
Assistant Professor, Division of Child and Adolescent Psychiatry, University of Minnesota Medical School. Attending Physician, University of Minnesota Hospitals and Clinics, Minneapolis, Minnesota.
Anxiety Disorders

Susan J. Bradley, M.D., F.R.C.P. (C.)
Associate Professor, Department of Psychiatry, University of Toronto Faculty of Medicine. Psychiatrist-in-Chief, Hospital for Sick Children. Consultant, Clarke Institute of Psychiatry, Toronto, Ontario, Canada.
Gender Dysphorias in Childhood and Adolescence

David A. Brent, M.D.
Associate Professor of Child Psychiatry, University of Pittsburgh School of Medicine. Attending Physician, Pittsburgh, Pennsylvania.
Suicide and Suicidal Behavior in Children and Adolescents

Gabrielle A. Carlson, M.D.
Professor of Psychiatry, Director of Division of Child and Adolescent Psychiatry, State University of New York at Stony Brook School of Medicine, Stony Brook, New York.
Bipolar Disorders in Children and Adolescents

Barry D. Garfinkel, M.D., F.R.C.P. (C.)
Associate Professor and Director, Division of Child and Adolescent
Psychiatry, Department of Psychiatry, University of Minnesota Medical
School, Minneapolis, Minnesota.
The Elimination Disorders

Paul E. Garfinkel, M.D., F.R.C.P. (C.)
Professor of Psychiatry, University of Toronto Faculty of Medicine.
Psychiatrist-in-Chief, Toronto General Hospital, Toronto, Ontario, Canada.
Eating Disorders: Anorexia Nervosa and Bulimia Nervosa

David S. Goldbloom, M.D., F.R.C.P. (C.)
Assistant Professor of Psychiatry, University of Toronto Faculty of
Medicine. Staff Psychiatrist, Toronto General Hospital, Toronto, Ontario,
Canada.
Eating Disorders: Anorexia Nervosa and Bulimia Nervosa

Laurence L. Greenhill, M.D.
Associate Professor of Clinical Psychiatry, Columbia College of Physicians
and Surgeons. Attending in Psychiatry, Columbia Presbyterian Medical
Center, New York, New York.
Attention-Deficit Hyperactivity Disorder in Children

James Halikas, M.D.
Professor of Psychiatry, Department of Psychiatry, University of Minnesota
Medical School, Minneapolis, Minnesota.
Substance Abuse in Children and Adolescents

Harry M. Hoberman, Ph.D.
Assistant Professor, Departments of Psychiatry and Pediatrics, and Adjunct
Assistant Professor, Departments of Child Development and Psychology,
University of Minnesota Medical School. University of Minnesota Hospitals
and Clinics, Minneapolis, Minnesota.
Multidimensional Psychotherapy for Children and Adolescents

Jonathan B. Jensen, M.D.
Assistant Professor and Director of Residency Education, Division of Child
and Adolescent Psychiatry, University of Minnesota Medical School,
Minneapolis, Minnesota.
Obsessive-Compulsive Disorder in Children and Adolescents

Charles F. Johnson, M.D.
Professor of Pediatrics, Ohio State University College of Medicine.
Director, Child Abuse Program, Children's Hospital, Columbus, Ohio.
Child Abuse and the Child Psychiatrist

Hiten Kisnadwala, M.D.
Instructor in Psychiatry, New York University Medical Center. Clinical
Assistant in Psychiatry, Bellevue Hospital Center, New York, New York.
Interviewing Children and Adolescents

David J. Kolko, Ph.D.
Associate Professor of Child Psychiatry, University of Pittsburgh School of Medicine. Staff, Western Psychiatric Institute and Clinic, Pittsburgh, Pennsylvania.
Suicide and Suicidal Behavior in Children and Adolescents

Len Leven, M.D.
Research Assistant Professor of Psychiatry, New York University School of Medicine. Attending Physician, Bellevue Hospital Center, New York, New York.
Interviewing Children and Adolescents

Dorothy Otnow Lewis, M.D.
Professor of Psychiatry, New York University School of Medicine. Attending Physician, Bellevue Hospital Center, New York, New York. Clinical Professor, Yale University School of Medicine. Attending Physician, Yale–New Haven Hospital, New Haven, Connecticut.
Conduct Disorders

Thomas R. Linscheid, Ph.D.
Associate Professor of Pediatrics and Psychology, Ohio State University College of Medicine. Director, Department of Psychology, Children's Hospital, Columbus, Ohio.
Sleep Disorders in Children and Adolescents

Wendy Ludman, Psy.D.
Assistant Clinical Professor of Psychiatry (Psychology), Mount Sinai School of Medicine, New York, New York.
Interviewing Children and Adolescents

Elaine Davidson Nemzer, M.D.
Clinical Assistant Professor, Ohio State University College of Medicine, Columbus, Ohio.
Psychosomatic Illness in Children and Adolescents

John D. O'Brien, M.D.
Clinical Associate Professor of Psychiatry, New York University School of Medicine. Director of Training and Education and Associate Director, Division of Child and Adolescent Psychiatry, New York University Medical Center, New York, New York.
Interviewing Children and Adolescents

Carol B. Peterson, B.A.
Predoctoral Student in Clinical Psychology, University of Minnesota. Eating Disorder Research Staff, Adult Psychiatry, University of Minnesota Hospital. University of Minnesota Hospital, Minneapolis, Minnesota.
Multidimensional Psychotherapy for Children and Adolescents

John C. Pomeroy, M.D.
Clinical Assistant Professor, State University of New York at Stony Brook School of Medicine. Attending in Child Psychiatry, University Hospital at Stony Brook, Stony Brook, New York.
Infantile Autism and Childhood Psychosis

Robert S. Pynoos, M.D., M.P.H.
Associate Professor, Department of Psychiatry and Biobehavioral Sciences, University of California, Los Angeles, School of Medicine. Director, Program in Trauma, Violence, and Sudden Bereavement, Neuropsychiatric Institute and Hospital, Los Angeles, California.
Post-Traumatic Stress Disorder in Children and Adolescents

Daniel J. Raiten, Ph.D.
Research Nutritionist, Children's Hospital National Medical Center, Washington, D. C.
The Medical Basis for Nutrition and Behavior

L. Kaye Rasnake, Ph.D.
Assistant Professor, Department of Psychology, Dennison University, Granville, Ohio.
Sleep Disorders in Children and Adolescents

Kitty W. Soldano, Ph.D.
Clinical Assistant Professor and Clinical Social Worker, Division of Child and Adolescent Psychiatry, Ohio State University, College of Medicine, Columbus, Ohio.
Divorce: Clinical Implications for Treatment of Children

Paul D. Steinhauer, M.D., F.R.C.P.(C.)
Professor of Psychiatry and Director of Training in Child Psychiatry, University of Toronto Faculty of Medicine. Senior Staff Psychiatrist, Hospital for Sick Children, Toronto, Ontario, Canada.
Adoption; Families and Family Therapy

Peter E. Tanguay, M.D.
Professor of Psychiatry, University of California, Los Angeles, Neuropsychiatric Institute, Los Angeles, California.
Mental Retardation

Abby L. Wasserman, M.D.
Director of Residency Training in Child Psychiatry, Washington University School of Medicine. Director of Consultation-Liaison Child Psychiatry, Children's Hospital. Active Staff, Barnes Hospital, St. Louis, Missouri.
Principles of Psychiatric Care of Children and Adolescents with Medical Illnesses

Elizabeth B. Weller, M.D.
Professor of Psychiatry and Pediatrics, Director, Division of Child and Adolescent Psychiatry, and Director of Training of Child and Adolescent Psychiatry, Ohio State University College of Medicine, Columbus, Ohio.
Depressive Disorders in Children and Adolescents; Grief in Children and Adolescents

Ronald A. Weller, M.D.
Professor and Director of Training and Education, Department of Psychiatry, Ohio State University College of Medicine. Attending Physician, Ohio State University Hospitals, Columbus, Ohio.
Depressive Disorders in Children and Adolescents; Grief in Children and Adolescents

Paul H. Wender, M.D.
Professor of Psychiatry, University of Utah College of Medicine, Salt Lake City, Utah.
Attention-Deficit Hyperactivity Disorder in Adolescents and Adults

J. Gerald Young, M.D.
Professor of Psychiatry and Associate Director, Division of Child and Adolescent Psychiatry, New York University School of Medicine. Attending Psychiatrist, Bellevue Hospital Center and University Hospital, New York University Medical Center, New York, New York.
Interviewing Children and Adolescents

Foreword

In reviewing the history of child as opposed to adult psychiatry, it can be seen that child psychiatry developed independently of adult psychiatry, not as an offspring. Whereas adult psychiatry had medical roots, this was not as true of child psychiatry. The Commonwealth Fund in 1922 encouraged the development of the Commonwealth Child Guidance Clinics. In these clinics, children were evaluated and treated by a multidisciplinary team of child psychiatrists, psychologists, and social workers. These clinics were mechanisms of clinical service, but they did not promote a scientific empirical approach to the study of the problems from which the children treated in these clinics suffered.

The American Association of Psychiatric Clinics for Children was formally established in 1946. To a large extent, these clinics became the training grounds for future child psychiatrists. It was not until 1953 that the American Academy of Child Psychiatry (now the American Academy of Child and Adolescent Psychiatry) was founded. And it was not until 1959 that the American Board of Psychiatry and Neurology established child psychiatry as a recognized medical specialty. However, Leo Kanner established the first major child psychiatry clinic in an academic pediatric department in 1930 at Johns Hopkins University. Kanner's *Child Psychiatry* in 1935 became the first textbook of child psychiatry in the English language.

This textbook of child and adolescent psychiatry differs in many ways from the majority of those that have preceded it. It is first and foremost a clinical textbook. The first three sections examine the common problems that children and adolescents experience—the internalizing disorders, the disruptive behavior disorders, and the developmental disorders. The fourth section deals with specific clinical issues that do not fit neatly under the first three general headings, such as child abuse, sleep disorders, suicidal behavior, and issues regarding divorce, nutrition, and adoption. Finally, section five covers issues having to do with assessment, including interviewing and neuropsychologic assessment as well as principles of psychiatric intervention and psychiatric care.

Kanner's first textbook was primarily based on the clinical lore that was available at the time. This textbook presents a much more empirical approach to the psychiatric disorders of childhood and adolescence. The various chapters emphasize the importance of careful clinical evaluation using state-of-the-art methods, careful clinical diagnosis and classification, and clinical intervention based on the most current methods with constant re-evaluation of the efficacy of the intervention.

The very effective use of clinical vignettes is also novel to this textbook. They systemically describe the nature of the child's problem, possible etiologic factors, the likely outcome, and interventions that may or may not have been effective.

The principles that underlie this empirical approach to child psychiatry have been discussed elsewhere. Among the most important of these principles are the following:

Child psychiatry is a medical specialty. Thus, a model found useful in other areas of medicine such as pediatrics is an entirely appropriate one, not only for research but also for clinical practice and for training.

This empirical model requires a primary focus on the disorder or disorders that the patients experience.

A further implication is that individual children and adolescents may present with many types of disorders that differ in their clinical phenomenology. However, it is important to recognize that these disorders differ from each other not only in clinical phenomenology but also in such important clinical parameters as untreated natural history and response to various therapeutic interventions. These disorders will most likely differ from each other in their etiology and pathogenesis; even if we do not know at the time what the etiology and pathogenesis are.

Another implication is that a valid classification system for psychiatric disorders of infancy, childhood, and adolescence is a necessary and essential step in the advancement of the field.

Last, the model also implies that because psychological processes and phenomena may be more subjective and thus more difficult to measure and quantify, it is important to adopt a tough-minded scientific approach in their investigation, enumeration, and clinical treatment. More, rather than less, in the way of systematically obtained data should be required when what we are attempting to measure is more subjective.

The empirical model, however, does not presuppose the existence of organically based disease entities, nor does it imply that biologic modes of intervention are the ones most likely to be effective. Current classification systems, such as DSM-III and DSM-III-R, which are based on phenomenologic criteria rather than on purported etiology, have highlighted the fact that an empirical approach to child psychopathology does not necessarily assume on an a priori basis any etiology for any disorder, nor does an empirical model a priori assume that any one type of intervention is better for one disorder than any other type of intervention. Whether or not a particular intervention is likely to be effective should be determined by empirical study rather than by dogmatic statement.

Nor does the empirical model diminish the importance of an individual child patient or an individual adolescent patient as a human being. Although the focus of clinical child psychopathology is on the disorders, it is recognized that every patient is unique and that this uniqueness must be taken into account in any doctor-patient relationship. This is part of the art of medicine, whether one is practicing pediatrics, neurology, child psychiatry, or other medical specialties.

The empirical model also points out that if one emphasizes only the unique aspects of each individual patient without recognizing common factors that are shared by patients with the same disorder, this will surely impede scientific advances. If patients have no common factors, then no amount of training and no amount of clinical experience is really meaningful, since working with each patient becomes a research project in itself. Such clinical empiricism has led to improved techniques for evaluation and diagnosis that originally began in research (such as *structured interviews* for parents and children, *standardized ways of evaluating* family interactions, *behavior rating scales,* and *reliable and valid classification systems*) that are now part of standard clinical practice and actually help make individual practitioners better clinicians.

The implications for training of such an empirical model are that those of us who are involved in the education of future child psychiatrists should produce scientifically minded artists rather than pure artists or pure scientists. Pure artists might be able to use currently available clinical skills to apply today's solutions to currently recognized clinical problems. However, those clinical problems and the solutions to them are often based on data that will be replaced in the future.

The pure scientist in the pursuit of ultimate truth may not be ready to take clinical action on clinical data and may provide only partial care for patients for this reason.

The scientifically minded artist, on the other hand, will think scientifically and empirically but will acquire and use clinical skills effectively. The scientifically minded artist accepts the fact that at the same time one is searching for ultimate truth, one must frequently take therapeutic action based on data that are known to be inadequate.

The clinician treating children must be a pragmatist. Patients are currently in treatment that is based on information from a scientific perspective, that may be incompletely and inadequately researched. Moreover, to be an effective clinician, one must deliver this treatment with therapeutic enthusiasm, even though the scientific mind says that we must be wary of accepting enthusiastic therapeutic claims.

During the training years, this scientifically minded artist must develop the capacity for critical evaluation of data and for making controlled observations in a clinical context. Most important, after training, the scientifically minded artist must be able to appreciate and critically evaluate new knowledge as it appears in the scientific literature and must integrate this with what is learned in clinical practice so that one can contribute to and complement the other.

From the standpoint of clinical practice, this empirical model emphasizes the fact that it should no longer be acceptable to have therapeutic interventions prescribed solely on the basis of what the therapist is able to deliver rather than on what the patient's needs are. There are many schools of thought regarding therapeutic intervention in child psychiatry, with multiple schools of individual dynamic psychotherapy, cognitive therapy, cognitive behavior therapy, family therapy, parent training, psychopharmacology, and others. Many of the tenets of these schools are based on personal biases, dogmatism, preconceived scientifically unsupported notions, or untested theory. These interventions are often delivered to the patient and his or her family on the basis of the therapist's years of "clinical experience."

The empirical approach presented in this book suggests that we need to strive to reach the highest standards of our discipline as a medical subspecialty. To do this with every patient, we must do a comprehensive diagnostic evaluation that will facilitate differential diagnosis. Based on this differential diagnosis using a modern classification system and knowledge of the current literature, we must be able to prescribe the most effective therapeutic intervention for a particular child with a particular disorder. Since most if not all child psychiatric disorders are multifactorial in origin, with dynamic, biologic, genetic, and other roots, it is most likely that a multimodality biopsychosocial approach to intervention will be necessary with most patients. During the course of therapeutic intervention, the child psychiatrist must constantly reappraise and evaluate the treatment plan that is being carried out.

In summary, this book represents a modern approach to the evaluation, diagnosis, and treatment of child and adolescent psychiatric disorders. I am happy to have the opportunity to introduce such a seminal work.

DENNIS P. CANTWELL, M.D.
Joseph Campbell Professor of Psychiatry
Director of Residency Education in Child Psychiatry
UCLA Neuropsychiatric Institute
Los Angeles, California

Preface

Increasingly, child and adolescent psychiatry is being conceptualized from a biopsychosocial perspective. This approach encompasses two models: the traditional environmental, interpersonal, and psychological and the more recent biological/medical. Our primary goal in writing this textbook is to integrate these approaches in terms of the current understanding of child and adolescent psychiatric disorders.

It is our view that the principal thrust of a medical model in adult and child psychiatry is the formulation of one or more diagnoses. This admittedly supposes the concept of an "illness" or "disorder." It also acknowledges that there may appear to be an overlap of symptoms and behaviors, which thus leads to "differential diagnoses."

The concept of a differential diagnosis is an important part of clinical medicine. It emphasizes that similar clinical pictures with minor variations in symptoms may have diverse etiologies, treatments, and outcomes. The purpose of the psychiatric evaluation from its broadest to its most specific aspects is to determine what diagnoses best explain the data obtained.

The third edition of the *Diagnostic and Statistical Manual of Mental Disorders* (1980) and its revision (1987) have as their goal the operationalization of the clinical phenomenology of the many problems with which clinicians come in contact. Some problems lend themselves more easily to such a system because the disorders have been recognized for a long time. Others are less convincing and may never be validated as true conditions or illnesses. Psychiatric disorders in children present even more complicated nosologic problems because the influence of development and the plasticity of children's behavior under different circumstances must be considered.

Previously published textbooks on child and adolescent psychiatry have presented a psychodynamic, psychoanalytical, and behavioral perspective to explain conditions affecting young persons. These viewpoints have been well formulated in these earlier volumes. Thus, in this book we wish to emphasize the importance and relevance of the empiric psychiatric model as it applies to the clinical disorders and problems affecting children and adolescents.

Another major goal is to define treatment in terms of specific disorders, with an emphasis on psychopharmacology, although several chapters address other treatment approaches. Unfortunately, the ability of mental health professionals to identify specific medical and psychosocial interventions for specific disorders is admittedly not yet nearly as good as it needs to be. It is obvious that most serious disorders afflicting children require an integration of medical, family, academic, and community approaches and resources. It is our contention that the relative value given to these modalities depends in part on the child's diagnosis.

We have designed this book to be a clear and practical guide to the diagnosis and treatment of children and adolescents with psychiatric disorders, and we hope that information presented will be of benefit for educational and clinical use.

B. D. G.

G. A. C.

E. B. W.

Contents

FIVE

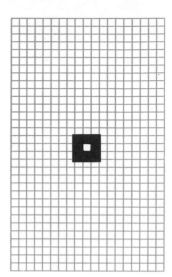

One

INTERNALIZING DISORDERS

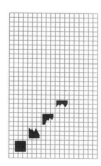
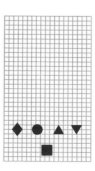

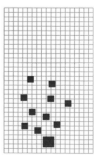

Depressive Disorders in Children and Adolescents

1

ELIZABETH B. WELLER, M.D.,
and RONALD A. WELLER, M.D.

Children and adolescents have depressive episodes with symptoms similar to those observed in depressed adults. As awareness of depression in this age group has increased, research activity has correspondingly increased. Descriptive studies and, more recently, biological studies have been undertaken, but the results of many of these studies are preliminary and await replication. New treatment strategies for depressive disorders are being developed and studied. However, additional information is needed before affective disorders in children and adolescents are fully understood.

DEFINITION

According to the *Diagnostic and Statistical Manual of Mental Disorders*, third edition, revised *(DSM-III-R)*, mood disorders occur in infants, children, and adolescents (American Psychiatric Association 1987). The diagnosis is made by the same criteria used to diagnose mood disorders in adults, with minor modi-

fications that take into account the different developmental levels observed in children. Although at one time bipolar disorders were not believed to occur in prepubertal children, evidence now indicates that children experience both unipolar and bipolar affective disorders. Symptoms of these disorders should be carefully evaluated and considered in the differential diagnosis of children and adolescents with depression both routinely and in complicated cases with unusual presentations and/or psychotic features.

Major Depressive Episode

The *DSM-III-R* lists the diagnostic criteria used to define psychiatric illness in the United States. It is a 1987 modification of the *DSM-III*, which was introduced in 1980. The *DSM-III* and *DSM-III-R* criteria for major depression are similar. A diagnosis of *major depressive disorder* requires five or more of the following signs and symptoms:

1. Depressed mood

2. Loss of interest or pleasure
3. Significant weight loss or weight gain (e.g., >5% of body weight in a month or failure to make expected weight gains in children
4. Insomnia or hypersomnia
5. Psychomotor agitation or retardation observable by others
6. Fatigue or loss of energy
7. Feelings of worthlessness or excessive/inappropriate guilt
8. Diminished concentration
9. Recurrent thoughts of death, suicidal ideation, suicide attempt, or specific plan for committing suicide.

These features should be present concurrently for at least 2 weeks. Depression is not diagnosed if an organic factor initiated or maintained the depression or if the depression was a reaction to the death of a loved one. Likewise, delusions or hallucinations in the absence of prominent mood symptoms cannot be present longer than 2 weeks. Finally, depression should not be diagnosed in those persons with a previous diagnosis of schizophrenia, schizophreniform disorder, delusional disorder, or another psychotic disorder.

Melancholia is a subtype of depression that indicates more severe psychopathology. It is diagnosed when a depressed person has at least five of the nine signs and symptoms specified in the *DSM-III-R*. These include the following:

1. Loss of interest or pleasure in all, or almost all, activities
2. Lack of reactivity to usually pleasurable stimuli (does not feel much better, even temporarily, when something good happens)
3. Depression regularly worse in the morning
4. Early morning awakening (at least 2 hours before usual time of awakening)
5. Psychomotor retardation or agitation (not merely subjective complaints)
6. Significant anorexia or weight loss (e.g., more than 5% of body weight in a month)
7. No significant personality disturbance before first major depressive episode
8. One or more previous major depressive episodes followed by complete, or nearly complete, recovery
9. Previous good response to specific and adequate somatic antidepressant therapy (e.g., tricyclic antidepressants, electroconvul-

sive therapy, monoamine oxidase inhibitors, lithium).

When diagnosing melancholia in children compared with adults, several considerations must be kept in mind. In the *DSM-III-R*, preexisting personality disorder is an exclusion criterion for melancholia. This criterion is not applicable to children since personality disorders are not diagnosed before the age of 16. Also, criteria such as previous affective episodes with complete recovery or good response to somatic treatment may not apply to some depressed children since many have not had prior episodes. Therefore, it is more difficult to diagnose melancholia in children because fewer than nine symptoms of melancholia are applicable, but nevertheless five symptoms are required to diagnose it.

Depression With Seasonal Pattern

Depression with a seasonal pattern is diagnosed when a temporal relationship exists between the onset of an episode of depression and a particular 60-day period of the year. In adults, seasonal depression typically occurs in October or November. In children, such a seasonal depression in October or November may be attributed to the start of a new school year. Thus, children who may have a seasonal affective disorder might be diagnosed as having an adjustment disorder with depressed mood, and the concurrence of a change of season and this particular stressor (start of school) for children makes it difficult to diagnose seasonal affective disorder. Further research is needed to clarify the relationship of seasonal factors to depression in children.

Dysthymia

Dysthymia is a depressed or irritable mood lasting at least a year. It occurs on an almost daily basis, with at least two of the following:

1. Decreased or increased appetite
2. Decreased or increased sleep
3. Fatigue
4. Low self-esteem
5. Poor concentration
6. Feelings of hopelessness.

Children with dysthymic disorder are not

without symptoms for more than 2 months during a year. As in adults, if dysthymia occurs in children a chronic course and future episodes of major depression can be predicted.

Depressive Disorder Not Otherwise Specified

Children with episodes of recurrent mild depression that do not meet the criteria for dysthmia or major depressive episode are included in the category of depressive disorder that is not otherwise specified, which also includes depressive episodes in children with residual schizophrenia.

Adjustment Disorder With Depressed Mood

Children with adjustment disorder with depressed mood present with tearfulness and feelings of hopelessness as a reaction to identifiable psychosocial stressor(s). This reaction occurs within 3 months of the onset of the stressor(s) and results in impairment in school functioning, in usual social activities, or in relationships with others. The duration of the disorder is less than 6 months. Persons with adjustment disorder with depressed mood should not meet criteria for any specific mental disorder in the *DSM-III-R*. Furthermore, uncomplicated bereavement is specifically excluded from this category.

Uncomplicated Bereavement

Often, a full depressive syndrome is a part of the expected reaction to uncomplicated bereavement. Decreased appetite, weight loss, and insomnia commonly occur. Psychomotor retardation and functional impairment are uncommon. Guilt, if present, is usually focused on things done or not done by the survivor for the deceased prior to the time of death. Usually, bereaved persons feel the depressed mood is normal. However, they may seek professional help for specific symptoms such as insomnia or anorexia. Uncomplicated bereavement usually occurs immediately after the death. Rarely is the onset more than 3 months after the death.

Weller and co-workers (1987) found that 39% of bereaved prepubertal children who had experienced the death of a parent met criteria for a major depressive episode during the first 3 months following the parent's death. Depression was predicted by preexisting psychiatric disorder in the child or a family history of affective disorder. However, follow-up studies are needed to determine the long-term effect of bereavement on psychopathology in children.

ETIOLOGY

Clinically, depressed children and adolescents are similar to depressed adults when differences in developmental stages are considered. Thus, it might be assumed that the etiology of the depressive disorders is also similar. However, it is premature to assume there is only one etiology for affective disorders in children. It is possible that numerous etiologies may lead to the expression of depressive symptoms (Kashani and Sherman 1988).

Genetic Model

In the genetic model, heredity is believed to be responsible for the development of depression. Twin studies have provided support for this model. Concordance for affective disorders in monozygotic twins is 76%, compared with 19% in dizygotic twins. When monozygotic twins are reared apart, the concordance rate drops only to 67%, indicating a more prominent role of heredity compared with that of the environment. However, monozygotic twins were not 100% concordant for affective disorders, implying that factors other than heredity play some etiologic role in depression (Akiskal 1986; Wender et al. 1986).

Children of affectively ill adults (so-called top-down approach) and the adult relatives of children with affective disorders (so-called bottom-up approach) have been evaluated for the occurrence of affective disorders. These studies found affective disorders clustered in families. Age-adjusted morbidity risk for affective disorders was higher in adult relatives of children and adolescents with affective disorders than in the general adult population. Children with one parent with an affective illness have double the risk of developing an affective disorder, and those with two parents with affective illness are four times more likely to have an affective disorder than children of parents without affective disorders.

The biological and adoptive relatives of adults with mood disorders (adopted when children) have been studied to determine the contribution of genetic and environmental factors in the etiology of mood disorders. They were matched with relatives of normal adoptees. The biological relatives of mood-disordered adult adoptees had an 8-fold increase in unipolar depression and a 15-fold increase in suicide. This study demonstrated a significant genetic contribution to the occurrence of unipolar depression and suicide.

A family study of first-degree relatives of children who met *DSM-III* criteria for major depression found 27% had unipolar depression and 14% had bipolar illness. Sixty-two percent of the probands' parents had affective illness. The mean ages at onset for major depression and bipolar illness among family members were 23.5 years and 19.5 years, respectively.

For 100 inpatient depressed children who met *DSM-III* criteria for major depression, family psychiatric history was determined by Weller and co-workers (1988) from standard structured diagnostic interviews of the parent (Psychiatric Diagnostic Interview [PDI]; Diagnostic Interview for Children and Adolescents [DICA]). Psychiatric disorders were more prevalent among relatives of these depressed children than among depressed families or normal families in the general population, as reported by Weissman and associates (1984). Major affective disorders were six and one-half times more frequent in probands' parents and were three and one-half times more frequent among second-degree relatives. Of 100 probands, 44 had first-degree relatives with affective disorders; 32 had both first- and second-degree relatives with affective disorders; and 8 had 20 relatives with affective disorders. Diagnosis of affective disorder was three times more frequent in mothers than fathers of probands. Schizophrenia, alcohol and drug abuse, sociopathy, anxiety disorders, and somatization disorder also occurred at higher rates among first- and second-degree relatives. This high rate of psychopathology and early age at onset of symptoms among family members are compatible with the theory that onset of illness in childhood indicates a severe form of the disorder.

Role of Environment

Children who had at least one biological parent with a depressive disorder (but not mania, schizophrenia, or schizoaffective disorder) were evaluated as to the effects of severity and chronicity of the parent's depression on the child. Severity and chronicity were both shown to have a significant association with impaired adaptation and presence of a *DSM-III* diagnosis in the children. Increased discord among married or separated parents had a similar effect. Depression in the mother was more strongly associated with increased psychopathology in the children than was depression in the father.

Poor relationships with parents, siblings, and peers are common in children with affective disorders. These social deficiencies in the child are more often obvious when one of the parents also has an affective disorder. In one study it was reported that some parents with affective disorders have at times mistreated or neglected their children (Weller et al. 1988). This was particularly true if the child also had an affective disorder. In this situation, irritability may be a strong factor in parent–child interactions. Parenting an irritable child is a difficult task and may be even more difficult when a parent(s) is also irritable. Benign neglect or even abuse may occur. Children usually do not seek psychiatric treatment. The adults in their lives (teachers, parents) refer or bring them to treatment. Depressed adults might fail to recognize depression in their children and fail to seek treatment for them. Children of adults with affective illness may need to be evaluated to identify such potential problems to allow prevention or early intervention.

Biological Factors

Since diagnosing children is more difficult and time consuming than diagnosing adults, the idea that a laboratory test could confirm a diagnosis is appealing. In many ways, biological studies are less complicated in children than in adults. Conditions such as drug or alcohol abuse, organic mental disorders, severe medical illnesses, and self-treatment with over-the-counter drugs that can limit the application of some biological tests are uncommon in children. In this sense, children are "purer" subjects than adults (Puig-Antich 1987).

Depression is an episodic disorder, and biological markers are classified as either trait or state markers. State markers are positive or abnormal during the episode and return to normal at some point during or following recovery. A trait marker is positive or abnormal prior to the onset of illness. Such a trait marker might be particularly useful in identifying children at risk for the development of a depressive episode.

NEUROENDOCRINE CHANGES IN CHILDREN

The most commonly studied biological test of depression in children and adolescents has been the dexamethasone suppression test (DST). Normally, an exogenously administered corticosteroid such as dexamethasone suppresses secretion of endogenous cortisol. This may not occur in some depressed persons. In endogenously depressed adults, 65% will have a nonsuppressed (i.e., positive) dexamethasone suppression test (DST). Of those patients who are not depressed, only 5% will have a positive DST. Children and adolescents have similar DST findings. Typically, the dexamethasone doses used are 0.5 mg for prepubertal and 1 mg for pubertal children. The drug is given orally at 11 PM. The next day, cortisol levels are measured at 8 AM and 4 PM. When studies performed in this manner are combined, approximately 50% of depressed children and adolescents do not suppress cortisol production when given dexamethasone (Casat et al. 1989; Weller and Weller 1988). Preliminary research indicates that patients who are shown by the DST not to suppress cortisol production are at a higher risk for relapse (Weller et al. 1986b) and are more likely to respond to pharmacologic intervention (i.e., tricyclic antidepressants) (Preskorn et al. 1987). The DST is usually considered a "state" marker.

GROWTH HORMONE

Prepubertal depressed children are reported to have increased growth hormone secretion during sleep compared with non-depressed psychiatric controls and normal controls (Puig-Antich 1987). Also, when given an insulin challenge test to assess growth hormone release, depressed children secrete less growth hormone compared with psychiatric controls. This abnormality is reported to remain following recovery and cessation of pharmacotherapy (tricyclic antidepressants). These findings await replication, and if they are confirmed, this growth hormone abnormality might be a trait marker of depression after an episode of illness has occurred.

POLYSOMNOGRAPHY

Shortened rapid eye movement (REM) sleep latency is often found in endogenously depressed adults. However, there are conflicting reports as to whether sleep electroencephalographic (EEG) changes occur in depressed children. In one study, children did not show any EEG changes during depression but depressed prepubertal children showed shortened REM latency during recovery from depression when they were drug free. If this finding can be replicated, such EEG changes might be useful as a marker of a past episode of depression. Unlike a true trait marker that is abnormal before the first depressive episode, it may be that persistent EEG changes are manifested only after the first episode (Puig-Antich 1987).

AUGMENTED AVERAGE EVOKED RESPONSE

In one study, a strongly augmented average evoked response to sensory stimuli in children with bipolar disorder indicated a good response to lithium. Also, urinary 3-methoxy-4-hydroxyphenylglycol (MHPG) excretion was altered during an affective episode. However, both of these biological markers appear to be state markers since levels return to normal once the child has recovered. Again replication of these findings is necessary (Cytryn and McKnew 1987).

PROBLEMS IN BIOLOGICAL STUDIES

There is still much to be learned about the biological aspects of depression in children. The lack of studies in children is in part related to the "invasive" nature of most biological studies. Techniques such as multiple blood samplings and/or lumbar puncture for cerebrospinal fluid are required. Collection of 24-hour urine samples in prepubertal children can be a challenge, particularly if the child is enuretic. Also, children and adolescents are less inclined than adults to participate in invasive studies. Thus, tests that are noninvasive and simple to perform are desired. This is especially important in prepubertal children, who perceive any unpleasant procedure as threatening rather than necessary. Currently, the possibility of substituting saliva samples for blood samples when measuring cortisol in children is being investigated (Bober et al. 1988).

Psychological Etiologies of Depression

PSYCHODYNAMIC

According to the psychodynamic theory, depression results from actual or perceived loss of a love object. Another related theory is that depression results from an inability to achieve one's ego ideal. Unfortunately, it is difficult to test these hypotheses systematically and there are no studies in children or adults that prove them.

LIFE STRESS MODEL

According to the life stress model, positive or negative life stressors may precipitate depression. Adults with depression report three times as many stressful life events as nondepressed controls. However, it is difficult to determine whether the converse is true, that is, whether depression precipitated the stress. For example, someone with an irritable depression may have marital problems that result in divorce. Later, the divorce is perceived as the cause of depression. For a depressed child, school failure may at times be similarly perceived as the cause, rather than the result, of depression.

COGNITIVE DISTORTION MODEL

Maladaptive cognition in the form of a negative view of self, the world, and the future may render a person vulnerable to depression. It is not clear whether these observations reflect causes or consequences of depression. Several studies have reported low self-esteem in depressed children. How-ever, low self-esteem is often found in nondepressed psychiatric patients, such as children with attention-deficit disorder. Therefore, low self-esteem does not seem specific to depression. Depressed children treated as outpatients reported a negative view of the future in one study. As of yet no studies have determined whether depressed children have a negative view of the world (Kashani and Sherman 1988).

SOCIAL SKILLS DEFICITS

In the social skills deficits model, depressed children do not have sufficient skills to elicit positive reinforcement from their environment. Lack of positive reinforcement results in depression. Depressed children are rated as less popular by their peers and less socially competent by their teachers. It is unclear whether deficits in social skills follow or precede depression (Kashani and Sherman 1988).

LEARNED HELPLESSNESS MODEL

Persons who experience life events beyond their control come to believe future outcomes cannot be controlled. This results in motivational, cognitive, and emotional deficiencies termed *helplessness deficits*. In the reformulated learned helplessness model, one's explanations for particular outcomes modulate expectations for future outcomes and reactions to the outcome (Kashani and Sherman 1988).

SELF-CONTROL

The self-control model assumes depressed persons have deficits in self-monitoring, self-evaluation, and self-reinforcement. Depressed patients focus on negative events and on short-term rather than long-term consequences of their actions. They have unattainable performance criteria and misattribute personal success and failure. There is a paucity of self-reinforcement and an excess of self-punishment (Kashani and Sherman 1988).

PARENT–CHILD RELATIONS MODEL

Depression has been theorized to result from poor parent–child interaction. Much of the evidence for this model comes from depressed adults who were questioned about early childhood experiences. Low paternal involvement and high maternal overprotectiveness were reported. In prospective studies depressed children often found their parents to be angry, punitive, detached, and belittling. Depressed parents' attitudes toward their children showed problematic mother–child relationships (Kashani and Sherman 1988).

EPIDEMIOLOGY

The reported prevalence of depression in children varies widely. This variation results in part from differences in samples studied, in sample sizes and associated characteristics, in the diagnostic criteria employed, and in the age of the subjects. Kashani and Sherman (1988), in a study of preschoolers drawn from the general population, reported a prevalence of 0.3%. These researchers concluded that depression diagnosed using adult criteria was not frequent in preschoolers. Investigators in the United States and New Zealand have found a population prevalence of depression of 1.8% in prepubertal children. This rate rose dramatically to 4.7% in 14- to 16-year-old adolescents. Increased prevalence of depression during adolescence was attributed to biological changes associated with puberty rather than to an increase in chronological age. Also, the incidence of depression in females increased with puberty.

In clinical samples, depression has been found in 28% of children attending a psychiatric outpatient clinic, 53% of those evaluated in an educational diagnostic center, 7% of general pediatric medical inpatients, and 40% of pediatric neurologic inpatients. The rate of depression among psychiatric inpatients ranged from 13% in a community mental health center to 59% in a psychiatric hospital.

The recent use of standardized diagnostic techniques, including structured and semistructured interviews, self-report and clinician rating scales, and reports from parents and teachers, has made it easier to diagnose depression. In general, researchers using these techniques have found childhood depression is not as rare as previously believed. A summary of recent epidemiologic studies of depression in children and adolescents is presented in Table 1–1.

CLINICAL PICTURE

Infants and Preschoolers

The natural course of an untreated affective disorder is not always episodic and can be chronic. The onset of affective disorders in children can be insidious. Studies of infants and preschoolers describe depressed children as having apathy, social withdrawal, sleeplessness, and weight loss. Anaclitic depression and hospitalism have been described in children separated from a primary caretaker. According to Poznanski (1982), nonverbal communication in this age group, particularly facial expression, body posture, tone of voice, tempo of language, and level of activity, take on an increased meaning since verbal skills are not fully developed. The varying cognitive and language skills children possess at different age levels affect both their interpretation of questions and their answers. When interviewing a child, specific questions should be asked in simple concrete language. For example, few preschoolers spontaneously volunteer they feel sad but will express sad feelings when carefully questioned. These children also have a poor sense of time. Thus, duration of symptoms should be clarified by parental figures to determine more accurately the length of the episode.

Unfortunately, most instruments to assess depression were not designed for use in preschoolers. Biological markers are of limited use since there have been almost no methodologically sound studies in this age group.

Children of adult unipolar and bipolar patients are at high risk to develop both affective and nonaffective psychiatric disorders. Rutter reported that 50% of children of depressed parents have a psychiatric disorder. These included conduct disturbances, mixed behavioral and emotional disturbances, and neurotic illnesses. None were diagnosed as depressed. However, in other studies, the incidence of depressive disorders ranged from 7% to 65%. Unfortunately none of these studies included normal controls for comparison. Controlled studies of depressed mothers and schizophrenic mothers found their children were more disturbed than children of normal controls. Types of disturbances assessed included impatience, defiance, disturbed classroom behavior, aggression, with-

Table 1–1. RECENT EPIDEMIOLOGIC STUDIES OF DEPRESSION IN CHILDREN AND ADOLESCENTS

Investigators(s)	Year	Country	Number of Children	Percent Depressed	Population Sampled
Ling et al.	1970	United States	25	40.00	Patients on a neurology ward with unexplained headaches
Rutter et al.	1970	United Kingdom	2,199	0.14	General population
Nissen	1971	Germany	6,000	1.80	Inpatients
Meierhoffer	1972	Switzerland	400	25.00	Children in residential nurseries
Bauersfeld	1972	Switzerland	400	13.70	Patients in school psychiatric center
McConville et al.	1973	Canada	141	53.00	Psychiatric inpatients
Weinberg et al.	1973	United States	72	58.00	Outpatients in educational diagnostic center
Pearce	1977	United Kingdom	547	23.00	Psychiatric inpatients
Petti	1978	United States	73	59.00	Psychiatric inpatients
Kashani and Simonds	1979	United States	103	1.90	Prepubertal children randomly selected from the general population
Carlson and Cantwell	1980	United States	102	28.00	Neuropsychiatric outpatients
Robins et al.	1980	United States		28.00	Adolescent inpatients
Kashani et al.	1982	United States	100	13.00	Prepubertal inpatients in community mental health center
Kashani et al.	1983	New Zealand		1.80	Prepubertal nonreferred sample
Kashani et al.	1983	United States	350	0.30	Preschoolers from general population
Kazdin et al.	1983	United States		15.00	Prepubertal inpatients
Kashani and Carlson	1987	United States	1,000	0.90	Clinical sample of preschoolers
Kashani et al.	1987	United States		4.70	Community sample of adolescents aged 14 to 16

drawal, unhappiness, and a lessening of creativity, initiative, and comprehension.

Prepubertal Children

With advancing age, children become more adept in using language to communicate problems. When this occurs, children must be interviewed individually. A combined interview with their parents is no longer sufficient. Children will be able to report inner experiences of sadness, suicidal thoughts, and sleep disturbances of which their parents may be unaware. On the other hand, parents will often provide better information on symptoms that the child would tend to minimize, such as poor social functioning. Irritable mood and lack of interest in activities may also be more frequently reported by parents. Of depressed children, approximately 25% will have enough symptoms reported independently by child and parent to diagnose depression. If information is taken only from the children, one fourth of cases of depression will be missed. If only parents are interviewed, half of the cases of depression will be missed.

After a child reaches 6 years of age, diagnostic interviews such as the Diagnostic Interview for Children and Adolescents (DICA) and the Kiddie Schedule for Affective Disorder and Schizophrenia (K-SADS), self-report rating scales such as the Children's Depression Inventory (CDI), and clinician rating scales such as the Childhood Depression Rating Scale—Revised (CDRS-R) can be used to assess depression (Table 1-2). Except for the CDI, use of these instruments is time consuming. They can be used for baseline evaluations during an index episode and for follow-up to provide systematic and objective information.

CASE HISTORY

Suzanne, age 10, presented to the outpatient child psychiatry clinic with episodic hypersomnia since the age of 6, severe weight loss, and suicidal attempts. Her most recent episode had lasted 2 months. The child was doing very poorly in school despite having A and B grades previously. She was talking about drowning herself by holding her breath under the water in a swimming pool. She thought that by doing this it would

Table 1–2. PSYCHOMETRIC AIDS		
Diagnostic Assessment	**Severity Rating Scales**	**Educational Assessment**
Diagnostic Interview for Children and Adolescents (DICA)—C/P	Children's Depression Inventory (CDI)	Wechsler Intelligence Scale for Children—Revised (WISC-R)
Kiddie-Schedule for Affective Disorder and Schizophrenia (K-SADS)—C/P	Childhood Depression Rating Scale—Revised (CDRS-R)	
DISC	Clinical-Global Impression Scale (CGI)	
ISC	PNID	
CAS		

Key: DISC: Diagnostic Interview Schedule for Children
ISC: Interview Schedule for Children
CAS: Child Assessment Schedule
PNID: Peer Nomination Index for Depression

be called an "accident" and her parents would not feel guilty that she had killed herself. She appeared emaciated and cachectic (she weighed 25 kg). The child was immediately hospitalized to prevent a suicide attempt since the family was not capable of doing so.

Results of a thorough organic workup including computed tomography were negative. There was no evidence of malignancy. On further evaluation, the child was found to have had four previous episodes of severe depression. These had been diagnosed as "school phobia" even though she did not have any of the severe anxiety symptoms when separated from home or significant caretakers. The mother denied that anxiety had been present in the previous episodes. The child was described as isolated, having no energy, and constantly wanting to sleep. The family history was positive for major depression for three generations on the mother's side and for two generations on the father's side. The child had an older brother who was diagnosed to have depression.

The child was scheduled for intensive individual therapy, family counseling, group therapy, and occupational and recreational therapy. She was always tired or sleepy and missed the majority of her treatments. Finally, imipramine, 100 mg/day at bedtime, was started. Within 10 days she was participating in school and all other activities and stated she had never felt better. Subsequently, her brother asked to be given the same medication since he was having similar problems. Suzanne was discharged with follow-up consisting of individual and family counseling and medication treatment pro-

vided by the referring community child psychiatrist.

Adolescents

A clear onset for an affective episode is more likely in adolescents than in prepubertal children. Adolescent-onset depression is more like adult depression than is prepubertal depression. In adolescents, drug and alcohol abuse may complicate affective symptomatology. Approximately 20% of adolescents with affective disorder present with drug abuse. In some, this may be an attempt to self-medicate. Longitudinal history and chronology of symptoms are key to separating depression and substance abuse. Diagnosis of primary affective disorder indicates that no other psychiatric disorders preceded the onset of the affective disorder. Diagnosis of secondary affective disorder indicates that another psychiatric disorder such as attention-deficit hyperactivity disorder, conduct disorder, separation anxiety disorder, obsessive-compulsive disorder, substance abuse, or a serious medical condition predated the affective disorder (Table 1–3). In cases of preexisting substance abuse, an affective disorder should not be diagnosed until the child is drug free and has completed withdrawal from the drug.

In primary conduct disorder with secondary depression, successful treatment of depression may not affect the conduct disorder. However, if the child has primary depression with some features of conduct disturbance, such as an inordinate amount of aggression due to irritability and provoc-

Table 1–3. COMORBIDITY IN DEPRESSION IN CHILDREN AND ADOLESCENTS

Study		Co-Diagnosis	Population
Carlson and Cantwell	1980	Attention-deficit disorder	
Puig-Antich et al.	1982	Conduct disorder	33% of depressed prepubertal children (conduct disorder disappeared with tricyclic antidepressant treatment)
Kovacs et al.	1984	Conduct disorder	Preceded depression in depressed children
Kovacs et al.	1984	Anxiety	33% of depressed children
McManese et al.	1984	Borderline	25% of inpatient adolescents with diagnosis of borderline had depression
Orvaschel et al.	1987	Attention-deficit disorder	Children of parents with unipolar depression (attention-deficit disorder preceded depression)
Ryan et al.	1987	Anxiety	33% of depressed adolescents
Kashani et al.	1987	Anxiety	33% of depressed children
Strober et al.	1988	Attention-derficit disorder	Is this precursor of mania?

ativeness or poor school attendance, then treatment of the depression usually alleviates these accompanying conduct problems.

Another diagnosis to be considered in the differential diagnosis is borderline personality disorder. This diagnosis is given to adolescents too frequently without a thorough evaluation. The incidence of borderline personality disorder drastically decreased in one adolescent psychiatric ward when diagnostic interviews were done to supplement routine admission clinical interviews. The majority of these youngsters fulfilled criteria for an affective disorder when examined this way. This observation is compatible with the theory that borderline personality disorder represents an atypical presentation of an affective disorder (Akiskal and Weller, 1989).

CASE HISTORY

Kelly, age 13, was brought to the outpatient clinic by her mother. The patient's chief complaint was "there is nothing wrong with me." The mother reported her daughter was extremely irritable and labile and had written two suicide notes in the previous 2 weeks. Kelly was admitted to the hospital and subsequently reported feeling miserable, wanting to sleep all the time, having no energy, and getting into fights with her best friends. Her concentration had diminished, and she had been getting Ds and Fs although she had been an A and B student. She had been suspended from school because of talking back to the teachers, getting into verbal fights with students, disrupting class, and sleeping in the classroom.

A dexamethasone suppression test (DST) was done 4 days after admission. The test was positive at both 8 AM and 4 PM. Individual psychotherapy was started, and imipramine, 150 mg, was given at bedtime. The patient and her family were also educated about affective disorders. She responded well and was discharged after 1 month. On follow-up, Kelly was doing well at school and was on the honor roll. She continued on imipramine therapy for 6 months. The medication was then tapered and discontinued, and she did well for 2 years. At age 15, she had a recurrence at which time she contacted her child psychiatrist and was treated as an outpatient. Thus, educating this patient and her parents about depression led to early recognition and treatment without rehospitalization.

DIFFERENTIAL DIAGNOSIS

In children and adolescents with depression the differential diagnosis is very important. Before a psychiatric diagnosis is made in a child or adolescent, organic conditions that mimic or cause psychiatric symptoms should be ruled out. The incidence of such conditions may vary according to age. Thus, knowledge of normal development and of physical illnesses with psychiatric manifestations is necessary to make an accurate diagnosis. For example, preschoolers presenting with depressive syndromes should also be evaluated for malignancies, child neglect/abuse, separation anxiety disorder, and adjustment disorder with depressed mood.

In prepubertal children, the differential diagnosis for depression includes separation anxiety disorder, overanxious disorder, and conduct disorder. It is also helpful to determine whether the affective disorder is primary or secondary. For adolescents, substance abuse, anxiety disorders, and early schizophrenia must be carefully ruled out. If it is unclear whether the patient has an affective disorder or schizophrenia, any error should be toward diagnosing and treating an affective disorder. Depending on response, the treatment strategy can be altered. As in adults, neuroleptic drugs have potentially serious side effects in children and adolescents. Neuroleptic drugs should only be used when clearly indicated, and duration of treatment should be minimized.

PROGNOSIS

For many illnesses, early age at onset indicates poorer prognosis than late onset of symptoms. This appears true for many psychiatric disorders in children. An early age at onset is frequently associated with a strong genetic predisposition. Often a psychiatrically ill child is cared for by psychiatrically ill adults who themselves may need treatment. Childhood affective disorders should be diagnosed and treated promptly. Otherwise, the illness may be further complicated by poor school performance, poor peer relationships, drug abuse, and suicide. A depressed child or adolescent is at high risk for recurrence of illness and at increased risk of developing bipolar illness.

ASSESSMENT

Structured diagnostic interviews have been widely used in adults. They have been helpful in standardizing information gathering. Now, diagnostic interviews and self-assessment scales are being used more frequently in evaluating children. Studies comparing parent and child versions of these instruments have demonstrated that information about the child's affective state was being missed by talking to parents alone. However, such instruments are not without problems. Many are lengthy and cumbersome to use. Sometimes major discrepancies between parent and child interviews occur. Until such problems with structured interviews can be fully resolved they should not be used as the sole basis for establishing a diagnosis. The diagnosis should be made by compiling information obtained from a detailed history of chief complaint, history of present illness, past medical history, developmental history, school history, family history of psychiatric disorders, mental status examination and physical examination of the child. Information from structured interviews can supplement and enhance this process.

TREATMENT

A biopsychosocial approach is commonly used to treat affective disorders in children (Table 1–4). In many situations, educating the child and family about the condition is of particular importance. Parents are often guilt ridden because they feel they may have caused the child's condition because of inadequate parenting skills. In the past, parents have been blamed for causing certain problems in their children. It is preferable to educate parents and elicit their help in providing care for the child since this leads to better results. In a severe episode of depression, intensive psychotherapy is rarely effective. However, a warm, caring, supportive clinician who sets limits for the child or adolescent may be particularly helpful. Sometimes medication will be indicated. Unfortunately, children and teenagers are frequently reluctant to take medications because they do not want to be different from their peers.

Doctor-patient confidentiality should be emphasized, except in situations when there is a possibility of suicide or homicide. Psychiatrists should assure a child that their role is to facilitate communication between the child and the family. However, this should be done in family sessions, not individually. Psychiatrists should not be messengers between a child and the parents. The average estimated length of an untreated major depressive episode is 8 months (Kovacs et al. 1984). Early treatment should be initiated

Table 1–4. TREATMENT OF CHILDHOOD DEPRESSION	
Individual psychotherapy	Group therapy
Play therapy	Out of home placement
Family therapy	Remedial education
Parent training	Pharmacotherapy

with the hope of avoiding school failure, which can exacerbate the already low self-esteem of depressed children.

Initially, it must be decided whether inpatient or outpatient treatment is needed. Treatment should be in the least restrictive environment. However, some situations require hospitalization. If a youngster is suicidal and the family is not able to provide constant monitoring, the child should be hospitalized for his or her protection. Children medicating themselves with drugs and alcohol may require hospitalization since outpatient treatment may not prevent their use of drugs or alcohol. Also, children with irritability as a major part of their depressive disorder may engage in self-destructive activities such as fights with peers or parents. Hospitalization may prevent harm to themselves or others. Diagnostic dilemmas, particularly first episodes of psychosis, may be resolved more quickly and safely in the hospital. Hospitalization provides a structured environment and gives the clinician frequent direct access to the patient. Additional behavioral observations by nursing staff, social workers, and school teachers are easily obtained and very valuable.

Pharmacotherapy

Most treatment studies have focused on pharmacotherapy. Tricyclic antidepressants, monoamine oxidase (MAO) inhibitors, and lithium carbonate have all been used to treat depressed children and adolescents. Frommer (1967) reported MAO inhibitors as the treatment of choice for children with uncomplicated depression, children with a depressive phobic anxiety state, and some enuretic depressed children. Annell (1969a, 1969b) reported lithium was successful in treating children with affective symptoms. However, the most commonly used medications in childhood depression have been the tricyclic antidepressants.

A variety of anecdotal reports have described the use of tricyclic antidepressants in children. In general, studies that have reported on a series of depressed children treated with tricyclic antidepressants fall into one of four categories: (1) diagnostic criteria for depression were not used and improvement was measured clinically; (2) diagnostic criteria were used but improvement was assessed clinically; (3) diagnostic criteria were

used and improvement was measured with structured rating scales; and (4) diagnostic criteria were used and structured rating scale scores were used to assess improvement in a double-blind, placebo-controlled fashion. Most of the studies in the third and fourth categories also employed monitoring of plasma tricyclic antidepressant levels.

An Early Study: No Diagnostic Criteria

Lucas and co-workers (1965) used amitriptyline to treat 14 children aged 10 to 17 in a residential treatment center. All were depressed and had an additional diagnosis of schizophrenia, personality disorder, or psychoneurosis. Subjects were randomly and blindly assigned to a fixed dose of amitriptyline or placebo for 6 weeks. Then the drugs were switched for an additional 6 weeks of treatment. In 6 of 10 subjects who completed the study, improvement occurred with amitriptyline when compared with placebo ($p < .05$). Children with chronically inadequate adjustment, negativism, and poor control of hostility had the worst response to amitriptyline.

Studies Using Diagnostic Criteria: No Structured Rating Scales

Ling and associates (1970) looked for depression in children aged 4 to 16 found to have unexplained headaches by the neurology staff of a large children's hospital. Of 800 consecutive children evaluated for headache, a total of 25 had unexplained headaches. Of these, 10 met Cassidy and colleagues' criteria for depression, which are similar to *DSM-III* criteria (Cassidy et al. 1957). These 10 depressed children were treated with varying doses of either amitriptyline or imipramine. Seven showed marked improvement and two showed mild improvement by clinical observation.

Kuhn and Kuhn (1972) treated 100 children and adolescents with clinical depression. Half received imipramine only, and half received imipramine plus another tricyclic antidepressant. Inpatient or outpatient status, dose of antidepressant, and duration of treatment were not specified. Improvement was determined by clinical observation. Response was rated good in 38%, 38% were improved, and 24% did not improve. Good treatment response was predicted by family history of depression, history of an episodic illness, and a mature electroencephalogram. Poor response was predicted by psychopathic personality.

A well-known study of depression in children was done by Weinberg and co-workers (1973). Children aged 6 to 12 years referred to an educational diagnostic center were evaluated for depression. Using the criteria of Feighner and co-workers (1972), modified for children, Weinberg and co-workers found 35 of 72 consecutive referral patients were depressed. Nineteen of the depressed children were treated by their primary physicians with amitriptyline (n = 3) or imipramine (n = 16). Doses ranged from 25 to 125 mg daily and were administered for at least 3 weeks. Fifteen depressed children did not receive tricyclic antidepressants. Both groups were reevaluated 3 to 7 months later. Ninety-five percent of those treated with amitriptyline or imipramine improved. Only 40% of untreated subjects improved.

Recent Studies: Diagnostic Criteria and Objective Assessment

Two methodologic advances have improved recent studies of tricyclic antidepressant efficacy in children: (1) the development of structured rating scales to assess severity of depression allowed more objective measurement of improvement than obtained by clinical judgment alone, and (2) assays that could accurately measure the plasma levels of tricyclic antidepressants were introduced. Thus, it became possible to determine equivalency of treatment and to evaluate important treatment parameters (e.g., the minimum therapeutic plasma drug level). This is important because a sevenfold variation in plasma tricyclic antidepressant levels has been reported in children taking the same dose of imipramine (Weller et al. 1982).

Puig-Antich and colleagues (1979) employed both of these new methodologies in prepubertal depressed children. Subjects were 13 outpatients aged 6 to 12 who met the Research Diagnostic Criteria (RDC) for depression. Severity was measured by combined mother and child ratings on the K-SADS. Children were treated with imipramine up to a maximum of 5 mg/kg/day. Plasma levels of the drug were measured weekly. After 6 weeks, 6 of 13 children (47%) had responded. Plasma imipramine levels

were significantly higher in responders than nonresponders: 231 ng/ml versus 128 ng/ml (p <.05). A cutoff of 146 ng/ml separated responders from nonresponders. The best response was reported at plasma levels above 200 ng/ml. No relationship was found between dose and clinical response, between dose and pretreatment rating of depression, or between plasma tricyclic antidepressant levels and baseline rating of severity of depression.

Staten and associates (1981) studied 11 children with "apparent biological depression." All met *DSM-III* criteria for major depressive episode, had a history of recurrent depressive illness, and had a first- or second-degree relative with depression and/or alcoholism. Amitriptyline (n = 10) or desipramine (n = 1) was started at a dose of 25 mg daily and increased until depression remitted. Plasma tricyclic antidepressant levels were monitored throughout treatment. All 11 children were rated as improved on the CDRS-R, the CDI, the Piers-Harris Self-Concept Scale, and the Conners' Parent Questionnaire.

Conners and Petti (1983) evaluated imipramine treatment in 21 depressed children aged 7 to 13. All were admitted to a university hospital during a 13-month period and were moderately to severely depressed on the Bellevue Index of Depression (BID). None had improved after 2 to 6 weeks of comprehensive milieu therapy. All had *DSM-II*: diagnoses of depressive neurosis, other reaction of childhood with depression, unsocialized aggressive reaction with depression, overanxious reaction, or runaway reaction.

All subjects were started on 25 mg of imipramine at bedtime. This dose was increased over 7 to 14 days to a maximum of 5 mg/kg/day or 200 mg, whichever was less. Treatment lasted 53 to 202 days. The Children's Behavior Inventory (CBI), which rates specific target behaviors in the child, was used to measure improvement. Two thirds of the subjects improved on at least one target behavior during imipramine treatment. Overall group scores improved on the CBI subscales for conceptual dysfunction, incongruous behavior, lethargy-dejection, and perceptual dysfunction and on the total score of all scales combined.

Preliminary results from a study of nortriptyline in 12 depressed children aged 6 to 11 were reported by Geller and co-workers (1983). All met both RDC and *DSM-III* criteria for depression and had a history of affective disorder or alcoholism in a first- or second-degree relative. The course of illness in these children was characterized as nonepisodic and unremitting. All were treated with nortriptyline. Each subject's dose was individually determined by predictive kinetic studies. Treatment lasted 16 weeks, and plasma drug level monitoring was used. Improvement was assessed with the CDI. The average pretreatment CDI score was 49. After treatment, all eight patients who completed the study had scores below 20, which was considered a good response.

Weller and co-workers (1982) studied the efficacy of imipramine in 31 prepubertal depressed children (23 males and 8 females) aged 6 to 12 who met *DSM-III* criteria for major depression. All had been depressed at least 30 days and required hospitalization. Depression was rated as moderate to severe. Treatment consisted of three phases:

Phase I: Two weeks of hospitalization without drug treatment. The child was observed and participated in individual, group, and family therapy.

Phase II: Three weeks of treatment with a fixed 75-mg bedtime dose of imipramine.

Phase III: Three additional weeks of imipramine treatment at an altered dose for those who had not responded at the end of Phase II.

At the beginning of phase III, the treating physician was allowed to make one dosage change based on the following guidelines. If the child had not responded, the dose was decreased to 50 mg if significant side effects were present, or the dose was increased if no significant side effects were present (maximum dose was 5 mg/kg/day).

Throughout the study, severity was assessed by three measures: (1) the CDI, a self-report scale similar to Beck's Depression Inventory for Adults; (2) CDRS, a scale similar to the Hamilton Depression Rating Scale in adults; and (3) a clinical-global impression scale in which severity of depression was rated on a 1–5 scale (1 = depression, 5 = severe depression). Also steady-state plasma monitoring of imipramine was performed using high-performance liquid chromatography.

None of the 31 children showed remission or significant improvement at the end of phase I (hospitalized, no drug treatment). At the end of phase II, 5 children (16%) were in

remission and 8 (20%) showed significant improvement. Six children were transferred to other facilities at the end of phase II and thus did not participate in phase III.

A total of 25 children completed phase III, in which children had an additional 3 weeks of imipramine therapy at an altered dose. At the end of phase III, 20 children (80%) were in remission and 2 (8%) showed significant improvement. Response was related to total plasma tricyclic antidepressant level (imipramine plus desipramine, the demethylated metabolite of imipramine). Patients whose total tricyclic antidepressant plasma levels were in the range 115 of 250 ng/ml had a response rate of 100%. Those whose levels were outside this range had a response rate of 50%. No patient with a steady-state plasma tricyclic antidepressant level above 250 ng/ml at the end of phase III had responded. Overall, 88% of those completing phase III were in remission or showed significant clinical improvement.

Other studies have reported the use of tricyclic antidepressants in the treatment of depressed children (Frommer, 1967; Stack, 1972; Polvan and Cebiroglu, 1972; Ossofsky, 1974). However, the results of these studies are more difficult to interpret. In some of the studies other medicines were given concurrently with tricyclic antidepressants. Several studies did not specify the number of subjects and/or the number who responded. Sometimes subjects who were not diagnosed as depressed were included. However, in general it was found that tricyclic antidepressants were useful in treating depressed children.

Double-Blind, Placebo-Controlled Studies

Two studies have used a double-blind, placebo-controlled methodology to assess the efficacy of imipramine in prepubertal depression. Somewhat different methodologies were employed, and different conclusions were reached. Because of the potential importance of these studies, they will be discussed in some detail.

The first study was published by Puig-Antich (1987). In this report, 38 prepubertal children completed a double-blind protocol. Twenty-two received placebo, and 16 received imipramine. All met RDC criteria for major depressive disorder as determined by two psychiatrists after a 2-week diagnostic assessment. Assessments were carried out using the K-SADS. Subjects included both inpatients and outpatients. Exclusion criteria were used to eliminate subjects with conditions that could interfere with the study. There were no differences in race, age, sex, socioeconomic status, body weight, or height between the imipramine and placebo groups. Assignment to placebo or imipramine was done in a random fashion.

After the 2-week drug-free diagnostic assessment, subjects were begun on imipramine or placebo given three times daily. The initial dose was 1.5 mg/kg/day. The dose was raised to 5 mg/kg/day in a stepwise fashion according to a predetermined schedule. After day 12, the dose was held constant until day 35, when the study ended. This schedule was monitored by a pediatrician who could alter the dosage schedule if there were significant side effects. The mean final imipramine dose was 136.8 mg (4.35 mg/kg), whereas all placebo-treated children received the maximum 5-mg/kg dose. Plasma level monitoring was employed throughout the study.

Improvement was rated using the K-SADS-P (parent version of K-SADS) for the entire fifth week of treatment, integrating information from all sources. Raters were blind to plasma levels and to the nature of the pills prescribed. Response was defined as a score on the scales for depressed mood and anhedonia of 2 (slight, of questionable significance) or less. Overall, 56% (9/16) of the imipramine-treated group responded and 68% (15/22) of the placebo-treated group responded. These response rates were not statistically different. Those who responded to imipramine had a higher mean plasma tricyclic antidepressant level (284 ng/ml) than those who did not respond (145 ng/ml).

The authors summarized their findings by stating that the hypothesis that imipramine is effective in prepubertal depression was not supported by their study. However, they further stated that their high placebo response rate made any other finding almost impossible. Imipramine and desipramine levels were linearly correlated with clinical response to the drug.

A preliminary report on another placebo-controlled study of imipramine in prepubertal depressed children has also been published. This study by Preskorn and colleagues (1987) used plasma level monitoring, the DST, structured rating scales, and a double-blind design. Subjects were 22 hospitalized depressed prepubertal children aged 6 to 12. All had been depressed for at least 30 days and met *DSM-III* criteria for major depressive episode. None had significant medical problems.

After a baseline evaluation of approximately 1 week, children who were unimproved were randomly assigned to imipramine or placebo. The severity of depression was rated with the CDI, CDRS-R, and CGI. The DST was performed for all subjects. Treatment was for 6 weeks. At the end of 2 weeks, plasma levels were used by a laboratory psychiatrist unaware of the patient's clinical state to make a dose adjustment so that the child's combined plasma desipramine and imipramine level was 125 to 250 ng/ml. Severity of depression was rated at 3 weeks and at 6 weeks. The results indicated that the response to imipramine treatment was better than with placebo at 3 weeks and 6 weeks of treatment. This finding was even more pronounced for subjects who had non-suppressed DST results.

Before a child is treated with a tricyclic antidepressant a complete blood cell count with differential; thyroid function tests; determination of blood urea nitrogen, serum creatinine, and electrolyte levels; liver function tests; and an electrocardiogram should be performed (Table 1–5). A properly performed DST in which the standard exclusion and inclusion criteria are carefully followed may prove useful in monitoring treatment. Children whose results of a DST remain abnormal despite clinical improvement may be at a greater risk for relapse.

Plasma tricyclic antidepressant monitoring is useful in children and adolescents (Table 1–6). It helps ensure compliance and helps monitor for cardiotoxicity and neurotoxicity. Children with plasma levels greater than 500 ng/ml are at a higher risk for developing increased PR interval, ST segment suppression, and increased diastolic blood pressure. A study by Preskorn and colleagues (1987) showed that children with high plasma tricyclic antidepressant levels can develop a toxic state that might be misinterpreted as unresponsiveness to drug treatment. This misinterpretation might result in incorrectly increasing the dose of tricyclic antidepressant when a reduction is needed. Unfortunately,

Table 1–5. LABORATORY TESTS	
Baseline	**Follow-up**
Blood urea nitrogen	Post dexamethasone: 20 μg/kg
Glucose	Cortisol: 8 AM, 4 PM
Sodium	Blood levels: tricyclic antidepressants, lithium
Potassium	carbonate
Chloride	Urine osmolality for lithium treatment
Carbon dioxide content	
Calcium	
Magnesium	
Cholesterol	
Triglycerides	
Creatine phosphokinase	
Alkaline phosphatase	
Serum glutamic pyruvic transaminase	
Serum glutamic oxaloacetic transaminase	
Bilirubin: direct and indirect	
Lactate dehydrogenase	
Total protein	
Albumin	
Triiodothyronine (radioactive uptake)	
Thyronine (radioimmunoassay)	
Thyroid-stimulating hormone	
Complete blood cell count	
Electrocardiogram	
Electroencephalogram	
Dexamethasone suppression test: 20 μg/kg at 11 PM (0.5 mg prepubertal children; 1 mg adolescents)	
Post DST Cortisol: 8 AM and 4 PM	

wide variations in plasma levels exist between children receiving the same fixed dose. Thus, actual dose is not a good measure of adequacy of treatment. For example, if the total daily dose of imipramine is 75 mg or less, 80% of depressed children will not respond.

If tricyclic antidepressants are to be used, parents should be informed that imipramine and other tricyclic agents have not been approved by the Food and Drug Administration for treating depressed children younger than 12 years old. Parents should also be taught to take the child's resting pulse and to carefully observe their children to spot potential complications. This is particularly important in the hot summer months when outdoor activities are frequent. Children can also be taught to monitor themselves for side effects without provoking undue concern on their part.

Imipramine has been given in a single dose at bedtime or in multiple doses throughout the day. The daily dose normally should not exceed 5 mg/kg. However, doses as high as 7 mg/kg have been used with close monitoring of electrocardiographic and vital signs. The average dose in one treatment study of prepubertal children was 150 mg/day, although some patients required doses of 200 mg/day or more. However, the plasma level and not the actual dose is most important in predicting response. Caution should be used in increasing the dose in obese children since they may tend to accumulate the drug in fatty tissue, which could cause complications. A typical dosing regimen is a starting dose of 1.5 mg/kg/day that is increased by 1.0 to 1.5 mg/kg every third day.

As mentioned earlier, the patient should be assessed for side effects. Both children and parents can be asked whether side effects are noted. Pulse, lying and sitting blood pressures, serial electrocardiograms, serial and plasma drug levels should be monitored. Prolongation of PR interval on the electrocardiogram should not exceed 0.21 second, QRS

Table 1–6. TRICYCLIC ANTIDEPRESSANT PLASMA LEVEL MONITORING RATIONALE

1. Check compliance.
2. Maximize clinical response.
3. Avoid toxicity.
4. Minimize cost.
5. Aid in avoiding medicolegal problems.

complex should not be prolonged by more than 30% over baseline, resting pulse should not exceed 130 beats per minute, and blood pressure should not exceed 140/90 mm Hg. If these parameters are exceeded, the dose can be altered as clinically indicated. Reported response rates of tricyclic antidepressants in adolescents are somewhat less (i.e., in the range of 40%). Some investigators have postulated that the high levels of sex hormones that occur during adolescence may decrease the efficacy of tricyclic agents.

Lithium carbonate is another medication that should be considered in the treatment of depressed children and adolescents. Although less studied than the tricyclic antidepressants in depressed children, lithium has been used to treat tricyclic antidepressant–resistant depression as well as bipolar illness and aggressive-impulsive behavior. A dosage guide for lithium carbonate for prepubertal children based on weight and body surface area can be used to select an appropriate dose (Weller et al. 1986a). Prior to initiation of lithium treatment, a complete blood cell count with differential, electrolyte studies, liver function tests, determination of blood urea nitrogen and creatinine concentrations, creatinine clearance, thyroid function tests, urine osmolality, and a pregnancy test in females should be done. Throughout treatment, lithium should be monitored very carefully since its long-term effect on growing children is unknown. It is also deposited in bone, but whether this is of clinical significance is not known. Lithium has the advantage of being less sedating than neuroleptic drugs. Fortunately, children and adolescents seem to tolerate lithium better than adults.

There are yet no published reports defining the optimal therapeutic range of lithium for children. However, lithium levels higher than 1.4 mEq/L should probably be avoided. Side effects and clinical response should be taken into account in deciding dosage changes. Once a good response has been obtained, treatment both with tricyclic antidepressants and lithium should be continued for 4 to 6 months following clinical response. The dose should then be tapered and discontinued. Some children show a flulike syndrome with nausea, vomiting, abdominal pain, and feelings of tiredness after abrupt withdrawal of a tricyclic agent. This is often misinterpreted by parents as recurrence of depression.

Treating children with affective disorders with medication alone may not always yield maximum improvement. Clinical experience indicates that concomitant group therapy, social skills training, family therapy, and individual therapy may also be of benefit. However, studies proving this have not been published.

CONCLUSIONS

Even though the criteria for diagnosing child and adolescent affective disorders are similar to those for adults, assessment can be difficult in this age group. Previously, child psychiatrists relied almost exclusively on parental reports to diagnose children and adolescents. Children were rarely directly questioned about their symptoms. It was assumed parents knew everything about their children. However, it is increasingly clear that children can be important informants regarding their symptomatology and provide information unknown to their parents. Age- and stage-relevant questions should be asked when probing for mood disorders. Among very young children, nonverbal communication such as sad or apathetic facies, stooped posture, and slow tempo of speech may play an important role in diagnosis.

Many researchers are now hypothesizing that unipolar depression may not exist in prepubertal children. Those children presenting with prepubertal unipolar depression may, in fact, have bipolar illness.

In the 1980s, child psychiatrists have shown increased interest in vigorously diagnosing mood disorders in children and adolescents. Clinical interviews, structured/semi-structured interviews, and, now in a preliminary fashion, biological markers can be used to aid in diagnosis. For example, cortisol secretion and the DST have been used to provide baseline measures prior to beginning pharmacologic treatment. Thus, the research of affective disorders in children and adolescents begun over the past 10 years is now providing useful information as to the diagnosis and treatment of affective disorders in children and adolescents, confirming the notion that "research of today is the treatment for tomorrow."

References

Akiskal, H. S. 1986. A developmental perspective on recurrent mood disorders: A review of studies in man. *Psychopharmacol. Bull.* 22:579.

Akiskal, H. S., and Weller, E. B. 1989. Mood disorders and suicide in children and adolescents. In Kaplan, H. I., and Sadock, B. J. (eds.): *Comprehensive Textbook of Psychiatry/V. Baltimore: Williams & Wilkins.* p. 1981.

American Psychiatric Association. 1987. *Diagnostic and Statistical Manual of Mental disorders*, 3rd ed., revised. Washington, D.C.: American Psychiatric Association.

Annell, A. L. 1969a. Lithium in the treatment of children and adolescents. *Acta Psychiatr. Scand. [Suppl.]* 207:19–30.

Annell, A. L. 1969b. Manic-depressive illness in children and effect of treatment with lithium carbonate. *Acta Paedopsychiatry* 36:292–301.

Bober, J. F., Weller, E. B., Weller, R. A., et al. 1988. Correlation of serum and salivary cortisol levels in prepubertal school-aged children. *J. Am. Child Adolesc. Psychiatry.* 27, 6:748–750.

Casat, C. D., Arana, G. W., and Powell, K., 1989. The DST in children and adolescents with major depressive disorder. Am. J. Psychiatry 146:503–507.

Cassidy, W. L., Flanagan, N. B., Spellman, N., et al. 1957. Clinical observations in manic depressive disease. *J.A.M.A.* 164:535–1545.

Conners, C. K., and Petti, T. 1983. Imipramine therapy of depressed children: Methodologic considerations. *Psychopharmacol. Bull.* 19:65–68.

Cytryn, L., and McKnew, D. H. Jr. 1987. Childhood depression: An update. In Call, J. D., Cohen, R. L., Harrison, S. I., et al. (eds.): *Basic Handbook of Child Psychiatry.* New York: Basic Books. vol. 5, p. 286.

Feighner, J. P., Robin, E., Guze, S. B., et al. 1972. Diagnostic criteria for use in psychiatric research. *Arch. Gen. Psychiatry* 26:57–63.

Frommer, E. A. 1967. Treatment of childhood depression with antidepressant drugs. *Br. Med. J.* 1:729–732.

Geller, B., Perel, J. M., Knitter, E. F., et al. 1983. Nortriptyline in major depressive disorders in children: Response, steady-state plasma levels, predictive kinetics, and pharmacokinetics. *Psychopharmacol. Bull.* 19:62–64.

Kashani, J. H., and Sherman, D. D. 1988. Childhood depression: Epidemiology, etiological models, and treatment implications. *Integrative Psychiatry.* 6(1):1–8.

Kovacs, M., Feinbert, T. L., Crouse, M. A., et al. 1984. Recovery in childhood depressive disorders: A longitudinal prospective study. *Arch. Gen. Psychiatry* 41:229.

Kuhn, V., and Kuhn, R. 1972. Drug therapy for depression in children. In Annell, A. L. (ed.): *Depressive States in Childhood and Adolescence.* New York: John Wiley & Sons.

Ling, W., Oftedal, G., and Weinberg, W. 1970. Depressive illness in childhood presenting as severe headache. *Am. J. Dis. Child.* 120:122–124.

Lucas, A. R., Lockett, H. J., and Grimm, F. 1965. Amitriptyline in childhood depression. *Dis. Nerv. Syst.* 26:105–110.

Ossofsky, H. J. 1974. Endogenous depression in infancy and childhood. *Compr. Psychiatry* 15:19–25.

Polvan, O., and Cebiroglu, R. 1972. Treatment with pharmacologic agents in childhood depressions. In Annell, A. L. (ed.): *Depressive States in Childhood and Adolescence.* New York: John Wiley & Sons.

Poznanski, E. O. 1982. The clinical phenomenology of childhood depression. *Am. J. Orthopsychiatry* 52:308.

Preskorn, S. H., Weller, E. B., Hughes, C. W., et al. 1987. Depression in prepubertal children: Dexameth-asone nonsuppression predicts differential response to imipramine vs. placebo. *Psychopharmacol. Bull.* 23:128.

Puig-Antich, J. 1987. Affective disorders in children and adolescents: Diagnostic validity and psychobiology. In Meltzer, H. Y. (ed.): *Psychopharmacology—The Third Generation of Progress*, p. 843. New York: Raven Press.

Puig-Antich, J., Perel, J., and Lupatkin, W. 1979. Plasma levels of imipramine and desipramine in clinical response in prepubertal major depressive disorder. *J. Am. Acad. Child Psychiatry* 18:616–627.

Stack, J. J. 1972. Chemotherapy in childhood depression. In Annell, A. L. (ed.): *Depressive States in Childhood and Adolescence.* New York: John Wiley & Sons.

Staten, R. D., Wilson, H., and Brumback, R. A. 1981. Cognitive improvement associated with tricyclic antidepressant treatment of childhood major depressive illness. *Percept. Mot. Skills* 53:219–234.

Weinberg, W. A., Rutman, J., Sullivan, L., et al. 1973. Depression in children referred to an educational diagnostic center: Diagnosis and treatment. *J. Pediatr.* 80:1065–1072.

Weissman, M. M., Gershon, E. S., Kidd, K. K., et al. 1984. Psychiatric disorders in the relatives of probands with affective disorders: The Yale–NIMH collaborative family study. *Arch. Gen. Psychiatry* 41:13.

Weller, E. B., Weller, R. A., and Fristad, M. A. 1984. Historical and theoretical perspectives on childhood depression. In Weller, E. B., and Weller, R. A. (eds.): *Major Depressive Disorders in Children.* Washington, D. C.: American Psychiatric Press, Inc., monograph series.

Weller, E. B., Weller, R. A., and Fristad, M. A. 1986a. Lithium dosage guide for prepubertal children: A preliminary report. *J. Am. Acad. Child Psychiatry* 25:92–95.

Weller, E. B., Weller, R. A., Fristad, M. A., et al. 1986b. Dexamethasone suppression test and clinical outcome in prepubertal depressed children. *Am. J. Psychiatry* 143:1469–1470.

Weller, E. B., Weller, R. A., Fristad, M. A., et al. 1987. Depressive symptoms in bereaved prepubertal children. American Academy of Child and Adolescent Psychiatry Annual Meeting, Washington, D. C., Oct. 21–25.

Weller, R. A., Weller, E. B., Cohen, L., et al. 1988. Family psychopathology in depressed children. Society of Biological Psychiatry. Annual Meeting, Montreal, Canada, May 7–11.

Weller, E. B., and Weller, R. A., Preskorn, S. H., and Glotzback, R. K. 1982. Steady-state plasma imipramine levels in prepubertal depressed children. *Am. J. Psychiatry* 139:506–508.

Weller, E. B., and Weller, R. A. 1988. Neuroendocrine changes in affectively ill children and adolescents. In Brown, W. (ed.): *Psychiatr. Clin. North Am.* 6(1):41–54.

Weller, R. A., Weller, E. B., Fristad, M. A., et al. 1988. Family psychopathology in depressed children. 141st Annual Meeting of the American Psychiatric Association, Montreal, Canada, May 7–11.

Wender, P. H. Kety, S. S., Rosenthal, D., et al. 1986. Psychiatric disorders in the biological and adoptive families of adopted individuals with affective disorders. *Arch. Gen. Psychiatry* 43:923.

Bipolar Disorders in Children and Adolescents

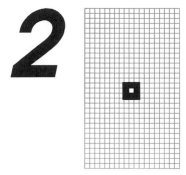

GABRIELLE A. CARLSON, M.D.

Kraepelin (1921) opens his famous treatise on manic-depressive insanity with the following definition:

Manic depressive insanity . . . includes on one hand the whole domain of so called *periodic and circular insanity*, on the other hand *simple mania*, the greater part of the morbid states termed melancholia and also a not inconsiderable number of cases of *amentia* (confusional or delirious insanity). Lastly we include here certain slight and slightest colourings of mood, some of them periodic, some of them continuously morbid, which on the one hand are to be regarded as the rudiment of more severe disorders, on the other hand pass over without sharp boundary into the domain of *personal predisposition*.

A review of the two most recent editions of the American Psychiatric Association's *Diagnostic and Statistical Manual of Mental Disorders (DSM-III* and *DSM-III-R)* (1980, 1987) reflects Kraepelin's categorizations. "Circular insanity" is called bipolar disorder and includes "simple mania"; "melancholia" alone is described under major depressive episodes. "Continuously morbid moods" are perhaps dysthymic disorders. The category "periodic colourings of mood," described both then and now as cyclothymia, is considerably less precise because the boundaries between disorder and "personal predisposi-

tion" require consensus about duration of episode and impairment of functioning. Current *DSM-III-R* nosology is summarized in Table 2–1.

In this chapter bipolar disorders are discussed as they specifically apply to children and adolescents. References to adult bipolar disorders are made where necessary, but the reader is encouraged to refer to textbooks of general psychiatry and cited reviews for more detail on this subject.

HISTORICAL BACKGROUND

The subject of depression and bipolar disorders in children and adolescents that has captivated mental health researchers over the past 15 years is not really new. Interest in juvenile bipolar disorders has waxed and waned over the years, and it appears that the tension between Kraepelinian empiricism and antidiagnostic and psychoanalytical theorizations has had an impact on which school of thought had ascendancy at any given time.

Several definitional issues have contributed to preventing meaningful progress in identifying and describing manic-depression in children. One was specifying whether

Table 2–1. MOOD DISORDERS CLASSIFICATION—DSM-III-R

Type	Description
Bipolar Disorders	
Bipolar disorder	One or more manic
Mild	episodes usually with
Moderate	major depression
Severe	
Without psychosis	
With psychosis	
Mood congruent	
Mood	
incongruent	
Cyclothymia	Hypomanic episode* and
	numerous periods with
	depressive symptoms
Bipolar disorder NOS†	Includes bipolar II–
	hypomanic episodes
	with full major
	depressive episodes
Depressive Disorders	
Major depression	One or more major
Mild	depressive episodes
Moderate	
Severe	
With or without	
psychotic features	
Melancholic type	
Chronic	
Dysthymia (in children)	One-year history of
	depressed more days
	than not

*Like mania but not severe enough to cause impairment and delusions never present.

†Not otherwise specified.

(From American Psychiatric Association. 1987. *Diagnostic and Statistical Manual of Mental Disorders*, 3rd ed., revised. Washington, D.C.: American Psychiatric Association.)

"childhood" included adolescence, and another was distinguishing cases in which *mania* occurred (until the relatively recent unipolar-bipolar dichotomy, all cases of serious depression were also considered manic-depressive illness). The final issue was establishing what constitutes a psychosis, since manic-depression was called a psychosis in contrast to a neurosis. By the time Anthony and Scott wrote their seminal paper in 1960, there was a range of views from one extreme, that is, that "manic-depression is a psychodynamic entity, recognizable in earliest infancy and merging with normal development" to the other psychoanalytical attitude that children's ego and superego structures were too immature to sustain either a severe depression or its defense, mania. There were, of course, still proponents of the notion that juvenile manic-depression was an early-onset

variant of the adult form occurring because of "heavy genetic loading and intense environmental experience" (Anthony and Scott 1960). Although it is the last assumption that currently prevails, it is not yet clear if there are age- and development-specific features of juvenile bipolar disorder with which clinicians treating children should be familiar.

Anthony and Scott (1960) advanced the cause of juvenile manic-depression by defining "childhood" as referring to prepubertal children and establishing a set of stringent criteria (Table 2–2) for manic-depression that were applied subsequently to a literature search dating back to 1884. Of 63 cases reviewed, only 3 met the criteria. All three of these patients were aged 11. (The remaining were rejected usually because only depres-

Table 2–2. JUVENILE MANIC-DEPRESSION CRITERIA

1. Evidence of an abnormal psychiatric state at some time of the illness approximating the classic clinical description as given by Kraepelin, Bleuler, Meyer, and others
2. Evidence of a "positive" family history suggesting a manic-depressive "diathesis"
3. Evidence of an early tendency to a manic-depressive type of reaction as manifested in:
   a. A cyclothymic tendency with gradually increasing amplitude and length of the "oscillations"
   b. Delirious manic or depressive outbursts occurring during pyrexial illnesses
4. Evidence of a recurrent or periodic illness. This entails the observation of at least two episodes, separated by a period of time (gauged in months or years) and regarded as clinically similar. There should be diagnostic agreement by different clinical judges on the nature of any one episode and diagnostic agreement by different clinical judges on the identity of different episodes
5. Evidence of diphasic illness showing swings of pathologic dimension from states of elation to states of depression and vice versa
6. Evidence of an endogenous illness indicating that the phases of the illness alternate with minimal reference to environmental events
7. Evidence of a severe illness as indicated by a need for inpatient treatment, heavy sedation, and electroconvulsive therapy
8. Evidence of an abnormal underlying personality of an extroverted type as demonstrated by objective test procedures
9. An absence of features that might indicate other abnormal conditions, such as schizophrenia or organic states
10. Evidence of current, not retrospective, assessments

(Modified from Anthony, E. J., and Scott, P. 1960. Manic-depressive psychosis in childhood. *J. Child Psychol. Psychiatry* 1:53–72.)

sions were reported or the severity criteria were not met. Anthony and Scott also described their own case, a 12-year-old prepubertal boy whose manic and depressive episodes continued into adulthood, confirming that classically defined childhood manic-depression is simply an early-onset variant of the disorder.

DEFINITION

In its clearest form, bipolar disorder can be diagnosed quite easily. The criteria and associated symptoms for mania and depression are obvious. Episodes of depression are marked by the relatively acute onset of a withdrawn, slowed, anergic state described by articulate patients as accompanied by feeling hopeless, dysphoric, and even occasionally dead inside. These periods are usually punctuated by states of exhilaration, which may proceed to frenetic energy, overcommitment, and volatile behavior. There may or may not be environmental events that trigger such behavior, and a minority of such patients may notice that seasonal changes are correlated with their high and low mood states. Although many personality components are exaggerated during manic and depressive episodes, there are clear distinctions between normality and disorder. Diagnostic confusion occurs at the boundaries of severity of the disorder. In milder forms in which mood oscillations never become extreme, episodes themselves are difficult to delineate. Impairment may be slight or difficult to differentiate from premorbid functioning. Relatively mild depressions are seen as "adjustment reactions" by many clinicians who are reluctant to diagnose affective disorder or who see such disorders as part of "adolescent turmoil." The distinction between personality disorder and cyclothymia is also difficult. If the person's behavior eventuates in substance abuse, as is sometimes seen, the complication overshadows the primary disorder. Finally, at the other end of the continuum, either the depression or the mania may be so severe that the patient is confused and psychotic such that the affective components of the episode pale by comparison to the other more flagrant aspects. At that juncture, confusion with schizophrenia and organic brain syndrome is common.

In the past 15 years several attempts have been made to refine and objectify what were essentially Kraepelin's observations. As can be seen from Table 2–3, there is considerable uniformity about the core symptoms of both manic and depressive phases. As noted above, divergence occurs at the boundaries where there is less certainty (e.g., how long symptoms need to be present to be considered truly an "episode"; how much impairment is necessary to be considered pathologic, and what the exclusionary criteria should be).

In addition to delineating specific diagnostic criteria, psychiatric researchers have also developed instruments called structured interviews. These instruments were constructed to increase the reliability of psychiatric diagnosis. The interview content makes certain that all psychiatric disorders are inquired after, that all informants are asked questions the same way each time, and, when possible, specific guidelines are established for counting whether a symptom was truly present or absent.

For children and adolescents, the two most commonly used interviews to diagnose bipolar disorders are the childhood version of the Schedule for Affective Disorders and Schizophrenia (K-SADS) and subsequent revisions (Chambers et al. 1985) and the Diagnostic Interview for Children and Adolescents (DICA) (Herjanic and Reich 1982). There are a number of other interviews as well (see Orvaschel 1985 for review). All are equally useful to diagnose episodes of depression, hypomania, or mania if they are occurring at the time of interview. In order to understand the relationship between maturation, the onset and offset of episodes, and the chronology of episodes, stressors, and euthymia, however, it is necessary to obtain a longitudinal history from both parent and child as well as ascertaining the presence of specific signs and symptoms.

EPIDEMIOLOGY

The determination of how frequently bipolar disorders occur in the general population depends on how rigorously one defines bipolar disorder. For example, in a study of 150 nonpsychiatrically referred 14- to 16-year olds using the DICA and the Research Diagnostic Criteria (RDC) for mania and bipolar disorder, Carlson and Kashani (1988) re-

Table 2–3. COMPARISON OF THREE CURRENT SETS OF CRITERIA FOR MAJOR MOOD DISORDERS

	Research Diagnostic Criteria (RDC) (Spitzer et al. 1978)	DSM-III (APA 1980)	DSM-III-R (APA 1987)
Major Depression			
Duration	At least 1 week (2 weeks—definite)	2 weeks	2 weeks
Mood	Dysphoric mood (prominent and relatively persistent) *or* pervasive loss of interest or pleasure	Dysphoric mood *or* loss of interest or pleasure	Depressed mood *or* loss of interest or pleasure
Depressive behavior	Poor appetite or weight loss *or* increased appetite and weight gain	Poor appetite or weight loss	Significant weight loss or gain without so intending
	Sleep difficulty or sleeping too much	Same as RDC	Same as RDC
	Loss of energy, fatigability	Same as RDC	Same as RDC
	Psychomotor agitation or retardation	Same as RDC	Same as RDC
	Loss of interest (including social contact or sex)	Loss of interest (need not be pervasive)	
	Feeling of self-reproach or excessive guilt	Worthlessness, self-reproach, guilt	Same as *DSM-III*
	Diminished ability to think or concentrate	Same as RDC	Same as RDC
	Recurrent thoughts of death or suicide or any suicidal behavior	Same as RDC	Same as RDC
Number of behaviors needed	Definite—5 Probable—4	4	5
Severity	Sought help; took medication; or impaired functioning at home, school, or family	Not described	Not described
Exclusion	Schizophrenia	Schizophrenia Organic brain syndrome	Schizophrenia
Mania			
Duration	1 week (any duration if hospitalized)	1 week (or any duration if hospitalization is necessary)	Not stated
Mood	Elevated or irritable, prominent and persistent	Elevated, expansive, or irritable mood	Elevated, expansive, or irritable mood
Concomitant behavior	More active than usual, more talkative, or pressure to keep talking	Increased activity or physical restlessness, more talkative or pressure to keep talking	Increased goal-directed activity or psychomotor agitation Same as *DSM-III*
	Inflated self-esteem (grandiosity that may be delusional)	Inflated self-esteem (grandiosity)	Same as *DSM-III*
	Flight of ideas or racing thoughts	Same as RDC	Same as RDC
	Decreased need for sleep	Same as RDC	Same as RDC
	Distractibility	Same as RDC	Same as RDC
	Excessive involvement in activities without recognizing potential for painful consequences	Excessive involvement in activities that have high potential for painful consequences	Excessive involvement in pleasurable activities that have high potential for painful consequences
Number of above items needed	3	3 (4 if mood only irritable)	Same as for *DSM-III*
Severity	Any 1 of the following: Social incapacitation Inability to communicate meaningfully Hospitalization	Not stated	Marked impairment in occupational functioning, social activities, or relationships; hospitalization
Exclusion	Drug-induced states, schizophrenia	Schizophrenia, organic mental disorder, drug-induced states	Schizophrenia, organic mental disorder, drug-induced states or organic factor that precipitated it

ported lifetime prevalence of bipolar disorder to be 0.6%. If severity of impairment were ignored (as in *DSM-III*), however (thus downgrading episodes of hypomania), the corresponding rate increased to approximately 7.3%. An even higher rate was obtained (13.3%) if duration of illness was ignored in making the diagnosis (*DSM-III-R*). The lifetime rate for adolescent major depression was 4.7%. This compares with general adult population rates of 0.6% to 1% for a manic episode (and thus, presumably, bipolar disorder) and 4.1% to 7.5% for a major depressive episode (Robins et al. 1984).

ETIOLOGY

The cause(s) of bipolar disorder is unknown. The considerable literature on biological markers in affective disorders (see Potter et al. 1986 for review) has not included children or adolescents. What data exist have focused on major depression and have been described in Chapter 1.

Although the etiology of bipolar disorder is unknown, it is clear that of all the psychiatric disorders, family genetic factors play a significant role and the relevance of this to children and adolescents is considerable. The familial nature of the disorder has been recognized almost as long as manic depression has been recognized. Specific attempts to understand the genetics have taken a number of approaches.

1. Twin studies have examined the higher concordance in monozygotic versus dizygotic twins. Nurnberger and Gershon (1982) summarize the results of studies examining 424 twin pairs and report an overall 65% concordance in monozygotic twins versus a 14% concordance in dizygotic twins.

2. Adoption studies have explored the higher rates of bipolar disorder in the biological versus adoptive relatives of probands with bipolar disorder reared by adoptive families from birth. Mendlewicz and Rainer (1977) reporting data exclusively from adoptees with bipolar illness found a rate of 31% of bipolar and bipolar spectrum disorders in biological parents versus 2% in adoptive parents of probands with bipolar disorder.

3. Studies of rates of bipolar and unipolar affective disorder in relatives of probands with bipolar disorder confirm the expectation that the number of relatives at risk for bipolar disorder will be concentrated in families of the probands. Rice and colleagues (1987) summarize data on morbidity risk for bipolar disorder from relatives of probands with bipolar probands and with unipolar disease. They report a range of 1.5% to 10.2% for relatives of probands with bipolar disorder and 0.3% to 4.1% for probands with unipolar disorder. (Morbidity risks for each in relatives of normal probands vary from 0.2% to 1.8% for bipolar disorder and 0.7% to 5.8% for unipolar depression.)

The National Institute of Mental Health Collaborative Study has reexamined the rates of psychiatric disorder among probands with bipolar disorder using systematic interviews of probands and relatives and specific diagnostic criteria (modified RDC) and separating out bipolar and bipolar spectrum disorders (Andreasen et al. 1987). A summary of these findings is presented in Table 2–4. One can conclude that bipolar disorder does occur more frequently in families of probands with bipolar disorder.

4. Risk studies examine offspring (rather than ancestors) of subjects with bipolar disorder with the hypothesis that these children will have higher rates of bipolar disorders than offspring of controls. Risk studies have suffered from small sample sizes, inadequate attention to polarity of parental affective disorder, and lack of control group. Findings range from high rates of specific affective disorders in offspring (LaRoche et al. 1981—23% of 39 children had dysthymic or anxiety disorders; Decina et al. 1983—26% of children with major and minor depressions compared with 6% in controls) to those with high rates of nonspecific disorders (Gershon et al., 1985).

5. Linkage studies attempt to isolate specific types of genetic transmission. Although a number of linkages have been tested (most notably X-linkage, HLA haplotype transmission, and C-Harvey-ras-1 and insulin gene segments on chromosome 11), none has been consistently replicated. The most precise studies using restriction fragment length polymorphisms (isolated DNA fragments whose inheritance can be identified as coming from a particular parent) have found convincing evidence for close linkage of a "gene" on chromosome 11 for bipolar disorder in family studies of the Old Order Amish. This has not been replicated with other family pedigrees, suggesting considerable het-

Table 2–4. FREQUENCY OF BIPOLAR SPECTRUM DISORDERS IN ALL RELATIVES OF COLLABORATIVE STUDY PROBANDS

Diagnoses in Relatives	Percent of Relatives			
	Bipolar I Probands	Bipolar II Probands	Schizoaffective Bipolar Probands	Unipolar Probands
No. of probands	151	76	37	330
No. of all relatives	867	392	179	1,872
Schizoaffective bipolar*	0.3	0	0	0.1
Bipolar I	5.8	2.9	2.8	0.6
Unipolar	22.3	30.9	22.3	25.7
Alcoholism	15.1	13.8	21.2	15.0
Never mentally ill	51.1	44.4	52.5	52.6

*Schizoaffective is defined in these data as meeting criteria for bipolar I disorder but with mood incongruent psychotic features.

(From Andreasen, N. C., Rice, J., Endicott, J., et al. 1987. Familial rates of affective disorder. *Arch. Gen. Psychiatry* 44:461–469. Copyright © 1987, American Medical Association.)

erogeneity in the transmission of bipolar disorders (see Blehar et al. 1988 for review).

6. There are undoubtedly other risk factors accruing to children who grow up with mentally ill parents. In fact, a small study comparing both rearing practices of parents with bipolar disorder and responses of their toddlers suggested differences from normal controls (see Cytryn et al. 1986 for review). Although the small sample size and inherent methodologic problems limit the impact of the findings, the study serves to demonstrate that the extent to which the environment interacts with genetic predisposition to covert vulnerability to disorder may be of considerable interest. For example, it is possible that environment–gene interactions account for the so-called cohort effect.

The cohort effect as it applies to both unipolar and bipolar disorders refers to the seemingly progressive increase in the lifetime rates of major depression observed over the past 70 years. Gershon and co-workers (1987) report that the lifetime prevalence of any affective disorder among relatives of probands with bipolar disorder born before 1940 is 21.7% versus 40.6% in those born after 1940. The cohort effect remains, even allowing for percent of relatives available for interview and without a change in rates of familial aggregation in families without bipolar disorder. Not only are there higher rates of disorder among relatives of probands with a younger age at onset, the age at onset per se was found to be decreasing in successively more recent cohorts. Although there are no unequivocal explanations of these findings, the implication is that bipolar disorder in

children and adolescents will be seen with increasing frequency and that this early age at onset is a hallmark of more severe disorder, at least as measured by its penetrance in other relatives.

The association between young age at onset and higher morbidity risk among relatives has been substantiated by several reports. For example, comparison can be made with the data presented in Table 2–4: (1) Dwyer and Delong (1987) found a lifetime rate of bipolar illness of 20% in their bipolar sample of 20 children aged 4 to 18, although relative diagnoses were not obtained blind to proband diagnosis and information about relatives was gathered by history from, rather than by direct interview of, purportedly ill relatives. (2) Data from the Old Order Amish reveal that 57% of 38 patients with bipolar illness experienced their first episode before age 20. The morbidity risk for all affective disorder in the first-degree relatives of this sample is 20.3%, and for bipolar I and bipolar II disorders it is 9.5% (Egeland et al. 1987). (3) The most convincing data come from a study of adolescent patients with bipolar illness by Strober and colleagues (1988). These investigators report that overall rates of major affective disorder in first-degree relatives of adolescents with bipolar illness were similar to those reported in the collaborative study (i.e., 29.6% and 28.1% in the study of Strober and colleagues and the collaborative study, respectively), but that the rates of bipolar disorder per se were significantly higher (i.e., 14.8% vs. 5.8%). More striking is the fact that those adolescents with the earliest age at onset (i.e., prepubertal) had the most affected relatives both for all affective disorders (44.1% vs. 23.5%) and for rates of bipolar disorder in first-degree relatives (29.4% vs. 8.6%). An indication of the severity of the disorder among adolescents with prepubertal onset of bipolar disease was their poor response to lithium. The findings of Strober and colleagues suggest the possibility of a different form of bipolar disorder (i.e., characterized by earlier onset, greater penetrance, and poor lithium response), a more severe disorder, or a disorder in which genetic and environmental effects interact to produce an earlier onset and poorer response to conventional treatment methods.

CLINICAL PICTURE AND DIFFERENTIAL DIAGNOSIS

Age at Onset

Although most studies report mean age at onset of bipolar disorder as being in the late 20s or early 30s, it is clear that this disorder is most likely to begin in adolescence and young adulthood. Loranger and Levine (1978) found that by age 19, 20% of their sample of 200 hospitalized patients had become symptomatic. This rate doubled over the next 5 years and by age 24, 33% of their sample had been hospitalized. The time between symptom onset and hospitalization is generally 3 years. Similar findings have been reported by Joyce (1984) (Fig. 2–1).

Symptom Characteristics Related to Age

The more closely episodes of mania and depression adhere to criteria presented in Tables 2–2 and 2–3, the less equivocal the diagnosis regardless of age. Several confounding features particularly bedevil clinicians in diagnosing bipolar disorders among younger subjects. For example, it is not always clear at the time of the first episode that a bipolar course will evolve. As was noted earlier, if the first symptoms are depressive, they may be mild and mistaken for adjustment reactions or adolescent "turmoil." Similarly, if somatic symptoms predominate, the episode may be misdiagnosed as a physical illness. The significance of these episodes, which frequently eludes psychiat-

ric attention, may be in recognizing their occurrence when obtaining a past psychiatric history (Carlson and Strober 1978).

The relationship of bipolar disorder to certain other psychiatric disorders also remains to be clarified. So-called school phobia occasionally appears in the early histories of patients with bipolar illness (Hassanyeh and Davison 1980), as do episodes of anorexia nervosa (Hsu et al. 1984) and episodes of what appear to be conduct disorders (Kovacs et al. 1988). The case history presented below embodies some of these diagnostic overlaps.

A 17-year-old girl presented with a relatively clear history of acute mania. It had been preceded 4 years earlier when beginning high school by an episode of school "phobia" marked by severe anxiety (including occasional panic attacks) about failing in school and not being liked by other children, but it did not occur in other contexts of separation. When forced to go to school, she hid in the bathroom, avoiding classes. This resolved, however, when the patient's school placement was changed. One year later, she responded to a critical remark about her pudginess by going on a diet and losing 40 pounds over 6 months. She eventually weighed 74 pounds at a height of 5 feet, 3 inches. The patient was preoccupied with her "fatness" and with not wanting to grow up (she repeatedly said she wanted to be a little girl). She was still premenstrual at the time of these symptoms. She was hospitalized, treated nutritionally for 6 weeks, and discharged with the diagnosis of anorexia nervosa. Her family refused any psychological follow-up. Prior to and between these periods of difficulty, she was an average, friendly student who experienced frequent conflicts with her rigid, unsympathetic parents. In the family was an older sister who was said to be schizophrenic but who had had two episodes of depression (with auditory hallucinations) successfully treated with tricyclic antidepressants. The family also contained a paternal aunt with a history of "nervous breakdown" and a paternal cousin who died by suicide.

The patient's mania at age 17 was classic. She was demanding, boastful, very argumentative, uninhibited, and quite intolerant of criticism and limit setting, being both caustic and verbally abusive. She was extremely distractible to sounds outside the building as well as noises on the ward where she was hospitalized. She claimed that she needed no rest, had no sense of fatigue, and was unable to stay in her room for any prolonged length of time. She was noted to decorate her body and clothes with drawings, dress provocatively, change clothes frequently, wear excessive makeup at times, and occasion-

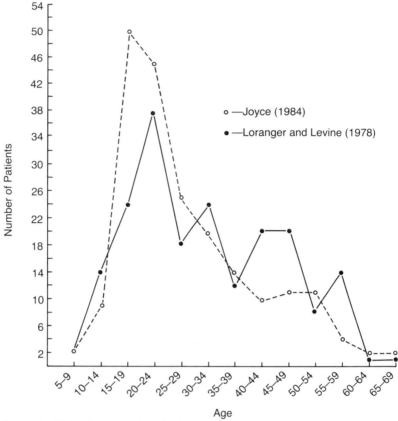

Fig. 2–1. Age at onset of bipolar disorder. (Data from Loranger, A. W., and Levine, P. M. 1978. Age of onset of bipolar affective illness. *Arch. Gen. Psychiatry* 35:1345–1348; and Joyce, P. R. 1984. Age of onset in bipolar affective disorder and misdiagnosis as schizophrenia. *Psychol. Med.* 14:145–149.)

ally throw all her belongings outside her room into the hallway. At times of excitement she was observed to bolt large quantities of food with complete disregard for manners. She often misidentified staff and other patients as former acquaintances. Her delusions focused primarily on her having a husband and a child named Joan (coincidentally, the name of her "schizophrenic" sister) and alternated between having a boyfriend, numerous boyfriends, or a husband. She also said her father was a communist and that he was out to punish her by hospitalizing her. Throughout the admission, she maintained that nothing was wrong with her. Her symptoms resolved on a daily combination of thiothixene, 60 mg, and lithium carbonate, 2100 mg. Following her recovery, she recalled her two previous spells as being marked by hypersomnia as well as feelings of worthlessness. Both were documented during her "anorexia nervosa" admission and were remarked on because the patient did not exercise like most anorexics. Neither her school "phobia" nor her "anorexia nervosa" were simply misdiagnosed depressive episodes since they contained clear

components of panic and abnormal attitudes toward food. On the other hand, the episodes were clearly more than an anxiety disorder or anorexia nervosa.

Since follow-up studies of school phobia and anorexia nervosa do not contain significant numbers of bipolar cases, it is unlikely that they all represent "masked manic depression." Although systematic symptom inquiry sometimes elucidates diagnosis, that is not always the case. As in the case of adjustment disorders, the clinical significance of these other disorders is at least recognizing their significance retrospectively. If they occur in the context of a positive family history, it is worth entertaining the possibility of an ultimate bipolar course.

Another diagnostic dilemma occurs when an older child or adolescent presents with psychotic symptoms. In spite of the fact that psychosis and mental confusion had been clearly described in cases of severe mania and depression among adults by Kraepelin and his early successors, those observations were neglected until the early 1970s. The tendency to consider schizophrenia as the diagnosis in any adolescent or young adult with hallucinations or delusions has been especially noteworthy. A review of the literature on adolescent bipolar disorders reveals both anecdotal and systematic evidence of this problem. Carlson and Strober (1978) reported on six young adolescents, all of whom had been diagnosed as schizophrenic but who, in fact, had bipolar disorder confirmed on follow-up. Some of the psychotic symptoms they reported are presented in Table 2–5. Confusion, delusions and hallucinations were the most confounding signs and symptoms.

Horowitz (1977) and Hassanyeh and Davison (1980) report similar findings in their adolescents with bipolar disorders. It is important to note that in all of these cases, the patients in question met accepted criteria for mania and/or depression. In most circumstances it appeared that had the subjects been between the ages of 30 and 40 rather than 10 and 20 there would have been less reluctance to ascribe a diagnosis of affective disorder.

Several investigators have examined the question of whether, in fact, psychotic symptoms occur more frequently among patients with early-onset bipolar disorders than among those with late-onset bipolar illness. Ballenger and co-workers (1982) reviewed records of manic patients younger than age 21 and older than age 30 and found that younger patients had significantly more delusions, ideas of reference, more than three "schizophrenic symptoms," and considerably (but not statistically significant) more confusion (55% vs. 25%), bizarre behavior or ideas (33% vs. 8%), and thought disorder (44% vs. 17%).

Rosen and co-workers (1983) systematically interviewed 71 patients with bipolar-I disease regarding lifetime history of psychotic symptoms and age at onset of the bipolar disorder. They found that patients with younger ages at onset were likely to report more psychotic symptoms ($r = -0.4$, $p < .001$). More specifically, 61.5% of subjects with onsets before age 20 reported a history of at least three psychotic symptoms, whereas none of those with onsets over age 40 had that high a number.

Finally, Joyce (1984) found a highly significant interaction between misdiagnosis as schizophrenia and age at onset in bipolar disorder. Thirty-eight percent of the depressives with onsets prior to age 20 versus none with onsets after age 30 were misdiagnosed as having schizophrenia. Seventy-two percent of young manics versus 24% of older manics were misdiagnosed.

It must be emphasized that schizophrenia and organic psychoses do, unfortunately, occur in young persons and it would be unfortunate if the diagnostic pendulum swings too far toward overdiagnosing affective disorder. Nevertheless, the occurrence of mood-congruent psychotic symptoms and occasionally mood-incongruent psychotic symptoms should prompt the examiner to look carefully for a history and other signs and symptoms of mania or depression. In addition, in the

Table 2–5. PSYCHOTIC SYMPTOMS REPORTED IN ADOLESCENTS WITH BIPOLAR DISORDER

From Depressive Episodes

Believes people are accusing her of being a drug addict, performing sexual acts, hating her parents.

Constant rumination and guilt over sexual matters; deluded that she is pregnant. Hears voices saying "you will die; you will live." Believes her insides are decaying. Hears voices calling her "a bitch and a dog." Wanted to wash dishes for the whole ward to atone for her sins. "I feel my brain is rotting and moving; it's making me dizzy." Incapacitated by confusion and lack of motivation. Suspects people are out to kill her.

Believes body is decaying and giving off foul odor; fears being raped and robbed by other patients.

States he is receiving communications from electronic media and that other patients are controlling him.

From Manic Episodes

"I feel I am the reincarnation of Newton or Jesus."

Patient claims "staff and patients are purposely making toilets flush louder than normal, changing the water temperature in the shower and pressurizing the room to wake me up."

States he is the Messiah; fears he will die because he has seen God; running around naked; speech so rapid it is incoherent.

Hears voices commanding her to kill people; believes she is having labor pains and will give birth to Moses; much laughing and preoccupied with pinups, prostitution, and homosexuality.

(From Carlson, G. A., and Strober, M. 1978. Manic-depressive illness in early adolescence: A study of clinical and diagnostic characteristics in six cases. *J. Am. Acad. Child. Psychiatry* 17:138–153.)

case of acute depression, Strober and Carlson (1982) found that psychotic symptoms co-occurring with hypersomnia and strong affective family histories predicted an ultimate bipolar course.

In the previous three considerations, the focus of discussion has been on diagnostic problems occurring because of misinterpretation of particular symptoms. In most cases, one of the features that should enable accurate diagnosis ultimately is the episodic nature of the psychopathology. Thus the final area of diagnostic confusion eventuates when the history of episodes is obscured by lack of a thorough past history, by episodes of affective disorder being superimposed on other behavior problems, or by the presence of rapid, mixed cycles. In adolescents and adults it is usually easier to identify mania because it represents a *change* in activity level and moods described by others as aversive and by the subject (perhaps) as euphoric. Those features are more difficult to distinguish in emotionally disturbed children.

For instance, without a clear history of episodes or the onset of a disorder that represents a distinct change in the person's behavior, distinguishing mania from attention-deficit hyperactivity disorder is very difficult. Both disorders are characterized by hyperactive, impulsive, and often volatile behavior. Moreover, garrulous, intrusive, silly, and disinhibited (and sometimes inappropriately sexual) behavior is both frequently part of a manic episode and characteristic of hyperactive children. Even decreased need for sleep does not distinguish the two groups. Children with attention-deficit hyperactivity disorder, however, have chronic behavior problems, have nonaffective family histories, respond to methylphenidate, and rarely improve with lithium. The most important discriminator, aside from episodes, is the not infrequent presence of hallucinations at some time during the course of a bipolar illness but that is never part of the clinical picture of attention-deficit hyperactivity disorder.

There are some investigators who believe in what is called the manic-depressive variant syndrome (Davis 1979). Clinicians who work with offspring of adults with bipolar illness have noticed that a minority of children present with hyperactivity, extreme emotional lability, explosive outbursts, and poor response to methylphenidate (see Carlson 1984 for a review). Unfortunately, children with this clinical picture have not turned up in systematic studies of offspring of adults with bipolar disease although admittedly the syndrome may be relatively rare even in a population at risk.

If the "variant" picture delineates an actual disorder, it may represent prodomata of a clear-cut bipolar disorder or be a part of the bipolar spectrum more likely to occur in younger children. In reviewing case reports of bipolar disorder in children younger than age 12, Carlson (1983) found that children with onsets before age 9 were more likely to have (1) chronic rather than episodic disorders, (2) other concurrent psychopathology, (3) less discrete episodes of profound depression or elated mania, and (4) irritability that was a constant feature across episodes. In children with onsets closer to puberty, symptoms of bipolarity were found to be more "classic" in their initial manic or depressive presentation. The confusion engendered by the "variant" syndrome's resemblance to other disorders might explain the high frequency of personality disorder diagnoses among Weller and colleagues' (1986b) sample of misdiagnosed prepubertal manics, the frequency with which Akiskal and co-workers (1985) found behavior disorders among the antecedent diagnoses of clinically referred siblings and children of parents with bipolar disease, and the similar frequency of hyperactive and conduct disorder diagnoses seen in the sample of Strober and associates (1988) of adolescent patients with prepubertal onset of bipolar disease. There thus appears to be circumstantial, albeit weak, evidence for a syndrome that occurs in young persons with a positive family history that itself does not appear classically bipolar.

Diagnoses mistaken for bipolar disorder in children are summarized in Table 2–6. The following case exemplifies the mixed diagnostic picture that may occur in prepubertal bipolar disorder.

A 9-year-old boy had been hospitalized elsewhere with what was recognized as a severe depression. His suicide attempt prompted admission, and he was clearly sad, disgusted with himself, irritable, and unable to think clearly. He had stopped eating, had frightening nightmares, and wanted to die. He heard voices saying he was bad, that no one liked him, and that he should kill himself. This had been going on for several weeks. He was treated with

Table 2–6. ISSUES IN MISDIAGNOSIS OF JUVENILE BIPOLAR DISORDERS

1. Mild episodes of depression or hypomania are attributed to adjustment disorders or adolescent turmoil.
2. Early episodes of affective disorder may be given other diagnoses (and may be other diagnoses). Among the more common are
   a. School phobia
   b. Anorexia nervosa
   c. Attention-deficit disorder
   d. Conduct disorder
3. Severe episodes of depression or mania are misdiagnosed as schizophrenia:
   a. Extreme flight of ideas looks like incoherence.
   b. Very slowed thinking is mistaken for thought blockage.
   c. Psychomotor retardation may be extreme enough to resemble catatonia.
   d. Paranoia and irritability that occurs in mania is mistaken for paranoid schizophrenia.
   e. Hallucinations and delusions are taken out of context of mood.

imipramine, but within several days he became so combative and wild, hallucinating, and irrational that he required almost constant restraints or seclusion. Medication was stopped, and it took several weeks before his sensorium cleared, although occasional hallucinations remained. Over the next several months, carbamazepine, neuroleptics, and lithium were tried. He developed a rash on carbamazepine therapy, ptosis on lithium therapy, and oversedation on neuroleptic therapy. He was transferred elsewhere and in the course of deciding how to proceed doctors found that his depression spontaneously remitted. One day he awoke, literally, with the announcement that he felt fine, that he felt like doing things again, and, in fact, was observed by staff and family to be fine. He was discharged on no medication.

By way of past history, this patient had always been sickly, frequently complaining of headaches that kept him out of school. He had been placed in a special education classroom at age 6 because of difficulties with math and reading and because of generally irritable, volatile, and oppositional behavior. He was described by his parents as extremely temperamental, never handling criticism well, and having frequent, severe tantrums both at home and at school. He had no friends because he was unpredictable and bossy. Although some of the above behavior remained with the remission of the depressive episode, the child was observed for the most part to be a likable, thoughtful youngster who related well to adults although he was still afraid of being teased by peers. Over the next year he had several periods of consecutive weeks when he was described

as "driven," refusing to go to bed before midnight, obsessed with doing things (e.g., fixing his bike, building a skateboard), and being extremely emotional, verbally abusive, and destructive of his own possessions during the raging tantrums that increased considerably over this time. His parents consented reluctantly to a trial of lithium, and it was administered without untoward effect. The lithium mitigated (but did not stop) depressive episodes (the psychotic symptoms that had occurred in his earlier depression did not return) and reduced the emotional volatility. During subsequent depressive episodes, which were characterized by physical complaints, school avoidance, self-denigration, and worsening appetite, trials of amitriptyline and phenelzine were undertaken. (It had never been clear if the prior response to imipramine was a toxic, anticholinergic response or a manic response or if a worsening of the depression occurred coincident with beginning the drug.) Even with concurrent lithium therapy, both antidepressants increased the patient's irritability, volatility, and oppositional behavior. Although neither obviously manic nor more depressed, he was worse on antidepressant therapy, though it took several months of observation before this became clear. Over the past year, the patient has been maintained on lithium alone. He continues to have moody periods but is fully mainstreamed into regular classrooms and has forged some tenuous peer relationships both due to better emotional and cognitive functioning.

The patient's family history is significant for bipolar II disorder in his maternal grandmother, alcohol abuse in his maternal grandfather, cocaine abuse and sociopathy in a maternal aunt and uncle, and driving phobia, morbid obesity, and major depression in his mother. There are also several cousins with a history of depression and suicidal behavior. His father's immediate family is without problems except for a granduncle, diagnosed "schizophrenic," who was released from a state hospital after 43 years when treated with lithium.

Although the patient has clear episodes of depression and brief periods of hypomania, it is not clear how to categorize either his life-long premorbid irritability that never totally remits or his aberrant response to antidepressant medication.

TREATMENT

In the previous section it has been clear that the core phenomenology of bipolar disorder is similar regardless of age although there are developmental variations that change the differential diagnosis. An equally important question is whether age at onset influences treatment response.

Although there are a number of anecdotal reports that extend the literature review of lithium use in children and adolescents by Youngerman and Canino (1978), the conclusions are essentially the same. Lithium appears to be equally effective in the treatment of juvenile and adult bipolar disorders. An overly optimistic view is likely from these reports, since lithium response is frequently used to validate the diagnosis of bipolar disorder. Moreover, relatively few investigators publish cases, especially if at all atypical, if the subject has not responded. When negative results have been published, they have been similar to those obtained in adults. For instance, in a small study of four young rapid cyclers only two were reported to respond to lithium (Jones and Berney 1987). This is in the range of response reported by Wehr and co-workers (1988) in describing the more typical older rapid cyclers.

There are no large-scale, systematic studies of lithium treatment for bipolar disorder in children or adolescents. There is considerable experience using lithium in young patients for other reasons (see Campbell et al. 1984 for review). The largest series of children are described by DeLong and Aldershof (1987) in their presentation of over 150 children and adolescents treated in clinical practice with lithium. Of their 59 bipolar subjects, two thirds were considered favorable responders. Other successfully treated groups were those with "emotionally unstable character disorders" (n = 11, 82% responders, although sample not described) and offspring of lithium responders (n = 7, 71% responders). Poor responders consisted of children with attention-deficit disorder and conduct disorders. Since these subjects were not systematically interviewed and diagnosed, treated under double-blind conditions, or rated systematically for response, conclusions must be considered tentative. Nevertheless, the data support the position taken by the American Academy of Child Psychiatry in 1977 that children and adolescents with manic-depression, emotionally unstable character disorder, and high-risk offspring of lithium responders are those for whom lithium might be helpful (Campbell et al. 1978). More specific indications for lithium treatment, in descending order of priority, are noted in Table 2–7.

Table 2–7. REASONS FOR INITIATING LITHIUM TREATMENT IN JUVENILE BIPOLAR DISORDER

1. Presence or history of disabling episodes of mania and depression
2. Episode(s) of severe depression with a possible history of hypomania
3. Presence of an acute, severe depression characterized by psychomotor retardation, hypersomnia and psychosis, positive family history for major, or bipolar disorder (Strober and Carlson 1982; Akiskal et al. 1985); young people with such histories are at risk for developing a manic episode when treated with tricyclic antidepressants and may develop a rapid cycling course (Wehr et al. 1988)
4. An acute psychotic disorder with affective features
5. Behavior disorders characterized by severe emotional lability and aggression when there is a positive family history of major affective or bipolar disorder or lithium responsiveness

---

Relative contraindications to lithium use include kidney and heart disease, diuretic use, and chronic diarrhea. Basic laboratory studies should include sodium and potassium levels to rule out electrolyte disturbances, blood urea nitrogen and creatinine levels (creatinine clearances on a 24-hour urine sample if a question of renal disease exists) to check kidney function, and thyroid function studies (serum thyroxine and thyroid-stimulating hormone, since lithium can produce overt hypothyroidism in persons with mildly impaired thyroid function).

Lithium pharmacokinetics in children have not been described but are assumed to be similar to those for adults. Lithium is rapidly absorbed (1–3 hours) and has a half-life of 17 hours. In children with efficient renal clearance, it may take higher doses of lithium to maintain levels within a therapeutic range of 0.7 to 1.2 mEq/L (drawn 12 hours after the last dose). In prepubertal children there was a significant positive correlation between weight and total daily lithium dosage. Children weighing less than 40 kg need 600 to 900 mg/day to achieve therapeutic levels, whereas children weighing more than 50 mg required 1200 to 1500 mg (Weller et al. 1986a). Neither the blood level needed for antimanic or prophylactic response nor the time necessary to achieve response to lithium in children and adolescents has been examined.

Campbell and co-workers (1984) report side effects in 36 children treated for behavior disorders with lithium. Less than half the sample experienced difficulties. Symptoms that occurred in descending order of frequency were weight gain, decreased motor activity, excessive sedation, gastrointestinal complaints, pallor, and headache. Although only 11% of Campbell and co-workers' sample complained of polyuria, this symptom has been reported as considerably more frequent. In addition, gastrointestinal disturbances can often be mitigated by giving the pill with meals.

As is known in adult treatment, signs of toxicity include slurred speech, muscle weakness and twitching, ataxia, and impaired consciousness. For some, diarrhea is also an indication of toxicity.

Effects of specific concern regarding children are proteinuria, the accumulation of lithium in bones, and the effect of lithium on the endocrine system (Jefferson 1982). Cognitive effects of lithium in adults and children have been documented (Campbell et al. 1984), but the implications in terms of learning are unknown.

Clinical issues in using lithium with children and adolescents require discussion. When young patients present at the beginning of a disorder, especially at the first serious episode, the question of when and whether to start lithium is a particularly cogent one.

The frequency, severity, duration of the episodes, and support system available to the patient largely determine when to start and how long to continue medication. On one hand, a teenager with an obvious, devastating manic episode should not have to wait for several more episodes before being offered acute and prophylactic treatment; on the other hand, a child who is receiving lithium to see if nonspecific symptoms respond may need to be taken off the medication (if response has not been clear cut) to evaluate if the child is better on or off medication. Even in the case of mild episodes of depression and mania, if they occur with frequency (at least two per year), the youngster may have a less stormy adolescence on medication and will be better able to cope with the other age-appropriate demands of making relationships, finishing school, and identifying himself or herself as other than flagrantly psychiatrically ill.

How long should lithium therapy be continued? Affective episodes, although muted, are still often discernible even on lithium. If this is the case, prophylaxis should be continued. Even if episodes are not obvious, one should try to convince teenagers and families to continue the medication through high school or college so those hurdles are crossed successfully. The possibility of drug holidays should be entertained, though they are best undertaken when major environmental changes are not anticipated, over the summer when school is not in session, and after at least 1 year of symptom control.

Treatment compliance is not just an issue with adolescents although frequently a teenager's need to feel in complete control of his or her life exacerbates the problem. Education of the youngster and family on the nature of the disorder is *imperative*. Long-term availability of a consistent treatment source is important. A person might need to experience several episodes before being convinced that a medication trial is helpful. Consultation with someone who has treated several episodes and whom the teenager trusts can help the teenager analyze the personal risk–benefit ratio and add immeasurably to treatment success.

The risk of suicide must be considered in treating young (and old) patients with bipolar disease. Eliminating or reducing the severity of future episodes is the most reliable way of accomplishing that end. Since medication cannot be forced on a person, it is preferable for both the clinician and family to know when a patient is refusing medication than to have that person lie and give everyone a false sense of comfort.

The addition of other treatment always depends on the individual case. Unless all problems subside with medication administration, one is left with all of the usual "bread and butter" issues of what is necessary for the specific child: school consultation, family therapy, individual therapy, hospitalization, residential placement, and so on. There is no question that psychotherapy in an adolescent whose mood swings are under some control is likely to be considerably more effective than the converse.

There have been few reports of other treatments of juvenile bipolar disorder. Carbamazepine, which seems to have some efficacy in adults (Ballenger and Post 1980), has been used successfully in one case report (Hsu 1986). Conversely, there is a report suggesting that this drug can produce mania in susceptible persons (Reiss and O'Donnell 1984). There is also one case report of elec-

Table 2–8. OUTCOME OF ADOLESCENT-ONSET BIPOLAR DISORDERS

Study	Sample Size	Age at Onset	Length of Follow-up	Clinical Picture	Outcome
Olsen (1961)	28 (13F, 15M)	15–16 years	About 25 years	15 with sudden onset 13 with childhood psychopathology (3 mentally retarded, 2 cycloid, 3 with periodic symptoms)	15 with acute onset (5 well, 1 suicide, 3 "late disability", 5 continued cycles, 1 ? schizophrenic) 13 childhood psychopathology (9 initially well, then 7 "ultimately disabled"; 4 chronically ill)
Landolt (1957)	60 (43F, 17M)	range, 15–22; $\bar{x} = 18$	5–25 years	50% of males and 25% of females showed "schizophrenic coloring"; 11 males and 17 females with "prepsychotic schizoid manifestations"	10 recovered (3M, 7F), including 6 with "schizophrenic coloring" 27 continued cycles 7 "schizophrenic" (2 recovered, 4 marginal adjustment) 11 inadequate information but not hospitalized 5 no information
Annesley (1961)	15	Adolescence	5 years		12 with good outcome 2 with fair outcome 1 with poor outcome
Carlson et al. (1977)	28 (12 M, 16 F)	$\bar{x} = 15.8$; range, 8–19	$\bar{x} = 19.3$; range, 3–46	18 with depression onset 10 with mania onset (2 rapid cyclers) Mean episode frequency per year, 0.38 No differences compared with those with onset after age 45	60% with good social outcome 20% significantly impaired but functional 20% chronically ill 1 suicide Outcome similar to adult onsets in terms of education and outcome although patients with early onset were earning less and were more often single.
Hudgens (1974) Welner et al. (1979)	13 (9F, 4M)	16.3 years for mania; 15.3 years for depression	9 years	11 admitted with mania 2 admitted with depression but prior mania Hudgens' description noted manic and mixed episodes predominated 45% with auditory hallucinations 45% with suicide 8 of 13 readmitted several times for initial episode	3 males suicide at 2½, 8, and 10 years after hospitalization 9 socially disabled, substance abuse, multiple suicide attempts 10/11 treated with lithium, as well as electroconvulsive therapy, neuroleptics, and tricyclics 1 not mentioned
McGlashan (1988)	35	Symptoms = 16 ± 3 years; first hospitalization, 21 ± 6 years	20 years later	Compared with those with onsets after age 20, patients had been ill longer prior to first hospitalization and had significantly more psychotic symptoms 83% originally called schizoaffective 30% had had trouble with the law 70% with "psychotic assaultiveness"	Compared with those with late onsets there were no more frequent hospitalizations or difference in treatment or suicide rate. Those with earlier onsets were performing significantly better regarding work and frequency of social contacts although specific ratings were not great for either group.

troshock therapy being the only successful therapeutic intervention in an 18-year-old girl whose rapid cycling was precipitated by a course of trimipramine (Berman and Wolpert 1987).

OUTCOME

The key consideration of outcome in juvenile bipolar disorders is whether the early age at onset also changes the prognosis of the disorder. Manic-depression as originally conceptualized by Kraepelin was distinguished by its course from dementia praecox with the implication being that it was a more benign illness. Its prognosis, however, is not necessarily benign.

Coryell and Winokur's (1982) review of adult bipolar disorder can be summarized as follows: Of 414 patients with bipolar disorder described in studies from 1942 to 1974, 15% to 53% (average about 32%) were considered chronically disabled. Of the 92 manic patients studied and followed after 40 years in the Iowa 500 study, the suicide rate was 11.1%, with excess mortality greatest in the first decade (Tsuang et al. 1978).

Although it is difficult to compare extant follow-up studies of patients with juvenile-onset bipolar disease with their adult counterparts because of variable diagnostic and outcome criteria and the effects of treatment, Carlson and co-workers (1977) and, more recently, McGlashan (1988) conclude that the prognosis of bipolar disorder with an adolescent onset is similar to that of adult onsets (Table 2–8). The presence of psychotic symptoms in episodes of mania and depression do not seem to worsen the prognosis if the disorder is clearly manic. There is some suggestion that children with a prepubertal onset may have a more stormy course than patients with adolescent- or adult-onset bipolar disorders.

If, in fact, the "cohort effect" described earlier in this chapter is a consistent and persistent finding, it may be possible to examine this hypothesis in the future, since the numbers of prepubertal children who are afflicted will increase.

CONCLUSIONS

Juvenile bipolar disorder represents the earliest onset of adult bipolar disorder. Although the data suggest greater genetic loading for the illness, the basic phenomenology, treatment, and outcome of the disorder, at least in its most classic presentation, do not appear to be affected by early age at onset. It is possible that a particularly severe form of bipolar disorder (severe in terms of a very high genetic loading, treatment resistance, and poor outcome) occurs with an onset in prepuberty. Accurate diagnosis of unusual presentations of bipolar disorder probably awaits the discovery of reliable and valid biological markers.

References

Akiskal, H. S., Downs, J., Jordan, P., et al. 1985. Affective disorders in referred children and younger siblings of manic-depressives. *Arch. Gen. Psychiatry* 42:996–1004.

American Psychiatric Association. 1980. *Diagnostic and Statistical Manual of Mental Disorders,* 3rd ed. Washington, D.C.: American Psychiatric Association.

American Psychiatric Association. 1987. *Diagnostic and Statistical Manual of Mental Disorders,* 3rd ed., revised. Washington, D.C.: American Psychiatric Association.

Andreasen, N. C., Rice, J., Endicott, J., et al. 1987. Familial rates of affective disorder. *Arch. Gen. Psychiatry* 44:461–469.

Annesley, P. T. 1961. Psychiatric illness in adolescence: presentation and prognosis. J. Ment. Sci. 107:268–278.

Anthony, E. J., and Scott, P. 1960. Manic-depressive psychosis in childhood. *J. Child Psychol. Psychiatry* 1:53–72.

Ballenger, J. C., and Fost, R. M. 1980. Carbamazepine (Tegretol) in manic-depressive illness: A new treatment. *Am. J. Psychiatry* 137:782–790.

Ballenger, J. C., Reus, V. I., and Post, R. M. 1982. The "atypical" presentation of adolescent mania. *Am. J. Psychiatry* 139:602–606.

Berman, E., and Wolpert, E. A. 1987. Intractable manic-depressive psychosis with rapid cycling in an 18-year-old woman successfully treated with electroconvulsive therapy. *J. Nerv. Ment. Dis.* 175:236–239.

Blehar, M. C., Weissman, M. M., Gershon, E. S., and Hirschfeld, R. A. 1988. Family and genetic studies of affective disorders. *Arch. Gen. Psychiatry* 45:289–292.

Campbell, M., Perry, R., and Green, W. H. 1984. Use of lithium in children and adolescents. *Psychosomatics* 25:95–105.

Campbell, M., Schulman, D., and Rapaport, J. 1978. The current status of lithium therapy in child and adolescent psychiatry. *J. Am. Acad. Child Psychiatry* 14:717–729.

Carlson, G. A. 1983. Bipolar affective disorders in childhood and adolescence. In Cantwell, D. P., and Carlson, G. A. (eds.). *Affective disorders in childhood and adolescence.* New York: S. P. Medical and Scientific Books, pp 61–84.

Carlson, G. A. 1984. Issues of classification in childhood bipolar disorder. *Psychiatr. Dev.* 4:273–285.

Carlson, G. A., Davenport, Y. B., and Jamison, K. 1977. A comparison of outcome in adolescent and late-onset bipolar manic-depressive illness. *Am. J. Psychiatry* 134:919–922.

Carlson, G. A., and Kashani, J. H. Manic symptoms in a non-referred adolescent population. *J. Affect. Dis.* 15:219–226.

Carlson, G. A., and Strober, M. 1978. Manic-depressive illness in early adolescence: A study of clinical and diagnostic characteristics in six cases. *J. Am. Acad. Child Psychiatry* 17:138–153.

Chambers, W. J., Puig-Antich, J., Hirsch, M., et al. 1985. The assessment of affective disorders in children and adolescents by semi-structured interview: Test–retest reliability of the K-SADS-P. *Arch. Gen. Psychiatry* 42:696–702.

Coryell, W., and Winokur, G. 1982. Course and outcome. In Paykel E. S. (ed.): *Handbook of Affective Disorders*. New York: Guilford Press.

Cytryn, L., McKnew, D. H., Zahn-Waxler, C., and Gershon, E. S. 1986. Developmental issues in risk research: The offspring of affectively ill parents. In Rutter, M., Izard, C. E., and Read, P. B. (eds.): *Depression in Young People: Clinical and Developmental Perspectives*. New York: Guilford Press.

Davis, R. E. 1979. Manic-depressive variant syndrome of childhood: A preliminary report. *Am. J. Psychiatry* 136:702–706.

Decina, P., Kestenbaum, C. J., Farber, S., et al. 1983. Clinical and psychological assessment of children of bipolar probands. *Am. J. Psychiatry*. 140:545–553.

DeLong, G. R., and Aldershof, A. L. 1987. Long-term experience with lithium treatment in childhood: Correlation with clinical diagnoses. *J. Am. Acad. Child Adolesc. Psychiatry* 26:389–394.

Dwyer, J. T., and DeLong, G. R. 1987. A family history study of twenty probands with childhood manic-depressive illness. *J. Am. Acad. Child Adolesc. Psychiatry* 26:176–180.

Egeland, J. A., Pauls, D. L., Morton, L. A., and Sussex, J. N. 1987. Presented at the American Academy of Child and Adolescent Psychiatry meetings, Washington, D.C.

Gershon, E. S., Hamovit, J. H., Guroff, J. J., and Nurnberger, J. I. 1987. Birth cohort changes in manic and depressive disorders in relatives of bipolar and schizoaffective patients. *Arch. Gen. Psychiatry* 44:314–319.

Gershon, E. S., McKnew, D., Cytryn, L., et al. 1985. Diagnoses in school-age children of bipolar affective disorder patients and normal controls. *J. Affect. Disord.* 8:283–291.

Hassanyeh, F., and Davison, K. 1980. Bipolar affective psychosis with onset before age 16: Report of 10 cases. *Br. J. Psychiatry* 137:530–539.

Herjanic, B., and Reich, W. 1982. Development of a structured psychiatric interview for children: Agreement between child and parent on individual symptoms. *J. Abnorm. Child Psychol.* 10:307–324.

Horowitz, H. A. 1977. Lithium and the treatment of adolescent manic-depressive illness. *Dis. Nerv. Syst.* 6:480–483.

Hsu, L. K. G. 1986. Lithium resistant adolescent mania. *J. Am. Acad. Child Psychiatry* 25:280–283.

Hsu, L. K. G., Holder, D., Hindmarsh, D., and Phelps, C. 1984. Bipolar illness preceded by anorexia nervosa in identical twins. *J. Clin. Psychiatry* 45:262–266.

Jefferson, J. W. 1982. The use of lithium in childhood and adolescence: An overview. *J. Clin. Psychiatry* 43:174–177.

Jones, P. M., and Berney, T. P. 1987. Early onset rapid cycling bipolar affective disorder. J. Child Psychol. Psychiatry 28:731–738.

Joyce, P. R. 1984. Age of onset in bipolar affective disorder and misdiagnosis as schizophrenia. *Psychol. Med.* 14:145–149.

Kasanin, J. 1931. The affective psychoses in children. *Am. J. Psychiatry* 6:897–926.

Kovacs, M., Paulauskas, S., Gatsonis, C., and Richards, C. 1988. Depressive disorders in childhood: III. A longitudinal study of comorbidity with and risk for conduct disorders. *J. Affect. Disord.* 15:205–217.

Kraepelin, E. 1921. Manic-depressive insanity and paranoia. Edinburgh: Livingstone.

Landolt, A. D. 1957. Follow-up studies on circular manic

depressive illness occurring in the young. *Bull. NY Acad. Med.* 33:65–73.

LaRoche, C., Cheifetz, P., Lester, E. P., et al. 1985. Psychopathology in the offspring of parents with bipolar affective disorders. *Can. J. Psychiatry* 30:337–343.

Loranger, A. W., and Levine, P. M. 1978. Age of onset of bipolar affective illness. *Arch. Gen. Psychiatry* 35:1345–1348.

McGlashan, T. H. 1988. Adolescent versus adult onset of mania. *Am. J. Psychiatry* 145:221–224.

Mendlewicz, J., and Rainer, J. D. 1977. Adoption study supporting genetic transmission in manic-depressive illness. *Nature* 265:327–329.

Nurnberger, J. I., and Gershon, E. 1982. Genetics. In Paykel, E. S. (ed.): *Handbook of Affective Disorders*. Edinburgh: Churchill-Livingstone.

Olsen, T. 1961. Follow-up study of manic-depressive patients whose first attack occurred before the age of 19. *Acta Psychiatr. Scand. [Suppl.]* 162:45–51.

Orvaschel, H. 1985. Psychiatric interviews suitable for use in research with children and adolescents. *Psychopharmacol. Bull.* 21:737–745.

Potter, W. Z., Rudorfer, M. V., and Goodwin, F. K. 1986. Biologic findings in bipolar disorder. *Ann. Rev. Psychiatry* 6:32–60.

Reiss, A. L., and O'Donnell, D. J. 1984. Carbamazepine-induced mania in two children: Case report. *J. Clin. Psychiatry* 45:272–274.

Rice, J., Reich, T., Andreasen, N. C., et al. 1987. The familial transmission of bipolar illness. *Arch. Gen. Psychiatry* 44:441–447.

Robins, L. N., Helzer, J. E., Weissman, M. M., et al. 1984. Lifetime prevalence of specific psychiatric disorders in three sites. *Arch. Gen. Psychiatry* 41:949–958.

Rosen, L. N., Rosenthel, N. E., VanDosen, P. H., et al. 1983. Age at onset and number of psychotic symptoms in bipolar I and schizoaffective disorder. *Am. J. Psychiatry* 140:1523–1524.

Spitzer, R. L., Endicott, J., and Robins, E. 1978. Research diagnostic criteria rationale and reliability. *Arch. Gen. Psychiatry* 35:773–782.

Strober, M., and Carlson, G. A. 1982. Bipolar illness in adolescents with major depression: Clinical, genetic, and psychopharmacologic predictors in a 3- to 4-year prospective follow-up investigation. *Arch. Gen. Psychiatry* 39:549, 555.

Strober, M., Morrell, W., Burroughs, J., et al. 1988. A family study of bipolar I in adolescence: Early onset of symptoms linked to increased familial loading and lithium resistance. *J. Affect. Disord.* 15:255–268.

Tsuang, M. T. 1978. Suicide in schizophrenics, manics, depressives and surgical controls. *Arch. Gen. Psychiatry* 35:153–155.

Wehr, T. A., Sack, D. A., Rosenthal, N. E., and Cowdry, R. W. 1988. Rapid cycling affective disorder: Contributing factor and treatment responses in 51 patients. *Am. J. Psychiatry* 145:179–185.

Weller, E. B., Weller, R. A., and Fristad, M. A. 1986. Lithium dosage guide for prepubertal children: A preliminary report. *J. Am. Acad. Child Psychiatry* 25:92–96.

Weller, R. A., Weller, E. B., Tucker, S. G., and Fristad, M. A. 1986b. Mania in prepubertal children: Has it been underdiagnosed? *J. Affective Disord.* 11:151–154.

Youngerman, J., and Canino, I. 1978. Lithium carbonate use in children and adolescents: A survey of the literature. *Arch. Gen. Psychiatry* 35:216–224.

3

Grief in Children and Adolescents

ELIZABETH B. WELLER, M.D.
and RONALD A. WELLER, M.D.

Despite the fact that 1.2 million (4%) children in the United States lose at least one parent by the age of 15 (Statistical Abstracts 1985), methodologically well-done prospective studies that look at the impact of this major life stressor on growth and development, pathologic consequences, or beneficial outcomes in youngsters are lacking.

According to Brandon (1974), attachment figures generate attachment behavior and threats of separation from such figures evoke anxiety and hostility. Since death is the ultimate separation, it provokes behaviors such as separation anxiety, searching behavior designed to restore contact with the attachment figure, and hostility when this is frustrated. Grieving adults have been repeatedly reported as being at high risk for increased morbidity and mortality. The morbidity includes increased rates of cancer and cardiac problems as well as exacerbation of preexisting affective disorders and increased incidence of the development of affective disorders (Osterweis et al. 1984).

DEFINITION

In any discussion of this topic, the terms *bereavement, grief* and *mourning* should be clearly defined.

Bereavement— deprivation, leaving a sad or lonely state due to loss or death.

Grief—keen mental suffering or distress over affliction of loss, deep sorrow, painful regret. This is mostly the *affect* resulting from bereavement.

Mourning—a psychological process set in motion by loss of a loved object; grief is the parallel subjective state in such a loss.

According to Freud (1917) in *Mourning and Melancholia*, "Although mourning involves grave departure from the normal attitude to life, it never occurs to us to regard it as a pathological condition and to refer it to medical treatment. We rely on its being overcome after a certain lapse of time and we look upon any interference with it as useless or even harmful." He then defines *melancholia* as "a lowering of the self regarding feeling to a degree that finds utterances in self-reproaches and culminates in a delusional expectation of punishment. An ambivalent and narcissistic relationship with the loved object predisposes to this outcome."

According to the *Diagnostic and Statistical Manual of Mental Disorders*, Third edition, revised (*DSM-III-R*, American Psychiatric Association, 1987), uncomplicated grief is a V code diagnosis; that is, it is a condition that has come to attention or treatment but is not considered a pathologic disorder:

A full depressive syndrome frequently is a normal reaction to such a loss. *Common symptoms include:* feeling depressed, poor appetite, weight loss, and insomnia. *Uncommon symptoms include:* morbid preoccupation with worthlessness, prolonged functional impairment, psychomotor retardation. If uncommon symptoms are present, it might suggest that bereavement is complicated by the development of a major depression.

CLINICAL PICTURE

The development of "normal grief" varies considerably among different cultural groups. It also varies depending on the preexisting relationship between the bereaved and the dead person. Losing a loved one is painful and difficult at any age. For a young child, the basic needs of caretaking and emotional nurturance are so important that disruption of these needs may lead to pathologic consequences in vulnerable children. Removal of young children from their mothers may initiate successive psychological phases of numbness, protest, despair, and detachment according to Bowlby (1960, 1961, 1963).

Manifestations of bereavement and consequences depend on the concept of death developed in the child at the time of death. Nagy (1948) reported three stages in the development of the concept of death after studying 387 Hungarian children. Stage I included children 6 years and younger who see death as a continuation of life under different circumstances. Stage II comprised children 6 to 9 years old who "personify" death as a phantom figure with human and superhuman qualities who causes a person to die. Finally, in stage III, children age 9 and older have an adult concept of death, that is, it is an irreversible and universal biological process of ultimate finality.

In Duffy's historical introduction to his second edition of *Child Psychiatry* (1977), he noted that one of the first hospital admissions of a child with emotional problems is documented in Morton's *History of Pennsylvania Hospital*. A letter written in 1765 by a German immigrant sought the release of his daughter from the Pennsylvania hospital:

To the manager of the Pennsylvania hospital.

The petition of Conrad I. Doer, the father of Mary Elizabeth Doer, a child of 13 years of age, a convalescent in your hospital. "Give me leave gentlemen to lay before you a true state of my case. To represent to you my deep concern for my said daughter and that I may. . . gratify the natural desire of a father by restoring to him his darling child which is now in a better condition than when she was committed to your charitable care. I embarked on board the ship *Hero* with my late dear wife and one child. My wife died when we were in the mouth of the river Maase and my unhappy daughter was at the moment of her parting with her dear mother seized with so violent a grief as would not yield to any comfort, her mind was disturbed and she cried day and night. In this condition we arrived in the Port of Philadelphia when Ralph Foster, the Commander of the ship told me she must be brought to the hospital.

Although this is a poignant description of grief resulting in hospitalization, it and most subsequent reports on grief in children have been anecdotal.

There are several schools of thought concerning grief in children and adolescents. Preadolescents are not capable of mourning because they lack sufficient ego functioning (Wolfenstein 1966, 1969). Children do mourn but "in a less complete or satisfactory way" than adults (Schowalter 1976). Children are as capable of mourning as adults by the developmental level of nursery school (Furman 1974, 1976).

GRIEF STUDIES IN CHILDREN

Retrospective Studies

Retrospective studies examine frequency of childhood loss among child and adult psychiatric patients (Barry and Lindeman 1960; Beck et al. 1963; Caplan and Douglas 1969; Tennant et al. 1980). However, each of these studies suffers from some of the following methodologic flaws:

1. Overestimating or underestimating frequency of bereavement in the "normal" population
2. Selecting nonrepresentative psychiatric and normal control groups
3. Lack of appropriate data-gathering techniques
4. Lack of accounting for demographic trends (such as differences in death rates among various sectors of the population)

5. Failure to consider possible effects of intervening variables such as

    a. Nature of the child's home environment before/after the death

    b. Special circumstances surrounding the death

    c. Reaction and adaptation of the surviving parent

Prospective Studies

Prospective studies follow bereaved and normal adolescents into adulthood (Gregory 1965; Markusen and Fulton 1971; Bendickson and Fulton 1976). In these studies three different groups of investigators used the same sample but interviewed them at different times: Gregory (1965) studied tenth graders and found a higher delinquency rate among the bereaved compared with age-matched controls. Markuson and Fulton (1971) studied these subjects in their early 20s and found the bereaved had a higher incidence of legal offenses. Bendickson and Fulton (1976) studied the sample in their 30s and found no relationship between bereavement and crime. However, bereaved subjects suffered from significantly more serious medical illnesses and more "emotional" distress than matched controls. In these studies, limitations include the fact that specific information regarding the course of bereavement for adolescents; that is, the frequency, duration, and types of symptoms manifested, was not included. Also, important variables such as age of child at bereavement, cause of parent's death, and reaction of surviving parent were not taken into account.

Studies of Psychiatrically Disturbed Children Who Have Experienced Parental Loss

Studies of psychiatrically disturbed children who experience the death of a parent are problematic in that mostly they are case reports and do not reflect on what normal grief is in children (Arthur and Kemme 1964; Furman 1974; Wolfenstein 1966). These studies tend to focus on severely abnormal grief reactions and do not provide information on children's normal grief processes. Some authors believe bereavement per se cannot exist in children because they lack mature person-

ality structure (Wolfenstein, 1966). Sample size is limited in most of these studies (many are individual case studies) (Greenberg 1975; Higgins 1977; Rosenthal 1980). Subjective ratings typically used in such reports reduce their generalizability (Furman 1974; Wolfenstein 1969).

Studies of Grief Reactions in Normal Children

Flaws or shortcomings of studies of grief reactions in normal children are numerous. Sample sizes are small (Kliman 1968). Several studies used subjects from a kibbutz (Elizur and Kaffman 1983; Lifshitz et al. 1977). The protected life of a kibbutz child cannot be compared with a child's life in a nuclear family in America. Studies often rely on information from ancillary sources (e.g., parent or teacher) rather than using information directly from the child (Van Eerdwegh et al. 1982). Some researchers assume parents know more about their children and are more reliable informants than the children themselves. Current research on interviewing psychiatrically disturbed children (particularly those with affective disorders) indicates parents accurately report overt signs and symptoms of behavioral changes in their children (Weller and Weller 1984). However, parents frequently are unaware of symptomatology such as guilt, anxiety, sleep disturbance, and suicidal thoughts in their children. It is more difficult to interview children: it takes an adept interviewer to establish rapport, to get meaningful information by asking age-relevant questions, and to be sensitive to nonverbal communication in the child. Adequate psychiatric diagnostic tools for use with children have only recently been available (Weller et al. 1984). Often the child tries to conceal such symptoms from the parent, particularly if the parent is also under stress. This could be expected in the grieving process.

CASE HISTORIES

Prepubertal

Johnny was 9 years old when his father died in a car accident on the way to work. The boy described that on the day of the death he was called out of classes in the middle of the morning. His aunt picked him up from school and drove him home, and although she would not tell him why he was being taken home, he knew something very bad had happened. At home his mother told him that his father had died. His initial reaction was sadness with much crying. He went to all the funeral activities and reported it made him very sad to see everyone cry. He did not like the way his father looked in the casket.

One month after the death he described missing his father a lot. He reported symptoms similar to those encountered in post-traumatic stress disorder (i.e., re-experiencing the events around the time of the death and funeral). He had some symptoms of anxiety about his mother, but they did not interfere with his current functioning. Johnny reported being more sad in the evenings, since this was the time he used to interact most with his father. He frequently had difficulty falling asleep. He reported he would lie in bed and think of his father. He had symptoms of psychomotor agitation and difficulty concentrating in school. He also reported feelings of guilt, wondering what he could have done to prevent the death. He had been thinking a great deal about death. His concept of death was that his father was living in much the same way but was in heaven. He did not think his father would ever return. Although he thought about death, he felt sometimes he would like to die so he could go be with his dad. However, he did not have plans to kill himself. On 6 months' follow-up, Johnny's depressive symptomatology had abated; however, he still had some problems with his school work. On 13 months' follow-up, he was functioning at his usual academic level.

Pubertal

Julie was a 16-year-old adolescent whose father died of cancer. The teenager showed hesitation in discussing some aspects of the death and her own current feelings and activities 1 month after her father's death. Often she cried or looked away and gave short answers. She was at home when her father died. Her first reaction was of sadness, with also some feelings of relief that he was out of pain. She did not like the funeral visitation and was concerned about her mother during this time. However, she liked the funeral service and was proud of how many people were there. She said the hardest part of the whole experience was "Just that he won't be around anymore."

Julie endorsed few psychiatric symptoms at 1 month after the death. She said she was still sad but had accepted the death. She had lost interest in school, including the sports team of which she was a member. She also reported some symptoms of social withdrawal. In terms of anxiety symptoms, she worried about her mother. This was mostly concern about the mother's social withdrawal and depression, rather than anxiety about the mother's life or about separation. She explained that she understood death, but she still thought it was unfair. She developed full-blown major depression that did not improve with individual and family therapy 1 year after her father's death. She eventually had to be treated with antidepressants in conjunction with psychotherapy and responded well. Julie's family history was positive for major depression over three generations.

CLINICAL COURSE

Unfortunately, there has been little systematic research on psychiatric symptoms experienced by children following parental death. For many years it was assumed very young children did not have the emotional sophistication to grieve about death.

Kranzler (1988), at Columbia University, found that grief and bereavement exist even in preschoolers. In bereaved children as young as 3 and 4 years old there was deep sadness and fear and anxiety just as in grieving adults. Kranzler felt that very young children experience grief in a less pervasive way than adults. Preschoolers did not hold on to emotions as persistently as adults: "There are spurts of intense emotion. Unexpected at moments when you'd least imagine it would occur, in the middle of play, while with friends. And at those moments there is very strong emotion. Lots of sadness, lots of anger. It will be there and it will go away. In between these bursts of emotion, what one sees is a child who looks like usual in many ways." Kranzler found in his preschool sample that not all emotional expression is associated with successful coping. Those children who were able to talk about being sad did well. Those children who said that they were angry or scared or even happy when thinking about their dead parent adjusted poorly.

Weller and co-workers (1988) examined depressive symptomatology in recently bereaved children and compared it with that found in normal and depressed control children. The recently bereaved children in their sample endorsed depressive symptoms more frequently than did normal control children. The bereaved children's dysphoria and loss of interest were the symptoms that best differentiated bereaved children from normal control children. The depressed children endorsed depressive symptoms more frequently than did the bereaved children. However, the difference between the bereaved and depressed children in reported loss of interest was not significant. Similar to findings in adults, feelings of guilt/self-depreciation and fatigue were less common in bereaved children and best differentiated bereaved children from depressed children. Bereaved children with preexisting psychiatric disorders or family history of depression were more likely to report depressive symptomatology following parental death.

Anxiety is a frequent symptom of bereavement in adults. However, the occurrence of anxiety symptoms in grieving children has not been well studied. Sanchez and colleagues (1988) evaluated bereaved children for anxiety symptoms 1 month after a parental death and compared them with normal and depressed control children. Anxiety symptoms were assessed using the Diagnostic Interview for Children and Adolescents— Child and Parent forms (DICA-C, DICA-P). Bereaved children reported more anxiety symptoms than normal controls, but this difference was not statistically significant. Bereaved children reported significantly fewer anxiety symptoms than depressed children. Parents of both bereaved and depressed children reported significantly fewer anxiety symptoms in their children than the children reported themselves. Age and sex of child, sex of surviving parent, and type of parental death (anticipated vs. unanticipated) were not significantly correlated with the total number of anxiety symptoms experienced. However, relationships between specific symptoms and certain key variables were noted among bereaved children: (1)

younger children were more likely to worry about their own safety; (2) girls worried more and were more phobic than boys; and (3) a positive family history of anxiety disorders tended to be associated with more anxiety symptoms.

Bereaved adults are reported to have increased somatic problems that lead to increased morbidity and mortality in the period after loss of a loved one. The effect of bereavement on children's health is unknown. Since children are more limited in their verbal expression than adults, perhaps they would tend to somaticize more in response to a loss. Furthermore, several additional variables have been hypothesized to be related to somatization in grieving children. Sood and associates (1988) studied 38 bereaved children who were evaluated 8 weeks after a parental death. All were assessed with standard structured diagnostic interviews and rating scales. In general, bereaved children reported few somatic complaints. Parental report of somatic problems in their children was even lower. Children who had anticipated their parent's death reported significantly more somatic symptoms than those who experienced an unanticipated loss. History of somatic complaints in a family member was significantly associated with increased symptoms in children as well as having a parent who was presently manifesting somatic complaints. Age, sex of child, or living parent did not impact on the presence of somatic symptoms. Although the mean number of somatic symptoms was not high, children with anticipated grief, family history of somatization, or a parent who was somaticizing during the bereavement period seemed at increased risk to develop somatic complaints.

Fristad and coworkers (1988) studied the effects of parental death on self-esteem, peer relations, and school performance in prepubertal bereaved children. Bereaved subjects were interviewed 1, 6, and 12 months after a parental death. Data were obtained from standard structured interviews (Diagnostic Interview for Children and Adolescents), clinical rating scales (Children's Depression Rating Scale—Revised), self-report inventories (Piers-Harris, Children's Depression Inventory), and teacher reports (Child Behavior Checklist, Conners Teacher Questionnaire). Bereaved children were significantly less interested in school and had more behavior problems at school than normal controls. Follow-up interviews at 6 and 12 months found that these problems did not improve significantly during the year. Bereaved children's age, sex, type of parental death (anticipated vs. unanticipated), and home environment factors had no effect on their functioning. When the surviving parent was a mother, significantly more problems were reported in (and by) the bereaved child. These included decreased interest in school and enjoyment of peer friendships. Thus bereaved children showed some impairment at school throughout the first year after their parent died.

Psychiatric symptomatology was prospectively and longitudinally assessed by Weller and co-workers (1988) in bereaved, prepubertal children aged 6 to 12 following the death of a parent when matched with depressed and normal controls. Children and parents were interviewed individually using standard structured interviews, clinical rating scales, and self-report inventories at 1, 6, and 12 months after the parental death. Compared with normal controls, bereaved children reported significantly more depressive symptoms, including sad affect, guilt, decreased school performance, psychomotor retardation, and morbid ideation. Bereaved children reported fewer depressive symptoms, anxiety symptoms, somatic symptoms, conduct problems, enuresis, and encopresis than depressed inpatients. When bereaved children's symptoms were compared at 1, 6, and 13 months, symptom endorsement was greatest at 1 month for almost all symptoms examined. Of the 24 symptoms assessed, 9 were experienced by over 40% of the children during the first month following parental loss. These included dysphoria, weeping, fatigue, loss of pleasure, trouble thinking/concentrating, social withdrawal, suicidal ideation, irritability, and separation anxiety. Although most symptom endorsement decreased over follow-up, 33% of children reported having each of the following symptoms: sad affect, weeping, headaches, and gastrointestinal complaints 13 months after the parental death.

For 18 of the 24 symptoms assessed, endorsement was highest at a statistically significant level for the depressed group and lowest for the normal controls, with the bereaved group at an intermediate level. Although bereaved children endorsed more symptoms than normal controls, these differences were often not statistically significant. Bereaved children reported significantly less depressive, anxiety, somatic, conduct, and enuresis/encopresis disorder symptoms than depressed inpatients.

The impact of six potential mediating factors on bereaved children's functioning were assessed: Age and sex of the child, type of death (anticipated vs. unanticipated), and sex of the surviving parent had minimal association with the presence or absence of psychiatric symptomatology. A better home environment and better parental adjustment were associated with fewer psychiatric symptoms in the children at 1 and 6 months after a parental death. Age and sex of the child, type of death (anticipated vs. unanticipated), and one measure of home environment had relatively little effect on bereaved children's functioning. When the surviving parent was a mother, however, significantly more problems were reported in and by the bereaved children, including decreased interest in school and enjoyment of peer friendships.

Bereaved children experienced significantly less interest in school and had more behavior problems in school than normal children; no other differences between the groups were significant. Compared with inpatient depressed children, bereaved children reported significantly more interest in school, more friendships and more enjoyment of those friendships, less guilt, and greater self-esteem. Contact with peers increased between 1 and 6 months after the death, although parents noted that the quality of these relations had diminished during that time. No other changes in self-esteem and peer relations were noted.

MODEL FOR STUDYING DEPRESSION

Several reports suggest the idea that bereavement in childhood may be a major risk factor for developing depression as an adult. This has been reported by Breier and associates (1988) and several other investigators. Breier and associates studied 90 adults between 18 and 55 years old who had experienced a "permanent" separation from one or both parents between the ages of 2 and 17. Sixty-four percent had experienced parental loss through death. Seventy-seven percent of this sample had a major psychiatric disorder, 86% of which was depression.

For a period of time, child and adolescent psychiatry in this country was strongly influenced by the psychoanalytic school of thought. It was believed that depressive disorders were rare in children and adolescents since their superego was not well formed and they can substitute "love objects" easier than adults. It was not until 1975 that a meeting of researchers sponsored by the National Institute of Mental Health concluded that depression in children and adolescents can exist. Schulterbrandt and Raskin (1977) summarized and published the findings of this meeting. In this book, Kovacs discussed studying bereaved children as a natural model of studying depression. She proposed to "define depression as the systematic description of grief reactions of different ages: list the number, type, and duration of symptoms for each age group. Examination of large populations of children who have lost a parent or a parent substitute may facilitate a description of clinical depression as a statistically deviant response to loss." This strategy may address (1) "normal" (± 1 1 SD) duration of dysphoria and other symptoms in view of objectively defined loss; (2) extent and type of associated behavioral impairments; (3) invariance of the symptoms as a function of exposure to different situations; (4) developmental variations in the syndrome as a function of age; and (5) actual prevalence of syndrome. She felt that "given a large enough population, it may be assumed that the various characteristics will be normally distributed." These "normal" grief reactions may be distinguished from "clinical" depressive reactions because depression is so much less frequent than bereavement.

LABORATORY FINDINGS

Psychometric Findings

When bereaved children are administered the DICA, 39% are diagnosed with the syndrome of major affective disorder 1 month after parental death. Other findings that are less common are decreased school performance, anxiety symptoms, and somatization (Weller, et al. 1988).

Biological Findings

The hypothalmic-pituitary-adrenal (HPA) axis has been studied in bereaved adults. Bereavement studies reveal abnormalities in the HPA axis with elevated cortisol levels. Weller and associates studied the HPA axis of bereaved children and adolescents using the dexamethasone suppression test (DST). All subjects were studied 4 weeks following the death of a parent. No child or family member had received psychiatric treatment in the previous 2 years. Eighteen children (8 prepubertal, 10 pubertal), aged 7 to 18 ($M \pm SD = 13.1 \pm 3.2$) without physical illness that might affect DST results were studied. All were administered the DICA and the Children's Depression Inventory (CDI) to assess depressive symptomatology 4 weeks after the parental death. Children were also given dexamethasone at 11 PM (0.5 mg, prepubertal; 1.0 mg, pubertal). Cortisol samples were drawn at 4 PM the next day, with levels determined by radioimmunoassay. The bereaved children's cortisol levels after dexamethasone ranged from 1.0 to 18.2 ($M \pm SD$ 4.9 ± 4.7). Overall, 50% of prepubertal children and 29% of pubertal children were nonsuppressors (cortisol ≥ 5 µg/dL). Nonsuppressors endorsed each *DSM-III* symptom of depression more frequently than did suppressors. For five depressive symptoms, endorsement by nonsuppressors was at least 25 percentage points higher than by suppressors. Additionally, absolute cortisol levels were significantly correlated with scores on both parent and child forms of the CDI. Further studies are necessary to clearly determine if there is a biological link between major depression and the depressive symptoms that occur during bereavement.

A study by Breier and associates (1988) looked at 90 adults who had lost a parent as a child between the ages of 2 and 17. They found nearly 80% had serious psychopathology as adults, and 86% of these had an affective disorder. Breier and associates also looked at the biology of bereavement and found that these adults with a history of affective disorder were not depressed at the time of the study but that they had abnormally high levels of cortisol and β-endorphin immunoreactivity. The group who had lost a parent but had not developed subsequent depressions did not have elevated cortisol and β-endorphin immunoreactivity. These investigators view the at-risk group as "walking wounded," vulnerable for the development of significant depression as adults and having abnormal responses to stress, all with antecedents in childhood. They state that there is a possibility that a severe early stress may not only temporarily alter the functioning of stress systems during the time of loss but that these changes might leave their mark on the brain and persist throughout the person's life.

Breier and associates wanted to identify factors that best predicted both high stress hormone levels and who will eventually experience depression as adults. Their analysis indicated the most important predictive factor was whether a stable adult figure was available to the child during the time of loss. It did not matter whether the mother or the father had died. The age of the child at the time of loss also did not predict later depression, nor how the loss occurred or even whether there was a history of depression in the family. They found that children who adapted poorly to the loss and who did not have a supportive environment were the ones who later in life had high cortisol and β-endorphin immunoreactivity and that these children were the ones who also became depressed.

DIFFERENTIAL DIAGNOSIS

Major Affective Disorders

Thirty-nine percent of children 2 months after a parental death satisfy criteria for major depression. There are no published data comparing symptomatology of grieving children with that of outpatient depressed children. Children who satisfy criteria for major depression are usually those who have had psychiatric diagnoses prior to the death of the parent and who have a high rate of family history of psychopathology, especially depression. There are no systematic data on short- and long-term follow-up of children as to the frequency of depressive symptomatology.

Very often grieving children have thoughts of death and dying. However, these thoughts center around the wish to visit with the dead person and are not probably true suicidal thoughts. A child who is actively suicidal (that is, who has a suicide plan or has attempted suicide) should be closely evaluated for the possibility of a coexisting depressive episode superimposed on grief.

Adjustment Disorder With Depressed Mood

Usually children with adjustment disorder with depressed mood have some signs and symptoms of depression but do not fulfill criteria for a major depressive disorder. When a child has lost a significant person through death the diagnosis of uncomplicated bereavement should be given rather than adjustment disorder with depressed mood according to the *DSM-III-R*.

Post-Traumatic Stress Disorder

The *DSM-III-R* describes post-traumatic stress disorder as a condition that follows an event that is outside the range of usual human experiences and that would be markedly distressing to almost anyone. Usually the traumatic event is reexperienced as an intrusive distressing recollection of the event, a repetitious play in which aspects of the trauma are experienced. There are recurrent distressing dreams of the event, a sudden feeling as if the traumatic event were necessary, and intense psychological distress at exposure to events that symbolize or resemble an aspect of the traumatic event.

Also, there is avoidance of stimuli associated with the trauma, such as efforts to avoid activities that arouse recollection of the trauma; inability to recall an important aspect of the trauma; regression in developmental skills; feelings of detachment from others; restrictive range of affect; sense of shortened future; persistent symptoms of increased arousal, such as difficulty falling or staying asleep; irritability; difficulty concentrating; and exaggerated startle response or physiological reactivity on exposure to events that symbolize or resemble an aspect of the traumatic event. The disturbance lasts at least 1 month. Children who experience death because of suicide or murder experience post-traumatic stress disorder symptoms more often than children who experience death due to natural causes. Since death is not outside the range of usual human experience, almost by definition grief should not be considered a post-traumatic disorder.

ATTENDANCE OF CHILDREN AT FUNERALS

Several theories have been proposed regarding children's participation in their parent's funeral. Some believe that school-aged children should be given the opportunity to attend the funeral, perhaps even be encouraged to go, but they should not be forced to go (Gardener 1983; Wessel 1983). There are also some reports that children who do not participate in funeral activities have a more difficult time accepting the death (Furman 1970; Grollman 1967; Bowlby 1963). Conversely, there are reports of children developing psychiatric symptoms as a result of funeral attendance (Schowalter 1976; Furman 1974, 1976). Schowalter (1976) described 12 patients (aged 3 to 15) who developed anxiety and phobic symptoms that directly followed a funeral or were associated with funeral attendance. Furman (1976) found similar symptoms in young children who reportedly did not cope well with the funeral experience. However, when the study was repeated with a control group, Furman noted the same symptoms in grieving children who had not attended a funeral.

These reports provide some systematic information. However, most reports are anecdoctal reports with little empiric data. A study by Weller and co-workers (1988) attempted to obtain objective information from prepubertal children to determine the extent of children's funeral participation and if participation is related to future psychopathology. After the death of a parent most children attended both the funeral home visitation and the funeral service. Most of them stated that they had been expected to go and wanted to go and reported being "basically in control" in both settings. Atypical reactions (i.e., the child was extremely agitated or very passive and withdrawn) were most often observed when the child helped with funeral arrangements, had gone to funeral activities despite not having wanted to go, and had known someone who had died before, and had reported that death meant that the parent "was buried." Funeral participation and/or atypical reactions were not associated with increased depressive or other psychiatric symptomatology assessed 2 months after parental death. Thus, if a child does not want to go and is forced to go to funeral activities, he or she could manifest atypical reactions. However, atypical reactions in themselves do not indicate the child would have been better off not going. Thus, it would appear that if a child wants to attend his or her parent's funeral there would be no reason to forbid attendance. One child reported that the funeral was the worst experience associated with the parent's death. This child went on to state, "It was really hard, but I'm glad I went. I think all kids should go to their parent's funeral . . . because it's a good way to send them off."

TREATMENT

A child who has lost a parent often has "lost" more than one parent. This is because the surviving parent is often engulfed in his or her own grief and hence is not emotionally available to meet the child's needs. Very often the bereaved parent puts excessive demands on the child and may come to emotionally depend on the child. This can be very upsetting for the child. To avoid this problem, an adult who can take over the care of the child both emotionally and physically until the bereaved parent is able to resume responsibilities should be identified. Children also are often scared because they think they might have caused the death. They may also wonder if it will happen to them or to their surviving parent and may worry about "who will take care of me." Encouraging children to verbalize their emotions and reassuring them that there will be someone to help them can help them deal with these concerns.

Following a parent's death, children face many changes in their lives. Such changes may include the surviving parent having to take a job to support the family and hence be less accessible to the child. The surviving parent might start to date and talk about marriage. This could result in the child feeling angry, since he or she might view this as the new parent-mate trying to replace the missing parent as well as taking the attention of the surviving parent away from the child. Families may move because they can no longer afford to live in their apartment or house due to decreased family income.

Sometimes, the surviving parent wants to move closer to relatives and thus disrupts the child's school and peer relationships. Children often feel they are like puppets and no one is paying attention to their needs. It is important that a responsible adult talk and listen to the bereaved child's wishes and concerns.

Some persons believe mutual support programs are helpful. Parkes (1975) states, "The person best qualified to understand and help with problems of the bereaved person is another bereaved person." However, few mutual support programs exist for children. Children with preexisting history of psychopathology may need to have psychiatric evaluation and treatment because of an exacerbation of preexisting problems or if new incapacitating symptoms develop. Furthermore, children who experience death in a traumatic manner such as murder and suicide might be at higher risk to develop depression and post-traumatic stress disorder. Professional intervention in these situations should be considered.

CONCLUSIONS

Because of immaturity and lack of well-developed coping mechanisms, bereaved children may be at a high risk to develop psychopathology. Depending on the developmental level, children might show different changes in behavior following the death of a loved one. In preschoolers, speech disturbances, altered eating patterns, sleeping changes, and bowel disturbances may occur.

By school age, children appear to experience depressive symptomatology similar to that seen in bereaved adults. Suicidal thoughts are common and may represent an attempt to unite with the missing parent. However, suicide attempts are rare and should receive immediate attention since this might signal a major depression rather than normal grieving. Anxiety symptoms and somatization are not very common. Also, bereaved children may have decreased scholastic performance as well as problems with peers. Adolescents who lose a parent often experience depressive symptoms. However, not all children who lose a parent manifest impairment. Some respond to the death of a loved one with increased academic performance, maturity, and sense of responsibility.

Children who seem to develop pathologic processes are those who had preexisting psychiatric disorders or family history of psychiatric disorder, especially depression in the surviving parent. A surviving parent who copes well with his or her grief and a good support system for the family seem to protect against the development of psychopathology. Conversely, if the surviving parent is dysfunctional in his or her coping with the grief and there is a lack of support for the parent and children, there may be an increased risk of the child developing psychopathology, particularly depression.

References

American Psychiatric Association. 1987. *Diagnostic and Statistical Manual of Mental Disorders*, 3rd ed., revised. Washington, D.C.: American Psychiatric Association.

Arthur, Kemme. 1964. Bereavement in childhood. *J. Child Psychol. Psychiatry* 5:37–49.

Barry, H. Jr., and Lindeman, E. 1960. Critical ages for maternal bereavement in psychoneuroses. *Psychosom. Med.* 22:166–181.

Beck, A. T., Sethi, B. B., and Tuthill, R. W. 1963. Childhood bereavement and adult depression. *Arch. Gen. Psychiatry* 9:295–302.

Bendickson, R., and Fulton, R. 1976. Death and the child: An anterospective test of the childhood bereavement and later behavior disorder hypothesis. In Fulton, R. (ed.): *Death and Identity*. Bowie, Md.: Charles Press.

Bowlby, J. 1960. Grief and mourning in infancy and early childhood. *Psychoanal. Study Child* 15:9–52.

Bowlby, J. 1961. Childhood mourning and its implications for psychiatry. *Am. J. Psychiatry* 118:481–498.

Bowlby, J. 1963. Pathological mourning and childhood mourning. *J. Am. Psychoanal.* 11:500–541.

Brandon, S. 1974. Grief. *Practitioner* 212:867–876.

Breier, A., Kelsoe, J. R., Kirwin, P. D., et al. 1988. Early parental loss and development of adult psychopathology. *Arch. Gen. Psychiatry* 45:987–993.

Caplan, M. G., and Douglas, U. I. 1969. Influence of parental loss in children with depressed mood. *J. Child Psychol. Psychiatry* 10:225–232.

Duffy, J. C. 1977. *Child Psychiatry*, 2nd ed. New York: Examination Publishing Co.

Elizur, E., and Kaffman, M. 1983. Factors influencing the severity of childhood bereavement reactions. *Am. J. Orthopsychiatry* 53:668–676.

Freud, S. 1917. Mourning and melancholia. In Strachey, J. (ed.): *The Standard Edition of the Complete Psychological Works of Sigmund Freud*, vol. 14. London: Hogarth Press and Institute for Psychoanalysis.

Fristad M., Galerston-Jedel, R., Weller, E., Weller, R., Hittner, J., and Preskorn, S.: Peer relationships, school performance, and self-esteem in bereaved children. 35th Annual American Academy of Child and Adolescent Psychiatry and Canadian Academy of Child Psychiatry Joint Meeting, Seattle, Washington, October, 1988.

Furman, R. 1970. The child's reaction to a death in the

family. In Schoenberg, B., Carr, A., Perentz, D., and Kutscher, A. (eds.): *Loss and Grief: Psychological Management in Medical Practice*. New York: Columbia University.

Furman, E. 1974. *A Child's Parent Dies*. New Haven, Conn.: Yale University Press.

Furman, E. 1976. Commentary. *J. Pediatr.* 89:143–145.

Gardener, R. A. 1983. Children's reactions to parental death. In Schowalter, J. E., Patterson, P. R., Tallmer, M., et al. (eds.): *The Child and Death*, New York: Columbia University Press.

Greenberg, L. I. 1975. Therapeutic grief work with children. *Social Casework* 56:396–403.

Gregory, I. 1965. Anterospective data following childhood loss of a parent: I. Delinquency and high school dropout. *Arch. Gen. Psychiatry* 13:99–109.

Grollman, E. 1967. *Explaining Death to Children*. Boston: Beacon Press.

Higgins, G. L. 1977. Grief reactions. *Practitioner* 218:689–695.

Kliman, G. 1968. *Psychological Emergencies of Childhood*. New York: Grune & Stratton.

Kranzler, E. 1988. Personal communication.

Lifshitz, M., Berman, D., Galili, A., and Gilad, D., 1977. Bereaved children: The effect of mother's perception and social system organization on their short-range adjustment. *J. Am. Acad. Child Psychiatry* 16:272–284.

Markusen, T., and Fulton, R. 1971. Childhood bereavement and behavioral disorders: A critical review. *Omega* 2:107–117.

Nagy, M. 1948. The child's theories concerning death. *J. Genet. Psychol.* 73:3–27.

Osterweis, M., Killilea, M., Greer, D., et al. 1984. Bereavement intervention programs. In Osterweis, M., Solomon, F., and Green, M. (eds.): *Bereavement: Reactions, Consequences, and Care*. Washington, D.C.: National Academy Press.

Osterweis, M., and Townsend, J. 1988. *Understanding Bereavement Reactions in Adults and Children*. DHHS publication No. (ADM 88-1555). Washington, D.C.: National Academy Press.

Parkes, C. M. 1975. Unexpected and untimely bereavement: A statistical study of young Boston widows. Schoenberg, B., et al. (eds.): *Bereavement: Its Psychosocial Aspect*. New York: Columbia University Press.

Rosenthal, P. A. 1980. Short-term family therapy and pathological grief resolution with children and adolescents. *Family Process* 19:151–159.

Sanchez, L., Fristad, M. A., Weller, E. B., and Weller, R. A. 1988. Anxiety symptoms in bereaved prepubertal children. Presented at the 141st annual meeting of the American Psychiatric Association, Montreal, Canada, May 7–11.

Schowalter, J. E. 1976. How do children and funerals mix? *J. Pediatr.* 89:139–145.

Schulterbrandt, J. G., and Raskin, A. 1977. *Depression in Childhood: Diagnosis, Treatment, and Conceptual Models*. New York: Raven Press.

Sood, B., Weller, E. B., Weller, R. A., Fristad, M. A., and Bowes, J. M.: Somatic symptoms in bereaved children. American Academy of Child and Adolescent Psychiatry Annual Meeting, Washington, D.C., October 21–25, 1987.

Statistical Abstracts of the United States. 1985. Washington, D.C.: U.S. Social Security Administration, Bureau of Census.

Tennant, C., Bebbington, P., and Hurry, J. 1980. Parental death in childhood and risk of adult depressive disorder: A review. *Psychol. Med.* 10:289–299.

Van Eerdewegh, M. M., Bieri, M. D., Parilla, R. H., and Clayton, P. J. 1982. The bereaved child. *Br. J. Psychiatry* 140:23–29.

Weller, E. B., and Weller, R. A. (eds.). 1984. *Current Perspectives on Major Depressive Disorders in Children*. Washington, D.C.: American Psychiatric Press.

Weller, E. B., Weller, R. A., and Fristad, M. A. 1984. Historical and theoretical perspectives on childhood depression. In Weller, E. B., and Weller, R. A. (eds.): *Current Perspectives on Major Depressive Disorders in Children*. Washington, D.C.: American Psychiatric Press.

Weller, E. B., Weller, R. A., Fristad, M. A., and Bowes, J. M.: Depressive symptoms in acutely bereaved children. 41st Annual Meeting of the American Psychiatric Association, Montreal, Canada, May 7–11, 1988.

Weller, E. B., and Weller, R. A.: Neuroendocrine changes in affectively ill children and adolescents. In Brown, W. (ed.): *Psychiatr. Clin. North Am.* 6(1):41–54, 1988.

Wessel, M. A. 1983. Primary care bereavement after tertiary care death. Paper presented at Palliative Care Conference on Bereavement: New Horizons, Philadelphia.

Wolfenstein, M. 1966. How is mourning possible? *Psychoanal. Study Child* 21:92–123.

Wolfenstein, M. 1969. Loss, rage, and repetition. *Psychoanal. Study Child* 24:432–460.

Post-Traumatic Stress Disorder in Children and Adolescents

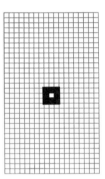

ROBERT S. PYNOOS, M.D., M.P.H.

Traumatic experiences in childhood and their consequences are important concerns in psychiatric practice. The diagnostic classification post-traumatic stress disorder (PTSD) recognizes that unusual human experiences of severe emotional impact induce a characteristic set of psychiatric symptoms. Beginning with the reports of "traumatic neurosis" among combat soldiers in World War I, psychiatrists have identified a similar clinical picture among adults exposed to war, disaster, and civilian violence. The clinical picture of this anxiety disorder has been classified in the revised third edition of the *Diagnostic and Statistical Manual of Mental Disorders (DSM-III-R)* of the American Psychiatric Association (1987) to include the following criteria:

1. The person has experienced an event that is outside the range of usual human existence that would be markedly distressing to almost anyone.

2. The traumatic event is persistently reexperienced.

3. There is continued avoidance of stimuli associated with the trauma or numbing of general responsiveness.

4. Symptoms of increased arousal persist that were not present before the trauma.

This anxiety disorder can occur at any age; recently, increased attention has been focused on the symptoms of PTSD in children who have experienced extreme stress. "Psychic trauma" had been the prevailing concept used to describe children's responses to severe adverse life events. Post-traumatic stress symptoms in children and adolescents have been reported in response to having experienced the stressors listed in Table 4–1.

PATHOGENESIS

PTSD is the only anxiety disorder whose etiology is associated with a known external event. Although controversy remains over defining traumatic stress, all theories, from the earliest formulations by Freud and Janet (cited in Van der Kolk 1987) to the most current (Van der Kolk 1987), focus on the experience of traumatic helplessness. As Freud (1926) noted, in a traumatic situation "external and internal, real and instinctual dangers converge." More recently, Kolb (1988) has postulated that PTSD results from "the intensity, recurrence and duration of fearful emotions from which there is no immediate escape or remedy . . . The central emotion is fear moving to levels of terror, horror, and helpless despair." Following the traumatic event, the person is left with the challenge of assimilating and tolerating the traumatic helplessness because a reality-based cognitive reappraisal only confirms the experienced life threat or danger to self or others.

The helplessness is experienced in several ways, each of which is related to the set of symptoms described in the *DSM-III-R*. First, there is an intense perceptual experience involving the sights, sounds, and actions before, during, and after the occurrence. Second, there is an internal, moment-to-moment appraisal of the threat involving conscious and unconscious meaning and unanswered fantasies of intervention. Third, there are overwhelming affective responses that are often coupled with a heightened, at times unbearable, awareness of autonomic arousal. As one school-age child declared, "I felt awful. My heart was beating so fast I thought it was going to break."

It is hypothesized that the memory of the event remains in prolonged active storage, constantly threatening to intrude, to disrupt normal information processing, as Horowitz (1976) emphasizes, and to cause shifts in attention. The mind, as if through remembering, repeating, and reexperiencing, searches for ways to offset the helplessness and alter the outcome in thought and fantasy. In addition, fear of being affectively overwhelmed leads to suppression of thought, avoidance, and affective inhibition or intolerance. As one child stated, "I never want to feel like that again." Furthermore, one remains in an aroused psychophysiological state as if the threat is ever-present. As Kardner (cited in Kolb 1987) observed, there is an enduring vigilance for and sensitivity to environmental threat. Van der Kolk (1987) has suggested that uncontrollable, terrifying experiences may have their most profound effects in children when the central nervous system's affect regulation and cognitive functions have not fully matured.

The first criterion of PTSD emphasizes the unusual and extreme nature of the stressor. Children's initial reactions are primarily determined by the degree of exposure, appraisal of threat, and personal impact or meaning. The two most likely stressors to induce post-traumatic stress symptoms are serious threat to the child's, family member's, or close friend's life and witnessing injury or death as a result of an accident or physical violence. Specific experiences, especially witnessing the grotesque or hearing cries of distress, appear to intensify the recall of the traumatic experience. The greater the personal impact, the more likely there will be a traumatic response; for instance, seeing a brother or sister rather than a stranger hit by a car.

Children as well as adults appear to respond more severely and their actions last longer if the traumatic event is associated with human accountability due to a violent act or human error, in contrast to a natural disaster. Furthermore, children's ability to assimilate the experience is usually strongly hindered when a family member is the agent of the trauma, as in cases of sexual or physical abuse, spousal murder, and, especially, parental suicide. Sometimes children are the perpetrators, causing injury or death to others because of an accidental shooting or automobile collision or, under duress or willfully, in committing a war atrocity. In these circumstances, the problem is compounded.

All the research evidence indicates the primacy of extent of exposure in children's post-trauma reactions (Pynoos et al. 1987). For instance, thousands of children may be in the region of a major disaster but not all children are equally at risk of developing PTSD. At highest risk are those who were in

---

Table 4–1. STRESSORS RESULTING IN POST-TRAUMATIC STRESS DISORDER IN CHILDREN

Kidnapping and hostage situations
Exposure to violence, including terrorism, gang violence, sniper attacks, and war atrocities
Witnessing rape, murder, and suicidal behavior
Sexual or physical abuse
Severe accidental injury, including burns and hit-and-run accidents
Life-threatening illnesses and life-endangering medical procedures
Train, airplane, ship, and automobile accidents
Major disasters

immediate threat of death (e.g., buried in rubble), who were present in the impact zone (e.g., at the epicenter of an earthquake or directly where a tornado hit), who suffered severe injury, and who witnessed or experienced the death or injury of family members or close friends. In addition, adolescents who serve as rescue workers, especially body handlers, may be especially at risk. A marked drop-off in post-traumatic stress symptoms can be expected just beyond the perimeter of immediate danger.

In life-threatening situations, very young children may be partially protected from the traumatic impact because they do not understand the extent of the danger. Their appraisal of threat is determined in large part by the actions and attitudes of the adult who is accompanying them. Even though adults may protect children from stress by trying to appear unalarmed, during horrifying and catastrophic situations they cannot be expected to remain calm. In many cases, children may be confused, disturbed, and potentially placed in greater jeopardy by adults who minimize an obvious threat (Pynoos and Nader, in press).

Although many untoward childhood events cause considerable distress, under typical circumstances (e.g., chronic parental or child illness, separation, divorce, or bereavement) PTSD is not likely to result. However, a traumatic experience may occur within these situations; for example, during a marital separation or custody battle, when a parent attempts suicide and is discovered by a child, when a psychotic parent becomes dangerously threatening to family members, or when a child witnesses the sudden, fatal heart attack of a parent. Moreover, this diagnosis does not include pathogenic environments and parental dysfunction that may result in severe disturbances in normal development and personality.

EPIDEMIOLOGY

At some time in their lives, approximately 1% of the adult population has suffered a sufficient number of symptoms to meet the diagnostic criteria of PTSD, while an additional 15% have experienced significant symptoms (Helzer et al. 1987). No similar estimates are available for children. However, data are available to suggest the poten-

tial extent of children's exposures to stressors associated with PTSD.

Disasters are one potential source. Since 1974, 798 major federal disasters and more than 3,000 federal emergencies have been declared in the United States. More than 8,000 deaths annually are attributed to natural and man-made disasters, and there are 50 estimated injuries for every death. Estimates of the psychiatric morbidity for adults vary greatly with differences in a disaster's overall impact on the community, the type and severity of exposure, and the percentage of the population affected. The same qualifications are likely to be true for exposed children (Pynoos and Nader, in press).

Domestic violence is a second source. In 1985, approximately 1.9 million cases of child abuse and neglect were reported in the United States, including 150,000 to 200,000 cases of child sexual abuse. Furthermore, estimates are that more than 3 million children witness spousal abuse annually (Eth and Pynoos 1985).

The witnessing by children of extreme violence places them at significant risk for PTSD. In 1985, there were 19,000 homicides in the United States; between 10% and 20% of all homicides are witnessed by children. In large urban areas, each year several hundred children witness the murder of a parent or sibling. Approximately 80,000 rapes are reported annually, an underreporting of perhaps 10 to 1. Hundreds of children each year are present during the sexual assault of their mothers. In addition, thousands of children are directly or indirectly exposed annually to the suicidal behaviors of their parents, siblings, and friends. Lastly, community violence, from gang warfare to sniper attacks, has increased in recent years, exposing large numbers of children, especially in the inner cities, to life-threatening violent situations (Eth and Pynoos 1985).

Refugee children from war-torn countries represent another population of children in whom PTSD symptoms are frequently present. These children have been exposed to war atrocities, as witnesses and participants, and some, such as Cambodian adolescents, have endured a holocaust. In addition, many recent child immigrants may have previously experienced major disasters in countries where the degree of destruction, morbidity, and mortality far exceeds those found following disasters in the United States (Eth and Pynoos 1985).

The recognition that PTSD can occur in response to life-threatening illnesses and life-endangering medical procedures places another group of children at risk, enlarging the scope of psychiatric concern to include medically ill children (Eth and Pynoos 1985).

CLINICAL PICTURE

In 1938, Levy suggested that children exhibited traumatic responses similar to those of adults. While adult diagnostic criteria are for the most part adequate in describing children's response to trauma, several modifications in the criteria more specifically portray symptomatology in children (Brett et al. 1988).

In this section the symptom criteria of PTSD as they pertain to children is discussed (Table 4–2).

Reexperiencing Phenomena

The whole set of reexperiencing phenomena demonstrate how elements of the traumatic experience remain active in children's mental life.

Table 4–2. SYMPTOM CRITERIA OF POST-TRAUMATIC STRESS DISORDER IN CHILDREN

1. Child experiences an unusual event that would be markedly distressing to almost anyone
   a. Life threat or harm to self or family/friend
   b. Sudden destruction of home or community
   c. Witnessing violent death or injury
2. Reexperiencing phenomena
   a. Intrusive recollections/images
   b. Traumatic dreams
   c. Repetitive play
   d. Reenactment behavior
   e. Distress at traumatic reminders
3. Psychological numbing/avoidance
   a. Avoidance of thoughts, feelings, locations, situations
   b. Reduced interest in usual activities
   c. Feelings of being alone/detached/estranged
   d. Restricted emotional range
   e. Memory disturbance
   f. Loss of acquired skills
   g. Change in orientation toward the future
4. Increased state of arousal
   a. Sleep disturbance
   b. Irritability/anger
   c. Difficulty concentrating
   d. Hypervigilance
   e. Exaggerated startle response
   f. Autonomic response to traumatic reminders

INTRUSIVE RECOLLECTIONS

Intrusive recollections can be in the form of recurrent thoughts, images, or sounds. They always remain unwelcome and distressing and are difficult to dispel. Intrusive recollections act as memory markers, indicating moments of extreme threat or helplessness during the traumatic experience that were associated with vivid perceptual input. Examples of intrusive recollections include a boy who sees in his mind the gun pointed directly at him at the moment he was taken hostage, a girl not being able to rid herself of seeing the rapist's cold impersonal facial expression that struck terror in her as he approached, or a boy privately suffering from the horrifying sight of his skin completely ripped off his knee as he lay on the street after being hit by a speeding truck. Children who witness violence may continue to picture a parent being shot, a sibling's body hanging by a rope, or a friend being hit and dragged by a car and to hear in their minds the sound of gunfire, sirens, or screams for help.

One should not expect that children will provide a detailed version of reexperiencing such scenes as adults report in describing a flashback. Typically, the younger the child, the more the recollection is confined to a single image or sound, which is usually what was the outstanding action for the child when immediate threat or injury occurred. In describing these images, the vocabulary of younger children may be especially limited and they may use expressions familiar to them. For example, after seeing his mother strangled, one boy said, "he squashed my mother's neck." The vividness of traumatic impressions can usually be elicited through drawings and redramatization.

TRAUMATIC DREAMS

Traumatic dreams, occurring when waking defenses are inoperative, are another example of unwelcomed intrusion. Often short and unelaborated, traumatic dreams depict the threat that the child experienced; for example, a child may dream that someone is once again shooting at him or that something is about to fall on him, or he may "recall" the scene as a family member is swept away by flood waters. At times, a child may even dream of his own death. These dreams are usually accompanied by a troubling sense of renewed fear or anxiety. They may actually occur during stage 2 or stage 4 sleep rather than rapid eye movement sleep and include motor restlessness, agitation, and vocalizations of fear. In younger children, these disturbing dreams may, within several weeks, change into generalized nightmares of monsters, of rescuing others, or of catastrophes that threaten oneself or others.

Mark Twain, who witnessed a murder as a child, provided a classic illustration of a traumatic dream in his description of Tom Sawyer's sleep after he had seen the murder in the graveyard.

"Tom, you pitch around and talk in your sleep so much that you keep me awake half the time.". . .

"And you do talk such stuff," Sid said. "Last night you said, 'it's blood, that's what it is!' You said that over and over." (Twain, 1881)

Because they renew traumatic anxiety, traumatic dreams can prolong the course of PTSD. Fear of dream recurrence can contribute to the often-reported, chronic need in children after trauma to sleep with a parent or sibling.

REPETITIVE PLAY

Children often compulsively express themes and aspects of the trauma in repetitive and often unrewarding play. After violent incidents, they may enact scenes of murder, kidnap, suicide, rape, or rescue of an injured party. For example, Bergen (1958) described how a young child who saw her mother murdered carefully painted her hands red and acted out a game of stabbing herself with a paintbrush. Children may play "tornado games" or "earthquake games." Children may also involve siblings or peers in their traumatic play. Much traumatic play goes unnoticed by parents. However, parents do get disturbed by some traumatic play, as for example when a child imitates in play a parent's suicidal behavior.

When examined closely, such play often entails some effort at denial in fantasy, in which the child attempts to mitigate the emotional pain, even while maintaining an accurate impression of what really happened. For example, a child may repeatedly play with a toy bus, always completing a safe bus ride, when in fact, the child's school bus had been kidnapped; or a child may use clay to apply bulletproof paneling to a truck after a bullet had pierced the window and killed a family member.

With time, the children's play may incorporate intrusive imagery or sound. After witnessing his father's assassination, a young boy was preoccupied with the sight of the blood. More than a year later, the only thing he drew on the coloring book illustration of a picnic basket was a catsup bottle that had spilled. Along with the intrusive image, he was also expressing a wish that it had only been fake blood and his father was still alive. As intrusive recollections become incorporated into traumatic play, children may report them less often. Therefore, as time passes, the clinical observation of persistent traumatic play may become more important than the self-report of intrusive imagery.

REENACTMENT BEHAVIOR

Reenactment behavior is repetition of some part of the traumatic experience, commonly in response to a traumatic reminder. More than 2 years after she had been raped and then shot at close range in the head, an adolescent girl ducked when a man with a hairstyle similar to that of her assailant raised a camera to take a picture at her apartment swimming pool.

Reenactment behavior often represents not only an overreaction to an environmental stimuli but, similar to traumatic play, also an effort to offset in action the original moments of traumatic helplessness. With closer examination, it became apparent that this teenager wished to eradicate the feeling of the gun against her head, to put the threat at a greater distance, and to imagine having time to take protective action.

Children or adolescents may actively seek out an opportunity to engage in a reenactment behavior. For example, a teenage boy had been in an accident that killed his close friend after their car rolled over from a blindside hit. Several weeks later, he found himself compulsively riding the "corkscrew" roller coaster. He later realized that he was repeating the sense of rolling in the car, only this time with a guaranteed safe outcome and with the opportunity to keep his eyes open and see all that was happening around him. With access to guns, automobiles, and drugs, reenactment behavior of adolescents can become dangerous and even life threatening.

DISTRESS AT TRAUMATIC REMINDERS

Children respond with renewed anxiety or distress to traumatic reminders as frequently as adults. The type of reminders are varied but are often closely associated with the details of the actual experience. After a tornado, children may become anxious any time it is windy, or after a flood, they may become frightened when it rains. Reminders include visual, auditory, tactile, and olfactory sensations; the actual trauma site or a similar place; physical attributes of persons that resemble an assailant; circumstantial reminders (e.g., the time of day, the day of the week, the season of the year, the activity one was doing beforehand, the clothes one was wearing); affects associated with the event (e.g., feeling terribly alone); somatic stimuli such as a stomachache, fast heart beat, or headache felt during or after the event; and human behaviors linked to the event, such as people arguing or someone coming into the room at night.

Children differ from adults primarily in the relative importance of concrete rather than symbolic reminders. After a violent occurrence, for example, children may feel anxious at seeing a knife in the kitchen, while watching violence on television, when hearing a siren or something that sounds like a gun, or when bleeding from an accidental cut. After a life-threatening illness "whenever one child felt aches in her legs, she thought of such aches as the first sign of her original cancer and experienced renewed fears and nightmares" (Pynoos and Eth 1986, p. 127). These everyday reminders as well as major events, like the anniversary of the event, are responsible for continued disruptions in mood and daily functioning. Traumatic reminders may seem minor to an outside observer; yet for traumatized children such stimuli trigger painful intrusive phenomena.

Psychological Numbing and Avoidance

The symptoms of psychological numbing and avoidance indicate how children continue to impose a restriction on themselves in the regulation of their emotions or behavior after the traumatic experience. The affects generated by traumatic incidents—intense fear, terror, horror, and helplessness—are especially difficult for a child's immature ego to tolerate. Children fear that any emotional response will reactivate a whole set of overwhelming traumatic affects. Whereas adults commonly will state, "I feel numb," after a traumatic experience, preschool and school-age children may not make such general comments about their emotional state, and therefore it is easy to underestimate such symptoms. Affect avoidance and reduced affective tolerance are key traumatic sequelae. Children are known to express one or more of the following complaints.

AVOIDANCE OF THOUGHTS, FEELINGS, LOCATIONS, OR SITUATIONS ASSOCIATED WITH THE TRAUMA

Typically, traumatized children will try to suppress thoughts about what happened, especially those moments that have remained intrusive. In doing so, a general inhibition in spontaneous thought or imagination may be observed as they try to avoid generating their own reminders. For example, a boy who had been watching television when his babysitter was killed omitted mention of a prominent television program when telling a story about his drawing. When asked to imagine the program on television, he said, "It was Bugs Bunny running out of the way of the pig shooting at him," and he cried while expressing his wish that the babysitter could have escaped unharmed.

Children will walk out of their way to avoid a house where a sniper had once shot at their school or a site where a person was injured or died. Such avoidances disrupt or alter children's normal daily life. They may avoid excitement, loud noises, or a hint of conflict, the latter out of fear that any conflict would escalate into violence or excite them to violence.

REDUCED INTEREST IN USUAL ACTIVITIES

A reduction in interest in usual activities is not simply a response to a depressed mood, although that may play a role, but indicates an effort to avoid further trauma by reducing involvement with the external world. School-age children will even discontinue pleasurable activities to avoid any chance of encountering another painful or frightening situation. Furthermore, children may exhibit marked inhibitions in play and stop playing familiar games (e.g., playing with toy guns).

FEELINGS OF BEING ALONE/DETACHED/ESTRANGED

Even while appearing to cling to their parents more, children may still feel a sense of estrangement, of being alone, feeling that others, including their parents, cannot fully understand or even recognize what they went through. They may appear more withdrawn and less outgoing to their friends and family.

RESTRICTED EMOTION RANGE

School-age children will often say they simply do not want to know how they feel. Even though they may obsessively retell others of the traumatic incident, it is an incomplete, journalistic recounting that is stripped of all relevant emotions. This need to regulate their emotions can inhibit pleasant as well as distressful feelings.

MEMORY DISTURBANCE

In recalling the event, children may demonstrate several different types of memory distortions. They may omit moments of extreme life threat, distort their proximity to the violence or the duration and sequencing of events, and in other ways minimize their life threat. In retrospect, they may start to feel that they had premonitions of the incident. To find clues as to why it happened, they may give undue emphasis to certain details in remembering the event. Preschool children may be mute or reluctant to discuss the trauma, but this should not be mistaken for amnesia. Whereas it is uncommon for single-incident trauma to result in amnesia or disavowal of the reality of what happened, multiple physical or sexual abuse may lead to dissociative reactions and major lapses in recall.

LOSS OF ACQUIRED SKILLS, REGRESSIVE BEHAVIOR, AND NEW FEARS

Recently acquired developmental achievements are especially prone to loss, and, with younger children, there may be noticeable regressive behaviors, including enuresis, anxious attachment, and reduced verbalization. Younger children often exhibit more generalized fear of being vulnerable and are more afraid of strangers, being in the dark, being alone, being in their own room or in the bathroom, or going to bed.

CHANGE IN ORIENTATION TOWARD THE FUTURE

Childhood trauma studies have consistently found a marked change in orientation toward the future, including a sense of foreshortened future, negative expectations, and altered attitudes toward marriage, career, and having children (Eth and Pynoos 1985; Terr 1984). One child whose mother was murdered exclaimed, "I am never going to get married or have children . . . and I am going to grow up and be a scientist and make sure no one ever dies and that there are no guns in the world." Some children attempt to avoid addressing the initial trauma by supplanting these memories with new fears, especially preoccupations with fantasies about future harm. Many children who have recovered from cancer are haunted by an omnipresent fear of relapse, many years after treatment has produced a cure.

Increased State of Arousal

The *DSM-III-R* establishes a separate criterion for the somatic symptoms of arousal, thus highlighting the physiological as well as psychological substrate to PTSD (Brett et al. 1988). The physiological reactions continue to keep the child focused on the traumatic incident. Laboratory evidence indicates that the physiological reactions reinforce the other PTSD symptoms, sometimes requiring psychopharmacologic intervention.

SLEEP DISTURBANCE

After a disaster or violent occurrence in a community, many children may exhibit a transient increase in anxiety at bedtime and difficulty going to sleep. However, the true sleep disturbance of PTSD reflects a more serious disturbance in sleep physiology that may persist for weeks, months, and even years. As stated earlier, there can be changes in the percentages of time in rapid eye movement, stage two and stage four sleep, and the occurrence of non–rapid eye movement sleep phenomena, including parasomnia symptoms of somnambulism, vocalizations, and night terrors. Children may fall asleep only to wake in the middle of the night or to sleep fitfully. Sometimes, children will describe that they do not awake feeling rested. These disturbances may be intermittent and associated with the occurrence of traumatic reminders at night. For example, one boy who witnessed a fatal industrial explosion suffered from the return of agitated sleep each year during summer thunderstorms.

IRRITABILITY/ANGER

Children may be more irritable and easy to anger. As a result, they may show a reduced tolerance of the normal behaviors, demands, and slights of peers and family members and produce a readiness to respond with aggression. Temporary difficulty in modulating aggression has been proposed as a typical traumatic sequela (Kolb 1988).

DIFFICULTY CONCENTRATING

Children commonly report acute difficulties in concentrating in school. There is frequently a transient deterioration in school performance during the first year. Both intrusive imagery and lack of sleep interfere with concentration and performance.

HYPERVIGILANCE

Children who remain "on alert," ready to respond to any sign of environmental threat, may appear fearful or anxious. They act as if the next time something happens they intend to be prepared to protect themselves or to intervene on someone's behalf. They may engage in constant behaviors to ensure their own personal security. An adolescent who had fought off an attempted rapist of his mother years afterward still answered the door from 10 feet away.

EXAGGERATED STARTLE RESPONSE

Children may startle in response to various sudden loud noises, including car backfires, firecrackers, thunder, a balloon bursting, or a dropped object. These startle reactions are often quite noticeable to family and peers.

AUTONOMIC RESPONSE TO TRAUMATIC REMINDERS

In addition to the distress caused by reminders, children may also become aware of their heartbeat or feel shaky, ill, lightheaded, or nauseated. The latency of these autonomic reactions has been demonstrated in children. Two years after terrorist bombings, exposed children, in contrast to nonexposed controls, evidenced significant signs of autonomic arousal while watching a film depicting a similar incident (Kristal 1982).

Age-Related Behavioral Changes

In addition to the general symptom profile noted above, each age group appears particularly vulnerable to certain behavioral changes. Preschool children are most likely to exhibit decreased verbalization and cognitive confusion, increased anxious attachment behavior, and other more immature symptomatology. The preverbal child, as Terr (1984) described, may demonstrate long-lasting perceptual "memories," entirely through his or her play or fears. School-age children are more apt to react to trauma with aggressive or inhibited behavior and psychosomatic complaints; their behavior may be both more inconsistent and more reckless, and they may also obsessively retell the event.

Adolescents often show a premature movement toward independence or an increased dependence. These changes can lead them to drop out of school, marry early, radically change their career choice, or decide never to leave home. Adolescents may also embark on a period of post-traumatic acting-out behavior in the form of school truancy, precocious sexual activity, substance abuse, delinquency, or self-endangering reenactment behavior. Van der Kolk (1987) has described the vulnerability of adolescents to trauma-induced narcissistic rage and the risk of their taking revenge into their own hands and, in war time, of responding to the killing of a combat friend by committing an atrocity. Therefore, prompt treatment of the traumatized adolescent can be imperative.

Associated Features

Reactions to a traumatic event may arise out of consequences other than direct exposure. Since these reactions alone do not usu-ally cause the core symptoms of reexperienc-ing, emotional constriction, or increased arousal, they are considered associative fea-tures of the disorder.

GUILT

A child need not be on site to experience guilt; for example, in the case of a sniper attack, one boy had sent his brother to fetch his cousin at school, only for the latter two to be caught under siege. School-age children have reported "feeling bad" because they were unable to provide aid, because they were safe when others were harmed, or be-cause they believed their actions endangered others (Pynoos et al. 1987). The presence of guilt is of diagnostic importance because it appears to increase the severity of children's post-traumatic stress reactions.

WORRY ABOUT A SIGNIFICANT OTHER

During the course of a disaster or violent episode, children may be separated from their parents or siblings and be worried about their welfare and survival. The waiting pe-riod to learn if a relative or friend is injured or dead or for the desired reunion can pro-duce intense agony in children as well as adults. In hostage situations, this worry can go on for days, weeks, or even longer. For all family members, worry about a significant other may persist even after a safe reunion, leading to chronic preoccupation about that person's whereabouts and safety or to an emotional detachment.

LOSS BY DEATH

Catastrophic situations often result in death. An important interplay exists between post-traumatic stress and grief reactions. Al-though both involve intrusive and avoidant phenomena, they differ. In contrast to trau-matic recollections, remembering or remin-iscing about a deceased family member may initially be painful, yet welcomed, and even-tually comforting. Intrusive images of the physical mutilation or horror over the man-ner of death may interfere with efforts to evoke more positive memories of the de-ceased.

Children may also be confused by two sets of dreams, traumatic dreams and grief

dreams, in which they once again see, hear, and/or interact with the deceased. There are also three types of reminders of a traumatic death: (1) of the circumstances of the death, (2) of the loss or absence of the deceased, and (3) of the secondary changes brought about in one's life. PTSD keeps the minds of children focused on the circumstances of the death and in doing so interferes with the full attention needed to address the loss and adaptation to subsequent life changes.

Children appear to be particularly vulner-able to the dual demands of trauma mastery and grief work. Efforts at relieving traumatic anxiety appear to take psychological priority over mourning. Furthermore, differences in exposure among family members may create different psychological agendas for each member. For example, a child may discover the body of a family member who committed suicide and remain preoccupied with the sight, while other family members may over-look this added demand on the bereavement process as experienced by the child. The mutual lack of appreciation of different psy-chological challenges may lead to estrange-ment or impatience between parent and child or sibling and sibling.

FEAR OF RECURRENCE

Fed by rumor, myth, and misinformation, fear of recurrence is a contagious anxiety within any community after major violence or disaster. In some cases, such fear may be justified, when, for example, a serial rapist or murderer has not been apprehended. In another instance, after a sniper had been killed, exposed and nonexposed children in the neighborhood equally feared that a sec-ond assailant had escaped and would return to shoot at them again (Pynoos et al. 1987). Without examining for specific PTSD symp-toms, this anxiety alone may be misconstrued as PTSD. Over time, those children most directly traumatized may continue to harbor this fear, whereas less exposed children usu-ally no longer do so.

RENEWAL OF SYMPTOMS FROM PRIOR EXPERIENCE

Children may be strongly reminded of a previous stressful life experience, such as other violent incidents, intrafamilial abuse, personal injury, or traumatic losses. As a result, there may be a recurrence of symptoms, including intrusive images, disturbing affect, incident-related fears, and disturbed sleep. In their own self-reports, children will often spontaneously comment on what they are reminded of and even distinguish between their primary reactions to the current event and the renewed ones based on past experience. For example, at a summer camp where a young child had drowned, only a few children who viewed at close range the resuscitation suffered from intrusive images of the dying boy, whereas many other children told of painful renewed memories (e.g., of a pet killed by a car).

Impact on Child Development

While more systematic studies are needed to examine the interaction between trauma and developmental stage, post-traumatic stress phenomena have been shown to influence the developmental process in the areas of cognitive functioning, trust, initiative, interpersonal relations, personality style, self-esteem, outlook, and impulse control. Intrusive, reexperiencing phenomena can affect cognitive functioning by altering attention either toward or away from concrete or symbolic traumatic reminders. The added importance of concrete reminders can restrict the child's use of symbolic expression. Children's imaginative play can become constricted and less enjoyable with the repetition of trauma-related themes in play (Terr 1984). Without resulting in a phobic disorder, traumatic avoidant behavior can lead to inhibitions or altered interests. Their irritability and diminished modulation of aggression can interfere with normal peer relationships.

Several researchers have reported prominent personality changes even in very young children, ranging from reduced impulse control to increased inhibition, from attraction to danger to a debilitating sense of fear, and from emotional withdrawal to exhibitionism. Changes in self-image may accompany the onset of PTSD, affecting children's sense of self-efficacy, self-confidence, or self-esteem. Experiencing the hyperarousal behaviors, especially, may disrupt children's emerging self-concept. It can be difficult to assess the degree of change and whether there is an actual discontinuity in personality development, or, as is common, an exaggeration of preexisting traits. Freud had observed how traumatic responses can play a significant role in shaping character and, as Greenacre (cited in Rothstein 1986) noted, leave children vulnerable to future life stresses because the traumatic episode is never fully mastered. One example is a profound change in the children's view of the world and their own future. Their search for omens may lead to a belief in their ability to prophesy future untoward life events. The influence on affective tolerance and emotional constriction may affect later parental behavior, as reported in observations of concentration camp survivors.

Children attempt to assimilate the external threat and interpret the internal threat by incorporating elements of the traumatic experience into developmentally appropriate psychosexual fantasies (e.g., fears regarding body integrity or fantasies of rescue or exile). As a result, these fantasies gain added meaning and are more easily reevoked by traumatic reminders. They may remain insufficiently worked through to permit normal intrapsychic developmental progression, and, in that sense, cause a "fixation to the trauma."

Little is known about the potential positive effects on character formation that are sometimes observed (e.g., an increased feeling of courage, increased capacity for empathy, and greater sense of purpose in life).

BIOLOGICAL CORRELATES

Traumatic experiences cause various neurophysiological disturbances of a transient or permanent nature. Freud (cited in Kolb 1987) proposed a breakdown in a "stimulus barrier" that protects an organism from excessive external stimulation. Kardner (cited in Van der Kolk 1987) was later to rename the disorder from "traumatic neurosis" to "physioneurosis" in order to emphasize long-lasting physiological changes. Kramer (cited in Van der Kolk 1984) has hypothesized that sleep disturbance is the critical reinforcer of the disorder, whereas Kolb (1988) has speculated that the exaggerated startle reaction is the central component to understanding the syndrome.

There may be two types of dysfunction of startle modulation. First, there is evidence of a "conditioned emotional response" in which the sights and sounds of the traumatic event serve as conditioning stimuli, which potentiate the innate startle response (Kolb 1987). Second, there may be an impairment of startle modulation that does not depend on the replication of actual traumatic stimuli (Ornitz and Pynoos 1989). The latter may reflect a long-standing alteration in the brain-stem circuits subserving startle modulation. Because inhibitory startle modulation is a developmentally acquired function, maturing at about 8 years of age, young children may have the greatest biological vulnerability to these neurophysiological changes.

PTSD appears to have a distinct biological profile that distinguishes it from depression, which shares a number of similar symptoms. Neuroendocrine studies of adult sufferers of PTSD have found (1) a tendency to excessive sympathetic arousal; (2) unusually high amounts of urinary norepinephrine and epinephrine and low levels of 24-hour urinary-free cortisol, best represented by an elevated ratio of urine norepinephrine to free cortisol; (3) reduced α_2- and β_2-adrenergic binding; (4) evidence suggesting a down-regulation of central adrenergic receptors; and (5) elevations in the release of cortisol releasing factor occurring without the dysregulation in the feedback from the adrenal gland to the hypothalamus and pituitary as seen in depression (Krystal et al. 1989). As a result, there are normal findings on the dexamethasone suppression test unless a concomitant depression is present. As yet, these neuroendocrine findings have not been replicated with children or adolescents, in whom they may affect a developing central nervous system, including the brain stem and higher cortical functions.

CLINICAL COURSE

The clinical course of PTSD in children and adolescents is variable, depending on the severity, duration, and personal impact of the original traumatic experience; the coping and resiliency of the individual child; the influence of previous trauma; the additive demands of grief and secondary stresses; the presence of adverse influences on recovery; and the impact on critical stages of development.

The *DSM-III-R* requires a duration of at least 1 month before the diagnosis is war-

ranted. This time interval was chosen to permit early detection of the disorder and, at the same time, exclusion of persons with only a transient stress reaction. For those with mild exposure or minimum personal impact, the symptoms usually diminish rapidly within days or weeks of the event. However, children who have faced severe threat to life or witnessed horrifying violence or injury to a family member are likely to suffer a more prolonged course. Studies of school-age and adolescent children have found no apparent delay in the onset of severe PTSD symptoms and that initial exposure is strongly predictive of later course (Pynoos and Nader, in press; Rothstein 1986). Five to 15 months after being kidnapped and buried alive, an entire group of 25 children had developed moderate to severe PTSD. At follow-up 4 years later, most of the children continued to suffer from prominent posttraumatic stress symptoms (Terr 1984).

The effect of multiple adversities (Rutter 1985), after major disasters or from massive trauma, greatly modifies the complex of symptoms, their duration, and their resolution, specifically by increasing the rate of co-morbidity, especially, concurrent PTSD and major depressive disorder or generalized anxiety disorder (in younger children, separation anxiety disorder). One disaster alone can lead to the experience of severe threat to life, death of a significant other, loss of residence and relocation, involuntary unemployment of a parent, and change in the family's financial status. The traumas inflicted by war involve a complex interplay of traumatic experiences superimposed on deprivation, malnutrition, and family disruption, loss, immigration, and resettlement. In a study of Cambodian adolescent refugees previously exposed to massive trauma and loss, 50% of the adolescents were found to suffer from chronic PTSD, 12% from major depressive disorder, 37% from intermittent depressive disorder, and 18% from generalized anxiety disorder, with a significant rate of co-morbidity (Anthony 1986).

A current debate concerns how to discriminate the effects of acute trauma from the debilitating effects of chronic or repetitive trauma (Garmezy 1983). Chronic situations appear to produce a profound and pervasive disturbance in emotional responsiveness, affect tolerance, modulation of aggression, and attachment behavior, and, in cases of traumatic deaths, persistent sadness. By the time children reach adulthood there may be a multiplicity of clinical presentations (Van der Kolk 1984). Even after a single traumatic experience, with time it becomes more difficult to ascertain the specific influence of the trauma. One reason is that the traumatic reminders responsible for recurrent anxiety become less obvious and the historical referents to current hypervigilant or other arousal behavior are no longer readily identifiable.

Child abuse is one example that does not usually involve a discrete trauma but rather a pattern of multiple molestations or beatings within a disturbed environment. There are several consequences. Each incident may cause immediate traumatic reactions from which there is only incomplete recovery. Therefore, there is an ongoing decrease in personality resources. The process of adaptation to repeated traumas within the family may lead to more primitive defenses, including severe disturbances in object relations, affective tolerance, and impulse control and the onset of dissociative states. Thus, a profound effect on the emerging personality may result, forming the antecedent to a clinical picture of a borderline or narcissistic personality disorder. Furthermore, chronic physical and sexual abuse both involve continued assaults on children's body integrity, increasing the likelihood of dissociative reactions and accounting for nearly all cases of multiple personality disorders. In addition, physical abuse can cause neurologic injury, leading to an organic impairment.

Child intrinsic factors also influence the clinical course. Influenced by their phase of development and prior experience, children vary widely in their attempts to interpret the event and their symptoms, to regulate their emotions, and to search for meaning, information, and assistance. Although effective coping reduces distress, maladaptive coping, such as drug abuse, may exacerbate it or become a problem itself.

To offset their traumatic helplessness, children imagine alternate actions that could have prevented the occurrence, interrupted the violence or disaster, reversed the physical harm, or gained safe retaliation. The dominant theme of these "inner plans of action" is direct intervention by the child or third party, and their content is developmentally guided. Fantasies of revenge or identification with the aggressor can seriously jeopardize children's impulse control and be debilitating.

Some children may interpret their post-traumatic stress reactions as an indication that something is wrong with them and may feel that other children are not similarly affected. They may unrealistically expect their recovery time to be shorter. These expectations can intensify children's distress and prevent them from seeking needed support. In addition, the way in which children process traumatic reminders, and manage the accompanying renewal of anxiety, may also significantly affect their recovery.

The task of assimilating the trauma and recovering from the acute post-traumatic reactions is demanding and requires considerable psychological effort and attention from children. Therefore, any factor that reduces children's capacity or opportunity to focus on this all-important task may lead to maladaptive resolution or prolongation of the symptoms. Child intrinsic factors may be operative. The presence of an attention-deficit disorder may interfere by distracting children from maintaining needed sustained attention, even within a therapeutic consultation. Pre-existing depression may predispose children to react with unjustified guilt, even when their exposure was minimal. The presence of significant psychopathology in children's parents or a guardian can jeopardize children's own efforts to achieve an adaptive resolution. Furthermore, the anxiety, fear, or depressive mood of a parent or guardian can easily be communicated to children, and a child's course of recovery may depend on the psychological well-being of parents and guardians. Finally, extrinsic factors, including all of the adverse stresses previously listed, may require children to turn their attention elsewhere in the acute aftermath or may interfere with spontaneous efforts to achieve some psychological closure.

DIFFERENTIAL DIAGNOSIS

The intense anxiety and avoidance related to reminders of the trauma are not diagnosed as a simple phobia because the identified stimuli relates to a specific extreme stressor. However, if the avoidance is generalized beyond the specific trauma-related stimuli, as occasionally happens, then a secondary diagnosis is warranted. The intrusive thoughts and images, and efforts to ignore or suppress, relate to an external event "outside the range of usual human experience" and therefore do not constitute an obsessive-compulsive disorder. The intensity of the intrusive phenomena may occasionally resemble hallucinations; however, PTSD can be differentiated from schizophrenia by the trauma-based origin of the precepts and the child's otherwise intact reality testing. Many generalized anxiety disorder symptoms, such as motor tension, autonomic hyperactivity, vigilance, and scanning, as well as symptoms of a major depressive episode (e.g., fatigue, depressed or irritable mood, diminished interest, insomnia, and diminished ability to concentrate) may be present. Symptoms of anxiety and depression are common to PTSD; however, a concomitant diagnosis is sometimes warranted, and co-morbidity is more likely if there has been a significant emotional impact from other factors, including multiple adversities and loss.

It is important to recognize the evidence of traumatic reenactment symptoms in the suicidal, self-mutilation, sexual, or aggressive behavior or play of physically abused or sexually molested children or in children who have witnessed violence. A history of multiple physical or sexual abuse should raise the suspicion of a dissociative disorder, including multiple personality disorder.

Acute deterioration in school performance, alterations in attention, and new-onset irritability or aggression should be attributed to the effects of the trauma and not be immediately diagnosed, either as an attention-deficit disorder or conduct disorder. However, symptoms of PTSD may tend to exaggerate disturbance in learning or behavior in children with a prior onset of these disorders. Adjustment reaction with mixed disturbance of emotion and conduct is differentiated from PTSD because (1) the stressor is less extreme and more ordinary; (2) there is a relative absence of reexperiencing phenomena; (3) increased states of arousal with physiological correlates are not found; and (4) there is the absence of significant distortions in basic personality development. A secondary diagnosis of substance abuse should be considered when maladaptive efforts at coping lead to the misuse of drugs or alcohol.

TREATMENT

Successful intervention requires triaging and screening for children at risk, reducing stress-induced disturbances in children undergoing normative reactions, and preventing the onset of disorders or reducing their duration and progression. Intervention strategies focus on strengthening individual and family coping capacities, as well as decreasing adverse influences on recovery. These strategies include fostering the continued adaptation of resilient children, as well as assisting those with severe post-traumatic stress and grief reactions. Short-term goals include preventing hazardous post-trauma behavior, such as recklessness, violence, or self-destructive acts. Long-term goals include preventing traumatic interference with normal child development and treating any resulting maladjustments.

All interventions must be tailored to the varying degrees of exposure and personal impact. In addition, the intervener has to adopt a preventive attitude that embraces a readiness for prompt intervention to avert more serious sequelae. Enhanced knowledge, both of post-traumatic stress reactions and therapeutic skills, should lead to better recognition of previously overlooked opportunities to provide assistance. Post-trauma interventions can be used: (1) in the emergency department where traumatized children wait while their parents receive medical attention after rape, suicidal behavior, or attempted murder or assault; (2) in pediatric inpatient units where children are being treated for life-threatening illnesses, for major injuries caused by car accidents, burns, shootings or other violent events, or with life-endangering medical procedures; and (3) on inpatient child psychiatry units where some children, especially from impulse-ridden families, have endured traumatic experiences. Primary care providers, including pediatricians and general practitioners, can play a pivotal role in identifying children with PTSD and making an appropriate referral.

Intervention with Individual Children

Children who have been severely exposed to life-threatening situations or who have witnessed injury or death may require individual intervention to avert serious psychiatric morbidity. Only preliminary investigations have been made regarding appropriate therapeutic techniques for children. However, investigators of adult PTSD have found that the optimal time for intervention is in the acute period when intrusive phenomena and incident-specific traumatic reminders are most identifiable and the associated affect is most available (Van der Kolk 1984). Adult investigators have concluded that increased tolerance of affect resulting from intrusive recollections or traumatic reminders is critical to successful recovery.

In the acute aftermath, school-age children and adolescents have participated in the same kind of clinical debriefing that has been a hallmark of adult trauma work (Pynoos and Eth 1986). For adults or children, almost all therapeutic approaches to PTSD incorporate some review and reprocessing of traumatic events. The emotional meaning is embedded in the details of the experience as well as the personal impact, and the therapist must be prepared to hear everything, however horrifying or sad. Special interview techniques may be necessary to assist children to thoroughly explore their subjective experience and to help them understand the meaning of their responses (Pynoos and Eth 1986). Encouraging children's expression through drawing, play, redramatization, and metaphor, the therapist attempts to understand the traumatic links and looks for ways to recruit children's fantasy and play actively into communication about their experience. The memory of young children may be especially improved when the original physical context is reinstated, so that going through the scene in drawing, redramatization, or even by in vivo return to the actual physical site can sometimes elicit important additional memories.

One goal is to bolster children's observing ego and reality testing functions, thus dispelling cognitive confusions and encouraging active coping. Children are assisted in identifying traumatic reminders that elicit intrusive imagery, intense affective responses, and psychophysiological reactions. A second goal is to help children to anticipate, understand, and manage everyday reminders, so that the intensity of these reminders and their ability to disrupt daily functioning recede over time. Enabling children to share these reminders with their parents increases the likelihood that they will receive essential parental support and understanding. Another goal is to assist the child in making distinctions between current life stresses and past trauma and to decrease the impact of

the trauma on present experience. One indication of the effectiveness of trauma exploration may be children's desire to discuss post-trauma changes in their lives.

It is expected and understandable that post-traumatic stress reactions will result from traumatic exposure. By using his or her authority, a primary care professional can legitimize children's feelings and reactions and assist them in maintaining self-esteem. Children can also be prepared to anticipate and cope with the transient return of unresolved feelings over time.

Although trauma debriefing and consultation will prove adequate for some children, many severely exposed children will require extended therapeutic interventions. There is an immediate need for investigations on the use of brief, focal psychotherapy with traumatized children. Studies have provided evidence on the effectiveness of such therapy with adults (Horowitz 1976). In the case of children, these methods need to be modified to reflect developmental considerations.

Even extended therapy may be required because of adverse influences on recovery. Factors that suggest the potential need for longer therapy include a history of previous trauma, concomitant loss and the dual demands of trauma and bereavement, preexisting psychopathology, parental disturbance; post-traumatic multiple adversities, continued participation in criminal proceedings, and the need for additional medical procedures due to trauma-related injuries. Even in situations of chronic or repetitive trauma, singular traumatic incidents that require special attention can be isolated. These unique experiences may hold such psychological priority in the child's mind that by addressing them in a timely fashion a therapeutic alliance is formed and the subsequent treatment is facilitated. Addressing the traumatic experience often restores sufficient functioning for children then to be able to address the less overt, yet substantial influences a disturbed environment or parental dysfunction has had on their lives.

Modifying arousal behavior may be an important aspect of an overall treatment plan. Laboratory and preliminary clinical data on adults indicate that this neurophysiological response can be attenuated by pharmacologic intervention (Krystal et al. 1989). A pilot investigation of persistent arousal behavior in children exposed to gunfire incidents is being conducted at the University of California at Los Angeles. Preliminary data suggest that abnormal sleep cycles, especially increased stage four sleep phenomena and loss of modulation of the acoustic startle response, are present and can be arrested by the use of clonidine. Clonidine, propranolol, and antidepressants may be useful as therapy for disorders of norepinephrine modulation. In one study of acute PTSD in children, arousal behavior, especially sleep disturbance, was associated with attention and learning difficulties (Pynoos et al. 1987). Early alleviation of these symptoms may decrease chronicity of PTSD and reduce functional impairment in severely exposed children.

Family Intervention

After trauma, family functioning strongly influences children's post-traumatic reactions and recovery (Raphael 1986). Studies have found a high symptom correlation between parents and children after shared traumatic experiences. Parental distress, parental disagreement about appropriate action during a catastrophic event, and changes in parenting after the incident all affect children. In particular, parents are often unsure how to respond to their children's temporary regressions, hypervigilance, reactions to traumatic reminders, and other new behaviors. Four parental attributes have been significantly associated with the persistence of symptoms in children: (1) preexisting psychopathology, (2) excessive dependence on children for support, (3) overprotectiveness, and (4) prohibitive attitude toward children's temporary regressive behavior or toward open expression and communication about the experience.

Adults often do not fully appreciate the post-trauma distress of children. Initially, children experience core symptoms, such as intrusive images, quite privately, and parents and teachers may not notice behavioral changes until weeks or months later. In addition, family members may be so preoccupied with their own reactions to the trauma that they overlook the special needs of children. Furthermore, the stigma attached to traumatic occurrences may result in family members providing misleading explanations, maintaining a conspiracy of silence, or prohibiting children from mentioning the incident. Children who do not receive adequate

emotional support may become more withdrawn or exhibit increased disturbances in conduct.

The goals for family intervention to assist the child are (1) to restore in children a sense of personal security; (2) to validate their affective responses rather than dismiss them; and (3) to anticipate and respond to situations in which they will need added emotional support, especially in managing traumatic reminders or handling feelings of vulnerability.

Before they can effectively help the children, family members often need support and guidance, and sometimes need therapeutic intervention to reduce their own levels of stress. Parenting skills can be enhanced if parents can be educated regarding post-traumatic stress reactions, realistic expectations about the course of recovery, differing psychological agendas among family members, and the importance of encouraging open communication with their children, not just in the immediate aftermath but in the months ahead when anniversary or other traumatic reminders may stimulate recollections.

School Intervention

Children commonly exhibit changes in cognitive performance and other school behavior that serve as key indicators of traumatic course and recovery. A coordinated plan between mental health professionals, teachers, and families can help to minimize the traumatic impact at school (Pynoos and Nader 1988).

Many disasters or incidents of community violence affect the whole school population. In these special circumstances, a school-wide mental health program having the following features can be pivotal in reducing psychiatric morbidity: (1) psychological first-aid to provide immediate emotional assistance at the school or evacuation site; (2) classroom exercises to reduce fears of recurrence, clarify cognitive confusions, normalize responses, and restore classroom functioning; (3) special programs to reintegrate injured, severely traumatized, or bereaved children back into the school setting; and (4) efforts to address the stressful impact on teachers and administrative staff. Care must be taken to conduct psychologically constructive classroom interventions. For example, children can be helped to redramatize an earthquake's destructive force, but then they need the opportunity to rebuild their neighborhood in play (Anthony 1986). Psychological crisis teams can foster a less anxious, more cohesive classroom environment that will promote the recovery of traumatized children.

CONCLUSIONS

Because PTSD is a new classification, the diagnosis should be approached conservatively until research provides more evidence about the condition in children of varying ages exposed to diverse experiences. However, there are many obvious cases. PTSD is a serious disorder with potentially profound effects on the intrapsychic, interpersonal, emotional, and cognitive development of the child. Time does not always heal, and sufferers from PTSD continue to live in the emotional atmosphere of the traumatic event (Van der Kolk 1987).

The therapeutic tools to assist children in the aftermath of these ordeals are being developed. Horowitz (1976) defined successful traumatic resolution as the capacity to recall the trauma at will while being equally capable of turning one's mind to other matters. The demonstrated capacity of children to engage in such challenging therapeutic work holds promise for the future.

References

American Psychiatric Association. 1987. *Diagnostic and Statistical Manual of Mental Disorders*, 3rd ed., revised. Washington, D.C.: American Psychiatric Press.

Anthony E. J. (ed.). 1986. Special section: Children's reactions to severe stress. *J. Am. Acad. Child Psychiatry* 25:299–392.

Bergen, M. 1958. Effect of severe trauma on a 4-year old child. *Psychoanal. Study Child* 31:3–32.

Brett, E. A., Spitzer, R. L., and Williams, J. B. W. 1988. *DSM-III-R* criteria for post-traumatic stress disorder. *Am. J. Psychiatry* 145:1232–1236.

Eth, S., and Pynoos, R. S. (eds.). 1985. *Post-traumatic Stress Disorder in Children*. Washington, D.C.: American Psychiatric Press.

Freud, S. 1926. Inhibitions, symptoms, and anxiety. In Strachey, J. (ed.): *Standard Edition of the Complete Psychological Works of Sigmund Freud*, vol. 20. London: Hogarth Press.

Garmezy, N. 1983. Stressors of childhood. In Garmezy, N., and Rutter, M. (eds.): *Stress, Coping, and Development in Children*. New York: McGraw-Hill.

Helzer, J., Robins, L., and McEvoy, L. 1987. Post-traumatic stress disorder in the general population. *N. Engl. J. Med.* 317:1630–1634.

Horowitz, M. J. 1976. *Stress Response Syndromes*. New York: Jason Aronson.

Kolb, L. C. 1987. A neuropsychological hypothesis explaining post-traumatic stress disorders. *Am. J. Psychiatry* 144:989–995.

Kolb, L. C. 1988. A critical survey of hypotheses regarding post-traumatic stress disorders in light of recent research findings. *J. Traumatic Stress* 1:291–304.

Kristal, L. 1982. Bruxism: An anxiety response to environmental stress. In Spielberger, C., Sarason, I., and Milgram, F. (eds.): *Stress and Anxiety*, vol. 5. Washington, D.C.: Hemisphere.

Krystal, J., Kosten, T., Perry, B., et al. 1989. Neurobiological aspects of PTSD: Review of clinical and preclinical studies. *Behav. Ther.* 20(2):177–193.

Levy, D. M. 1938. Release therapy in young children. *Psychiatry* 1:387–390.

Ornitz, E. M., and Pynoos, R. S. 1989. Startle modulation in children with post-traumatic stress disorder. *Am. J. Psychiatry* 147:866–870.

Pynoos, R. S., and Eth, S. 1986. Witness to violence: The child interview. *J. Am. Acad. Child Psychiatry* 25:306–319.

Pynoos, R. S., Frederick, C., Nader, K., et al. 1987. Life threat and post-traumatic stress in school-age children. *Arch. Gen. Psychiatry* 44:1057–1063.22.

Pynoos, R. S., and Nader, K. 1988. Psychological first aid and treatment approach to children exposed to community violence: Research implications. *J. Traumatic Stress* 1:445–471.

Pynoos, R. S., and Nader, K. Mental health disturbances in children exposed to disasters: Prevention intervention strategies. In Goldston, S., Yager, J., Heinecke, C., and Pynoos, R. S. (eds.): *Preventing Mental Health Disturbances in Children*. Washington, D.C.: American Psychiatric Press (in press).

Raphael, B. 1986. *When Disaster Strikes: How Individuals and Communities Cope with Catastrophe*. New York: Basic Books.

Rothstein, A. (ed.). 1986. *The Reconstruction of Trauma: Its Significance in Clinical Work*. Madison, Wis.: International Universities Press.

Rutter, M. 1985. Resilience in the face of adversity. *Br. J. Psychiatry* 147:598–611.

Terr, L. C. 1984. Children at acute risk: Psychic trauma. In Grinspoon, L. (ed.): *Psychiatry Update: The American Psychiatric Association Annual Review*, vol. 3. Washington, D.C. American Psychiatric Press.

Twain, M. 1881. *The Adventures of Tom Sawyer*. Toronto: Bantam Books.

Van der Kolk, B. A. (ed.). 1984. *Post-Traumatic Stress Disorder: Psychological and Biological Sequelae*. Washington, D.C.: American Psychiatric Press.

Van der Kolk, B. A. 1987. *Psychological Trauma*. Washington, D.C.: American Psychiatric Press.

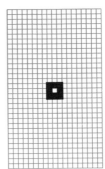

Anxiety Disorders

GAIL A. BERNSTEIN, M.D.

Symptoms of anxiety in children are often diverse and confusing. Anxiety symptoms appear frequently as somatic complaints, a presentation that is a common part of the phenomenology of childhood anxiety disorders. A child may also have separation anxiety disorder manifested as school refusal. A characteristic pattern of symptom flare-up is distress prominent on school days when separation from parents and home is anticipated but not on weekends when the child can remain close to family and home.

The *Diagnostic and Statistical Manual of Mental Disorders,* third edition, revised (*DSM-III-R*) (American Psychiatric Association 1987) defines three childhood anxiety disorders. Anxiety is the predominant feature in all three disorders. In the first two, anxiety is situation specific. In separation anxiety disorder, anxiety occurs when separation from home and parental figures is anticipated. In avoidant disorder, the essential feature is anxiety about contact with strangers that is sufficiently severe to interfere with social functioning. A child with avoidant disorder has a clear desire for social involvement only with family and familiar persons. On the other hand, overanxious disorder is characterized by generalized anxiety that is not specific to particular situations but rather is apparent in a variety of settings and generalized throughout a child's daily experience.

DEFINITION

Anxiety is the affective or feeling state of dread, apprehension, worry, or uneasiness that something ominous will happen. The affective state of anxiety is often associated with a physiological or motor response to the perception of danger. Physiological concomitants of anxiety may include sweaty palms, rapid heart rate, feeling of "butterflies" in the stomach, or shortness of breath. The motor response is often the subjective need to flee.

Anxiety disorders are among the oldest and most commonly recognized emotional disorders. Sigmund Freud, one of the earliest theorists to define anxiety, described several models of anxiety (Michels et al. 1985). In the neurophysiological model, anxiety was hypothesized as resulting from sexual excitement without adequate discharge of energy. The psychological model explained anxiety as a reaction to memories of real or imagined dangers. The evolutionary model emphasized the adaptive value of anxiety, whose origin and form were believed to be related to experiences of birth, copulation, and dangerous situations during the prehistory of the species. Lastly, the learning theory model described a hierarchy of childhood situations whose anxiety-eliciting properties were enhanced through learned association with earlier traumatic experiences.

A modern explanation of anxiety attempts to integrate some or all of Freud's models. For example, by viewing anxiety as a signal of fantasies of imagined dangerous situations provoked by internal drives or external events, Freud's psychological and learning theory models are probably the easiest to apply to the modern view of anxiety.

Other theorists presented differing explanations of anxiety. Anna Freud (1946) explained anxiety as resulting from a fear of disintegration due to excessively strong drives. Klein (1952) described anxiety as a child's response to destructive rage within one's self projected onto the mother. Sullivan (1953) suggested a social transmission of anxiety as the infant copies the mother as a learned response. Mahler (1968) stated anxiety originated from a psychological fear of loss of someone or separation anxiety. Bowlby (1973) regarded anxiety as originating from a psychological fear of loss of a significant individual and described anxiety as an innate response to the disruption of attachment behavior.

Although it is difficult for one theory to explain all aspects of anxiety, a contemporary explanation may attempt to integrate aspects of several models. As anxiety is discussed in this chapter from clinical and research viewpoints, the reader may reflect on the theories of Freud and others and weigh the data as to which theory or combination of theories is most valuable.

ETIOLOGY AND PATHOGENESIS

Adult anxiety disorders have been shown to be familial. The familial patterns are likely due to a combination of genetic and environmental factors. Several studies support a genetic etiology. Slater and Shields (1969) demonstrated that 50% of monozygotic twins show concurrent anxiety disorders, as opposed to only 2% to 3% of dizygotic twins. In a study by Surman and co-workers (1983), two pairs of HLA-identical siblings were concordant for panic disorder with satisfactory response to tricyclic antidepressants; this suggests a possible association between panic disorder and major histocompatibility gene complexes. Additional indirect evidence supporting a genetic hypothesis stems from biochemical abnormalities in patients with panic disorder. Research shows that lactate infusion or inhalation of carbon dioxide is a precipitant of panic attacks in patients with panic disorder but not in normal controls.

Family history and interview studies demonstrate that anxiety disorders are more frequent in certain families. Three sets of data exist for examination of familial patterns in adult anxiety disorders: (1) family studies of probands with panic disorder, (2) family studies of probands with anxiety plus depression, and (3) family studies of probands with agoraphobia.

A number of family studies of panic disorder demonstrated an increased morbidity risk for panic disorder in first-degree relatives of probands with panic disorder compared with the relatives of controls (Table 5–1). In general, these studies describe subjects with psychiatric disorders that are similar to the concept of panic disorder in *DSM-III*. However, since five of the studies were reported prior to publication of the *DSM-III*, one wonders whether systematic inclusion criteria were employed and whether these studies included only probands with panic disorder or if a more heterogeneous population was investigated.

Two studies by Leckman and colleagues (1983a, 1983b) demonstrate a different pattern: a familial relationship between anxiety disorders and major depressive disorder. In the first study (1983a), these researchers demonstrated an increased risk of anxiety disorder and major depression in first-degree relatives of probands with anxiety disorder plus major depression compared with the relatives of probands with major depression only. This suggests that depression alone and depression plus anxiety disorders are different entities. Another study by Leckman and colleagues (1983b) compared the first-degree relatives of probands with major depressive disorder plus panic disorder with the first-degree relatives of probands with only major depression. The combination of major depression plus panic disorder accounted for twice the risk of the following: major depression, panic disorder, simple phobia, and alcoholism. A similar pattern is apparent in the offspring of the probands (Weissman et al. 1984). Depression in a parent increased the risk of depression in the children. Depression plus anxiety disorder increased the risk of depression and of anxiety disorder in the children. Specifically, panic disorder in the parent increased the risk of separation anxiety disorder in the children threefold.

Table 5-1. MORBIDITY RISK OF PANIC DISORDER IN RELATIVES OF PROBANDS
WITH PANIC DISORDER

Author (Year)	Type of Study	Inclusion Criteria	Number of Probands	Results*
McInnes (1937)	Family history	Anxiety neurosis	50	14% Controls: 4.5%
Brown (1942)	Family history with 22% direct interviews	Anxiety state	63	15.1% Controls: 0% Second-degree relatives: 2.7% Controls: 0.7%
Cohen et al. (1951)	Family history	Neurocirculatory asthenia	111	15.8% Controls: 0.4%
Noyes et al. (1978)	Family history	Anxiety neurosis	112	18% Controls: 3%
Pauls et al. (1979)	Family history	Panic disorder (*DSM-III* criteria)	19	Second-degree relatives: 9.5% Controls: 1.4%
Crowe et al. (1983)	Family interview	Panic disorder (*DSM-III* criteria)	41	17.3%; 24.7% if definite *and probable* panic disorder Controls: 1.8%
Harris et al. (1983)	Family interview	Panic disorder (*DSM-III* criteria)	20	20.5% if definite *and probable* panic disorder Controls: 4.2%

*Results indicate morbidity of panic disorders in first-degree relatives.

In a recent study researchers compared the morbidity risk for first-degree relatives of agoraphobic, panic disorder patients with a control population (Noyes et al. 1986). There was an increased risk of anxiety disorders in the relatives of the persons with agoraphobia and panic disorder compared with relatives of controls. The pattern was different in each case. The morbidity risk for agoraphobia was increased among relatives of agoraphobics but not among relatives of panic disorder patients. However, the morbidity risk for panic disorder was increased among relatives of both anxiety disorder relatives. The probands and relatives with agoraphobia reported earlier onset, more severe symptoms, and less favorable outcome than probands and relatives with panic disorder. This suggests that agoraphobia may be a more severe variant of panic disorder.

In anxiety disorders of childhood, one study compared the family histories of children with severe anxiety disorders and those of children with depression. Livingston and co-workers (1985) showed that children with depression and children with severe anxiety disorders have similar family histories, with increased depression and alcoholism in first-

degree relatives. Bernstein and Garfinkel (1988) described the family pedigrees of six children with severe school refusal resulting from both anxiety and depressive disorders and the pedigrees of a matched group of families of children with other psychiatric disorders (Fig. 5-1). Blind and independent family histories and structured interviews of parents and siblings showed a higher rate of depressive and anxiety disorders in first-degree relatives of children with school refusal. In four of the six families of children with school refusal, anxiety and depressive disorders were present in both maternal and paternal relatives and across three generations of family members. Fourteen (17%) of the 82 first- and second-degree relatives of children with school refusal had anxiety disorders only, 10 (12%) had depressive disorders only, and 10 (12%) had both anxiety and depressive disorders; in the 57 relatives of control children, however, 9 (16%) had anxiety disorders only, 2 (4%) had depressive disorders only, and 3 (5%) had both. The evidence indicates that there is an increased familial risk for anxiety disorders in relatives of patients with agoraphobia and panic disorder. More studies are needed of children with

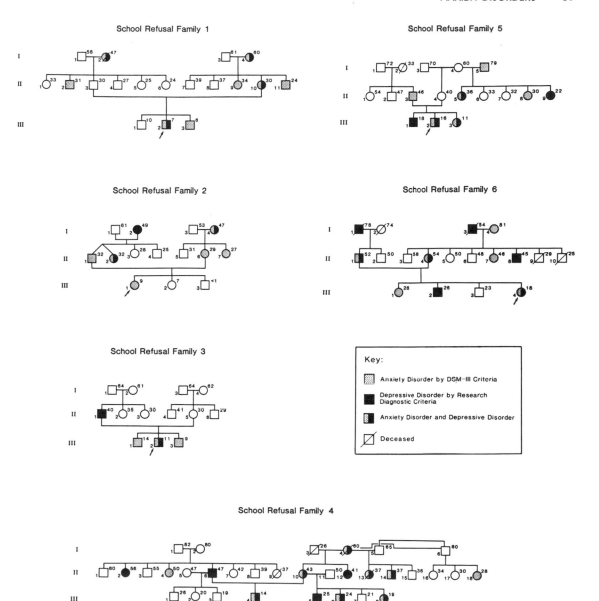

Figure 5–1. *Family pedigrees of six children with severe school refusal resulting from anxiety and depressive disorders.*

anxiety disorders as probands to ascertain the familial patterns for the childhood anxiety disorders.

Environmental influences on the development of childhood anxiety disorders have not been studied. However, clinical observation suggests that certain precipitants may be associated with the initiation or exacerbation of anxiety disorders. Precipitating factors may include initial entry into school, move to a new home and school, pregnancy of the mother, birth of a sibling, illness of the child,

loss of a friend, and a family crisis such as death, divorce, or parental illness.

One study of anxiety symptoms in adolescents indicates that the nature of life event stressors is similar in anxious and nonanxious teenagers (Bernstein et al. 1989). These stressors included trouble with a sibling, increased number of arguments with parents, trouble with classmates, receiving failing grades, losing a friend, breaking up with a boyfriend or girlfriend, and increased arguments between parents. However, there is a significant difference between the number of stressors experienced in the 1 month prior to evaluation by anxious adolescents ($\bar{x} = 3.33$) compared with nonanxious adolescents ($\bar{x} = 1.76$). It appears that anxiety symptoms in adolescents are not linked to specific stressors but instead are related to an increased number of stressors.

EPIDEMIOLOGY

Adult anxiety disorders have a relatively high prevalence. A review of the literature found that estimates for prevalence were 3% for panic disorder, 6% for agoraphobia, 3% for generalized anxiety, 2.5% for simple phobia, and 1.5% for social phobia (Reich 1986). The female-to-male ratio for anxiety disorders is approximately 2:1.

A review of seven community surveys showed that anxiety symptoms are quite common in children of all ages (Orvaschel and Weissman 1986). Anxiety symptoms were more common in girls than boys, in black children than white children, and in children from lower socioeconomic families than those from upper-class families.

An anonymous questionnaire study of 988 students in the 9th through 12th grades in a rural public high school was conducted (Bernstein et al. 1989). Anxious teenagers compared with nonanxious teenagers were more likely to be female than male. Other characteristics associated with anxiety symptoms in adolescents included frequent somatic complaints, a history of physical and/or sexual abuse, street drug usage, and poor grades. Statistical analyses showed that the score on the Beck Depression Inventory, history of street drug usage, history of physical abuse, and history of somatic complaints were most likely to predict anxiety symptoms in adolescents. There was a significant correlation ($r = .59$) between teenagers' scores on the Beck Depression Inventory (Beck 1978) and on the Revised Children's Manifest Anxiety Scale, supporting the overlap of anxiety and depressive symptoms in adolescents.

PATHOLOGY

There is evidence for a biological contribution to anxiety. Currently there are three areas of investigation of the biological substrates of anxiety: the dexamethasone suppression test, lactate infusion as a precipitant of panic attacks, and the association with mitral valve prolapse.

Dexamethasone Suppression Test

The dexamethasone suppression test (DST) has served as a useful biological marker in endogenous depression. Fifty percent of endogenously depressed persons show nonsuppression of serum cortisol levels after taking oral dexamethasone. Several studies of adults with anxiety disorders demonstrate that the DST is not sensitive for identifying adult patients with anxiety symptoms. However, one study with children suggests that the DST may be helpful in identifying prepubertal children with separation anxiety (Livingston et al. 1984).

An uncontrolled study of the DST in 15 prepubertal children aged 6 to 12 on an inpatient unit suggested that this test may be positive in children with separation anxiety (Livingston et al. 1984). Each subject was interviewed by two psychiatrists and one psychologist and was observed by ward staff for 2 weeks before a diagnosis was given. Diagnoses were made before obtaining DST results. Seven positive DSTs identified three children with depression, three children with separation anxiety disorder, and one with simple phobia. Two borderline positive DSTs identified one child with depression and one with separation anxiety. With these results, the DST is 75% sensitive to depression and 60% sensitive to separation anxiety. The results suggest a neuroendocrinologic similarity between children with depression and children with separation anxiety.

Lactate Infusion

Physical exercise produces anxiety symptoms and increased blood lactate levels. Pitts and McClure (1967) and subsequent researchers have shown that patients with panic disorder manifest symptoms of acute panic attacks during lactate infusion while normal subjects do not. The lactate infusion technique has been used to investigate physiological and biochemical responses during panic attack. The technique has also been used to monitor the effects of drug pretreatment. It has been suggested that the abnormality in panic disorder patients that is corrected with tricyclic antidepressants or monoamine oxidase inhibitors is the same as that responsible for susceptibility to lactate-induced anxiety.

It has been shown that adrenocorticotropic hormone (ACTH) and cortisol levels are elevated during fear responses. To explore alterations of the hypothalamic-pituitary axis, ACTH and cortisol levels were measured in patients with panic disorder and controls during lactate infusion. There was no difference in the hormone secretion patterns of patients with panic attacks and those without attacks (Levin et al. 1987). Thus, the neurobiological mechanism that is responsible for panic attacks is different than that which mediates fear responses.

Mitral Valve Prolapse

There is an epidemiologic association between mitral valve prolapse (MVP) and panic disorder. The prevalence of MVP in the general population is approximately 6% (De-Vereux et al. 1976), with the prevalence of MVP in panic disorder patients being about 45% (Crowe et al. 1982). It has not been possible to differentiate between patients with panic disorder with and without MVP. Several theories have been offered to explain this finding: (1) there are two separate types of panic disorder, one with MVP and one without MVP; (2) panic disorder and MVP are both secondary to an underlying autonomic abnormality; and (3) panic disorder results from an autonomic vulnerability activated by different factors, including MVP. In this last case, palpitations secondary to MVP serve as a precursor of panic attacks, which progress to panic disorder in persons with this predisposition.

Results of one study cast doubt on the third hypothesis that suggests that MVP is etiologically related to the pathogenesis of panic disorder. Mazza and colleagues (1986) investigated the prevalence of anxiety disorders in patients with MVP and in controls. There was no significant difference between the two groups in the prevalence of panic disorder or other anxiety disorders. No individuals in either group met *DSM-III* criteria for panic disorder or phobic disorder. One person in the MVP group and no one in the control group met criteria for generalized anxiety disorder. The MVP patient group scored significantly higher than control subjects on the Zung Anxiety Scale. To evaluate the hypothesis that the presence of palpitations in patients with MVP accounted for the symptoms that differentiated this group from the control group on the Zung Anxiety Scale, the scores for palpitations were compared with the scores for other symptoms. Dizziness was the only symptom whose variance was attributed to the presence of palpitations. The authors concluded that palpitations in the patients with MVP did not account for the anxiety that differentiated the patients from control subjets.

CLINICAL PICTURE

Separation Anxiety Disorder

The essential feature in separation anxiety disorder is excessive anxiety about separation from parents or major attachment figures. The diagnosis is considered when separation anxiety is extreme and the separation reaction is beyond that expected for the child's developmental level. Thus, when severe separation anxiety persists beyond the early school years, the diagnosis is considered.

Separation anxiety is a normal developmental phenomenon from age 6 months through preschool. At 6 to 7 months of age, infants begin to show distress on their mothers' leaving, especially in unfamiliar surroundings. By this age, strong specific attachments are formed. The degree of the separation reaction may indicate the strength of the attachment. An infant's separation anxiety may be manifested by increased crying and decreased activity and exploration. A toddler's normal separation anxiety may be characterized by trying to follow the mother out of the room, calling her name, irritability, or whining. Normal separation anxiety peaks at about 18 months of age but is not usually abnormal throughout the toddler and preschool years. At age 3 most children have the cognitive capacity to perccive that separation is temporary and are able to maintain an internal image of the mother during her absence. Thus, usually between the ages of 3 and 5, separation anxiety decreases. Boys tend to have more separation anxiety than girls at all ages, since boys lag behind girls developmentally.

In order to diagnose separation anxiety disorder the *DSM-III-R* requires that three of the following nine criteria be met:

1. Unrealistic, persistent worry about harm to major attachment figures during periods of separation
2. Unrealistic worry about harm to self during separation
3. School refusal in order to remain with parental figures or to remain home
4. Reluctance to sleep without major attachment figures nearby or to sleep away from home
5. Avoidance of being alone
6. Recurrent nightmares about separation
7. Somatic complaints
8. Signs of extreme distress in anticipation of separation
9. Signs of extreme distress at times of separation.

The symptoms have an onset before age 18 and must be present for a minimum of 2 weeks.

Children with significant separation anxiety refuse to sleep at a friend's house, will not go on errands alone, will not attend summer camp, and frequently will not attend school.

Separation anxiety disorder appears to be familial, with an increased incidence in family members compared with the general population. There is some evidence that this disorder may precede panic disorder or agoraphobia in adulthood.

School Refusal

School refusal (school phobia) may be associated with separation anxiety disorder. Up to 60% to 80% of school phobics have separation anxiety disorder, especially younger children, who have acute, short-duration school refusal. In school refusal, physical complaints are common. The pattern of symptom flare-up is characteristic, with symptoms more common in the fall than in the spring, more common on Mondays than on Fridays, and more prevalent in the morning when separation is anticipated and less common as the day progresses, especially if the child convinces the parent that he or she should stay home. Symptoms are absent on weekends and during summer. Exacerbations are common after holidays or after legitimate illnesses requiring absence from school.

While the separation fears are usually irrational, they may be based on realistic concerns. For example, a child may worry about a depressed, suicidal parent making a suicide attempt while the child is at school or a child may have concern about one parent physically abusing the other if a history of this is present. In these or similar situations, role reversal may occur, with the child staying home to care for a parent who is depressed, anxious, or dependent.

School refusal occurs in approximately 5% of a referred clinical population. It occurs with the same frequency in males and females. There is a bimodal age distribution, with the first peak occurring between ages 5 and 7 when a child enters school for the first time. The second peak occurs between ages 12 and 14 with the transition from grade school to junior high. Children with school refusal tend to have average intelligence.

There are two different presentations of school refusal. First, there are younger patients with acute-onset separation anxiety. These children are often recognized by family physicians and school personnel. With intervention supporting the need to get the child to school and keep the child there through rewards for appropriate independent behavior, the outlook is usually positive. The second group with school refusal is the 12- to 14-year-old students with a chronic, insidious presentation. These adolescents may present with a mixed picture of anxiety and depressive symptoms. Half of these teenagers meet full criteria for a major depressive episode and an anxiety disorder (usually separation anxiety disorder) (Bernstein and Garfinkel 1986). Outlook in this group is more guarded.

There have been two different presentations of family issues observed in families with children who refuse to attend school. The older literature describes a hostile-dependent relationship between parent (usually mother) and child. The father is described as distant and uninvolved. Interaction between parent and child highlights separation issues. Parents encourage dependency and less mature behavior. They collude in supporting the child's fears. The child often assumes a pivotal, oppositional, controlling role in the family.

The second pattern is that of a chaotic family with many problems. In this situation there is usually an unreliable mothering figure who has been physically or emotionally unavailable to her children. There may be a history of poor attachment between mother and child in the first year of life. There is a history of significant episodes of difficult separation, such as a parent with physical or psychiatric disorder being hospitalized repeatedly, a parent who is unable to care for the child with placement of the child outside of the home, or separation or divorce of parents. These children have trouble forming a consistent internal representation of their mother or may form an image of a rejecting unavailable mother.

The General Scale of the Family Assessment Measure has been used to assess family relationships and interactions in a small sample of families with a child with school refusal. Seven clinical subscale scores of family interaction were obtained. The parents of school phobics compared with parents of children with other psychiatric diagnoses reported dysfunction in the areas of role performance, communication, affective expression, and control (Bernstein and Garfinkel 1988).

Avoidant Disorder

The primary feature of avoidant disorder is the avoidance of contact with strangers; yet there is a desire for warm, close relationships with family members and familiar persons. The *DSM-III-R* requires a minimum of 6 months of psychopathology. Furthermore, the avoidance of strangers must be severe enough to interfere with social adaptation in peer relationships. The child must be at least 2½ years old since stranger anxiety is a normal developmental phenomenon up to this age. In addition, the symptomatology should not be generalized and should be persistent enough to warrant the diagnosis of avoidant personality disorder.

Children with avoidant disorder are frequently perfectionistic and self-condemning. They may present as unassertive children with decreased self-confidence. Very little is known about the demographics of this disorder. Clinically, it appears to be uncommon. It is believed that perhaps this disorder is more common in females.

The understanding of etiology and predisposing factors to this disorder is still at a speculative stage. However, temperamental difference such as shyness, devastating experiences or losses (such as the experiencing of physical abuse or death of a parent), chronic medical illness, or moves from foreign countries may be contributing factors. Specific developmental disorders may contribute to development of avoidant disorder. There is a suggestion that mothers of children with this disorder have a higher prevalence of anxiety disorders.

Overanxious Disorder

In overanxious disorder there is excessive anxiety and fearful behavior not focused on a specific situation or object and not resulting from a recent stressor. These children are "worriers." They worry about future events, such as doctor appointments, school tests, or group activities. They also worry about past events and may harbor guilt that they have done something wrong. These children worry about competence and performance in the areas of academics, athletics, and social situations. Children with overanxious disorder are perfectionistic, obsessional, and filled with self-doubt. Physical concomitants of anxiety are often apparent, such as butterflies in the stomach, a lump in the throat, headaches, or shortness of breath.

To diagnose overanxious disorder, the *DSM-III-R* requires 6 months of symptoms. Four of the following seven symptoms must be present:

1. Worry about future events
2. Concern about past behavior
3. Concern about competence
4. Physical complaints
5. Significant self-consciousness
6. Continual need for reassurance
7. Feelings of tension or the inability to relax.

Overanxious disorder is not uncommon. Children with overanxious disorder compared with children with separation anxiety disorder are more likely to have another anxiety disorder, especially simple phobia or panic disorder (Last et al. 1987). It is believed that the disorder affects males and females with equal frequency.

With respect to predisposing factors, this

disorder seems to be more common in eldest children. It may occur more often in children from upper socioeconomic status families and is more prominent in families that value performance or encourage competition. There is some evidence to suggest that anxiety disorders are more common in mothers of children with overanxious disorder than in mothers of children with other psychopathology.

CASE HISTORIES

Case 1

Peter, a 6½-year-old first grader, presented to the School Refusal Outpatient Clinic with a history of reluctance to attend school. On school days he complained of headaches and stomachaches. The pattern of symptom flare-up was characteristic, with symptoms more prominent earlier in the school week and after holidays or absences for legitimate illnesses. If Peter was able to convince his mother to let him stay home, somatic complaints dissipated as the day progressed. He verbalized fears of leaving home and concern about the safety of his mother. At the time of leaving for school, he would have tantrums, cry, and scream that he was too sick to go. After arriving at school, he cried for 1½ hours.

In kindergarten, he was absent 29 days from school, with similar complaints and behaviors. Prior to evaluation in November, he missed 20 days of first grade. He had stopped attending school 2 weeks before the evaluation. At school he was afraid to go with the teacher and his schoolmates across the street to the playground because he imagined that he would get hit by a car. Peter described concerns that on the way home from school the bus driver would leave him at the wrong bus stop and that he would subsequently get lost or kidnapped. He also expressed fears that while he was at school his mother would get hit by a car, be attacked by strangers, or commit suicide by overdosing. He stated that he wanted to stay home to care for and protect his mother.

He was above average in abilities and was described as precise and perfectionistic. Prior to starting first grade, the family had moved from the city to the suburbs, necessitating a change of schools for Peter. The parents noticed exacerbation of symptoms in October, when Peter's mother was hospitalized for depression.

The past medical history was remarkable for hospitalization at age 14 months for *Haemophilus influenzae* arthritis for 2 weeks. During the hospitalization he was in isolation; he recovered fully.

The family history was significant for his mother having depression. She had attempted suicide on two occasions by overdosing on antidepressants. The paternal grandfather had a history of agoraphobia. A paternal uncle had panic disorder. The patient had a 13-year-old brother with school refusal secondary to major depressive disorder and separation anxiety disorder.

While the parents' marriage was seemingly intact, when the mother was depressed there were marital conflicts and family stress and Peter appeared more anxious and symptomatic. In the spring of the year preceding referral, she was treated with antidepressants with clinical improvement. Peter simultaneously appeared less anxious and symptomatic.

On mental status examination, Peter was an attractive, appropriately dressed, well-groomed boy. There were no abnormalities of speech or motor behavior. Thinking was coherent. There was no evidence of psychotic thought process. Thought content focused on worries about leaving his mother and home. He reported concern that something ominous would happen to himself or to his mother during periods of separation. He reported recurrent nightmares about separation; for example, he described a dream about getting on a bus, being driven to a desert, and never being able to return home. He related a dream in which he went to school and when he returned his mother had turned into a skeleton. Mood was anxious, and affect was appropriate. He showed age-appropriate interests in the toys in the playroom. When playing with puppets, he portrayed a sad boy puppet who refused to go out with other children and instead stayed home with his mother. Intellect was judged to be above normal. No deficits during cognitive testing were noted.

On the Diagnostic Interview for Parents of Children and Adolescents (Herjanic and Campbell 1977), Peter met criteria for separation anxiety disorder. Peter's score on the Children's Depression Rating Scale was 37, with a score of greater than 40 consistent with clinical depression. His score on the Children's Depression Inventory was 10, indicating mild symptoms of depression. On the Revised Children's Manifest Anxiety Scale, his anxiety score was 19 with a Lie scale score of 3. The mean for a group of adolescent school refusers with an anxiety diagnosis is 12 (Bernstein and Garfinkel 1986). On the Anxiety Rating for Children, his score was 16. The mean for a group of adolescent school refusers with an anxiety diagnosis is 12 (Bernstein and Garfinkel 1986). Scores of both tests for anxiety were elevated.

Peter's history, clinical presentation, and test results emphasized significant symptoms of separation anxiety. His fears focused on concerns about his mother's health and safety. While at times irrational, it appeared likely that some of the fears were secondary to his mother's history of psychiatric disorders and suicide attempts.

Feedback of results of the evaluation and testing was provided to the family. Consultation was provided to the school, and a behavioral school reentry program was designed with rewards for returning to school and for continued school attendance. Weekly individual play therapy for Peter was initiated. The therapist coordinated Peter's treatment with his mother's treatment in the Adult Outpatient Psychiatry Clinic. Family therapy sessions were held. Imipramine was given at a dose of 75 mg at bedtime, and a therapeutic serum level was achieved. There was gradual improvement, with a decrease in symptoms of separation anxiety over 6 months, with the above-described program.

Case 2

Susan, a 14-year-old white female in the eighth grade, was referred to the School Refusal Outpatient Clinic by her school counselor. She had a long history of poor school attendance, dating back to the fifth grade. In the fifth and sixth grades, she missed 20 days of school per year. Poor attendance was more apparent after entry into the seventh grade with transition into junior high. In the seventh grade, she missed 35 days of school. In the eighth grade, she missed more than 40 days, including nonattendance for 1 month prior to referral to the clinic. Susan's parents

were divorced while she was in the seventh grade. This event seemed to be stressful for Susan and was temporally related to an exacerbation of symptoms.

The patient was described as a "worrier." She was quite anxious about her school performance. She worried about being called on by the teacher and about presenting in front of the class. She spent a great deal of time obsessing about whether she had made the correct decision regarding past circumstances. She always worried about events prior to their occurrence.

At the time of evaluation, she was dysphoric. She described vegetative symptoms of depression, including initial insomnia lasting an hour, anorexia with weight loss, decreased concentration, and hopelessness. She had intermittent suicidal ideation without a definite plan. She also described significant intense anxiety symptoms, including marked feelings of nervousness/inner tension and somatic complaints of abdominal pain and dizziness. These complaints were most prominent in the morning on school days. At times, she had experienced symptoms of panic attacks prior to getting on the school bus or before entering the classroom, including tachycardia, increased respiratory rate, a "queasy" sensation in her stomach, dizziness, and thoughts of death or doom. She avoided riding the school bus, stating that she felt very self-conscious.

The past medical history showed a medical workup for abdominal pain, including upper and lower gastrointestinal series that were negative. A medical evaluation for the complaint of dizziness, including a CT scan of the cranium, was negative.

The past psychiatric history was remarkable for the history of a depressive episode. In the seventh grade, she was treated with psychotherapy and antidepressants for depression. Susan's depressive episode followed the divorce of her parents, and she made two suicide attempts. On the first occasion, Susan overdosed on a week's supply of imipramine. She told her mother right away and was given ipecac. The second time, she took half a bottle of imipramine. She emptied the ipecac at home before taking the pills. She did not tell her mother for a half hour. She had a grand mal seizure at home and was transferred to the intensive care unit of a local hospital. She had electrocardiographic changes and was intubated. After medical stabilization, she was transferred to an inpatient adolescent psychiatric unit for 2 weeks. At the time of evaluation, she was in group psychotherapy at a local mental health center.

The family history was significant for Susan's father having a history of recurrent major depressive episodes. Susan had three siblings, including a 25-year-old married sister with a history of chemical dependency, a 23-year-old brother with a history of depression who had been treated with antidepressants and had attempted suicide 3 years prior to Susan's evaluation, and a 16-year-old brother with a history of school refusal secondary to separation anxiety disorder.

On mental status examination, Susan presented as a casually dressed, well-groomed young female. Eye contact was poor, with Susan looking at the floor for much of the interview. She answered questions in a low, barely audible voice when directly questioned. Psychomotor retardation and increased latency of response were evident. Mood was anxious and depressed. Affect was appropriate and consistent with mood. Thinking was logical and coherent. Thought content focused on anxiety about going to school. She denied current suicidal ideation. Results of a cognitive examination were within normal limits.

On the Diagnostic Interview for Children and Adolescents (Herjanic and Campbell 1977), Susan met criteria for major depressive episode (recurrent) and overanxious disorder. Susan's score on the Children's Depression Rating Scale was 56. Her score on the Children's Depression Inventory was 17. Both of these scores were elevated and consistent with clinical depression. Her score on the Revised Children's Manifest Anxiety Scale was 19 with a Lie scale score of 3. The score on the Anxiety Rating for Children was 15. Scores of both rating scales for anxiety were elevated.

The patient began weekly individual psychotherapy sessions. Family sessions were held once a month. Imipramine was started and titrated to a therapeutic level. A gradual school reentry program was designed and initiated with input from Susan's school counselor.

Over the course of several weeks there was partial remission of Susan's depressive symptoms. Her anxiety symptoms including panic symptoms improved somewhat. The patient made progress with the school reentry program. However, she still missed school after holidays and legitimate illnesses throughout the course of her high school years. The course of her illness had exacerbations and remissions. Eventually, she was transferred to a high school with a full-time program for emotionally disturbed students from which she graduated. She subsequently entered junior college and had a successful freshman year without psychiatric symptoms and with excellent grades and attendance.

CLINICAL COURSE

Separation Anxiety Disorder

Young children (5–7 years old) with acute-onset school refusal often have pure separation anxiety and a good prognosis. They tend to respond well to behavioral intervention. A directive, limit-setting approach emphasizing rapid return to school with emotional support for the child and rewards for appropriate school directed behavior is usually effective. Many of these children can have mild exacerbation of symptoms at times of stress. Some will have no recurrence of symptoms; a small percentage as young adolescents may progress to the chronic, severe form of school refusal with both anxiety and depressive symptoms. The insidious presentation of school refusal seen in early adolescence has a much more guarded prognosis. Many of these teenagers experience exacerbations and remissions over a number of years, with the development of a chronic disorder.

Functional consequences include loss of normal peer friendships, academic losses, and dysfunctional parent–child relationships. In the severe form, symptomatology from school refusal may be very incapacitating.

Longitudinal outcome studies indicate that at least one third of children who refuse to attend school continue to manifest significant psychiatric symptomatology. Most of these studies were completed prior to publication of *DSM-III* diagnostic criteria, and thus diagnoses at follow-up are not clearly and consistently defined. However, it is still possible to identify symptom-complexes and look at the number of patients with ongoing dysfunction.

The longitudinal outcome studies indicate that the majority of school refusers return to school (Table 5–2). Rodriguez and co-workers (1959) demonstrated that the prognosis for successful return to school is better with the younger children. Eighty-nine percent of children younger than 11 years old at the time of initial presentation were attending school regularly at follow-up. Only 36% of the children older than age 11 demonstrated a successful return to school. The treatment program employed in this study involved brief psychotherapy, focusing on rapid return to school. Baker and Wills (1979) showed that whether or not a child returned to school or the time spent out of school showed no

correlation to future work or educational performance. Berg and Jackson (1985) evaluated 168 children with school refusal 10 years after inpatient treatment. Predictors of favorable outcome included intelligence, treatment prior to age 14, and those who were asymptomatic or substantially better at the time of discharge. Those children and adolescents who manifest dysfunctional outcomes as adults have diagnoses of phobic states, other anxiety disorders, or depression.

Avoidant Disorder

The clinical course of those with avoidant disorder is variable. Some children recover

Table 5–2. OUTCOME OF CHILDREN AND ADOLESCENTS WITH SCHOOL REFUSAL

Author	Number of Patients	Years at Follow-up	Results
Rodriguez et al. (1959)	41	3	71% attending school 89% of children <11 years 36% of children >11 years
Coolidge et al. (1964)	49	10	96% returned to school 50% still symptomatic
Warren (1965)	16 inpatients	6	44% phobias (25% severe, 19% mild–moderate) 18% neurotic symptoms 38% asymptomatic
Weiss and Burke (1967)	16	5–10	33% anxiety, depression, or phobias
Berg (1970)	27 inpatients	1	59% satisfactorily attending school or work 33% well adjusted in family and peer relationships 41% poor family and peer adjustments
Berg (1976)	100	3	33% "severe dysfunction" anxiety, depression, phobias, or obsessional traits 33% symptomatic anxiety, depression, or obessional traits 33% marked to full improvement
Waldron (1976)	24 with SAD*; 18 with other neuroses		29% of SAD vs. 6% neurotics are "dependent" 42% of SAD vs. 11% neurotics are somatizers 25% of SAD vs. 6% neurotics have trouble finishing school
Berg and Fielding (1978)	32 inpatients	1	53% well or much improved 47% slightly improved or ill
Baker and Wills (1979)	67	Evaluated after reaching the age of high school graduation	85% at work or school; length of time away from school was not important
Berg and Jackson (1985)	168	10	50% well or much improved 30% disturbed

*SAD, separation anxiety disorder.

spontaneously; others fail to form friendships and social bonds outside the family and have ongoing feelings of isolation and depression. How often this disorder becomes chronic and persists into adulthood is unknown. In adults corresponding disorders are avoidant personality disorder and social phobia. Avoidant personality disorder is characterized by adults who have no friends outside their family and are unwilling to become involved with others. They are reticent to meet persons and avoid social situations. They tend to be easily embarrassed and are very sensitive to criticism. Persons with social phobia have persistent fear of situations in which they will be exposed to possible scrutiny and will be humiliated or embarrassed.

Overanxious Disorder

The onset of overanxious disorder may be gradual or sudden. The clinical course of overanxious disorder is characterized by exacerbations associated with stress. Complications include unnecessary medical workups, poor school performance, and failure to engage in age-appropriate activities. This disorder has some similarities to generalized anxiety disorder in adults. Persons with generalized anxiety disorder manifest excessive unwarranted anxiety about two or more life circumstances for a minimum of 6 months. They show physiological symptoms of anxiety, including motor tension, autonomic hyperactivity, and vigilance.

PSYCHOMETRIC EVALUATION

Psychometric evaluation of anxiety symptoms in children is in a very early stage of development. This area of assessment has lagged behind the study of adult anxiety. There are several explanations for this: it is difficult to define, recognize, and rate anxiety symptoms in children; anxious children tend to be internalizers (i.e., they keep their symptoms inside and external manifestations of the symptomatology are not usually readily apparent); and anxious children are often compliant, cooperative, "eager-to-please" children who do not cause difficulties in the home and classroom. Thus, parents, teachers, and clinicians are less aware of the symptoms. When the symptoms are recognized,

adults are less invested in identifying and treating the manifestations.

Since anxiety is often a diffuse, difficult-to-define phenomenon, it is challenging to create assessment questions. In addition, the symptom presentation of anxiety disorders frequently overlaps with the presentation of depressive disorders. Whether this is explained by the hypothesis that severe anxiety disorders and major depression have a common underlying diathesis (Leckman et al. 1983b) or by the idea that anxiety disorders and major depression are distinct conditions with common characteristics resulting in diagnostic errors remains open to speculation. In either case, creating instruments that are capable of differentiating anxiety symptoms from symptoms of depression is an important, yet difficult goal. Since the symptom presentation of anxiety often overlaps with, or is concurrent with, depression, it is useful to evaluate children with anxiety disorders with both anxiety and depression scales.

In the School Refusal Outpatient Clinic at the University of Minnesota, a comprehensive protocol is followed for assessing anxiety disorders in children and adolescents. The evaluation of each child includes a clinical family diagnostic interview, a family psychiatric history, an individual interview with the child, a structured interview with the child, and self-report and clinician rating scales for anxiety and depression.

Interview

When interviewing a child or adolescent and his or her parents for assessment of childhood anxiety disorder, a careful developmental history is essential. Attachment and relationship history in the child's first year of life is essential for assessment of the quality of bonding and secure versus anxious attachment. Documentation of developmental milestones is necessary to mark normal versus abnormal progression of development and cues the examiner if specific or pervasive developmental disorders are to be considered in the differential diagnosis. A history of traumatic life events should be evaluated, such as physical or sexual abuse of the child, repeated difficult separations between child and parent as the result of parental separation or divorce, or psychiatric or physical illness of a parent necessitating recurrent hospitalization of the parent or temporary foster placement of the child.

To assess the type and quality of separation reactions a child has experienced, useful areas to pursue include (1) the number of caretakers or babysitters a child had in the first 5 years of life and the child's reaction to being left by the primary attachment figure and (2) information about day-care and/or preschool settings and the child's reactions and experiences in such settings.

Specific fears and phobias that are not characteristic for the youngster's age should be noted. Overanxious concerns and personality traits of perfectionism are also noted.

The nature of the anxious symptomatology should be described, including age at onset of specific anxiety symptoms, duration of symptoms, symptom interference, episodic versus continuous nature, precipitants or random occurrence of symptoms, and success versus failure of practical intervention methods.

Family history of psychiatric illness in first- and second-degree relatives should also be noted. There appears to be an increased incidence of depression, alcohol dependency, and anxiety disorders in relatives of probands with severe school refusal (Bernstein and Garfinkel 1988).

Structured Interviews

A child psychiatric structured interview systematically surveys the symptom presentation of the child and adolescent psychiatric diagnoses and thus defines the presence or absence of full *DSM-III-R* criteria for specific disorders, including anxiety disorders. By the methodical, straightforward format, the structured interview eliminates the clinician's bias in making diagnoses. A structured interview can suggest associations between related disorders (e.g., anxiety disorders and affective disorders) since multiple diagnoses are possible with such an interview.

A structured interview can serve as an initial data base. Since a structured interview can be repeated at different times, it can serve to document the change in symptomatology with the passage of time and treatment. Structured interviews may also be helpful in evaluating the longitudinal outcome of child and adolescent disorders since some child-structured interviews are paired with a counterpart adult-structured interview. It is important to note that a structured interview should not be relied on alone to establish definitive clinical diagnoses. It is one source of assessment information to be used in conjunction with clinical interviews and anxiety and depression rating scales.

Revised Children's Manifest Anxiety Scale

The Revised Children's Manifest Anxiety Scale (RCMAS), which is also called "What I Think and Feel" (Reynolds and Richman 1978), is a self-report instrument of anxiety. This instrument assesses the child's general state of anxiety across a variety of situations. The RCMAS contains 28 items and 9 Lie scale items. The test–retest reliability of the items of the RCMAS was found to be .83 (Reynolds and Richman 1978). Girls have been found to score significantly higher than boys on the anxiety questions and on the Lie scale. Validity studies have demonstrated that children in classes for the emotionally and behaviorally disturbed (Kitano 1960) and children in residential treatment (Montgomery and Finch 1974), compared with age- and sex-matched normal children, receive significantly higher scores on the CMAS.

This self report rating scale is very easy to administer. The questions are easy to read and understand, and the responses require a "yes" or "no" answer. The Lie scale is particularly useful. With younger children an elevation of the Lie scale may suggest an attempt to give socially desirable responses, while with older children and adolescents it may be an indication of defensiveness (Reynolds and Richman 1978).

A difficulty with the RCMAS is that a number of the items overlap with symptoms of depression. For example, items on the RCMAS include "it is hard for me to get to sleep at night," "other children are happier than I," and "I feel alone even when there are people with me." Thus, when interpreting the total score, it is equivocal whether the score reflects pure anxiety or anxiety and depression.

State–Trait Anxiety Inventory for Children

The State–Trait Anxiety Inventory for Children (STAIC) (Spielberger 1973) comprises two independent 20-item subscales: the anxiety–state subscale, which assesses situational symptoms or transitory anxiety, and the anxiety–trait subscale, which describes generalized anxiety across a variety of situations, similar to what is presumed to be measured with the RCMAS.

Interestingly, test–retest reliability over a 3-month period is only fair, especially for the anxiety–trait subscale. For the anxiety–state subscale $r = .63$, and for the anxiety–trait subscale $r = .44$ (Finch et al. 1974). These data are the opposite of what would be expected, with the expectation that trait anxiety would be more stable over time with greater fluctuations in state anxiety. A validity study showed that emotionally disturbed children obtain significantly higher scores on the anxiety–state and anxiety–trait subscales of the STAIC compared with normal children (Montgomery and Finch 1974).

Visual Analogue Scale for Anxiety

The Visual Analogue Scale for Anxiety (Garfinkel et al. 1984) is a self-report instrument. This scale consists of two faces depicting "steady" and "jittery/nervous" with the associated words at opposite ends of a line. The child is instructed to place a mark on the line to indicate his or her current level of anxiety. It is scored by measuring the number of centimeters from the "steady" end, which is a zero-point to the mark placed by the child.

The original Visual Analogue Scale for Anxiety has been revised into an 11-item battery of visual analogues for identifying and quantifying potential anxiety associated with anxiety-producing situations in childhood and adolescence. The Visual Analogue Scale for Anxiety—Revised consists of sets of faces ("steady" versus "jittery/nervous") accompanied by a phrase describing a specific situation that may produce anxiety. In a small sample of school refusers (N = 15) and their siblings (N = 7), correlations between the subjects' total scores on the Visual Analogue Scale for Anxiety—Revised and the RCMAS and between the Visual Analogue Scale for Anxiety—Revised and the trait anxiety subscale of the STAIC suggest construct validity of the new instrument (Bernstein et al. 1986).

Anxiety Rating for Children

The Anxiety Rating for Children (ARC) (Erbaugh 1984) is a clinician rating scale of anxiety. This scale includes seven subscales, rated by the clinician, based on a semi-structured interview. Some of the subscales overlap with depression items. The instrument takes 30 to 45 minutes to administer. Preliminary data show that the mean and standard deviation for a group of school phobic children and adolescents who met criteria for a *DSM-III* anxiety diagnosis is $12.1 \pm .4.2$ compared with 8.0 ± 4.4 ($p \leq .05$) for a group of school phobics who did not meet criteria for an anxiety disorder (Bernstein and Garfinkel 1986).

DIFFERENTIAL DIAGNOSIS

Separation Anxiety Disorder

Children and adolescents with separation anxiety disorder, manifested as school refusal, need to be differentiated from children who are truant from school because of conduct disorder behavior. Children with conduct disorder manifest behaviors such as lying, stealing, running away from home, or violating rules at home and school. Children with school refusal generally show a high standard of work and behavior at school in contrast to children with conduct disorder whose standard of work is often poor and who behaviorally are careless and defiant. Children with conduct disorder compared with those with school refusal have a higher frequency of learning disabilities and organic or neurologic findings (Torma 1975). The patterns of nonattendance between the two groups are distinct. While children with school refusal are at home with their parents' knowledge during school time, children with conduct disorder are in the community without their parents' knowledge roaming alone or in groups. Truant children and adolescents enter the front door of the school and quickly exit through the back or side doors. School phobic children never even go in the front door.

Children with avoidant disorder or overanxious disorder may be confused with those with separation anxiety disorder since children in all three groups may have discomfort in social settings. All may be reticent, may be unsure of themselves, and may have difficulties with peer relationships. However, only with separation anxiety disorder is the anxiety focused on fears tied to separation. While children with pervasive developmental disorders or schizophrenia may manifest separation anxiety, the anxiety is overwhelming, generalized, pervasive, and secondary to the underlying disorder; thus, the diagnosis of separation anxiety is not made.

Symptoms of major depression and separation anxiety disorder may overlap. When full criteria for both disorders are met, both diagnoses should be made.

In a study of 26 young adolescents with chronic school refusal, 69% met *DSM-III* criteria for a depressive disorder, 62% met *DSM-III* criteria for anxiety disorder (usually separation anxiety disorder), and 50% had both depressive and anxiety disorders (Bernstein and Garfinkel 1986) (Fig. 5–2).

Avoidant Disorder

Avoidant disorder is differentiated from the other two childhood anxiety disorders because only this disorder results from anxiety related to contact with strangers. In schizoid disorder of children and adolescents (DSM-III), the child is a loner rather than has a fear of strangers. While children with avoidant disorder have a desire for affection and acceptance from peers, children with schizoid disorder do not enjoy peer relationships and have little desire for social involvement.

Persons with avoidant personality disorder shy away from social situations because of extreme sensitivity to rejection. They are unwilling to enter into friendships unless there is a strong guarantee of acceptance. Avoidant personality disorder should only be diagnosed if the behavior patterns are of long standing and the person is older than 18 years of age. In adjustment disorder with withdrawal, the behaviors of withdrawal clearly follow a psychosocial stressor within the previous 3 months.

Overanxious Disorder

In overanxious disorder, there is generalized anxiety and worry in multiple situations, whereas the other two childhood anxiety disorders are situation specific. Generalized anxiety disorder in adults is similar to overanxious disorder, characterized by motor tension, autonomic hyperactivity, apprehensive expectation, vigilance, and scanning. Individuals must be at least 18 years old to qualify for a diagnosis of generalized anxiety disorder. In attention-deficit hyperactivity disorder (ADHD), a child has excess motor activity and is constantly moving or "on the go"; thus, a child with ADHD may appear tense. However, children with ADHD do not pre-

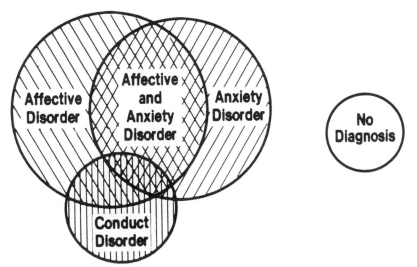

Figure 5–2. Overlap of affective and anxiety disorders in school refusers. (From Bernstein, G. A., and Garfinkel, B. D. 1986. School phobia: Overlap of affective and anxiety disorders. J. Am. Acad. Child Psychiatry 25:235–241.

sent with multiple worries. In adjustment disorder with anxious mood, the anxiety symptoms follow a recent psychosocial stressor.

TREATMENT OF SCHOOL REFUSAL

A three-pronged approach, including consultation to the school to design a behavioral school reentry program, medication, and psychotherapy, is recommended.

It is important to detect symptoms early and intervene quickly. Temporarily excusing a child from school validates and supports the fears. The longer a school phobic child remains at home, the harder it is for the child to return to the classroom. There may be secondary gain associated with staying at home, such as more attention and free time. It is necessary to lessen the attraction of staying home and increase the attraction of going to school. Children who remain at home fall behind academically, and the farther behind they get the harder it is to make up the school work. In addition, these children lose the opportunity for normal peer relationships, lose friends, and become socially isolated. Homebound tutoring is contraindicated for the following reasons: (1) receiving schooling at home becomes too comfortable for an anxious child and (2) returning to school is often more difficult after tutoring at home. As a child returns to school and overall functioning improves, the relationship between parents and child also improves.

Behavioral Treatment

Intervention strategies have not been well studied. The literature consists primarily of single-case studies or multiple-case history reviews reporting success with one type of treatment. A variety of approaches have been cited as effective.

Reentering a child into school is accomplished with a behavioral program. When school avoidance is motivated by high anxiety, a classical conditioning approach may be used. In this model, the child identifies the stimuli for fears and anxiety. A hierarchy of fears is constructed. For example, a child may rank the following situations as anxiety producing from most to least: (1) walking out of the house to leave for school; (2) riding the school bus; (3) changing clothes in the locker room for gym; (4) eating in the lunchroom; (5) passing between classes; and (6) being called on by the teacher. With classical conditioning, fears are treated by desensitization. Desensitization involves relaxation therapy. The child learns to substitute a relaxation response while gradually introducing thoughts and images that previously elicited anxiety. The next step is in-vivo desensitization in which the child "walks" through anxiety situations with support in order to decrease anxiety. The anxiety-producing situations are gradually increased to include those that are most anxiety laden. The therapist will usually spend time at school with the patient before handing the responsibility over to the parents.

The operant behavioral approach is employed when the anxiety is somewhat less than that which requires a classical conditioning approach. A behavioral analysis identifies contingencies supporting a child's maladaptive behavior. With the operant method, desired behavior is positively reinforced and undesirable behavior is not rewarded. For example, returning to school (however accomplished) is rewarded. Other desirable behaviors, including separation from the mother, adequate performance after return to school, and maintenance of school attendance, are rewarded. Thus, the reinforcement system is rearranged to decrease the child's fear of leaving his or her mother, to encourage school attendance, and to maintain school attendance.

The classical conditioning and operant behavioral approaches are often combined. Classical conditioning may be used to accomplish getting a child to school and may help the child stay comfortably for brief periods of time. Subsequently, an operant reward system is employed for continued attendance.

Blagg and Yule (1984) evaluated different treatments for school refusal. In their study 30 patients received behavioral treatment, 16 received inpatient treatment, and 20 received psychotherapy and home tutoring. Subjects ranged in age from 11 to 16. The behavior therapy included an in-depth clarification of the child's problems, realistic discussion of child, parental, and teacher concerns, contingency plans to ensure maintenance, in-vivo flooding, and follow-up. The behavioral therapy was most effective for decreasing separation anxiety and facilitating a return to and maintenance in school. Twenty-nine of 30 subjects in the behavioral group were attending school regularly at follow-up. Behavioral therapy was most economical, faster, and less intrusive than the other two treatments.

School Consultation

Consultation to the school is an integral part of treatment. A school official (social worker, counselor, special education teacher, nurse, or administrator) should be involved with the designing and instituting of a behavioral reentry program. It is helpful to designate a key person at school whom the child can go to if emotional support is needed. It is advisable to allow a student with high anxiety or panic symptoms to leave the classroom for a brief period, at which time the student can go to the school support person for reassurance, if necessary. Then the student is encouraged to return to the classroom.

If symptoms are extreme and the child or adolescent is not able to function full-time in a mainstream classroom, referral for placement in a classroom for the emotionally or behaviorally disturbed is recommended. The teachers in these classrooms are trained to work with children having special emotional needs. Sometimes all that is needed is 1 hour in a classroom for emotionally and behaviorally disturbed students to allow the student to receive emotional support and academic guidance, after which he or she joins the regular classes for the remainder of the day. Other adolescents may require up to 3 to 4 hours per day of instruction for the emotionally and behaviorally disturbed. Time in the emotionally and behaviorally disturbed classroom can be decreased and hours in mainstream classes can be increased as the child's symptoms improve and the child regains comfort and confidence in the normal school setting. Referral for full-time instruction in a special school or for residential treatment is reserved for children who do not improve in the less restrictive settings.

Pharmacologic Studies

Several studies have evaluated the efficacy of medication in children with school refusal.

Frommer (1967) studied 14 depressed and phobic children. She employed a double-blind, crossover design that compared phenelzine and chlordiazepoxide to phenobarbital. The combination treatment proved superior to phenobarbital alone. Diagnosis and therapeutic outcome were not systematically obtained. The results from this study are encouraging but must be viewed cautiously.

Gittelman-Klein and Klein (1973) reported a double-blind, placebo-controlled study of 35 children aged 6 to 14 with school refusal refractory to psychotherapy. All children had separation anxiety without significant depression. Imipramine (100–200 mg/day) was significantly better than placebo in leading to return of the children to school. Imipramine induced school return in 81%; placebo was effective in 47%. This high placebo response rate demonsrates a very high remission rate without any psychoactive medication. Although 47% returned to school while on placebo, these children were often still symptomatic. Psychiatrists, mothers, and children rated the imipramine group as showing significantly greater improvement, including a decrease in fearfulness and somatic complaints. The authors concluded that imipramine was more effective than placebo in returning children to school because the drug targeted the patients' separation anxiety symptoms.

Abe (1975) reported on the open administration of sulpiride to 21 school phobic children with depressive symptoms who had failed in psychotherapy or behavioral treatment. In this uncontrolled study, 13 children returned to school within the first week of drug treatment with a decrease in symptoms of anxiety and depression, 3 improved clinically but remained at home, and 5 showed no improvement. Of the 8 not returning to school, 6 subsequently were placed on imipramine therapy with 2 eventually showing a response.

Berney and co-workers (1981) using a double-blind, placebo-controlled trial of a tricyclic antidepressant, clomipramine, 40 to 75 mg/day, in school refusers, reported no significant difference between placebo and clomipramine in decreasing symptomatology or facilitating a return to school. Criticism of the study is the low dose of clomipramine used.

The two tricyclic antidepressant studies had conflicting results. Several variables may explain the contrasting findings. The antidepressant dosage in the study of Gittelman-Klein and Klein (1973) was higher than that achieved in the study of Berney and co-workers (1981). Patient populations differed between the two studies. Patients in Berney and co-workers' study were slightly older and more depressed than patients in Gittelman-Klein and Klein's study. These two factors may predict nonresponse at the lower end of the dose range for a tricyclic antidepressant medication. The studies also differed in psychosocial therapies concurrent with medication. Gittelman-Klein and Klein used persuasive and desensitization techniques; Berney and co-workers employed concurrent individual psychotherapy for the child and casework with the parents.

Clinical experience at the School Refusal Clinic suggests that both alprazolam, a new benzodiazepine, and imipramine are useful in the treatment of school refusal secondary to anxiety and depression.

Psychotherapy

Individual and/or family therapy may be indicated with a focus on role functioning, communication, and problem-solving among family members. In family therapy the theme of the family as an interacting system that maintains the ongoing problem can be pursued. It may be necessary to change the overprotective role of the family by reestablishing the proper parent–child hierarchy. The family's goal must be returning the child to school.

Legal Involvement

Truancy petitions were present in 50% of the school refusers referred to the School Refusal Clinic at the University of Minnesota. Truancy petitions effect change differently in different school refusers. In some families, court involvement is often what is needed to effect a return to school, since the petition provides a firm, clear message to student and parents that school refusal is against the law. However, other families respond differently and become more noncompliant and anxious owing to fears that the child will be punished and possibly removed from the home. The courts often recognize school refusal as resulting from psychiatric difficulties and therefore mandate psychiatric evaluation and treatment. After age 16, the schools usually do not file truancy petitions because, at this age, it is legal to drop out of school with parental permission.

Coordination of Efforts/ Multidisciplinary Approach

Mental health professionals, the family, school officials, and the courts need to coordinate efforts in treating children with school refusal. Otherwise, certain disciplines may not be adequately informed and subsequently different persons or agencies may be working in different directions. By coordinating all of the above institutions, one can hope to identify and treat a greater number of children and adolescents now suffering from school refusal.

References

Abe, K. 1975. Sulpiride in school phobia. *Psychiatr. Clin.* 8:95–98.

American Psychiatric Association. 1987. *Diagnostic and Statistical Manual of Mental Disorders*, 3rd ed., revised. Washington, D.C.: American Psychiatric Association.

Baker, H., and Wills, U. 1979. School phobia in the children of agoraphobic women. *Br. J. Psychiatry* 135:561–564.

Beck, A. T. 1978. *Depression Inventory*. Philadelphia, Center for Cognitive Therapy.

Berg, I. 1970. A follow-up study of school phobic adolescents admitted to an inpatient unit. *J. Child Psychol. Psychiatry* 11:37–47.

Berg, I., Butler, A., and Hall, G. 1976. The outcome of adolescent school phobia. *Br. J. Psychiatry* 128:80–85.

Berg, I., and Fielding, D. 1978. An evaluation of hospital inpatient treatment in adolescent school phobia. *Br. J. Psychiatry* 132:500–505.

Berg, I., and Jackson, A. 1985. Teenage school refusers grow up: A follow-up study of 168 subjects, ten years on average after in-patient treatment. *Br. J. Psychiatry* 147:366–370.

Berney, T., Kolvin, I., Bhate, S. R., et al. 1981. School phobia: A therapeutic trial with clomipramine and short-term outcome. *Br. J. Psychiatry* 138:110–118.

Bernstein, G. A., and Garfinkel, B. D. 1986. School phobia: Overlap of affective and anxiety disorders. *J. Am. Acad. Child Psychiatry* 25:235–241.

Bernstein, G. A., and Garfinkel, B. D. 1988. Pedigrees, functioning, and psychopathology in families of school phobic children. *Am. J. Psychiatry* 145:70–74.

Bernstein, G. A., Garfinkel, B. D., and August, G. J. 1986. Visual analogue scale for anxiety, revised. In *Scientific Proceedings for the Annual Meeting*, vol. 2. American Academy of Child and Adolescent Psychiatry.

Bernstein, G. A., Garfinkel, B. D., and Hoberman, H. 1989. Self-reported anxiety in adolescents. *Am. J. Psychiatry* 146:384–386.

Blagg, N. R., and Yule, W. 1984. The behavioural treatment of school refusal: A comparative study. *Behav. Res. Ther.* 22:119–127.

Bowlby, J. 1973. *Attachment and Loss,* Vol. 2, *Separation: Anxiety and Anger.* New York: Basic Books.

Brown, F. W. 1942. Heredity in the psychoneuroses. *Proc. R. Soc. Med.* 35:785–790.

Cohen, M. E., Badal, D. W., Kilpatrick, A., et al. 1951. The high family prevalence of neurocirculatory asthenia (anxiety neurosis, effort syndrome). *Am. J. Hum. Genet.* 3:126–158.

Coolidge, J. C., Brodie, R. D., and Feeney, B. 1964. A ten-year follow-up study of sixty-six school phobic children. *Am. J. Orthopsychiatry* 34:675–684.

Crowe, R. R., Gaffney, G., and Kerber, P. 1982. Panic attacks in families of patients with mitral valve prolapse. *J. Affective Disord.* 4:121–125.

Crowe, R. R., Noyes, R., Pauls, D. L., and Slymen, D. 1983. A family study of panic disorder. *Arch. Gen. Psychiatry* 40:1065–1069.

DeVereux, R. B., Perloff, J. K., Reichek, N., et al. 1976. Mitral valve prolapse. *Circulation* 54:3–14.

Erbaugh, S. E. 1984. Anxiety rating for children (personal communication).

Finch, A. J., Jr., Montgomery, L. E., and Deardorff, P. A. 1974. Reliability of State–Trait anxiety with emotionally disturbed children. J. Abnorm. Child Psychol. 2:67–69.

Freud, A. 1946. *The Ego and the Mechanisms of Defense.* New York: International Universities Press.

Frommer, E. A. 1967. Treatment of childhood depression with antidepressant drugs. *Br. Med. J.* 1:729–732.

Gittelman-Klein, R., and Klein, D. F. 1973. School phobia: Diagnostic considerations in the light of imipramine effects. *J. Nerv. Ment. Dis.* 156:199–215.

Harris, E. L., Noyes, R., Crowe, R. R., et al. 1983. Family study of agoraphobia. Report of a pilot study. *Arch. Gen. Psychiatry* 40:1061–1064.

Herjanic, B., and Campbell, W. 1977. Differentiating psychiatrically disturbed children on the basis of structured interview. *J. Abnorm. Child Psychol.* 5:127–134.

Kitano, H. I. 1960. Validity of the Revised Children's Manifest Anxiety Scale and the modified revised California inventory. *Child Devel.* 31:67–72.

Klein, M. 1952. On the theory of anxiety and guilt. In Riviere, J. (ed.): *Developments in Psychoanalysis.* London: Hogarth Press.

Last, C. G., Hersen, M., Kazdin, A. E., et al. 1987. Comparison of DSM-III separation anxiety and overanxious disorders: demographic characteristics and patterns of comorbidity. *J. Am. Acad. Child Adolesc. Psychiatry* 26:527–531.

Leckman, J. F., Merikangas, K. R., Pauls, D. L., et al. 1983a. Anxiety disorders and depression: Contradictions between family study data and *DSM-II* conventions. *Am. J. Psychiatry* 140:880–882.

Leckman, J. F., Weissman, M. M., Merikangas, K. R., et al. 1983b. Panic disorder and major depression: Increased risk of depression, alcoholism, panic, and phobic disorders in families of depressed probands with panic disorder. *Arch. Gen. Psychiatry* 40:1055–1060.

Levin, A. P., Doran, A. R., Liebowitz, M. R., et al. 1986. Pituitary adrenocortical unresponsiveness in lactate-induced panic. *Psychiatr. Res.* 21:23–32.

Livingston, R., Nugent, H., Rader, L., and Smith, G. R. 1985. Family histories of depressed and severely anxious children. *Am. J. Psychiatry* 142:1497–1499.

Livingstone, R., Reis, C. J., and Ringdahl, I. C. 1984. Abnormal dexamethasone suppression test results in depressed and nondepressed children. *Am. J. Psychiatry* 141:106–108.

Mahler, M. 1968. *On Human Symbiosis and the Vicissitudes of Individuation.* New York: International Universities Press.

Mazza, D. L., Martin, D., Spacavento, L., et al. 1986. Prevalence of anxiety disorders in patients with mitral valve prolapse. *Am. J. Psychiatry* 143:349–352.

McInnes, R. G. 1937. Observations on heredity in neurosis. *Proc. R. Soc. Med.* 30:895–904.

Michels, R., Frances, A., and Shear, M. K. 1985. Psychodynamic models of anxiety. In Tuma, A. H., and Maser, J. D. (eds.): *Anxiety and the Anxiety Disorders.* Hillsdale, N. J.: Lawrence Erlbaum Associates.

Montgomery, L. E., and Finch, A. J., Jr. 1974. Validity of two measures of anxiety in children. *J. Abnorm. Child Psychol.* 2:293–298.

Noyes, R., Clancy, J., Crowe, R. R., et al. 1978. The familial prevalence of anxiety neurosis. *Arch. Gen. Psychiatry* 35:1057–1059.

Noyes, R., Crowe, R. R., Harris, E. L., et al. 1986. Relationship between panic disorder and agoraphobia. *Arch. Gen. Psychiatry* 43:227–232.

Orvaschel, H., and Weissman, M. M. 1986. Epidemiology of anxiety disorders in children: A review. In Gittelman, R. (ed.): *Anxiety Disorders of Childhood.* New York: Guilford Press.

Pauls, D. L., Noyes, R., and Crowe, R. R. 1979. The familial prevalence in second-degree relatives of patients with anxiety neurosis (panic disorder). *J. Affective Disord.* 1:279–285.

Pitts, F. N., and McClure, J. N. 1967. Lactate metabolism in anxiety neurosis. *N. Engl. J. Med.* 277:1328–1336.

Reich, J. 1986. The epidemiology of anxiety. *J. Nerv. Ment. Dis.* 174:129–136.

Reynolds, C. R., and Richman, B. O. 1978. What I think and feel: A revised measure of children's manifest anxiety. *J. Abnorm. Child Psychol.* 6:271–280.

Rodriguez, A., Rodriguez, M., and Eisenberg, L. 1959. The outcome of school phobia: A follow-up study based on 41 cases. *Am. J. Psychiatry* 116:540–544.

Slater, E., and Shields, J. 1969. General aspects of anxiety. In: *Studies of Anxiety* (Special Publication 3). *Br. J. Psychiatry* 139:62–71.

Spielberger, S. 1973. Manual for the State–Trait anxiety inventory for children. Palo Alto, CA: Consulting Psychologists Press.

Sullivan, H. S. 1953. In Perry, H. S., and Gawel, M. L. (eds.): *Interpersonal Theory of Psychiatry.* New York: W. W. Norton.

Surman, O. S., Sheehan, D. V., Fuller, T. C., and Gallo, J. 1983. Panic disorder in genotypic HLA identical sibling pairs. *Am. J. Psychiatry* 140:237–238.

Torma, S., and Halsti, A. 1975. Factors contributing to school phobia and truancy. *Psychiatria Fennica* 75:209–216.

Waldron, S. 1976. The significance of childhood neurosis for adult mental health: A follow-up study. *Am. J. Psychiatry* 133:532–538.

Warren, W. 1965. A study of adolescent psychiatric inpatients and the outcome six or more years later: II. The follow-up study. *J. Child Psychol. Psychiatry* 6:141–160.

Weiss, M., and Burke, A. G. 1967. A five- to ten-year follow-up of hospitalized school phobic children and adolescents. *Am. J. Orthopsychiatry* 37:294–295.

Weissman, M. M., Leckman, J. F., Merikangas, K. R., et al. 1984. Depression and anxiety disorders in parents and children. *Arch. Gen. Psychiatry* 41:845–852.

Obsessive-Compulsive Disorder in Children and Adolescents

JONATHAN B. JENSEN, M.D.

As I was Going to St. Ives

As I was going to St. Ives,
I met a man with seven wives.
Every wife had seven sacks,
Every sack had seven cats,
Every cat had seven kits.
Kits, cats, sacks and wives,
How many were going to St. Ives?

DEFINITION

Encountering the diagnosis of obsessive-compulsive disorder (OCD) in children can be an experience like that of the man who is on his way to St. Ives. It is possible to become so engrossed with the symptoms, confounding factors of personality traits, family interactions, associated affective states of anxiety and depression, and possible precipitating events that the direction of the diagnostic assessment can be lost. Similarly, the child with OCD can become so preoccupied with counting kits, cats, sacks, and wives that the purpose of the evaluation, and what one set out to do in the first place, is lost. The answer to these riddles is to understand the biological substrate of OCD. There are other conditions that may be associated but differ in etiology. These disorders need to be understood more from a behavioral and dynamic perspective and require different treatment interventions.

During the course of a child's development a variety of repetitive processes stabilize the child's life. A feeding schedule is established based on the child's needs and the parents' response to them. Similarly, putting the child down for a nap or for bedtime becomes a habitual set of behaviors and stimuli from which the child learns. During the latter part of the first year of life, the child develops repeated gestures and vocalizations with which the child attempts to effect control on objects and persons in his or her environment. The child learns from the repeated gestures and vocalizations his or her effect on the environment (Piaget 1952).

As the child enters the toddler years (with an emphasis on toilet training and cleanliness), the pattern for some of the later rituals of washing and fears about dirt can become established. Overly demanding and controlling adults may contribute to the child's inability to behave freely. Finch (1960) suggested that children who had preoccupation with thoughts and who practiced rituals were believed to be "pseudomature." These children respond to both parents and other adults with overcompliance and worry about being outwardly correct while maintaining angry and ambivalent feelings toward the adults. They exhibit a tendency toward smearing, being dirty, messiness, and stubbornness. As conscience develops in the grade school years, the child is very good and compliant. This has been called the mechanism of "reaction formation." That is, the child acts opposite to his or her inner desires. The child knows right from wrong and attempts to develop strategies to prevent himself or herself from doing these wrong things. The developing obsessive-compulsive personality appears as an overly compliant, worrying child, often with ritualistic behaviors. The ideas and/or ritualistic behaviors are seen as unreasonable but nonetheless continued. Typical thoughts are fears of dirt, sexual misbehavior, and disorderliness. Commonly occurring behaviors include rearranging, throwing out dirty or marred articles, excessive washing of hands and clothes, repeated counting and checking of light switches and stoves, and, in older children, turning off/on and locking the family car.

The importance of a ritual in decreasing inner worry and fear is readily seen in a number of street games and bedtime behaviors. Being able to keep "monsters in the closet" by the use of a night light and closing of closet doors are quite common experiences of the preschool and grade school child. Similarly, the superstitions of "step on a crack, break your mother's back, step on a line, break your mother's spine" are often repeated by schoolchildren. Chance associations between stimulus and response not only occur to preschool children, who are using preoperational cognitive constructs of irrational cause and effect associations, but also to older children, who associate uncomfortable events through stimulus generalization with the circumstances of a trauma. The child has recurring thoughts and ritualistic behaviors that may help to establish regularity and reduce tension. Specific stimuli or upsetting events may result in an abnormal reliance on obsessions and compulsions. The child's personality may be strongly flawed by these symptoms.

A distinction must be made between the obsessive personality traits of punctuality, perfectionism, frugality, and resistance to new ideas and the more serious, dysfunctional symptoms of OCD. In adults OCD often results in persons who concentrate so much on the symptoms and habits that they are dysfunctional in work, are socially withdrawn, and are often surrounded by their own messiness and disorder. These patients have been described as maintaining small islands of vigilant orderliness in a sea of stubbornly resistant disorder. In adolescents, this is often manifested in the area of homework. So much attention is given to reading and re-reading material that the overall purpose of the work is lost and grades suffer.

The diagnostic criteria as presented in the *Diagnostic and Statistical Manual of Mental Disorders*, third edition, revised (*DSM-III-R*) (American Psychiatric Association 1987) for the obsessive-compulsive personality disorder and for true OCD are found in Tables 6–1 and 6–2.

The emerging obsessive-compulsive personality of a child likely results from a very severe, punishing conscience. In order to manage the aggressive, sexual ideas and feelings the child has, he or she develops a plethora of thoughts and ritualistic behaviors to fight against the emergence of these ideas. A traumatic event, such as parental divorce with an overly attentive remaining parent or the death of an important adult figure, may be the stimulus that contributes to the development of this type of personality.

Moral development is integral to the development of an obsessive-compulsive personality disorder. In Kohlberg's schema, the first response of a preschool child is to obey the parents' superior force. As a child develops relationships there is a sense of responding for positive rewards that develops into the desire to be liked by others and to behave well to gain approval. Later stages of moral development involve understanding the need for rules in order to maintain the structure of society, followed by adherence to contracts, and, finally, as a person reaches adolescence and adulthood, behavior based on ethical principles that are complied with voluntarily. The person with an obsessive-compulsive personality, in attempting to be liked by others and do things correctly, may be overly shaped by the environment in which he or she has been raised. This same environment may be a precipitating factor in true OCD. In a study of 44 families of adults with OCD there was an interesting finding

---

Table 6–1. DIAGNOSTIC CRITERIA FOR OBSESSIVE-COMPULSIVE PERSONALITY DISORDER

A pervasive pattern of perfectionism and inflexibility, beginning by early adulthood and present in a variety of contexts, as indicated by at least *five* of the following:

1. Perfectionism that interferes with task completion, e.g., inability to complete a project because own overly strict standards are not met.
2. Preoccupation with details, rules, lists, order, organization, or schedules to the extent that the major point of the activity is lost.
3. Unreasonable insistence that others submit to exactly his or her way of doing things, *or* unreasonable reluctance to allow others to do things because of the conviction that they will not do them correctly.
4. Excessive devotion to work and productivity to the exclusion of leisure activities and friendships (not accounted for by obvious economic necessity).
5. Indecisiveness: decision making is either avoided, postponed, or protracted, e.g., the person cannot get assignments done on time because of ruminating about priorities (do not include if indecisiveness is due to excessive need for advice or reassurance from others).
6. Overconscientiousness, scrupulousness, and inflexibility about matters of morality, ethics, or values (not accounted for by cultural or religious identification).
7. Restricted expression of affection.
8. Lack of generosity in giving time, money, or gifts when no personal gain is likely to result.
9. Inability to discard worn-out or worthless objects even when they have no sentimental value.

From American Psychiatric Association. 1987. Diagnostic and Statistical Manual of Mental Disorders, 3rd ed., revised. Washington, D.C.: American Psychiatric Association, p. 247.

---

that the religious background of most of the subjects was strict, orderly, and inflexible (Rasmussen 1986). While for many persons this may result in a conservative way of life that is comfortable, this may well be one of the contributing factors to OCD.

Conflicts between parent and child can be resolved positively (Anthony 1967) if the child has had normal premorbid development. Personality traits of ambivalence toward others, magical thinking, and an unforgiving conscience can cause coping mechanisms of isolation, reaction formation, and undoing (Moore and Fine 1968). Obses-

sive personality traits provide stability and order that make a person less anxious. Symptoms of OCD represent an overwhelming of a person's response capacity, resulting in a highly uncomfortable disorganized state. Researchers had reasoned, therefore, that a premorbid obsessive personality might mitigate the maladjustment of the symptoms of OCD. It was found, however, that obsessive-compulsive patients who had an obsessional personality (orderly, parsimonious, and obstinate) were not better adjusted than patients who had a low degree of these features (Solyom et al. 1986). This study again lends

---

Table 6–2. DIAGNOSTIC CRITERIA FOR OBSESSIVE-COMPULSIVE DISORDER

A. Either Obsessions or Compulsions:

Obsessions:

1. Recurrent and persistent ideas, thoughts, impulses, or images that are experienced, at least initially, as intrusive and senseless, e.g., a parent's having repeated impulses to kill a loved child, a religious person's having recurrent blasphemous thoughts.
2. The person attempts to ignore or suppress such thoughts or impulses or to neutralize them with some other thought or action.
3. The person recognizes that the obsessions are the product of his or her own mind, not imposed from without (as in thought insertion).
4. If another Axis I disorder is present, the content of the obsession is unrelated to it, e.g., the ideas, thoughts, impulses, or images are not about food in the presence of an eating disorder, about drugs in the presence of a psychoactive substance use disorder, or guilty thoughts in the presence of a major depression.

Compulsions:

1. Repetitive, purposeful, and intentional behaviors that are performed in response to an obsession, or according to certain rules or in a stereotyped fashion.
2. The behavior is designed to neutralize or to prevent discomfort or some dreaded event or situation; however, either the activity is not connected in a realistic way with what it is designed to neutralize or prevent or it is clearly excessive.
3. The person recognizes that his or her behavior is excessive or unreasonable (that may not be true for young children; it may no longer be true for people whose obsessions have evolved into overvalued ideas).

B. The obsessions or compulsions cause marked distress, are time consuming (take more than an hour a day), or significantly interfere with the person's normal routine, occupational functioning, or usual social activities or relationships with others.

From American Psychiatric Association. 1987. Diagnostic and Statistical Manual of Mental Disorders, 3rd ed., revised. Washington, D.C.: American Psychiatric Association, p. 247.

support to the idea that, while obsessional coping styles may become a part of a personality, there is a distinct and separate biological condition of OCD.

The family plays an especially important role in adolescent OCD. In one study (Hoover and Insel 1984), data were collected on 174 relatives of severe obsessive-compulsive patients. Family entrapment was found to be common. Parents were often unable to say no to the OCD child; there was an excessive need for closeness; and there was an absence of marital intimacy. The child was perceived as being unable to cope with the outside world; the family experienced exhaustion in response to the rituals and tantrums of the OCD child; and there was guilt about their own parenting style. The authors concluded that the obsessive-compulsive patient's symptoms acted as a barrier against too much closeness with a parent.

The child's OCD had a profound effect on the family. The elaborate thought patterns and rituals of the child were not found in other family members; therefore, the child's disorder was different and could not be the same as obsessional personality traits. The child's relationships to other persons, responses to events, traumatic experiences, and family environment were affected by the OCD.

ETIOLOGY AND PATHOGENESIS

In children, there is evidence that biological and genetic causation is important. Indirect studies include the association of obsessive-compulsive symptoms with other conditions that are known to be neurologic (such as Tourette's syndrome), family history studies examining the incidence of other psychiatric conditions in relatives of patients with OCD, and pedigree studies.

Direct examination of the nervous system through animal studies, particularly manipulations in the region of the cingulate gyrus, have produced obsessive-compulsive symptoms. Nonspecific neurologic findings in children and adults with OCD such as galvanic skin response differences and electroencephalographic (EEG) changes have been observed. A further indirect way of examining the nervous system in these children is through the use of the dexamethasone suppression test and growth hormone chal-

lenge response. Site-specific investigations that examine overall brain organization have also been employed. Neuropsychological tests and learning and auditory discrimination tasks show differences in patients with OCD compared with normals. The recent development of positron emission tomography (PET) has allowed comparison between anatomical localization of altered metabolic processes in patients with OCD and normals.

Support for an organic basis for OCD can be found through response to pharmacologic probes, such as clomipramine. From pharmacologic studies, neurotransmitter hypotheses have evolved that implicate serotonin dysregulation, with or without dopamine dysregulation.

In 1896, Gadelius, in Sweden (also Schilder 1938), thought that OCD had a neurologic basis. He noticed that patients with OCD often had mild neurologic abnormalities, including very mild tremors, decreased movement of the arms, rigid face, akinesias, and hyperkinesis. In adults, neurologic symptoms have been correlated with obsessive-compulsive symptoms. In adolescents (Rapoport 1986), a rather sudden onset of OCD was noted in some patients. Since there was no history of obsessive traits for the majority of these children, these observations support the notion that OCD is a manifestation of an organic event and not a worsening of a personality disorder.

In children and adolescents, there are increased rates of OCD symptoms in patients with Tourette's syndrome. In 1885, Tourette described obsessions in a woman with tics and vocalizations. More recently, 74% of Tourette's syndrome patients were found to have prominent obsessive-compulsive symptoms. The families of Tourette's syndrome patients demonstrated a rate of OCD among first-degree relatives that was significantly higher than that in the general population and control samples of adoptive relatives. Tourette's syndrome and OCD are probably etiologically related (Pauls et al. 1986). Genetic studies indicate that Tourette's syndrome results from a single major gene, with a gene frequency of 0.006, suggesting that 1.2% of the population carry the gene and that more than half may express it in some form (Biederman et al. 1986). Grad and coworkers (1987) found that 28% of the Tourette's syndrome group had OCD, while 10% of a comparison control group had OCD.

Parents and teachers reported children with Tourette's syndrome as having significantly more obsessive-compulsive symptoms.

There is also an association between OCD and anorexia nervosa. One of the diagnostic criteria for anorexia nervosa includes a preoccupation with weight, which is manifested as obsessional thinking about eating calories and the forms of food. Likewise, adult women with OCD often report a past history of anorexia nervosa.

In adults, the syndrome is associated with depressive disorders in as many as 71% of the cases. However, Rapoport (1986) reported only a 10% concordance with major affective disorder in children.

A pedigree study demonstrated affective psychosis, obsessive-compulsive phenomena, panic attacks, and eating disorder clustering in over three generations of relatives of a 17-year-old girl with schizoaffective disorder, bulimia, panic attacks, and interepisode OCD. From this pedigree it was argued that these various disorders may represent "the multifactorial transmission of vulnerability." That is, the presentation of any one of these disorders may be different phenotypic expressions of the same gene. The severity of pathology and number of different symptoms would indicate genetic loading (Dilsaver and White 1986).

For 24 pairs of twins with OCD, 7 dizygotic pairs were discordant for OCD. Of the 17 pairs of monozygotic twins, 12 twin pairs were concordant for OCD and 5 were discordant (Lieberman 1984).

In addition to the evidence of a genetic predisposition, there are correlations between central nervous system trauma and the development of obsessive-compulsive symptoms. In World War I, soldiers who sustained brain injuries were noticed to have OCD; the outbreak of von Economo's encephalitis (1917–1919) was followed not only by Parkinson's disease in adults and hyperactivity in children but also by OCD symptoms in some patients. Grimshaw found that "OC neurotic" patients had about 2½ times the incidence of neurologic illness as did control patients. Kettl and Marks described the onset of OCD in two patients just after the onset of epilepsy.

Neurologic and Neuropsychological Investigations

The reported incidence of EEG abnormalities in patients with OCD is between 11%

and 65%. Similarly, visual evoked potentials were abnormal when compared with schizophrenic or other psychiatric patients. In nine children studied by Rapoport and co-workers (1981), however, there was only one abnormal EEG. Sleep EEG changes were found to be similar to those in middle-aged patients with major depression. The OCD children had short rapid eye movement latency with reduced sleep efficiency. The EEGs of these adolescents were similar to adult OCD sleep EEG patterns.

Nonspecific findings suggest a hemispheric imbalance. Dysfunction in the left hemisphere was inferred from the finding that 44% of patients studied by Rapoport and co-workers (N = 9) were left handed for writing, eating, and sports (incidence in the total population 10% to 20%). Similarly, speech perception tests showed that the adolescents with OCD did not have the usual advantage of right ear greater than left ear. There was probably less dominance of the left hemisphere for speech perception in patients with OCD compared with controls. The patients with OCD had a higher "two-flash threshold"; that is, they could not distinguish single and double flashes as readily as could controls. There may not be as much cortical arousal in children with OCD.

Evidence of localization of areas in the brain that may be associated with OCD is found in electrical stimulation and lesion studies. Grey-Walter (1966) determined that overactivity of the cingulate system led to OCD. Stimulation studies by Talairach (1973) found that stimulation of the anterior cingulate gyrus in an awake patient produced compulsive repetitive movements. Psychosurgical techniques have demonstrated that anterior cingulate lesions are very often successful in treating OCD patients (Kelly 1980).

The use of brain imaging techniques has allowed direct examination of children with OCD. Behar and colleagues (1984) found that the ventricular-to-brain ratios of adolescents with OCD were significantly higher than in controls. Differences were found mostly in posterior brain regions. While there were also neuropsychologic deficits in these patients involving the inability to mentally rotate themselves in space, or to discern and follow unstated rules and patterns during maze learning, the ventricular enlargement and cognitive deficits did not necessarily occur in the same subjects.

Positron emission tomography (PET) scans

have provided further evidence of hemispheric involvement. Baxter and co-workers (1987) used radioactive-labeled glucose to determine metabolic activity of the brain (Fig. 6–1). Patients with OCD had significantly more glucose metabolism in the left orbital gyrus compared with groups with depression or normal controls. Not only did the left orbital gyrus exhibit higher activity than the rest of the left and right hemispheres in these patients, it remained high even after treatment with an antidepressant that had improved symptoms. A further finding was that the obsessive-compulsive patients all had abnormal activity in the dominant hemisphere. The caudate nuclei demonstrated an increased glucose metabolism only in patients

with OCD who showed a positive response to medication. In unmedicated patients with OCD and in patients with OCD who did not show an improvement to medication, there was no difference in caudate nuclei activity compared with normals. These results are interpreted to mean that the caudate region does have a role in processing of thoughts.

In cortical blood flow studies of 12 adults with OCD, Insel discovered slight increases in cortical blood flow when patients directed their thoughts to their obsessions. However, when they were actually exposed to the object of their obsession (such as dirt or something that might be contaminated), the cortical blood flow decreased significantly, while measures of general autonomic arousal (gal-

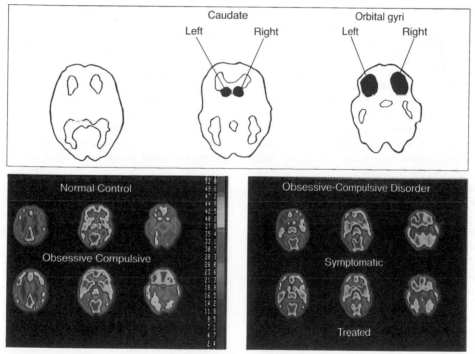

Figure 6–1. Positron emission tomographic scans of patients with OCD. Top. *Location of heads of caudate nuclei and orbital gyri in scans shown below.* Bottom left. *Scan of patient versus that of age- and sex-matched normal control. Colors of scans correspond to glucose metabolic rates, which are indicated in color bar to right (in micromoles of glucose per minute per 100 g of brain tissue; 1 mg of glucose equals 5.56 μmol). Glucose metabolic rates in OCD are especially high in caudate nuclei and orbital gyri (particularly on left) compared with normal controls.* Bottom right. *Scan of patient with OCD before and after successful drug treatment. Scan has been coded to reflect metabolic rate of each area of brain, divided by that of brain as whole. As in center illustration, red indicates highest values and blue, lowest. Note how value of ratio for head of caudate nuclei increased with successful treatment. Patients who did not respond did not show increase in ratio. Note how ratio value does not change in left orbital gyri; despite symptomatic improvement, it remains high when compared with normal controls. (From Baxter, L. R., Phelps, M. E., Mazziota, J. C., et al. 1987. Local cerebral glucose metabolic rates in obsessive-compulsive disorder: A comparison with rates in unipolar depression and in normal controls. Arch. Gen. Psychiatry 44:211–218. Copyright © 1987, American Medical Association.)*

vanic skin response and heart rate) were increased significantly. Combining the findings of the PET scanning and the cortical blood flow, it can be seen that the subcortical areas of the dominant hemisphere (orbital gyrus and caudate nuclei) are directly involved with the symptoms of OCD. Conscious cortical control becomes lessened as these areas are activated.

Neuroanatomical-Neurochemical Theories

Three theories of neurotransmitter dysfunction are suggested that may be responsible for the OCD symptoms. The hypothesis that there is a dysfunction in serotonin regulation has received the most attention. However, all of the findings cannot be explained by this system alone. Dysregulation of norepinephrine, as well as possible contributions from dopaminergic sites, has also been entertained. The serotonin hypothesis is supported by the success of serotonergic agonists, such as clomipramine, in treating OCD symptoms. It is more effective than placebo, nortriptyline, amitriptyline, and clorgyline. While the major effect of clomipramine is to inhibit serotonin reuptake into presynaptic nerve terminals, the first breakdown product, desmethylclomipramine, acts as a potent uptake inhibitor of norepinephrine. In studies by Stern and Wright (1980), it was found that clomipramine correlated highly with an improvement in compulsive rituals, while improvement in depression correlated highly with plasma levels of desmethylclomipramine. This again favors primary serotonin effect. However, zimelidine, which is supposedly serotonergic only, does not show consistent success in treatment of patients with OCD. The evidence that serotonin dysregulation underlies obsessive-compulsive symptoms is found indirectly in studying the orbital gyri and caudate nuclei, which are rich in serotonergic fibers. These are the brain areas that have shown altered activity in PET scans. Animal research has shown that depletion of limbic serotonin results in marked perseverative behavior and a decreased rate of behavioral habituation. Another measure of serotonin activity is platelet imipramine binding sites. These sites have been shown to be related to presynaptic uptake for serotonin. Weizman (1986) showed that the imipramine binding was significantly lower in patients with OCD than in control subjects. These findings are similar to those seen in patients with major depressive disorders. Hypoactive serotonergic systems may be responsible for the continued response to serotonin agonists seen in OCD. The binding sites may be lower nonspecifically in any chronic disabling psychiatric disorder. In a related study, Flament and colleagues (1987) demonstrated that (1) high platelet serotonin was a strong predictor of favorable clinical response to clomipramine and (2) a decrease in platelet serotonin content after treatment with clomipramine was highly correlated with improvement. An interesting additional finding was that there was a 10% decrease in monoamine oxidase (MAO) functioning. Furthermore, this decrease in MAO functioning was correlated with a decrease in the OCD symptoms.

In addition, there are reports that serotonergic agonists, such as L-tryptophan, lithium, fluoxetine, fluvoxamine, and trazodone, are also effective in treating obsessive-compulsive patients. In recent studies, the trazodone metabolite metachlorophenylpiperazine (mCPP), which is presumed to be a postsynaptic serotonin receptor agonist, was given to adult patients with OCD, and obsessions and compulsions increased (Zohar et al. 1987). Furthermore, the serotonin antagonist metergoline did not produce a worsening of OCD symptoms. On the basis of this finding, it was suggested that the medications that improve OCD symptoms and are believed to increase serotonergic function indirectly (clomipramine, fluvoxamine, fluoxetine) might work by down-regulating postsynaptic serotonin receptor sites when given regularly. This theory was supported by unpublished reports from an inpatient study that showed that during the first 3 to 5 days of clomipramine treatment, patients with OCD showed an increase in symptoms. In a follow-up study, the group of clomipramine-treated patients received an mCPP stimulation test. As predicted, the mCPP did not significantly increase obsessive-compulsive symptoms, anxiety, or depression in these clomipramine-treated patients. The hyperthermic response to mCPP was also abolished by treatment with clomipramine. These findings are consistent with clomipramine effecting an adaptive hyporesponsivity of the serotonergic system.

However, Charney and associates (1988) challenged a group of adult patients with mCPP and found no difference between patients and healthy subjects. The patients were also challenged with tryptophan, and there were no differences between patients and controls in behavioral response. These researchers found a decrease in baseline prolactin levels in female OCD patients and a diminished prolactin response to mCPP in female OCD patients. It was concluded that lower prolactin release may result from either reduced serotonin neuronal activity or from another abnormal function, such as excessive dopamine activity.

Cerebrospinal fluid (CSF) studies in adult patients with OCD have yielded higher levels of 5-hydroxyindole acetic acid (5-HIAA), which is the major breakdown product of serotonin. Furthermore, in those patients with OCD who show improvement with clomipramine, there is a decrease in CSF levels of 5-HIAA. Low CSF levels of 5-HIAA are correlated with marked aggression, suicide, and homicidal aggression. In a clinical trial of clomipramine on 30 adolescents, there were 5 who developed aggressive tendencies, showed much more impulsiveness, and were involved in such acts as striking their fathers. These findings are consistent with the down-regulation of the serotonin system.

Dopaminergic involvement is suggested by patients' response to other medications. Trimipramine was reported to have a good effect in a 12-year-old boy with OCD symptoms. Trimipramine and clomipramine both exhibit dopamine D_2-receptor blockade, which may explain the efficacy of these medications. Improvement in adult patients with OCD following the administration of dextroamphetamine may result from the release of dopamine. It is also a powerful blocker of dopamine reuptake.

Norepinephrine has been partially implicated by the finding that clonidine, in three cases, improved the effectiveness of clomipramine in treating OCD. Clonidine is a specific noradrenergic agonist that operates both presynaptically and directly postsynaptically. Adult patients with OCD have been found to have higher levels of plasma 3-methoxy-4-hydroxyphenolglycol (MHPG) and norepinephrine, suggesting presynaptic release of norepinephrine and down-regulation of postsynaptic receptors.

It is unlikely that a single neurotransmitter controls OCD, but what is important is the interaction of several neurotransmitters. There are data that mCPP interacts with a number of nonserotonergic receptors (Peroutka, reported in Charney 1988) including α-adrenergic, β-adrenergic, dopamine, and muscarinic receptors. Further evidence for the implication of other systems is that significant increase in baseline prolactin concentrations with clomipramine treatment has been demonstrated by Zohar and colleagues (1988).

EPIDEMIOLOGY

Underreporting likely exists in the incidence and prevalence of OCD in children and adolescent populations. Typical young and mid adolescents are not comfortable describing personal and private thoughts. They hide these symptoms from their peers and especially from adults. In sampling large high school populations it is likely that the most severely disturbed children may not be in school or may not be able to answer questionnaires that are distributed.

The onset of OCD can occur during childhood. Hollingsworth and co-workers, in a 1980 review of OCD in childhood, found an average age at onset of 9.6 years with a range of 3 to 15 years in age (Table 6–3). Rapoport and colleagues (1981) described a similar average age of onset of 9.5 ± 4.1 years, while Judd (1965) concluded that the average age at onset was 7.5 years and was often associated with a significant precipitating event.

In a child psychiatry sample, Hollingsworth and co-workers discovered that 76% of children with OCD were male. Rapoport (1986) reported two thirds of the children were male. The males became ill significantly earlier than the females (2.5 years). The age at onset in that sample was between 3 and 14 years of age. In contrast to these studies, the adult ratios of men and women are almost identical. One third to one half of adults had the onset of a full OCD by the time they were 15 years old. Furthermore, this OCD syndrome varies little between children and adolescents. Early identification of these children with appropriate intervention can greatly diminish the secondary depression, anxiety, social dysfunction, and academic failures that can ensue.

Table 6–3. EPIDEMIOLOGY OF OBSESSIVE-COMPULSIVE DISORDER

Author	Date	Incidence (%)	Prevalence (%)	Comment
Rudin	1953	0.5		Child psychiatric inpatients
Judd	1965	1		Child psychiatric inpatients
Rutter	1970	0.3		10- and 11-year-olds, Isle of Wight, mixed obsessive and anxiety features
Hollingsworth	1980	0.2		Clinical population—children
Helzer	1985		0.3	Adult general population
Flament	1985	0.33		General high school population
Perse	1988		2–3	Lifetime prevalence

CLINICAL PICTURE

A number of investigators have reported that adolescents often hide the symptoms of obsessional thinking and minimize the compulsive rituals in which they engage. Therefore, in children and adolescents with OCD it is necessary to talk with members of the family as well as the child. Some families report that the only way they are able to tell how many of these rituals are being performed is to count the number of bars of soap used daily in a bathroom or the number of rolls of toilet paper used each day. Adults with OCD report that they kept the symptoms and rituals to themselves as much as possible during their teenage years to avoid criticism and ostracism by others. Another factor that makes detection difficult is the habituation and adaptation of the family environment to these children. In a clomipramine clinical trial, one family reported at the end of the seventh week of active medication that the child now slept in his bed. The child, not wanting to wrinkle the bed, had been sleeping on the floor next to the bed for 2 years. This had become so commonplace that the family had not recognized this behavior as truly abnormal until after the child began again sleeping in the bed. They also noted that they were able to take the vacuum cleaner out of the room. The patient no longer needed to vacuum up footprints after walking on the carpet. Another family had to check the garbage daily since their 13-year-old boy would remove any books from the bookshelf that had turned corners, worn bindings, ink marks, or tears and put them in the garbage. Similarly, tools that were nicked or dirty were removed from the father's workshop and piled into the garbage. This same person changed clothes so often that, in this family of three, there were eight loads of wash daily.

Improvements, on the other hand, are sometimes upsetting and bothersome to families. Family members have become accustomed to the children's habituations to the point that they feel uncomfortable when the rituals are not carried out.

For these children, there may be frank denial of any obsessive thinking. The parents' report of compulsive behavior may be the only reliable information that can be used to establish the diagnosis and to follow clinical response. Other children are agonizingly aware of symptoms and report in great detail the kind of burdensome thoughts that they experience. Interference with schoolwork (the need to re-read paragraphs and do problems over) is a part of their daily lives and, as such, is extremely frustrating. In general, older adolescents are more ready to report thoughts and behaviors than younger adolescents. Similarly, children 11 or 12 years of age may be very good historians. In the child of 10 or 11 with OCD the symptoms often take on the quality of an alien thought and might be misdiagnosed as hallucinations of a psychotic child. With a careful evaluation, mood disorders and schizophrenia can be effectively ruled out.

There are three clinical subgroups of OCD in children and adolescents. The first group includes compromised, isolated, withdrawn persons with anxious affect and unusual thinking that at times borders on suspicious and delusional thoughts. Their associations are not truly loosened or disjointed, as in schizophrenia, nor do they have a hypomanic, tangential, or rambling quality, as in bipolar illness. The child may have features of Asperger's syndrome (normal intelligence autism) with or without the avoidance of social interaction that is characteristic of autism. They can also present as mute children who appear to have an agitated depression.

The differential diagnosis may be best made by careful review of prior psychiatric records, parental history, structured interviews, and rating scales such as the Yale Brown Obsessive-Compulsive Scale.

A second group of children with OCD are rather appealing, are normal in appearance, and have a range of affect from anxiety to confusion and despair regarding their symptoms. These children appear to be interested in interactions with others and frustrated by the presence of their symptoms. Some of them have oppositional behavior and, at times, minor conflicts with their family.

The third group consists of what have been termed the *supernormals* (Rapoport 1986). These children have exemplary functioning in school and often are outstanding athletes, political leaders, and extremely accomplished students. One sixth grade boy with straight "A's" and early accomplishments in track and soccer stoutly denied his symptoms. His parents described the propping of an open Bible on the toilet tank, exact rearranging of silverware at each meal, and precise arrangement of stuffed animals. This child was forced by his rituals to go into the basement and perform a certain number of physical exercises each time he passed the door to the basement stairs. Overall, these children are quite likable and concerned about their symptoms, and, while many of them are anxious and may have secondary depressions, these symptoms are understandable in terms of the obstacles in thought and action that they are attempting to overcome.

Obsessions often take the form of fears of aggression, sexual behavior, contamination, disorderliness, or noncompletion of tasks. Angry and aggressive thoughts are so tightly controlled that the child may become withdrawn from others. Concern about actually hitting others, using knives in the household as weapons, or even expresssing the fact that they are angry results in often docile, restricted children. Interestingly, with treatment some of the newly assertive children are a surprise to their parents; children sometimes overreact in their expression of aggression once the obsessions are removed.

Sexuality is a major source of concern. For boys, homosexual fears are often the basis of a great deal of rumination, may lead to paranoia about other boys and men, and can result in compulsive rituals to clean hands or arms where they have been touched by parents or other children. Heterosexual fantasies and masturbation can likewise become the center of a great deal of mental activity and physical undoing. One 16-year-old Catholic girl sought the advice of ten different priests on her masturbatory activity. She could never receive consolation about her guilt.

Fear of contamination by dirt and germs and rigid rules of hygiene are very common in children with OCD. One child was so careful about his food that any food that touched the periphery of the plate could not be eaten. Toilet rituals can become the center of attention, resulting in a child spending several hours in the bathroom, using eight to ten rolls of toilet paper a day, and using as many as five to six bars of soap. One child who was hospitalized had a sink ritual. He would wash his hands for 5 to 10 minutes, discover he had contaminated his hands by turning off the water, again feel the need to wash his hands, the faucets, and the sink and to wipe up water from the floor, and then begin the ritual all over again since the contact with these contaminated areas had dirtied his hands.

Task completion is another major concern. Turning off gas jets and lights, exiting the family car, and prolonged bedtime rituals cause significant interference in these children's lives. However, one of the more difficult processes is the reading and re-reading of material for school, imposing a great burden on classroom work and studying at home.

CASE HISTORIES

Case 1

Jane is a 17-year-old girl who remembers vividly that at age 5 or 6 she was washing her hands often. She said that she needed to "cover each spot" and would wash her hands again and again because of an inner urge to be certain that her hands were clean. This gradually improved over the next few years, but by age 7 or 8 the obsession and compulsion had changed. Jane had enuresis at night until well into the third grade. She would shower but would not feel clean and would have to take two or three more baths per day. The subjective feeling of lack of cleanliness and of being contaminated did not wash away. As a result she had to change her clothes two or three times per day.

When she was 9 years old, Jane experienced a specific precipitating event. While approaching the end of a book, she felt uncertain about whether she understood it. As she finished the last paragraph, she had a terrible feeling that she had not read the book correctly and began to slowly re-read the book. She would read and re-read each paragraph carefully, going over and over sentences, paragraphs, chapters, and the entire book. Her schoolwork was especially impaired if she had to read out loud. Her pervasive thoughts were that she was not doing her work correctly.

In the summer following the ninth grade, Jane attempted to make herself read and socialize more. She, however, became increasingly more anxious and uncertain. She decided to lose weight so that she would become more acceptable to others. She became markedly depressed. She noticed her heart would beat fast, she was short of breath, and she felt desperate and suicidal. During the early fall of the tenth grade, she found herself overwhelmed with anxiety, unable to concentrate at all on her work, and completely unable to function at school. She was hospitalized in a psychiatric hospital for 6 months. The first 3 months of that hospitalization were in a "short-term" acute care ward. She was told her diagnosis was "free-floating anxiety." She said that talking in group and individual therapy did little to help. She was placed on haloperidol, 5 mg twice daily, with no improvement. Nortriptyline and imipramine were both given brief clinical trials. She reported that while the drugs helped with the anxiety, they did not ameliorate her major depression, suicidal thoughts, thoughts of guilt, and listlessness. The medication did not help the almost constant thoughts with which she struggled. Finally, she was referred to a behavioral medicine clinic during the last 3 months of the hospital stay, where a therapist gave her cognitive behavioral therapy. She was told to focus on her feelings, instead of her thoughts, and this appeared to help in distracting her from the obsessions. By January of the tenth grade year, at age 16, she was back in school and seeing her therapist weekly for individual cognitive therapy.

The therapy continued for a year and a half, with more family-oriented focused therapy. The family history included a ruminative, obsessive father. The father, who had impulsive temper outbursts, would often physically assault the mother, twisting her arm, kneeing her in the chest, throwing crystal in the house, and forcing himself sexually on his wife. Jane had been very frightened of him and had been "kidnapped" by him when she was 6 years old. However, he was also a man who was noted to be very hardworking, a studious person who was at times quite likable.

At the time that Jane was seen for an evaluation for clomipramine, her main obsession continued to be with reading. She would often stop, repeat the reading, and not be able to go on. There was almost constant preoccupation with checking her schoolwork that required her to spend two or three times longer doing her homework or schoolwork. She became afraid that she would hurt children whom she was babysitting, although she had spent the previous summer babysitting from 12 to 13 hours per day. She would ruminate about suicide and what she was doing to prevent self-destruction. As she remembered her wrongdoings, she became more certain that she might harm herself; while having these distressing thoughts, she found that her heart was beating fast and that she could not breathe. She attempted to control these thoughts, although she had very little control. Compulsions were limited to reading and re-reading. She said that she became very distressed if anyone interrupted her.

Jane responded poorly to a clinical trial of clomipramine. She continued to have marked difficulty with obsessions and compulsions. Plans for treatment included a trial of exposure in vivo and response prevention as well as a medication trial with fluoxitine. Jane and her mother were very depressed that the clomipramine had not been successful. Day hospitalization was arranged while the cognitive therapy and new medication trial was arranged. Her symptoms were so distressing that she continued to have occasional suicidal ideation of a moderate to severe degree.

Case 2

According to his parents, Charles, a 13-year-old boy, was different from his siblings from infancy onward. He would often cry as an infant and continue for 2½ hours. He would not be soothed unless his parents walked with him or rubbed his back. By the time he was in first grade, he had developed checking procedures to see that he had opened or closed doors; the checking seemed to be in response to worries about his mother. His mother had a number of abnormal bleeding spells and had been hospitalized for a hysterectomy following the birth of his youngest sibling. He developed constant worries about his mother and was very worried and tearful at school. The school did not inform the father of Charles' anxiety and worries, and he eventually began resisting attending school, so that his parents had to push him onto the school bus in the mornings. Soon after, he developed fears about being contaminated; when his father would put gas into the car, Charles would not allow his father to touch him. Similarly, any food that was not in the center of his plate but rather ended up touching the edge or actually falling off would not be touched again. If there was any question about a package of food having been opened, he would not eat any of the contents. He would often check and inspect packages to be certain they were intact. By the time he was 10, he had developed frequent, repetitive hand washing, especially in association with gasoline or being touched by somebody who had been near gasoline or dirt. In the fall of 1986, when he was 11 years old, both of the mother's parents died within 3 days of each other. He began to hear a "little voice" inside his head. This voice would repeatedly tell him to hurt himself. The parents were not aware of this until he was seen for an evaluation for treatment.

Initially, this symptom was first recorded as evidence of psychosis. However, on further questioning about this auditory experience, it was discovered that it was the 12-year-old's perception of repetitive obsessive thoughts. He could recognize this as a product of his own mind, yet one that was certainly not comfortable to him.

Charles improved almost immediately while on clomipramine. In 2 weeks, he went from being a constantly obsessed, very frightened boy who would not let his parents leave him alone to being able to tolerate getting on the bus and going to school. He also did not question his parents' whereabouts all of the time and became less withdrawn and more socially active. By the summer following sixth grade, he was ready to go away to camp for the first time in his life. He tolerated the first day well until there was a contest between two groups of children. The group that won would receive a food reward, and the group that lost the game was to clean the bathrooms. When Charles heard of this, he immediately became anxious, started to cry, and demanded to be returned to his home. The parents rescued him from this camp and his emotional state again reached equilibrium.

By the end of that summer, the parents were planning a vacation away from home without the children. Charles began to cry and protest. This behavior continued for 5 hours one evening and then, on awakening the next day, he demonstrated marked anxiety. He pleaded to be included because he feared the absence of his parents; the parents eventually conceded and took him with them on vacation. As he went back to school, the symptoms of school phobia returned with marked anxiety. Clomipramine was increased to the maximum (3 mg/kg) and the school phobia improved markedly. In September of that year, Charles began to be very petulant, crying and complaining when his brother got a present and he did not. The parents were able to use the local police both as a resource to calm and counsel him and be available when both of them were away from the immediate community. Much practice was required by the father as well as relearning for the entire family to be able to tolerate Charles' rituals, worries, and obsessional thinking differently.

Charles was very sensitive to the medication. On one weekend, he missed one day's dosage and also had very little sleep because he had slept over at another child's house; the next day, he was crying, excessively demanding, and acting in a very controlling manner. The parents responded in a firm, yet kindly manner. They eventually persuaded him to take his medication. With this new family response to his illness and consistent medication, he again improved to the point that he had no more obsessions or compulsions.

The family history was significant. A maternal grandfather was reported to have been a person with many fears. There was a pattern of overeating and compulsive eating in both the father's and mother's families. The father's maternal grandfather had been hospitalized in a state hospital with paranoid features; several of the father's half-brothers had problems with alcoholism.

The father was a high school teacher and the mother a nurse at the local community hospital. The marriage was stable and the other children, both younger boys, were doing well in school, had normal friendships, and had no psychiatric symptoms.

CLINICAL COURSE

In a review of over 8,000 medical records from the University of California at Los Angeles (UCLA) Neuropsychiatric Institute from 1959 through 1975, Hollingsworth (1980) discovered 50 children with the diagnosis of obsessive-compulsive neurosis. When these children were further defined by present OCD criteria, and lack of other major psychiatric disorders, only 17 patients were included. This group of 17 children often had serious medical illness. Eighty-two percent of their parents had both serious medical illness and severe psychopathology. Ten of these subjects were located and agreed to be studied. Treatment of these patients had consisted of an average of 17.7 months of mostly outpatient psychotherapy, without the use of medication, on a once- or twice-weekly basis. Only 10% received behavior modification. Three of 10 had received inpatient therapy as well. Seven of 10 continued to have OCD symptoms, although symptoms were less frequent following treatment. On follow-up, these patients were found to have difficulty forming close interpersonal relationships and a tendency to dislike occupations in which the obsessive-compulsive symptoms would surface. The prognosis for the complete resolution of OCD in later life was poor.

In Israel, Apter (1984) found improvement in seven of eight adolescents with OCD. These teenagers, like adolescents with OCD studied by Bolton and co-workers (1983), did response prevention and in vivo exposure. Insight psychotherapy plus clomipramine (two cases), supportive therapy alone (two cases), or support plus clomipramine (two cases) was provided. There was marked improvement in 3 to 4 months in seven of the eight children. Four remained symptom-free at follow-up 2 to 3 years later.

On follow-up, Goodwin (1969) found that not all adults with OCD have a poor prognosis. Only 10% of the patients have further deterioration in functioning. Three groups of patients were identified in this study. There were those with a chronic, unremitting course; another group had a phasic course with periods of complete remission; the last were patients who only had episodes of OCD with incomplete remission that permitted normal functioning.

Prognosis is predicted by the severity of symptoms and the degree of premorbid adjustment, with less severe, healthier patients having a better prognosis. Treatment with behavior modification techniques using exposure and response prevention demonstrated remarkable improvement in rituals, mood, and social adjustment when evaluated 2 years after treatment. Over 80% of patients showed a favorable outcome on follow-up. Although some authors did not find clomipramine to be effective for the treatment of rituals, other groups studying the effect of various treatments (Quality Assurance Project 1985) found that exposure and response prevention and clomipramine therapy were powerful treatment modalities. Graded exposure with response prevention was believed preferable since patients rated improvement after that treatment more highly than with clomipramine. Furthermore, when therapy with clomipramine was stopped, symptoms returned while improvement with exposure and with response prevention persisted. Clomipramine in children and adolescents will be one important aspect of a treatment regimen for OCD. It was found that once children were relieved of their symptoms, their functioning improved in other areas (Flament 1985; Rapoport 1986).

Therefore, the clinical outcome for OCD children is not likely to be as difficult as portrayed by the UCLA study. Treatments of exposure and of response prevention and the use of clomipramine offer promise for changing the course of what was once considered to be a difficult and chronic condition.

LABORATORY FINDINGS

To investigate a possible link between depressive disorders and OCD, two different laboratory examinations have been performed. The dexamethasone suppression test

(DST) in a variety of studies showed mixed results. Insel (1982) found that the DST did not suppress cortisol levels in 6 of 16 patients, yielding a 37.5% positive response rate. Many of those patients had secondary depressive symptoms. A trend was demonstrated between higher depression rating scale scores and the positive DST response. A positive family history for depression and a positive DST were also noted. Cottraux (1984) found a 30% rate of DST nonsuppression in an adult sample of OCD. Major depressive disorder did not correspond to the positive findings in this study. In contrast, Lieberman (1984) found none of 18 patients with a nonsuppressing DST. Monteiro (1986) found only 2 of 50 (40%) of their patients with "uncomplicated" OCD had positive DSTs. Another 11 patients who had anorexia nervosa history, abused alcohol, were working nights, had cancer, or had a major depressive disorder showed nonsuppression. Finally, Jenike (1987) showed a 0% rate of DST nonsuppression in their nondepressed OCD sample with an 80% abnormal DST in their depressed patients with OCD. Therefore, there is a legitimate controversy about whether the DST is a useful laboratory tool to support the diagnosis of OCD. The majority of the evidence indicates that the DST will most likely be positive in patients who have associated conditions and that OCD alone will not demonstrate nonsuppression.

Growth hormone challenge studies have been performed in a small group of adult patients (Siever 1983). Obsessive-compulsive patients showed a significantly decreased growth hormone response compared with control patients. While a lower growth hormone response may be characteristic of OCD, it may also be representative of a depressive disorder since growth hormone hyposecretion in response to clonidine stimulation may be a trait instead of a state marker of depression. It is also possible that growth hormone hyposecretion is part of a more generalized, nonspecific mental disorder state.

Rating Scales

The Hopkins Symptom Checklist, developed between 1954 and 1974, is 58 self-report items. In a recent analysis (Steketee 1985), this instrument was found to discriminate adult obsessive-compulsive patients from anxious patients. It was not demonstrated to have adequate diagnostic utility or a reliable cutoff score. The obsessive-compulsive cluster was only weakly related to other measures of OCD. The Maudsley Obsessive-Compulsive Questionnaire, developed in 1977, is a 30-item questionnaire that has been used with adult patients. These questions fall into four general categories: (1) checking (i.e., "I frequently have to check things"; (2) doubting and ruminating (i.e., "I find that almost every day I am upset by unpleasant thoughts that come into my mind against my will"); (3) cleaning (i.e., "I take rather a long time to complete my washing in the morning"); and (4) obsessional slowing. In children and adolescents the Maudsley Obsessive-Compulsive Inventory only discriminated obsessive-compulsive adolescents from normal adolescents in terms of total score and checking factors (Clark and Bolton 1985).

A third self-report instrument, the Leyton Obsessive Inventory, which is a card sort self-report scale, was found not to discriminate between adolescent patients with OCD and normal persons. Obsessional adolescents probably underestimated the presence and severity of their symptomatology. Berg (1986) modified the adult form for children. The Leyton Obsessional Inventory—Child Version (LOI-CV) was able to discriminate between adolescents with OCD and controls. It was found to be a valid and reliable measure of improvement while on clomipramine therapy. The LOI-CV has a sensitivity of about 50%. The LOI-CV at baseline does not correlate well with other measures of obsessive behavior, however. It was concluded that while the LOI-CV was more sensitive to the number of symptoms, a more subjective, general rating scale is a better measure of the severity of obsessive-compulsive symptoms. In order to accomplish two goals, distinguishing patients from controls and quantifying changes in the OCD symptoms during treatment, a combination of measures should be used. A global rating scale that has been developed by the National Institutes of Mental Health (NIMH) is useful in discriminating patients from normals and measuring change (Table 6–4). A 15-point range is used. Groupings within each 3-point interval describe a range from mild and insignificant symptoms to very severe manifestations. The definitions are based on how much interference this causes in the patient's life, how

Table 6–4. GLOBAL RATING SCALE FOR OBSESSIVE-COMPULSIVE DISORDER*

CIRCLE THE NUMBER (1 TO 15) THAT BEST DESCRIBES THE PRESENT CLINICAL STATE OF THE PATIENT BASED ON THE GUIDELINES BELOW:
1   2   3 | 4   5   6 | 7   8   9 | 10   11   12 | 13   14   15

	LEGEND *(for reference only)*
1–3	Minimal within range of normal, mild symptoms. Person spends little time resisting them. Almost no interference in daily activity.
4–6	Subclinical obsessive-compulsive behavior, mild symptoms that are noticeable to patient and observer, cause mild interference in patient's life and which he may resist for a minimal period of time. Easily tolerated by others.
7–9	Clinical obsessive-compulsive behavior. Symptoms that cause significant interference in patient's life and which he spends a great deal of conscious energy resisting. Requires some help from others to function in daily activity.
10–12	Severe obsessive-compulsive behavior. Symptoms that are crippling to the patient, interfering so that daily activity is "an active struggle." Patient *may* spend full time resisting symptoms. Requires much help from others to function.
13–15	Very severe obsessive-compulsive behavior. Symptoms that completely cripple patient so that he requires close staff supervision over eating, sleeping, etc. Very minor decision making or minimal activity requires staff support, "worst I've ever seen."

IS THE PATIENT'S SCORE ON THE GLOBAL NIMH SCALE FOR MANIA, DEPRESSION, PSYCHOSIS OR ANXIETY GREATER THAN THE RATING SCORE ON THE GLOBAL NIMH OBSESSIVE-COMPULSIVE SCALE?:
1. No   2. Yes *(If "Yes," Patient Is Ineligible For The Study)*

*From Murphy, D. L., Pickar, D., Alterman, I. S. 1982. Methods for the quantitative assessment of depressive and manic behavior. In Burdock, E. L., Sudilovsky, A., Gershon, S. (eds): *The Behavior of Psychiatric Patients.* New York: Marcel Decker.

much they resist these symptoms, and the degree to which others need to assist them in their daily function.

The Yale Brown Obsessive-Compulsive Scale (YBOCS) was developed as a clinician rating scale and used in clinical trials of clomipramine (Table 6–5). The Yale Brown Scale considers the patient's obsessions and rituals separately. In each of these two categories, a rating from 0 to 4 is made for five different characteristics. These five categories include (1) the amount of time spent per day; (2) the interference in the patient's life that is caused by thought or behavior; (3) distress induced by the thoughts or the amount of distress experienced if the ritual were to be interrupted; (4) the effort needed to resist the symptom, with much resistance receiving a score of zero and yielding completely scored highest; and (5) the control that the patient is able to exert over the symptoms. Both the NIMH Global and the Yale Brown Obsessive-Compulsive Scale give a quantitative assessment of the severity of obsessive-compulsive symptoms. The Yale Brown Scale has been shown to be valid and reliable for adult subjects (Goodman et al. submitted 1988).

PSYCHOLOGICAL TESTING

Relatively few studies have been done with psychological tests in patients with OCD. Using the Willoughby Personality Schedule, Turner (1983) found that 68% of obsessive-compulsive patients had clinically significant levels of social anxiety. This same dimension of anxiety was found when Frost (1986) examined "checkers" as against "noncheckers" using the Minnesota Multiphasic Personality Inventory (MMPI-168) and the Symptom Checklist-90 Revised (SCL-90R). Checkers reported higher levels of anxiety, depression, social introversion and withdrawal, aggressive impulses, confusion, and feelings of loss of control. In this same study, the checkers were found to eat more often in response to feelings of loneliness and to have a higher frequency of binge eating. However, an eating attitudes test in 16 adult patients with OCD by Joffe (1987) suggested patients with OCD did not have the worries and behaviors that are commonly seen with anorexia nervosa patients.

A third area of study is psychosis and OCD. Thirty-two men and women patients with OCD, meeting *DSM-III* criteria for OCD,

Table 6–5. YALE BROWN OBSESSIVE-COMPULSIVE SCALE*

FOR EACH ITEM CIRCLE THE NUMBER IDENTIFYING THE RESPONSE WHICH BEST CHARACTERIZES THE PATIENT:

1. TIME OCCUPIED BY OBSESSIVE THOUGHTS How much time do you spend thinking about these things? How frequently do these thoughts occur? [Be sure to exclude ruminations and preoccupations which, unlike obsessions, are ego-syntonic and rational (but exaggerated).]	0 = None. 1 = Mild, occasional intrusion (less than 1 hr/day). 2 = Moderate, frequent intrusion (1 to 3 hrs/day). 3 = Severe, very frequent intrusion (greater than 3 to 8 hrs/day). 4 = Extreme, near constant intrusion (greater than 8 hrs/day).
2. INTERFERENCE DUE TO OBSESSIVE THOUGHTS How much do thoughts get in the way of school or doing things with friends? Is there anything that you don't do because of them? [If currently not in school determine how much performance would be affected if school was in session.]	0 = None. 1 = Mild, slight interference with social or school activities, but overall performance not impaired. 2 = Moderate, definite interference with social or school performance, but still manageable. 3 = Severe, causes substantial impairment in social or school performance. 4 = Extreme, incapacitating.
3. DISTRESS ASSOCIATED WITH OBSESSIVE THOUGHTS How much do these thoughts bother or upset you? [Only rate anxiety that seems triggered by obsessions, not generalized anxiety or anxiety associated with other symptoms.]	0 = None. 1 = Mild, infrequent, and not too disturbing. 2 = Moderate, frequent, and disturbing, but still manageable. 3 = Severe, very frequent, and very disturbing. 4 = Extreme, near constant, and disabling distress.
4. RESISTANCE How hard do you try to stop the thoughts or ignore them? [Only rate effort made to resist, not success or failure in actually controlling the obsessions.]	0 = Makes an effort to always resist or symptoms so minimal doesn't need to actively resist. 1 = Tries to resist most of the time. 2 = Makes some effort to resist. 3 = Yields to all obsessions without attempting to control them, but does so with some reluctance. 4 = Completely and willingly yields to all obsessions.
5. DEGREE OF CONTROL OVER OBSESSIVE THOUGHTS When you try to fight the thoughts, can you beat them? [For the more advanced child ask:] How much control do you have over the thoughts?	0 = Complete control. 1 = Much control, usually able to stop or divert obsessions with some effort and concentration. 2 = Moderate control, sometimes able to stop or divert obsessions. 3 = Little control, rarely successful in stopping obsessions, can only divert attention with difficulty. 4 = No control, experienced as completely involuntary, rarely able to even momentarily divert thinking.
6. TIME SPENT PERFORMING COMPULSIVE BEHAVIORS How much time do you spend doing habits you can't stop? How frequently do you do these habits? [When rituals involving activities of daily living are chiefly present, ask:] How much longer does it take to complete your daily routines because of the habits? [In most cases compulsions are observable behaviors (e.g., hand washing), but there are instances in which compulsions are not observable (e.g., silent checking).]	0 = None. 1 = Mild, spends less than 1 hr/day performing compulsions, or occasional performance of compulsive behaviors. 2 = Moderate, spends from 1 to 3 hrs/day performing compulsions, or frequent performance of compulsive behaviors. 3 = Severe, spends more than 3 and up to 8 hrs/day performing compulsions, or very frequent performance of compulsive behaviors. 4 = Extreme, spends more than 8 hrs/day performing compulsions, or near constant performance of compulsive behaviors.

Table continued on following page

Table 6–5. YALE BROWN OBSESSIVE-COMPULSIVE SCALE Continued	
FOR EACH ITEM CIRCLE THE NUMBER IDENTIFYING THE RESPONSE WHICH BEST CHARACTERIZES THE PATIENT:	
7. INTERFERENCE DUE TO COMPULSIVE BEHAVIORS How much do the habits get in the way of school or doing things with friends? Is there anything that you don't do because of them? [If currently not in school determine how much performance would be affected if school was in session.]	0 = None. 1 = Mild, slight interference with social or school activities, but overall performance not impaired. 2 = Moderate, definite interference with social or school performance, but still manageable. 3 = Severe, causes substantial impairment in social or school performance. 4 = Extreme, incapacitating.
8. DISTRESS ASSOCIATED WITH COMPULSIVE BEHAVIOR How would you feel if prevented from carrying out your habits? [Pause] How upset would you become? [Rate degree of distress patient would experience if performance of the compulsion were suddenly interrupted without reassurance offered. In most, but not all cases, performing compulsions reduces anxiety. If, in the judgment of the interviewer, anxiety is actually reduced by preventing compulsions in the manner described above, then ask:] How upset do you get while carrying out your habits until you are sure they are done?	0 = None. 1 = Mild, only slightly anxious if compulsions prevented, or only slight anxiety during performance of compulsions. 2 = Moderate, reports that anxiety would mount but remain manageable if compulsions prevented, or that anxiety increases to manageable levels during performance of compulsions. 3 = Severe, prominent and very disturbing increase in anxiety if compulsions interrupted, or prominent and very disturbing increase in anxiety during performance of compulsions. 4 = Extreme, incapacitating anxiety from any intervention aimed at modifying activity, or incapacitating anxiety develops during performance of compulsions.
9. RESISTANCE How much do you try to fight the habits? [Only rate effort made to resist, not success or failure in actually controlling the compulsions.]	0 = Makes an effort to always resist, or symptoms so minimal doesn't need to actively resist. 1 = Tries to resist most of the time. 2 = Makes some effort to resist. 3 = Yields to almost all compulsions without attempting to control them, but does so with some reluctance. 4 = Completely and willingly yields to all compulsions.
10. DEGREE OF CONTROL OVER COMPULSIVE BEHAVIOR How strong is the feeling that you have to carry out the habits? [Pause] When you try to fight them, what happens?	0 = Complete control. 1 = Much control, experiences pressure to perform the behavior, but usually able to exercise voluntary control over it. 2 = Moderate control, strong pressure to perform behavior, can control it only with difficulty. 3 = Little control, very strong drive to perform behavior, must be carried to completion, can only delay with difficulty. 4 = No control, drive to perform behavior experienced as completely involuntary and overpowering, rarely able to even momentarily delay activity.

*From Goodman, W. K., Rasmussen, S. A., Price, L. H., et al. 1986. Children's Yale-Brown Obsessive-Compulsive Scale. Submitted for publication.

were evaluated with the MMPI. Elevations on scales 7, 2, 8, and 4 were found. Patients in this group who had been previously diagnosed with schizophrenia showed additional variation. Men in this group had elevations on scales F, 6, 7, and 8. Females with previous diagnosis of schizophrenia showed elevations on scales F, 4, and 6 (Carey 1986).

The difficulty of using a structured interview in children with OCD has been addressed by Breslau (1987). While Erdman (1987) found that the Diagnostic Interview

Schedule (DIS) showed good agreement for OCD diagnosis between the DIS diagnosis and chart review diagnosis, Breslau found that the administration of the Diagnostic Interview Schedule for Children (DISC) by a non–child psychiatrist resulted in overreporting of symptom rates for obsessions and compulsions. When the initial DISC was reexamined by a child psychiatrist to discover misunderstandings of the questions, it was found that the children's initial reports of obsessions and compulsions were approximately double that of the edited DISC. Suggestions were that the DISC be modified further to use longer questions with more detail, give specific examples that children would understand, instruct the interviewers in the intent of the DISC questions, and have the interviewer record examples of positive answers.

DIFFERENTIAL DIAGNOSIS

The differential diagnosis of OCD includes Tourette's syndrome, anorexia and bulimia, schizoaffective disorder, panic attacks, major depressive disorder, Asperger's syndrome, autism, and separation anxiety disorder. In fact, Welner and associates (1976) proposed that there are seven subgroups of patients with OCD based on the existence of anorexia, psychotic symptoms, and the presence of primary or secondary depressive symptoms. Rasmussen and Tsuang (1984) proposed the addition of more subgroups that are characterized by generalized anxiety disorder, panic disorder, and Tourette's syndrome. While anxiety is frequently seen in these patients, it is not certain how many of them have these traits, nor has the presence of OCD in groups of patients with primarily panic disorder, phobic disorder, or generalized anxiety disorder been studied. This group of primarily anxious patients, however, must be carefully delineated from those patients with OCD who have simply overwhelming anxiety generated by the thoughts and frustration of their daily activities.

A second distinction is the differential diagnosis of aberrant and unusual thoughts. Tourette's syndrome is often characterized by bizarre sexual thoughts and acts. In Asperger's syndrome and in autism there is pervasive lack of interaction with others as well as an unusual perseverative thought pattern with atypical thinking. Studies of patients with schizoaffective or schizophrenic disorders have noted obsessive thoughts. In cross-sectional studies, between 1% and 3.5% of schizophrenics demonstrated obsessional symptoms (Jahrreiss 1927). Fenton (1986) discovered that schizophrenic adults with obsessive-compulsive symptoms had a poor long-term outcome in the areas of social relations, employment, psychopathology, and global functions compared with schizophrenics without obsessive-compulsive symptoms. Goodwin's review (1969) of studies of schizophrenia and OCD suggest that obsessionals probably do not have a higher probability of developing schizophrenia than do normals. Finally, when adult OCD patients who were refractory to treatment were studied (Jenike 1987), it was found that obsessive-compulsive patients with concomitant schizotypal personality disorder had a much higher rate of treatment failure.

A third major area is depression. Patients with a major depressive disorder (MDD) may have repetitive thoughts associated with guilt as well as perseveration in speech. Major differences between the obsessive-compulsive patients and those with MDD are that patients with MDD have changes in patterns of eating, changes in sleep, psychomotor slowing, pervasive lack of energy, and anhedonia. Patients with OCD often have mild to moderate levels of secondary depression. There are recurrent thoughts of guilt, worrying over minor matters, somatic preoccupations, feelings of sadness and hopelessness, and at times thoughts of suicide. Thus, a secondary depression has been frequently associated with OCD and is a typical report (up to 71%) in adult studies (Welner 1976). However, studies with child and adolescent patients with OCD find as few as 10% of subjects meet criteria for major affective disorder. It may well be that the children have not had the longstanding frustrations and failures that adults with OCD have had to experience.

TREATMENT

Children and adolescents with OCD have been treated with psychoanalytically oriented insight psychotherapy, family therapy, behavioral therapy, and medication. Psychosurgery has not been used in the child and adolescent population but has been studied in adults.

In individual anecdotal case reports, patients with classic symptoms of obsessive counting and tapping behaviors have responded to insight-oriented psychotherapy. Hollingsworth's study showed 9 of 10 patients thought their obsessive-compulsive symptoms were less frequent and less disabling after psychotherapy, although 7 of the 10 continued to have some degree of symptom manifestation. In contrast, there are many more treatment failures with insight-oriented approaches.

Behavioral treatments have been more successful, especially the techniques of exposure in vivo and response prevention. In adults, in vivo exposure consists of up to 6 hours a day of contact with the feared or disliked stimuli that produces discomfort. Two hours per day of this is done with the aid of a therapist, while the remaining 4 hours are assigned as "homework." In a typical paradigm, these daily sessions are continued for 10 days at a time. Response prevention consists of not doing the behaviors that are characteristic of the ritual. For instance, if a person were a ritual hand washer, there would be no contact allowed with water or soap. A third component of this method involves imagined exposure. This is accomplished by imagining situations that are feared by the person. The fear of disastrous consequences from phenomena, such as death, natural catastrophes, and abhorrent acts, can be best treated by imagining being exposed to these events. In controlled studies, it has been shown that all three procedures are necessary for the most effective treatment response. The in vivo exposure mainly reduces worry and fears that are associated with rituals, while response prevention helps to minimize subsequent rituals. Imagined exposure is important in maintaining the effects of the in vivo exposure and response prevention, since patients who did not receive imagined exposure had a greater return of symptoms following treatment than those who received this additional training. Follow-up studies by Foa and Goldstein (1978) found that 80% of 23 patients who used these techniques showed improvement at a 15-month follow-up.

The family is often involved with the illness of the child or adolescent with OCD. These behavioral techniques must include the family in order to have some therapeutic success. Bolton and co-workers (1983), in a treatment report of 15 cases of adolescent OCD, found that the child's anxiety was linked with parental anxiety. The child often would ask for reassurance and, at times, would dominate the family by shouting instructions and inducing guilt in the parents (Quality Assurance Project 1985). Family therapy was initiated to ensure response prevention; to help the parents reestablish appropriate control over the child; and to help the parents feel personally more confident, thus reducing anxiety for the child. The family therapy included modifying the parents' perceptions so that they no longer believed the child would come to harm or die. Response prevention was achieved by the parents refusing to participate in the child's ritual or actively restraining the child from performing the rituals; when this procedure did not work on an outpatient basis, an inpatient setting was employed. Flooding (i.e., encouraging the patients to expose themselves to the feared objects) was not often successful with adolescents. Follow-up assessment of the children demonstrated that 13 of 15 patients (87%) improved. Forty-seven percent of the patients experienced complete relief of symptoms and in 40% the symptoms were reduced to a mild level.

Single case reports of family treatment for obsessive-compulsive children concentrate on expression of feelings, separation of the child from the parents (Hafner 1981), or ignoring compulsive behaviors and concentrating on more positive behaviors (Dalton 1983). The treatment of adolescents differs from that of adults mainly in that family factors must be considered. Some considerations are the parents' confidence and esteem, the parents' involvement in rituals, their adaptation to the life style imposed on them by the adolescent's obsessive-compulsive rituals, or the family milieu that focuses only on these behaviors rather than their feelings.

In adults, a variety of medications have been used to treat OCD. Treatment attempts have largely involved the use of antidepressants and have emerged from the hypothesis that a dysregulation in the serotonin neurotransmitter system may be responsible for OCD. Clomipramine for a group of 19 adolescents exhibited highly significant improvement at 5 weeks of treatment (Flament et al. 1985b). Clinical response did not correlate with the plasma concentration of either the drug or its metabolites. A decrease in platelet serotonin levels, however, was associated with symptom improvement.

For adults, there have been equally good improvements with the use of clomipramine in five double-blind studies. Improvements were found at between 4 and 6 weeks, and clomipramine was demonstrated to be superior to placebo, nortriptyline, amitriptyline, clorgyline, and imipramine. Case reports suggest that MAO inhibitors such as phenelzine and tranylcypromine are also effective. Additional case reports have found that addition of L-tryptophan may potentiate clomipramine and that clonidine may enhance the antiobsessive effects of clomipramine. Fluoxetine has been effective in clinical use with OCD adults.

Zimelidine, a potent serotonin reuptake blocker, was reported to be effective in reducing adult OCD symptoms when compared with imipramine; however, it was not effective in a case report with a young adolescent. Use of trazodone has been reported in single case studies, including one older adolescent boy, in which it was effective. An open study of combined trazodone and tryptophan in 11 adult patients, however, showed little benefit. It was concluded that increasing central serotonergic activity was not necessarily related to improvement in this group of patients. Fluvoxamine, a unicyclic antidepressant that inhibits reuptake of serotonin and reportedly has little effect on norepinephrine or MAO systems, has been shown to be effective in two adult controlled studies. Price (1987) found a 60% improvement rate with 10 patients, and Perse (1988), in a double-blind, placebo-controlled, crossover study of 20 patients, found 81% improvement.

Other medications that have been used in adults include lithium carbonate, which has been reported to be helpful in case reports but has not been demonstrated to be effective in two different placebo-controlled trials. Neuroleptics have been used in patients with associated auditory hallucinations to good effect (Perse 1988). Patients with more psychotic symptoms perhaps belong in a different diagnostic category and may require antipsychotic medication. Anxiolytic medication has been used in adults with mixed results. Case reports mention specifically that alprazolam was effective in patients with coexisting anxiety and depression. Lastly, dextroamphetamine was used successfully in a group of 12 patients. There was significant improvement in clinical ratings, which was correlated with the patients' improvement on attentional tasks (Insel 1983). Psychosurgery has been reported to be effective in treatment-resistant adults with OCD. Stereotypic limbic leukotomy is performed with lesions made through the cingulate gyrus. Various authors report between 50% and 84% improvement with this procedure. It is noted that intelligence scores increase significantly following the leukotomy in these adult patients.

CONCLUSIONS

The biopsychosocial model is the basis of understanding the etiology of this disorder. This is especially true regarding the treatment of children and adolescents with OCD. In child and adolescent OCD the most effective treatment has been administration of clomipramine. A published study and empiric data indicate that from 70% to 80% of children are responsive to this medication.

Because the family is impacted by the child with OCD, family therapy and individual therapy are required in order for optimal functioning to be achieved. Some patients have responded to a variety of nonmedical treatments; intensive psychotherapy has been helpful for some; behavioral techniques, most notably response prevention and exposure in vivo have been shown to be effective for many; and, lastly, family therapy designed to promote emotional expression and effect the parents' control of the child's behavior has achieved success. Pathologic disorders and faulty interactional patterns in family members must always be addressed when treating OCD.

Children with concurrent depression or bipolar illness may require the addition of another antidepressant and/or lithium. Alprazolam has been an effective antianxiety agent that can be used safely in conjunction with clomipramine. Patients who are resistant to clomipramine would most likely benefit from a trial of fluoxetine or tranylcypromine. Trimipramine remains a further option that has yet not been fully studied. Further research is needed to clarify the underlying neurochemical mechanisms of OCD and to identify pharmacologic subgroups within this heterogeneous disorder. More effective treatment and more predictable response patterns will ensue.

References

American Psychiatric Association. 1987. Diagnostic and Statistical Manual of Mental Disorders, 3rd ed., revised. Washington, D.C.: American Psychiatric Association.

Andrews, G., Christensen, H., Hadzi-Pavlovic, D., et al. 1985. Treatment outlines for the management of obsessive-compulsive disorders: The quality assurance project. *Aust. N. Z. J. Psychiatry* 19:240–253.

Anthony, J. E. 1967. Psychiatric disorders of childhood. II. Psychoneurotic disorders. In Freedman, M., and Kaplan, H. (eds.). *Comprehensive Textbook of Psychiatry.* Baltimore: Williams & Wilkins.

Apter, A., Bernhout, E., Tyano, S. 1984. Severe obsessive-compulsive disorder in adolescence: A report of eight cases. *J. Adolescence* 7:349–358.

Baxter, L. R., Phelps, M. E., Mazziota, J. C., et al. 1987. Local cerebral glucose metabolic rates in obsessive-compulsive disorder: A comparison with rates in unipolar depression and in normal controls. *Arch. Gen. Psychiatry* 44:211–218.

Behar, D., Rapoport, J. L., Berg, C. J., et al. 1984. Computerized tomography and neuropsychological test measures in adolescents with obsessive-compulsive disorder. *Am. J. Psychiatry* 141:363–369.

Berg, C. J., Rapoport, J. L., Flament, M. 1986. The Leyton Obsessional Inventory—child version. *J. Am. Acad. Child Psychiatry* 25:85–91.

Biederman, J., Munir, K., Knee, D., et al. 1986. High rate of affective disorders on probands with attention deficit disorder and in their relatives: A controlled family study. *Am. J. Psychiatry* 144:330–333.

Bolton, D., Collins, S., and Steinberg, D. 1983. The treatment of obsessive-compulsive disorder in adolescents: A report of fifteen cases. *Br. J. Psychiatry* 142:456–464.

Breslau, N. 1987. Inquiring about the bizarre: False positives in the D.I.S.C. ascertainment of obsession, compulsions and psychotic symptoms. *Am. Acad. Child Adolesc. Psychiatry* 26:639–644.

Brown, F. W. 1942. Heredity in the psychoneuroses. *Proc. R. Soc. Medicine* 35:785–790.

Carey, R. J. 1986. MMPI correlates of O.C.D. *J. Clin. Psychiatry* 47:371–372.

Charney, D. S., Goodman, W. K., Price, L. H., et al. 1988. Serotonin function in obsessive-compulsive disorder. *Arch. Gen. Psychiatry* 45:177–185.

Clark, D. A., and Bolton, D. 1985. An investigation of two self-report measures of obsessional phenomena in obsessive-compulsive adolescents: Research note. *J. Child Psychol. Psychiatry* 26:429–437.

Cottraux, J. A., Bouvard, M., Claustrat, B. 1984. Abnormal dexamethasone suppression test in primary obsessive-compulsive patients: A confirmatory report. *Psychiat. Res.* 13:157–165.

Dalton, P. 1983. Family treatment of an obsessive-compulsive child: A case report. *Fam. Process* 22:99–108.

Dilsaver, S. C., and White, K. 1986. Affective disorders and associated psychopathology: A family history study. *J. Clin. Psychiatry* 47:162–169.

Erdman, H. P. 1987. A comparison of the D.I.S.C. diagnosis. *Am. J. Psychiat.* 144:1477–1480.

Fenton, W. S., and McGlashan, T. H. 1986. The prognostic significance of obsessive-compulsive symptoms in schizophrenia. *Am. J. Psychiatry* 143:437–441.

Finch, S. 1960. *Fundamentals of Child Psychiatry.* New York: W. W. Norton.

Flament, M., Rapoport, J., Whitaker, A., et al. 1985a. Obsessive compulsive disorders in adolescents: An epidemiological study. Presented at the 32nd meeting of the *American Adademy of Child Psychiatry*, 27 October, San Antonio, Texas.

Flament, M. F., Rapoport, J. L., Berg, C. J., et al. 1985b. Clomipramine treatment of childhood obsessive-compulsive disorder. *Arch. Gen. Psychiatry* 42:977–983.

Flament, M. F., Rapoport, J. L., Murphy, D. L., et al. 1987. Biochemical changes during clomipramine treatment of childhood obsessive-compulsive disorder. *Arch. Gen. Psychiatry* 44:219–225.

Flor, H. 1975. Psychiatric surgery evolution and current perspectives. *Can. Psychiat. Assoc. J.* 20:157–167.

Foa, E., and Goldstein, A. 1978. Continuous exposure and complete response prevention in treatment of obsessive compulsive neurosis. *Behav. Ther.* 9:821–829.

Frost, R. O. 1986. Psychopathology and personality characteristics of nonclinical compulsive checkers. *Behav. Res. Ther.* 24:133–143.

Gadelius, B. 1896. Om Tvangstankar. Stockholm. Quoted by G. Skogg (1959), *Acta Psychiatrica Scandinavia* Supplement, 134.

Goodman, W., Rasmussen, S., Price, L. 1988. *Children's Yale-Brown Obsessive-Compulsive Scale (CY-BOCS).* New Haven, CT: Clinical Neuroscience Research Unit, Connecticut Mental Health Center.

Goodwin, D. W. 1969. Follow-up studies in obsessional neurosis. *Arch. Gen. Psychiatry* 20:182–187.

Grad, L. R., Pelcovitz, D., Olson, M., et al. 1987. Obsessive-compulsive symptomatology in children with Tourette's syndrome. *J. Am. Acad. Child Adolesc. Psychiatry* 26:69–73.

Grey-Walter, W. 1966. Appendix A. In Smythies, R. (ed.): *The Neurological Foundation of Psychiatry.* Oxford: Blackwell.

Hafner, J. 1981. The treatment of obsessional neurosis in a family setting. *Aust. N. Z. J. Psychiatry* 15:145–157.

Helzer, J., Robins, L., McEnvoy, L., et al. 1985. A comparison of clinical and diagnostic interview schedule diagnosis. *Arch. Gen. Psychiatry* 42:657–666.

Hollingsworth, C. E., Tanguay, P. E., Grossman, L., and Pabst, P. 1980. Long-term outcome of obsessive-compulsive disorder in childhood. *J. Am. Acad. Child Psychiatry* 19:134–144.

Hoover, C. F., Insel, T. R. 1984. Families of origin in obsessive-compulsive disorder. *J. Nerv. Ment. Dis.* 172:207–215.

Insel, T. R., Kalin, N. H., Guttmacher, L. B., et al. 1982. The dexamethasone suppression test in patients with primary obsessive-compulsive disorder. *Psychiatry Res.* 6:153–160.

Insel, T. R., Donnelly, E. G., Lalaken, N. L., et al. 1983. Neurological and neuro-psychological studies of patients with obsessive-compulsive disorder. *Biol. Psychiatry* 18:741–751.

Insel, T. R., Mueller, E. A., Gillin, J. C., et al. 1985. Tricyclic response in obsessive compulsive disorder. *Prog. Neuropsychopharmacol. Biol. Psychiatry* 9:25–31.

Jahrreiss, W. 1927. Paranoische und paraphrene erkrankungen. *Arch. Psychiat.* 80:39–54.

Jenike, M. A., Baer, L., Brotman, A. W., et al. 1987. Obsessive-compulsive disorder, depression, and the dexamethasone suppression test. *J. Clin. Psychopharmacol.* 7:3.

Joffe, R. T. 1987. Caring attitudes: Test scores of patients with O.C.D. *Am. J. Psychiatry* 144:1510–1511.

Judd, L. L. 1965. Obsessive compulsive neurosis in children. *Arch. Gen. Psychiatry* 12:136–143.

Kelly, D. 1980. *Anxiety and emotions: Physiological basis and treatment.* Springfield, IL: Charles C Thomas.

Kettl, P. A., and Marks, I. M. 1986. Neurological factors in obsessive compulsive disorder. *Br. J. Psychiatry* 149:315–319.

Kohlberg, L. 1969. Stage and sequence: The cognitive-developmental approach to socialization. In Goslin, D. A. (ed.), *Handbook of Socialization Theory and Research.* Chicago: Rand McNally.

Lieberman, J. 1984. Evidence for a biological hypothesis of obsessive-compulsive disorder. *Neuropsychobiology* 11:14–21.

Loeb, L. R. 1986. Traumatic contributions in the development of an obsessional neurosis in an adolescent. *Adolesc. Psychiatry* 13:201–217.

Monteiro, W., Marks, I. M., Noshirvani, H., et al. 1986. Normal dexamethasone suppression test in obsessive-compulsive disorder. *Br. J. Psychiatry* 148:326–329.

Moore, B., and Fine, H. 1968. *A Glossary of Psychoanalytic Terms and Concepts.* New York: American Psychoanalytic Association.

Murphy, D. L., Pickar, D., Alterman, I. S. 1982. Methods for the quantitative assessment of depressive and manic behavior. In Burdock, E. L., Sudilovsky, A., and Gershon S. (eds.). *The Behavior of Psychiatric Patients.* New York: Marcel Dekker, pp 355–392.

Pauls, D. L., Towbin, K. E., Leckman, J. F., et al. 1986. Gilles de la Tourette's syndrome: An obsessive-compulsive disorder—Evidence supporting a genetic relationship. *Arch. Gen. Psychiatry* 43:1180–1182.

Perse, T. 1988. Obsessive compulsive disorder: A treatment review. *J. Clin. Psychiatry* 49:48–55.

Piaget, J. 1936. *The Origins of Intelligence in Children* (M. Cook, trans.). New York: International Universities Press, 1952.

The Quality Assurance Project. 1985. Treatment outlines for the management of obsessive-compulsive disorders. *Aust. N. Z. J. Psychiatry* 19:240–253.

Rapoport, J., Elkins, R., Langer, D., et al. 1981. Childhood obsessive-compulsive disorder. *Am. J. Psychiatry* 138:1545–1554.

Rapoport, J. L. 1986. Childhood obsessive compulsive disorder. *J. Child Psychol. Psychiatry* 27:289–295.

Rasmussen, S. A., and Tsuang, M. T. 1984. The epidemiology of obsessive-compulsive disorder. *J. Clin. Psychiatry* 45:450–457.

Rasmussen, S., Tsuang, M. 1986. Clinical characteristics and family history in DSM-III obsessive-compulsive disorder. *Am. J. Psychiatry* 143:317–322.

Rudin, E. 1953. Ein Beitrag zur Frage der Zwangskrankheit, insobesondere ihrere hereditaren Beziehungen. *Arch. Psychiat. Nervenk.* 191:14–54.

Runck, B. 1983. Research is changing views on obsessive compulsive disorder. *Hosp. Community Psychiatry* 34:597–598.

Rutter, M., Tizard, J., Whitmore, K. 1970. *Education, Health and Behavior.* London: Longmans.

Schilder, P. 1938. The organic background of obsessions and compulsions. *Am. J. Psychiatry* 94:1397–1416.

Siever, L. J., Insel, T. R., Jimerson, D. C., et al. 1983. Growth hormone response to clonidine in obsessive-compulsive patients. *Br. J. Psychiatry* 142:184–187.

Solyom, L., Ledwidge, B., and Solyom, C. 1986. Obsessiveness and adjustment. *Compr. Psychiatry* 27:234–240.

Steketee, G., Foa, E. B., Grayson, J. B. 1982. Recent advances in the behavioral treatment of obsessive-compulsives. *Arch. Gen. Psychiatry* 39:1365–1371.

Steketee, G. 1982. Recent advances in behavioral treatment of obsessive compulsives. *Arch. Gen. Psychiatry* 39:1365–1371.

Steketee, G. S., Grayson, G. B., Foa, E. B. 1985. Obsessive-compulsive disorders: Differences between washers and checkers. *Behav. Res. Ther.* 23:197–201.

Stern, R. S., and Wright, J. 1980. Clomipramine: plasma levels, side effects and outcome in obsessive-compulsive neurosis. *Postgrad. Med. J.* 56:134–139.

Talairach, J., Bancaud, S., Geier, S. 1973. The cingulate gyrus and human behavior. *Electroenchephalogr. Clin. Neurophysiol.* 34:45–51.

Turner, R. M. 1983. Assessment of social anxiety: A controlled comparison among O.C.D., agoraphobics, sexual disorders and simple phobics. *Behav. Res. Ther.* 21:181–183.

Weizman, A., Carmi, M., Hermesh, H., et al. 1986. High-affinity imipramine binding and serotonin uptake in platelets of eight adolescent and ten adult obsessive-compulsive patients. *Am. J. Psychiatry* 143:335–339.

Welner, A., Reich, T., Robins, E., et al. 1976. Obsessive compulsive neurosis: Record of follow-up and family studies: Inpatient studies. *Comp. Psychiatry* 17:527–539.

Zohar, J., Insel, T. R., Zohar-Kadouch, R. C., et al. 1988. Serotonergic responsivity in obsessive-compulsive disorder: Effects of chronic clomipramine treatment. *Arch. Gen. Psychiatry* 45:167–172.

Zohar, J., Mueller, E. A., et al. 1987. Serotonergic responsivity in obsessive-compulsive disorder: Comparison of patients and healthy controls. *Arch. Gen. Psychiatry* 44:946–951.

7

Eating Disorders: Anorexia Nervosa and Bulimia Nervosa

DAVID S. GOLDBLOOM, M.D.
PAUL E. GARFINKEL, M.D.

DEFINITION

Anorexia nervosa (AN) is an eating disorder characterized by self-imposed starvation due to the relentless pursuit of thinness and the morbid fear of fatness; this engenders varying degrees of emaciation, accompanied by significant medical and psychiatric sequelae. The term anorexia nervosa itself is a misnomer that reflects common misconceptions about the nature of the disorder; unlike the anorexia of depression or malignancy, there is no true loss of appetite until the more severe stages of the illness are reached. On the contrary, a determined struggle is waged against internal sensations of hunger to achieve an illusory mastery.

Various diagnostic criteria have been proposed over the past 20 years to rigorously characterize a disorder that has been described clinically for hundreds of years. The current criteria of the *Diagnostic and Statistical Manual of Mental Disorders*, third edition, revised (*DSM-III-R*) for AN (Table 7–1) provide a clinically useful, inclusive definition for both case identification and research purposes (American Psychiatric Association 1987).

Yet, a reality of psychiatric illness is that formal diagnostic classifications impose arbitrary boundaries on the spectrum of clinical phenomenology. As a result, less than ideal diagnoses such as "partial syndrome of AN" or "subclinical AN" have been generated. In

Table 7–1. DIAGNOSTIC CRITERIA FOR ANOREXIA NERVOSA

A. Refusal to maintain body weight over a minimal normal weight for age and height, e.g., weight loss leading to maintenance of body weight 15% below that expected; or failure to make expected weight gain during period of growth, leading to body weight 15% below that expected.

B. Intense fear of gaining weight or becoming fat, even though underweight.

C. Disturbance in the way in which one's body weight, size, or shape is experienced, e.g., the person claims to "feel fat" even when emaciated, believes that one area of the body is "too fat" even when obviously underweight.

D. In females, absence of at least three consecutive menstrual cycles when otherwise expected to occur (primary or secondary amenorrhea). (A woman is considered to have amenorrhea if her periods occur only following hormone, e.g., estrogen, administration.)

(From American Psychiatric Association. 1987. *Diagnostic and Statistical Manual of Mental Disorders*, 3rd ed., revised. Washington, D.C.: American Psychiatric Association.)

some respects, these categories reflect overlap between the clinical disorder and socioculturally sanctioned beliefs. However, both the significant medical and psychiatric manifestations of AN and the characteristic psychological features (Garner et al. 1983a) argue for a definition of AN as a distinct psychiatric disorder and not as a mere exaggeration of Western social values.

The definition of bulimia nervosa (BN) is

Table 7–2. DIAGNOSTIC CRITERIA FOR BULIMIA NERVOSA

A. Recurrent episodes of binge eating (rapid consumption of a large amount of food in a discrete period of time).
B. A feeling of lack of control over eating behavior during the eating binges.
C. The person regularly engages in either self-induced vomiting, use of laxatives or diuretics, strict dieting or fasting, or vigorous exercise in order to prevent weight gain.
D. A minimum average of two binge eating episodes a week for at least 3 months.
E. Persistent overconcern with body shape and weight.

(From American Psychiatric Association. 1987. *Diagnostic and Statistical Manual of Mental Disorders*, 3rd ed., revised. Washington, D.C.: American Psychiatric Association.)

complicated by the existence of bulimia as a symptom in a variety of medical disorders and the frequent coexistence of BN and AN. The symptoms of bulimia describe binge eating per se—the rapid consumption of a large amount of food in a discrete period of time. Criteria for defining a binge with regard to quantity and duration are problematic and to date have not been elucidated; clinically, however, patients are almost always able to distinguish between a normal meal and a bulimic episode. Purely as a symptom, bulimia may present in a variety of medical disorders from the Prader-Willi syndrome to Parkinson's disease. In BN, however, the definition of the disorder extends beyond binge eating to include a sense of loss of control, post-binge self-deprecation, and usually the wish to purge the ingested food through a variety of means; there is an accompanying and characteristic preoccupation with weight and shape. Within the context of AN, BN may occur in about 50% of cases (Garfinkel et al. 1980). Importantly, BN may also occur in persons who are neither emaciated nor medically ill. This autonomous disorder in those at normal weight has been recognized only recently (Russell 1979). *DSM-III-R* criteria for BN (Table 7–2) describe not only a variety of techniques used to counteract caloric consumption but also the typical psychological disturbances. This definition of BN represents a more restrictive and clinically more severe conceptualization of the disorder than previous diagnostic criteria and has received broad acceptance.

ETIOLOGY

The etiologies of AN and BN are unknown. Most clinicians and researchers embrace a multidetermined model of etiology that acknowledges risk factors at several levels (Table 7–3) (Garfinkel et al. 1987). Culturally, prejudice against obesity is strong and emphasis on thinness is high. Conflict between pressures on women to perform professionally and to be nurturing may highlight concerns about personal control that are manifested in weight regulation. Furthermore, some career choices link thinness and achievement, and special populations (notably dancers and fashion models) have been shown to be at unusually high risk for the development of eating disorders. It is important to note that these disorders were fully described clinically long before thinness achieved its current high social desirability.

At the level of the family, a history of depression, alcoholism, obesity, or AN may augment risk for the development of an eating disorder through unknown means. Families may magnify dominant cultural attitudes or imbue food, weight, or shape with undue symbolic significance. At a genetic level, there is evidence for a 50% concordance rate for AN among monozygotic twins versus a 10% concordance among dizygotic twins (Holland et al. 1984), the latter rate is equivalent to the rate for non-twin siblings. Even here, however, it is difficult to tease apart issues of genetic vulnerability from obstacles to the establishment of individual psychological identity. Similarly, the nature of the as-

Table 7–3. PURPORTED RISK FACTORS FOR EATING DISORDERS

Cultural
Idealization of a thin form
Pressures to perform, to please others

Familial
Magnification of cultural attitudes
Family history of eating disorder
Family history of affective disorder or alcoholism
Family relationships that discourage autonomy in adolescence

Individual
Defective autonomous functioning
Disturbances in self-perception
Personality features
Obesity
Cognitive style
Chronic medical illness

sociation between AN or BN and a family history of affective disorder or alcoholism is unclear.

At an individual level, predisposing factors include a sense of personal helplessness, fear of losing control, self-esteem highly dependent on the opinions of others, and an all-or-nothing thinking style (Garfinkel and Garner 1982). Beyond these individual psychological characteristics, a history of premorbid obesity may also heighten risk, particularly for BN. Furthermore, medical illness may serve as a foundation, trigger, or perpetuant for eating disorders. A systematic study of female juvenile-onset diabetics revealed an unusually high prevalence of AN and BN, with the latter associated with poor metabolic control (Rodin et al. 1986). Chronic medical illnesses of childhood and adolescence may lead to body image distortion and heightened preoccupation with body control through eating; food may become symbolically overvalued in power struggles between adolescents and their families or physicians in illnesses in which nutritional regulation is important.

While research survey studies can identify populations at risk, this provides an incomplete understanding of etiology, since AN and BN do not appear in all or even the majority of such high-risk subjects. Historically, concepts of etiology in eating disorders have evolved in tandem with dominant theoretical trends in general psychiatry. The early years of this century featured a renewed interest in neuropsychiatry. In that context, observation of an association between cachexia and adenohypophyseal destruction in a patient spawned a variety of biological treatments for AN. Then the ascendant model of psychoanalytic theory assumed dominance, and AN was formulated as a defense against oral impregnation fantasies. The subsequent evolution of object relations theory, cognitive psychology, and family systems theory have likewise influenced etiologic models for eating disorders. Bruch (1973) emphasized both faulty interactional patterns between the infant and the mother in AN and resultant perceptual and conceptual disturbances; her emphasis on disturbances in body image, interoceptive awareness, and a sense of personal ineffectiveness has received extensive research validation. The significance of patterns of familial interaction has been recognized and has led to

enhanced therapeutic modalities (Minuchin 1978; Russell et al. 1987). The renaissance of biological psychiatry over the past 2 decades has rekindled interest in the biological disturbances in AN and BN, with a special focus on the biology and psychology of human starvation. It is hoped that acceptance of a multifactorial model of etiology (Andersen 1985) will prevent such extreme oscillations of the theoretical pendulum.

EPIDEMIOLOGY

At least 90% of cases of AN and BN occur in females. Current accepted prevalence rates among Western adolescent and young adult women are 1% for AN and 2% to 4% for BN. Descriptions of prepubertal AN, while well documented in case reports and series, have not been subject to epidemiologic scrutiny. Semantic and diagnostic confusion over the term *bulimia* until recently has generated gross overestimates of its prevalence that have limited clinical significance. Nevertheless, various attitudinal and behavioral characteristics of eating disorders may be detected in child and adolescent samples. Whether such findings are truly predictive awaits prospective research. A sample of over 1,300 high-school students indicated a prevalence of about 1% of *DSM-III-R* criteria for BN among the girls, while 9.6% of the girls met far less stringent criteria for simple bulimia (Gross and Rosen 1988). In this adolescent sample, there was no correlation between eating disorder and social class. Disturbed eating behavior was accompanied by the typical attitudes and preoccupations seen in adult samples. Another large-scale survey of nearly 2,000 school girls revealed that by age 12, 25% of the sample was concerned about their weight and by age 18 this percentage reached over 60% (Crisp 1984). For some, this generated dieting and purging behavior. The low prevalence rates for AN and BN in comparison with the degree of weight preoccupation and dieting among adolescents reflects the multidetermined nature of these disorders and argues against etiologic reductionism.

CLINICAL PICTURE

The focal point of AN is the patient's marked pursuit of thinness and the associated conviction that her body is too large (Garfinkel and Garner 1982). This may originate from a variety of sources, such as a past history of obesity and the social humiliation and failure associated with it; children and adolescents display negative attitudes toward and negative associations with obesity. Alternately, AN may reflect a symbolic focus in the search for personal mastery that in turn reveals a sense of ineffectiveness. AN may also provide a retreat from the maturational processes of adolescence as typified by the development of secondary sexual characteristics (Crisp 1980).

The initial clinical manifestations of AN are often deceptively benign; AN frequently begins with a diet. Early symptoms of AN are listed in Table 7–4. Although dieting is commonplace in our society, dieting in the context of AN is decidedly different. Normal dieting typically features a fixed weight goal, variably successful restraint, enhancement of social interaction, a relinquishing of prohibitions once the goal is reached, and usually a gradual return to prediet weight. In AN, dieting is characterized by a continuing downward drift of new weight goals as old ones are reached and an augmented sense of being overweight as weight loss occurs. Abstention from high-calorie foods becomes a more global food aversion. Despite periodic frenzied physical activity—as a distraction from hunger sensations and a further mode of weight loss—social contacts diminish. While the family becomes alarmed at the evolving emaciation, the patient typically denies being thin or ill and is uninterested in professional help to reverse her weight loss.

A characteristic but not universal feature of AN is a disturbance in body image by which the person actually overestimates her current body size significantly, believing herself to be fat even in stages of advanced emaciation. Its origins are unknown; hypotheses include regression from the maturational meaning of menarche, the linkage of self-worth with body fat in an inversely proportional relationship, and fixation at a concrete operational stage of piagetian development. This disturbance of body self-perception is closely linked to feelings of loathing of the body and anhedonia.

Clinical accompaniments to these beliefs and pursuits include a repertoire of eating and dieting behaviors familiar to both patients' families and their physicians. Food is secretly disposed of or toyed with rather than eaten. Patients skip meals for a variety of seemingly plausible reasons. An obsessional system of rules and rituals regarding food and its consumption develops, accompanied by a seemingly encyclopedic awareness of caloric content and magical beliefs about different food groups. Typically, there is a long list of forbidden foods; if BN is a concomitant disorder, it is often precisely these foods that are consumed in binges. Such binges are then followed by efforts to counteract the ingestion of calories by vomiting, laxative or diuretic abuse, severe food restriction, and intensive exercise.

Increasing preoccupation with food parallels diminishing consumption. Patients may seek work as waitresses or cooks or simply collect recipes and articles on food. This intensifies the fear of yielding to the impulse to eat and further heightens the prohibitions against it. Characteristic thinking patterns, which are often present premorbidly, take on a new and dangerous significance; dichotomous thinking, a style of all-or-none reasoning, leads to the conclusion that a pound gained signifies a transition from normal to fat (Garner and Bemis 1982). This cognitive pattern extends beyond issues of food and weight to intrapsychic and interpersonal beliefs. It is accompanied by a profound sense of self-mistrust, whether it relates to biological signals of hunger and satiety or to affective states.

Initially, because the disorder is congruent with one's personality, patients rarely present to physicians complaining of weight loss. Rather, they may want help for dieting in the absence of obesity or they may complain of the secondary features of their AN, which may include (1) constipation with a request for laxatives, (2) bloating or frank edema with a request for diuretics, (3) weakness or leg cramps due to hypokalemia as a result of vomiting, (4) amenorrhea, (5) depression, or (6) anxiety.

Table 7–4. PRESENTING SIGNS AND SYMPTOMS OF ANOREXIA NERVOSA

Changing weight goals
Dieting that leads to increased body dissatisfaction
Dieting that leads to social isolation
Amenorrhea
Vomiting
Misuse of laxatives, diuretics, and diet pills

The clinical picture of BN has only recently been determined in a systematic manner (Fairburn and Cooper 1984). Much like its sister disorder, a morbid fear of fatness is the overriding psychological preoccupation. Although BN is frequently diagnosed in persons at actuarially normal body weights, a past history of AN or obesity or both is a frequent finding. With regard to eating attitudes, subjects with BN do not differ from those with AN. In addition to past histories of weight and eating difficulties, there may be previous personal or family history of depression or substance abuse.

Initial descriptions of the BN subgroup of AN patients (Garfinkel et al. 1980) documented distinctive clinical features reflecting possible global disturbance in impulse control: stealing, self-mutilation, suicidal thoughts, and substance abuse. This subgroup also displayed more prominent social and sexual activity. More recently, there is recognition that BN encompasses a broad spectrum of psychopathology; for some patients, BN is but a fleck of paint on a large canvas of chaotic impulse dyscontrol and character pathology. For others, BN may be a relatively isolated but disturbing area of dysfunction. In terms of psychopathology, current empiric research indicates little difference between patients with BN at normal weight and those with coexistent AN (Garner et al. 1985). They all share characteristic attitudes and beliefs about food, shape, and weight.

The patient with BN may binge up to several times per day and often describes cognitive preoccupation with food. Secrecy and shame associated with the disorder can culminate in social isolation and impaired professional functioning. Unlike in AN, there are few aspects of this disorder that are in keeping with one's personality, and thus the patient may be more inclined to seek help; working against this are the humiliation and revulsion associated with bulimic behaviors. Patients often wait several years before divulging their difficulties to a professional.

Binges may occur spontaneously or habitually or can be triggered by unpleasant feelings, such as anger, anxiety, depression, and loneliness. Patients frequently describe a sense of loss of control during binges and a sense of frenzy, as well as frank dissociation at times. They eat quickly, often describing it as "inhaling rather than tasting." Binges can last from minutes to hours and may

Table 7–5. PRESENTING SIGNS AND SYMPTOMS OF BULIMIA NERVOSA

Hypochloremic hypokalemic metabolic alkalosis
Parotid hypertrophy
Loss of dental fillings and enamel
Alternating diarrhea and constipation
Calluses on dorsum of hand
Depression and weight preoccupation

involve consumption of 3,000 to 5,000 calories in an hour. Binges are terminated by running out of food, physical fullness, abdominal pain, fatigue, social interruption, or self-loathing. The usual internal cues for satiety are notably absent. Post-binge guilt and dysphoria are common sequelae, although some patients experience the binges as soothing or anxiolytic.

The binges are typically followed by efforts to counteract them. The most common sequela is vomiting, often induced with a finger or by manual pressure on the abdomen; some patients can eventually vomit simply by bending over. Some use the potentially toxic serum of ipecac to induce vomiting. Laxative, diuretic, diet pill abuse, as well as compulsive exercising, may be alternatives or adjuncts to vomiting.

As is the case with AN, BN may present to the clinician only in the form of associated symptoms and sequelae (Table 7–5); unlike the personality-compatible aspects of AN, bulimic behaviors may result in shame and self-loathing, which induces concealment of the disorder from clinicians.

CLINICAL HISTORIES

Anorexia Nervosa

L. C. was referred by her general practitioner because of a refusal to eat and subsequent weight loss. She was 11½-years old at consultation and had lost 13 pounds from her previous high of 73 pounds at age 9; she was 4 feet, 8 inches tall. She reported to have restricted her intake following the onset of epigastric pain that occurred after dinner. She noticed that if she ate less the pain would not occur so over several months she gradually cut out all high-carbohydrate foods and meats. She then eliminated fatty foods. After several months she developed a terror of any weight gain. She would weigh herself at least twice daily and if the scale recorded an increase she would withdraw, force herself to exercise more and restrict her intake for the remainder of the day. She was convinced that she was too fat in her waist, buttocks, and thighs but regarded her arms, neck, and legs as being "skin and bones" and hid regularly in bulky sweaters. She had primary amenorrhea. Physical examination revealed lanugo hair growth and bradycardia as well as the gross wasting.

Historical information revealed that L. C. was the second child of a family of central European background. Her parents were relatively old at the time of marriage and birth of their children. L. C's older brother, 2 years her senior, developed a serious case of asthma when he was 11 months old that required several admissions to hospital. L. C.'s mother became increasingly preoccupied with her son's health and possible dietary contributors. L. C.'s father was a passive accountant with a marked sweet tooth and history of a depressive episode shortly after arriving in Canada. He never achieved the occupational or financial success his wife demanded, which was a source of chronic marital friction. L. C.'s mother had been married previously; her first husband died in his early 30s of a myocardial infarction, and she had polycystic kidney disease and was very preoccupied with health and well-being.

The family was never well integrated in the community and L. C.'s father developed a very close tie with his daughter as a main support. He and his wife also emphasized academic achievement for the children as a means of restoring the status they had achieved in Europe. L. C. had begun playing the piano with her father's enthusiastic support and displayed excellent grades until the onset of the diet. Just prior to the onset of dieting L. C. had been informed that she had no real abilities at the piano and she was perceiving her school work to be more difficult.

L. C. was admitted to hospital with a diagnosis of anorexia nervosa. She was treated with a weight restoration program and prior to discharge the family began therapy, which continued for 6 months after discharge. L. C resumed a normal weight, and development in adolescence was normal. She was well on follow-up 6 years later.

Bulimia

I. V. was referred by her pediatrician after she finally revealed to him that she had been bulimic for 4 years. At the time of consultation, she was 19 years old. She dated the onset of her eating disorder to a suicide attempt at age 15. This attempt had occurred in the context of chronic physical abuse from her older brother and father as well as chronic parental verbal conflict. After she recovered from her overdose, her brother stopped hitting her but her father forced her to apologize to her mother for the suicide attempt. Following that, she recalled beginning to hate the way she looked. She weighed 135 pounds at a height of 5 feet, 4 inches. She began dieting intensively and after several weeks began to binge on food. She learned about vomiting from a popular magazine article on bulimia, and this quickly became part of her repertoire. Her weight oscillated between 93 and 125 pounds, and her menses became irregular. She alternated between bulimic episodes and fasting.

At the time of consultation, the patient weighed 125 pounds and avoided scales assiduously. She was bingeing and vomiting three to eight times per day and was consuming up to 24 Ex-Lax tablets at a time. She also took occasional over-the-counter diuretics and had experimented with diet pills. She performed an hour of aerobics daily. She had significant dental enamel loss, documented hypokalemia, episodes of hematemesis, frequent dizziness, and leg cramps. She admitted to constant cognitive preoccupation with food. She continued to see 93 pounds as an ideal weight for herself. She had a self-imposed upper limit for daily dietary intake of 1200 calories. Exceeding this often triggered a binge. She was consuming up to a loaf of bread, a box of cereal or pasta, and several meals from fast-foot outlets in binges.

She was the youngest child of Italian immigrants. She developed pneumonia at birth, requiring extended hospitalization, and her childhood recollections are colored by chronic lung infections. The atmosphere at home was strict and protective, with meal completion a rigidly enforced rule. She was only allowed to play with children of her own ethnicity and recalled that her school performance never satisfied her parents. Her father teased her about her secondary sexual characteristics and restricted her adolescent social activity. She described him as a "charmer," whom she had caught several times in sexually compromising situations. Her mother, on chronic disability for back pain, had attempted suicide on three occasions, usually related to her marital situation.

She was referred to a group therapy program for eating disorders but did not keep her appointment, fearing her parents might find out and interfere.

CLINICAL COURSE

AN and BN are usually gradual, secretive, and often chronic. Methodologic problems (sampling bias, diagnostic vagaries, varying outcome criteria, sample attrition, and length of follow-up) have hampered research on course and prognosis (Theander 1985). Nevertheless, Theander's follow-up of 94 Swedish patients with AN for up to 24 years revealed that fewer than one third recovered within 3 years and that more than one third were ill for more than 6 years. Of the sample, 13% died of AN and a further 4% committed suicide. This speaks to the significant mortality associated with these disorders. Although it has been argued that an earlier age at onset of AN heralded better outcome (Garfinkel and Garner 1982), more recent longitudinal studies have called this conclusion into question.

In addition to mortality, there is significant psychological and physiological morbidity associated with AN; the long-term clinical course, however, of BN has been less well described. A longitudinal study of 60 Canadian women 5 to 14 years after initial presentation of AN revealed significant psychopathology in comparison with a control group (Toner et al. 1986). Both restricting and bulimic AN patients had markedly elevated life-time prevalence of affective disorder (chiefly major depression) compared with controls; the same held true for anxiety disorders. Of particular significance, the high prevalence of anxiety and affective disorders bore no relation to whether the eating disorder was still active or in remission.

The precise nature of the evident clinical relationship between affective symptoms and eating disorders still awaits elucidation. It must be recognized that starvation itself induces many of the classic vegetative symptoms of depression as well as neuroendocrine disturbances similar to those seen in affective disorders. Similarly, with regard to anxiety symptoms, the confound of nutritional chaos and the affects elicited by threats to the pursuit of thinness must be considered in context.

Personality dysfunction as a component of the clinical picture of eating disorders, while well recognized, has received little systematic appraisal. Generally, compulsive, passive-aggressive, avoidant, and dependent personality traits have been clustered in the profile of AN subjects. BN has been associated with borderline, histrionic, narcissistic, and antisocial features. Whether these traits precede the eating disorder, are awakened from a subclinical level by the eating disorder, or are a secondary reflection of the chaos induced by the eating disorder is unknown. A study of 68 patients with AN or BN, using both clinical and psychometric evaluation, confirmed a high prevalence of avoidant personality disorder (60%) in restricting AN and an equally high prevalence of borderline personality disorder (55%) in the BN group (Piran et al. 1988). However, there is significant overlap between the bulimic state and the diagnostic criteria for borderline personality disorder and some evidence exists that improvement in bulimic behaviors leads to a diminution in borderline symptomatology. What remains to be determined is the nature of personality function long after the acuity of the eating disorder has passed.

Links between eating disorders and substance abuse (in particular, alcohol) have been made on clinical, familial, biological, and psychodynamic grounds. In the case of BN, there is a higher prevalence of substance abuse in both subjects and their families than for the general population. Many of the cognitive and behavioral preoccupations of alcohol abuse can be seen in eating disorders; dieting and drinking are behaviors that are normally under conscious control and practiced in moderation but eating-disorder and alcoholic patients practice them to excess. Both the longitudinal relationship of eating disorders and substance abuse and the meanings of their coexistence await elucidation.

With regard to BN, particularly at normal weight, few studies exist that document the course of this recently characterized disorder. Nevertheless, it is a clinical reality that patients may suffer from BN for several years prior to seeking professional help. The follow-up of one sample 1 to 3 years after a brief behavioral and dietary treatment indicated an outcome strikingly similar to that seen in AN (Hsu and Holder 1986): half the patients had marked improvement, while one fourth demonstrated an intermediate response and one fourth were doing poorly. Another sample of BN subjects treated by a variety of means was followed at 3 years (Normal and Herzog 1986). This study revealed that the greatest gains in terms of eating attitudes and behaviors were made within a year of diagnosis; the subsequent 2 years did not lead to further improvement. Other longitudinal studies have followed the usual "rule of thirds" with regard to good, intermediate, and poor results.

In considering the clinical course of eating disorders as women traverse adolescence and young adulthood, it is important to consider the impact of this pathology on normative life events; pregnancy in patients with AN and BN has been studied in this context. Outcome studies indicate, not surprisingly, a low pregnancy rate for AN subjects. For those who do conceive, however, continuation of the AN may have adverse consequences for the pregnancy. Our follow-up of AN patients through pregnancy indicates that among those who are still symptomatic there is an association of lower birth weights and lower Apgar scores for the infants (Stewart et al. 1987). Clinically, a range of reactions to pregnancy occurs. Some patients are able to "eat for the baby," while others may intensify dieting practices. Similarly, in BN, the occurrence of pregnancy with its attendant weight gain and body shape distortion may be threatening or therapeutic. A recent follow-up of 20 women with BN at normal weight who became pregnant indicated a mixed outcome (Lacey and Smith 1987). The prevalence of bulimic behaviors declined over each trimester, and 15 subjects remained in remission post partum, but most returned to their preconception level of bulimic activity. Of particular concern was the transgenerational transmission of weight preoccupation; one third of subjects were worried their infants might be overweight, and several had been placed on low-carbohydrate diets.

Finally, the self-perpetuating factors of eating disorders must be acknowledged; some of these are listed in Table 7–6. The clinician must identify these in the clinical course of

Table 7–6. SELF-PERPETUATING FACTORS OF EATING DISORDERS

Effects of starvation on thinking, feeling, and behavior
Use of bulimia and vomiting to modulate affect
Reinforcing properties of weight reduction
Loss of social skills and friendships
Loss of vocational skills
Changes in the family
Depression
Secondary gain: power over the others, specialness derived from illness
Lack of resolution of predisposing factors

the disorder in order to intervene in a globally effective manner. These self-perpetuating factors speak to the interwoven biopsychosocial features of eating disorders.

LABORATORY FINDINGS

Psychometric

A wide variety of psychopathologic traits has been measured in eating disorders and compared with other psychiatric disorders and normal states. In general, these tests confirm the presence of features of depression, anxiety, obsessionality, dependency, and impulsivity. At the same time, in the past decade there has been the evolution of a number of psychometric instruments that identify attitudinal and behavioral features characteristic of eating disorders; these tests may be of particular value in screening populations for eating disorders as well as in providing a conceptual framework for understanding individual patients. The Eating Disorder Inventory (Garner et al. 1983b) and the Eating Attitudes Test (EAT) (Garner and Garfinkel 1979) are two such measures; the former assesses psychological and behavioral traits in the areas of drive for thinness, bulimia, body dissatisfaction, ineffectiveness, perfectionism, interpersonal distrust, interoceptive awareness, and fears of maturity. Significant differences have been described in these areas among eating-disorder subjects compared with controls. Similarly, the EAT measures symptoms of AN and BN in three clusters: dieting, bulimia, and oral control. Newer measures continue to appear, operationalizing hypotheses of etiology and improving the quality of research. With the use of a variety of quantification techniques from calipers to a distorting photograph, unequivocal evidence of body image distortion in AN and BN has been demonstrated; about half of the patients consistently overestimate their actual body size and idealize a markedly thinner form.

Biological

A panoply of biological changes occurs in the context of AN and BN and may reflect either starvation or the consequences of other means to prevent weight gain (Kaplan and Woodside 1987). As such, there are no primary or trait biological markers for these disorders; it is hoped that work in molecular genetics may yield indices for those persons with biological vulnerability to the development of these disorders. The biological complications of AN and BN are summarized in Table 7–7. Ultimately, no body system is spared from these disorders and clinicians must be familiar with the protean biological manifestations of AN and BN.

DIFFERENTIAL DIAGNOSIS

Children, adolescents, and young adults may lose weight for various reasons. The etiology of such weight loss may be medical or psychiatric. Ultimately, the diagnoses of AN and BN are based on a careful clinical interview to elicit the important psychological features of the drive for thinness, fear of weight gain, and the fear of losing control over eating. While heightened public awareness has led to increasing clinical diagnosis of eating disorders, there remains a risk of inadequate consideration of differential diagnosis.

Psychiatric Disorders

The characteristic features of psychiatric disorders to be considered in the differential diagnosis of AN are summarized in Table 7–8 (Garfinkel et al. 1983). Starvation may be a final common pathway producing similar signs in persons suffering from a variety of psychiatric disorders. Such signs may include food preoccupation, unusual eating habits, obsessional and hoarding behavior, disruption of sleep, cessation of menses, mood changes, absence of sociability, and frank

bulimia. These may obscure the underlying disorder that generates the starvation process. Schizophrenia, depression, and conversion disorder may mimic eating disorders in terms of weight loss and certain eating behaviors, but they all lack the crucial drive for thinness that is central to AN.

Depression is increasingly recognized among children and adolescents. Here, a true anorexia may occur, although there is no struggle against appetitive drives. A genuine loss of interest in food is contrasted to the systematic avoidance of and magical beliefs about food in AN. Depression is not characterized by vomiting and laxative abuse, and in general the activity level is reduced. Bulimia is uncommon, although at times there may be evidence of hyperphagia in the context of "atypical depression," accompanied by hypersomnia and hypersensitivity to rejection.

In conversion disorder, vomiting may be a prominent feature of the clinical picture and is usually not seen by the patient as a means of counteracting caloric ingestion. Indeed, these patients do not describe preoccupation with being thin, distortions in body image, or conscious food restriction. Rather, there is more commonly a symbolic context to swallowing difficulty or vomiting that results in caloric deprivation. Acute precipitants in the form of psychological trauma are often uncovered and translated into behavioral manifestations.

Schizophrenia is another disorder of adolescence and young adulthood that may manifest as unusual eating habits, weight loss, and purging behavior; here, the central psychological issue is not a pursuit of thinness but delusions regarding food or somatic delusions. Paranoia that food is poisoned will lead to avoidance; belief that the stomach is sealed or malformed may lead to vomiting. These beliefs are in contrast to disturbances in body perception that are commonly seen in AN, that respond to weight restoration, and that do not respond to antipsychotic medication. Case reports and longitudinal outcome studies clearly indicate that the co-prevalence of eating disorders and schizophrenia is extremely low.

Medical Disorders

Most cases of eating disorders reflect a primary psychological disturbance, perhaps

Table 7–7. BIOLOGICAL COMPLICATIONS OF ANOREXIA NERVOSA AND BULIMIA NERVOSA

	Frequency	Cause	Treatment
Cardiovascular Changes			
Bradycardia	Common	Starvation	Weight restoration
Hypotension	Common	Starvation, fluid depletion	Weight restoration
Arrhythmias	Infrequent	Usually provoked by exercise in starvation; may be due to hypokalemia	Weight restoration or potassium supplements
Cardiomyopathy	Rare	Emetine toxicity from ipecac	Stop the ipecac
Central Nervous System Changes			
Nonspecific EEG changes	Common	Starvation	Weight restoration
Reversible cortical atrophy	Uncommon	Starvation	Weight restoration
Renal/Electrolyte Changes			
Hypokalemia	Common	Loss of potassium from multiple routes (vomiting, diarrhea, and diuretics)	Prevent purging; may need a potassium supplement
		Salt restriction and water intoxication (to meet weight goals)	Well-balanced diet with appropriate amount of fluids
Increased blood urea nitrogen	Uncommon	Dehydration	Rehydration
Hypochloremic metabolic alkalosis	Common	Purging	Prevent purging
Edema	Common	Not clearly understood	Elevate feet for 1 hour three times a day; avoid salt; do not use diuretics
Gastrointestinal Changes			
Parotitis	Common	Mechanical trauma; starvation	Stop binges and vomiting
Early satiety	Common	Delayed gastric emptying	Domperidone, 20 mg, three times a day
Gastric dilatation	Rare	Rapid refeeding	Avoid oral feeding; use intravenous feeding
Constipation	Common	Starvation; reliance on laxatives	Use diet: emphasis on dietary bulk, fruits, vegetables and try to avoid laxatives
Dental caries	Common	Acidic nature of vomitus	Dental consultation
Hyperamylasemia	Common in bulimia	Salivary ± pancreatic hypersecretion	Prevent purging
Gastric rupture	Rare	Bingeing	Surgery
Superior mesenteric artery syndrome	Rare	Weight loss	Weight restoration
Musculoskeletal Changes			
Myopathy	Uncommon	Starvation; hypokalemia; emetine myotoxicity of ipecac	Weight restoration; stop ipecac abuse
Osteoporosis and pathologic fractures	Rare	Starvation	Weight restoration
Neuroendocrine Changes			
Decreased serum triiodothyronine and increased reverse triiodothyronine	Common	Starvation	Weight restoration
Hypercortisolism	Common	Starvation	Weight restoration
Primary or secondary amenorrhea	Infrequent	Low weight; emotional stress	Restore weight to 90% of average
Hypothermia	Infrequent	Low weight	Weight restoration
Cortisol escape from dexamethasone suppression	Common	Unknown	Weight restoration
Prepubertal luteinizing and follicle stimulating hormone	Common	Starvation	Weight restoration
Hematologic Changes			
Anemia	Infrequent	Bone marrow hypoplasia; due to starvation	Weight restoration; may need iron
Thrombocytopenia	Rare	Starvation	Weight restoration
Hypercholesterolemia	Common	Unknown	Balanced diet
Hypercarotenemia	Infrequent	Ingestion of high carotene foods	Balanced diet
Dermatologic Changes			
Dry, cracking skin	Common	Dehydration, loss of subcutaneous fat	Weight restoration
Lanugo hair development	Common	Unknown	Weight restoration
Callus on dorsum of hand	Common	Friction against teeth in inducing vomiting	Stop vomiting

Table 7–8. CLINICAL FEATURES OF ANOREXIA NERVOSA, CONVERSION DISORDER, SCHIZOPHRENIA, AND DEPRESSION*

Feature	Anorexia Nervosa	Conversion Disorder	Schizophrenia	Depression
Intense drive for thinness	Marked	None	None	None
Self-imposed starvation	Marked (due to fear of body size)	None	Marked (due to delusions about food)	None
Disturbance in body image	Present (lack of awareness of change in body size and lack of satisfaction or pleasure in the body)	None	None	None
Appetite	Maintained (but with fear of giving in to impulse)	Variable	Maintained	True anorexia
Satiety	Usually bloating, nausea, early satiety	Variable	Variable	Variable
Avoidance of specific foods	Present (for carbohydrates or foods presumed to be high in "calories")	None	Present (of foods that are thought to be poisoned)	Loss of interest in all food
Bulimia	Present in 30% to 50%	May occur	Rare	Rare
Vomiting	Present (to prevent weight gain)	Present (expresses some symbolic meaning)	Rare (to prevent undesirable effects on the body)	None
Laxative abuse	Present (to prevent weight gain)	Infrequently present (expresses some symbolic meaning)	None	None
Activity level	Increased	Reduced or no change	No change	Reduced
Amenorrhea	Present	Present	Present	Present

*From Garfinkel, P. E., Garber, D. M., Kaplan, A. S., et al. 1983. Differential diagnosis of emotional disorders that cause weight loss. *Can. Med. Assoc. J.* 129:939–945.

intensified by biological vulnerability and magnified by cultural preoccupation. Medical illnesses may simulate certain features of AN and BN, but while it is important to rule out a medical etiology it is also essential to avoid dichotomous thinking that leads to an "either/or" approach to diagnosis. For instance, diabetes mellitus may induce weight loss and appetitive changes but the prevalence of true AN and BN in a diabetic population far exceeds normal rates (Rodin et al. 1986). Where a medical disorder explains all the presenting features suggestive of an eating disorder, the etiology will usually be apparent to the astute clinician via the physical stigmata as well as the psychological state. Medical disorders that may potentially mimic eating disorders are listed in Table 7–9.

TREATMENT

Although much has been written about the treatment of eating disorders, particularly in the past decade, two facts of treatment stand out: (1) many of the basic recommendations made by physicians a century ago still have clinical utility today and (2) few of the many available treatments have been subject to rigorous outcome research. Detailed discussions of therapeutic modalities are available (Garner and Garfinkel 1985; Garfinkel and Garner 1987; Andersen 1985).

Persons suffering from AN are often mistrustful of physicians, whom they perceive

Table 7–9. MEDICAL DISORDERS THAT MAY PRESENT WITH FEATURES OF EATING DISORDERS

Tumors of the central nervous system
Anterior pituitary insufficiency
Hyperthyroidism
Diabetes mellitus
Addison's disease
Gastrointestinal malabsorption
Regional enteritis
Gastrointestinal ulcers

to be interested only in refeeding them or making them lose the will to control their weight. Thus, the physician must encourage normal eating habits and weight gain without this becoming the sole focus of treatment or a battle of wills. In the past, some clinicians have even recommended that openly addressing eating and weight-related issues be avoided, focusing instead on psychological contributors. However, this approach is not useful since attitudes concerning weight and foods must ultimately be discussed. Furthermore, the patients need to be aware of the medical and psychological sequelae of the disorder that may be distressing to them. Also, the physician must convey a commitment to stand by the patient through difficult times in the treatment process.

During therapy, some problems may develop as a result of the feelings these patients induce in the physician. One must, for example, avoid the natural tendency either to condone some of the patients' aberrant eating behaviors or, more commonly, to become angry at these patients because of their apparently manipulative or self-destructive behaviors. These feelings can inevitably result in punitive reactions; the goal of the therapy is not control of the patient but rather the relief of suffering.

The initial step of treatment is clearly a careful diagnostic assessment with emphasis both on origins and evolution of the disorder as well as on the potential medical complications described earlier. When the patient remains involved with her family, a family assessment is appropriate. Diagnostically, it allows evaluation of how relationships and attitudes within the family may predispose the patient to perpetuate the illness. Therapeutically it offers an opportunity to reduce tensions, blame, and guilt for all involved and provide frequently needed education about eating disorders. The first controlled trial of family therapy in eating disorders indicates this modality may be the psychotherapy of choice in the treatment of non-chronic AN in younger patients (Russell et al. 1987).

Educational input is extremely valuable. Basic information about the epidemiology of and contributing factors to eating disorders, as well as teaching about the sequelae of starvation, helps patients to feel better understood and less alone. For families who have usually exhausted their own resources in dealing with their affected member, it provides reassurance and explanation regarding a phenomenon that has overwhelmed them. A number of highly accessible publications for patients and families are helpful in this education process.

Outpatient Treatment

All patients with AN and BN should have at least a consultation with a physician knowledgeable about eating disorders. However, continuing treatment can be carried out by a family physician, pediatrician, psychiatrist, psychologist, or internist, often in collaboration with a nutritionist.

For patients with AN, a weight range must be set as a goal. This is usually 90% of average for the person's age and height. A range of 3 to 5 pounds, rather than a precise weight, is selected, both to recognize natural fluctuations in body weight and to counter the tendency of anorexics to focus on precise numbers. Beyond the use of actuarial tables, it is important to know the patient's weight prior to the onset of the anorexic episode and the weight at which secondary amenorrhea developed; these weights will provide further guidance toward restoration of an appropriate weight for that person.

For patients with BN, the issue is not so much weight regulation as eating regulation; this will lead more to a diminution of characteristic weight fluctuations than weight gain per se.

These patients must relinquish their subjugation to their body weight, which includes discarding the scales at home and being weighed weekly by the physician. At the same time, patients must be taught the importance of being at a higher body weight. They must confront the phobia regarding body size, relieve the symptoms of starvation, and ultimately resume control of the disorder that has seized control from them.

The next step is prescription of a regular eating plan. A daily diary of eating and of associated thoughts, feelings, and behaviors helps to reveal the idiosyncratic rules, beliefs, and restrictions of the anorexic and the dietary chaos of the bulimic. Simple recommendations in terms of frequency, setting, and quantity of meals allow the patient to gain weight gradually or regulate urges to binge.

For patients with AN, an initial intake of

1,500 calories per day is usually adequate to initiate weight gain without inducing gastric dilatation associated with intensive refeeding. This is usually increased by 200 to 300 calories per week toward a goal of 2,400 calories per day. A rate of weight gain of 0.5 to 1.0 kg per week is desirable; more precipitous weight gain can be associated with medical complications, including gastric dilatation, fluid overload, and edema, as well as fear and distrust in patients who remain, at best, ambivalent about weight gain. Given the propensity of these patients to think in catastrophic extremes, it is important to reassure them that while they have relinquished control of their weight, they will not be allowed to gain weight too quickly.

For patients with BN, there is often a history of significant daily dietary restriction between binge episodes. The prescription of three structured daily meals of adequate caloric value goes some way toward reducing the chaos of their eating patterns and the intensity of their urges to binge. In addition, individualized recommendations of pleasurable alternatives to bingeing behaviors when the patient feels out of control may be helpful.

Comprehensive outpatient treatment involves both psychological and caloric input. Psychotherapy involves the cognitive processes of learning, which may be impaired in starvation. Important goals of such psychotherapy include learning to recognize feeling states, trusting oneself, and untying one's sense of self-worth from the scales. Whether these goals are best achieved by cognitive, psychodynamic, or behavioral therapies awaits research investigation; at a practical level, elements of all three are often employed.

In terms of medications, the only recommended pharmacotherapy for the outpatient treatment of AN is food. Appetite stimulants such as cyproheptadine are not effective. No controlled studies in AN indicate a role for antipsychotics, antidepressants, or anxiolytics. Drug studies of zinc and gastric prokinetic agents await further confirmation before they can be endorsed for AN.

In contrast to AN, there is more reason to be optimistic about the pharmacotherapy of BN. At the same time, a review of the evidence reveals that it is likely only a subset of BN patients will respond to drugs; the response is reflected more in behavioral change

Table 7–10. PRACTICAL GUIDELINES FOR THE USE OF DESIPRAMINE IN BULIMIA NERVOSA

Initial Dose	50–75 orally at bed time
Dose Increase	25–50 mg every 3–4 days as tolerated
Therapeutic Dose	Up to 250 mg/day in outpatients
Maintenance Dose	Same as therapeutic dose
Response Lag	2–4 weeks after initiation of treatment
Response Failure	Check plasma level for evidence of poor absorption or noncompliance
Complications	Anticholinergic toxicity Overdose potential
Maintenance Dose Duration	4–6 months (as in depression)

than in underlying beliefs about weight and shape. In the past 5 years, double-blind, placebo-controlled trials have demonstrated the efficacy of several antidepressants in diminishing bingeing frequencies; these include imipramine, desipramine, fluoxetine, and phenelzine, which may improve the bulimic condition even in the absence of coexistent depression. Desipramine is an ideal choice because of its relatively low anticholinergic toxicity, and guidelines for its use are presented in Table 7–10. This is a burgeoning area of research to find which drugs work best and what are their putative mechanisms of action.

Abuse of medications in AN and BN emanates from both the patients' drive for thinness and the physicians' misunderstanding of symptoms and complications. A number of drugs to be avoided in the management of eating disorders are listed in Table 7–11.

Inpatient Treatment

Although these disorders are being managed increasingly on an outpatient basis, there remains a set of indications for hospitalization (Table 7–12). Inpatient management usually demands a team approach, including physicians, nurses, psychologists,

Table 7–11. DRUGS TO AVOID IN MANAGEMENT OF EATING DISORDERS

Insulin	Laxatives
Thyroxine	Appetite stimulants
Diuretics	Benzodiazepines (in bulimics)

occupational therapists, and nutritionists. Ideally, following a preadmission interview with the patient and other family members when appropriate, a target weight range is set. Treatment begins with bed rest and supervised meals. In the first week of hospitalization, physical, psychological, and nutritional assessment allows tailoring of an individualized program.

Bed rest serves several purposes: it tends to counter the patient's denial by emphasizing she is ill, it restricts compulsive exercising, and it acts as a starting point for behavioral rewards to encourage weight gain. Close nursing monitoring both fosters a trusting relationship and limits the degree of food concealment and vomiting. Because inpatients with AN are often particularly emaciated, a weight gain of 1 to 2 kg per week and a gradual increase in intake up to 3,500 calories per day is acceptable. It is rare that patients require either nasogastric feeding or total parenteral nutrition. These methods should be used only in life-threatening circumstances or when all other means have failed; while they restore weight, they do not reflect the normalization of eating behavior that treatment should encourage.

In the initial phases of hospitalization, severe anticipatory anxiety may interfere with the patient's beginning to eat. When the patient fails to respond to peer and nursing support or relaxation techniques, the short-term use of lorazepam, 0.5 to 1.0 mg given an hour prior to meals, may be helpful. Patients are weighed three times per week at a standard time and in standard clothing. They are provided with information about their weight changes and are encouraged to discuss their perceptions and reactions.

Reaching a goal weight may take 6 to 8 weeks. Treatment then shifts to a consolidation of gains made and a transfer of autonomy back to the patient. Psychotherapy may then play a more prominent role.

For the inpatient with BN, treatment must go beyond mere environmental constraint. Regular meals, the introduction of foods associated with binges into those meals, and working on other problems with impulse control are also important.

Before insulin was used in the treatment of diabetes mellitus, hundreds of treatments were advocated for that multisystemic disorder. In AN and BN, virtually every form of psychiatric and psychological therapy has been described, from psychoanalysis to psychosurgery. Unlike diabetes mellitus, it is highly unlikely there will be a single treatment for eating disorders with such widespread benefit. Nevertheless, the next decade of research on treatment will include comparative trials of different psychotherapies as well as trials of pharmacotherapy versus psychotherapy. For the clinician, it is likely that the challenge will be how to combine a number of treatment modalities to help these patients.

References

American Psychiatric Association. 1987. *Diagnostic and Statistical Manual of Mental Disorders*, 3rd ed., revised. Washington, D.C.: American Psychiatric Association.

Andersen, A. E. 1985. *Practical Comprehensive Treatment of Anorexia Nervosa and Bulimia*. Baltimore: Johns Hopkins University Press.

Bruch, M. 1973. *Eating Disorders: Obesity, Anorexia Nervosa, and the Person Within*. New York: Basic Books.

Crisp, A. H. 1980. *Anorexia Nervosa: Let Me Be*. London: Academic Press.

Crisp, A. H. 1984. The psychopathology of anorexia nervosa: Getting the "heat" out of the system. In Stunkard A. J., Stellar E. (eds.): *Eating and Its Disorders*. New York: Raven Press.

Fairburn, C. G., and Cooper, P. J. 1984. The clinical features of bulimia nervosa. *Br. J. Psychiatry* 144:238–246.

Garfinkel, P. E., and Garner, D. M. 1982. *Anorexia Nervosa: A Multidimensional Perspective*. New York: Brunner/Mazel.

Garfinkel, P. E., and Garner, D. M. (eds.). 1987. *The Role of Drug Treatments for Eating Disorders*. New York: Brunner/Mazel.

Garfinkel, P. E., Garner, D. M., and Goldbloom, D. S. 1987. Eating disorders: Implications for the 1990's. *Can. J. Psychiatry* 32:624–631.

Garfinkel, P. E., Garner, D. M., Kaplan, A. S., et al. 1983. Differential diagnosis of emotional disorders that cause weight loss. *Can. Med. Assoc. J.* 129:939–945.

Garfinkel, P. E., Moldofsky, M., and Garner, D. M. 1980. The heterogeneity of anorexia nervosa: Bulimia

---

Table 7–12. INDICATIONS FOR HOSPITALIZATION

Rapid weight loss of greater than 30% over 6 months

Signs of severe energy loss and cognitive dysfunction

Evidence of marked electrolyte imbalance (hypokalemia of less than 3.0 mEq/L or electrocardiographic changes despite potassium supplements)

Cycle of bingeing, purging, and restricting that cannot otherwise be interrupted

Uncontrolled coexistent diabetes mellitus

Concomitant depression and/or suicidality

Persistent substance abuse

Failure of outpatient treatment

as a distinct subgroup. *Arch. Gen. Psychiatry* 37:1036–1040.

Garner, D. M., and Bemis, K. M. 1982. A cognitive behavioural approach to anorexia nervosa. *Cognitive Ther. Res.* 6:1–27.

Garner, D. M., and Garfinkel, P. E. 1979. The eating attitudes test: An index of the symptoms of anorexia nervosa. *Psychol. Med.* 9:273–279.

Garner, D. M., and Garfinkel, P. E. (eds.). 1985. *Handbook of Psychotherapy for Anorexia Nervosa and Bulimia.* New York: Guilford Press.

Garner, D. M., Olmsted, M. P., and Garfinkel, P. E. 1983a. Does anorexia nervosa occur on a continuum? Subgroups of weight-preoccupied women and their relationship to anorexia nervosa. *Int. J. Eating Disord.* 2:11–19.

Garner, D. M., Olmsted, M. P., and Garfinkel, P. E. 1985. Similarities among bulimic groups selected by different weights and weight histories. *J. Psychiatr. Res.* 19:129–134.

Garner, D. M., Olmsted, M. P., and Polivy, J. 1983b. Development and validation of a multidimensional eating disorder inventory for anorexia nervosa and bulimia. *Int. J. Eating Disord.* 2:15–34.

Gross, J., and Rosen, J. C. 1988. Bulimia in adolescents: Prevalence and psychosocial correlates. *Int. J. Eating Disord.* 7:51–61.

Holland, A. J., Hall, A., Murray, R., et al. 1984. Anorexia nervosa: A study of 34 twin pairs and 1 set of triplets. *Br. J. Psychiatry* 145:414–419.

Hsu, L. K. G., and Holder, D. 1986. Bulimia nervosa: Treatment and short-term outcome. *Psychol. Med.* 16:65–70.

Kaplan, A. S., and Woodside, D. B. 1987. Biological aspects of anorexia nervosa and bulimia nervosa. *J. Consult. Clin. Psychol.* 55:645–653.

Lacey, J. H., and Smith, G. 1987. Bulimia nervosa: The impact of pregnancy on mother and baby. *Br. J. Psychiatry* 150:777–787.

Minuchin, S., Rosman, B. L., and Baker, L. 1978. *Psychosomatic Families: Anorexia Nervosa in Context.* Cambridge, Mass.: Harvard University Press.

Norman, D. K., and Herzog, D. B. 1986. A 3-year outcome study of normal-weight bulimia: Assessment of psychosocial functioning and eating attitudes. *Psychiatr. Res.* 19:199–205.

Piran, N., Lerner, P., Garfinkel, P. E., et al. 1988. Personality disorders in anorexic patients. *Int. J. Eating Disord.* 7:589–599.

Rodin, G. M., Johnson, L. E., Garfinkel, P. E., et al. 1986. Eating disorders in female adolescents with insulin-dependent diabetes mellitus. *Int. J. Psychiatr. Med.* 16:49–57.

Russell, G. F. M. 1979. Bulimia nervosa: An ominous variant of anorexia nervosa. *Psychol. Med.* 9:429–448.

Russell, G. F. M., Szmukler, G. I., Dare, C., and Eisler, I. 1987. An evaluation of family therapy in anorexia nervosa and bulimia nervosa. *Arch. Gen. Psychiatry.* 44:1047–1056.

Stewart, D. E., Raskin, J., Garfinkel, P. E., et al. 1987. Anorexia nervosa, bulimia, and pregnancy. *Am. J. Obstet. Gynecol.* 157:1194–1198.

Theander, S. 1985. Outcome and prognosis in anorexia nervosa and bulimia: Some results of previous investigations, compared with those of a Swedish long-term study. *J. Psychiatr. Res.* 19:493–508.

Toner, B. B., Garfinkel, P. E., and Garner, D. M. 1986. Long-term follow-up of anorexia nervosa. *Psychosom. Med.* 48:520–529.

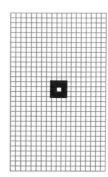

Gender Dysphorias of Childhood and Adolescence

SUSAN J. BRADLEY, M.D.

The gender dysphorias discussed in this chapter will encompass the broad range of gender-related disorders as they present in children and adolescents. Those that arise in childhood are confined largely to the broad category of gender identity disorder of childhood (GIDC). In adolescence, however, these disorders appear much more similar to their adult counterparts and will be dealt with under the headings transsexualism, homosexuality, and transvestic behavior. It is becoming increasingly clear that GIDC is a precursor of adolescent/adult homosexuality and transsexualism (Green 1987). However, because many persons with transsexual or homosexual concerns will not present to the clinician until adolescence and not all children with gender identity problems display difficulties in adolescence, the presenting concerns will be described as though they were distinct entities. The connections among these disorders will be discussed in the section on the clinical course of GIDC.

The following terms and their definitions are used in this chapter: *Gender identity:* the subjective awareness of one's self as male or female; and *gender/sex role:* the behaviors that are understood to reflect masculinity or femininity in our society.

GENDER IDENTITY DISORDER OF CHILDHOOD

Definition

The Diagnostic and Statistical Manual of Mental Disorders, third edition, revised (*DSM-III-R*) provides the following definition (American Psychiatric Association 1987):

The essential features of this disorder are persistent and intense distress in a child about his or her assigned sex and the desire to be, or insistence that he or she is, of the other sex. (This disorder is not merely a child's nonconformity to stereotypic sex-role behavior as, for example, in "tomboyishness" in girls or "sissyish" behavior in boys, but rather a profound disturbance of the normal sense of maleness or femaleness.) In addition, in a girl there is either persistent marked aversion to normative feminine clothing and insistence on wearing stereotypic masculine clothing, or persistent repudiation of her female anatomic characteristics. In a boy, there is either preoccupation with female stereotypic activities, or persistent repudiation of his male anatomic characteristics. This diagnosis is not given after the onset of puberty.

Tables 8–1 and 8–2 list the *DSM-III-R* criteria for identifying this disorder.

Etiology

There is no adequate and tested explanation concerning the origins of this disorder. Biological factors are suggested as etiologically relevant by several areas of investigation (for reviews see Rutter 1980; Meyer-Bahlburg 1984; Gladue 1987). Animal studies in which the female fetus is exposed to androgens in utero have established that masculine behaviors can be induced in this way. These behaviors include higher levels of aggressivity,

Table 8–1. DIAGNOSTIC CRITERIA FOR FEMALES WITH GENDER IDENTITY DISORDER OF CHILDHOOD

A. Persistent and intense distress about being a girl and a stated desire to be a boy (not merely a desire for any perceived cultural advantages from being a boy), or insistence that she is a boy.
B. Either 1 or 2:
  1. Persistent marked aversion to normative feminine clothing and insistence on wearing stereotypical masculine clothing (e.g., boys' underwear and other accessories)
  2. Persistent repudiation of female anatomical structures, as evidenced by at least one of the following:
    a. An assertion that she has, or will grow, a penis
    b. Rejection of urinating in a sitting position
    c. Assertion that she does not want to grow breasts or menstruate
C. The girl has not yet reached puberty.

(From American Psychiatric Association. 1987. *Diagnostic and Statistical Manual of Mental Disorders,* 3rd. ed., revised. Washington, D.C.: American Psychiatric Association.)

rough-and-tumble play, as well as increased frequency of mounting behavior. These changes cannot be induced through androgen administration later in life, thus suggesting a critical period effect. The behavioral effects are also quantitative in that there is a shift toward more masculine behaviors.

Table 8–2. DIAGNOSTIC CRITERIA FOR MALES WITH GENDER IDENTITY DISORDER OF CHILDHOOD

A. Persistent and intense distress about being a boy and an intense desire to be a girl or, more rarely, insistence that he is a girl.
B. Either 1 or 2:
  1. Preoccupation with female stereotypical activities, as shown by a preference for either cross-dressing or simulating female attire, or by an intense desire to participate in the games and pastimes of girls and rejection of male stereotypical toys, games, and activities
  2. Persistent repudiation of male anatomical structures, as indicated by at least one of the following repeated assertions:
    a. That he will grow up to become a woman (not merely in role)
    b. That his penis or testes are disgusting or will disappear
    c. That it would be better not to have a penis or testes
C. The boy has not yet reached puberty.

(From American Psychiatric Association. 1987. *Diagnostic and Statistical Manual of Mental Disorders,* 3rd. ed., revised. Washington, D.C.: American Psychiatric Association.)

These female animals still display heterosexual behavior in adult life. These studies have led to the theory that the presence/absence of testosterone in utero produces a male/female differentiation of a hormonal regulating center in the hypothalamus (Goy 1968). This center is believed to be responsible for the cyclic control of luteinizing and follicle stimulating hormones.

Although empirical work to directly test such an hypothesis in humans cannot be carried out because of ethical constraints, natural experiments in humans support the animal findings. The most significant studies have been done in girls with congenital adrenal hyperplasia (CAH) (Ehrhardt and Baker 1974). In this genetically determined abnormality, the adrenal gland fails to produce normal amounts of corticosteroids. The resultant increase in ACTH secretion causes an increase in testosterone production. Masculinization of the external genitalia and higher levels of tomboyish activity in childhood are considered the result of increased testosterone production in utero. Studies that followed these girls into adulthood have found increased homoerotic fantasy and reduced heterosexual activities and interests. Gender identity in these girls is, however, female (Money et al. 1984). Nevertheless, they may be at increased risk for gender difficulties based perhaps on their tomboyish orientation (Zucker et al. 1987).

Based on the above studies, Dorner (1983, 1988) has proposed that homosexuality and transsexualism are the result of a hormonal abnormality in utero that produces a differentiation of the hypothalamic center contrary to the person's biological sex. Support for this position has come from estrogen challenge studies that show that homosexual men have a luteinizing hormone response that is intermediate between heterosexual men and women (Dorner 1976). These findings have been replicated in one study (Gladue et al. 1984), but more recently three studies have failed to find differences (Gooren 1986; Hendricks et al. in press; Gladue et al. 1988). The relevance of this theory must await further study. Even if confirmed, this theory can provide only a partial explanation of gender disorders and homosexuality since there is considerable overlap between results in homosexual and heterosexual persons.

Based on the above studies it is reasonable

to assume that biological factors may be contributory in GIDC since most GIDC boys are very avoidant of rough-and-tumble activities (Green 1974). GIDC girls, to the contrary, appear interested in rough-and-tumble activities (Bradley 1980). Assessment of brain-regulated hormonal function has not been done in children since hormone levels prior to the onset of pubertal changes are low. Physical examination of these children generally reveals no abnormalities. A further biologically related factor found in GIDC children is marked sensitivity to parents' feelings. Although not well studied, this sensitivity may be explained by the relatively heavy loading in these families of affective disorder (Bradley 1985).

Money and co-workers (1957) have shown that in most instances psychological factors override biological factors in the determination of one's gender identity. These authors studied children born with ambiguous genitalia from CAH and other types of hermaphroditism. Regardless of their chromosomal sex or appearance of their genitals, these children, if clearly assigned to one sex before the age of 18 months, had a gender identity consonant with their sex of assignment and rearing. This view of the overriding importance of the sex of assignment and rearing continues to be generally accepted despite some recent studies that cast doubt on its applicability in all cases. Imperato-McGinley and colleagues (1979) have provided evidence that persons with 5α-reductase deficiency, initially reared as girls, because of female-appearing genitalia, have reversed their gender identity at puberty when typical male secondary sexual characteristics appear. No adequate explanation has been provided for this anomalous finding, although questions have been raised about the expectations for consistency of the rearing situation, since these persons are all from related families in rural Dominican Republic (Ehrhardt and Meyer-Bahlburg 1981). Similar findings have been reported within the Arab population in Israel in persons with 17β-hydroxysteroid dehydrogenase deficiency (Rosler and Kohn 1983).

Psychosocial factors have been posited as particularly salient in the development of this disorder. Stoller (1968) stated that some boys had an overclose, very involved relationship with mothers who themselves are conflicted about their own gender identity. Others have suggested that these boys are anxious about separation and identify with their mothers because of fear of her loss (Coates and Person 1985). Maternal depression and hostility toward men during the first few years of the child's life have been considered contributory in clinical descriptions of these boys and their families (Bradley 1985). Green (1974, 1987), who has undertaken the only large-scale, longitudinal, comparative study in this area, could define only lack of parental discouragement of cross-sex behaviors and parental unavailability as distinguishing GIDC boys from normal boys.

Since GIDC girls present less frequently than GIDC boys, there is less information on etiologic factors. However, Bradley (1980) reported on clinical experience with several GIDC girls where maternal depression, paternal violence, or threats of violence were seen as contributing to the daughter's reluctance to identify with women. Devaluation of the child's sex by caretaking persons is also thought to be contributory (Bradley 1985).

Intrapsychic factors in the child such as undue sensitivity, poor anxiety tolerance, and borderline-type personality traits have been noted (Bradley et al. 1980). Children with GIDC have been shown to score as highly as psychiatric controls on scales that measure psychological disturbance (Zucker 1985). Because this disturbance factor appears more significant in older children, some authors have suggested that the disturbance is a reaction to parental frustration and peer isolation (Green et al. 1980). Validation of the importance of many of these factors must depend on further empirical work; to date, no one factor has been shown to discriminate children with GIDC from other children with psychiatric problems.

With the above cautions in mind, the following is provided to give a conceptual framework to integrate these diverse factors. The situation for a cross-gender-identified boy may be as follows. A sensitive boy is born to parents, each of whom have unresolved gender-related conflicts. During the first year after the child's birth his mother feels depressed and overwhelmed over her own difficulty dealing with the demands of parenting, her husband's nonsupportiveness, or difficulties related to illness in the child or members of her family. Typically, this mother has ambivalent feelings toward males, which her son perceives. This child may also observe his mother as preferring female siblings or experience a sense that his mother would prefer him as female and as nurturing or supportive to her. In this context, the child who is in the midst of consolidating his gender identity may, in an effort to obtain his mother's attention, begin to act feminine. Parental conflict often about the father's absence or nonsupport of the mother further increases the child's insecurity. Difficulty with affect tolerance reinforces the child's need to diminish his sense of inner stress and find ways of feeling more secure, a function that cross-dressing and feminine behaviors appear to serve. When this behavior is not discouraged, the child begins to develop a sense of himself being valued for the female characteristics and devalued for the male aspects of himself. As the child interacts with peers his innate discomfort with rough-and-tumble activities and his interest in feminine activities directs him to female peers. Parental reactions, such as the father's withdrawal (from this son who both confuses and threatens him), further his sense of devaluation. Usually parents begin to feel uncomfortable with what they perceive as a phase that the child has not outgrown. Their discouragement of the behavior at this point, if not accompanied by others' valuing of the child, may drive the behavior underground, leaving the child clinging to an internal but valued female self. As the child moves through middle childhood, he becomes increasingly isolated because of peer rejection and may spend considerable time fantasizing about his female self.

The following may serve as a conceptual framework for understanding this disorder in girls. The GIDC girl is sensitive but oriented to activity and motion. She is raised in a family in which the mother is seen as depressed or inadequate, while the father tends to be aggressive or to view women as inadequate. There may be overt conflict interpreted as being threatening to the mother who is seen as being unable to defend herself. The GIDC girl whose sensitivity and anxiety make her vulnerable to the parental dysfunction appears to identify with the aggressor, her father, as a way of defending herself against overwhelming anxiety. She may then, in fantasy, protect both herself and her mother. If the need for this defense continues and is not discouraged, this girl will develop an internal self-concept that is partially male. She will show this in her choice of activities and peers. Because of a greater societal acceptance of tomboyish behavior she will not experience the same negative effect on her self-esteem (related to peer rejection) that GIDC boys endure.

Epidemiology

There are no studies that have attempted to examine the prevalence of this disorder in the general population. Based on the connection with adult homosexuality, one can speculate that this disorder or subclinical variations of it may occur in 3% to 4% of children. This is consistent with symptom surveys of cross-gender behaviors carried out by various authors on normative samples of children (Zucker 1985). Cross-gender behaviors are reported infrequently and tend to be considerably less frequent in older children. The proportion of males to females with this disorder is not well documented, but in our clinic population it appears to be about 7:1. This may be falsely skewed in the direction of more males to females since it is harder to discriminate girls with GIDC because cross-gender behavior in girls is more acceptable than it is in boys.

Clinical Course

Most parents report onset of cross-gender behavior within the first 3 to 5 years (Green 1976). The behaviors are often described as always having been there, but careful questioning will usually reveal onset in conjunction with events affecting parental availability, such as maternal depression or illness in a family member. Occasionally these disorders will appear following a traumatic event such as hospitalization or surgery. With the GIDC girl, onset is sometimes more difficult to identify because the behaviors appear less obvious. Most typically, early behaviors for boys consist of interest in and wearing of the mother's clothes, shoes, jewelry, and purses. For girls, initial difficulties may emerge as the child learns anatomical differences between the sexes. She may insist she has a penis or does not have a vagina.

As the boy with GIDC grows older and is exposed to other children, he prefers playing with female peers and avoids rough-and-tumble activities typically associated with boy's play. Play interests include role play, particularly as the mother or other females, and doll play where hair combing is a prominent activity. Fantasy heroines, such as Wonder Woman, are admired. Dressing up, if permitted, often displays creativity with the use of objects such as towels for hair. With the GIDC girl her interests focus on more typical male activities such as competitive sports, play with guns, and muscular activities, such as climbing. Fantasy dress-up tends to be less prominent. These girls dislike being expected to wear typically feminine clothing, such as dresses. Some of these children will pretend to be boys when playing and may adopt a boy's name.

These children often state they wish to be the opposite sex. Some, when younger, may even have claimed to be the opposite sex. Occasionally, boys try to reinforce their femininity by hiding their genitalia between their legs; infrequently girls will claim to have a penis. Most, at the time they present, by age 5 to 6 know to which sex they belong but still present confusion with respect to gender constancy. They continue to be uncertain whether changing certain aspects of one's appearance (e.g., clothing, hair) will also change one's gender (Zucker 1985).

GIDC children are often first identified when they enter school. Skilled teachers will report concern to the parents regarding the extent of cross-sex interests. Confusion may exist for some teachers and parents because of liberalizing trends deemphasizing rigid gender stereotyped behaviors. Mannerisms such as a high-pitched voice and exaggerated dorsiflexion of the wrist tend to make GIDC boys obvious when observed with other children. Frequently the behaviors are extreme enough to lead to social isolation. When name calling and peer ostracism become a problem, many GIDC boys (whose behaviors have been tolerated within the family) are referred for consultation. This usually occurs between the ages of 8 and 12. At this point, these boys may not meet all of the criteria for GIDC since the more overt behaviors and statements tend to diminish with age. Careful history taking will usually reveal the presence of a previous GIDC.

The course of GIDC in girls tends to be less obvious for the reason mentioned earlier, that is, tolerance of tomboyish behavior by parents and peers. Generally, these girls continue to be very involved in competitive sports and play with boys and, unless they come to adult attention through overt attempts to pass as a boy or statements about growing up to be male, many pass unnoticed, at least by clinicians.

As the GIDC boy moves into adolescence, he generally has failed to develop male peer-related skills or interests, may continue to exhibit some mannerisms (high-pitched voice, limp wrist), and has been the butt of name calling or teasing for many years. These boys often spend many hours fantasizing themselves as females or engrossed in female-oriented television programs. Friends, if they exist, may be other nonaggressive boys or girls. Parents may mistakenly assume this friendship with girls is heterosexual. For most of these boys it is the only kind of companionship with which they are comfortable.

The GIDC girl entering adolescence is, again, less obvious. However, her continued disinterest in feminine clothes and preference for traditionally masculine activities and males as buddies begin to set her apart from most tomboys. Emerging homosexual interests may cause her to associate with one or two close girl friends. Whereas most tomboys gradually relinquish their masculine interests as heterosexual interests emerge, GIDC girls fail to develop interests in dating and other heterosocial pursuits.

Which GIDC children will become transsexual, homosexual, or heterosexual is not clear. However, it was observed that about 75% of GIDC children will declare themselves homosexually oriented by late adolescence (Green 1987). A small number will be transsexual, and some will be heterosexual. Those GIDC children most likely to be transsexual in adolescence or adulthood have been in a family with a high level of tolerance for cross-sex behaviors. Generally, this has meant either no referral or a late referral for consultation. This lack of intervention by parents allows for the development of a fixed cognitive attribution and self-image as being of the opposite sex. When this occurs, request for sex reassignment is seen by the person as the only solution to his or her discomfort. Homosexuality is likely on a continuum with transsexualism. Some homosexuals with an earlier history of GIDC will continue to display gender confusion or uncertainty, but not usually to the degree warranting a request for sex reassignment. These persons display their cross-gender identification in behaviors ranging from very subtle feminine mannerisms to full-blown cross-dressing (e.g., "drag queens").

Case 1

The patient, a boy aged 5, presented to the clinic with parental concern expressed about "girlish behaviors." Since age 3 the patient had been interested in girls' toys such as dolls, playing house (in which he invariably played the mother or the baby but never the father), and used the mother's clothes, makeup, and jewelry. He was in kindergarten and preferred girls to boys as playmates. When the father encouraged him to play outside, he would find many excuses, the most persistent of which was that the boys played rough. His mother sympathized that the neighborhood boys were rough and generally not the kind she wanted her son to play with. Preferred activities at home were Barbies and dressing up. The parents acknowledged that they had initially thought his behavior amusing and had not discouraged it. They expected he would grow out of it when he went to school, but he did not seem to be changing; after the teacher commented on his rather intense feminine interests, they sought a referral. Their earlier inquiries with the family doctor about the normality of this behavior had reinforced their belief that it was just a phase through which he was passing.

History taking revealed that the mother experienced depressive episodes earlier in her life, the first related to her father's death when she was a teenager. She had had a rather distant relationship with her mother and a somewhat ambivalent relationship with her father, who seemed to prefer her older brother. The patient's father was an anxious, hard-working man who had difficulty understanding his wife's periods of depression and spent most of the early years of the marriage working overtime. The mother was particularly stressed in the early years of the son's development because of her mother's illness. She resented her husband's absence but was unable to discuss her feelings with him. Instead, the couple fought about chores, money, and their son. She became moderately depressed when her son

was age 2½, the time at which her mother's illness had worsened; she did not, however, seek treatment. It was the clinician's impression that she had been less than optimally available to her son over this period.

The patient, a slim and somewhat pretty boy, when seen individually, was able to clearly state that he was a boy but acknowledged feeling that he would like to be a girl. When asked what would be good about it, he talked about being pretty and wearing nice dresses that swirl. He did not know whether his mother wanted him to be a boy or not, although he knew his father did. He said that he thought his mother was sometimes mad at him but he did not know why. He thought maybe his father could help him in some way. He appeared sad when talking about his parents. These parents were very concerned about the possibility of a homosexual outcome and readily agreed to treatment. They were advised to discourage the cross-gender behaviors and to look for ways of enhancing their son's sense of value to them as a boy. They were supported to find ways of diminishing their conflict, which was felt to be worsening their son's anxiety and sadness. The father was encouraged to spend more time with his son. Because of the extent of this boy's cross-gender identification, he was referred for individual play therapy. Follow-up after 2 years revealed that the cross-gender behavior had almost disappeared and the patient had succeeded in making friends with several quieter boys at school. The parents' marital difficulties had also diminished. Whether internal difficulties have truly been resolved will have to await longer-term follow-up.

Case 2

A 4-year-old girl was brought to the clinic when her mother felt unable to convince her that she was a girl. The patient, a stubborn child, insisted on being called Bobby. Although the mother initially went along with this, she became increasingly concerned that it indicated more than a passing interest in playing as a boy. This girl persistently refused to wear dresses, insisting on jeans and sneakers as the only comfortable clothing. She constantly sought out male playmates at nursery school with whom she engaged in competitive and rough-and-tumble games.

She would occasionally stick an object between her legs pretending to have a penis. She insisted she did not have a "gina" despite her mother's efforts to educate her in this respect.

Relevant background history revealed a stormy marriage with at times violent fighting. The patient had been witness to some of the fighting and had expressed fears that her mother would be hurt. The mother felt very put down by her husband, whom she saw in general as denigrating to women. The father acknowledged a rather violent temper. He was considerably less concerned about what he regarded as tomboyish behavior on his daughter's part. He had in the past encouraged her involvement and interests in sports and rough-and-tumble play; he was proud that she could stick up for herself with the boys.

In the individual interview the patient, a sturdy-looking little girl with short hair, expressed confusion about whether she really was a boy or a girl. She seemed to believe that anatomy was less relevant than clothes or hair in determining one's sex, a phase typical of children up to this age. She indicated that males were better because they were stronger. She expressed concern that she did not want to be like her mother and get hurt. Treatment recommendations included play therapy for the patient to help her relinquish the defensive identification with males. Her parents were advised that failure to deal with the open marital conflict would make resolution of their daughter's cross-gender identification very difficult.

Differential Diagnosis

Making the diagnosis of GIDC in boys is relatively straightforward for those children who meet all the criteria, that is, who display abnormalities in several aspects of function such as statements of wanting to be the opposite sex, role play, and peer and activity preferences. For a list of dimensions to evaluate see Table 8–3. For girls, the diagnosis is also relatively simple in the young child who may insist that she is a boy and who clearly prefers the company and play activities of boys. The distinction between normality and pathology is more difficult as the symptoms become less numerous or persistent. For slightly older girls, the confusion with tom-

Table 8–3. CORE CROSS-GENDER BEHAVIORS	
Identity statements	Mannerisms
Toy preference	Anatomical dysphoria
Peer preferences	Rough and tumble play
Cross dressing	

(Adapted from Zucker, K. J. 1985. Cross-gender-identified children. In Steiner, B. W. (ed.): *Gender Dysphoria: Development, Research, Management*. New York: Plenum.)

boyish behavior and the wish not to over-determine these behaviors as clinical symptoms leads to more difficulty. Zucker (1985) has suggested that extreme avoidance of dresses and cosmetics may be a useful distinguishing factor. Earlier history of more extreme/less guarded statements about wishing to be or being a boy may be helpful. The family doctor or pediatrician will see children who present with less extreme manifestations of these behaviors. Children with isolated or single cross-sex behaviors that are not persistent are probably at less risk than those whose behaviors affect function or who have a history of GIDC. This impression has not, however, been documented through a follow-up study of a large normative population. Follow-up of GIDC children referred to clinics who display significant variation in cross-gender behavior may provide information in this regard.

The older child is more guarded about open expression of feelings and behaviors that are known to be unacceptable to adults; so, a history of earlier cross-sex behaviors or preoccupations may be particularly important for assessing these children. Although many 8- to 12-year-old children referred because of gender concerns may not meet the criteria for GIDC, those with an earlier history of GIDC who are having peer-related difficulties should be regarded as unresolved cases of GIDC and treated as such. Those children presenting at this age with minimal symptomatology and no earlier cross-gender history are problematic from a diagnostic point of view but deserve monitoring.

The other cross-gender behavior that presents relatively rarely and only in boys is use of maternal undergarments such as pantyhose and underpants. This behavior, if persistent and occurring in the context of disturbances in the mother–child relationship, may be a precursor of transvestic fetishism. It is not usually accompanied by other indices of GIDC.

Tests

Physical examination seldom reveals anomalies, although girls with CAH and other causes of ambiguous genitalia may be at increased risk for GIDC (Zucker et al. 1987). Despite the finding of abnormalities during estrogen challenge in adult homosexual subjects, this test has not been used in children; in fact, it has been suggested as clinically unusable in adults because of its broad range of overlap.

Psychological tests such as the It-Scale, Draw-a-Person Test, and free play tasks distinguish GIDC children from psychiatric controls and normal children. The It-Scale, which requires a child to respond to questions about feelings, activities, and preferences of a neutral-appearing figure will generally provide data confirmatory to the clinical signs and symptoms (Green et al. 1972). GIDC children, in comparison with controls, are more likely to draw an opposite sex figure than a figure of the same sex (Zucker et al. 1983), but about 20% of boys and girls in normative studies may also do so (Jolles 1952). GIDC children, when placed in a room with both male and female stereotypic toys, will tend to play with cross-sex toys (Zucker et al. 1982). A variety of sex-typed activity preference scales have been developed that again provide confirmatory evidence of cross-sex interests and behaviors (Zucker 1985).

Tests such as the Child Behavior Checklist (Achenbach 1978) tend to reveal symptomatology in a number of domains that might be taken as an overall disturbance rating (Zucker 1985).

Treatment

For the very young child (aged 3–4) with GIDC, intervention is most appropriately focused on the parents. Efforts should be made to understand why the child feels devalued or threatened. Has the parent been unavailable to or rejecting of the child? Do the parents argue or fight? Is the child unduly sensitive? If the parents can accept their role in contributing to how the child feels, they may well be able to institute changes that promote a healthier, more secure child. The parents should be encouraged to actively, but not punitively, limit the child's cross-sex

activities and promote more appropriate activities and friendships. Parental intervention is often sufficient for younger children and for children with milder variants of GIDC. For the older child, aged 5 to 12, especially those who clearly meet all criteria for GIDC, individual psychotherapy is usually necessary to allow the child to understand the feelings that have led to the cross-sex behaviors. These children frequently manifest fears of being hurt, concerns about their own goodness/badness, and significant anxiety related to expressions of anger toward parents. Some parents require intensive individual and/or marital therapy to resolve the conflicts that have contributed to their child's difficulties.

GENDER DYSPHORIAS OF ADOLESCENCE

The *DSM-III-R* does not adequately provide a helpful classification of gender disorders that present in adolescence. In our Child and Adolescent Gender Identity Clinic in which we have seen and followed over 120 adolescents with gender problems, a practical classification based largely on presenting symptoms or concerns has been devised (Table 8–4). As mentioned in the section on GIDC, many of the adolescents with gender concerns have an earlier history of GIDC. It is not clear, therefore, whether these cases should be regarded as unresolved forms of GIDC or treated as syndromes that are unique. In some instances, such as transsexualism, the presentation in adolescence may be sufficiently well defined to meet the adult criteria for this disorder. In other cases in which persons present with concerns about

Table 8–4. CLARKE CHILD AND ADOLESCENT GENDER IDENTITY CLINIC CLASSIFICATION OF ADOLESCENT GENDER DYSPHORIAS

Classification	Presenting Concern
Uncertain	Effeminate mannerisms and peer ostracism
Transsexual	Expressed wish for sex reassignment
Homosexual	Their own/other's concern regarding their sexual orientation
Transvestitic behavior	Use of female undergarments often with erotic arousal

sexual orientation or effeminate behaviors, the syndromes are less clearly defined.

The rationale for these classifications is that adolescents who present with these concerns tend to fall into different groups with respect to their management. As well, the transvestitic group appears distinct from the other three groups with respect to developmental and background variables such as history of cross-gender activities and interests, expressive language difficulties, and school difficulties (Bradley and Zucker 1984).

Although homosexuality per se is not defined as a psychiatric disorder in *DSM-III-R*, adolescents and their parents frequently present with concerns about sexual orientation. Such cases comprise the category "Homosexual."

Uncertain Orientation

These adolescents (median age 14.1) are referred because of teasing and social isolation and have an earlier history of cross-gender behaviors and interests. Some would have met the criteria for GIDC while others would not; however, in early adolescence, they continue to manifest feminine behaviors such as dorsiflexion of the wrists when talking, hands on hips with palms facing backward when angry, high-pitched voice during periods of excitement, and a marked lack of ability and interest in sports. Their interests tend to be directed towards traditional homemaking activities such as cooking and sewing. Their heroines are frequently soap opera and comic figures. They spend extreme amounts of time in solitary activities such as watching "soaps" on television or reading romantic stories. Generally, they have few or no male friends and are regularly referred to as "gay" or "fag."

Typically, at the time of assessment, these boys are seen as unassertive. Despite feeling poorly about their social ostracism, they deal with their distress through retreat into a fantasy world. Few will acknowledge gender concerns despite their mannerisms and obviously feminine interests. Almost none will be able to discuss concerns about sexual feelings, although it is believed that many of them have even in early adolescence begun to self-identify as homosexual.

Differential diagnosis includes transsexualism, which can only be clarified by following the individual over time. Homosexuality appears to be the most typical outcome. Transvestitism is distinguished by the lack of feminine mannerisms and interests both in current and past history.

Treatment is not often desired, since aside from the peer ostracism most of these adolescents do not regard their behavior as problematic. Some adolescents choose to work on reducing their mannerisms with the aim of making themselves less obvious targets for teasing; assertiveness training and group exposure designed to improve social skills with same-sexed peers can be helpful. Very few are candidates for individual psychotherapy, although in particularly motivated or distressed adolescents this intervention may lead to an exploration of their identity as a male and ultimately allow them to look at the factors that may influence their sexual object choice.

CASE 3

A 13-year-old boy was referred for evaluation at the request of the school because of daydreaming in class, teasing by peers, and refusal to participate in gym. The patient came to the clinic with his mother and younger sister, both of whom described the patient as "nice and quiet." All agreed that the boys in his class were unfair and rough. There was little acknowledgement that the boy's effeminate behaviors were the reason for his ostracism by peers.

The patient expressed frustration at the way he was treated by classmates but said he did not really care. His best friend was a girl in his apartment building with whom he would spend long hours listening to records and talking. He was not aware of sexual feelings toward either boys or girls. When asked what he daydreamed about, he divulged fantasies of being a rich and famous entertainer. He enjoyed watching soaps and sitcoms on television. He denied concerns about himself, his family, or his father, who had left the family several years previously.

The patient was offered individual counseling to help him deal with his effeminate mannerisms, which were believed to be the cause of the peer ostracism. The patient and family declined help.

Transsexual

Approximately one fourth of the adolescents seen in our clinic present with a request for sex reassignment (median age, 15.8 years). As with the adult transsexual population, many of the adolescents appear to wish for sex reassignment in order to deal with unacceptable homosexual feelings. Some of these persons will, with support, accept themselves as homosexuals and relinquish the cross-sex wish. Others, despite therapy, will decide that, no matter why they feel the way they do, being able to "be" who they feel they are inside is the only way they can live comfortably.

Most adolescents who present with the desire for sex reassignment have a history of early cross-gender behaviors and would meet the *DSM-III-R* criteria for GIDC. Those adolescents with the most persistent desire for sex reassignment have experienced more parental tolerance of cross-gender behaviors. This lack of discouragement by parents may have allowed these persons to develop a cross-gender sense of self such that these adolescents cannot imagine life in any form other than as the opposite sex. These adolescents manifest significant difficulties with depression and are at risk for suicide. Assessment should include exploration of the reasons for reassignment, sexual experience (including erotic fantasy), and, if sexually active, whether they derive pleasure from their genitals. If these adolescents are persistent in their cross-sex wishes, management becomes the same as that of the adult transsexual (Steiner 1985).

CASE 4

A 14-year-old girl was referred to the clinic by a community psychiatrist with the presenting concern of the belief that she should have a sex reassignment. The patient was the younger of two children from an immigrant family, the elder sibling being a brother. Her father brought her to the clinic, hoping that she would be talked out of this idea. Thoughts about being the opposite sex were of long standing but had become pressing over the previous 2 years and seemed connected with the awareness of intense feelings of attraction toward a neighborhood girl. Earlier history of cross-gender behaviors was difficult to elicit because the father was not a good historian and the patient was unwilling to recall her past. Physical examination revealed no abnormalities nor history of genital anomalies; she was, at the time of assess-

ment, moderately well developed pubertally, having begun her menses 2 years earlier.

A family interview was accomplished with some difficulty since the father could not see the point of his wife coming to the assessment. A story evolved of long-standing marital conflicts, with the mother being chronically depressed and the father having multiple affairs and never being home. The patient complained of the way her mother was treated by her father but also complained of the family expectation that she should pick up after her brother. It was clear that, in the patient's eyes, being female in this family meant being depressed, overburdened, and devalued.

The patient was seen in individual therapy to see if insight into the reasons for her wish for sexual reassignment would allow any other options. Despite developing some awareness of the underlying reasons for her behavior, she has been very resistant to change. She continues as an isolated adolescent who experiences frequent bouts of depression related to feelings that even sex change is no answer since her family cannot accept that solution. She is, however, unable to see herself as lesbian or heterosexual; she spends significant amounts of her leisure time fantasizing about herself as a male interacting with an admired female. She has begun the process of referral to an adult gender identity clinic.

Homosexual

Adolescents in this category (median age, 16.0) typically are seen because either they or their parents are concerned that they are homosexual. This concern may arise in connection with homosexual behavior or occur when an adolescent experiences unwanted homosexual feelings. Those adolescents who decide that they are homosexual and are comfortable with that decision are seldom seen in the clinic unless their parents can coerce them into coming. Frequently, an early history of cross-gender behavior is reported, although many homosexual adolescents may not have met the full criteria for GIDC. Some male adolescents who experience homosexual attractions have, however, had little earlier cross-gender history except for avoidance of rough-and-tumble activities and competitive sports. Often they become socially isolated in late childhood and early adolescence because of timidity and gradually become convinced they are different. If involved in homosexual activity, some of these persons may become quite confused, feeling some arousal, but also not feeling much comfort with the idea of being homosexual. Normatively, adolescents without previous cross-gender history may experience crushes or intense feelings of attraction to persons of the same sex and not interpret these feelings as homoerotic. Particularly for the anxious or obsessive adolescent, these feelings may become the source of intense concern about being homosexual.

Assessment of these adolescents involves exploration of (1) the extent of their earlier cross-gender history, (2) their present and past erotic fantasizing, and (3) sexual behavior. Persons with an earlier history of GIDC, and present erotic arousal, which is predominantly homosexual, seem more likely to move to a homosexual orientation. For the adolescent who is comfortable with a homosexual orientation but whose parents cannot accept the idea of a homosexual son or daughter, intervention efforts are directed at helping the family deal with their reaction to homosexuality; the aim of this effort being to promote as positive an ongoing interaction between parent and child as possible.

For those adolescents uncomfortable with homoerotic feelings or who experience an admixture of heterosexual erotic arousal or interest, therapy (usually individual) focuses on helping the adolescent understand the meaning of his or her feelings of attraction to same-sexed persons, which may be a desire for closeness and not necessarily purely erotic. For some persons, supportive psychotherapy is directed to help them find what sexual orientation is best. The approach developed by Masters and Johnson (1979) for treatment of homosexual adults can be used for adolescents wishing to establish heterosexual behaviors.

CASE 5

A 17-year-old male was brought to the clinic by his parents after he had acknowledged that he felt "gay." The patient had recently broken up with a gay lover, following which he had taken an overdose of sleeping pills. The history of homosexual involvement emerged during the psychiatric assessment related to the suicide attempt. The patient, a high achiever, had kept his homosexual relationship a secret from his family and friends but following the suicide attempt decided to tell his family, who were puzzled and upset over this.

Past history revealed a history of GIDC, the importance of which the parents had minimized, although indicating their displeasure at his dressing as a girl. The parents' relationship had been particularly difficult and stormy when the child was younger but appeared to have stabilized in the boy's adolescent years. He continued to feel close but uncomfortable with his mother; their relationship in the previous years had been one of intermittent conflict. He felt distant from his father, whom he admired but was unable to talk to. He had difficulty forming close friendships in early adolescence and felt "different" from other boys. He did well at school but always avoided competitive sports. He was seen as a pleasant and hardworking young man who had a few school friends, largely members of a group of high achievers.

On examination, he presented as a bright, articulate young man who was clearly and comfortably self-identified as homosexual. He displayed no cross-gender mannerisms and denied gender dysphoria. His past sexual experiences and erotic imagery were almost entirely homosexual. His worries centered largely on his depression and sensitivity. He expressed a desire for help with his depression but did not wish to alter his sexual orientation. His parents were very distressed at what they felt their son's choice of a homosexual life style meant. Concerns about the Acquired Immunodeficiency Syndrome (AIDS), loneliness, and the "seamy side" of the gay life were paramount. The family was offered supportive counseling with respect to dealing with their son's sexual orientation. The patient was offered psychotherapy to deal with his tendency toward depression.

CASE 6

The patient, a 16-year-old female, was referred by a psychiatrist treating her for depression when she acknowledged that the reason for her depression was the presence of recurrent, intrusive homosexual thoughts and feelings. The patient reported extreme disgust at the thought of being homosexual but could not rid herself of these thoughts. She had had no homosexual experience; there was no earlier cross-gender history. She clearly wished to be "normal" and rid of these thoughts. The patient reported that these thoughts, which had begun 2 years previously, worsened when she would attempt any heterosexual relationship. When not involved in such a relationship, she could be relatively free of homosexual thoughts. This was problematic since she very much wanted to be able to enjoy heterosexual relationships.

Therapy focused on the understanding of these obsessive thoughts (which were part of a poor self-image) along with the building up of a positive, competent heterosexual self-image. Cognitive behavior strategies were used to stop the escalation of thoughts promoted by her anxiety, which then led to a more intense depression.

Transvestitic Behavior

Adolescents exhibiting transvestitic behavior (median age, 15.0) are brought to the clinician when they have been discovered using female undergarments. Often these undergarments are stolen and frequently have been used for masturbation. Occasionally, more often in younger adolescents they may simply be put on or kept near the adolescent, for example, under the mattress. Some report dressing up fully in female clothing and becoming erotically aroused when doing so. For some adolescents these behaviors appear transient, while for others the behaviors appear to be the early manifestation of adult transvestitism.

In addition to the presenting behaviors, these boys tend to have past and present externalizing behavioral symptoms, many of which meet the criteria for conduct disorder. Almost all of those referred have evidence of language difficulties. Some have had long-standing school-related difficulties with formal diagnoses of learning disabilities. Others have obvious expressive language difficulties, which may be clearly manifest in their difficulty communicating (especially around affectively laden material) in the interview. These adolescents do not have earlier cross-gender histories, although some may have shown interest in female undergarments

when younger. They do not, however, display other evidence of being uncertain about their gender identity. When asked about current sexual interests, they nearly always are heterosexual and do not acknowledge any real homosexual interest or arousal. Conflicts with mothers and difficulties dealing with this conflict have been typical findings. These boys have considerable difficulty standing up for themselves, especially in relationship with their mothers, whom they often perceive as impossibly dominating (Bradley and Zucker 1984). Earlier reports in the adult literature that these boys were cross-dressed by older female siblings or other females as an act of denigration have not been found in all samples. The presence of temporal lobe abnormalities in some forms of fetishistic behavior requires that history taking include inquiry with respect to head injury and seizures (Hoenig 1985).

Therapy, when the adolescent is motivated, consists of efforts to assist in finding more appropriate ways to deal with feelings of anger and assertiveness. Counseling is directed at indicating the need to keep separate the development of erotic arousal from the use of transvestitic garments. When practiced extensively with little effort at inhibiting this behavior, a full-blown transvestitic picture with arousal dependent on cross-dressing may ensue. Often warning of this outcome can help some adolescents attempt to contain this behavior.

CASE 7

A 15-year-old boy was referred by the social worker from the group home at which he had been staying for the past year. The presenting complaint was that the patient had been taking underwear belonging to female staff and was believed to have been using it for masturbation. Soiled and mutilated female underwear had been found stashed in his closet. The patient had been confronted about this behavior on two previous occasions with no apparent effect; he was very reluctant to discuss this behavior in the interview.

History revealed that the patient had been placed in the group home at his mother's request because she felt unable to control him. He had had behavioral problems at home and in the community, which worsened at age 12 when his father left the family;

there had been a history of academic and school-related difficulties for many years. There was no history of cross-gender behavior. There was concern that the patient may have sustained some brain damage due to marked physical abuse as a small child.

In the individual interview, the patient was anxious, with some difficulty talking about feelings, but he could acknowledge feelings of anger and frustration because of rejection by his mother. He had never been able to talk to her when angry and felt powerless in dealing with her. He was aware that his use of the female undergarments occurred at times of anger, particularly at his mother; he felt very confused and overwhelmed whenever he felt angry at her. His sexual orientation was heterosexual.

Intervention consisted of individual work with the patient to help him deal with his angry feelings and to explore alternate ways of self-soothing unconnected with erotic arousal. Work with the group home was directed at improving the patient's relationship and assertiveness skills with his mother and helping the group home staff in dealing with the transvestitic behaviors.

References

Achenbach, T. M. 1978. The Child Behavior Profile: Boys aged 6–11. *J. Consult. Clin. Psychol.* 46:759–776.

American Psychiatric Association. 1987. *Diagnostic and Statistical Manual of Mental Disorders*, 3rd. ed., revised. Washington, D. C.: American Psychiatric Association.

Bradley, S. J. 1985. Gender disorders in childhood: A formulation. In Steiner, B. W. (ed.): *Gender Dysphoria: Development, Research, Management*. New York: Plenum.

Bradley, S. J. 1980. Female transsexualism: A child and adolescent perspective. *Child Psychiatry Hum. Dev.* 11:12–18.

Bradley, S. J., Doering, R. W., Zucker, K. J., et al. 1980. Assessment of the gender-disturbed child: A comparison to sibling and psychiatric controls. In Samson, J. (ed.): *Childhood and Sexuality*. Montreal: Editions Etudes Vivantes.

Bradley, S. J., and Zucker, K. J. 1984. Gender dysphoric adolescents: Presenting and developmental characteristics. Paper presented at the joint meeting of Canadian and American Academies of Child Psychiatry, Toronto, October.

Coates, S., and Person, E. S. 1985. Extreme boyhood femininity: Isolated behavior or pervasive disorder? *J. Am. Acad. Child Psychiatry* 24:702–709.

Dorner, G. 1983. Hormone-dependent brain development. *Psychoneuroendocrinology* 8:205–212.

Dorner, G. 1988. Neuroendocrine response to estrogen and brain differentiation in heterosexuals, homosexuals, and transsexuals. Arch. Sex. Behav. 17:57–75.

Dorner, G., Rohde, W., Siedel, K., et al. 1976. On the evocability of a positive estrogen feedback action on LH secretion in transsexual men and women. *Endokrinologie* 67:20–25.

Ehrhardt, A. A., and Baker, S. 1974. Fetal androgens, human central nervous system differentiation and behavior sex differences. In Friedman, R. C., Richart, R. M., and VanDewiele, R. L. (eds.): *Sex Differences in Behavior*. New York: John Wiley & Sons.

Ehrhardt, A. A., and Meyer-Bahlburg, H. F. L. 1981. Effects of prenatal hormones on gender-related behavior. *Science* 211:1312–1318.

Gladue, B. A. 1987. Psychobiological contributions. In Diamant, L. (ed.): *Male and Female Homosexuality: Psychological Approaches*. Washington, D.C.: Hemisphere.

Gladue, B. A., Green, R., and Hellman, R. G. 1984. Neuroendocrine response to estrogen and sexual orientation. *Science* 225:1496–1499.

Gladue, B. A., Larson, J., Bakken, J., and Staton, R. D. 1988. Hormones, neuroendocrine response and sexual orientation in men and women. Presented at the International Academy of Sex Research, Fourteenth Annual Meeting, Minneapolis, August.

Gooren, L. 1986. The neuroendocrine response of luteinizing hormone to estrogen administration in heterosexual, homosexual and transsexual subjects. *J. Clin. Endocrinol. Metab.* 63:583–588.

Goy, R. W. 1968. Organizing effects of androgen on the behavior of rhesus monkeys. In Michael, R. P. (ed.): *Endocrinology and Human Behavior*. London: Oxford University Press.

Green, R. 1976. One hundred ten feminine and masculine boys: Behavioral contrasts and demographic similarities. *Arch. Sex. Behav.* 5:425–446.

Green, R. 1974. *Sexual Identity Conflict in Children and Adults*. New York: Basic Books.

Green, R. 1987. *The "Sissy Boy Syndrome" and the Development of Homosexuality*. New Haven, Conn.: Yale University Press.

Green, R., Fuller, M., and Rutley, B. 1972. It-Scale for children and Draw-A-Person Test: 30 feminine vs. 25 masculine boys. *J. Pers. Assess.* 36:349–353.

Green, R., Williams, K., and Harper, J. 1980. Cross-sex identity: Peer group integration and the double standard of childhood sex-typing. In Samson, J. (ed.): *Childhood and Sexuality*. Montreal: Editions Etudes Vivantes.

Hendricks, S. E., Graber, B., and Rodriguez-Sierra, J. F. Neuroendocrine response to exogenous estrogen in heterosexual and homosexual men. *Psychoneuroendocrinology* (in press).

Hoenig, J. 1985. Etiology of transsexualism. In Steiner, B. W. (ed.): *Gender Dysphoria: Development, Research, Management*. New York: Plenum.

Imperato-McGinley, J., Peterson, R. E., Gautier, T., and Sturla, E. 1979. Androgens and the evolution of male gender identity among male pseudohermaphrodites with 5 alpha-reductase deficiency. *N. Engl. J. Med.* 300:1233–1237.

Jolles, I. 1952. A study of validity of some hypotheses for the qualitative interpretation of the H-T-P for children of elementary school age: I. Sexual identification. *J. Clin. Psychol.* 8:113–118.

Masters, W. H., and Johnson, V. E. 1979. *Homosexuality in Perspective*. Boston: Little, Brown & Co.

Meyer-Bahlburg, H. F. L. 1984. Psychoendocrine research on sexual orientation: Current status and future options. *Progr. Brain Res.*, 61:375–398.

Money, J., Hampson, J. G., and Hampson, J. L. 1957.

Imprinting and the establishment of gender role. *Arch. Neurol. Psychiatry* 77:333–336.

Money, J., Schwartz, M., and Lewis, V. G. 1984. Adult erotosexual status and fetal hormonal masculinization and demasculinization: 46,XX congenital virilizing adrenal hyperplasia and 46,XY androgen-insensitivity syndrome compared. *Psychoneuroendocrinology* 9:405–414.

Rosler, A., and Kohn, G. 1983. Male pseudohermaphroditism due to 17β-hydroxysteroid dehydrogenase deficiency: Studies on the natural history of the defect and effect of androgens on gender role. *J. Steroid. Biochem.* 19:663–674.

Rutter, M. 1980. Psychosexual development. In Rutter, M. (ed.): *Scientific Foundations of Developmental Psychiatry*. London: Heinemann Medical Books.

Steiner, B. W. 1985. The management of patients with gender disorders. In Steiner, B. W. (ed.): *Gender Dysphoria: Development, Research Management*. New York: Plenum.

Stoller, R. J. 1968. *Sex and Gender*. New York: Science House.

Zucker, K. J. 1985. Cross-gender-identified children. In Steiner, B. W. (ed.): *Gender Dysphoria: Development, Research, Management*. New York: Plenum.

Zucker, K. J., Bradley, S. J., and Hughes, H. E. 1987. Gender dysphoria in a child with true hermaphroditism. *Can. J. Psychiatry* 32:602–609.

Zucker, K. J., Doering, R. W., Bradley, S. J., and Finegan, J. K. 1982. Sex-typed play in gender-disturbed children: A comparison to sibling and psychiatric controls. *Arch. Sex. Behav.* 11:309–321.

Zucker, K. J., Finegan, J. K., Doering, R. W., and Bradley, S. J. 1983. Human figure drawings of gender-problem children: A comparison to sibling, psychiatric and normal controls. *J. Abnorm. Child Psychol.* 11:287–298.

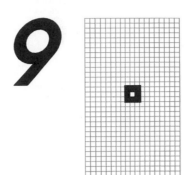

Psychosomatic Illness in Children and Adolescents

ELAINE DAVIDSON NEMZER, M.D.

Medical science has long recognized that psychosocial and emotional factors can lead to the development of physical symptoms. All disorders, from cancer and the common cold to anorexia nervosa and conduct disorders, have biological, psychological, and sociocultural components. These components play a role in the initiation, exacerbation, and/or maintenance of the disorder. The relative contribution of each will vary from disorder to disorder, between persons with the same disorder, and in the same person over time.

The interaction between mind and body is complex. Psychogenic factors can produce or exacerbate organic disease states. Conversely, organic disease, especially in children, often results in secondary emotional problems and family disturbance. Given the complexity of the interaction between biological and psychosocial factors, it is not surprising that psychosomatic illnesses in children and adolescents are relatively common disorders.

DEFINITIONS

A disorder is called "psychosomatic" if psychological factors contribute significantly to the development, exacerbation, or maintenance of a physical symptom or disorder.

There are three main categories of psychosomatic illness described in the *Diagnostic and Statistical Manual of Mental Disorders*, third edition, revised *(DSM-III-R)*. In all three, there are prominent physical symptoms associated with significant psychological components (Fig. 9–1). In *psychophysiological disorders* (psychological factors affecting physical condition) there is clear evidence of organic pathology or a known pathophysiological mechanism that is associated with the symptom. In *somatoform disorders* (including conversion disorder, hypochondriasis, somatization disorder, and somatic pain disorder) there is no identifiable organic cause that explains the symptom and the symptoms are not voluntarily maintained. In *factitious disorders* (including the chronic form, Munchausen's syndrome), the physical symptoms are consciously produced for psychological reasons.

Psychosomatic disorders in children and adolescents are discussed in this chapter. In some disorders the general diagnostic criteria are modified to fit the different ways that these disorders present in children and adolescents.

ETIOLOGY

Several theories have been developed regarding the etiology of psychosomatic disorders. The biological model, psychodynamics, theory of personality types, learning theory, emotions and communication, and family systems model are discussed. These paradigms should not be seen as mutually exclu-

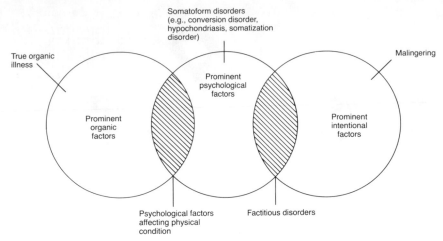

Figure 9–1. DSM-III-R disorders with physical symptoms.

sive. Rather, they are different factors that may interact in a given patient to produce psychosomatic illness.

Biological Model

There is clear evidence that genetic factors contribute to vulnerability to many physical conditions. Temperamental and constitutional characteristics also predispose persons to various disorders. However, the expression of these vulnerabilities may depend on environmental factors. The tendency to gastric hypersecretion may only manifest as an ulcer in an adolescent undergoing emotional stress.

It is well known that emotions can influence many biological indices, especially those controlled by the autonomic nervous system. These include heart rate, blood pressure, respiratory rate, and galvanic skin response. Emotional state is known to alter brain wave patterns. Less recognized is the effect of emotional state on other biological parameters such as blood sugar levels, growth hormone levels, and clotting factors.

The hypothalamic-pituitary-adrenal cortical axis is one pathway that responds to physical and emotional stress by hormonal changes. Chronic alterations of this pathway are proposed to lead to organ damage or dysfunction. This could explain the psychosomatic aspect of certain diseases such as ulcerative colitis, rheumatoid arthritis, and diabetes mellitus.

Research has uncovered associations between acute and chronic stress and immunologic changes (Calabrese et al. 1987). These changes could lead to increased vulnerability to infection, autoimmune disease, and cancer.

Psychodynamics

Alexander, following a Freudian psychodynamic model, proposed that psychophysiological disorders were the result of unconscious repression of certain specific intrapsychic conflicts. Although out of conscious awareness, the repressed conflict results in autonomic tension. If chronic, it can cause physiological disorders and an organic pathologic process. The organ system involved would be determined by genetic vulnerability.

This theoretical approach has been criticized. There is little evidence that specific conflicts lead to specific diseases or even produce specific physiological changes. Unconscious conflict is considered to have some role in psychosomatic disease, but further research needs to be done.

Theory of Personality Types

Another theory is that persons with certain personality types are more susceptible to certain diseases. For example, "type A" personalities (aggressive, time-conscious, hardworking) are believed to be more prone to heart disease. Depressed persons, who deny or repress emotions, may be at higher risk for cancer.

This approach has not found specific, identifiable personality characteristics in children prone to develop psychosomatic disorders. It is especially difficult in children to identify premorbid personality traits from those characteristics that are reactions to illness or stress.

Learning Theory

Learning theory has been applied to the etiology and maintenance of psychosomatic disorders. Both classical and operant conditioning may be involved. An example of classical conditioning is a child who having experienced nausea after chemotherapy becomes nauseated on entering the hospital. An example of operant conditioning is a child who manages to avoid a dreaded math test or piano recital by having an asthma attack. Avoidance of a painful situation reinforces the physiological response and makes it more likely to occur again.

Vicarious learning is also involved in the development of psychosomatic illness. The child who sees a sick sibling receiving extra maternal attention may well imitate the sibling's symptoms. Having a role model for illness in the family has been highly correlated with the development of psychosomatic disorders (Kriechman 1987).

Emotions and Communication

Physical symptoms may be seen as a form of communication of emotional distress. The term *alexithymia* was coined to explain a quality observed in psychosomatic adults, in which there is an apparent lack of the ability to verbalize feelings. Emotional distress becomes manifested in physical symptoms.

This theory, while having much intrinsic appeal, has not been found applicable to all psychosomatic patients. Many patients with psychosomatic illness can communicate their emotional distress quite clearly. On the other hand, some persons with alexithymia never develop a psychosomatic illness (Kaplan and Sadock 1985).

Children, by virtue of their developmental stage, have concrete thinking and a limited vocabulary for expressing emotional needs. The symptom-as-communication concept may have special applicability to young children.

Family Systems Model

The family systems model to describe psychosomatic illness in children was first proposed by Minuchin (1975). In family systems theory, the child and his or her illness are viewed in the context of a family network with reciprocal interactions. According to Minuchin, certain types of family functioning are associated with the initiation and maintenance of psychosomatic symptoms in children. In addition, the child's symptoms play a role in maintaining family homeostasis. Patterns of family interaction reinforce somatization. Three factors are believed to be necessary for the development of severe psychosomatic illness:

1. The child has a physiological predisposition for or existing organ dysfunction.
2. The family manifests four specific transactional patterns: enmeshment, overprotection, rigidity, and lack of conflict resolution.
3. The sick child and his or her illness enable the family to avoid conflict.

Enmeshment is a pattern of family interaction in which family members are excessively "close" and too involved in each other's activities. Individual boundaries and identities are blurred. Little respect is given for privacy. Overprotection is evident in a family system where the members show a high degree of concern for each other's health and safety. This excessive concern is not limited to the ill child. All family members tend to worry too much about each other's welfare. Rigidity as a familial trait is manifest in the strong aversion to change. Transition points such as a child attaining school age or reaching adolescence are usually accompanied in healthy families by adjustment in rules, privileges, and responsibilities. Pathologically rigid families find it very difficult to alter their patterns of interaction to allow for age-appropriate change and increased autonomy. Lack of conflict resolution is another characteristic of families with a psychosomatically ill child. These families have a low tolerance for conflict. Since they find even low levels of conflict unbearable, much energy is devoted to denying or avoiding issues of conflict. As a result, conflict is rarely resolved. The child's illness or symptom is reinforced because it provides a powerful means to avoid conflict. This reinforcement is believed to be a major factor in maintaining the symptom.

The family systems model of psychosomatic illness in children has many ramifications for treatment, which will be discussed in a later section of this chapter.

EPIDEMIOLOGY

There are few studies that document the incidence or prevalence of psychosomatic disorders in children. In a multicenter study involving primary care facilities, Starfield and co-workers (1980) found that 8% to 10% of outpatient pediatric visits were for some form of psychosomatic condition. That study also found a higher prevalence of psychosomatic illness among children from lower socioeconomic groups.

Conversion disorder has been estimated to occur in 4% to 8% of inpatient pediatric referrals to child psychiatry (Folstein 1986). Although there is a predominance of females among adults and adolescents diagnosed with conversion disorder, most studies find an approximately equal sex distribution among childhood cases (Williams 1985).

CLINICAL PICTURE

Psychological Factors Affecting Physical Condition

Certain physical illnesses and disorders have long been recognized as having close links between emotional states and psychosocial factors and the course of the disorder. These disorders include eating disorders (e.g., failure to thrive, obesity, bulimia), bronchial asthma, tension headache, gastric ulcers, epilepsy, diabetes mellitus, ulcerative colitis, Crohn's disease, and migraine. These disorders were called "psychophysiological disorders" in the *DSM-II*. In the *DSM-III*, the term was replaced by *psychological factors affecting physical condition*. The physical condition or illness is recorded on Axis III.

One such disorder, asthma, will be discussed in detail because it is one of the most common pediatric disorders with a significant psychosomatic component. Childhood asthma is caused by a congenital tendency toward overreactivity of the bronchi. Periodic "attacks" of bronchial narrowing result in wheezing, respiratory distress, and sometimes death. Asthma attacks can be triggered by a number of agents. These include allergens (e.g., pollen, mites, dust, or cat dandruff), infection, exercise, as well as anxiety or excitement. Some children learn to self-induce attacks by coughing or hyperventilating.

Children with asthma generally do not have higher rates of psychopathology than children with other chronic illness. Some researchers have noted an association between severity of the asthma and emotional disturbance, although this has not been consistently seen. Others have hypothesized that the weaker the allergic component, the more marked is the psychological component (Graham 1985).

Understandably, asthma attacks are frightening for both the child and the child's family. Recurrent attacks engender overprotection on the part of the parents and overdependence on the part of the child. Frequent absences from school and the need, in some cases, to avoid exertion tend to lead to social isolation from peers. Self-esteem often suffers. Age-appropriate developmental tasks may not be mastered, resulting in social and cognitive immaturity. The symptoms may be used for secondary gain (e.g., to control parents, defuse marital conflict, or avoid responsibilities). Often the pattern of family interaction promotes or maintains the symptom.

Somatoform Disorders

Somatoform disorders show physical symptoms that have no known pathophysiological process or that do not have sufficient organic findings to explain the physical complaints. The initiation or exacerbation of these physical problems is presumably because of psychological factors. This category includes a number of diagnoses in the *DSM-III-R*: conversion disorder, hypochondriasis, body dysmorphic disorder, somatization disorder, and adjustment disorder with physical complaints (Table 9–1).

Table 9–1. DIAGNOSES WITH PROMINENT PHYSICAL COMPLAINTS*

Psychological Factors Affecting Physical Condition
A. Psychologically meaningful environmental stimuli are temporally related to the initiation or exacerbation of a specific physical condition or disorder (recorded on Axis III).
B. The physical condition involves either demonstrable organic pathology (e.g., rheumatoid arthritis) or a known pathophysiological process (e.g., migraine headache).
C. The condition does not meet the criteria for a somatoform disorder.

Adjustment Disorder with Physical Complaints
This category should be used when the predominant manifestation is physical symptoms (e.g., fatigue, headache, backache, or other aches and pains) that are not diagnosable as a specific Axis III physical disorder or condition.

Factitious Disorder
A. Intentional production or feigning of physical or psychological symptoms.
B. A psychological need to assume the sick role, as evidenced by the absence of external incentives for the behavior, such as economic gain, better care, or physical well-being.
C. Occurrence not exclusively during the course of another Axis I disorder, such as schizophrenia.

Malingering (not a mental disorder)
Intentional production of false or grossly exaggerated physical or psychological symptoms, motivated by external incentives such as avoiding military conscription or duty, avoiding work, obtaining financial compensation, evading criminal prosecution, obtaining drugs, or securing better living conditions.

Somatoform Disorders
Body Dysmorphic Disorder
Preoccupation with some imagined defect in appearance in a normal-appearing person. If a slight physical anomaly is present, the person's concern is grossly excessive.

Conversion Disorder
A. A loss of, or alteration in, physical functioning suggesting a physical disorder.
B. Psychological factors are judged to be etiologically related to the symptom because of a temporal relationship between a psychosocial stressor that is apparently related to a psychological conflict or need and initiation or exacerbation of the symptom.
C. The person is not conscious of intentionally producing the symptom.
D. The symptom is not a culturally sanctioned response pattern and cannot, after appropriate investigation, be explained by a known physical disorder.
E. The symptom is not limited to pain or to a disturbance in sexual functioning.

Hypochondriasis
A. Preoccupation with the fear of having, or the belief that one has, a serious disease, based on the person's interpretation of physical signs or sensations as evidence of physical illness.
B. Appropriate physical evaluation does not support the diagnosis of any physical disorder that can account for the physical signs or sensations or the person's unwarranted interpretation of them, *and* the symptoms in A are not just symptoms of panic attacks.
C. The fear of having, or belief that one has, a disease persists despite medical reassurance.
D. Duration of the disturbance is at least 6 months.

Somatization Disorder
A. A history of many physical complaints or a belief that one is sickly, beginning before the age of 30 and persisting for several years.
B. At least 13 symptoms from a given list. To count a symptom as significant, there must be no organic pathologic process to account for it, and it must have caused the person to take medicine, see a doctor, or alter life style. Highly suggestive symptoms on the list are vomiting, pain in extremities, shortness of breath, amnesia, and difficulty swallowing.

Somatoform Pain Disorder
A. Preoccupation with pain for at least 6 months.
B. Either no organic pathologic process to account for the pain, or else the pain or resulting impairment is grossly in excess of what would be expected from the physical findings.

*Diagnostic criteria from American Psychiatric Association. 1987. *The Diagnostic and Statistical Manual of Mental Disorders*, 3rd ed., revised. Washington, D.C.: American Psychiatric Association.

CONVERSION DISORDER

The description of conversion disorder, which was traditionally defined in a narrow way to describe alterations of sensorimotor function (as opposed to visceral/autonomic function), has been broadened in the *DSM-III-R*. Children with conversion disorder can present with a mixture of symptoms of both sensorimotor and autonomic system dysfunction (Loff 1970). The symptom in conversion disorder (e.g., temporary blindness, aphonia, or lower limb paralysis) classically was thought of as an unconscious intrapsychic conflict, wish, or need, which has been "converted" to a somatic manifestation. The symptom provides both primary and secondary gain in that it keeps the underlying conflict from conscious awareness (minimizing anxiety) and provides escape from aversive activities or responsibilities. An example of this is a teenage boy who both desires and fears striking back at his abusive father and subsequently is unable to move his right arm.

Although the literature on conversion disorder in childhood and adolescents is sketchy and conflicting, a consensus on some of the issues has emerged (Volkmar et al. 1984). Conversion disorders in children tend to occur after a significant psychosocial stressor, often one of a sexual nature. There are usually significant family problems. The presence of "la belle indifference" (inappropriate lack of concern regarding the disability) is variable in children and should not be relied on to make the diagnosis. Many studies have noted the presence of a family model for the illness or disability, indicating that imitation and learning may play a role in the initiation of this disorder. Some conversion disorders develop after a minor illness or injury. Conversion disorder is considered rare in children younger than 5 years of age (Green 1984).

HYPOCHONDRIASIS AND BODY DYSMORPHIC DISORDER

The rapid physical changes that occur with the onset of puberty can be a source of stress for even a well-functioning young person. Early and mid adolescence is associated with an increase in body awareness, preoccupation with somatic concerns, acute self-consciousness, and the tendency to question normalcy of one's body and appearance. This is especially true when puberty occurs either much earlier or much later than same-age peers. *Body dysmorphic disorder* is defined as preoccupation with an imagined physical defect, such as excessive facial hair or imperfectly shaped nose. *Hypochondriasis* is preoccupation with the fear of having a serious illness, such as cancer or heart disease. It is commonly associated with anxiety, depression, and compulsive and narcissistic personality traits (Williams 1985). Clinical judgment is needed to differentiate between normally heightened adolescent somatic preoccupation, hypochondriasis, and body dysmorphic disorder.

SOMATIZATION DISORDER

Somatization disorder is characterized by recurrent multiple somatic complaints over several years' duration, which are not explainable by a physical disorder. These complaints are usually presented in a dramatic and exaggerated way and often include those of a reproductive and sexual nature. *DSM-III-R* criteria require 13 symptoms from a defined list. Although the characteristic symptoms usually begin during adolescence, the full criteria are not usually met until early adulthood (Cloninger 1986).

There has been controversy over whether somatization disorder can be diagnosed in prepubertal children. There is at least one series of case reports (Livingston and Martin-Connici 1985) that supports the validity of prepubertal diagnosis. Adoption and family studies suggest that both genetic and environmental factors contribute to the risk of developing somatization disorder. There are genetic links to antisocial and hysterical personality disorder and alcoholism. Somatization disorder is also associated with histrionic personality (Cloninger 1986).

ADJUSTMENT DISORDER WITH PHYSICAL COMPLAINTS

Adjustment disorder with physical complaints is diagnosed when there is an acute overwhelming stressor that is an obvious precipitating factor in the onset of physical symptoms and another diagnosis (e.g., conversion disorder) is not appropriate. This is believed to be common in children and adolescents and may not be associated with significant individual or family problems. The development of unexplained stomachaches by a child shortly after a move to a new town is a typical example of this disorder.

Factitious Disorder

Factitious disorder is the diagnosis given to a usually confusing clinical presentation: a patient who seems to be cooperative with medical treatment actually is inducing the signs and symptoms of the illness. Examples of this behavior have included injecting fecal material under the skin to produce abscesses, putting blood (from a pricked finger) into a urine specimen to simulate hematuria, rubbing a thermometer to increase the apparent temperature, and ingesting toxic substances. Unlike malingering, in factitious disorder there is no obvious recognizable goal (other than to maintain the patient role). Chronic factitious disorder (Munchausen's syndrome) can have onset in adolescence, but it is not often diagnosed until adulthood. The childhood history often reveals severe abuse, neglect, and frequent abandonment. There is often the history of a childhood illness or injury that required a hospital stay. Psychological motives hypothesized to be underlying this disorder include striving for nurturance, need for control, and relief of guilt. A person with Munchausen's syndrome has frequent hospitalizations and usually undergoes multiple surgical procedures. There is often a concurrent histrionic or borderline personality disorder.

Factitious disorder by proxy describes the situation in which a parent or caregiver induces illness in a child. There is no obvious recognizable goal or incentive. The parent, who often seems loving and devoted, is later found to have a severe character disorder. The use of a sick child to gain entry into a caregiving milieu, to re-create a traumatic event, and/or to control and manipulate medical professionals are a few of the proposed psychological explanations for this uncommon and baffling phenomenon (Palmer and Yoshimura 1984).

Malingering refers to symptoms or apparent signs of illness that are voluntarily induced to obtain a recognizable goal. Generally, the symptoms make the goal evident, such as avoidance of work or school or obtaining money, shelter, or drugs. Malingering in adults is often associated with other antisocial behaviors. It is not considered a mental disorder.

CASE HISTORIES

Case 1: A Child With Conversion Disorder

A 10-year-old boy from a low-income rural family presented with a 2-year history of inability to use his right leg after suffering a mild sprain. Because he needed crutches and his school building had three stories with no elevator, he was given a medical excuse from school and was tutored at home. Over the past 2 years he had been hospitalized three times for extensive diagnostic studies at different medical centers. Despite a physical examination that revealed muscular atrophy and roentgenograms that showed demineralization of the bones of the affected leg, no organic cause had been identified for his continued disability.

The diagnosis of conversion disorder was made, and he was admitted to the psychiatric unit of a university hospital.

The psychosocial history revealed that he was the youngest child of a large family and 10 years younger than the next older sibling. The mother was chronically depressed. The father was an alcoholic who was abusive to his wife. It became apparent that the boy felt a need to stay home from school in order to protect his mother from the father's physical and verbal abuse. Identifying the family dynamics, and providing the possibility that the situation could be changed, enabled the boy to give up his symptom. Within 3 days of admission, he was walking without assistance.

Case 2: An Adolescent With Asthma

A 15-year-old girl, the only child of professional parents, presented with a 4-year history of intractable asthma. Despite intensive treatment (including use of corticosteroids) and close follow-up, she had frequent severe asthma attacks. She presented at the emergency department on a regular basis and required frequent hospitalizations. Shortly after an admission her symptoms would resolve. She was a good student but shy with peers. She had few friends and engaged in no extracurricular activities.

A psychiatric consultation uncovered the fact that there was considerable marital conflict between her parents. The mother treated her daughter as an ally and confidante. She tended to overprotect the child and discouraged her attempts toward emancipation.

Therapy was aimed at improving the marital relationship, decreasing the mother–daughter enmeshment, encouraging age-appropriate responsibilities, and increasing socialization with peers. These therapeutic efforts led to a marked decrease in emergency department visits and decreased the need for corticosteroids and bronchodilators. Further hospitalizations were not required.

CLINICAL COURSE

The course and prognosis of psychosomatic illness in children and adolescents vary widely. The type of disorder, the severity, and the degree of psychopathology of the child and family are all contributing factors. Most children with conversion disorder recover quickly, especially if treatment is instituted promptly. Some conversion symptoms remit spontaneously even without treatment. Others may become chronic. Some studies have suggested that conversion disorder in childhood foreshadows the development of other psychiatric disorders in adulthood such as somatization or anxiety disorders (Pomeroy and Stewart 1981). In particular, boys with conversion disorder are believed to develop personality disorders as adults (Chess and Hassibi 1978).

One long-term follow-up study (Caplan 1970) of children diagnosed with conversion disorder emphasizes the need for a careful evaluation. In this study of 28 patients, 46% were found at follow-up 4 to 11 years later to have a medical diagnosis that could have explained their presenting symptom. This was especially the case when visual loss was the initial complaint.

Somatization disorder in children and adolescents usually has a fluctuating course and often develops into a chronic adult form. Thus early identification and treatment are important before symptoms become entrenched. Hypochondriasis also usually has a waxing and waning course with exacerbations and remissions, often persisting into adulthood. These patients are especially resistant to psychotherapeutic intervention. Chronic factitious disorder with onset in adolescence can also be a persistent, severely debilitating disorder with frequent hospitalizations. This prevents steady employment or the maintaining of stable interpersonal relationships. Treatment of this disorder is often difficult. Adjustment disorder with physical complaints, like other adjustment disorders, tends to have a good prognosis if environmental stressors can be ameliorated.

LABORATORY FINDINGS

Psychometrics

The diagnosis of psychosomatic illness depends mainly on the results of the physical examination, on pertinent radiologic and laboratory findings, and on the psychiatric interview. In addition, psychometric tests have been used to identify children with psychosomatic illness.

The Diagnostic Interview for Children and Adolescents (DICA), a structured interview for children and parents, comprehensively reviews the *DSM-III* diagnostic criteria, including those for psychophysiological and somatoform disorders.

The Child Behavioral Checklist, a rating scale developed by Achenbach, can be most helpful when completed by parents (Achenbach and Edelbrock 1983). There is also a teacher's version. It has nine scales, including a "somatic complaints" scale. Those children receiving a T-score above 70 on this scale are rated to have significantly more somatic symptoms than peers of the same age and sex. It is best used as a screening instrument, not to confirm a diagnosis. This is also true for the Personality Inventory for Children (PIC), which is standardized for the age range 6 to 16 and has a "somatic concern" scale (Goldman et al. 1983).

Results of projective testing such as the Rorschach Inkblot Test or the Children's Thematic Apperception Test may add to the findings in the clinical interview but, again, cannot be relied on to make the diagnosis. Projective testing of this type has not provided a consistent set of results and must not be regarded as central to the diagnostic workup.

Biological

When the results of the physical examination and the psychiatric interview strongly suggest psychosomatic illness, confirming evidence may come from hypnosis and/or a sodium amobarbital interview. True organic dysfunction tends to worsen or stay the same under the effects of hypnosis or sodium amobarbital, while psychosomatic disorders can improve or disappear altogether, either transiently or permanently (Weller et al. 1985).

DIFFERENTIAL DIAGNOSIS

Before a diagnosis of psychosomatic disorder is made in a patient presenting with vague or unusual somatic complaints, other possibilities should be considered. On the one hand, the patient might have "true" organic illness in which psychological factors do not play a significant role. On the other hand, the symptoms might indicate a psychiatric disorder such as affective disorder (including depression), anxiety disorder (such as separation anxiety with school refusal), or psychosis (such as schizophrenia). These are considered under the differential diagnosis.

"True" Physical Illness

Many conditions that are entirely organic can present as transient, unusual, and confusing complaints that can be mistaken for psychosomatic illness. A few examples of these diagnostically challenging conditions are multiple sclerosis, lupus erythematosus, and temporal lobe epilepsy. Factors weighing in favor of a physical diagnosis include supportive findings on physical examination and laboratory studies, chronicity, and appropriate concern about the disability. Factors weighing against a physical diagnosis include temporal association with stressors, reasons for secondary gain (such as school avoidance), and the presence of characteristic "psychosomatogenic" family patterns (such as enmeshment).

Of course, true organic illness often engenders apparent secondary gain, is exacerbated by stress, and alters family interaction. Stoic persons can appear inappropriately unconcerned. Differentiating "functional" disorders from organic ones can be difficult, especially since aspects of both often coexist.

Affective Disorder

Affective disorders in children, as in adults, can present initially as somatic complaints. Some complaints are vague: mild aches and pains, weakness, low energy level. Others are dramatic: severe headaches, chest pain, acute abdominal pain. Since these symptoms may result from an underlying mood disturbance, the clinician should perform a thorough psychosocial history and mental status examination.

Symptoms confirming a diagnosis of depression include dysphoric mood, tearfulness, irritability, low self-esteem, guilt, hopelessness, suicidal ideas, poor concentration, lack of interest in usual activities, sleep disturbance, and appetite disturbance. In most cases, if the underlying depression is treated, the somatic complaints resolve.

Anxiety Disorder

Physical symptoms are also common in children with anxiety disorders. Headaches, stomachaches, and even nausea and vomiting can occur in children with separation anxiety when they anticipate separation from a parent or other attachment figure. Overanxious children can develop similar symptoms in situations in which their competence is challenged, such as athletic competitions, examinations, or social events.

The diagnosis of anxiety disorder is generally apparent if there is a temporal relationship between the symptoms and clearly defined circumstances, for example, vomiting in the morning occurring only on school days or headaches only before mathematics examinations. The somatic symptoms resolve when the underlying anxiety disorder is treated.

Psychosis

Although it is uncommon, a physical symptom or somatic delusion can be the presenting complaint for an adolescent with incipient psychosis. The delusional belief that one has a vile or incurable disease may be a symptom of major depression with psychotic features, schizophreniform disorder, or schizophrenia. This kind of delusional belief can also be seen in delusional (paranoid) disorder, somatic type.

Finding other evidence of thought disorder (hallucinations, delusions, inappropriate affect, social withdrawal, and impaired functioning) differentiates psychosis from psychosomatic disorders.

Differentiating between somatic delusional disorder and hypochondriasis may be difficult. It depends on the intensity of the belief and on the fixed nature of the delusional disorder. In hypochondriasis, the person can acknowledge the possibility that he or she does not have a serious illness.

TREATMENT

In nearly all cases of psychosomatic illness, the presenting complaint is a physical one, so the first professional to deal with the symptomatic child is usually the pediatrician or family practitioner. Even before therapy itself begins, proper procedures are needed for diagnosis and psychiatric referral (if appropriate).

Diagnosis

Ideally, the primary physician will take a complete medical and psychosocial history and will perform a thorough physical and mental status examination. At the onset, the physician should explain to the child and the parents that all possible causes of the symptoms will be pursued, both physical and psychological. This balanced approach reassures the patient and the family that psychological factors are legitimate areas of investigation and are important to the diagnostic process. It removes much of the stigma of a psychological etiology and minimizes resistance to exploring psychosocial concerns.

During the diagnostic process, when there is sufficient evidence to confirm a psychosomatic diagnosis (negative workup for physical illness and positive indicators of significant psychogenic factors), this should be clearly presented to the patient and the parents. Obvious environmental stressors should be pointed out, such as school-related difficulties, parents' marital problems, the birth of a sibling, or the death of a close relative. Sometimes merely making the diagnosis and linking it to these stressors can be therapeutic. Parents may have been unaware of the degree of their child's distress. The symptoms might be alleviated by simple environmental changes, such as individual time with a parent, or a change in school placement. Authoritative reassurance and judicious use of placebos may also be helpful.

If motor impairment is present as part of a conversion disorder, then physical therapy and rehabilitation are often used. This encourages the patient to take an active role in his or her recovery and also provides a face-saving way to give up the symptom. If the symptoms are not alleviated by these basic interventions, then a prompt psychiatric referral should be made.

Psychiatric Referral

If at all possible, the primary care physician should continue to be involved in the treatment process and have close contact with the treating psychiatrist. The patient and the family need to feel a sense of continuity of care. Resistance to mental health treatment will be increased if the patient or the family believe that a referral was made out of frustration or that they have been abandoned by their primary physician. They may need ongoing reassurance that psychological factors are underlying the symptoms and that psychiatric treatment is necessary and will be beneficial. This is especially true if the symptom waxes and wanes or if new symptoms develop.

Unfortunately, the diagnosis of psychosomatic illness is often delayed by extensive or repeated workups. Multiple referrals to medical specialists and "doctor shopping" also delay an accurate diagnosis. Any delay can prolong and reinforce the symptoms, making therapy more difficult. There may also be extensive resistance to treatment if the family comes to psychiatric treatment under duress, such as court-ordered therapy due to school absence or through the involvement of children's welfare agencies.

Modes of Psychotherapy

Psychotherapeutic intervention may take many forms. The choice of therapeutic modality (or modalities) will depend on the specific circumstances of each case. Modalities available include individual psychotherapy, group therapy, family therapy, and parent guidance. Individual psychotherapy for psychosomatic disorders is similar to that for other childhood psychiatric conditions. Psychodynamic principles may be used, especially in the case of conversion disorders. Goals of therapy include helping the patient to gain insight into how psychological factors can exacerbate physical symptoms and to identify unconscious conflicts or mechanisms of secondary gain.

Cognitive and behavioral therapies are also important. Many psychosomatic children are shy, unassertive, and lack self-confidence. One goal of therapy is to increase self-esteem. Another goal is to learn more appropriate ways to express distress. Role playing and assertiveness training may be helpful. Eliminating the secondary gain of the symptom is crucial. Providing rewards for mastery over the symptom can be a further incentive to quick recovery.

Educating the child about psychophysiological mechanisms of anxiety, and concomitant physical symptoms, can help to prepare the patient to cope with anxiety. Relaxation training and desensitization may also be useful. Biofeedback has been shown to be effective in controlling some psychophysiological symptoms, such as asthma, or tension headaches.

Hypnotherapy can be a very useful modality in the treatment of psychosomatic illness in children. Children are often considered more receptive to hypnosis than adults because of their greater use of fantasy and increased suggestibility. They also appear to learn voluntary control over autonomic function more easily than do adults (Olness 1986). Hypnosis can be used to remove or alleviate conversion symptoms. It is also helpful adjunctive treatment of many disorders with a psychophysiological component such as asthma, hypertension, hemophilia, and diabetes mellitus.

Group therapy can be a valuable modality, especially if the group members share a common disorder (e.g., asthma, diabetes mellitus, ulcerative colitis, obesity). Group therapy provides a source of peer support and a forum for improving social skills and peer interaction. The group can explore issues such as excessive dependency, parental overprotection, manipulative use of symptoms, compliance with medical treatment, and need for control.

Participation of the parents in parent guidance and/or family therapy is often necessary for successful treatment of all psychosomatic disorders in children. Parents and children need to recognize the patterns of interaction that have promoted enmeshment, overprotection, rigidity, and conflict avoidance. The child's illness can be seen in the context of maintaining homeostasis (e.g., keeping parents together, avoiding conflict, preventing emancipation). The family can be helped to develop healthier modes of interaction, thus freeing the psychosomatically ill child from having to maintain the symptoms to meet the family's needs. Other goals of family therapy include strengthening the marital dyad and fostering generational boundaries. Sometimes marital therapy will also be necessary for successful outcome.

In certain cases, medication for specific disorders (e.g., antidepressants, anxiolytics) and hospitalization or out-of-home placement may be necessary. Removing the child from the aversive environment and ameliorating the symptoms of a specific disorder can be crucial for recovery.

To summarize, psychosomatic disorders in various forms are commonly seen in children and adolescents. Accurate diagnosis of the particular disorder and its contributing factors, followed by prompt institution of appropriate treatment, will lead to the best chance for successful outcome.

References

Achenbach, T. M., and Edelbrock, C. S. 1983. *Manual for the Child Behavior Checklist and Revised Guide Profile.* Burlington, Vt.: Department of Psychiatry, University of Vermont.

Calabrese, J. R., Kling, M. A., and Gold, P. W. 1987. Alterations in immunocompetence during stress, bereavement, and depression. *Am. J. Psychiatry* 144:1123–1134.

Caplan, H. L. 1970. Hysterical "conversion" symptoms in childhood, dissertation, University of London; cited in Levine, M.D., Carey, W. B., Crocker, A. C., and Gross, R. T. 1983. *Developmental-Behavioral Pediatrics.* Philadelphia: W. B. Saunders Co.

Chess, S., and Hassibi, M. 1978. *Principles and Practice of Child Psychiatry.* New York: Plenum Press.

Cloninger, C. R. 1986. Somatoform and dissociative disorders. In Winokur, G. (ed.): *Medical Basis of Psychiatry.* Philadelphia: W. D. Saunders Co.

Folstein, S. E. 1986. Emotional disorders in children. In Winokur, G. (ed.): *Medical Basis of Psychiatry.* Philadelphia: W. B. Saunders Co.

Goldman, J., Stein, C. L. E., and Guerry, S. 1983. *Psychological Methods of Child Assessment.* New York: Brunner/Mazel.

Graham, P. F. 1985. Psychosomatic relationships. In Rutter, M., and Hersov, L. (eds.): *Child and Adolescent Psychiatry: Modern Approaches,* 2nd. ed. Oxford: Blackwell Scientific Publications.

Green, M. 1984. *Ambulatory Pediatrics.* Philadelphia: W. B. Saunders Co.

Kaplan, H. I., and Sadock, B. J. (eds.). 1985. *Comprehensive Textbook of Psychiatry,* 4th. ed. Baltimore: Williams & Wilkins.

Kriechman, A. 1987. Siblings with somatoform disorder in childhood and adolescence. *J. Am. Acad. Child Psychiatry* 2:226–231.

Livingston, R., and Martin-Connici, C. 1985. Multiple somatic complaints and possible somatization disorder in prepubertal children. *J. Am. Acad. Child Psychiatry* 24:603–607.

Loof, D. H. 1970. Psychophysiological and conversion reactions in children. *J. Am. Acad. Child Psychiatry* 9:318–331.

Minuchin, S. et al. 1975. A conceptual model of psychosomatic illness in children. *Arch. Gen. Psychiatry* 32:1031–1038.

Olness, K. N. 1986. Hypnotherapy in children: New

approach to solving common pediatric problems. *Post-grad. Med.* 79:95–105.

Palmer, A., and Yoshimura, G. J. 1984. Munchausen syndrome by proxy. *J. Am. Acad. Child Psychiatry* 23:503–508.

Pomeroy, J. C., and Stewart, M. A. 1981. Conversion symptoms. In Stewart, G. (ed.): *Behavioral Problems in Childhood: A Primary Care Approach.* New York: Harcourt Brace Jovanovich.

Starfield, B., Gross, E., and Wood, M. 1980. Psychosocial and psychosomatic diagnoses in primary care of children. *Pediatrics* 66:159–166.

Volkmar, F. R., Poll, J., and Lewis, M. 1984. Conversion reactions in childhood and adolescence. *J. Am. Acad. Child Psychiatry* 23:424–430.

Weller, E. B., Weller, R. A., and Fristad, M. A. 1985. Use of sodium amytal interviews in prepubertal children: Indications, procedure and clinical utility. *J. Am. Acad. Child Psychiatry* 24:747–749.

Williams, D. T. 1985. Somatoform disorders. In Shaffer, D., Ehrhardt, A. A., and Greenhill, L. L. *The Clinical Guide to Child Psychiatry.* New York: Free Press.

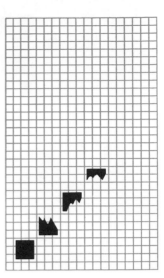

Two

DISRUPTIVE BEHAVIOR DISORDERS

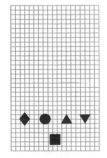 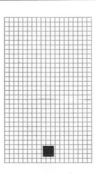 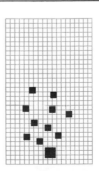 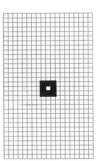

Attention-Deficit Hyperactivity Disorder in Children

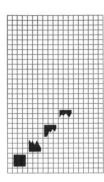

10

LAURENCE L. GREENHILL, M.D.

Over the past 25 years in the United States attention-deficit disorder has grown into one of the most used clinical concepts in child psychiatry. This disorder has appeared under a number of different aliases, including hyperkinesis, hyperkinetic syndrome, minimal brain dysfunction (MBD) (Wender 1971), attention-deficit syndrome with hyperactivity (ADDH), and now attention-deficit hyperactivity disorder (ADHD) (American Psychiatric Association 1987) (Table 10–1). One cannot assume that these terms are synonymous, having been based on different concepts of the dysfunction that emerged at different periods in the development of child psychiatry. Indeed, one study indicates that different populations are chosen when ADDH and ADHD are used. As a result, this chapter will use the abbreviation appropriate to the work being cited.

For the clinician, however, any treatment suggestions in this chapter will use the latest ADHD criteria for case selection. Case histories, global rating forms, structured interview techniques, and behavioral observation clues are presented to help identify these children and track their progress in treatment.

DEFINITION

Although some degree of hyperactivity is found in normal school-age boys (Lapouse and Monk 1953), the diagnosis of attention-deficit hyperactivity disorder (ADHD) should be limited to a developmentally inappropriate degree of gross motor activity, impulsivity, and inattention in the school or home setting (American Psychiatric Association 1987). Boys are affected much more often than girls. Girls may present more often with academic underachievement, whereas boys are referred for behavioral problems. Tasks that are sedentary, are repetitive, and require self-instruction (independent classwork or homework) can produce the most intense signs of the disorder.

The *Diagnostic and Statistical Manual of Mental Disorders,* third edition, revised *(DSM-III-R)* (American Psychiatric Association 1987) provides an operationalized definition of ADHD that is directly applicable to patients and their families. Eight of 14 items listed in the manual must be answered affirmatively for a child to be diagnosed ADHD. Most of these items will reveal a lack of productive functioning in situations in which the affected child will be unable to finish classwork in the classroom or function smoothly on a sports team. The child's behavior will not only interfere with his or her own goal-directed activity, but it will also seriously interfere with others.

ETIOLOGY AND PATHOGENESIS

Brain Damage

Although the ADHD syndrome presents as a classroom behavioral disorder, the con-

Dimension	MBD	Hyperkinetic Syndrome	ADDH	ADHD
DSM version	None (1971)	*DSM-II* (1965)	*DSM-III* (1980)	*DSM-III-R* (1987)
Duration of problem criterion	None	None	6 months	6 months
Onset criterion	None	None	None	Before age 7
Operationalized criteria	None	None	Yes	Yes
Signs of disorder (must be present in several situations?)	No	No	No	No
Exclusion criteria	No	No	Mental retardation; schizophrenia; mania	Mental retardation severe; schizophrenia; mania
Concept	Polythetic: 7 to 14 different problem areas: learning disability, clumsy, handwriting, family history, etc.	Polythetic: 7 to 14 different problem areas: learning disability, clumsy, handwriting, family history, etc.	Polythetic: 3 areas: attention, impulsivity, hyperactivity; multiaxial	Strict count 8/14 questions answered yes; multiaxial
Severity	No measure	No measure	No measure	Yes, plus Global Assessment Score, Axis V
Problems with system	Overinclusive	Overinclusive	Specific, but dimensions not empirical	Overinclusive
Arena of dysfunction (primary)	School, home	School, home	School	School

Table 10–1. COMPARISON OF VARIOUS DIAGNOSES OF HYPERACTIVITY

dition was first classified often as a medical disorder of the central nervous system. More recently, a diverse group of classroom misbehaviors were merged under a common etiologic rubric called minimal brain dysfunction (MBD) (Wender 1971). In a critique, Shaffer and Greenhill (1979) found the concept of MBD conceptually weak for lack of diagnostic specificity. It was overinclusive, because it identified a widely diverse and heterogeneous group of children quite dissimilar in their etiologic precedents and current clinical features. The MBD criteria were too broad to help identify a common etiology, a single response to treatment, and an outcome for both treated and untreated groups with acceptable levels of specificity and sensitivity. In addition, MBD implied direct damage to the brain, an unproven etiologic mechanism of brain dysfunction, which caused a very broad type of behavioral dysfunction. This produced very poor construct validity.

A specific etiologic link between frank brain damage and the hyperkinetic syndrome has not been supported by diverse lines of evidence. Factor-analytical studies failed to find relationships between overactivity or inattention and brain damage. Population surveys (Rutter et al. 1970) and direct measurement studies of brain-damaged children have shown no disproportionate incidence of inattention, motor activity, or impulsiveness in brain-damaged children over rates seen in children with psychiatric disorders without brain damage.

Environmental Causation

Social disadvantage, large family size, and overcrowding have been associated with the overactive and inattentive signs of the hyperkinetic syndrome (Rutter et al. 1970). These social factors have broad etiologic influences on behavior, which may greatly affect outcome whether the child is treated or not. The efficacy of drug treatment or special classroom placement can also be hampered by poverty, overcrowding, and large family size. These factors should be inquired about during any diagnostic inquiry.

Catecholamine Hypothesis

Biochemical models of ADHD have been the driving force behind a number of psychopharmacological investigations (Zametkin and Rapoport 1987). In order to bring together observations from the basic sciences, the hyperactive behavior of these children, and the beneficial effects of dopamine agonists (dextroamphetamine and methylphenidate), an etiologic dopamine hypothesis of this disorder has been formulated (Wender 1971). This, in turn, has promoted the search for an animal model, involving biochemical abnormalities.

The dopamine-deficiency model itself has evolved from several key observations. One comes from a similarity between animal operant conditioning and the presence or absence of prosocial behavior in the school-age child (Wender 1971). Another is the demonstration of animal hyperkinesis after treatment with a neuronal toxin, 6-hydroxy-dopamine (6-OHDA), which destroys dopamine neurons and lowers intrasynaptic dopamine concentrations in rodent cortex.

Some investigators have been concerned that children with ADHD, who may have such postsynaptic denervation hypersensitivity, may show side effects of amphetamine overdosage at lower oral intake than other children, including dyskinesias, tics, and psychoses. Increased sensitivity, with the development of stereotyped behavior, to the same dose of methylphenidate has been observed in guinea pigs and in one patient, suggesting that there may be a kindling effect with these dopaminergic drugs. Sokol points out that hyperkinesis has been associated with dopamine system hyperfunctioning, and hypokinesis with decreased dopamine system functioning. Seamens (pers. com. 1987) noted that the relatively low doses of stimulant required to produce control in behavior suggests that stimulants may exert their action on the dopamine system through an inhibitory feedback loop involving dopamine autoreceptor terminals on the presynaptic neuron.

The dopamine deficiency model predicts certain findings in ADHD children. First, one would expect low concentrations of dopamine, either as abnormal dopamine turnover in the central nervous system or low dopamine concentrations in cerebrospinal fluid (CSF). A relative deficiency in intrasynaptic dopamine concentrations would produce a denervated, supersensitive postsynaptic dopamine receptor, resulting in an enhanced behavioral response to amphetamine. Second, dopamine agonists should produce clinical improvement while dopamine antagonists should worsen clinical behavior.

Actual psychopharmacologic research, however, has not supported the dopamine hypothesis of ADHD. No other laboratory beside Shaywitz's has reported abnormally low homovanillic acid concentrations in the central nervous system. Although the stimulants are dopamine agonists, simply increasing central nervous system dopamine concentrations does not alleviate the clinical syndrome. Experimental trials with pure dopamine agonists such as carbidopa/levodopa and piribedil only make ADHD children nauseated without decreasing their activity or increasing their attention span. The dopamine agonist amantadine, given in doses of 200 mg/day, produced no significant improvement in nine children with ADHD. As a corollary, the dopamine-deficiency hypothesis predicts that dopamine-blocking drugs should increase the target signs of the disorder, when, in fact, these drugs actually improve the children's overactive and impulsive behaviors (Gittelman-Klein et al. 1980a) and may be additive when combined with methylphenidate. At the low doses of antipsychotics used in clinical practice with children with ADHD the noradrenergic blockade of these drugs may be the main action, not dopaminergic blockade (Zametkin and Rapoport 1987).

The other primary catecholamine implicated in the etiology of ADHD is norepinephrine. Drugs that positively affect children with ADHD alter the primary metabolite of norepinephrine, 3-methoxy-4-hydroxyphenyl-glycol (MHPG). Both dextroamphetamine and desipramine reliably lower the urinary concentration of MHPG. Yet a number of psychopharmacologic trials have failed to specifically show that norepinephrine is affected selectively during successful treatment of children with ADHD. Mianserin, a presynaptic α-adrenergic receptor blocker, failed to ameliorate the signs of ADHD in five males, despite the fact that plasma levels of norepinephrine were increased. Clonidine, an α-adrenergic, presynaptic autoreceptor agonist affecting the locus ceruleus, has been shown to be effective in children with ADHD. Although tricyclic antidepressants affect the noradrenergic system, they are not as effective as the stimulants. In addition, the clinical improvement of children with ADHD does not correlate with changes in their urinary MHPG concentrations (Zametkin and Rapoport 1987).

The indoleamine serotonin has also been suggested as a possible area of disturbance in children with ADHD. Results of basic studies of animals with altered serotonin have suggested nonspecific changes in levels of activity and aggressivity. Pharmacologic studies in humans, however, have been inconclusive. Fenfluramine, an appetite suppressant that raises then reduces concentrations of brain serotonin, did not prove useful in the treatment of dextroamphetamine–responsive males with ADHD. Only modest changes in school were found in males treated in a 7-day, placebo-controlled study of the serotonin precursor L-tryptophan.

It appears that most of the effective agents used in the treatment of ADHD affect more than one neurotransmitter system. Methylphenidate and dextroamphetamine produce changes in a wide range of neurotransmitter systems. Studies show that all three classes of monoamine oxidase (MAO) inhibitors produce strong ameliorative effects on attention and impulsivity in boys with ADHD. MAO inhibitors indirectly affected the levels of norepinephrine and serotonin (clorgyline affecting only MAO-A enzyme), dopamine (clorgyline for MAO-A and deprenyl for MAO-B), and the β-phenylethylamines (mixed MAO-A and MAO-B enzymes, as suppressed by tranylcypromine). A controlled study (Zametkin 1987) showed that all three drugs had efficacy and suggested that no one neurotransmitter system is either selectively deficient or can be selectively aided during a successful pharmacologic drug treatment program of ADHD.

Food Additives

Feingold originally hypothesized that chemically synthesized food additives could produce disturbed behavior in some children or exacerbate hyperactive behavior in children who already have ADHD. Other workers have criticized Feingold's reports saying they are entirely anecdotal and uncontrolled. As Sobotka noted, two basic types of studies have emerged to examine Feingold's obser-

vation: the dietary crossover design and the specific challenge design. In crossover studies (Conners 1980), carefully diagnosed hyperkinetic children were randomly assigned to either a control dietary program or to a specific elimination diet and then switched to the opposite diet. Crossover studies failed to show conclusive advantages for the elimination diet. A second mode of investigation was to use food additive challenges. Using cookies or drinks supplied by the Nutrition Foundation or by Nabisco Corporation, hyperactive children were placed on long-term elimination diet programs and randomly given challenges or placebo. The concentration of additives in the challenge vehicle were kept low, and very few children showed behavioral changes related to challenge state.

Abnormalities in Cortical Arousal

Cortical arousal problems have been related to the basic mechanism of ADHD and have been based on a large body of literature, including electroencephalographic activation data, evoked-potential data collected on and off stimulant medication, reaction-time studies, and galvanic skin responses. Overall, the physiological data appear equivocal, with untreated children with ADHD appearing underaroused in some studies and overaroused in others, when compared either to normal controls or to treated children with ADHD. Gittelman-Klein and associates (1980a) suggested the relevant aspects of cortical arousal for ADHD may not be testable with present laboratory approaches.

Dysregulation of Attention

A critical concept for the development of a unitary etiology for ADHD was employed in the nosologic conceptualization of *DSM-III*. This model specified that the primary deficit behind all the signs of the hyperkinetic disorder was attentional dysregulation; impulsive behavior and motor hyperactivity were only secondary effects. On the other hand, Gittelman-Klein and co-workers (1980a) found that attention, impulsivity, and motoric hyperactivity are probably independent dimensions of the disorder, with complex, not simple, causal interrelationships. They use the phrase a "problem in the regulation of appetitive behaviors," which, in turn, creates an inability to maintain attention for even a short period of time without experiencing habituation and boredom.

Other Etiologies

Many other etiologies have been proposed for the appearance of this disorder in the school-age population. These include general nervous system dysfunction, chromosomal abnormalities (genetic transmission), and birth complications. Social-learning effects were implicated by other workers, including the traumatic influences of severe family discord.

EPIDEMIOLOGY

Cantwell (1977) accurately points out that the prevalence reported for the hyperkinetic syndrome depends on a number of factors, including the population studied, methods of investigation, and diagnostic criteria employed. In addition, the base rate of motor hyperactivity in normals is high, with mothers reporting overactivity in 57% of boys and 42% of girls (Lapouse and Monk 1958). The same investigators reported first- and second-grade teachers found 49% of boys and 24% of girls could not sit still and a slightly lower percentage had attentional difficulties.

Direct observation methods, such as those used in the Isle of Wight study (Rutter et al. 1970), find fewer children with this disorder than those uncovered by rating scale screening instruments.

When multiple observers or raters are asked to agree on a diagnosis, the numbers may drop further. In some ways, this requirement was generated by the British investigators, who felt the strongest construct validity for the diagnosis would be met if the child were hyperactive in all situations, showing "cross-situational hyperactivity." Lambert and colleagues (1978) found a prevalence of 1% when a consensus among the parents, teachers, and the physicians was required. A study using the Diagnostic Interview Schedule for Children (DISC) and DISC–Parent found only 2 of 144 children 9 years of age who met the ADDH criteria of the *DSM-III* on both DISC and DISC–P, but only 55% of the questionnaires had been completed

(Lahey et al. 1987). Likewise, Shapiro and Garfinkel (1986) found only 2.3% of a rural, nonreferred elementary school population of 315 children met the inattentive-overactive signs of the ADDH disorder when screened using a combination of teacher rating scales, clinical interviews, and laboratory performance measures.

Screening with a single simple teacher rating form can produce much higher prevalence rates for the hyperactive disorder. Trites and co-workers (1982) reported more than 14.3% of a large Ottawa sample of 14,000 school-age children met the criteria of having a score of 1.5 or greater on the Conners Teacher Questionnaire (Factor 4), while the Isle of Wight sample yielded only 2 hyperkinetic children in a population of 2,199 children aged 10 and 11. Other studies, using teacher's reports, have figures of 5% or greater in samples of school-age populations from Vermont, Maryland, and Missouri. Using an abbreviated five-item rating scale, Satin and colleagues identified 294 boys ages 6 through 9 of a population of 1,884 boys (12%); interviews of a subsample of 92 established the accuracy of the *DSM-III* diagnosis with 91% sensitivity and 73% specificity. Wender (1971) believes that clinical samples have an even greater preponderance of children with a hyperactive disorder, making it the most common diagnosis in school referred samples.

Certain biases concerning criteria for the hyperactive disorder have influenced reported prevalences. For a number of years, a number of British investigators suggested that the concept of "minimal brain dysfunction" might be overinclusive, drawing in a diverse grouping of children with all sorts of externalizing disorders (Shaffer and Greenhill 1979). In addition, a number of British investigators used more stringent inclusion criteria for hyperkinesis, demanding that the overactivity be severe and be present across several situations (Schachar et al. 1981; Shekim et al., 1985). Prevalence figures from these studies have ranged from 1% to 1.5% (Rutter et al. 1970), far below the 3% to 5% quoted by American authors. In the United States, both *DSM-III* and *DSM-III-R* allow for the overactivity, restlessness, and inattention to be present in only one situation, usually school. In Great Britain, these children with impulsivity, restlessness, and single-situation inattention might be diagnosed as having conduct disorder. As late as 1986, an editorial in the *Lancet* titled, "Does Hyperactivity Matter?" suggested that the risk for adolescent and early adult life psychopathology may not reside in being hyperactive but in other aspects of poor social and academic adjustment. More recent work by American-trained researchers working in London has suggested that prevalence estimates run higher when hyperactive children are diagnosed using American criteria (Taylor 1986).

The preponderance of males over females with hyperactive disorder is an area of agreement across the various population studies, regardless of diagnostic criteria or survey method. Boys predominate in both epidemiologic and clinical samples, with boy-to-girl ratios ranging from 4:1 to 9:1 (Cantwell 1977). No clear explanation has emerged from any area of research to shed light on this seeming vulnerability of males. Rather, rates of other central nervous system problems predominate in preadolescent males, whether it be retardation, learning disabilities, epilepsy, cerebral palsy, or psychiatric disorders in general.

PATHOLOGY

The term *pathology* denotes an invaluable tool in clinical medicine that greatly assists the diagnostic process. The abnormal tissue change or the result of the blood test or the bacterial culture can help identify the etiology of the disorder. In child psychiatry, *pathology* often has another, less clear, meaning and may refer to the mechanism of the disturbance, the original psychological trauma, or the current trigger for the major disturbance of the child. The most current positron emission tomography results suggest that there may be areas in the anteromedial frontal cortex of adult males who were hyperactive as children that may function at different metabolic rates than in normals (Zametkin, pers. com.). This suggests that brain areas classically linked by Flor-Henry and others with the attentional processes may be dysfunctional. At this stage, however, the results of positron emission tomography provide only a lead for future research.

Clinical Picture

The ADHD child's behavioral traits often seem to be exaggerations of normal childhood inattention and overactivity. These traits unpredictably interact with the environmental setting and are somewhat age-dependent. The younger the child, the more pervasive is the motor restlessness, being somewhat less dependent on setting. The young preschooler rapidly moves about the room, getting into everything in a chaotic, haphazard manner. He climbs, jumps, and runs as if "driven by a motor." Birthday parties and peer-group get-togethers are dreaded by parents because the child becomes wild, driven, and unmanageable if the occasion is unstructured.

The school-age boy shows a wide range of impulsive and overactive behaviors, with large group settings bringing out the most severe disturbances. In class, inattentiveness predominates, for the child often appears not to be listening, to be daydreaming, and/or to be preoccupied while squirming or moving restlessly in his seat. The inattentiveness may seriously degrade the child's academic performance, as evidenced by sloppy handwriting, careless errors, and messy papers. At home, parents accuse the children of "not listening," failing to follow through on even the simplest requests, and being unable to complete homework.

Past history of these children usually indicates long-standing difficulties with impulse control, high levels of motor activity, and disruptiveness in groups. These behaviors represent the maximum expression of the disorder. Yet, the variability of these signs within a given child must be emphasized. In a one-to-one situation with a professional, a boy with ADHD could be calm, organized, and appropriate. On the playground during recess, the same child will also be indistinguishable from his playmates, although the other children rapidly find that the child's impulsivity and inattentiveness make him a poor team-mate. Peer situations involving self-paced work (Whalen et al. 1987) exert the greatest stress. Activity levels in children with ADHD are generally higher, even during sleep. In gym class, levels may be lower, since children with ADHD have trouble modulating their behavior downward (in academic class) or upward (during a soccer game) as the social setting demands. Because of this variability, most school-age children do not demonstrate the cardinal signs of ADHD in every setting (American Psychiatric Association 1987).

The clinical picture of this disorder emerges first and foremost through a history gathered during evaluation. As with epilepsy, the clinician depends a great deal on parents' and relatives' accounts for signs of the hyperactive disorder. It must be stressed that the child will not complain about his or her disorder and will often deny being symptomatic. As a result, the clinician must rely on parental reports, phone calls to teachers, and general observation of the patient in the waiting room and office. Even after gathering a "classic" history of ADHD, the clinician may actually see little chaos and mayhem in the first one-to-one exchange with the child. If the clinician expects "Attila the Hun" to come tearing into his examining room, he will be surprised if he sees a well-related, lively, but not restless, young man with a charming manner. So, how can the clinician make a diagnosis if he or she cannot validate the disorder in the office?

As mentioned previously, the history-taking procedure is critical. Several criteria can be sought out. Despite the changes in the formal diagnostic manuals over the past 10 years, the syndrome has three key elements: (1) a developmentally inappropriate level of motor hyperactivity, (2) inattention in school, and (3) impulsive behavior as regards rule-governed behavior (Barkley 1982). The clinician's history-taking approach becomes optimal when the inquiry touches on the positive signs of the disorder, exclusion conditions, severity measures, associated conditions, and family history. Such information can be best collected if both parents are present.

Positive histories of the disorder in relatives can strengthen the diagnosis, since most investigators agree that the disorder aggregates in families. If asked, fathers may say, "I was just like Benny when I was in the first grade." This yields a positive family history and may alert the clinician to explore the father's attitude about his son's treatment—will he be helpful if he himself had the problem?

ADHD is one of the externalizing disorders of childhood, and its most salient sign is gross motor hyperactivity. This trait may subside at an early age, leaving a child with a developmentally short attention span, impulsivity, and restlessness, so the clinician should begin by taking a developmental history of inattentiveness. The age of the patient

will determine the approach. For the preschooler, parental home observations will provide the best data. Can the child entertain himself or herself for 30 minutes looking through a book or playing with building blocks? Hyperkinetic preschoolers will race through all activities, finishing none, and beg for attention from the parent, all within several minutes.

School-age children display inattentiveness at home by not completing homework or chores or by not seeming to listen. Classically, the hyperactive school-age child forgets what he or she was sent to do. In addition, the child may have difficulty carrying out multistep tasks, such as building models, finishing needlepoint, or cooking projects. During these times, parents will report that they must literally stand over their children, refocusing their wandering attention, or else the task is never completed.

In particular, behavior during homework may be the most distressing of the ADHD child's "invisible handicaps." Even bright children with this disorder report the rapid onset of boredom during homework and a strong feeling that "I work in school so why should I have to continue this stuff at home?" Unfortunately, teachers may insist that uncompleted classwork, an inevitable outcome of the ADHD child's low productivity, be finished at home, further burdening the child with the very tasks that are found to be most difficult. Unsupervised, such a child will start three other activities and end up finishing neither the schoolwork nor the other projects. Secondary behavior patterns often develop around the homework struggle, particularly avoidance routines, such as "forgetting" assignments, leaving important books at school, and even dashing through the homework unconcerned about errors. Parents quickly get discouraged, taking much of their leisure week-time evening hours to hover over the child while he or she struggles with the homework. The parents find themselves checking the work once it is completed and occasionally doing the work themselves.

School provides the ultimate provocative test for attentional problems. Although biased, parents are often capable of rendering a very complete academic history. It is important to ascertain which teachers did well or did poorly with the child and why. The current teacher's name, attitude toward the child, and relationship with the parents should be obtained. Particular behaviors in the classroom that have caused trouble over the years should be listed. Parents can facilitate information gathering from the teacher as well. As part of the initial interview, self-addressed envelopes containing teacher's rating forms should be handed to the parents. Once the teacher has completed these reports on the child, the papers should be returned directly to the clinician by mail. A set of teacher's ratings should contain the original 39-item Conners Teacher Questionnaire (CTQ) and the Child Behavioral Checklist (Achenbach Teacher's Report Form). This rating instrument covers attentional, academic, impulsive, and prosocial behaviors; it appeals to teachers because of its comprehensive view of the child, and it yields a visual profile, akin to the Minnesota Multiphasic Personality Inventory with the scoring sheets containing built-in norms.

SPECIFIC INQUIRY ABOUT SIGNS OF ADHD

Inattention

The *DSM-III-R* attempts to operationalize the concept of inattention, but, to date, there is no widely accepted instrument or standardized procedure to measure inattention. One can only abstract from the excellent work of those who directly studied the minute-by-minute classroom behavior of these children. When a child is inattentive, he or she can neither process the classwork nor rapidly produce goal-directed work without refocusing from another person. These children spend more time off-task and are over solicitous with the teacher (calling out more often or answering questions that they do not understand) than other children. While other children are completing class assignments, very little "product" results from the ADHD child's work, even if he or she is the brightest child in the class. Nothing frustrates teachers more than the marked contrast between the ADHD child's high verbal output and the low quality of his or her written classwork.

At home, the school-age child with ADHD often has trouble listening to adults, often looks away, does not make eye contact, and is restless. The child always seems preoccupied, distracted, or "on the way in a hurry"

to some other activity, even though this is not the case.

The *DSM-III-R* attempts to operationalize these clinical expressions of inattention into a series of helpful (to the clinician) questions:

1. Is the patient easily distracted by extraneous stimuli?
2. Does the patient have difficulty following through on instructions from others (not due to oppositional behavior or failure of comprehension), such as failing to finish chores?
3. Does the patient have difficulty sustaining attention in tasks or play activities?
4. Does the patient often shift from one uncompleted activity to another?
5. Does the patient often not seem to listen to what is being said to him or her?
6. Does the patient often lose things necessary for tasks or activities at school or at home (e.g., toys, books, assignments)?

At best, these questions by themselves will not distinguish between normal children and those with a true clinical disorder. The clinician must be aware of normal levels of behavior in order to use these guidelines, which, unfortunately, the *DSM-III-R* does not provide. In order to make the diagnosis with some specificity, the clinician tries to obtain evidence that the inattention causes the patient serious impairment in academic and social functioning.

Impulsivity

Another key dimension of the ADHD child's behavior is impulsivity. This trait leads the child with ADHD to act without forethought of the consequences; he or she appears to be unaware of danger and of the relationship between cause and effect and shows a willingness to "take dares" other children would walk away from. During the early years, this impulsivity drives toddlers from one toy to the next, disrupting all objects in their path; during school-age years, they constantly interrupt others and refuse to wait their turn. The thoughtless, nonpremeditated quality of the hyperkinetic child's rule breaking often leads such children to get caught "holding the bag," while the real instigators are not caught. With characteristically poor judgment, the child then denies that he or she has the stolen object. As a result, the child with ADHD can get in trouble and be confused with children who have long histories of conduct problems. The *DSM-III-R* uses the following questions to tap impulsivity in this population:

1. Does the patient have difficulty awaiting his or her turn in games or group situations?

2. Does the patient often blurt out answers to questions before they have been completed?

3. Does the patient have difficulty playing quietly?

4. Does the patient interrupt or intrude on others (e.g., butts into other children's games)?

5. Does the patient often engage in physically dangerous activities without considering possible consequences and not for the purpose of thrill-seeking (e.g., runs into street without looking)?

Overactivity

Gross motor activity forms the final part of the clinical triad necessary to make the diagnosis of ADHD. The clinician should inquire about activities in which the child must employ some type of motor inhibition to complete an age-appropriate task. In class, children are asked to sit still, remain quiet, and work; children with ADHD end up squirming in their chairs, humming, making noises, and disturbing other children. When quizzing parents about the less-structured home environment, the interviewer should ask about routine pursuits that are not well structured, such as asking about seated behavior during television viewing or during meals. A more tedious chore, such as practicing the piano, gives even a better indication of ability to control activity. This motor activity makes the child with ADHD so restless that he or she appears to be driven and never tires out. Parents, in turn, are "run ragged."

The *DSM-III-R* asks about hyperactivity by inquiring if the child often fidgets with hands or feet or squirms in seat (in adolescents, may be limited to subjective feelings of restlessness) and has difficulty remaining seated when required to do so.

CASE HISTORIES

The following case history of a 6-year old illustrates some frequently reported findings in the school-age child:

Jimmy was born prematurely with a birth weight of 4 pounds, 2 ounces, at 33 weeks of gestational age. His Apgar scores were good. He remained in the nursery for the first month of life until he gained enough weight to go home. He was colicky during the first few months of life, crying continuously between the hours of 3 PM and 6 PM. He seemed to reverse day and night, sleeping from 4 AM to 2 PM, when he awoke to feed. By 6 months of age, he was no longer crying during the afternoon. By 8 months he was crawling vigorously and putting all kinds of objects in his mouth. His parents were surprised to discover him walking by 11 months, and from then on he was always on the go. In comparison with his older brother, the mother found Jimmy far more active, always climbing, and needing constant supervision. By his second year, he seemed to be ignorant of danger, walking on the edge of counters and hanging from the top shelf of the bookcase. If his mother did not watch him closely in the park, he would wander off. On one occasion, she became involved in discussion with another mother and later found Jimmy on another block, staring in a window and seemingly unaware that he had become lost. Temperamentally, he could be described as a child with a high level of motor activity, fluctuating mood, intensity of reaction, and difficulty adapting to new situations.

Early school experiences did not go well for Jimmy. His day-care supervisor reported that he was very difficult, often fighting with the other children and grabbing their toys. Nursery school turned into a pitched battle between the teacher and Jimmy, who seemed to be unresponsive to her cajoling, threats, and punishments. He would jump up on the tables and throw blocks at the other children when he became irritable or was told to comply. First and second grade went a bit better because he had male teachers, which seemed to help. All in all, Jimmy's mother was not optimistic about third grade, but Mrs. Johnson's classroom appeared to be more structured than other classrooms, so both Jimmy's mother and the school counselor requested he be placed there. This turned out to be a good decision, although Jimmy did have his good and bad days in class.

In his third grade class Jimmy sat near the front of the room, where the teacher could quietly direct him and answer his endless stream of questions. As usual, Jimmy made noise (squirming in his seat, humming, and drumming with two pencils) while the teacher was working at the board. His desk was disorganized, with papers falling out and crayons under the seat that occasionally were ground into the floor. He often did not sit in his seat but positioned himself on his knees and leaned out into the aisle. Mrs. Johnson gave up ordering him to be quiet because threats each day had been greeted with verbal agreement but no change in Jimmy's behavior. She reluctantly agreed with the school psychologist that Jimmy had a "chemical imbalance" and that he could not help his restlessness.

In an attempt to distract him from his humming and drumming, Mrs. Johnson called on Jimmy to come to the board to do a simple problem in addition. He edged out of his seat, brushed against another desk, toppling the books onto the floor. The other student began to protest when the teacher quieted him with a gesture. Jimmy remained oblivious, crawling around and trying to pick up the books. The teacher called his name three times and he finally answered. She reminded him he was to come to the board. He got up, went to the board, took the chalk she handed him, and began to copy the problem. He wrote slowly and with great effort. The pressure applied broke the long piece of chalk he was using. Frustrated, Jimmy yelled, marked up the board, and threw the chalk on the floor.

Jimmy, like many children with ADHD, seems to ignore the "formality" of the classroom. He makes noises, moves around in an uninhibited fashion, and does not seem to be bothered by the teacher's requests, her withholding of social praise, or her threats. Even when the other kids call him names, he seems pleased to get the attention (no matter how negative) and will increase his silly noise-making, prodded on by his classmates. This negative attention-seeking behavior makes him the "class clown."

The adolescent with ADHD may seem to be less jumpy and "motor driven" but continues to be an unproductive student. The academic failure assumes a nasty chronicity by this stage, with school officials and parents angry and impatient with the adolescent's "lack of motivation" and "seeming laziness." Psychological testing done at this stage may report poor self-esteem, chronic anger, and pessimism about the future. Take for example, the case of John, now almost 13 years old:

John was referred for psychological testing after failing half of his seventh grade subjects. The school psychologist was concerned because John had been reported to have looked sad for several days after the report cards had come out. That week the gym teacher found him banging his head against the locker repeatedly. When he was stopped, he said, "My father will be so angry. He's already taken all the toys and

books out of my room and made me stay with a relative when my family went to Florida because of my bad grades. What will he do now?"

John was observed in his history class as part of the psychologist's psychological assessment. He arrived late, as usual. His teacher had stopped making his late arrival a public issue, after John banged his head on the wall while being reprimanded. John sat down and spent longer than necessary rummaging through his papers to "catch up" with the lesson. When the teacher asked for the homework to be passed in, more rummaging occurred, but the homework did not turn up. The psychologist noticed, as did the teacher, when John slapped his own forehead. The teacher said, almost under her breath, "Left the homework in your other jacket again, John?" He nodded affirmatively.

The lesson began again. Soon after the teacher began to read from her notes, John was observed drawing his cartoon figures. He later told the psychologist that he hoped to become a cartoonist as an adult and showed off his drawings from history class. The messy, much erased sheet depicted a birdlike superhero figure firing both his laser pistols at a variety of enemies, who, in turn, had turned a clearly lethal amount of firepower on the bird figure. In any case, John worked intensely on the cartoon and seemed dazed and unsure when the teacher called on him. After stumbling around, he asked the teacher to repeat the question, at which time he answered the question correctly.

The psychologist tested John. The Wechsler Intelligence Scale for Children—Revised (WISC-R) showed a performance IQ of 142 and a verbal IQ of 123, with a full scale IQ of 133, clearly in the superior range. Besides the discrepancy between verbal and performance scores, there was much variability in the other test scores, which the psychologist recognized as the same type of "interest scatter" he found in younger boys with ADHD. The projective tests yielded a number of results. The psychologist interpreted them and noted a good deal of internal loneliness and isolation. John's judgment was found to be faulty, and his major defense mechanism seemed to be denial. A good deal of internal depression and stress was also seen.

John's history revealed him to have the classic signs of ADHD as a small youngster. He was always on the go, was always climbing, and never seemed to listen to his mother or father, even when he was 10 years old. He had consistently done poorly in school; he had great difficulties staying in his seat, paying attention, and following the rules of the classroom.

He had been sent for psychotherapy, but this did little to sharpen his academic skills, because he continued to have problems with teachers and peers. Even so, he seemed like a "happy extrovert," laughing, being the class clown, and denying the negative reports from school. He became less pleased when his classmates stopped laughing at his class pranks about the fifth grade.

CLINICAL COURSE

The clinical course of this disorder has been detailed in the clinical description above. The externalizing aspects of motor drivenness, overactivity, disruptiveness, and inability to sit still appear often within the first 4 years of life and are a prominent feature of the child's behavior prior to adolescence. The inattentiveness and academic underachievement become more evident by the end of primary school. Associated problems with poor peer relationships and clumsiness in athletics also appear about this time. Adolescence for the child with ADHD is marked by continued problems with school; approximately one fourth of these patients will continue to show inattentiveness, restlessness, and hyperactivity by the age of 18 (Gittelman et al. 1985). Conduct problems appear during the end of the preadolescent period and may become severe in adolescence. The hyperactive boy with a "versatile" pattern of conduct disorder, including aggressivity, is at risk for being in trouble with the law by the age of 16. Treatment has been shown to be helpful within the first 3 years if medication and therapy are combined, but longer-term studies of those children treated with stimulants alone do not necessarily show an advantage in the academic area.

The adult outcome, as with many childhood disorders, has been open to some debate. Some of the early retrospective follow-up studies suggested that ADHD was a true risk factor for adult maladjustment. A large body of published work has shown that most ADHD children followed for 15 years or more do not have more trouble with the law or poorer jobs than controls, but the hyperactive sample had an attrition rate greater than 25% (Hechtman et al. 1985). Gittelman's later, prospective follow-up study with controls from a medical clinic had a much higher retrieval rate of 98% and showed that approximately 60% had no psychiatric diagnosis by the age of 18. On the other hand,

approximately 25% of the ADHD sample developed a diagnosis of conduct disorder, although they had originally been selected not to have that diagnosis at the study's inception (Gittelman et al. 1985). The relative outcomes from a number of these studies are shown in Table 10–2.

LABORATORY FINDINGS

Psychological testing can be most helpful in the clinical workup of a child with ADHD. Barkley (1982) suggests that psychometric tests cover four key areas of psychological functioning: language skills, visuospatial skills, sequential-analytical skills, and motor planning and execution skills. Complete testing will also involve tests of intelligence and academic achievement. The test report should give the clinician some indication of the child's restlessness, inattentiveness, and ability to focus in a one-to-one test situation. Among the tests of intelligence, the WISC-R and the McCarthy Scales of Children's Abilities are most often used. Barkley (1982) notes that a discrepancy of more than 15 points between the results of the verbal and performance WISC-R tests often goes with academic underachievement. Low scores on coding, information, digit span, and arithmetic may be found as well.

Although a large number of academic achievement tests are available, many clinicians prefer to use the Wide Range Achievement Test (WRAT), the Peabody Individual Achievement Test (PIAT), and the Gray Oral Reading Test. The WRAT is simple and easy to administer, although it may estimate reading skills limited solely to word recognition and decoding; it may provide some estimate of problems in written expression, particularly handwriting difficulties that show up on the written spelling section. The PIAT goes further, adding silent reading paragraphs for comprehension. The Gray Oral Reading Test is timed and involves oral reading of paragraphs, and as Barkley (1982) points out, will show up word recognition problems, inversions, substitutions, mispronunciations, and other types of difficulties.

Projective tests have been used in many types of assessments. The Thematic Apperception Test (TAT), the Child's Apperception Test (CAT), and the Rorschach Inkblot Test

Table 10–2. OUTCOME: HYPERKINETIC CHILDREN

Study	Number ADDH	Attrition Rate	Age at Start	Follow-up Interval	Prospective?	Controls	Outcome ADHD
Ackerman	23	21%	9–11	4	Yes	Normals	Most well
Blouin	23	45%	9	5	No	Students	Alcoholism
Borland and Hechtman	20	46%	7	25	No	Siblings	Bad grades
Gilberg	39	17%	6	7	Yes	Normals	General ADD, bad prognosis
Gittelman	101	2%	9	9	Yes	Normals	31% still ADD at 18
Hechtman et al.	53	49%	9	12	Yes	Normals	Poor self-esteem
Hechtman and Weiss	61	41%	9	15	Yes	Normals	No difference
Howell and Huessay	102	17%	7–13	14	Yes	Normals	20% legal trouble
Laufer	100	44%	8	12	No	None	39% legal trouble
Loney, et al.	124	8%	8	5	No	None	Aggression a risk
Loney, et al.	22	NA	4–12	9	No	Siblings	NA
Mannuzza	52	2%	9	9	Yes	Normals	Formerly ADDH, OK at 18, males OK
Mattes and Gittelman	84	50%	NA	4	Yes	None	Methylphenidate dose level explains 2% of height variance
Mendelson	83	41%	13	2–5	No	None	MBD, poor risk
Menkes and Rowe	14	22%	7	25	No	None	MBD, poor risk
Minde, et al.	91	22%	9	5	Yes	Normal	MBD, kids repeat more grades
Miller	70	?	5–16	5	No	None	10% risk seizures, psychosis
Oettinger	25	?	5–16	1–10	No	None	Dextroamphetamine shows no long-term growth delay
Satterfield, et al.	110	27%	9	8	Yes	Normal	ADD boys at risk for arrest
Stewart, et al.	83	41%	10	2–5	No	None	MBD at risk
Weiss, et al.	75	28%	9	10	Yes	Normal	MBD more impulsive

(Adapted from Gittelman, R., Mannuzza, S., Shenker, R., and Bonagura, N. 1985. Hyperactive boys almost grown up. *Arch. Gen. Psychiatry* 42:937–947. Copyright ©1985, American Medical Association.)

are often employed. In terms of children with ADHD, these measures have limited value in making a diagnosis or predicting future outcomes or responses to treatment. Some authors do not find these measures useful in making a diagnosis (Gittelman-Klein et al. 1980b). Thus, the psychological measures most useful to the clinician are the "objective tests" that estimate intelligence and academic strengths and weaknesses.

Children with ADHD should be evaluated medically, which constitutes the only formal "laboratory testing." The children's immaturity, motor clumsiness, or academic problems may bring them to a child neurologist or pediatrician, even if the somewhat rarer associated conditions (enuresis, encopresis, allergies) do not. A standard physical exam-

ination might reveal major problems in the sensory areas, since children with partial deafness or very poor vision will appear inattentive and restless to a teacher. Careful neurologic testing may turn up some non-specific signs, such as minor physical anomalies (Waldrop et al. 1978) or so-called soft neurologic signs (Shaffer 1978). Imbalances in reflex findings, nonlocalizing signs of minor choreoathetoid movements, inability to carry out rapid alternating movements, and generally poor coordination have all become known as "soft signs" and are used by certain clinicians to make the diagnosis of ADHD. Soft signs, however, proved to show great variability and interrater unreliability, and, to date, their prognostic significance is unclear (Shaffer 1978).

The child's height and weight should be measured prior to any medication trials, particularly if the child is to begin therapy with stimulant medication, which may cause a temporary slowdown in weight or height velocity. Furthermore, recent concerns about methylphenidate producing a decrease in white blood cell count, in rare instances, makes it necessary to have a complete blood cell count on record before a clinical trial. Finally, it would be useful to have an electroencephalogram on record. As noted by Wender (1971), a positive electroencephalogram does not make the diagnosis of hyperactivity, nor does it predict the response to any particular type of therapy; still, it is useful to identify children with a seizure disorder, because some of the drugs used to treat ADHD may lower the seizure threshold slightly. Other tests, such as computed tomography or magnetic resonance imaging add no useful diagnostic or treatment information unless the neurologist suspects a space-occupying lesion in the child.

DIFFERENTIAL DIAGNOSIS

Age-appropriate overactivity may occur in children who show no impulsive or attentional problems. The high level of activity found in ADHD differs from other clinical states by its intense, non-goal-directed quality. Children who have a co-morbid Axis I diagnosis of conduct disorder will have all the features of the ADHD syndrome, but their high propensity for aggressivity differs from the more typical hyperactive child's behavior. The impulsivity of the conduct-disordered child has more of a calculating, premeditated quality not found in the reactive and impulsive misbehaviors of the hyperactive child.

Children with other psychiatric diagnoses may display the chaotic, stimulus-bound motor drivenness of the ADHD child, yet be excluded from a formal hyperactive diagnosis. Severe and profoundly mentally retarded children may be quite hyperactive but have been excluded by the *DSM-III-R* criteria. Schizophrenic children and those with other affective disorders (manic type) display impulsivity, overactivity, and inattentiveness but only secondarily to the primary illness. *DSM-III-R* also excludes cases when the disorder is of short duration, when it appears after the age of 7, and when there is a clear psychosocial stressor. The negative, uncooperative child with oppositional disorder may also resemble a child with ADHD.

There can be medical problems that may cause a child to be overactive and inattentive that should be mentioned for completeness. Children with poor vision or deficient hearing may show typical ADHD behavior in the classroom. Severe language disorders will produce very aberrant behavior, and, at times, these children can show motor drivenness and severe inattentiveness. Dermatologic conditions, such as eczema and even pinworms, may produce restlessness and disruptiveness in first graders, which may appear to be a pure behavior disorder to the teacher. Even more rare, Sydenham's chorea will generate intense restlessness in children and require careful workup and treatment. Finally, Tourette's syndrome is often associated with a behavioral syndrome much like ADHD; it should not be treated with stimulants alone because they exacerbate the motor tics of Tourette's syndrome.

Studies have shown that adults who had severe ADHD as children can run the risk of showing similar symptoms in their late teens and early 20s (Gittelman et al. 1985). As a result, the concept of a purely inattentive (but not motorically active) "residual" ADHD state has not been supported in the current *DSM-III-R*. In some ways, this cautious approach to adult disorders is justified, because patients with substance abuse are aware that "adult hyperactives" are often treated with pemoline, methylphenidate, or even methamphetamine and will mimic the history and behavior in order to secure stimulant treatment. Second, patients with schizophrenia or schizotypal and/or borderline personality disorders can show all the signs of impulsivity and inattentiveness necessary to fulfill criteria. Stimulant treatment of such schizophrenia-spectrum patients could induce or exacerbate a psychotic episode. Finally, patients with conduct disorders may be brought in by hopeful parents who would like to believe that their children actually have the potentially treatable diagnosis of ADHD, which, theoretically would respond to a course of stimulant medication.

What about the child with attentional problems who does not show the high levels of motor drivenness associated with the ADHD syndrome? The 1980 *DSM-III* allowed for a diagnosis of attention-deficit disorder without hyperactivity. Such children were characterized as having high levels of anxiety and low levels of academic performance (Lahey et al. 1987). Early studies of children with pure learning and reading difficulties suggested that stimulants did not ameliorate the disabilities nor did they necessarily directly boost the remediation process (Gittelman-Klein et al. 1980a).

DECISION-MAKING PROCESS

Historical items can be used in making the diagnosis of ADHD but do not make up all the necessary and sufficient conditions for the diagnosis or decision to treat. The clinician must see the child, speak to the parent, discuss the school behavior with the teacher, and then make the diagnosis. Most clinicians speak with several teachers and review the Conners Teacher Questionnaire prior to any diagnostic decision. The reporting by multiple observers of similar behaviors in more than one situation truly raises the confidence level about the diagnostic process.

The child must have had the problem at least 6 months with the onset of externalizing behavior problems before 7 years of age. There must be no other Axis I diagnoses of severe mental retardation, major affective disorder, or schizophrenia. Eight of the 14 items listed in the *DSM-III-R* manual must be answered positively. Finally, it would be wise to require that the child show these problems in at least two different situations, such as at school and at home, in order to rule out disorders that present in the classroom but are not ADHD.

PRESENCE OF ASSOCIATED CONDITIONS

It is good medical practice to investigate the associated conditions, even though they may not help, by themselves, in making the diagnosis. These conditions can be the source of much functional impairment and, as such, may be susceptible to early intervention. Poor academic performance often accompanies the ADHD syndrome and appears to remain a stable characteristic of the disorder; remedial education may be indicated. Satterfield and colleagues (1980) during a prospec-

tive, 3-year follow-up of children with ADHD, have shown that an individual, multimodal treatment plan involving tutoring and medication produces better outcomes than giving medication alone. Specific learning disabilities may be revealed during history-taking. Questions regarding impulsivity may reveal more fights with peers than one would anticipate in a child who does not have a primary conduct disorder. Poor coordination may also be noted during the interview. The clinician may eventually advise the parents to enroll the child in swimming and horseback riding programs, which emphasize gross motor skills over fine ones. Finally, the clinician may be able to explain the child's irritability and mood lability as an aspect of the disorder, which may be ameliorated by stimulant medication.

APPROPRIATE TREATMENT PLANNING

The timing of the referral should always be investigated. Did the school simply process the referral at the end of a regular marking period as an administrative reaction to a chronic, unchanging classroom disturbance? Did the child's hyperkinesis suddenly worsen with the occurrence of a new stressor at home? Had the school been ignoring signs of serious impulsive behavior until some threshold had been crossed (e.g., setting a fire in the boys' bathroom)?

Previous environmental approaches employed by the school and the parents are critical for treatment planning. Was the hyperkinetic patient referred to a smaller structured class or to a resource room where there was increased supervision? Did the teacher simply move the child's seat up to the front of the class to lower distractions and increase the ability to manage the child? Was the child sent home after becoming too disruptive in class? Was a special working desk with built-in blinders provided to help the child concentrate? Did any of these techniques prove helpful in any situation?

At home, were the parents consistent in their limit setting? Was the household routine kept regular and predictable? Did the parents respond to the hyperkinetic child's behaviors inconsistently, or did they use operant conditioning approaches (time outs and ignoring negative behaviors)?

There is evidence that consistent behavioral modification techniques help a hyperkinetic child behave more calmly at home. In addition, if the child's room is kept simple, uncluttered, and organized by the use of easily accessible storage boxes, the child often will be less distractible.

Previous treatment regimens, both with medication and behavioral modification, must be looked into. What drugs did the child take and what were the doses? The most common reason for treatment failure with medication comes from poor compliance and underdosing. Occasionally, a child receives a stimulant at a young age and shows an equivocal or negative response, only to do very well on the same dose several years later. Tolerance also may explain the failure of previous drug treatments with methylphenidate or dextroamphetamine. Reinstitution of the previously successful drug to which the child had become tolerant may prove helpful if several months off the drug have elapsed.

Side effects can also interdict an otherwise successful stimulant medication program. The clinician should ask about headaches, stomachaches, weight loss, and insomnia. Did the parents become worried about a particular reaction and stop the medication without telling the physician or returning for appointments? Even though a dosage adjustment might have solved the entire problem, the family may have been chagrined about the treatment and not returned for followups with the child's first doctor. In such circumstances, they may initially be reluctant to reveal a former treatment failure.

Previous special treatments are most valuable to investigate. Were megavitamin or special elimination diets employed? Although the research data suggest that the Feingold additive-free diet produces no significant benefits in controlled studies, an individual child can show powerful positive placebo effects, particularly when the entire family rallies behind the diet. If the parents did carry out the full dietary program, it indicates a willingness to follow a professional's instructions in detail, even at some inconvenience to the household.

On the other hand, the phenomenon of compulsively "shopping around," trying a number of new, exotic, and unproven treatment programs in quick succession, may turn up as a "driven" pattern of "help" seeking with certain parents. From the beginning,

the professional must address such a pattern if discovered, but in a tactful, supportive manner. The parents can be advised to stick to the treatment program for a minimum of 2 months before moving on to the next doctor. A written contract may prove useful and supportive in helping them cope with impatience, anxiety, and the pressure for instant results.

Other data can be obtained from parents that will greatly aid the implementation of a treatment plan. Does the child staunchly refuse to take pills, insisting that he or she will take only liquid medications? A chewable tablet, such as is available for pemoline, or a liquid, such as that for dextroamphetamine, may be required. Will the school be cooperative with midday medication and with behavioral modification programs? Another area to explore is the presence of drug abuse in family members. A physician should carefully account for the number of pills prescribed if someone in the household has had a drug-addiction problem. In that case, the doctor probably should begin treatment with pemoline, a medication that is a class IV drug, has no street exchange value, and has low abuse potential.

Finally and most crucial is the parent's attitude toward treatment. Many adults today are deeply worried about the use of stimulant drugs and their impact on physical and neurologic development. Even if questions are not raised, parents should be engaged in an open discussion concerning their attitudes toward medication and behavior modification. Do they fear that such interventions will suppress their child's natural spontaneity, creativity, or enthusiasm? They may harbor fears of drug dependence or addiction, or that the child will develop the habit of turning to pills instead of solving his or her own problems.

The physician will be asked to review follow-up data, evidence of addiction, and signs of "suppressed creativity" in stimulant-treated hyperactive children. Extensive follow-up data from a number of separate, independent investigators have shown no increase in drug abuse in hyperkinetic children treated previously with stimulants. Direct observation studies by Whalen and co-workers (1987) show no decrease in the spontaneous rate of classroom interactions for hyperkinetic children treated with stimulants compared with untreated controls. These facts will prove helpful during discussions with the parents, but, most important, one should let parents ventilate their fears and anxieties concerning drug treatment before handing them a prescription.

GLOBAL RATING FORMS

Conners (1985) has developed several global rating forms for research on hyperkinetic children. One scale, the Conners Parent Questionnaire (CPQ), consists of 93 items, and is administered to patients' parents (Appendix 10–1). It can be useful during history gathering for assessing the severity and variety of a particular patient's symptomatology. Repeated use of this instrument becomes impractical owing to this rating scale's length. The Conners Teacher Questionnaire (CTQ) is also very useful (Appendix 10–2). Factor analysis with principal components analysis yielded four main factors (Conners and Barkley 1985). Since the CTQ appears to be sensitive to drug effects, particularly demonstrating changes in factor IV (hyperactivity), much work has centered around tracking factor IV during treatment. Early epidemiologic work suggests that the CTQ factor IV may prove useful as an early screening tool.

The CTQ may be used in the following manner. Answers to each question can be scored according to item scale scores. A check in the "Not at All" column should be scored as 0, a check in the "Just a Little" column receives a score of 1, "Pretty Much" gets a 2, and "Very Much" gets a 3. To arrive at the factor IV score, just add the weighted scores of questions 1, 2, 5, 6, 14 and 29, then divide by 6 to obtain the average. Since the mean score of the males in the primary school system without psychiatric diagnoses is 0.56 ± 0.65, a score of 1.5 or more has been taken as 2 standard deviations from the norm and held to be significantly deviant. For screening purposes, however, it is probably safer to use a score of 2.2 or more to reduce the false-positive results (Trites et al. 1982). During treatment, a factor IV score that drops 0.5 below the baseline score generally heralds success. One more point: at least two CTQs should be done on the same child during the pretreatment phase. The factor IV score tends to drop spontaneously because of scoring changes that could be mistaken as a treatment response. During longer periods of maintenance drug therapy, it probably would be wise to obtain CTQs trimonthly.

Conners has also developed an Abbreviated Symptom Questionnaire (1985) (CAPTQ) that includes ten items that are common to both the CTQ (items 1, 3, 5, 6, 7, 8, 13, 14, 16, and 21) and the Conners Parent Questionnaire (see Appendix 10–1). The CAPTQ has been used as a repeatable rating scale and has proven treatment-sensitive in controlled studies when administered weekly to parents, teachers, and ward personnel. It can be quickly filled out and scored. Dividing the sum by ten to obtain the average yields a number comparable to factor IV. The CAPTQ probably should be used with parents on a weekly basis during dose-adjustment periods, then trimonthly during maintenance.

Since these rating scales have shown sensitivity to treatment in controlled studies and demonstrate interest reliability, the clinician can employ them as a convenience to attain greater rigor in his or her practice. When the treatment produces a drop in CAPTQ score or in factor IV CTQ score and these numbers remain low throughout therapy, the professional can be confident that this measure is tracking a real change.

AVAILABLE TREATMENTS

Pharmacotherapy

Many different types of psychoactive preparations have proven useful for treating the hyperkinetic syndrome, but more than 31 controlled studies involving over 1,800 children have shown stimulants to be more effective than placebo (Barkley 1982). Stimulants have become the most common form of treatment for these children, inhibiting impulsivity and hyperactivity while generally improving performance on attentional measures (Rapoport et al. 1980).

DEXTROAMPHETAMINE SULFATE

Dextroamphetamine sulfate has had the longest usage, beginning in 1937 with the open studies of Bradley. More recent studies, since 1960, using the appropriate placebo controls have shown this drug to be highly effective in reducing impulsivity and inattentiveness. Available in liquid suspension, tablet, or slow-release capsule (spansule), dextroamphetamine shows a 5- to 6-hour duration of action due to its plasma half-life of 10.5 hours in children. The drug can usually be given in a dose range of 10 to 40 mg/day in divided doses. The stimulant side effects of anorexia, insomnia, and mild increases in blood pressure and pulse rate occur most often with dextroamphetamine since its action occurs throughout the body. Adult abuse of the amphetamine derivatives, particularly methamphetamine ("speed"), and the drug's poor performance in controlling adult weight problems have led to restrictions on use of this drug by the Food and Drug Administration. Currently, indications are limited to the childhood hyperkinetic syndrome and to narcolepsy.

METHYLPHENIDATE

Methylphenidate (Ritalin) has become the most popular psychostimulant used in the United States. The methyl ester of ritalinic acid methylphenidate enters the plasma in minute amounts but is highly effective in low plasma concentrations. The parent compound is metabolized to ritalinic acid in the gastrointestinal tract and the liver. As many as 22 controlled treatment studies have shown methylphenidate to be highly effective in the treatment of children with ADHD and to work in both moderate (Rapoport 1980) and high doses (60 mg/day) (Table 10–3).

More recent reports by Gittelman-Klein and associates (1980a) have shown that parents, teachers, and professionals blindly rate over three fourths of the children as improved while on active methylphenidate for at least 4 weeks. If a favorable response occurs, it does so within the first 10 days of treatment; the clinician can begin most children on 5 mg twice a day, at 8 AM and noon, and increase the drug by 5 mg per dose every 3 days. The dosage range extends from a total daily intake of 20 mg to a maximum of 60 mg. Currently, methylphenidate is dispensed in 5- and 10-mg tablets; a liquid formulation is not available. Twenty-milligram sustained-release tablets, which peak at 4.7 hours and show a disappearance half-life of 8 hours, are now available. This formulation avoids involvement of school personnel in medication administration.

Methylphenidate's site of action tends to be the central nervous system, so that blood pressure and pulse changes are less marked than with dextroamphetamine; still, children can develop anorexia and insomnia on the drug. Tolerance to methylphenidate may develop if treatment extends much past 1 year. This lack of response may be treated with a switch to another psychostimulant.

MAGNESIUM PEMOLINE

Magnesium pemoline (Cylert) is a dopamine agonist with proven psychostimulant effects in hyperkinetic children. A relatively long half-life of 12 hours in children means that once-a-day administration is possible; since pemoline is not a controlled drug, it may be prescribed without the restrictions associated with methylphenidate. Both these features make the drug a promising clinical tool. A large controlled, lengthy study of 238 children showed that pemoline exerts its strongest action from the third week on. Pemoline's dosage has been set by the manufacturer in pills or chewable tablets in multiples of the 18.75-mg lowest-dose tablet. Treatment follows a regimen of weekly increases up to 112.5 mg/day. Children often begin to show improvement at dose levels above 50 mg/day. Some irritability, insomnia, and anorexia may be seen during therapy; rare reports of elevated liver enzyme levels suggest that the clinician should carry out routine liver function tests and complete blood cell counts every 6 months. Pemoline's ability to be given once per day makes it an

Table 10–3. METHYLPHENIDATE: EFFICACY OF TREATMENT

Reviewer	Number or Studies	Subjects (N)	% Subjects Better on MPH	% Subjects Better on Placebo
Gittelman, 1975	5	261	73–94%	Not given
Gittelman, 1980	22	715	30–90%	10–37%
Barkley, 1982	14	866	77%	25%
Cantwell and Carlson, 1978	31	NA	75%	25%

ideal drug for hyperkinetic children who may be teased by classmates for taking pills in school, have trouble with drug rebound, or have difficulty with insomnia from late-afternoon stimulant doses.

OTHER DRUGS

Besides the stimulants, other drugs have shown some efficacy in the treatment of ADHD. Clonidine (Catapres) has been given in at least two controlled clinical studies and seems promising as a drug for use in children with Tourette's syndrome who also have ADHD. It can be used in a skin-patch formulation, but the patient must be watched carefully for allergic reactions. In addition, children with ADHD seem driven to tear off the patches, regardless of their location. Because clonidine has not been approved for children, and because of its marked effect on blood pressure and potential for producing moodiness and depression, children on this drug must be watched carefully. Desipramine (Norpramin) has been considered a useful drug in the treatment of children with ADHD, and recent controlled studies have shown it to be effective for this disorder. It is used in doses of up to 3 mg/kg/day and may be given at night time in older children. Earlier studies have suggested that children with ADHD may become tolerant to its effects. Still, it is a very useful drug in those children who cannot tolerate the stimulants. Carbamazepine (Tegretol) is an anticonvulsant that has received attention as a drug for externalizing behavior disorders in childhood. Unfortunately, there have been no controlled studies of its efficacy in childhood behavior disorders. One report of carbamazepine-induced mania in an adolescent make it, at best, a secondary drug for ADHD.

Lithium has been shown to be useful in the treatment of aggressive, hospitalized boys with conduct disorder, but reviews have shown no particular efficacy of lithium in treating those with ADHD (Greenhill et al. 1973). An early double-blind controlled study comparing amphetamines with lithium carbonate in treatment-refractory boys with hyperkinetic syndrome showed a major advantage for the amphetamines. Still, good controlled studies of lithium in the treatment of children with ADHD need to be done. Deanol has been given in several controlled studies but seems to have minimal therapeutic activity for hyperkinesis. Caffeine does show specific effects on attention span but has failed to control the impulsive or hyperactive behaviors that cause hyperkinetic children to have difficulty in the classroom. According to five of the seven controlled studies, no effect was seen with caffeine treatment.

ANTIPSYCHOTIC MEDICATIONS

Overall, the neuroleptic drugs reduce the cardinal signs of the hyperactive syndrome in children. Studies by Gittelman-Klein and co-workers (1980a) and other investigators have shown that children with ADHD respond positively to antipsychotics, especially in the area of motor hyperactivity. Clinicians as a group, however, hesitate to use neuroleptics because of concerns about sedating side effects interfering with cognitive activities in school and the development of involuntary motor problems. These side effects may be transient, as are the withdrawal emergent symptoms seen with sudden discontinuation of high-dose neuroleptic medication. More persistent late-appearing buccal-lingual-masticatory symptoms have been reported in adults (tardive dyskinesia), which may be irreversible in certain cases and are a reason to be cautious about neuroleptic drug use in childhood.

Behavior Modification

The use of behavior modification to treat the hyperkinetic child has been advocated as an alternative to stimulants in the treatment of children with ADHD. Reasons for this include (1) stimulants do not work in roughly 20% of cases; (2) some children develop limiting side effects, including insomnia, weight loss, severe behavioral "rebound," headaches, and, in rare cases, reduced white blood cell count; (3) some parents do not want their children on medication, no matter how convinced their doctor is of the value of medications; (4) some children cannot take a drug holiday during the summer without ruining their camp stay; and (5) medication has not shown convincing evidence of being able to positively affect grades when the child has a learning disorder or has a long-standing problem with completing homework. Behavior modification may also be an excellent adjunct to the use of medication, particularly in overcoming the inertia certain children with ADHD have about starting and completing work, or to deal with secondary "diversionary" problems in families of children with ADHD, such as extreme sibling rivalry. Gittelman-Klein and co-workers (1980) compared an 8-week course of behavior modification alone to combined medication (methylphenidate) and behavior modification; all were significantly better than placebo. The children on combined treatment were nondistinguishable from normals, while those children treated with methylphenidate alone could be easily separated from nonafflicted classmates. Behavior modification requires much professional time to be effective, which can be costly in comparison to medication alone. Also, the teacher must devote a great deal of time and effort to any behavior modification program for it to be successful, which is not always possible.

Other Psychological Therapies

Psychotherapy has often been recommended for the hyperkinetic child, but there is little evidence to support its efficacy. More focused psychological interventions have included the "stop, look, and listen" approach, used by Douglas et al. (1976), to teach hyperkinetic children to refocus attention and the cognitive behavior modification (CBM) system, as advocated by Meichenbaum (1977, 1979). This latter technique teaches troubled children to use self-verbalization and self-instruction to help themselves focus on the problem and develop better coping styles. Some evidence exists indicating the CBM may be a promising technique because it has been used successfully to treat the disruptive behavior of hyperactive boys, aggressive children, and unruly preschoolers. More recent work (Abikoff and Gittelman 1985) has not substantiated the value of cognitive therapy.

Tutoring and remedial education may help some of the academic difficulties that occur in hyperactive children, but the training does not generalize into the behavioral area. A final approach involves parent education. Many clinicians routinely set up 10-week, 2-hour workshops to teach behavior modification management techniques to parent groups.

PRACTICAL GUIDE TO TREATMENT

Assessment of Severity

The clinician must first assess the severity of the disorder. Then, for those children with the mild form, environmental manipulation would be the first approach. Such steps involve appropriate class placement in small, structured academic settings with a teacher who can deliver a good deal of structured supervision and one-to-one attention. In addition, the parent should be counseled in parental management techniques involving the establishment of a regular, consistent home routine for the child, as well as consistent parental response to good behaviors (praise and attention) and to undesirable behaviors (ignore, take away reinforcer, or use time out). These techniques may be taught in a parental workshop or in individual office visits.

The child might enter into a behavior modification program whose aim is the reduction of certain target behaviors. Parental counseling will also help the clinician evaluate the strengths of the parent–child relationship, relieve feelings of guilt in the parent, and help the parent to view the difficulties more objectively. For those children with a moderate to severe disorder, the treatment plan should be supplemented with pharmacotherapy.

Assessment for Pharmacotherapy

First and foremost, one should learn the parents' attitudes toward the use of medications for their child. An open discussion of risks and benefits might lead the way to a sharing of the parents' fears and misconceptions about drugs. One should also take a drug history, gathering data on past treatment for behavior problems, looking particularly for unfavorable reactions to stimulants, allergic reactions, and a history of severe exacerbation of hyperactivity after being given phenobarbital. The latter drug reaction often occurs in children who will respond well to stimulants.

Explanation to the Patient

Finally, time should be set aside to explain the treatment plan to the child. If there is to be a class change, it must be negotiated with the patient, who may be initially against it. The child may not understand the need for remediation or for increased focus on and tracking of his or her behaviors for a behavior modification plan. In addition, the child may have strong feelings about medication. Often it is helpful to explain that the medication is a "crutch" that will be of help in doing classwork but does not control him or her. The timing of doses frequently becomes critical for compliance, since a child may decide unilaterally to stop his or her schooltime doses if ridiculed by the other children; here, pemoline (Cylert) or dextroamphetamine (Dexedrine) spansules are recommended.

Initiating Drug Therapy

Starting doses for all the stimulants are minimal and consist of a once-daily, early morning ingestion of 5 mg of methylphenidate, 2.5 mg of dextroamphetamine, or 18.75 mg of pemoline. The parent should begin to give the medication on the weekend so the onset and duration of action can be recorded over a week's time. Then, as dosing increments occur, the timing of the crucial early morning dose can be changed to cover the toughest times (getting dressed, getting on the school bus, or starting class work at school). Doses are generally titrated up to the maximum (60 mg of methylphenidate, 40 mg of dextroamphetamine, and 112.5 mg of pemoline) or to the point of troublesome side effects, whichever occurs first.

Management of Drug Treatment

Drug rebound can occur either on arising in the morning or during the late afternoon and is characterized by a withdrawal-like state in which the child becomes unusually irritable and hyperactive. This can be managed by giving an additional small dose on arising or when the child first comes home. Long-acting medication (pemoline) may avoid rebound because of its prolonged action. Tolerance rarely develops with chronic psychostimulant therapy and shows itself when the child becomes unresponsive to ever-increasing doses of medication after a long stable period of drug response. This can

be handled by switching to another stimulant.

Monitoring the child's progress is best done through teacher reports, both in the form of rating scales like the CTQ and through direct phone contact with teachers to assess the child's progress in academics and in peer relationships, distractibility and inattentiveness, impulsiveness and gross motor hyperactivity, and ability to respond to limit setting and do unsupervised tasks. Teachers will provide the information needed in planning medication change (both dose level and timing of each dose) by noting the time of classroom behavior deterioration. Teacher's reports will also be invaluable for placebo trials during the school year, since teachers should be the first to detect a major change in behavior off active drugs.

Drug Vacations

Children should be taken off psychostimulant therapy at least once a year, preferably during the summer. They can then be observed in a more active summer camp program at a time when they have the maximum growth period and are able to catch up to any height and weight losses that may have occurred. A subgroup of hyperkinetic children have been shown to be sensitive to the growth-inhibiting effect of stimulants, particularly dextroamphetamine. Withdrawal should involve decreasing doses over 1 week's time to avoid the rebound from a 1-day discontinuation. Before reinstituting medication, a 3-week period should be allowed to pass to ascertain whether the child still demonstrates enough behavior problems in the new class to merit continued drug therapy. Follow-up should occur even if the child does not currently meet criteria for medication, since the need for continued support and guidance will go on throughout the school year.

GENERAL RULES FOR SUCCESSFUL MANAGEMENT

Hyperkinetic children are best managed by a multidisciplinary team, comprising a physician, a psychologist, a social worker, and an educational specialist, to provide for the many needs these children have. Psychostimulants are the drugs of choice, and chronic drug therapy should be carried out with once-a-day dosing, if possible. Close communication with school personnel is absolutely necessary to work out the dosage and time of administration, both of which must be tailored to each individual case. Drug vacations, preferably placebo controlled, should be regularly planned to evaluate the need for continuation and to allow for physical growth. Tutoring may be necessary to teach children compensatory skills if learning difficulties are present. Children should be followed on a once-weekly to once-monthly schedule during treatment and a once-per-year schedule (at minimum) even after the intense part of the treatment plan is completed and medications are stopped.

TELLING PARENTS ABOUT THE FUTURE

There has been some evidence that a proportion of hyperkinetic children go on to become inattentive, labile, impulsive adults with psychiatric diagnoses and problems. Unfortunately, it is impossible to predict the future for each individual child. The unknown outcome of the attention deficit disorder can be helpful in persuading the family to maintain follow-up on a regular yearly basis, even if drug treatment has been stopped.

References

Abikoff, H., and Gittelman, R. 1985. Hyperactive children treated with stimulants: Is cognitive training a useful adjunct? *Arch. Gen. Psychiatry* 42:953–961.

American Psychiatric Association. 1987. *Diagnostic and Statistical Manual of Mental Disorders*, 3rd. ed., revised. Washington, D.C.: American Psychiatric Association.

Barkley, R. A. 1982. *Hyperactive Children: A Handbook for Diagnosis and Treatment*. New York: Guilford Press.

Cantwell, D. 1977. The hyperkinetic syndrome. In Rutter, M., and Hersov, L. (eds.): *Child Psychiatry: Modern Approaches*. London: Blackwell Scientific Publications.

Cantwell, D. P., and Carlson, G. A. 1978. Stimulants. In Werry, J. S. (ed.): *Pediatric Psychopharmacology: The Use of Behavior Modifying Drugs in Children*. New York: Brunner/Mazel.

Conners, C. K. and Barkley, R. 1985. Rating scales and checklists for child psychopharmacology. In: *Psychopharmacology Bulletin* (DHEW publication No. [ADM] 86–173), *Pharmacotherapy of Children* (special issue): 21(4):55–66.

Conners, C. K. 1980. *Food Additives and Hyperactive Children*. New York: Plenum Press.

Does Hyperactivity Matter. 1986. *Lancet* 1–73.

Douglas, V. I., Parry, P., Maron, P., and Garson, C. 1976. Assessment of a cognitive training program for hyperactive children. *J. Abnorm. Child Psychol.* 4:389–410.

Feingold, B. F. 1974. *Why Your Child is Hyperactive*. New York: Random House.

Gittelman-Klein, R. 1975. Review of clinical psychopharmacological treatment of hyperkinesis. In Klein, F., and Gittelman-Klein, R. (eds.): *Progress in Psychiatric Drug Treatment*. New York: Brunner/Mazel, 1975, pp. 661–674.

Gittelman, R., Mannuzza, S., Shenker, R., and Bonagura, N. 1985. Hyperactive children almost grown up. *Arch. Gen. Psychiatry* 42:937–947.

Gittelman-Klein, R. 1980. Diagnosis and drug treatment of childhood disorders: Attention-deficit disorder with hyperactivity. In Klein, D. F., Gittelman, R., Quitkin, F., and Rifkin, A. (eds.): Diagnosis and Drug Treatment of Psychiatric Disorders: Adults and Children, 2nd. ed. Baltimore: Williams & Wilkins.

Gittelman-Klein, R. 1980b. The role of psychological tests for differential diagnosis in child psychiatry. *J. Acad. Child Psychiatry* 19:413–437.

Gittelman-Klein, R., Abikoff, H., Pollack, E., et al. 1980. A controlled trial of behavior modification and methylphenidate in hyperactive children. In Whalen, C., and Henker, B. (eds.): *Hyperactive Children: The Social Ecology of Identification and Treatment*. New York: Academic Press.

Greenhill, L. L., Reider, R. O., Wender, P. H., et al. 1973. Lithium carbonate in the treatment of hyperactive children. *Arch. Gen. Psychiatry* 28:636–640.

Gualtieri, T., Wafgin, W., Kanoy, R., et al. 1982. Clinical studies of methylphenidate serum levels in children and adults. *J. Am. Acad. Child Adolesc. Psychiatry* 21:19–26.

Lahey, B., Schaughency, E. A., Hynd, G. W., et al. 1987. Attention-deficit disorder with and without hyperactivity: comparison of behavioral characteristics of clinic-referred children. *J. Am. Acad. Child Adolesc. Psychiatry* 26:718–723.

Lambert, N. M., Sandoval, J., and Sassone, D. 1978. Prevalence of hyperactivity in elementary school children as a function of social system definers. *Am. J. Orthopsychiatry* 48:446–463.

Lancet editorial. 1986. Does hyperactivity matter? *Lancet* January 11, 1986, p. 73.

Lapouse, R., and Monk, M. 1958. An epidemiologic study of behavioral characteristics in children. *Am. J. Publ. Health* 48:1134–1144.

Methylphenidate (Ritalin) revisited. 1988. *Med. Lett.* (in press).

Michenbaum, D. 1977. *Cognitive-Behavior Modification: An Integrative Approach*. New York: Plenum Publishing Corp.

Michenbaum, D. 1979. Application of cognitive-behavior modification procedures to hyperactive children. *Int. J. Mental Health* 8:83–94.

Pelham, W. E., Bender, M. E., Caddell, J., et al. 1985. Methylphenidate and children with attention-deficit disorder. *Arch. Gen. Psychiatry* 42:948–952.

Perel, J. M., and Dayton, P. G. 1976. Methylphenidate. In Usdin, E., and Forrest, I. (eds.): *Psychotherapeutic Drugs, Part II*. New York: Marcel Dekker.

Rapoport, J. L. The "real" and "ideal" management of stimulant drug treatment for hyperactive children. Recent findings and a report from clinical practice. In Whalen, C. K., and Henker, B. (eds.): *Hyperactive Children: The Social Ecology of Identification and Treatment*. New York: Academic Press, 1980.

Rapoport, J., Buchsbaum, M., Weingartner, H. 1980. Dextroamphetamine: Its cognitive and behavioral effects in normal and hyperactive boys and normal men. *Arch. Gen. Psychiatry* 37:933–943.

Rutter, M., Tizard, J., and Whitehouse, K. 1970. *Education, Health and Behavior: Psychological and Medical Study of Childhood Development.* New York: Longman Group, distributed by John Wiley & Sons.

Satin, M., Winsberg, B., Monetti, C., et al. 1985. A general population screen for attention deficit disorder with hyperactivity. *J. Am. Acad. Child Psychiatry* 24:756–764.

Satterfield, J. H., Cantwell, D. P., and Satterfield, B. T. 1979. Multimodality treatment: A one year follow-up study of 84 hyperactive boys. *Arch. Gen. Psychiatry* 36:965–974.

Satterfield, J. H., Satterfield, B. T., Schell, A. M. 1987. Therapeutic interventions to prevent delinquency in hyperactive boys. J. Am. Acad. Child. Adolesc. Psychiatry Jan. 26(1):56–64.

Schachar, R., Rutter, M., and Smith, A. 1981. The characteristics of situationally and pervasively hyperactive children: Implications in syndrome definition. *J. Child Psychol. Psychiatry* 22:375–392.

Shapiro, S. K., and Garfinkel, B. D. 1986. The occurrence of behavior disorders in children: The interdependence of attention-deficit disorder and conduct disorder. *J. Am. Acad. Child Adolesc. Psychiatry* 25:809–819.

Shaffer, D. 1978. Annotation: Soft neurological signs and later psychiatric disorder—a review. *J. Child Psychol. Psychiatry* 19:63–66.

Shaffer, D., and Greenhill, L. 1979. A critical note on the predictive validity of the hyperactive syndrome. *J. Child Psychol. Psychiatry* 20:61–72.

Shekim, W. O., Kashani, J., Beck, N., et al. 1985. The prevalence of attention deficit disorders in a rural midwestern community sample of nine-year-old children. *J. Am. Acad. Child Adolesc. Psychiatry* 24:765–770.

Sobotka, T. J. 1978. Update on studies of the relationship between hyperkinesis in children and food additives.

In Reatig, N. (ed.): *Proceedings of the National Institute of Mental Health on the Hyperkinetic Behavior Syndrome.* Doc. Number PB-297804 (code A12). Springfield, VA: National Technical Information Service, pp. 39–47.

Sokol, M. S., Campbell, M., Goldstein, M., et al. 1987. Attention deficit disorder with hyperactivity and the dopamine hypothesis: Case presentations with theoretical background. Grand Rounds in Child Psychiatry. *J. Am. Acad. Child Adolesc. Psychiatry* 26:428–433.

Sprague, R. L., and Sleator, E. K. 1977. Methylphenidate in hyperkinetic children: Differences in dose effects on learning and social behavior. *Science* 198:1274–1276.

Taylor, E. A. 1986. Overactivity, hyperactivity, and hyperkinesis: problems and prevalence. In Taylor, E. (ed.): The Overactive Child. Oxford: S.I.M.P./Blackwell.

The Medical Letter. 1988. Methylphenidate (Ritalin) revisited. 26:97–98.

Trites, R. L., Blouin, A. G., Ferguson, H. B., and Lynch, G. M. 1982. The Conners Teacher Rating Scale: An epidemiological interrater reliability and follow-up investigation. In Gadow, K., and Loney, J. (eds.): *Psychosocial Aspects of Drug Treatment for Hyperactivity.* Boulder, Colo.: Westview Press.

Waldrop, M. F., Bell, R. Q., McLaughlin, B., and Halverson, C. F., Jr. 1978. Newborn minor physical anomalies predict short attention span, peer aggression and impulsivity at age 3. *Science* 199:563–564.

Wender, P. H. 1971. *Minimal Brain Dysfunction in Children.* New York: John Wiley & Sons.

Whalen, C. K., Henker, B., Swanson, J. M., et al. 1987. Natural social behaviors in hyperactive children: Dose effects of methylphenidate. *J. Consult. Clin. Psychol.* 55:187–193.

Zametkin, A. J., and Rapoport, J. L. 1987. Neurobiology of attention-deficit disorder with hyperactivity: Where have we come in 50 years? *J. Am. Acad. Child Adolesc. Psychiatry* 26:676–687.

APPENDIX 10–1

PARENT SYMPTOM QUESTIONNAIRE

The Parent Symptom Questionnaire (PSQ) is a 93-item check list of symptoms most commonly associated with behavior disorders of childhood. The symptoms are rated on a 4-point scale by either one or both parents of a child. Instructions are simply to rate the presence and severity of symptoms in the child as *he is currently functioning* (not as he functioned earlier, i.e., more than one month prior to the evaluation).

Scoring is achieved in the following manner. The item weights (0, 1, 2, 3) are summed to give a total symptom score. This should be prorated for items not answered or mentioned by the parent as not applicable.

The list has been factor analyzed on a sample of clinic outpatients and normal children (N = 683) and has been shown to give relatively stable factor structure across ages and a wide social class range (Conners 1970*). The list has been slightly revised and reworded to include 10 items in common with the *School Symptom Questionnaire* (SSQ). These 10 items are among those most frequently checked by parents and teachers of outpatient children and have been found to be relatively sensitive to drug changes. The brief 10-item scale [Abbreviated Symptom Questionnaire (ASQ)] is useful when frequent reports from parents or teachers need to be assessed during the course of study. The ASQ consists of items 52, 53, 49, 54, 80, 79, 85, 88, 91, and 55 from the PSQ.

Factor scores are obtained by summing the weights for 42 of the PSQ items according to the Table below.

These factor scores will be relatively independent since items were selected so as to have minimal overlap in loadings on other factors. (But some correlation among scales can be expected since only factor scores derived by using actual loadings will be orthogonal to other factors.)

Parents are also asked to indicate those "target symptoms" of most concern. Those items should be scored **separately** for analyses of drug effects if maximal sensitivity to change is to be obtained.

Factor Title	Items to be Summed	No. of Items
I. Conduct Problem	39, 40, 41, 47, 48, 51, 69	7
II. Anxiety	8, 9, 10, 11, 42, 64, 43	7
III. Impulsive-Hyperactive	79, 80, 81, 82, 83, 84, 89, 90	8
IV. Learning Problem	45, 62, 63, 67	4
V. Psychosomatic	6, 21, 22, 23, 24	5
VI. Perfectionism	76, 77, 78	3
VII. Antisocial	71, 72, 73, 75	4
VIII. Muscular Tension	12, 13, 14, 36	4
		42

36 items with loadings > .40
4 items with loadings > .35
*Conners, C. K. 1970. Symptom patterns in hyperkinetic, neurotic, and normal children. *Child Dev.* 41:667.
(From Conners, C. K., and Barkley, R. 1985. Rating scales and checklists for child psychopharmacology. In: *Psychopharmacology Bulletin*, DHEW publication No. [ADM] 86–173, *Pharmacology of Children* [special issue] 21(4):55–66.)

PARENT SYMPTOM QUESTIONNAIRE

OFFICE USE
Patient No.
Study No.

Name of Child _____ Date _____

Your Name _____ Relationship _____

I. Instructions: Listed below are items concerning children's behavior or the problems they sometimes have. Read each item carefully and decide how much you think your child has been bothered by this problem *during the past month*—NOT AT ALL, JUST A LITTLE, PRETTY MUCH, or VERY MUCH
Indicate your choice by placing a check mark (√) in the appropriate column to the right of each item.

ANSWER ALL ITEMS

Observation	Not at all	Just a little	Pretty much	Very much
PROBLEMS OF EATING				
1. Picky and finicky				
2. Will not eat enough				
3. Overweight				
PROBLEMS OF SLEEP				
4. Restless				
5. Nightmares				
6. Awakens at night				
7. Cannot fall asleep				
FEAR AND WORRIES				
8. Afraid of new situations				
9. Afraid of people				
10. Afraid of being alone				
11. Worries about illness and death				
MUSCULAR TENSION				
12. Gets stiff and rigid				
13. Twitches, jerks, etc.				
14. Shakes				
SPEECH PROBLEMS				
15. Stuttering				
16. Hard to understand				

<table>
<tr><td colspan="3">**PARENT SYMPTOM QUESTIONNAIRE (Continued)**</td><td colspan="2">OFFICE USE</td></tr>
</table>

PARENT SYMPTOM QUESTIONNAIRE (Continued)

	OFFICE USE
	Patient No.
	Study No.

ANSWER ALL ITEMS

Observation	Not at all	Just a little	Pretty much	Very much
WETTING				
17. Bed wetting				
18. Runs to bathroom constantly				
BOWEL PROBLEMS				
19. Soiling self				
20. Holds back bowel movements				
COMPLAINS OF FOLLOWING SYMPTOMS EVEN THOUGH DOCTOR CAN FIND NOTHING WRONG				
21. Headaches				
22. Stomach aches				
23. Vomiting				
24. Aches and pains				
25. Loose bowels				
PROBLEMS OF SUCKING, CHEWING, or PICKING				
26. Sucks thumb				
27. Bites or picks nails				
28. Chews on clothes, blankets, or other items				
29. Picks at things such as hair, clothing, etc.				
CHILDISH OR IMMATURE				
30. Does not act his age				
31. Cries easily				
32. Wants help doing things he should do alone				
33. Clings to parents or other adults				
34. Baby talk				

	OFFICE USE
PARENT SYMPTOM QUESTIONNAIRE (Continued)	Patient No.
	Study No.

ANSWER ALL ITEMS

Observation	Not at all	Just a little	Pretty much	Very much
TROUBLE WITH FEELINGS				
35. Keeps anger to himself				
36. Lets himself get pushed around by other children				
37. Unhappy				
38. Carries a chip on his shoulder				
OVER-ASSERTS HIMSELF				
39. Bullying				
40. Bragging and boasting				
41. Sassy to grown-ups				
PROBLEMS MAKING FRIENDS				
42. Shy				
43. Afraid they do not like him				
44. Feelings easily hurt				
45. Has no friends				
PROBLEMS WITH BROTHERS AND SISTERS				
46. Feels cheated				
47. Mean				
48. Fights constantly				
PROBLEMS KEEPING FRIENDS				
49. Disturbs other children				
50. Wants to run things				
51. Picks on other children				
RESTLESS				
52. Restless or overactive				
53. Excitable, impulsive				
54. Fails to finish things he starts— short attention span				

PARENT SYMPTOM QUESTIONNAIRE (Continued)				

OFFICE USE
Patient No.
Study No.

ANSWER ALL ITEMS

Observation	Not at all	Just a little	Pretty much	Very much
TEMPER				
55. Temper outbursts, explosive and unpredictable behavior				
56. Throws himself around				
57. Throws and breaks things				
58. Pouts and sulks				
SEX				
59. Plays with own sex organs				
60. Involved in sex play with others				
61. Modest about his body				
PROBLEMS IN SCHOOL				
62. Is not learning				
63. Does not like to go to school				
64. Is afraid to go to school				
65. Daydreams				
66. Truancy				
67. Will not obey school rules				
LYING				
68. Denies having done wrong				
69. Blames others for his mistakes				
70. Tells stories which did not happen				
STEALING				
71. From parents				
72. At school				
73. From stores and other places				
FIRE-SETTING				
74. Sets fires				

	OFFICE USE
PARENT SYMPTOM QUESTIONNAIRE (Continued)	Patient No.
	Study No.

ANSWER ALL ITEMS

Observation	Not at all	Just a little	Pretty much	Very much
TROUBLE WITH POLICE				
75. Gets into trouble with police				
Why?				
PERFECTIONISM				
76. Everything must be just so				
77. Things must be done same way every time				
78. Sets goals too high				
ADDITIONAL PROBLEMS				
79. Inattentive, easily distracted				
80. Constantly fidgeting				
81. Cannot be left alone				
82. Always climbing				
83. A very early riser				
84. Will run around between mouthfuls at meals				
85. Demands must be met immediately—easily frustrated				
86. Cannot stand too much excitement				
87. Laces and zippers are always open				
88. Cries often and easily				
89. Unable to stop a repetitive activity				
90. Acts as if driven by a motor				
91. Mood changes quickly and drastically				
92. Poorly aware of surroundings or time of day				
93. Still cannot tie his shoelaces				

II. Please add any other problems you have with your child

_____

_____

_____

PARENT SYMPTOM QUESTIONNAIRE (Continued)

OFFICE USE
Patient No.
Study No.

ANSWER ALL ITEMS

Observation	Not at all	Just a little	Pretty much	Very much

III. How serious a problem do you think your child has at this time?
    (   ) No Problem   (   ) Minor Problem   (   ) Serious Problem

IV. Indicate the items you are most concerned about or those you think are the most important problems your child has by placing a circle around the number (1-93) of those items.

APPENDIX 10–2

TEACHER QUESTIONNAIRE

The Teacher Questionnaire (TQ) is a 39-item symptom list to be filled out by the child's home-room teacher. Two forms for initial and follow-up ratings are identical except for background information included on the preliminary school report. The items are divided into three large groupings: classroom behavior, group participation, and attitude toward authority. Ten items (5, 6, 14, 8, 1, 7, 3, 13, 16, and 21) are also included in the Parent Symptom Questionnaire (PSQ) and may be used as a separate, brief scale (abbreviated symptom scale) for more frequent assessments of behavior during the course of study.

The factor analysis of the TQ (Conners 1969*) was based on a slightly reworded version of the scale. Factor scores may be obtained from the present version by summing item weights (0, 1, 2, 3) according to the table below.

Factor scores will have some degree of intercorrelation, especially between Factors I and IV. (These two Factors might be summed together for some analyses to attain greater reliability of scores.)

Factor Title	Items to be Summed	No. of Items
I. Conduct Problem	12, 15, 17, 18, 19, 20, 21, −30†, 25, 31, 32, 36, 38	13
II. Inattentive-Passive	4, 7, 8, 11, 24, 26	6
III. Tension-Anxiety	9, 10, 30, 33, 34, −39†	6
IV. Hyperactivity	1, 2, 5, 6, 14, 29	6
		31

*Conners, C. K. 1969. A teacher rating scale for use in drug studies with children. *Am. J. Psychiatry*, 126:884–888.

†Note that these scores are subtracted from the sum.

(From Conners, C. K., and Barkley, R. 1985. Rating scales and checklists for child/psychopharmacology. In: *Psychopharmacology Bulletin*, DHEW publication No. [ADM]86–173, *Pharmacology of Children* [special issue] 21[4]:809–843.)

	OFFICE USE
TEACHER QUESTIONNAIRE	Patient No.
Preliminary School Report	Study No.

Name of Child _____ Date _____

School Attended _____ Grade _____

School Address _____
Number and Street   City   State   Zip

Name of Principal _____

I. How long have you known this child? _____ In your own words describe briefly this child's main problem.

_____
_____
_____
_____

II. STANDARDIZED TEST RESULTS
  A. Intelligence Tests

Name of Test	Date	C.A.	M.A.	I.Q.

  B. Most Recent Achievement Tests

Subject	Grade When Tested	Achievement Grade Level
Reading		
Spelling		
Arithmetic		

III. ACHIEVEMENT IN SCHOOL SUBJECTS
  A. List subjects in the appropriate category

Very Good	Average	Barely Passing	Failing

TEACHER QUESTIONNAIRE (Continued)

Preliminary School Report

III. ACHIEVEMENT IN SCHOOL SUBJECTS *Continued*
  B. Check special placement or help this child has received
( ) Ungraded   ( ) Sight-Saving ( ) Special Class ( ) Remedial Reading ( ) Speech Correction

( ) Tutoring, specify subjects _____

( ) Other, specify _____

IV. Listed below are descriptive terms of behavior. Place a check mark in the column which best describes this child.
  ANSWER ALL ITEMS

Observation	Degree of Activity			
	Not at all	Just a little	Pretty much	Very much
CLASSROOM BEHAVIOR				
1. Constantly fidgeting				
2. Hums and makes other odd noises				
3. Demands must be met immediately—easily frustrated				
4. Coordination poor				
5. Restless or overactive				
6. Excitable, impulsive				
7. Inattentive, easily distracted				
8. Fails to finish things he starts— short attention span				
9. Overly sensitive				
10. Overly serious or sad				
11. Daydreams				
12. Sullen or sulky				
13. Cries often and easily				
14. Disturbs other children				
15. Quarrelsome				
16. Mood changes quickly and drastically				
17. Acts "smart"				
18. Destructive				
19. Steals				
20. Lies				
21. Temper outbursts, explosive and unpredictable behavior				

TEACHER QUESTIONNAIRE (Continued)

Preliminary School Report

OFFICE USE
Patient No.
Study No.

Observation	Degree of Activity			
	Not at all	Just a little	Pretty much	Very much
GROUP PARTICIPATION				
22. Isolates himself from other children				
23. Appears to be unaccepted by group				
24. Appears to be easily led				
25. No sense of fair play				
26. Appears to lack leadership				
27. Does not get along with opposite sex				
28. Does not get along with same sex				
29. Teases other children or interferes with their activities				
ATTITUDE TOWARD AUTHORITY				
30. Submissive				
31. Defiant				
32. Impudent				
33. Shy				
34. Fearful				
35. Excessive demands for teacher's attention				
36. Stubborn				
37. Overly anxious to please				
38. Uncooperative				
39. Attendance problem				

V. FAMILY OF CHILD
   A. Do other children in the family who attend your school present any problem?
If YES, please explain. _____

_____

_____

_____

_____

	OFFICE USE
	Patient No.
	Study No.

TEACHER QUESTIONNAIRE (Continued)

Preliminary School Report

B. Please add any information concerning this child's home or family relationships which might have bearing on his attitudes and behavior, and include any suggestions for improvement of his behavior and adjustment. (Use reverse side if more space is required.)

_____

_____

_____

How would you rate this child's behavior compared to other children the same age?

much worse
_____

worse
_____

about the same
_____

better
_____

much better

_____

_____

_____

_____

_____

| Signature | Title | Date Signed |

Attention-Deficit Hyperactivity Disorder in Adolescents and Adults

11

PAUL H. WENDER, M.D.

Attention-deficit hyperactivity disorder (ADHD) is the term the *Diagnostic and Statistical Manual of Mental Disorders*, third edition, revised *(DSM-III-R)* has designated for what the *DSM-III* had termed attention-deficit disorder (ADD) (American Psychiatric Association 1987). Although the *DSM-III* divided ADD into a childhood form and a residual type (ADD, RT), the *DSM-III-R* has recognized that the natural history of ADD is analogous to that of infantile autism: both persist into adult life. In addition, the *DSM-III-R* has changed the diagnostic criteria. The ADD criteria were attentional problems and impulsivity, with or without hyperactivity; these general diagnoses could be assessed in both adults and children. In the *DSM-III-R*, however, many of the diagnostic criteria are inapplicable to adolescents and adults (e.g., "has difficulty awaiting turn in games or group situations" or "has difficulty playing quietly"). While these characteristics may have been present in the childhood of the adult with persisting ADHD, they are clearly not useful in describing the signs and symptoms of a more mature person. Finally, it is important to note that in the past the disorder has had several other, now obsolete, appellations, including hyperactivity, hyperkinesis, minimal brain dysfunction, minimal brain damage, among others.

ETIOLOGY AND PATHOGENESIS

Some psychiatrists advanced the hypothesis that "minimal brain dysfunction," as it

has been called, was a genetically transmitted disorder of monoaminergic (probably dopaminergic) underactivity (Wender 1971, 1978). The data that suggest genetic transmission come from family studies of "hyperactive" children in which investigators found an increased prevalence of certain forms of psychopathology in the subjects' biological relatives. Morrison and Stewart (1971) reported that approximately 55% of hyperactive children, versus 10% of the controls, had a parent with a diagnosis of alcoholism, sociopathy, or hysteria. Interestingly, 60% of the relatives who had been hyperactive in childhood received one of these diagnoses as an adult. Cantwell (1972), replicating these studies, reported that approximately 35% of the hyperactive boys' parents, versus 10% of the controls, received a diagnosis of alcoholism, sociopathy, and hysteria; moreover, 10% of the parents of ADHD children had been hyperactive themselves and all had received one of these three adult diagnoses. These findings are of twofold significance: (1) they demonstrate an increased incidence of familial psychopathology and (2) they reveal a particular clustering of psychiatric disorders. Collateral studies have shown that male alcohol abuse, sociopathy, and Briquet's syndrome run in families and that there is an increased frequency of each of these illnesses in the families of persons with one of the other two (Arkonac and Guze 1963).

Although such family studies do not discriminate between genetic and psychosocial transmission, adoption studies do. A variation on this type of study is to look at siblings or half-siblings who have been reared in different homes. Using this method, Safer (1973) examined the full siblings and the maternal half-siblings of a cohort of children with "minimal brain dysfunction" and found that approximately 50% of the full siblings and only 10% of the half-siblings were given the same diagnosis. These figures are close to the 50% and 25% prevalence one would expect if the disorder were transmitted by a dominant gene. Applying the "adoptive parents' method," Wender and co-workers (1968), Morrison and Stewart (1973), and Cantwell (1975) compared the adopting parents of "hyperactive children" with biological parents who had reared their own "hyperactive children" and with the parents of controls. The reasoning behind this approach was that if psychopathology per se (alcohol abuse, antisocial personality disorder, somatization disorder) in the biological parents produces hyperactivity in the offspring, such psychopathology should be present in the adopting parents of hyperactive children. If psychopathology in the biological parents is a manifestation of the genetic disorder they have transmitted to their children (which would be analogous to an abnormal glucose tolerance curve in the parent of a diabetic), then the adoptive parents should be free from that psychopathology. All three studies found a significantly increased prevalence of alcoholism and antisocial personality in the biological fathers and an increased frequency of Briquet's syndrome in the biological mothers of the hyperactive children compared with the other two groups. None of the studies revealed more psychopathology in the adoptive parents of the hyperactive children than in the parents of the controls. These results are consonant with genetic transmission and suggest that psychological abnormalities in the rearing parents are not necessary to produce hyperactivity in their children. The major difficulty in interpretation, in both the family and adoption studies, has been that the diagnoses of the children were not precise. In retrospect, it is now apparent that the groups undoubtedly consisted of children with varying mixtures of ADHD, conduct disorder, and specific developmental disorder. In order to clarify this issue, these studies will need to be replicated, paying close attention to current diagnostic criteria.

A second body of data, coming from studies done in the first part of the century, suggests that dopaminergic symptoms are involved in ADHD. Following World War I, there was a worldwide epidemic of a viral encephalitis called either encephalitis lethargica (descriptively) or von Economo's encephalitis (eponymically). The disorder was frequently fatal; however, when adults recovered from the acute illness, they often manifested symptoms of postencephalitic parkinsonism; when children recovered from the acute illness, they often manifested marked behavioral changes deemed postencephalitic behavior disorder. The illness produced similar lesions in children and adults, with the most marked involvement in the basal ganglia, an area known to be rich in dopaminergic neurons. The finding of damage to dopaminergic neurons in postencephalitic Parkinson's disorder is in keeping with more recent studies of the idiopathic form of the illness: patients with idiopathic Parkinson's syndrome have been found to have a decreased level of homovanillic acid (HVA), the principal metabolite of dopamine, in cerebrospinal fluid. Taken together, the above suggest that decreased dopaminergic functioning might be involved in the pathogenesis of idiopathic ADHD. Accordingly, one would predict decreased HVA in the cerebrospinal fluid of patients with ADHD. Two studies have been conducted in ADHD children and one in adults: decreased HVA levels were found in one study of children and changes (probably dopamine receptor supersensitivity) in the other. The study of ADHD in adults showed decreased HVA in methylphenidate-responsive women and a higher-than-normal level of HVA in ADHD men who were methylphenidate nonresponders (Reimherr et al., 1984).

Further data supporting the dopaminergic hypothesis come from an examination of the mechanisms of action of the psychoactive drugs that are effective in the treatment of ADHD in children and adults. The most effective drugs have been found to be the amphetamines, methylphenidate, and pemoline, all of which increase dopaminergic activity. The striking feature of these drugs is they often produce profoundly positive psychological effects that enable the person to function more effectively than he or she ever has before. This clinical observation leads one to suspect that the disorder is being remediated at the beginning of its causal chain. (An analogy, in cardiac disease, would be a drug that relieved angina pectoris by reversing atherosclerosis rather than a drug, such as nitroglycerin, that eases the pain by temporary vasodilatation.) If dopaminergic activity plays a major role in ADHD, one would predict that the monamine oxidase (MAO) inhibitors would be effective in the treatment of the disorder. Brain MAO occurs in at least two forms: (1) MAO-A, which degrades norepinephrine, dopamine, and serotonin, and (2) MAO-B, which degrades dopamine and is selectively inhibited by the MAO-B inhibitors pargyline and deprenyl. Two open trials of these drugs found them to be effective in the treatment of ADHD in adults (Wender et al. 1983; Wood et al. 1983). Although this finding is interesting, it is not conclusive, since the drugs were given within a dose range that may have inhibited MAO-A as well. In contrast to the effectiveness of the MAO inhibitors is the relative ineffectiveness of the tricyclic antidepressants in the treatment of ADHD. Consistent with the hypothesis that decreased dopaminergic activity may play a role in the ADHD syndrome is the fact that the tricyclic antidepressants increase noradrenergic and serotonergic activity but not dopaminergic activity. In one study of amino acids that are precursors of neurotransmitters (Wood et al. 1985), adults with ADHD showed a substantial therapeutic response to pharmacologic doses of tyrosine, the precursor of dopamine (but *also* the precursor of norepinephrine).

EPIDEMIOLOGY

There are no data on the prevalence of ADHD in the older population, but an estimate can be made on the basis of a number of longitudinal studies. Reviewing such studies, Cantwell (1985) concluded that the core ADD symptoms continue into adolescence in 50% to 80% of ADHD children and that "in adolescents, low self-esteem, poor academic performance, and antisocial behavior are relatively common occurrences, with antisocial behavior occurring in 10% to 50% of different samples." The most intensively studied prospective sample is that of Weiss and Hechtman (1986), who indicated that in two thirds of the population the problems continued into early adulthood with complaints of rest-

lessness, poor concentration, impulsivity, and explosiveness. It should be emphasized that all of this is difficult to interpret because of the heterogeneity (the possible mixture of ADD and conduct disorder) of the samples studied.

Nevertheless, even with the problems of interpretation, an order-of-magnitude estimate can be calculated. If the prevalence of ADHD in childhood is 3% to 10%, and, if approximately 50% have significant residual symptoms, then the prevalence of ADHD in adults could be as high as 5%. It should be noted that the childhood figures are based on a fairly arbitrary quantitative cutoff because the abnormalities of ADHD are quantitative, not qualitative (e.g., being "considerably" more active or "considerably" less attentive than "normal"). Obviously, defining criteria based on the magnitude of a normal attribute leads to ambiguous estimates of prevalence. An analogy may be drawn with a case of hypertension in which a blood pressure of 141/91 mm Hg is hypertensive, while one of 139/89 mm Hg is not.

The other important epidemiologic datum is the sex ratio of the ADHD population. In clinical samples, the male:female ratio ranges from 6:1 to 9:1; in community samples, the ratio is about 7:1. Experience with older ADHD persons has been different; in the Utah studies of methylphenidate (Wood et al. 1976; Wender et al. 1985a), pemoline (Wender et al. 1981), pargyline (Wender et al. 1983), and deprenyl (Wood et al. 1983), the sex ratio has been approximately 1:1. This discrepancy may be due, in part, to the treatment of patients with symptoms troublesome to themselves that women seem to acknowledge more readily. In addition, males with antisocial personality or current alcohol or substance abuse were excluded, and both groups were likely to have a high concentration of ADHD subjects.

CLINICAL PICTURE

The *DSM-III-R* provides no information regarding the signs and symptoms of the disorder beyond childhood. Although the *DSM-III* stated that the usual developmental course of ADD was for hyperactivity to disappear while attentional difficulties and impulsivity might persist, it provided no further adolescent and adult diagnostic criteria.

The first requirement for an assessment of ADHD in an adult population was that the subject have had ADHD in childhood. Most patients have not been evaluated as children and hence the diagnosis must be made retroactively and might be based "narrowly" on the *DSM-III* criteria or on the "broad criteria" listed in Appendix 11–1. The critical information was derived from either the patient or relatives. Because patients' memories of their childhood were frequently skimpy and parents could not always be interviewed, an adjunctive rating scale was employed. This was the Conners Abbreviated Teacher's Rating Scale (CTRS), which was sent to the patients' mothers with the instruction that they describe their adult child as he or she had been between the ages of 6 and 10 (Appendix 11–2 and called the Parents Rating Scale [PRS]). Each of the items was scored on a 0–3 scale, with a maximum of 30 points. In a normative sample of over 400 (Wender et al. 1981), scores of 12 or greater placed an individual in the 95th percentile of hyperactivity in the normal population. The PRS was used as an independent check on the accuracy of clinical diagnosis of "formerly ADD." The question of reliability (i.e., does the scale really measure what it purports to measure?) had been raised because of the lack of contemporaneous ratings with which to compare it; in particular, mothers might exaggerate or whitewash.

One way of validating a rating scale is to see if it correlates with other measures. A diagnosis of ADHD in childhood (and a high score on the PRS) is a good predictor of responsivity to stimulant medication; therefore, one needs to examine the relationship between high scores on the PRS and a response to medication in adults; it was found that ADHD patients with high scores were more likely than those with low scores to respond to pemoline or methylphenidate (Wender et al. 1981, 1985a). Since current theory is that the PRS does not discriminate between ADD and conduct disorder, it would be useful to employ refined scales that would differentiate between ADHD and conduct disorder.

In addition to the criteria for ADD in childhood, postchildhood ADHD requires the following signs and symptoms: (1) the continuing presence of attentional difficulties *and* motoric hyperactivity and (2) two of the following five symptoms: affective lability, hot temper, impulsivity, disorganization, and stress intolerance. The exact cues are as follows:

1. *Hyperactivity:* persistent excessive motor activity as manifested by restlessness, inability to relax, "nervousness" (meaning inability to settle down—not anticipatory anxiety), inability to persist in sedentary activities (e.g., watching movies, television, reading a newspaper), being always on the go, and dysphoric when inactive.

2. *Attentional deficits:* manifested by inability to keep one's mind on conversations, distractibility (being aware of other stimuli when attempts are made to filter them out), inability to keep one's mind on reading materials, difficulty keeping one's mind on a task, and "forgetfulness" (often losing or misplacing things, forgetting plans, etc.).

3. *Affective lability:* described as antedating adolescence and in some instances extending as far back in time as the patient can remember and manifested by definite shifts from a normal mood to depression or to mild euphoria and excitement; The depression is described as a state of being "down," "bored," or "discontented"; the mood shifts usually last several hours to a few days, are present without significant physiological concomitants, and may occur spontaneously or be reactive.

4. *Inability to complete tasks:* the patient reports a lack of organization on the job, running a household, or in performing school work; tasks are frequently not completed and the subject may switch from one task to another in haphazard fashion; problem solving is disorderly, as is organizing time.

5. *Hot temper, explosive short-lived outbursts:* the patient reports transient outbursts that may be accompanied by a loss of control; he or she may be frightened by his or her own behavior, admit to being easily provoked, and is constantly irritable; temper problems often impair personal relationships.

6. *Impulsivity:* the patient makes decisions quickly without reflection, often on the basis of insufficient information and to his or her own disadvantage; the patient often has an inability to delay acting without experiencing discomfort; manifestations of impulsivity include poor occupational performance, abrupt initiation or termination of relationships (e.g., multiple marriages, separations, divorces), antisocial behavior, (joy-riding, shoplifting), and excessive involvement in

pleasurable activities without recognizing consequences (e.g., buying sprees, foolish business investments, reckless driving).

7. *Stress intolerance:* the patient cannot take ordinary stresses in stride and reacts excessively or inappropriately with depression, confusion, uncertainty, anxiety or anger; emotional responses interfere with appropriate problem solving; repeated crises are experienced in dealing with routine life stresses.

It should be emphasized that many patients with antisocial personality disorder also meet criteria for ADHD and that the *DSM-III-R* permits coding of both diagnoses (like one can simultaneously diagnose ADHD and conduct disorder in children). It appears there is a greater-than-chance association between ADHD and other psychiatric syndromes, particularly antisocial personality disorder and borderline personality disorder, but from the formal standpoint of *DSM-III-R* coding of diagnosis, one may simply code both. It appears that ADHD occurs along a continuum, a "spectrum" of severity, as do schizophrenia, the major affective disorders, and probably antisocial personality disorder.

Other features associated with ADHD in adults include marital instability; academic or vocational underachievement despite adequate intelligence, education, and opportunity; substance dependence or abuse; atypical response to psychoactive medications; family histories of ADHD in childhood; and family histories of alcoholism, drug abuse, antisocial personality, and somatization disorder.

DIAGNOSIS AND DIFFERENTIAL DIAGNOSIS

The disorder appears to be quite common, although its diagnosis is frequently overlooked. There are several practical indicators whose presence suggests ADHD in adolescents and adults. The first is a family history of alcoholism, substance abuse, or antisocial traits in biological relatives. The second indicator is the presence of two symptoms: lability of mood and anger. The ADHD mood problems differ from those seen in major affective disorder and dysthymic disorder; that is, they antedate adolescence, have a duration that ranges from hours to days, are clearly reactive, and are not accompanied by

vegetative signs. The lack of temper control is also distinctive. These patients have a "short fuse," a "low boiling point." They flare rapidly and calm down rapidly and are not characterized by the brooding seen in borderline personality disorder or the constant irritability frequently seen in major affective disorders. The last indicator is a life course of underachievement in school and less adequate functioning in vocational, familial, and parental roles than one would anticipate.

MANAGEMENT

The only systematic treatment studies, both open and controlled, have been of stimulant medications. Two of three placebo-controlled trials of methylphenidate have found this drug to be effective (Wender et al. 1985a); and one placebo-controlled trial of pemoline found that drug to be effective (Wender et al. 1981). The percentage of patients with ADHD who sustain a moderate-to-marked degree of improvement on stimulant medication is somewhere between 50% and 70%. The desired and the untoward drug effects are similar to those seen in children. Overall, methylphenidate and dextroamphetamine appear to be more effective than pemoline, but, as in children, any individual patient may respond best to any one of these drugs. When the medications are effective, concentration improves, motor activity decreases, moods become stable, patients' "fuses" lengthen, temper outbursts diminish and often disappear, impulsivity subsides, organization improves, and patients develop increased stress tolerance. The potency of the stimulants differ. As a rough approximation, 1 mg of dextroamphetamine or methamphetamine is equivalent to 2 mg of methylphenidate or 4 mg of pemoline. The duration of action of the drugs varies: single doses of dextroamphetamine last 3 to 5 hours, and the medication is usually given two or three times a day. Methylphenidate's duration of action is generally 2 to 3 hours, and the drug is given three and sometimes four times a day. Pemoline has a long duration of action and in some instances need be given only once a day. Long-acting forms of methylphenidate and the amphetamines are marketed, but their effectiveness is open to question. The usual ranges of the medications are dextroamphetamine, 10 to 45 mg/day; methylphenidate, 30 to 90 mg/day; and pemoline, 37.5 to 150 mg/day. Side effects of the medications are anorexia, irritability, and, if given too late in the day, insomnia. These symptoms can usually be controlled by diminishing the dose and giving the last dose no later than 3 or 4 PM. Insomnia can sometimes be controlled by giving a small dose of a sedative antipsychotic (e.g., thioridazine, 10 to 25 mg, at bedtime). Idiosyncratic reactions and allergies to the amphetamines and methylphenidate are rare. Two to 3% of patients receiving pemoline have developed liver function abnormalities, so that periodic liver function tests are mandatory.

The only other class of drugs that seem effective in the treatment of ADHD is the MAO inhibitors. The MAO inhibitors can be used safely only in patients who are willing to abide by the dietary restrictions (foods low in tyramine), so that the impulsivity of the ADHD patient may constitute a contradiction. The MAO inhibitors that have been systematically studied (openly) are pargyline (Wender et al. 1983) and deprenyl (Wood et al. 1983). Pargyline is marketed as an antihypertensive but was developed as an antidepressant. Although it does produce orthostatic hypotension, it is generally well tolerated. The onset of action, the side effects, and the necessary precautions are similar to those of the other MAO inhibitors. Deprenyl is currently an investigational drug and not available in the United States. It was chosen because in low doses it produces no "cheese effect." The dose ranges employed were pargyline, 30 to 150 mg/day, and *l*-deprenyl, 10 to 50 mg/day. These drugs have usually been given in the morning and at noon. Anecdotal reports are that tranylcypromine may be an effective agent. Problems with the MAO inhibitors include orthostatic hypotension, dependent edema, insomnia, and the development of tolerance.

Other drugs have been tried in patients with ADHD. Some clinicians have reported tricyclic antidepressants to be effective, but most have not. Lithium and the benzodiazepines are likewise rarely of benefit.

Good clinical management requires the presence of an "other." As was mentioned earlier, patients with postchildhood ADHD are not only unaware of their behavior patterns but generally fail to perceive changes that are produced by medication. Like children with ADHD, they may sustain marked improvement but report minimal or no improvement. A further aid in assessing treatment response is to employ the seven defining symptoms (hyperactivity, attentional problems, affective lability, hot temper, impulsivity, disorganization, and stress intolerance) as "target symptoms" to be rated on each visit (with an ordinal scale, such as: 0 = none, 1 = slight, 2 = moderate, 3 = marked improvement or worsening).

There have been no studies of psychosocial intervention in the management of adolescent and adult ADHD. Nonetheless, clinical experience has found certain approaches useful. The first is education. The patients must be taught which of the symptoms are biological and can be suppressed only with the aid of medication. They must learn how to assess the severity of these symptoms, using both introspection and reports from their "other." They then may be gradually helped to see how their biological difficulties have psychological, occupational, and interpersonal symptoms. Once the biologically produced symptoms have been suppressed, therapy is directed at modifying the maladaptive and possibly autonomous behavior patterns. Only individual and couple therapy have been used to date. It is probable that group therapy would be an effective modality.

CASE HISTORIES

The following are two cases of adults with ADHD. They were treated in an early placebo-controlled study that did not exclude patients with a concurrent diagnosis of antisocial personality disorder. "RDC" refers to the Research Diagnostic Criteria, a diagnostic scheme that antedated and has been incorporated into the *DSM-III* and *DSM-III-R* criteria.

Case 1

This 26-year-old, divorced man was self-referred with complaints of violent temper, inability to maintain relationships with women, and marked affective lability. His PRS score was 12, which placed him in the 95th percentile of childhood "hyperactivity," and his Global Assessment Scale (GAS) score was 50. In childhood he was very hyperactive, had marked concentration problems, and flunked out of high school despite an IQ of 106. He was chronically moody, had frequent temper outbursts, had numerous fights, and had been arrested for drunkenness, assault, car theft, and stealing credit cards.

In his early 20s he became completely law abiding, obtained a high school equivalency diploma, and took a job as a skilled mechanic; however, his relationships with his wife of 3 months and several women thereafter were compromised by his violent temper, unpredictable moodiness, stubbornness, alcohol and marijuana abuse, and inability to "cope." Impulsivity was very evident. During the course of the study (while taking placebo), he married a woman he had known for 3 days. Of his mood difficulties, which dated from childhood, he stated, "One minute I feel good and the next minute I feel depressed . . . sometimes for a reason, sometimes not . . . It usually lasts for hours, sometimes (rarely) days." He met RDC for the following diagnoses:

1. Mood disorders (chronic and intermittent depressive disorder, cyclothymic personality, and labile personality)
2. Alcohol abuse
3. Drug abuse (marijuana)
4. Generalized anxiety disorder
5. Briquet's syndrome (probable)
6. Antisocial personality (probable)

When treated with placebo, he showed no response. He was later offered an open trial of pemoline, and over a 6-week period he sustained a dramatic response. He decided it was not "worth" fighting his bosses, began to attend work regularly (rather than calling in sick), stopped fighting with his wife, and abandoned his "six-pack-a-night" alcohol habit. After 3 months, the results of his liver function tests showed questionable abnormalities (a mildly elevated serum glutamic oxaloacetic transaminase level) and pemoline therapy was discontinued. His symptoms recurred and he failed for over a year to respond to treatment with methylphenidate, imipramine hydrochloride, amitriptyline hydrochloride, tranylcypromine sulfate, and lithium carbonate. He was given pemoline therapy and again showed a good response with no liver abnormalities as his problems resolved.

Case 2

Another example of a seriously disturbed person showing a marked response was that of a 31-year-old, twice-divorced woman. Her PRS score was 14, which placed her in the 95th percentile of childhood "hyperactivity," and her GAS rating was 50. She had been "nervous" her whole life and so restless when lying in bed with a broken ankle that "it nearly drove me insane." She had lifelong attentional difficulties, difficulty completing tasks, and episodes of crying, guilty feelings, and withdrawal. As a child, she tersely described herself as "a little rebel with frequent temper tantrums who was disobedient, stole a good deal, truanted frequently, became a runaway during adolescence, fought a lot, did not like any of the other girls, and was a real tomboy." She was "locked up a few times" in juvenile homes during adolescence. She stated that she used to have a bad temper in childhood and related an episode with her first husband when he had pushed her and browbeat her and she had "nearly beaten him to a pulp . . . it took five people to pull me off him."

"Most of my life, until I entered [technical training], I didn't like women or vice versa . . . their backstabbing and frivolousness . . . I get along well with men [despite two horrendous marriages] . . . Both my marriages were rotten . . . I decided not to go to bed with men. The thought passed my mind that I was a lesbian . . . I almost gave up . . . My first husband almost killed me . . . he was only interested in sex . . . my second husband was an alcoholic and beat me up so badly that I went to the hospital twice." She chronically overreacted to stress. "Things get to me . . . I get upset when I can't do something about a situation . . . I get frustrated very easily . . . I swear, talk to myself, get very restless, mad, sad . . . go get drunk." She had multiple somatic symptoms from early childhood, including chronic multiple aches and pains, a loss of central vision, headaches, chest pains, dyspnea, palpitations, menstrual cramps, dyspareunia, and tingling and numbness in her hands for a year after the violent fight with her husband.

Her RDC diagnoses included the following:

1. Mood problems (chronic and intermittent minor depressive disorder, cyclothymic personality, and labile personality)

2. Alcohol abuse (definite) for a period of 3 years

3. Generalized anxiety disorder (probable)

4. Antisocial personality (definite)

5. Briquet's syndrome (probable)

(Her multiple conversion symptoms were insufficient to meet the RDC operational criteria.)

She was randomly assigned to placebo and showed no change. After completion of the study, she requested treatment and received an open trial of methylphenidate. During a 3-month period while receiving medication she stabilized her relationship with her boyfriend, got her "act" together, and obtained a high school equivalency diploma and a steady job; she also performed well, received praise, promotion, and increased recompense. As is true of many of the persons treated successfully, she then discontinued taking the medication. Such patients frequently return when they encounter life stresses, which are usually self-generated.

References

American Psychiatric Association. 1987. *Diagnostic and Statistical Manual of Mental Disorders*, 3rd ed., revised. Washington, D.C.: American Psychiatric Association.

Arkonac, O., and Guze, S. B. 1963. A family study of hysteria. *N. Engl. J. Med.* 268:239–242.

Cantwell, D. P. 1972. Psychiatric illness in the families of hyperactive children. *Arch. Gen. Psychiatry* 27:414–4172.

Cantwell, D. P. 1975. Genetic studies of hyperactive children: Psychiatric illness in biologic and adopting parents. In Fieve, R. R., Rosenthal, D., and Brill, H. (eds.): *Genetic Research in Psychiatry*. Baltimore: Johns Hopkins Press.

Cantwell, D. P. 1985. Pharmacotherapy of ADD in adolescents: What do we know, where should we go, how should we do it? *Psychopharmacol. Bull.* 21:251–257.

Morrison, J. R., and Stewart, M. A. 1971. A family study of the hyperactive child syndrome. *Biol. Psychiatry* 3:189–195.

Morrison, J. R., and Stewart, M. A. 1973. The psychiatric status of the legal families of adopted hyperactive children. *Arch. Gen. Psychiatry* 28:888–891.

Reimherr, F. W., Wender, P. H., Ebert, M. H., and Wood, D. R. 1984. Cerebrospinal fluid homovanillic acid and 5-hydroxyindoleacetic acid in adults with attention deficit disorder, residual type. *Psychiatr. Res.* 11:71–78.

Safer, D. J. 1973. A familial factor in minimal brain dysfunction. *Behav. Genet.* 3:175–186.

Weiss, G., and Hechtman, L. T. 1986. *Hyperactive Children Grown Up*. New York: Guilford Press.

Wender, P. H. 1971. *Minimal Brain Dysfunction in Children*. New York: John Wiley & Sons.

Wender, P. H. 1978. Minimal brain dysfunction: An overview. In Lipton, M. A., DiMascio, A., and Killam, K. F. (eds.): *Psychopharmacology: A Generation of Progress*. New York: Raven Press.

Wender, P. H., Rosenthal, D., and Kety, S. S. 1968. Psychiatric assessment of adoptive parents of schizophrenics. In Rosenthal, D., and Kety, S. S. (eds.): *The Transmission of Schizophrenia*. New York: Pergamon Press.

Wender, P. H., Reimherr, F. W., and Wood, D. R. 1981. Attention deficit disorder ("minimal brain dysfunction") in adults: A replication study of diagnosis and drug treatment. *Arch. Gen. Psychiatry* 38:449–456.

Wender, P. H., Reimherr, F. W., Wood, D., and Ward, M. 1985a. A controlled study of methylphenidate in the treatment of attention deficit disorder, residual type, in adults. *Am. J. Psychiatry* 142:547–552.

Wender, P. H., Wood, D. R., Reimherr, F. W., and Ward, M. 1983. An open trial of pargyline in the treatment of attention deficit disorder, residual type. *Psychiatr. Res.* 9:329–336.

Wender, P. H., Wood, D. R., and Reimherr, F. W. 1985b. Pharmacological treatment of attention deficit disorder, residual type (ADD, RT, "minimal brain dysfunction," "hyperactivity") in adults. *Psychopharmacol. Bull.* 21:222–231.

Wood, D. R., Reimherr, F. W., and Wender, P. H. 1976. Diagnosis and treatment of minimal brain dysfunction in adults. *Arch. Gen. Psychiatry* 33:1453–1461.

Wood, D. R., Reimherr, F. W., and Wender, P. H. 1983. The use of *l*-deprenyl in the treatment of attention deficit disorder, residual type (ADD,RT). *Psychopharmacol. Bull.* 19:627–629.

Wood, D. R., Reimherr, F. W., and Wender, P. H. 1985. Amino acid precursors for the treatment of attention deficit disorder, residual. *Psychopharmacol. Bull.* 21:146–149.

APPENDIX 11–1

UTAH CRITERIA FOR THE DIAGNOSIS OF ADHD IN CHILDHOOD

Narrow Criteria (DSM-III) (Childhood)

The child displays, for his or her mental and chronological age, signs of developmentally inappropriate inattention, impulsivity, and hyperactivity. The signs must be reported by adults in the child's environment, such as parents and teachers. Because the symptoms are typically variable, they may not be observed directly by the clinician. When the reports of teachers and parents conflict, primary consideration should be given to the teacher's reports because of greater familiarity with age-appropriate norms. Symptoms typically worsen in situations that require self-application, as in the classroom. Signs of the disorder may be absent when the child is in a new or a one-to-one situation.

The number of symptoms specified (below) is for children between the ages of 8 and 10, the peak age range for referral. In younger children, more severe forms of the symptoms and a greater number of symptoms are usually present. *The opposite is true of older children.*

1. *Inattention*—At least three of the following:
   a. Often fails to finish things he or she starts
   b. Often does not seem to listen
   c. Easily distracted
   d. Difficulty concentrating on schoolwork or other tasks requiring sustained attention
   e. Difficulty sticking to a play activity

2. *Impulsivity*—At least three of the following:
   a. Often acts before thinking
   b. Shifts excessively from one activity to another
   c. Difficulty organizing work (unrelated to cognitive impairment)
   d. Needs a great deal of supervision
   e. Often calls out in class
   f. Difficulty awaiting turn in games or group situations

3. *Hyperactivity*—At least two of the following:
   a. Runs about or climbs on things excessively
   b. Difficulty sitting still or fidgets excessively
   c. Difficulty staying seated
   d. Moves about excessively during sleep
   e. Is always "on the go" or acts as if "driven by a motor"

4. *Onset* before age of 7

5. *Duration* of at least 6 months

6. *Not due* to schizophrenia, affective disorder, or severe or profound mental retardation

Broad Criteria (Adult)

Both characteristics of Nos. 1 and 2 and one characteristic of Nos. 3 through 6.

1. More active than other children, unable to sit still, fidgetiness, restlessness, always on the go, talking excessively

2. Attention deficits, sometimes described as "short attention span," characterized by inattentiveness, distractibility, and inability to finish school work

3. Behavior problems in school

4. Impulsivity

5. Overexcitability

6. Temper outbursts

APPENDIX 11–2

PARENTS' RATING SCALE

Patient's Name _____ Date _____ Physician _____

To be filled out by the *mother* of the subject (or father only if mother is unavailable).

Instructions: Listed below are items concerning children's behavior and the problems they sometimes have. Read each item carefully and decide how much you think your child was bothered by these problems when he/she was between 6 and 10 years old. Rate the amount of the problem by putting a check in the column that describes your child at that time.

	NOT AT ALL	JUST A LITTLE	PRETTY MUCH	VERY MUCH
1. Restless (overactive)				
2. Excitable, impulsive				
3. Disturbs other children				
4. Fails to finish things started (short attention span)				
5. Fidgeting				
6. Inattentive, distractible				
7. Demand must be met immediately; gets frustrated				
8. Cries				
9. Mood changes quickly				
10. Temper outbursts (explosive and unpredictable behavior)				

12

Conduct Disorders

DOROTHY OTNOW LEWIS, M.D.

Conduct disorder, with its subtypes (group, solitary aggressive, and undifferentiated), is the term used to describe children and adolescents with a multitude of different kinds of behaviors and a multitude of different kinds of biopsychosocial vulnerabilities underlying these behaviors. These behaviors can range from running away from home to rape and murder. Perhaps what distinguishes youngsters diagnosed as having conduct disorder most from those given other diagnoses is the fact that the signs of their disturbance are of greater concern to persons around them than they are to the youngsters themselves. Their behaviors infringe on the rest of society in especially unpleasant ways. In fact, when psychiatrically hospitalized adolescents who were ever diagnosed as having conduct disorder were compared with psychiatrically hospitalized adolescents never having been so diagnosed, symptoms and signs in the two groups were remarkably similar (Lewis et al. 1984). The most significant factor distinguishing the two groups was aggressive behavior. It would seem that aggressive behaviors, in spite of the presence of other symptomatology, strongly influence the diagnosis. The negative responses that behaviorally disordered children and adolescents evoke not only in family, friends, and teachers but also in the clinicians charged with evaluating them often result in perfunctory clinical examinations in which other underlying potentially treatable disorders are overlooked. In this chapter not only the behavioral characteristics that define the syndrome but also the underlying psychiatric, neurologic, psychological, educational, family, and social vulnerabilities that are found so frequently in children and adolescents who are given the diagnosis conduct disorder are discussed.

DEFINITION

The *Diagnostic and Statistical Manual of Mental Disorders*, third edition, revised (*DSM-III-R*) defines conduct disorder as follows: "The essential feature of this disorder is a persistent pattern of conduct in which the basic rights of others and major age-appropriate societal norms or rules are violated." In order to fulfill criteria for the diagnosis, the child or adolescent must have had a disturbance of conduct lasting at least 6 months. During this period of time, three of the following behaviors must have been present:

1. Has stolen without confrontation of a victim on more than one occasion (including forgery)
2. Has run away from home overnight at least twice while living in parental or parental surrogate home (or once without returning)
3. Often lies (other than to avoid physical or sexual abuse)
4. Has deliberately engaged in firesetting
5. Is often truant from school (for older person, absent from work)
6. Has broken into someone else's house, building, or car

7. Has deliberately destroyed others' property (other than by firesetting)

8. Has been physically cruel to animals

9. Has forced someone into sexual activity with him or her

10. Has used a weapon in more than one fight

11. Often initiates physical fights

12. Has stolen with confrontation of a victim (e.g., mugging, purse-snatching, extortion, armed robbery)

13. Has been physically cruel to persons

According to the *DSM-III-R*, a person over 18 years of age can also be diagnosed as having a conduct disorder if his or her symptomatology does not meet criteria for antisocial personality disorder. On the other hand, children younger than 18 years of age cannot be diagnosed antisocial personality disorder, with the assumption being that before age 18 years, character is not yet fixed.

The current diagnosis conduct disorder is divided into three subtypes: (1) group type, in which most of the above behaviors occur in the company of peers; (2) solitary aggressive type, in which there is a predominance of aggressive behavior that is initiated by the child or adolescent alone; and (3) undifferentiated type, for children or adolescents with a mixture of clinical features that are not easily classified in the previous two subtypes.

The severity of conduct disorder in the *DSM-III-R* is assessed on a scale of mild, moderate, and severe, according to the numbers of conduct problems in excess of those needed to make the diagnosis and according to the degree of harm or actual physical injury that has been inflicted on others.

The term *conduct disorder* should be distinguished from the term *delinquent*. *Delinquent* is a legal term rather than a diagnostic term. In the United States, a delinquent is a child or adolescent who has been found guilty by a juvenile court or family court of having engaged in some form of legally proscribed behavior. Sometimes the offense can be as minor as truancy. On the other hand, a child who has committed murder may also be adjudicated delinquent.

Of note is that the severity of youngsters' offenses is not necessarily a good indicator of whether the diagnosis of conduct disorder is appropriate. For example, the child who is truant from school, hangs around with his pals, and occasionally participates in petty thefts, and who has no other serious emotional or intellectual problems, may qualify for the diagnosis of conduct disorder. On the other hand, the recurrently aggressive youngster who gets into serious, seemingly unprovoked fights and who, on occasion, does extreme physical harm may prove to be extremely paranoid and far more psychiatrically disturbed than the diagnosis of conduct disorder would indicate. In fact, it is fair to state that the more seriously and repeatedly aggressive the youngster is, the more likely he or she is to be suffering from more serious psychopathology than that subsumed under the diagnostic category of conduct disorder. Thus, the diagnostician must be careful not to dismiss recurrently violent children or adolescents as suffering simply from a conduct disorder unless he or she has ruled out the other kinds of serious neuropsychiatric conditions that often underlie such behaviors. Since many of the behaviors included in the conduct disorder category are also characteristic of children and adolescents with other kinds of psychiatric disorders (e.g., psychosis, mood disorders, brain damage) and since there is no specific effective treatment for conduct disorder itself, the clinician should make the diagnosis of conduct disorder cautiously and only after having ruled out the existence of other potentially treatable conditions.

EPIDEMIOLOGY

In 1986, of all arrests in the United States 5% were of persons younger than 15 years of age, 17% were of persons younger than 18 years of age, 31% were of persons younger than 21 years of age, and 49% were of persons younger than 25 years of age. Persons younger than 18 years of age accounted for 9% of those arrested for murder and 15% of those arrested for rape; persons from 18 to 24 years of age accounted for approximately 33% of all arrests for murder and 30% of all arrests for rape (Federal Bureau of Investigation 1987).

These statistics from the Federal Bureau of Investigation represent the extremes of behavioral disturbance. Clearly, most children and adolescents with the diagnosis of conduct disorder do not become violent antisocial aggressors. What then is the actual prevalence of conduct disorder? The answer to this question depends not only on the criteria used for the diagnosis but also on the sources of data. It would seem that certain kinds of antisocial behaviors are characteristic of many young children. For example, such behaviors as lying, disobedience, and even destruction of property have been reported to occur in roughly 50% of young children younger than 5 or 6 years of age (Achenbach and Edelbrock 1981; Kazdin 1987). The point is that these behaviors diminish as children mature into adolescents and are far less common after 12 years of age. However, there have been self-report studies of youngsters from 13 to 18 years of age that call into question the diminished prevalence of antisocial behaviors in adolescence. In some of these studies, 50% of adolescents admitted to theft, 45% to destruction of property, and a surprisingly high 35% to assault. Moreover, more than 50% of the subjects admitted to more than one kind of antisocial behavior. Were one to rely on self-reports to make diagnoses, clearly a higher proportion of adolescents would qualify for inclusion in the category of conduct disorder than if one relied on parent or teacher reports only.

Conduct disorder is of particular interest and concern to clinicians because between 33% and 50% of outpatient referrals to clinics are for antisocial, often aggressive behaviors. Aggression toward others is also one of the major reasons why adolescents are hospitalized. Antisocial behavior in childhood is also of great clinical concern because it is so often a precursor of adult antisocial behaviors. In fact, it is unusual to find adult antisocial behavior in the absence of a history of similar childhood disturbance. It would seem that the variety of different kinds of antisocial behaviors in childhood, and the failure of these behaviors to diminish appreciably over time with maturation, bode ill for adult normal socialization.

Delinquency statistics reflect the fact that although some delinquent behavior is relatively common during adolescence, only a small percentage of arrested youths go on to become chronic offenders. In a follow-up study of almost 10,000 persons born in the Philadelphia area in the same year, approximately 35% were arrested at least once during childhood or adolescence (Wolfgang et al. 1972). Of this group of arrested youths, however, only 18% (or 6% of the original birth cohort) became chronic offenders. This small percentage of the birth cohort, however, was responsible for more than 50% of the reported delinquencies in the area. It is, therefore, this fraction of behaviorally disordered youth that is of greatest concern.

Conduct disorder, as well as officially documented delinquency, is far more common in males than females. The greater prevalence of antisocial behavior in males is also reflected in crime statistics. Males account for four of five arrests; moreover, they account for 89% of violent crimes. They are also more likely to be arrested for drunken driving. When women are arrested, it is commonly for larceny or theft (Federal Bureau of Investigation 1987).

The rate of arrests of females seems to be increasing. From 1981 to 1985 there was a 2% increase in male arrests but a 13% increase in arrests of females (Federal Bureau of Investigation 1987).

ETIOLOGY

There is no single etiology for conduct disorder. Children and adolescents have a limited repertoire of behaviors with which they can respond to internal and external stresses. Therefore, a multiplicity of different kinds of biopsychosocial stressors or vulnerabilities, and combinations thereof, seem to be associated with antisocial behaviors. One of the most useful ways of looking at the etiology of conduct disorder is to consider the extrinsic and intrinsic factors associated with it and the interaction of the two.

EXTRINSIC FACTORS

Sociocultural Factors

That sociocultural factors play a role in the expression of antisocial behaviors there can be little doubt. The greater violence in the United States compared with the countries of Western Europe alone attests to this fact. Furthermore, in the United States the majority of delinquent youngsters come from the most economically deprived sectors of society. Among incarcerated delinquents as well as incarcerated adults, certain racial minorities, such as blacks, are overrepresented. The explanation for these facts, however, is unclear.

In the 1940s, 1950s, and 1960s sociological theories regarding the greater prevalence of antisocial behaviors in socioeconomically disadvantaged youngsters flourished. Among the most influential was the theory that antisocial behavior occurred in lower socioeconomic classes because of the frustration generated when impoverished persons lacked legitimate access to the material goods and social status of the wealthier members of society (Merton 1957). Others hypothesized that those raised in poverty subscribed to different social norms, that within the delinquent subculture antisocial behavior was permissible (Cloward and Ohlin 1960). Another sociologic theory hypothesized that antisocial behavior was only apparently more common in the lower socioeconomic sectors of society because youngsters from those sectors were more likely to be caught by the police (Becker 1963). There are, however, certain correlates of social class that are probably more important than socioeconomic status per se in the etiology of antisocial behavior. For example, family size, poor supervision, and a high prevalence of parental mental and physical illness are associated with low socioeconomic status. These kinds of factors, rather than poverty alone, would seem to be of importance. A lack of access to social, medical, and psychiatric services must also be considered.

Studies have documented a tendency for emotionally disturbed, aggressive black adolescents to be incarcerated, while their emotionally disturbed aggressive white adolescent counterparts are more likely to be given treatment (Lewis et al. 1980). Thus, mental illness, manifested by antisocial behavior, in black children is often dismissed as culturally expectable. The very same behaviors and symptoms in white children are much more likely to be recognized as possible signs of significant psychopathology and to receive appropriate attention.

There is a good likelihood that different kinds of child-rearing practices in different sociocultural groups contribute to or inhibit the development of antisocial behavior (Loeber and Dishion 1984; Patterson 1982). For example, there is good evidence that extremely severe corporal punishment contributes to a child's aggressive behaviors. Thus an ethnic or cultural group in which such a practice is common may, in part, account for more destructive behaviors in its children and adolescents. Similarly, the ways in which

alcohol or drugs are used (or *not* used) in different cultures probably contribute to the rate at least of alcohol- or drug-related antisocial behavior in youngsters.

Suffice it to say that the role of society in the etiology of antisocial behavior is complex. For the clinician, however, it is essential that he or she not jump to the conclusion that recurrent stealing, lying, carrying dangerous weapons, or assaultiveness are normal adaptive behaviors in minority youths or in youths raised in conditions of poverty. Most minority children, most socioeconomically deprived children, do not repeatedly come in conflict with the law; and certainly most are not recurrently aggressive. Therefore, any child who repeatedly indulges in seriously antisocial behavior deserves a careful clinical assessment.

Parental Factors

The role of parents in the etiology of children's problematic behaviors has been long recognized. Just how parental characteristics and behaviors affect children's behaviors, however, is far from clear.

There are studies that suggest the possibility that genetic factors play a role in the development of antisocial behaviors. For example, studies of adopted-away children of antisocial fathers suggest that such children have a higher likelihood of acting in antisocial ways than adopted-away children of nonantisocial fathers (Mednick and Hutchings 1978). The children most likely to behave antisocially are those with both an antisocial biological father and an antisocial adoptive father, a finding indicative of an interplay between inherited and environmental factors.

Other studies have documented specific kinds of antisocial behaviors in succeeding generations (Huesmann et al. 1984). Such symptoms and behaviors as alcoholism, truancy, and even aggressiveness itself have been reported in antisocial youngsters and their parents.

These kinds of findings must be interpreted with caution. For example, studies that rely on registered criminality and not on actual clinical assessment do not take account of the fact that criminality can be the most obvious manifestation, the final common pathway, of the interplay of a variety of different kinds of neuropsychiatric disorders and environmental stressors. Similarly, truancy in parents and children can reflect the interaction of intellectual or cognitive deficits and a lack of intellectual stimulation or cultural opportunities. In short, just because certain antisocial behaviors occur in succeeding generations does not mean that they are inherited traits.

PARENTAL VIOLENCE AND PHYSICAL ABUSE

The most serious kind of antisocial behavior, namely, aggressive behavior, has been well documented to be characteristic of the parents of many very aggressive antisocial youngsters (Lewis 1981). In fact, aggressive behaviors in four generations have been documented (Huesmann et al. 1984). There is also a wealth of data documenting the fact that abused persons often become violent and abusive themselves. Nevertheless, evidence to date suggests that it is unlikely that the mode of transmission of aggression is genetic.

Although the mode of transmission of violence and abusiveness from generation to generation has not been exhaustively researched, clinical experience and well-established psychological principles shed light on these questions. First of all, it is well recognized that children imitate the behaviors they witness. Whether this phenomenon is called modeling, identification with the aggressor, or something else is irrelevant. It happens.

Second, physical abuse often leads to brain injury, which, in turn, is often associated with impulsivity and fluctuations of mood and temper. Abusive parents are also often alcoholic parents, and exposure to alcohol in utero can itself contribute to central nervous system dysfunction and problem with temper and control.

Finally, from a psychodynamic point of view, physical abuse of a child instills rage, a rage that is often displaced onto others in the child's environment. All of these factors associated with abuse—modeling, central nervous system injury, and the engendering of rage—contribute to a child's own aggressive behaviors. Thus, what may appear at first to be the genetic transmission of aggressive behavior can usually be explained in other ways.

Aggression within a family, even when it is not directed at the child, has also been associated with children's antisocial behavior and violence (Rutter and Giller 1983). Broken homes, in and of themselves, do not seem to be related specifically to children's behavior problems. On the other hand, severe parental discord and physical violence has been associated with seriously delinquent behaviors in children. Evidence of the importance of abuse and family violence in the genesis of seriously antisocial behavior is seen in the results of a study comparing a matched sample of delinquent and nondelinquent adolescents (Lewis et al. 1987). As can be seen in Table 12–1, significantly greater numbers of delinquents had been seriously physically abused and had witnessed extreme violence between parents and other relatives.

Even when parents are not violent, studies have shown that their inadequacies in terms of simply providing appropriate structure and supervision are associated with their children's disordered conduct (Patterson 1982). They are inconsistent in their responses to antisocial behavior and often ignore or even criticize socially desirable behavior. Perhaps most important has been the observation that the parents of antisocial youngsters, for whatever reasons, do not seem to display the kind of emotional investment and support, the kind of consistent affection that children require to adapt appropriately to society.

INTRINSIC FACTORS

Physiologic, Biochemical, and Genetic Etiologic Theories

From the time of Lombroso onward, investigators have searched for some kind of biological predisposition to antisocial behavior. It was Lombroso who believed that criminals represented a kind of biological throwback to more primitive stages of human development. He also believed that criminality was transmitted genetically from generation to generation. Although this kind of perspective fell into disfavor as psychoanalytical and sociologic theories gained prominence in the 1930s, 1940s, and 1950s, in the past 20 years we have witnessed a renewed interest in the subject of possible biological predispositions to criminality.

As mentioned in the section on parents of

Table 12–1. COMPARISON OF ABUSE AND FAMILY VIOLENCE IN DELINQUENTS AND NONDELINQUENTS

Abuse and Family Psychopathology Variables	Delinquents		Nondelinquents		x^2	p Value
	No.	%	No.	%		
Abuse by mother	13	41.9	3	9.7	8.42	0.0037
Abuse by father	14	45.2	3	9.7	9.81	0.0017
Abuse by others	15	48.4	1	3.2	16.5	0.0001
Ever abused	24	77.4	4	12.9	26.05	0.0001
Witness to family violence	19	61.3	7	22.6	9.54	0.0020

(Parts of this table were published in Lewis, D. O., Pincus, J. H., Lovely, R., et al. 1987. Biopsychosocial characteristics of matched samples of delinquents and nondelinquents. *J. Am. Acad. Child Adolesc. Psychiatry* 26:744–752.)

delinquents, epidemiologic studies have reported a higher prevalence of antisocial behavior in adopted-away offspring of criminal fathers than in adopted-away children of noncriminal fathers. Other studies have noted a greater concordance for antisocial behavior in monozygotic than dizygotic twins (Christiansen 1977). However, even in these kinds of studies, environmental factors have been recognized as important influences. Efforts to document chromosomal abnormalities in antisocial persons have failed to demonstrate a significant association between such abnormalities and criminal behavior (Mednick and Gabrielli 1983).

Others have hypothesized that antisocial youngsters have an inherent autonomic hyporeactivity reflected in a slow electrodermal recovery time, making such youngsters difficult to condition with positive reinforcement (Mednick 1977). These findings are hard to interpret, given the variety of different kinds of neuropsychiatric vulnerabilities found in delinquent youngsters. Thus, at this time, it would seem to be extremely doubtful that a particular genetic or physiologic factor specific for the transmission of antisocial behavior exists.

Efforts to identify biochemical abnormalities in antisocial persons are still in their infancy. There is, however, a growing literature on the relationship of levels of certain neurotransmitters such as serotonin and norepinephrine and their metabolites to aggressive behaviors (Sahakian 1981; Alpert et al. 1981). Diminished serotonin levels in the cerebrospinal fluid of rats and of humans have been associated with high levels of aggression.

The fact that in most societies males are more aggressive than females has led investigators to consider the role of hormones in antisocial behavior, particularly in violent behavior. Findings related to testosterone levels in adolescence and aggression have been equivocal (Mattsson et al. 1980). There have also been reports of associations between endogenous and exogenous fetal androgens and increased aggressive behavior in childhood. However, hormonal studies remain inconclusive. At this time, therefore, there are no chromosomal, hormonal, physiological, or biochemical tests for conduct disorder or antisocial behavior.

Medical Histories and Neurologic Vulnerabilities

There was a time in the recent past when delinquents were believed to be physically healthy, muscular (mesomorphic) youngsters; medical problems seemed unrelated to their adaptational problems.

Our more recent epidemiologic studies (Fig. 12–1) have documented the fact that seriously antisocial youngsters, at least those who come before the juvenile court, have many more accidents, injuries, and illnesses than their demographically similar nondelinquent peers and make greater use of all hospital facilities (Lewis and Shanok 1977). Of note, differences between the medical histories of white delinquents and white nondelinquents (Table 12–2) are greater than those between black delinquents and black nondelinquents (Table 12–3). The fact, however, that black nondelinquents have almost as poor medical histories as black delinquents probably reflects especially adverse environmental conditions and, as such, sheds further light on the disproportionate number of black youngsters in the juvenile justice system.

Cumulative Hospital Contacts and Medical Problems of Delinquent and Nondelinquent Children**

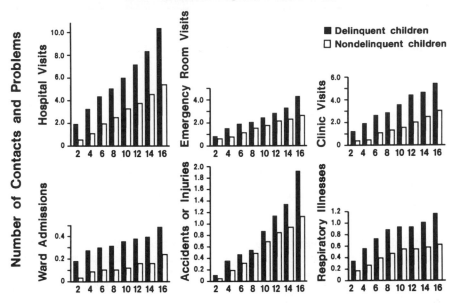

Results of Two-Tailed t Tests of Cumulative Hospital Contacts and Medical Problems of Delinquent Versus Nondelinquent Children

Item	Age of Child (years)							
	2	4	6	8	10	12	14	16
Hospital visits								
t	4.402	3.001	2.610	2.296	2.345	2.615	2.518	2.787
Significance	p=.015	p=.004	p=.010	p=.023	p=.020	p=.010	p=.013	p=.004
Emergency room visits								
t	1.757	2.366	2.023	1.548	1.588	1.578	1.787	2.411
Significance	p=.081	p=.019	p=.045	p=.124	p=.114	p=.117	p=.076	p=.017
Clinic visits								
t	2.067	2.354	2.102	2.039	2.237	2.253	2.170	2.913
Significance	p=.041	p=.020	p=.037	p=.043	p=.027	p=.026	p=.032	p=.053
Ward admissions								
t	2.625	2.675	2.355	2.429	2.636	2.215	2.370	2.295
Significance	p=0.10	p=.009	p=0.20	p=.017	p=.010	p=.028	p=.019	p=.023
Accidents or injuries								
t	1.545	1.718	1.136	0.370	0.972	1.290	1.513	2.449
Significance	p=.124	p=.088	p=.258	p'.500	p=.332	p=.199	p=.132	p=.016
Respiratory illnesses								
t	1.458	1.632	1.222	1.238	1.161	1.184	1.273	1.620
Significance	p=.147	p=.105	p=.224	p=.217	p=.248	p=.238	p=.205	p=.107

Figure 12–1. Cumulative hospital contacts and medical problems of delinquent and nondelinquent children. (Parts of Figure 12–1 were published in Lewis, D. O., Shanok, S. S. 1977. Medical histories of delinquent and nondelinquent children: An epidemiological study. Am. J. Psychiatry 134:1020–1025.)

Table 12–2. HOSPITAL USE AND NUMBER OF ACCIDENTS OF WHITE DELINQUENTS VS. WHITE NONDELINQUENTS

Hospital Service Used and No. of Accidents	Mean No. of Contacts		t Test*	p Value	Degrees Freedom
	White Delinquents	White Nondelinquents			
Total visits before age 17	9.531	2.934	3.056	<0.005	123
Emergency department visits before age 17	2.781	1.148	3.518	<0.001	123
Clinic visits before age 17	6.156	2.484	1.798	$0.10 > p > 0.05$	124
Ward admissions before age 17	0.563	0.197	2.252	<0.050	123
Accidents before age 17	1.714	0.869	2.490	<0.050	122
Total visits before age 4	2.734	0.918	1.997	<0.050	123
Emergency department visits before age 4	0.734	0.246	2.209	<0.050	123

*Results of a two-tailed t test.
(From Lewis, D. O., Feldman, M., Barrengos, M. A. 1985. Race, health and delinquency. *J. Am. Acad. Child Psychiatry* 24:161–167.)

There is considerable disagreement in the literature regarding the prevalence of neurologic impairment in antisocial children and adults. There is, however, a growing body of evidence that certain kinds of episodic violence may be associated with disorders of the central nervous system, particularly the limbic system.

One of the reasons that there is so much controversy regarding the relationship of antisocial behavior and neurologic impairment is that whatever neurologic vulnerabilities exist they are not of an immediately obvious nature. In fact, it is relatively rare to encounter a repeatedly antisocial youngster with evidence of cerebral palsy or with a history of frequent uncontrolled seizures. Nevertheless, many seriously behaviorally disturbed youngsters, on careful history and examination, will be discovered to have a multiplicity of nonspecific signs and symptoms indicative of brain dysfunction of one sort or another. A history of hyperactivity and of difficulties concentrating is a frequent accompaniment of conduct disorder.

Among the most commonly found signs of central nervous system dysfunction in youngsters with behavior problems are choreiform movements and an inability to skip. Awkward rapid alternating movements are also commonly elicited. Although, as stated, grand mal seizures are relatively uncommon, it is not unusual for a child with a conduct disorder to have a history of early febrile seizures or a diffusely abnormal electroencephalogram.

Whether complex partial seizures are more common in antisocial children or adults than in socially well-functioning persons remains an area of disagreement. Although the full

Table 12–3. HOSPITAL USE AND NUMBER OF ACCIDENTS OF BLACK DELINQUENTS VS. BLACK NONDELINQUENTS

Hospital Service Used and No. of Accidents	Mean No. of Contacts		t Test*	p Value	Degrees Freedom
	Black Delinquents	Black Nondelinquents			
Total visits before age 17	12.300	8.463	1.442	NS	79
Emergency department visits before age 17	6.282	4.390	1.260	NS	78
Clinic visits before age 17	5.333	3.707	1.056	NS	78
Ward admissions before age 17	0.462	0.341	0.780	NS	78
Accidents before age 17	2.410	1.707	1.082	NS	78
Total visits before age 4	4.700	1.244	2.695	<0.010	79
Emergency department visits before age 4	2.200	1.024	1.842	$0.10 > p > 0.05$	79

*Results of a two-tailed t test.
(From Lewis, D. O., Feldman, M., Barrengos, M. A. 1985. Race, health and delinquency. *J. Am. Acad. Child Psychiatry* 24:161–167.)

picture of complex partial seizures may not be present, it is common for seriously antisocial adolescents to reveal a history of a multiplicity of different kinds of psychomotor symptoms, including lapses of awareness, episodes of *déjà vu*, olfactory hallucinations, and impaired memory for aggressive and nonaggressive behaviors. A comparison of very violent delinquents with less aggressive delinquents is presented in Table 12–4. The kinds of symptoms characteristic of the violent sample suggest the possibility that in antisocial youngsters some kind of limbic system dysfunction may exist (Lewis et al. 1979).

In summary, the kinds of neurologic vulnerabilities characteristic of youngsters with conduct disorder tend to be subtle. As such, they will come to light only if a painstaking neurologic evaluation is performed, with special time devoted to a history of symptoms and behaviors.

Psychiatric Vulnerabilities

The extent to which behaviorally disturbed children or adults suffer from psychopathology other than characterologic defects remains another area of disagreement. One of the earliest and most influential psychodynamic theories hypothesized that antisocial children had deficient superegos, or what was termed *superego lacunae* (Johnson and Szurek 1952). These characterologic defects were believed to occur when children unconsciously lived out their parents' antisocial proclivities. Others hypothesized ego deficiencies to account for their antisocial behaviors. More recently, some interest has focused on what have been called "borderline" states in antisocial youngsters.

These rather subtle concepts regarding the psychopathology underlying children's antisocial behaviors probably reflect the fact that most antisocial youngsters, on the surface, do not appear to be seriously psychiatrically impaired. Just as it is uncommon to come across a grossly neurologically impaired youngster in this group, so it is unusual to encounter one who is flamboyantly psychotic. Had obvious neuropsychiatric disturbances other than behavior problems been present, such youngsters would undoubtedly have been recognized as emotionally disturbed, treated appropriately, and not diagnosed conduct disorder.

Ironically, antisocial youngsters, while not necessarily overtly psychotic or brain impaired, usually have long-standing histories of maladaptation affecting every area of their lives—at school, at home, and in the community. In fact, it is common to find that youngsters whose behaviors fit the diagnostic criteria for conduct disorder have had many different evaluations over the years and that at different times they have carried different diagnoses. Most common among these diagnoses is hyperactivity with attention-deficit problems, although many youngsters have histories of having been diagnosed as borderline psychotic.

It is not uncommon for the most behaviorally disturbed youngsters to have been in multiple placements during childhood, including psychiatric hospitals and residential treatment centers. In fact, there is reason to believe that, as young children, they often appeared to be more disturbed than they do during adolescence (Bender 1959). It is hard to know for sure whether the symptomatology itself changes over time or whether the very same kinds of signs and symptoms recognized in childhood as evidence of brain dysfunction or psychosis are ignored in adolescence or reinterpreted by clinicians as simply signs of behavioral problems. Unfortunately, adolescence is often erroneously expected to be a time of great emotional upheaval and rebelliousness, even though studies reveal that normal adolescents do not behave that way (Rutter et al. 1976). Thus, during adolescence, extreme or bizarre behaviors that may be signs of significant psychopathology are often dismissed by clinicians as developmentally normal.

Comparisons of incarcerated delinquents with a matched sample of nondelinquents and comparisons of especially violent delinquents with ordinary delinquents have shown that the more aggressive the youngster the more likely he or she is to have experienced a multiplicity of different kinds of serious psychiatric symptoms (Lewis et al. 1979; Lewis et al. 1987). The most prevalent of these symptoms is paranoid ideation. Many have also had episodic hallucinatory experiences as well. These kinds of symptoms have also frequently contributed to aggressive behaviors. Recurrently aggressive antisocial youngsters tend to feel threatened

Table 12–4. SPECIFIC NEUROLOGIC SIGNS: COMPARISON OF MORE VIOLENT AND LESS VIOLENT DELINQUENT BOYS

	More Violent		Less Violent			
	No.	%*	No.	%*	x^2	p Value
One or more major neurologic signs	31	46.3	1	6.7	6.499	.011
Abnormal electroencephalogram	19	29.7	0	0	2.590	.108
Positive Babinski sign	11	15.9	1	5.6	0.569	>.5
One or more minor neurologic signs	71	98.6	12	66.7	16.275	.001
Inability to skip	26	43.3	2	11.1	4.926	.027
Choreiform movements	40	60.6	5	31.1	3.375	.067
Psychomotor symptomatology	46	71.9	6	37.5	5.223	.023
Greater than 10% discrepancy between right and left palm strike	40	61.5	6	37.5	2.123	.115
Greater than 10% discrepancy between right and left finger taps	26	44.8	7	50.0	0.002	>.5

*Percentages are based on the actual number of children for whom data were available for each category.
(From Lewis, D. O., Shanok, S. S., Pincus, J. H., and Glaser, G. H. 1979. Violent juvenile delinquent: Psychiatric, neurological, psychological, and abuse factors. *J. Am. Acad. Child Psychiatry* 18:307–319.)

and to feel a need to protect themselves and carry dangerous weapons even when others in their neighborhoods do not. They often misperceive the behaviors and intentions of others and lash out when minimally provoked or when not provoked at all.

The bravado and grandiosity of many seriously antisocial, aggressive youngsters is often part of their paranoid symptomatology. Unfortunately, this bravado is so obnoxious that it is often misinterpreted by clinicians as evidence of coldness and lack of empathy. Thus the underlying paranoia and insecurity are missed.

CASE 1

A tall, black youth was incarcerated because of having raped and beaten a teenaged girl. The boy had an extensive record of other aggressive offenses, including robbery, and came from a family in which his brothers had similar histories of antisocial behavior. In addition, his mother had been psychiatrically hospitalized but her diagnosis was unclear. During interviews with this youngster, he showed no particular remorse. He was boastful and claimed to earn hundreds of dollars nightly and to have no need to rob people. On the secure unit, where he was placed, he tended to keep to himself, to walk close to the walls, and to refuse to attend class. Unfortunately, he also got into frequent physical fights with staff and peers. He had a history of occasional auditory misperceptions when he thought he or his mother was being insulted, at which times

he retaliated. It seemed to the consulting psychiatrist that many of this youngster's maladaptive aggressive behaviors were related to his paranoid orientation.

It took considerable tact to enable this youngster first to acknowledge his great psychological discomfort on the secure unit and then to agree to take some medication to try to feel more comfortable. Low doses of antipsychotic medication were started and gradually increased; every effort was made to avoid creating side effects that might have caused this very suspicious boy to discontinue treatment. As the antipsychotic medication began to take effect, this youngster became increasingly comfortable and relating. What is more, his recurrently aggressive behaviors diminished in intensity and frequency and eventually stopped. Only at this point was it possible to obtain an accurate history, perform other kinds of evaluations, including a psychoeducational assessment and begin to address the other kinds of intrinsic and extrinsic vulnerabilities contributing to his antisocial behaviors.

This case is typical of many seriously antisocial youngsters, boys and girls, whose paranoid orientations contribute to their assaultiveness. It should be stressed that the paranoid ideation and orientation of many antisocial youngsters is not necessarily indicative of a schizophrenic process. Any number of different kinds of disorders, including brain dysfunction, mood disorders, and the effects of alcohol and drugs, can be manifested as paranoid thinking. When, however, the cause is identified and the symptom is addressed, the youngster is then able to respond to whatever other aspects of treatment are also indicated.

Suicide and Conduct Disorders

It is currently fashionable in some clinical settings to categorize disturbed youngsters as either internalizers or externalizers, according to the nature of their signs, symptoms, and behaviors (Achenbach and Edelbrock 1981). From this perspective, children with conduct disturbances tend to be categorized as externalizers. However, suicide, suicide attempts, and self-mutilation, all acts against the self, are common among delinquent youngsters. What is more, several studies have reported high prevalences of major depressive disorders in seriously antisocial delinquents. It is a mistake, therefore, to dismiss suicide attempts among such youngsters as merely histrionic or manipulative acts. It is especially important not to overlook the significance of suicidal ideation and attempts because there is evidence that when depressive symptoms are treated, antisocial behavior diminishes.

Psychological, Educational, and Intellectual Vulnerabilities

There is ample evidence that behaviorally disordered children and adolescents tend to score lower on tests of intelligence than do their nondelinquent counterparts (Hirische and Hindelang 1977). These findings reflect a variety of different factors, including cultural deprivation, the consequences of central nervous system trauma, nutritional deficiencies, innate intellectual limitations, lack of schooling, test bias, and combinations of these factors. Intellectual limitations probably also influence which behaviorally disturbed youngsters will be caught and designated delinquent and which will not.

Whatever the causes, limited intelligence alone does not account for behavioral problems. Clearly, most intellectually limited children are not antisocial. Moreover, even severely retarded children, when raised with affection, understanding, and structure, behave in loving and socially acceptable ways. The degree of intellectual limitation in chil-

dren and adolescents with conduct disorder is usually minimal and is often but one of the many different kinds of vulnerabilities that make social adaptation more difficult.

Learning disabilities, however, are very prevalent in youngsters with conduct disorders, and the degree of disability, particularly in verbal skills, often corresponds to the degree of overall maladaptation of the youngsters. This may be in part because such youngsters have problems putting thoughts and feelings into words rather than actions.

The prevalence and severity of learning disabilities cannot be explained simply in terms of poor educational opportunities. Nor can these difficulties be dismissed as a reflection of the child's conscious or unconscious resentment of the system. When such young persons drop out of school early, it is usually because of the chronic frustration they experience when they tackle certain kinds of academic tasks and the lack of satisfaction they get from the work. The combination of perceptual-motor difficulties, attention problems, problems sitting still, and sometimes mild intellectual limitations together combine to make school an unhappy experience for youngsters with conduct disorders. Indeed, these very vulnerabilities, and the negative responses they elicit from teachers and peers, contribute to the development of behavioral problems. Children with conduct disorders rarely receive positive reinforcement; there is reason to believe that at least some of their disruptive behaviors represent an effort to obtain some kind of attention, even if that attention is of a negative kind.

There is a tendency among clinicians to minimize the importance of intellectual deficits or learning disabilities among minority behaviorally disordered youngsters, to dismiss poor performance on tests as evidence primarily of cultural bias in the testing materials. Unfortunately, these attitudes often deprive such youngsters of the kinds of special educational services that would enhance their academic and social functioning. The extent of cognitive dysfunction and learning disabilities in seriously antisocial youths was revealed in a study of 14 persons condemned to death as juveniles. As can be seen in Table 12–5, the majority of subjects demonstrated significant brain dysfunction, were learning disabled, and had IQs in the low and borderline ranges of normal.

Table 12–5. NEUROPSYCHIATRIC AND PSYCHOEDUCATIONAL SCORES OF 14 JUVENILES CONDEMNED TO DEATH

	WAIS-R IQ			Halstead-Reitan Battery			Woodcock-Johnson Battery		
Subject	Verbal	Performance	Full-Scale	Categories (errors)*	Tactile Performance (minutes)†	Impairment Index‡	Reading Comprehension (grade equivalent)	Calculation (grade equivalent)	Concept Formation Score
1	67	63	64	113	37.0	1.0	2.3	3.0	1.0§
2	85	84	85	57	9.4	0.4	7.6	3.3	5.8§
3	76	82	77	57	10.8	0.7	6.6	7.5	1.0§
4	75	76	74	96	23.3	0.7	5.8	7.5	2.2§
5	88	88	86	90	9.5	0.6	12.9	5.0	12.8
6	80	87	82	93	27.3	0.9	10.6	6.6	8.6
7	84	71	77	93	25.0	0.7	5.6	5.0	4.6§
8	75	85	77	66	18.6	0.7	8.6	5.3	3.0§
9	84	85	83	38	21.6	0.7	8.6	8.0	5.8§
10	112	99	106	15	8.4	0.1	12.9	12.9	7.1§
11	68	91	81	23	12.7	0.4	1.1	6.6	3.6§
12	71	77	73	91	15.6	0.5	2.0	2.6	1.0§
13	86	94	88	11	6.4	0.0	9.5	6.2	10.8
14	115	125	121	19	8.9	0.0	12.9	12.9	19.9

*More than 50 errors indicates significant brain dysfunction.
†More than 15 minutes indicates significant brain dysfunction.
‡An overall index of .07 or greater indicates brain damage.
§Subject functions significantly below appropriate grade level.
(From Lewis, D. O., Pincus, J. H., Bard, B., et al. 1988. Neuropsychiatric, psychoeducational and family characteristics of 14 juveniles condemned to death in the United States. *Am. J. Psychiatry* 145:584–589.)

CLINICAL PICTURE

As this description of the medical, neurologic, psychiatric, and psychoeducational characteristics of children and adolescents with conduct disorders has revealed, these youngsters usually do not have flamboyant symptoms or deficits that would necessarily justify their placement in other distinct diagnostic categories. Nevertheless, they have a multiplicity of vulnerabilities, all of which place them on the border of other diagnostic categories.

Youngsters with conduct disorders are not so seriously neurologically impaired that a neurologist would diagnose localized brain damage or epilepsy; still, they have numerous signs and symptoms, which may include attentional problems, cognitive impairment, psychomotor symptoms, and "soft" neurologic signs, suggestive of some central nervous system dysfunction. They are not overtly psychotic, and their mood problems rarely meet criteria for a diagnosis of depression; still, they may have considered or attempted suicide. Although few of these youngsters are overtly schizophrenic, many have histories of occasional psychotic symptomatology, especially paranoid ideation and misperceptions, that contribute to their ag-

gressive behaviors. Antisocial youngsters have numerous educational difficulties, but they are usually not retarded. Their intellectual limitations, when present, usually place them in the borderline retarded category. This category often excludes them from receiving placement in special schools and, often, even from being recognized as in need of special educational services. In short, children with behavior problems tend to have symptoms and signs that place them on the border of several different neurologic, psychiatric, and psychoeducational diagnostic categories.

CASE 2

The following case is an example of the multiplicity of vulnerabilities characteristic of behaviorally disordered children and adolescents:

A 13-year-old white boy was adjudicated delinquent and remanded to a correctional school because of outrageous behaviors, which included stealing his uncle's car and sideswiping six other cars parked near the pavement and threatening teachers and students with sticks and bats. At other times, he ran into the streets, during apparent temper tantrums, and shouted threats that he would kill himself.

This youngster was extremely reluctant to share any information with corrections staff or psychiatrists. He was provocative and inappropriate during interviews and did not endear himself to evaluators. He refused to participate in psychological testing. On admission, all that was known was that he was the child of drug-addicted, alcoholic parents and that at 6 years of age custody had been given to his grandmother. Clearly, it was essential to interview a close relative.

When his grandmother was finally located, she provided the following history. The boy had been in the custody of his addicted mother until age 6 when he fell from the third floor of a housing project while his mother was unconscious from a heroin overdose. He had suffered severe head injury, was comatose for 2 weeks, and subsequently had several grand mal seizures. Of note, his behavior changed markedly after the accident. He was unable to sit still in class, got into frequent fights, and could not learn to read. His teachers complained that he was often lost in his own world and unresponsive to questions. They thought he was simply daydreaming.

When his hospital records were reviewed and a comprehensive neuropsychiatric assessment completed, it became evident that the boy not only was cognitively impaired, with severe word-finding difficulty and poor short-term memory but his apparent daydreaming was really a manifestation of a previously overlooked seizure disorder.

In addition to his severe neuropsychological problems, scars and bruises on his body revealed that he had also been severely physically abused by a male relative. His impulsive, often violent behaviors seemed to have resulted from the combination of his central nervous system (CNS) impairment and his upbringing in a violent, abusive household. Because of the severity of his CNS trauma at age 6, the contribution to his CNS dysfunction of his mother's addictions during her pregnancy with him could not be assessed.

Of note, it took many weeks to determine just what kinds of medications would be of help. Trials of carbamazepine (Tegretol) and methylphenidate (Ritalin) were not especially helpful. Eventually, treatment with phenytoin (Dilantin) and small amounts of amphetamine (Dexedrine) and amobarbital (Amytal)

greatly improved his functioning. Once he was able to sit still and concentrate, his response to a remedial education program was dramatic and after several months, from total illiteracy, he was able to read at a second- or third-grade level.

Unfortunately all of the gains achieved during his period of intensive evaluation and treatment were lost when he was placed in a group home and his medications discontinued.

Thus, a diagnostic evaluation of a behaviorally disordered child or adolescent must be a search for a variety of different kinds of subtle but potentially treatable vulnerabilities rather than a search for single causes.

DIFFERENTIAL DIAGNOSIS AND DIAGNOSTIC EVALUATION

There is no specific treatment for conduct disorder. Furthermore, longitudinal studies of behaviorally disturbed children indicate that prognosis without treatment is poor. In addition, the diagnosis of conduct disorder has, over the years, acquired negative connotations for clinicians as well as those in the legal profession dealing with juvenile offenders. (One of the recently discarded synonyms for the aggressive type of conduct disorder was unsocialized aggressive reaction.) Because of these connotations, which imply hopelessness, the clinician must be extremely careful about making the diagnosis of conduct disorder and must rule out other potentially treatable disorders before settling on it. It is essential to keep in mind the fact that almost any of the other psychiatric conditions found in childhood and adolescence, including thought disorders, mood disorders, organic impairment, intellectual deficits, learning problems, and combinations thereof, may present as antisocial behaviors.

When evaluating an antisocial child or adolescent, the search is never for a single cause. After all, even if neurologic problems exist, most neurologically impaired children are not antisocial; even if many youngsters with conduct disorder have had episodic psychotic symptoms, most psychotic children are not antisocial; even if intellectual deficits or learning disabilities are discovered, most retarded or learning-disabled children are not antisocial. From an environmental perspective, even if parents are abusive, or if social conditions are extremely adverse, most abused children, and certainly most socioeconomically disadvantaged children, are not seriously behaviorally disturbed.

Therefore, when evaluating youngsters whose behaviors correspond to the criteria in the *DSM-III-R* for conduct disorder, one should be searching for constellations of vulnerabilities that together contribute to unacceptable behavior. When this approach is used, the clinician will almost invariably discover a variety of different kinds of problems, each of which must be addressed if the child is to function optimally.

There are certain principles that should guide such an evaluation. Primary is the enormous responsibility inherent in evaluating a child presenting with behavioral problems. The failure to recognize potentially treatable vulnerabilities in such a child may result in the child's being dismissed as simply bad. When evaluations are performed for courts, findings will often be used to determine whether a child or adolescent is found guilty or innocent of an offense, and whether he or she is incarcerated, receives treatment, or is simply sent home.

Given the multiplicity of different kinds of vulnerabilities characteristic of children with behavior problems, it is essential that assessments be thorough and multidisciplinary. Psychological, psychoeducational, neuropsychological, pediatric, and neurologic assessments can be expected to document certain kinds of vulnerabilities untapped in even the most careful psychiatric examination.

The most important part of the neurologic assessment of the behaviorally disordered child is the history. Much more is learned talking with the youngster than testing reflexes. Because such is the case, the neurologic history can be obtained by clinicians other than neurologists, including psychiatrists, psychologists, social workers, nurses, and even specially trained probation staff. In fact, the well-trained paraprofessional who is willing to spend 2 or 3 hours taking a history is more likely to document relevant data than the rushed neurologist, who may spend but half an hour with a delinquent youngster. The person, whatever his or her discipline, who takes the time to ask about accidents, injuries, illnesses, dizzy spells, headaches, memory impairment, and so on, will be able to make a more focused referral to a neurologist should it become evident

that a complete neurologic examination needs to be performed. A sophisticated referral will almost invariably elicit a more sophisticated evaluation and a more useful clinical report from the neurologist.

A focused referral, in which the neurologist is presented with all of the different reasons why the referring clinician or agency suspects that a problem exists (e.g., a history of severe head injuries, a report of episodic lapses of awareness, dizzy spells or headaches, olfactory hallucinations) requires the neurologist to look into these areas of functioning. Unfortunately, such detailed neurologic histories are not usually part of the routine neurologic examination and hence risk being overlooked.

In fact, whenever any part of a diagnostic evaluation is considered "routine," there is evidence that it is less than thorough, at least in the case of behaviorally disordered youths. A study of the documentation of medical problems and symptomatology by different clinicians examining the very same delinquent youngsters revealed how frequently important medical and family problems are overlooked by different specialists. In Figure 12–2, which is from a study of 20 incarcerated delinquents, comparison is made of the clinical findings gathered by professionals in several different clinical fields and data from hospital records. Given this evidence of how much relevant data was overlooked by each specialist, it is vital for the clinician seeing a child with behavior problems to assume that he or she is the only caring, competent clinician who will ever spend time with the child. The likelihood that someone else will pick up relevant signs and symptoms missed by the first clinician is small.

TREATMENT AND PROGNOSIS

There is no recognized effective treatment specifically for conduct disorder. In fact, Martinson et al. (1976), after reviewing hundreds of different programs for delinquents and adult criminals, reported that nothing seemed to be very effective.

The reason that·no single treatment modality has proven effective is most likely because conduct disorder is not really a single homogeneous entity. Given the myriad of different kinds of intrinsic and extrinsic vulnerabilities characteristic of children and ad-

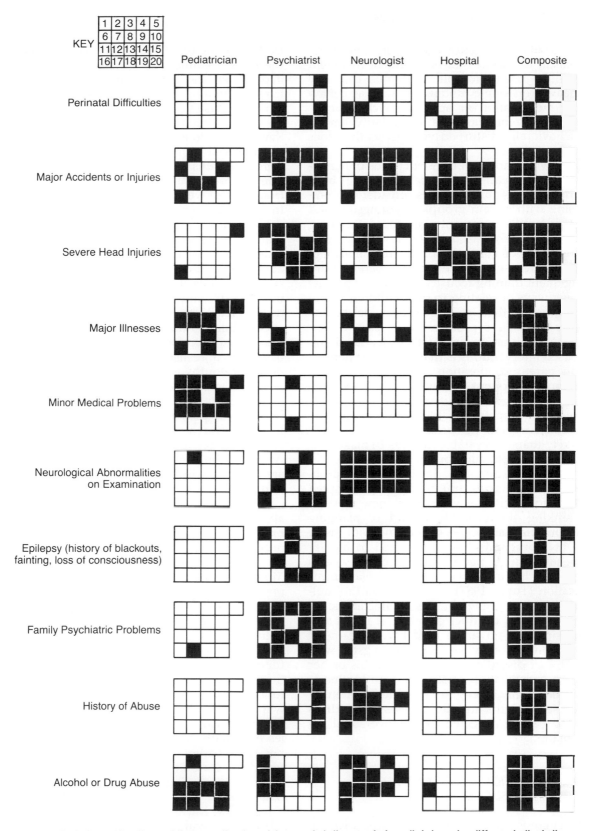

Figure 12–2. Identification of the medical problems of delinquents by clinicians in different disciplines. (Reprinted by permission of Elsevier Science Publishing Co., Inc., from Lewis, D. O., Shanok, S. S., Pincus, J. H., and Giammarino, B. A. 1982. The medical assessment of seriously delinquent boys. J. Adol. Health Care 3:160–164. Copyright 1982 by The Society for Adolescent Medicine.)

olescents with conduct disorder, there is no reason to expect that one kind of treatment will be useful for all. Programs that rely heavily on single modalities, such as behavior modification or specific psychopharmacologic agents, assume a similarity among behaviorally disturbed youngsters that does not exist.

A wide variety of different kinds of family-oriented treatment modalities have been tried. One of the strategies considered promising with certain groups of youngsters and their families is parent management training (Kazdin 1985). Based on the assumption that disorders of conduct spring from maladaptive parent–child interactions, parent management training focuses on teaching parents new ways of relating to their children and of reinforcing their children's prosocial behavior. One of the problems with parent management training and with other family-focused interventions is that they must depend on parent cooperation. For the families of many delinquent youngsters, this expectation is unrealistic. Outcome studies have already demonstrated that socioeconomically disadvantaged, discordant families are less likely than more stable families to make lasting gains from such programs.

Other treatment modalities, such as problem-solving skills training, have attempted to teach antisocial youngsters new ways of thinking about problems and of planning appropriate strategies for dealing with them. Other programs have attempted to modify behavior with psychopharmacologic agents such as lithium carbonate or stimulant medication (Tupin 1987). Again, given the multiplicity of vulnerabilities characteristic of youths with conduct disorder, it is not surprising that no single modality of treatment has proven effective. Each youngster with conduct disorder is unique, with his or her own constellation of strengths and vulnerabilities. Only a program designed to identify those strengths and deficiencies and address each can be expected to enhance social adaptation.

TIME LIMITATIONS IN RELATION TO TREATMENT SUCCESS

There is another common characteristic of treatment programs as they exist today that further diminishes the chances that they will lead to lasting functional gains. That is, even the finest treatment programs are time limited. Given the pervasiveness of the problems of children with conduct disorder, these limits are usually unrealistic. For example, residential treatment, even in institutions that attempt to address a multiplicity of biopsychosocial problems, is usually limited to from 6 months to 2 years. Similarly, parent training programs are described as requiring from several weeks to 50 or 60 sessions (only from 1 to 2 years) (Kazdin 1985).

The kinds of intrinsic and environmental vulnerabilities of children with conduct disorder and their families described previously are chronic. Such vulnerabilities as paranoid misperceptions, learning disorders or cognitive deficits, and neurologic impairment are usually responsive to specific kinds of therapeutic interventions. They rarely, however, disappear. Therefore, any treatment program based on a realistic comprehension of the needs of youths with serious conduct disorder must appreciate the need to build ongoing supports into the program. It may be necessary to plan for such sustained supports to last throughout the youngsters' adolescence and on into their early adult years. After all, the years between ages 18 and 24 are those in which antisocial youngsters get into greatest difficulty.

A good way for readers of this chapter to appreciate the ongoing needs of multiply handicapped youngsters with conduct disorder is to look back at their own support systems during their late teens and early 20s. Most readers will find that they had certain institutional supports (e.g., college) as well as family supports, and chances are the average reader did not suffer from the kinds of vulnerabilities characteristic of the youngsters described previously. If ordinary, well-functioning children and adolescents require these kinds of ongoing supports in order to function as competent adults, can youths with conduct disorder be expected to function well with considerably less? Since adolescents with conduct disorder usually do not have parental supports, ways must be found to create at least partial ongoing substitutes for missing emotional and physical sustenance.

Ironically, the knowledge that children and adolescents with conduct disorder have a multiplicity of neuropsychiatric and psychoeducational vulnerabilities is not necessarily bad news, because the nature of these handicaps is identifiable. What is more, each of the identified vulnerabilities underlying conduct disorder, in contrast to the diagnosis of conduct disorder itself, has implications for specific treatment interventions. Thus there is reason to be hopeful that effective multimodal treatment programs with ongoing support systems can be developed to meet the needs of the multiply handicapped youngsters diagnosed as having conduct disorder.

References

Achenbach, T. M., and Edelbrock, C. S. 1981. Behavioral problems and competencies reported by parents of normal and disturbed children ages four through sixteen. *Monographs of the Society for Research in Child Development* 46:188. Chicago: University of Chicago Press.

Alpert, J. E., Cohen, D. J., Shaywitz, B. A., et al. 1981. Neurochemical and behavioral organization: Disorders of attention, activity, and aggression. In Lewis, D. O. (ed.): *Vulnerabilities to Delinquency*. New York: Spectrum Publications, Inc.

Becker, H. S. 1963. *Outsiders: Studies in the Sociology of Deviance*. New York: Free Press.

Bender, L. 1959. The concept of pseudopsychopathic schizophrenia in adolescents. *Am. J. Orthopsychiatry* 29:491–509.

Christiansen, K. O. 1977. A review of studies of criminality among twins. In Mednick, S. A., and Christiansen, K. O. (eds.): *Biosocial Bases of Criminal Behavior*. New York: Gardner Press.

Cloward, R. A., and Ohlin, L. E. 1960. Differential opportunity and delinquent subcultures. In Cloward, R. A., and Ohlin, L. E. (eds.): *Delinquency and Opportunity: A Theory of Delinquent Gangs*. New York: Free Press.

Federal Bureau of Investigation. 1987. *Uniform Crime Report*. Washington, D.C.

Hirische, T., and Hindelang, M. J. 1977. Intelligence and delinquency: A revisionist review. *Am. Sociol. Rev.* 42:571–587.

Huesmann, L. R., Eron, L. D., Lefkowitz, M. M., et al. 1984. Stability of aggression over time and generations. *Devel. Psychol.* 20:1120–1134.

Johnson, A. M., and Szurek, S. A. 1952. The genesis of antisocial acting out in children and adults. *Psychoanal. Quart.* 21:323.

Kazdin, A. E. 1985. *Treatment of Antisocial Behavior in Children and Adolescents*. Homewood, IL: Dorsey Press.

Kazdin, A. E. 1987. *Conduct Disorders in Childhood and Adolescence*. Newbury Park, Beverly Hills, London, New Delhi: Sage Publications.

Lewis, D. O. (ed.): 1981. *Vulnerabilities to Delinquency*. New York: Spectrum Publications, Inc.

Lewis, D. O., and Shanok, S. S. 1977. Medical histories of delinquent and nondelinquent children: An epidemiological study. *Am. J. Psychiatry* 134:1020–1025.

Lewis, D. O., Shanok, S. S., Pincus, J. H., et al. 1979. Violent juvenile delinquents: Psychiatric, neurological, psychological, and abuse factors. *J. Am. Acad. Child Psychiatry* 18:307–319.

Lewis, D. O., Shanok, S. S., Cohen, R. J., et al. 1980. Race bias in the diagnosis and disposition of violent adolescents. *Am. J. Psychiatry* 137:1211–1216.

Lewis, D. O., Lewis, M., Unger, L., and Goldman, C. 1984. Conduct disorder and its synonyms: Diagnoses of dubious validity and usefulness. *Am. J. Psychiatry* 141:514–519.

Lewis, D. O., Pincus, J., Lovely, R., et al. 1987. Biopsychosocial characteristics of matched samples of delinquents and nondelinquents. *J. Am. Acad. Child Adolesc. Psychiatry* 26:744–752.

Loeber, R., and Dishion, T. J. 1984. Boys who fight at home and school: Family conditions influencing crosssetting consistency. *J. Consult. Clin. Psychol.* 52:759–768.

Martinson, R., Palmer, T., and Adams, S. 1976. *Rehabilitation, Recidivism, and Research*. Hackensack, N.J.: National Council on Crime and Delinquency.

Mattsson, A., Schalling, D., Olweus, D., et al. 1980. Plasma testosterone, aggressive behavior, and personality dimensions in young male delinquents. *J. Am. Acad. Child Psychiatry* 19:476–490.

Mednick, S. A. 1977. A bio-social theory of learning of law-abiding behavior. In Mednick, S. A., and Christiansen, K. O. (eds.): *Biosocial Bases of Criminal Behavior*. New York: Gardner Press.

Mednick, S. A., and Hutchings, B. 1978. Genetic and psychophysiological factors in asocial behavior. In Hare, R. D., and Schalling, D. (eds.): *Psychopathic Behavior: Approaches to Research*. Chichester, England: John Wiley.

Mednick, S. A., and Gabrielli, W. F. 1983. Biological, psychological, and sociofamilial factors in crime: Part II. In Mednick, S. A., et al. (eds.): *Longitudinal Study of Social and Biological Factors in Crime*. Washington, D.C.: Department of Justice.

Merton, R. K. 1957. *Social Theory and Social Structure*. New York: Free Press.

Patterson, G. R. 1982. *Coercive Family Process*. Eugene, OR: Castalia.

Rutter, M., and Giller, H. 1983. *Juvenile Delinquency: Trends and Perspectives*. New York: Guilford Press.

Rutter, M., Graham, P., Chadwick, O., et al. 1976. Adolescent turmoil: Fact or fiction? *J. Child Psychol. Psychiatry* 17:35–56.

Sahakian, B. J. 1981. The neurochemical basis of hyperactivity and aggression induced by social deprivation. In Lewis, D. O. (ed.): *Vulnerabilities to Delinquency*. New York: Spectrum Publications, Inc.

Tupin, J. P. 1987. Psychopharmacology and Aggression. In Roth, L. H. (ed.): *Clinical Treatment of the Violent Person*. New York: Guilford Press.

Wolfgang, M. E., Figlio, R., and Sellin, T. 1972. *Delinquency in a Birth Cohort*. Chicago: University of Chicago Press.

Substance Abuse in Children and Adolescents

JAMES HALIKAS, M.D.

Substance abuse, the use of alcohol, illegal psychoactive chemicals, and psychoactive natural products, or the inappropriate use of prescribed psychoactive drugs among children and adolescents, has been a major problem in our society for more than 25 years. There is no historical information with which to compare this quarter century for precedents and solace. From anecdotal, descriptive information, it would appear that alcohol abuse has been present among adolescents of all economic levels wherever alcoholic beverages existed. Abuse of the other major naturally occurring substances, while present, is not well documented. These substances include marijuana, cocoa leaf or cocaine, hallucinogenic mushrooms or mescaline, opium, tobacco, and caffeine-containing products. These substances appear to have been commonly used in all societies where available. There is scant evidence that persuasively documents the existence of any culture or society over any historical time period that did not have at least one psychoactive drug in use.

Part of the dearth of specific information regarding the use of such substances by children and adolescents in past eras is the general lack of historical differentiation between children and the adult culture. Historically, children and adolescents, unless they are major players in historical events, are largely invisible. In the United States, there is substantial support indicating that alcohol abuse has been a major problem and a major component of our adult society throughout our history, from colonial days to the present (Rorabaugh 1979). There was no particular focus on adolescent versus adult substance abuse in U.S. historical writings. When early 19th century authors do mention it, they describe children imitating or being trained in adults' drinking patterns: "It is no uncommon thing to see a boy of twelve or fourteen years old . . . walk into a tavern in the forenoon to take a glass of brandy and bitters . . . " (Rorabaugh 1979).

Alcohol has been the drug of choice for American society from earliest days. Tobacco, also, has been a ubiquitous substance from early colonial days. Marijuana use can be traced to colonial days, although it never enjoyed the popularity or persistence of alcohol and tobacco use. There is no indication that opium was a significant problem in the United States for any group, other than immigrant Chinese laborers imported in the 19th century to work on the railroads. Injectable narcotics became a problem after the Civil War because of the convergence of the discovery of the hypodermic needle and the creation of a generation of maimed veterans with chronic pain. With the development of the proprietary pharmaceutical industry, the use of tinctures of various drugs such as opium, cocaine (Vin Mariani and the original Coca-Cola), and marijuana came into widespread use (Musto 1973). Intermittently, other drugs, including belladonna and ether, have enjoyed relatively brief popularity. Because of the absence of systematic demographic and epidemiologic data from previous generations, we are at a loss to know whether the drug "epidemic" of the past 25 years is a historical aberration, a presage of things to come, or merely a new wrinkle in an old tale.

Tobacco use, mostly in the form of cigarettes or chewing tobacco, and alcohol use, in many forms, have been part of adolescent culture in the United States since the late 1800s. What is not known for the past is what percentage of youngsters tried these substances, at what ages, or with what effect. For tobacco, it has been suggested that upward of 75% of persons who smoke a total of one pack (20) of cigarettes before the age of 21 will become dependent on tobacco use at some point in their lifetime. Given the enormous addiction potential of nicotine, it was not surprising that the entire culture was soon overwhelmed with tobacco addiction once an acceptable form of tobacco use became available by the invention of prerolled cigarettes. The only groups of society who appear to have survived the tobacco epidemic of the 1920s to 1950s unscathed were those protected by strong religious beliefs, ethnic isolation, antifeminist conservatism, or idiosyncratic physiological intolerance to early experimentation. It would appear that most persons who eventually became dependent on tobacco learned to use it as children or teenagers. Alcohol use was probably also learned in adolescence, although at somewhat later ages than tobacco use. Marijuana and injectable forms of opiates (primarily heroin) have had cycles of epidemic use in the United States beginning in the early 1900s.

In the late 1940s, Glueck and Glueck (1950) extensively studied delinquent behavior in white male adolescents in Boston. It is noteworthy that they thought so little of drug and alcohol problem usage that they failed to collect epidemiologic data on use in this population. Robins collected similar, fragmentary data on black males in St. Louis. Her data indicated that while few black adolescents of that era used heroin, those who used it more than six times were at very high risk of eventual addiction to heroin (Robins and Murphy 1967).

Beginning in the early 1960s, there has been an epidemic of substance abuse among young adults and adolescents in all parts of U.S. society. From the early 1960s through the mid-1970s, this epidemic followed the pattern of the spread of other innovative sociologic phenomena. It began in the larger cities and spread by social contact from current user to future user. It spread from adult users to young adult users to late adolescent and earlier adolescent users and finally to child users. A clinically apparent characteristic that was eventually verified by careful research was that the spread was first among more antisocial and risk-taking populations. Depending on their local leadership position, use then spread to more mainstream, more normal, potential users. Over the past 25 years, what began as adult behavior among more antisocial and dissocial elements became mainstreamed into the general population and moved down chronologically to younger and younger more normal adolescents and children.

With the spread to wider segments of the population, however, has come the virtual disappearance of several previous descriptive characteristics of the drug-using population; that is, prevalence among males, among lower class populations, among minority populations, and among antisocial populations. Those characteristics have become progressively less useful in identifying populations at risk for substance abuse (Kardel 1978).

Several childhood and adolescent diagnoses are associated with an increased incidence of drug and alcohol abuse. Although controversial, several authors believe "hyperactivity" (attention-deficit disorder) predisposes children to substance abuse. More recently, research efforts have suggested that aggression and other conduct disorder symptoms often associated with hyperactivity may be the actual predisposing variables. There is, for example, no convincing evidence that hyperactivity in the absence of aggression puts a child at increased risk for substance abuse. Concern that treatment of hyperactive children with medications such as stimulants may lead to later abuse of drugs has also abated after rigorous study. Conduct disorder and associated symptoms, on the other hand, are likely predisposing variables in the development of substance abuse. Aggressivity, delinquent behavior, low self-esteem, and poor scholastic performance have all been supported as precursors of substance abuse (Barcai and Rabkin 1974; Kaplan 1975;

Jessor and Jessor 1977; Weiss et al. 1979; Loney et al. 1981).

Multiple studies conclude that family history is the strongest predictor of future alcoholism in adolescents. The majority of research on genetic factors in the etiology of alcoholism has come from adoption studies in men. In North America and Western Europe 20% to 25% of the sons of alcoholics become alcoholic. Goodwin and colleagues (1977) failed to find the same vulnerability in adopted daughters of biological alcoholic mothers, but Bohman and co-workers (1981) found alcoholism three times as likely in proband than control daughters. It has been proposed that familial risk for alcoholism can result from heredity or environment or from a significant interaction of both factors. Cloninger (1983) identified two types of genetic predisposition to alcoholism: male-limited, which is characterized by early onset, usually adolescence, and severe behavioral consequences; and milieu-limited, which tends to have a variable, later adult onset, proceeds along a more benign behavioral course, occurs in women as well as men, demonstrates addiction features, and is influenced by environmental factors. The diagnosis of conduct disorder or associated symptoms in addition to a family history of alcoholism increases a child's risk for later abuse.

Cloninger et al. (1986) found that the risk of developing alcoholism by age 25 rose dramatically in the first-degree relatives of alcoholic probands in comparing 1969 and 1983 studies. Therefore, even a strong predictor such as family history may be rapidly changing.

Thus, substance abuse among children and adolescents continues to be a challenging area without historical precedence and with changing dimensions.

EPIDEMIOLOGY

Alcohol

Almost all adolescents have tried alcohol (as a nonparentally sanctioned behavior) at least once at some point prior to graduation from high school. In 1985, 37% of senior high school students reported that they had drunk heavily at least once during the preceding 2 weeks. This was a slight drop from 1983 when 41% had indicated at least one episode of recent heavy drinking. In 1985, nearly 5% of high school seniors reported that they drank every day; this was a slight decline from 7% among high school seniors in 1979 (National Institute on Alcohol Abuse and Alcoholism 1987).

Alcohol is a factor in nearly half of all deaths from motor vehicle accidents. Adolescents appear to be particularly vulnerable to serious drunk driving automobile accidents. Because of this, 26 states raised their minimum drinking age between 1975 and 1984. These states showed an average reduction of 13% in night-time fatal automobile crashes among 18-year-old and 19-year-old drivers.

Overall Drug Use

According to the most recent National Household Survey of Drug Abuse (1985) 70 million Americans, or 37% of the total U.S. population aged 12 and above, have used some illicit drug at some time in their lives. At the time of the survey, 23 million persons, or 12% of the total U.S. population, had used some illicit drug within the past 30 days. They were considered "current" users. While the use of marijuana and some drugs had declined since the comparable 1982 survey, the use of cocaine increased markedly (National Institute on Drug Abuse 1985).

Among adolescents, there has been a continuing downward trend in drug use in recent years, as found by the 1986 National High School Senior Survey by the National Institute on Drug Abuse (1986b). The proportion of high school seniors who reported any lifetime experience with illicit drugs dropped from 61% in 1985 to 58% in 1986 and to 57% in 1987. Current use of any illicit drug, that is, use within the past 30 days, decreased from 30% to 27% of the high school seniors surveyed.

Marijuana

Marijuana use among high school seniors peaked at just over 60% in the survey year 1979–1980. Among 1986 high school seniors, 51% had used marijuana at some time. Current use of marijuana was acknowledged by 23% of the high school seniors surveyed, down from 26% the year before and down from the peak of 37% found in 1978. Daily marijuana use continued to decline from a high of 11% in 1978 to 4% in the 1986 surveyed group and 3.3% among 1987 seniors (National Institute on Drug Abuse 1987).

From 1982 to 1985, current use of marijuana decreased from 11% to 10% of the total population over 12 years old. Among 12- to 17-year olds, the proportion who had ever tried marijuana declined from 27% to 24% and among 18- to 25-year olds, the proportion who had ever tried marijuana declined from 64% to 61% (National Institute on Drug Abuse 1985). Attitudes among high school seniors regarding marijuana use have also changed in recent years. By 1986, the proportion of high school seniors who believed that regular marijuana use involved great risk had more than doubled to 71% compared with the proportion of high school seniors in 1978 who had this belief (National Institute on Drug Abuse 1986a).

Cocaine

Unfortunately cocaine experimentation and use went up dramatically from 1982 to 1985. There were 4.2 million persons in the United States in 1982 who had used cocaine during the prior 30 days ("current"); this rose to 5.8 million in 1985, a 38% increase (National Institute on Drug Abuse 1985). Between 1985 and 1986, the proportion of high school seniors who had ever tried cocaine remained static at 17%. Use of a smokeable form of cocaine, "crack," was surveyed for the first time in 1986 among the high school seniors, and it was found that 4% of the seniors had tried this form of cocaine during the year prior to the interview (National Institute on Drug Abuse 1986a). Overall, the percentage of teenagers (aged 12–17) who had ever used cocaine decreased from 6.5% in 1982 to 5.2% in 1985.

In 1986, 6.2% of seniors were "current" users of cocaine. In 1987, that rate dropped to 4.3%. Among college students during this same interval, there was a decline from 17% to 14%. Among the 1987 high school seniors, use in the previous year declined from 12.7% to 10.3% and lifetime use declined from 16.9% to 15.2%. "Crack" was tried by 5.6% of seniors at some time and 4% in the past year (National Institute on Drug Abuse 1987).

Paralleling the widespread increase and availability of cocaine has been a parallel increase in publicity about the dangers and consequences of its use. High school seniors in 1986 were readily aware of harmful effects of "regular" cocaine use (82% vs. 70% in 1979), however this recognition of risk decreased to 54% for occasional cocaine use; furthermore, 34% believed that there was not much risk associated with trying cocaine once or twice (National Institute on Drug Abuse 1986a).

The illicit use of stimulants and sedatives continues to decline among young persons generally. For example, current use of stimulants among high school seniors went from 5.5% in 1986 to 5.2% in 1987. Current use of sedatives dropped from 2.2% to 1.7% during the same interval.

Other Drugs

The proportion of high school seniors who had ever used PCP remained at 5% in the 1986 survey. While use in the past year decreased from 3% in 1985 to 2% in 1986, use within the past 30 days decreased from 2% in 1985 to 1% in 1986. Unfortunately, 9% of teenagers aged 12 to 17 have experimented with inhalants and 4% were current users (National Institute on Drug Abuse 1986a). Among the 1986 high school seniors, 1% had at one time tried heroin (National Institute on Drug Abuse 1986b).

Multiple Drug Use

Most current illicit drug users are multiple drug users. Among young adults aged 18 to 25, more than a fourth of current marijuana users are also current cocaine users. Among those who had not used marijuana in the past month, only 2% had used cocaine (National Institute on Drug Abuse 1985).

In 1987, there was no decline in use of alcohol by high school seniors for the third straight year, with 66% being current users, 5% daily users, and more than 37% reporting at least one occasion of heavy drinking (five or more drinks in a row) in the past 2 weeks. Cigarette smoking has not dropped since 1984 among high school seniors. Nearly 20% are daily smokers before they leave high school, a group almost certain to become addicted users, based on past comparable populations (National Institute on Drug Abuse 1987).

Among teenage current cigarette smokers aged 12 to 17, 74% also drink alcohol, 47% use marijuana, and 9% use cocaine. Among teenagers who drink, 37% also use marijuana and 5% also use cocaine. Among teenagers who use marijuana, 60% smoke cigarettes, 84% drink alcohol, and 12% use cocaine. Thus, cigarette use appears to have a gate-keeper function for most teenagers, even those who do not continue its use. In addition, for many youngsters there appears to be a common progression, or stepping stone, from cigarettes to alcohol to marijuana to cocaine and other drugs (National Institute on Drug Abuse 1986b).

Methodologic Limitations of These Data

Unfortunately, all large-scale adolescent substance abuse surveys are school based, of necessity. School dropouts are therefore lost beyond the point that they leave school, and this group is particularly vulnerable and at particular risk for ongoing drug use exposure and personal drug use. The proportion of ongoing drug use in this population is probably significantly higher than in those teenagers who remain in high school. This national data base is therefore significantly flawed and should be considered a minimum estimate. A summary of the lifetime prevalence and recent use of 16 types of drugs by the 1987 senior cohort studied by the National Institute on Drug Abuse is presented in Table 13–1.

DIAGNOSIS

The Concept of the Diagnosis of Substance Abuse

Substance abuse as a diagnosis, whether labeled chemical dependency, alcoholism, alcohol dependence, or identified by a particular named drug, such as cocaine dependence, is a relatively new concept. Osler, and others, defined the various syndromes of "morphinism" and alcoholism by (1) their presenting intoxicated states, (2) their tendency to relapse and readdiction, and (3) the intense craving noted for the particular substance. No early investigator considered that an underlying disease process dictated the course of the illness.

In the 1940s and 1950s Jellinek (1952) described the natural history of the alcoholic patient as a descending life curve lined with behavioral problems until the patient "hits bottom." From that point, the patient could begin his recovery with analogous landmarks. As part of his descending curve, Jellinek listed a series of adverse life events in what he considered the appropriate chronological sequence to characterize the natural history of the alcoholic.

While the specific chronology and sequence of problems were not necessarily accurate or even present for any single patient, a crucial leap forward had been made by this conceptualization of the disease of alcoholism. Until that point there was no coherent formulation on which to base the disease concept of alcoholism. There were clinicians who believed that the pathognomonic characteristic of the alcoholic was "looking forward to a drink" and others who believed that tolerance was the sine qua non of the illness or that inability to remain abstinent was the salient characteristic. Jellinek moved the field forward by focusing on multiple behavioral events and consequences of use.

Investigators at Washington University provided the theoretical formulation for the definition of the disease of alcoholism. Collecting adverse life events and behavioral consequences of the use of the psychoactive substance and organizing them by appropriate life categories, they developed the proposition that a substance abuser was someone who had problems in multiple life areas as a consequence of his or her drug use. Thus, the crucial underlying concept that has defined substance abuse from that time on is the appearance of *adverse consequences or life problems directly related to the elective use of a substance occurring in multiple areas of the person's life.* As summarized by this group, alcoholism involved an adverse consequence or problem in two or more of four groups of symptoms (Feighner et al. 1972):

1. Biomedical complications
2. Control, or the loss of control, of the use of the substance
3. Psychosocial complications
4. Subjective opinions of significant others.

Within each of these four life areas were five

Table 13–1. LIFETIME PREVALENCE (PERCENT EVER USED) AND RECENCY OF USE OF 16 TYPES OF DRUGS BY CLASS OF 1987 (APPROX. N = 16,300)

Drug	Ever Used	Past Month	Past Year, Not Past Month	Not Past Year	Never Used
Marijuana/hashish	50.2	21.0	15.3	13.9	49.8
Inhalants*	17.0	2.8	4.1	10.1	83.0
Inhalants adjusted†	18.6	3.5	4.6	10.5	81.4
Amyl and butyl nitrites‡	4.7	1.3	1.3	2.1	95.3
Hallucinogens	10.3	2.5	3.9	3.9	89.7
Hallucinogens adjusted§	10.6	2.8	3.9	3.9	89.4
LSD	8.4	1.8	3.4	3.2	91.6
PCP‡	3.0	0.6	0.7	1.7	97.0
Cocaine	15.2	4.3	6.0	4.9	84.8
"Crack"‖	5.6	1.5	2.5	1.6	94.4
Other cocaine‡	14.0	4.1	5.7	4.2	86.0
Heroin	1.2	0.2	0.3	0.7	98.8
Other opiates¶	9.2	1.8	3.5	3.9	90.8
Stimulants adjusted¶**	21.6	5.2	7.0	9.4	78.4
Sedatives¶	8.7	1.7	2.4	4.6	91.3
Barbiturates¶	7.4	1.4	2.2	3.8	92.6
Methaqualone¶	4.0	0.6	0.9	2.5	96.0
Tranquilizers¶	10.9	2.0	3.5	5.4	89.1
Alcohol	92.2	66.4	19.3	6.5	7.8
Cigarettes	67.2	29.4	(37.8)††		32.8

*Data based on four questionnaire forms. N is four fifths of N indicated.
†Adjusted for underreporting of amyl and butyl nitrites.
‡Data based on a single questionnaire form. N is one fifth of N indicated.
§Adjusted for underreporting of PCP.
‖Crack users may have used other forms of cocaine.
¶Only drug use that was not under a doctor's orders is included here.
**Based on the data from the revised question, which attempts to exclude the inappropriate reporting of nonprescription stimulants.
††The combined total for the two columns is shown because the question asked did not discriminate between the two answer categories.
‡‡Data based on two questionnaire forms. N is two fifths of N indicated.
(From the National Institute on Drug Abuse, 1987, National High School Senior Survey. Alcohol, Drug Abuse, and Mental Health Administration, Public Health Service, U.S. Department of Health and Human Services. Conducted by the University of Michigan Institute for Social Research.)

to ten individual problems, consequences, or pathologic behaviors that had been noted in previous literature as being common clinical manifestations and characteristics of individual alcoholics.

This separation into specific life areas is very similar to the traditional "review of systems" used in the rest of medicine. Using this life areas model, and depending on how narrowly one might define a life area, it is possible to generate many life areas, each of which has a specific array of problems and pathologic behaviors related to the effect and use of alcohol. It is therefore this fundamental proposition that the diagnosis of substance abuse is based on adverse consequences having occurred in *multiple* life areas that is crucial to identification of the individual substance abuse syndromes.

The Theoretically Based Diagnosis of Substance Abuse

The first life area for alcoholism, as the prototypical substance abuse disorder, is *biomedical complications*, a series of medical problems and conditions such as gastritis, ulcers, diarrhea, liver problems, Wernicke-Korsakoff syndrome, cerebellar dysfunction, and, most commonly, memory blackouts.

The second life area, *control, or the loss of control*, acknowledged the apparent importance of loss of control or partial loss of control that the substance abuser or alcoholic experiences that normal drinkers do not face: an inability to stop drinking once begun; an inability to maintain abstinence; an inability to abstain from use in dangerous or socially inappropriate situations; an inability to moderate one's use in specific social situations; and craving, an internal urgency or need for the substance, that dominates periods of nonuse. Loss of control includes being unable to stop drinking once one has begun, making attempts to control one's drinking, placing artificial rules on occasions or types of alcohol used, going on binges or benders of continuous drinking with default on responsibilities, drinking nonbeverage alcohol, and drinking on first arising or before the first meal.

The third life area, *psychosocial complications*, involves vehicular problems, work problems, problems with the law, and other acting-out behaviors. Default on responsibilities, decrease in productivity, disciplinary issues, and missed time are all considered examples of job problems. Driving problems involve automobile accidents, moving violations, or any other complication of driving because of being intoxicated in this or other dangerous circumstances. Other acting-out consequences of intoxication might have included public intoxication, disorderly conduct, or fighting.

The fourth life area, *subjective opinions of significant others*, reflects negative comments from those persons important to the patient. For example, family members may have objected to the patient's drinking or complained about problems that arose from the drinking; complaints or concerns expressed by important persons in the patient's life, such as physicians, neighbors, clergy, parents, and friends, are also considered in this category. Patients, themselves, may have felt that they were drinking too much, or had occasions of overuse, or may have even begun to move toward treatment, such as by attending an Alcoholics Anonymous meeting or attempting a period of abstinence from use, to demonstrate (falsely) that they are not alcoholics.

The Diagnosis of the Adolescent or Child

For purposes of characterizing the behavior as harmful, inappropriate, and not socially sanctioned, it is acceptable to define any use of tobacco, alcohol, or any of the psychoactive substances as abuse in this population. However, that characterization is very different from a diagnosis for that same youngster. Diagnosis carries with it information about

etiology, natural history, clinical course, and so on. There is some importance attached to being able to differentiate between youngsters who may be following social peer pressure, whose natural caution and responsiveness to normal societal rules will limit their involvement in such unacceptable behaviors, and those youngsters whose use of substances is either symptomatic of larger problems or representative of a progression of developmentally deviant social behaviors. This differentiation has a significant impact on management and treatment.

With the use of the theoretical principles and criteria required to formulate a diagnosis as just presented, diagnostic criteria for substance abuse in adolescents have been developed based on the presence of problems in each of three adolescent life areas: biomedical complications, school problems, and psychosocial complications (Halikas et al. 1984). These criteria are presented in Table 13–2 and were initially described relative to alcohol abuse characteristics. A second set of criteria was derived from drug abuse syndromes. Subsequently, modifications to the original alcohol criteria that make them "drug neutral" and can be used to represent either alcohol or illicit substances or both were made (Blum 1987).

In these adolescent criteria, biomedical complications include a history of behavior changes such as memory blackouts, morning drinking, hallucinations, or shakes because of alcohol use. Any of these behaviors or problems need have occurred only once to be counted. While shakes, hallucinations, and morning drinking may be related to withdrawal or tolerance effects, the presence of tolerance or a withdrawal syndrome from the substance is not required for adolescents. There are no data regarding the frequency of tolerance or actual physical dependence in populations of adolescents fulfilling these or any diagnostic criteria.

The second adolescent diagnostic life area defined is school problems. Here, drinking while truant, ever drinking on school grounds, school absences because of alcohol, drinking in a school building, kept or carried alcohol in school, needed a drink before going to school, and ever saw a school social worker or guidance counselor because of drinking are each considered adverse behavioral events or complications related to the use of the substance affecting this particular life area of the adolescent.

Table 13–2. DIAGNOSTIC CRITERIA FOR SUBSTANCE ABUSE IN ADOLESCENTS

Symptom	Percent Positive of Those Who Drink (N = 976)
Psychosocial complications	
Family member expressed concern	26
Drinking at home in front of parents	23
No nondrinking friends	21
Drinking patterns causing family fights or arguments	15
Problems with parents of friends because of alcohol	7
Treatment for alcohol ever	5
Arrest was alcohol related	4
Any psychosocial complication	55
Biomedical complications	
Behavior changes due to alcohol use	43
Memory blackouts due to alcohol	23
Morning drinking	15
Hallucinations due to alcohol	9
Shakes due to alcohol	9
Any biomedical complication	52
School problems	
Drinking while truant	17
Drinking on school grounds	17
School absences due to alcohol or its effects	13
Drinking in school building	9
Kept or carried alcohol in school	8
Needed a drink before going to school	3
Has seen school social worker or counselor because of drinking	2
Any school problem	34

The third life area defined for this adolescent population is psychosocial complications. In many ways this life area might alternatively be characterized as alcohol related complications from interactions with adults, since only one of the complications is focused entirely in the adolescent's world of peers. The problems identified in this life area include a family member has expressed concern about drinking patterns, drinking at home in front of parents, drinking patterns causing fights or arguments within the family, no nondrinking friends, problems with parents of friends because of subject's alcohol use, treatment for alcohol, and any alcohol-related arrests.

There are a great number of parallels between these criteria developed for adolescents and the original formulation for adult alcoholics. The differences are noteworthy, however. In designing these criteria, it was concluded on clinical grounds that tolerance, dependence, and withdrawal were not significant (or frequent) enough problems to be explicitly included. Furthermore, the entire area of control, or lack thereof, was essentially eliminated because it was too early in the natural history of the disease process in

this population to occur with any frequency. A further difference is the use of school and school problems as a separate area. This was done because so much of an adolescent's life involves school and school-related activities, and interactions derived from school activities, that school problems merit consideration as a separate and crucial life area. It was felt that school was, in fact, the "full-time job" of the adolescent and therefore default in responsibility in school was analogous to default on the job or in housework responsibilities for the adult.

Additional symptoms and consequences for the drug abuse diagnostic criteria that were developed in parallel for biomedical complications included drugs injected, mixing drugs and alcohol, drug overdose, vomiting caused by drugs, passing out from drug use, or drug addiction. Behavioral changes, morning use, and shakes were eliminated as being either idiosyncratic to alcohol use, or, in the case of behavior changes, an expectation of drug use rather than an adverse consequence of it.

The life complications categorized as school problems were identical whether related to alcohol use or drug use. Psychosocial complications were also essentially identical for both drug and alcohol use. Differences in the criteria are related to ascribing appropriate pharmacologic, psychological, and social consequences to the specific chemical rather than any wholly different set of life consequences. This diagnostic template is therefore useful in assessing the significance of any type of drugs used by the adolescent. The fundamental diagnostic principle prevails: does the youngster have problems or adverse consequences from his or her drug use that affect each of these three main life areas, biomedical problems, psychosocial problems, and school problems?

Using these criteria, and requiring at least one problem in each of the three areas, results in a very clear separation between adolescent substance abusers with many additional and associated problems and adolescent users with substantially fewer drug-associated life issues. In a clinical setting, however, the requirement for fulfilling the diagnostic criteria could be reduced from three symptoms in three life areas to two symptoms in two life areas. This would be concordant with the original criteria requirement of life problems in two of four groups for a diagnosis of "probable" alcoholism and three of four groups for a diagnosis of "definite" alcoholism.

The *DSM-III* (American Psychiatric Association 1980) used this one-symptom-in-each-of-two-groups principle to diagnose "abuse" and required one symptom plus evidence of tolerance or dependence to qualify for a "dependence" diagnosis. More recently, the *DSM-III-R* returned to three symptoms positive for any substance abuse diagnosis, eliminated the "abuse" category in favor of "dependence," but reduced the reliability of each of the individual symptoms by making them less precise and behavioral and more judgmental, as in "a great deal of time spent in activities necessary to get the substance (e.g., theft), taking the substance (e.g., chain smoking), or recovering from its effects." (American Psychiatric Association 1987).

A second clinical modification that could be appropriate in the use of these specific adolescent criteria is the use of a "mixed" drug abuse diagnosis that could require three problems positive in the three life areas but derived from all of the drugs abused by the youngster. For example, the adolescent may have had blackouts from alcohol use, missed school because of hangover effects from PCP use, and had fights or arguments with family because of marijuana use and therefore qualify for the mixed drug abuse diagnosis. Because there are no long-term studies using these diagnostic criteria, just as there are no long-term studies using the *DSM-III* or the *DSM-III-R* criteria, clinicians should feel free to modify and elaborate on the criteria as long as they carefully document the modifications and the justification for the modifications.

Drug and alcohol experimentation is clearly a high-risk behavior on the part of adolescents. Unfortunately, experimentation with drugs, alcohol, and even cigarettes appears to approach almost universal proportions. As noted earlier, there are some indications that this social pressure to experiment may be diminishing and there may be increasing numbers of adolescents who succeed in refusing all experimental opportunities. However, the bulk of adolescents appear to experiment with one or more substances with little impact on their lives.

Some youngsters, like adults, incorporate tobacco addiction readily into what otherwise is normal adolescent growth and development. Some adolescents appear to incorporate regular but limited use of alcohol into their normal development. There probably are youngsters who incorporate occasional drug use into their lives without significant consequence. Of all the experimental behaviors, drug use is the most fraught with potential short-run problems. Using these adolescent criteria, it was found that problems from the use of drugs increased linearly with duration of use, frequency of use, and number of different drugs used. Thus, drug experimentation followed the pattern of all other high-risk behaviors: the more often one does something that is very risky, the more likely one is to have adverse consequences or accidents from that behavior. This pattern appeared to hold true whether the youngster was having problems from the use of alcohol or not.

Patterns of adverse consequences from alcohol use in adolescence appear analogous to adult patterns. That is, most adults use alcohol relatively safely, while some adults use it more often, in greater quantities, and with substantially more adverse consequences to their lives, (i.e., become alcoholics). This appears to be the pattern observed in adolescents. Most adolescent alcohol experimenters appear to have few if any adverse consequences from their use of alcohol. However, they also do not appear to use alcohol either in very large quantities or very frequently. Rather, they appear to use it in more or less peer-approved social situations. Some youngsters, conversely, have substantial numbers of adverse consequences from the use of alcohol that begin appearing in their lives very soon after they have initiated use of alcohol. Those youngsters with early-appearing adverse consequences have a substantially higher frequency and quantity of alcohol use compared with the majority of their peers. They seem to qualify almost immediately for a diagnosis of alcoholism using the presented criteria. They also have larger numbers of drug problems than their peer group, although the drug problems develop linearly over time.

Characteristics of the Diagnosis in a High-Risk Population

A population of 1,185 high-risk adolescents was interviewed at the Milwaukee County Juvenile Court using a systematic structured interview that focused on symptoms and consequences of alcohol and drug use. Of these, 976 had used alcohol. The incidence of positive symptoms in this population of drinkers as they were grouped in the three diagnostic life areas is shown in Table 13–2. Not surprisingly, psychosocial complications were the most frequently encountered life problems that resulted from their alcohol use, with 55% of adolescent drinkers reporting at least one symptom in this life area. Some biomedical complication was reported by 52% of those who drink. Some school problem as a consequence of alcohol use was reported by 34%. The most frequent positive symptoms noted in each life area were family members expressing concern about the subject's drinking, significant behavior changes because of alcohol use, and drinking while truant or on school grounds.

Of the 1,185 high-risk adolescents interviewed, the proposed criteria identified 19% who qualified for the diagnosis of alcohol abuse by having one symptom positive in each of the three life areas. When these subjects fulfilling the diagnostic criteria were compared with those 81% who did not fulfill

the diagnostic criteria, it was found that the adolescent alcoholics had a mean number of 7.0 life problems or symptoms compared with the nonalcoholic, who had a mean of 1.1 symptoms. When subjects having a minimum of 3 symptoms were compared, those who qualified for the diagnosis were found to have an average of 6.9 positive symptoms, while those who did not qualify for the diagnosis were found to have an average of 4.0 symptoms. Both of these symptom splits were highly significant. Thus the criteria successfully separated out those adolescents with a preponderance of symptoms and a much broader spectrum of problems affecting their lives resulting from alcohol abuse from other comparable adolescents who had used alcohol but with few problems.

Memory blackouts because of alcohol use occurred in 23% of the drinkers in this population. That means that almost one fourth of these youngsters, whose average age was 15½, have drunk so much, so rapidly, that they developed an anterograde amnesia. This age group has not yet developed substantial tolerance. There are no data available on whether the rate of rise or the level of blood alcohol required to achieve these memory blackouts might be close to a level that could cause death in a nontolerant population when compared with tolerant adults. The margin of safety that develops through tolerance is not yet present. Drinking in the morning, that is, before the first meal after arising, was tried by 15% of these drinkers. Hallucinations and withdrawal shakes occurred in 9% of this population. Clearly, these youngsters were having serious symptoms of alcohol use.

While family members expressed concern in over 25% of the instances, almost 25% of the youngsters persisted in drinking at home in front of their parents, and for 15% drinking was causing family fights or arguments.

School problems were less frequent. Drinking while truant, drinking on school grounds, and school absences because of alcohol or its effects happened to about one in eight drinkers. While some of these youngsters were clearly drinking in and around school and during school time, virtually none of them (2%) had ever seen any school official because of alcohol problems.

Symptoms, behaviors, or life characteristics that were associated with the diagnosis were examined. For example, youngsters with the diagnosis were significantly more frequent drinkers, with 48% having used alcohol in the 30 days prior to interview, whereas only 6% of the nondiagnosed had used alcohol that often in the prior 30 days.

As shown in Table 13–3, the substance use historical landmarks were dramatically different in the two groups. Those destined to be diagnosed as being alcoholics by these criteria had been intoxicated from the use of alcohol at an average age younger than their same-sexed nondiagnosed control group. As can be seen, their cigarette and alcohol use landmarks were fully a year and a half earlier than those destined not to have a diagnosis of alcohol abuse by these criteria.

This diagnosis of alcohol dependence provides a very clear indication of similar alcohol and drug problems among parents and siblings. Mothers and fathers of these youngsters were twice as likely to be involved in alcohol or drug use, and, overall, 51% of those with the diagnosis had at least one parent with an alcohol or a drug problem. With regard to their siblings, those teenagers with a positive diagnosis were two to four times as likely to have a brother or a sister with an alcohol or drug problem, and, overall, about a third of these youngsters (31%) had at least one sibling with an alcohol or drug problem.

Thus, these adolescent diagnostic criteria provide a shorthand way of communicating much descriptive information regarding the breadth and number of alcohol-related problems and adverse consequences in this population and also provide much information about associated descriptive features involving the youngster and his or her family.

A diagnosis of alcohol abuse using these criteria appeared to have an enormous impact on drug use patterns. Teenagers with the diagnosis were six times as likely to have tried five or more different drugs and nine times as likely to have tried five or more

different drugs at least three times each. These youngsters were three times as likely to have engaged in heavy and frequent drug use for at least three days per week during the prior 30 days and at least three times as likely to have mixed drugs and alcohol in an effort to boost the effect. All of the biomedical complications of drug use were five to ten times as likely to occur in the alcohol-diagnosed youngster compared with the youngster with no alcohol abuse diagnosis. These symptoms included overdose from drugs, vomiting because of drugs, memory blackouts because of drugs, hallucinations due to drugs, passing out from drugs, addiction to drugs, and treatment for drugs. Involvement with drugs in school was also found to be substantially more likely in the alcohol abusers and to be predicted by the alcohol abuse diagnosis. Drug use on school grounds, getting high while being truant, drug use in school, and having drugs hidden in school were all at least three times as likely to have occurred in those with the alcohol abuse diagnosis.

In terms of psychosocial complications related to drug use, drug use at time of arrest, having had drug-related arrests, having family concerned about the youngster's drug use, and drug use in front of parents were all three to five times as likely to have occurred in the youngster with alcohol abuse and to have been determined by that diagnosis.

It was possible to identify three key questions that could be used to screen youngsters and identify those likely to have alcohol abuse problems when interviewed thoroughly. These three questions are listed in Table 13–4. It should be noted that each of the three questions involves school behavior: (1) has the subject ever been drinking on school grounds; (2) when truant, has the subject ever gone drinking; and (3) has the subject ever missed school because of drink-

Table 13–3. SUBSTANCE USE HISTORICAL LANDMARKS BY DIAGNOSTIC STATUS*

	Diagnostic (N = 174)		All Others (N = 736)	
	M (n = 148)	F (n = 26)	M (n = 653)	F (n = 83)
Mean Age First Cigarette†	10.7	10.4	11.9	11.5
Mean Age First Alcohol Use†	11.2	11.5	12.9	13.1
Mean Age First Drunk†	12.2	12.7	13.5	13.9

*Based on first 910 subjects.
†Of those in which the event has occurred.

Table 13–4. KEY CLINICAL SCREENING QUESTIONS

Alcohol Abuse
1. Has subject ever been drinking on school grounds?
2. When truant, has subject ever gone drinking?
3. Has subject ever missed school because of drinking or hangovers or from being sick from drinking?

Drug Abuse
1. Has subject ever mixed alcohol with drug to boost its effect?
2. Has family ever expressed concern about subject's drug use?
3. When truant, has subject ever gotten high on drugs?

ing or hangovers or from being sick from drinking? Ninety-four per cent of the teenagers who fulfilled the diagnostic criteria for alcohol abuse answered yes to one of these three questions. Six per cent of the known alcohol abusers were negative on all three of those selected variables. Among those not diagnosed as alcohol abusers by the criteria, only 10% were positive on any one of these three selected items, in effect, false positives. Thus, these three questions can act as an effective screening instrument when incorporated into a routine clinical or behavioral review of systems.

Key questions to identify drug-related problems are also listed in Table 13–4. Being positive on any one of these three symptoms—mixing alcohol and drugs, family being concerned about the person's drug use, or getting high while truant—predicted with great reliability the presence of a drug abuse diagnosis, that is, having at least one symptom positive in each of the three life areas when the questions were focused on drug-related consequences and adverse effects. Of those who had a drug abuse diagnosis alone or in addition to an alcohol abuse diagnosis, using the criteria as specified, 88% were found to have at least one of these drug symptoms positive. Conversely, of those with neither a drug abuse diagnosis nor an alcohol abuse diagnosis, only 15% were found to be positive on at least one of these selected variables, (i.e., false positives).

If these three drug symptoms, as well, are included in a screening instrument or are part of a routine clinical interview, it would appear that only about 10% of teenagers having significant numbers of problems from alcohol use or drug use would fail to be identified. Conversely, by including these six

symptoms in all routine adolescent assessments, only 10% to 15% would be subjected unnecessarily to a more extensive review of alcohol- and drug-related problems and behaviors.

Those missed because they have not yet developed a positive symptom among these six screening items and those who are not yet positive in three life categories but who are positive on at least one of these six symptoms are in a transitional group. With time, they are likely to have increasing numbers of problems from their substance use. Frequent follow-up of these youngsters, if not outright intervention on clinical grounds, is appropriate.

Clinical Diagnosis and Co-morbidity

Using these screening questions, 95 youngsters were referred for full psychiatric and psychological assessment. About three fourths of the group were male, two thirds of the group were white, the average educational level was tenth grade, and the average age was 15½. Most lived in families of four or five members, and almost a third were still living with both biological parents. In their lifetime they had moved an average of four to five times. About 10% had at one time been placed in a foster home.

Forty-four per cent of the boys and 46% of the girls had symptom clusters of either inattention, impulsivity, hyperactivity, or some combination of the three based on the DSM-III criteria, while 19% qualified for the full diagnosis of attention-deficit disorder. Based on the source of the patient population (i.e., court), essentially all qualified for a diagnosis of conduct disorder or oppositional disorder.

Only *one* person did *not* qualify for an Axis I psychiatric diagnosis. The average number of psychiatric diagnoses, including attention-deficit disorder, oppositional disorder, conduct disorder, or major depressive disorder, among the boys was 2.4, with a range of 0 to 6 diagnoses. Among the girls, the average number of diagnoses was 2.9, with a range of 1 to 6. Two thirds of the girls and about half of the boys qualified for a diagnosis of oppositional disorder.

Depression, either current or past, was found in 36% of the girls and 11% of the boys. Phobic, obsessive-compulsive, or psychotic symptoms were found in about 5% of the boys and in 10% to 20% of the girls, but these symptoms did not qualify by diagnostic criteria for diagnosis.

Chemical dependency diagnoses were considered separately from these psychiatric diagnoses. About one fourth of the girls and 10% of the boys had only a diagnosis of alcohol abuse. Marijuana abuse was the most common drug diagnosis, occurring in three fourths of the boys and two thirds of the girls. Almost half of the girls and almost a third of the boys also qualified for another drug abuse diagnosis as well. Use of the hallucinogens, stimulants, sedatives, and inhalants were all more common in the girls than in the boys. Cocaine and the opiates were used in about equal proportions by both the boys and the girls, and marijuana use was more prevalent in the boys. Overall, alcohol abuse was present in 78% of the girls and 61% of the boys.

To summarize, careful systematic psychiatric assessment of this representative population of alcohol- and drug-abusing adolescents, diagnosed using systematic behavioral criteria, revealed an "onion skin" of diagnoses, beginning with the most adult or most current diagnosis, that of depressive disorder, beneath which was the adolescent diagnosis of substance abuse. When both of these are stripped away, there was the pubertal and postpubertal diagnosis of conduct disorder; beneath that was oppositional disorder. Finally, when these diagnoses, too, were stripped away, the strong presence of major childhood diagnoses involving the constellation of attention-deficit disorder (inattention, hyperactivity, and impulsivity) was observed. It would appear that these childhood diagnoses, coupled with the genetics or biology of alcoholism and substance abuse in the family, propel and direct the youngster forward into the particular sequence and pattern of acting-out behavior and substance use behavior.

CASE HISTORIES

Case 1

Josh was a 17-year-old white single male charged with burglary. He was found intoxicated on the roof of a sporting goods store where he had been celebrating. Nothing had been stolen. He had no recollection of the incident. He had one previous police contact at age 12 when he and some friends were arrested for stealing beer. After that incident he was placed on probation for 6 months. He had also had two moving traffic violations in the past.

His parents, health care professionals who had retired early to a rural home setting, were considered eccentrics. Josh had three brothers, all away at college or boarding school. Josh was living in the metropolitan area with two roommates while attending college in an advanced placement. He had lived away from home intermittently since age 14 when he was placed in a boarding prep school. After four high school semesters he had been accepted at the local college.

When seen, Josh was a sophomore in that college. His enrollment had occurred rather spontaneously when he visited the college to discuss later career plans. He was invited to take placement exams and was enrolled within the week. He had always been a gifted student. While in junior high he had assisted in science classes, and throughout school he had always been allowed to study independently because he was ahead of his class.

Behavioral problems in his early school years depended greatly on the personality and approach of the teacher. Because he was bright and verbal he was capable of intimidating some teachers and interfering with their normal lesson plans. Beginning in second grade he had been in independent study or accelerated classes. His first college semester had gone well, and he had made the dean's list. Thereafter his grades began to slip. At the time he was seen he intended to drop out.

He remembered little of his grade school years. He recalled no symptoms compatible with attention-deficit disorder, hyperactivity, impulsivity, oppositional disorder, or conduct disorder.

Josh qualified for a diagnosis of alcohol dependence. He was 12 years old when he first drank on his own and got drunk. He had been drinking virtually daily in the 30 days prior to evaluation. He often drank as much as 15 shots, generally in bars. He had never had any trouble being served. He had had the following adverse consequences from his drinking: hangover, vomiting, memory blackouts, tolerance, drinking in the presence of ulcer disease, going on binges or benders, drinking early in the day just after arising, drinking to help him forget his troubles, drinking alone, drinking at home in front of his parents since age 15, trying to drink only at special times to limit his drinking, drinking as much as a fifth of liquor on one occasion, drinking on school grounds, drinking in the school building, keeping liquor on him at school, drinking at the time of his arrest, having been arrested for stealing some alcoholic beverage at some time, having an automobile accident when drinking, thinking that he drinks too much, having his family object to his drinking, feeling guilty about his drinking, and feeling that he has a drinking problem.

Josh qualified for a diagnosis of marijuana abuse, sedative/hypnotic (diazepam [Valium]) abuse, codeine abuse, and mixed drug abuse. Josh smoked marijuana since the age of 12 on numerous occasions but only twice in the past 30 days. He used LSD and psilocybin on fewer than 20 occasions, beginning at age 16, and once or twice in the past 30 days. He used cocaine on three occasions and "speed" on two occasions. He used diazepam on more than 50 occasions from the age of 15 but none in the past 30 days (this drug had originally been prescribed). He had abused codeine, opium in marijuana, oxycodone (Percodan), and propoxyphene (Darvon). He first used opiates at the age of 14 and used them on more than 50 occasions. During the past 30 days he used codeine daily for 1 week but quit when he felt that he was becoming addicted to it, a feeling he had in the past. Josh had used the following inhalants: amyl nitrite, butyl nitrite, ether, nitrous oxide, and ethyl chloride beginning at age 13.

Josh had the following adverse symptoms from his drug use: nausea or vomiting from codeine and ether; hallucinations from LSD and from codeine; feelings of anxiety, panic, or fear from marijuana, cocaine, and stimulants; memory blackouts from hallucinogens; using marijuana before breakfast; feeling suspicious on hallucinogens; feeling "spacey" on sedatives, opiates, and inhalants; losing coordination on sedatives; trembling hands, tongue, and eyelids on cocaine and stimulants; racing heartbeat on cocaine and stimulants; diarrhea; being unable to sleep when using hallucinogens, cocaine, or stimulants; feeling overactive and unable to calm down on hallucinogens, cocaine, stimulants, or inhalants; developing tolerance to marijuana,

sedatives, and opiates; feeling addicted to codeine; mixing alcohol with all of these drugs to boost their effect; using marijuana and codeine daily for at least 2 weeks; bingeing marijuana and codeine; using sedatives and codeine just after arising; using marijuana, hallucinogens, sedatives, and codeine when alone; using marijuana, stimulants, and codeine on school grounds; using marijuana, stimulants, and codeine in the school building and carrying these drugs on him in school; having his use of marijuana cause fights or arguments in the family; and thinking that he used marijuana and codeine too much.

Josh qualified for a diagnosis of major depressive disorder. He had the following symptoms of depression: having trouble falling asleep at night, nightmares, sleeping at odd times during the day, feeling more tired than usual, having a low appetite and eating less than usual for several days, noting that his body was slowed down as he moved from place to place, feeling tired all the time or easily fatigued, feeling that life was not worth living, feeling that life was hopeless and there was nothing good for him in the future, thinking a lot about death and dying, wishing he were dead, and thinking about killing himself. Josh had never attempted suicide. He recalls a 1-week period at age 16 when he was having conflicts with girlfriends and studying for finals that he felt people were out to get him. He lost control, threw a telephone against a wall, began crying uncontrollably, and was very suspicious of others. He was taken back to his parents' home where he met up with an old friend and went on an alcoholic binge. Thereafter he dropped out of school and hitchhiked around the country.

Josh recalled discrete episodes of depression beginning in childhood on at least seven different occasions. He had never been treated for depressive illness. The diagnosis of depression was made in spite of the obvious constraint that he had not been free of psychoactive chemicals for more than a few days at any time in the past 4 to 5 years.

Josh was unable to provide sufficient symptomatology of alcohol abuse in either parent, but there was some likelihood that his father at least was a problem drinker. Apparently his paternal grandfather was a problem drinker and a paternal uncle was an alcoholic, now abstinent. One of Josh's older brothers had a continuing problem with alcohol and drugs. Another paternal uncle had been treated at the state mental hospital at some point in the past. The paternal grandfather was also considered an eccentric recluse. Mental status examination revealed a bright, verbal, handsome young man who looked and acted older than his stated age of 17. Examination was otherwise unremarkable.

Diagnostic formulation suggested that Josh had suffered from major depressive disorder of a recurrent variety for much of the time since age 14, for which he had been self-medicating with alcohol and other drugs. He did not have the emotional maturity to deal with the college environment or with his forced independent life. It was decided that he be treated on an outpatient basis with antidepressant medications (desipramine, 150 mg/day) and in individual, ongoing psychotherapy. He responded well to this treatment plan. He spontaneously gave up all drug use and virtually all alcohol use. He started working steadily and developed more realistic plans for himself both in the short-term and in the intermediate-term. He was seen in regular therapy on a biweekly basis for 8 months and then was followed for medication management on a less frequent basis. His personal life stabilized, and he made realistic decisions about furthering his education.

Case 2

Kathy was a 15-year-old black female charged with assault and battery that occurred when she and two other girls were drinking wine. She had two prior police contacts but no juvenile court contacts before. She had been reprimanded at age 13 by the police for conduct problems on a public bus, evidently for talking loudly and using profanity. The police removed her from the bus and took her home. At age 14 while fighting with another girl she threw a rock and broke a window of the girl's house. She saw a counselor once for this vandalism.

Kathy lived at home with her 61-year-old mother, two older half-sisters, younger nieces and nephews, and one older nephew. Outside the home there were an additional six brothers and two sisters. Income was from General Assistance and Social Security

Widows and Orphans Income. Kathy had no awareness or information about her biological father's identify or whereabouts. Other than two brief periods when she lived with older siblings while her mother cared for her own ill mother, Kathy had always lived with her mother.

Kathy was currently a tenth grader in the public school. While she had never been in special classes because of her behavior, she acknowledged conduct problems going back as far as the fourth grade, with the school's response being to send her to the principal's office (often) and being put in the coat room. She had been suspended from school approximately 20 times beginning in the sixth grade. These suspensions were usually because of "fighting, cussing, and losing my temper." She had never repeated a grade nor been in classes for slow learners, although for 2 years she was in special reading classes.

Kathy qualified for a diagnosis of attention-deficit disorder. She acknowledged that she tended to leave projects unfinished; she acknowledged particularly having trouble finishing her assignments in school when she was in a bad mood. She had had considerable past difficulty with paying insufficient attention in school. This was more of a problem in early grades at least as far back as third grade. She acknowledged having difficulty keeping her mind on school assignments, even interesting ones. She acknowledged a tendency to rush from one activity to another even though she had not completed the first one. She acknowledged that her mother was "on my case a lot." Frequently the teachers would have to tell her what to do after the rest of the class had already begun doing it. Often she got into trouble at school for speaking out of turn. Until seventh grade she was frequently in trouble for trying to push ahead in lines and get in before her turn. She acknowledged that teachers frequently complained because of her failure to remain in her seat at school. She was frequently on the move, unable to sit still very well. "I don't like to sit for long." This was often a source of problems with teachers.

Kathy met criteria for a diagnosis of conduct disorder, undersocialized, aggressive type, with some nonaggressive features as well. It is noteworthy that she had strong oppositional features. She noted that she was inclined to do just the opposite of what she had been told because she did not like being told to do anything. She frequently got upset and showed her temper when things did not go her way. She was frequently in trouble because of talking back to teachers or the principal. She acknowledged breaking rules such as going out when she was told to stay in or not coming back when she was told to. She had had some difficulty in keeping friends. The longest friendship with any particular person was 1 year. Were she in trouble, she acknowledged that there would not be any friend she could turn to in confidence. She denied guilt or shame unless someone would find out about a misdeed. If a friend of hers were to get into trouble with the police, she would figure that it was none of her business. However, were she to get into trouble with friends, she would stick with them and share the consequences.

Aggressive features were obvious in this young woman. She acknowledged having a reputation as a fighter. She acknowledged having bitten five different people on different occasions, some requiring medical attention. On three occasions she threatened persons with a knife, but "I only used it once and that was because he stole my money."

Kathy qualified for a *DSM-III* diagnosis of alcohol abuse but not alcohol dependence, because of lack of tolerance or withdrawal symptoms. She noted visual hallucinations, increased violence when drinking, and derealization and depersonalization while drinking alone. She first drank and first got drunk at age 13. She drank whenever she had money, three to five times per week, generally four to six beers per occasion. She acknowledged the need to drink daily to function. She acknowledged drinking before going to school, drinking to help forget her troubles, drinking alone, drinking while truant, and drinking at the time of her arrest. She had been in fights after drinking. She had some insight into her drinking problem because of its acceleration of her violence. Kathy had had no other problems with substance abuse, having used no other drugs except two diazepam (Valium) pills on one occasion at age 13.

Kathy qualified for a diagnosis of major depressive disorder and also for dysthymic disorder. She noted affective feelings of being sad and "down in the dumps" that waxed and waned over several days or so, as well as periods lasting weeks where she thought she would be better off dead and thought about killing herself. She noted that the longest such time when she felt depressed was 1 month. During those times she had difficulty initiating sleep, had trouble sleeping with interval insomnia, was sleeping during the day at school, and felt more fatigued. Her appetite would decrease and she would lose 3 to 4 pounds. She stopped seeing friends, she stopped activities, and her grades dropped. Kathy believed her first such episode of depression occurred in eighth grade while her mother was away. When depressed she was self-deprecatory. Her personal appearance deteriorated; she was more irritable without reason. Her thoughts slowed, and she had difficulty concentrating and paying attention. She felt her body slowed down and she moved more slowly, although she still had ongoing trouble staying still. She sometimes thought that life was not worth living, that her family would be better off without her, and that life was hopeless and there was no future for her. She thought about killing herself, wished to be dead, and thought a lot about death and dying without having ever made any suicide attempts.

Following these episodes she usually improved in the space of about a month. She indicated at least seven episodes or more of feeling depressed. She had never been treated for it. Her frequent, short-lived periods of depression were without return to a normal euthymic state. During episodes of depression she acknowledged obsessive thoughts about dying with the repetitive thought "you need to die, you need to die."

A 28-year-old half-brother was hospitalized for an unknown psychiatric disorder. A younger half brother had had police problems. There was no known family history of alcohol or drug abuse.

Mental status examination revealed an adolescent black girl who appeared her stated age. She fidgeted frequently during the course of the interview, picking at her clothes, picking at the table, and shifting her body position frequently. She appeared somewhat sad. She tended to mumble at times. All other parts of the mental status were intact. She read at a seventh grade level.

The diagnostic impression included (1) major depressive disorder; (2) dysthymic disorder; (3) attention-deficit disorder; (4) alcohol abuse; and (5) conduct disorder, undersocialized, aggressive type, with strong oppositional features.

It was concluded that this 15-year-old girl had a considerable problem with depression that needed to be treated. It was thought that she would benefit from individual and/or group therapy aimed at improving her self-concept and improving her self-esteem through cognitive therapy, which might also serve to alleviate her depression. In addition, she should have a trial of antidepressant medication.

Some success and mastery through graded task assignments would help by giving her a sense of her own ability to be more effective in her daily life. A behavioral modification training program was designed as a means of acquiring and maintaining more socially acceptable behaviors and perhaps extinguishing the socially unacceptable behaviors.

A MODEL TREATMENT PROGRAM FOR THE ADOLESCENT SUBSTANCE ABUSER

Thorough Assessment and Differential Diagnosis

The importance of a complete differential diagnosis has been stressed throughout this chapter. An accurate and precise differential diagnosis is the key to maximizing the imperfect therapeutic capability that is the current state of treatment. Thorough assessment will take at the very least a full day and more likely several days. It includes interviews with parents, possibly with siblings, and certainly systematic structured interviews with the patient, along with opportunities to observe the patient in a milieu setting.

Systematic psychiatric diagnostic evaluation is best done using a structured instrument such as the Diagnostic Interview for Children and Adolescents (Herjanic and Reich 1982), the Kiddie–Schedule for Affective Disorders and Schizophrenia (Orvaschel et al. 1982), or the Diagnostic Interview Schedule for Children (Costello 1987). As new clinical instruments are developed and become known, the treatment team will have the opportunity to select one that works best in their setting. In the absence of a systematic structured interview, the key to differential diagnosis is the collection of criteria symptoms and behaviors that reflect the major diagnostic groups discussed in this chapter.

Careful and thorough assessment of the alcohol and drug use patterns of each young-ster must be obtained. The key to obtaining the information is asking the most specific and precise questions possible. The more numerous and precise the questions, the more honest and thorough are the answers. Overview, open-ended, and nonspecific questions tend to be least reliable. Specific behavioral questions tend to be the most reliable.

The theoretical basis of the substance abuse diagnosis, multiple problems and multiple consequences related to the use of the substance affecting multiple life areas, indicates the presence of a substance dependence. As presented earlier, the three basic life areas on which behavioral consequences have been identified for adolescents and a behavioral diagnosis has been generated are biomedical complications, school problems, and psychosocial problems. Adverse behavioral consequences and problems should be assessed for each drug used separately. A first step might involve identifying what drugs and substances have been used by the youngster at any one time and then what drugs and substances have been used by the youngster more than five times in a lifetime. Those substances used more than five times in a lifetime should be evaluated separately for resultant behavioral problems and medical consequences. In this way, a precise assessment of the degree of impairment and disruption attributable to each separate substance and to each combination of substances can be made.

As was seen earlier, underlying alcohol dependence is often a crucial but frequently ignored problem. This is because of the presence of what often appears to be substantially more dangerous or frightening drugs, such as hallucinogens or stimulants. The role of alcohol dependence as an underlying physiological mechanism facilitating the development of dependence syndromes with other substances is not yet clear at a pharmacologic or physiological level. Clinically, however, it is apparent from work with adult drug addicts that alcohol dependence is usually the final common pathway as the individual ages beyond the ability to maintain abuse of illegal substances. Thus, an accurate and thorough evaluation of the role of alcohol both as a gatekeeper drug and an ongoing abuse problem is essential.

As part of this evaluation of substance abuse, a thorough evaluation of abuse and dependence patterns in the nuclear family and in the extended family is important. It is likely that the youngster has a genetic predisposition to the abuse of substances that can be determined from careful assessment of the family history, in addition to possible environmental loading based on the presence of other conditions, psychosocial problems, and maladaptive behaviors. Again, this underlying familial predisposition is important because it affects the treatment of the adolescent directly and because of the long-term prognostic implications.

As part of the initial assessment of an adolescent, issues of tolerance, withdrawal, physiological addiction, and intravenous or other parenteral drug use all need to be assessed. The parenteral administration is clearly of importance because of the acquired immunodeficiency syndrome (AIDS). If there is any question regarding the possibility of a patient being positive for the human immunodeficiency virus, this should be ascertained, if at all possible, prior to admission to a facility. All these youngsters are at high risk both for surreptitious drug use behavior while inpatients and also for inappropriate sexual acting out as well, which could put everyone on the unit at risk for this illness. If assessment prior to admission is not possible, and there is some likelihood of transmission or contagion, appropriate precautions must be taken until results of antibody studies are known. Likewise, other routes of administration need to be addressed. Inhalation, snorting, and smoking substances, all may bring with them medical complications and problems that need to be evaluated and treated.

Issues regarding intoxication and withdrawal need to be addressed at admission. If the patient is likely to develop a withdrawal syndrome, this takes first priority. If the sensorium is not clear, the youngster cannot benefit from a rehabilitation program that is largely verbal and cognitive. Appropriate medical and pharmacologic withdrawal treatment should be instituted concomitantly while the ongoing in-depth assessment occurs.

Careful assessment for major depressive disorder and all of the dysphoric states should be done. This is a diagnosis that is often lost in the youngster because of acting-out behavior. While the presentation of depression in teenagers is often acting out,

rebellion, and indirect self-destructive behavior, careful probing, systematic collection of signs and symptoms, and history will often identify an underlying affective syndrome. Again, family history is very relevant and very helpful. A positive family history of affective disorder should provide a substantial clue that an adolescent affective syndrome may be present in the patient.

In the adolescent dysphoric population, overeating is often seen rather than undereating and hypersomnia is more likely to be seen than forms of insomnia. If insomnia is seen in this population it is generally initial insomnia, which is masked by a shift in the biological clock such that the youngster tries to go to bed as late as possible and sleep through as much of the morning as possible. While psychomotor agitation and restlessness are the more common presentations in this age group, psychomotor retardation can sometimes be seen along with intense hypersomnia.

Sex drive is sometimes increased rather than decreased. This may be manifested as an increase in masturbation or as the development of poor social judgment or outright sexual promiscuity. Generally, the combination of depression and substance abuse leads to frequent and dangerous sexual activity. Often adolescent females in substance abuse treatment programs report rape and even gang rape as a function of their substance abuse (primarily alcohol) behavior and their association with other acting-out adolescents. When seen, the increase in sex drive is often, in boys, a tension release mechanism and, in girls, a need for closeness and protection. The accompanying decrease in social judgment that attends depression in this age group may manifest itself also as a higher likelihood of becoming pregnant or of getting someone pregnant.

The increased appetite with accompanying weight gain, decrease in social judgment and increased sexual acting out, and loss of energy and sense of productivity all worsen the sense of lowered self-esteem and feelings of worthlessness that are ever-present in this population. A striking characteristic of the substance abuser is the presence of this lowered self-esteem. This is likely related to an ongoing history of failure that dates back to childhood and the presence of an attention-deficit disorder. Hopelessness and suicidal tendencies in this adolescent population are generally represented by a sense of futility and disregard for the future and, occasionally, by outright statements of a desire for a "killer-hit," a maximal overdose experience.

The assessment for affective disorder in this population should include a careful chronologic history. Often a cycling of interpersonal and school problems that waxes and wanes will become apparent. There may be times of the year during which younger adolescent patients act out and other times when they are relatively comfortable. As the adolescent becomes more embedded in multiple life problems, however, the bad times create an ongoing dysphoria and overwhelm what possible remissions might be otherwise apparent. In later grade school and even in early junior high school, cycling may still be apparent. Self-destructive talk or actions, futility, or passive comments about the future should also alert the clinician about the possibility of an affective disorder. Surreptitious suicide attempts never reported to adults need to be assessed. This question is usually asked as "Have you ever tried to kill yourself and no one ever found out about it?" Childhood overdoses with aspirin or other pain reliever or some other such attempt will often be uncovered. This can then be used to unlock other behavior of a depressive nature that may have occurred at that same time.

Another major area of assessment involves early-onset antisocial behavior and antisocial personality. In children this is conduct disorder. An identification of this disorder is most helpful when it occurs prior to puberty and prior to the onset of any drug or alcohol abuse. When the syndrome of conduct disorder is in place before first substance abuse has occurred, it indicates a particular pathway of treatment and behavioral management that is useful. This can be most easily assessed by using the school grades as landmarks. Generally questioning the youngster about behavior in kindergarten through fifth grade allows the youngster to focus on early childhood for behavioral and academic problems and acting out. It is a manageable historical segment that the youngster can reflect on and remember. Beginning in sixth grade, with the additional freedom of moving among classes and having multiple teachers, later antisocial behavior appears to surface.

Neuropsychological testing is often valuable. Self-esteem issues will become apparent; learning disabilities may become apparent;

personality issues that were not apparent on systematic interview may be identified; and mild organic deficits may be picked up. Medical issues that are not yet well characterized should be noted. These include hypoglycemia, sugar sensitivity or dependence, the tension fatigue syndrome, behavioral and environmental allergies including food dyes, the possibility of occult lead poisoning or other such toxic pollutants, and the presence of minimal or subtle brain injury present from infancy or before. For this, careful neurologic and neuropsychological assessment is essential.

A careful differential diagnosis should assess (1) particular alcohol and substance use problems; (2) the presence of any underlying alcohol dependence or positive family history of alcohol dependence; (3) the presence of an affective disorder or positive family history of affective disorder; (4) the presence of a childhood conduct disorder or adolescent antisocial behavior disorder; (5) the presence of chronic long-term low internal and behavioral self esteem; (6) the presence of past attention-deficit disorder or any of its subtypes; and (7) the presence of any additional biological problems. The identification of each of these provides the building blocks for a differential treatment program.

General Principles of Treatment

The "glue" that allows the treatment program to function smoothly is built around a behavioral program format using a token economy, step system, and a cognitive behavioral approach. This is most useful in dealing with youngsters who have a propensity for acting out. Positive reinforcement should be readily available, both by interpersonal interactions and by rewards.

The basis of the treatment program should be a focused substance abuse rehabilitation format that relies on recovering counselors, education about the effects of substances, group therapy led by facilitators and counselors, individual counseling and therapy, and the use of self-help organizations such as ALATEEN and Alcoholics Anonymous.

Low self-esteem should be addressed by the use of social skills training and behavioral approaches that work on specific issues raised by individual adolescents. Treatment should be the opportunity to teach adolescents new coping skills such that their need to rely on drugs is eliminated. Part of self-esteem training should also be the use of non-drug-taking coping skills in handling the vicissitudes of adolescence.

Biological problems identified at assessment, such as behaviorally related allergies, occult lead poisoning, and minimal brain dysfunction, should be sorted out and treated concomitantly.

Youngsters with conduct disorder or early-onset antisocial personality require a vigorous behavioral modification program and token economy. If they have also qualified for a diagnosis of oppositional disorder, a particular interactional strategy to deal with them is needed. Confrontation with those youngsters should be minimized in lieu of enlisting their cooperation. Awareness of the underlying conduct disorder or antisocial personality will alert the team and the ward staff to anticipate "acting-out" behaviors, such as arguments or fights with other patients or staff members, splitting behavior, and possible petty criminality on the ward (stealing from other patients, selling cigarettes, attempting to smuggle drugs onto the unit, or bringing contraband materials in from outside trips).

Frequently, treatment must address the adolescent with the concomitant affective syndrome. Aggressive management of this youngster using a variety of modalities simultaneously will often produce very dramatic behavioral and personality changes. The use of cognitive behavior therapy is quite useful in helping the youngster take control of what appears to be an out-of-control life situation. The use of tricyclic antidepressant medications, usually desipramine or nortriptyline, often make a dramatic difference in the outcome of substance abuse treatment. Efforts at educating the youngster and the family about the presence of the affective syndrome will be useful in achieving their cooperation and compliance and also in the prevention of relapse in later years. Individual and group psychotherapies that are supportive as well as cognitive will also be of assistance in dealing with the affective syndrome.

Family therapy is crucial in dealing with the adolescent substance abuser. The family is usually in turmoil, either directly because of the problems engendered by the adolescent and his or her behavior or because of additional problems that the family brings to the situation. This family turbulence often includes the presence of another substance abuser in the family, either one of the siblings or one of the parents. Often there is marital discord, either present or past (or both) that surfaces frequently during therapy and in the naturalistic setting. Not uncommonly the youngster is being raised by one parent or the other and becomes enmeshed in his or her disputes. Occasionally the issue of adoption and other similar issues may surface that need to be managed. Issues of physical abuse and sexual abuse, which occur often in families of alcoholics, need to be assessed routinely and, when they arise, need to be handled promptly. Engagement of family members in family therapy and maintaining their cooperation is a difficult and delicate, but crucial, therapeutic task. Substance abuse is not an individual problem. It is a family problem and must be managed with all family members involved in the rehabilitation process.

Treatment of the Adolescent Substance Abuser

Prior to 1980, treatment of the adolescent substance abuser was largely confined to enrollment in alcohol and drug abuse treatment programs designed for adults. Little systematic attention was paid to designing specific programs for the developmental needs of adolescents. What data existed on the treatment outcome of such populations were derived from a few pioneering treatment programs supported by government efforts (Beschner and Friedman 1979).

The conclusion from that work, and the continuing observation based on more recent assessments of treatment efficacy, indicate that virtually all treatment is helpful in the short term to slow the progression of, or in fact to reverse, the substance-using behavior of adolescents. Further conclusions as to efficacy of treatment have to do with good outcome features. Not surprisingly, the greater number of good prognosis features a youngster brings to treatment, the more likely he or she is to succeed or have a relative efficacy obtained from treatment. For example, the youngster still in school prior to treatment is more likely to be in school after treatment. The youngster from an intact home prior to treatment is more likely to be in an intact home after treatment. The youngster who had a job before treatment is more likely to have a job afterward. The youngster who has not had, or who has few, police contacts prior to treatment is likely, on follow up, to continue to have no or few police contacts.

Currently, there are many adolescent substance abuse treatment programs in existence. Generally, they are limited by philosophical constraints and a treatment belief system absorbed from the adult treatment community that remains untested and unstudied. This treatment philosophy has face validity and seems plausible, but its efficacy cannot be assessed because there are no substantially different alternative models in existence.

The standard treatment model proposes that the primary components of treatment are (1) education as to the consequences and effects of alcohol and substance use in the person's life; (2) group therapy led by specially trained counselors who are generally recovering past substance abusers themselves; (3) a focus on the function, use, and effect of substances in the patient's own life; (4) the development of alternative coping skills for management of stress, anger, sadness, and boredom; (5) and the development of independence and utilization of a non-substance-using peer group for support, generally in the form of Alcoholics Anonymous, and equivalent self-help fraternal organizations. The youngster and his or her family are encouraged to work together during the latter part of the treatment program to manage the ever-present conflicts that exist in family interactions.

The physician's most prominent role in the management of the early treatment phase may involve supervision of the detoxification and assessment of intercurrent medical and psychiatric problems. Often, though, this is all handled with minimal medical input. Treatment is largely psychosocial and includes guided self-help (Felter et al. 1987).

Adolescent treatment outcome data on a multisite basis have been collected through the Chemical Abuse/Addiction Treatment Outcome Registry (CATOR) (Hoffmann et al. 1984). Their most recent data are based on follow up of more than 1,800 adolescents treated between 1984 and 1986 in 12 different treatment programs. The average length of stay in treatment for this adolescent sample is 36 days. Over two thirds of patients complete treatment; boys are more commonly discharged for behavioral reasons than girls. On discharge from treatment, about two thirds return home. The remainder are referred to halfway houses, group homes, other relatives, or other chemical dependency programs. The most frequent postdischarge referrals are to Alcoholics Anonymous or Narcotics Anonymous (88%), peer support groups (65%), family therapy (54%), and individual therapy (42%) (Harrison and Hoffmann 1987).

At time of follow-up, interviews had been completed at both 6 months and 12 months. Legal problems at admission reduced the likelihood of successful follow-up; adolescents not in school at admission to treatment were significantly less likely to be located for follow-up interviews than those still in school. Those who completed treatment were more likely to be found than those who did not. Significant predictors of failure to even complete follow-up included a history of sexual abuse for the girls, physical abuse or parental substance abuse for both boys and girls, and school and legal problems for the boys. Unfortunately, this most extensive follow-up is therefore based on youngsters with the fewest problems and the most stable backgrounds and probably reflects the best possible outcome.

Of 493 patients contacted for both 6-month and 12-month follow-up interviews, 44% reported total abstinence from all drugs for the first year following treatment. An additional 22% reported at least 3 months of abstinence during each of the two 6-month intervals. The remaining third reported using chemicals during at least 4 of the 6 months in one or both of the follow-up intervals. There was a trend for 18- and 19-year olds to have a higher rate of total abstinence than younger teenagers. Girls were significantly more likely than boys to report total abstinence for the year.

The most statistically significant association with poor outcome was that of a suicide attempt during the year prior to treatment for girls. Girls reporting a pretreatment suicide attempt had a 35% abstinence rate compared with 58% for those without a suicide attempt. Physical abuse was also a predictor of poor outcome for girls; girls who had been physically abused had a 37% abstinence rate compared with 59% for girls not physically abused. In boys, neither suicide attempt nor intrafamiliar physical abuse was associated with outcome.

A history of legal problems before treatment was negatively associated with outcome for both boys and girls. The presence of depression prior to treatment also was negatively associated with abstinence outcome for girls. Denial in boys, as indicated by the absence of any self-deprecatory or self-denigrating statements when questioned about self-concept, indicated a much higher rate of relapse than in those who were willing to make more negative self-statements. Sexual abuse history, learning disability, lack of intimacy, relationship with parents, court-ordered evaluation, and school status were factors that were not significantly associated with treatment outcome.

Treatment completion was significantly associated with abstinence outcome. Of those who completed treatment, 48% reported total abstinence compared with 29% of the treatment noncompleters. Almost half of the noncompleters fell into the multiple or prolonged relapse category, and since treatment noncompleters were also less likely to be interviewed at follow-up, the beneficial impact of treatment completion is clear.

Regular participation in Alcoholics Anonymous or similar peer support groups was significantly associated with post-treatment abstinence success. Adolescent patients involved in at least one support group throughout the year were almost six times as likely to report total abstinence as those who never attended. Adolescents who attended for only a portion of the year were also much more likely to relapse than those who continuously attended. While the highest abstinence rates were achieved by adolescents who attended two or more meetings per week, it is only after attendance drops below two meetings per month that there are dramatic reductions in sobriety. Of the totally abstinent patients, 81% attended group continuously all year, 13% attended only a part of the year, and 6% did not attend at all. Involvement of parents in ALANON or a similar group was strongly associated with the child's sobriety.

In summary, it would appear from these outcome data that for girls a suicide attempt or depressive syndrome before treatment is associated with a greater tendency to relapse and for boys greater legal problems and use of denial are more likely associated with relapse.

Treatment completion was significantly associated with recovery, with almost half of the adolescents who completed treatment reporting total abstinence. Regular attendance at Alcoholics Anonymous and other support groups was significantly associated with post-treatment sobriety, and continued involvement by parents with support groups was also strongly correlated with post-treatment sobriety. The need for careful assessment of the multiple life problems affecting these youngsters and the importance of a differential diagnosis so that proper and thorough treatment can be provided are indicated by these follow-up data.

References

American Psychiatric Association. 1980. *Diagnostic and Statistical Manual of Mental Disorders*, 3rd. ed. Washington D.C.: American Psychiatric Association.

American Psychiatric Association. 1987. *Diagnostic and Statistical Manual of Mental Disorders*, 3rd. ed., revised. Washington D.C.: American Psychiatric Association.

Barcai, A., and Rabkin, L. 1974. A precursor of delinquency: The hyperkinetic disorder of childhood. *Psychiatr. Q.* 48:387–389.

Beschner, G. M., and Friedman, A. S. (eds.). 1979. Youth Drug Abuse: Problems, Issues, and Treatment. Lexington, Mass.: D.C. Heath and Co.

Blum, R. W. 1987. Adolescent substance abuse: Diagnostic and treatment issues. *Pediatr. Clin. North Am.* 34:523–537.

Bohman, M., Sigvardsson, S., and Cloninger, C. R. 1981. Maternal inheritance of alcohol abuse: Crossfostering analysis of adopted women. *Arch. Gen. Psychiatry* 38:965–969.

Cloninger, C. R. 1983. Genetic and environmental factors in the development of alcoholism. *J. Psychiatr. Treat. Eval.* 5:487–496.

Cloninger, C. R., Reich, T., and Sigvardsson, S. 1986. The effects of changes in alcohol use between generations on the inheritance of alcohol abuse. In Bose, R. (ed.): *Alcoholism: A Medical Disorder*. New York: Raven Press.

Costello, E. J. 1987. Structured interviewing for the assessment of child psychopathology. In Noshpitz, J. (ed.): *Basic Handbook of Child Psychiatry: Advances and New Directions*. New York: Basic Books.

Feighner, J. P., Robins, E., Guze, S. B., et al. 1972. Diagnostic criteria for use in psychiatric research. *Arch. Gen. Psychiatry* 26:57–63.

Felter, R., Izsak, E., and Lawrence, S. 1987. Emergency department management of the intoxicated adolescent. *Pediatr. Clin. North Am.* 34:399–421.

Glueck, S., and Glueck, E. 1950. *Unravelling Juvenile Delinquency*. New York: Commonwealth Fund.

Goodwin, D. W., Schulsinger, F., Knop, J., et al. 1977. Alcoholism and depression in adopted-out daughters of alcoholics. *Arch. Gen. Psychiatry* 34:751–755.

Halikas, J. A., Kemp, K., Kuhn, K., et al. 1989. Carbamazepine for cocaine addiction? *Lancet* (letter) March 18, pp. 623–624.

Halikas, J. A., Lyttle, M., Morse, C., et al. 1984. Proposed criteria for the diagnosis of alcohol abuse in adolescence. *Compr. Psychiatry* 25:581–585.

Harrison, P. A., and Hoffmann, N. G. 1987. *CATOR 1987 Report*. St. Paul, Minn.: Chemical Abuse/Addiction Treatment Outcome Registry.

Herjanic, B., and Reich, W. 1982. Development of a structured psychiatric interview for children: Agreement between child and parent on individual symptoms. *J. Abnorm. Child Psychol.* 10:307–324.

Hoffmann, N. G., Harrison, P. A., and Belille, C. A. 1984. Multi-dimensional impact of treatment for abuse. *Adv. Alcohol. Substance Abuse* 3:83–94.

Jellinek, E. M. 1952. Phases of alcohol addiction. *Quart. J. Stud. Alcohol* 13:673–684.

Jessor, R., and Jessor, S. 1977. *Problem Behavior and Psychosocial Development: A Longitudinal Study of Youth*. New York: Academic Press.

Kaplan, H. 1975. Increase in self-rejection as an antecedent of deviant responses. *J. Youth Adolesc.* 4:281–292.

Kardel, D. 1978. Convergences in prospective longitudinal surveys of drug use in normal populations. In Kardel, D. (ed.): *Longitudinal Research on Drug Use—Empirical Findings and Methodological Issues*. New York: John Wiley & Sons.

Loney, J., Kramer, J., and Milich, R. 1981. The hyperkinetic child grows up: Predictors of symptoms, delinquency, and achievement at follow-up. In Gordon, K. D., and Loney, J. (eds.): *Psychosocial Aspects of Drug Treatment for Hyperactivity*. Boulder, Colo.: Westview Press.

Musto, D. F. 1973. *The American Disease: Origins of Narcotic Control*. New Haven, Conn.: Yale University Press.

National Institute on Drug Abuse. 1985. National Household Survey on Drugs. Washington, D.C.: Alcohol, Drug Abuse, and Mental Health Administration, Public Health Service, U.S. Department of Health and Human Services.

National Institute on Drug Abuse. 1986a. Annual Data from Drug Abuse Warning Network. Washington, D.C.: Alcohol, Drug Abuse, and Mental Health Administration, Public Health Service, U.S. Department of Health and Human Services.

National Institute on Drug Abuse. 1986b. National High School Senior Survey. Washington, D.C.: Alcohol, Drug Abuse, and Mental Health Administration, Public Health Service, U.S. Department of Health and Human Services.

National Institute on Drug Abuse. 1987. National High School Senior Survey. Washington, D.C.: Alcohol, Drug Abuse, and Mental Health Administration, Public Health Service, U.S. Department of Health and Human Services.

National Institute on Alcohol Abuse and Alcoholism. 1987. Sixth Special Report to Congress on Alcohol and Health. Washington, D.C.: Alcohol, Drug Abuse and Mental Health Administration, Public Health Service, U.S. Department of Health and Human Services.

Orvaschel, H., Puigh-Antich, J., Chamber, W., et al. 1982. Retrospective assessment of prepubertal major depression with the Kiddie SADS-E. *J. Am. Acad. Child Adolesc. Psychiatry* 21:393–397.

Robins, L. N., and Murphy, G. E. 1967. Drug use in a normal population of young Negro men. *Am. J. Public Health* 57:1580–1596.

Rorabaugh, W. J. 1979. *The Alcoholic Republic*. New York: Oxford University Press.

Weiss, G., Hechtman, L., Perlman, T., et al. 1979. Hyperactives as young adults: A controlled prospective ten-year follow-up of 75 children. *Arch. Gen. Psychiatry* 36:675–681.

APPENDIX 13–1

SUBSTANCES OF ABUSE

Alcohol

Alcohol intoxication in adolescence results in slurred speech; staggering gait; slowed reflexes; and personality change, including argumentativeness, belligerence, melancholia, irritability, euphoria, social disinhibition, and a variety of other significant personality changes. Memory blackouts, related to the rapidity of the rise in blood alcohol level, which in turn is related to the rapidity of ingestion coupled with the lack of other food contents in the stomach, are the most common medical consequence. (Memory blackouts are a fragmentary or total amnesia for a period of time in minutes to hours during which time the person is awake and alert.) Alcohol overdose, especially in this nontolerant population, can result in death. Therefore a youngster who is nonarousable and believed to have ingested significant quantities of alcohol (or any other drug for that matter) should be considered a medical emergency and hospitalized for close management. There, appropriate intervention including support, gastric lavage, and dialysis, if necessary, can be instituted.

Marijuana

Marijuana, or hashish, is generally smoked but occasionally eaten. It has a relatively rapid onset of action by inhalation and the intoxication lasts 15 to 30 minutes unless renewed. Intoxication is generally sedating with a euphoriant quality. Time is slowed down, the senses seem heightened, the person is happy, and everyone is "mellow." The most consistent physiological concomitant is hunger, and snacking is common ("the munchies"). Occasionally, novice users develop symptoms of a panic anxiety attack because of tachycardia or sensory effects. Sensory effects that are generally perceived as pleasurable but can be seen as frightening include visual distortions with trails or streaks of light following movement of objects across the field of vision and misperceptions of textural changes (e.g., shimmering of walls or waving of light or air). These misperceptions can become frightening and reach the proportion of hallucinations in the panicked user. A marijuana toxic delirium exists but is rarely seen. In the face of a marijuana-induced panic attack, benzodiazepines might be used to provide some sedation. In the face of a toxic delirious state, brief hospitalization and supportive care would be appropriate, since the active constituents of marijuana, the cannabinoids, are fat soluble and can have impact over several days.

Stimulants

Stimulants, or amphetamines, are generally taken orally by adolescents, although in an earlier epidemic, and occasionally today, injectable amphetamine preparations are still used. The acute effects are generally those of stimulation, with increased energy, euphoria, grandiosity, increased irritability, increased physical activity, and decreased sleep. A higher proportion of girls than boys use stimulants, probably related to the side benefit of appetite reduction. Acute toxicity generally includes paranoid symptoms and can easily include spontaneous violence. For that reason caution should be exercised in dealing with an adolescent intoxicated with amphetamines. Any rapid movement or any movement in the direction of the patient is likely to be misinterpreted as an aggressive act, and the patient may become violent very rapidly. Use of injections may be seen as particularly threatening. Intervention must include a great deal of supportive talk and calming agents such as benzodiazepines. Chronic amphetamine use generally requires hospitalization for withdrawal because of the withdrawal depression that occurs uniformly.

Cocaine

Cocaine is generally snorted or smoked, although injectable forms are also occasionally used. The acute intoxication is in many ways similar to the amphetamines but more subtle and more reinforcing. Apparently there are fewer adverse acute effects. This drug has a rapid onset of action by the routes used. This is probably the hardest single drug in which to achieve abstinence and stable remission. The relapse rate is almost universal. Withdrawal cannot hope to be achieved on an outpatient basis. Inpatient withdrawal should include therapy with amantadine and desipramine. There is some recent interest in carbamazepine as an adjunct to control craving (Halikas et al. 1989). Many drugs are being tried in the management of this resistant condition.

Sedatives and Tranquilizers

Sedatives and tranquilizers, including barbiturates, methaqualone, sleeping pills, and the benzodiazepines, are occasionally used by youngsters. These drugs also seem of more interest to girls than boys. Intoxication with these substances, not unexpectedly, includes sedation, somnolence, or sleep. The state sought and achieved, while awake, is that of a "mellow," oblivious neutrality. These drugs are sometimes used in conjunction with one or another of the stimulants to counteract harshness or adverse effects. Overdose with these drugs is a medical emergency. The barbiturates and barbiturate-like compounds can cause death. The benzodiazepines, when combined with alcohol, can also be lethal. Unresponsive patients should be hospitalized and treated aggressively. Withdrawal from the benzodiazepines can last up to 2 weeks because of their fat solubility. Therefore, it is not surprising that patients addicted to these substances become irritable and paranoid and demand discharge at day 10 to 14 of hospitalization. Withdrawal from these drugs should proceed at about a 10% reduction per day after switching the patient to a seconal or diazepam withdrawal schedule.

Hallucinogens

The hallucinogens PCP (phencyclidine), LSD, mescaline, and the "designer" drugs are not commonly used by this generation of adolescents, although they are occasionally used by that portion of the population that uses multiple drugs. Intoxication from these drugs will vary from mild stimulation, euphoria, sensory enhancement, and increased energy to delirious states with hallucinations, fluctuating sensorium, and disorientation. Acute intoxication with the hallucinogens that results in a "bad trip" can be managed generally with verbal supportive care and the use of calming agents such as the benzodiazepines.

PCP is, however, an extremely troublesome drug. It has an unfathomable appeal to some youngsters. Toxic psychotic states associated with its use seem to occur among chronic users of it, while the acute delirious toxic state occurs among more irregular or novice users. This chronic toxic state requires long-term inpatient management and has been known to last several months. It clears very slowly. Hallucinations and delusions, confusion and bewilderment, and an overall decrease in mental functioning are hallmarks of this chronic state. It is often misdiagnosed as a schizophrenic condition when seen in adolescents. Treatment of the acute intoxication includes acidification of the urine with ammonium chloride in an effort to accelerate the excretion of the substance from the body. Management of the long-term condition generally includes major neuroleptics, which unfortunately are not very useful but are commonly used for behavior control.

Narcotics

Heroin and other narcotics are not often used by this age population. Oral narcotics are occasionally used with regularity and are frequently at least tried among multiple drug users in this group. Narcotic overdose is a medical emergency requiring aggressive management. Any adolescent brought to an emergency department in a comatose state should receive an intravenous narcotic antagonist, naloxone hydrochloride, because of the possibility of a narcotic overdose. Should the patient be roused by this medication, it would indicate that at least one of the drugs that this person has overdosed with was a narcotic. Multiple drugs are generally involved, however, so that the management is

not just for narcotics. Also, illegal availability of the long-acting narcotic methadone in large cities means that some youngsters will overdose with that substance. While they will be aroused by naloxone, left to themselves they will soon become unconscious again. They therefore should be watched closely for at least 24 hours.

Hydrocarbons

Glue sniffing, toluene sniffing, and the inhalation of other volatile hydrocarbons are ongoing problems. The sniffing of any of the volatile hydrocarbons, whether directly from cans of gasoline or from glue or other substances placed into plastic bags, is a particularly distressing phenomenon among youth. For one thing, this tends to be a habit or behavior that is likely to occur at grade school and junior high school age and is, in the Third World, the most common type of adolescent drug abuse after alcohol. In recent years, for example, the sniffing of typewriter-correcting chemicals became popular among grade school children. It would appear that any volatile hydrocarbon has the potential for inducing an altered state that is regarded as pleasurable by the young. These youngsters are only brought to the attention of the medical community in an acute state when toxic and delirious. At that time they have all of the usual signs and symptoms of an acute delirium. Hospitalization is usually required. Supportive care, close observation, and close protection, as with all of the other drug intoxication states, are necessary here. Aggressive treatment for the longer-term problem is crucial. It would appear, after 20 years of experience with these drugs in our society, that the volatile hydrocarbons have the worst long-term impact on the user. A chronic organic state can result that will include decreased cognitive functions, hallucinations, irritability and aggressiveness, and a persistent drive for an altered euphoric mental state. Because of their youth, this drive, and their aggresiveness, these patients often require chronic hospitalization in state hospital systems, generally mislabeled as "young chronic schizophrenics."

Three

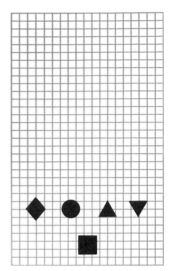

DEVELOPMENTAL
DISORDERS

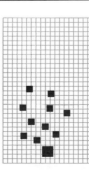

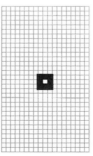

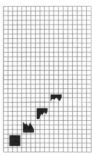

14

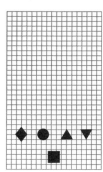

Learning Disorders

L. EUGENE ARNOLD, M.Ed., M.D.

The clusters of deficits generally referred to as learning disorder (LD) or learning disability (LD) are for the most part diagnosed in the *Diagnostic and Statistical Manual of Mental Disorders*, third edition, revised *(DSM-III-R)* (American Psychiatric Association 1987) as specific developmental disorder (SDD). Educators also tend to include attention-deficit disorder (ADD) and attention-deficit hyperactivity disorder (ADHD) as attentional learning disorders. Certainly, there is great overlap between these concepts: individual children frequently meet the diagnostic criteria for both attentional disorder and SDD, the net results are often similar, and proposed etiologies and even suggested treatments are similar. However, since ADHD is treated in a separate chapter, this chapter will focus on SDDs.

DEFINITION, DIAGNOSIS, AND EPIDEMIOLOGY

The terms *learning disabilities* (LDs) or *learning disorders* (LDs) are roughly synonymous and used interchangeably, but "disabilities" emphasizes the handicap/habilitation/education aspect while "disorders" emphasizes the pathology/etiology/treatment aspect. Both

Parts of this chapter were excerpted/adapted with permission from a chapter by W. J. Bates and L. E. Arnold, in Gregory, I., and Smeltzer, D. (eds.) in press. *Psychiatry: Essentials of Clinical Practice.* Third edition. Boston: Little, Brown & Co.

terms are used rather loosely. In the broadest sense, they can include not only specific developmental disorders (SDDs) but also mental retardation (MR) and any specific neurologic disorder that interferes with learning. For example, there is literature referring to fragile X syndrome as a cause of LD, and LDs are sometimes discussed as if they were attenuated forms of MR. Actually, it would not be inaccurate to characterize some cases of LD (those that do not disappear with maturation) as *partial forms* of MR. In fact, many British authors refer to "reading retardation." However, many LDs spontaneously remit with maturation and others seem highly responsive to treatment, while MR, once established, is generally accepted to be life long and unremitting even with treatment. As generally used, the term LD excludes MR and pervasive developmental disorder. Sometimes the preface "specific" is used to distinguish from MR: specific learning disability (SLD) or specific learning disorder (SLD). Another term sometimes used is developmental LD. The concept is generally congruent with SDD, although some experts would also include ADHD.

The legal definition of specific learning disability in Public Law 94–142 (1975 Education for all Handicapped Children Act) is "a disorder in one or more of the basic psychological processes involved in understanding or using language, spoken or written, which may manifest itself in an imperfect ability to listen, think, speak, read, write, spell, or do mathematical calculations." To determine eligibility for publicly funded LD programs, schools commonly evaluate a child's functioning in seven areas: reading basic skills, reading comprehension, written expression, oral expression, listening comprehension, math calculation, and math reasoning.

A *developmental disorder* is a failure of some skill or ability to develop by the appropriate age. There are three main categories: (1) general developmental disorders, best known as mental retardation (MR); (2) pervasive developmental disorders, best known as autism; and (3) specific developmental disorders (SDDs), known as learning disabilities. A child with an SDD, in contrast to MR or pervasive developmental disorder, shows an impairment in only one or a few areas of development and is usually normal otherwise. Like MR, SDDs are quantitative rather than qualitative diagnoses. The *DSM-III-R* diagnosis requires a judgment, aided by individual standardized tests, as to whether the patient falls significantly short of the expected performance for mental age on some identified ability or skill.

Specific developmental disorders come in three main types: (1) academic skills disorders (reading disorder, arithmetic disorder, expressive writing disorder); (2) speech and language disorders (articulation disorder, expressive language disorder, receptive language disorder); and (3) motor skills disorder (coordination disorder).

This is a very common group of disorders. Although it is hard to find definitive prevalence data, some estimates range as high as 20% of elementary schoolchildren, and estimates of 10% are common. Silver (1986) very conservatively estimates up to 7%. Two to four times as many boys as girls are affected: 3.5 boys to 1 girl for reading retardation in the Isle of Wight study (Rutter and Yule 1977). These disorders are often associated with each other and with ADHD, conduct disorder, and functional enuresis. Thus the prevalence in a child psychiatric population is even higher than the figures above suggest (McClelland 1986). Some of these relationships are shown in Figure 14–1.

A given child may meet the criteria for more than one SDD. If so, each disorder should be diagnosed. The following are descriptions and diagnostic criteria for each of the eight SDDs.

Academic Skills Disorders

For the *DSM-III-R* diagnosis, each of the three academic skills disorders require performance "markedly below the expected level" for schooling and mental age, both on standardized individual achievement tests and on academic or other tasks requiring the skill in question (reading, arithmetic, or expressive writing). To determine performance markedly below the expected for purposes of LD program eligibility, schools follow a statewide federal formula with some local modifications: generally, a 2-standard-deviation gap between standard achievement scores and IQ qualifies. (A standard score is like an IQ, with 100 being normal achievement for chronologic age.) Thus if the standard deviation (σ) of a given test is 16, a standard score of 108 on that test is $+0.5\sigma$ and 88 is -0.75σ. The gap between these two is 1.25σ. A gap of 2σ or greater between achievement and IQ scores would qualify as LD. In addition, an "override" mechanism, invoked at local discretion, can qualify children with gaps between 1.0σ and 2.0σ who are considered high risk or greatly in need of service or whose IQ scores are suspected to be artificially depressed and who "would have met" the 2σ criterion if their true IQ were available. Commonly used achievement tests are listed in Table 14–1. Some examples of markedly low reading performance would be a 14-year-old eighth grader of normal intelligence reading at fifth grade level; an 8-year-old third grader of normal intelligence reading at first grade level; a 7-year-old first grader with an IQ of 140 reading at first grade level in a school where most first graders are reading above second grade level; and a mildly retarded 16-year-old with a mental age of 10 who is reading at second grade level.

In a school where the average is below grade level, or in cases where the child has missed a lot of school or changed schools repeatedly, some of the poor performance must be attributed to poor schooling. In such cases more stringent criteria of performance impairment should be used. For the *DSM-III-R* diagnosis, the poor performance cannot be explained by sensory end organ or peripheral nerve impairment (deafness, refractive error) or a neurologic disorder. However, it can involve constitutional perceptual deficits at the level of central nervous system inte-

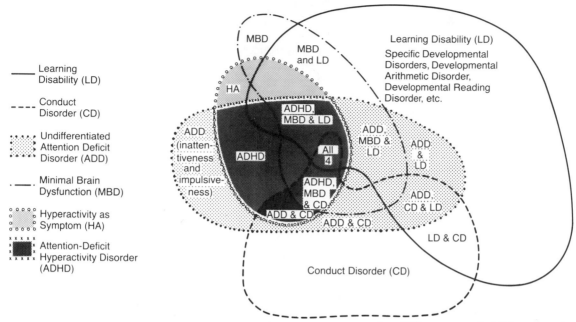

Figure 14–1. *Overlap of related terms, concepts, and diagnoses in the 10% or more of children (mostly boys) who have chronic learning and classroom behavior problems besides mental retardation (3%), pervasive developmental disorder, and depression. Minimal brain dysfunction (MBD) is not a diagnosis, but with enough evidence, an organic mental disorder can sometimes be diagnosed. (Reproduced with permission from Gregory, I., and Smeltzer, D., in press.* Psychiatry: Essentials of Clinical Practice. *Third edition. Boston: Little, Brown & Co.)*

gration and coordination, such as visuomotor dysfunction. More specific features of the three disorders are detailed below.

Developmental reading disorder is frequently called dyslexia and has at times been called congenital word blindness, strephosymbolia, specific reading disorder, or (specific) reading retardation. The reading problem may involve impairment of word discrimination, difficulty with word sequencing, difficulty with phonetic audiovisual integration, or other language difficulties. Many experts distinguish a dysphonetic, auditory form (with difficulty sounding out words), a dyseidetic, visual form (with difficulty discriminating, recognizing, and organizing graphemes), and a combined dysphonetic/dyseidetic form. The dysphonetic form may also be called perceptual or P-type, with accurate but slow reading and mistakes due to hesitation and repetition. The dyseidetic may be called the linguistic or L-type, with fluent but inaccurate reading riddled with substitutions and deletions.

Developmental reading disorder affects 2% to 8% of elementary schoolchildren, mostly boys. Many of the affected children also

warrant diagnoses of language or expressive writing disorder. As with other SDDs, expression of the reading disorder may be rather specific to circumstances. There is even speculation that some children may show a reading disorder in one language but not another. Certainly some may show it when taught by the phonetic method but not when taught by the holistic method, while others may show it when taught holistically but not when taught phonetically. There is also a familial tendency.

Developmental expressive writing disorder involves impairment in spelling, organization, punctuation, or grammar, not merely in penmanship. Children with expressive writing disorder often also have reading, language, arithmetic, or coordination disorder.

Developmental arithmetic disorder has one or more of the following four kinds of impairment: (1) linguistic problems, involving math terminology, concepts, operation naming, encoding, and decoding; (2) perceptual problems, involving recognition of symbols or signs or organization of things into groups or sets; (3) attention problems, including correct copying or carrying; and (4) math prob-

Table 14–1. EXAMPLES OF COMMONLY USED ACHIEVEMENT TESTS

Name of Test	What is Measured (Subtests or Scores)	How Reported
Group Screening Tests Given All Children Periodically		
California Achievement Test (CAT)	All Group Tests Include:	
	Reading	Percentile rank*
Iowa Test of Basic Skills (ITBS, grades K–9) or Test of Achievement and Proficiency (TAP, grades 9–12)	Spelling	Stanine†
	Languages	Standard scores‡
Metropolitan Achievement Test (MAT)	Mathematics	Scaled scores§
	Social Studies	Grade equivalent
Stanford Achievement Test Series (STAN)	Science	
Individually Administered Tests (by Special Request, With Parent's Permission)		
Wide Range Achievement Test (WRAT)	Reading recognition Arithmetic Spelling	Grade equivalent Percentile Standard scores by age
Peabody Individual Achievement Test (PIAT)	Mathematics Reading recognition Reading comprehension Spelling General information	Age equivalent Grade equivalent Percentile Standard scores by age Standard scores by grade
Peabody Picture Vocabulary Test-Revised (PPVT-R)	Receptive language	Standard scores Percentile Stanine Age equivalent
Kaufman Test of Educational Achievement (K-TEA)	Reading decoding Reading comprehension Math application Math computation Spelling	Age equivalent Grade equivalent Percentile rank by age and grade Standard scores by age and grade
Woodcock-Johnson Psycho-Educational Battery (WJPEB), Part II (Part I measures ability/aptitude; Part III measures interests)	Letter-word identification Word attack Passage comprehension Calculation Applied math Dictation Proofing Science Social studies Humanities	Age equivalent Grade equivalent and instructional range Percentile by age and grade Standard scores Stanines
Key Math Diagnostic Arithmetic Test	Content Operations Applications	Grade equivalent Percentile ranks Norm curve
Test of Written Language (TOWL) (Can also be administered in group)	Thematic maturity Spelling Vocabulary Word usage Style Handwriting	Percentiles Standard scores

Percentile = the percent of test takers (of same age or grade) who scored lower. Thus a child scoring in the 87th percentile performed better than approximately 87% of peers. The 50th percentile is median. (This is not an exact statistical definition, but close enough for clinical interpretation.)

†*Stanine* is short for "standard nines." Each stanine (except the first and ninth) spans half a standard deviation (σ). Stanine 5 is centered on the mean. Thus a child scoring in stanine 5 is within ¼ σ of the mean; a score in stanine 7 is ¾ to 1¼ σ above the mean. Stanine 9 is 1¾ σ or more above the mean.

‡*Standard scores* are understood like IQ scores, with 100 being average achievement for age/grade.

§*Scaled scores* are a type of standard score used for subtests.

(This table was compiled with the assistance and consultation of Mary T. Sidman, M.A., Clinical Instructor in Psychiatry, Ohio State University.)

lems, involving count, sequential math procedures, or multiplication tables. With so many different possible deficits, it should not be surprising that many patients with this diagnosis also have developmental language, reading, expressive writing, or coordination disorder, or ADHD. Patients with Tourette's syndrome are believed especially vulnerable to arithmetic disorder.

"Nonverbal learning disability" (Tranel et al. 1987) presumably results from right hemisphere damage, with the following characteristics: depression, shyness, impaired eye contact, impaired gesture communication, impaired prosody (intonation and rhythm of speech), lower performance IQ than verbal IQ, math impairment, acceptable reading achievement but with lower reading comprehension, and failure of social conduct despite academic success in some subjects. In the extreme form this is sometimes called Asperger's syndrome. It does not have a separate *DSM-III-R* category; it should be diagnosed by the same criteria as other LDs. Some will qualify for other SDDs. They may also qualify for an Axis I diagnosis (e.g., organic affective syndrome or major depression) or for a pervasive developmental disorder diagnosis, even though more attention has been paid to left hemisphere impairments in autistic patients.

Language and Speech Disorders

Developmental articulation disorder is one type of speech disorder; others include stuttering, cluttering, and spastic or anatomical impediments. It is the most benign of the developmental disorders and perhaps the most common, affecting 10% of children younger than age 8 and 5% of those older than age 8. The *DSM-III-R* diagnosis requires consistent failure to articulate age-appropriate consonants, not because of mental retardation, pervasive developmental disorder, hearing impairment, anatomical defect, or neurologic disorder. Examples of failure to articulate age-appropriate consonants would be an 18-month old not using m or d, a 3-year old not using b, p, or t, and a school-age child not using r, l, sh, ch, th, f, or z. Variants are lisping (substituting th for s), lalling, and baby talk. The disorder tends to run in families. Language milestones are usually normal. However, children with this

disorder often also have a developmental language disorder, reading disorder, coordination disorder, or functional enuresis.

Developmental language disorder is delayed language acquisition, not loss of language already acquired or failure to acquire it at all. It is the most common language disorder (others being mutism associated with hearing loss, traumatic aphasia, and pervasive developmental disorder) and the most crippling LD, often underlying the academic skills disorders. It affects 3% to 10% of schoolchildren. This diagnosis should not be made if the problem seems due to hearing impairment, neurologic disorder, pervasive developmental disorder, or MR.

The expressive and receptive types are diagnosed separately even though they have the same *DSM-III-R* code number, and most patients with receptive language disorder also have the expressive type. Thus, a patient may appropriately be given two diagnoses with the same code number. Diagnosis of either type requires a score on an individual standardized language test "substantially below" the score on an individual standardized test of nonverbal intelligence, along with disruption of academic achievement or activities of daily living. There is usually normal nonverbal communication (gestures and facial expressions), both receptive and expressive. In many cases, an additional diagnosis of articulation disorder is warranted.

Developmental expressive language disorder is an inability to encode language in an age-appropriate way. There may be limitations of vocabulary, sentence length and complexity, tense, or other grammatical repertoire. Essential parts of sentences may be left out, or words may be substituted or arranged in an unorthodox order. There may be circumlocutions, jargon, tangentiality, or overgeneralization. Milder cases may show only hesitations on certain words, recall errors, or problems with long, complex sentences. Expressive language disorder affects 3% to 10% of schoolchildren, manifesting by age 3 in severe cases. Expressive language disorder is often associated with developmental articulation disorder, coordination disorder, and functional enuresis. Because of perceptual or sequencing deficits, learning problems are common at school age, which may also bring emotional and behavioral problems. There is a familial tendency.

Developmental receptive language disorder is

the failure to develop language decoding abilities (comprehension) at the appropriate age. The disturbance can vary from mere inability to understand one type of word or understand long complex sentences to a severe pervasive inability to comprehend basic words and simple sentences or even to discriminate phonemes or associate sounds and symbols. There may be deficits in auditory storage, recall, sequencing, or other auditory processing. These predispose to academic skills, expressive language, and articulation disorders. Some patients have coordination disorder, functional enuresis, ADHD, or other behavioral disorder. There is a higher than normal rate of electroencephalographic abnormality. Receptive language disorder may well be the most disabling of the SDDs.

Motor Skills Disorder

Developmental coordination disorder is the only motor skills disorder listed in the *DSM-III-R.* Diagnosis requires coordination "markedly below" the expected level for age and intelligence, interfering with academic achievement or activities of daily living (including sports customary for age and culture). The incoordination cannot be attributable to cerebral palsy, hemiplegia, myasthenia gravis, muscular dystrophy, or other diagnosed physical disorder. The afflicted children are often noted to be clumsy as toddlers or delayed in attaining motor milestones. They have difficulty learning to run, manage eating utensils, button or zip clothes, tie shoelaces, assemble puzzles or models, throw or hit a ball, print, or write. They may also be delayed in attaining non-motor milestones. Illegible penmanship is diagnosed under this category, not under expressive writing disorder. Coordination disorder is associated with developmental language and speech disorders. It is estimated to affect as many as 6% of 5- to 11-year olds.

Specific Developmental Disorder Not Otherwise Specified

Specific developmental disorder not otherwise specified allows for diagnosis of developmental problems of speech, language, academic, or motor skills that do not meet the criteria for one of the previous disorders. For example, developmental spelling problems could be diagnosed here if they do not seem to be part of a developmental expressive writing disorder. Another example would be a skill impairment associated with a long-standing physical disorder.

ETIOLOGY

Although a few LDs may be psychogenic or secondary to an Axis I disorder, the vast majority are neurophysiological and rise independently. Of course, they may be aggravated by an Axis I or other disorder. Very likely there are several etiologies for each of the LDs.

There is some evidence for a genetic predisposition: there is a higher rate of SDD among first-degree biological relatives than in the general population. If the familial linkage is genetic, there appears to be some variation in expression. For example, those with developmental expressive language disorder are likely to have relatives with developmental articulation disorder; those with developmental expressive writing disorder are likely to have relatives with developmental language disorder as well as academic skills disorders. Nevertheless, developmental reading disorder and developmental articulation disorder seem to "breed true." For example, in the Isle of Wight study, 60% of children with reading retardation had a positive family history. The variability may be a spurious result of incomplete study of the familial patterns of these disorders. The observed familial tendencies could be compatible with a dominant transmission with variable penetrance, sex influenced. If so, the genes involved may operate through effects on testosterone or immune function, or the disorder could be of the homeotic type, affecting the growth of brain areas such as the left planum temporale.

There is often a history of perinatal brain injury or at least insult. There is an association with low birth weight, gestational maternal smoking and alcohol use, and other gestational exposure to toxins, infection, or other stresses. Early deprivation is another possible cause. Iron deficiency and frank malnutrition, where they occur, are believed to contribute. Postnatal toxins, notably lead, have also been implicated.

The Geschwind hypothesis (Behan and Geschwind 1985; Geschwind and Galaburda 1985) is that prenatal excess testosterone or an autoimmune reaction (possibly maternal antibodies) disrupts cortical cell migration in the later-developing left hemisphere, or otherwise suppresses its development. Although the right hemisphere is completed ahead of the left, and not as susceptible to testosterone or autoimmune disruption, the disruption on the left could affect the wiring of both sides. Alternately, the right could even be directly affected. These points are important in preventing a simplistic assumption that LDs are merely left hemisphere problems. Most learning involves both hemispheres (Swanson 1987), and in some cases the problem seems to be mainly right hemisphere. It has been speculated that such a hormone effect could be the mechanism by which some gestational toxins exert their effect. In this context, there may be overdevelopment of the right hemisphere and even outstanding talents or skills associated with right hemisphere development. An excess of left-handedness has been noted not only among learning disabled and autistic patients but also among medical students, art students, and math geniuses. It is not clear what determines whether genius or learning disorder results from left hemisphere suppression with right hemisphere hypertrophy.

Other "hemispheric" hypotheses (Rourke et al. 1983) include Satz's, which postulates delayed left-hemisphere specialization. Supposedly the left hemisphere normally specializes in fine motor control about age 5, perceptual skills about age 8, and language about age 11; dyslexics would thus have reading problems related to these three delays at the respective ages. Masland postulated a failure to transfer visual symbol analysis from the right to the left hemisphere at the appropriate age. In normal beginning readers, visual symbols, including words, are decoded/analyzed in the right hemisphere. About third grade this function transfers to the left hemisphere for efficient proximity to language and speech centers. Reading development could thus be arrested by either relatively poor right-hemisphere visuospatial function (dyseidetic, L-type dyslexia) or by overdeveloped right hemisphere function, which resists transfer to the left (dysphonetic, P-type dyslexia). These three hypotheses, of course, are not mutually exclusive.

As in ADHD, with which LDs are sometimes grouped, there are many popular etiologic hypotheses and corresponding treatments, most of which are not well documented. These include dietary allergies or hypersensitivities (Feingold hypothesis), relative vitamin or trace mineral deficiencies (orthomolecular medicine), maturational lag, mixed laterality or incomplete dominance, repeated otitis media affecting the cerebellar-vestibular system, other causes of cerebellar-vestibular dysfunction, deficient eye tracking, and abnormality of sphenoid and temporal bones with "ocular lock" and "cloacal reflexes" (Beauchamp and Kosmorsky 1987). Certainly, anything affecting general health, zest, attention, energy, or neurologic integrity can affect the complex process of learning. Therefore, it should not be surprising to find individual anecdotes in which one or more of the problems listed are contributing to an LD. Such anecdotes do not establish a generalizable cause. Unfortunately, in many cases the etiology remains unclear.

PATHOLOGY

Cortical areas of learning-disabled children generate excessive alpha rhythm compared with normal controls (Fig. 14–2). Excess alpha rhythm presumably reflects hypofunctioning in these areas, which are the medial frontal lobe on both sides, the left lateral frontal lobe, the left midtemporal lobe, the left posterior quadrant (including Wernicke's area), and the right posterior quadrant (Duffy et al. 1980).

Twenty per cent of dyslexic children have been reported to be left handed, significantly more than the general population. This is questioned by other authors (Obrzut and Boliek 1986). If valid, it is presumably related to left hemisphere damage of some kind (Bakker 1984). CT brain scans suggest absence of the normal finding of slightly larger left posterior quadrant than right posterior quadrant. Normal brains are asymmetrical, generally with the left posterior quadrant larger, but sometimes with the right larger. LD patients have greater symmetry. The planum temporale, which is normally larger on the left than on the right in right-handed persons, is often of similar size on both sides in LD.

Postmortem study of a few dyslexic brains

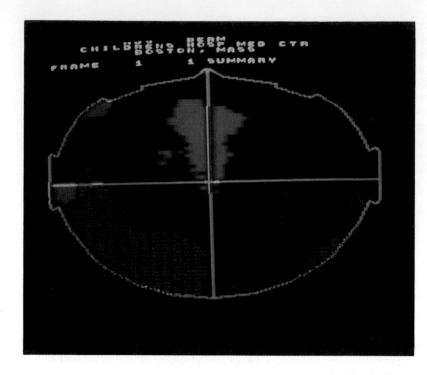

Figure 14–2. Summary topographic brain electrical activity map showing the areas of dyslexics that were significantly different from normal controls. (Reproduced with permission from Torello, M. W., and Duffy, F. H. 1985. Using brain electrical activity mapping to diagnose learning disabilities. Theory Into Practice 26:95–99.)

(Behan and Geschwind 1985) suggests perisylvian ectopia (clusters of cortical cells where they should not be) and dysplasia (pockets of abnormal small cells disrupting the cortical layers) mostly in the left temporal lobe. Micropolygyria has also been noted more on the left than on the right. These phenomena are likely to have dated from early in gestation. The ectopia and dysplasia presumably resulted from interference with prenatal cell migration, mostly on the left. Another reported finding is that both the Purkinje cells of the cerebellum and temporal cortical cells seem sparser.

CLINICAL PICTURE

Many elements of the clinical picture are already described under definitions and diagnosis. The specific impairment shown by the child will vary according to which disorders are present. The speech and language disorders may be obvious from interview, especially in the more severe cases. However, milder cases may be more subtle and require some probes or even formal testing. Coordination disorder becomes obvious on subtle (soft) sign neurologic examination (Bax and Whitmore 1987). Even children with

other SDDs without coordination disorder may show some subtle signs. According to the Satz model, early dyslexics should have fine-motor impairments and primary-grade dyslexics should have perceptual deficits. The academic skills disorders may not be obvious at clinical interview unless the child is asked to read or write something or work age-appropriate math problems. Like ADHD children, learning-disabled children habituate rapidly to a stimulus, encode fewer features than do normal controls, and seem to attend only to the most salient differences between stimuli, thus giving the appearance of seeking novel stimuli.

Typically, a learning-disordered child is referred to a psychiatrist for associated behavior problems or secondary depression rather than for the LD per se. A high proportion have ADHD and/or conduct disorder, possibly secondary to the frustration. There are often secondary emotional problems from the frustration, failure, and disappointment. At interview, many of the children show a reluctance to attempt tasks or tests, possibly even verbalizing an expectation of failure or poor performance (e.g., "I can't."). Some develop obsessive-compulsive symptoms as a means of coping with their impairment. The parents may vary from supportive to frustrated and rejecting at one extreme or overprotective and crusading at the other extreme.

CASE HISTORIES

Case 1

A 7-year-old first grade boy was brought for testing by his adoptive parents because of "auditory processing dysfunction" found on school testing. His parents were concerned about prognosis and behavioral management. He was already scheduled to repeat the first grade. His Weschler Intelligence Scale for Children (WISC) IQ scores were performance, 111; verbal, 90; and full scale, 101. He had good scores in general knowledge and was weakest in auditory memory. Language testing showed significant delay in auditory processing and memory consistent with a developmental receptive language disorder. His reading readiness skills were at a beginning kindergarten level even though he had just finished a year in the first grade. In class he was easily distracted, with difficulty staying on task, understanding directions, and expressing himself. In a special resource room for reading and speech he had begun to make slow but steady progress. His behavior was worse in his regular class than in the smaller LD resource room class. He was noted to do well in a group of two or three.

Because of neglect by his drug-abusing, alcoholic mother, who had a diagnosis of schizophrenia following use of LSD, he was put in a foster home at age 6 months. There he was rarely held. He was therefore moved to a second foster home until he was adopted at age 2½. The parents attributed some of his delayed ability to several hospital stays during his first 2½ years, when he suffered from neutropenia, colds, and ear infections. Because of the latter, he underwent tonsillectomy and adenoidectomy and had ear tubes inserted three times. He also had corrective eye surgery for strabismus.

On interview he was a well-groomed thin boy who was overactive, restless, oppositional, and easily frustrated. He did not finish activities unless closely supervised. He was inattentive and fidgeted constantly. He seemed most oppositional and even whiny between 10 and 11 AM (after a cornflakes breakfast). He had numerous soft neurologic signs, including problems with fine coordination, balance, tapping, stereognosis, graphesthesia, and pencil grip. He showed crossed laterality. Eye tracking was jerky. In attempting to repeat "puh-tuh-kuh," he had trouble with sequencing and auditory-motor ability. His fantasy material showed depression, thoughts of death, and aggressive themes, including shooting persons.

On a vigilance task, he got 16 correct with 29 omission and 60 commission errors, all abnormal scores consistent with inattentiveness and impatience. His Bender Gestalt test showed 7 Koppitz errors, borderline for his age. His parents rated him 27 (probable hyperkinetic) on the Davids scale and 9 (borderline) on the Conners Hyperactivity Index. On physical examination, he had bilaterally slightly retracted tympanic membranes and mild right exophoria. His pulse was 100 beats per minute and his blood pressure was 105/60 mm Hg. He was taking no medication.

Discussion. As with most LD children who come to the attention of a child psychiatrist, this boy had a wealth of diagnoses and possible etiologies. In addition to developmental receptive and expressive language disorders, developmental reading disorder, and developmental coordination disorder, he also had oppositional disorder, possibly secondary to the learning problems, and probably ADHD. The learning problems and ADHD may have been caused by fetal alcohol effects, other chemical toxicity, early deprivation, infectious insult of the central nervous system, or allergic or other immune problems, possibly superimposed on a genetic predisposition.

Case 2

A 12½-year-old seventh grade boy was referred by the school special education resources center because the boy related, "I can't keep my mind on one thing . . . I'm hyper." He and his parents agreed that he had suffered lifelong difficulties with inattentiveness, limited ability to sit still, and easy frustration. However, they had not considered this a problem until a recent school psychological report said that the child might be hyperactive. In the past his mother helped him with his homework because by himself he would get so easily frustrated he would wad up the paper and throw it away. The current year he had requested to try it alone, and it was not getting done or turned in. In one of his classes, two chairs were provided for him because of his constant movement. His worst time of school was about 11 or 11:30 AM until lunch. At that time he would begin to feel tired, restless, and unable to concentrate. His usual breakfast was cinnamon toast.

His early development was unremarkable except for many ear infections, for which he had tubes placed. Kindergarten went well except that he became anxious during test situations. School through the third grade was fairly smooth, but in the fourth grade he rode the school bus across town and had difficulty adjusting to the new school. His fourth grade teacher categorized him as lazy. His grades had been a concern since then.

In the sixth grade he was tested and found to have a verbal Weschler Intelligence Scale for Children—Revised (WISC-R) IQ of 105, performance IQ of 121, and full-scale IQ of 113. On the Woodcock-Johnson Achievement Test, he received standard scores of 89 in reading, 97 in written language, and 91 in mathematics (106 in calculation and 79 in applied problems). His SLD tutor noted "poor concentration, inattentive in class, moves continually with whole body, whether sitting or standing, does not complete work."

He wrote a letter at the beginning of seventh grade stating, "I am a tutored student. My handicaps are spelling, punctuation, comprehension, vocabulary, listening, and study skills. I have trouble organizing, completing homework, and studying. I need to write my assignment every day. I read better when I am moving, and I learn better when I am moving, too." His most recent report card showed F in language arts, C in math, D in social studies, F in science, and As in physical education and chorus.

His mother scored him 18 on the Conners Hyperactivity Index, significant, and 34 of 36 on the Davids Hyperkinetic Rating Scale, probably hyperkinetic. On the ADHD Checklist, she endorsed 8 of the 14 items as "often," with a total score of 24, compatible with mild ADHD. A teacher scored him 16 on the Conners Hyperactivity Index, significant.

At interview and in a small group with other children, he appeared a normal robust pubescent boy, cooperating constructively with the evaluation and with the group activities. His three wishes were for improvement in grades, a Lamberghini, and three more wishes, which he used for money, to grow taller, and to sit still. His human figure drawing had the top of the head missing. His subtle sign neurologic examination was normal except for mild overflow on some of the tapping tests. He accurately completed the Bender Gestalt with no Koppitz errors but did turn the paper to the reverse side for the last figure. He scored 6 on the Children's Depression Inventory, which was unremarkable.

Discussion. This bright boy's insight highlights a not unusual mix of learning problems. All of his problems appear to have been mild enough that his good intelligence and strong family support allowed him to lurch along undiagnosed until middle school. In a less supportive family, or with 20 points lower IQ, he would probably have been identified and diagnosed by fourth grade. His academic problems seem attributable to several diagnosable entities. His low grades in the face of an above-average IQ, coupled with low reading and applied math scores on an individual test, warrant diagnoses of developmental reading disorder and developmental arithmetic disorder. A standard reading score of 89 does not sound bad in itself, but when compared with his IQ of 113, it is 24 standard points too low, representing over two grade levels of deficiency. Along with his F in language arts, the 16-point shortfall in verbal IQ compared with performance IQ suggests the possibility of mild language disorder underlying the reading and arithmetic disorders. However, this could not be diagnosed without an individual language test, which was not done. It is likely that the arithmetic disorder resulted partly from the reading disorder since the deficiency was in applied problems, which depends partly on reading comprehension at this age. In fact, an argument might be made that there is not an arithmetic disorder, only a reading disorder that spilled over into arithmetic achievement. For optimization of his learning potential, this boy needs treatment of all three disorders (ADHD, reading disorder, and arithmetic disorder).

Case 3*

A consulting psychiatrist was asked to talk with a 14-year-old eighth grade boy because

---

*This case is reprinted by permission of Elsevier Science Publishing Co., Inc. from *Case Studies in Child Psychiatry* by Coddington, R. D., Arnold, L. E., Leaverton, D. R., and Rowe, M. R., p. 208. Copyright 1973 by Medical Examination Publishing Company, Inc.

he insisted on dropping out of school. The boy was interviewed in the presence of his father and the school counselor who had requested the consultation. He stated that he wanted to drop out of school because he did not know how to read. On further inquiry, he said that he had been told in the second grade he had a reading disability. He had understood from this that he would never be able to read. When asked what he had tried to read lately, he replied that he had not bothered trying to read anything because he knew he could not. When handed a popular magazine and asked to demonstrate his incapacitating disability, he began reading aloud fluently. After two sentences he stopped in mouth-gaping amazement that was matched only by that of his father and the counselor. He decided to continue in school on a half-day basis, which the counselor had already offered to arrange with the vice-principal's permission.

Follow-up 2 months later revealed that he had begun specializing in looking things up and reporting back to the class. In fact, he was beginning to get into trouble because all he wanted to do was read.

Discussion. This unusual case illustrates several points, including the danger of labeling and the child giving up. Unfortunately, the school records were not checked to make sure that the original label was confirmed by an individualized achievement test. However, it is not likely that a school would classify someone as having an LD without such tests, not only for legal reasons but also because such classification costs the school for special services. The *DSM-III-R* states that the prognosis for mild reading disorders is good with appropriate intervention, but this boy had not read the *DSM-III-R* (presumably because he was unaware that he could read). One of the lessons from this case is that there is hope even for teenagers with LDs. Another is that many SDDs have a good prognosis if the child and parents can take a long view. However, it should not be concluded from this exceptional case either that one can sweep through the schools miraculously curing reading disorders by handing students popular magazines and challenging them to read or that spontaneous remission should be counted on without intervention and practice.

Case 4

A 5½-year-old transnational adoptee of Asian ancestry was referred by his therapeutic preschool because of apparent hyperactivity. According to his adoptive parents, since the age of 2 he had been in constant motion, unable to complete most activities, and verbally loud and disruptive. In school he was described as easily frustrated, restless, excitable, impulsive, inattentive, impatient, distractible, unpredictably disruptive, and in need of constant prompting to follow through with tasks. In his native land he had taken phenytoin (Dilantin) and other medications for a history of febrile seizures but had stopped these a year ago, with a normal electroencephalogram. A week-long trial of methylphenidate by his pediatrician had not helped. Testing disclosed a mild receptive and expressive language disorder despite good English vocabulary. He also had some memory problems. His Conners Hyperactivity Index score by his teacher was 17.

On interview, he was inattentive, distracted, and fidgety, with rapid speech and poor articulation, possibly related to change of language. He was unable to participate in fantasy play. He could not draw a square or triangle, and his Bender Gestalt, taking 8 minutes, suggested severe visuomotor dysfunction, with much perseveration and rotations. He could not engage in vigilance testing because of his extreme inattentiveness. On subtle neurologic signs examination he had difficulty balancing, dysrhythmia on tapping and finger succession, and inability to foot-tap. Twenty-four-hour urinary homovanilic acid (3.0 mg), 5-hydroxyindole acetic acid (1.4 mg), metanephrine, epinephrine, norepinephrine, dopamine, and total catecholamine levels were all normal.

Because of his age, he was given a trial of an elimination diet before attempting another medication trial. With the diet he showed dramatic improvement in behavior, attention, and academic performance. His speech and language became clearer and more to the point. The occupational therapist who was working with his coordination problems discontinued treatment because it suddenly no longer seemed necessary. Repeated challenges established milk as a precipitant of inattentiveness, disorganized speech and behavior, and poor academic performance.

Discussion. This case is presented as an exception to the rule. It should not be taken as a basis to conclude a generalized benefit of elimination diets, even in the preschool age group where they are most likely to help. Less than 5% of children with LD might be expected to show enough benefit to make continued dietary eliminations worthwhile. Evidence for efficacy of dietary eliminations is, like this case, anecdotal.

CLINICAL COURSE

The age at onset varies by the type of disorder and its severity. Since academic skills disorders by definition cannot be recognized until school age, articulation disorder and language disorders are likely to be the first noted. Expressive language disorder is generally manifested by age 3 in severe cases, although milder cases may not manifest until the increasing language complexity of early adolescence. Receptive language disorder usually manifests by age 4 (age 2 in severe cases), but in some cases not until age 7. Coordination disorders are often first noted in toddlerhood, when the patient may be clumsy or delayed in attaining motor milestones. Developmental reading disorder usually manifests by second grade, but bright children may compensate well enough to cover it up until age 9 or 10. Developmental arithmetic disorder occasionally manifests by third grade, but usually not until after age 10.

Once the problem is noted, the child begins experiencing frustration, discouragement, perhaps failure, and perhaps teasing or ostracism. These bring secondary emotional problems, such as depression. In some cases, there is an avoidance reaction, with rejection of academic work. Many affected children develop disruptive behavior problems (conduct disorder, ADHD, oppositional-defiant disorder) and may eventually even turn to delinquent behavior, presumably as a means of succeeding at something. There is often a "domino" tendency, with one disorder leading to another. For example, a language disorder may lead to a reading or other academic skills disorder, which may predispose to a disruptive behavior disorder. When academic problems first become obvious, parents may misinterpret the problems as laziness or stubbornness. Denial is common. Once the parents understand the problem, they may either become appropriately supportive, reject the damaged child, blame the school or obstetrician, or overprotect and run interference for the child in all activities.

The disorders vary in prognosis. Articulation disorder has an almost 100% remission with therapy, and many cases, especially the mild ones, remit spontaneously by age 8. At the other extreme, some of the more severely affected children with receptive language disorder never develop normal language abilities. The prognosis is better for expressive language disorder, from which up to 50% of the patients may spontaneously recover by school age; even most of the patients with more severe cases of expressive language disorder develop normal language by late adolescence. Coordination disorder has a variable prognosis, with some cases continuing into adulthood (in muted form). The outcome for academic skills disorders depends largely on the intervention provided. For example, reading disorder usually responds well enough to remediation that mild cases often show no adult impairment. Without treatment, most dyslexics fall farther and farther behind their age mates.

LABORATORY FINDINGS

By definition, the academic skills disorders and language disorders must show on individual tests significant impairment as compared with the level of performance expected for the child's mental age. For convenience, achievement and language scores are expressed in standard scores, which can be compared directly with IQ rather than needing to compare grade level or language age level with mental age. The LDs that have an attentional component may show impairment on vigilance and distractibility tests. Those that have perceptual-motor deficits may show these on such tests as the Bender Gestalt, the Graham Kendall, or appropriate tests of the Halstead-Reitan Battery. Ten per cent of reading disorders have visuomotor dysfunction.

Electroencephalograms are often diffusely abnormal, especially in receptive language disorder, but many appear normal on routine standard electroencephalography. Becker et al. (1987) did report abnormal focal activity as well as high-amplitude alpha. Specialized procedures such as evoked potential and brain electrical activity mapping are now claimed to be more diagnostic (Sutton et al. 1986). Learning-disabled children have been reported to show greater interregional evoked potential synchrony than controls. Brain electrical activity mapping is reported to show differences from normals in the medial frontal lobe on both sides of the brain, the left lateral frontal lobe, the left midtemporal lobe, the left posterior quadrant (including Wernicke's area), and the right posterior quadrant. Brain scans are reported to show more symmetry than in normals. These are not routine tests for LD.

Abnormalities in urinary catecholamine metabolites have been reported. For example, boys with arithmetic disorder compared with normal controls had significantly less 3-methoxy-4-hydroxyphenylglycol (MHPG), believed to reflect brain norepinephrine turnover, and significantly more normetanephrine, believed to reflect peripheral norepinephrine. However, the standard deviations indicated considerable overlap between the LD and normal ranges.

DIFFERENTIAL DIAGNOSIS

The SDDs are inadequacies in development of particular academic, language, speech, or motor skills, not due to known physical or neurologic disorder, pervasive developmental disorder, MR, or deficient schooling. Thus the main differential diagnostic problems are with each other and with MR, pervasive developmental disorder, neurologic disorders, ADHD/ADD, depression, anxiety, substance abuse, and other Axis I disorders that can interfere with academic performance (Table 14–2).

Distinctions among the SDDs are sometimes obvious, such as between articulation disorder and arithmetic disorder, but many of them have overlapping symptoms. They sometimes require formal testing to tell the difference, for example, among the academic skills disorders or between one of these and a language disorder. The distinction between coordination disorder and expressive writing disorder may be difficult if coordination problems make writing laborious and distracting for the child. Generally, illegible penmanship is properly diagnosed under coordination

disorder rather than expressive writing disorder. The essential elements for each SDD can be reviewed in the *DSM-III-R* or in the Definition section at the beginning of this chapter. Frequently a child with one SDD has others. Therefore, multiple diagnoses are common and appropriate. Although not necessarily coded differently, nonverbal LD (or right-hemisphere LD) is distinguished by impairments of prosody, gesture, social skills, eye contact, mood (depression), math, and performance IQ as compared with verbal IQ. Rarely some cases may also warrant a diagnosis of pervasive developmental disorder.

The distinction from mental retardation (MR) is made by comparing the specific ability to mental age (IQ). MR requires subnormal IQ (<70) as well as impaired adaptive functioning. If the specific ability in question is commensurate with general intelligence (IQ), SDD is not diagnosed. If however, the specific ability is impaired more than general intelligence, the additional diagnosis is justified and desirable. For example, if a moderately retarded 5-year-old child with a mental age of 2 shows the language ability or coordination of a 2-year-old child, the impairment is covered by the MR diagnosis. However, if a moderately retarded 10-year-old child with a mental age of 4 shows the coordination or language ability of a 2-year-old child, the additional specific developmental diagnosis is warranted. A mildly retarded child with an IQ of 60, a reading standard score of 62, a spelling standard score of 57, and an arithmetic standard score of 54 does not have an academic skills disorder, but an IQ of 60 with an achievement standard score of 30 would qualify for both diagnoses (assuming that the patient meets the other diagnostic criteria). Articulation disorder is not usually diagnosed with mental retardation unless the misarticulation is especially severe.

Although academic skills disorders can be diagnosed in the presence of pervasive developmental disorder, the latter preempts the diagnosis of articulation or language disorder, and usually coordination disorder. Pervasive developmental disorder itself usually includes language impairments (both expressive and receptive), articulation problems, delays in attaining motor milestones, and abnormal gaits, all of which are considered part of the pervasive developmental disorder and not separately diagnosed. The distinc-

Table 14–2. DIAGNOSTIC DECISION TREE FOR LEARNING PROBLEMS
(FAILURE TO DEVELOP AGE-APPROPRIATE SKILLS OR ABILITIES)

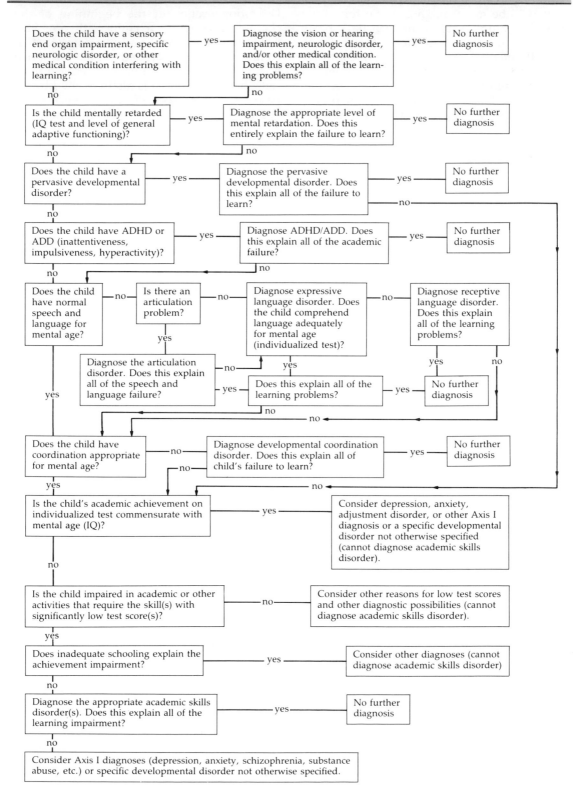

tion between the pervasive disorders and SDDs is easily made by the other symptoms of pervasive developmental disorder: impairment of gesture and other nonverbal communication, impairment of reciprocal social interaction, restricted repertoire of interests and activities, and in many cases impairment of imagination or fantasy. SDDs, even a combination of several of them, usually do not have these additional symptoms. ("Nonverbal LD," which includes impaired gesture, prosody, and social skills, is considered by some experts a variant of pervasive developmental disorder.)

There is some overlap of symptoms between the SDDs and ADHD/ADD (Allen 1986). The academic skills disorders, and even language disorders, often seem to have an attentional component. In some cases there may also be some impulsiveness, although not usually to the extent found in ADHD. The net results of either type of disorder can be underachievement in terms of grades: an obviously bright or normally intelligent child who is flunking, or at least "not working up to potential." However, an optimized individual achievement test will show the ADHD/ADD child without specific developmental disorder to have achievement test scores commensurate with IQ. A child who has deficient achievement test scores may have either an SDD without ADHD/ADD or may have both. The additional ADHD or ADD diagnosis is based on careful assessment of the signs of ADHD/ADD. Of course, if the child is very restless and impulsive as well as inattentive, having 8 of the 14 signs listed in the *DSM-III-R* present for over 6 months dating from before age 7, the diagnostic decision for ADHD becomes easy. In the absence of restlessness and impulsiveness, the decision as to whether the inattentiveness should be diagnosed as undifferentiated ADD becomes much more difficult in the presence of an SDD. A judgment is based on how prominent a symptom the inattentiveness is. Both developmental coordination disorder and ADHD can result in accident proneness (e.g., bumping into things, falling), but careful observation will show that the ADHD children are doing this impulsively, restlessly, and inattentively, while the coordination-disordered children are just clumsy no matter how much care they exercise.

In elective mutism, the child may give the impression of a language disorder because of the restricted output. However, careful history will disclose that the child speaks normally with a few intimates, such as the mother. If there is any doubt, normal comprehension on formal language testing will confirm elective mutism rather than language disorder.

Other Axis I problems can interfere with academic performance through emotional interference. Adjustment disorders and reactive depression can usually be identified by history of a stressor followed by academic decline. As with anxiety disorders, careful interview may elicit from the child that preoccupations interfere with schoolwork. Endogenous depression can also occur in schoolchildren. Substance abuse is common in secondary schools and in many places reaches down into elementary school. All of these disorders can be diagnosed by their *DSM-III-R* criteria and can accompany specific developmental disorders or occur as the sole cause of academic problems.

Poor school experience—absences, transfers, or attendance at an ineffective school where most of the children are underachieving—can mimic the academic skills disorders. This possibility is ruled out by careful history, perusal of school records, comparison with other children in the same school, and knowledge of the community schools.

Vision or hearing impairment can cause difficulty with academic subjects, and hearing impairment can cause speech and language problems. These can be ruled out by ordinary vision and hearing tests. In many cases such tests will have already been done, with the results available on the child's school records. Acquired aphasia can show speech and language problems, but it dates from head trauma or seizure onset (or at least electroencephalographic abnormalities) rather than being lifelong. It is often associated with having paresis, paraplegia, or other hard neurologic signs. The articulation problems of dysarthria or apraxia can be distinguished from articulation disorder by the associated muscle weakness, drooling, abnormal speech rate, problems with chewing, sucking, or other oral mechanisms, or other evidence of a neurologic disorder.

Coordination problems can result from specific neurologic disorders such as progressive degenerative diseases, cerebral palsy, lesions of the cerebellum or associated tracks, or other conditions with definite neurologic damage. These generally show hard abnormal findings on neurologic examination, in contrast to developmental coordination disorder, which usually has many subtle signs without hard signs.

PREVENTION

Prenatally and perinatally, prevention opportunities include good prenatal (and preconception) care, including maternal nutrition, education about the effects of even moderate tobacco, alcohol, and other drug use; prevention of prenatal and perinatal infection; and education of new parents about the importance of infant stimulation and nutrition. At the preschool/kindergarten stage, numerous studies have demonstrated the value of Head Start and other programs for training readiness skills before the child is subjected to the academic demands that bring out full-blown academic skills disorders. At least two studies have shown that even as late as the first grade, academic skills disorders can be prevented by identifying vulnerable children and giving them special individual training in basic specific perceptual skills rather than academic tutoring. The strategy is to start at the level of the child's current ability and build increasingly difficult perceptual readiness skills before expecting academic performance (Arnold et al. 1977). The same strategy can be used as a treatment option even after the disorder has been identified.

TREATMENT

Treatment should be comprehensive and multidisciplinary (Table 14–3). The first priority is *education/habilitation*. Several remedial strategies are possible: one choice is whether to work directly on academic skills or to lay a foundation first by working on readiness skills (as explained under Prevention above). Another choice is whether to strengthen weak areas by focused training and practice or to teach the child to use strong areas to compensate. Freides and Messina (1986) produced significant memory enhancement through motor enactment (possibly by recruiting cerebellar memory mechanisms). Sometimes simply switching from phonetic

to holistic instruction or from holistic to phonetic instruction may be effective. One author reported improvement in P-type (dysphonetic) dyslexia from presenting words to the right half visual field (left cortex) and in L-type (dyseidetic) from presenting words to the left visual field (right cortex), presumably by activating the less functional hemisphere.

Articulation disorder does not usually require the intensity and duration of treatment that the other developmental disorders do. Speech therapy is provided in most public schools and is usually curative in a year or so. The children referred to the "speech teacher" usually continue in a regular classroom for academics unless they also have another developmental disorder. If the school does not provide this service, the child should be referred to a speech therapist or clinic. Language disorders may also receive attention from a school-provided speech and language specialist, but these usually require also special academic remediation, often in a special class or resource room. The treatment is more arduous and prolonged than for articulation disorder.

For coordination disorder, extra physical education (especially "adaptive physical education") and even some physical medicine rehabilitative approaches or occupational therapy sensory integration activities can help such children develop an acceptable level of coordination. In all remediation, small increments of improvement need to be recognized and reinforced.

Psychosocial Therapy

In all habilitative efforts, the child's and family's psychosocial context and reaction to the handicap need attention. Parent guidance (usually brief) is often indicated to help the parents understand and accept the child's handicap rather than assuming laziness, stubbornness, or lack of motivation. Some parents need guidance to modulate protectiveness or a tendency to blame the school. In many cases, the prognosis for improvement with maturation is good if children can be kept motivated in the meantime. They need support from parents and teachers, with an optimistic expectation of gradual improvement through small steps. One of the dangers is that they will give up and quit trying, thus losing the opportunity to learn.

Table 14–3. PREVENTION AND TREATMENT OF LEARNING DISABILITIES			
Intervention Category	Documented Efficacy or Accepted/Established	Questionable or Unproven	Denounced or Inadvisable

Educational/ Habilitative	Head Start and other preschool
	Channel-specific perceptual training
	Remedial education:
	  learning disability tutoring,
	  resource room, small classes
	Adaptive physical education
	Speech and language therapy
	Operant reinforcement
		Vestibular stimulation
		Sensory integration
		Nonspecific perceptual training
			Optometric eye training
			Doman-Delacato patterning

Medical/Chemical	Prenatal care/toxin abstinence Adequate nutrition Prompt treatment of childhood illness/preventive immunization Stimulants Piracetam (not yet available)	Antinauseants/ Antihistamines Elimination diets Other special diets Megavitamins Lecithin Vasopressin ACTH fractions	Rebreathing expired air Restriction of fluids
Psychosocial	Parent guidance Supplemental supportive psychotherapy Success experiences		

Their circumstances need to be arranged so they can experience some success at their level of ability. This can be done through either special classes or resource rooms (e.g., LD classes or learning and behavior disorder classes) or special tutoring adjunctive to a regular class taught by a flexible, understanding teacher who can help structure the child's activities in the direction of experiencing success. Psychotherapy is sometimes necessary either to resolve secondary depression or anxiety or to facilitate adjustment to the handicap. Children who are teased or ostracized may benefit from assertion or other social skills training. Failure of the child to cooperate with remedial efforts should be one indication for psychotherapy.

Somatic Treatments

Somatic treatments have received increasing attention, especially for children who do not respond promptly to educational interventions. Even some educational interventions, such as visual half-field presentations and adaptive physical education, could be considered somatic. However, the efficacy of most somatic treatments has not been well documented by controlled studies, and some of them are rather suspect. Among the latter

is optometric visual training as advocated by some optometrists, which has been denounced by the American Academy of Pediatrics as a waste of time and money that can delay effective treatment for the child. Another treatment so denounced is the Doman-Delacato type of patterning, which consumes great amounts of family time, with guilt induction for not maintaining the rigorous schedule. It may be coupled with bag rebreathing and restriction of sugar, salt, and fluids.

A more reasonable approach to psychoneurological patterning is the sensory integration or sensorimotor integration advocated by Ayers and other occupational therapists. This has intuitive appeal, overlaps considerably with adaptive physical education (an accepted, reputable discipline), seems anecdotally useful by clinical observation, and does not run the risk of delaying other treatments because it is usually part of a comprehensive treatment approach. However, even Ayers points out that it has not been proven effective by studies. Its effectiveness is indirectly supported by two controlled studies suggesting positive effects on attention and behavior from rotational vestibular stimulation, closely related to one type of stimulation provided in sensory integration. It appears to have commonsense validity for developmental coordination disorder, but its value for other SDDs would be more questionable.

Nutritional and other dietary treatments have received perhaps the greatest attention, at least in the popular press. Megavitamin treatment, despite the fervent claims made in the past, has not been established. It appears that a megadosage cocktail of many vitamins is no better than placebo in a controlled study. There is still the possibility that an individual vitamin in megadosage may help a few individual cases, although this has not been demonstrated to the satisfaction of most scientists. In one study of 100 hyperkinetic and learning-disabled children, 6 or so were believed to benefit from high doses of pyridoxine (vitamin B_6) and made worse by high doses of thiamine (vitamin B_1), while another 6 or so were believed to have been helped by thiamine but made worse by pyridoxine. These findings have not been replicated in a controlled fashion. In a small sample of hyperkinetic children selected for low serotonin levels, a placebo-controlled comparison showed more benefit from pyridoxine, 600 mg/day, than from methylphenidate. Naturally, any child found to be suffering a vitamin, iron, other mineral, or other nutritional deficiency should have that deficiency corrected, and it would not be unreasonable to expect that any learning problems would benefit from such correction. However, this is quite different from providing hypersupplementation to children who are not noted to have a deficiency.

Elimination diets have been strongly advocated, but it is sometimes difficult to decide what substances should be eliminated. The original Feingold treatment eliminated salicylates but was then extended to food dyes, preservatives, flavorings, and other additives. Much of the research effort was focused on dyes. A National Institutes of Health Consensus Development Conference in 1982 was unable to find convincing evidence from controlled studies that dyes are important in the majority of children with hyperactivity. Other possible dietary culprits included refined sugars and classic immune reactions to milk, wheat, corn, chocolate, and so on. For none of these have there been controlled studies convincing enough to win general acceptance of such a mechanism as explanation for the majority of LDs. However, for a few children a dietary hypersen-

sitivity seems anecdotally important. These children seem to be mainly preschool age and may have a strong allergy history. Since a 1-week elimination diet trial is not risky and would not significantly delay more effective treatments, it can be justified when the clinician feels, on the basis of history, that it would be worth a try. If it seems to help, a series of challenges should establish which dietary components, if any, make the difference. A complete elimination diet is onerous in time, work, and expense, as well as possibly deficient in calcium or other nutrients if maintained over a long period. Some dietary advocates warn that challenges may not show obvious responses when delayed more than a week or so beyond the beginning of elimination. This treatment is highly dependent on the child's cooperation; no parent should feel guilty for giving up on it.

Medication

Stimulant drugs have not been shown as helpful for LDs as for ADHD and other behavior problems, but some authors recommend them for even *hypoactive* learning-disabled children. They do seem to help coordination, including visuomotor coordination, reaction time, and other motor skills. Such effects are perhaps best documented for dextroamphetamine, whereas there is a suspicion that methylphenidate may be better for academic skills disorders involving memory, association, and verbal retrieval. Despite increasing attention in the literature to stimulant effects on learning (Ashman and Schroeder 1986; Famularo and Fenton 1987; Schroeder et al. 1983), the picture is not entirely clear. Whether a stimulant benefit is found seems to depend largely on what measure is used.

Aman and Rojahn (in press) reviewed 18 well-controlled studies of stimulant treatment of LD, employing 129 perceptual/cognitive measures and 130 achievement/academic application measures. They found that 40% of perceptual/cognitive measures and 29% of achievement measures showed improvement; studies including ADHD subjects showed improvement on 53% of achievement measures compared with 18% for studies excluding ADHD; only 22% of achievement measures in high-dose studies but 45% of such measures in other studies showed improvement; short-term studies (4 weeks or less) showed improvement in 44% of achievement measures compared with 27% for longer studies; subjects with less stringent criteria of LD improved on 40% of measures compared with 21% for stringently defined severe LD.

There seems little doubt that stimulants improve short-term academic productivity, in the sense of improving grades on homework and tests. However, there has been question whether increased learning is associated with the improved grades; the latter could be merely a manifestation of improved output. Richardson et al. (1988) and Kupietz et al. (1988) report convincing data supporting methylphenidate enhancement of reading achievement, especially recognition of more difficult words, in hyperactive reading-disabled children. They believed the mechanism was improvement of attention, recall, and verbal retrieval. The improvement in reading achievement correlated only poorly with dose or plasma level but dramatically with behavioral improvement. It is not clear whether nonhyperactive reading-disabled children would have shown similar improvement. One early concern was the fear of state-dependent learning (that children who learn while taking drugs would forget what they learned after they stopped taking the drugs), but studies suggest that this phenomenon does not occur in children taking stimulants.

On balance, the literature suggests that low-to-moderate doses of stimulants have a possibility of helping a learning-disabled child, especially if the disability includes impairment of attention, recognition, or recall. Therefore, a trial is justified in patients who do not seem to respond satisfactorily to the more usual educational/habilitative approaches. The dose optimal for learning seems to be 0.3 to 0.7 mg/kg methylphenidate twice daily. Some authors report decrements in learning at doses above 0.7 mg/kg. The general guideline is to start low and cautiously titrate, monitoring progress by direct teacher (as well as parent) reports. The clinician should be alert to the possibility of a child outgrowing the need and/or benefit if a child previously doing well on a stable dose deteriorates.

A more promising drug is piracetam, which is structurally related to γ-aminobutyric acid and vasopressin. It has shown not only mild benefit in laboratory measures but also significant benefit in clinical trials (Rapoport 1987). In 12 double-blind studies with dyslexic boys, it brought improvement in verbal learning, single word reading, short-term memory, and reading rate. However, only about one third of the dyslexics made significant gains (compared with practically none of the placebo controls). Piracetam has not yet been approved for release in the United States.

Because LDs do not lend themselves well to medical treatment, clinical desperation has justified trials of various other drugs. One of these is diphenhydramine (Benadryl), one of the components of Dramamine (the other component being caffeine), which has been advocated for dyslexia on the hypothetical basis of vestibular-cerebellar dysfunction. Diphenhydramine has anecdotally shown some encouraging results. In fact, the boy in Case 1 was given a trial of this drug on the basis of prominent vestibular-cerebellar signs and recurrent early otitis. At 6-month follow-up he showed much improved concentration, academic performance, and peer relations on a dose of 37.5 mg administered twice daily. Efficacy for LDs has not been established by controlled studies. The appeal of this drug is its relative safety. If tried, it may be needed and tolerated in fairly large doses; for example, up to 50 mg three times a day may be used in a 40-kg 10 year old child with no seizure history (starting lower).

Anticonvulsants, major and minor tranquilizers, and most tricyclics have generally not shown favorable effects on learning and often tend to impair it. An important exception would be an appropriate anticonvulsant for a child with petit mal. Another exception would be the anecdotally reported benefit of tricyclic antidepressants for nonverbal (right-hemisphere) LD, especially when accompanied by symptoms of a mood or anxiety disorder.

Some more natural "medications" have been shown to have transient benefit. Vasopressin has shown mild benefit in laboratory learning tasks. Lecithin, which can supply choline for synthesis of acetylcholine, has shown transient benefit in LDs with memory impairment. Learning effects have also been found with adrenocorticotropic hormone (ACTH) and fractions thereof. These do not appear to be practical treatments at this time.

As pharmacologic research progresses, the

future may bring more effective medical help for those children with LDs for whom educational help alone seems unsatisfactory.

References

Allen, T. W. 1986. Styles of exploration in control, attention-deficit disorder with hyperactivity and learning disabled children. *J. Learn. Disab.* 19:351–353.

Aman, M. G., and Rojahn, J. (in press). Pharmacological Intervention. In N. N. Singh and I. L. Beale (eds.): *Current Perspectives in Learning Disabilities: Nature, Theory, and Treatment.* New York: Springer-Verlag.

American Psychiatric Association. 1987. *The Diagnostic and Statistical Manual of Mental Disorders,* 3rd. ed., revised. Washington, D.C.: American Psychiatric Association.

Arnold, L. E., Barnebey, N., McManus, J., et al. 1977. Prevention by specific perceptual remediation for vulnerable first-graders. *Arch. Gen. Psychiatry* 34:1279–1294.

Ashman, A., and Schroeder, S. R. 1986. Hyperactivity, methylphenidate, and complex human cognition. *Adv. Learn. Behav. Disab.* 5:299–320.

Bakker, D. J. 1984. Hemispheric specialization and specific reading retardation. In Rutter, M. (ed.): *Developmental Neuropsychiatry.* New York: Guilford Press.

Bax, M., and Whitmore, K. 1987. The medical examination of children on entry to school: The results and use of neurodevelopmental assessment. *Dev. Med. Child Neurol.* 29:40–55.

Beauchamp, G. R., and Kosmorsky, G. 1987. Learning disabilities: Update comment on the visual system. *Pediatr. Clin. North Am.* 34:1439–1446.

Becker, J., Velasco, M., Harmony, T., et al. 1987. Electroencephalographic characteristics of children with learning disabilities. *Clin. Electroencephalogr.* 18:93–101.

Behan, P. O., and Geschwind, N. 1985. Hemispheric laterality and immunity. In Guilleman, R., et al. (eds.): *Mental Modulation of Immunity.* New York: Raven Press.

Duffy, F. H., Denckla, M. B., Bartels, P. H., and Sandini, G. 1980. Dyslexia: Regional differences in brain electrical activity by topographic mapping. *Ann. Neurol.* 7:412–420.

Famularo, R., and Fenton, T. 1987. The effect of methylphenidate on school grades in children with atten-tion-deficit disorder without hyperactivity: A preliminary report. *J. Clin. Psychiatry* 48:112–114.

Freides, D., and Messina, C. A. 1986. Memory improvement via motor encoding in learning disabled children. *J. Learn. Disab.* 19:113–115.

Geschwind, N., and Galaburda, A. M. 1985. Cerebral lateralization: Biological mechanisms, associations, and pathology: a hypothesis and a program for research. *Arch. Neurol.* 42:428–459.

Kupietz, S. S., Winsberg, B. G., Richardson, E., et al. 1988. Effects of methylphenidate dosage in hyperactive reading-disabled children: I. Behavior and cognitive performance effects. *J. Am. Acad. Child Adolesc. Psychiatry* 27:70–77.

McClelland, A. 1986. Psychological and psychiatric aspects of learning difficulties. *Br. J. Hosp. Med.,* July, pp. 35–44.

Obrzut, J. E., and Boliek, C. A. 1986. Lateralization characteristics in learning disabled children. *J. Learn. Disab.* 19:308–314.

Rapoport, J. L. 1987. Pediatric psychopharmacology: The last decade. In Meltzer, H. Y. (ed.): *Psychopharmacology: The Third Generation of Progress.* New York: Raven Press.

Richardson, E., Kupietz, S. S., Winsberg, B. G., et al. 1988. Effects of methylphenidate dosage in hyperactive reading-disabled children: II. Reading achievement. *J. Am. Acad. Child Adolesc. Psychiatry* 27:78–87.

Rourke, B. P., Bakker, D. J., Fisk, J. L., et al. 1983. *Child Neuropsychology.* New York: Guilford Press.

Rutter, M., and Yule, W. 1977. Reading difficulties. In Rutter, M., and Hersov, L. (eds.): *Child Psychiatry: Modern Approaches.* Oxford: Blackwell Scientific.

Schroeder, S. R., Lewis, M. H., and Lipton, M. A. 1983. Interactions of pharmacotherapy and behavior therapy among children with learning and behavioral disorders. *Adv. Learn. Behav. Disab.* 2:179–225.

Silver, L. B. 1986. Controversial approaches to treating learning disabilities and attention-deficit disorder. *Am. J. Dis. Child.* 140:1045–1052.

Sutton, J. P., Whitton, J. L., Topa, M., and Moldofsky, H. 1986. Evoked potential maps in learning disabled children. *Electroencephalogr. Clin. Neurophysiol.* 65:399–404.

Swanson, H. L. 1987. The combining of multiple hemispheric resources in learning-disabled and skilled readers' recall of words: A test of three information-processing models. *Brain Cogn.* 6:41–54.

Tranel, D., Hall, L. E., Olson, S., and Tranel, N. N. 1987. Evidence for a right-hemisphere developmental learning disability. *Dev. Neuropsychol.* 3:113–127.

15

Specific Communication Disorders

LORIAN BAKER, PH.D.

DEFINITION

Children suffering from specific disorders involving communication are characterized by inadequate development of some particular aspect of communication and, at the same time, absence of any demonstrable etiology of physical disorder, neurologic disorder, global mental retardation, or severe environmental deprivation. Impairments in communication also exist as symptoms of more general syndromes, including mental retardation, pervasive developmental disorders (infantile autism), genetic disorders (sex chromosome abnormalities), neurologic disorders, (acquired aphasia, apraxia), and organic impairments (cleft palate, hearing impairment). However, the specific or "developmental" disorders are the most common form of childhood communication disorders.

The subcategorization of the specific communication disorders is controversial (Cantwell and Baker 1987). This work uses the *Diagnostic and Statistical Manual of Mental Disorders*, third edition, revised *(DSM-III-R)* classification system, which subcategorizes the specific communication disorders into three major subtypes: (1) developmental articulation disorder, (2) developmental expressive language disorder, (3) and developmental receptive language disorder (American Psychiatric Association 1987). Similar subcategorizations are specified in the most recent

draft of the World Health Organization's system (*International Classification of Diseases*, tenth edition).

It should be noted that a number of professionals believe that the *DSM-III-R* category called developmental expressive writing disorder (viewed in the *DSM-III-R* as a type of learning or "academic skills" disorder) should also be considered a subtype of specific communication disorder (Baker and Cantwell, in press). Insofar as little is currently known about this disorder, it will not be discussed in detail here.

As stated previously, all of the specific communication disorders share certain features. These include the presence of a specific delay or deficit in some aspect of communication development and normal functioning in other (noncommunication) areas such as general cognition, physical development, and adaptive function. In addition, all of the specific communication disorders have in common the following: an onset in childhood; long duration of the disorder; clinical features representing the functional levels of younger normal children; resulting impairments in adaptive functioning, particularly within the school setting; tendency to "run in families"; predisposition toward males; common presumed etiologic factors; increased prevalence among the younger (elementary school) age range; diagnosis requiring the use of standardized (psychometric) techniques; tendency toward certain specific

257

Table 15–1. FEATURES OF THE SPECIFIC COMMUNICATION DISORDERS

Features Common to All the Specific Communication Disorders

1. Inadequate development of some aspect of communication
2. Absence of any demonstrable etiology of physical disorder, neurologic disorder, global mental retardation, or severe environmental deprivation
3. Onset in childhood
4. Long duration
5. Clinical features representing the functional levels of younger normal children
6. Resultant impairments in adaptive functioning, particularly within the school setting
7. Tendency to "run in families"
8. Predisposition toward males
9. Presumed etiology
10. Increased prevalence in younger age range
11. Diagnosis requiring a range of standardized techniques
12. Tendency toward certain specific associated problems
13. Wide range of subtypes and severities of impairments

Features Unique to Various Subtypes of Specific Communication Disorders

Subtype	*Unique Features*
Developmental articulation disorder	Impairment in the ability to produce speech sounds
Developmental expressive language disorder	Impairment in the ability to formulate spoken utterances
Developmental receptive language disorder	Impairment in the ability to understand language
Developmental expressive writing disorder	Impairment in the ability to formulate written sentences or paragraphs

associated problems; and a wide range of subtypes of deficits and severities of impairments.

The subtypes of specific communication disorders differ primarily according to the area of communication that is impaired. In developmental articulation disorder, the ability to produce speech sounds is impaired. In developmental expressive language disorder it is the ability to formulate spoken utterances that is impaired. (In developmental expressive writing disorder the ability to formulate written sentences or paragraphs is impaired.) And, in developmental receptive language disorder, the ability to understand language is impaired.

The features that all of the subtypes of specific communication disorders have in common as well as the features that uniquely characterize each of the different subtypes are summarized in Table 15–1.

ETIOLOGY AND PATHOGENESIS

The etiology of the specific communication disorders is unknown. A number of possible etiologic mechanisms have been hypothesized; these hypotheses fall into four general groups: (1) neurologic impairments, (2) spe-

cific perceptual or cognitive abnormalities, (3) environmental factors, and (4) a multifactorial or heterogeneous etiology. The various hypotheses regarding the etiology of the specific communication disorders are summarized, along with the evidence in Table 15–2.

The first group of hypotheses about the etiology of specific communication disorders suggest that the disorders are the result of some type of brain damage. These hypotheses may be traced back to the late 1800s and the work of the first neurologists and aphasiologists, who observed that the subtypes of specific failures of language development in children were somewhat similar to the subtypes of damaged language seen in adults with aphasia. Thus, they postulated that focal lesions in the left hemisphere of the brain were responsible for the specific communication disorders of childhood. These lesions were conceived of as the result of either (prenatal or postnatal) brain injury or congenital brain defects. This hypothesis led to several decades of futile attempts to verify the cerebral trauma and to localize the brain damage.

The inability to establish cerebral trauma or damage in the vast majority of cases of specific communication disorders led to a variant of neurologic hypotheses postulating subclinical or "minimal" brain damage. Such damage was considered to have originated prenatally or as the result of genetically determined left-sided brain abnormalities. The increased prevalence of mild abnormal neurologic difficulties or "soft signs" (motor coordination problems, oral stereognosis) and the increased prevalence of dominance problems (mixed handedness, footedness, or eyedness; abnormal performance on dichotic listening tests) in children with specific communication disorders have been cited as support for this hypothesis. The relatively high incidence of family histories positive for language, speech, and learning disorders found in children with specific communication disorders has been cited as evidence for a genetic component. However, research has not established brain pathologic processes or even consistent evidence of neurologic impairment in children with specific communication disorders, nor has any causative relationship between language development and cerebral dominance or lateralization been proven.

The second group of hypotheses about the etiology of the specific communication disorders postulate the existence of very specific perceptual or cognitive deficits. Because children with specific communication disorders tend to perform better on visual than auditory tasks, most of the perceptual deficits postulated have had to do with areas of auditory perception or processing. These include deficits in auditory discrimination (the ability to discriminate speech sounds or acoustic signals generally, in context, or at particular rates of speed); auditory attention span; auditory figure–ground (the ability to sort out background versus significant auditory signals); auditory memory (or sequential memory); auditory-visual association (the ability to scan and associate between auditory and visual stimuli); and deficits in the processing of specific linguistic units (such as words or sentences). Cognitive deficits have been postulated in symbolic or concept development, in anticipatory imagery, in sorting and/or categorizing abilities, and in hierarchical processing skills.

In at least certain cases of specific communication disorder, experimental efforts have produced convincing evidence of some perceptual or cognitive deficits. However, it has not been shown that all children with specific communication disorders have such

deficits, nor has it been established that such deficits actually produce language disorder. In fact, the subprocesses involved in the acquisition and processing of linguistic materials by normal children are ill understood.

A third class of hypotheses has to do with environmental factors playing a role in the etiology of specific communication disorders. The two types of evidence involved are parent–child interaction studies and longitudinal "risk factor" studies. The parent–child interaction studies have shown correlations between the rate of language acquisition in normal children and the type of parent–child interactions the children have received. The longitudinal studies of children have identified certain environmental factors having to do with socioeconomic status and medical history that seem to put children "at risk" for specific language and/or learning disorders. The factors that have been shown to be associated with specific communication disorders are large family size, lower social class, later birth order, prematurity, environmental deprivation, and early history of recurrent otitis media. The association between these socioeconomic or medical factors and language disorders are that the factors are themselves associated with deprived auditory or linguistic input.

Currently, there is insufficient evidence to warrant the conclusion that any of these environmental factors are the sole or unique cause of the specific communication disorders. Nonetheless, the symptomatology, course, outcome, and various correlates clearly indicate that the specific communication disorders represent true disorders, rather than simply the "low end" of normal acquisition. Although there is no convincing evidence for a unique etiology, it is nonetheless possible that combinations of the above factors may be responsible for the specific communication disorders.

The evidence supporting each of the above types of hypotheses, along with the inability of any one hypothesis to account convincingly for all cases of specific communication disorders, has led to the postulation of a multifactorial etiology. Thus it is reasonable that multiple factors including biological and psychological mechanisms, processing systems, environmental circumstances, and language experiences may interact to produce the specific communication disorders.

The heterogeneity of clinical features

Table 15–2. HYPOTHESES ABOUT THE ETIOLOGY OF SPECIFIC COMMUNICATION DISORDERS	
Types of Hypotheses	**Specific Hypotheses**
Neurologic impairments	1. Specific localizable brain damage 2. Subclinical (minimal) brain damage
Perceptual deficits	1. Deficits in auditory discrimination 2. Deficits in auditory attention 3. Deficits in auditory figure–ground 4. Deficits in auditory memory 5. Deficits in auditory-visual association 6. Deficits in the processing of specific linguistic units
Cognitive deficits	1. Deficits in symbolic or concept development 2. Deficits in anticipatory imagery 3. Deficits in sorting and/or categorizing 4. Deficits in hierarchical processing
Environmental factors	1. Inadequate parent–child interaction 2. Socioeconomic factors (large family size, lower social class, late birth order, environmental deprivation) 3. Medical factors (e.g., prematurity, history of recurrent otitis media)
Multifactorial etiology	Combinations of all of the above

across and within subtypes of specific communication disorders, the differing courses and outcomes seen, and the variety of external factors that may be associated are further evidence for the heterogeneous or multifactorial hypothesis.

EPIDEMIOLOGY

The literature shows a wide range of prevalence estimates for specific communication disorders. This range is due to methodologic differences in the various epidemiologic studies involved, including differences in subclassifications and definitions of the disorders; cut-off criteria for normal versus abnormal functioning; and age, sex, or other aspects of the samples of children studied. The estimated prevalence in the literature is that 3% to 32% of children have developmental articulation disorder and 1% to 13% have some type of developmental language disorder.

According to the most recent report to Congress (U.S. Department of Education 1987), speech or language impairments are currently second only to learning disabilities in prevalence among the "handicapping conditions" found in schoolchildren. They are thus more prevalent than all other classifications of handicaps requiring special help (including mental retardation, emotional disturbance, deafness, orthopedic impairments, visual handicaps, deafness-blindness, and multiple handicaps). Thus, for the 1985–1986 school year, approximately 1 million children in the United States were sufficiently impaired to qualify for special services under speech or language impairment.

Despite the lack of agreement between the various epidemiologic studies of speech and language disorders, one consistent finding is that almost all of specific communication disorders are more common in males than in females.

CLINICAL PICTURE

The clinical features of developmental articulation disorder, developmental expres-

Table 15–2. *HYPOTHESES ABOUT THE ETIOLOGY OF SPECIFIC COMMUNICATION DISORDERS* Continued

Evidence for Hypotheses	Evidence Against Hypotheses
1. Similarities with damage found in adult aphasia 2. Presence of neurologic soft signs in some cases 3. Abnormal laterality in some case 4. Increased prevalence of disorders within families	1. Inability of research to document or localize damage 2. Absence of neurologic soft signs or abnormal laterality in many cases 3. Inability of research to demonstrate effects of laterality on language development
1. Presence of perceptual deficits in some cases 2. General tendency for inferior performance on auditory tasks	1. Inability of research to establish deficits in many cases 2. Inability of research to document that perceptual deficits can result in language deficits
1. Limited parent–child interaction associated with slower language acquisition 2. Certain environmental factors are risk factors for language disorders.	1. No evidence that limited interactions actually cause language disorders 2. The environmental factors are only weakly associated with the development of language disorders.
1. Evidence for and against all other hypotheses 2. The heterogeneity of subtypes, outcomes, and associated features	1. As yet there is no "head" evidence

sive language disorder, and developmental receptive language disorder are described below. The separate descriptions of the clinical features of each specific communication disorder are summarized in Table 15–3. The associated features of the specific communication disorders are described below and then summarized in Table 15–4. The associated features for each of the specific communication disorders are described together because they tend to have the same associated features.

When reading the separate descriptions of the clinical features of the three subtypes of specific communication disorders, the reader should keep in mind that these three subtypes frequently co-occur. The reader should also keep in mind that, particularly with regard to developmental receptive language disorder and developmental expressive language disorder, language disorders tend to be heterogeneous rather than uniform.

Developmental Articulation Disorder

The cardinal feature of developmental articulation disorder is defective articulation of developmentally expected speech sounds. The defective articulations are not attributable to deficits or abnormalities in intelligence, hearing, or physiology of the speech mechanism.

Typically, the speech sounds that are defective are those acquired later in the developmental sequence (those sounds represented by the letters s, z, sh, ch, dg, th, and r). However, in severe cases, some of the sounds that are acquired earlier in the developmental sequence may be affected (those sounds represented by the letters b, m, t, d, n, and h). Misarticulations of vowel sounds are signs of organic impairment and are therefore not found in this disorder.

The misarticulated speech sounds produced in developmental articulation disorder may be omitted, replaced by another sound, or produced in a distorted but recognizable fashion. Typical examples include "car" becomes "ka," "house" becomes "ow," and "blue" becomes "bu" (omissions); "sick" becomes "thik," "red" becomes "wed," "thumb" becomes "fum," and "this" becomes "dis" (substitutions); and "slurping"

Table 15-3. *CLINICAL PICTURE OF THE SPECIFIC COMMUNICATION DISORDERS*

Disorder	Major Deficit	Manifestations of the Deficit	Specific Examples
Developmental articulation disorder	Acquisition of articulation of speech sounds	Omissions of speech sounds, substitutions of speech sounds, distortions of speech sounds	"Car" becomes "ka" "Blue becomes "bu" "Tree" becomes "twee" "Thumb" becomes "fum" Producing "s" sound with a "slurp"
Developmental receptive language disorder	Acquisition of comprehension of the meaning of language	Comprehension of words, comprehension of grammatical units (morphemes), comprehension of word order, comprehension of language usage	Does not understand meaning of words Does not understand meaning of verb tense, plural forms, adjective degrees Does not understand "he is here" vs. "is he here?" Does not understand meaning of slang or polite forms
Developmental expressive language disorder	Acquisition of language expression	Expressive vocabulary	Limited vocabulary, word-finding problems, word substitution, functional descriptions, overgeneralization, jargon
		Expressive grammar	Word omissions, morpheme omissions, limited range of grammatical constructions, incorrect word order, inappropriate combinations
		Expressive usage	Tangential/inappropriate responses, limited range of speech acts, difficulty with topicality, limited conversational assertion, problems with dialectical forms

Table 15-4. *FEATURES ASSOCIATED WITH THE SPECIFIC COMMUNICATION DISORDERS*

General Type	Examples
Neurologic problems	"Soft signs" on neurologic examination Clumsiness and motor problems Cerebral asymmetry/mixed dominance Inconsistent electroencephalographic abnormalities
Developmental problems	Delayed motor milestones Delayed speech/language milestones Other specific communication disorders Other developmental disorders Familial loading for specific learning and communication disorders
Psychiatric problems	Social/emotional problems: Peer relationship problems Anxiety disorders Adjustment disorders Affective disorders Behavioral problems: Attention deficit/hyperactivity disorder
Learning problems	Developmental expressive writing disorder Developmental reading disorder Developmental arithmetic disorder

lisped production of "s" (distortion). Generally, omissions are found in the speech of younger children and distortions occur in the speech of older children. However, it is not uncommon for a child with developmental articulation disorder to have each of these types of misarticulation.

In developmental articulation disorder misarticulations of speech sounds are not random but rather are governed by various "conditioning factors." Thus a sound may be produced correctly at one time, omitted at another time, and substituted at yet another time. Some of the conditioning factors that affect the articulation of sounds are the position in the word where the sound occurs (initially, between vowels, or at the end of a word); the type of utterance being made (long sentences vs. single-word utterances); the rate of speech (rapid vs. slow); and the length of time a child has known a word (new words vs. familiar words).

Developmental articulation disorder has a considerable range in severity; one sound or many sounds may be misarticulated, one type of misarticulation or all three types of misarticulations may occur, or the child's speech may be completely intelligible, semi-intelligible, or unintelligible. In milder forms of developmental articulation disorder, the child's speech will resemble the speech of a younger normal child.

The recognition of the disorder is dependent on its severity. Thus, in more severe cases, the disorder is apparent before the age of 3 years; in milder cases, the disorder may not be identified until the child is 7 years old.

Developmental Receptive Language Disorder

The cardinal feature in developmental receptive language disorder is a specific impairment in the development of language comprehension skills. Any area or all areas of language comprehension may be affected: comprehension of vocabulary, grammatical units, word ordering, or aspects of language usage.

A deficit in the area of vocabulary comprehension may be manifested by lack of understanding of the meaning of words or by misinterpreting the meaning of words. Such difficulties are most likely to occur with prepositions, adjectives, adverbs, demonstratives, and abstract nouns. However, in severe cases, even simple nouns and verbs may be affected.

A deficit in the area of comprehension of grammatical units may be manifested by complete lack of understanding of, or by misinterpreting of, the meaning of grammatical units (or "morphemes"). Examples of morphemes include noun plurals (pencil vs. pencils), verb tenses (sit vs. sat), and comparative and superlative degrees of adjectives ("small" vs. "smaller" vs. "smallest").

A deficit in the area of comprehension of word ordering rules (or syntax) is manifested by difficulty understanding those linguistic structures in which meaning is indicated to some degree by word order. Two examples of such structures are the difference between statements versus questions ("he is here" vs. "is he here?") and the difference between the active versus passive state ("the car was hit by the bus" vs. "the car hit the bus").

A final area of comprehension that may be affected in developmental receptive language disorder involves the comprehension of aspects of language usage. For example, there may be difficulty understanding the significance of "polite" forms ("it is cold here" used to mean "shut the window"), slang forms, or even paralinguistic aspects of communication such as facial expression, intonation patterns, and tone of voice.

As in the other specific communication disorders, the deficit involved in developmental receptive language disorder may appear with a wide range of severity. Recognition of the disorder is correlated with severity: more severe forms of the disorder can be apparent by 2 years of age, whereas milder forms may go unrecognized until the child is in an educational setting.

As stated above, the language problem in developmental receptive language disorder tends to be heterogeneous. Some children will show deficits in all of the areas of comprehension mentioned, whereas others will show deficits in only some of the areas of comprehension. Furthermore, the deficits in each of the areas of comprehension may be either narrow or broad. For example, a child with a deficit in the area of vocabulary may have trouble understanding the meaning of all types of words, or he or she may have trouble understanding only certain types of words such as abstract nouns or complex verbs. In those cases in which the child has deficits that cross all areas in uniform severity, the child will appear to be functioning linguistically the same as a younger normal child.

Developmental Expressive Language Disorder

The primary feature of developmental expressive language disorder is a specific deficit in the development of expressive language abilities. As was the case with developmental receptive language disorder, the language problem is heterogeneous and may involve a range of impairments in various areas of expressive language. The areas of expressive language that may be affected include vocabulary, morphology, grammar, word order, and language usage.

Deficits in the area of expressive vocabulary include limited vocabulary size, word retrieval or "word-finding" difficulties, word substitutions (saying "table" when meaning "chair"), functional descriptions (saying "thing to sit on" instead of "chair"), overgeneralizations (saying "thing" instead of "chair"), or jargon (saying "pabim" for "chair").

Deficits in the area of expressive grammar may be manifested by omissions of words, especially prepositions, indefinite pronouns, or verbal auxiliaries ("he sitting," "mommy car," "where we going?"), and morphemes ("dad wear white shoe," "she sleep"); the use of a limited selection of grammatical structures (using only the present tense of verbs); the use of incorrect word order ("car Mommy have"); and the use of inappropriate combinations of forms ("they was reading," "two foots").

Deficits in the area of expressive usage include tangential or inappropriate responses to questions and limitations in the range of speech acts produced (requests, imperatives, questions). Difficulty maintaining and/or changing topics and initiating interactions are also problems. Lack of assertiveness in the conversational situation and inability to use dialectical forms when needed (polite forms or slang) are other limitations of expressive language disorder.

As in the other specific communication disorders, developmental expressive language disorder shows a wide range of severity of impairment. Usually all areas of expressive language are affected to some degree, but the degree of involvement may vary. Within a particular area of language functioning, deficits may be widespread or limited. For example, vocabulary deficits may affect the child's entire lexicon or may be limited to only certain types of words. In the latter case, the child may appear to have a large vocabulary, but specific deficits, such as with abstract nouns or with words having to do with spatial-temporal concepts, will be discovered on systematic testing.

As in the other specific communication disorders, the more severe forms of developmental expressive language disorder are recognized earlier than the less severe forms. Severe forms of the disorder are typically apparent by 3 years of age, but milder forms may remain undetected until the later elementary school grades. In these less severely impaired children the deficits may be limited to "higher level" (later-learned) language structures (such as passives, embedded sentences, or abstract concepts) that are not used frequently in speech.

Features Associated With the Specific Communication Disorders

As stated above, the various subtypes of specific communication disorders all share the same associated features (see Table 15–4). The features associated with the various specific communication disorders fall into four general areas: neurologic problems, developmental problems, psychiatric problems, and learning problems. The presence of any of these associated features is most likely for children with developmental receptive language disorder, least likely for children with developmental articulation disorder, and of intermediate likelihood for children with developmental expressive language disorder.

No clear association has been established between neurologic disorders and specific communication disorders. However, the literature contains numerous case histories documenting the existence, in at least some of the children with specific communication disorders, of inconsistent electroencephalographic abnormalities, "soft signs" on neurologic examination, mixed dominance or abnormal performance on tests of lateralization, and finally clumsiness and motor coordination problems.

Similarly, developmental difficulties have been reported in a number of children with specific communication disorders. These include minor delays in reaching motor milestones (sitting, standing, crawling, walking) as well as delays in speech/language milestones (babbling, saying first word, saying first sentence). As stated previously, specific communication disorders tend to co-occur. Also, the specific communication disorders are frequently associated with other developmental disorders, such as enuresis, encopresis, developmental coordination disorder, and specific learning disabilities. Furthermore, children with specific communication disorders tend to have family histories that are positive for both specific communication disorders and other specific developmental disorders among first-degree relatives.

The psychiatric disorders associated with the specific communication disorders include both social-emotional disorders and overt behavioral disorders. Numerous case reports (Baker and Cantwell 1985; Cantwell and Baker 1985) have documented the existence of a variety of social and emotional problems in children with specific communication disorders. Peer relationship problems are common among children with specific communication disorders, as are anxiety disorders (especially separation anxiety disorder and avoidant disorder), adjustment disorders, and affective disorders.

By far the most commonly occurring psychiatric disorders found in children with specific communication disorders are the behavioral psychiatric disorders. In a study of 600 children with communication disorders (Cantwell and Baker 1985), it was found that approximately one fourth of the children had a diagnosis of some type of behavioral psychiatric disorder. The most common disorder (within the *DSM-III* classification system) was attention-deficit disorder with hyperactivity, which occurred in approximately one fifth of the sample. The association between the attention-deficit hyperactivity syndrome and disordered language has also been documented in a number of articles in the hyperactivity literature.

The association between specific communication disorders (especially the developmental language disorders) and specific learning disorders has also been well documented in the literature. Difficulties in reading, spelling, mathematics, and formulation of written language are common in children with specific communication disorders. In the above study of children with communication disorders, the majority were in the preschool age range. Nonetheless, 7% of the sample met the *DSM-III* diagnostic criteria for a specific learning disorder.

The interrelationship between specific communication disorders and learning disorders is so close that it is often difficult to draw a line between them. In fact, the new *DSM-III-R* category of developmental expressive writing disorder, which includes disabilities in spelling and in the formulation of written language (punctuation, paragraph organization), is considered by some to be a type of specific communication disorder.

Those children whose communication disorder involves comprehension of language are most at risk for learning disorders. Those children whose communication disorder is limited to developmental articulation disorder have the lowest risk for learning disorders. Nonetheless, even they show a greater risk of learning disorders than children in the general population without communication disorder.

CASE HISTORIES

Case 1

Jimmy was referred by his pediatrician for psychiatric evaluation because, at 3½ years of age, he was unable to function appropriately in a preschool classroom setting.

Jimmy's mother outlined an essentially normal medical history but with various developmental delays and numerous behavioral problems. Jimmy was an only child, the product of a full-term pregnancy and normal delivery. Developmental milestones, which had been carefully recorded, consisted of sitting at 7 months, crawling at 8 months, standing at 9 months, walking aided at 11 months, and walking alone at 15 months.

Jimmy's first word, "babi" (referring to "Batty," the family cat), was spoken at age 12 months. From that time until his second birthday, Jimmy had a limited vocabulary of "approximately ten words, different words at different times" and all of them "pronounced only partially." At age 2 years, the mother had become concerned that Jimmy's speech lagged behind that of his peers and sought advice from the pediatrician. She reported that she had been assured that Jimmy was a normal child and that there was no cause for concern. When Jimmy reached his third birthday and still was using only a limited number of single-syllable words, the mother bypassed the pediatrician and took him to a speech clinic. There he was diagnosed as having "functional aphasia" and had been enrolled in speech therapy three times a week. The mother observed that as a result Jimmy "still had limited speech, but at least what he does say is easier for other people to understand."

When asked about the behavior problems that had resulted in Jimmy's psychiatric referral, the mother stated that it was "essentially a matter of self-discipline." Jimmy was unable to sit still in the classroom, became overly excited, failed to respond to the teacher's commands, and was given to having tantrums or fighting with the other children when things were not going his way. Apparently there were also problems in the home with being restless, impulsive, easily frustrated, and disobedient.

Observations. Jimmy separated from his mother without noticeable anxiety and headed straight for the toy box, completely ignoring the examiner's greeting. His play consisted of appropriate manipulation of the small people, cars, and buildings. During this solitary play, Jimmy showed considerable distractibility, stopping play several times to stare in the direction of various environmental sounds. At these times, however, the examiner was able to redirect to the play activities.

Eventually, Jimmy began interacting in play with the examiner. He responded intermittently to commands such as "get the red car," "put the man in the car," and "drive the car over here." Sometimes Jimmy would respond appropriately to such commands; other times he would respond inappropriately (for example, to "get the red car" Jimmy handed the examiner the yellow car while smiling happily); and at other times he would just stare at the examiner doing nothing. Attempts to engage Jimmy in conversation were less than successful. Jimmy told his name but refused to answer simple questions about his age, whether he went to school, what toys he liked, and where his

mother was. When the examiner held out a new toy and told Jimmy he could have the toy if he asked for it, Jimmy proceeded to stamp his feet, shriek, and throw toys at the examiner. Jimmy would not respond to questions such as "what is this?" However, he would attempt to repeat the responses if the examiner supplied them. Under Jimmy's repetitions, sentences were reduced to single words, which were often abbreviated. For example, "this is a cup" became "cu" and "this is my foot" became "foo."

Discussion. Jimmy exhibited typical symptoms of developmental receptive language disorder (inability to understand directions), developmental expressive language disorder (inability to answer questions, name things, or repeat utterances), and developmental articulation disorder (omission of age-appropriate consonants). The history of delays in achieving speech and language milestones and behavioral problems involving attention and concentration are also typical of a child with specific communication disorders.

Case 2

Mark was referred by the school psychologist for evaluation of learning difficulties, dysphoric mood, and problems with social skills and relationships. His early medical history had been normal, and developmental motor milestones, while slightly delayed, were also within normal limits. Development of both speech and language had been somewhat more delayed, although this had not been the focus of professional attention in the preschool years.

The educational history had included nursery school at age 4, kindergarten at age 5, and regular classroom placement in the primary grades. Although Mark had had some difficulties learning phonics, his report cards in the first and second grades had been average. Learning problems became more obvious in the latter part of the third grade, finally leading to educational testing in the fourth grade. Mark was found to have developmental receptive language disorder, developmental expressive language disorder, and developmental learning disorder manifested by vocabulary, auditory processing, and sentence comprehension and processing difficulties. His intelligence was found to be in the high average range overall, although there was a discrepancy between verbal and performance intelligence levels. Speech/language therapy and educational assistance were provided in "pull out" classes, while keeping Mark in the regular classroom setting throughout elementary and junior high school.

Current Functioning. Now in high school, Mark has had continuing problems with language and learning. Abstract concepts and concepts involving spatial or temporal relationships such as are frequently used in social studies, sciences, and mathematics, were particular problems.

In spontaneous speech, Mark tended to overuse a limited, concrete vocabulary and a restricted set of syntactic structures. However, no grammatical errors or dysfluencies were observed in Mark's speech. Nonverbal responses such as smiling and head nodding were present to an excessive degree.

Mark complained that he was "dumb," did not understand what was expected in social situations, frequently said the wrong thing, and found himself the victim of ridicule from his peers.

Discussion. Milder forms of developmental expressive language disorder and developmental receptive language disorder are often not detected until third or fourth grade. Subtle forms of developmental language disorder, although apparent with systematic language testing, may not be apparent in conversations or informal interactions.

Nonetheless, such subtle language disorders produce difficulties in listening and learning skills in the intermediate grades. Around the end of third grade, the classroom demands for listening skills increase as teachers depend more on verbal presentations, directions, and responses while decreasing

their use of manipulative materials and visual aids. Subtle deficits in language processing and formulation at this point affect reading comprehension skills, writing dictation skills, and the acquisition of mathematical concepts.

Because of inconsistent terminology in the educational field, children such as Mark may not receive diagnoses of developmental language disorder. However, symptoms including auditory processing difficulties, concept and vocabulary limitations, and diminished sentence length and syntactic complexity are all clues of an underlying language disorder. Often, these children's difficulties are sufficiently subtle that they will not qualify for placement in language-disordered classes. Unfortunately, learning-disabled classes may not provide sufficient specific language help for them. In such cases, difficulties are highly likely in the area of social interaction.

In summary, impairments in communication skills invariably result in impaired interpersonal interactions and educational achievement. Unsuccessful experiences in interpersonal interactions and in educational achievement during adolescence may have long range effects in psychosexual identity, self-image, and vocational goals. Various psychiatric problems, including a demoralization syndrome, are common in adolescents with language disorders. Whether the secondary psychiatric consequences of developmental language disorder can be prevented with early intervention is not yet known.

CLINICAL COURSE

The course of specific communication disorders varies considerably according to their

Table 15–5. COURSE AND OUTCOME OF THE SPECIFIC COMMUNICATION DISORDERS

Disorder	Short-Term Course	Long-Term Course
Developmental articulation disorder	Delayed acquisition of articulatory skills; catch-up is common by third grade	Normal speech articulation skills; usually no residual problems
Developmental expressive language disorder	Delayed acquisition of expressive language; catch-up usual by age 18; associated problems are common and persistent	Normal expressive language in most cases; severe cases may have residual expressive problems; associated problems may persist
Developmental receptive language disorder	Delayed acquisition of comprehension skills; catch-up usual by age 18; associated problems common and persistent	Normal or mildly impaired comprehension; associated psychiatric problems may persist for years

Table 15–6. LABORATORY FINDINGS FOR THE SPECIFIC COMMUNICATION DISORDERS

Findings Common to All the Specific Communication Disorders	Findings Specific to Certain Specific Communication Disorders	
	Disorder	*Finding*
Audiometric testing is within normal limits	Developmental articulation disorder	Articulation skills are below levels expected for age and nonverbal IQ
Performance intelligence (from standardized test) is within normal limits	Developmental expressive language disorder	Expressive language skills are below levels expected for age and nonverbal IQ
	Developmental receptive language disorder	Receptive language skills are below levels expected for age and nonverbal IQ

severity and is summarized in Table 15–5. Generally, these disorders have a long course, although the prognosis is excellent for the ultimate acquisition of speech/language within normal limits. Developmental articulation disorder has the shortest and least complicated course. For the developmental language disorders, the course is usually chronic. Developmental receptive language disorder has a poorer prognosis than developmental expressive language disorder.

LABORATORY FINDINGS

The laboratory findings (including those of psychometric tests) for specific communication disorders are summarized in Table 15–6. For all of the specific communication dis-

orders, assessments in all of the nonlinguistic areas will produce findings that are grossly within normal limits. This includes audiometric assessment of hearing and standardized psychometric testing of nonverbal (or "performance") intelligence.

For each of the specific communication disorders, speech or language testing will reveal functioning in the deficit area that is significantly below the level of acquisition expected from the child's chronologic age and mental abilities. As specified in the *DSM-III-R*, the speech or language tests should be standardized for the child's age, social class, and linguistic background (bilingual or monolingual). A large number of such standardized tests are available for the assessment of each of the various areas of speech/language functioning. These have been described in

Table 15–7. EXAMPLES OF STANDARDIZED TESTS FOR ASSESSMENT OF SPEECH/LANGUAGE FUNCTIONING

Test	Areas Covered	Ages	Deviations to Look For
Goldman-Fristoe Test of Articulation (Goldman and Fristoe 1972)	Speech articulation	All	Total score below 20th percentile for age level
Test of Auditory Comprehension of Language (TACL) (Carrow 1978)	Language comprehension (English and Spanish)	3–7 years	Total score below 20th percentile; errors in specific word types only
Test of Language Development (Newcomer and Hammill 1977)	Language comprehension and expression	4–9 years	Score 2 standard deviations below mean on total test and/or any specific subtests
Illinois Test of Psycholinguistic Abilities (Kirk et al. 1968)	Language comprehension, expression, and processing	2–10 years	"Psycholinguistic age" 1 year below chronologic age; significant difference between auditory and other subscores
Clinical Evaluation of Language Functions (CELF) (Semel and Wiig 1980)	Language comprehension, expression, and processing	K–12th grades	Processing, production, or total scores below 20th percentile; deviant error patterns as specified in test manual

detail elsewhere (Cantwell and Baker 1987; McCauley and Swisher 1984; Stephens and Montgomery 1985; Wiig and Semel 1980); however, examples of some of the more commonly used tests are provided in Table 15–7.

Because even standardized test results can be unreliable, the *DSM-III-R* requires that a diagnosis of any of the specific communication disorders must demonstrate a deficit through testing as well as clinically. Such a demonstration could include either clinical observation of the problem or of reliable report provided by a parent or teacher.

DIFFERENTIAL DIAGNOSIS

The disorders that must be ruled out when making the differential diagnosis of one of the specific communication disorders and the criteria for ruling out each disorder are summarized in Table 15–8. The relevant disorders include deafness or significant hearing loss, mental retardation, pervasive developmental disorder or infantile autism, organically based communication disorders (cleft palate, apraxia, cerebral palsy, or childhood acquired aphasia), elective mutism, or childhood schizophrenia. Generally, each of these disorders can be ruled out by nonlinguistic data. However, there are also specific language features that characterize each of these other disorders. These are described in detail elsewhere (Cantwell and Baker 1987). The differential diagnosis between subtypes of specific communication disorders requires linguistic data of the type specified in Table 15–6.

TREATMENT

The treatment of choice for any of the specific communication disorders is speech/language therapy administered by a certified speech/language pathologist. Because associated educational and/or psychiatric problems are common in children with specific communication disorders, educational tutoring, social skills training, and/or psychiatric intervention may also be necessary.

There is no scientific evidence supporting other forms of intervention. Some of these, such as the currently very popular "neurolinguistic programming," may be harmful by keeping the child away from appropriate treatment.

References

American Psychiatric Association. 1987. The Diagnostic and Statistical Manual of Mental Disorders, 3rd ed., revised. Washington, D.C.: American Psychiatric Association.

Baker, L., and Cantwell, D. P. 1985. Psychiatric and learning disorders in children with speech and language disorders: A critical review. *Adv. Learn. Behav. Disabil.* 4:1–28.

Baker, L., and Cantwell, D. P. (in press). Specific language/learning disorders. In Ollendick, T. H., and Herson, M. (eds): *Handbook of Child Psychopathology*. Second Edition. New York, Plenum Press.

Cantwell, D. P., and Baker, L. 1985. Psychiatric and learning disorders in children with speech and language disorders: A descriptive analysis. *Adv. Learn. Behav. Disabil.* 4:29–47.

Cantwell, D. P., and Baker, L. 1987. *Developmental Speech and Language Disorders*. New York: Guilford Press.

Carrow, E. 1978. *Test of Auditory Comprehension of Language (TACL)*. Austin, Tex.: Learning Concepts.

Goldman, R., and Fristoe, M. 1972. *Goldman-Fristoe Test*

Table 15–8. DIFFERENTIAL DIAGNOSIS OF SPECIFIC COMMUNICATION DISORDERS

Diagnoses to be Ruled Out	Criteria for Ruling Out This Diagnosis
Deafness, significant hearing loss	Normal results on audiometric testing
Mental retardation	Normal results on standardized intelligence testing
Pervasive developmental disorder (autism)	Absence of gross abnormalities in nonlinguistic areas (social relationships, social play, object usage)
Organically based communication disorders (cleft palate, apraxia, cerebral palsy, acquired aphasia)	Absence of organic speech mechanism (cleft palate), neuromuscular (apraxia, cerebral palsy) or cerebral (acquired aphasia) abnormalities
Elective mutism	Use of speech/language does not vary significantly depending on listener
Childhood schizophrenia	Absence of psychotic symptoms (hallucinations, delusions, thought disorder)

of Articulation (GFTA), rev. ed. Circle Pines, Minn.: American Guidance Service.

Kirk, S. A., McCarthy, J. J., and Kirk, W. D. 1968. *The Illinois Test of Psycholinguistic Abilities (ITPA)*, rev. ed. Urbana: University of Illinois Press.

McCauley, R., and Swisher, L. 1984. Psychometric review of language and articulation tests for preschool children. *J. Speech Hear. Disord.* 49:34–42.

Newcomer, P. L., and Hammill, D. D. 1977. *Test of Language Development (TOLD)*. Austin, Tex.: Empiric Press.

Semel, E., and Wiig, E. 1980. *CELF: Clinical Evaluation of Language Functions: Diagnostic Battery*. Columbus, Ohio: Charles E. Merrill.

Stephens, M. I., and Montgomery, A. A. 1985. A critique of recent relevant standardized tests. *Top. Language Disord.* 5(3):21–45.

U.S. Department of Education. 1987. *Ninth Annual Report to Congress: 1987*. Washington, D.C.: U.S. Government Printing Office.

Wiig, E. H., and Semel, E. M. 1980. *Language Assessment and Intervention for the Learning Disabled*. Columbus, Ohio: Charles E. Merrill.

16

Infantile Autism and Childhood Psychosis

JOHN C. POMEROY, M.D.

In his seminal 1943 paper, Kanner introduced the term *autism* in his description of 11 severely disturbed children whose "autistic disturbance of affect" was a descriptive accompaniment to the "extreme aloneness" he observed. The term, however, has other connotations that are not synonymous. Webster's dictionary defines autism as an "absorption in self-centered subjective mental activity (daydreams, fantasies, delusions, and hallucinations) especially when accompanied by marked withdrawal from reality." Psychopathologists consider autistic thinking to range from the normal preoccupation with one's own fantasies (particularly noticeable in shy, withdrawn persons) to the uncontrolled absorption in more unusual thoughts observed in schizophrenia, usually occurring in predisposed schizoid individuals (Bleuler 1911). Hence, autism has been used to describe a range of thought patterns from preoccupation with daydreams to florid psychosis, in addition to its more recent use as a diagnostic term that refers specifically to the behavioral manifestation of severe withdrawal and social dysfunction. The term *autistic* has also become an adjective applied to a variety of behaviors (e.g., repetitive, perseverative movements or acts) that are observed in this disorder.

Historically, in keeping with the primary definition of autism, there has been a belief that the mute, withdrawn behavior observed in autistic children is a consequence of a psychotic process and that the child is preoccupied with internal thoughts. This is one reason why infantile autism has been considered a psychosis and/or a childhood form of schizophrenia. However, psychosis more appropriately refers to a deterioration in functioning in which symptoms of hallucinations, delusions, and disordered thinking predominate in some phase of the process. Children with infantile autism are not only typically characterized by a wide variety of developmental delays and deviations in which severe language impairment probably precludes hallucinations and delusions, there is also no evidence that the disorder proceeds to a psychotic state. This clinical differentiation has been upheld by empirical studies of large groups of children designated psychotic (e.g., Kolvin et al. 1971), which have revealed that the age at onset discriminates between disorders that are developmental (an onset usually before age 3 years) and those that are more likely to resemble adult psychoses (an onset after age 5 years). Recently, there has been renewed discussion of the clinical and etiologic overlap between the early- and late-onset disorders, but the majority of clinical studies confirm that infantile autism and late-onset (schizophrenic-like) childhood psychoses should be considered as clearly separate conditions.

INFANTILE AUTISM

Definition

Considerable controversy about the diagnosis and definition of the autistic syndrome has occurred in the past 40 years. Definitional problems have occurred for several reasons: (1) there is wide variation in the severity of the disorder; (2) the prominence of certain symptoms alters with age; and (3) associated intellectual ability can range from profound retardation to normal intelligence. Other characteristics such as phenomenal memory and good motor skills once suggested that these children had innately normal or supernormal intellectual abilities that were being repressed by severe emotional disturbance.

The American Psychiatric Association in its latest *Diagnostic and Statistical Manual of Mental Disorders* (*DSM-III-R* 1987) has taken an innovative approach to the classification of these disorders and (in keeping with the developmental nature of their origin) has designated a category of pervasive developmental disorders (PDD), of which autism is the most well-defined syndrome within the group. There appears to be unanimity among all workers on a triad of abnormalities in language development, social functioning, and flexibility of behavior patterns that characterize autism and are apparent in autistic children before age 3 years. (It should be noted that the abnormal developmental problems are not merely *delays* in acquisition of skills, but they are also *deviant* in nature.) The possibility of this disorder occurring after 3 years of age is usually retained in popular diagnostic schemes so that the extremely rare situation of a childhood onset (age 3 to 5 years) does not require a different diagnostic category if the full syndrome is apparent. Children who share many but not all of the required symptoms are diagnosed as having "PDD not otherwise specified." The presence of florid psychotic symptoms (hallucinations or delusions) is generally considered to be an exclusion to the diagnosis. To clarify the diagnostic criteria, it is helpful to review the developmental and behavioral problems that are observed in autistic children.

LANGUAGE AND COMMUNICATION

Because most autistic children show marked delay in language development and as many as 50% do not develop useful speech, developmental language dysfunction has been proposed as the central deficit. However, communication, in a broader sense, is also severely disturbed. These characteristics are markedly different from children with pure developmental language disorders (see Differential Diagnosis). The early language development is characterized either by delay in onset or lack of progress (or regression) after initial acquisition of some language. This may be preceded by a lack of communicative babbling as a baby. If speech does develop, it is often perseverative and echolalic and commonly includes a confusion in using personal pronouns (e.g., talking of self in the third person). Communication problems (which often become more apparent in late childhood and early adolescence) include an inability to reciprocate in conversational speech, a lack of flexibility in expressive language, an inability to understand or respond to other's verbal and nonverbal social cues, and an impaired modulation of speech to provide emphasis and appropriate tone.

SOCIAL DEVELOPMENT

All autistic children show deviant social relationships. Many parents report a failure of the child to accept or give physical affection as a baby. However, a few children are affectionate with, and even extremely anxious if separated from, one or other parent. The essential social deficits are seen in inappropriate responses to social cues, a lack of empathy for others emotions, and an inability to modify behavior to a social context. Typical early characteristics are avoidance of eye-to-eye gaze, rarely seeking comfort or affection from others, rarely initiating play with others, rarely greeting others, and no peer friendships with mutual interaction in activities.

INFLEXIBLE BEHAVIORAL PATTERNS

This group of abnormalities reflect a need to impose rigidity and routine on everyday functioning and is also characterized in the inflexible, unimaginative style of thinking. These behaviors include preoccupation with restricted and stereotyped interests, attachments to unusual objects, rituals, repetitive mannerisms, noncreative play with toys (e.g., taking apart, lining up), and extreme reactions to changes in small details of the environment.

ABNORMAL PERCEPTUAL RESPONSES

Not all researchers consider this group of symptoms to be crucial to the diagnosis of autism. However, a number of unusual reactions to auditory, visual, olfactory, tactile, and pain stimuli are commonly observed (e.g., apparent deafness to loud sounds but extreme sensitivity to ordinary noise levels or special sounds, lack of reaction to pain and even apparent pleasure in self-infliction of pain, fascination with certain tactile stimuli, and apparent confusion or difficulty with visual recognition).

OTHER SYMPTOMS

There are a number of symptoms that are commonly seen in autistic children but that are not considered pathognomonic because they are not universally observed and can be seen in other developmentally delayed or psychiatrically disturbed children. These include hyperactivity, sleep problems, food fads, intermittent behavioral problems, unusual gait (particularly toe-walking), clumsiness, and self-destructiveness (e.g., head banging, scratching, biting). The latter is often included among a number of different repetitive motor movements (e.g., flapping hands, particularly when excited), which tend to be termed *self-stimulating behaviors*. In truth, they may reflect neurologic dysfunction or manneristic or attention-seeking behavior.

The three groups of clinical items for a diagnosis of autistic disorder from the *DSM-III-R* are listed in Table 16–1. At least one half of the symptoms must be present, and one symptom (two for group A) must be observed in each of the three categories. A subclassification of infantile onset (before age 3 years) and childhood onset (after age 3 years) is to be made. This approach to diagnosis appears to be an improvement over previous attempts, but it is unclear if this will tighten the diagnostic grouping or include an inappropriately wide range of developmentally disordered children. Some clinicians have proposed other subclassifications based on such features as associated organic disorders, presence or absence of mental retardation, and qualitative differences in the core deficits (e.g., degree and types of social withdrawal). Only further research will help clarify the value, if any, of more precise classification and subdivisions of the autistic and autistic-like syndromes.

Epidemiology

PREVALENCE

Epidemiologic studies in England, Denmark, Sweden, and the United States have all found between four and five clear cases of autism per 10,000 children. However, as implied previously, when children with autism are grouped with those with autistic-like symptoms (usually a combination of language and social impairment), considerably higher rates are observed, for example, 21 per 10,000 children in a United Kingdom study and 69 per 10,000 children in a Swedish study. One Japanese study reported a rate of "true autism" at 16 per 10,000 children. Differing rates most probably represent different diagnostic criteria. Mental retardation with associated language, social, and behavioral problems appears to account for the majority of the higher prevalence figures. However, the possibility of geographic variation in prevalence has to be considered, and there is some evidence that the rates of both mental retardation and autism may be greater in rural areas. Most workers, therefore, conclude that the figure of 4 cases per 10,000 children is the age-specific prevalence of true autism. Approximately one half of this group are typical of Kanner's original description, in which social aloofness and elaborate repetitive routines were the predominant symptoms.

SEX RATIO

Boys outnumber girls in all studies of autism, but the ratio has ranged from 1.5 to 4.8 boys to every girl. There is some evidence that the overrepresentation of boys is more marked in the presence of higher IQ and more classic autistic symptoms. The more equal sex ratio in the profoundly retarded group implies that girls with autism are more severely brain damaged than autistic boys.

SOCIAL CLASS

Kanner's first account of autism suggested that higher social class was related to the disorder. However, further study suggests that social class has no bearing on the course or epidemiology of autism.

SIBLING RANK

Although the relationship between sibling rank and autism is by no means well sub-

---

Table 16–1. DIAGNOSTIC CRITERIA FOR AUTISTIC DISORDERS

A. *Qualitative impairment in reciprocal social interactions*, as manifested by the following:
1. Marked lack of awareness of the existence or feelings of others
2. No or abnormal seeking of comfort at times of distress
3. No or impaired imitation
4. No or abnormal social play
5. Gross impairment in ability to make peer friendships

B. *Qualitative impairment in verbal and nonverbal communication, and in imaginative activity*, as manifested by the following:
1. No mode of communication, such as communicative babbling, facial expression, gesture, mime, or spoken language
2. Markedly abnormal nonverbal communication, as in the use of eye-to-eye gaze, facial expression, body posture, or gestures to initiate or modulate social interaction
3. Absence of imaginative activity
4. Marked abnormality in the production of speech, including volume, pitch, stress, rate, rhythm, and intonation
5. Marked abnormalities in the form and content of speech, including stereotyped and repetitive use, irrelevance, idiosyncratic speech, and lack of use of personal pronouns
6. Marked impairment in the ability to initiate or sustain a conversation with others despite adequate speech

C. *Markedly restricted repertoire of activities and interests*, as manifested by the following:
1. Stereotyped body movements
2. Persistent preoccupation with parts of objects or attachment to unusual objects
3. Marked distress over changes in trivial aspects of environment
4. Unreasonable insistence on following routines in precise detail
5. Restricted range of interests and a preoccupation with one narrow interest.

(From American Psychiatric Association. 1987. *Diagnostic and Statistical Manual of Mental Disorders*, 3rd. ed., revised. Washington, D.C.: American Psychiatric Association.)

---

stantiated, there is some evidence to suggest that a higher than expected number of autistic children are first born or late-born (fourth or more in sibling rank).

SEASON OF BIRTH

One study has shown a seasonal birth excess in spring and early summer for nonverbal, retarded autistic boys (Konstantareas et al. 1986).

MENTAL RETARDATION

There is a consistent agreement among the findings of all epidemiologic studies that the vast majority of autistic children test in the mentally retarded range (IQ score below 70). Specific rates do vary, but about 50% of the autistic population have scores in the moderate to profound range of mental retardation and only 10% to 20% of children have IQ scores within the normal range. Unusual skills (often called *idiot savant* or *splinter skills*) can be present and include exceptional rote memory, artistic, or musical abilities. However, these should generally be considered islets of special ability and not an indication of unrealized superior intellect.

Etiology and Pathology

Kanner originally considered autism to be a constitutional disability, but he and others came to believe that parents played a significant part in the causation of the disorder. Due to referral biases in this early research, autistic children were disproportionally represented among the families of professional classes and more commonly had testable intelligence in the normal range. Psychogenic theories of withdrawal from a "cold," noxious environment prevailed. However, a biological etiology was considered a more appropriate explanation when it was observed that there was an increased incidence of mental retardation, epilepsy, and clear-cut medical disorders in autism. The search for the biological basis of infantile autism has subsequently proceeded in many directions.

ASSOCIATED DISORDERS

Autism has been associated with numerous disease entities. In no instance does any specific disease universally produce autism nor is there necessarily an obviously shared neuropathology. The list of case reports of clinical associations is constantly growing.

However, many of these reports could be chance findings, and only established associations are considered here.

Congenital rubella was one of the first disorders shown to lead to an increased incidence of autism. The severity of the associated defects of this illness are not important, but the presence of auditory and possibly visual loss is relevant. This is in keeping with some reports that congenital deafness and blindness increase the risk of autism. Rubella-related autism is often associated with a delayed onset, and recovery from the syndrome has also been observed. Other congenital infections have been described in autistic patients, but none has been substantiated as causative. These include cytomegalovirus infection, syphilis, toxoplasmosis, varicella, and rubeola.

Postnatal central nervous system infections may also be related to autism. For example, herpes encephalitis and mumps have preceded the onset of autistic syndromes. The latter may be due to hydrocephalus, a potential complication of mumps encephalitis. More unusual are reports of reversible (and sometimes irreversible) autistic syndromes occurring in older children and adolescents who have encephalitis, most probably due to herpes simplex infection.

A number of metabolic disorders have been associated with autism. Phenylketonuria, hyperuricuria ("purine autism"), lactic acidosis, and storage diseases (e.g., lipidosis) are the most common. In addition, some autistic children have low urinary calcium excretion or low levels of serum magnesium, which have led to evaluation for malabsorption syndromes and bowel disease. However, celiac disease is probably not the cause of these findings despite some case reports.

The congenital neurocutaneous disorders (tuberous sclerosis and neurofibromatosis) do appear to be associated with autism. This may be due to structural defects as seen with other intracerebral space-occupying lesions (e.g., arachnoid cysts). Other congenital syndromes that have been observed in autism are Cornelia de Lange's, Moebius', Noonan's, Coffin-Siris, and Biedl-Bardet syndromes, Duchenne's muscular dystrophy, and achondroplasia. Also there are a number of reports of the coexistence of Tourette's syndrome and autism.

Seizure disorders show a complex relationship with autism. Seizures are observed in at least one third of the autistic population. The age at onset is usually during the adolescent years, and it is more common in the mentally retarded. However, one particular seizure disorder, infantile spasms, which is also associated with numerous neuropathologic causes and characterized by hypsarrhythmia on the electroencephalographic pattern, can lead to autism. Psychomotor seizures have been observed in young autistic children, and reports exist of the cessation of the autistic characteristics with appropriate antiepileptic drug treatment.

GENETICS

Family and twin studies leave little doubt that familial factors play a part in the transmission of autism. Siblings of autistic children have 50 times the risk of normal population for developing the disorder. Monozygotic twins have an 80% to 90% concordance for autism as opposed to a 15% to 25% concordance for dizygotic twins. It should be noted that the inherited component may not be autism per se but rather a predisposition to language or cognitive abnormalities. In fact, language-related difficulties among relatives have been observed in approximately 25% of the families with an autistic child.

Chromosomal disorders may be a very significant factor in the familiality of autism. The fragile X syndrome (which refers to a fragile site on the X chromosome when observed in a folate-deficient medium) has been found in as many as 16% of some autistic populations. Affected males have distinctive facial features with large ears, macro-orchidism (detectable at puberty), and impairment of cognitive and language skills. Although surveys vary in their findings, it seems apparent that an excessive number of affected males and some carrier females will exhibit autism. In addition, the fragile X syndrome probably accounts for 50% of the X-linked mental retardation. Other fragile sites on the autosomes have been reported, but none has yet proven to be associated with a recognizable set of clinical features (Bregman et al. 1987).

BIRTH FACTORS

Although many studies have suggested that birth trauma may be a significant factor in the causation of autism, few studies are well controlled. The only pregnancy and birth factor (other than congenital viral infection) that shows a reliable association with autism is midtrimester uterine bleeding. However, certain prenatal abnormalities have emerged as potential factors in the manifestation of autism. These include increased rates of parental exposure to chemical toxins, parental thyroid disorders, and histories of infertility and possibly spontaneous abortions. The importance of these factors is unclear, but one line of research links immunologic disorders with autism. This may connect the parental propensity for thyroid disorders (which are often autoimmune) with autism. More specifically, it is claimed that the parents of autistic children have significantly higher rates of shared HLA antigens, which may decrease the protection of the fetus from the mother's immune system, and some autistic patients have also been reported to have a relative T-cell deficiency and possibly a cell-mediated immune response to brain tissue.

NEUROCHEMISTRY

Studies of neurochemical abnormalities in autism have produced few consistent findings, but their findings are pointing to potential biological subgroups. More research is necessary before firm conclusions can be made.

Serotonin. Numerous studies have shown that a large proportion of autistic children have higher levels of whole blood and platelet-bound serotonin. Assessing measures of uptake and excretion of serotonin have not led to a full explanation of this finding, nor is there complete understanding of the relationship between blood levels of serotonin and brain functioning. Elevated serotonin levels are also found in other mental retardation disorders and in congenital hypothyroidism. These findings have led to treatment approaches that have attempted to reduce serotonin levels (see Treatment). One unusual finding in some autistic persons is an increased urinary level of an atypical breakdown product of serotonin, bufotenin, which implies an excessive turnover of serotonin. This finding appears to be familial, because the abnormality is observed in some healthy relatives. An additional unexplained observation is that some autistic children show

significantly low levels of peripheral serotonin.

Catecholamines. A number of abnormalities in the catecholamine synthetic pathway have been observed in autistic persons. The congenital abnormality in the primary metabolic step (phenylalanine to tyrosine) that leads to phenylketonuria has already been mentioned. Some researchers have found evidence for increased turnover of dopamine because there are raised levels of cerebrospinal fluid and urinary homovanillic acid, the most common excretory product. An atypical breakdown product, homoprotocatechuic acid, has been found in excess in the urine of some autistic probands as well as some of their relatives. This substance is potentially produced when there is an accompanying decrease in the catalytic enzyme dopamine β-hydroxylase, which facilitates the formation of norepinephrine from dopamine. Other enzymes in the catecholamine breakdown process (catechol-O-methyltransferase and monoamine oxidase) are not altered in autism, but vitamin B_6 deficiency has been proposed as a potential cause of some features of autism. This vitamin is a co-enzyme in a number of steps of the catecholamine and serotonin pathways. There has also been evidence of increased levels of plasma cyclic adenosine monophosphate, which is believed to act as the "second messenger" inside the cell for these neurotransmitters.

Amino and Organic Acids. Although no conclusive observations have been made in urinary and cerebrospinal fluid studies of amino and organic acids (except for phenylketonuria), there have been distinct chromatographic patterns that suggest that some autistic children may have specific metabolic abnormalities. Raised levels of cerebrospinal fluid arginine and ethanolamine have been reported as well as unexplained patterns of urinary peptides. Brain opioids are believed to modulate systems associated with social affect and intent, and one study has shown raised cerebrospinal levels of endorphins in autistic children who are self-destructive and somewhat insensitive to pain.

ELECTROPHYSIOLOGY

The majority of younger autistic children have normal electroencephalographic patterns, unless there is a specific syndrome (infantile spasms) or a localized lesion. Abnormal electroencephalographic patterns, when present, do not have specific characteristics. These are generally bilateral or a mixture of diffuse and localized abnormalities. Evoked potential studies have generally found a subgroup of children with abnormalities in both brain-stem and cortical measures. In the brain-stem auditory evoked response, prolonged reaction times have been associated with hypotonia in some autistic children. The cortical measures have usually shown less frequent, smaller amplitudes or even missing potentials of which the auditory evoked potential is usually more abnormal than the visual evoked potential.

NEUROPATHOLOGY

Postmortem brain studies of autistic children are rare, and in many reports diagnostic criteria have not been rigidly applied to the clinical history. Abnormalities that have been observed (and have led to promising research) are lesions in the forebrain, hippocampal, and cerebellar regions. The latter, which includes a loss of Purkinje cells in the neocerebellum, has been likened to an animal model in which mutant mice (autosomal recessive inheritance) with deficient Purkinje cells also have abnormal sperm morphology and decreased photoreceptors in the retina. An ongoing multicenter study has shown that a considerable number of autistic persons do have decreased visual rod functioning as measured by electroretinography (Ritvo et al. 1988).

Neuroradiology is the major method available to study gross neuroanatomy in live humans. Initially, pneumoencephalography was used, then computed tomography. Magnetic resonance imaging (MRI) is likely to supersede all of these procedures. In essence, the findings to date are confusing. Occasionally, gross abnormalities (e.g., hydrocephalus or structural lesions, often temporal or frontal) are found. Some other studies suggest a reversal of the normal asymmetry of right and left parietal occipital regions as well as ventricular enlargement (which is often more severe on the left side of the brain). The first MRI studies of higher-functioning autistic subjects have revealed either cerebellar abnormalities or more widespread abnormality of structures that define the fourth ventricle (Gaffney et al. 1987; Courchesne et al. 1988).

SYNTHESIS

This long, often contradictory and complex description of associated pathology in autistic disorders suggests that a considerable amount of further research is required to understand how these pathologic entities interrelate to produce the autistic syndrome. For example, it is unclear if some of these biological characteristics are associated with mental retardation in general or infantile autism specifically. Certainly, the more cognitively impaired autistic patient has an increased likelihood of revealing an associated disorder or gross pathology. Suggestions have been made that the inherited component of autism may be a predisposition to a developmental cognitive/learning disability that produces autism when additional biological insults of a specific nature are present.

Two major approaches have been taken to synthesize the literature. The first is a neuropsychologic/cognitive model that pays less attention to the biomedical features and highlights the primary deficits shown by all autistic persons. These deficits are separated into abnormalities in language/symbolic processing and dysfunction in social perception and integration, probably combined with a disorder in those brain systems that regulate affect. At present, the cognitive theorists are in dispute about which system (language or social/affective) represents the primary disturbance. Either way, these workers would suggest that whatever the underlying biology, this combination of cognitive problems (or cerebral processing abnormalities) are required for autism to manifest.

Because these cognitive skills are controlled by cortical structures of the brain, much of the associated research has focused on these higher level skills. However, the other models are more neuropathologically oriented and take into account the range of dysfunction from brain stem to cortex. Anatomically, it has been proposed that autistic behaviors could be caused by bilateral dysfunction in the mesolimbic cortex, which includes mesial temporal and frontal lobes, neostriatum, and thalamus. This particular area of the brain is developmentally and neurochemically distinct and represents the major target area of brain-stem dopaminergic neurons. This has led to an integration of the brain-stem abnormalities, excess dopamine turnover, and some of the neuropathologic findings. In this theory, dysfunction of the brain-stem dopaminergic neurons, which may have many causes, occurs early in development and leads to abnormal formation and innervation of mesolimbic cortical structures. This theory could also allow for other destructive events occurring along this pathway or in appropriate cortical areas, all of which may cause a clinical picture of infantile autism.

Clinical Picture and Course

Many factors influence the clinical presentation. These include the degree of associated neurodevelopmental dysfunction, specific syndromes, and the presence of a normal period of development. The more biologically damaged the child, in general, the more obvious are the developmental problems. This may result in significant problems in the first year, such as poor eating and sleeping patterns, excessive crying, lack of attachment to the mother, and resistance to being picked up or played with. Alternatively, the first year is often unremarkable except parents occasionally note that the child was an exceptionally good, rather quiet baby.

For many parents, the first indication of their child's abnormality is his or her unusual social behavior and lack of speech or a sudden change between 18 and 30 months of age that denotes the beginning of the same problems. Pediatricians commonly reassure parents at this early stage of development because they observe wide variation in the acquisition of these cognitive and behavioral skills. Somewhere between 24 and 36 months, however, the aberrant characteristics usually become obvious to all.

Clinical history from the parents reveals many, if not all, of the characteristics listed in Table 16–1. The typical presentation is of a toddler or preschooler who looks healthy (often relatively attractive), wanders aimlessly around the room or is immediately attracted to certain parts of the room (e.g., fans, fire extinguishers, electrical outlets), avoids eye contact, appears to look at objects with peripheral field of vision, does not respond to questions or commands, and may be extremely active. Verbalizations may be absent or idiosyncratic, perseverative, and echolalic. If the child is interested in toys, he or she will usually play in a repetitive, nonimaginative manner or take the toys apart.

A number of unusual motor movements may be seen (e.g., toe-walking, hand-flapping, finger extensions), and some of the movements have choreoathetoid qualities. Other more complex rituals (e.g., systematically smelling objects) may be observed. The number and severity of symptoms vary from child to child as well as depend on the age at evaluation. The history of the first 3 years of development is critical in making the clinical diagnosis in older children. Unfortunately, the reliability of such retrospective information is always limited.

The course of the disorder has some predictability based on a number of clinical features. Essentially, the children who have a better prognosis have a higher testable intelligence (above 60 on IQ tests), develop useful speech before age 5 years, and have less severe overall symptomatology. Appropriate schooling from an early age may also improve the prognosis. About two thirds of the autistic population remain mentally retarded and withdrawn, have limited language (if any), and maintain the whole range of abnormal behaviors. Most of these children become institutionalized adults. Of the better prognosis group, some (about one third) lose their autistic qualities and may become socially outgoing and jovial, although shallow and lacking in empathy. Most, however, are reserved, cool, socially inept, and have speech abnormalities that include echolalia and pronoun reversal. If more normal speech develops, it generally seems formal, pedantic, and lacks intonation. Reports exist of autistic children who develop more normally and may even complete higher education. Such persons probably represent less than 1% of the total autistic population. Of relevance to the second part of this chapter is the observation that none of the major follow-up studies have revealed evidence of schizophrenia occurring in reliably diagnosed autistic children.

Over the years, not only may some symptoms change, but different problems may arise. Those children who appear hyperactive may have a reduction in their extreme activity level in adolescence. However, new problems in adolescence are common. In this regard, the onset of seizures has already been discussed. Between 10% and 30% of autistic adolescents show a significant deterioration in performance and behavior. This may include loss of skills, self-harm, increased aloofness, and stereotypic behaviors, as well as loss of verbal skills. Many of these children also show cyclic behavioral disturbance, with hyperactive, aggressive, or more withdrawn, apathetic periods. It has been proposed that there is increased risk for this change in female patients and in the presence of a family history of affective disorder.

Other problems that are related to pubescence itself, include adjustment to sexual development, which can lead to inappropriate public sexual behavior, and, for many higher functioning autistic adolescents, increasing insight into their differences from their nonautistic peers, which can lead to marked depression. The following case histories describe the clinical presentation of an autistic preschooler, a grade-schooler, and an adolescent. The latter two patients have relatively good intellectual functioning on individually administered intelligence tests.

Case Histories

CASE 1

D.C. was a 3-year-old boy referred to the clinic by a speech pathologist to help in diagnostic classification. The parents had already obtained a number of evaluations from different professionals but seemed angry with the speech pathologist's suggestion that their son had infantile autism.

Until 18 months of age, D.C. appeared to be developing normally. He had been walking from 11 months and had sounded words (e.g., mama, clock) at 9 months. He was already repeating numbers and some letters when there was a sudden deterioration and regression in language and social skills. There was no acute illness prior to this, and the only medical history was an episode of severe dehydration during an upper respiratory tract infection at 6 months.

There had been little progress in the previous 2 years. D.C. had no socialization with peers and would shy away from them; his eye contact was poor; he tended to run in circles and flap his hands; and he was not toilet trained, lacked a sense of danger, and was extremely sensitive to loud noises. He had fixations on certain body parts, first ears then toes, and would perseveratively examine them. He tended to line up objects on the floor and if given a doll would bite it. He did not know how to use crayons and was not able to master more complex age-appropriate motor tasks.

More positive characteristics were that D.C. allowed affection and physical contact with his family and he was beginning to show some interest in books and TV and was starting to use some single words. He also did not seem to be upset by changes in routine.

In the family, there was a history of alcoholism and depression and a maternal cousin had "learning disabilities." A step-brother by the father's previous marriage had a growth hormone deficiency.

Observation of D.C. revealed an extremely attractive, bright-eyed young boy who was well-dressed, seemed physically adept, and looked his age. Although accepting separation from parents, he had no verbal interchange and no eye contact and purposely avoided any close proximity with the examiner. He flicked through books but paid no attention to content. He would not mimic any actions or comply with direct requests. Given crayons, he pulled them out of the box and threw them over the floor. He clearly did not understand how to use pencil and paper. Left alone, he tore up books. With his parents, he sat cuddled in his father's lap.

D.C. received a thorough neurologic examination, including electroencephalogram, brain computed tomographic scan, urinary screen for organic and amino acids, and karyotyping. No cause was elicited for his autistic disorder. The parents seemed to understand D.C.'s problem more clearly after long discussion and placed him in a preschool program for children with developmental disorders. The prognosis for D.C. is uncertain because it is too early to assess his intellectual potential.

CASE 2

M.N. was evaluated at 9 years of age when the major concerns were his inability to relate to others. He preferred to be alone, spending hours counting or doing mathematic problems, talking to himself, laughing for no apparent reason, and observing and playing with his hands for many hours if undisturbed. In addition, M.N. was restless; he had walked away from the house and become lost on a number of occasions. Although not deaf, he commonly did not respond to others speaking to him, he made unrelated irrelevant statements; and he was extremely resistant to interruption of his activities, going to new places and going to bed. On these occasions, he would commonly yell, stamp his feet, and rub his face in agitation. He had recently become preoccupied with maps and highways.

M.N. was born 3 weeks prematurely and had a brief period of hypoxia at birth. He was a quiet, easy baby who showed a delay in acquisition of motor skills (sitting at 9 months, walking at 19 months) and language. He said words at 3 years of age, and his language improved to forming sentences within a few months, but he was echolalic and talked to himself. He was resistant to change, showed no interest in peers, and had no affection for his family. He would be absorbed by moving objects and would play for hours spinning wheels on a toy car, watching records turn, or observing other moving objects. Placed in preschool classes for the mentally retarded, he began to show some awareness of surroundings and peers by 4½ years of age. Temper tantrums were observed commonly at home and at school. At the time of the evaluation, he was placed in a program for the trainable mentally retarded, with a recently tested IQ on the Weschler Intelligence Scale for Children—Revised (WISC-R) of 59. However, it was believed that he actually functioned at a higher level than this.

M.N. was the product of the mother's second marriage, and the parents were divorced. Both parents had received psychiatric treatment for unspecified emotional problems. The father had been a loner in school, received special education, and only completed eighth grade. There was a 5-year-old brother who had Down syndrome.

When observed, M.N. was cooperative but had limited eye contact, giggled without reason, and asked numerous irrelevant questions (e.g., What would happen if I crossed my hands?). He was echolalic and perseverative, and he would become "stuck" on one word. His voice was monotonous and high pitched. He made sounds and grimaces and flapped his hands. When asked to draw a person, he drew a head connected to legs and feet. He started drawing and counting the toes on the foot up to 20, then 30, and then wanted only to draw a foot with many toes. He started crying at the end of the examination and repetitively rubbed his nose, eyes, and whole face.

Physical and laboratory investigations were unremarkable. A speech and language assessment revealed normal receptive language skills but an expressive delay of approximately 4 years. He had confusion with personal pronouns plus severe communication deficits, suggesting a desire to interact, but very inappropriate speech production. Psychological evaluations revealed marked variability with full-scale IQ ranging from 56 to 80 on different testing occasions. The scores were notable for discrepancy between strengths in some organizational, arithmetic, and memory tasks and deficiencies in language and higher-order comprehension skills. Despite some evidence of a high overall intelligence, it was apparent that M.N. was extremely handicapped in areas of social functioning, pragmatic language, and self-sufficiency. During treatment, M.N. showed some response to a behavioral program designed to increase appropriate speech and socialization plus decrease his unusual behaviors and tantrums. This had little generalization to settings outside the treatment center.

CASE 3

M. was first evaluated at 5 years of age when a diagnosis of mental retardation and autism was made. He was noted to have communication deficits and echolalia and did not initiate interaction with others. Peculiarly, he had been able to recite the alphabet and numbers when 3 years old, but even by age 5 years, he had little useful, social speech. He did not react to affection and engaged in ritualistic twirling of objects. Developmental history revealed a pregnancy that was complicated by some bleeding in the first trimester, medication given for a maternal sinus infection, and spontaneous delivery 3 weeks before the due date. In addition to the abnormal language development, M. did not begin walking until 20 months. M. was the second child of well-educated parents who appeared warm and committed and had no relevant medical or psychiatric history.

M. received play therapy, with little benefit, and was placed in a regular kindergarten program that was unsuccessful because of his restlessness and inattention. After 4 years in a special education program for learning disabilities, he was spending one half his day in a regular school class. A reevaluation at 10 years noted odd ritualistic behavior, lack of peer interaction, inappropriate and non-sensical language, inability to think abstractly and generalize from experience, and lack of academic progress.

At 15 years, M. was attending regular classes in a junior high school with one class a day in special education. At this time, the major problems were his inability to express himself adequately (particularly with complete sentences), stammering, disorganization, difficulty with abstraction, poor reading comprehension, and continuing social problems. The latter were a consequence of his inability to appreciate or understand humor and the ease with which he could be teased and provoked into fits of laughter and overactivity when peers discussed his favorite preoccupations such as television commercials. Although M. generally had good self-help skills, he was unable to use money, would not organize his spare time, nor perform more than one task at a time (e.g., could not talk and dress himself at the same time). When frustrated, he returned to his room and bounced on his bed.

On examination, M. was neatly and appropriately dressed. He had a habit of becoming more rapid in his movements as he progressed with a task (e.g., climbing stairs or writing) and repetitively patted his hand and stroked his body. His affect was appropriate. His speech showed initial delay in response, monotony, perseveration, and occasional echolalia, but was often more appropriate in social interaction with adults. His gross cognitive skills were normal. Physical examination revealed a few minor physical anomalies (high-arched palate, malocclusion, and curved fifth fingers), as well as poor coordination of fine movements.

Psychometric study, at 15 years, showed his full-scale IQ scores on the WISC-R to be 89 (verbal, 91; performance, 90). Although this showed a normal intelligence, there was considerable scatter on subtests, with significantly impaired comprehension, picture completion, and coding, as well as idiosyncratic approaches to solving problems. A very extensive neuropsychological assessment found only subtle abnormalities in stereognosis, incidental learning, and memory for auditory information. An electroencephalogram was abnormal because of excessive slow wave activity, mostly localized to right parietal and posterior temporal regions.

Clearly, M. had much more significant social handicaps than biological or psychological studies could reveal. Future management of his needs would focus on vocational skills and training with a recommendation of using a school-based job to help him develop independent work skills.

Physical and Laboratory Findings

To the extent that autism has already been shown to have an association with numerous medical conditions, the physical findings will reflect this. The important issue in assessment of the child is, therefore, to investigate all the potential causes of autism. However, the number of investigations applied to each child should reflect good clinical judgment. Exhaustive and expensive investigation is only appropriate based on a thorough physical examination and if likely to produce an explanation for the condition that has treatment or intervention value. These benefits may not always be specifically for the patient. For example, chromosomal analyses that reveal disorders such as the fragile X syndrome have important implications for parental genetic counseling.

Physical examination should focus on general physical health and growth (e.g., height, weight, head circumference), and particular attention should be paid to minor physical anomalies, skin lesions (e.g., café au lait spots, adenoma sebaceum), and cardiac abnormalities, all of which may be indicators of structural defects, metabolic disorders, or specific genetically determined syndromes. The full list of laboratory investigations that are recommended by Coleman and Gillberg (1985) is presented in Table 16–2. It is debatable whether some of these studies, which relate to research findings of unknown clinical value (e.g., platelet serotonin levels and urinary homovanillic acid), are really required. Priority should be given to eliciting potentially treatable structural and metabolic defects. These workers also list a number of optional studies, including a 72-hour stool collection for lipid and occult blood, examination of cerebrospinal fluid, and evoked potential studies. A decision about the investigations to be performed should be discussed fully with the parents, possibly in accompaniment with a pediatric neurologist

Table 16–2. LABORATORY STUDIES IN INFANTILE AUTISM

Blood Studies
Phenylalanine
Serotonin and platelet count
Uric acid
Calcium
Phosphorus
Magnesium
Lactic acid
Pyruvic acid
Herpes virus
Cytomegalovirus } titers
Mumps virus
Chromosomal culture: folate-deficient media
Blood urea nitrogen

Urine Studies (24-hour sample)
Uric acid
Magnesium
Calcium
Phosphorus
Creatinine
Homovanillic acid
Metabolic screen (amino and organic acids, mucopolysaccharides)

Other Studies
Electroencephalogram
Computed tomography or magnetic resonance imaging of brain
Ophthalmologic evaluation
Auditory evaluation
Otologic examination, including test of vestibular functioning

(Data from Coleman, M., and Gillberg, C. 1985. *The Biology of the Autistic Syndrome.* New York: Praeger.)

who has performed a full neurologic examination.

The psychological evaluation requires a very experienced evaluator who has knowledge of a number of appropriate tests and has learned to obtain (often with aid of reinforcing techniques) the optimal skills from developmentally delayed children. The measures that are used should be able to test intellectual ability that is not influenced by language such as the performance scales from traditional IQ tests (for example, the age-appropriate Wechsler Scales) or specific nonverbal tests such as the Leiter International Performance Scale (Arthur adaptation). Developmental assessments can include parent and/or teacher reports (e.g., Vineland Social Maturity Scale) as well as specific neurodevelopment tests (e.g., Visual Motor Integration Task). In addition, a full assessment of speech and language functioning is required.

There is considerable dispute about the value of measuring intelligence in autistic children even though follow-up studies have tended to substantiate the predictive quality of such measures. Although the range of IQ scores is very wide, the profile is more notable for its pattern of strengths and weaknesses. Typically, there are relative strengths in non-language-based skills such as visuospatial abilities. This pattern is, however, more complex, and the central cognitive deficit that defines autism is inadequately defined. It does appear that autistic children have a deficit in abstracting information that is necessary for sequencing material and then transforming this information into symbolic representation. As stated earlier, there is argument between the cognitive theorists on the primary source of dysfunction, namely language, social cognition, or the affective systems. The latter is of importance because psychological testing can be severely affected by motivational and attentional factors. Whatever the appropriate theory, neuropsychological findings consistently reflect the marked differential skills.

Differential Diagnosis

Although a number of disorders may resemble autism in certain ways, they rarely cause significant diagnostic difficulty. More problematical is the value and difficulty in separating mentally retarded children with significant autistic features from infantile autism. Similarly, the designation of such diagnostic categories as Asperger's syndrome, schizoid personality, borderline disorder, and symbiotic psychosis has not been determined. Essentially, children who have been described in these categories all function in the higher intellectual range.

Some further classification of the range of pervasive developmental disorders may be required. For example, Asperger's syndrome is typified by many of the behavioral features of infantile autism and marked abnormalities in motor development but much less severe language disability. In this example, there is also a clinical overlap with disorders described in the neurologic literature that may relate to neuropsychological deficits (either developmental or due to brain damage) that are assumed to associate with localized cortical dysfunction, probably in the nondominant hemisphere (e.g., developmental dyspraxia or clumsy child syndrome, right hemisphere deficit syndrome).

Most workers involved in the classification of autistic disorders, however, do not feel that there are important distinctions between these different syndromes and suggest that higher-functioning autistic persons resemble the description of these other disorders too closely. It is therefore presumed that most children with psychotic-like disorders that are not degenerative can be adequately grouped by the early/autistic and late/schizophrenic dichotomy. Certain other clinical disorders should be considered in differential diagnosis.

Rett's syndrome (Olsson and Rett 1987) is a degenerative neurologic disorder that affects only females. There is a slow progressive deterioration of acquired behavioral, social, motor, and communication skills from 18 months of age. Classic symptoms include handwringing stereotypies, gait disorder, truncal apraxia, and deceleration of head growth. By age 11 years, severe spasticity and akinesia are apparent. In the toddler years, an incorrect diagnosis of infantile autism is commonly made. The cause is unknown.

Progressive disintegrative psychosis (Corbett et al. 1977) is characterized by normal development for the first few years of life followed by a gradual loss of social and language skills, often accompanied by overactivity and stereotypic, and possibly psychotic, symptoms (hallucinations, delusions). Typically, there is a progressive dementing process that commonly leads to death. Causes include a number of neurodegenerative processes (e.g., storage diseases), often not accurately diagnosed until after death.

Developmental language disorders are disorders of the acquisition of language and are generally subclassified by the nature of speech problems (e.g., receptive, expressive, or motor disorders). Although some social difficulties may be apparent, children with these disorders wish to communicate, interact, and play with peers. Recent work has proven that children who have central processing language deficits have an extremely high rate of psychiatric disturbance that covers the full spectrum of clinical diagnoses.

Mental retardation provides a major diagnostic difficulty, particularly among the severely mentally retarded, who often do not develop the cognitive ability for imaginative skills and may have stereotypic behaviors. Sociability is usually the key clinical feature that helps differentiate global mental retardation from the specific deficits that characterize autism.

Sensory impairment, the early behavior of children with congenital or early-onset blindness or deafness can cause diagnostic difficulties, but careful assessment of social, communicative, and cognitive skills helps differentiate these disorders from autism.

Developmental disorders of motor and/or visuospatial skills may cause social problems, and the overlap with Asperger's syndrome has been mentioned. Most children with these problems, however, do not show gross deficits of an autistic nature.

Elective mutism is a disorder in which children are mute in certain situations but may talk in other environments, usually at home. Occasionally, minor speech disorders are present, and the child may appear withdrawn. Clinical evaluation should easily rule out autism.

Psychosocial deprivation refers to children raised in deprived, hostile, or institutional environments and who show characteristic patterns of abnormal behavior, regression, and failure to grow. Environmental manipulations often lead to significant improvement. In addition, infants who have developed normally can show a reversible but specific depressive reaction if separated from their parents or major caregiver. This may resemble, but is rarely confused with, an autistic regression.

Other psychiatric syndromes that share clinical characteristics with autism include hyperactivity (attention-deficit disorder), Tourette's syndrome, and obsessional disorders. The first two disorders may coexist with autism, but opinion differs on whether older, higher-functioning autistic adolescents have true obsessional symptoms or merely more elaborate repetitive routines.

Treatment

Unfortunately, despite many enthusiastic claims, a major breakthrough in treatment of infantile autism has not yet materialized. Some therapies, such as megavitamin treatment, physical or sensory stimulation, and dietary interventions have produced considerable public interest, but none of these has received scientific scrutiny. There has been recent interest in the degree of success that can be achieved by very early (under 3 years) intensive behavioral and educational programming, which includes parent training to provide virtually 24-hour intervention. This approach, which is a sophistication of the only proven beneficial treatments, has produced claims that as many as two thirds of the treated children can be placed in regular school programs by second or third grade, with highly significant improvement in IQ scores as compared with control groups (e.g., Lovaas 1987). However, these findings have also been criticized for possible selection biases and exaggeration of the degree of clinical improvement.

PHARMACOTHERAPY

There is no evidence that drug treatment can alter the basic autistic disorder. A number of drugs have been shown to improve some aspects of the disorder, for example, reducing tension, overactivity, stereotypies, and sleep disturbance. Such medications include phenothiazines, butyrophenones, and tricyclic antidepressants, as well as more experimental therapies such as vitamin B_6 in pharmacologic doses (200 to 500 g daily in combination with vitamin B-complex supplement) and folate supplement, which has been particularly advocated for children with fragile X syndrome.

Following the finding of raised serotonin levels in autistic children, treatment with fenfluramine has been intensively studied. This drug reduces serotonin levels, but any positive effects appear unrelated to this property, and its benefits for some children resemble the psychostimulant effect on hyperactive children. In addition, studies have shown a number of unpleasant side effects (e.g., irritability, bowel problems, insomnia), and the drug has been claimed to have neurotoxic effects.

In the adolescent years, pharmacotherapy may become more crucial, particularly for the children who show deterioration. Major tranquilizers may be required for behavioral disturbance; antidepressant treatment may help mood-related symptoms; and for periodic disorders, lithium carbonate or carbamazepine may be considered. Propranolol has reduced severe aggressive behavior disorders in some autistic adolescents.

STRUCTURED BEHAVIORAL PROGRAMMING AND EDUCATION

This is clearly the most effective intervention, and the best models provide appropriate, structured educational services in combination with a supportive, behaviorally based counseling for parents to implement similar intervention at home. Goals include increasing useful communication and socialization and reduction of inappropriate, maladaptive, or stereotypic behaviors. There has been disagreement about the appropriate use of reinforcing procedures (i.e., should punishment be included), and most programs accentuate positive reinforcements (e.g., food, praise) with intensive intervention to eliminate the abnormal behaviors that often occur when the child is not stimulated. Newer ideas have included integrating autistic children with their normal peers at school in an attempt to reduce their overall abnormal environment.

OTHER TREATMENTS

Social skills programming despite its logical application has not been very successful, but some workers are trying treatment approaches that help autistic children integrate their obvious possession of social skills (smiling, eye contact, verbal responses) with the appropriate social setting. Alternatively, approaches have been tried to modify the child's environment so that they receive more appropriate demands for and reinforcement of existing skills. Some schools have, therefore, accentuated the individual autistic child's strengths (e.g., music or art), in accompaniment with physical therapies and specially trained teachers and healthy peers to provide a very different and less structured program. The benefits of these approaches have not been adequately studied.

LATE-ONSET (SCHIZOPHRENIC) PSYCHOSES OF CHILDHOOD

The classic phenomenologic symptoms of psychosis (hallucinations, delusions, thought disorder) are clearly observable in children as young as 5 years of age. Although these phenomena are relatively easily distinguished from such age-specific and normal ideas as imaginary playmates or fear of monsters, their prognostic and diagnostic significance is less clear. For example, as many as 5% of the children referred to child psychiatrists report experiencing hallucinations (usually auditory), but the accompanying diagnoses are very varied. It appears that normal or retarded children may hallucinate secondary to chronic deprivation or severe stress or in accompaniment with anxiety or depression (Burke et al. 1985).

It is proposed that children with nonpsychotic illnesses can be differentiated from youngsters with psychotic disorders because the former's psychopathology is coherent, understandable, and congruent with their circumstances. Interestingly, there is some evidence that nonpsychotic hallucinating children have relatively high familial rates of psychosis. Whatever the underlying diagnosis, mood changes are relatively common in children who experience hallucinations, and childhood suicide attempters frequently experience command hallucinations. In studies of depressed children, between 18% and 40% report hallucinations (Freeman et al. 1985). Historically, many of these children would have been considered schizophrenic, but increasing interest in affective and anxiety disorders of childhood has helped delineate other psychotic or psychotic-like conditions. Affective, anxiety, and stress-related disorders are discussed elsewhere in this text.

From the time that schizophrenia (or dementia praecox) was first delineated at the beginning of this century, it was suggested that a very small number of these disorders had their origin in the prepubescent years (Kraepelin 1919). Indeed, as research focused on childhood psychosis, it became apparent that after excluding children with autistic conditions, there was a group of children with schizophrenic-like psychoses, often beginning in the so-called latency period of childhood development. Study of these children has lagged far behind that of autistic children, and this is reflected in the briefer presentation in this chapter. Because schizophrenia itself is an immense topic in adult psychiatry, no attempt is made to address this larger issue, but readers are suggested to review the appropriate texts.

Definition

Schizophrenic psychoses of childhood should logically fulfill the requirements for diagnoses that are applied to any age group. The important features are a deterioration from previous levels of functioning, the manifestation of florid psychotic symptoms, a prolonged history of disturbance (at least 6 months by the *DSM-III*), a lack of any predisposing organic or toxic cause for the psychopathology, and no evidence of marked affective (depressive or manic) symptoms (Table 16–3).

Although these criteria are reasonable for a schizophrenic diagnosis in adults, they are often less meaningful for children. For example, some researchers are unable to document a true deterioration, and more typically see a chronically disturbed child who begins to develop psychotic symptoms at 7 to 8 years of age, often in association with bizarre behavior and regression. Also, some children who have similarities to those called schizophrenic more typically resemble adult schizotypal or borderline personality disorders (i.e., only fleeting psychotic-like symptoms are seen in addition to age-inappropriate magical thinking, mood lability, social problems, and mild delusional phenomena). A number of centers are working on appropriate diagnostic criteria for these childhood disorders, but no separate definition has been published. DSM-III-R has made some minor changes to the diagnostic criteria for the active and prodromal symptoms of schizophrenia (A and C in Table 16–3) but also two specific statements that are relevant to childhood schizophrenia. The first is that for children and adolescents, the deterioration criteria can be adapted to a "failure to achieve expected level of social development" and second, that if there is a history of autistic disorder, an additional schizophrenic diagnosis should be made only if prominent delusions or hallucinations are also present.

Epidemiology

The exact incidence of childhood schizophrenia has not been determined. In the prepubescent years, the disorder is believed to be rarer than infantile autism and to predominate among boys. More problematic for definition or classification are reports that some autistic children develop schizophrenic illnesses (e.g., Petty et al. 1986). These reports have all been anecdotal and retrospective, and it is generally agreed that if such

Table 16–3. DIAGNOSTIC CRITERIA FOR SCHIZOPHRENIA

A. Presence of characteristic psychotic symptoms in the active phase: either (1), (2), or (3) for at least 1 week (unless the symptoms are successfully treated):
  1. Two of the following:
      a. Delusions
      b. Prominent hallucinations (throughout the day for several days or several times a week for several weeks, each hallucinatory experience not being limited to a few brief moments)
      c. Incoherence or marked loosening of associations
      d. Catatonic behavior
      e. Flat or grossly inappropriate affect
  2. Bizarre delusions (i.e., involving a phenomenon that the person's culture would regard as totally implausible, such as thought broadcasting, being controlled by a dead person)
  3. Prominent hallucinations [as defined in (1)(b) above] of a voice with content having no apparent relation to depression or elation, or a voice keeping up a running commentary on the person's behavior or thoughts, or two or more voices conversing with each other
B. During the course of the disturbance, functioning in such areas as work, social relations, and self-care is markedly below the highest level achieved before onset of the disturbance (or, when the onset is in childhood or adolescence, failure to achieve the expected level of social development).
C. Continuous signs of the disturbance for at least 6 months. The 6-month period must include an active phase (of at least 1 week, or less if symptoms have been successfully treated) during which there were psychotic symptoms characteristic of schizophrenia (symptoms in A), with or without a prodromal or residual phase, as defined below.

Prodromal phase: A clear deterioration in functioning before the active phase of the disturbance that is not due to a disturbance in mood or to a psychoactive substance use disorder and that involves at least two of the symptoms listed below.

Residual phase: Following the active phase of the disturbance, persistence of at least two of the symptoms noted below, these not being due to a disturbance in mood or to a psychoactive substance use disorder.

Prodromal or residual symptoms:
  1. Marked social isolation or withdrawal
  2. Marked impairment in role functioning as wage-earner, student, or homemaker
  3. Markedly peculiar behavior (e.g., collecting garbage, talking to self in public, hoarding food)
  4. Marked impairment in personal hygiene and grooming
  5. Blunted or inappropriate affect
  6. Digressive, vague, overelaborate, or circumstantial speech; poverty of speech or of content of speech
  7. Odd beliefs or magical thinking, influencing behavior and inconsistent with cultural norms, e.g., superstitiousness, belief in clairvoyance, telepathy, "sixth sense," "others can feel my feelings," overvalued ideas, ideas of reference
  8. Unusual perceptual experiences, e.g., recurrent illusions, sensing the presence of a force or person not actually present
  9. Marked lack of initiative, interests, or energy
D. It cannot be established that an organic factor initiated and maintained the disturbance.
E. If there is a history of autistic disorder, the additional diagnosis of schizophrenia is made only if prominent delusions or hallucinations are also present.

(Modified from American Psychiatric Association, 1987. *Diagnostic and Statistical Manual of Mental Disorders III-R.* Washington, D.C.: American Psychiatric Association.)

an illness progression does occur, it is extremely uncommon. However, clinical experience and some research suggests that prepubertal and pubertal schizophrenic disorders are often clinically and developmentally different. Whether this merely represents a factor of severity or increased genetic loading is unknown.

Etiology and Pathology

Given the rarity, diagnostic problems, and limited research into childhood schizophrenia, it is not surprising that there is little information on etiology and pathology. Two lines of research are of relevance. The first would consider that schizophrenia is a genetically determined disorder that can manifest at any age but the age at onset determines the type and severity of pathology. It is then assumed that a similar central disintegration of neurologic functioning is present in all schizophrenic subjects (Fish 1977). (For the advocates of this theory, infantile autism might be considered the most severe form of schizophrenia.)

Such a theory has had a reevaluation, partly because of continuing studies of childhood schizophrenics, but also because of work that describes the premorbid characteristics of adult schizophrenics (Nuechterlein 1986) and an awareness that schizophrenia might really be a developmental disturbance relating to brain damage occurring very early in life (Weinberger 1987). Overall, present research suggests that many childhood schizophrenics, children who are at genetic risk to become schizophrenic, and adult schizophrenics share the same abnormalities in specific attentional tasks, sensorimotor functioning (soft neurologic signs), social interaction and communication, and on measures of neurophysiological functioning (evoked potentials). These findings support the neurodevelopmental theory, which suggests that schizophrenia can manifest at any age.

A second approach would be to consider prepubertal schizophrenia as a separate entity. In this situation it would be likely that different organic abnormalities lead to the manifestation of psychosis. Such abnormalities may include an organic insult (e.g., viral infection) (Nunn et al. 1986), and there could be a clinical overlap with the disintegrative psychoses or pervasive developmental disorders. One researcher has suggested that the neurologic dysfunction in childhood schizophrenia may relate to a disorder in the cholinergic system (Cantor et al. 1980). The answers to these clinical and diagnostic issues await further study.

Clinical Picture and Course

Clinical descriptions of childhood schizophrenics (e.g., Kolvin, 1971; Green et al. 1984; Cantor et al. 1982) show that these children have very high rates of hallucinations, delusions, and thought disorder, and these are comparable between study groups. Equally, these symptoms can be as easily detected as they are in adult schizophrenics. However, the associated pathology and type of onset is often difficult to elicit from these papers. Despite many authors' claims that a deterioration from previous level of functioning is present, it is apparent that many of these children have marked social, motor, or speech impairments prior to the diagnosis of schizophrenia.

Eggers (1978) has provided the most complete description and follow-up of children diagnosed as schizophrenic. He studied 57 children (mean follow-up 15 years) aged 7 to 14 years with psychosis beginning after 5 years. Although a paranoid-hallucinatory state was the most common clinical picture, under the age of 10 years hallucinations were uncommon, "negative symptoms" were typical, and the prognosis was very poor. Negative symptoms included social isolation, diminished interests, stereotypy, hyperkinesis, severe emotional changes, speech disturbances, and often totally disinhibited behavior. When the disorder began after 10 years, over 50% showed recurrent illness with a favorable outcome. This was not necessarily related to the manic-depressive characteristics, which some of them exhibited. Eggers stated that all of these children had relatively normal development prior to the onset of their psychoses. The case histories attest to the different clinical pictures that can be seen in the early (before 10 years) and later (after 10 years) onset of schizophrenia. It is of interest to speculate whether these differences are related to the maturational process of puberty.

Case Histories

CASE 4

J. was a 9-year-old boy who was evaluated because of unusual behavior (e.g., purposely urinating on the eyes of his sister's teddy bear because he thought the bear was staring at him), abnormal affect with bouts of unprovoked laughter, inappropriate sexual activity with his peers (inserting crayons in their anus), aggressive behavior, and poor social functioning (essentially no interactive play).

Developmentally, J. was the product of a prolonged labor that led to a cesarean section. He required surgery for congenital abnormality of his genitourinary system and was noted to have significant delay in language development as well as early social problems. When speech began at 2 years, it was often echolalic, perseverating on his own peculiar interests, and, at times, robot-like.

At 5 years of age a formal evaluation revealed marked deficits in expressive and receptive language. At 6½ years of age, he was observed to be hyperactive and impulsive as well as encopretic. A trial of psychostimulants was ineffective. In special education settings, his communication skills were said to improve but his behavior was very peculiar, and this had clearly exacerbated in the few months prior to evaluation. Psychological testing revealed a verbal IQ (on WISC-R) of 69 with a performance IQ of 129. His speech was dysfluent, illogical, and not always related to current reality. Educational testing showed him to be functioning at a 6-year level in reading and math.

J. is from an intact family with a 3-year-old sister. This family had made numerous moves because of the father's employment. Neither parent had formal psychiatric illness. There was a history of alcoholism in paternal grandparents, and the grandmother had been hospitalized for a "nervous breakdown." A maternal cousin had a seizure disorder, and a maternal aunt had been treated for anorexia nervosa, which was later followed by hospitalization for bipolar affective disorder.

On examination, J. was a mildly overweight boy who looked his age. Initially in the interview he was appropriately, but softly spoken. However, he would rapidly become more strange, with his affect ranging from flat or bland to inappropriate bouts of laughter, even when talking of unpleasant events. His eye contact was poor. His thought processes were impoverished, illogical, and tangential. He would admit to paranoid ideas (e.g., persons or toys staring at him) and auditory command hallucinations (e.g., voices telling him to set fires). He would talk of strange and silly ideas. He often said that he took his "red brain out of his head and tasted it." He also talked excessively of sexual acts, particularly oriented toward his sister.

On inpatient evaluation, he appeared restless and somewhat isolated. If stimulation increased, he became extremely active and impulsive. Around peers, he was antagonistic and provocative. Full physical, neurologic, serologic, electroencephalographic and computed tomographic brain scan studies were negative. Experimental neuroendocrine studies revealed possible evidence of hypothalamic pituitary dysfunction (exaggerated thyrotropin response to thyrotropin releasing hormone stimulation and no response to luteinizing hormone–releasing hormone stimulation).

Pharmacologic intervention associated with behavioral modification produced only limited change. Haloperidol, fluphenazine, lithium carbonate, and amitriptyline were ineffective in altering the psychotic symptomatology. A major tranquilizer, loxapine (which is a dibenzoxazepine), at 50 mg daily, had a more beneficial effect behaviorally and cognitively. However, shortly after discharge and placement in a day hospital, J. developed orofacial dyskinesia and this medication had to be withdrawn. The clinical picture has remained essentially unchanged, and consideration is being given to a long-term residential placement.

CASE 5

R. was a 13-year-old postpubertal girl who had exhibited a 6-month deterioration in functioning that initially consisted of avoidance of group activities, deterioration in school performance, and refusal to complete school assignments. Later she began to refuse to prepare herself for school, and for 6 weeks she had exhibited even more unusual behavior. She would sit, laughing for no apparent reason, and appear to be listening to something. She felt people watched her and laughed at her. She believed she smelled and took numerous showers. Within the family, she became increasingly hostile, particularly toward her younger sister. Her handwriting deteriorated. She wrote notes to her friends remarking on her persecution and torment. A few days prior to admission to a psychiatric hospital, she suddenly refused to enter the bathroom, believing that she was being spied on from outside. She gradually became increasingly upset and tearful, talked of God and the Devil speaking to her, and wished to die to end her persecution.

R. was the product of a liaison her mother had outside the marriage while separated from her husband. R. was, therefore, a half-sister to three of her siblings (30-year-old brother, 28-year-old sister, 26-year-old brother) and had a full sister 1 year younger than herself. R.'s mother later reconciled with her husband. The mother was a high school graduate. She was overtalkative, bossy, and irritable with R. The maternal grandmother had received psychiatric treatment. The natural father was a convert to fundamentalist religion who lived with his own family in another state. He was not in contact with R. The step-father was a railroad foreman who seemed calm and appropriate in managing the family situation.

Although the birth history was unremarkable, R. had respiratory problems at 2 weeks of age, which almost led to a crib death. She was cyanotic and required resuscitation. In a nonspecific way, she had always been considered "weak" and sensitive. For example, she required to be walked to sleep throughout her toddler years. She had been placed on tranquilizers for hyperactivity from 18 months to 4 years. There were no reported delays in development, and R. was a competent student prior to her illness. However, she had appeared less mature and "sillier" compared with her peers. Psychological testing (after her illness began) revealed a WISC-R full-scale IQ of 90 with verbal and performance scales identical at 91.

Examination of her mental state showed a tall, heavy 13-year-old girl with a slow, rigid gait and an air of confusion. Affect was mostly flat, but she had bouts of inappropriate giggling. Her thought patterns showed marked blocking, but other than a slow and deliberate speech she did not exhibit other thought disorders. She described numerous psychotic symptoms. She felt controlled by God and the Devil, and believed she was being watched. She had auditory, olfactory, tactile, and possibly visual hallucinations. She believed thoughts were inserted into her head and that others would read her mind. The only significant physical findings were orthopedic abnormalities (thoracic kyphosis, lumbar lordosis, spina bifida occulta).

Pharmacologic therapy with haloperidol significantly reduced the psychotic phenomena, and behavioral management techniques were used to address continuing unusual behaviors secondary to her delusional ideas. Because of extrapyramidal side effects, pharmacotherapy was changed to trifluoperazine. On discharge from the hospital, R. continued to have a flat affect and occasional psychotic experiences. In addition, family stresses were apparent. She was referred to a therapist who focused on these family problems and withdrew the medication. R. rapidly returned to her earlier psychotic state and did not respond at the time of follow-up to reinstitution of neuroleptic therapy.

Physical and Laboratory Findings

The most important aspect of laboratory work is to exclude any treatable neurologic or toxic condition that could lead to psychotic symptoms. Some of the investigations would be indicated by history and physical examination, but full hematologic, serologic, neurophysiologic, and neuroradiologic studies are required. Although abnormalities on psychological testing may be present (possibly due to the poor attention and disorganization), most schizophrenic children have IQ scores in the normal or dull-normal range.

Differential Diagnosis

The major differential diagnoses are between transient (stress-related) psychotic states, organic psychoses (including substance-induced disorder), seizure disorder (e.g., psychomotor, petit mal status), affective disorder, pervasive developmental disorder, or atypical personality development (e.g., schizoid or schizotypal).

Treatment

Little is known about outcome and treatment. Clinical experience suggests that the neuroleptics do not have dramatic effect on the schizophrenic psychoses in prepubescence. However, they are often required for behavioral control. Occasionally, trials of lithium or carbamazepine can be considered when mood changes are marked. In adolescent psychoses, the treatment responses are more typical of adult schizophrenia.

Given the degree of disturbance, consideration must be given to school placement, family support and intervention, structured behavioral intervention, and individual therapy, which may need to focus on impulse control and anxiety reduction. Many children require specialized residential settings because their behavior problems are not manageable in home or school. Both Eggers' work and clinical reports suggest that there can be some stabilization of the disorder in late adolescence and young adulthood, although continuing pharmacologic and psychologic interventions are usually required.

References

Infantile Autism

Cohen, D. J., Donnellan, A. M., and Paul, R. (eds.). 1987. Handbook of Autism and Pervasive Developmental Disorders. New York: John Wiley & Sons.

Cohen, D. J., and Volkmar, F. R. (eds.). 1986. Special

Section: Issues in the diagnosis and phenomenology of the pervasive developmental disorders. *J. Am. Acad. Child Psychiatry* 25:158–220.

Coleman, M., and Gillberg, C. 1985. *The Biology of the Autistic Syndrome.* New York: Praeger.

Corbett, J., Harris, R., Taylor, E., and Trimble, M. 1977. Progressive disintegrative psychosis of childhood. *J. Child Psychol. Psychiatry* 18:211–219.

Eisenberg, L., and Kanner, L. 1956. Early infantile autism 1943–55. *Am. J. Orthopsychiatry* 26:556–566.

Fein, D., Braverman, M., Pennington, B., et al. 1986. Toward a neuropsychological model of infantile autism: Are the social deficits primary? *J. Am. Acad. Child Psychiatry* 25:198–212.

Kanner, L. 1943. Autistic disturbances of affective contact. *Nervous Child* 2:217–250.

Olsson, B., and Rett, A. 1987. Autism and Rett syndrome: Behavioral investigation and differential diagnosis. *Dev. Med. Child Neurol.* 29:429–441.

Rumsey, J. M., Rapoport, J. L., and Sceery, W. R. 1985. Autistic children as adults: Psychiatric, social and behavioral outcomes. *J. Am. Acad. Child Psychiatry* 24:465–473.

Rutter, M., and Schopler, E. 1987. Autism and pervasive developmental disorders: Concepts and diagnostic issues. *J. Autism Dev. Dis.* 17:159–186.

Rutter, M. 1983. Cognitive deficits in the pathogenesis of autism. *J. Child Psychol. Psychiatry* 24:513–531.

Rutter, M. 1985. The treatment of autistic children. *J. Child Psychol. Psychiatry* 26:193–214.

Rutter, M., and Lockyer, L. 1967. A five to fifteen year follow-up study of infantile psychosis: I. Description of sample. *Br. J. Psychiatry* 113:1169–1182.

Rutter, M., Greenfield, D., and Lockyer, L. 1967. A five- to fifteen-year follow-up study of infantile psychosis: II. Social and behavioral outcome. *Br. J. Psychiatry* 113:1183–1199.

Childhood Schizophrenia

Cantor, S., Evans, J., Pearce, J., and Pezzot-Peace, T. 1982. Childhood schizophrenia present but not accounted for. *Am. J. Psychiatry* 139:758–762.

Eggers, C. 1978. Course and prognosis of childhood schizophrenia. *J. Autism Childhood Schizophrenia* 8:21–36.

Fish, B. 1977. Neurobiologic antecedents of schizophrenia in children. *Arch. Gen. Psychiatry* 36:1297–1313.

Green, W. H., Campbell, M., Hardesty, A. S., et al. 1984. A comparison of schizophrenic and autistic children. *J. Am. Acad. Child Psychiatry* 23:399–409.

Kolvin, L., Ounsted, C., Humphrey, M., and McNay, A. 1971. Studies in the childhood psychoses: II. The phenomenology of childhood psychoses. *Br. J. Psychiatry* 118:385–395.

Tanguay, P. E., and Cantor, S. L. (eds.). 1986. Special Section: Schizophrenia in childhood. *J. Am. Acad. Child Psychiatry* 25:591–630.

Other References

American Psychiatric Association. 1987. *Diagnostic and Statistical Manual of Mental Disorders,* 3rd. ed., revised. Washington, D.C.: American Psychiatric Association.

Bleuler, E. 1911. *Dementia Praecox in the Group of Schizophrenias.* Vienna. 1911. Zimkin, J. (trans.). 1950. New York: International University Press.

Bregman, J. D., Dykens, E., Watson, M., et al. 1987. Fragile-X syndrome: Variability of phenotypic expression. *J. Am. Acad. Child Adolesc. Psychiatry* 26:463–471.

Burke, P., Del Vaccaro, H., McCauley, E., and Clark, C. 1985. Hallucinations in children. *J. Am. Acad. Child Psychiatry* 24:71–75.

Cantor, S., Trevenen, C., Posturia, R., et al. 1980. Is childhood schizophrenia a cholinergic disease? *Arch. Gen. Psychiatry* 37:658–667.

Courchesne, E., Yeung-Courchesne, R., Press, G. A., et al. 1988. Hypoplasia of cerebellar vermal lobules VI and VII in autism. *N. Eng. J. Med.* 318:1349–1354.

Freeman, L. N., Poznanski, E. O., Grossman, J. A., et al. 1985. Psychotic and depressed children: A new entity. *J. Am. Acad. Child Psychiatry* 24:95–102.

Gaffney, G. R., Kuperman, S., Tsai, L. Y., et al. 1987. Mid-saggital magnetic resonance imaging of autism. *Br. J. Psychiatry* 151:831–833.

Konstantareas, M., Hauser, P., Lennox, C., and Homatidis, S. 1986. Season of birth in infantile autism. *Child Psychiat. Hum. Dev.* 17:53–65.

Kraepelin, E. 1919. *Dementia Praecox and Paraphrenia.* Translated by R. M. Barclay from the 8th German edition of the *Textbook of Psychiatry.* Edinburgh: Livingstone.

Lovaas, O. I. 1987. Behavioral treatment and normal education and intellectual functioning in young autistic children. *J. Consult. Clin. Psychol.* 55:3–9.

Nuechterlein, K. H. 1986. Childhood precursors of adult schizophrenia. *J. Child Psychol. Psychiatry* 27:133–144.

Nunn, K. P., Lask, B., and Cohen, M. 1986. Viruses, neurodevelopmental disorder and childhood psychosis. J. Child Psychol. Psychiatry 27:55–64.

Petty, L. K., Ornitz, E. M., Michelman, J. P., and Zimmerman, E. G. 1986. Autistic children who become schizophrenic. *Arch. Gen. Psychiatry* 41:129–135.

Ritvo, E. R., Creel, D., Realmuto, G., et al. 1988. Electroretinograms in autism: A pilot study of b-wave amplitude. *Am. J. Psychiatry* 145:229–232.

Weinberger, D. R. 1987. Implication of normal brain development for the pathogenesis of schizophrenia. *Arch. Gen. Psychiatry* 44:660–669.

17

Mental Retardation

PETER E. TANGUAY, M.D.

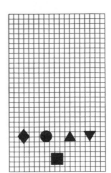

Child psychiatrists, trained as they are in understanding developmental issues, have an important and specific professional responsibility to persons who are mentally retarded. The child psychiatrist should be fully prepared to evaluate, diagnose, and recommend treatment for mental disorders in retarded persons. Why then, do few child psychiatrists feel comfortable with the notion of diagnosing and treating persons who are retarded? There may be many reasons for this, among which are the myths and misconceptions that persons often hold about the mentally retarded: the "retarded" cannot learn, they lack the capacity to feel lonely or depressed, they have very different aspirations and hopes from you or I, or they are incapable of enjoying life.

A more cogent reason why a child psychiatrist might hesitate to evaluate and treat retarded persons is the fact that very few child psychiatrists learn much about the manifestations and treatment of mental illness in mentally retarded persons during their training. Those child psychiatry trainees who meet retarded persons often do so in sterile, long-term hospitals for the profoundly retarded. Today, however, following the trend of deinstitutionalization of the 1960s and 1970s, most mild and many moderately retarded persons reside at home or in residential settings in the community. The emotional needs of these persons are, for the most part, similar to those of the general population. They are even more susceptible to the same psychiatric disorders as nonretarded per-

sons. In mildly retarded persons the signs and symptoms of psychiatric disorders are not particularly different from those described in the *Diagnostic and Statistical Manual of Mental Disorders*, third edition, revised *(DSM-III-R)* (American Psychiatric Association 1987) and, like normal disorders, can be effectively treated. The usual diagnostic criteria may require modification for use with moderately and severely retarded persons, and in some instances (notably schizophrenia) it may be difficult to decide if the patient actually suffers from the disorder.

Many professionals serve the needs of retarded persons, including social workers, employment counselors, rehabilitation therapists, teachers, psychologists, pediatricians, speech pathologists, and child psychiatrists. In general, the child psychiatrist does not provide services aimed at helping retarded persons learn to live in the community or reach their maximum potential. The child psychiatrist should be a consultant in regard to the diagnosis and treatment of mental illness. His or her services are offered to the retarded person, sometimes at the latter's request, but usually at the request of those who provide the retarded person's everyday care, including parents, guardians, or members of other professional disciplines.

The goal of this chapter will be to present answers to the questions of who are the retarded, what are their mental health problems, and how are these problems best treated. Because few psychiatrists have been active in working with retarded persons in the past several decades, there is still much to be learned about the manifestations of mental illness in retarded persons, especially in the moderately and severely mentally handicapped. Scientific studies of mental disorders started in the field of general psychiatry long before they did in the field of child psychiatry. Now that more studies are being carried out in child psychiatry, we can hope that in the next decade or so we will see a movement in this direction in the field of developmental disability.

WHO ARE THE MENTALLY RETARDED?

Severe mental retardation has, of course, been known for thousands of years, but it is only in the past 100 years that society has become particularly interested in identifying persons who have milder forms of the disorder. In the days when few persons went to school for many years and most jobs required few intellectual skills (such as reading or writing), mild or even moderate degrees of intellectual handicap were not likely to be noticed. In the latter half of the 19th century, universal education became more of a reality and educators could not avoid observing that there was a fairly wide range of talent for learning classroom materials. In the early 1900s the French Government commissioned Binet and Simon to construct tests that would enable the educational authorities to identify those students who would be unlikely to benefit from the regular course of instruction in school. From this work came the first "intelligence test." Within very few years the test developed by Binet and Simon had been translated and standardized for use in the United States and other English-language countries and many more instruments were designed for a similar purpose.

The concept of mental retardation can be quite difficult to define, or, more to the point, it can easily be oversimplified and misunderstood. The definition provided in 1977 by the American Association on Mental Deficiency (AAMD) (Grossman 1977) is a widely accepted point of departure in discussing the subject:

Mental retardation refers to *significantly subaverage general intellectual functioning* existing concurrently with *deficits in adaptive behavior* and manifested *during the developmental period*.

Significantly Subaverage Intellectual Functioning

One of the most important questions in the field of intelligence testing in the past 50 years has been how to measure human "intellectual functioning." Intellectual functioning is an extremely complicated matter. Historically, intellectual functioning has been defined as the ability to learn or to profit from experience, to reason, and through reasoning to adapt to novel situations. But when one begins to study how persons go about this, one appreciates how poorly we understand how this takes place. An early attempt to describe intellectual development was made by Piaget. Although his ideas have been much refined by cognitive psychologists in the past 2 decades (see Flavell and Markman 1983), Piaget recognized the intellectual operations of children appeared to represent a set of different skills, each qualitatively quite different from the other; the degree to which the child was capable of using the various skills varied with age and experience. The youngest children, those below 18 months of age, appeared to solve problems largely through what Piaget termed *sensorimotor* operations. These were largely trial-and-error attempts to solve problems through motor activity guided by feedback from the senses. The children did not appear to "think out" a solution "in their head" as they would come to do increasingly well after 18 months of age. Beyond 18 months of age Piaget noted that children began to exhibit a capacity for "internal operations," including symbolic representation and, eventually, rational thought. Between 2 and 7 years of age, Piaget noted that children's thought was illogical and inconsistent; only after 7 years of age did logical cause-and-effect and syllogistic thinking become evident. It has been argued elsewhere (Tanguay 1987) that what Piaget described as "preoperational" thinking in the child younger than 7 years appears to be similar to what has been called "gestalt" operations by modern neuropsychologists, in which what one perceives leads to an immediate understanding, without further logical operations being invoked. An example of such a gestalt operation would be facial recognition. A parallel example from Piaget would be if one pours water from a short, wide container to a tall, narrow one, the water appears to have changed in volume, even though an algebraic tall by wide solution would give a different (and logically correct) solution. The algebraic solution of the latter example may be similar to what neuropsychologists have termed *sequential thought*. Thus, in the Piagetian scheme, there is evidence of three distinct types of intellectual operations: sensorimotor, gestalt, and logical (sequential). Although Piaget believed that children do not use logical operations much before 7 years of age, later work has demonstrated that the capacity to think logically may be seen, at least in rudimentary form, as early as 4 years of age (see Flavell and Markman 1983). This is hardly surprising since 4-year-old children are already beginning to master the grammar of language, which is itself a "sequential" code.

More recently, information-processing theorists have added new dimensions to understanding intellectual functioning, both in normal and retarded persons (Sternberg and Gardner 1982). The latter describe intellectual functioning as composed of several components. There are executive components for "sizing up" a situation, considering alternatives, and planning a response. There are performance components that retrieve information items from memory, compare them with other relevant items, note the possible higher and lower correlations between items ("A" and "a" are physically different but represent the same alphabetical letter), select the correct meaning, compare options, justify the choice, and respond. Additional components acquire and encode new information in memory and allow information to be "generalized" from one situation to another. The model is highly theoretical and subject to change, but it illustrates the complexity of the operations that are called intellectual functioning.

There is another aspect of human endeavor that is extremely important to the question of intellectual performance. This aspect is motivation. Motivation may be as important to individual test performance as previously learned information and basic intellectual skills.

Intelligence tests do not tell us very much about intelligence. They measure a selected set of skills, not all of which may fully encompass intellectual functioning to the same degree. In general, modern intelligence tests measure such things as rote knowledge, perceptual-motor (gestalt) skills, and logical op-

erations. As such, they are adequate for measuring intellectual functioning in a general way. Their greatest strength is that the most popular tests have been well normed on representative populations of the dominant culture. These norms may not apply to other populations, however.

Three intelligence tests most used in assessing retarded adults and children are the Wechsler Adult Intelligence Scales (WAIS), the Wechsler Intelligence Scales for Children—Revised (WISC-R; age range, 6 to 16 years), and the revised Stanford-Binet (age range, 2 to 18 years). The Stanford-Binet yields a single composite IQ score and mental age score; the Wechsler scales yield both verbal and performance IQ and mental age scores, as well as a number of individual subtest scores within each of the latter domains.

Tests of intellectual capacity do not, in and of themselves, define who should be diagnosed as mentally retarded. In order to classify persons in terms of their intellectual skills so that decisions can be made in regard to placement into special school programs, cut-points (below which a person is classified as retarded) must be devised. In practice, these cut-points have almost always been stated in statistical terms. It was recommended by the AAMD (Grossman 1977) that subjects scoring more than 2 standard deviations below the mean on one or other of the usual intelligence tests would be officially classified as retarded; degrees of increasing handicap would be further defined by increasingly large standard deviation scores. A similar definition was adopted by both the *DSM-III* and the *DSM-III-R*. An example of this is shown in Table 17–1 for the Wechsler scales. Several very important facts should be stated about Table 17–1. The first is that the vast majority of retarded persons (the percentages in the third column are derived from the report of the President's Commission on Mental Retardation; see Grossman 1977) are no more

Table 17–1. CLASSIFICATION OF MENTALLY RETARDED BY IQ SCORES		
Level of Retardation	Wechsler Scores	Approximate Percent of Retarded Population
Mild	55–69	89
Moderate	40–54	7
Severe	25–39	3
Profound	0–24	1

than mildly retarded. Persons who fall within the mild category are capable of learning considerable self-help and social skills. Those scoring in the upper end of this range should be able to be employed in nontechnical work, that is, if they do not have an untreated mental illness such as an affective disorder or are not victims of community prejudice. Second, the cutoff points (2 SD, 3 SD, 4 SD below the mean) are purely arbitrary choices. The upper cutoff point could just as well have been 1.5 SD or 2.5 SD. In fact, in an earlier version of the AAMD definition the upper cutoff point was 1 SD and an additional category of borderline retardation existed above the mild level. This effectively classified 16% of the American population (32 million at the time) as retarded. This was considered unreasonable, and the category of borderline was dropped. A third point that should be understood is that the IQ scores that represent the standard deviation cutoff points are different between IQ tests. For the Stanford-Binet, the mild range is represented by IQ scores between 52 and 67, a slightly lower set than for the Wechsler scale.

For the psychiatrist, the question of specific IQ scores is of less importance than it might be for a school administrator, who may be required to apply a set of fixed criteria in determining who receives what service. The psychiatrist will understand the score as a general indication of the person's developmental level, knowing that the person may have certain useful social skills not measured by the IQ test, that the person's performance in the outside world might be enhanced by a high level of motivation, and that the score may underrepresent capacity in someone whose sociocultural background is different from those for whom the tests were normed.

Deficits in Adaptive Behavior

This second criterion of the AAMD (Grossman 1977) and *DSM-III-R* definitions of retardation takes into account that IQ score alone, especially if that score is in the mild range, may be an inadequate representation of how a person will adapt to home, school, or workplace. In addition to the factors listed previously, which may decrease the validity of the IQ score, there are skills that are either poorly measured or not measured at all by

intelligence tests but that may play an important role in the degree to which one is able to function in society. One of the more important of these are social-communication skills. From a linguistic viewpoint, these skills, which are called pragmatic and prosodic functioning, are quite different from the skills of what linguistically is considered semantic and syntactic discourse. Syntactic discourse is defined as the capacity to learn the words that make up a language and the ability to learn to understand or convey meaning using grammatical constructs. Pragmatic skills comprise the social rules that govern language—the ability to sense what another person may be trying to convey in conversation, to tailor one's utterances to fit in with this topic, and to smoothly enter a conversation and engage in turn-taking behavior. Prosodic skills involve the melody of speech—the ability to encode information by changes in tone, tempo, rate, and rhythm of speech. Unfortunately, it is only recently that attention has been turned to the latter topics, and there are as yet few studies of prosodic or pragmatic functioning in mentally retarded persons (see Mundy et al 1985). Study of referential communication (describing elements in a visual display to another speaker from whom the display is hidden) indicate that mentally retarded children and adolescents may be fairly adept at understanding a referential message when they receive it from a normal subject. They do poorly, however, as senders of messages to normal subjects. Also, in ordinary conversation, moderately and severely retarded persons are often relatively passive listeners, seldom asking for clarification or modification of ambiguous material. The authors commented that this may be as much a function of social constraints learned by the retarded person as it is a function of cognitive deficit.

Other important adaptive functions include self-help skills of daily living and knowledge of social routines. Testing adaptive functioning has a short history compared to testing intelligence. At present there are several tests that are used for this purpose, although none is accepted with the degree of enthusiasm and confidence currently accorded the leading intelligence tests. They do not, for the most part, test for specific pragmatic or prosodic social-communication skills, but there are a few linguistic tests that do. Two popular instruments for measuring adaptive functioning are the AAMD Adaptive Behavior Scale for Children and Adults (Nihira et al. 1974) for persons with a mental age of 7 or older and the AAMD Adaptive Behavior Scale for Infancy and Early Childhood (Nihira et al. 1974) for those with a mental age of younger than 7 years. The 1975 version of the Adaptive Behavior scales is divided into two parts. Part I measures 10 behavioral domains necessary for independent life: independent functioning, physical development, economic activity, language development, numbers and time, domestic activity, vocational activity, self-direction, responsibility, and socialization. Part II measures 14 domains focusing on maladaptive behavior.

Despite the good intentions of the multi-dimensional definitions of retardation, it must be admitted that whether someone is labeled as retarded is much more likely to depend on his or her IQ scores than on anything else. Experience teaches that research investigators, social service agencies, hospitals, and clinics continue to use IQ tests as the sole instrument in determining intellectual capacity. Use of adaptive scales is more likely to be found in rehabilitation settings and good residential facilities. Use of an adaptive behavioral screen is important for epidemiologists who wish to measure the prevalence of mental retardation in the general population. Without such an additional screen, the prevalence, based solely on IQ scores, would be overestimated by 100% or more, as will be shown in the section on epidemiology.

ETIOLOGY AND PATHOGENESIS

Only with the introduction of modern genetic techniques and the availability of neurochemical analysis in the late 1950s and 1960s have science researchers begun to unravel a few of the complex biological factors that result in mental retardation. The landmark discovery that Down's syndrome is a result of an identifiable chromosome anomaly was made in 1959, which emphasizes how new our study is of the subject. A few of the chromosome anomalies, such as Down's syndrome and the sex-chromosome abnormalities, are found with sufficient frequency to be of practical clinical interest. Unlike phenylketonuria, many of the more

recently identified inborn errors of metabolism are extremely rare. We can expect that with the application of the techniques of developmental biology, an ever-greater number of putative causes of retardation will come to light in the form of small chromosome deletions or replications of neurodevelopmentally important sites. Each discovery is important in that it raises the possibility for future prevention through prenatal intrauterine diagnosis (although much more efficient methods of intrauterine screening will need to be found before it will be practical to identify very rare anomalies), and even, treatment through genetic engineering in the future. At present, the known genetic causes of mental retardation (including the inborn errors of metabolism) account for approximately 5% of all cases.

Genetic Factors

It is not within the scope of this chapter to present a detailed discussion of all of the currently known genetic causes of mental retardation and their clinical features. Readers interested in the topic should consult a more comprehensive and specialized text (Baroff 1986). A list of the most frequently found genetic syndromes associated with mental retardation is given in Table 17–2. There would perhaps be many more cases of retardation associated with genetic syndromes were it not that many chromosomal additions and deletions are fatal to the fetus.

Other Physical "Causes"

Many other factors have been implicated in the etiology of mental retardation (Table 17–3). While the majority of these factors may produce mental retardation, there are some that are less likely to do so unless they are present to a severe degree. In the aftermath of learning that one's child is mentally retarded, parents are emotionally shocked and their initial response (other than denying that the diagnosis may be correct) may be to try to "fix the blame" on some untoward event that may have occurred during pregnancy or at birth. Most premature children, even ones who are markedly so, do not become mentally retarded, nor do children who suffer mild episodes of anoxia at birth.

Table 17–2. MAJOR GENETIC SYNDROMES ASSOCIATED WITH MENTAL RETARDATION

Autosomal Chromosomes: Trisomies, Additions, Deletions

1. Down's Syndrome
   Frequency: 1 in 700 live births
   Anomaly: trisomy 21; translocation-15; mosaicism
   Degree of retardation: moderate to severe
   Additional features: skeletal, muscle, facial, joint and organ abnormalities, symptoms of Alzheimer's disease by age 30
2. Edwards' Syndrome
   Frequency: 1 in 5,000 live births
   Anomaly: trisomy 18
   Degree of retardation: severe
   Additional features: many skeletal and organ anomalies; 90% die within first 12 months
3. Cri-du-chat (cat cry)
   Frequency: unknown
   Anomaly: deletion of short arm of chromosome 5
   Degree of retardation: moderate to severe

Sex Chromosomes: Anomalies

1. XXY male (Kleinfelter's)
   Frequency: 1 in 600 live male births
   Anomaly: extra X chromosome (sometimes seen as XXYY, XXXY)
   Degree of retardation: low normal IQ to mild retardation
   Additional features: hypogonadism, enlarged breasts in adolescence
2. XYY males
   Frequency: 1 in 700 live male births
   Anomaly: extra Y chromosome
   Degree of retardation: not associated with retardation
   Additional features: tall stature, elbow abnormalities; increased impulsivity
3. XXX females
   Frequency: approximately 1 in 850 births
   Anomaly: extra X chromosome in females
   Degree of retardation: may or may not be present; the larger the number of extra X chromosomes, the more likely is there to be retardation.
4. XO female (Turner's)
   Frequency: 1 in 2,200 live female births
   Anomaly: absence of X chromosome in female
   Degree of retardation: not retarded, though may have some specific learning deficits in space–form perception
   Additional features: small stature and sexual infantilism; congenital heart disease; webbing of neck, elbow deformity
5. Fragile X syndrome
   Frequency: Estimated as 1 in 1,000 births
   Anomaly: a constriction near the end of the long arms of one X chromosome, with detachment of small pieces of chromosome; seen best when cells cultured in a folic acid–deficient growth medium
   Degree of retardation: in males, moderate retardation (though sometimes only mild); in females, usually mild retardation and sometimes no retardation
   Additional features: macro-orchidism in males

Gene Abnormality—Dominant Inheritance

1. Tuberous sclerosis
   Frequency: 1 in 200,000 or less
   Anomaly: specific gene abnormality not known
   Degree of retardation: mild to moderate in 60% of affected persons; normal IQ in 40%
   Additional features: in full-blown syndrome, butterfly rash on face, cerebral calcifications epilepsy
2. Neurofibromatosis
   Frequency: 1 in 3,000 births
   Anomaly: unknown gene abnormality
   Degree of retardation: Less than 25% mildly retarded, remainder normal
   Additional features: café-au-lait spots on skin, neurofibromas in central and peripheral nervous system, endocrine and growth disturbances

Gene Abnormality—Recessive Inheritance

1. Phenylketonuria (PKU)
   Frequency: approximately 1 in 11,500 with disorder, although as many as 1 in 54 may carry the defective gene
   Anomaly: deficiency of the enzyme phenylalanine hydroxylase needed for metabolism of phenylalanine to tyrosine
   Degree of retardation: severe to profound if untreated; if treated by diet beginning before 15 weeks of age, no retardation or mild degree of retardation may be found later.
2. Galactosemia
   Frequency: approximately 1 in 200,000 births
   Anomaly: inability to metabolize galactose, a constituent of milk
   Degree of retardation: no retardation if treated by diet
   Additional features: none
3. Lesch-Nyhan syndrome
   Frequency: unknown
   Anomaly: unknown
   Degree of retardation: children appear normal for first 6 to 8 months. Later, child develops moderate retardation, although some persons have mild retardation or even normal IQ.
   Additional features: development of severe loss of motor control after 8 months and occurrence of self-mutilating behavior

Table 17–3. SOME PRENATAL, PERINATAL, AND POSTNATAL CAUSES OF MENTAL RETARDATION

Prenatal
    Maternal diseases: toxemia, hypothyroidism
    Drug or alcohol abuse
    Infections; cytomegalovirus, sexually transmitted
      disease, rubella
    Poor prenatal care

Perinatal
    Prematurity
    Asphyxia
    Birth trauma
    Infections: herpes virus
    Kernicterus

Postnatal
    Infections: viral or bacterial; postimmunization
      encephalopathy
    Brain trauma
    Environmental toxins: lead, mercury
    Anoxia: drowning, status epilepticus
    Extremely deficient nutrition
    Endocrine abnormality: hypothyroidism

The fact is that for a large majority of children who are retarded, even ones who are moderately or severely so, identification of any biological cause with certainty is not possible. For those persons who are in the upper range of mild retardation, many may represent the left-hand tail of the normal gaussian curve of the distribution of intellectual skills, which are a result of both polygenic and environmental influences.

Sociocultural Factors

In the literature of the past several decades there is discussion of a specific form of poor intellectual performance found in the children of some families of low socioeconomic status, resulting in IQ scores in the mildly retarded range as well as in school failure beginning as early as the first and second grade. The implication of these reports was that these children suffered from a lack of adequate intellectual challenge and experience at home, as well as from a lack of verbal stimulation. Their parents, it was suggested, failed to motivate their children to achieve intellectually. A more thorough study of the matter has revealed that while children who come from severely deprived socioeconomic circumstances, in particular from urban ghettos, are more likely to have difficulties in school, the concept of "familial retardation"

or "sociocultural retardation" (as it also has been termed) is largely incorrect. The vast majority of children born into a low socioeconomic family are not intellectually retarded. What failures children from economically deprived backgrounds may show can be due to a number of factors outside the family. IQ tests administered to children from culturally different backgrounds may incorrectly label children as retarded. Schools in disadvantaged urban areas are more likely to have teachers who are overwhelmed and demoralized by the social and behavioral problems that some of the children bring to the school, further decreasing the likelihood that students will be able to learn. Nonetheless, it must be admitted that families can be found in which one or both of the parents are mildly retarded, the household environment is disorganized and intellectually barren, and the children are doing poorly in school and therefore test as retarded. In such instances it is often very difficult to untangle genetic and environmental influences and assign the children's failure to any single circumstance.

EPIDEMIOLOGY

From a statistical viewpoint, 2.28% of a normally distributed curve lies 2 SD below the mean. On that basis, 2.28% of the population would be retarded according to the IQ criteria of the 1973 AAMD definition and the DSM-III-R. The distribution of IQs is not normal, however. There are an unknown number of persons whose retardation is due to organic factors who must be added to the expected distribution. When this is done it has been estimated (Zigler and Hodapp 1986) that the statistical prevalence should be approximately 3% of the population. In fact, not all recent surveys have agreed with this estimate. Some have shown that the estimate is much too high, by at least a factor of 2. In a study of the entire population of 9- to 11-year olds on the Isle of Wight, Rutter and co-workers (1970) reported that when IQ criteria alone were used, 2.53% of the children were retarded, a figure similar to that estimated from statistical analysis. When adaptive behavior criteria are added (either through actual testing or by counting only those persons who were receiving special services), the estimates are lower. When

Birch and associates (1970) retrospectively surveyed an entire city population of 22-year-olds who had, before they were 15 years of age, received special services for the retarded, they found a prevalence of 1.6%. In another community study (Mercer 1973), which used both IQ and adaptive behavior test scores, the overall prevalence of mental retardation was slightly less than 1%.

A second factor that must be considered in studies of the prevalence of mental retardation is the age of the persons being studied. Before 5 years of age, the prevalence has been reported to be 0.7% (Tarjan et al. 1973). Only those children who have moderate and severe degrees of retardation will be likely to be identified before age 5, although the increasing numbers of children attending preschools may bring about earlier identification of milder forms of mental handicap.

After age 5 the prevalence rises, since more children are identified who cannot meet academic demands; but after 18 years of age the prevalence falls once more, reflecting the fact that persons with milder forms of retardation become employed and are no longer labeled as retarded. Richardson (1978) reported that in the study by Birch and associates (1970), by 22 years of age 89% of the males were in full-time jobs and two thirds were no longer receiving special services. Once the demands of school are passed, it would appear that the level of adaptive functioning achieved by most mildly retarded persons is sufficient for at least a marginally successful existence in the community.

PSYCHIATRIC DISORDERS

Prevalence

There have been a number of investigations of the prevalence of psychiatric disturbances among retarded persons (see Russell 1985 and Table 17–4). In general, these studies have had many shortcomings. Varying diagnostic criteria make it difficult to state what specific psychiatric disorders might be present in retarded persons and whether the symptoms of the disorders might differ from those found in the general population. What these studies do state with some certainty, however, is that the incidence of emotional and behavioral disturbances in mentally re-

tarded persons is quite high, more so than in the nonretarded population. There are a number of reasons for this: retarded persons are likely to experience negative attitudes from others, to be rejected socially, to feel isolated, and to feel less capable in school and at work. The studies also appear to tell us that the range of disorders is not unlike that seen in the nonretarded population.

Evaluation and Diagnosis

REFERRAL PROCESS

The mentally retarded person may have been urged to seek psychiatric help by a family member, a caretaker at a residential center, or another person directly involved in his or her life. There are several important issues that need to be addressed in terms of the referral: what are the manifest problems that prompted the referral, why is it being made now (supposing that the problem has existed for some time), and what are the hidden issues for which help is being sought. In some instances the manifest problems may be relatively simple and indicate the recent onset of an affective disorder or schizophrenia, but usually they are more insidious, longstanding, and indicative of more complex interpersonal difficulties, with or without superimposed psychiatric disorder. Families may be hoping that a diagnosis other than mental retardation will be made, or they may be extremely fearful about what will become of their retarded son or daughter in the future. The parents may be in disagreement as to how they should deal with their child's temper tantrums, schooling, or sexual behavior, or a different family member may be depressed and in need of individual help. The timing of the referral may reflect the fact that the referred person is at a transition point: between preschool and regular school, grade school and high school, or school and the work place. Such transitions can be very frightening and stressful to a person who has a poor self-image or who has experienced many past failures; the stress may in turn trigger onset of an affective disorder, anxiety state, or acting-out behavior.

Referrals from the work place or residential living center are very often for antisocial and aggressive behaviors. The staff who must deal with the person may be angry, believe they have failed, and hope that the referral

---

Table 17–4. SELECTED STUDIES OF THE PREVALENCE OF PSYCHIATRIC DISORDERS
IN THE MENTALLY RETARDED

Unselected Population Surveys
1. Isle of Wight Study
    Reference: Rutter et al. 1970
    Subjects: Entire population of 9- to 11-year-olds; mental retardation diagnosed using IQ scores
    Methods: Standardized assessment and diagnostic instruments
    Incidence of psychiatric disorders: prevalence rate for emotional disorders among retarded was 30.4% with
        teacher questionnaire and 41.8% with parent questionnaire. Rates for the nonretarded children were 7.7%
        and 9.5%.
2. British longitudinal birth cohort study
    Reference: Koller et al. 1983
    Subjects: 22-year-old mentally retarded persons who had been studied earlier as part of 5-year birth cohort
        who had been receiving services for the retarded prior to age 16.
    Methods: Comprehensive interviews of retarded subjects and nonretarded controls; earlier records from
        service agencies
    Incidence of psychiatric disorders: 61% of the retarded showed behavioral disturbance in childhood, and 59%
        in the postschool period. This compared with 24% behavioral disturbance in the control sample. Types of
        disturbance: 29% emotional disturbance, 33% aggressive conduct disturbance, and 27% antisocial behavior
3. New York Developmental Disabilities Information Survey
    Reference: Jacobson 1982
    Subjects: 30,000 persons receiving developmental disability services in the state; those with greater disability
        somewhat overrepresented
    Methods: Raters asked to code a maximum of 3 problem behaviors from a list of 29, as well as indicate their
        frequency; absence of problem behaviors also must be indicated
    Incidence of psychiatric disorders: 47.7% of the population had some type of behavior problem; 13.7% of
        children and 17.1% of adults classified as psychiatrically impaired

Clinic Population Surveys
1. Chess and Hassibi study
    Reference: Chess and Hassibi 1977
    Subjects: 52 mildly retarded middle-class children living at home
    Methods: Patient and caretaker interviews
    Incidence of psychiatric disorders: 60% had some incidence of psychiatric disorder at time of study and 40%
        on follow-up 6 years later; 35% of the sample were said to have reactive behavior disorder reflecting
        environmental stress, one child had a neurotic disorder, and one was psychotic.
2. Philips and Williams study
    Reference: Philips and Williams 1975
    Subjects: 100 consecutive referrals of mentally retarded children to a psychiatric clinic
    Methods: Interviews of parents and children
    Incidence of psychiatric disorders: 80% of referrals had emotional disturbances; 26 children had a behavior
        disturbance, 16 had personality disturbances, 5 had neurosis, and 2 had transient situational disorder
3. Reid study
    Reference: Reid 1980
    Subjects: 60 retarded children and adolescents referred to a clinic
    Methods: Use of a multiaxial classification scheme somewhat similar to *DSM-III*
    Incidence of psychiatric disorders: Most common diagnosis was conduct disorder (45% of sample), followed
        by neurotic disorders (42%), hyperkinetic syndrome (15%), childhood psychosis (8%), adjustment reaction
        (4%); one child was diagnosed as having manic-depressive psychosis.

---

will lead to some hitherto untried treatment (perhaps medication) or to the person being removed from their care. The goal of the evaluation must not only be to identify whether a specific psychiatric condition may exist to account for the problem behaviors but also to identify and deal with interpersonal issues between the retarded person and other workers or residents at the center that may be complicating the situation. Tactful patient advocacy may be necessary in some situations, such as when normal curiosity and independent strivings are seen as aggressive behavior by caretakers in an understaffed setting.

DIAGNOSTIC PROCESS

The diagnostic evaluation should provide a comprehensive survey of the symptoms of psychiatric disorders through interview and use of structured diagnostic instruments and ancillary tests. Three general diagnostic instruments are available for use: the Kiddie—Schedule for Affective Disorders and Schizophrenia (K-SADS) (Orvaschel et al.

1982), the Diagnostic Interview for Children and Adolescents (DICA) (Herjanic and Campbell 1977), and the Interview for Childhood Disorders and Schizophrenia (ICDS) (Russell and colleagues 1985). These instruments have the advantage of having both patient and parent (caretaker, schoolteacher) versions, are fairly comprehensive, and yield information generally applicable to the *DSM-III* and *DSM-III-R* systems of diagnoses. The instruments were primarily designed for use in research. Clinicians may wish to use only parts of the interviews in their everyday diagnostic work. It has been the experience at the University of California at Los Angeles Child Psychiatry Clinical Research Center that the instruments are not valid for direct use with persons whose mental age is younger than 8 years, which translates roughly to an IQ of 50 to 60 in an adult. The parent versions may provide useful information even if the patient-instrument cannot be employed. Kazdin and colleagues (1983) have published a scale specifically designed for the assessment of depression in mentally retarded persons.

INTERVIEW

The retarded person is likely to have experienced failure in test situations or to have had medical examinations in the past that were frightening and painful. It is important that the examiner carefully explain the nature of the examination and encourage questions from the outset. Before proceeding to a review of the current complaints, the examiner should "tune in" to the person being interviewed, learning his or her current living situation, level of language use and self-help skills, and what the person does best. The person may see the examination as a punishment for bad behavior or may fear that it will result in removal from his or her place of residence.

Retarded persons require direction, structure, and support. Leading questions should be avoided or worded so that the various alternatives are voiced (e.g., are you happy or unhappy in the workshop?). Remarks and praise should be appropriate and in keeping with the person's mental age. In general the entire pace of the interview may be slower than with a nonretarded person. It may also be necessary to set limits in a clear and unequivocal way. Toys, games, dolls, and other props should be used as appropriate to the mental age of the person. Drawing is also useful as a projective technique and a way of getting the person to feel more at ease. Szymanski (1980) commented that with adult retarded persons, games and toys appropriate for a younger person can be usefully employed. He advises offering the toys carefully, perhaps making them just visible, and, if the person shows interest, using some type of face-saving permission such as "I like to play this game myself."

There is a lack of detailed study of how various psychiatric disorders manifest in persons who are moderately and severely mentally retarded. For mildly retarded persons, the symptoms of the various disorders described in the *DSM-III* are not very different than those seen in nonretarded persons. Many persons have commented on the imperfections of the *DSM-III* criteria, which are no greater or less when the *DSM-III* criteria are used in the diagnosis of retarded persons.

Treatment

PSYCHOTHERAPY

Outcome studies of psychotherapy with mentally retarded persons are few, marred by methodologic short comings, and contradictory in results (see Sigman 1985). At the University of California at Los Angeles, where, over the past 20 years many psychiatric disorders in young retarded persons have been seen, the major therapeutic techniques employed have been behavioral (token economy, positive reinforcement, social skill teaching). Occasionally, however, it has been found useful to use psychotherapy (loosely defined as one-to-one interactions aimed at decreasing symptoms, raising self-esteem, and providing alternate means of expressing anger) with some of the retarded patients, particularly with adolescents. Sigman (1985) has reviewed ten of these cases. The patients ranged in age from 12 to 22 years, while the patient's IQ scores on the WISC-R varied between 45 and 77. The initial goal of the therapist was to build rapport, and in two cases, this was as far as the therapy went. The development in these persons of the capacity to trust another was, however, considered a major accomplishment. The patients were seen two or three times a week for 40-minute sessions for periods ranging from 4 to 10 months. Among the issues dealt with in therapy were the need of the patient to separate from an overprotective family and regulate his or her own life; the need to develop greater impulse control and to express anger in other than destructive ways; the need to learn to avoid exploitative peer relationships; and the need to resolve fears about moving into a more independent living situation. In general, the therapists felt that treatment was helpful because it permitted the patients to make better use of the special school, vocational, and rehabilitation services available to them.

MEDICATION

Surveys have indicated that both stimulant and psychotropic medications are frequently prescribed for retarded children and adults, especially those who are in hospitals or community placements (Gadow 1986). In some instances, as many as 50% of some hospital's populations were receiving medication (mostly neuroleptics), often in very high doses. The reasons advanced for this form of treatment were "overactive behavior," "noisiness," "perverseness," and control of agitated behavior and aggression. Although there is justification for use of medication to treat certain specific disorders such as attention-deficit disorder, depression, or schizophrenia, use of medication solely to control aggression and agitation can only be understood as a form of chemical straitjacket. In some instances the situation comes about because there is a serious shortage of staff and because the residents have little to do all day.

Although there have been many surveys of the use of medication with retarded persons, the number of well-designed studies of specific medications used in specific psychiatric disorders (with the exception, perhaps, of hyperactivity and attention-deficit disorder) are few. As far as is known, the response of retarded persons to psychotropic, antidepressant, and psychoactive medication is the same as that of nonretarded persons (the same holds for lithium use). Hence, medications should be used to treat psychiatric disorders in retarded persons along the lines recommended in other chapters in this book. Already, new uses for old medications are being suggested for some psychiatric disorders of children and adults and new medi-

cations are being introduced. It is important that as new pharmacologic approaches are found effective, careful clinical trials be extended to populations of retarded persons.

Specific Psychiatric Disorders

ATTENTION-DEFICIT DISORDER

Some retarded children and adolescents may be impulsive and restless and have a short attention span for school activities. Whether such persons should be judged as having the syndrome of attention-deficit disorder or whether their symptoms are more a manifestation of the person's lack of understanding of more complex activities coupled with a degree of social isolation may not be easy to decide. If the impulsivity and restlessness are fairly severe and exhibited in many settings, a trial of stimulant medication should be instituted. The effects of the medication should be carefully monitored and medication continued only if the symptoms show clear improvement as measured by the Conners rating scale for attention-deficit disorder. Drug holidays should also be considered. Although attention-deficit disorder has been little studied in retarded adults, it is likely that it does exist (since it has been described in nonretarded adults) and may be effectively treated with stimulants.

AFFECTIVE DISORDERS

In clinical experience at the University of California at Los Angeles, depression is a frequent disorder in mentally retarded persons. For patients with an IQ above 50, the illness is manifested with many of the same signs and symptoms seen in nonretarded persons. Persons who are moderately and severely retarded may also be depressed, but one needs to rely on such symptoms as sad facial expression, psychomotor slowing, irritability, affectual volatility, and loss of appetite and weight to make the diagnosis. A family psychiatric history should always be taken to evaluate the likelihood that a patient's symptoms represent an affective disorder. Depressed retarded persons respond to antidepressant medication much as nonretarded persons do.

Case 1. Although manic illness is seen much less frequently in mentally retarded patients than is depression, the following case history describes one such person:

James was a 14-year-old boy living with his biological parents and attending special education classes in the public school system. His father was a school principal, and his mother worked part time in a bank. James had a brother who was 2 years younger and a sister who was 4 years younger, both of whom were normal. As a young child James did not walk until age 18 months and did not use two-word sentences until age 28 months. At age 4 he was taken to a psychiatric clinic for evaluation of his slowness and found to be mildly retarded. His IQ score on the Stanford-Binet was 64. It was also noted that James had some features of infantile autism; he seemed socially withdrawn and was preoccupied with mechanical objects and subjects such as car washes. He would also tilt his head and make writhing movements with his hands. While his language development was in keeping with his overall intellectual functioning, he had a severe articulation deficit that made it difficult for him to make himself understood by persons other than his immediate family. He did make emotional contact with adults, however, and was not sufficiently withdrawn to be given a diagnosis of autism. It was recommended that James be placed in classes for the mildly retarded and receive speech therapy.

Over the next several years James lost the autistic-like symptoms, his speech became clearer, and he began to learn more social skills. His progress in school was fairly even until he reached 13 years of age. At that time his teacher reported that his school performance was deteriorating and he had become preoccupied with thoughts of nuclear war, flood, fires, and murderers. He frequently became aroused and overstimulated, jumping up and down, hyperextending his limbs, and slapping his hands. He began to fight and attack other children without provocation. After several months of worsening behavior, the school asked James' parents to bring him to the psychiatric clinic for reevaluation.

When seen by the child psychiatrist, James exhibited overactivity, short attention span, racing thoughts, and mood lability. Physical examination revealed a boy who was postpubertal with no medical illnesses. A structured diagnostic assessment was carried out by means of the Interview for Childhood Disorders and Schizophrenia (Russell and colleagues 1985). James was found to meet the criteria for schizotypal personality disorder and for possible manic disorder. The mother reported that her uncle had been diagnosed with what she believed might be schizophrenia at 20 years of age. Based on this family history and the diagnosis of schizotypal personality, a trial of haloperidol (Haldol) was initiated at a starting dose of 1 mg twice daily, later raised to 2 mg three times a day. Side effects (severe drowsiness and lethargy) led to termination of the trial. Although the symptoms of racing thoughts and overactivity had diminished while on haloperidol, they quickly returned when the drug was stopped. A trial of lithium was instituted next. At a blood level of 0.8 mEq/L there was a pronounced improvement in all symptoms, and within several weeks James' school work improved, his attention span lengthened, and his mood swings disappeared.

After 6 months of lithium treatment, coincident with the summer vacation, a drug holiday was instituted. Within 2 months many of James' manic symptoms reappeared and remained until the lithium therapy was started again.

James has been followed at the psychiatric clinic on a monthly basis. It is currently planned to begin another drug holiday with the hope that James' manic disorder will remain in remission for a longer period of time.

SCHIZOPHRENIA

For the past 10 years, investigators at the University of California at Los Angeles Child Psychiatry Clinical Research Center have been studying childhood-onset schizophrenia (*DSM-III* type schizophrenia whose onset begins before the age of 12 years). In addition, they have diagnosed and treated mentally retarded adolescents in the clinic population having schizophrenia. It has been their experience that persons can be found (both among the retarded and the nonretarded) who show sufficient *DSM-III* signs of schizophrenia for the diagnosis to be made. Below a mental age of 8 years (IQ of 50 to 60 in late adolescents and adults), it is often difficult to obtain sufficiently convincing evidence of delusions or hallucinations to reach a diagnosis. One may suspect that such symptoms are present, but one is unable to identify any good method of resolving the issue. While no large clinical studies of the effects of psychotropic medication on schizophrenia in children or in retarded persons have been conducted it is the impression that these medications are not always effective in banishing the symptoms of the disorder. Some persons are helped, but not all. Clearly, this is an issue that deserves study.

Case 2. The following case history illustrates the manner in which the diagnosis of schizophrenia may be difficult; the response of a patient to a neuroleptic may be dramatic; and even if the treatment may not keep a moderately to severely retarded person out of an institution indefinitely, it may allow him or her to remain at home for a longer time than would otherwise be possible.

Jerry was a 10-year-old black boy admitted for the first time to a psychiatric hospital for marked aggression (hitting, kicking, pulling hair) against children in his foster home, severe agitation, yelling and shouting, and visual hallucinations. He had been diagnosed as moderately to severely retarded at age 4, at which time his mother had given him up and he was placed in a good foster home. Until age 7 he appeared to be progressing fairly well, but following Halloween and being greatly frightened by "ghosts" at a "haunted house" he began to be extremely fearful, withdrawn, and regressed. His regression later remitted, but 1 year before admission he began to complain that he could "see creatures in his room" who he believed were going to attack him. At the time of his admission his foster parents said they could no longer care for him and the authorities were contemplating sending him to a local state hospital for the mentally retarded.

His behavior on admission to the child psychiatry service was so violent that the staff described him as one of the most out-of-control children they had ever seen. On testing, his mental age was 40 months, with language comprehension and production at 36 months. Because of his language handicaps, it was not possible to obtain sufficient symptom history to make a diagnosis of schizophrenia. On the basis of his continuing hallucinations and his extreme fear and agitation he was given a tentative diagnosis of atypical psychosis. He was placed in the structured milieu program on the ward, put

in one-to-one nursing care, and enrolled in the therapeutic school and recreational therapy program of the hospital. His behavior was so disturbed, however, that he could not take part in any of these programs and initially made little progress. Based on his diagnosis, a trial of thorazine was started. After 3 weeks, when the medication level was 400 mg/day, there was a dramatic improvement in his condition. He became calmer, much less agitated, stopped attacking other children, and no longer complained of visual hallucinations. He began to participate in all of the ward programs to a much greater degree. As a result of his improvement, it was possible to return him to his foster home, though with a guarded future prognosis.

Over the next 5 years he had several drug holidays, during each of which he again became agitated, fearful, and hallucinated. Larger doses of thorazine or other neuroleptics were needed to produce remission, and at one point he showed transient signs of tardive dyskinesia. During his third hospitalization it was felt unwise to give him more than a moderate dose of neuroleptic. His behavior did not improve sufficiently for him to return to his foster parents so he was sent to a state hospital program. It was hoped that when his behavior stabilized he could be returned to a residential program in the community.

EARLY INFANTILE AUTISM AND PERVASIVE DEVELOPMENTAL DISORDER

Autistic children have been extensively studied over the past 30 years. Seventy per cent of autistic persons are also retarded. Their autism represents a severe failure to learn social-communication skills (both pragmatic and prosodic), to learn to use emotionally communicative gestures (putting one's arm around another in a comforting gesture), and to see that others can be "agents of contemplation" (persons who can share ideas) rather than simple "agents of action" (someone who can get a cookie). Their retardation is represented by their failure to develop good semantic and syntactic language, to learn to reason, and to do school work.

Some autistic persons are not retarded: they score above 70 on intelligence tests, some even above 100. These persons are autistic in that they have all of the social-communication deficits described above but they have fairly good syntactic and semantic language, can reason fairly well, and do reasonably well on their school work (at least until they attempt more complex high-school subjects).

Based on the above, it would seem that a very different set of core capacities must underlie the autistic and the retarded domains of mental handicap. What these capacities are will be an important topic for future research investigators to contemplate.

ANXIETY DISORDER AND PHOBIAS

Although many retarded persons often feel anxious, clinical experience has been that there is usually good reason for them to feel this way, given their inexperience in many social situations and in everyday outside-the-home activities. *DSM-III* anxiety disorders are rarely diagnosed and very few patients with panic attacks or phobias have been observed. Milieu experiences, social skills training, and psychotherapy are used as a means of reducing anxiety in retarded patients.

CONCLUSIONS

Mentally retarded persons have a greater likelihood of having serious psychiatric disorders than do the general population. In persons having a mental age of 8 years or more (adult IQ of 50 to 60), the signs and symptoms of specific psychiatric disorders are similar to those described in the *DSM-III* or the *DSM-III-R*. Child psychiatrists, with their experience in working with parents and with teams of other professionals and their understanding of developmental issues, are well prepared for evaluating, diagnosing, and prescribing treatment for psychiatric disorders in retarded persons. Although the symptoms of psychiatric disorders are more difficult to identify in persons who are moderately and severely retarded, affective disorders and attention-deficit disorders may be diagnosed in such persons through behavioral observations. The treatment of psychiatric disorders in retarded persons is not very different from that used for nonretarded populations. There is a limited, but important, place for psychotherapy. Psychotherapy with retarded persons should be goal directed and initially aimed at establishing rapport. When

rapport is established it can be used to help the retarded person resolve issues of separation from family, to learn better methods of handling feelings, and to reduce anxiety in social and work situations.

References

American Psychiatric Association. 1987. *Diagnostic and Statistical Manual of Mental Disorders*, 3rd. ed., revised. Washington, D.C.: American Psychiatric Press.

Baroff, G. S. 1986. *Mental Retardation, Nature, Cause, and Management*, 2nd. ed. Washington, D.C.: Hemisphere Publishing Corporation.

Birch, H. G., Richardson, S. A., Baird, D., et al. 1970. *Mental Subnormality in the Community: A Clinical and Epidemiological Study*. Baltimore: Williams & Wilkins.

Russell, A., Bott, L., Sammons, C. 1989. The phenomenology of schizophrenia occurring in childhood. 1973. *J. Am. Acad. Child Adolesc. Psychiatry* 28:399–407.

Chess, S., and Hassibi, M. 1977. Behavior deviations in mentally retarded children. *J. Am. Acad. Child Psychiatry* 9:282–297.

Flavell, J. H., and Markman, E. M. 1983. *Handbook of Child Psychology*, Vol. III, *Cognitive Development*. New York: John Wiley & Sons.

Gadow, K. D. 1986. *Children on Medication*, vol. 1. San Diego, Calif.: College-Hill Press.

Grossman, H. J. (ed.). 1977. *Manual on Terminology and Classification in Mental Retardation*, rev. ed. Washington D.C.: American Association on Mental Deficiency.

Herjanic, B., and Campbell, W. 1977. Differentiating psychiatrically disturbed children on the basis of a structured interview. *J. Abnorm. Child Psychology* 5:127–134.

Jacobson, J. W. 1982. Problem behavior and psychiatric impairment within a developmentally disabled population: Behavior frequency. *Appl. Res. Ment. Retard.* 3:121–139.

Kazdin, A. E., Matson, J. L., and Senatore, V. 1983. Assessment of depression in mentally retarded adults. *Am. J. Psychiatry* 140:1040–1043.

Koller, H., Richardson, S. A., and Katz, M. 1983. Behavior disturbance since childhood among a 5-year birth cohort of all mentally retarded young adults in a city. *Am. J. Ment. Defic.* 87:386–395.

Mercer, J. R. 1973. The myth of 3 per cent prevalence. In Tarjan, G., Eyman, R. K., and Meyers, C. E. (eds.): *Sociobehavioral Studies in Mental Retardation*. Washington, D.C.: Monographs of the American Association on Mental Deficiency.

Mundy, P. C., Seibert, J. M., and Hogan, A. E. 1985. Communication skills in the mentally retarded. In Sigman, M. (ed.): *Children with Emotional Disorders and Developmental Disabilities*. New York: Grune & Stratton.

Nihira, K., Foster, R., Shellaus, M., and Leland, H. 1974. *Manual for AAMD Adaptive Behavior Scale*. Washington, D.C.: American Journal on Mental Deficiency.

Orvaschel, H., Puig-Antich, J., Chambers, W., et al. 1982. Retrospective assessment of prepubertal major depression with the kiddie-SADS-E. *J. Am. Acad. Child Psychiatry* 21:392–397.

Philips, I., and Williams, N. 1975. Psychopathology and mental retardation, *Am. J. Psychiatry* 132:1265–1271.

Reid, A. H. 1980. Psychiatric disorders in mentally

handicapped children: A clinical and follow-up study. *J. Ment. Defic. Res.* 24:287–298.

Richardson, S. A. 1978. Careers of mentally retarded young persons: Services, jobs and interpersonal relationships. *Am. J. Ment. Defic.* 82:349–358.

Russell, A. T. 1985. The mentally retarded, emotionally disturbed child and adolescent. In Sigman, M. (ed.): *Children with Emotional Disorders and Developmental Disabilities.* New York: Grune & Stratton.

Rutter, M., Graham, P., and Yule, W. 1970. *A Neuropsychiatric Study in Childhood.* London: Spastics International Medical Publications and Heinemann.

Sigman, M. 1985. Individual and group psychotherapy with mentally retarded adolescents. In Sigman, M. (ed.): *Children with Emotional Disorders and Developmental Disabilities.* New York: Grune & Stratton.

Sternberg, R. J., and Gardner, M. K. 1982. A compo-

nential interpretation of the general factor of human intelligence. In Eysenck H. J. (ed.): *A Model for Intelligence.* Berlin-Springer-Verlag.

Szymanski, L. S. 1980. Psychiatric diagnosis of retarded persons. In Szymanski, L. S., and Tanguay, P. E. (eds.): *Emotional Disorders of Mentally Retarded Persons.* Baltimore: University Park Press.

Tanguay, P. E. 1987. Cognition and psychopathology. In Noshpitz, J. D. (ed.): *Basic Handbook of Child Psychiatry*, Vol. 5, *Advances and New Directions*, New York: Basic Books.

Tarjan, G., Wright, S. W., Eyman, R. K., et al. 1973. Natural history of mental retardation: Some aspects of epidemiology. *Am. J. Ment. Defic.* 77:369–379.

Zigler, E., and Hodapp, R. M. 1986. *Understanding Mental Retardation.* New York: Cambridge University Press.

18

Tics and Other Stereotyped Movements*

L. EUGENE ARNOLD, M.Ed., M.D.

Psychiatric movement disorders of child-hood include tic disorders and stereo-type/habit disorders. These two categories differ in numerous ways. For example, tics are involuntary while stereotyped habits are under voluntary control. Tics are intermittent and random while stereotyped habits are often rhythmic. Tics are distressing to the patient while stereotyped habits often seem pleasurable or at least consoling. Because of such differences, the two disorders will be discussed in separate sections. Either cate-gory can include some self-injurious behav-iors.

TIC DISORDERS

Definition and Diagnosis

Tics are intermittent, rapid, involuntary, nonrhythmic, stereotyped, recurrent, usually purposeless contractions of a functionally re-lated skeletal muscle group. They may in-volve vocal muscles, resulting in sounds or even words, including obscenities. Although involuntary, they can often be postponed for minutes to hours by concentrated effort. They are often distressing, with shame and self-consciousness. The prototypical tic dis-order is Tourette's disorder, which is also called tic de Gilles de la Tourette, maladie des tics, multiple tic disorder, or (Gilles de la) Tourette syndrome. With multiple motor and vocal tics and a chronic course, it is often socially and functionally disabling. At the opposite extreme are transient simple tics with a benign course and prognosis. Al-though Tourette's disorder is relatively rare, most of the discussion below will focus on it because of its severe consequences for the patient. Some experts believe that all tic dis-orders constitute a spectrum, with the main distinction among disorders being severity and/or chronicity (e.g., Bruun 1984).

The *Diagnostic and Statistical Manual of Men-tal Disorders*, third edition, revised *(DSM-III-R)* (American Psychiatric Association 1987) operationally defines Tourette's disorder as a syndrome having onset before age 21 of multiple motor tics and at least one vocal tic at some time during the illness (not neces-sarily concurrently), a duration of over a year (perhaps intermittently), occurrence of tics many times a day (usually in bouts), and varying location, number, frequency, com-plexity, and severity ("waxing and waning"). Tics occurring only during psychoactive sub-stance intoxication or central nervous system (CNS) disease do not qualify for a Tourette's disorder diagnosis. The synonym Tourette's syndrome is often used interchangeably and equivalently but technically covers a broader referent, including a Tourette's-like clinical picture resulting from CNS disease or sub-

---

*Some short sections of this chapter were ex-cerpted/adapted with permission from the author's chapter in Gregory, I., and Smeltzer, D. J. (in press). *Psychiatry: Essentials of Clinical Practice*, third edition. Boston: Little, Brown & Co.

stance intoxication or withdrawal. An example is neuroleptic-induced "tardive Tourette's syndrome," with a course similar to other forms of tardive dyskinesia.

Chronic motor or vocal tic disorder is essentially a mild form of Tourette's disorder, from which it is distinguished technically by having only motor or only vocal tics but not both (not even successively). It is not necessary for the anatomical location, number, frequency, complexity, or severity of tics to change over time. Otherwise the diagnostic criteria are similar to those for Tourette's disorder.

The *DSM-III-R* describes *transient tic disorder* as onset before age 21 of single or multiple motor or vocal tics occurring many times a day nearly every day for at least 2 weeks but no longer than 12 months, without a history of Tourette's disorder or chronic motor or vocal tic disorder and not occurring exclusively during intoxication or CNS disease. Although transient tics are usually simple facial tics, such as eye blinks, they can include any tic found in the more serious disorders. Therefore, the distinction is made on the basis of time course rather than type of tic.

Any tic that does not meet the *DSM-III-R* criteria for one of these three disorders can be diagnosed as *tic disorder not otherwise specified*.

A variety of technical terms are used in describing various tics or associated symptoms. *Coprolalia* is uttering obscenities involuntarily. *Mental coprolalia* is involuntarily thinking of obscenities; this is subtly distinguished from obsessions by its spasmodic, meaningless quality. *Echolalia* and *palilalia* are meaningless repetitions of words, the former of other's words, the latter of one's own words. *Copropraxia* or *copropraxis* is making obscene gestures or signs, the motor equivalent of coprolalia. *Palikinesia* is pathologic repetition of movements (usually the patient's own). *Echopraxis* and *echopraxia* refer to meaningless repetition of movements of others or initiated by others. *Echokinesis* is spasmodic, involuntary imitation of movements. (*Echomotism* and *echomimia* are imitation of movements, voluntary or involuntary.) *Echomatism* is purposeless imitation of an act.

Etiology

A genetic predisposition to Tourette's disorder has been reasonably established by several family studies (e.g., Pauls et al. 1984), which suggest an autosomal dominant with variable penetrance. The gene seems related also to some forms of attention-deficit hyperactivity disorder and obsessive-compulsive disorder. Vulnerable persons may be further predisposed by some sort of brain insult. Tourette's syndrome has been associated with gestational complications, low birth weight, head trauma, carbon monoxide poisoning, chronic neuroleptic exposure, and encephalitis lethargica.

There is general agreement that patients with Tourette's disorder suffer an excess of catecholamine neurotransmission, probably from receptor supersensitivity (Leckman et al. 1987). The favorite culprit is dopamine excess, but some investigators suspect that norepinephrine is equally important. Serotonin has also been implicated. Williams and associates (1987) suggest that motor tics may reflect dopamine overactivity while disinhibition (coprolalia, distractibility) reflects norepinephrinergic or serotonergic problems. Cholinergic mechanisms may be involved, at least secondarily. Endogenous opioids and gamma aminobutyric acid (GABA) have also been suspected. Since adrenergic stimulants are known to aggravate tics and even to cause reversible tics as a side effect, there has been suspicion that stimulant treatment of attention-deficit hyperactivity disorder may be instrumental in bringing on Tourette's disorder in those patients who have both disorders. More recent data are reassuring: stimulant treatment prior to tic onset does not appear to be an important cause of Tourette's disorder, though it aggravates many cases, usually reversibly (Shapiro and Shapiro 1981; Comings and Comings 1987).

Epidemiology

Tourette's disorder is rather rare, but not as rare as once believed. It affects between 0.05% and 0.1% of persons at some time in their lives. In contrast, transient tics affect up to one fifth of the population at some time. Three fourths of the victims are males. Many experts believe that Tourette's disorder is more common in whites than other races, especially blacks. About half of children with Tourette's disorder also have attention-deficit hyperactivity disorder, which usually precedes the manifestation of Tourette's disorder (Comings and Comings 1987). (The converse is not true: nowhere near half of the children with attention-deficit hyperactivity disorder eventually develop Tourette's disorder.) Another disorder commonly associated with Tourette's disorder is obsessive-compulsive disorder. Both of these are also found in greater than expected frequency among first-degree relatives of patients with Tourette's disorder. These findings have led to a suspicion of a common gene. Increased rates of arousal disorder (somnambulism and night terrors), depression, and anxiety disorders have also been reported (Barabas et al. 1984). The depression and anxiety are suspected in some cases to be related more to neuroleptic treatment than to Tourette's disorder. Details of suspected linkage can be found in Table 18–1. One pervasive developmental disorder sample was reported to have a 20% incidence of Tourette's disorder (Burd et al. 1987), but the opposite risk has not been reported, probably because pervasive developmental disorder is usually diagnosed at a younger age than Tourette's disorder.

Neuropathology

There is general agreement at this time that patients with Tourette's disorder have excessive brain dopamine activity (probably receptor supersensitivity), but it is not clear whether this is a primary genetic manifestation or whether it is a secondary finding, resulting from a more primary defect. There are also reports of serotonin abnormalities and equivocal reports of norepinephrine abnormalities. Pathogenesis may well result from relations among several neurotransmitters, including possibly even acetylcholine. Sweeney and associates (1972) reported an inverse correlation in a single patient of tic frequency with the amount of 24-hour urinary excretion of 3-methoxy-4-hydroxyphenolglycol (MHPG), a norepinephrine metabolite, and suggested that decreased norepinephrine activity may release dopamine-precipitated tics.

The literature reports evidence for midbrain and basal ganglia localization of the defects. The basal ganglia have long been known to be implicated in such dopamine disorders as parkinsonism. The two main ascending dopaminergic pathways arise in the locus ceruleus and the ventral tegmental area. Devinsky (1983) marshalled evidence supporting periaqueductal gray and midbrain tegmental damage. Such lesions could account for the motor and nonverbal phonic

Table 18–1. DISORDERS ASSOCIATED WITH TOURETTE'S DISORDER

| Disorder | In Same Patient | | Familial-Genetic Link | Pharmacologic Data (Neurotransmitter Inferences) |
	Clinical Samples	*General Population Samples*		
Other tic disorders	N.A.	N.A.	+ +	Generally same as Tourette's syndrome
Attention-deficit hyperactivity disorder	+ + + + (esp. younger)	+ +	+ (not twin support)	Stimulants exacerbate about 20% of Tourette's syndrome cases
Obsessive-compulsive disorder	+ + + + (esp. older)	+ +	+ + + (some twin support)	Chlorimipramine has no clear effect on tics. Serotonin precursor may help tics (not established treatment)
Other anxiety disorders	+ +	?	?	Benzodiazepines sometimes help tics, but variable
Depression	+ +	?	?	Effect of antidepressants on tics not clear; may be beneficial
Substance abuse	?	?	Anecdotal	No evidence of widespread successful self-medication. ? effects of narcotic antagonists
Arousal disorders (sleepwalking, terrors)	+ +	?	?	
Migraine	+	?	?	
Arithmetic disorder	+	?	?	

Acknowledgement: This table could not have reached its final form without the invaluable consultation and revision of James Leckman, M.D., of Yale Child Study Center.

tics and perhaps even affect-laden simple verbal tics. However, it seems reasonable to suspect cortical involvement in the more complex verbal tics; the frontal lobe and cingulate gyrus might be reasonable sites for localizing some of the pathologic processes involved in verbal tics. One report of a pineal tumor affecting the midbrain may have been a coincidental finding (Lakke and Wilmink 1985). Patients with Tourette's disorder often have associated subtle neurologic abnormalities (soft signs) (Caine 1985).

Clinical Picture

The presentation of a tic disorder can vary considerably, even within those who meet the diagnostic criteria for Tourette's disorder. Not only can the constellation of symptoms vary from one patient to another, but also the particular symptoms evident at any one time may vary within the same patient. In fact, one characteristic of Tourette's disorder is its pleomorphic waxing and waning of individual symptoms and shifting of anatomical location of the "tic of the month." Another variable affecting the clinical picture is the length of time from onset of symptoms to the time of diagnostic assessment. The longer this has been, the more severe are learning problems and secondary emotional symptoms, particularly depression and deterioration of social skills. Also, the longer the time elapsed, the more likely the patient is to have progressed to verbal tics. Tics can affect any body part, including abdominal muscles. Four kinds are distinguished:

1. Simple motor tics, such as eye blinking, grimacing, and shoulder shrugs, appear at a mean age of 7. They are darting, rapid, spasmodic, and purposeless. More examples can be found in Table 18–2.

2. Complex motor tics, usually appearing shortly after simple motor tics, are slower and appear more purposeful. They include hopping, touching self or others, clapping, copropraxia (such as "flipping the finger"), and some rather bizarre things, such as pulling back on a pencil while writing, as well as some rather compulsive appearing ritual-like behaviors (which can be distinguished from compulsions only by careful interview regarding the subjective experience). They can also include biting or hitting oneself,

picking at scabs, or other self-destructive actions.

3. Simple phonic tics (also called simple vocal tics), appearing at a mean age of 11, are nonverbal sounds such as coughing, grunting, barking, or clicking. In one sense, these could be considered a special subcategory of complex motor tics because they can be easily explained by involuntary contracture of respiratory and vocal muscles. However, they have been traditionally distinguished from nonvocal motor tics.

4. Verbal tics, or complex phonic/vocal tics, usually appear after simple phonic tics. They are explosive words, phrases, or expressions that seem to have a meaning, although they are not usually uttered with the intent to convey the semantic meaning. The classic prototype is an obscenity, often the word "fuck" or "shit," from which the term *coprolalia* derives. These may be interjected unexpectedly in the middle of otherwise normal conversation or may escape explosively during silence and often have a staccato quality. There are often attempts to camouflage them, perhaps by dropping out vowels or one or more consonants, or even changing them into some other kind of sound. Verbal tics need not be obscene but are often insulting or hostile in content and sometimes in affect. Some authors extend the term *coprolalia* to include hostile outbursts or insults without obscenity. Although coprolalia was at one time considered essential for diagnosis, it is now realized, with increased diagnostic sensitivity, that considerably fewer than half of the victims of Tourette's disorder suffer this particular symptom.

Because the experienced ticquer usually learns to camouflage tics, the tics may not be obvious to an inexperienced observer. For example, a head-touching tic might be camouflaged as straightening or brushing the hair. A head-tossing tic might be camouflaged as flipping the hair out of one's eyes. The camouflage may extend occasionally to taking a brazen attitude about verbal or other tics, as if the patient is cussing on purpose or is merely being a macho tough guy with his insulting interjections. Empathic interviewing is often required to elicit an admission that the tics are not under control of the patient. Furthermore, the tics can be suppressed or postponed for a period of time with extreme effort, which many children

Table 18–2. TYPES OF TICS WITH EXAMPLES

Simple Motor	Complex Motor	Simple Phonic (Simple Vocal)	Complex Vocal (Complex Phonic/Verbal)
Abdominal tensing	Adjusting clothing	Barking	Coprolalia
Arm jerking	Arranging things	Belching	Counting rituals
Echokinesis	Biting (lip, arm, etc.)	Blowing	Echolalia
Eye blinking	Body rocking	Chewing	Hostile interjections
Finger movements	Clapping	Clicking	Inarticulateness
Frowning	Copropraxia	Clucking	Insults
Grimacing	Dystonic postures	Coughing	Laughing
Hand jerking	Echopraxia	Grunting	Mental coprolalia
Head jerking	Fist clenching	Gurgling	Nonsensical interjections
Head rolling	Gyrating and bending	Hawking	Partial words
Jaw snapping	Head banging	Hiccoughing	Stammering
Lip pouting	Hitting (self or others)	Hissing	Stereotyped expressions
Nose twitching	Holding funny expressions	Screeching	Stuttering
Palikinesis	Hopping/jumping/skipping	Shrieking	
Rapid kicks	Kicking ("purposeful")	Sighing	
Shoulder shrugging	Kissing	Sneezing	
Teeth clicking	Knee bending	Sniffling	
Teeth grinding	Picking (nose, scab)	Snorting	
	Pinching	Spitting	
	Smelling	Squealing	
	Squatting	Sucking sounds	
	Striking out	Swallowing	
	Tearing paper or books	Throat clearing	
	Thigh rubbing	Whistling	
	Throwing		
	Thrusting arms		
	Tongue protruding		
	Touching objects, genitals (self or others)		
	Writing same word over		

exert in the presence of a strange diagnostician; therefore extended observation may be necessary to confirm tics reported historically.

In addition to the tics, many afflicted children exhibit behavioral and temperamental problems, which may actually be the chief complaint. These can include impulsiveness, easy frustration, irritability, obsessive argumentativeness, restlessness, impairment of concentration, and other attention-deficit hyperactivity disorder symptoms. They often precede the tics. Many patients have obsessive-compulsive symptoms, and these sometimes constitute the chief complaint.

Besides the techniques the patient may have tried to suppress or modify the tics, the parents may also have resorted to a number of aversive (and occasionally reinforcement) paradigms to suppress the undesirable behavior. The failure of these leads to a good bit of tension in the parent–child relationship, sometimes with mutual blaming. Occasionally the parent–child conflict is the presenting complaint: "I can't get him to stop making those noises. Before I kill him I thought I better get some professional advice." At the other extreme, as with any chronic handicap, parental overprotectiveness may have developed.

Case Histories

The following case histories illustrate the variety of possible clinical presentations.

CASE 1

A 7-year-old first grader was referred by a general psychiatrist because his attention-deficit hyperactivity disorder failed to respond to trials of methylphenidate and pemoline. He had difficulty concentrating in school and difficulty keeping friends. He would get exceptionally loud in a classroom and frequently make strange noises. He was in a learning disorders class where there was suspicion that his distractibility, inattentiveness, and hyperactivity were contributing to his suboptimal performance. He frequently punched, pinched, hit, and pushed other children when he was frustrated.

He and his teacher described the noises as involuntary vocalizations occurring three to four times per day without associated motor activity. Sometimes he would repeat lines over and over, speaking in a progressively louder tone. His peers would ask the teacher to make him be quiet. He said that he could be quiet but then he would be unable to do his work because he would have to concentrate instead on being quiet and not making the noises. His classmates did not believe him when he said he could not help making the sounds; they felt he was being purposefully disruptive. He was frequently teased by classmates, leading to the aggressive behavior. By the time of evaluation, he considered himself "dumb" despite normal intelligence on individual IQ tests by the school.

During the interview, he showed two whole-body tics, one right arm tic while writing, and several head-turning tics, especially when stressed by performance demands. He also described "bad thoughts" nightly for the previous several months and difficulty falling asleep because of the bad thoughts. He tried to get rid of these by good thoughts. He was so motivated to get rid of the bad thoughts that he stopped eating candy because he thought that was bringing the bad thoughts on. He also felt that he had to step over cracks. He was squirmy and fidgety throughout the interview, with impulsiveness and inattentiveness. Results of standard rating scales by teachers and parents were consistent with attention-deficit hyperactivity disorder. Children's Depression Inventory taken by the patient scored 23, consistent with moderate depression.

Review of *DSM-III-R* criteria indicated that this patient warranted the following diagnoses: Moderate attention-deficit hyperactivity disorder, mild Tourette's disorder, obsessive-compulsive disorder, dysthymic disorder, developmental reading disorder, and developmental arithmetic disorder.

CASE 2

An 8-year-old boy was brought by his mother because several times a day he blurted out "the F word." Both he and his mother were embarrassed about this, and both resisted saying the actual word in giving the history. Actually, for a long time he had left the F off the "F word." The problem had begun more than a year earlier, with repetition several times a day at home and school of "Uck, uck, uck." Only in the last month had he put the F on the F word. He attempted to camouflage it by turning it into a cough or other noise. Nevertheless, it came out clearly enough that in a supermarket a woman stopped him and told him he should not say it. He did not know what to say to her, and his mother felt so sorry for him that she decided to bring him for an evaluation on the advice of a teacher who had read about Tourette's syndrome.

His behavior otherwise was good, and he had enjoyed good peer relations until his friends began to object to his verbal tic. He had been an A and B student until the past year, when his arithmetic and social studies grades declined concomitant with the waxing of his tics. Although he and his mother denied motor tics, several eye blinks, lip pouts, and head jerks were noted during the interview. His father was a reformed alcoholic who used to swear a lot, including the F word when he was drunk, but quit drinking 5 years earlier. The boy's mental status examination, neurologic examination, and history were otherwise benign, and he was of normal intelligence.

CASE 3

An 11-year-old boy in a class for the developmentally handicapped was brought by both parents because of increased aggression. When greeted in the waiting room, the father quipped, "We're the lucky parents," in an ironic manner. The parents related that he was "born hyperactive" and medication trials were begun by the age of 2. Therapy with pemoline and dexedrine was unsuccessful, but imipramine seemed for a couple of years to control his inattention, overactivity, and impulsiveness until school age, when he "became immune." A combination of methylphenidate and thioridazine seemed to work for a couple of years, but these were discontinued when his tics surfaced.

At age 8 he began having many vocal tics, with squealing and other odd noises, shuddering of his shoulders, drawing up of his fingers and hands into a semi-obscene posture, and ptosis. These attenuated somewhat when thioridazine and methylphenidate were stopped. A trial of pimozide was unsuccessful. Haloperidol helped his tics "half way," but left behavior intolerable. Clonazepam also helped the tics immensely, but not the behavior. Clonidine seemed to help his behavior. Violence became a problem only in the last half-year, while taking a combination of clonazepam and clonidine.

He manifested appetite and weight problems. Although he had a hospitalization at age 2 because of refusing to eat, he suddenly developed a ravenous appetite at the onset of his tics and was overweight since then. There was a strong family history of chemical dependency (most relatives on both sides) and suicide attempts. He rated himself 26 (significant) on the Children's Depression Inventory, which had to be read to him.

At interview he showed many frequent facial grimaces, lip pouting, and squirming. He picked almost continually at his own hand and repeatedly looked to the side in a manner that appeared to be camouflaged side-glancing tics. His parents several times had to set limits on his getting into things in the office. He was not currently having vocal tics, but his parents reported them historically. His speech and language sounded immature, and he seemed of borderline intellectual function. During joint interview with parents, he tried to sit on his mother's lap and hug her but did it in a way that obviously hurt her, even after she cautioned him to take it easy.

Fear seemed to be an important dynamic in this patient and his family. Not only was his mother afraid *of* him, but she was also afraid *for* him and was protective. The patient also suffered numerous fears. He was afraid to go outside and play since being bitten by a dog many months before. Even when the family went camping, away from the neighborhood where he had been bitten, he would hang around his parents instead of going off to play with other children. He also attempted to refuse school, preferring to stay home with his mother. Some of his aggression, both toward mother, teacher, and peers, appears to have been partly motivated by fear or anxiety, in a "fight or flight" reaction. It may also have resulted partly from benzodiazepine disinhibition, because withdrawal of the clonazepam while retaining the clonidine decreased his aggressiveness without changing the tic frequency and severity. However, his separation anxiety/agoraphobic symptoms increased and he also developed night terrors.

CASE 4

A 10-year-old middle-class boy with a diagnosis of Tourette's disorder was referred by a neurologist because he continually harangued his younger brother and parents. He would argue quickly about anything. He would take the opposite side of whatever issue his parent, brother, or doctor would take. His tics were largely unnoticed by teachers and classmates. The main current tic was an abdominal tensing. A few facial tics and a few noises occurred earlier in the course of his disorder, a year before.

He seemed almost diabolical in his disruption of the family's peace and enjoyment of life and would hardly lose any opportunity to harass the other family members. His peer relations also suffered somewhat from his argumentative hostility. He reacted negatively to any attempts to help or to facilitate his social skills. He denied the diagnosis, about which it must be admitted there was some doubt, even though both a neurologist and a child psychiatrist concurred. He would become vitriolic at the suggestion of participating in a Tourette's disorder support group. Prior to the onset of his tics, he had seemed well adjusted, with the same benign temperament as the rest of his family. History could elicit no convincing psychosocial or developmental explanation for his spiteful attitude. Low doses of haloperidol relieved the abdominal tensing but only slightly helped the argumentative attitude.

CASE 5

A 25-year-old housewife was referred by the Tourette's Association for diagnostic clarification. She dated her symptoms from age 4 when she experienced eye blinks, leg jerks, and an involuntary need to touch her genitals. At that age she was evaluated by a pediatrician who scolded her, telling her she was a "crazy nut." Her symptoms waxed and waned throughout childhood as old motor tics disappeared and new tics replaced or added to preexisting tics. Vocal tics were limited to clearing of her throat and palilalia. By fourth grade she was able to voluntarily suppress her tics for minutes to hours. In high school her tics were considered a nervous habit and she learned to camouflage them. As a teenager she smoked pot, drank beer, and took diazepam and noted that her tics were suppressed by downers.

At age 23, she read a newspaper article about Tourette's syndrome and wondered if this were her problem. She presented a written list of multiple involuntary motor tics that she had experienced: shoulder, leg, arm, and neck jerks; abdominal and other muscular contractions; and a need to touch an object repeatedly. Her tics got better during pregnancy and for almost a year after delivery, except for a week of worsening post partum. They were worsened by birth control pills and stress and increased 8 days prior to menses. She had been diagnosed as having premenstrual syndrome. Trazodone, prescribed by a psychiatrist, had made her too drowsy, but Limbitrol (a combination of chlordiazepoxide and amitriptyline) helped her considerably on an as needed basis. Other medical history included mitral valve prolapse, a knee repair, and allergy to sulfa, aspirin, and antibiotics. She gave a history of claustrophobia.

When asked about depression she began to cry. When she was young she cried alone often because there was no one to talk to. Her father was an alcoholic and had Crohn's disease and was verbally and physically abusive to her mother, who suffered from anxiety attacks and depression. Her parents were divorced when she was 10 years old. Although she had considered suicide in the past, she did not currently because of her religion and because she wanted to live. Her husband tried to be supportive, but ineffectively: he tried to cheer her up by making light of her tics and assuring her that God would heal a good Christian. She had not confronted him with the fact that his approach was not comforting.

During the interview she showed a few shoulder tics and a head toss and the shuddering that she said is her way of suppressing tics. Despite all her misfortunes she maintained an optimistic attitude, with a friendly, appealing manner. Changing her Limbitrol to a regular dosage rather than as needed gave her 80% relief from her tics. Attendance at a Tourette's Association meeting helped her stop worrying about the remaining tics. However, she began to worry that her 3-year-old daughter was beginning to tic. Observation of both together suggested that the daughter was imitating the mother's tics. Explanation that mommy could not help jerking but that no one should do it on purpose "cured" the daughter.

Clinical Course

The symptoms of Tourette's disorder typically first appear prepubertally, possibly as young as age 1 or 2, and by age 7 in at least half the cases. A few cases may first manifest as late as teen age. Often the first symptoms are behavioral rather than tics. In about half the cases, tics begin with a single simple motor tic, usually facial, such as blinking, and at this stage cannot be distinguished from a transient tic disorder. Other cases begin with squatting, sniffling, hopping, skipping, stuttering, barking, grunting, snorting, yelping, or other tics. Up to 30% begin with phonic (vocal) tics. A few begin with verbal tics, perhaps obscenities (coprolalia). However, those who manifest coprolalia usually begin first with a nonverbal phonic tic (e.g., barking or grunting) or a partial word. For example, the patient may start repeating "uck, uck, uck," then add the "f" on later. The tics typically change over time regardless of the initial presentation. Over the course of several years, the whole tic complex may completely change, by gradual addition and subtraction of individual tics. The variety of tics possible can be reviewed in Table 18–2. Some authors (e.g., Leckman and Cohen 1985) report a natural progression from simple motor to complex motor to simple phonic to verbal tics and from head/neck to limbs to trunk. Of course, there are many individual exceptions to this typical progression. Even in patients with typical progression, the original tics can recur later. Most patients have not been noted to tic while sleeping. In addition to change in the type and location of tic, intensity can vary, sometimes with periods of complete remission.

As the disorder progresses, the patient's problems are compounded by secondary and associated problems. The motor tics can interfere with various academic and other tasks, aggravating the impairment of function that often results from an associated arithmetic disorder or other academic skills disorder. According to Bornstein and associates (1985), cognitive deficits themselves, including written arithmetic, verbal IQ, and visuomotor deficits, seem to worsen with age in the Tourette's patients who have such deficits (Table 18–3). It should be noted that Bornstein's study was cross-sectional; an age skew of the sample could have resulted if younger patients who have no cognitive deficits recover from Tourette's disorder by the older age and are therefore not included at the older age. A longitudinal study is necessary to confirm age deterioration. In any event, this worsening on standard age-normed tests seems more an arrest of certain types of cognitive development than loss of skills already learned.

Restlessness, impulsiveness, easy frustration, impaired concentration, other behavior problems, or obsessive argumentativeness may develop early or late, and more often than not are the first symptoms to be noted, even when mild tics are also present. Behavior and social problems may be aggravated by tics that consist of blurting insults, which may be obscene. Of the patients who also have attention-deficit hyperactivity disorder, the latter often precedes the tics but may appear simultaneously or later. Obsessive-compulsive symptoms are usually more synchronous with the development of tics but can also precede them. Anxiety disorders and sleep disorders (sleepwalking, sleep terrors) may appear sporadically, usually after the onset of Tourette's disorder. In addition to the possibility of primary depression, there is often secondary depression from socially or functionally disabling tics. Coprolalia and copropraxia are especially troublesome socially, but even nonobscene tics may elicit teasing or accusations from peers or authorities. Some patients repeatedly get in trouble for these and may withdraw from attempts to socialize, at least with new acquaintances.

Tics may cause physical self-injury: Orthopedic injuries can result from jerking or twisting spasmodically. Some patients pick at themselves or bite themselves enough to cause chronic or permanent skin injuries, or even mutilate deeper structures. Blindness has resulted, usually by retinal detachment, from headbanging or self-hitting, an unusual but serious tic.

Medications used to treat symptoms can add side effects to the clinical picture, including depression, anxiety (including school phobia or agoraphobia), akathisia, hostility, aggression, seizures, cognitive or affective

Table 18–3. RELATIONSHIP BETWEEN AGE AND TEST PERFORMANCE (AGE-CORRECTED) FOR PATIENTS WITH TOURETTE'S SYNDROME

Test	r	Test*	r	Test*	r
Verbal IQ (VIQ)	−0.36†	HCT	−0.72‡	Peg-D	0.10
Performance IQ (PIQ)	−0.22	TPT-D	−0.10	Peg-ND	0.01
Wide Range Achievement Test—Reading (WRATR)	−0.13	TPT-ND	−0.14	Tap-D	−0.04
Wide Range Achievement Test—Spelling (WRATS)	−0.22	TPT-Tot	−0.06	Tap-ND	−0.35§
Wide Range Achievement Test—Arithmetic (WRATA)	−0.57‡	TPT-Mem	0.03	Grip-D	−0.20
Peabody Picture Vocabulary Test (PPVT IQ)	−0.11	TPT-Loc	0.23	Grip-ND	−0.20§
Knox IQ	−0.57‡	SSPT	−0.12	FNW-D	−0.45†
		TMTA	−0.61‖	FNW-ND	−0.42§
		TMTB	−0.66‡	TFR-D	0.05
				TFR-ND	−0.08

*Abbreviations of test variables: HCT, Halstead Category Test; TPT, Tactual Performance Test; Mem, memory component; Loc, Localization component; SSPT, Speech Sounds Perception Test; TMTA, TMTB Trail Making Test parts A and B; Peg, Grooved Pegboard Test; Tap, Finger-Tapping Test; Grip, grip strength; FNW, finger tip number writing; TFR, tactile finger recognition; D, dominant hand trial; ND, nondominant hand trial. Negative correlation means the neuropsychological deficit was worse in older patients than in younger.
† $p < 0.05$.
‡ $p < 0.005$.
§ $p < 0.10$.
‖ $p < 0.01$.
(Reproduced with permission from Bornstein, R. A., Carroll, A., and King, G. 1985. Relationship of age to neuropsychological deficit in Tourette's syndrome. *J. Dev. Behav. Pediatrics* 6:284–286. © by Williams & Wilkins, 1985.)

blunting, dizziness, sedation, tardive dyskinesia, or even worsening of tics.

Tourette's disorder may disappear completely by early adulthood, persist lifelong (usually with reduced severity), or remit and recur repeatedly. Transient tic disorder, by definition, does not have such a chronic course, and the tics themselves are usually milder. The associated emotional problems are also milder. However, transient tics can progress to Tourette's disorder or to chronic motor or chronic vocal tics. The latter, of course, can also progress to full-blown Tourette's disorder.

Laboratory Findings

There is no pathognomonic laboratory test for Tourette's disorder. Patients often have nonspecific diffuse electroencephalographic (EEG) abnormalities (up to 85%). These are mostly sharp waves and slowing without localization or epileptic signs. EEG abnormality seems to be associated with younger age at onset. Computed tomography may also show nonspecific abnormalities in a minority of patients. Sleep studies are equivocal, with a claim of decreased delta sleep (reversed by haloperidol) balanced by a claim of increased delta sleep. Patients manifesting motor tics show no cortical or electrical potentials preceding the tics but do have negative potentials when they mimic the same movements voluntarily.

Psychometric findings include decreased verbal IQ, deficits in written arithmetic, and deficits in visual attention, psychomotor problem solving, fine motor tasks, and visuospatial/visuomotor/visuographic tasks in general. The neuropsychological measures in Table 18–3 showing significant negative age correlations are in general those reported deficient in Tourette's disorder.

The cerebrospinal fluid of Tourette's disorder patients has shown decreased amounts of homovanillic acid (HVA), the main metabolite of brain dopamine, and of 5-hydroxyindoleacetic acid (5-HIAA), the main metabolite of serotonin (5-HT). The main metabolite of norepinephrine, 3-methoxy-4-hydroxyphenylglycol (MHPG), has been reported to be both increased and decreased. Neuropsychological (psychometric cognitive) deficits correlated with 24-hour urinary excretion of HVA (positively), 5-HIAA (negatively),

HVA/5-HIAA ratio (positively), MHPG/5-HIAA ratio (positively), and HVA/MHPG ratio (positively) (Bornstein and Baker 1988). In other words, the higher the HVA and the lower the 5-HIAA excretion, the worse were the neuropsychological deficits.

Differential Diagnosis

A diagnostic decision tree for tics and other abnormal movements is presented in Table 18–4.

Tics are distinguished from tremors by their irregular pacing and the fact that tics are usually coarser, involving larger movements than tremors. They are distinguished from chorea by the stereotyped similarity of successive tics and by the complexity of some of the tics. They are distinguished from athetosis by the slow writhing character of the latter. Dystonia is a slow twisting movement interspersed with prolonged muscle tension. Myoclonus is a brief shock affecting only a single muscle or a group of muscles. Hemiballismus is coarse unilateral limb jumping; ballistic movements may occur in Tourette's disorder, but they are not confined to one side nor an isolated symptom. In a sense, ballismus may be considered one type of tic if it occurs in the constellation of a tic syndrome, but as an isolated symptom it is not considered a tic. Spasms are slower and more prolonged than tics.

Dyskinesia, hemifacial spasm, and synkinesis are sometimes difficult to distinguish from tics. Hemifacial spasm is repetitive, irregular, unilateral facial jerks; the distinction from Tourette's disorder is made by the absence of other symptoms. Synkinesis is mouth movements on attempting to close the eyes or eye movements on moving the mouth; the distinction from tics is made by the temporal association with a specific voluntary movement. Dyskinesia usually involves chewing and other oral, buccal, or lingual movements or choreoathetosis of limbs, trunk, or head. Some of the more spasmodic movements of dyskinesia resemble simple motor tics. Interestingly, both tardive dyskinesia induced by neuroleptics and Tourette's disorder are believed to result from a similar mechanism: dopamine receptor supersensitivity. Also, Tourette's syndrome has been reported to follow chronic neuroleptic exposure. Even the same initials,

Table 18–4. DIAGNOSTIC DECISION TREE FOR STEREOTYPED MOVEMENTS

Are the abnormal movements and/or sounds a recognized nonpsychiatric disorder (tremor, athetosis, chorea, dystonia, myoclonus, etc.)? —yes— Diagnose the neurologic disorder. Does this explain all the symptoms? —yes— No further diagnosis

—no—

no

Are the movements and/or sounds repetitive, stereotyped, and nonfunctional? —no— Consider other diagnosis

yes

History of neuroleptic before any abnormal movements? —yes— Can entire clinical picture be explained by tardive dyskinesia? —yes— Diagnosis tardive dyskinesia

no

no

Is part of clinical picture consistent with tardive dyskinesia?

yes

Are the recurrent movements tics (rapid involuntary nonrhythmic contractions of functionally related muscles)? ← Consider diagnosing both tardive dyskinesia and tic or stereotypy

—no— Pervasive developmental disorder? —no— Cause injury or interfere with normal activities? —yes— Diagnose stereotypy/habit disorder

yes

Diagnose only pervasive developmental disorder

no

Search for other diagnosis

yes

Present only during intoxication or central nervous system disease? —yes— Diagnose only the basic disease or psychoactive substance intoxication

no

Many times/day most days? —no— Diagnose tic disorder not otherwise specified

yes

Onset before age 21? —no—

yes

no

Present over 1 year? —no— Previous history Tourette's or chronic motor/vocal tic? —no— Present at least 2 weeks?

yes —yes— yes

Both motor and phonic tics? —no— Diagnose chronic motor tic disorder or chronic vocal tic disorder

Diagnose transient tic disorder

yes

Diagnose Tourette's disorder

T.D., have been used (in different contexts) to refer to both disorders. The presence of complex tics or phonic tics suggests Tourette's disorder; athetotic components and a history of neuroleptics help distinguish tardive dyskinesia.

Tics may develop as a side effect or toxic effect of adrenergic stimulants. If they remit on cessation of stimulants, they are not usually diagnosed as a tic disorder but rather as a toxic or side effect.

The motor restlessness of Tourette's disorder may be confused with attention-deficit hyperactivity disorder, and some cases of Tourette's disorder are misdiagnosed as attention-deficit disorder. In half the cases both diagnoses are warranted. If the patient has inattentiveness and impulsiveness in addition to restlessness and meets the *DSM-III-R* criteria for attention-deficit hyperactivity disorder, it should be diagnosed, but the motor restlessness can also be counted in assessing the severity of Tourette's disorder if the patient also meets the *DSM-III-R* criteria for Tourette's disorder.

A more difficult differential diagnosis occurs with obsessive-compulsive disorder, because some of the Tourette's disorder tics resemble rituals and because mental coprolalia is similar to obsessions. Also, the argumentativeness often gets obsessive. Careful interviewing is necessary to determine the distinctions. Tics are done impulsively and involuntarily, without thinking, while rituals are usually done voluntarily for some subjective purpose, such as getting rid of an obsession or making sure that the door is really locked or that the hands are really clean. Obsessions are usually more complex than mental coprolalia, are often described as an act or as visual imagery, may sometimes be enjoyable even though the patient feels guilty about having them, and sometimes have an obvious psychodynamic significance. On the other hand, mental coprolalia is generally couched in words rather than images, is very distressing to the patient, and is more simple and unexpectedly intrusive. Nevertheless, in some cases a firm distinction cannot be made. If the patient seems to meet the *DSM-III-R* diagnostic criteria for both Tourette's disorder and obsessive-compulsive disorder, both should be diagnosed.

Self-injurious tics (hitting, picking, biting) need to be distinguished from other self-injurious behavior, such as suicide attempts or suicide equivalents. The patient's description of the act and the reasons for it are usually sufficient for this distinction: self-injurious tics are involuntary and are not done for any purpose that the patient can think of. Other self-injurious behavior is usually deliberate and motivated by guilt, anxiety, delusion, or grief, which the patient can usually verbalize, or which (in the case of nonverbal patients) is obvious from the context. The distinction from self-injurious stereotypy/habit disorder is that the latter is not diagnosed in the presence of a tic disorder.

Treatment

The Tourette Syndrome Global Scale (TSGS) (Harcherik and associates 1984) can quantify baseline symptomatology for later comparison of treatment effectiveness. The first half of the TSGS quantifies the four types of tics by multiplying frequency times disruptiveness; the last half quantifies behavioral, academic, and occupational problems. Since different treatments differentially affect tics and behavioral symptoms, it is desirable to monitor the subscores as well as the total. Interpretation of any score change or other indication of treatment effectiveness needs to be qualified by knowledge of the natural waxing and waning of Tourette's symptoms. Because of this waxing and waning, multiple baseline measures may be desirable if there is not an urgent need to start treatment. Discontinuation of any stimulant should ordinarily be done first. A careful history of previous medicines tried, dosage, length of trial, and results (benefits, side effects) forms part of the necessary data base for effective clinical management.

For a long time the treatment of choice was haloperidol (Haldol), a potent dopamine-blocking major tranquilizer (neuroleptic). It was reported to be most effective at serum levels between 1 and 4 ng/mL. Unfortunately, this dose also induces unacceptable side effects, mainly lethargy, dysphoria, sedation, akathisia, extrapyramidal symptoms, and weight gain. Therefore clinical management often involves a compromise between symptoms and side effects (as with most drugs used for Tourette's disorder). The dose ordinarily used is lower than for treatment of psychosis. Bruun (1988) reports a "threshold dose" varying from one patient to another and ranging from 0.5 to 3 mg twice daily, above which dysphoria (depression, anxiety) commonly occurs. At escalating doses akathisia may drive the Tourette's symptoms. Therefore, if the Tourette's disorder seems to worsen while taking a neuroleptic, dose reduction should be considered before a dose increase. Besides haloperidol, other dopamine-blocking neuroleptics have also been used. Pimozide (Orap) has been claimed to be more specific with less side effects (e.g., Shapiro and Shapiro 1984) and has been especially approved for use in Tourette's disorder. It is reported to benefit the majority of patients who tried it. Unfortunately, it carries significant cardiac risk (bradycardia, QT interval lengthening, and inverted T waves) compared with other neuroleptics, and some sudden deaths have been reported. Therefore it is justified mainly when safer drugs have not been satisfactory. A baseline electrocardiogram is advisable, with follow-up monitoring. Dosage starts at 1 to 2 mg/day in divided doses and should never exceed 0.3 mg/kg/day. Usually 0.2 mg/kg/day is the upper limit. Titration for either neuroleptic should be slow, increasing by not more than the initial dose every 3 to 7 days.

Clonidine (Catapres) is an α_2-adrenergic agonist, which damps catecholamine activity (norepinephrine and possibly dopamine) by stimulating adrenergic inhibitory presynaptic autoreceptors in the locus ceruleus. It also is believed to inhibit serotonin transmission somewhat. The mechanism of benefit in Tourette's disorder is not clear, but studies showed it efficacious for at least half of Tourette's disorder patients, including many not helped by haloperidol. Some clinicians have begun to prefer it over the neuroleptics. One advantage is that it is not believed to carry the risk of tardive dyskinesia, as a neuroleptic might. Another is that patients with Tourette's disorder and attention-deficit hyperactivity disorder can have both disorders simultaneously treated because clonidine has also been reported effective for the latter. The standard adrenergic stimulant treatment for attention-deficit hyperactivity disorder is believed to aggravate tics in many patients (Caine et al. 1984). However, some authors have claimed benefit for both disorders from combining a stimulant and a neuroleptic (Shapiro and Shapiro 1981; Comings and Comings 1987). Clonidine dosage usually starts at 0.05 mg once or twice daily and is titrated to 0.2 or 0.3 mg/day over a few weeks. Up to 3 months may be needed to assess full benefits. A large obese 13-year-old adolescent took 1.3 mg a day in divided doses. The main side effects are drowsiness, fatigue, and dry mouth, but hypotensive dizziness and irritability should be checked for at high doses. Some generic clonidine has been reported less effective than Catapres.

Other drugs reported beneficial in Table 8–5 include the GABA-agonist benzodiazepine, clonazepam (Klonopin). The anticonvulsant carbamazepine (Tegretol) may help or worsen tics. The serotonin precursor L-5-hydroxytryptophan seemed effective in two studies but not another. Both physostigmine, a cholinergic central cholinesterase inhibitor, and scopolamine, a central anticholinergic agent, have been reported helpful in individual patients. Acetylcholine precursors (lecithin, choline, deanol) showed equivocal results. Low-dose apomorphine to stimulate presynaptic inhibitory dopamine autoreceptors showed some promise in preliminary trials. Selective D_2 receptor blockers and calcium channel blockers also show promise. Opioid antagonists have shown inconsistent results. Lithium reportedly caused acute exacerbation followed by improvement (Leckman et al. 1987).

A tricyclic antidepressant such as imipramine sometimes helps, especially for the patients with obsessive-compulsive symptoms, significant depression, attention-deficit hyperactivity disorder, and/or other associated disorders usually responsive to tricyclic agents. Compared with the adrenergic stimulants, a tricyclic agent seems less likely to worsen tics, and in some cases seems to help them. Because some patients seem responsive to a serotonin precursor and because of the strong association with obsessive-compulsive disorder, which is believed serotonergic responsive, a more serotonergic tricyclic or the new serotonergic bicyclic fluoxetine may be preferable. However, this has not been established, and it is not clear whether the symptoms of attention-deficit hyperactivity disorder would respond as well to a strongly serotonergic antidepressant. Unfortunately, tricyclic antidepressants have been reported to interfere with clonidine action on blood pressure and platelet aggregation (Silverstein et al. 1985). Presumably, this interference could extend to the ameliorating effect on Tourette's disorder.

Table 18–5. DRUGS USED FOR TOURETTE'S DISORDER

Drug and Mechanism	Indications	Starting Dose	Therapeutic Daily Dose Range	Maximum Safe Daily Dose	Side Effects
Haloperidol (Haldol) and other dopamine-blocking neuroleptics	Tics, behavior	0.5 mg	0.5–6.0 mg	?	Usual neuroleptic side effects, including lethargy, dysphoria, akathisia, tardive dyskinesia, worsening of Tourette's disorder
Pimozide (Orap), a special dopamine-blocking neuroleptic	Tics, behavior, with failure of other drugs	1.0 mg	1–10 mg	0.2–0.3 mg/kg	Bradycardia, QT interval lengthening, sudden death
Clonidine (Catapres), an α_2-agonist	Tics, behavior, attention-deficit hyperactivity disorder	0.05 mg	0.1–0.3 mg	<1.0 mg? Monitor BP	Drowsiness, ↓ BP dizziness, dry mouth
Tricyclic antidepressants (except protriptyline)	Attention-deficit hyperactivity disorder, obsessive-compulsive signs, sleepwalking or terrors, separation anxiety, depression	10–25 mg	1–3 mg/kg	3–5 mg/kg Monitor ECG	Dry mouth, ↓ BP dizziness, may ↑ tics, may antagonize clonidine
Clonazepam (Klonopin), a GABA agonist and serotonin-active	Tics, spasms, anxiety	0.01–0.03 mg/kg/day in two to three doses	Titrate by effects every 3 days	0.3 mg/kg	Sedation, cognitive blunting, aggression
Carbamazepine (Tegretol)	Tics, behavior, depression, irritability	Low	Titrate serum level	Titrate serum level	Sedation, rarely hyperactivity; possible worsening
Serotonin precursors	Tics, depression, behavior				Sedation
Cholinergic agents and precursors	Tics, behavior				Cholinergic side effects
Scopolamine (anticholinergic)	Tics, behavior				Dry mouth, cognitive blunting

Education of patient and family about the tic disorder should include appropriate cautions about adrenergic agents, including over-the-counter decongestants. Patient education about symptoms can be a two-edged sword: a few patients, especially younger ones, are suggestible enough that expectation may help bring on described additional symptoms. There may also be a temptation to feel licensed to swear or argue voluntarily, excusing it as a symptom. Nevertheless, education about the disorder and referral to the Tourette's Syndrome Association support services are generally helpful.

Behavior therapy has been reported help-ful in suppressing the more disabling manifestations of tic disorders by channeling symptoms, substituting less disabling tics, and training social skills. Hypnotherapy with relaxation training showed significant tic reduction within days in a sample of four (Kohen and Batts 1987). Supportive psychotherapy can help the patient learn to live with the problems, which are seldom completely controlled by chemotherapy or other means. Family therapy may help families adjust to their family member's symptoms. (Siblings, for example, may be embarrassed by the patient's tics.)

Parent guidance is usually indicated for

home management and to assist the parents in being appropriately supportive. Some parents tend to become overprotective, and some children exploit their disorder by blaming any misbehavior or other lapse onto their diagnosis. Dealing with this can be very challenging because the manifestations of Tourette's disorder are so pleomorphic. A helpful principle is to remember that everyone is responsible for the consequences of his or her own behavior whether or not it was intentional or his or her "fault." For example, the child who breaks a sibling's toy because of a tic is still responsible for replacing it. This principle helps to prevent exploitation of the diagnosis. As with any other chronic disabling neurologic or medical disorder, the patient must be expected to adjust and learn how to cope despite the handicap.

STEREOTYPY/HABIT DISORDERS AND SELF-INJURIOUS BEHAVIORS

Definition and Diagnosis

Stereotyped habits are generally rhythmic, habitual, purposeless, repeated motions. They are usually self-stimulating or self-soothing. The prototype is head banging, but other variants are rocking, hand flapping, teeth grinding, or even such self-injurious behaviors as self-hitting, self-biting, or self-picking.

The DSM-III-R diagnosis requires intentional, repetitive, nonfunctional behaviors that either physically injure the child or interfere with normal activities in a patient who does not meet the criteria for either tic disorder or pervasive developmental disorder. The behaviors are usually rhythmic but do not have to be to meet the diagnostic criteria. The most noteworthy stereotyped habits are the self-injurious behaviors, and the following discussion will focus on these.

Etiology and Pathogenesis

Stereotyped habit disorders may result from either strictly organic causes, from psychodynamic or operant behavioral causes, or from some combination of these. The best known example of organic causation is the Lesch-Nyhan syndrome, with repetitive self-biting. This syndrome is believed to result from an abnormality of purine metabolism. Other organic causes include temporal lobe epilepsy and encephalitis (which can also cause a tic disorder, in which case the stereotypy is not diagnosed). Some experts suspect that stereotypies are associated with excess dopamine activity. This would be compatible with occurrence in autism and Tourette's disorder, both of which are reported to have excess dopamine activity.

On the operant-behavioral side, repetitive self-injurious behaviors can result from perverse reinforcement. For example, it has been demonstrated in experimental animals that self-induction of pain can be produced by first subjecting the animal to an avoidance paradigm and then switching to a fixed punishment schedule. At a more credible level, pain or other associated sensations may be perceived as better than the alternative of boredom or confusion. In many cases, the stereotyped behavior seems to be a form of self-stimulation. When this occurs in a child with sensory handicaps (blindness, deafness), it may be an attempt to provide tactile, kinesthetic, or other sensory input to compensate for insufficient auditory or visual clarity or meaning.

Behavioral theory and biochemistry are combined in the hypothesis that the reinforcement for self-injury is induction of endogenous opioids. In this hypothesis, the patient may be considered addicted to his or her own opioids. Certainly, patients addicted to exogenous narcotics can be just as self-destructive in their pursuit of a fix.

In many cases, especially where the activity does not seem to be self-injurious, it may be merely a bad habit that the child has acquired. In the case of rocking or mild head banging, the child might be meeting a need for vestibular stimulation, either constitutional or resulting from early deprivation.

Epidemiology

The disorder seems to occur with more frequency in patients who have mental retardation, deprivation of social stimulation, sensory handicaps ("blindisms"), CNS disorder, schizophrenia, obsessive-compulsive disorder, or stimulant intoxication, but it can also occur as an isolated phenomenon. The disorder is also more likely in the severely retarded than in the mildly retarded, and in institutional settings with lack of stimulation. In such settings, self-injurious stereotyped behaviors have been reported in up to one fifth of the mentally retarded.

Pathology

Since the diagnosis is phenomenologic and is often made in the presence of more serious disorders, such as schizophrenia, psychotic depression, or mental retardation, there is not a specific pathology. Neuropathology varies widely, ranging from a reasonably intact nervous system with a psychogenic/behavioral etiology to severe brain damage with profound mental retardation, cerebral palsy, or other gross brain disorder. In most of the more serious cases, there is some degree of brain damage.

Clinical Picture

The clinical picture also varies widely, being dominated by the frequently associated more serious disorders. The stereotyped movement can involve any part of the body. Examples are headbanging; teeth grinding; rocking of the body or any part of it; self-hitting; self-slapping; self-biting; picking at skin or nose; self scratching; hair pulling; poking at eye, anus, mouth, or other body orifice; eating or mouthing various things; repetitive vocalizations; hyperventilation; breath holding; air swallowing; hand rotation; finger flipping; and so on. With mentally retarded or developmentally disabled patients there is often a tendency for the activity to occupy a large proportion of waking hours. In many cases, it seems to be a rhythmic form of self-stimulation, and the patient typically seems to take pleasure in it, or at least to be preoccupied or engrossed with it. Sometimes there is a trancelike state, but the patient's attention can usually be attracted. The stereotyped behavior often stops when attending to something interesting, but in some cases it may continue even while engaging in another activity. It tends to increase under stress. There may be idiosyncratic postures that facilitate the stereotyped behavior.

Sometimes, particularly with self-abusive behavior, the patient may look at the caretaker or examiner while doing it as if watching for a reaction. At times, patients may even seem to sneak to engage in the stereotyped habit. They do not seem to be distressed by it. However, some patients, when subjected to a behavioral paradigm to extinguish the behavior, seem grateful for relief from the habit and may even indicate a desire for continued access to a punishment device that suppresses the self-injurious behavior.

On physical examination there may be bruises, scars, wounds, or deformities if the stereotyped habit is self-injurious. Head bangers or head rubbers may have bald patches at the point of contact. There may also be stigmata of associated disorders such as mental retardation, cerebral palsy, postencephalitic syndrome, congenital syndromes, or substance-induced organic mental disorder.

Case Histories

CASE 6

A 14-year-old high school freshman, Rocky, was brought by his mother because of mild misbehavior, crying, and rocking constantly. He had seemed normal in development, behavior, and emotional adjustment until 4 years before when his brother developed leukemia and consumed all of the parents' financial, emotional, and time resources. For months at a time, both parents spent all of their available time in the hospital with the leukemic brother. He and his sister had been relatively neglected. The sister had been admitted to the adolescent psychiatric unit several months before because of emotional adjustment problems she had developed. This shifted the parents' focus of attention to her, leaving Rocky even more neglected. At this time his rocking and other behavior problems increased to the place at which he developed peer relation problems as well as getting in trouble with school authorities and his parents. Eventually, he told his parents that he thought he was sick, too.

On interview he was a depressed-looking young adolescent appearing about his stated age and of normal intelligence. On beginning the interview, he rocked mildly in his seat. As he began telling about his troubles, the rocking increased in amplitude and intensity. On being enrolled in group therapy with peers, he continued to rock throughout the group sessions, and this rocking increased whenever the topic touched on parent–child relations or issues of security. He had no history of head banging as an infant. None of his rocking seemed self-injurious. Rather, it seemed a means of working off anxiety and depression.

CASE 7

A 9-year-old girl with cerebral palsy and borderline intelligence was referred by her psychologist because of frequent temper tantrums resistant to behavioral management. During her tantrums, she cried, screamed, postured, and repeatedly bit her forearm. Her parents reported mood swings with depression followed by excitability and increased tantrums. Times of excitement, such as holidays, led to increased tantrums. She had developed suicidal thoughts without a plan. She ate "anything she can find—crayons, glue, sand, etc." She had functional encopresis and wore diapers, although at school and at her aunt's she did not soil her clothes. She demanded so much of her parents' time and energy that they did not have enough time for their two other daughters. A trial of thioridazine (Mellaril), 25 mg twice daily, by a previous physician was discontinued because of sedation.

She presented as an obese, neatly dressed girl with red bruises on her left forearm from biting herself. She walked with crutches and had little fine motor control. She readily admitted the behaviors described by her parents but refused to cooperate with other interview questions, such as projective questions, or to make any drawings. In fact, when asked to draw a person, she became agitated and tearful, put her head on the desk, and began crying and screaming for her parents. Having her father return to the room calmed her temporarily, but further attempts to engage her in activities or conversation resulted in loud screeching and repeated biting of her left forearm and wrist.

The differential diagnosis included major depression, bipolar disorder, organic affective disorder, and oppositional disorder as well as stereotypy (self-biting), pica, functional encopresis, and borderline intellectual function.

Clinical Course

The course is influenced by the type of accompanying disorder. In the few cases where there is no underlying disorder, the prognosis is good. The stereotypy may disappear with maturation or with minimal intervention. Stereotyped behavior that is associated with an underlying acute episode of schizophrenia, major depression, or other episodic disorder may disappear as the underlying disorder abates. If the underlying disorder is chronic, the stereotyped behavior also tends to be chronic, especially with frank neurologic disorders. It is usually chronic in severe or profound retardation, but in some mentally retarded patients it responds to treatment or even abates spontaneously in later childhood or adolescence. On the other hand, it may worsen during adolescence.

The self-injurious behaviors can result in self-mutilation, blindness from retinal detachment, scarring, wound-induced septicemia, crippling, self-induced amputation, disfigurement, or even life-threatening injuries. Even without physically self-injurious behavior, stereotyped behavior can disrupt activities of daily living and self-care or elicit social rejection.

Laboratory Findings

Laboratory findings are generally those of the underlying disorder, such as low IQ in mental retardation or the purine abnormalities of Lesch-Nyhan syndrome.

Differential Diagnosis

The diagnostic decision tree in Table 18–4 includes stereotypy/habit disorder. This disorder is distinguished from normal developmental self-stimulating behaviors, such as infantile thumbsucking and rocking oneself to sleep, by the fact that it is inappropriate for age or is self-injurious or interferes with functioning in some way. Tic disorders, especially Tourette's disorder, can have stereotyped behavior that looks strikingly similar to stereotyped habits but are involuntary. The *DSM-III-R* diagnostic rule is that if a tic disorder is present, the tic disorder is diagnosed and the stereotyped behavior is considered part of it, not diagnosed as stereotypy/habit disorder.

Self-injurious behaviors can be tics, stereotyped habits, or psychodynamically induced sporadic self-injuries. The latter would include suicide attempts; the self-punishment of a guilt-ravaged, depressed, or schizophrenic patient; and the bizarre self-injuries or mutilations of a psychotic or borderline patient. Although stereotypy/habit disorder can be diagnosed in a depressed or schizophrenic patient, it is only diagnosed when the self-injurious behavior is repeated in a stereotyped, often rhythmic fashion. For example, repeatedly poking oneself in the eye would qualify for the additional diagnosis but a one-time self-enucleation without previous eye poking would not qualify as stereotypy/habit disorder.

Treatment

When there is a treatable associated disorder, such a disorder should be optimally treated as the first step in eliminating self-injurious or other stereotyped habits. Because so many patients with stereotypy are mentally retarded to an extent that distorts the usual presentation of psychiatric syndromes, the family history is important in ferreting out possible treatable disorders. Family history may be especially helpful in guiding or supporting appropriate therapy. For example, if another family member has had major depression or bipolar disorder and responded well to a certain antidepressant or lithium, this can justify a trial of the same treatment in a mentally retarded patient with a puzzling clinical presentation. An extreme example is the report of highly beneficial electroconvulsive therapy for a severely retarded man with a long history of head banging and self-mutilation and a family history of major depression.

In cases in which no suggestion of a specific underlying disorder can be elicited by history, family history, or examination of the patient, empiric trials of various psychotropic drugs can be justified if the potential for self-injury is severe. Baclofen, a GABA-like muscle relaxant, has been reported beneficial for some self-injurious behaviors. The serotonin precursor 5-hydroxytryptophan at first seemed effective, but replications were equivocal, with probable development of tolerance. Neuroleptic trials have been justified on the hypothesis of excess dopamine activity analogous to tics. Naltrexone has been reported helpful for some cases, tried on the hypothesis that the perpetuating reinforcer

was release of endogenous opioids, with which the naltrexone interferes (Bernstein et al. 1987). Lithium also has some promising case reports. In an excellent review, Farber (1987) concluded that lithium and naltrexone show the most promise for self-injurious behavior.

Any drug tried should be given a fair trial over a period of several months to check the results. Once the target behavior has disappeared for several months, an attempt should be made to withdraw the drug and see if it is still necessary. Doses may be rather idiosyncratic, especially in the mentally retarded; and a broad range of doses, including very low ones, should be tried while monitoring side effects, but each dose should be given a sufficient trial (e.g., a month).

Chemotherapy, of course, does not take place in a vacuum. Restraints to prevent injury may be necessary during an interim before an effective treatment is found. Behavioral paradigms have been found very effective for many self-injurious behaviors and other stereotyped habits and ordinarily would be preferred over chemotherapy if the situation is not urgent. Even if chemotherapy is tried, behavioral treatments should not be abandoned. Sometimes chemotherapy provides immediate relief, to be reinforced behaviorally, with later drug withdrawal.

In the case of isolated stereotypy/habit disorder without a more serious associated disorder, one of the most appropriate interventions may be to provide or encourage more appropriate forms of rhythmic stimulation, such as a rocking chair, swing, or hammock, or even some constructive activity such as sawing wood or hammering a nail. Pleasurable sensations other than rhythmic stimulation can also be encouraged to fill up the time previously taken by stereotyped habits, thus crowding them out. If attention seeking seems an important dynamic, other means of seeking and receiving attention need to be devised.

References

American Psychiatric Association. *Diagnostic and Statistical Manual of Mental Disorders*, 3rd. ed., revised. Washington, D.C.: American Psychiatric Association.

Barabas, G., Matthews, W. S., and Ferrari, M. 1984. Disorders of arousal in Gilles de la Tourette's syndrome. *Neurology* 34:815–817.

Bernstein, G. A., Hughes, J. R., Mitchell, J. E., and

Thompson, T. 1987. Effects of narcotic antagonists on self-injurious behavior: A single case study. *J. Am. Acad. Child Adolesc. Psychiatry* 26:886–889.

Bornstein, R. A., and Baker, G. B. 1988. Neuropsychological correlates of urinary amine metabolites in Tourette's syndrome. *Int. J. Neurosci.* Sept. 42 (1–2):113–120.

Bornstein, R. A., Carroll, A., and King, G. 1985. Relationship of age to neuropsychological deficit in Tourette's syndrome. *J. Dev. Behav. Pediatrics* 6:284–286.

Bruun, R. D. 1984. Gilles de la Tourette's syndrome: An overview of clinical experience. *J. Am. Acad. Child Psychiatry* 23:126–133.

Bruun, R. D. 1988. Subtle and underrecognized side effects of neuroleptic treatment in children with Tourette's disorder. *Am. J. Psychiatry* 145:621–624.

Burd, L., Fisher, W. W., Kerbeshian, J., and Arnold, M. E. 1987. Is development of Tourette disorder a marker for improvement in patients with autism and other pervasive developmental disorders? *J. Am. Acad. Child Adolesc. Psychiatry* 26:162–165.

Caine, E. D. 1985. Gilles de la Tourette's syndrome: A review of clinical and research studies and consideration of future directions for investigation. *Arch. Neurol.* 42:393–397.

Caine, E. D., Ludlow, C. L., Polinsky, R. J., and Ebert, M. H. 1984. Provocative testing in Tourette's syndrome: *d*- and *l*-amphetamine and haloperidol. *J. Am. Acad. Child Psychiatry* 23:147–152.

Comings, D. E., and Comings, B. G. 1987. A controlled study of Tourette syndrome: I. Attention-deficit disorder, learning disorders, and school problems. *Am. J. Hum. Genet.* 41:701–741.

Devinsky, O. 1983. Neuroanatomy of Gilles de la Tourette's syndrome: Possible midbrain involvement. *Arch. Neurol.* 40:508–514.

Farber, J. M. 1987. Psychopharmacology of self-injurious behavior in the mentally retarded. *J. Am. Acad. Child Adolesc. Psychiatry* 26:296–302.

Harcherik, D. F., Leckman, J. F., Detlor, J., and Cohen, D. J. 1984. A new instrument for clinical studies of Tourette's syndrome. *J. Am. Acad. Child Psychiatry* 23:153–160.

Kohen, D. P., and Botts, P. 1987. Relaxation-imagery (self-hypnosis) in Tourette's syndrome: Experience with four children. *Am. J. Clin. Hypnosis* 29:227–237.

Lakke, J. P. W. F., and Wilmink J. T. 1985. A case of Gilles de la Tourette's syndrome with midbrain involvement. *J. Neurol. Neurosurg. Psychiatry* 48:1293–1296.

Leckman, J. F., and Cohen, D. J. 1985. Tourette's disorder and other stereotyped movement disorders. In Michels, R., and Cavenar, J. (eds.): *Psychiatry*, vol. 2. Philadelphia: J. B. Lippincott.

Leckman, J. F., Walkup, J. R., Riddle, M. A., et al. 1987. Tic disorders. In Meltzer, H. Y. (ed.): *Psychopharmacology: The Third Generation of Progress.* New York: Raven Press.

Pauls, D. L., Kruger, S. D., Leckman, J. F., et al. 1984. The risk of Tourette's syndrome and chronic multiple tics among relatives of Tourette's syndrome patients obtained by direct interview. *J. Am. Acad. Child Psychiatry* 23:134–137.

Shapiro, A. K., and Shapiro, E. 1984. Controlled study of pimozide vs. placebo in Tourette's syndrome. *J. Am. Acad. Child Psychiatry* 23:161–173.

Shapiro, A. K., and Shapiro, E. 1981. Do stimulants provoke, cause, or exacerbate tics and Tourette's syndrome? *Compr. Psychiatry* 22:265–272.

Silverstein, F., Smith, C. B., and Johnston, M. V. 1985. Effect of clonidine on platelet alpha$_2$-adrenoreceptors and plasma norepinephrine of children with Tourette's syndrome. *Dev. Med. Child Neurol.* 27:793–799.

Sweeney, D., Pickar, D., Redmond, D. E., Jr., and Maas, J. 1978. Noradrenergic and dopaminergic mechanisms in Gilles de la Tourette syndrome. *Lancet* 1:872.

Williams, D. T., Pleak, R., and Hanesian, H. 1987. Neuropsychiatric disorders of childhood and adolescence. In Hales, R. E., and Yodofsky, S. C. (eds.): *Textbook of Neuropsychiatry.* Washington, D.C.: American Psychiatric Press.

19

The Elimination Disorders

BARRY D. GARFINKEL, M.D.[*]

Included in the category of elimination disorders are enuresis and encopresis. These disorders are disturbances associated with the involuntary elimination of urine or feces at inappropriate times. The term *elimination disorder* indicates that the divergence from normal behavior can be viewed from multiple etiologies but is specifically associated to bladder or bowel functioning. An alternate way of viewing these two disorders has been to regard them as developmental delays. This type of developmental delay implies that the failure to acquire appropriate control over bladder and bowel functioning is contrary to the normal developmental maturation that usually occurs. During normal development children start acquiring control over bladder function most frequently between the second and third years of life. Night-time control usually is completed between the third and fourth years. The age at which bowel control occurs overlaps to a large extent with these ages. The inability to gain control of either bowel or bladder functioning within an appropriate time period of these ages suggests that there are undetermined factors that have prevented the normal developmental control over these functions.

These disorders have been studied as arising from a functional abnormality of the bladder or bowel or a developmental failure to achieve control at an age-appropriate stage of development. These observations suggest a number of important issues to be addressed. Is the symptom a reflection of an underlying psychiatric disorder, is it a nonspecific response to general stressful life events, or does it signify an abnormality in the functional anatomy or physiology of these organ systems? The view that the elimination disorders are symptoms of an underlying condition mainly arises out of a psychanalytical perspective, in which the symptoms indicate a larger and substantially more important psychodynamic condition. Most often enuresis has been associated with passive aggressive behavior, depression, and the inability to resolve or contain high levels of anxiety. Others have suggested that it reflects direct hostility toward one's parents and that the elimination symptoms are a metaphor for this anger as well as being a plea for nurturance and care (Breger 1963; Binderglas and Dee 1978; Daniels 1971). Psychoanalysts have viewed the symptoms as expressing a child's wish to return to a more immature stage of development when pleasure is derived from direct bodily functions. This "regression" model suggests that a formerly continent child may subsequently lose control of bladder functioning in response to a birth of a sibling, parental/marital discord, and/or physical illness. Finally, psychoanalytical thinking (Freud 1938) associated enuresis with masturbation, stating that when masturbation commonly appeared, enuresis receded. Encopresis has also been viewed as

[*]The research on enuresis was completed with the collaboration of Andrea Bond, B.A., and J.P. Fournier, M.D., F.R.C.P.(C).

reflecting poor parental toilet training; a possible symptom of some underlying psychodynamic factor in the youngster's relationships primarily with parents; an abnormal response to environmental stress in which the youngster expresses a response to a harmful event through defecation at inappropriate times; and an abnormality of the physiological functioning of the bowel.

Although there is considerable overlap between these two disorders, each will be treated separately in this chapter. In general, the presentation of these disorders has emphasized three recurring observations that are supported by empiric studies:

1. The lack of control of bowel and bladder functioning is part of normal development, but as maturation occurs, greater control during the day and night replaces the involuntary release of urine or feces.

2. Occasionally, soiling and wetting can reflect a systemic nonspecific response to environmental stress.

3. There are separate functional disorders of unknown etiology in which bedwetting and soiling are the primary characteristics. It is this third condition that is described in greater detail in this chapter.

ENURESIS

The history of enuresis is indeed ancient and transcends many different cultures. The description of enuresis extends over 3500 years. In 1544, in the *Boke of Children,* Thomas Phaer, a British pediatrician, described a condition "of pissing in the bedde." His understanding of enuresis indicates that there is an intrinsic bladder and kidney problem that can extend well beyond childhood that is most frequently observed in males. His treatment included "cock trachea and hedgehog testicle,'" which would eliminate and ultimately control the bedwetting (McLain 1979). Earlier in central medieval Europe, enuresis was believed to be controlled through ancient cultural practices and by prayer. There were two patron saints for the relief of enuresis, Saint Catherine of Alexandria and Saint Vitas. In 1751, *Sharp's Surgery* described an unusually severe form of treatment for bedwetting that included an iron yoke with a velvet covering that fitted over the penis and was removed only during urination. This treatment persisted for approximately 100 years and was stopped only when a case of gangrene was reported (McLain 1979).

Various treatments were used by different cultures at different times. The earliest report of a specific treatment for bedwetting was found in the *Papyrus Ebers* in 1550 BC. The treatment was primarily pharmacologic, including one juniper berry, one cyprus leaf, and one measure of beer (Garrison 1923). Another reported treatment was to give infants boiled mice in their food (Salmon 1975). Glicklich (1951) reported numerous other naturalistic treatments, including hot wine, fragrant drinks made from chrysanthemums, and a drink made of the shaved testicle of the hare administered in wine. Navaho Indians were reported to have the naked enuretic child stand over a burning bird's nest, at which time a magical rite was performed (Leighton and Khuckholm 1947).

Developments in the latter part of the 19th century demonstrated that although pediatrics was becoming more enlightened this was not the case regarding the treatment of enuresis. Treatment included a number of measures, specifically the elimination of fluids, changes in diet and exercise, silver nitrate cauterization of the urethra to guarantee painful and difficult urination, and application of something cold to the perineum. The other movement in medical knowledge at that time involved psychoanalytical explanations of enuresis, suggesting that it was a symptom substitute for masturbation. This theory also suggested that persons who were enuretic were emotionally disturbed and that this disturbance was a result of some abnormal parent–child relationship (Gerard 1939). By examining the historical literature concerning enuresis it is obvious that a number of accurate as well as inaccurate conclusions were made. Correct observations identified that enuresis extended beyond childhood and could be observed in adolescents as well as adults. Unfortunately, however, treatment included both dangerous and harmful pharmacologic substances (e.g., strychnine and belladonna derivatives) as well as devices and trauma to the urethra. Most inaccurate, however, was the implausible depiction of enuretic children as having a psychiatric disturbance or problem in their relationship with their parents. Bedwetting, in an indirect way, attempted to signify this underlying conflictual relationship. The enuresis would not disappear unless the problematic issues, which were symbolized by the symptom of bedwetting, were treated and resolved. Neither this psychoanalytical treatment of bedwetting nor its association with specific psychopathology has been corroborated by empiric studies.

Definition

Functional enuresis can be defined by four primary features:

1. The release of urine either at night, during the daytime, or both into one's clothing or bed, either unwittingly or purposefully

2. For children between the ages of 5 and 6 there must be two documented involuntary voidings per month and for older children at least one involuntary voiding per month.

3. The child must be at least 5 years of age or have a mental age of 4.

4. There can be no identifiable physical ailment such as diabetes, seizure disorder, or urinary tract infection that can explain or be causative of the wetting.

There are two types of enuresis: a primary type and a secondary type. For the primary type there was no previous period when the child was continent for at least 1 year. In the secondary type the bedwetting follows a period of urinary continence that lasted for at least 1 year. It is believed that 75% to 80% of all enuretic children have primary enuresis, indicating that 20% to 25% had experienced a period of urinary continence for at least 1 year (Cohen 1975). By age 12, however, 57% of enuretic children have been identified as secondary enuretics, that is, children who had previously been continent but have experienced relapse (Oppel et al. 1968). The distinction of primary and secondary enuresis has not been associated with any significant clinical or treatment factor. Older children are proportionately more secondary enuretics. Age appears to be the important and determining precondition that may predict higher rates of emotional responses to still being enuretic when peers have long ago been trained. The discrepancy between the enuretic child and his or her peer group is much more pronounced and therefore interferes with normal social interaction, such as overnight camp, sleepovers, and other activities.

Epidemiology

Klackenburg (1981) identified the prevalence rate for enuresis according to different age groups. Those findings, along with those of McLain (1979) and others, indicate a declining rate of enuresis from childhood throughout the adolescent years. A rate of 26.1% has been identified at age 4, whereas by age 8 a rate of 8.9% is observed and by age 12 a rate of 2.8% can be identified. Depending on the study, somewhere between 1% and 2% of teenagers 18 years or older continue to be enuretic (Fig. 19–1). There is a generally steep and steady decline until late adolescence in the actual rate of enuresis. Shaffer and co-workers (1978b) identified that boys were enuretic more often than girls. Rutter and colleagues (1970) demonstrated that the boy–girl ratio of enuresis at age 5 was approximately 1.5 boys for every 1 girl and that by the age of 12 there were approximately 4.5 boys for every 1 girl. These observed gender differences have never been fully explained, but different theories have been suggested that boys mature more slowly and show more frequent developmental lags as well as being less responsive to parental toilet training.

Essen and Peckham (1976) showed that socioeconomic status and stressful life events predicted higher rates of enuresis. Difficult living situations including overcrowding and poor housing also created a greater rate of enuresis in children who experienced these environmental circumstances. Particular stressful life events characteristic of family dysfunction are also more frequently associated with enuretic children and they include marital problems, parental alcoholism, and hospitalization and removal of a family member from the home. McLain (1979) demonstrated that enuresis does run in families, with children of former enuretic parents being more likely to be enuretic themselves (Bakwin and Bakwin 1972). There is no association between intellectual functioning or mental retardation and enuresis (Hallgren 1956). Rutter and colleagues (1970) demonstrated that in older children who were enuretic there was a higher rate of psychiatric disorder. This finding does not suggest however that enuresis is a result of the psychopathology. It is primarily the older enuretic children who demonstrate more psychosocial symptoms and academic difficulties (Essen and Peckham 1976).

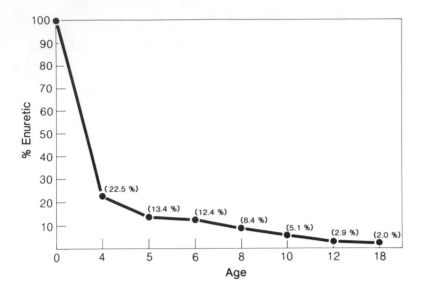

Figure 19–1. Frequency of enuresis at selected ages.

Pathogenesis

A number of investigators have demonstrated the familial occurrence of enuresis. Bakwin (1973) studied monozygotic and dizygotic twins and showed that in the monozygotic pairs there is a 68% concordance rate for enuresis compared with a 36% concordance rate in dizygotic twins (Table 19–1). The familial occurrence of enuresis has been associated with socioeconomic disadvantage, race, immigrant status, familial psychopathology, and poor toilet training techniques. These observations have not been replicated in different empiric studies.

There are no studies consistently demonstrating abnormalities in either urinary tract functioning or morphology. In contrast, however, the rate of urinary tract infection in enuretic children was found to be five times higher than that of children who were not

enuretic (Shaffer et al 1968; Dodge et al 1970). In one study it was demonstrated that approximately one fourth of the group of enuretic girls responded to antibiotic treatment of their urinary tract infection and thus stopping the bedwetting (Jones et al 1972). There are also no consistent well-established obstructive lesions interfering with micturition. Mahoney (1971) suggested that because of obstruction to outflow there was a hypertrophy and irritability of the detrusor muscle. Others have suggested that the musculature surrounding the vesicourethral junction was immature and provided an inadequate control of the vesicourethral junction. This poor musculature would lead to problems with continence, especially when there was high intravesicle pressure. Frequently, anterior urethral valves or meatal stenosis was identified as producing the obstruction. If these results were observed in multiple clinical studies it would suggest that surgery and urethral dilation would be appropriate treatment for enuresis. These findings, however, have not been replicated by others, especially using voiding cystourethrography. Gardner and Shaffer (1984) observed that there was a smaller functional bladder volume in enuretic children compared with normal children. This finding suggests that enuretic children urinate more frequently, never allowing the bladder to accommodate to a larger fluid volume, and with each urination smaller amounts are passed. Those children who had smaller bladder capacities were also found to have speech and language developmental

Table 19–1. ENURESIS CONCORDANCE IN SELECTED FAMILY RELATIONSHIPS

Relationship	Enuretics
Monozygotic twin, with twin	67.8
Both parents with biological child	77.3
Father with biological child	42.5
Mother with biological child	43.5
Dizygotic twin with twin	35.7
Enuretic twin with nontwin sibling	25.2
Neither parent enuretic with biological child	15.2

(From Bakwin, H., and Bakwin, R. M. 1972. Clinical Management of Behavior Disorders in Childhood, 4th ed. Philadelphia: W. B. Saunders.)

delays as well as more psychosocial symptoms. Mikkelsen and associates (1980) demonstrated that enuresis occurred throughout all sleep stages and that bedwetting was not associated with a deeper stage of sleep or a particular period when the child was less arousable. These observations are in contrast to parental reports that suggest that enuretic children are especially difficult to arouse.

Others have suggested that enuresis results from abnormal toilet training methods. When training is attempted at too young an age and in too punitive and harsh a fashion there can be a failure to develop continence (Breger 1963; Sears et al. 1957). It has also been noted that passive and inconsistent toilet training can also lead to incontinence. Stressful life events, although associated with a relative increase in the occurrence of enuresis, may be a result of parental socioeconomic status, family breakdown, and other parental medical and psychiatric hospitalizations. Although these events have been linked to enuresis, the overwhelming factor may simply be socioeconomic status of the child and family (Heisel et al. 1973).

Although the evidence is inconclusive, it does support the notion that enuresis reflects a maturational delay in developing urinary continence. The observations supporting this conclusion include the following: reduced functional bladder capacity of enuretic children; frequent voiding and urgency in enuretic children; the hereditary predisposition to enuresis; and with maturation, the dramatic decrease in enuresis (Binderglas and Dee 1978). Other environmental factors that may complicate and may further delay maturational control include the emotional response of others, the family context in which the enuresis is occurring, and the efficacy of the toilet training that the parents are providing.

Problems with toilet training encompass three issues: (1) training too early, before the child is maturationally "ready"; (2) inconsistent reinforcement for appropriate voiding behavior; and (3) punitive punishment for errors or incontinence. The most frequent parental mistake is to begin training too early, often within the first year (Lovibond 1964). If training is delayed to a more optimal time the actual amount of time spent in training is less (Sears et al. 1957). In contrast, if training is delayed too long there is an increased rate of enuresis (Kaffman and Eli-

zur 1977). Reinforcement influences the early acquisition of bladder control by positively using food, social learning (e.g., praise, hugs), and special equipment (e.g., child's own commode) (Foxx and Azrin 1973). A severe, stern, punitive response to incontinence or to the training experience itself may lead to difficulties in training or in other areas of the child's functioning (Sears et al. 1957).

Case History

Alex is a 12-year-old boy who was referred for an evaluation of his learning disability and possible attention-deficit disorder. At the time of his evaluation there was marked marital discord between the parents, indicating that separation and eventually a divorce were imminent. Alex was very large for his size, very awkward, and poorly coordinated. He exhibited many specific learning disabilities affecting reading comprehension, auditory decoding, and penmanship. His poor fine motor control contributed to an almost illegible handwriting. Printed words were also very difficult to identify because of reversals, indicating severe visuomotor integration problems.

During the course of the history-taking, his mother indicated that Alex has always been severely enuretic, never having achieved night-time bladder control for longer than 6 months. There were two periods of 6 months each, when he was 8 and 10 years old, respectively, when he was substantially continent. Even during these periods, he would be incontinent three to four times each month. Since age 5 until the present, he has had complete bladder control during the daytime. There were no episodes of soiling reported.

On examination, Alex appeared as an obese 12-year-old boy who looked somewhat older, primarily because of his obesity. There were no positive findings on the standard mental status examination. He appeared mildly dysphoric and had very low self-esteem. He did not show any other criteria for an affective disorder. He related that he was overly active, distractible, impulsive, and restless. He also had a number of temper outbursts each week. He was very evasive and used much denial when describing his bedwetting. He indicated that all forms of help, including alarms, changes in drinking habits, and parental awakenings in the first few hours of sleep, were ineffective.

Alex was started on 50 mg of imipramine at bedtime and required an eventual dose of 200 mg before there was a moderate cessation of his enuresis. Wet nights decreased from nightly to 3 to 4 times per month. His parents agreed that they did not want any further treatment for the enuresis, since they felt that this was a sufficient improvement. They also noted good improvement in Alex's behavior, as well as a positive change in his affect and self-esteem.

Differential Diagnosis

In considering functional enuresis as a possible clinical diagnosis, the clinician must be reassured first that other physical explanations for the continued incontinence have been ruled out. One must systematically eliminate congenital anatomical abnormalities, sickle cell anemia, neurologic disorders (e.g., seizures), urinary tract infections, allergies, and an abnormal consumption of fluids in the evening hours. Similarly, specific endocrinologic diseases, such as diabetes insipidus and diabetes mellitus, can present as bedwetting.

The evaluation of enuresis must quickly determine whether it is primary or secondary, in order to ascertain whether there has been a period of time (usually 1 year) when the youngster was continent. If it was this continent period that was subsequently lost, it indicates that training techniques had been effective at one time. A complete psychiatric history must include the following:

1. Marital and family relationships
2. Physical and sexual abuse
3. Separations and removal from the home
4. Episodes of depression
5. The impact of new siblings
6. Bereavement and loss
7. Developmental delays/learning disabilities
8. Disruptive behavioral disorders (e.g., oppositional/defiant/conduct disorder)
9. Separation anxiety disorder symptoms
10. Ineffective toilet training practices

These ten factors have been associated with enuresis from various studies conducted over the past 30 years. The psychiatric disorders most often linked to enuresis have been depression (Frommer 1968) and developmental delays (Shaffer 1973). Appropriate treatment must be directed at the associated psychiatric disorder as well as the enuresis. Remedial educational programs, including other forms of intervention and treatment, should be provided in conjunction with either an alarm system or imipramine. In the cases of depressed enuretic children, the clinician may prefer to use imipramine, rather than an alarm system, because the imipramine may have a dual therapeutic purpose. Enuresis can emerge following traumatic life events, especially bereavement, abuse, and family breakdown. Effective counseling for these associated precipitants should be started directly. An environment that is safe for the child is mandatory and is always the initial form of intervention.

Although the youngster may be vulnerable because of developmental delays, often the onset of enuresis can be precipitated by an environmental event. Similarly, a very thorough history of training methods used by the parents must be taken to see if they have used a consistent, positive reinforcing approach.

Frequently, youngsters temporarily revert to bedwetting in response to a need for more attention, especially with the birth of a younger sibling. Providing the youngster with appropriate attention over a period of time and with reinforcement of previous training techniques, one can see an improvement in the symptoms of enuresis. These general factors can act independently from or in association with the delay in the development of bladder control.

Treatment

Treatment has been thoroughly studied over the past 30 years and has been broadly categorized into three main orientations: (1) psychodynamic, (2) psychopharmacologic, and (3) behavioral. Werry and Cohrssen (1965) and DeLean and Mandrell (1966) demonstrated that psychodynamic psychotherapy alone is not effective in ameliorating enuresis. Furthermore, psychoanalytical theoretical explanations of the etiology of why enuresis is present are not generally helpful in directing a management program for an individual child. Viewing enuresis as a result of conflict over masculinity/femininity, masturbation, or aggressive impulses may obscure a better understanding of the developmental delays and of providing a compassionate, effective rehabilitation program.

By a chance observation, a psychiatrist observed that geriatric patients on imipramine for depression had hesitancy on voiding. It occurred to him that it may similarly delay micturition in enuretic children. It was attempted in 1960 and has led to numerous studies replicating its efficacy, as well as the efficacy of other medications. There have been well over 20 double-blind, placebo-controlled studies of the efficacy of tricyclic antidepressants for the treatment of enuresis. This class of drugs has been regularly shown to be superior to placebo. Other drugs (e.g., sympathomimetic agents, anticonvulsants, and anxiolytics) have not been shown to be effective (Blackwell and Currah 1973). The reason why tricyclic antidepressants are effective is still unknown, but most researchers agree that the improvement in enuresis is not a result of the treatment of an underlying or associated depression (Rapoport et al. 1978). Unlike treating depression with tricyclic antidepressants, in which there is a long latency, there is a relatively immediate response of the enuresis within the first 2 weeks. With cessation of treatment after a short period of treatment, enuresis returns. In one study, treatment was necessary for at least 5 months to ensure that a relapse did not occur (Fournier et al. 1987).

All antidepressants appear to be equally effective. The newer tetracyclics, such as maprotiline, also appear to be helpful in treating enuresis (Simeon et al. 1981). Pure anticholinergic drugs, such as belladonna and methylscopolamine, have not been shown to have a therapeutic efficacy (Rapoport 1980). These findings are significant, since they suggest that the therapeutic effect of tricyclic antidepressants is not mediated through anticholinergic side effects of these drugs. Most side effects of tricyclic antidepressants are primarily associated with the anticholinergic properties and include dry mouth, constipation, tachycardia, hypertension, arrhythmias, and problems with accommodation. Although there are a few studies showing the efficacy of amphetamines and other nonspecific medications, presently the evidence supporting the single use of tricyclic antidepressants is so overwhelming that no other medication

should be considered. Because serum tricyclic antidepressant levels have not been established for enuresis, current treatment should be judged by clinical response alone and not by a therapeutic serum level (Jorgensen et al. 1980).

One study (Fournier et al. 1987) compared imipramine therapy with seven other treatment methods, including an alarm system, awakening at night, and a placebo. Each therapy was given alone or in combination with others. By the second week, the imipramine therapy alone was the most efficacious treatment. The alarm device took longer to show a therapeutic effect. By the end of 6 active weeks of treatment, the alarm device, either alone or in combination with imipramine therapy, was superior to the other methods. Imipramine therapy was very close in its efficacy to the alarm device, and both were superior to placebo and awakening at night (Fig. 19–2). The conclusion of the investigators was that for rapid cessation of symptoms imipramine would be the drug of choice and that for overall improvement both the alarm device or medication would be effective. The relapse rates over a 5-month period were approximately equal for these two treatments, in contrast to other studies that demonstrated a high relapse rate associated with imipramine. The difference with this study is that imipramine was continued for 5 months in those patients who did not suffer relapse. Too brief a drug trial (i.e., for less than 5 months) or too low a dosage (i.e., under 2.5 mg/kg) may explain treatment failures or relapse. Moderate to complete improvement is observed in 30% to 85% of the treated youngsters.

Alarm Device

Studies have shown a consistently positive therapeutic effect of an alarm device in the range of 60% to 85% (Med. Lett., 1982). After consistent application of the treatment for 6 weeks, few children experience relapse. The relapse rate is believed to be less than 35% on the alarm device. Occasional "booster" sessions, in which the device is applied again, have been found to decrease relapse.

The alarm device is successful because it creates a situation that allows for either classical conditioning or operant conditioning to occur. In classical conditioning, the uncon-

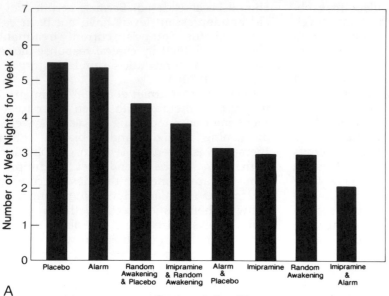

A

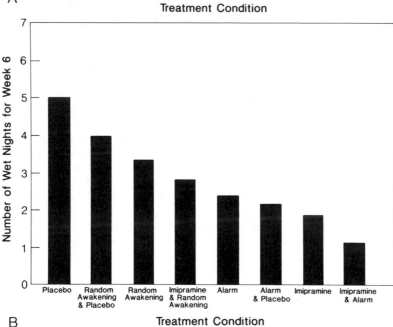

B

Figure 19–2. Comparison of imipramine therapy with other methods of treatment. A. Frequency of enuresis during week 2. B. Frequency of enuresis during week 6.

ditioned stimulus is the alarm (or bell) and the conditioned stimulus is bladder distention and/or micturition. The bell or alarm becomes coupled with bladder distention, with the resulting behavioral response of awakening. For operant conditioning, the response is bladder distention/micturition that results in the stimulus (i.e., the alarm), followed by awakening. In effect, both theoretical perspectives explain why bladder distention results in the training of awakening the child who is about to micturate. Alarm

devices in association with other techniques, such as "overlearning," "booster sessions," and "rehearsal" or practice have all proved useful in improving the therapeutic efficacy of this type of treatment (Wagner et al. 1982; Azrin and Thienes 1978). "Retention control training," or having the child practice retention after fluid loading along with appropriate micturition, has been shown to have limited positive results but may be an additional procedure to add to the alarm device protocol (Fielding 1980). Optimally these behavioral procedures can be combined with medication (i.e., imipramine) to ensure on-going continence. Other psychological treatments, such as hypnosis, have been shown to be effective in single studies (Olness 1975). Replication studies are necessary in order to substantiate a broader application of such treatment.

ENCOPRESIS

Encopresis is defined as defecation at inappropriate times and places, either on purpose or in an involuntary manner. Encopresis includes situations in which the youngster passes feces as a result of overflow incontinence because of fecal retention or impaction. The fecal soiling must occur at least once per month for a minimum of 6 months. The youngster must have attained a mental and chronologic age of 4, and there can be no other psychiatric or physical disorder (such as aganglionic megacolon) to explain the symptoms. Like enuresis, there is a primary type in which the child never had a period of fecal continence of 1 year's duration and a secondary type, in which there had been fecal continence for 1 year but the child has reverted to fecal soiling afterward.

Various studies have indicated that the majority of children attain bowel control sometime between 2 and 2½ years of age. Developmental research has suggested that approximately 100% of children studied had bowel control by age 4; therefore, if bowel control is not present by this age, the functional disorder, encopresis, is believed to be present (Bellman 1966). From two studies of elementary school-aged children, the prevalence of encopresis showed rates of between 1.3% and 1.5% (Rutter et al. 1970; Davie et al. 1972). Boys have encopresis three times more commonly than do girls (Bellman 1966). There are no reliable demographic characteristics found in the families of encopretic children; however, some studies show it to be more commonly observed in lower socioeconomic families (Olatawura 1973). Other associated clinical and developmental characteristics that have been noted are delayed language development, "soft" neurologic signs, below normal intelligence, and poor coordination (Olatawura 1973). Infrequently, there is a neurologic basis, as observed in cerebral palsy, spina bifida, and mental re-

tardation. In a number of cases, a fear of defecation, because of an anal fissure, can result in impaction and overflow soiling. Rarely, obsessive-compulsive disorder has led to retention and soiling because of a fear of germs on toilet seats.

Pathogenesis

One study found that two thirds of all encopretic children soil because of constipation with overflow incontinence (Coekin and Gairdner 1960). The remaining third are encopretic children who defecated in unusual places, not because of constipation/overflow but because of serious psychological problems. The feces were meant to be left on the floor, wastebasket, sink, sofa, and bed. It is this latter group who are most often believed to represent the classic cases of encopresis.

Parks (1975) demonstrated that pressure and distention in the lower rectum produces the urge to defecate and the corresponding sense of control. Control results from the contraction of the striated muscle (voluntary) of the puborectalis sling and of the external sphincter and the internal sphincter, made up of smooth muscle (involuntary) (Nixon 1975). Children who have severe and chronic constipation have a poorly functioning weak internal anal sphincter (Loening-Baucke and Younoszai 1982). The other major physiological factor involves poor or weak peristaltic contraction of the lower colon.

The role of bowel training has much greater significance as an etiologic factor for encopresis than bladder training has for enuresis. Training that may be punitive and critical can in part contribute to the child retaining stools, with the result being the associated constipation/overflow soiling. Harsh, unrewarding, and punitive training can create a response in a vulnerable child that can set into motion the pattern of events leading to encopresis (Sears et al. 1957; Caldwell 1964). The problematic training procedures of some parents are not sufficient alone to produce encopresis in a particular child. Often there must also be present a preexisting developmental delay in other areas (such as speech) or some constitutional vulnerability (neuromuscular delays) that amplify the deficits in training practices. By eliminating the situations in which fecal impaction is present, 75% of all encopretics will show a marked improvement (Levine 1975). The most difficult patients to treat and to investigate are those children who defecate in unusual places. These youngsters tend to be older, have more generalized psychological and behavioral symptoms, and frequently reflect some stressful life event, such as a move to a new home, the birth of a sibling, and an environment of marital and/or family discord. A number of these children will have enuresis, learning disabilities, and conduct disorder symptoms (Berg and Jones 1964; Rutter 1975).

The study of encopresis was dominated by psychoanalytical thinking. The main component of this viewpoint was that a problematic parent (e.g., mother)–child relationship at the time of bowel training resulted in encopresis. Anthony (1957) described power struggles with the noncompliant child and others, and he assumed that children became passive-aggressive, withholding feces in response to forceful training (Pinkerton 1958). Kessler (1960) equated constipation as the child's wish to become pregnant. There is no empiric evidence to suggest that parents of encopretic children have a specific psychological profile or a specific problem with the bowel training practices they use.

Differential Diagnosis

Many of the associated behavioral and psychiatric disorders associated with encopresis are summarized in Table 19–2. Each of these conditions must be investigated to determine their presence or absence. Also identified are key physiological disorders that have been frequently observed as well.

Case History

Terry is a 10-year-old boy with marked hyperactivity and mild learning disabilities. He was adopted at 6 weeks of age. At age 6 years he was first diagnosed as having attention-deficit hyperactivity disorder. He was treated for the past 4 years with methylphenidate, currently on a dosage equivalent of 0.6 mg/kg. Some of the behavioral problems subsided with medication, especially the hyperactivity and impulsive behavior.

Starting at age 8, Terry began to soil three to four times per month. Feces were found in the living room and den. This fecal incontinence has continued to the present time. It was also associated with overflow incontinence that occurred approximately once every 10 days. The soiling at this time was of watery and poorly formed stools that were not placed in inappropriate situations but left in underwear and the bed. Symptoms of encopresis were associated with the onset of severe discord between his parents that eventually led to their separation. Management consisted of a very thorough workup of both physical and psychological factors. Stool softener and regular enemas for the first 8 to 10 weeks broke the soiling/overflow pattern. Family and individual psychotherapy was helpful in reducing Terry's generalized stress response. Also helpful were a remedial educational program to help with deficient classroom learning and an individual cognitive behavioral approach to psychotherapy that gave Terry coping strategies for difficult and stressful situations.

Treatment

For the first 4 to 8 weeks of treatment, management initially consists of stool softeners, mineral oil, enemas, or suppositories. The goal is to remove the obstruction and eliminate the origin of overflow soiling. It is imperative that defecation become painless (Levine 1982). A number of studies have used either direct conditioning of the anal sphincter or biofeedback based on balloon pressures in the anus at the internal sphincter (Kohlen-

---

Table 19–2. DISORDERS FREQUENTLY ASSOCIATED WITH ENCOPRESIS

Functional
1. Developmental disorders
   a. Specific language/communication disorders
   b. Learning disabilities
2. Obsessive-compulsive disorder
3. Oppositional-defiant disorder
4. Conduct disorder
5. Phobias
6. Enuresis
7. Generalized systemic reaction to stress (e.g., marital, family)
8. Deficient bowel training

Organic
1. Spina bifida
2. Cerebral palsy
3. Hirschsprung's disease
4. Anal fissure
5. Mental retardation

burg 1973; Engel et al. 1974; Olness et al. 1980). Treatment employing a basic pediatric approach, focusing mainly on bowel cleansing and the training of normal bowel habits, produces a therapeutic response rate of between 80% and 90% (Levine and Bakow 1976). In the more severe, older, and behaviorally disordered group, additional psychotherapy must also be provided. The long-term outcome, however, is very positive, with almost all showing an amelioration of symptoms by 16 years of age (Berg et al. 1983). Too often one parent alone becomes overly drawn into the many issues concerning the soiling child. The soiling gets the parent's attention, whereas other accomplishments and activities are overlooked. Psychotherapy frequently results in much more parental involvement and attention with the child, especially by the father. Toilet training rituals and monitoring often are best handled by the father, with good success. Generally, although much more disruptive than enuresis, encopresis has a much better outcome, with complete cessation of symptoms by late adolescence in almost all children.

References

Anthony, E.J. 1957. An experimental approach to the psychopathology of childhood: Encopresis. *Br. J. Med. Psychol.* 30:146–175.

Azrin, N.H., and Thienes, P.M. 1978. Rapid elimination of enuresis by intensive learning without a conditioning apparatus. *Behav. Res. Ther.* 9:342–354.

Bakwin, H. 1973. The genetics of bed-wetting. In Kolvin, I., MacKeith, R.C., and Meadow, S.R. (eds.): *Bladder Control and Enuresis.* London: Heinemann/SIMP.

Bakwin, H., and Bakwin, R.M. 1972. *Clinical Management of Behavior Disorders in Childhood,* 4th ed. Philadelphia: W.B. Saunders.

Bellman, M 1966. Studies on encopresis. *Acta Paediatr. Scand.* (Suppl. 170).

Berg, I., Forsythe, I., Holt, P., and Watts, J. 1983. A controlled trial of "Senokot" in faecal soiling treated by behavioural methods. *J. Child Psychol. Psychiatry* 23:543–549.

Berg, I., and Jones, K.V. 1964. Functional faecal incontinence in children. *Arch. Dis. Child.* 39:465–472.

Binderglas, P.M., and Dee G. 1978. Enuresis treatment with imipramine hydrochloride: A 10-year follow-up study. *Am. J. Psychiatry* 135:1549–1552.

Blackwell, B., and Currah, J. 1973. The psychopharmacology of nocturnal enuresis. In Kolvin, I., MacKeith, R., and Meadow, S.R. (eds.): *Bladder Control and Enuresis.* London: Heinemann/SIMP.

Breger, E. 1963. Etiological factors in enuresis: A psychobiological approach. *J. Child Psychiatry* 2:667–676.

Caldwell, B.M. 1964. The effects of infant care. In

Hoffman, M.L., and Hoffman, L.W. (eds.): *Review of Child Development Research,* vol. 1. New York: Russell Sage Foundation.

Coekin, M., and Gairdner, D. 1960. Faecal incontinence in children. *Br. Med. J.* 2:1175–1180.

Cohen, M. 1975. Enuresis. *Pediatr. Clin. North Am.* 22:545–560.

Daniels, M. 1971. Enuresis, body language, and the positive aspects of the enuretic act. *Am. J. Psychother.* 25:564–579.

Davie, R., Butler, N., and Goldstein, H. 1972. *From Birth to Seven.* London: Longman.

DeLean, G., and Mandrell, W. 1966. A comparison of conditioning and psychotherapy in the treatment of functional enuresis. *J. Clin. Psychol.* 22:326.

Dodge, W.F., West, E.F., Bridgforth, M.S., and Travis, L.B. 1970. Nocturnal enuresis in 6- to 10-year old children. *Am. J. Dis. Child.* 120:32–35.

Electronic bed-wetting alarm. 1982. *Med. Lett.* 6(32).

Engel, B.T., Nikoomanesh, P., and Schuster, M.M. 1974. Operant conditioning of rectosphincter responses in the treatment of faecal incontinence. *N. Engl. J. Med.* 290:646–649.

Essen, J., and Peckham, C. 1975. Nocturnal enuresis in childhood. *Dev. Med. Child Neurol.* 18:577–589.

Fielding, D. 1980. The response of day and night wetting children and children who wet only at night to retention-control training and the enuresis alarm. *Behav. Res. Ther.* 18:305–317.

Fournier, J.P., Garfinkel, B.D., Bond, A., et al. 1987. Pharmacological and behavioral management of enuresis. *J. Am. Acad. Child. Adolesc. Psychiatry* 26:849–853.

Foxx, R.M., and Azrin, M.H. 1973. Dry pants: A rapid method of toilet training children. *Behav. Res. Ther.* 11:435–442.

Freud, S. 1938. *The Basic Writings of Sigmund Freud.* New York: Modern Library.

Frommer, E.A. 1968. Depressive illness in childhood. In Coppen, A., and Walk, A. (eds.): *Recent Developments in Affective Disorders. Br. J. Psychiatry* special publication 2:117–136.

Gardner, A., and Shaffer, D. 1984. Expected values for the Starfield test of functional bladder volume in children. (Unpublished manuscript)

Garrison, F.H. 1923. In Abt, I.A. (ed.): *Abstracts of Pediatrics.* Philadelphia: W.B. Saunders.

Gerard, M. 1939. Enuresis: A study in etiology. *Am. J. Orthopsychiatry* 15:81–88.

Glicklich, L.B. 1951. An historical account of enuresis. *Pediatrics* 8:859–876.

Hallgren, B. 1956. Enuresis: I. A study with reference to the morbidity and symptomatology. *Acta Psychiatr. Neurol. Scand.* 31:379–403.

Heisel, J.S., Ream, S., Raitz, T., et al. 1973. The significance of life-events as contributory events in the diseases of children. *J. Pediatr.* 83:119–123.

Jones, B., Gerrard, J.W., Shokeir, M.K., and Houston, C.S. 1972. Recurrent urinary infection in girls: Relation to enuresis. *Can. Med. Assoc. J.* 106:127–130.

Jorgensen, O.S., Lober, M., Christiansen, J., et al. 1980. Plasma concentration and clinical effect in imipramine treatment of childhood enuresis. *Clin. Pharmacokinet.* 5:386–393.

Kaffman, M., and Elizur, E. 1977. Infants who become enuretics: A longitudinal study of 161 kibbutz children. *Monogr. Soc. Res. Child. Dev.* 42:170.

Kessler, J.W. 1960. *Psychopathology of Childhood.* Englewood Cliffs, N.J.: Prentice-Hall.

Klackenburg, G. 1981. Nocturnal enuresis in a longitudinal perspective. *Acta. Paediatr. Scand.* 70:453–457.

Kohlenberg, R.J. 1973. Operant conditioning of human anal sphincter pressure. *J. Appl. Behav. Anal.* 6:201–208.

Loening-Baucke, V.A., and Younoszai, M.K. 1982. Abnormal anal sphincter response in chronically constipated children. *J. Paediatr.* 100:213–218.

Leighton, D., and Khuckholm, C. 1947. *Children of People.* Cambridge, Mass. Harvard University Press.

Levine, M.D. 1975. Children with encopresis: A descriptive analysis. *Paediatrics* 56:412–416.

Levine, M.D. 1982. Encopresis: Its potentiation, evaluation and alleviation. *Pediatr. Clin. North Am.* 29:315–330.

Levine, M.D., and Bakow, H. 1976. Children with encopresis: A study of treatment outcome. *Paediatrics* 58:845–852.

Lovibond, S.H. 1964. *Conditioning and Enuresis.* Oxford: Pergamon.

Mahoney, D.T. 1971. Studies of enuresis: I. Incidence of obstructive lesions and pathophysiology and enuresis. *J. Urol.* 106:951–958.

McLain, L.G. 1979. Childhood enuresis. *Curr. Probl. Pediatr.* 9:1–36.

Mikkelsen, E.J., Rapoport, J.L., Nee, L., et al. 1980. Childhood enuresis. I. Sleep patterns and psychopathology. *Arch. Gen. Psychiatry* 37:1139–1144.

Nixon, H. 1975. The diagnosis and management of faecal incontinence in children. *Arch. Chir. Neerlandicum* 27:171–177.

Olatawura, M. 1973. Encopresis: A review of thirty-two cases. *Acta Paediatr. Scand.* 62:358–364.

Olness, K. 1975. The use of self-hypnosis in the treatment of childhood nocturnal enuresis. *Clin. Pediatr.* 14:273–279.

Olness, K., McParland, F.A., and Piper, J. 1980. Biofeedback: A new modality in the management of children with fecal soiling. *J. Pediatr.* 96:505–509.

Oppel, W.C., Harper, P.A., and Rider, R.V. 1968. Social, psychological and neurological factors associated with enuresis. *Pediatrics* 42:627–641.

Parks, A. 1975. Anorectal incontinence. *Proc. R. Soc. Med.* 68:21–30.

Pinkerton, P. 1958. Psychogenic megacolon in children: The implications of bowel negativism. *Arch. Dis. Child.* 33:371–938.

Rapoport, J.L., Mikkelson, E.J., and Zavadil, A.P. 1980. Childhood enuresis: Psychopathology, tricyclic concentration in plasma, an antienuretic effect. *Arch. Gen. Psychiatry* 5:386–393.

Rapoport, J.L., Mikkelson, E.J., and Zavadil, A.P. 1978. Plasma imipramine and desmethylimipramine concentration and clinical response in childhood enuresis. *Psychopharmacol. Bull.* 14:60–61.

Rutter, M. 1975. *Helping Troubled Children.* Harmondsworth, England: Penguin.

Rutter, M., Tizard, J., and Whitmore, K. 1970. *Education, Health and Behavior: Psychological and Medical Study of Childhood Development.* New York: John Wiley & Sons.

Salmon, M.A. 1975. An historical account of nocturnal enuresis and its treatment. *Proc. R. Soc. Med.* 68:443–448.

Sears, R.R., Maccoby, E.E., and Levin, H. 1957. *Patterns of Child Rearing.* Evanston, Ill.: Row Peterson.

Shaffer, D. 1973. The association between enuresis and emotional disorder: A review of the literature. In Kolvin, I., MacKeith, R.C., and Meadow, S.R. (eds.): *Bladder Control and Enuresis.* London: Heinemann/SIMP.

Shaffer, D., Costello, A.J., and Hill, I.D. 1968. Control of enuresis with imipramine. *Arch. Dis. Child.* 43:665–671.

Shaffer, D., Turgeon, L., and Hedge, B. 1978b. Psychiatric disturbance and enuresis. Paper presented at 25th Annual Meeting of the American Academy of Child Psychiatry, San Diego, California.

Simeon, J., Maguire, J., and Lawrence, S. 1981. Maprotiline effects in children with enuresis and behavioral disorders. *Prog. Neuropsychopharm.* 5:495–498.

Wagner, W., Johnson, S.B., Walker, D., et al. 1982. A controlled comparison of two treatments for nocturnal enuresis. *Pediatrics* 101:302–307.

Werry, J.S., and Cohrssen, J. 1965. Enuresis: An etiologic and therapeutic study. *J. Pediatr.* 67:423–431.

Four

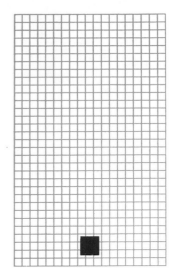

SPECIFIC
CLINICAL
ISSUES

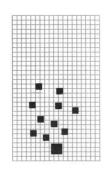
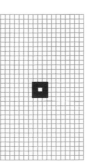
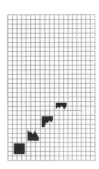
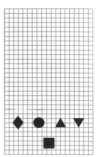

Child Abuse and The Child Psychiatrist

20

CHARLES F. JOHNSON, M.D.

CHILD ABUSE IN THE UNITED STATES: A CAPSULE HISTORY

Although child abuse is an affliction that has its roots in antiquity (Helfer and Kempe 1968; Solomon 1973), it has only received serious consideration in medicine since 1946 when Caffey, a radiologist, reported the frequent association of chronic subdural hematomas and multiple fractures of long bones in children (Caffey 1946). Caffey was uncertain about the cause of the injuries he described. In 1961, Kempe addressed the American Academy of Pediatrics and offered the phrase "the battered child" to describe injuries intentionally caused by parents (Helfer 1987); he coauthored a landmark text on the subject in 1962 (Kempe et al. 1962). Media attention to issues of child abuse followed, and between 1963 and 1967 all states and the District of Columbia passed laws requiring the reporting of child abuse (Nelson 1984). Twenty-six years after Caffey's discovery, he labeled his findings the parent–infant stress syndrome (Caffey 1972). The First International Congress of Child Abuse was held in Geneva in 1976 (Steele 1987). Between 1973 and 1980 (National Library of Medicine 1975, 1980), over 800 publications about child abuse appeared in the medical literature. A text dedicated to medical aspects of child abuse appeared in 1981 (Ellerstein 1981) and, in 1987, the *Journal of the International Society of Child Abuse and Neglect* was dedicated to Brand Steele, M.D., who was honored as the pioneer psychiatrist in the field. Many states have legislated Childrens' Trust Funds, which are supported by surcharges on birth and marriage certificates, to support prevention programs.

As questions involving diagnosis, incidence, and treatment of physical and sexual abuse are being answered, there has been a shift of research focus toward studying the *dynamics* of abuse to facilitate prevention. Emotional abuse and neglect (Brassard et al. 1987) and unusual manifestations of abuse such as Munchausen's syndrome by proxy (Rosenberg 1987) are also receiving increased attention.

CHILD ABUSE LAWS VERSUS PATIENT CONFIDENTIALITY: A DILEMMA FOR THE CHILD PSYCHIATRIST?

Each state has laws that define child abuse and neglect and that direct professionals to report *suspected* cases. Failure to report can result in legal consequences. Stressful malpractice litigation may be instituted against the professional if a child, who was recognized as being at risk, becomes reinjured. It is unlikely that judges, the lay public, and the juries on which the public serve would look favorably on a professional whose concern about confidentiality overrode obedience of the law and the safety of a child abuse victim.

It is noteworthy that legislation specifies

339

that physician–patient privilege or confidentiality does not free a child psychiatrist from reporting suspected abuse. Although the state laws are basically the same, familiarity with the nuances of the law in one's own state is necessary. Copies of state laws can be obtained from county prosecutors, children services, or county welfare offices. Reports can be made to the police department or the designated social services department. In most states, all counties are required to have a "plan of cooperation" for the reporting and investigation of abuse. In Franklin County, Ohio, for example, children services and the police department must notify each other when a case is reported to them or uncovered by their own agencies. If "criminal activity" is suspected, the police may wish to be involved early in the investigation to ensure that evidence is not disrupted. Organized communities will attempt to assess the situation in a "one stop" interview, physical examination, and laboratory examination to avoid overwhelming the child. This requires that a medical evaluator, in addition to other abuse team members, be available 24 hours a day. This situation generally is only available in an emergency department, which may not be the ideal place to perform a comprehensive assessment.

A state law may not delineate clearly what constitutes abuse. Lawmakers have often stated that they purposefully left an ambiguous boundary, in order to leave the decision to report up to the observer and, ultimately, the judge or jury. There is disagreement among professionals, as well as parents, about what constitutes physical abuse and discipline or physical neglect and appropriate care. If one moves into the arena of emotional abuse and neglect, the ability to draw a defensible line from consensus becomes even more difficult.

Physical abuse is the result of an action that leaves a measurable and observable consequence, that is, a nonaccidental injury or an injury that is not compatible with the history of the injury or the child's level of development. The physician's skills are tested when the history is devious, elaborate, and sophisticated. For example, a child who falls down a flight of stairs can receive a variety of injuries that are similar to those from being struck repeatedly with a blunt object of similar size and shape as a segment of stair edge. Developmentally, this type of

fall would have been impossible if the child were at a precrawling state or the devious parent, who is trying to mask abuse, might claim that the injury occurred when he or she "tripped and dropped the child." A home visit might reveal that the stairs were heavily padded, if an investigation was launched as the result of a report. The physician may need to report strong concerns about such incompatible descriptions in order to instigate an investigation of the home by the police or children services agency.

ABUSE VERSUS HARSH DISCIPLINE: PHYSICIAN BIAS

When an injury occurs in the course of discipline, the issue of reporting becomes more complicated. Physicians disagree about what constitutes acceptable discipline (Morris et al. 1985). This may be one reason why physicians have been considered remiss in reporting of abuse. In 1981, of the 16,314 cases of suspected child abuse reported to the Ohio Central Registry of Child Abuse, 202 (1.2%) were made by physicians. Physicians indicated that their reporting behavior is influenced by (1) personal attitudes toward the seriousness of the injury, (2) presence of other injuries, (3) their familiarity with the family, (4) appropriateness of parental concern about the child, (5) compatibility of the history and physical examination, and (6) the child's behavior (Morris et al. 1985). Of all the reasons given, only a compatibility of the results of the history and physical examination with the injury is medically acceptable for not reporting the injury. Physicians fear that reporting will cause them to lose patients; they are uncomfortable with speculative diagnoses and lack confidence in community social service agencies (Morris et al. 1985). Physicians do not routinely consider the level of the child's development in accessing the possibility of abuse (Johnson and Showers 1985) and are uncomfortable with parents who may have abused their children (Sanders 1972). The child psychiatrist, although less likely than a pediatrician or emergency department physician to be confronted with acute physical injuries as a chief complaint or as the result of a physical examination for another complaint, is also influenced by personal attitudes and values. Concern for maintaining rapport with a family in therapy, or breaking the confidence of a young patient, may be a cause of considerable consternation as one tries to balance the ethics of the therapeutic situation with the requirements of the law. It is likely that the child psychiatrist, heavily involved with children who are being seen for delinquency, emotional disturbance, or behavior problems, will be dealing with families who have exhausted nonphysical methods of behavioral management and have turned to physical discipline. It is also possible that physical discipline, emotional abuse or neglect, or sexual abuse is the underlying cause of the behavior for which the child was referred.

PHYSICAL ABUSE

Definitions

One definition of child abuse is the use of an instrument on a child. Parents Anonymous, a support group for parents who have abused their children, has modified that definition to allow the use of physical punishment for "discipline." By their definition, those "disciplinary" actions that cause any visible injury or death would be immune for required reporting. From the child's point of view, the reason for an injury may be immaterial. In addition, most physical abuse is in reaction to a child's behavior and intended to stop the behavior. In the ideal society there would be no need to use physical punishment to influence behavior. Parents would all be experts in managing behavior, and all children would respond appropriately. In the United States, attitudes toward the use of physical discipline are reflected by the existence of corporal punishment in the schools and surveys that indicated that 20% of clergy, police, and teachers favor the use of instruments in discipline. Surveys of school teachers, whose profession models behavior management for children and their parents, indicate that nearly 50% wish to maintain the option of physical punishment in the classroom. Mothers have indicated that 30% use physical punishment before their infants reach 6 months of age. Obviously, if one is to avoid reporting much of the parent population for child abuse, standards must be relaxed to allow normally developing children, after 12 months of age, to be struck once or twice with the parent's hand on the child's buttocks or hand. Ideally, adversive conditioning should relate to the offending anatomical area of the body; however, the face should never be struck and shaking, which has the potential to injure the child's brain, must be eliminated. Studies of high school and college students indicate that shaking is not considered a harmful form of discipline by the majority (Johnson et al. 1982; Showers and Johnson 1984). Just as some parents should never be allowed to use physical discipline, some children should never receive physical discipline. Studies of corporal punishment in the schools indicate that children with developmental difficulties, who require more sensitive treatment, are those who are most frequently paddled. Of concern to the child psychiatrist are the children whose parents or teachers choose emotional abuse in lieu of physical punishment. Parents who are reported for abuse and teachers whose school systems eliminate corporal punishment may turn to emotional abuse if they are not taught acceptable alternatives.

Abuse is an act of commission; neglect is an act of omission. If the commission or omission affects the body, this is physical abuse or neglect; if the psyche is affected, there is emotional abuse or neglect. Sexual abuse has been separated into a special category. The term *sexual failure to protect* has been applied to children who are exposed to pornography or sexual experiences that are inappropriate for their level of development. The appropriateness of childhood sexual experiences is controversial among physicians (Ladson et al. 1987) and often avoided as an issue among parents. Only those physicians who find themselves involved in abuse issues will realize how widely accepted are assaults on children and neglect of their rights. Children themselves are often shocked to learn, in programs designed to prevent their abuse, that their bodies belong to themselves and not to their parents. How various types of abuse are on a continuum is represented in Figure 20–1. Abuse and neglect are represented as polar behaviors, as are physical and emotional consequences. Sexual abuse is represented as physical abuse of specific anatomical areas. Prudence and research would suggest that emotional abuse and neglect are the end results of physical abuse and neglect. Frequency of abuse and relationship of the incident to critical stages of de-

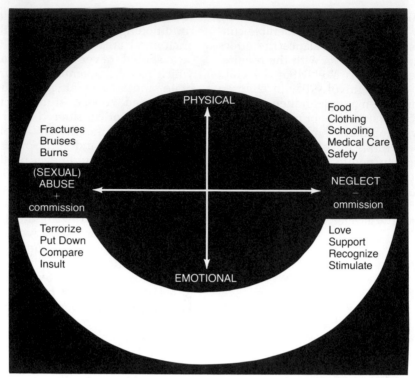

Figure 20–1. *Continuum of various types of abuse.*

velopment are important elements associated with the injury.

Emotional neglect in early infancy, an aspect of nonorganic failure to thrive, is an example of an insult that has profound effects because it occurs during early bonding (Gagen et al. 1984). The term *nonorganic failure to thrive* also emphasizes the visible effect of the syndrome on the child's weight. The term *emotional neglect syndrome of early infancy* has been suggested as an alternative. The former term brings the child to the pediatrician; the latter term emphasizes the psychological pathology. The frustration experienced among physicians in trying to reach a consensus definition of abuse may be overshadowed by the realization that abuse is "in the eye of the beholding judge or jury too." Despite physicians' efforts to recognize, report, and testify about the strength of their convictions, the ultimate disposition of a case will be decided in the courtroom (Showers and Apolo 1986). The criminal court deals best with severe and life-threatening events of commission, which are usually physical in nature. The criminal court requires proof, beyond doubt, for "conviction." The juvenile court, more concerned with protecting the child than punishing an offender, requires less definitive proof. As a result, most cases of abuse do not reach the criminal court because of an inability to establish proof, especially when the witness is a child victim facing an adult perpetrator.

Incidence: National and Regional

Several agencies track the incidence of child abuse in the United States. The National Committee for Prevention of Child Abuse surveys 50 states annually. The American Association for Protecting Children, in Denver, releases regular reports, and the National Center on Child Abuse and Neglect (NCCAN), in Washington, D.C., applies standardized definitions of child abuse and neglect to all cases known to child welfare, social service, health, and law enforcement agencies. According to the National Committee, these latter data provide more reliable estimates of the scope of abuse than do studies that rely on reported cases. The definitions and sources of information can influence conclusions. For example, the NCCAN study of 1986 data (National Clearinghouse 1988) uses information gathered from cases known to professionals and does not identify cases known to friends or relatives or the victims themselves. Changes in definitions and methodology may make it difficult to interpret trends in abuse. Reported cases may not be "confirmed" as abuse by the investigating agency or may not be "adjudicated" as abuse in the court. For example, the 1986 NCCAN study (National Clearinghouse 1988) indicated that fewer than one third of the child abuse cases identified by law enforcement officials, medical personnel, educators, and social service providers are reported to them and substantiated by child protective service agencies. Professionals may react to these figures with decreased confidence in social service agencies and less willingness to report (Curran and Johnson 1987). The 1986 data indicated that social service agencies have increased their success in "substantiating" abuse to 53%, an increase of 10% over that of 1980. Reported abuse does not equal actual abuse. It is probable that reported numbers of cases of abuse is "much" lower than the actual incidence. With the use of a definition that included children who had suffered observable harm as the result of abuse or neglect, more than 1 million children, or 16.3 per 1,000, are estimated to be abused annually. If abuse refers to those children who were endangered but not "obviously harmed," the numbers increase to 1.6 million children, or 25.2 per 1,000 (National Clearinghouse 1988).

The question "Is child abuse on the rise?" is the subject of several studies and controversies (Knudsen 1988). Agencies funded to decrease the incidence of child abuse may "interpret" data to enhance the credibility of the effectiveness of their programs. Programs intended to decrease abuse incidence may increase the incidence of reporting, thus skewing data. For example, programs that train children to recognize the sanctity of their bodies by saying no to sexual importuning and reporting "uncomfortable" touches may result in children reporting abuse who were previously unknown. The 1986 NCCAN study reflects a 66% increase in incidence over the 1980 study. The largest increases were noticed in moderately severe physical abuse and all forms of sexual abuse. Nonsignificant increases were noted in the

rates of fatal and serious physical abuse, all forms of emotional abuse, abandonment, and educational and medical neglect. Nationally in 1986, 1,110 children died of child abuse, a 10% increase over 1980. Since there are no accepted definitions of seriousness of abuse (Fouras and Johnson 1988) these data must be interpreted carefully. The issue of increased incidence versus increased sensitivity and subsequent increased reporting has yet to be resolved.

Physical Abuse as Seen in a Children's Hospital

Local data may be more revealing and meaningful to the practitioner. In one pediatric hospital there is a team of 14 professionals, including physicians, social workers, a psychologist, data coordinator, and nurse practitioner, to study child abuse. A child psychiatrist is available to the team for consultation. Data from 1 year (1986–1987) (*Child Abuse Program Annual Report* 1987) is illustrated in Tables 20–1 and 20–2.

Of the 1,115 children assessed in 1987 for abuse, 852 (76%) were reported. The reasons why abuse was not reported in 24% included inability to gather information from preverbal children, insufficient evidence, or other conditions that masked child abuse. As professional sensitivity to the possibility of abuse has increased, dermatologic conditions such as diaper dermatitis have been confused with possible sexual abuse and impetigo (Brown and Melinkovich 1986) has been reported as

Table 20–1. SUSPECTED CHILD ABUSE IN 1987	
Number of Children Assessed for Possible Child Abuse	1115
Total Child Abuse Cases Reported	**852**
Physical	313
Sexual abuse/assault	464
Neglect/failure to thrive	52
Combination	23
Male	332
Female	520
White	539
Black	285
Other	28
Total children hospitalized	80
Total children who died because of abuse/neglect	5
Children reported for abuse/neglect under the age of 6	46%
Average age of the abused/neglected child	7.39

Table 20–2. INITIAL REFERRAL SOURCE FOR SUSPECTED ABUSE: 1987

Referral	No. Cases
Children services	398
Children's hospital	214
Parents	242
Law enforcement	104
Private physician, medical	50
Facility	17
Other relatives	9
School/daycare	72
Other	

cigarette burns. Conversely, physicians are being sensitized to unusual manifestations of child abuse such as Munchausen's syndrome by proxy (MBP). In a 3-year period 21 cases of MBP were reported by the hospital, including 3 cases of previously unrecognized intentional ipecac poisoning (McClung et al. 1988). Of the 852 total reports in 1987, 313 (37%) were reported for suspected physical abuse and 464 (54%) were reported for suspected sexual abuse. There has been a trend, over the period beginning in 1983, for an absolute and relative increase of sexual abuse as compared with physical abuse. The 93% rise in sexual abuse reports between 1983 and 1984, shown in Figure 20–2, may have resulted from media-influenced public awareness of sexual abuse issues and heightened professional concern about the existence of sexual abuse in preschools across the country.

The number of children admitted to a hospital varies with the seriousness of the abuse and hospital policy. Children with sexual abuse are frequently admitted only if surgical exploration or repair is necessary. Admission for "social reasons" is not encouraged because of third-party payment restrictions and a desire to provide the abused child with a more "normal" alternative placement, if the home environment is not considered to be safe. The latter requires immediate court-ordered temporary commitment to a social services agency and ready availability of a relative or quality foster care placement. Admissions for abuse in 1987 included skin trauma (38.9%), head trauma (12.8% and the most common cause of death), nonorganic failure to thrive (12%), burns (10.2%), fractures (7.2%), injury due to neglect (6.6%), illness due to neglect (5.4%), trauma from intercourse (2.4%), and MBP (1.8%). Depending on the role of the child psychiatrist in the hospital, psychiatric consultation may be indicated in all admitted cases. In some places, a special unit has been developed to which abused children can be admitted for assessment by hospital staff. Children are protected while community agencies investigate the home environment. Hospitalization gives various members of a team, which may include a child psychiatrist, more opportunity to provide input. Hospitalization obviously should be based solely on the needs of the child.

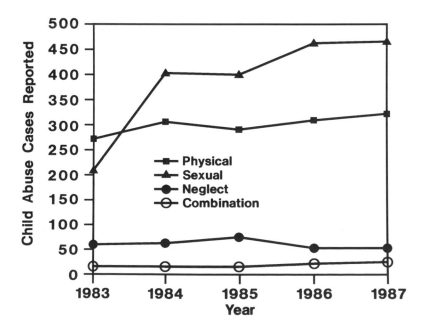

Figure 20–2. Trends in child abuse for the years 1983 through 1987 in one pediatric hospital.

Minor injuries may not require a medical assessment and may be evaluated by children services. Relatively few assessments are done by private physicians because of the county plan, ready availability of a special team and the pediatric emergency department staff. The availability of "experts" who may need to testify in court also facilitates local, as well as out of county, referral.

Of the 80 children admitted to Children's Hospital, Columbus, Ohio, in 1987, five (6%) died. Considering other admission diagnoses and their outcomes, the death rate for child abuse admissions indicates the magnitude and seriousness of the problem in one hospital. Abuse deaths bring the problem from a national statistic to a local and personal source of angst. The physical and psychological morbidity of the survivors continues to be a therapeutic challenge to a variety of professionals, emphasizing the need for primary, secondary, and tertiary prevention.

Physical Abuse and the Child Psychiatrist: Looking Beyond the Psyche

Emergency department physicians, pediatricians, and family practitioners are most likely to see children who are physically injured. It is unlikely that a parent will bring a child to a child psychiatrist with a chief complaint of physical injury. If the psychiatrist performs physical examinations on his or her patients, injury manifestations will be present that must be explained. An appropriate adage when evaluating injuries is to ask oneself, for each injury, *is this injury compatible with the child's development and the history being given?* If the answer is negative, a suspect abuse referral must be made to an appropriate agency. Familiarity with the manifestations of physical trauma and conditions that may be confused with abuse (Brown and Melinkovich 1986) is crucial as well as knowledge about the relative incidence of accidental and nonaccidental injuries. In 1967 it was estimated that 1.75 million infants had sustained a fall in the first year of life (Kravitz et al. 1969). An estimated 15 million children are injured annually (Iznat and Hubay 1966). These injury statistics must be considered to reflect the risk of childhood encounters with the environment and the inability of parents to protect their children

from all harm; however, studies of hospital charts have indicated that as many as 10% of injured children, seen in an emergency department, have been abused and another 10% may have been neglected (Holter and Friedman 1968). The main problem with chart studies is the lack of adequate written information that would help one draw a definitive conclusion! Audits of inpatient charts have indicated that 60% of the charts have inadequate information to rule out abuse as a cause of injury (Solomons 1980). In addition, critical questions about child development are rarely documented in the emergency department chart (Johnson et al. 1986). Although the child may not present to the child psychiatrist with a complaint of abuse, the child may have visible injury on the hand or face. Alternatively, the child may manifest the consequences of a beating by an inability to sit comfortably. Other injuries, covered by clothing, may also result in "protective" posturing or gait. The child psychiatrist has a legal duty and moral responsibility to inquire about the cause of any visible or suspected injury and to perform an examination as a physician.

If rapport has been established with the child, the child psychiatrist may have less trouble eliciting a history of the cause of injury than an unknown examiner, especially if the examination is to take place in a busy emergency department. Rapport established with the parent may work to a disadvantage. Physicians have reported a tendency to believe that the (middle class, clean, friendly, literate, cooperative) parents of their patients are not abusers. There is also a tendency to believe that these (bright, sensitive, motivated) parents will respond to simple counseling or admonishment. These same parents who are not reported can decide to sue the "forgiving" child psychiatrist if they reabuse the child! If the child psychiatrist is working in a unit in which pediatric consultation is available, an emergency referral for examination should be requested. If the child is sent to another institution, the child psychiatrist must protect himself or herself from litigation by reporting the suspicion to the appropriate agency. There is no guarantee that the child will be taken to the consultant. Familiarity with common manifestations of physical abuse should be part of the diagnostic repertoire of any professional dealing with children. A slap mark on the face is indicative of child abuse. The parallel marks of erythema make a hand print over the soft tissues. The erythema is between the fingers and results from blood being pressed away from the fingers by the force of the blow. Any object with a hard geometric shape, such as a belt buckle, will leave its imprint on the skin. Heated objects will do likewise. Spiral fractures in pre-toddlers, metaphyseal injuries, adult bite marks, genital injuries, immersion burns, banding injuries, cigarette burns, injuries in various stages of healing, and multiple types of injuries are likely to result from child abuse and must be reported unless the injury explanation and circumstances are satisfactory (Johnson and Showers 1985). If abuse is not suspected, the answers to the questions about injuries and reasons for not reporting should be clearly indicated in the patient's chart. When unsure, any professional should report or obtain a consultation. Heightened suspicion is necessary when an injury is on symmetrical parts of the body. Two black eyes and no injury to the nose or forehead suggests nonaccidental trauma. Rarely does nature present itself, except microscopically, in a perfect geometric pattern. A target-shaped, 2-cm geometric burn is more likely to result from a car cigarette lighter than from "erythema annulare." Paired blisters separated 1 to 2 cm from each other and scattered over the body are not from compulsively traveling and biting scabies or fleas: they are more likely from the child being attacked with a heated cooking fork.

Some of the answers parents give to explain an injury approach the humorous in their creativity. Parents have claimed that a 6-month-old infant received a third-degree burn by "stepping on a hot knife." Developmental sophistication is not required to question the ability of a 6-month old to stand, but what is a hot knife doing on the floor? The child psychiatrist may relax his or her vigilance by falsely believing that patients will describe the true cause of an injury. The verbal child may fear reprisal from the offender if the offender is a parent, caretaker, teacher, peer, or sibling. Children generally prefer to remain in a situation that is known to them. The promise of removal to foster care or potential for imprisonment of a breadwinning parent may hinder revelation. These variables are known to sexual abusers, who take advantage of the child's fears to engage them and keep them engaged in sexual activity (Budin and Johnson 1989).

Who Physically Abuses Children, and What Do They Do?

A review of the injuries suffered by children who were reported by a hospital-based abuse team is weighted toward more serious injuries; however, one is assured that the medical diagnosis is likely to be accurate. A review of the records of 616 children seen by one such team revealed that boys were referred for assessment more frequently than girls and that black children were reported disproportionately more often than were white children. Preschool children made up 53% of the population studied. Since bruises were the most common type of abuse manifestation reported, the number of dark-skinned children who escaped early detection may be higher than that of fair-skinned children, whose skin is more likely to show bruising. Mothers were the most frequent perpetrators of abuse. It is theorized that this does not result from an increased propensity for violence but rather from their exposure to the child. The types of injury, injury site, and types of instrument used varied with the age and race but not the sex of the child. A wide range of instruments were used to injure children. The most common instrument was a belt or strap (23%); an open hand to choke, grab, pinch, or slap (22%); followed by the fist (11%). Children were propelled by being thrown, dropped, pushed, pulled, and dragged (8%); hit with switches (8%), paddles and boards (6%), and cords (4%); and burned with hot liquids (3%). This was followed in frequency by injuries from a perpetrator's foot and burns from grids, heaters, stoves, and cigarettes. Knives were used to injure 1% of the children, and 1% were bitten. The items used to injure children were so extensive that it appeared that the instrument at hand was the instrument of choice. The primary target of injury was the buttocks and hips (12%), followed by face (11%), arms (10%), back (10%), and thighs (9%). If one adds the injuries to the scalp (7%), skull (1%), brain (1%), mouth (1%), nose (1%), and eye (5%) together, the head and its contents was the most common site of injury. This frequently injured anatomical area is readily visible to the child psychiatrist.

The child psychiatrist may not be confronted with specific injuries because of the age profile of his or her practice. Children from birth to 3 years of age were more likely to have fractures, hemorrhages, and burns. The burns and other injuries to the buttocks and genitalia of toddlers may be related to frustrated attempts to toilet train and during diaper changes, ready access to both the anatomical areas and hot water. Marks and erythema were most common among children 6 to 12 years of age. The larger and more physically durable adolescents, who could also *escape*, were more likely to report pain and tenderness from injury. This suggests that these symptoms in adolescents warrant investigation by the child psychiatrist. The adolescent age group was most likely to manifest injury of the scalp, nose, or neck. Why caretakers choose specific targets is unknown. Perhaps the head is a target because that is where the "child lives," perhaps it is because the unsettling sounds come from the mouth—be they the night cries of infants or the back-talking of adolescents. The finding that infants from birth to 12 months of age have a higher incidence of injuries to the skull and brain may result from the anatomical and structural susceptibility of this area to injury by impact and shaking.

Cultural and racial differences were also noted. Blacks were most likely to be injured with a cord, belt, strap, switch, stick, knife, or iron on the arms and legs, whereas whites were more likely to be injured with boards, paddles, and the open hand on their buttocks and faces. If the choice of the instrument is a matter of convenience, homes with limited electrical outlets are likely to provide electrical extension cords for injury. The instrument choice may not result from cultural or racial traditions but rather from poverty. Although one might theorize that girls would be disciplined more gently, the sex of the child did not influence the type of injury suffered.

The most common perpetrators of physical abuse in hospital-based data were the mother (28%) and father (17%). Of the perpetrator for whom sex was known, 49% were female and 51% were male. The caretaker of the child, at the time of "crisis," is most at risk for being the abuser. It is not known if males are more likely to abuse when they are in the caretaker role. Documented risk factors are listed in Table 20–3 (Johnson 1983).

Efforts are being made to predict abuse potential (Tsujimoto and Berger 1988). Little knowledge exists about why high-risk parents do not abuse. The role of the child-victim is a new and very sensitive topic (Ney 1988). One formula indicates that abuse results from the addition of three variables: the parents plus the child plus stress. It has been much more acceptable to place complete blame for physical and sexual abuse on the perpetrator (Steele 1980).

Transcultural Differences

Familiarity with the disciplinary approaches, dietary habits, and health care approaches of the various cultures in the community in which the child psychiatrist practices is necessary when providing services to children from these cultures. This is especially necessary when the children's parents are recent arrivals to the country and unfamiliar with the country's laws.

A young Asian couple, recently arrived in the United States, were apprised that their infant had bilateral retinoblastomas. They refused to allow the eyes to be removed, and an emergency court order was obtained to perform the surgery. Friends and relatives created a diversion in the hospital while the parents fled with the child. A police search was instituted at the insistence of frustrated professionals. Because of a large influx of Asian immigrants to the city, a special social services agency had been established to serve their needs. The agency accused the involved professionals of lacking understanding. They explained that the parents believed that the removal of the child's eyes would endanger the child's spirit or soul. The parents believed that they were acting in the child's best interest. Should they be prosecuted for their behavior? Should the recommended procedure be done?

A six month old Asian infant was seen for a scheduled appointment in the pediatric clinic for follow-up of a strep throat. The parents, recent immigrants, had brought the child to the emergency department 5 days previously. The examining physician noted a series of parallel abrasions overlying the ribs on the anterior and posterior chest. The interpreter stated that these were the marks of *cia gao*, a treatment used in Vietnam and Cambodia, in which a coin is rubbed against the skin to heal underlying affliction (Muecke 1983). The parents were reported for physical abuse. The parents could not un-

Table 20–3. RISK FACTORS IN PHYSICAL ABUSE: A CHECKLIST FROM CONTROLLED STUDIES	Mother	Father	Child
Risk Factor			
(Mother) lacked parental affection	X	?	
Parents abused	X		
(Mother) rejected as a child	X	?	
Father's age 16–21 at child's birth			
Adolescent mother (controversial)	X		
Unplanned pregnancy	X	?	
No preparation for child's arrival	X	?	
Chose one sex name prior to child's birth	X	?	
Father's reaction poor to pregnancy news			
Delivery problems (forceps, presentation, cesarean section)	X		
Difficult/bad birth experience	X		
Prematurity/postmaturity			X
Neonatal/bonding problems? (respiratory distress syndrome, apnea, infection)			X
Low Apgar			X
Not breast-fed	X		
Saw as below average or poor baby	X		
Did not enjoy caring for the child	X		
Early toilet training (<1 year)	X		
Punitive toilet training	X	?	
Frequent physical punishment	X	?	
Told bad or unloved	X	?	
Scream, hit for temper tantrums	X	?	
Rare praise for good behavior	X	?	
Strict disciplinarian	X	?	
Infrequent supervision	X		
Father not fond of child, rejects	X	X	
Mother thinks poorly of spouse/partner	X		
Do not share decision-making	X	X	
Disagreement in child rearing	X	X	
Not discuss child rearing	X	X	
"Limited" contact with others (controversial)	X		
"Limited" use of babysitter(s)	X		
Four or more children	X	?	
Church attendance, never or rare	X	?	
Financial stress	X	X	
Housing stress	X	X	
Domestic stress	X	X	
Parent's health a problem	X	X	
Family's health a problem	X	X	
Alcohol or drug use (controversial)	X	X	
Developmental Delay (2 or more delays on Denver)			
Personal social			X
Fine motor-adaptive			X
Language			X
Gross motor			X
Other Risk Factors			
Child with actual: mental retardation, physical abnormalities, learning disability, or hyperactivity; twins			X
Mother (76%) or father (64%) has personality disorders	X	X	
Mother has below-average (<85) IQ	X	?	
Mother (11%) or father (29%) has criminal record	X	X	
Ignorance about child health (controversial)	X	X	
Ignorance about child rearing	X	X	
Aggressive tendencies in mother	X	?	
Lack of empathy (related to own childhood)	X	?	
Lack of control	X	?	

? Studied in mothers, probable significance in father/caretaker.

derstand why they were being investigated for providing what was considered, in their country, to be appropriate care. Should they be reported for abuse? If they had substituted their folk remedy for the prescribed penicillin, would this have constituted medical neglect?

One may take a strict approach and say that immigrants should be made aware of local standards. We may choose to temper our conclusions with memories of chicken soup, mustard plasters, and other folk remedies used by our own, well-meaning relatives. If education is not offered, is the responsibility for the child's welfare shifted to immigration authorities and society? What does one do when the immigrant does not come through "appropriate immigration channels"?

Behavioral Consequences

The behavioral consequences of physical abuse will vary with the type of injury, injury location, chronicity of injury, developmental stage of the child, specific strengths and weaknesses of the child, and the relationship of the perpetrator to the child. It is much easier to predict the physical consequences of a blow of a particular force against an object of particular susceptibility. The intellectual and motor consequences that can occur (Martin et al. 1974) are less easy to predict and are complicated by the lack of developmental measurements made prior to the injury of young infants. In addition, an abused infant, who is tested as "normal" following a head injury, may have been "destined" for above-average performance. The older child may have school records that can serve as a baseline for pre-abuse brain functioning. Complicating the issue of predictability further is the effect of removal from the home, placement in a different school, and separation from peers, siblings, and foster parents on a child's behavior. The acute physical abuse that brings the child to the attention of authorities may be less damaging than chronic emotional and physical abuse and deprivation that may have been suffered by the child over time. Certainly one can appreciate the feeling of terror experienced by a child when a trusted caretaker injures him or her. A single event, with temporary pain and no disfigurement, may be "absorbed" with minimal detectable effect; chronic terror and pain will have invariable consequences. Observed from a psychodynamic perspective, the actual or threatened acute physical and psychological assault may result in disorganization, personalized injury, and a painful affective state, which, in turn, activates primitive coping mechanisms and a compulsion to repeat the trauma (Green 1983). The behavior of children who are chronically abused ranges from overcompliant and overactive, hypervigilant to withdrawn, depressed, and underactive. The victims may identify with the abuser and become abusive or resign themselves to being passive victims. Their defenses and mistrust of adults may prevent them from facile and open communication during initial assessments.

Expressions of anger, frustration, fear, and terror may be more readily revealed in play or with drawings. Cases reaching the psychiatric literature in which "disorganization and suspension of reality testing" are reported do not reflect the majority of abused children. These extreme cases result from the "filtering system," which places mildly afflicted or asymptomatic children in nonpsychiatric settings for therapy.

In the ideal situation, each new case of abuse would receive an initial multidisciplinary evaluation, including psychological/psychiatric, social, educational, nutritional, speech and hearing, and medical services. A multidisciplinary plan would be prescribed directed at serving all uncovered needs. The team members would then follow the progress of the child and family and would periodically adjust their recommendations. The number of abused children, combined with limited financial and professional resources, makes this an unlikely situation in all but the most wealthy communities, or in those communities with unusual sensitivity to the needs and welfare of children. The child psychiatrist should ensure that the community services for abused and neglected children are at least adequate and should advocate for improvement when needed. Guidelines should exist that ensure that the most seriously affected children will be recognized and served. It is likely that the screening will be done by physicians and social workers who are involved with initial assessment and not by child psychiatrists.

Treatment

The services offered to the abused child and the family will vary with the personality characteristics of the child and family. Quality diagnostic services must be linked to quality and available therapeutic services. A treatment plan, developed by a multidisciplinary team, will be needed to serve the social, medical, educational, and psychological needs of the child and family. The child psychiatrist must realize that a number of psychotherapeutic and educational techniques have been successfully applied to the abused child. These include play therapy, environmental manipulation, structuring, and support. Goals of treatment may include strengthening of coping mechanisms, improving reality testing, increasing frustration tolerance, and substituting verbal expression of aggression for physical expression (Green 1983). Treatment approaches for the child may include teaching relaxation skills, problem-solving skills, social skills, peer relations, and anger management (Walker et al. 1988). Family-centered treatment requires coordination with the various agencies involved in serving the child and family. Treatment is hampered when the perpetrator is removed from contact with the family by jailing or court-ordered restricted visitation. Treatment goals in family therapy include efforts to prevent re-abuse; improve the functioning of the parents; reduce frustration, stress, and conflict that may have contributed to or precipitated the abuse; improve self-esteem and parenting skills; decrease emotional isolation; and improve problem-solving skills (Gentry and Brisbane 1985). Education to improve parenting skills must be coupled with teaching stress management. Parents, like any students, may attend prescribed parenting classes and not change their behavior. When confronted with stress, be it the loss of the job or the management of a frustrating behavior in a child, they may revert to child abuse. Parent groups, available in most large cities, provide support and emergency services such as "drop-in nursery care" and hot lines. Often these groups are more acceptable to parents who mistrust professionals who have labeled them as child abusers, removed their children, and inveigled into their lives and homes. Families who are reported to the social system for child abuse may be known to the agencies for other reasons. Child abuse may be but one consequence of poverty, teenage pregnancy, drug abuse, parental abuse experience in their own childhood, and other risk factors that are difficult to isolate from each other.

Treatment trials in lieu of permanent placement are likely to be supported by the court in all but the most serious and blatant child abuse cases. How long treatment should be tried before the child is permanently placed in a healthy, skilled, and nurturing environment will be influenced by a balance between the needs of the child and the rights of the parents. For the child's sake, the treatment period should be short, with well-defined goals and measurable objectives. Early decision making will help ensure that permanent placement, if recommended, can be accomplished. The older child is less likely to be adopted. In addition, the child who suffers through multiple placements, while the parents' ability to parent is tested, may be damaged as much by the system as by the abusive parents. The therapist who fails to participate in a network of multiple disciplinary services, or who holds unrealistic optimism for changing the behavior of multiproblem, uncooperative, and rigid parents, may not be serving the best and long-term interest of the child.

SEXUAL ABUSE

Our early knowledge about the sexual abuse of children tended to come from studies of adult rape (Groth 1979). As the sexual abuse of children has received increasing attention, several myths have been eliminated. These include that the child offender is a "dirty old man" who is a stranger, sexually frustrated, insane, and liable to become more violent in time and that the victims are likely female and retarded. (Groth 1979). It is possible that our early conceptions about sexual abuse came from those children who entered the system as a result of perpetrators who were caught, confessed, or were guilty of especially heinous assaults. Studies have indicated that the number of males who are abused is higher than previously believed (Showers et al. 1983; VanderMey 1988) and that the dynamics of abuse of males and females is surprisingly similar (Farber et al. 1984). Males may be more reluctant to report abuse. The perpetrator is more likely to be a male, and this may result in fears of homosexuality to the male victim. In addition, males are expected to be able to avoid victimization. There is no uniform profile describing the perpetrator of incest or pedophilia (Finkelhor 1986). The two major categories appear to be different, and two types of pedophilia, fixated and regressed, have been described (Groth 1982). Sex with a relative before the age of consent is both incest and pedophilia.

Generalizations that can be applied to both types of sex abuse are that the perpetrator is likely to be young, male, and known to the child. Data from 464 cases of sexual abuse investigated in one year at a Children's Hospital (Child Abuse Program Annual Report 1987) indicated that 22% were male victims. Ages of victims ranged from 5 months to 18 years and averaged 9 years. The most common perpetrator was the father (15%), followed by the stepfather (8%) and uncle (7%). Female perpetrators totaled 2.3%. Because children are less likely to recognize inappropriate contact from a caretaker female, it is speculated that the incidence of female perpetrators may be higher. The types of sexual abuse included finger manipulation (25%), intercourse (18%), oral genital contact (17%), genital contact (11.5%), anal intercourse (11%), and fondling (5%). The preadolescent children were less likely to be penetrated. Only 24% of the children reported had positive physical findings. This increases the importance of the interview in the investigation of suspected sexual abuse. Girls are more at risk for sexual abuse. Increased risk is associated with employed or disabled mothers, witnessing parental conflict, poor relationship with a parent, and living with a stepfather (Finkelhor 1986).

Symptoms of Sexual Abuse

The initial and long-term physical and emotional symptoms of sexual abuse vary with the trauma resulting from the abuse and the age and the sex of the child (Finkelhor 1986). Infants and toddlers may have general irritability from oral or rectal abrasions that cannot be localized by the parent or physician. Dysuria from genital trauma may suggest a urinary tract infection. Trauma resulting in laceration to the anus, vestibule, or hymen should be associated with bleeding; however, an anal fissure from penetration may be misdiagnosed or misrepresented as being due to passing large stools or from falling on an object. Rarely does an object accidentally penetrate the rectum or vagina. Trauma to the genitalia of preverbal children should be reported as possible sexual abuse unless the incident was witnessed. Any venereal disease in a child should be reported as suspected sexual abuse since non-sexually-transmitted venereal disease is extremely rare (White et al. 1983).

Behavioral changes from sexual abuse are more likely to bring the child to the child psychiatrist. Symptoms vary with the age and sex of the child (Cavaiola and Schiff 1988) and the abuse experience. Symptoms may be overt, such as fear and avoidance of the perpetrator, or general and nonspecific, as indicated in Table 20–4. Symptoms may present in adulthood and can include medical complaints (Cunningham et al. 1988), including bulimia (Downs et al. 1987) and alcoholism (Root and Fallon 1988) in women and sexual compulsiveness, masculine identity confusion, and relationship confusion in men (Dimmock 1988).

The older child may have the verbal ability to relate about abuse but may be reluctant because of fear of reprisals, guilt associated with the act or acceptance of bribes, or fear of dissolution of the family. The child must ultimately testify in court and face the accu-

---

Table 20–4. PHYSICAL AND BEHAVIORAL OBSERVATIONS ASSOCIATED WITH SEXUAL ABUSE

Sleep disorders
Developmental delay
Venereal disease
Frequent urinary tract infections
Rectal, vaginal, or penile bruise/bleeding/laceration/ discharge
Sexual acting out
Generalized anxiety
School behavioral problems
Avoid physical contact
Fear of dying
Run away
Prostitution
Poor self-esteem
Role reversal
Lying, stealing
Fire setting
Suicide attempt
Fatigue, dysmenorrhea, low energy, low appetite
Sore throat
Dyspareunia
Bulimia
Alcoholism
Identity/relationship confusion

ser. Anticipation of this trauma engendered by the legal system (Tedesco and Schnell 1987) may cause a child to recant. Courtroom reforms to make the experience less traumatic for children have been recommended (Whitcomb 1986) and adopted in some states. Recent studies have attested to the credibility of young children to recall unpleasant events and effectively testify (Nurcombe 1986).

Who is Best Qualified to Collect the History of Sexual Abuse?

In communities, such as Columbus, Ohio, with an established child abuse team, suspected children will be referred to them for assessment. Abuse that is less than 72 hours old is considered a medical emergency and is seen "immediately" in the emergency department. The social worker who assists in the assessment is a trained team member, whereas the medical staff of the emergency department will vary in degrees of experience with abused children and sensitivity to social and behavioral issues. The child may need to wait in the emergency department until "higher priority" cases are seen. This upsets the parents and the professionals accompanying the child. The local children services agency considers every case of abuse to be an emergency and they are charged with making an immediate decision about placement to ensure the child's safety. This need conflicts with the reality of the emergency department case load and the availability of appointments in clinics. The private physician, although more likely to have rapport with the child, may not have the resources or equipment to perform the assessment, which may take 2 hours. In addition, the children service agency, interested in serving the needs of the child in court, is more likely to seek consultation from "recognized experts."

It is unlikely that the child psychiatrist will see children referred to the emergency department, unless the child's psychological reaction to the abuse is obvious and serious. Suicide, or suicide attempts, are uncommon after sexual abuse experiences or revelations. In addition, the report may follow the incident by weeks or years to be precipitated by an unrelated event such as a television program, abuse prevention program in school, or question to the parent about sexual practices. Recent reports indicate that the interval between the time of revelation by the child and the abuse event is shortening just as the reported incidence is increasing. Both changes may be secondary to increased sensitivity on the part of parents or professionals rather than because of an increase in abuse severity or ability of children to reveal events.

The child psychiatrist may be part of an established diagnostic team or may serve as a consultant to the team or community. Complicated cases, especially those in which custody is at issue (Paradise et al. 1988), may result in a request for a second opinion. A child who is reluctant to communicate with a team during a "one stop" interview may become more comfortable with a therapist in a longer team relationship. The purpose of the "therapy" may be to help establish a diagnosis. The child psychiatrist who is trained to interview children of various developmental levels, and who is interested in sexual abuse issues, has an important role to play in serving the needs of abused children.

How to Perform the Interview in Suspected Sexual Abuse

Although there are no standardized approaches to interviewing a child about any issue, there has been an effort to organize the sex abuse interview to ensure the court that the child has not been prompted or asked leading questions (Sgroi et al. 1985; Burgess et al. 1978; Johnson and Showers 1985). Many of the techniques used in younger children, including the use of dolls and drawings to help the younger child explain possible sexual abuse events, have not been studied with control groups and are controversial (Cohn 1988; Sivan et al. 1988).

The child psychiatrist is familiar with the need to vary interviews according to the developmental and temperamental disposition of the child. Clinicians may mistakenly believe that the child is only frightened of the potential for a "shot" in a hospital clinic and that reassurance that no shots will be given in the clinic is adequate in some situations to allay a child's anxiety and reluctance. The child may not desire to discuss the incident(s) again because the recollection is painful and the parents may appropriately support the child in this resistance.

Preparation for the interview is continued

when the child is asked to complete a series of nonverbal tasks, which includes drawing a person, family, scary place, and nice place. A series of situational drawings are given to the child to color. The drawings include a picture of a child being examined, being put to bed, being shaken by an adult, and being approached by a adult with a beltlike object. The child may be given an opportunity to play with a doll house, which may be used in the interview, and other toys. The interview takes place in a room with a one-way mirror. Parents, when appropriate, students, and other professionals watch the interview while a team physician and social worker begin the interview with a review of the child's drawings and the child's description of the actions taking place in the situational drawings. Anatomical drawings of a child and suspected perpetrator of the same sex, age and race are then introduced. The child is asked to identify body parts on the child drawing, to identify the "private parts," to state what they would do if a private part was touched, hurt, tickled, or looked at, and to state what they would do if requested to do "something" to another individual's private parts. If the child indicates any inappropriate activity, he or she is asked for details about the event(s) and perpetrator(s). Younger children may respond better with the help of time charts, the doll house, and anatomically correct dolls.

The police are interested in more details than the clinician. Each sexual abuse event is a "count" that effects plea bargaining and sentencing of a perpetrator. If the interview is "incomplete," according to the desires of other professionals who are observing the interview, written messages or "bug-in-the-ear" electronic receivers can be used to communicate with the interviewers. This obviates the need to perform multiple interviews that may decrease the child's credibility to the court because of an assumed "practice" effect.

There is no agreement about how many times a child should be interviewed. Interviews that go beyond the child's attention span may appear to be coercive to the court as the interviewer tries to focus the child on the topic. Substantiation of abuse charges and determination of the credibility of the child become especially challenging when parents are involved in custody or visitation disputes (Paradise et al. 1988). Children must

be reminded that they are going to be protected, believed, brave, good, and not guilty (Johnson 1986). They are reassured that they have done what they are supposed to do—tell about invasions of their privacy. The child may not have seen the invasion as painful, discomforting, or bad; the interviewer must therefore be careful in word choices. The adjective used to describe the event (e.g., *bad* touch) could result in a negative answer. A physical examination by the physician who is present during the interview decreases the child's anxiety and resistance for this necessary procedure. Internal genital examinations should only be performed in instances of internal genital bleeding. The colposcope, when available, improves lighting and proves magnification and photographic documentation of the examination. Cultures for *Chlamydia* and *Neisseria gonorrhoeae* are obtained. Generally the throat culture is considered to be the most traumatic part of the examination by the child. The results of the assessment are recorded on a standardized form to ensure that all information has been gathered and documented.

Who Receives Therapy?

The interviewers must decide if the effects of the abuse warrant referral for therapy. The child psychiatrist may become involved with the child for the first time when asked to determine if therapy is needed. If resources are limited, priorities must be developed to determine which children receive therapy. Generally, a single, "nonpainful" experience with a stranger (exposure, frottage, fondling) is more traumatic to the child's parents and the neighborhood than it is to the child. This may also be said of sexual play, which is defined as nonintercourse sexual behavior, without threats or bribes, between preadolescent children who are separated by not more than 4 years in age. When a young child displays seductive, inappropriate, or sophisticated sexual behavior, the professional must determine how the child learned the behavior. Often the source of the behavior proves to be sexual abuse.

Treatment will vary with the seriousness of resultant behavior. The sexual abuse may be but one aspect of physical and emotional abuse and neglect; psychotherapy should not overshadow other services needed by the child and family. The identity of the perpetrator will affect therapeutic approaches since treatment of incest is best conducted when the entire family is involved (Sgroi et al. 1985). Special approaches may be indicated in the most common type of sexual abuse, sibling incest (Sgroi et al. 1985). Other techniques include art therapy and group therapy (Sgroi et al. 1985). Incarceration precludes treatment of the offending parent and causes guilt within the child and possible anger from siblings and relatives who are affected by the economic and emotional consequences of the incarceration. Countering this is the possible "benefit" that incarceration with therapy may have. Typically, referred children and families are assessed with a battery of instruments before a decision is made about which of the many available programs is to be offered. If the children services agency obtains custody of the child, its plan for reuniting the family may dictate the therapeutic approach and agencies involved. A child psychiatrist should be a member of the team that writes reunification plans and evaluates their efficacy. Ultimately, this team will need to decide if the incest perpetrator can be allowed back into supervised and unsupervised contact with the child. Re-abuse of a child, who has been reported and served, causes the community to lose faith in therapeutic approaches and increases their demand for harsh punishment of perpetrators. Criminal prosecution places emphasis on proving who perpetrated the event (Mac-Murray 1988), an eventuality that may be impossible depending on the type of abuse on and the development and motivation of the child.

NEGLECT

Neglect is a failure to provide for a child's emotional or physical needs. As an act of omission, neglect may not have a dramatic and readily visible or measurable impact on the child. This lack of objective "evidence" and the age of the child (Powers and Eckenrode 1988) may make it more difficult to recognize and document neglect; this will adversely affect the facility with which an agency can influence the court to grant temporary custody. Medical neglect includes inadequate care (missed appointments, incomplete immunizations, lack of or delay in obtaining medical or dental care) or a failure to follow medical advice about treatment. Medical neglect may begin *in utero* when a mother's failure to maintain adequate nutrition, avoid drugs, or follow medical advise may adversely affect the fetus. The physician may be accused of neglect if he or she fails to serve the needs of the normal or abnormal newborn (Lund 1985). Emotional neglect involves a failure to provide those emotional supports that are necessary if a child is to develop to his or her maximum potential. This can include a failure to supervise, love, protect, and support. Education neglect includes a failure to obtain schooling for a child and a lack of stimulation to learn. Failure to protect may result in ingestions and accidents. Social neglect, in a hospital setting, could include reluctance to take a discharged child home, inadequate number of visitations, and inaccessibility of the parents to the medical staff. The cause of the neglect, be it intellectual deficit, emotional disturbance, or substance abuse is immaterial to the child who suffers the consequences. Planned neglect (or an intentional lack of concern for the child's welfare) may have the same physical effect on the child but a more adverse effect on the child's psyche and on the attitudes of involved professionals toward the parents.

Physical neglect is the most common type of child abuse seen by the social service departments in the community. These agencies are involved with families at risk for failure to supply shelter, education, and food. Medical neglect is more likely to be diagnosed and reported in a medical setting. There are no standardized definitions of what constitutes failure to provide for a child's emotional needs. The ability of a family to serve their children's needs is influenced by their own emotional, intellectual, and economic resources. Acquired basic resources such as food, housing, and clothing may make neglect the easiest type of child abuse to resolve, unless complications are formed by parental inability or lack of desire to change priorities and behaviors. The same may be said for medical neglect when resources can be made available but are not used by the parents who disagree with medical standards for care or are intellectually or emotionally unable to follow through with recommendations. The child psychiatrist may become involved in the evaluation of a parent's qualifications to parent in cases of neglect.

Documentation of medical neglect includes assurance that the caretakers understood what was expected. Efforts to instruct parents about the health needs of their children should be documented in the hospital records. When the parent's religious conviction prevents a child from receiving necessary health care, this may not be considered "neglect" in some states. Efforts are being made to protect children from unfavorable consequences resulting from their parent's religious beliefs. Medical care can be provided to the child by court order. Those instances of medical neglect, in which the child's life is at stake, are easier to document for the court than less dramatic and possibly controversial issues, such as the need to be immunized. Poor care of a child's hygiene and clothing needs may be more easily recognized and comprehended when the court is approached to intervene.

Efforts have been made to more precisely define emotional neglect and emphasize the psychological effects of physical and sexual abuse (Brassard et al. 1987). Psychological abuse and neglect have been expanded to explore the effects of racism, social systems, and dangerous environments including the school environment on a child's emotional development (Brassard et al. 1987). In 1987, 52 cases of neglect and failure to thrive were evaluated. The average age was 2.34 years, making this the youngest group of children seen for abuse. Mothers were reported for neglect in 47 of the cases. Neglect cases included nonorganic failure to thrive (17.87%), medical neglect (33.33%), failure to protect (13%), lack of supervision (11.9%), and physical neglect (5.95%). Emotional neglect was documented in 11 cases (11.9%).

Nonorganic Failure to Thrive

The term *nonorganic failure to thrive* (NOFTT) emphasizes the visible or measurable effect of maternal failure to provide. The term *maternal deprivation* has been suggested as a substitute (Gagen et al. 1984). There are instances in which a child fails to grow because of lack of calories in the diet, because of ignorance or a lack of economic resources. This condition is readily recognized in the clinic and easily resolved with education and provision of resources. Of most concern is the child who is suffering the consequences of maternal deprivation. The deprivation may be intentional, because the child was unwanted or related to a postpartum depression or other mental illness. The infant may "fail to stimulate maternal responses" in the mother. NOFTT (Goldson et al. 1976) and physical abuse (Klein and Stern 1971) are seen more frequently in prematures, where bonding opportunities and infant responses are limited, than in full-term infants. The extent of the pathologic dynamics of infant nurturing will dictate the course and type of treatment of this life-threatening condition.

Emotional Abuse

Emotional abuse can be an isolated event or chronic behaviors and can include ignoring, rejecting, terrorizing, isolating, and corrupting (Gabarino et al. 1986). It is rarely reported and difficult to document. In order to prove that a child has suffered permanent disability from the willful "emotional attack" of a caretaker, one must prove that the attack had an effect that is independent from other painful childhood experiences. One must also prove willfulness. Parents, in their sincere attempts to rear healthy children, use methods of behavior control that are psychologically harmful to the child. As with any other forms of abuse, factors within the child, the child's success in seeking alternative support systems, and the chronicity of insult will influence the outcome of the child's behavior. The child psychiatrist, involved with a child over time, is in a unique position to document parental behaviors that are adversive to the child. The documentation is best obtained through direct observation and not through hearsay from the child or others. As in other cases of abuse, a child's recounting of events may not be adequate to convince the legal system of the need to protect the child. Emotional abuse in the classroom, reported by a series of parents, is one instance in which the amount of objective data collected can result in sufficient documentation to effect change. Intervention in emotional abuse and neglect is designed to reduce environmental stress on the family and intrapersonal conflict and to mobilize community resources for treatment (Gabarino et al. 1986). Child psychiatry has an important role to play in clarifying what constitutes emotional abuse and neglect of children, how to document that they are taking place, and how to convince protective agencies that these non-physical adverse influences on a child are important and worthy of immediate and serious attention.

MUNCHAUSEN'S SYNDROME BY PROXY

Munchausen's syndrome by proxy (MBP) is the most recent form of child abuse to receive attention in the medical literature. Named after Baron Von Munchausen, an 18th century mercenary known for his tall tales, the syndrome of factitious illness was first described in adults. In MBP the parent, invariably the mother, causes disease in the child (Rosenberg 1987). Psychotherapy has been described for the perpetrator (Nicol and Eccles 1985); however, engaging the denying perpetrator in therapy, and effecting change, remain as formidable challenges.

PREVENTION

The morbidity and mortality of child abuse and neglect, coupled with the expense and unpredictable success of therapy, has resulted in research and resources being shifted to prevention (Smith and Kunjukrishnan 1985). The child psychiatrist who recognizes and reports abuse will provide tertiary prevention or prevention of re-abuse. Secondary prevention is directed at those known populations at high risk for abuse. Obviously children who have been abused should be of highest priority for therapy to prevent them from becoming abusers to the next generation. Primary prevention is aimed at the population in general and is focused on larger and more abstract arenas such as teaching parenting and stress management and reducing teenage pregnancy, physical and mental handicaps, prematurity, and poverty. Because the antecedents of child abuse may begin in childhood and are often multifactorial, the efficacy of primary and secondary prevention is difficult to prove (Steele 1980).

The subject of abuse prevention was the topic of a 1988 national conference (Daro 1988). Recommendations included the following:

1. Educational and support services for all new parents

2. Continuing parenting education
3. Adequate child care facilities
4. Diagnostic services to detect health and developmental problems
5. Treatment for maltreatment consequences
6. Life skill training to improve ability of children to protect themselves
7. Increasing self-help groups

Topics for future research are listed below:

1. The impact of social systems
2. Culture and race of families and their definitions of adequate parenting
3. Study of treatment based on family as well as child developmental stages
4. The effect of acute versus chronic family violence
5. Victim factors that increase susceptibility to sexual abuse
6. Substance abuse and emotional maltreatment
7. Testing and improvement of methodologies and assessment measures

For the child psychiatrist interested in research, the fields of abuse diagnosis, especially emotional abuse and neglect, and abuse treatment and prevention are frontiers of opportunities. For the clinician, child abuse will continue to exist as a diagnostic and therapeutic challenge until a myriad of changes are wrought by society and results of quality research in diagnosis, treatment, and prevention are effectively applied.

References

Brassard, M. R., Germain, R., and Hart, S. N. 1987. *Psychological Maltreatment of Children and Youth.* New York: Pergamon Press.

Brown, J., and Melinkovich, P. 1986. Schönlein-Henoch purpura misdiagnosed as suspected child abuse: A case report and literature review. *J.A.M.A.* 256:617–618.

Budin, L., and Johnson, C. F. 1989. Sex abuse prevention programs: Offenders' attitudes about their efficacy. *Child Abuse and Neglect* 13:77–87.

Burgess, A. W., Groth, A. N., Holmstrom, L. L., and Sgroi, S. M. 1978. *Sexual Assault of Children and Adolescents.* Lexington, Mass.: Lexington Books.

Caffey, J. 1946. Multiple fractures in long bones of children suffering from chronic subdural hematoma. *A.J.R.* 56:163–71.

Caffey, J. 1972. The parent–infant traumatic stress syndrome (Caffey-Kempe syndrome, battered baby syndrome). *A.J.R.* 218–219.

Cavaiola, A. A., and Schiff, M. 1988. Behavioral sequelae of physical and/or sexual abuse in adolescents. *Child Abuse and Neglect* 12:181–188.

Child Abuse Program Annual Report 1986–1987. Columbus, Ohio: Children's Hospital.

Cohn, D. C. 1988. Play activity with anatomically correct dolls: Is there a difference between children referred for sexual abuse assessment and controls? Dissertation, Ohio State University.

Cunningham, J., Pearce, T., and Pearce, P. 1988. Childhood sexual abuse and medical complaints in adult women. *J. Interpersonal Violence* 3:131–144.

Curran, C., and Johnson, C. F. 1987. Mistrust of children services agencies: One reason why physicians fail to report child abuse. Poster Session at Landacre Conference, Ohio State University, Columbus, Ohio.

Daro, D. 1988. *Enhancing Child Abuse Prevention Efforts for the 1990's*. Chicago: National Center on Child Abuse Prevention.

Dimmock, P. T. 1988. Adult males sexually abused as children: Characteristics and implications for treatment. *J. Interpersonal Violence* 3:203–221.

Downs, W. R., Miller, B. A., and Gondoli, D. M. 1987. Childhood experiences of parental physical violence for alcoholic women as compared with a randomly selected household sample of women. *Violence and Victims* 2:225–240.

Ellerstein, N. 1981. *Child Abuse and Neglect: A Medical Reference, 3*. New York: John Wiley & Sons.

Farber, E. D., Showers, J., Johnson, C. F., et al. 1984. The sexual abuse of children: A comparison of male and female victims. *J. Clin. Child Psychol.* 13:294–297.

Finkelhor, D. 1986. A sourcebook on child sexual abuse charges when parents dispute custody or visitation. *Pediatrics* 81:835–839.

Fouras, G., and Johnson, C. F. 1988. Measurements of the severity of physical abuse. *J. Trauma* (submitted)

Gabarino, J., Guttman, E., Seeley, J. W. 1986. *The Psychologically Battered Child*. San Francisco: Jossey-Bass.

Gagen, R. J., Cupoli, J. M., and Watkin, A, H. 1984. Families of children who fail to thrive: Preliminary investigations of parental deprivation among organic and nonorganic cases. *Child Abuse Neglect* 8:93–103.

Gentry, T., and Brisbane, F. L. 1982. The solution for child abuse rests with the community. *Children Today* (November/December):22–24.

Goldson, E., Cadol, R. V., Fitch, M. J. 1976. Nonaccidental trauma and failure to thrive: A sociomedical profile in Denver. *Am. J. Dis. Child.* 130:490–492.

Green, A. H. 1983. Child abuse: Dimension of psychological trauma in abused children. *J. Am. Acad. Child Psychiatry* 22:231–237.

Groth, N. A. 1979. Men who rape: The psychology of the offender. New York: Plenum Press.

Groth, N. A. 1982. The incest offender. In Sgroi, S. M. (ed.): *Handbook of Clinical Intervention in Child Sexual Abuse*. Lexington, Mass.: Lexington Books.

Helfer, R. E. 1987. Back to the future. *Child Abuse Neglect* 11:11–14.

Helfer, R. E., and Kempe, K. (eds.). 1968. *The Battered Child*. Chicago: University of Chicago Press.

Holter, J. C., and Friedman, S. B. 1968. Child abuse: Early case finding in the emergency department. *Pediatrics* 42:128–138.

Iznat, R. J., and Hubay, C. 1966. The annual injury of 15,000,000 children: A limited study of childhood accidental injury and death. *J. Trauma* 6:65–74.

Johnson, C. F. 1983. Sudden infant death syndrome v. child abuse: The teenage connection. *The Journal of Pedodontics* 7:196–208.

Johnson, C. F. 1986. *The Sexually Abused Child: A Pediatrician's Approach to the Interview*. Columbus, Ohio: Children's Hospital Press.

Johnson, C. F., Apolo, J., Joseph, J. A., and Corbitt, T. 1986. *Pediatr. Emerg. Care* 2:6–9.

Johnson, C. F., Loxterkamp, D., and Albanese M. 1982. Effect of high school students' knowledge of child development and child health on approaches to child discipline. *Pediatrics* 69:559–563.

Johnson, C. F., Showers, J. 1985. *Diagnosis and Management of Physical Abuse of Children: A Self-Instructional Program, Case #6*. Child Abuse Program, Children's Hospital, Columbus, Ohio.

Kempe, C. H., Silverman, F. N., Steele, B. F., et al. 1962. The battered child syndrome. *J.A.M.A.* 181:17–24.

Klein, M., and Stern, L. 1971. Low weight and the battered child syndrome. *Am. J. Dis. Child.* 122:15–18.

Knudsen, D. D. 1988. Child maltreatment over two decades: Change or continuity. *Violence Victims* 3:129.

Kravitz, H., Driessen, G., and Gomberg, R. 1969. Accidental falls from elevated surfaces in infants from birth to one year of age. *Pediatrics* 44:869–876.

Ladson, S., Johnson, C. F., and Doty R. E. 1987. Do physicians recognize sexual abuse? *Am. J. Dis. Child* 141:411–415.

Lund, N. 1985. Infanticide, physicians, and the law: The "Baby Doe" amendments to the child abuse prevention and treatment act. *Am. J. Law Med.* 2:1–29.

MacMurray, B. K. 1988. The nonprosecution of sexual abuse and informal justice. *J. Interpersonal Violence* 3:197–202.

Martin, H. P., Beealey, P., Conway, E. F., and Kempe, H. C. 1974. The development of abused children: I: A review of the literature. *Adv. Pediatr.* 21:25–73.

McClung, H. J., Murray, R., Braden, N. J., et al. 1988. Intentional ipecac poisoning in children. *Am. J. Dis. Child.* 142:637–639.

Morris, J. L., Johnson, C. F., and Clasen, M. 1985. To report or not to report: Physicians' attitudes toward discipline and child abuse. *Am. J. Dis. Child.* 139:194–197.

Mueke, M. A. 1983. Caring for Southeast Asian refugee patients in the U.S.A. *Am. J. Public Health* 73:431–438.

National Clearinghouse on Child Abuse and Neglect. *Study of the National Incidence and Prevalence of Child Abuse and Neglect*. Washington, D.C. 1988.

Nelson, B. J. 1984. Making an issue of child abuse: Political agenda setting for social problems. Chicago: University of Chicago Press.

Ney, P. G. 1988. Triangles of abuse: A model of maltreatment. *Child Abuse Neglect* 12:363–373.

Nicol, A. R., and Eccles, M. 1985. Psychotherapy for Munchausen's syndrome by proxy. *Arch. Dis. Child.* 60:344–348.

Nurcombe, B. 1986. The child as witness: Competency and credibility. *J. Am. Acad. Child Psychiatry* 254:473–480.

Paradise, J. E., Rostain, A. L., and Nathanson, M. 1988. Substantiation of sexual abuse charges when parents dispute custody or visitation. *Pediatrics* 81:835–839.

Powers, J. L., and Eckenrode, J. 1988. The maltreatment of adolescents. *Child Abuse Neglect* 12:189–199.

Root, M. P. P., and Fallon, P. A. 1988. The incidence of victimization experiences in a bulimic sample. *J. Interpersonal Violence* 3:161–163.

Rosenberg, D. A. 1987. Web of deceit: A literature review of Munchausen syndrome by proxy. *Child Abuse Neglect* 11:547–563.

Sanders, R. 1972. Resistance to dealing with parents of battered children. *Pediatrics* 50:853–857.

Sgroi, S. M., Porter, S. F., Blick, L. C. 1985. Validation of child sexual abuse. In Sgroi, S. M. (ed.): *Handbook of Clinical Intervention in Child Sexual Abuse.* Lexington, Mass.: Lexington Books.

Showers, J., and Apolo, J. 1986. Criminal disposition of 72 cases of fatal child abuse. *Med. Sci. Law* 26:243–247.

Showers, J., Farber, E. D., Joseph, J. A., et al. 1983. The sexual victimization of boys: A three year survey. *Health Values* 7:15–18.

Showers, J., and Johnson, C. F. 1984. Students' knowledge of child health and development: Effects on approaches to discipline. *Journal of School Health* 54:122–125.

Sivan, A. B., Shor, D. P., Koeppl, G. K., and Noble, L. D. 1988. Interaction of normal children with anatomical dolls. *Child Abuse Neglect* 12:295–304.

Smith, A. M., and Kunjukrishnan, R. 1985. Child abuse: Perspectives on treatment and research. *Psychiatr. Clin. North Am.* 8:665–683.

Solomon, T. 1973. History and demography of child abuse. *Pediatrics* [Suppl.] 51:773–776.

Solomons, G. S. 1980. Trauma and child abuse: The importance of the medical record. *Am. J. Dis. Child.* 134:503–505.

Steele, B. F. C. 1987. Henry Kempe Memorial Lecture. *Child Abuse Neglect* 11:313–318.

Steele, B. 1980. Psychodynamic factors in child abuse. In Kempe, C. H., and Helfer, R. E. (eds.): *The Battered Child.* Third Edition. Chicago: University of Chicago Press.

Tedesco, J. F., and Schnell, S. V. 1987. Children's reactions to sex abuse investigation and litigation. *Child Abuse Neglect* 11:267–272.

Tsujimoto, R. N., and Berger, D. E. 1988. Predicting/preventing child abuse: Value of utility maximizing cutting scores. *Child Abuse Neglect* 12:397–408.

VanderMey, B. J. 1988. The sexual victimization of male children: A review of previous research. *Child Abuse Neglect* 12:61–72.

Walker, C. E., Bonner, B. L., and Kaufman, K. L. 1988. The physically and sexually abused child: Evaluation and treatment. New York: Pergamon Press.

Whitcomb, D. 1986. Prosecuting child sexual abuse: New approaches. Natural Institute of Justice Reports, SN1 197:1–6.

White, S. T., et al. 1983. Sexually transmitted diseases in sexually abused children. *Pediatrics* 72:16–21.

Sleep Disorders in Children and Adolescents

21

THOMAS R. LINSCHEID, Ph.D.
L. KAYE RASNAKE, Ph.D.

Sleep problems are not uncommon in children and adolescents and can present as isolated disorders or in combination with other physiological or behavioral manifestations of emotional disturbance. Schroeder (1979), for example, found that 8% to 10% of all concerns expressed by parents to their child's pediatrician were related to sleep problems. Bixler and co-workers (1976) surveyed 4,358 physicians nationwide, including pediatricians and child psychiatrists. Pediatricians reported a prevalence rate for sleep disturbances of 0.2% to 7.8%, while child psychiatrists reported ranges from 0.2% to 19.4%. Sleep disturbances, whether physiologically, emotionally, or behaviorally based, comprise a significant proportion of problems encountered by pediatricians and child psychiatrists. Problems with sleep affect not only the child experiencing the problem but the entire family and can have a significant impact on family functioning. Sorting out the various reasons for the sleep problem, discriminating cause and effect, is an important function for the child psychiatrist. A thorough knowledge of physiologically based sleep disturbances, behavioral etiology for sleep problems, and effects of various emotional disorders (e.g., depression) on sleep are necessary prerequisites.

In this chapter an overview of the physiology of sleep in children and adolescents is presented with emphasis on development of sleep patterns and common sleep problems and their treatment are reviewed.

NORMAL SLEEP AND ITS DEVELOPMENT

Adult sleep can be divided into two main categories, rapid eye movement (REM) sleep and non–rapid eye movement (NREM) sleep. The development of physiological recording equipment, primarily the electroencephalograph, has allowed dramatic progress in the understanding of sleep over the past 40 years. It is now known that NREM sleep is composed of up to four stages differentiated by their characteristic electroencephalographic (EEG) patterns (Anders and Weinstein 1972; Coates and Thoresen 1981; Parkes 1985). Stage 1 sleep is thought of as the lightest sleep stage and is characterized by slow, mixed-frequency EEG activity (3–7 cycles per second). During this stage, rolling eye movements can occur and mental and physiological activity is quite pronounced. Stage 2 sleep is a somewhat deeper stage of sleep than stage 1 and is characterized by short bursts of higher-frequency EEG activity called sleep spindles (13–18 cycles per second; duration, 0.5–2 seconds). Stages 3 and 4 are represented by the occurrence of delta waves, which are slow, high-amplitude patterns signaling a reduction in overall brain activity. Stage 3 is scored when 20% to 50%

of the overall EEG is composed of delta wave patterns, while stage 4 is defined as more than 50% delta waves. On falling asleep, a person progresses from stage 1 to stage 4 sleep, showing an increasing pattern of reduction in physiological activity and responsiveness to the environment.

REM sleep generally occurs after the first progression from stage 1 through stage 4 sleep, approximately 90 minutes after the onset of sleep. REM sleep is characterized by a high-frequency, low-amplitude EEG pattern and the presence of strong eye movements, as indicated by electro-oculograms. An interesting component of REM sleep relates to the absence of muscle tension as measured by electromyographic recordings. As the night progresses there is a decreasing amount of time spent in sleep stages 3 and 4, with REM sleep predominating as morning approaches, as shown in Figure 21–1 (Coates and Thoresen 1981; Ware and Orr 1983).

Unlike adults, infants spend a much greater proportion of their time in REM sleep, shown in Figure 21–2. With maturation of the nervous system, sleep spindles occur at around 3 months of age. This pattern gradually shifts to a more adult distribution of REM and NREM sleep, and by 1 year of age infants are generally capable of sleeping for periods of 5 hours or more during the night with predominant waking periods during the day. Moore and Ucko (1957) found that 70% of infants sleep through the night by 3 months of age, and 83% do so by 6 months of age. By the first year of life 90% are consistently sleeping for 5-hour periods or longer. "Sleeping through the night" is not

defined by actual physiological sleep but by the length of time during which the child does not awaken and summon parents by crying or calling out. Most infants awaken frequently during the night, and this can continue well into the second year of life. This phenomenon of frequent night-time awakening during infancy is discussed later as it relates to the development of behaviorally based sleep problems.

As children mature they require less sleep and the percentage of time in REM sleep decreases. By the end of their first year of life, children spend 30% of their 12 to 13 hours of sleep in REM sleep. By adolescence, sleep duration decreases to an average of 8 hours per night, 20% of which is REM sleep. The number of REM periods decreases from 6.7 in 3- to 5-year old children to 4 in 16- to 19-year old adolescents (Coates and Thoresen 1981; Parkes 1985). Knowledge of normal child and adolescent sleep patterns is important when assessing the abnormality of observed patterns in children referred for sleep disorders. Most parents have a poor understanding of the development of children's sleep patterns, and often simple reassurance that a sleep pattern is normal is sufficient to solve the problem.

Children's cognitive development is also important in understanding sleep-related problems. For example, the child's loss of egocentric thinking allows him or her to ponder such questions as "what happens to my parents when I am asleep or what if I don't wake up" and to more accurately interpret the content of nightmares. These changes in cognitive abilities are consistent with often-seen increases in bedtime-related problems in the 2- to 5-year-old child (Anders and Weinstein 1972; Ware and Orr 1983). The onset of nightmares occurs around this age as well, with the highest incidence occurring at the ages of 3 to 7 years (Hartmann 1980). The causes of nightmares are unknown. Explanations that have been considered include stress and emotional strain (Bakwin and Bakwin 1972), sensitive personalities (Hartmann 1980), ego immaturity (Scharfman 1985), and nervous system immaturity (Bakwin and Bakwin 1972). By age 5, children are able to recall the dream vividly (Bakwin and Bakwin 1972) and possess cognitive abilities necessary to see cause and effect relationships between dream content and emotional responses.

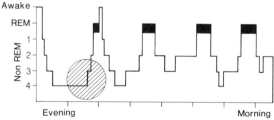

Figure 21–1. *An idealized child's sleep pattern indicating the initial progression through sleep stages 1 through 4 followed by the first REM period. The shaded area represents the time that disorders of arousal tend to occur. (From Coates, T. J., and Thoresen, C. E. 1981. Sleep disturbances in children and adolescents. In Mash, E. J., and Terdal, L. G. [eds.]:* Behavioral Assessment of Childhood Disorders. *New York: Guilford Press.)*

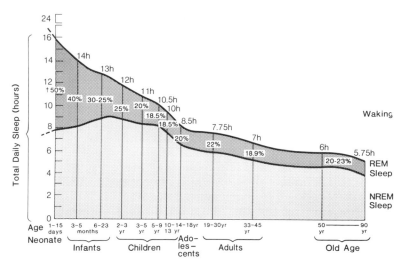

Figure 21–2. Changes in total sleep time and proportion of REM sleep with age. (From Parkes, J. D. 1985. Sleep and Its Disorders. London: W. B. Saunders.)

BEHAVIOR AND DEVELOPMENTALLY RELATED SLEEP PROBLEMS IN CHILDREN

During the first year of life, parents' concerns regarding sleep generally focus on sleeping through the night. This is actually a misnomer since few children actually sleep consistently for extended periods of time similar to adult sleep. As mentioned earlier, approximately 80% of children sleep for 5-hour periods by age 6 months. Moore and Ucko (1957) refer to this period as "settling" rather than sleeping since the child may frequently awaken but does not cry out and returns to sleep after a brief period of minor motor activity or fussiness. This is a very normal pattern and related to the development of REM–NREM relationships during the first year of life. The settling phenomenon, however, is often the root of many behavior-based sleep problems that go unreported until the child is several years older. A common practice of new parents is to have their new infant sleep in the bedroom with them. Sometimes this is actually in bed with them, but more likely it is in a crib in the parents' room. Night-time awakenings in which the infant fusses only slightly are heard by the parents because of the physical proximity and are likely to be interpreted as the child needing reassurance or feeding. If the child is picked up, fed, or rocked during these brief awakening periods, the child may actually become more alert than if left to return to sleep on his or her own. If the child is sleeping in another room, parents may not hear the child rustling and the child learns

to fall back to sleep without parental intervention.

Parents who bring children to professionals with the complaint of frequent night-time awakenings in the 2- to 5-year age range often have a history of allowing the child to sleep in their room during the infancy period. If this pattern continues, the child develops a habitual awakening pattern, learns to expect comfort from the parent in the form of affection or feeding, and becomes distressed when this expectation is not fulfilled. A study (Lozoff et al. 1985) revealed that in a sample of 28 children described as having sleep problems, 68% had a history of sleeping with the parents. Parents often ask the question about having their infants, toddlers, or children sleep with them. While this is generally not a good practice for a number of reasons (see Ferber 1985), the professional must be careful not to recommend against certain cultural practices where the communal bed is accepted and deviations may create greater social problems for the parents.

Although not technically a sleep problem, infant colic can often be associated with the development of sleep problems in children. Colic occurs between birth and 3 to 4 months of age and is primarily expressed by an infant showing signs of inconsolable distress, frequently accompanied by the child doubling up as if experiencing gastrointestinal problems. The lack of sleep combined with frustrations experienced by parents unable to console their child despite numerous efforts can produce great stress. Keener and co-workers (1988) reported that both mothers' and fathers' perceptions of the temperament of their infants at 6 months of age were related to the infant's sleep pattern, especially those factors that reflect sleep continuity. While colic seems in almost all cases to resolve simply with the passage of time, the perceptions of the infant engendered in the parent during colicky stages certainly can influence their perception of the child and his or her needs in the future.

Schmidt (1981), while recognizing that there is no definitive and universally effective treatment for colic, recommends overfeeding and not allowing the child to sleep for extended periods during the day. Schmidt further suggests that rhythmic activity and gentle stroking may be helpful in comforting the colicky child. Interestingly, Loadman and associates (1987) reported research on the development of a device capable of calming crying, colicky infants. Invented by a father who noticed his colicky infant would cease crying and fall asleep while riding in the car on the highway, the device re-creates the vibrations and wind sounds of a car traveling at 55 miles per hour.

During the latter part of the first year of life and through toddlerhood, nocturnal awakening and crying episodes present as major problems with some children. Causes can be related to the infant or child's medical history, temperament, colic, family distress, or simply poor sleep habits or sleep environments.

Rickert and Johnson (1988) investigated two methods for treating spontaneous awakening and crying episodes in infants and toddlers. A procedure derived from pediatrician advice to simply ignore the child's crying was compared with a technique in which the child was awakened at a time just prior to when he or she might normally awaken with parents responding as they would if the child awakened on his own. This might include feeding, holding, or rocking. Systematic ignoring involved instructing parents to immediately check their child's safety with the onset of crying in a stereotypic, mechanical manner without providing any soothing or comfort. Once the parents had determined that the child was not ill or physically hurt they were to leave the room and continue to ignore the crying regardless of the duration. If diaper changes were necessary, this was allowed but were to be done in a very matter of fact, rapid manner with as little interaction as possible.

Comparison of the systematic ignoring and scheduled awakening procedures with a control condition revealed that systematic ignoring produced the most rapid and most complete reduction of night-time spontaneous awakening. Scheduled awakenings were effective in reducing night-time awakenings beyond the control group level, and at a 6-week follow-up systematic ignoring and scheduled awakenings produced similar results.

In the Rickert and Johnson study (1988) the failure to provide "reinforcement" in the form of bottle feedings, holding, or rocking contingent on night-time awakenings produced a decrease in these behaviors. Thus, the argument can be made that night-time awakenings are learned habits that may have started for legitimate medical reasons but are maintained by their own consequences. Christophersen (1982) provides guidelines for bedtime problem crying for use by parents. These guidelines suggest the establishment of a reasonable bedtime that is followed strictly. About 30 minutes before bedtime, parents should begin what Christophersen calls "quiet time," during which the child and parents engage in quiet activities such as reading or doing a puzzle and should avoid roughhousing and exercising. A regular bedtime routine should include a visit to the bathroom, a drink of water if desired, kisses, and a story. Once this routine is completed the child should be placed in bed and the parents should leave the room and not return even if their child continues to cry. Parents are told that the child may cry for extended periods of up to 1 or 2 hours but that returning to the room after this extended period will simply give the child the message that persistent crying will result in the parent's return. This procedure usually works well with bedtime crying diminishing in one or two nights. Once the child has been regularly going to bed without crying parents may feel more secure responding to their child should he or she awaken and cry during the night.

This same concept can be used to treat children who leave their bed during the night for the purpose of entering the parents' bed. While some parents embrace the concept of a family bed, most parents tolerate the child coming to their bed in the night not because it is preferred but because it is easier than teaching the child to stay in his or her own bed. The most successful treatment for a child who comes to the parents' bed in the night is to immediately return the child to bed with as little verbal interaction as possible. The parents should place the child back in bed and return to their own bed. In a case example, this technique was suggested to a mother whose 30-month-old child, following a bout of severe gastrointestinal illness, developed a habit of awakening during the night and coming into the parents' room. During the first night of treatment, the child attempted to leave his room 66 times. The mother, dutifully following instructions, was ready each time he attempted to enter the parents' room and without comment picked him up and placed him back in bed, leaving immediately. The second night the mother was prepared for another long night, however, the child slept through the night without a single attempt to enter the parents' room.

Bedtime and night-time behavioral problems appear in most cases to be habit based. Although these behaviors may begin for legitimate reasons such as acute illness or colic, they can also be taught through parental mismanagement, usually arising from a lack of knowledge regarding infant and children's sleep habits or from excessive parental anxiety. Children who do not respond to simple behavioral management suggestions should be evaluated for physiologically based sleep disturbances.

PHYSIOLOGICALLY BASED SLEEP DISORDERS

With the increase in our knowledge about sleep and sleep disorders came a need for a classification system to promote communication between clinical and research-oriented professionals working with sleep. In 1979 the Association of Sleep Disorders Centers (ASDC) devised such a classification system, comprising four major categorizations. The first category, disorders of initiating and maintaining sleep (DIMS), includes the insomnias and disorders related to early morning awakenings. Also contained within this category is childhood-onset DIMS, which designates those patients with insomnia who had onset prior to puberty and whose difficulties initiating sleep persist into adulthood. Childhood-onset DIMS is believed to be

closely related to a new diagnostic term under this category called *psychophysiological insomnia*. This term defines those patients whose insomnia is not primarily associated with a known or underlying organic disorder or the result of a psychopathologic process such as depression. The suggestion is that childhood-onset DIMS is not related to depression or other emotional disturbances of childhood.

The next major category in the ASDC system is disorders of excessive somnolence (DOES). These disorders have as their main focus complaints of daytime sleepiness. This category also contains conditions that produce excessively long night-time sleep with full alertness during the day. The third major category is disorders of the sleep–wake schedule (DSWS) and includes disturbances of the timing of sleep. These disorders are rarely seen in children or adolescents and will not be discussed here. The final major category is parasomnias, which includes dysfunctions associated with sleep, sleep stages, or partial arousal. These disorders occur during the main sleep period and include somnambulism, sleep terrors, nightmares, and sleep-related enuresis. Some of the parasomnias have a very distinct correlation with specific sleep stages or occur exclusively during REM sleep.

The American Psychiatric Association's *Diagnostic and Statistical Manual of Mental Disorders*, third edition, revised (*DSM-III-R*) (1987) proposes two categories of sleep disorders, dyssomnias and parasomnias. Dyssomnias include the various types of insomnias, hypersomnias, and sleep–wake schedule disorders. Included under parasomnias are dream anxiety disorder, sleep terror disorder, and sleep walking disorder. It is interesting to note that in the *DSM-III* (1980) the only sleep disorders noted were sleep terror and sleep walking disorders, both predominantly childhood problems.

DISORDERS OF INITIATING AND MAINTAINING SLEEP

One of the subtypes of DIMS is entitled childhood-onset DIMS and appears to be rare. Research has suggested that childhood-onset insomniacs when compared with adult-onset insomniacs take longer to fall asleep and sleep less. There is also evidence of increased amounts of REM, which is poorly defined (Hauri and Olmstead 1980). These children appear to have insomnia almost from birth, and difficulty falling asleep does not appear to be related to stressful incidents in their life. Interestingly, persons with childhood-onset DIMS also show a higher than normal incidence of hyperkinesia, dyslexia, and attention-deficit disorder. They also appear to be overly sensitive to stimulants.

While childhood-onset DIMS appears to be rare, insomnia in postpubertal adolescents is more frequent (Lacks 1987). Adolescent insomnia can be of several types. Psychophysiological DIMS is what most persons think of when they hear the term insomnia. It is characterized primarily by difficulty falling asleep but also includes difficulty remaining asleep and premature morning awakening. This disorder can be diagnosed through sleep laboratory assessment or through the exclusion of the other forms of insomnia related to psychiatric disturbance, drug and alcohol abuse, or insomnia related to respiratory impairment.

Psychophysiological DIMS is subdivided into two types. The first, transient and situational, refers to brief periods of disturbed sleep usually associated with specific, emotionally laden events. Factors such as divorce, serious mental illness in a family member, and child-related stress can lead to transient insomnia. According to the ASDC categorization system, the disturbed sleep does not persist more than 3 weeks past the end of the precipitating emotionally laden event.

The second subcategory is called persistent psychophysiological DIMS. Persons with persistent insomnia are described as tense, rigid, obsessive personality types who have multiple somatic complaints (Lacks 1987). Persistent insomnia is often preceded by transient and situational psychophysiological insomnia. It is thought that this disorder is a result of the person's personality type combined with a negative conditioning process that occurs when anxiety about being able to fall asleep produces actual difficulties in falling asleep.

In depressed adolescents, although sleep onset may be affected, sleep maintenance and early morning awakenings are the primary problems. Lacks (1987) reports that the severity of depression and the severity of insomnia often show a strong relationship.

Insomnia in adolescents can also be related to the use of drugs and alcohol either through a direct effect of the drug on sleep or from drug withdrawal.

There are three main categories of treatment for insomnia. The first includes commonsense remedies such as counting sheep or drinking warm milk; the second involves the use of hypnotics or sedating medications, and the third and newest is the treatment of persistent insomnia with behavioral procedures.

The most common category of medications for treating insomnia are the hypnotics. While their use appears to be decreasing, it remains high in certain populations such as older persons in nursing home settings (Lacks 1987). Within this category, benzodiazepines (e.g., alprazolam, diazepam, lorazepam, triazolam) are the most widely used. The reason for the predominant use of the benzodiazepines over other categories such as barbiturates, antidepressants, and tranquilizers lies in the safety of the benzodiazepine group (Dement et al. 1984). While hypnotics, especially the benzodiazepines, can be effective in rapidly treating both sleep onset and sleep regularity problems, there are some reasons to carefully consider their use. First, withdrawal phenomenon can occur with the cessation of benzodiazepine use. This has been related more to the use of the longer-acting as opposed to the shorter-acting substances. Benzodiazepines are generally well tolerated compared with other traditional hypnotics such as barbiturates and chloral hydrate; however, they do have interactive effects with alcohol and other central nervous system depressants. There is evidence to suggest that social judgment and performance skills such as reaction time and alertness can be decreased in persons concurrently taking benzodiazepines, alcohol, or psychoactive medications (Hindmarch and Ott 1984).

Dement and co-workers (1984) suggest that the single most appropriate use of hypnotics is for the treatment of transient insomnia. The hypnotics may be prescribed prophylactically to prevent transient and situational psychophysiological insomnia from developing into persistent psychophysiological insomnia. These authors suggest that hypnotics should not be recommended for long-term use unless thorough evaluation is conducted in a qualified sleep laboratory.

Contraindications for hypnotics include suspicion of sleep apnea or excessive alcohol use, pregnancy especially in the first trimester, or the possibility of night-time arousal requiring the person to perform and think clearly. A clinician should not only consider the effectiveness of the drug in alleviating the sleep onset or sleep irregularity symptoms but also the effect it may have on daytime behaviors and performance. Benzodiazepines have been shown to have a detrimental effect on perceptual motor performance, especially in the elderly (Morgan 1984).

Behavioral treatments for insomnia are based primarily on the supposition that difficulties in initiating sleep or maintaining sleep are because of arousal factors (i.e., somatic, emotional, or cognitive), performance anxiety, or issues of stimulus control. Somatic arousal refers to the possibility that persons with insomnia have increased physiological arousal and muscle tension. This theoretical explanation has resulted in treatments directed at physiological arousal reduction such as progressive relaxation, biofeedback, and hypnosis. Emotional arousal refers to the theory that insomnia is related to a personality style characterized by an anxious, perfectionistic approach. These persons are believed to be introverted and inhibited and engage in much nonproductive worry. Lacks (1987) correctly points out the dilemma of cause and effect when viewing insomnia from the emotional arousal standpoint. Chronic difficulties with sleep may lead to an introverted, mildly depressed state. Somewhat related to the emotional arousal theory is the performance anxiety and low self-efficacy concept. In this theory, persons suffer from anxiety regarding their ability to perform in school, sports, or on the job and generally have a poor self-concept.

The theoretical approaches of stimulus control and cognitive arousal, perhaps the most promising, have led to successful behavioral treatments. Stimulus control refers to the environmental control of behavior. Persons who, for one transitory reason or another, may have had difficulty falling asleep begin to associate the bed, bedroom, and other objects within the sleep environment with the lack of sleep. These objects then begin to signal nonsleep. Cognitive arousal theory suggests that persons with difficulty sleeping do so because they are unable to control their cognitions or thoughts while preparing for sleep. Treatments derived from these behavioral explanations of insomnia include teaching progressive relaxation techniques to control physiological and somatic arousal, stimulus control changes to prevent the sleep environment from acquiring nonsleep signals, paradoxical intention strategies in which a person is instructed to act as if he or she does not intend to go to sleep, and cognitive control strategies such as thought stopping and reframing thoughts.

While the behavioral approaches to the treatment of insomnia are promising, little research has been done with children and adolescents using these techniques. The bulk of the research involves chronic adult insomniacs with sleep latency as the main treatment effectiveness criteria (Lacks 1987).

DISORDERS OF EXCESSIVE SLEEP

Daytime drowsiness or sleepiness can be caused by many factors, including psychiatric disorders of depression and anxiety. The physiological sleep disorders associated with daytime drowsiness are narcolepsy and sleep apnea.

Narcolepsy

Daytime sleepiness per se is not an indication of narcolepsy. Specifically, persons with narcolepsy present with frequent day naps and one or more of the following: cataplexy, sleep paralysis, and hypnagogic hallucinations. This disorder is considered to have a hereditary component (Anders and Weinstein 1972; Karacan and Howell 1988; Parkes 1985). Parkes (1985) reports a prevalence rate of 4 cases per 10,000, with estimates ranging from 2 to 6.7 cases per 10,000. Roth (1980) found 23 cases of narcolepsy onset before age 10 in 360 cases studied; however, age at onset is generally in the adolescent to early adult years (Fig. 21–3).

Definitive diagnosis of narcolepsy is made only through referral to a certified sleep disorders laboratory. Persons who exhibit narcolepsy frequently show a disturbed sleep cycle pattern in which there is an initial prolonged REM period both in the daytime attacks and during regular night-time sleep. This pattern interestingly is more characteristic of newborn sleep (Anders and Weinstein

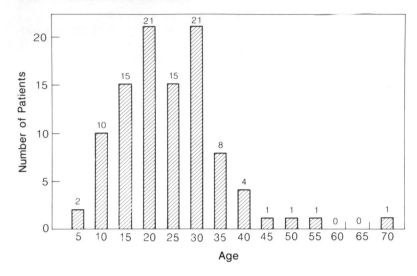

Figure 21–3. Age at onset of narcolepsy as reported in 100 patients. (From Parkes, J. D. 1985. Sleep and Its Disorders. London: W. B. Saunders.)

1972; Karacan and Howell 1988). One of the difficulties in diagnosing narcolepsy in the absence of EEG recordings is the fact that onset of the disorder is usually gradual and may take several years to develop. Even when developed, symptoms can show minor fluctuations and do not always occur in consistent clusters. In addition to the characteristic daytime, rapid-onset sleep periods, there are three additional features referred to as the "narcolepsy tetrad": cataplexy, sleep paralysis, and hypnagogic hallucinations. Cataplexy refers to a sudden loss of muscle tone and can result in the person actually falling to the ground while remaining conscious, triggered almost exclusively by events such as laughter, fright, and surprises (Parkes 1985). Cataplexy is not a form of seizure since the person remains conscious throughout the episode. Sleep paralysis occurs either while a person is falling asleep or during the night. It is characterized by feeling that any type of motor or verbal activity is not possible. Occurring with sleep onset, hypnagogic hallucinations can be both visual or auditory and are usually very vivid. Sleep attacks are most commonly associated with cataplexy and to a lesser degree with hypnagogic hallucinations and sleep paralysis.

Treatment for this disorder is usually confined to measures that minimize the effect of the disorder on the patient's life. Treatment is generally conservative, especially pharmacologic treatments, including the use of stimulants for daytime sleepiness and tricyclic antidepressants for cataplexy episodes. Because it is a life-long disorder, the lowest

effective dose should be used in order to avoid development of tolerance, drug abuse, or side effects. Karacan and Howell (1988) note the need for a close relationship between patient and physician in order to provide accurate information to minimize the resentment, guilt, or family disruptions that can occur because of the symptoms. In addition, behavior modification methods are recommended to assist the patient in developing behavioral habits that can reduce the effect of the disorder on his or her life (Karacan and Howell 1988). Parkes (1985) describes narcoleptics as normally intelligent and generally free of pathologic personality traits. They frequently suffer, however, from a distorted self-image, from social withdrawal, and from the stresses often incurred because of difficulties in maintaining employment. Parkes' review of the literature suggests that there is perhaps a 20% incidence of mild depression and anxiety in narcoleptics, with sexual problems somewhat more common. The sexual or psychotic-like problems in narcoleptics should be carefully evaluated since they may stem from tricyclic antidepressant or amphetamine treatments.

Sleep Apnea

Sleep apnea disorder involves two major symptoms, disturbed night-time sleep and excessive daytime drowsiness. It is often difficult to diagnose in children because the most obvious symptom, daytime sleepiness, results in quiet, even-tempered children who do not present with behavior or emotional problems. Indeed it is more common to receive referrals initiated by persons outside the family, such as teachers (Guilleminault and Dement 1988). An objective definition of sleep apnea relates to the number of 10-second or longer periods during which there is a total or near-total cessation of air exchange at the nose and mouth. Typically, the total number of apneic episodes is divided by total sleep time and multiplied by 60. This yields an index of apnea episodes per hour. Guilleminault and Dement (1978) consider an apnea index of greater than 5 per sleep hour abnormal. Two major types of sleep apnea include obstructive sleep apnea, which is the most common and more prevalent in males, and central sleep apnea. Obstructive sleep apnea syndrome occurs in persons who experience intermittent airway obstruction during sleep, often caused by factors such as obesity, enlarged tonsils, or micrognathia. Central sleep apnea syndrome refers to the condition in which there is no physical obstruction of the airway but rather a central nervous system failure to maintain respiratory movements (Parkes 1985).

Prevalence of sleep apnea in children and adolescents is not known. However, it is known that the syndrome occurs in this population. Obese patients with daytime sleepiness whose parents report restless and noisy sleep should be considered possible candidates for this disorder. Briefly, treatments include medication, mechanically augmented oxygen flow, and in some cases, surgery.

PARASOMNIAS

Parasomnias are disorders of arousal rather than disorders of sleep. These disorders are generally associated with sleep state changes in which the sleep pattern is moving toward arousal. They can be associated with REM sleep or with periods of NREM but lighter sleep. Generally these disorders are more frequent in children and are not signs of serious physiological or psychological pathology per se. Parasomnias are often treated by providing information and support and by preventing the child from harming himself or herself if the problem involves sleep walking or head banging. Parasomnias usually disappear with maturation (Anders and Weinstein 1972; Ware and Orr 1983).

Sleep Terrors (Pavor Nocturnus)

Pavor nocturnus or night terrors are often confused with nightmares. Although these two phenomena differ electrophysiologically and behaviorally, most parents do not differentiate the two. Bixler and colleagues (1976) found that pediatricians and child psychiatrists reported nightmares in 7.8% and 18.3% of their patients, respectively. Night terrors were reported in 2.4% and 5.5%. These data suggest that nearly one fourth of child psychiatry patients report either nightmares or night terrors. Nightmares appear to be especially common in children diagnosed with anxiety and affective disorders (71.4%) (Simonds and Parraga 1984).

Night terrors are particularly frightening to parents since the child characteristically wakes up with a start, stares blankly forward, and exhibits a great deal of emotional behavior, including screaming, crying, and agitated movements. Of particular distress to parents is that the child is generally inconsolable during these episodes and regardless of what the parents do the episode appears to run its course. When the episode ends the child generally falls back asleep and is unable to remember the event if awakened immediately or on awakening in the morning. Physiological changes such as tachycardia and rapid breathing occur during night terrors, and episodes are associated with NREM sleep, generally stages 3 and 4.

Onset of night terrors usually occurs between ages 4 and 12, with a gradual decrease in the number of occurrences. While not common, night terror attacks may occur as frequently as every night. There appears to be a higher incidence of sleep terrors in children with somnambulism than in the general population, and some evidence suggests that conditions that increase stage 3 and 4 sleep (e.g., fatigue, medications) tend to increase night terrors. The incidence of night terrors appears to be slightly higher in males and is estimated at approximately 4% of the population (Karacan 1988).

Nightmares can be differentiated from night terrors electrophysiologically, since they are a REM-related phenomenon, and they can also be differentiated behaviorally. While night terrors occur earlier in the sleep period, nightmares occur more frequently as morning approaches when sleep is less deep and the content of dreams appears to be more vivid. Parents are usually awakened by the child at the end of the nightmare rather than by the onset as is the case with night terrors. Following a nightmare children are more arousable and consolable and can often describe the content of the nightmare. During the nightmare itself, there is little physical movement by the child in contrast to the agitated and emotional behaviors observed during a night terror. The factors that differentiate nightmares from night terrors according to *DSM-III-R* categories of dream anxiety and sleep terror disorders are summarized in Table 21–1.

Unfortunately there has been little research on the treatment of night terrors (Karacan 1988). Benzodiazepines have been used to treat night terrors since they have a suppressive effect on stage 3 and 4 sleep. There has been no correlation found, however, between the degree of stage 3 and 4 sleep suppression and the clinical response (Parkes 1985). Despite this, there are claims that both benzodiazepines and imipramine have been used successfully in the treatment of night terrors (Karacan 1988). Drug treatment is not considered to be a true cure, and it has been suggested that psychotherapy should be considered for children who are experiencing severe anxiety (Kales et al. 1980).

Somnambulism and Somniloquy

Sleepwalking and talking are perhaps two of the most common physiologically based sleep problems in children. The problem is particularly troubling to parents because they fear for the safety of their child during the episode and there is a great deal of folklore as to all sorts of undesirable consequences occurring if a sleepwalking child is awakened. Somnambulism and somniloquy are positively associated with a history of nocturnal enuresis and family history of sleepwalking (Anders and Weinstein 1972; Parkes 1985). While called sleepwalking, the most common manifestation of this phenomenon is for the child to sit up in bed or perhaps sit on the edge of the bed while engaging in repetitive and seemingly purposeless actions. Spontaneous verbalizations, which are often slurred and unintelligible, occasionally occur during the episode. Interestingly, sleepwalkers generally return to their bed if they do leave. Duration of the sleepwalking episode is usually short, ranging from 10 to 15 seconds up to, in rare cases, 30-minute episodes. Sleepwalking generally occurs in the first 1 to 3 hours of sleep and is a stage 3–4 NREM sleep phenomenon (Karacan 1988). Parent's concern over possible harm in awakening the sleepwalker is probably related to the brief period of disorientation and confusion that is seen immediately following awakening. Generally there is amnesia for the event on morning awakening or when awakened during the episode.

Anders and Weinstein (1972) suggest that there is no single constellation of personality disorders associated with childhood somnambulance. There are data, however, to

---

Table 21–1. DIAGNOSTIC CRITERIA FOR DREAM ANXIETY DISORDER AND SLEEP TERROR DISORDER

Dream Anxiety Disorder	Sleep Terror Disorder
A. Repeated awakenings from the major sleep period or maps with detailed recall of extended and usually frightening dreams, usually involving threats to survival, security, or self-esteem. The awakenings generally occur during the second half of the sleep period.	A. A predominant disturbance of recurrent episodes of abrupt awakening (lasting 1–10 minutes) from sleep, usually occurring during the first third of the major period and beginning with a panicky scream.
B. On awakening from the frightening dreams, the person rapidly becomes oriented and alert (in contrast to the confusion and disorientation seen in sleep terror disorder and some forms of epilepsy).	B. Intense anxiety and signs of autonomic arousal during each episode, such as tachycardia, rapid breathing, and sweating, but no detailed dream is recalled.
C. The dream experience or the sleep disturbance resulting from the awakenings causes significant distress.	C. Relative unresponsiveness to efforts of others to comfort the person during the episode and, almost invariably, at least several minutes of confusion, disorientation, and perseverative motor movements (e.g., picking at pillow).
D. It cannot be established that an organic factor initiated and maintained the disturbance (e.g., certain medications).	D. It cannot be established that an organic factor initiated and maintained the disturbance (e.g., brain tumor).

(From American Psychiatric Association. 1987. *Diagnostic and Statistical Manual of Mental Disorders*, 3rd. ed., revised. Washington, D.C.: American Psychiatric Association.)

suggest that it is associated with personality disorders (Association of Sleep Disorders Centers 1979). The diagnostic criteria for sleepwalking disorder as defined by the *DSM-III-R* are presented in Table 21–2. Several factors should be considered in the diagnosis and prognosis of sleep walking disorders (Kales et al. 1980). Later onset is associated with increased probability that the disorder will continue. Psychopathology is associated with sleep walking episodes occurring early in the sleep period, more potentially dangerous activity during the episode, and greater recall. While children typically do not show abnormal daytime behavior, this may not be true for adult sleep walkers. Also, unlike adults, sleep walking episodes in children are generally unrelated to stress.

There seems to be a consensus indicating that sleepwalking in adults is much more indicative of emotional disturbance and psychopathologic states. Children with sleepwalking appear to show a more benign course and can be expected to show a decrease in the number of episodes as they mature. Most children outgrow the condition between the ages of 7 and 14 years. Estimates of the frequency of sleepwalking can run as high as 15% of children between the ages 5 and 12 years (Parkes 1985). The major differential diagnosis in sleepwalking in children is to rule out the possibility of temporal lobe or psychomotor seizures. Once this is done, treatment should be conservative.

While medications and psychotherapy have been shown to be effective for adults, their use in children, especially those who show no other psychological symptoms, is questionable. Unfortunately, often when medication treatments are used for sleepwalking children the purpose is more to placate the parents, who have become extremely anxious over the possibility that the child might be injured or wander off during a sleepwalking episode. Parents should be counseled on how to decrease the likelihood of injury and given reassurance that the behavior will decrease in frequency over time. Parents need to be told that the almost "zombie-like" appearance of sleepwalkers does not reflect a major neurologic or psychological disorder. Sleepwalkers can be protected from injury by securing doors and windows, removing dangerous objects from the environment, and having the child sleep in a bed on the ground floor (Parkes 1985). Although hypnotics are not always successful, small doses of diazepam or other benzodiazepines, through their effect on stage 3–4 sleep, can sometimes assist in preventing sleepwalking episodes. For those patients in whom sleepwalking is associated with psychological problems, antidepressants (e.g., imipramine) may be helpful (Karacan 1988; Parkes 1985).

Table 21–2. DIAGNOSTIC CRITERIA FOR SLEEPWALKING DISORDER

A. Repeated episodes of arising from bed during sleep and walking about, usually occurring during the first third of the major sleep period.
B. While sleepwalking, the person has a blank, staring face, is relatively unresponsive to the efforts of others to influence the sleepwalking or to communicate with him or her, and can be awakened only with great difficulty.
C. On awakening (either from the sleepwalking episode or the next morning), the person has amnesia for the episode.
D. Within several minutes after awakening from the sleepwalking episode, there is no impairment of mental activity or behavior (although there may initially be a short period of confusion or disorientation).
E. It cannot be established that an organic factor initiated and maintained the disturbance (e.g., epilepsy).

(From American Psychiatric Association. 1987. *Diagnostic and Statistical Manual of Mental Disorders*, 3rd ed., revised. Washington, D.C.: American Psychiatric Association.)

Jactatio Capitus Nocturna (Sleep Rocking or Head Banging)

Jactatio capitus nocturna is an interesting and somewhat rare phenomenon that can range from the benign to the very serious. The phenomenon is best described as rhythmic movements of the child's head or body during sleep. It can take the form of the child simply rocking the head back and forth, rocking the entire body in a rhythmic fashion, or actually banging, thumping, or otherwise making rhythmic contact of the head with an object (e.g., headboard, pillow). Onset usually occurs around 6 months of age and may be initiated after sleep has begun or as the child is falling asleep (Ware and Orr, 1983). Many researchers believe that the behavior is self-stimulatory and may serve as a quieting function during sleep onset. It appears that this behavior may be as close as possible to the conceptual idea of a "sleep habit," which likely begins in infancy and the toddler years and may be used as an anxiety-reducing mechanism.

Treatment of the disorder depends on the severity and intensity and the degree to which others in the child's environment are aware of the behavior. In two cases of jactatio capitus nocturna, treated by the senior author, behavioral techniques were successful in rapidly eliminating the behavior (Linscheid et al. 1981). The first case occurred in a 12-year-old boy with a long-standing history of nightly episodes (three to four per night) in which he laid on his stomach and rhythmically banged his head into his pillow. Each episode contained 20 to 30 head hits. His parent and others judged him to be asleep during these episodes since he was difficult to arouse and had no awareness of headbanging on arousal. This child had a history of sleepwalking and sleeptalking, and, by history, the child had exhibited the behavior since infancy. However, he was not referred for treatment until the child's parents were divorced and the family moved into a small apartment that necessitated the boy sleeping in the same room with his father. The father was unable to sleep peacefully through the night since each of these episodes awakened him and thus sought treatment for his son.

In another case, a 6-year-old girl had a long-standing history of rocking her head back and forth from side to side while lying on her back. In her case it was more difficult to ascertain whether the child was asleep, however, the behavior did occur at all stages during the night and it was difficult to arouse her even when the rocking was at its most intense. The behavior was so severe that the back of her head was bald. The girl had a history of emotional neglect early in her life but had been adopted by a warm and supportive family and had been living with them for 2 to 3 years prior to treatment.

Both children were treated successfully using an overcorrection behavioral technique in which they were made to practice alternative and incompatible responses on the occurrence of the behavior. The children were watched throughout the night and as soon as the behavior began were awakened immediately and told to roll into a position in which the behavior never occurred and to hold perfectly still for 15 seconds. This pro-

cedure was repeated 15 to 20 times each time the behavior occurred. In both cases, the behaviors were eliminated after 4 nights of treatment. Other interventions to be considered include further evaluation for psychological or physiological pathology and the institution of measures to protect against injury (Ware and Orr 1983).

Sleep Bruxism

Sleep bruxism or the "gnashing" of teeth occurs in an estimated 15% of children 3 to 17 years of age. The condition appears to be maturational in that it tends to decrease in frequency with the passage of time. While often assumed to be a result of anxiety in the child, there are no proven etiologies for sleep bruxism. Treatment, in severe cases, is usually accomplished with a dental prosthetic device (Ware and Orr 1983).

ASSESSING SLEEP PROBLEMS IN CHILDREN AND ADOLESCENTS

In assessing complaints of sleep disturbance, Coates and Thoresen (1981) suggest a four-part assessment, including medical examination, assessment of drug use, all-night sleep recordings, and behavioral analysis. Medical and psychological examination is necessary to rule out organic or major psychiatric conditions, which may themselves affect sleep, and should include a thorough review of past or present drug use. Family histories of sleep, neurologic, or psychiatric conditions can be very important.

Behavioral analysis refers to measures designed to give an accurate picture of the child or adolescent's sleep environment, sleep times, and sleep habits. This can be important in differentiating sleep problems as either behavioral (based on parental responses or sleep habits) or physiological (consistent with known characteristics such as the inconsolability seen in night terrors). Sleep logs kept by parents and all-night video recordings of sleep behaviors can be used to determine if referral to a sleep laboratory is warranted.

CONCLUSIONS

Sleep disorders or disturbances in children and adolescents can be based in behavioral, emotional, or physiological etiologies. Behavioral etiologies generally have their roots in infancy and toddler years and usually arise as an interaction between parental anxiety, parental lack of knowledge regarding normal sleep patterns, and, in some cases, legitimate medical conditions leading to disruption of the development of normal sleep. Physiological sleep disturbances can take the form of problems attaining and maintaining sleep, excessive daytime sleepiness, and periods of arousal during sleep (parasomnias). Emotional factors such as depression can affect both behaviorally and physiologically based sleep problems. Indeed, throughout the discussion of sleep problems, behavioral, psychotherapeutic, and pharmacologic treatments have all been referred to as necessary or useful in the treatment of the various disorders. Knowledge of the physiological sleep disorders is crucial for initial assessment, as is careful history taking and documentation of the child's current sleep habits, including place, timing, and parental response.

References

American Psychiatric Association. 1980. *Diagnostic and Statistical Manual of Mental Disorders*, 3rd. ed. Washington, D.C.: American Psychiatric Association.

American Psychiatric Association. 1987. *Diagnostic and Statistical Manual of Mental Disorders*, 3rd. ed., revised. Washington, D.C.: American Psychiatric Association.

Anders, T.F., and Weinstein, M.S. 1972. Sleep and its disorders in infants and children: A review. Pediatrics 50:312–323.

Association of Sleep Disorders Centers. 1979. Diagnostic classification of sleep and arousal disorders. *Sleep* 2:1–137.

Bakwin, H., and Bakwin R.M. 1972. *Behavior Disorders of Children*, 4th. ed. Philadelphia: W.B. Saunders.

Bixler, E.O., Kales, J.D., Scharf, M.B., et al. 1976. Incidence of sleep disorders in medical practice: A physician survey. *Sleep Res.* 5:62.

Christophersen, E.R. 1982. Incorporating behavioral pediatrics into primary care. *Pediatr. Clin. North Am.* 29:261–296.

Coates, T.J., and Thoresen, C.E. 1981. Sleep disturbances in children and adolescents. In Mash, E.J., and Terdal, L.G. (eds.): *Behavioral Assessment of Childhood Disorders*. New York: Guilford Press.

Dement, W., Seidel, W., and Carskadon, M. 1984. Issues in the diagnosis and treatment of insomnia. In Hindmarch, I., Ott, H., and Roth, T. (eds.): *Sleep, Benzodiazepines and Performance*. New York: Springer-Verlag.

Ferber, R. 1985. *Solve Your Child's Sleep Problems.* New York: Simon & Schuster.

Guilleminault, C., and Dement, W.C. 1988. Sleep apnea syndromes and related disorders. In Williams, R.L., Karacan, I., and Moore, C.A. (eds.): *Sleep Disorders: Diagnosis and Treatment.* New York: John Wiley & Sons.

Hartmann, E.R. 1980. Sleep Disorders. In Kaplan, H., Freedman, A., and Sadock, B. (eds.): *Comprehensive Textbook of Psychiatry.* Baltimore: Williams & Wilkins.

Hauri, P., and Olmstead, E. 1980. Childhood-onset insomnia. *Sleep* 3:59–66.

Hindmarch, I., and Ott, H. 1984. Sleep, benzodiazepines and performance: Issues and comments. In Hindmarch, I., Ott, H., and Roth, T. (eds.): *Sleep, Benzodiazepines and Performance.* New York: Springer-Verlag.

Kales, J.D., Kales, A., Soldatos, C.R., et al. 1980. Night terrors: Clinical characteristics and personality patterns. *Arch. Gen. Psychiatry* 37:1413–1417.

Karacan, I. 1988. Parasomnias. In Williams, R.L., Karacan, I., and Moore, C.A. (eds.): *Sleep Disorders: Diagnosis and Treatment.* New York: John Wiley & Sons.

Karacan, I., and Howell, J.W. 1988. Narcolepsy. In Williams, R.L., Karacan, I., and Moore, C.A. (eds.): *Sleep Disorders: Diagnosis and Treatment.* New York: John Wiley & Sons.

Keener, M.A., Zeanah, C.H., and Anders, T.F. 1988. Infant temperament, sleep organization, and nighttime parental interventions. *Pediatrics* 81:762–771.

Lacks, P. 1987. *Behavioral Treatment of Persistent Insomnia.* New York: Pergamon Press.

Linscheid, T.R., Copeland, A.P., Jacobstein, D.M., and Smith, J.L. 1981. Overcorrection treatment for nighttime self-injurious behavior in two normal children. *J. Pediatr. Psychol.* 6:29–35.

Loadman, W., Arnold, K., Volmer, R., et al. 1987. Reducing the symptoms of infant colic by introduction of a vibration/sound based intervention. *Pediatr. Res.* 21:182A.

Lozoff, B., Wolf, A.W., and Davis, N.S. 1985. Sleep problems seen in pediatric practice. *Pediatrics* 75:477–483.

Moore, T., and Ucko, L.E. 1957. Night waking in early infancy. *Arch. Dis. Child.* 32:333–342.

Morgan, K. 1984. Effects of two benzodiazepines on the speed and accuracy of perceptual-motor performance in the elderly. In Hindmarch, I., Ott, H., and Roth, T. (eds.): *Sleep, Benzodiazepines and Performance.* New York: Springer-Verlag.

Parkes, J.D. 1985. *Sleep and Its Disorders.* London: W. B. Saunders.

Rickert, V., and Johnson, C. 1988. Reducing nocturnal awakening and crying episodes in infants and young children: A comparison between scheduled awakenings and systematic ignoring. *Pediatrics* 81:203–212.

Roth, B. 1980. *Narcolepsy and Hypersomnia.* Basel: Springer-Verlag.

Scharfman, M.A. 1985. The preschool child. In Simons, R., (ed.): *Understanding Human Behavior in Health and Illness*, 3rd ed. Baltimore: Williams & Wilkins.

Schmidt, B.D. 1981. Infants who do not sleep through the night. *J. Behav. Dev. Pediatr.* 2:20–23.

Schroeder, C.S. 1979. Psychologist in a private pediatric practice. *J. Pediatr. Psychol.* 4:5–18.

Simonds, J., and Parraga, H 1984. Sleep behaviors and disorders in children and adolescents evaluated at psychiatric clinics. *Dev. Behav. Pediatr.* 5:6–10.

Ware, J.C., and Orr, W.C. 1983. Sleep disorders in children. In Walker, C.E., and Roberts, M.C. (eds.): *Handbook of Clinical Child Psychology.* New York: John Wiley & Sons.

Suicide and Suicidal Behavior in Children and Adolescents*

22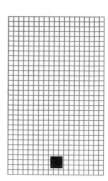

DAVID A. BRENT, M.D.
DAVID J. KOLKO, Ph.D.

Suicide is now the second leading cause of death among adolescents aged 15 to 19 and accounts for 12% of the mortality in the adolescent and young adult age group (Centers for Disease Control 1985). Suicidal behavior has also become increasingly common (Hawton and Goldacre 1982). As many as 4% of high school students have made a suicide attempt within the previous 12 months, and 8% have made a suicide attempt sometime in their lifetime (Smith and Crawford 1986). It is of particular concern that as few as one in eight of suicide attempts ever come to medical attention (Smith and Crawford 1986).

A high proportion of child psychiatric patients have problems related to suicidality (Brent et al. 1986; Carlson and Cantwell 1982; Pfeffer 1986), and a substantial number of adolescents who attempt suicide will seek medical attention within 1 month prior to their attempt (Hawton and Catalan 1987). Therefore, given the major contributions that suicide and suicidal behavior make to morbidity and mortality in this age group, the proper identification, referral, and management of youngsters at risk for suicidality should be a concern of every physician who cares for young patients.

In this chapter, the descriptive epidemiology and risk factors for suicide, suicidal be-

havior, and suicidal ideation are reviewed. On the basis of this review, guidelines for the identification, referral, and management of young patients at risk for suicide and suicidal behavior are provided. Finally, we will discuss the prevention of suicide and areas of current research.

SUICIDE

Descriptive Epidemiology

Not only is suicide the second leading cause of death among adolescent youth, but the rate has tripled in the past 3 decades from 2.7 per 100,000 in 1950 to 8.5 per 100,000 in 1980 for 15- to 19-year olds (Centers for Disease Control 1985; Shaffer and Fisher 1981; Fig. 22–1). The increase appears not to be the result of coroners' increasing willingness to certify an adolescent death as a suicide but due to a real increase in the suicide rate (Brent et al. 1987b). The reasons for this dramatic increase are unclear but may be linked to parallel increases in rates of alcohol abuse and depression in youth born after World War II (Brent et al. 1987b; Klerman et al. 1985), increased availability of firearms (Boyd and Moscicki 1986), an increased divorce rate, an increase in mobility, a decrease in religious affiliation (McAnarney 1979), and an increased number of adolescents relative to the number of adults associated with the

*This work was supported by grants from the William T. Grant Foundation #86-1063-86 and an NIMH Clinical Investigator Award #K08 MH00581.

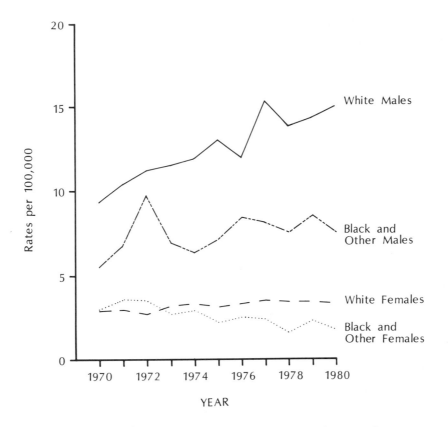

Centers for Disease Control: Youth Suicide in the United States, 1970–1980 Issued November 1986. (Reproduced with permission)

Fig. 22–1. Suicide rates for all persons 15 to 19 years of age by race and sex, United States, 1970–1980. (Centers for Disease Control: Youth Suicide in the United States, 1970–1980, issued November 1986.)

post-war "baby boom" (Holinger and Offer 1982).

Age

Although suicidal impulses are not uncommon in prepubertal children, actual completed suicide is extremely rare (Shaffer and Fisher 1981). Most studies indicate that the increase in the suicide rate has not occurred in the 10- to 14-year age range, but only among 15- to 19-year olds (Brent et al. 1987b; Shaffer and Fisher 1981). Within the child and adolescent age range, the suicide rate increases with increasing age (Shaffer and Fisher 1981). Prepubertal and young adolescent children may be protected against suicide by their cognitive immaturity, which prevents them from actually planning and executing a lethal suicide attempt (Shaffer and Fisher 1981).

Sex

The suicide rate among males is much higher than among females, perhaps due to males' propensity to resort to more violent and irreversible means of suicide (Shaffer and Fisher 1981).

Race

The suicide rate is higher among whites than among blacks, although the suicide rate among young black males has also shown a dramatic increase in recent years (Centers for Disease Control 1985). The black suicide rate is closest to that of whites in the Northeastern and Midwestern United States (Shaffer and Fisher 1981). Young Native American males show a suicide rate even higher than that of whites, but the rate varies greatly by tribe and seems to be most prominent in those tribes that have experienced erosion of traditional cultural values and have high rates of delinquency, alcoholism, and family disorganization (Berlin 1987).

Method

In the United States, firearms are the most common method of suicide for both sexes in adolescents, followed by hanging, jumping, carbon monoxide intoxication, and self-poisoning (Centers for Disease Control 1985; Shaffer and Fisher 1981). The suicide rate by firearms appears to be increasing faster than the suicide rate by other methods (Centers for Disease Control 1985; Boyd 1983; Brent et al. 1987b; Fig. 22–2) and is a particularly common method of suicide when the victim has also been drinking alcohol (Brent et al. 1987b). There is evidence that the suicide rate by firearms is correlated directly with the production, sale, and ownership of guns (Boyd and Moscicki 1986; Kellerman and Reay 1986) and inversely with the restrictions of gun control laws (Lester and Murrell 1982). Moreover, the homes of suicide victims are much more likely to contain firearms than those of psychiatrically hospitalized suicidal adolescents, even after controlling for demographic and diagnostic variables (Brent et al. 1988a). The view that the restriction of the availability of the means for suicide may favorably influence the suicide rate is supported by a decline in suicide by carbon monoxide following detoxication of domestic gas in Great Britain (Kreitman 1976).

Precipitants

Frequent precipitants for suicide among adolescents include disciplinary and legal crises, interpersonal loss, interpersonal conflict, exposure to suicide or suicidal behavior, and an accumulation of life stressors (Brent et al. 1988a; Shaffer 1974; Shafii et al. 1985).

Circumstances of the Suicide

Youthful suicide victims are frequently intoxicated with alcohol at the time of death (Brent et al. 1987b; Friedman 1985). Many adolescent suicide victims show evidence of high intent (i.e., a strong wish to die), as manifested by timing the suicide so as not to be discovered, planning ahead, leaving a note, choosing an irreversible method, and stating intent to die prior to the actual suicide (Brent et al. 1988a; Shaffer 1974). However, high intent notwithstanding, many adolescent suicides are highly impulsive acts (Brent et al. 1988a).

Psychiatric and Social Difficulties

The majority of adolescent suicide victims appear to be suffering from at least one major, debilitating psychiatric disorder (Brent et al. 1988a; Shaffer 1974; Shafii et al. 1985, 1986a). Both affective and antisocial symptomatology appear to play a role in adolescent suicide, often concurrently (Brent et al. 1988a; Shaffer 1974; Shafii et al. 1985, 1986a). Interviews with relatives and friends of the victims indicate that between 63% and 76% of adolescent suicide victims had an affective disorder (Brent et al. 1988a; Shafii et al. 1986a), with over a fifth of the victims in one series showing evidence of bipolar disorder (Brent et al. 1988a). About one third of the victims had difficulties with substance abuse, often in combination with an affective disorder (Brent et al. 1988a; Shafii et al. 1986a). At least half had made suicidal threats or attempted suicide in the past (Brent et al. 1988a; Shafii et al. 1985, 1988). A substantial minority have shown academic and behavioral difficulties at school, antisocial problems in the community, and personality problems of inhibition, perfectionism, and explosiveness (Shaffer 1974; Shafii et al. 1985). Only a minority (30%–45%) of the victims had ever been referred to a mental health professional, and, in one series, only 2 of 27 were in treatment at the time of the suicide (Brent et al. 1988a; Shaffer 1974).

Family History of Psychiatric Disorder

The families of suicide completers appear to have very high rates of psychiatric disorder, particularly unipolar and bipolar affective disorders, antisocial disorders, attempted suicide, and completed suicide (Brent et al. 1988a; Shaffer 1974; Shafii et al. 1985).

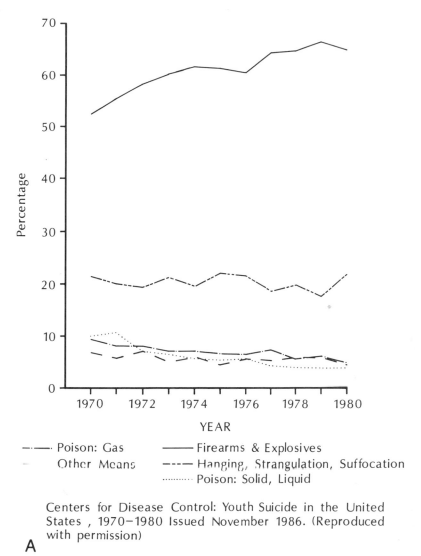

Fig. 22–2. A. *Percent of suicides for males 15 to 19 years of age by method of suicide, United States, 1970–1980.*

Illustration continued on following page

Family Environment

Shaffer (1974) noted a high prevalence of marital breakdown among the parents of young suicide victims. Suicide victims have been noted to experience more parental absence and abuse than controls (Shafii et al. 1985). These associations are probably nonspecifically related to an increased risk for a variety of psychiatric disorders that subsequently predispose to suicide and may also be a consequence of the high rates of psychiatric disorder among the parents of young suicide victims.

Exposure to Suicide

In light of the dramatic and epidemic upswing in the adolescent suicide rate, experts have questioned whether exposure to, and publicity about suicide, in and of itself may predispose to suicide and suicidal behavior (Shaffer and Fisher 1981). In fact, there are reports of outbreaks of suicide and suicidal behavior far in excess of the expected frequency in several communities (i.e., suicide clusters; Robbins and Conroy 1983; Ward and Fox 1977). Adolescent suicide completers are much more likely to have been exposed to a suicide than demographically matched close

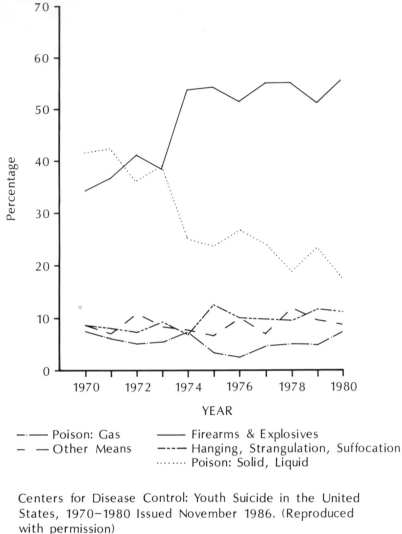

Centers for Disease Control: Youth Suicide in the United States, 1970–1980 Issued November 1986. (Reproduced with permission)

B

Fig. 22–2 Continued B. *Percent of suicides for females 15 to 19 years of age by method of suicide, United States, 1970–1980. (Centers for Disease Control: Youth Suicide in the United States, 1970–1980, issued November 1986.)*

friends, and the rate of suicide among those close friends so exposed is increased over the expected frequency (Shafii et al. 1985, 1986a). Additionally, there is evidence that media publicity about suicide is followed by an increase in the suicide rate, regardless of whether the source of such publicity are newspaper headlines (Phillips 1974), fictional television docu-dramas (Gould and Shaffer 1986), or television news stories (Phillips and Carstensen 1986). The increase in the suicide rate following publicity about suicide is greatest in the adolescent age group, according to one study (Phillips and Carstensen 1986).

Although the issue of vulnerability to exposure has not been systematically researched, those adolescents who become suicidal as part of a suicide cluster do seem to have had serious psychiatric difficulties that antedate the exposure to suicide (Robbins and Conroy 1983; Ward and Fox 1977), so that exposure to suicide may be more of a precipitant than a cause of suicidality per se.

Medical Illness

The only medical illness that has been conclusively linked with suicide and suicidal behavior in the pediatric age group is that of epilepsy (Brent 1986; Matthews and Barabas 1981). The use of phenobarbital as an anticonvulsant, particularly in those epileptic patients with a family history of affective disorder, is associated with depression and suicidal ideation and may contribute to the high risk for suicidal and suicidal behavior among young epileptic patients (Brent et al. 1987a). One study has also indicated that adolescent suicide victims were more likely than controls to have experienced perinatal distress (Salk et al. 1985). As the acquired immunodeficiency syndrome (AIDS) becomes more prevalent among the adolescent population, this disorder may contribute to the suicide rate as it has in adults (Marzuk et al. 1988).

EPIDEMIOLOGY AND RISK FACTORS FOR SUICIDAL BEHAVIOR

Relationship Between Suicide and Suicidal Behavior

Suicide attempters and completers are two distinct, but overlapping populations (Tables 22–1 and 22–2). The two groups are distinct insofar as attempters tend to be female and only a maximum of 10% of youthful attempters go on to complete suicide (Goldacre and Hawton 1985; Otto 1972). However, the two groups overlap insofar as both groups show high rates of psychiatric disturbance, prior suicidal behavior, and family psychopathology and discord, and the risk for suicide is elevated 100- to 1,000-fold in suicide attempters relative to the population (Brent et al. 1988a; Goldacre and Hawton 1985; Otto 1972; Shaffer 1974; Shafii et al. 1985, 1988).

Descriptive Epidemiology

The prevalence of suicidal behavior is very difficult to assess in the United States, due to the lack of registries or centralized regional medical facilities. However, emergency department visits for self-poisoning in Oxford, Great Britain, in 1979 were 131 per 100,000 for 12- to 15-year olds and 343 per 100,000 for 16- to 20-year olds (Hawton and Goldacre 1982). Epidemiologic studies from public schools and medical clinics indicate that suicide attempts may be even more common

Table 22–1. RISK FACTORS FOR SUICIDE

	vs. Controls	vs. Suicidal Patients
Demographic		
Sex	Male	Male
Age	Older	Older
Ethnic group	White	–
	Native American	–
Psychiatric Characteristics		
Any disorder	+	o
Affective disorder	+	o
Affective disorder with co-morbidity	+	+
Bipolar disorder	+	+
Psychosis	+	+
Substance abuse	+	o
Conduct problems	+	?
Personality disorder	+	?
Past suicidal threats or behavior	+	o
Past psychiatric treatment	+	–
High suicidal intent/ lethality	?	+
Family/Environmental Characteristics		
Family history of psychiatric disorder		
Any disorder	+	o
Suicide	+	+
Suicidal behavior	+	o
Affective disorder	+	o
Other environmental characteristics		
Parental absence	+	o
Parental abuse	+	?
Numerous life stressors	+	?
Availability of firearms	?	+
Exposure to suicide	+	o
Medical Characteristics		
Epilepsy	+	?
Perinatal stress	+	?

Key:
+ = risk factor more common in completed suicide
– = risk factor less common in completed suicide
o = no association
? = association not yet investigated

than this, with the 12-month and lifetime prevalence of such behavior being 4% and 8%, respectively (Robins, in press; Smith and Crawford 1986). A very significant issue for all physicians who care for at-risk youth is the rarity with which such behavior comes to medical attention (12% according to Smith and Crawford, 1986). Based on emergency department records, the rate of suicide attempts has increased markedly, particularly in the adolescent age group (Hawton and Goldacre 1982).

Sex

The reported ratio of female-to-male attempters ranges from 3:1 to 9:1 (Garfinkel et al. 1982; Hawton and Catalan 1987). The reason for the female preponderance is unknown but may relate to females' preference for less lethal methods of suicidal behavior, their greater willingness compared with males to engage in covert help-seeking behavior, and the higher rate of affective disorder noted among postpubertal females (Shaffer and Fisher 1981).

Age

Suicidal behavior can be observed in children as young as preschool age, although in these cases it almost invariably is associated with physical abuse (81% in one series, Rosenthal et al. 1986). Suicidal thoughts are common in psychiatrically referred patients of school age, although actual suicidal behavior is rare until adolescence (Brent 1987; Garfinkel et al. 1982; Hawton and Catalan 1987).

Race and Socioeconomic Status

Few epidemiologic studies have surveyed young populations with large minority populations. In emergency department–based studies, which may draw from poorer areas, there is evidence that economic distress distinguishes the families of young suicide attempters from those of medical controls (Garfinkel et al. 1982).

Precipitants

The precipitants for suicidal behavior among children and adolescents are similar to those for adolescent suicide. Frequently, interpersonal conflict, either with a parent or romantic attachment, are prominent; and other significant contributors include interpersonal loss, physical and sexual abuse, and family discord (Brent et al. 1988a; Cohen-Sandler et al. 1982a; Hawton and Catalan 1987).

Motivation and Intent

About two thirds of adolescent suicide attempters engage in suicidal behavior for reasons other than a desire to die (Hawton and Catalan 1987). Most suicide attempts by adolescents are impulsive and result in little threat to life (Brent et al. 1988a; Hawton and Catalan 1987). Often the motivation is a desire to influence others, to gain attention, to communicate love or anger, or simply to escape a noxious situation. If one can achieve an understanding of the motivation of the adolescent attempter and help the patient to influence others, gain attention, or communicate feelings in a more appropriate manner, then the adolescent may not need to resort to suicidal behavior when under stress in the future.

Method

By far, the most common method of suicide attempt in adolescents is that of intentional overdose (Brent 1987; Garfinkel et al. 1982). Wrist-cutting is the second most common method in most North American series (Brent 1987; Brent et al. 1988a; Garfinkel et al. 1982). There is some evidence that those suicide attempters who resemble completers in lethality (e.g., with a high degree of planning, use of a lethal method such as hanging) also resemble completers in psychiatric diagnoses and family history and are, in fact, more likely to eventually complete suicide (Brent 1987; Garfinkel et al. 1982; Otto 1972). However, the converse is not invariably true—given children and adolescents' modest knowledge about the lethality of most suicidal methods, a patient may make a psychologically serious attempt of high intent that results in little danger to the patient's life (Beck et al. 1975; Carlson et al. 1982).

Psychiatric Disorder and Psychological Traits

There is convergent evidence from studies of child and adolescent suicide attempters sampled from inpatient units, psychiatric clinics, medical clinics, and public schools that depressive symptomatology, substance abuse, and conduct disorder are most closely related to suicidal behavior (Brent et al. 1986, 1988a; Brent 1987; Garfinkel et al. 1982; Pfeffer 1986; Robbins and Alessi 1985; Robins in press; Smith and Crawford 1986).

Table 22–2. RISK FACTORS FOR SUICIDAL BEHAVIOR

	vs. Controls	vs. Nonsuicidal Psychiatric Patients	Repeated Attempts	High Intent/ High Lethality
Demographic				
Sex	Female	Female	o	Male
Age	Older	Older	?	Older
Socioeconomic status	Lower	?	?	?
Psychiatric Characteristics				
Any disorder	+	o	o	o
Chronic, severe disorder	+	+	+	+
Affective disorder	+	+	o	+
Substance abuse	+	+	o	+
Conduct disorder	+	+	o	o
Psychosis	?	?	?	?
Personality disorder	+	+	+	?
Past suicidal threats or behavior	+	+	+	?
Past psychiatric treatment	+	?	–	?
Psychological Characteristics				
Hostility	+	+	+	?
Hopelessness	+	+	+	+
Poor social skills	+	+	+	?
Poor school performance	+	?	+	–
Impulsivity	+	+	+	?
Cognitive distortion/poor coping strategies	+	+	?	?
Family/Environmental				
Family history of psychiatric disorder				
Any psychiatric disorder	+	o	?	o
Suicide/suicidal behavior	+	+	?	+
Affective disorder	+	+	?	?
Alcohol/drug abuse	+	o	?	o
Other Environmental Characteristics				
Physical/sexual abuse	+	+	+	?
Discord	+	+	?	?
Parental absence/loss	I	o	+	?
Exposure to suicide behavior	+	?	?	?
Total life stressors	+	+	?	?
Medical Characteristics				
Epilepsy (with use of phenobarbital)	+	?	+	+

Key:
+ = risk factor associated with category
– = risk factor less common in completed suicide
o = no association
? = association not yet investigated

Psychological Traits

In addition, or perhaps as a correlate of frank psychiatric disorder, adolescent suicide attempters show a number of dysfunctional psychosocial characteristics, including hopelessness, impulsivity, external locus of control, poor affective modulation, and poor interpersonal problem-solving and social skills (Asarnow et al. 1987; Brent et al. 1986; Kazdin et al. 1983; Smith and Crawford 1986; Topol and Reznikoff 1982). Specifically, hopelessness has correlated with the severity of the suicidality and is predictive of future attempts (Brent et al. 1986; Hawton and Catalan 1987; Pfeffer 1986; Smith and Crawford 1986). Psychosocial interventions that specifically target these deficits are believed to be likely to decrease the risk for further suicidal behavior, although this has yet to be empirically demonstrated in children and adolescents (Hawton and Catalan 1987).

Family History of Psychiatric Disorder

There is evidence that the relatives of adolescent suicide attempters, like those of completers, have high prevalences of affective disorder, alcohol and drug abuse, suicide, and suicidal behavior (Brent et al. 1988a; Garfinkel et al. 1982; Pfeffer 1986). Moreover, such family members are likely to be depressed and suicidal at the time of the child's presentation (Pfeffer 1986; Tischler et al. 1981; Tischler and McKenry 1982).

Family Environment

In addition to familial psychopathology, there is substantial evidence that family discord and disruption serve both as correlates and key antecedents to suicidal behavior (Brent et al. 1988a; Cohen-Sandler et al. 1982a; Garfinkel et al. 1982; Hawton and Catalan 1987; Robins, in press; Smith and Crawford 1986). Suicide attempters have been noted to have experienced the loss of a parent due to divorce or death more frequently than medical (Garfinkel et al. 1982) or psychiatric controls (Kosky 1983), particularly if the loss occurred prior to age 12 (Stanley and Barter 1970). The family environments of suicidal children and adolescents, when compared with psychiatric controls, have been reported to be less supportive and more conflicted (Asarnow et al. 1987; Topol and Reznikoff 1982) and are often characterized by hostility and enmity (Kosky 1983; Smith and Crawford 1986). In fact, suicide attempters have been exposed to family violence and have been the victims of physical or sexual abuse more often than psychiatric or community controls (Cohen-Sandler et al. 1982a; Hibbard et al. 1988; Kosky 1983; Smith and Crawford 1986), and the severity and recency of the abuse is correlated with the severity of suicidality (Hibbard et al. 1988). The relationship between abuse and suicidal behavior appears to be strongest among very young children (Rosenthal et al. 1986). Adolescents who have run away from home, a group quite likely to have experienced abuse (Hibbard et al. 1988), have also been noted to be at high risk for suicidal behavior (Hibbard et al. 1988; Robins, in press).

Other Environmental Influences

Exposure to suicide and suicidal behavior may increase the risk for suicidal behavior.

The airing of television docu-dramas about suicide was followed by an increase not only of suicide but also of suicide attempts in the New York area (Gould and Shaffer 1986). High school students who themselves are suicide attempters are more likely than non-attempters to have known someone who has completed or attempted suicide, both within and outside their family (Harkavy-Friedman et al. 1987; Smith and Crawford 1986).

Medical Illness

Children with epilepsy appear to have an increased risk for suicidal behavior (Brent 1986), and this risk may be heightened and may be even in part attributable to the use of phenobarbital as an anticonvulsant (Brent et al. 1987a).

Although no other medical condition has been specifically associated with suicidal behavior, it should be of interest to pediatric and family practitioners that about half of the adolescents visit a physician within the month prior to their suicide attempt (Hawton and Catalan 1987).

Risk of Repetition of Suicidal Behavior

There is substantial risk among adolescent suicide attempters for reattempts (see Table 22–2). In follow-up studies ranging from 1 to almost 3 years in length, the reattempt rate was between 6% and 15% per year (Cohen-Sandler et al. 1982b; Goldacre and Hawton 1985; Hawton and Catalan 1987; McIntire et al. 1977; Stanley and Barter 1970). The risk for repetition seems greatest within 3 months of the initial attempt (Hawton and Goldacre 1985). Some of the risk factors that have been found to predict reattempts are previous suicidal behavior, high suicidal intent, serious psychopathology (either depression or substance abuse), hostility and aggression, hopelessness, noncompliance with treatment, social isolation and poor school performance, family discord, abuse and neglect, and parental psychiatric illness (Cohen-Sandler et al. 1982b; Hawton and Catalan 1987; McIntire et al. 1977; Pfeffer 1986; Stanley and Barter 1970).

Risk Factors for Completed Suicide Among Suicide Attempters

Our knowledge about risk factors for completed suicide among attempters is derived from both case-control and prospective studies (see Table 22–1). One comparison of completers with psychiatrically hospitalized suicidal adolescent inpatients indicates that the following are more common among the completers: high suicidal intent, lack of prior psychiatric treatment, affective disorder with co-morbidity, bipolar disorder, and availability of firearms in the homes of the victims (Brent et al. 1988a).

Prospective studies of adolescent psychiatric inpatients and suicide attempters validate the above-noted findings. Welner and co-workers (1979) noted that 7.7% of 77 adolescent psychiatric inpatients (some of whom were initially suicidal) died of suicide on an 8- to 10-year follow-up and that the risk was most marked among bipolar and schizophrenic patients. Otto (1972), in a 10- to 15-year follow-up of adolescent and young adult suicide attempters found that 2.9% of female and 10% of male attempters had died by suicide. The period of greatest risk for suicide during the follow-up was the first 2 years after the initial attempt. The characteristics of those most likely to have completed suicide were as follows: male sex, no apparent precipitant, high suicidal intent, "active" method (e.g., jumping, hanging, as compared with overdose), and "manic-depressive" or "psychotic" disorders.

SUICIDAL IDEATION

Suicidal ideation, or thoughts about suicide, are even more common than suicidal behavior. Suicidal ideation is a spectrum from nonspecific (e.g., "Life is not worth living", "I wish I was dead"), specific (ideation with intent, ideation with a plan), and, finally, actual suicidal behavior (Brent et al. 1986; Pfeffer 1986; Table 22–3). Any child who is suspected of being "at risk" should be questioned as to suicidal ideation moving from nonspecific questions to more specific ones, if the answers to the nonspecific ones are positive.

Community-based surveys indicate that between 12% and 25% of primary and high school children have some form of suicidal

Table 22–3. INTERVIEWING FOR SUICIDAL IDEATION
1. Have you ever thought that life was not worth living?
2. Have you ever wished you were dead?
3. Have you ever thought about trying to hurt yourself?
4. Do you intend to hurt yourself?
5. Do you have a plan to hurt yourself?
6. Have you ever attempted suicide?

ideation (Hibbard et al. 1988; Pfeffer 1986). Suicidal ideation and behavior are about four times more common among psychiatrically referred patients than in the population at large (Brent et al. 1986; Pfeffer 1986). The correlates of suicidal ideation are quite similar to those for more serious forms of suicidality; suicidal ideation is associated most closely with depression but is related to substance abuse and conduct disorder as well (Pfeffer 1986; Smith and Crawford 1986). The severity of suicidality has been correlated with the severity of depressive symptoms, hopelessness, and severity and recency of physical abuse (Brent et al. 1986; Hibbard et al. 1988; Pfeffer 1986; Smith and Crawford 1986). Given the clinical overlap between those with specific suicidal ideation (i.e., with intent to attempt suicide and/or with an actual plan) and those who actually attempt suicide (Brent et al 1986), it follows that those patients with specific suicidal ideation should be considered to be at high risk to act on their suicidal thoughts.

GUIDELINES FOR THE NONPSYCHIATRIC PHYSICIAN

Screening for At-risk Youth

Given the prevalence of suicidal behavior among the young, as well as the associated morbidity and mortality, all physicians who see adolescent patients should be able to competently detect and appropriately triage suicidal youth. Table 22–4 includes the four broad categories of inquiry: (1) psychiatric (serious handicapping conditions, including depression and hopelessness, substance abuse, conduct problems, psychosis, past suicidal threats or attempts); (2) social adjustment (legal problems, school dropout or failure, social isolation and/or interpersonal conflict, living away from parents [especially

Table 22–4. SCREENING FOR YOUTH AT RISK FOR SUICIDALITY

Psychiatric Difficulties
Depression
Substance abuse
Conduct problems
Psychosis
Past suicidal threats/attempts

Poor Social Adjustment
School failure/dropout
Legal problems
Social isolation
Interpersonal conflict

Family/environment
Interpersonal loss
Family problems
  Abuse/neglect
  Family history, psychiatric disorder or suicide
Exposure to suicide (in those already psychiatrically
  vulnerable)

runaways]); (3) life stressors (close friend or relative of a suicide victim, victim of physical or sexual assault, interpersonal loss); and (4) family problems (family violence, particularly physical or sexual abuse, family history of psychiatric disorder).

After Identification of Suicidality

It is important to listen to the patient in a nonjudgmental way. The physician should avoid becoming entrapped in promises of confidentiality that may have to be broken to protect and treat the child. The child's parents should always be given some feedback about the assessment, because the parents are going to have a great deal to say about the child's compliance with any subsequent recommendations for evaluation and treatment. When the physician discovers that a patient is suicidal, it is important to obtain a no-suicide contract, in which the patient promises not to hurt himself or herself, and, if suicidal impulses recur, to notify the physician or a caretaking adult. Firearms should be removed from the homes of all at-risk youngsters.

Once a patient has been identified as potentially suicidal, the physician should obtain a psychiatric consultation and then the physician, psychiatrist, and family can conjointly make a decision about the next appropriate step. If psychiatric treatment is recommended, the physician can play a critical role in monitoring compliance and satisfaction

with treatment, since 50% of suicide attempters fail to attend the first outpatient appointment (Hawton and Catalan 1987). Referrals to a therapist are much more likely to go smoothly if the following conditions are met: (1) the patient and family are given a definite appointment; (2) the therapist meets the family and, preferably, is introduced to the family by the referring professional; and (3) the patient and family are seen within 48 hours (and sooner if clinically indicated) of the initial assessment and triage. Physicians who treat young patients should be familiar with the referral resources in the area of practice, in order to be able to refer the patient in the midst of a potential crisis. Referral to a psychiatrist, as compared with referral to other mental health professionals, is specifically indicated if the patient is psychotic, has a serious affective disorder, requires detoxification, has a complicating medical condition that may contribute to the psychiatric presentation, or may require psychopharmacologic intervention.

Management of Suicide Attempters

Regardless of medical condition, no suicide attempter should ever be discharged directly from an emergency department. While a small number of highly suicidal and psychiatrically disturbed patients should be admitted directly to a psychiatric inpatient unit, most attempters will not require such intensive or restrictive treatment. For this less disturbed remainder, a 48-hour admission to an adolescent or general medical ward is indicated to evaluate the patient and family. Even though the medical lethality alone might not warrant admission, the decision to admit to the hospital communicates to the family that the suicide attempt has been noticed and taken seriously. Many of the families of these attempters are chaotic, and a substantial minority are abusive or neglectful. It is both critical and almost impossible, in the emergency department setting, to make an accurate determination of the precipitants, motivation, mental status, and family environment of the attempter, hence the recommendation to admit.

Referral for Inpatient Psychiatric Treatment

Suicidal children and adolescents who are judged to be at serious risk for committing or attempting suicide are most appropriate for inpatient hospitalization. The indications for psychiatric hospitalization are listed in Table 22–5 and include inability to commit to a no-suicide contract, active suicide ideation and/or lethal or high-intent suicide attempt, serious psychopathology (e.g., psychosis, serious depression, bipolar disorder in mixed state, substance abuse, serious aggressive conduct disorder), previous noncompliance or failure of outpatient treatment, unsupportive, abusive, and/or chaotic family. However, it is important to remember that hospitalization is but a temporary respite from the risk for suicidality and, in fact, the risk for patients recently discharged from psychiatric hospitals is especially high (Pokorny 1960; Roy 1982). Therefore, it is critical to have the outpatient and inpatient teams work closely together so that continuity of treatment can be presented during the transition from inpatient to outpatient care.

General Psychiatric Treatment Strategies

Certain broad treatment strategies should be followed in the treatment of suicidal patients, regardless of the specific types of interventions recommended. These strategies include (1) maintenance of a no-suicide contract; (2) availability of 24-hour clinical back-up; (3) steps to maintain compliance; and (4) removal of firearms from the home of the at-risk patient.

Table 22–5. INDICATIONS FOR PSYCHIATRIC INPATIENT HOSPITALIZATION

Characteristics of Suicidality
Inability to maintain a no-suicide contract
Active suicidal ideation (with plan and intent)
High intent or lethality suicide attempt

Psychiatric Disorder
Psychosis
Severe depression
Substance abuse
Bipolar illness
Serious aggression
Previous attempts
Previous noncompliance or failure with outpatient
   treatment

Family Problems
Abuse
Severe parental psychiatric illness
Family unable to monitor or protect patient or
   unwilling

NO-SUICIDE CONTRACT

The forging and maintenance of a no-suicide contract is a key component of outpatient treatment of suicidal patients (Rotheram 1987). In fact, the inability to agree to a no-suicide contract, in conjunction with other risk factors, is often the reason for inpatient referral. The no-suicide contract is an agreement between patient and therapist that the patient will not hurt himself or herself, and if the patient does experience suicidal urges that he or she will notify the therapist, a parent, or another responsible adult (Drye et al. 1984). At the outset of treatment, it is helpful to review with the patient the precipitants for the initial suicidality and rehearse alternate ways of coping with these stressors (Rotheram 1987). The extent of the patient's suicidality should be assessed in every subsequent clinical session as part of an overall mental status. This can be accomplished without calling undue attention to suicidality, particularly if a cognitive mode of treatment is used, since an exploration of dysfunctional cognitions and the manner in which the patient copes with stressful situations is central to this mode of treatment (Bedrosian and Epstein 1984).

AVAILABILITY OF 24-HOUR CLINICAL BACK-UP

The clinician also has responsibilities as a result of the no-suicide contract. Paramount among these is that if the patient is told to contact the therapist or someone covering for the therapist, there should be a trained clinician available to respond to the patient day or night. It is a rare psychiatrist who is truly available 24 hours a day, so that the patient should be given the number of a hospital with 24-hour emergency psychiatric coverage in addition to that of the treating professional.

STEPS TO INCREASE COMPLIANCE WITH TREATMENT

Suicidal patients are particularly noncompliant with treatment recommendations, with only about half of adolescent and young adults keeping the first outpatient appointment, and only 32% completing as many as three outpatient sessions (Hawton and Catalan 1987; Taylor and Stansfeld 1984b; Trautman et al. 1984). This noncompliance is of particular concern given evidence that noncompliant suicidal patients are more likely to have more severe psychopathology, higher suicidal intent, and more disturbed parents (Taylor and Stansfeld 1984b; Trautman et al. 1987) and, in follow-up studies of adolescent and young adult suicide attempters, more likely to reattempt and to commit suicide as well (Greer and Bagley 1971; Kennedy 1972; Motto 1976; Welu 1977).

Therefore, certain steps should be taken that are known to increase compliance in a variety of outpatient psychiatric settings (Baekeland and Lundwall 1975; Table 22–6). These steps include (1) having the patient seen for treatment by the same person who does the initial evaluation, or at least having the patient meet the person who will provide treatment at the time of the initial assessment; (2) giving the patient a definite appointment at the time of intake; (3) calling the patient to remind him or her of the appointment the day before; (4) scheduling the patient in a timely fashion (i.e., within a week of intake); (5) aggressively pursuing no-shows by phone calls and letters; (6) eliciting from the patient and family what type of treatment is desired, and contracting with them what will be provided; and (7) involving significant others such as family, professionals, and friends as necessary in the treatment.

RESTRICTION OF THE AVAILABILITY OF LETHAL AGENTS

There is considerable evidence to suggest that the availability of firearms in the home increases the risk for suicide for the occupants (Brent et al. 1988a; Kellerman and Reay 1986; Markush and Bartolucci 1984). Therefore, parents of potentially suicidal adolescents should be instructed to remove all fire-

---

Table 22–6. STEPS TO MAINTAIN COMPLIANCE WITH OUTPATIENT TREATMENT

1. Continuity between evaluation and treatment
2. Patient given a definite appointment for follow-up at the time of intake
3. Patient called to remind them of the appointment
4. Patient scheduled in a timely fashion
5. No-shows pursued by phone calls and letters
6. Explicit contracting between patient, family, and therapist about the type of treatment that is desired and what can be provided
7. Involvement of family members and other significant adults (e.g., teachers, physicians)

---

arms from the home. The availability of firearms appears to be a more significant risk factor than the accessibility, so that storage of the gun in a more "secure" fashion is probably not as protective as simply removing the gun from the home environment of the suicidal or at-risk adolescent (Brent et al. 1988a).

Since the lethality of impulsive suicide attempts in adolescents appears to be related to the availability of potentially lethal, prescribed agents, such as tricyclic antidepressants (Brent 1987), clinicians who prescribe such agents for children and adolescents should do so only for a clear indication of an affective disorder and should limit the quantity that is prescribed at any one time. If other household members have such agents prescribed, then these medications should be securely stored.

Psychiatric interventions

Treatment of suicidal youngsters should proceed on three levels: (1) treatment of the underlying psychiatric illness; (2) remediation of social and problem-solving deficits; and (3) family psychoeducation and conflict resolution.

TREATMENT OF THE UNDERLYING PSYCHIATRIC ILLNESS

As noted previously, the majority of seriously suicidal youth have difficulties with affective disorders and/or substance abuse. The treatment of these disorders is detailed elsewhere in this textbook and includes psychopharmacology (antidepressants, lithium) and detoxification, respectively. One disorder that may be particularly lethal in adolescence is bipolar affective illness (Brent et al. 1988a). This disorder may go undiagnosed because of co-morbid conditions of conduct disorder and substance abuse and because of a tendency for many of the patients to present in a mixed state. Such patients may be resistant to lithium therapy and require detoxification from substance abuse and augmentation of lithium treatment with carbamazepine (Himmelhoch and Garfinkel 1986). A more detailed discussion of the management of bipolar and unipolar affective disorder is available elsewhere in this text (see Chapters 1 and 2).

Case 1. Robbie, a 16-year-old male, presented with irritability, dysphoria, hopelessness, insomnia, distractibility, loss of appetite, racing thoughts, grandiosity, and paranoid ideation. In addition, he had a long history of conduct problems, school expulsion, and legal problems. He had made a serious suicide attempt and was admitted to a psychiatric inpatient unit. At first, he was diagnosed as having a major depressive disorder because of his predominantly dysphoric and irritable affect, but treatment with a tricyclic antidepressant seemed to exacerbate his explosiveness and led to increased insomnia, grandiosity, paranoia, and racing thoughts. Therefore, his diagnosis was changed to bipolar disorder and mixed state. Lithium was added to his treatment regimen, and the tricyclic antidepressant was withdrawn. This resulted in some clinical improvement, but a significant residue of dysphoria, lability, and irritability remained. Addition of carbamazepine resulted in remission of his symptoms and caused his mother to remark, "this is the best I've seen him in 9 years."

REMEDIATION OF SOCIAL AND PROBLEM-SOLVING DEFICITS

Figure 22–3 illustrates a common constellation of deficits that may lead to suicidal behavior under stress. Each deficit, if remediated, may protect the attempter against future suicidality when under stress.

Case 2. Judy is a 14½-year-old female who made an impulsive overdose after a fight with her best friend. She felt that she was unable to tell her friend how she really felt (inability to influence others, lack of assertiveness) and that if she and her friend did not get along, then she might as well be dead (cognitive distortion). As a result, she became so upset that she was unable to think clearly (poor affect regulation), and before she knew what she was doing she had taken an overdose (impulsive problem solving). She took her mother's tranquilizers in hopes that her friend would feel guilty and apologize (inability to influence others). She ended up in intensive care, a possibility she did not consider before taking the overdose (impulsive problem solving).

Judy's treatment targeted these deficits. She was taught how to regulate her affect through positive self-statements and relaxation techniques. She learned how to assert herself with her friend and express her own needs and concerns more directly. Judy also explored with her therapist her view that "without my friend, I'm nothing" and came to the conclusion that this was incorrect. She practiced responses to similar stresses and learned to generate alternative solutions to social problems and assess their potential consequences *before* enacting them. A 6-month follow-up disclosed that Judy had, in fact, weathered subsequent, qualitatively similar stresses without resorting to suicidal behavior.

FAMILY INVOLVEMENT

Familial involvement in the treatment of suicidal children and adolescents is key to the success of the treatment of such patients. Family conflict is one of the most frequent precipitants for suicide and suicidal behavior (Brent et al. 1988a; Cohen-Sandler et al. 1982a, 1982b; Hawton and Catalan 1987; Kosky 1983; Kosky et al. 1986; Pfeffer 1986; Taylor and Stansfeld 1984a). Therefore, the source of this conflict must be addressed to prevent recidivism of the suicidal behaviors. If the conflict is extensive, as in the case of physical or sexual abuse, then the child may need to be removed from the home.

Sometimes a major contributor to the conflict is the irritability associated with affective illness in the parent (Weissman et al. 1973), child (Ryan et al. 1987), or both. In this case, psychoeducation about the effects of living with an affectively ill family member may buy time while the parent and/or child is treated with antidepressants.

Not only do suicidal children frequently have parents with active affective illness (Pfeffer 1986; Tischler et al. 1981; Tischler and McKenry 1982), but the children of psychiatrically ill parents are more likely to drop out of treatment (Taylor and Stansfeld 1984b; Trautman et al. 1987). Therefore, the diagnosis and treatment of psychiatric illness in the parents of suicidal children is critical not only for the reduction of tension in the home but also for the maintenance of compliance with treatment recommendations.

Family psychoeducational approaches that educate family members about the nature and course of the psychiatric illness that affects a given family member have been shown to increase compliance with medica-

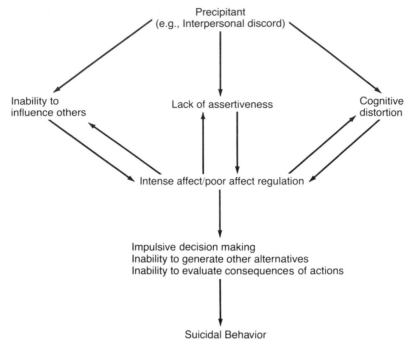

Fig. 22–3. *Pathways to suicidal behavior: prescriptions for psychosocial interventions.*

tion and clinic attention and symptomatic recovery in affectively disordered adults (Frank and Kupfer 1986; Haas et al. 1986; Miklowitz et al. 1986) and are likely to be equally effective for psychiatrically ill adolescents as well. Compliance is also likely to be maintained if the family, clinician, and patient are all in agreement about the treatment to be prescribed.

Therefore, it is vital to give the parents specific feedback about the patient during the assessment and throughout the treatment process. Additionally, psychoeducation of the family about the psychiatric illness of the child can enable the family to detect early signs of recurrences of psychiatric illness (e.g. affective disorder, substance abuse) and enable referral for treatment before the situation has become emergent.

Case 3. Felicia is a 17-year-old female who made a suicide attempt after a fight with her father, who was often openly critical of Felicia's withdrawal and social ineptness. After assessment, it became apparent that Felicia's withdrawal was part of a chronic dysthymic disorder and attendant social skill deficits and that her father's criticism was in part a response to this and partly due to irritability secondary to an undiagnosed and untreated major depression. As her father became

aware of the source of Felicia's difficulties and received pharmacotherapy for his own depression, the conflict was much diminished. Felicia received social skills training and cognitive-behavior treatment and was discharged from treatment much improved. Four months later, we received a call from Felicia's father that he thought Felicia was becoming depressed—not sleeping, not eating, looking sad all the time—and he wanted her to get help before the situation deteriorated. On evaluation, Felicia was at the beginning of a full-blown major depressive episode, which responded to antidepressant medication. Felicia's father had become an important ally in Felicia's recovery.

It can be seen that attendance to the familial component of treatment in this and many other cases is critical and that failure to do so might result in the patient and family dropping out of treatment and not returning at a critical point in the recurrence of the disorder.

Efficacy of Treatment for Suicidal Behavior

There have been no published studies on the treatment of children and adolescents who have attempted suicide. The results of studies of adult suicide attempters are mixed (reviewed in Brent et al. 1988b) but suggest that aggressive outreach (Welu 1977) and a cognitive-behavior orientation (Liberman and Eckman 1981) may reduce the risk of subsequent suicidal behavior and/or suicidal thoughts. One study of adult, personality-disordered, recurrent suicide attempters indicates that depot-injected neuroleptic medication was effective in reducing recidivism. The cognitive-behavioral approach shows promise in the treatment of children and adolescents (Trautman and Shaffer 1984). While no published accounts document the efficacy of this approach in adolescent attempters, cognitive-behavioral treatment has been shown to be effective in children and adolescents with related conditions, such as depression (Reynolds and Coates 1986) and conduct disorder (Kazdin et al. 1987a, 1987b).

PREVENTION OF SUICIDE

By Nonpsychiatric Physicians

Physicians have an important role to play in the identification and screening of youth at risk for suicide. Robins (in press) showed that in medical clinics one could identify with four questions asked of 66% of all patients who had made previous suicide attempts: (1) chief complaint includes psychological concerns; (2) patient does not live with a relative or spouse; (3) patient has been drunk three or more times in the past year; and (4) patient has had a history of running away from home.

It is essential that those physicians who work with adults consider that the risk for suicide and suicidal behavior is quite high if their adult patients show signs of an affective disorder and the offspring of all such patients should be evaluated. Prescription of large amounts of potentially lethal medication, particularly psychotropic medication, should be avoided.

In Schools: Primary Prevention

Teachers are in an excellent position to identify students at risk for suicidal behavior with the proper training (Kerr et al. 1987). Therefore, inservice education should be pro-

vided for teachers on the identification and referral of students who show behavior problems, preoccupation with death, or frank suicidal thoughts and behavior. Moreover, close links between schools and mental health treatment centers are important in order to facilitate referrals and consultation.

After a Suicide has Occurred

Little is known about the effects of a suicide on other students, but with the report of a number of suicide clusters within schools and communities it behooves schools to develop a postvention policy. It is recommended that schools avoid sensationalizing or memorializing the student through memorial services, flying the flag at half-mast, or large group assemblies. The evidence at hand appears to indicate that those students most vulnerable to the influence of another pupil's suicide are those with psychiatric vulnerability (e.g., conduct disorder, substance abuse, depression) that antedated the exposure regardless of the closeness of the relationship to the victim (Brent et al. in press). Therefore, it is best after a student suicide to offer small group therapy to those who are upset and to use these groups to screen those students who would benefit from further evaluation. In addition, those close friends and other students known to have prior psychiatric difficulties should be screened by a skilled counselor to determine if they might benefit from further evaluation and treatment.

Hotlines

One difficulty in evaluating the efficacy of suicide prevention services is that they are not used by the group at highest risk for suicide—older, white males. Another problem is that the outcome of interest is a very rare event. On the other hand, the clients of suicide prevention centers appear to be at higher risk than the population at large (Dew et al. 1987). Meta-analysis could not confirm that such programs have an impact on the suicide rate (Dew et al. 1987), although one study did indicate a decrease in the suicide rate among the group most likely to use such services—young, white females (Miller et al. 1984). However, there have been no studies of the effectiveness of prevention services that specifically target adolescent populations. General recommendations for improving the efficacy of prevention services include specific training of personnel in the assessment and counseling of suicidal patients and close ties to psychiatric facilities (Dew et al. 1987).

FUTURE AREAS OF RESEARCH

Biology of Suicide and Suicidal Behavior

The biology of suicide and suicidal behavior has not been carefully investigated in younger populations. However, several convergent lines of evidence in adults suggest that suicide and suicidal behavior are related to changes in central serotonergic functioning. Violent suicide attempters are noted to have low cerebrospinal fluid levels of 5-hydroxyindole acetic acid and these attempters are especially likely to complete suicide (Asberg et al. 1986). Postmortem examination of the brains of suicide completers has revealed a decreased number of presynaptic and increased number of postsynaptic serotonergic receptor binding sites (Stanley et al. 1986). However, these findings have not been examined in parallel studies of younger subjects, nor have the nosologic correlates of these findings been well established. Puig-Antich and colleagues have found that depressed suicidal (suicidal ideation with a plan or an actual attempt) children and adolescents differ from depressed nonsuicidal patients on a number of biological markers (unpublished data). The suicidal patients show decreased sleep rapid eye movement latency, decreased nocturnal growth hormone secretion, and increased growth hormone secretion after desipramine challenge (Ryan et al. 1988).

Familial Aggregation of Suicide and Suicidal Behavior

A number of studies of suicide and suicidal behavior in both adolescents and adults indicate that the relatives of suicide victims have high rates of both suicide and suicidal behavior (Brent et al. 1988a; Garfinkel et al. 1982; Roy 1986; Shaffer 1974). It is unclear if this familial tendency represents the aggregation of psychiatric disorders or if suicidality is transmitted separately or interactively from an Axis I disorder, perhaps as a tendency to impulsive violence. Finally, the possibility that suicidality occurs as a consequence of modeling or aberrant family interactions needs to be explored (Pfeffer 1986).

Impact of Exposure to Suicide

While there is evidence that exposure to suicide may increase the likelihood of imitation (e.g., Gould and Shaffer 1986), it is unknown which youth are most vulnerable to the effects of exposure. Prospective investigations into the effects of exposure to suicide may clarify this issue and enable school and mental health professionals to identify those students most vulnerable to the contagion effects subsequent to a student suicide.

Treatment of Suicide Attempts

Both pharmacologic and cognitive-behavioral approaches to suicide attempters should be evaluated formally by use of clinical trials. Currently the clinician has no empirically established guidelines to recommend treatment for suicidal adolescents.

CONCLUSIONS

Suicide and suicidal behavior among youth are serious public health problems. Psychiatric and psychosocial risk factors include disorders of affect, substance abuse, conduct disorders, disorders of personality, family history of psychiatric disorder and suicide, family discord, and exposure to suicide. The success of suicide prevention and early intervention for "at-risk" youngsters most likely to succeed will depend on the ability of teachers, physicians, and parents to identify psychiatrically ill youngsters and refer them for psychiatric treatment.

References

Asarnow, J.R., Carlson, G.A., and Guthrie, D. 1987. Coping strategies, self-perceptions, hopelessness and perceived family environments in depressed and suicidal children. *J. Contemp. Clin. Psychol.* 55:361–366.

Asberg, M., Nordstrom, P., and Traskman-Bendz, L. 1986. Cerebrospinal fluid studies in suicide: An overview. In Mann, J.J., and Stanley, M. (eds.): *Psychobiology of Suicidal Behavior*. New York: Annals of the New York Academy of Sciences.

Baekeland, F., and Lundwall, L. 1975. Dropping out of treatment: A critical review. *Psychol. Bull.* 82:738–783.

Bedrosian, R.C., and Epstein, N. 1984. Cognitive therapy of depressed and suicidal adolescents. In Sudak, H.S., Ford, A.B. and Rushforth, N.B. (eds.): *Suicide in the Young*. Boston: John Wright Publishing.

Berlin, I.N. 1987. Suicide among American Indian adolescents: An overview. *Suicide Life-Threat. Behav.* 17:218–232.

Boyd, J.H. 1983. The increasing rate of suicide by firearms. *N. Engl. J. Med.* 76:1240–1242.

Boyd, J.H., and Moscicki, E.K. 1986. Firearms and youth suicide. *Am. J. Public Health* 308:872–874.

Brent, D.A. 1986. Overrepresentation of epileptics in a consecutive series of suicide attempters seen at a children's hospital, 1978–1983. *J. Am. Acad. Child Psychiatry* 25:242–246.

Brent, D.A., Kalas, R., Edelbrock, C., et al. 1986. Psychopathology and its relationship to suicidal ideation in childhood and adolescents. *J. Am. Acad. Child Psychiatry* 25:666–673.

Brent, D.A. 1987. Correlates of the medical lethality of suicide attempts in children and adolescents. *J. Am. Acad. Child Psychiatry* 26:87–89.

Brent, D.A., Crumrine, P.K., Varma, R.R., et al. 1987a. Phenobarbital treatment and major depressive disorder in children with epilepsy. *Pediatrics* 80:909–917.

Brent, D.A., Perper, J.A., and Allman, C. 1987b. Alcohol, firearms and suicide among youth: Temporal trends in Allegheny County, PA, 1960–1983. *J.A.M.A.* 257:3369–3372.

Brent, D.A., Perper, J.A., Goldstein, C.E., et al. 1988a. Risk factors for adolescent suicide: A comparison of adolescent suicide victims with suicidal inpatients. *Arch. Gen. Psychiatry* 45:581–588.

Brent, D.A., Kerr, M.M., Goldstein, C.G., et al. An outbreak of suicide and suicidal behavior. *J. Am. Acad. Child Adolesc. Psychiatry*. in press.

Brent, D.A., Kupfer, D.J., Bromet, E.J., et al. 1988b. The assessment and treatment of patients at risk for suicide. In Francis, A.J., and Hales, R.E. (eds.): *Review of Psychiatry*. Washington, D.C.: American Psychiatric Press.

Carlson, G.A., Cantwell, D.P. 1982. Suicidal behavior and depression in children and adolescents. *J. Am. Acad. Child Psychiatry* 4:361–368.

Centers for Disease Control. 1985. *Suicide Surveillance 1970–1980*. Atlanta: U.S. Department of Health and Human Services, Public Health Service, Violent Epidemiology Branch, Center for Health Promotion and Education.

Cohen-Sandler, R., Berman, A.L., and King, R.A. 1982a. Life stress and symptomatology: Determinants of suicidal behavior in children. *J. Am. Acad. Child Psychiatry* 1982b. 21:178–186.

Cohen-Sandler, R., Berman, A.L., and King, R.A. 1982b. A follow-up study of hospitalized suicidal children. *J. Am. Acad. Child Psychiatry* 21:398–403.

Dew, M.A., Bromet, E.J., Brent, D.A., et al. 1987. A quantitative literature review of the effectiveness of suicide prevention centers. *J. Contemp. Clin. Psychol.* 55:1–6.

Drye, R.C., Goulding, R.L., and Goulding, M.E. 1984. No-suicide decisions: Patient monitoring of suicidal risk. *Am. J. Psychiatry* 130:170–174.

Frank, E., Kupfer, D.J. 1986. Psychotherapeutic approaches to the treatment of recurrent unipolar depression: Work in progress. *Psychopharmacol. Bull.* 22:558–563.

Friedman, I.M. 1985. Alcohol and unnatural deaths in San Francisco youths. *Pediatrics* 76:191–193.

Garfinkel, B., Froese, A., and Hood, J. 1982. Suicide attempts in children and adolescents. *Am. J. Psychiatry* 139:1257–1261.

Goldacre, M., and Hawton, K. 1985. Repetition of self-poisoning and subsequent death in adolescents who take overdoses. *Br. J. Psychiatry* 146:395–398.

Gould, M.S., and Shaffer, D. 1986. The impact of suicide in television movies: Evidence of imitation. *N. Engl. J. Med.* 315:690–694.

Greer, S., and Bagley, C. 1971. Effect of psychiatric intervention in attempted suicide: A controlled study. *Br. Med. J.* 1:310–312.

Haas, G.L., Glick, F.D., Spencer, J.H., et al. 1986. The patient, the family and compliance with post-hospital treatment for affective disorders. *Psychopharmacol. Bull.* 22:999–1005.

Harkavy-Friedman, J.M., Asnis, G.M., Boeck, M., et al. 1987. Prevalence of specific suicidal behaviors in a high school sample. *Am. J. Psychiatry* 144:1203–1206.

Hawton, K., and Goldacre, M. 1982. Hospital admissions for adverse effects of medical agents (mainly self-poisoning) among adolescents in the Oxford region. *Br. J. Psychiatry* 141:166–170.

Hawton, K., and Catalan, J. 1987. *Attempted Suicide. A Practical Guide to its Nature and Management*, 2nd. ed. Oxford: Oxford University Press.

Hibbard, R.A., Brack, C.J., Rauch, S., et al. 1988. Abuse, feelings, and health behaviors in a student population. *Am. J. Dis. Child.* 142:326–330.

Himmelhoch, J.M., and Garfinkel, M.E. 1986. Sources of lithium resistance in mixed mania. *Psychopharmacol. Bull.* 22:613–620.

Holinger, P.C., and Offer, D. 1982. Prediction of adolescent suicide: A population model. *Am. J. Psychiatry* 139:302–307.

Kazdin, A.E., Esveldt-Dawson, K., French, N.H., et al. 1987a. Effects of parent management training and problem-solving training combined in the treatment of antisocial child behavior. *J. Am. Acad. Child Adolesc. Psychiatry* 26:416–424.

Kazdin, A.E., Esveldt-Dawson, K., French, N.H., et al. 1987b. Problem-solving skills training and relationship therapy in the treatment of antisocial child behavior. *J. Contemp. Clin. Psychol.* 55:76–85.

Kazdin, A.E., French, N.H.Y., Unis, A.S., et al. 1983. Hopelessness, depression, and suicidal intent among psychiatrically disturbed impatient children. *J. Contemp. Clin. Psychol.* 51:504–510.

Kellerman, A.L., and Reay, D.T. 1986. Protection or peril? An analysis of firearms-related deaths in the home. *N. Engl. J. Med.* 314:1557–1560.

Kennedy, P. 1972. Efficacy of a regional poisoning treatment centre in preventing further suicidal behavior. *Br. Med. J.* 4:255–257.

Kerr, M.M., Hoier, T.S., and Versi, M. 1987. Methodological issues in childhood depression: A review of the literature. *Am. J. Orthopsychiatry* 57:193–198.

Klerman, G.L., Lavori, P.W., Rice, J., et al. 1985. Birth-cohort trends in rates for major depressive disorder among relatives of patients with affective disorder. *Arch. Gen. Psychiatry* 42:689–695.

Kosky, R. 1983. Childhood suicidal behavior. *J. Child Psychol. Psychiatry* 24:457–468.

Kosky, R., Silburn, S., and Zubrick, S. 1986. Symptomatic depression and suicidal ideation: A comparative study with 628 children. *J. Nerv. Ment. Dis.* 174:523–528.

Kreitman, N. 1976. The coal gas story: United Kingdom suicide rates, 1960–1971. *Br. J. Prev. Soc. Med.* 30:86–93.

Lester, D., and Murrell, M.E. 1982. The preventive effect of strict gun control laws on suicide and homicide. *Suicide Life-Threat. Behav.* 12:127–138.

Liberman, R.P., and Eckman, T. 1981. Behavior therapy vs insight-oriented therapy for repeated suicide attempters. *Arch. Gen. Psychiatry* 38:1126–1130.

Markush, R.E., and Bartolucci, A.A. 1984. Firearms and suicide in the United States. *Am. J. Public Health* 74:123–127.

Marzuk, P.M., Tierney, H., Tardiff, K., et al. 1988. Increased risk of suicide in persons with AIDS. *J.A.M.A.* 259:1333–1337.

Matthews, W., and Barabas, G. 1981. Suicide and epilepsy: A review of the literature. *Psychosomatics* 22:515–524.

McAnarney, E.R. 1979. Adolescent and young adult suicide in the United States: A reflection of societal unrest. *Adolescence* 14:765–774.

McIntire, M.S., Angle, C.R., Wikoff, R.L., et al. 1977. Recurrent adolescent suicidal behavior. *Pediatrics* 60:605–608.

Miklowitz, D.J., Goldstein, M.J., Nueckterlein, K.H., et al. 1986. Expressed emotion, affective style, lithium compliance, and relapse in recent onset mania. *Psychopharmacol. Bull.* 22:628–632.

Miller, H.L., Coombs, D.W., Leeper, J.D., et al. 1984. An analysis of the effects of suicide prevention facilities on suicide rates in the United States. *Am. J. Public Health* 74:340–343.

Motto, J.A. 1976. Suicide prevention for high-risk persons who refuse treatment. *Suicide Life-Threat. Behav.* 6:233–241.

Otto, U. 1972. Suicidal acts by children and adolescents: A follow-up study. *Acta. Psychiatr. Scand. Suppl.* 233:1.

Pfeffer, C.R. 1986. *The Suicidal Child*. New York: Guilford Press.

Phillips, D.P. 1974. The influence of suggestion on suicide: Substantive and theoretical implications of the Werther Effect. *Am. Soc. Rev* 39:340–354.

Phillips, D.P., and Carstensen, L.L. 1986. Clustering of teenage suicides after television news stories about suicide. *N. Engl. J. Med.* 315:685–689.

Pokorny, A.D. 1960. Characteristics of forty-four patients who subsequently committed suicide. *Arch. Gen. Psychiatry* 2:314–323.

Reynolds, W.M., and Coates, K.I. 1986. Comparison of cognitive and behavioral therapy and relaxation training for treatment of depression in adolescents. *J. Contemp. Clin. Psychol.* 54:653–660.

Robbins, D., and Conroy, R. 1983. A cluster of adolescent suicide: Is suicide contagious? *J. Adolesc. Health Care* 364:253–255.

Robbins, D.R., and Alessi, N.E. 1985. Depressive symptoms and suicidal behavior in adolescents. *Am. J. Psychiatry* 142:588–592.

Robins, L.N., Earls, F., Stiffman, A.R., et al. Suicide attempts in teen-aged medical patients. Proceedings of NIMH/CDC Conference in Youth Suicide, Washington, D.C.: U.S. Public Health Service. (in press)

Rosenthal, P.A., Rosenthal, S., Doherty, M.B., et al.

1986. Suicidal thoughts and behaviors in depressed hospitalized preschoolers. *Am. J. Psychotherapy* 40:201–212.

Rotheram, M.J. 1987. Evaluation of imminent danger for suicide among youth. *Am. J. Orthopsychiatry* 57:102–110.

Roy, A. 1982. Risk factors for suicide in psychiatric patients. *Arch. Gen. Psychiatry* 39:1089–1095.

Roy, A. 1986. Genetic factors in suicide. *Psychopharmacol. Bull.* 22:666–668.

Ryan, N.D., Puig-Antich, J., Ambrosini, P., et al. 1987. The clinical picture of major depression in children and adolescents. *Arch. Gen. Psychiatry* 44:854–861.

Ryan, N.D., Puig-Antich, J., and Rabinovich, H.R. 1988. Growth hormone response to desmethylimipramine in depressed and suicidal adolescents. *J. Affect. Disord.* (in press)

Salk, L., Lipsitt, L.P., Sturner, W.Q., et al. 1985. Relationship of maternal and perinatal conditions to eventual adolescent suicide. *Lancet* 1:624–627.

Shaffer, D. 1974. Suicide in childhood and early adolescence. *J. Child Psychol. Psychiatry* 15:275–291.

Shaffer, D., and Fisher, P. 1981. The epidemiology of suicide in children and young adolescents. *J. Am. Acad. Child Psychiatry* 20:545–565.

Shafii, M., Carrigen, S., Whittinghill, J.R., and Derrick, A. 1985. Psychological autopsy of completed suicide in children and adolescents. *Am. J. Psychiatry* 142:1061–1064.

Shafii, M., Steltz-Lenarsky, J., Derrick, A.M., Beckner, C., Whittinghill, J.R. 1988a. Comorbidity of mental disorders in the post-mortem diagnosis of completed suicide in children and adolescents. *J Affect. Disord.* 15:227–233.

Shafii, M. 1986b. Reply to "Handling Threats in Children and Adolescents." *Am. J. Psychiatry* 143:1061–1063.

Smith, K., and Crawford, S. 1986. Suicidal behavior among "normal" high school students. *Suicide Life-Threat. Behav.* 16:313–325.

Stanley, E.J., and Barter, J.T. 1970. Adolescent suicidal behavior. *Am. J. Orthopsychiatry* 40:87–96.

Stanley, M., Mann, J.J., and Cohen, L.S. 1986. Serotonin and serotonergic receptors in suicide. In Mann, J.J., and Stanley, M. (eds.): *Psychobiology of Suicidal Behavior*. New York: Annals of the New York Academy of Sciences.

Taylor, E.A., and Stansfeld, S.A. 1984a. Children who poison themselves: I. A clinical comparison with psychiatric controls. *Br. J. Psychiatry* 145:127–135.

Taylor, E.A., and Stansfeld, S.A. 1984b. Children who poison themselves: II. Prediction of attendance for treatment. *Br. J. Psychiatry* 145:132–135.

Tischler, C.L., McKenry, P.C., and Morgan, K.C. 1981. Adolescent suicide attempts: Some significant factors. *Suicide Life-Threat. Behav.* 11:86–92.

Tischler, C.L., and McKenry, P.C. 1982. Parental negative self and adolescent suicide attempts. *J. Am. Acad. Child Psychiatry* 21:404–408.

Topol, P., and Reznikoff, M. 1982. Perceived peer and family relationships, hopelessness and locus of control as factors in adolescent suicide attempts. *Suicide Life-Threat. Behav.* 12:141–150.

Trautman, P.D., Lewin, N., and Krauskopf, D. 1987. Home visits with non-compliant adolescent suicide attempters—a pilot study. Presented at the 34th annual meeting of the American Academy of Child and Adolescent Psychiatry, Washington, D.C.

Trautman, P.D., Rotheram, M.J., Chatlos, C., et al. 1984. Differences among normal, psychiatrically disturbed and suicide attempting adolescent females. Presented at the American Child Psychiatry meeting.

Trautman, P.D., and Shaffer, D. 1984. Treatment of child and adolescent suicide attempters. In Sudak, H.S., Ford, A.B., and Rushforth, N.B. (eds.): *Suicide in the Young*. Boston: John Wright Publishing.

Ward, J.A., and Fox, J. 1977. A suicide epidemic on an Indian reserve. Can. Psychiatr. Assoc. J. 22:423–426.

Weissman, M.M., Fox, K., and Klerman, G.L. 1973. Hostility and depression associated with suicide attempts. *Am. J. Psychiatry* 130:450–455.

Welner, A., Welner, Z., and Fishman, R. 1979. Psychiatric inpatients: Eight-to-ten year follow-up. *Arch. Gen. Psychiatry* 36:689–700.

Welu, T.C. 1977. A follow-up program for suicide attempters: Evaluation of effectiveness. *Suicide Life-Threat. Behav.* 7:17–30.

Divorce: Clinical Implications for Treatment of Children

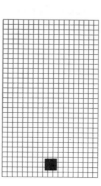

23

KITTY W. SOLDANO, Ph.D.

There is no question that family instability, divorce, and remarriage represent major life stressors for children with significant implications for development. Physicians and mental health professionals working with children and their families should be well acquainted with divorce-related issues as they attempt to facilitate family adjustment during the divorce process as well as treat the long-term emotional problems experienced by many children. Although much research on the effects of divorce has been methodologically limited by small, nonrepresentative samples with primarily white, middle-class subjects in a clinical rather than nonclinical setting, there have been several good longitudinal studies using larger national samples with appropriate comparison groups (Guidubaldi and Perry 1985; Hetherington et al. 1985; and Kurdek 1986). Along with valuable longitudinal clinical research elucidating the experience of divorce from the child's point of view, clinical work with these children and their families can draw from a fairly firm data base, which suggests that while most children eventually adjust to their parents' marital rearrangements, many experience both short-term and long-term emotional and behavioral problems related to divorce (Table 23–1). Such findings are mirrored by the greater representation in child and adolescent psychiatric clinics from divorced families as compared with intact

families (Kalter and Rembar 1981) and by recognition in the *Diagnostic and Statistical Manual of Mental Disorders*, third edition, revised *(DSM-III-R)*, of divorce as a severe, acute stressor that often precipitates a variety of symptoms in children (American Psychiatric Association 1987). It is currently projected that one of every two marriages will end in divorce and that approximately 39% of all children will experience marital disruption by their 15th birthday (Kurdek 1986; NBC 1986). Furthermore, it is estimated that approximately 85% of divorced parents marry and that 40% of these marriages will end in a second divorce (Guidubaldi and Perry 1985). A large number of children are going to continue to grow up in new family situations, adjusting to life in single parent families or blended remarriage families complicated by various types of custody arrangements and visitation agreements. As clinicians, it is crucial to have a clear understanding of how divorce can affect development at different ages, as well as appreciate the constraints that the level of development may place on the cognitive understanding and emotional working through of divorce-related events. Similarly, professionals need to be familiar with a variety of intervention strategies that have been effective in working with children and families of divorce so that treatment goals can be thoughtfully formulated based on an understanding of factors

Table 23–1. SUMMARY OF REPRESENTATIVE RESEARCH ON IMPACT OF DIVORCE ON CHILDREN

Investigators	Title	Sample and Design	Variables Assessed	Summary of Findings
Guidubaldi and Perry (1985)	Divorce and Mental Health Sequelae for Children: A Two-Year Follow-up of a Nationwide Sample	2 year follow-up of 110 (of 699 at time 1) elementary school boys and girls in divorced and intact families. Average time since divorce was 6 years at follow-up.	Academic functioning School behavior Peer acceptance Locus of control General mental health	Children from divorced families performed more poorly than intact family children; boys showed more negative effects than girls.
Hetherington et al. (1985)	Long-term Effects of Divorce and Remarriage on the Adjustment of Children	6 year follow-up of 124 (of 144 at time 1) middle class families including 60 divorced and 64 intact families. Mean age of children at time of follow-up was 10.1 years.	Behavioral observation of home adjustment Academic performance Teacher/peer evaluation Level of family stress Social competence Locus of control	Divorce has more adverse effects for boys, whereas remarriage is more difficult for girls.
Kalter and Rembar (1981)	The Significance of a Child's Age at the time of Parental Divorce	144 children of divorced families ranging in age from 7–17 years who presented for evaluation in a child psychiatry outpatient clinic	Presenting complaints; overall degree of emotional adjustment based on clinical evaluation	When divorce occurs in a child's life it is unrelated to overall level of adjustment but associated with characteristic patterns of problems at different stages of development.
Wallerstein and Kelly (1980)	Surviving the Breakup: How Children and Parents Cope with Divorce	60 middle-class families with 131 children between 2–18 years who participated in divorce counseling at time of divorce and were evaluated again at 18 months post separation and again at 5 years post divorce	Assessment of child's response to and experience of divorce; assessment of parent child relationships; assessment of support systems outside the home (including school)	The initial decision to divorce is associated with acute distress including anxiety, depression, and anger at parents. At 18 months, preadolescent boys seemed to be having most difficulty adjusting at home and school; 30% of children presented as clinically depressed at 5-year evaluation. Good adjustment depended on quality of life in the postdivorce family.
Wallerstein (1985)	Children of Divorce: Preliminary Report of a Ten-Year Follow-up of Older Children and Adolescents	40 young adults between 19 and 29 who were between 9–19 years at time of divorce	Clinical evaluation of young adults (continuation of the earlier study)	Subjects continued to view divorce as major influence on their lives; most were very committed to lasting marriage, but women tended to fear repeating parents' mistakes

most often associated with healthy adjustment.

It is the purpose of this chapter to (1) discuss the initial impact of divorce on children as they adjust to parental separation and the decision to divorce; (2) examine the impact of divorce on children of different developmental stages; (3) discuss adjustment in the post-divorce family and review various forms of custody arrangements; and (4) present a number of therapeutic strategies that may be helpful in working with both children and their families as they adjust to the aftermath of divorce.

FACTORS IMPACTING ON CHILDREN'S INITIAL REACTIONS AND ADJUSTMENT TO DIVORCE

Longitudinal studies examining the impact of divorce confirm that most children initially experience divorce as an extremely stressful life event and may exhibit developmental disruptions, emotional distress, and behavior disorders as well as long-term emotional problems related to the divorce and the continued family disruption that follows. Hetherington and colleagues (1985) note that a number of studies found increased incidences of antisocial and acting-out disorders, more aggression and noncompliance, dependency, academic difficulties, depression, and anxiety in children of divorced parents compared with those living in intact families. Guidubaldi and Perry (1985) assessed 110 school-aged children in a 2-year follow-up study using a national sample and confirmed that children of divorce performed more poorly on several social and academic adjustment indices than did intact family children; elementary school age boys exhibited the most adverse effects. Studies by Wallerstein and Kelly (1980) also examined how children and their parents reacted to and are affected by divorce. This study examined the lives of 131 children in 60 middle-class families as they adjusted to divorce at 18 months, 5 years, and 10 years after separation. The first 18 months after separation were typically confused and chaotic for both children and parents; there were increases in a variety of acute symptoms in children, ranging from separation anxiety and phobias to sleep disturbances and mourning reactions. Children were often able to settle into new patterns of

family functioning before parents had completely resolved their own emotional issues. There appeared to be a diminishing of acute symptoms by the 18-month post-separation evaluation for most children. Yet, it was noted that some children were left with a profound sense of loss and vulnerability, which they continued to report at the 5- and 10-year assessment points (Wallerstein and Kelly 1980; Wallerstein 1985).

Factors Motivating Parental Decision to Divorce

Wallerstein and Kelly (1980) found that children's initial responses to their parents' decision to divorce were often colored by the couples' motivation for separation. Children who were told and perceived that parents had made a rational decision to divorce seemed best able to cope. For these children the decision to divorce did not come as a surprise. Many had witnessed years of conflict between their parents and felt that divorce would end the unhappiness. Many of these parents and children had already divorced emotionally and thus did not experience the initial shock and profound sense of loss that often was felt deeply by children whose parents divorced more impulsively. For these children and their parents, the legal separation and divorce process followed rather than preceded the emotional disengagement, affording them the opportunity to have alternative support systems in place as they began the task of emotional adjustment in the post-divorce family.

A decision to divorce made impulsively by parents was much more problematic for children to understand and tolerate. These divorces were often precipitated by involvement of one spouse in an affair or brought on by an inability of the family to adjust to some kind of stressor such as unemployment, mental illness in a family member, or death of a loved one. Children were left angry and confused by the decision with no one to turn to for clarification. Parents were so involved in their own pain that they did not respond adequately to their children's needs for reassurance and stable, consistent care.

Factors Contributing to Family Instability in the Newly Divorced Family

A parental decision to separate sets in motion a number of changes for all family members. At a time when children (and their parents as well) would find comfort in a stable environment, most must face a number of extrafamiliar changes that intensify their pain. Perhaps most significant is the economic impact of divorce (NBC 1986). Statistics suggest that 60% of children growing up in poverty are children of divorce. Although custody laws are changing in many states and joint custody as well as sole paternal custody is increasing, 90% of children are still in the custody of their mothers following divorce. Estimates are that 50% of noncustodial parents do not pay child support. The harsh reality remains that women do much worse economically after divorce (NBC 1986). During this difficult post-separation and divorce period, many of these mothers return to full-time work, change jobs, and/or increase the number of hours worked per week. Child care planning often changes dramatically as personal and financial resources are diminished; and parents, preoccupied by their own concerns, are not motivated or emotionally able to support joint planning. Children often experience the compounded pressure of adjusting to both a physically absent and an emotionally unavailable parent simultaneously. With family relationships in a state of flux, children may turn to sources outside their families for a sense of continuity. However, many of these sources of support are also likely to change. In the Wallerstein and Kelly study (1980), one fifth of the children in a predominately middle-class sample moved within the first 6 months following divorce. Many other families talked about an anticipated move, thus increasing their children's anxiety about changing schools, neighborhoods, and peer groups. Guidubaldi and Perry (1985) confirmed the relationship between altered family income and post-divorce adjustment, particularly for girls. When family income was controlled, responses of girls in intact families and those from divorced families were similar on 28 of 30 mental health and behavioral measures. Although more differences appeared for boys, post-divorce family income remained a powerful predictor of adjustment.

DEVELOPMENTAL IMPLICATIONS OF DIVORCE: LONG-TERM SEQUELAE AND CHARACTERISTIC RESPONSES OF CHILDREN AT DIFFERENT STAGES

Although children's initial responses to divorce are fairly well understood, as time goes on overt symptoms diminish and more chronic patterns of behavior develop in an attempt to adjust to the continued changes in family life. To understand more clearly the impact of divorce on children of different ages, researchers and clinicians have suggested three different theoretical formulations (Kalter and Rembar 1981). The *cumulative effect hypothesis* maintains that the earlier divorce occurs in a child's life, the more vulnerable the child will be as he or she meets developmental demands and the more likely is it that problems will develop. The *critical stage hypothesis*, espoused primarily by psychoanalytical theorists and clinicians, suggests that children between the ages of 3 and 6 (especially boys) are most vulnerable to divorce because parental separation interferes with appropriate resolution of oedipal fantasies, leaving the child consumed with guilt over victory (if they are the same sex as the absent parent) or without appropriate parental involvement to facilitate good identification (if they are the same sex as the custodial parent). The *recency hypothesis* postulates that divorce has short-term impact only and suggests that most children recover from trauma within 1 or 2 years. Kalter and Rembar (1981) have examined the significance of a child's age at the time of divorce using a sample of 144 children from divorced families who presented for outpatient evaluation between ages 7 and 18 years. They attempted to find support for each of these hypotheses and concluded that "the total sample yielded a dearth of significant findings. The critical stage and recency hypotheses failed to find support with respect to the extent of distress experienced later by children of divorce. The cumulative effect view received minimal support." What did emerge, however, was a distinct pattern of emotional-behavioral difficulties experienced by children of different ages. Studies by Wallerstein and Kelly (1980), Kalter and Rembar (1981), Kalter (1987), and Kurdek (1986) support these findings. A discussion of characteristic cognitive, emotional, and behavioral responses of children at different developmental stages follows. Table 23–2 summarizes these findings.

Preschool–Kindergarten

COGNITIVE UNDERSTANDING OF DIVORCE

Preschoolers' emotional experience of divorce is overdetermined by their limitations in cognitive development. Children between ages 3 and 5 are typically unable to understand the concept of finality and view divorce as temporary. Their logic is also basically linear and dyadic—they perceive themselves as having the power to cause their parents' behavior (Neal 1983). Their omnipotence is further fueled by their inability to separate themselves subjectively from their parents and clearly differentiate between parents' internal motives and their own. When asked, "What does it mean when parents say they are getting divorced?", children in this age group defined divorce in terms of one parent being physically separated from another. They were confused by parental assurances of love and their decision to separate and move away (Kurdek 1986).

EMOTIONAL AND BEHAVIORAL RESPONSE

It is no wonder, then, that these children's characteristic emotional response to separation includes fear, bewilderment, and guilt as they attempt to grapple with the cognitive complications and emotional pain of divorce. Wallerstein and Kelly (1980) described preschoolers in their sample as emotionally needy with preoccupation about their own replaceability. More immature behavior was typical. At a time when mothers themselves were depressed and emotionally less available to children, separation anxiety often increased, blankets and bottles reappeared, and toileting accidents became a daily occurrence. Level of aggression in many of these children also changed. For some, aggressive outbursts increased as their emotional energy to tolerate daily frustrations was diminished by preoccupation with loss. In others, aggression was inhibited either in an unconscious hope that good behavior might bring resolution or in an attempt to support an already fragile mother. Some children coped by use of fantasy, developing their own explanations for the divorce. Wallerstein notes that these somewhat violent "macabre" fantasies

provided some children with a way of making sense of the complexities of events around them. Still other children denied the divorce altogether. For most, play was disrupted and no longer enjoyed (Wallerstein and Kelly 1980).

LONG-TERM SEQUELAE

Hetherington and colleagues (1985) reviewed some long-term effects of divorce when separation occurred during the preschool years. They examined children who had problems adjusting in the 2 years after divorce to determine if problems persisted 4 years later when these children were age 10. Data suggest that sex differences emerge with regard to internalizing or externalizing behavior with boys being more typically aggressive and girls characterized more frequently as anxious or depressed. Hetherington and colleagues' data suggest that "preschool boys who are viewed by peers, teachers and parents as socially unskilled and insensitive at two years post divorce are less competent and show more antisocial behaviors as ten year olds." Although aggressive behavior was much less typical of preschool girls, it also served as a stable predictor of inept social behavior in girls at age 10. Social competence in preschool girls, however, showed only a modest relationship to social skills at age 10. Hetherington and colleagues conclude that early externalizing behavior is generally a more stable predictor of later behavioral characteristics than is early withdrawal and anxiety.

Kalter and Rembar (1981) provide data on the long-term impact of divorce when separation and divorce occur in the preschool years. They examined outpatient evaluation data from 144 children of divorce and correlated presenting problems to the age of the child when the divorce occurred. Their data suggest that when parental separation occurs prior to age 2½, elementary school age boys and girls show significantly fewer nonaggressive disturbances with parents than expected. Early divorce was also significantly associated with increased aggression against peers in elementary school age girls and nonaggression with peers and academic problems in adolescent boys. Data on 3- to 5-year-old children indicated higher rates of school behavior problems and "subjective symptoms" occurring in elementary school

Table 23–2. SUMMARY OF FINDINGS: CHARACTERISTIC RESPONSES TO DIVORCE AT DIFFERENT DEVELOPMENTAL STAGES

Developmental Stage	Cognitive Understanding	Emotional/Behavioral Responses (0–2 yr post divorce)
PRESCHOOL-KINDERGARTEN: *Infancy (0–2½ yr)* *Preschool (3–5 yr)*	(4–5 yr olds) • Understand divorce in terms of physical separation • Perceive divorce as temporary • Are confused by parents' positive and negative feelings about each other • Understand divorce in dyadic terms and believe they could cause behavior of parent (Kurdek, 1986)	(3–5 yr olds) • Fear • Regression • Macabre fantasy • Bewilderment • Replaceability • Fantasy denial • Disruption/inhibition of play • Increase in aggression • Inhibition of aggression • Guilt • Emotional neediness (Wallerstein and Kelly, 1980, Chapter 4)
ELEMENTARY SCHOOL AGE: *Early (6–8 yr)* *Late (9–12 yr)*	(6–8 yr olds) • Understand the finality of divorce • Appreciate psychological and physical effects of parental conflict • Find it difficult to interpret ambivalent feelings toward one person • May interpret divorce egocentrically and believe their behavior impacts on parental decision (9–12 yr olds) • Understand psychological motives for divorce • Appreciate each parent's perspective of divorce • Do not blame themselves • Believe cessation of conflict will be a benefit of divorce for them (Kurdek, 1986)	(6–8 yr olds) • Grief • Fear leading to disorganization • Feeling of deprivation • Yearning for departed parent • Inhibition of aggression at father • Anger at custodial mother • Fantasies of responsibility and reconciliation • Conflicts in loyalty (9–12 yr olds) • Initially well defended • Attempted mastery by activity and play • Anger • Shaken sense of identity • Somatic symptoms • Alignment with one parent
ADOLESCENCE: *Early adolescence (12–14 yr)* *Late adolescence (15–18 yr)*	(12–14 yr olds) • Appreciate complexity of communication and can recognize incongruence between verbal and nonverbal cues • Understand stability of personality characteristics • Express concern about "parental intention" and believe that negative responses are a result of malevolent motives (15–18 yr olds) • Explain divorce in terms of parental incompatibility and feel it was a mature decision • Detach from parental conflict and focus on personal concerns (Neal, 1983; Kurdek, 1986)	(13–18 yr olds) • Change in parent-child relationships • Worry about sex and marriage • Mourning • Anger • Perceptions in flux • Loyalty conflicts • Strategic withdrawal • Greater maturity and moral growth • Changed participation within the family

Table continued on following page

Table 23–2. SUMMARY OF FINDINGS: CHARACTERISTIC RESPONSES TO DIVORCE AT DIFFERENT DEVELOPMENTAL STAGES Continued

Long-Term Sequelae
(Greater Than 2 Years After Divorce)

When separation/divorce occurred between birth and 2½ years of age:
- Separation-related difficulties increased during latency.
- Nonaggression with parents for both boys and girls is evidenced.
- Aggression with peers is noted in elementary school-aged girls.
- Nonaggression with peers/academic problems is associated in adolescent boys (Kalter and Rembar 1981).

When separation/divorce occurred between 3 and 5 years of age:
- Increase in subjective symptoms in elementary school boys is reported.
- Increase in aggressive behavior with parents in adolescent boys and girls is noted.
- Increase in academic problems is reported for adolescent girls (Kalter and Rembar 1981).
- Increase in externalizing behavior in elementary school boys and girls who were aggressive as preschoolers is reported (Hetherington 1985).

- Both girls and boys from divorced families emerged as performing more poorly on mental health measures than children from intact families (Guidubaldi 1985).
- Boys' performance was significantly worse than girls', and boys evidenced more behavior problems in school and at home (Guidubaldi and Perry 1985; Hetherington 1985).
- Girls living in single mother custody homes were as well adjusted as girls living in intact homes 6 years after divorce (Hetherington et al. 1985).
- Girls living in remarriage families have more difficulty adjusting than boys who showed good adjustment 2 years after remarriage (Hetherington 1985).*
- Father's absence seems to contribute more significantly to cognitive development in boys than girls (Radin 1985).

(13- to 18-year-olds)
*Adolescent girls and young women appear to be vulnerable to problems with feminine self-esteem and heterosexual development (Kalter et al. 1985; Kalter 1987; Wallerstein 1985.)

age boys and more aggressive behavior with parents, peers, and siblings in both adolescent boys and girls (Kalter and Rembar 1981).

Finally, studies suggest that preschoolers may be especially vulnerable to development of behavioral disorders since they have an increased probability of encountering "multiple negative life changes." There may be less continuity in the adjustment of these children than in children from intact families. Economic changes, changes in family members' physical and mental health, as well as changes in family dynamics may all contribute to the increased risk that many of these children face (Hetherington et al. 1985; Wallerstein and Kelly 1980).

Elementary School Age

COGNITIVE UNDERSTANDING

The typical 6- to 8-year-old child begins to develop the cognitive capacity to assess more accurately the emotional dynamics of divorce and to understand finality. Young children begin to recognize both the psychological and physical effects of parental conflict although they continue to be unable to tolerate ambivalent feelings toward this, usually blaming either one parent or the other. These children continue to interpret divorce egocentrically but begin to accept parental conflict and incompatibility as reasons for divorce. Kurdek (1986) noted that these children believed decreased parental conflict could be a benefit of divorce but worried that they would not be able to visit with the noncustodial parent frequently enough. By later elementary school age (9 to 12 years), children understood psychological motivation for divorce and accepted reasons for divorce from each parent's perspective. These children were much less likely to blame themselves for the divorce, but many became loyal to one parent with strong ambivalence toward the other. Like their younger counterparts these children also acknowledged cessation of parental conflict as a benefit of divorce and continued to express concern about the frequency of visits with their noncustodial parent (Kurdek 1986).

EMOTIONAL AND BEHAVIORAL RESPONSES

Wallerstein and Kelly (1980) described 6- to 8-year olds as frightened, disorganized children grieving for the departed parent. Fantasies of responsibility and reconciliation remained a preoccupation. These children, who were typically in the mother's custody, expressed anger toward the mother and inhibited aggression toward the father. Loyalty conflicts between parents emerged in this age group and became far stronger for older elementary school-age children. Custodial mothers may find this an especially trying age to parent children through divorce since anger and aggression are most often directed at them while keeping the noncustodial parent "good."

Wallerstein and Kelly (1980) suggest that older elementary school-age children initially appear much better defended than younger children, directing much of their emotional energy into mastering skills in activity and play. As they continued to talk, however, they became less well defended and some openly expressed anger while others presented somatic symptoms. These children often aligned with one parent against the other and loyalty conflicts increased. They also expressed some concerns about identity issues. Their identity seemed to be based on their understanding of themselves in relation to parents, peers, and broader supportive environment. These youngsters were especially troubled by changes of friends, schools, and neighborhoods, since they often identified themselves in terms of them.

LONG-TERM SEQUELAE

Strong differences emerged in functioning between elementary school-age children living in divorced families and those from intact homes. As has been noted, the long-term impact of divorce is clearly evident when children who experienced divorce during their preschool years were followed and assessed again during elementary school age. Several studies comparing nonclinical divorced and intact family children suggest that children of divorce have more difficulties adjusting than do those from intact families. Divorced family boys are especially vulnerable. Guidubaldi and Perry (1985) compared responses of first, third, and fifth graders from divorced and intact families on a 30-item mental health measure. Results from the total sample indicate that children of divorce performed more poorly on 9 of the 30 indices than did children from intact homes. They showed increased frequency of dependency, irrelevant talk, withdrawal, blaming, and inattention; decreased work effort; and increased inappropriate behavior.

When sex differences were analyzed, boys' responses continued to show significant differences with very little difference in performance between girls from divorced families and girls from intact homes. These findings continued to emerge when intelligence and socioeconomic status were controlled.

Hetherington and colleagues (1985) support these findings and suggest that girls' better adjustment during elementary school age stems from more girls living with a single mother and benefiting from a close relationship with a same-sex custodial parent. Girls from families with divorced nonmarried mothers were very similar in adjustment to girls in nondivorced families 6 years after divorce. Elementary school-age boys, however, showed much more externalizing and sometimes more internalizing, as rated by peers, teachers, and investigators in a number of home-based observation periods. Kalter and Rembar (1981) also support these findings and indicate that elementary school-age boys in their clinical sample presented with "subjective psychological symptoms," "problems with aggression with parents, siblings, and peers," as well as "school-related problems."

A different picture emerges, however, for children living with a parent who has remarried. Both boys and girls living in these families (parent married less than 2 years) self-reported and were seen by parents as having more externalizing problems than children in intact families. Stepfathers expressed particular concern over their stepdaughters, reporting them as having poor self-concepts and perceiving them to internalize more than girls in intact families (Hetherington et al. 1985). When children from families in which the parents have been remarried more than 2 years were compared with those with never-divorced parents, no differences were found for boys while stepdaughters seemed to remain more vulnerable, with continued difficulty noted in relationship with stepfathers. Thus, the combined data suggest that divorce has more detrimental effects for boys while remarriage is more difficult for girls.

The hypothesis that elementary school-age boys living in homes with a single mother are especially vulnerable to academic problems receives further support in the literature on the role of the father in cognitive development. Radin (1981) reviewed a number of studies on children living in "father absent homes" (absent through divorce, death, or desertion) and found that paternal nurturance appears to be closely associated with cognitive competence in boys but not girls; that a close relationship between father and son seems to foster an analytical cognitive style; and that a father's absence before age 5 appears to be most damaging to intellectual functioning. In conclusion, all these studies point to the relative difficulty encountered by elementary school-age children as they continue to face adjustment problems in the aftermath of divorce. The difficulties appear to be more profound for boys than for girls during this period.

Adolescence

COGNITIVE DEVELOPMENT

Neal (1983) described young adolescents as having the cognitive capacity to view parents as having stable personality characteristics that exist independently of social context. They no longer are limited to a linear, dyadic understanding of divorce motivated by parental actions and reactions but can appreciate the complexity and incongruence of verbal and nonverbal cues. They are likely to verbalize concern about parents' motives with regard to divorce and may err in assuming good intentions can ensure stable and committed relationships. As is evidenced by their relationships with peers, early adolescents continue to have an immature understanding of intimacy and seem "to believe that parents have an awareness of willful control over how they affect other persons." Older adolescents, on the other hand, appreciated parental limitations and interpreted divorce in terms of parental incompatibility. They often felt the decision to divorce was a mature and sensible one. Many seemed both emotionally and cognitively detached from parental conflict and focused instead on their own life events (Kurdek 1986; Neal 1983).

EMOTIONAL AND BEHAVIORAL RESPONSES

The response of adolescents to parental divorce must be addressed within the context of normal developmental tasks. Their tremendous distress and angry outbursts represent an awareness, on some level, that the stability they so desperately need to facilitate independence and foster identity development is compromised. Wallerstein and Kelly (1980) described adolescents in their sample as mourning the death of their parents' marriage and grieving the loss of stable family relationships. They often expressed concern about their own ability to have lasting marriages and were preoccupied with understanding the divorce from each parent's point of view, sometimes siding with one and then the other. As they attempted to resolve their own feelings about the divorce, loyalty conflicts were common. Many reported they were "put in the middle" by parents who both felt the need for their allegiance and relied on them for emotional support and help with daily household chores. Some felt overwhelmed by these demands, while others seemed to meet the demands of the post-divorce period with increased maturity. Some seemed to enjoy their more responsible role in family life. Still others responded by "strategic withdrawal," detaching themselves from parental conflict and turning to peers and contemporary issues to provide a more stable context to facilitate development.

LONG-TERM SEQUELAE

Adolescent children of divorce evaluated in Kalter and Rembar's (1981) study presented with increased aggression toward parents, academic problems, and subjective psychological symptoms. Boys who experienced early divorce (birth to age 2 years) continued to be nonaggressive with peers in adolescence and experienced some academic problems, while those experiencing divorce during ages 3 to 5½ were aggressive with parents and peers. Increased school refusal characterized adolescent boys whose parents divorced during elementary school age. Adolescent girls whose parents divorced during preschool years did not evidence remarkable symptoms; however, problems seemed especially remarkable for adolescent females whose parents had divorced during ages 3 through 5. These girls showed increased aggression with parents and peers in addition to marked academic problems. Thirty-five percent of adolescent girls in the sample were involved with drugs.

Kalter et al. (1985) take a more in-depth look at the impact of divorce on female development. They review data from three studies that suggest girls become more vulnerable to the effects of divorce in adolescence and young adulthood than boys. Issues associated with feminine self-esteem and heterosexual development are most cogent. Studies have shown that girls benefit from close same-sex parenting during elementary school age. Boys' relatively poorer adjustment in single parent, mother custody homes also supports these hypotheses. However, for many girls of divorce, the relatively tranquil relationship with mother during elementary school age gives way in adolescence to increased hostility, power struggles at home, and antisocial rebelliousness in peer relationships. Kalter et al. (1985) note that in a study on delinquency based on a national sample, adolescent daughters of divorce reported engaging in more delinquent behavior than did daughters from intact families. These data support the supposition that the father's role is crucial in the separation-individuation and identification processes of adolescence. Wallerstein's (1985) follow-up data also suggest that problems in female self-esteem and concern over heterosexual functioning complicate adjustment for many young women. She examined 40 young women at age 9 to 19 years at the time of divorce. Thirty percent of them continued to have problems with commitment 10 years later. Their relationships with men were characterized by a number of short-lived sexual encounters. Over one half of these women, however, continued to be strongly committed to marriage and family life. These daughters continued to affirm the value of the divorce experience in fostering increased independence and maturity.

In general then, data from studies examining the long-term impact of divorce on children do not fully support any of the previously held theories. The cumulative-effect hypothesis fails to explain the initial positive adjustment of girls followed by their increased vulnerability at adolescence. The critical stage hypothesis accounts for these findings as well as the fact that elementary school age boys experienced increased difficulty in homes in which the mother had custody. However, it does not speak to problems experienced by children whose parents divorced during preschool years. The recency hypothesis is rejected since long-term impact is clearly validated in both clinical and nonclinical populations. What emerges instead is a framework that suggests that not only do children at different developmental stages react initially to divorce with similar emotional concerns and behavioral patterns, but that there are long-term developmental vulnerabilities expressed in a variety of emotional, behavioral, and cognitive constellations. An awareness of these interacting concerns greatly facilitates evaluation and clinical understanding when working with these children and their families over time. The divorce experience can best be defined as the process beginning prior to the crisis of initial separation (when marital tensions are generally high) and continuing to influence the child's functioning through each developmental passage (Kalter and Rembar 1981; Wallerstein and Kelly 1980).

ADJUSTMENT AFTER DIVORCE

As has been noted previously, the initial decision to divorce often brings with it a dramatic change in family dynamics, accompanied by ambivalent feelings for both children and their parents. Optimally, the pain of the initial crisis, which sets in motion a myriad of emotions from anger to mourning, begins to resolve after about 18 months to 2 years as family members settle into newly organized relationships. In general, children of divorce have the same physical and psychological needs as children living in intact families. In Wallerstein's (1980) 5-year follow-up study, she confirmed that childrens' overall adjustment tended to reflect the quality of parenting after the divorce. Kalter (1987), Ahrons and Rodgers (1987), and Shiller (1986) also discuss factors that facilitate adjustment. In general, the following factors serve to enhance adjustment after divorce:

1. The ability of parents to meet their own emotional needs in a healthy way, while maintaining an emotionally open and stimulating environment for children

2. The ability of parents to continue effective and consistent parenting

3. The ability of parents to resolve past marital conflict and successfully negotiate problems with children when they arise

4. The ability of the child to adjust during the predivorce period

5. The ability for the child to have an ongoing relationship with the nonresidential parent

6. The ability to maintain stability in the family's physical environment, minimizing the number of changes in family support systems

Custody Options and Concerns

Clearly the factors mentioned in the previous section represent what is optimal and valuable for healthy family adjustment in the post-divorce period. However, parents, children, and the courts are often faced with the realities of limited financial, physical, and emotional resources when determining custody and support arrangements that formally elucidate and validate expected parental roles. At the present time, custody options that mandate how the child will be both physically and legally cared for are determined by state statutes and, therefore, differ in both the form and process from state to state. In general, *sole custody*, in which one parent (usually the mother) has both physical and legal custody, continues to be awarded most frequently. However, in response to parental demand and the recognition of children's need for continued involvement of both parents, a variety of other custody arrangements have become options within the past 15 years. Some states provide for *divided custody*, in which each parent retains physical and legal custody when the child is living with them. The child often resides alternatively with one parent for part of the year, then with the other. The nonresidential parent maintains visitation rights. *Joint custody or shared parenting* has emerged as an option in 30 states and was initially believed by many courts and mental health professionals to be the best for children since it requires, by definition, that both parents remain physically and legally responsible for the child with neither one superior. Joint custody does not presume, however, that the child spends equal amount of time with each parent. Hagen (1987) reviewed joint custody practices in different states and noted that it is awarded in several different ways. In many states, joint custody is considered only at the request of both parents, although in at least four states it may also be awarded at the request of only one parent. As Hagen notes, this may be particularly problematic for battered women or others fighting for sole cus-

tody to avoid continued abuse and therefore may not be in the best interests of children.

In about half of the states with joint custody, there is a *presumption of joint custody*. In these states, joint custody is the preferred custody arrangement with other forms of custody considered only after the feasibility of joint care has been ruled out. At the present time there is a trend toward awarding joint custody in many states. With this trend comes the demand for research to help us more adequately understand the implications of all types of custody arrangements for families so that guidelines can be developed based on what kind of arrangements work best for which families under what conditions.

Custody Options: Research Findings

Research studies that examine family adjustment in different types of post-divorce situations have begun to provide us with a better understanding. Johnston and co-workers (1985) provide a review of studies indicating that children who are the subject of lengthy post-separation conflict between parents are the most vulnerable children of divorce. Wallerstein and Kelly (1980) found that approximately one third of parents remain actively hostile 5 years after divorce. For these children, the major benefit of divorce, cessation of parental conflict, did not occur. Johnston et al. (1985) studied 44 elementary school-age children who were subjects of lengthy post-separation and post-divorce disputes over their custody and care. These children witnessed numerous parental conflicts, and both younger and older children reported being acutely distressed by parental fighting. Parents often seemed so intensely involved in their battles that they were unaware of children's needs or responses. Younger children often seemed immobilized by conflict and tried by their own behavior to distract the fight. Older children were more likely to become involved with their parents' battles and, as has been suggested previously, many became intensely involved with loyalty conflicts. Many parental conflicts occurred during the transition time when children visited with the other parent. Johnston notes that although children found this constant threat of parental conflict particularly painful, they continued to want visitation and enjoyed frequent contact with the nonresidential parent. In general, children did not like changes in the visitation schedule, seemingly finding comfort in any structure provided. These children developed a number of different coping strategies to defend themselves in the face of parental conflict. They often chose passive alternatives with marked absence of aggressiveness and conduct problems. Johnston et al. note that approximately two fifths of children presented with fairly severe somatic problems and "many were prone to anxiety, tension, depression and psychosomatic illness." They also state that these children showed problems with ego integration and concluded that their capacity for secure, intimate, yet autonomous relationships with one or both parents was severely compromised. Finally, they estimate that as many as one ninth of all children of divorce are likely to be caught between parents in ongoing custody disputes. It is likely that parental conflict in these families will be ongoing despite changes in custody arrangements and visitation since battles are fueled by unresolved past conflicts and parental inability to place children's needs before their own. In terms of factors that promote good adjustment, these parents' problems interfered with their ability to effectively parent; fear of impending conflict pervaded the emotional context of family life, and freedom to maintain an open relationship with the noncustodial parent was significantly limited.

There are other circumstances as well in which parental psychopathology impairs adjustment after divorce. Parents who are themselves mentally ill, are addicted to drugs or alcohol, or have a history of family violence, child abuse, or neglect are at risk and may require help before they can function appropriately as parents. For them, custody options and visitation arrangements must be carefully considered. For these families as well as for those in which conflict blatantly continues between parents, children may not benefit from joint custody—in fact, joint custody may contribute to their vulnerability.

Under what circumstances is joint custody most likely to promote healthy post-divorce adjustment? Joint custody allows continued ongoing physical and emotional involvement of children with both parents. Parents must, therefore, have the flexibility in their schedules as well as the economic resources to meet the demands of two separate households. Hagen (1987) suggests that research to date on the experience of joint custody has been primarily with middle- to upper middle-class families who are more likely to have employment conditions and income necessary to meet the increased demands of maintaining two primary residences. Steinman (1981) examined parents in 24 families who were firmly committed to joint custody and reported that their experience with co-parenting generally had been positive. Two thirds of these parents had maintained their joint custody arrangement more than 4 years. These parents valued each other as parents and were strongly valued by their children. In general, these parents could tolerate differences in each other and marital conflict had been controlled during the marriage and continued to be controlled or resolved. The children did not provide a battleground for unresolved marital issues. Shiller (1986) studied post-divorce adjustment in boys aged 6 to 11 years in maternal and joint custody situations. In 20 joint-custody situations, all but one set of parents had reached the decision to maintain joint custody mutually. Children spent on the average of 2 full days each week with each parent. In a matched sample of 20 maternal custody homes, over one half visited the noncustodial parent at least once a week and all visited at least once a month. Shiller found that whereas both groups showed more behavioral problems as rated by parents and teachers than same-aged boys from intact families, boys in joint custody homes had fewer problems than those living in sole custody with the mother. However, she noted that mothers involved with joint custody evidenced more strengths in parenting than did mothers with sole custody, presenting some confusion as to whether outcome is a result of custody arrangements or of preexisting strengths in parenting. It is possible that the kinds of parents who opt for joint custody and have the resources to implement it logistically have more psychological resources in parenting as well.

Steinman (1981) also provides one of the few studies that examines joint custody from the child's point of view. She examined the experience of 32 children living in joint custody and concluded that although parents generally found the arrangement satisfying, children's experiences were more mixed. These children continued to verbalize their preference for marriage over divorce but accepted joint custody as evidence that both their parents valued continued relationships with them. This parental commitment enhanced the children's self-esteem. Although they complained about the practical problems of joint custody, most (75%) were able to cope with the difficulties presented by shuffling back and forth between homes. These children were able to differentiate between expectations in their two homes and easily defined their separate relationships with parents. There did not appear to be major differences in child-rearing in these families. In general, children did not appear to experience strong loyalty conflicts although some seemed especially concerned about "fairness" between the two homes. They also did not report fear of rejection and/or abandonment typical of many children of divorce, although about one third of these children did appear overwhelmed by the psychological demands of two homes. Again, it is unclear as to whether the custody arrangement was responsible for their difficulty or simply exacerbated it. Finally, most of these children continued to go to the same school and stated that the continuity of peer relationships was important to them. Steinman concludes that the benefits of joint custody for children seem to lie in the message to the child that each parent is committed to their continued care and values the other parent's continued relationship with the child as well.

It is painfully clear that while custody arrangements can physically and legally define expectations for continuing parent–child relationships, such arrangements cannot determine the emotional climate within which they unfold. These data suggest that childrens' adjustment is enhanced by good parenting and that it is parental commitment to the child and the parents' ability to provide a healthy emotional climate, not the type of custody arrangements per se, that are most important to good adjustment.

PSYCHOPATHOLOGY AND TREATMENT

The framework presented thus far suggests that the child's divorce experience can best be understood in terms of the interaction of the child's level of cognitive and emotional development with family dynamics. In healthy families, parents are able accurately to understand children's concerns and respond to them in developmentally appropriate ways. They also can manage their own adult relationships and have skills to resolve conflict. In general they convey to their children a strong sense of commitment and value; children, in turn develop a firm sense of identity, which serves them as they confront normal developmental demands as well as the pain and confusion of divorce.

As clinicians and researchers in mental health, we are much more likely to come into contact with those children and families more vulnerable to the deleterious effects of divorce. These families, many of whom have experienced multiple traumas and may have biological vulnerabilities to specific illnesses as well, are asking for help as they attempt to face life's continued demands. It is within the context of this developmental framework and with an understanding of normal functioning, that we evaluate, diagnose, and develop treatment plans sensitive to the realities of patients' lives and those in their families.

That children of divorce are more vulnerable to psychiatric illness is attested to by the percentage of children referred for evaluation and treatment in child and adolescent psychiatric clinics who are either currently, or have in the past, experienced the breakup of their family. As Kalter and Rembar (1981) have suggested, these children present a variety of problems from depression and separation anxiety to conduct disorder and drug abuse. Guidubaldi and Perry (1985) and others have also noted concomitant psychiatric disorders in parents of these children. At 2 years after divorce, parents continued to report problems with adjustment. Parental lethargy was correlated significantly with negative classroom behavior, including less independent learning. Similarly, parental report of low self-esteem predicted increased dependency and behavior problems in children. Parental psychopathology is often an indicator of increased problems in children. The divorce experience serves both to exacerbate already existing pathology as well as to precipitate new symptoms in the post-divorce readjustment period.

Kalter (1987) suggests that children of divorce are particularly vulnerable to problems with gender identity, modulating aggression and achieving emotional separation from parents. The most typical post-divorce custody arrangements—children living in sole maternal custody with a visiting father—may serve to promote rather than discourage such problems. Often, parents must become aware of their own issues and meet their own needs before they can encourage separation and individuation in their children. At a time of increased stress for both mother and father, parents may need guidance and encouragement before they can develop or resume appropriate limit setting and/or the emotional openness necessary to deal with the child's anger and pain. Similarly, parents may need help in understanding the special roles played by both in gender identity formation and the need for a continued psychological relationship with each parent. The therapeutic task with parents is as important for the parents as for the child and is crucial to the success of any intervention made with the child.

Wallerstein (1983) has outlined six psychological tasks that should be confronted by children adjusting to parental divorce. Goals of psychotherapy with children should reflect not only age-appropriate developmental concerns but the child's need to resolve these issues as well. Wallerstein suggests that work on divorce issues begin with *acknowledging the reality of marital rupture.* Second, children must be encouraged to *disengage from parental conflict* and deal with their own issues. It is only after disengagement that children are free to *resolve* not only the *loss* of the *nonresidential parent* but also the loss of the "ideal family life" and familiar family dynamics. Dealing with issues around loss often raises concerns over *self-blame* and *feelings of anger* with self and parents that need to be confronted before the child can *psychologically accept the permanence* of divorce and achieve *realistic hope of establishing meaningful relationships* in the future.

Treatment plans should be developed to manage the needs of both parents and children as they confront not only divorce-related issues but other problems as well. These plans must be developed with regard to realistic alternatives for family members. For some families, treatment goals will need to be limited to deal with the immediacy of a crisis situation and/or limitations in financial resources or lack of commitment to longer-term therapy. For other children and families, longer-term child psychotherapy with parent guidance or individual psycho-

therapy for the parent may be the treatment of choice. Whatever intervention is chosen, however, it is important to recognize that children will continue to deal with divorce-related concerns as they mature both cognitively and emotionally and reevaluate the impact of divorce as they master each developmental task. Therapists and parents as well need to be open to children's continued need to explore these issues. They may indeed benefit from several short-term courses of therapy over a number of years (Kalter 1987).

Alternative Treatment Approaches

The treatment approach decided on reflects a number of different factors, including the kind of setting in which the patient is being seen (availability of different types of treatment), the nature of the presenting problems and etiology, when the divorce occurred and family members' recognition of it as problematic, parents' and childrens' emotional resources, as well as financial concerns. For example, the needs of family members in the midst of divorce are very different from those of a depressed child with a divorced mother suffering from recurrent depression. Although divorce-related issues are salient for both, the first requires immediate response to these issues. In the second, depression must be treated before other concerns can be confronted. The following represent several different treatment approaches that have been used to deal with problems of divorce. Theoretical assumptions, rationale for treatment, and clinical indications as well as specific treatment goals are discussed for each.

FAMILY THERAPY

Nichols (1985) provides a helpful discussion of family therapy as a treatment modality for children of divorce. Family therapy is based on systems theory and explains the child's problems as a product of dysfunctional family dynamics. In families in which the child presents as the "identified patient," the first task of the therapist is to reframe the problem in terms of family dysfunction and help develop alternative, more healthy ways of dealing with these issues. Nichols suggests that family therapy can be most helpful at two major stress points for children, the initial family breakup and again when parents decide to remarry. In terms of particular treatment goals, family therapy can be especially useful just prior to divorce to help all family members begin the process of acknowledging marital breakup and confront and work through the anger and self-blame that often accompanies initial separation. Subsequent to divorce, the therapist may want to meet with different family members conjointly so that children have an opportunity to deal with mother and father separately. Such sessions may be helpful in dealing with painful feelings of loss and clarifying expectations of individual households and visitation. Sometimes it may be necessary to include both parents and children in family sessions after divorce, but the obvious complication of fostering reunion fantasies should be taken into account. Nichols also suggests that family sessions that include biological parents and intended or new spouses and children may be helpful in working on practical and emotional problems of remarriage. Contraindications of family therapy include situations in which parents continue to be hostile with each other and are invested in ongoing conflicts that involve the child. Such dynamics inhibit the child from disengaging from parents and reinvesting in individual concerns. In this situation, individual psychotherapy with parent guidance is clearly the treatment of choice.

PLAY THERAPY

Play therapy is often recommended as the treatment of choice for preschool- and elementary school-age children experiencing developmental interference after divorce (Mendell 1983). This approach, theoretically based in either Freudian or Kleinian theory, focuses on the child's play as a representation of unconscious conflicts and uses play as a vehicle for expression of the child's inner world. Whereas short-term supportive therapy and parent guidance may be most helpful during the crisis of divorce, children who continue to be symptomatic or become symptomatic years later need more intensive longer-term psychotherapy to rework divorce-related issues. Mendell suggests that play therapy may be very helpful in dealing with fear of abandonment, grief, reunion fantasies, and problems with identification. Chethik and Kalter (1980) suggest that ther-

apists can serve as an important "developmental facilitator" for the child, providing a stable, consistent, and supportive relationship in which the child can deal with unresolved issues. For children dealing with object loss, they recommend that a therapist of the same sex as the absent (noncustodial) parent be assigned to enhance effectiveness.

INSIGHT-ORIENTED PSYCHOTHERAPY

Insight-oriented psychotherapy is appropriate for adolescents who have the capacity to make an alliance with the therapist and work within a therapeutic framework to examine past conflicts as well as present concerns with parents and their relationships with peers of the opposite sex. As Kalter and co-workers (1985) have pointed out, adolescent girls may be particularly vulnerable to low feminine self-esteem and have difficulty with heterosexual relationships. As for younger children, the therapeutic relationship can become the vehicle through which the adolescent can work through the psychological tasks of divorce using his or her newly acquired cognitive ability to abstract and more fully develop the capacity for emotional insight to understand the dynamics of divorce.

PARENT GUIDANCE OR INDIVIDUAL PSYCHOTHERAPY

Parent guidance or individual psychotherapy for one or both parents may also be integral to the child's treatment. Perhaps one of the most important issues for parents to address before treatment begins is the importance of making a commitment to the child's therapy and to their own. For children who have already experienced major object loss, premature termination of the therapeutic relationship is clearly not in the child's best interests. Gardner (1976) discusses the importance of working closely with the parent and suggests that it may be valuable to have parents join play therapy sessions with young children to observe therapist–child interaction in order to learn to interpret more accurately children's behavior and understand their concerns. He reports that parental involvement during sessions with elementary school-age children did not raise confidentiality concerns and contributed positively to parental investment in treatment.

This practice is not recommended for adolescent patients for whom confidentiality is frequently an issue. Parents of these patients can either be seen by another therapist or be seen in a session with the patient so that the adolescent has an opportunity to voice his or her own concerns. In addition to addressing immediate parenting concerns, Gardner suggests that goals for parent guidance should include keeping lines of communication open between parent and child particularly with regard to divorce-related issues; helping parents understand children's need to deal with these issues at different stages of development; encouraging parents to be flexible with regard to visitation with the other parent; communicating directly with the other parent with minimal conflict so that using the child as a "middle man" can be avoided; and, perhaps most difficult, helping parents and children accurately interpret pathologic behavior in family members so that they can better cope with problems when they arise.

Case 1. Billy, a white 7½-year-old boy, was brought for evaluation by his mother after referral from school, where he was having both academic and behavior problems. Billy's parents had separated 3 years previously and were divorced within a year of the separation. Billy's mother continued to be angry with her husband for having a series of affairs prior to their divorce. She expressed her rage openly to Billy. Billy's father traveled frequently on his job and had visited only sporadically since the divorce. Billy described himself as very similar to his father in physical appearance and interests. "I'm sort of tall, just like my dad. We both like fast cars, football, and dogs." When asked about his parents' divorce, Billy explained that "you've just got to tough it out" and acknowledged that the only painful part of the divorce was "we had to move to an apartment and give my dog away."

Treatment. Billy was seen in weekly play therapy for 10 months. His mother was seen for a year, initially for parent guidance that focused on problems with parenting and difficulties dealing with the school and conflicts with her own family. Discussion of these issues led to exploration of many individual concerns and she began working through her own unresolved feelings about the divorce. Billy quickly made an attachment with the therapist and worked intensively in early sessions reenacting with puppets the scene in which his dog was given away. This important loss served as a metaphor for the loss of his father and facilitated expression of anger and self-blame. He clearly expressed his worry that he had not treated his dog with enough care and worried if the new owners were able to take good care of him. Resistance to dealing with the disappointing reality of his current relationship with father characterized mid-treatment sessions. During this time, play was often restricted and there were increased periods of silence and depression. Billy fluctuated between angry outbursts with the therapist for not providing more interesting toys in the playroom and for missing a session for vacation and periods of tearfulness when he acknowledged that he missed his dog and wished to see his father more frequently. During this time, Billy began talking about the divorce with mother and there was an improvement in school behavior and academic performance. After 8 months of treatment, his mother requested a joint session with Billy and his therapist to discuss divorce-related issues that she was uncomfortable dealing with at home. Billy was prepared for the session and asked to think about any questions he might have about the divorce. Billy opened the family therapy session with the statement "can we move into a new house so I can get a dog?" After two family sessions in which many details of the divorce were clarified for Billy, individual sessions resumed and focused on the acceptance of the divorce. The sadness rapidly abated and termination was planned. Billy returned to therapy 5 years later for a 6-month period at age 13 following the death of his grandmother and a breakup with a girlfriend he had been seeing for 1 year. He explained to the therapist that "some of the old feelings are coming back and I don't want to get depressed again." Certainly this child's initial experience in treatment facilitated his ability to deal more effectively with significant later losses. His mother's support of, and commitment to, her own treatment also were essential for a good prognosis.

Case 2. Martha was an attractive 16-year-old white girl presenting with clinical depression, academic problems, and intense conflict with father and stepmother around her boyfriend of 2 years. Martha's parents were separated when she was aged 4, reunited for 1 year, and then divorced when Martha was aged 6. Martha had lived with mother until she was 13 years old when her mother was hospitalized for treatment of depression and alcohol abuse. Martha then moved to her father's home shortly before he was married to her stepmother, who had three children aged 11, 8, and 4 years from a previous marriage. Martha indicated at evaluation that she had "never intended to be part of father's family" and put all her emotional energy into her relationship with her boyfriend. She continued to visit her mother on weekends if visits did not conflict with plans with her boyfriend. She described her relationship with her mother as "very conflictual" and "always making me feel guilty, but I don't know why."

Treatment. Martha was seen in individual insight-oriented psychotherapy for 1 year with intermittent family sessions. With her father's permission, the mother was contacted and asked to participate in her daughter's treatment. Her mother met initially with a social worker so that further family history could be taken. Evaluation indicated a three-generation history of recurrent depression in the mother's side of the family. The mother had experienced three severe depressive episodes, the first in adolescence, the second at the time of divorce, and the third just prior to her hospitalization. She had good response to antidepressant medication. Family history also was positive for drug and alcohol abuse. Martha was subsequently begun on imipramine therapy, and vegetative signs of depression cleared within 2 months. The mother and the social worker joined Martha and her therapist on two occasions for family sessions. In the first meeting, problems with visitation were discussed, which led to expression of both mother and daughter's anger with each other and the rejection that both felt. In the second session, which occurred about 2 months later, Martha discussed similarities between her relationship with her boyfriend and her mother's marital relationship with father. She worried that she would lose her boyfriend as her mother "lost" her father. Visitation had become more regular, and both mother and daughter were able to talk more openly about mutual concerns. During the later phase of treatment, Martha and her therapist met with her father, stepmother, stepbrothers, and stepsister for two sessions and with her father only for one session. These sessions helped family members clarify expectations of each other and gave each an opportunity to express their frustrations within a safe context.

Individual treatment focused initially on her anger that she had been "robbed of my family and my childhood." Martha focused on her own feminine identity and critically came to understand her behavior in her relationship with a boyfriend in terms of emotional efforts to heal past wounds. At one point she stated that her inability to let go of the present relationship was because of her fear of loss of any kind. She terminated treatment after 12 months of individual sessions and a 9-month course of antidepressant medication. She was visiting regularly with mother and had made a commitment to work on problems in her family and was more realistic regarding her relationship with her boyfriend. Follow-up 1 year later indicated continued maturation with good adjustment at home, in school, and in her continued relationship with her boyfriend.

COGNITIVE/BEHAVIORAL TREATMENT

Cognitive/behavioral approaches to treatment of children of divorce are aimed at helping children develop a more realistic appraisal of their own situation while modifying behaviors that contribute to maladaptive responses to that situation. Based on the presumption that a change in cognitions and altered behavior will be followed by a change in feelings, this approach seeks to help children modify maladaptive irrational beliefs that contribute to negative feelings. Although cognitive approaches have not been used widely with this population in the past, Kurdek (1987) suggests that they can be blended with behavioral modalities to help children deal with problem identification and examine the "cause of feelings," learn "effective problem solving and communication," as well as develop "anger resolution skills." Cognitive-behavioral techniques are well adapted to short-term treatment plans and can be useful in conjunction with other modalities, such as family therapy.

In conclusion, individual psychodynamically oriented treatment has been the treatment of choice for children and adolescents who continue to experience psychiatric symptoms related to developmental inhibition some years after divorce. Family therapy and supportive psychotherapy may be appropriate during the crisis following separation and during the post-divorce adjustment phase. Cognitive-behavioral modalities may be best used when short-term intervention is planned. Finally, it should be noted that supportive group therapy for parents has long been helpful to parents and that community resources such as "Parents Without Partners" can provide a valuable adjunct to child treatment.

CONCLUSIONS

Studies suggest that while most children eventually adjust to their parents' divorce, a significant minority continue to experience symptoms related to unresolved divorce conflicts that inhibit normal development. Children's understanding of divorce, their emotional and behavioral responses to their parents' separation and divorce as well as long-term sequelae experienced can best be explained in developmental terms. Developmental stages are associated with different constellations of behavior and emotional concerns. Factors that contribute to increased vulnerability include poverty, parental psychopathology, poor pre-divorce adjustment, multiple family changes, post-divorce conflict between parents, and emotional-physical absence of the noncustodial parent. Similarly, factors associated with good prognosis include adequate financial resources, good pre-divorce adjustment, minimal post-divorce family change, continued involvement with both parents, and availability of extrafamiliar support systems. The impact of divorce on presenting symptomatology should be assessed during the evaluation of any child with a history of divorce. Psychotherapy is recommended for those patients who need to work through the "psychological tasks" related to divorce in order to resume normal development.

References

Ahrons, C.R., and Rodgers, R.H. 1987. *Divorced Families.* New York: W.W. Norton & Co.

American Psychiatric Association. 1987. Diagnostic and Statistical Manual of Mental Disorders, 3rd. ed., revised. Washington, D.C.: American Psychiatric Association.

Chethik, M., and Kalter, N. 1980. Developmental Arrest Following Divorce: The Role of Therapist as Developmental Facilitator. *J. Am. Acad. Child Psychiatry* 2:281–289.

Gardner, R. 1976. *Psychotherapy with Children of Divorce.* New York: Jason Aronson.

Guidubaldi, J., and Perry, J.D. 1985. Divorce and mental health sequence for children: A two-year follow-up of a nationwide sample. *J. Child Psychiatry* 24:531–537.

Hagen, J.L. 1987. Proceed with caution: Advocating joint custody. *Social Work,* January-February, 26–30.

Hetherington, E.M., et al. 1985. Long-term effects of divorce and remarriage on the adjustment of children. *J. Child Psychiatry* 24:518–530.

Johnston, J.R., et al. 1985. Latency children in post-separation and divorce disputes. *J. Am. Acad. Child Psychiatry* 24:563–574.

Kalter, N., et al. 1985. Implications of parental divorce for female development. *J. Am. Acad. Child Psychiatry* 24:538–544.

Kalter, N. 1987. Long-term effects of divorce on children: A developmental vulnerability model. *Am. J. Orthopsychiatry* 57:587–599.

Kalter, N., and Rembar, J. 1981. The significance of a child's age at the time of parental divorce. *Am. J. Orthopsychiatry* 51:85–100.

Kurdek, L.A. 1986. Children's reasoning about parental divorce. In Ashmore, J.R.D., and Brodzinsky, P.M. (eds.): *Thinking About the Family: Views of Parents and Children.* 233–276.

Mendell, A.E. 1983. Play therapy with children of divorced parents. In Schaefer, C.E., and O'Conner, K.J. (eds.): *Handbook of Play Therapy.* New York: John Wiley & Sons, 312–354.

NBC White Paper. Jane Pauley, *Divorce is Changing America,* May 3, 1986.

Neal, J.H. 1983. Children's understanding of their parents' divorce. In Kurdek, L.A. (ed.): New Directions for Child Development, vol. 19. *Children and Divorce.* San Francisco: Jossey Bass, 3–14.

Nichols, W.C. 1985. Family Therapy with children of divorce. In Sprenkle, D. (ed.): *Divorce Therapy.* New York: Haworth Press, 55–68.

Radin, R. 1985. The role of the father in cognitive, academic, and intellectual development. In Lamb, M. (ed.): *The Role of the Father in Child Development,* New York: John Wiley & Sons, 237–276.

Shiller, V.M. 1986. Joint versus maternal custody for families with latency age boys: Parent characteristics and child adjustment. *Am. J. Orthopsychiatry* 486–489.

Steinman, S. 1981. The experience of children in a joint-custody arrangement: A report of a study. *Am. J. Orthopsychiatry* 51:403–414.

Wallerstein, J.S. 1985. Children of divorce: Preliminary report of a ten-year follow-up of older children and adolescents. 24:545–553.

Wallerstein, J.S., and Kelly, J.B. 1980. *Surviving the Breakup.* New York: Basic Books.

Wallerstein, Judith. 1984. Children of divorce: The psychological tasks of the child. *Am. J. Orthopsychiatry* 54: 444–458.

24

The Medical Basis for Nutrition and Behavior

DANIEL J. RAITEN, Ph.D.

Historically there are two major eras in the evolution of the field of nutrition (Guthrie 1986). The first era, often called the chemical-analytical era, was known for the discovery and chemical characterization of the major essential nutrients and their respective roles within biological systems. This was closely followed by investigations of those clinical events associated with a deficiency of a given nutrient. Once nutritionists discovered the cause and treatment of the classic deficiency syndromes (i.e., scurvy and beriberi), they then began to turn their energies toward the establishment of dietary standards that, once implemented, would provide safeguards for the largest percentage of the population. The creation of the recommended daily allowances (RDAs) and extensive educational efforts constitute the second major era in the maturation of the nutrition field. These latter efforts, along with a diversified and readily accessible food supply, have largely eliminated the classic deficiencies in most of the industrialized world.

While the efforts of those involved in these earlier eras continue (as reflected by the periodic process of revising the RDAs), there is a new era evolving, the examination of the functional impact of nutrition on the individual. Nutrition is defined as the sum total of the processes involved in the taking in and utilization of food substances by which growth, repair, and maintenance of activities in the body as a whole or in any of its parts are accomplished. Within this context, func-tionality refers to the impact that nutritional status, as reflective of the processes of nutrition and dietary adequacy, has on a person's ability to perform the normal functions of life to an optimal level. In 1977, the National Academy of Sciences ushered in this new era with its identification of five areas of functionality that can be affected by nutrition: (1) disease response (immunity), (2) reproductive competence, (3) physical activity/work performance, (4) social-behavioral performance, and (5) cognition.

The questions facing clinicians and researchers are how does the interaction between nutrition and function occur, what are the causes, and how are they identified? To those of us involved in the study and treatment of childhood psychopathology, of paramount concern is how these questions may be applied to the last three areas of functionality associated with behavior and cognition delineated by the National Academy of Sciences. There are several ways in which nutrition is associated phenomenologically with behavioral or neurologic disorders: etiologically, through modulations in behavior via the aggravation of preexisting biochemical problems, or through modulations in behavior as a result of fluctuations in the intake of specific nutrients. In our zeal to address these issues we must not lose sight of nutrition in the larger sense, as an integral component in the normal growth and development of children. The role of clinical nutrition in the chronic care of developmentally disabled

410

children has been addressed (Raiten 1987). The concern here is to describe what is known about how nutrition can effect behavior and to review some of the work examining the role of nutrition in childhood psychopathology.

It is important to view the impact of nutrition on behavior as one aspect in a sociopsychological milieu. As shown in Figure 24–1, there are a myriad of interacting features in the child's environment that have an impact on his or her behavior. The focus will be on those elements within the context of the "medical model" that can interact and affect behavior. Table 24–1 is a general list of those mechanisms by which nutrition and/or dietary components may affect behavior and cognition and will serve as an outline for the rest of this chapter.

NUTRITION AND DEVELOPMENT

There is a vast body of research that contributes to our understanding of the role of adequate nutrition in neurologic development and behavior (Winick 1979). Situations such as suboptimal nutrient intake during the periods of gestation or lactation have been shown to influence central nervous system (CNS) development in terms of anatomical and neurophysiological integrity. Changes in either brain size or organizational features, such as synaptic formation and orientation, have been reported to result from prenatal and postnatal undernutrition. Are these changes associated with functional "brain damage"? Do these anomalies have long-term implications for behavior and cognition? These questions form the basis for a continuing debate about the role of nutrition in development.

The use of animal models has provided much of the useful information regarding the impact of undernutrition on the growth and development of the CNS. For example, Jones and Dyson (1981) observed changes in the morphologic or structural development of postsynaptic terminals in both the offspring of protein-deprived rats and in perinatal rats fed a deficient diet. While there were major compensatory gains after nutritional rehabilitation, significant differences in brain weights and other structural features remained.

Delaney and co-workers (1981) have shown that young undernourished rats have reduced synthesis of the lipid myelin, which surrounds motor nerve fibers and is essential for the rapid transmission of motor impulses. These authors found that the defect was apparently not mediated by a reduction in the number of myelin-producing oligodendrocytes, but rather by a failure of these specialized cells to function normally. Since the period of rapid myelination occurs late in the development of the CNS (Wiggins 1982), it is not surprising that the effects seen in the Delaney study occurred in postnatal rats. Consistent with these findings in animals is the suspicion expressed by Bartel and co-workers (1986) that their finding of abnormal brain-stem auditory evoked response (BAER) in malnourished infants was reflective of a defect in the myelination of the auditory pathways.

Nutrition and Neurochemistry

Aside from the processes of myelination, another way nutrition can have an impact on the ontogeny of CNS metabolism is through its role in neurochemistry. In addition to their structural components, each neuronal system is identified with a specific transmitter, a chemical messenger responsible for the initiation of communication and eventual propagation of the electrical signal from one neuron to another. There are an estimated 30 to 40 of these transmitters (Anderson 1981), described as low-molecular-weight substances that are amino acids (e.g., γ-aminobutyric acid, glycine, histidine, or taurine) or amine derivatives of amino acids (e.g., dopamine, norepinephrine, serotonin, or acetylcholine). The amount and availability of these neurotransmitters are inherently and undeniably linked to the nutritional status of the organism. Anything that can influence absorption and transport of their dietary precursors or the biosynthetic machinery required for their production can influence neurotransmitter availability and viability.

Dietary precursors are those substances that serve as the basic units for the eventual synthesis of the neurotransmitter. Examples of precursors include tyrosine, which is the parent component for the catecholamines (dopamine, norepinephrine, and epinephrine), and tryptophan, which is the core component of serotonin. Because they are

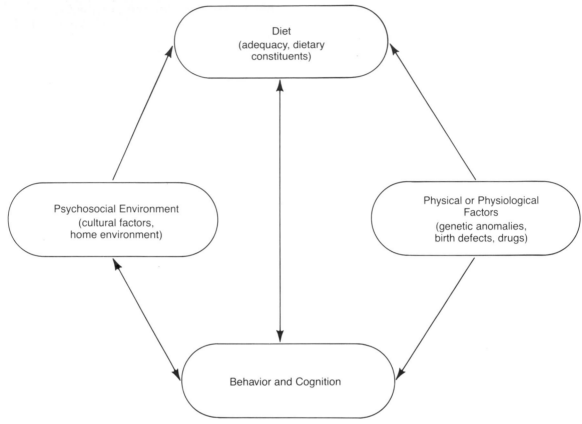

Figure 24–1. Factors affecting behavior and cognition.

essential nutrients, both tyrosine via its dietary precursor phenylalanine and tryptophan must be supplied through the diet as amino acid constituents of protein. The rate of synthesis and the availability of these derivative neurotransmitters are dependent on the availability of their dietary precursors. Animal studies have shown that brain levels of serotonin (Fernstrom and Wurtman 1971), acetylcholine (Cohen and Wurtman 1976), and the catecholamines (Wurtman et al. 1974) can be altered or raised with dietary supplementation.

There are many elements that influence both the accessibility of these precursors to the brain and their eventual conversion into neurotransmitters. For instance, the availability of circulating compounds to the brain is subject to a finely controlled selective filtering system known as the blood–brain barrier (Spector 1977). Circulating substances encountering this barrier may pass through depending on their size, the concentration gradient on either side of the barrier, or the nature of the specific transport mechanism required for a given compound. The precursors for serotonin and the catecholamines, tryptophan and phenylalanine, compete for a blood–brain barrier transport system with several other amino acids: tyrosine, valine, leucine, and isoleucine. Collectively these

Table 24–1. MECHANISMS BY WHICH NUTRITIONAL FACTORS AFFECT BEHAVIOR AND COGNITION

I. Dietary Adequacy
   A. Prenatal effects of nutritional insults
   B. Postnatal effects of nutritional insults
   C. Nutrition and neurochemistry
   D. Genetically mediated inborn errors of metabolism
II. Food Reactions
   A. Reactions to normal dietary constituents
     1. Sugar
     2. Aspartame
   B. Toxicologic reactions to dietary constituents
     1. Food additives
     2. Lead
   C. Food allergies

amino acids are known as large neutral amino acids. The ratio between any one of the precursors and the other large neutral amino acids will dictate how much will enter the brain.

There are several things that can influence this ratio, including dietary imbalance and the ratio of protein to carbohydrate in the diet (Fernstrom 1981). In the case of tryptophan, a high-carbohydrate, low-protein meal will result in increased insulin, which in turn will clear the blood of the other large neutral amino acids thus creating a favorable ratio for tryptophan's subsequent entry across the blood–brain barrier and eventual increase in brain serotonin levels. Similar relationships hold for other precursors (Fernstrom 1981). While these relationships have been defined under ideal circumstances (with animal models, and specifically defined acute dietary challenges), a definitive connection between these descriptive studies and functional changes has not been established.

Wurtman and colleagues (1981) noted that while dietary supplementation with tyrosine can result in increased tyrosine concentrations in the brain, norepinephrine levels increased only when their dependent neurons were active, for example during stress. Reinstein and associates (1985) found that prior tyrosine administration eliminated not only the depletion of norepinephrine but also the accompanying behavioral depression in acutely stressed rats. On the other hand, Trulson (1985) found that while he was able to produce significant changes in brain serotonin content with dietary manipulation of the precursor tryptophan, he found no evidence of any functional changes in the animals studied. An additional question confronting this precursor hypothesis is the differential responses in acutely versus chronically fed animals to changes in protein-carbohydrate ratios (Peters and Harper 1984). While many questions remain about the precursor model, it nevertheless offers, for the first time, evidence that specific nutrients can directly alter the chemistry of the brain.

Another way that nutrition may impact on neurotransmission is via the conversion of metabolic substrate or dietary precursors into neurotransmitters. The conversion of substrate to end product in any biological system is dependent on genetics and environmental influences. The production of neurotransmitters involves a multicomponent system that consists of substrates which are usually amino acids like tyrosine or tryptophan, enzymes, and coenzymes. This process occurs in a sequential manner, with each step requiring a specific enzyme. Each enzyme consists of a genetically coded protein portion called the apoenzyme. The apoenzyme is activated by a cofactor, which is usually a vitamin such as vitamin B_6 (pyridoxine) or vitamin B_2 (riboflavin), or a trace mineral such as iron, zinc, or magnesium. The protein cofactor combines with the cofactor or coenzyme to form the functional holoenzyme. The actual function of the coenzyme may be structural, changing the configuration of the enzyme to its biologically active shape, or the cofactor may actively interact with the substrate in the reaction process. The relationship between specific cofactors and enzyme systems involved in the biosynthesis of neurotransmitters is shown in Figure 24–2. A partial list of some of the neurologic and behavioral effects associated with vitamin deficiencies is given in Table 24–2. Several studies have shown a connection between vitamin and trace mineral status in developmentally disabled children (Thatcher and Lester 1985; Raiten et al. 1984; Massaro et al. 1983; Capel et al. 1981). Unfortunately, there have been no valid attempts at discerning the functional relevance of these findings or investigating the effects of nutritional intervention.

Changes in the availability of these cofactors may occur as a result of insufficient or irregular dietary intake, a physical problem such as a malabsorption syndrome, a genetic error in metabolism, or iatrogenically as in the case of a drug–nutrient interaction (Raiten 1987). Neurophysiological changes often accompany a frank nutritional deficiency, or they may be a consequence of a nutrient-responsive disorder. Examples of the former and the nutrients involved include the neuropathies associated with pellagra (niacin, pyridoxine, and riboflavin), beriberi or Wernicke-Korsakoff syndrome (thiamine), and scurvy (vitamin C). In the case of a vitamin-dependency syndrome, a person may not show direct biochemical signs of a nutrient deficiency even though he or she may respond to large doses of the nutrient involved, as in the case of vitamin B_6–dependent seizures in infants. In this case the defect is in a vitamin B_6–dependent enzyme involved with the production of γ-aminobutyric acid,

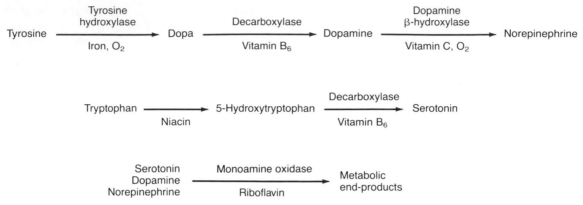

Figure 24–2. *Representation of the role of nutrients in neurochemistry.*

the major inhibitory neurotransmitter. Measurement of the usual parameters associated with vitamin B_6 status (e.g., plasma pyridoxal 5'phosphate) would not reveal this problem.

The major class of nutrient-responsive dis-

orders are the genetic inborn errors of metabolism. Although there are several types of these disorders that differ in their particular biochemical manifestations, they are all characterized by several common features; they

Table 24–2. NEUROLOGIC AND BEHAVIORAL EFFECTS OF SOME VITAMIN DEFICIENCIES

Vitamin	Neurologic	Behavioral
Thiamine (B_1)	Wernicke's encephalopathy, peripheral neuropathy, polyneuritis	Mental depression, apathy, anxiety, irritability, Korsakoff's psychosis
Riboflavin (B_2)	Electroencephalographic abnormalities, peripheral neuropathy	Depression, anxiety, personality disorders
Niacin, nicotinic acid, niacinamide (B_3)	Neurologic degeneration; tremor; spasticity; loss of position sense; exaggerated tendon reflexes; progressive paralysis of lips, tongue, mouth, pharynx, and larynx; abnormally increased skin sensitivity; abnormal sensations such as burning or prickling	Apathy, anxiety, mania, hyperirritability, memory deficits, delirium, organic dementia, emotional lability
Pyridoxine, pyridoxal, pyridoxamine (B_6)	Lack of muscle coordination, convulsions, electroencephalographic changes, hyperacousia, altered amino acid and catecholamine levels, changes in central stimulus conduction, decreased dendritic branching	Depression, nervous irritability
Pantothenic acid	Neuritis, lack of motor coordination, staggering gait, numbness, paresthesia	Restlessness, fatigue, irritability, depression
Biotin	Abnormally increased skin sensitivity	Depression, extreme lassitude, somnolence
Cyanocobalamin (B_{12})	Diminished vibratory and position sense, abnormal electroencephalogram, motor weakness, myelopathy associated with impaired myelin peripheral neuropathy	Mania, organic psychosis, irritability, depression, confusion, paranoia, delusions, memory loss, hallucinations
Folic acid, folacin, pteroylglutamic acid	No central nervous system symptoms reported after second year of life; in infants: mental retardation, lack of muscle coordination, continuing writhing movements	Forgetfulness, apathy, insomnia, irritability, depression, psychosis, delirium, dementia
Vitamin C (ascorbic acid)	Impaired nerve transmission	Lassitude, personality changes such as those occurring in physically ill persons (e.g., hypochondriasis, depression, and hysteria)

(From Raiten, D. J. 1988. Nutrition and developmental disabilities: Clinical assessment. In Schopler, E., and Mesibov, G. B. [eds.]: Diagnosis and Assessment in Autism. New York: Plenum Press.)

are genetic in origin, they are usually caused by a problem in the absorption, transport, or metabolism of an essential metabolic substrate, and they are usually remediated with a nutritional intervention (Fernhoff 1982). Historically, these types of disorders have been well documented (Albright 1937; Hunt et al. 1954) and include pyridoxine-dependent seizures, thiamine-responsive maple syrup urine disease, and pyridoxine- and vitamin B_{12}–responsive forms of homocysteinuria.

The mechanisms for the abnormal brain development in these or any of the other types of inborn errors of metabolism such as phenylketonuria appear to be multifactorial, with possible causes including toxic reactions to metabolites arising from incomplete or impaired precursor metabolism. In phenylketonuria it may be the combination of elevated phenylalanine levels and the toxic by-products of an otherwise little-used pathway of phenylalanine metabolism. An important feature of these disorders is the timing of the insult. If these conditions are diagnosed and treated early enough, then a relatively normal course can ensue; however, if they are undiagnosed, the damage to the developing nervous system is severe and irreversible.

Nutrition and the Critical Period Hypothesis

The kind and extent of the damage to the nervous system may depend to a large degree on the stage of development of the young animal. Within this context, one must be aware of the presumed critical periods in the development of the nervous system when the developing animal is most susceptible to environmental insults. In the human, nutritional insults during early or late gestation or during early postnatal development can result in changes in the cell number and cell size, whereas insults occurring 2 to 4 years postnatally may result in changes in dendritic branching and synaptic formation (Read 1982).

The three periods, early gestation, late gestation, and postnatal, coincide with the three critical periods of growth in the rat described by Winick (1975). In the first period there are increases in the number of cells as reflected quantitatively by increases in DNA. Both cell size (hypertrophy) and number (hyperplasia)

increase during the second phase. In the third stage there is only an increase in hypertrophic cell growth that occurs at roughly 65 to 86 days postnatally in the rat. Winick (1975) demonstrated the relative impact of malnutrition during these three periods when he found that rats malnourished during the first hyperplastic phase and subsequently rehabilitated had a decreased number of cells. Even after refeeding, the number of cells remained lower. A second group of rats malnourished during phase two of development also had a reduced number of cells in all organs except the brain and the lungs, which had reached their full complement of cells prior to the initiation of the experiment. However, there was a reduction in the size of both the brain cells and the lung cells before refeeding. After refeeding, the brain cells and lung cells recovered to normal size. In the final group, the number of cells was normal before the start of the experiment, but the nutritional stress resulted in an eventual reduction in the size of the cells. Refeeding in these animals resulted in a compensatory recovery to normal size of all cells. The study by Jones and Dyson (1981) also included a group of rats fed adequately and then placed on an inadequate diet at day 75 post partum, coinciding with Winick's third phase of development. These animals had alterations in brain weight, consistent with Winick's earlier study (Winick 1975), suggesting that even in an animal whose development has been normal, the imposition of a deficient diet during a critical period in growth can cause structural changes.

As a logical correlate to the critical period paradigm, it follows that an animal malnourished during any of these phases without rehabilitation would not have the plasticity or compensatory potential to withstand further insults to its developing nervous system. In other words, the insult would predispose the animal to the effects of further insults. In the human, changes associated with insults during the first period might include those resulting in structural or "hard wiring" problems seen in the severely brain-damaged child.

Househam and De Villiers (1987) found cerebral atrophy in computed tomographic scans of children with severe protein–calorie malnutrition. Stoch and colleagues (1982) reported that infants who were severely malnourished in infancy had significantly smaller head circumference, deficits in visuomotor integration, and a higher incidence of abnormal computed tomograms indicative of organic brain damage when compared with matched controls. Similarly, Nelson (1959) described abnormal electroencephalograms in severely malnourished infants that continued even after rehabilitation. Likewise, Barnet and associates (1978) found disturbances in auditory reception as indicated by changes in brain-stem auditory evoked potentials (BAEP), which measure the latency of the response to sound stimuli and reflect the ability of appropriate areas of the brain to communicate with each other. More recently, Bartel and co-workers (1986) found unilateral abnormalities in BAEP in malnourished infants that deteriorated even after 3 weeks of treatment.

Insults in the latter stages of CNS development, which are more likely to occur in lactationally dependent mammals such as humans, have been associated with such structural and spatial aberrations as decreased synaptic formation (Dobbing and Sands 1973) or decreased dendritic branching (Read 1982) seen in undernourished infants. The implication is that changes in the structures or morphology of the brain that occur during critical periods of development will have functional ramifications (i.e., changes) perhaps irreversible, in behavioral or cognitive development. Consistent with this theory are the suggestions of Thatcher and associates (1986), who linked physical evidence with psychological theory by stating that hemispheric lateralization may occur in stages such that there are critical periods in this process that coincide with the developmental stages in behavior and cognitive skills described by Piaget (1971).

There are no studies that have made a definitive link between functional changes consequent to nutritional insults and the presumed critical periods of brain growth and development in humans. Moreover, there is evidence to suggest that the developing brain can compensate for transient insults. Freed and associates (1985) reviewed the evidence to support the concept of plasticity after neuronal injury. In addition, as suggested by Winick (1976), there may be a sufficient excess of neurons to allow for loss without permanent functional change. In discussing his reservations about the emphasis on cell size and number, Dobbing (1984), noted that there may be no association between intellect

and cell number or size. While the possibility that losses in cell number or size may have no functional ramifications, depending on the location of the losses, it is equally possible that there may be yet unidentified functionally significant areas of the brain that have differing vulnerabilities to nutritional problems. Similarly, such organizational or "fine wiring" changes as decreased dendritic arborization or symptogenesis may be associated with yet undefined changes in behavior and cognition.

Advocates of the critical period theory linking physical development to functional changes cite the example of the acquisition of language skills as one domain that is developmentally susceptible to insults. One case that is often cited is "Genie," an example of a "wild child." Genie was isolated in an unlit room, deprived of essentially any social interaction, and severely malnourished from the age of 20 months until her discovery at the age of 12 years. Nutritional rehabilitation and intensive special education produced only marginal language or social skills (Pines 1981).

The example of Genie raises several interesting questions regarding not only the concept of nutritional insults during critical periods but also their potential interaction with environmental insults such as isolation. A literal interpretation of the animal studies discussed previously would seem to support the notion that malnutrition during early development produces anatomical-physiological changes that are responsible for the deficits in an animal's ability to interact or function within its environment. Studies such as those in which primates were shown to have not only behavioral problems but also concurrent morphologic changes when raised in isolation provide evidence for a lesion associated with environmental stress (Heath 1972; Floeter and Greenough 1979).

One theory that melds the ideas of plasticity with the early insult paradigm was proposed by Levitsky and co-workers (1979). These authors suggested that it is not the physical changes but rather the adaptation to the stress of the malnutrition that in effect limits the young animal's inclination to interact with its environment, thus isolating it for intents and purposes from that environment. This "functional isolation" paradigm evolved as a result of a series of experiments that showed a generalized effect best described as a decrease in exploratory behavior in nutritionally deprived animals (Frankova and Barnes 1968; Massaro et al. 1974; Massaro et al. 1977b; Gallo 1982). This limited interaction may be explained eventually in terms of energy conservation or selective survival behaviors. A neurochemical correlate of this theory by Lehnert and colleagues (1984) demonstrated an amelioration of the stress-induced depletion of norepinephrine and consequent decrease in exploratory behavior in rats supplemented with tyrosine. Perhaps it is the combination of malnutrition and stress that results in alterations in neurotransmitters that is responsible in part for the functional isolation phenomena. Irrespective of the eventual explanation, the consequences of this decreased interaction with the surrounding environment are limitations in the malnourished animal's exposure to different experiences, and an eventual inability to cope with novel experiences, the so-called neophobic response (Zimmerman et al. 1975). As a result, the animal lacks the early experiential opportunities necessary to develop normal behavioral and cognitive strategies.

Many questions remain about the impact of nutritional insults on functional outcomes. For example, does the insult cause irreversible structural or metabolic damage associated with either short-term or long-term problems or is the damage the result of a synergism between nutrition and either another environmental (e.g., socioeconomic status) or endogenous factor (e.g., a defect in neurotransmitter metabolism such as that associated with attention-deficit hyperactivity disorder [ADHD])? Equally important is the issue of irreversibility as it pertains to the timing of the insult. If there is damage of any kind, is it irreversible, and if it is, does that mean there will be no long-term problems? If Levitsky is correct, there may be problems whether the damage is irreversible or not if it occurs during a period of development that is essential for the acquisition of skills needed for future cognitive and behavioral growth.

Questions about the relationship between structure and function are essential to our understanding of nutrition and development and ultimately our capacity to influence the outcome in malnourished children. Whether the insult's effects are primarily the result of structural or metabolic changes or are secondary to the behavioral adaptation or environmental influences, there is no doubt that adequate nutrition is essential to healthy development.

Applications of Theory—Treatments

Clearly, specific nutrients play essential roles in the structure and integrity of the CNS as proven by the neurologic complications of both the classic deficiency diseases and the inborn errors of metabolism and by laboratory studies of individual nutrients. However, even though the manifestations of deficiencies of many vitamins have been well documented, the exact mechanism or specific roles, if any, that these nutrients may play in specific disorders such as specific learning disabilities, mental retardation or in pervasive developmental disabilities such as autism have yet to be determined. Moreover, the previous examples of the essentiality of nutrition to CNS function and development should not be construed to imply a direct cause-and-effect relationship between deficiency of any specific nutrient and mental disease. Any blanket recommendations regarding large doses of either vitamins or any other nutrients is, at this time, ill advised and should be tempered by reports of toxicity from nutrients such as the water-soluble B vitamins previously presumed to be innocuous (Evans and Lacey 1986; Miller and Hayes 1982).

The following case is an example of the potential harm of "megavitamin" therapy.

At the time of the initial consult Timothy was an 18-year-old autistic boy in his ninth year living in a full-time residential care facility. During the course of a clinical rounds attended by pediatricians, psychiatrist, and residential personnel, the residential nurse noted that Timothy had been having episodes of skin "flushing" and hyperirritability. Since this was a boy with a severe behavioral-neurologic disorder the focus of the discussion was on appropriate treatment modalities within the accepted model (i.e., behavioral modification and/or psychopharmacology). When asked if anything had changed in Timothy's environment that might have initiated these changes, the nurse said "no" but wondered if it could have anything to do with his vitamins.

It turned out that before coming to the residential program, Timothy's parents took him to a well-known advocate of megavitamin or "orthomolecular" therapy who, without the benefit of any apparent biochemical or dietary assessments, started Timothy on a vitamin program. This daily program consisted of 500 mg of niacin, 500 mg of pyridoxine, 500 mg of vitamin B_{15} (also known as pangamic acid, a substance that has no known biological value and that has as a core component dichloroacetate, a hepatotoxin), and 2000 mg of vitamin C. The RDAs for an 18-year-old male for niacin, vitamin B_6 and vitamin C are 18 mg, 2.0 mg, and 60 mg, respectively. Timothy had taken this regimen for 9 years without any questions by anyone regarding its safety or utility. A review of his recent routine blood analyses revealed that Timothy had elevated liver enzyme levels indicative of possible early signs of damage. No one, including the psychiatrist and pediatricians in charge of Timothy's care, had ever thought to ask about these vitamins even in the face of evidence suggesting potential liver damage. Timothy was eventually slowly weaned off of the vitamins and the somatic problems subsided.

There is increasing evidence that the water-soluble vitamins can be toxic. Aside from the toxicity, this case points out two major issues. First, the prescription of these vitamins was done without any evidence of either dietary deficiency or biochemical anomaly that would suggest such a clinical course. Furthermore, the individual who prescribed the vitamins, who is highly visible in the lay community because of his many books, journal articles, and very successful practice based on this use of megavitamins, never followed up with this patient after the initial consultation. Second, the caregivers charged with the health of this boy, who although autistic was otherwise normal, were derelict in their responsibility by paying absolutely no attention to matters other than those directly related to the disability.

Besides toxicity, one should be aware that nutrients such as the large neutral amino acids and vitamins interact within biological systems so that by creating a possible imbalance with oversupplementation, one may seriously interfere with basic metabolic processes. Finally, as noted with the amino acid precursors, vitamins are also subject to many of the same or similar controls that limit their availability to the brain (i.e., gastrointestinal absorption, transport mechanisms, peripheral metabolism, the blood–brain barrier, and interactions with other nutrients). Thus, the promotion of nutritional interventions such as megavitamin or orthomolecular therapy (Pauling 1969) should be viewed with skep-

ticism in the absence of any concrete evidence of their efficacy in the treatment of childhood psychopathology (Raiten and Massaro 1987).

Malnutrition and Development: Human Studies

Malnutrition has long been assumed to be associated with impairments in cognitive development and performance in humans (Cravioto and DeLicardie 1970). Some of the best efforts at addressing the relationship between CNS changes associated with malnutrition and function have been those studies that have examined the effects of environmental manipulations on previously malnourished subjects. Several animal studies have shown a reversal in those behavioral deficits that may have occurred as a result of malnutrition (Barnes et al. 1975; Massaro et al. 1977a). Moreover Crnic (1983) found that environmental enrichment resulted in a reversal of the behavioral manifestations of malnutrition while having no effect on the changes in brain structure.

Unlike the animal model, the study of the effects of malnutrition in the human is problematic in that it is exceedingly difficult to control for the confounding effects of other factors that may interact with the dependent variable. Malnutrition often occurs within an ecologic milieu consisting of several elements, all of which can in some way contribute to a depression in cognitive-behavioral performance. It is, therefore, difficult to attribute specific effects solely to nutritional insults that may have occurred to infants or children during the so-called critical periods of development. Time also becomes an issue when one considers that the identification of developmental problems such as poor attention or learning difficulties may not occur until many years after the insult. As a result, the nutritional insult has been far removed and its influence compounded by other features within the child's experience. Other methodologic issues such as the sensitivity of nutritional assessment techniques and the use of global measures of cognitive ability (e.g., IQ) have prevented us from making any definitive associations between diet and development. Despite these formidable obstacles there have been several concerted efforts to glean some useful information about the interactions of nutrition and environment on intelligence and behavior in children.

Prenatal Nutrition

The most well-recognized examination of the effects of prenatal malnutrition on humans was the study of the effects of the Netherlands famine (Smith 1947). Here, wartime shortages placed severe restrictions on the availability of food for roughly 2 years. Children from malnourished mothers were studied and found to have reduced birth weight, length, and head circumference. The effects of malnutrition were greatest in children exposed during the third trimester of gestation. In 19-year-old boys exposed to malnutrition in utero there were no apparent detriments in cognitive ability. The interpretation of these results is tempered by the lack of sensitive measures of neurophysiology. This study was unique in that the independent variable, malnutrition, occurred in an otherwise healthy, enriched environment and it occurred over a brief time without extending into the postnatal period in those subjects studied.

The small-for-gestational-age (SGA) infant is another example of the potential impact of prenatal malnutrition on development. In the absence of other possible causes (e.g., drug use, smoking, alcohol use, or infection), malnutrition is assumed to be a primary cause of SGA infants. Crane and Kopta (1979) noted reduced anthropometric indices of length, weight, and head circumference when compared with appropriate-for-gestational-age (AGA) infants. Sann and associates (1986) found a higher percentage of short stature and reduced head circumference in SGA as compared with AGA infants. They also found that growth outcome at 5 years in SGA infants was significantly correlated with perinatal factors. Calame and co-workers (1986) found a significantly higher incidence of neurodevelopmental abnormalities in their SGA group. The SGA group also had a higher incidence of school failure than the AGA group. Unfortunately, none of these studies specifically focused on nutrition as an etiologic variable and as is often the case with longitudinal studies there were many uncontrolled factors that could have influenced the dependent variables.

Premature infants as a general group, of which SGA infants are but one segment, are at high risk for the development of neurologic problems (Fuller et al. 1983). Premature infants are also at risk for deficiencies of several nutrients because of the interruption of normal intrauterine accretion. In addition, the severe medical problems associated with prematurity, the immaturity of the bowel, and developmental lags in the absorptive and enzymatic capacity for nutrient utilization further compromise these infants by the prohibition of enteral feeding and necessitate the use of intravenous or total parenteral nutrition for the very low birth weight infant (Hay 1986). Studies have shown that very low birth weight infants receiving total parenteral nutrition may be at risk for deficiencies of several essential nutrients (Raiten et al. 1987; Lucas and Bates 1984). The functional relevance of these deficiencies has yet to be determined.

Postnatal Nutrition

The ability of environmental stimulation to overcome the effects of postnatal malnutrition in children was investigated by Winick (1976). In this study Korean children who had suffered severe malnutrition unbeknown to their adoptive parents, performed equal to or better than non-Korean control children. The authors concluded that it was the enriched environment of their adoptive homes that had overcome the effects of the malnutrition. This interpretation has been challenged by the studies of Grantham-McGregor and co-workers (1983), who found that while psychosocial stimulation improved developmental outcomes of previously malnourished children, they remained behind normal controls in locomotor development. In a series of studies Galler and colleagues (1984, 1986) found that while early malnutrition was clearly related to poorer cognitive and behavioral outcomes, it probably did so in synergy with other environmental factors. Cravioto and Arrieta (1986) have addressed those issues and obstacles related to our present knowledge and the future investigation of the relationships between nutrition and development.

BEHAVIORAL EFFECTS OF NORMAL DIETARY CONSTITUENTS

The emphasis of the preceding discussion has been on questions directed at the potential long-term consequences of dietary inadequacy. Another way by which nutrition may affect behavior is via a toxicologic influence of dietary components on those systems involved in behavior. Hathcock (1982) defined nutritional toxicology as the study of the interaction between toxic agents in the food system and the various processes of nutrition and health. He included the following in his list of potential toxins: amino acids, vitamins and minerals, food additives such as preservatives, food colorings and dyes, and artificial sweeteners. A subspeciality of this field that is of specific interest to those of us concerned with childhood psychopathology is behavioral teratology. As defined by Hutchings (1983), this is the study of the neurobehavioral effects of exposure to environmental toxins.

Food Additives and Food Allergies

There is considerable controversy surrounding the impact of dietary constituents, such as natural and synthetic sweeteners and food additives, in the various childhood psychopathologies, particularly ADHD. The question of whether these substances can affect behavior has two primary components, the acute response to a "challenge" and the chronic effects of habitually high consumption.

Dr. Benjamin Feingold, an allergist by training, originally proposed that naturally occurring salicylates and artificial food colorings and additives were to a large extent responsible for some cases of learning disability and most cases of hyperactivity (Feingold 1975). This hypothesis stirred considerable debate, culminating in a report by the National Advisory Committee of the Nutrition Foundation (1980) that concluded that there was no need for further funding of this hypothesis. The basis for this finding was a series of selected studies that met certain design criteria established in an earlier report by this same committee (1975). A listing and brief discussion of these studies are provided in Table 24–3.

The problems with the Feingold hypothesis and the later studies it inspired have been discussed in great detail (Conners 1980; Weiss 1986). The research, although marred by methodologic flaws, clearly indicates a subgroup of children who are affected by food additives. Among the many obstacles

---

Table 24–3. STUDIES USED IN THE 1980 NATIONAL ADVISORY BOARD REPORT ON DIET AND HYPERKINESIS AND AN INTERPRETATION OF THE RESULTS

1. Harley et al. (1978): 36 school-aged males and 10 preschool-aged children; the Feingold diet was found superior based on parent ratings; significant improvement based on parent ratings for preschoolers
2. Conners et al. (1976): in a series of studies, a total of 68 primarily school-aged children. In the first study (n = 15), regular diet was compared with Feingold diet. Other studies used "responders" who were challenged. The first study found significant effect on parent ratings. The subsequent challenge studies produced "nonsignificant" differences.
3. Conners (1980): used nine definite responders and found possible dose–time effect, which they dismissed as a nonsignificant difference.
4. Swanson and Kinsbourne (1980): studied 40 children; used a larger challenge dose, 100 mg, than any other study; found significant impairment of paired associated learning.
5. Weiss et al. (1980): studied 22 children diagnosed as "behaviorally disturbing" to parents and teachers. Children were given a placebo or 36 mg/day challenge given 1 day per week for 8 weeks. Behavior was measured for 24 hours after the challenge. One child was found who consistently responded to challenge.
6. Mattes and Gittleman-Klein (1978): studied 14 school-aged children from the local Feingold association. One child has consistent response to challenge.
7. Williams et al. (1978): studied 26 children comparing Feingold diet with control diet and challenge versus medication. They found that the Feingold diet plus medication gave maximum results. The diet effect alone reached statistical significance, but there were inconsistent results between parent and teacher ratings.
8. Levy et al. (1978): studied 22 children and found significant diet effects. The challenge effects were nonsignificant. The study used FD & C yellow #5 (tartrazine). Differences were found between the challenge and the placebo in parent ratings of behavior.

(National Advisory Committee on Hyperkinesis and Food Additives. 1980. *Final Report to the Nutrition Foundation.* New York: Nutrition Foundation.)

---

to the understanding of this phenomenon, perhaps the most critical is the continued lack of a valid conceptualization about the mechanism by which food additives might affect behavior. The vast majority of the studies of food additives focused on the diet rather than the possibility that these substances may be causing a physiological change and how that change may occur in a given child. There have been suggestions supported by animal studies that these substances may interfere with neurotransmitter metabolism (Shaywitz et al. 1979; Kaplita and Triggle 1982). Neurophysiological changes as reflected by changes in electroencephalography in hyperactive children have also been reported (Salamy et al. 1982). Perhaps with the use of more sensitive measures, such as those suggested in the model proposed by Conners and Blouin (1982), the question of the effects of these substances could be reconceptualized and examined.

Another point of confusion in this area is the lack of a consistent terminology in the discussion of adverse reactions to foods (Anderson 1986). The distinction between a sensitivity and an allergy is rarely made, and the two terms are often used interchangeably. They are, however, quite different phenomena. This is more than a semantic issue, because it bears a heavy influence on both the identification of the problem and the treatment. A food sensitivity may be broadly defined as a clinically abnormal reaction to a food or food additive, whereas a food allergy is an immunologic response.

Food allergies are generally associated with somatic complaints, including skin reactions, respiratory effects, gastrointestinal complications, and neurologic complaints (Sampson 1986). Conceivably, the behavioral manifestations of food allergies may occur as a direct effect of chemical changes in the brain or, more likely, as the secondary effect of somatic complaints. Crook (1975) outlined the possible sequence of events leading to behavioral problems associated with food allergies. There is considerable debate about the most appropriate diagnostic methods. Table 24–4 is a listing of some of the most commonly used methods for diagnosis of food allergies. The reliability of the available tests for food allergy and the differential diagnosis of adverse reactions to foods have been reviewed (Dockhorn 1984; Metcalfe 1984; Sampson 1986).

One issue of particular concern clinically is the use of an elimination diet in the treatment of both food sensitivities (e.g., the Feingold diet) and food allergies. While studies of the dietary adequacy of the Feingold diet showed it to be adequate (Harper et al. 1978), concerns about this practice in the treatment of food allergies have been expressed (David et al. 1984).

David was a 10-year-old boy who was referred by a school psychologist for a nutritional eval-

---

Table 24–4. DIAGNOSTIC TESTS FOR IMMUNOLOGICALLY MEDIATED FOOD SENSITIVITY

1. *Food Challenge:* In children younger than 5 to 6 years of age the challenge may be hidden in some tolerated food. Children older than 6 years old can receive a coded capsule containing a powdered form of the challenge. The challenge may also be administered in liquid form sublingually.
2. *Elimination Diet:* Care must be taken to ensure the nutritional adequacy of the diet after the suspected food(s) have been eliminated.
3. *Skin Tests:*
   a. Puncture test
   b. Scratch test
   c. Intradermal test
4. *Radioallergosorbent Test (RAST):* uses a serum sample for a radioimmunoassay designed to measure circulating levels of IgE antibody in response to specific allergen. The RAST is probably the most commonly used in vitro test.
5. *Cytotoxic Testing:* uses blood sample and measures reduction or destruction of white cells after exposure to a suspected allergen.
6. Other tests less commonly used:
   a. Enzyme-linked immunosorbent assay (ELISA)
   b. Basophil histamine release
   c. Leukocyte migration inhibition test
   d. Lymphoblastogenesis

---

uation. After having previously done well in school, his performance had begun to deteriorate. He often complained of tiredness and an inability to concentrate. He was evaluated and found to be of normal intelligence without any emotional problems (other than a developing anxiety about school) and without either a specific learning disability or attention-deficit disorder. During the course of the evaluation the psychologist found out that David had been diagnosed as having food allergies and placed on a special diet. At this point he was referred for a consultation to ascertain whether there was any way in which the food allergies could be causing his problems.

It turned out that he had been diagnosed as being allergic to eggs, milk, and wheat products. The diagnosis had been made by an allergist in the community, who subsequently placed David on a restricted diet. Unfortunately, while the diet eliminated all of the problem foods, neither David nor his parents were adequately counseled about making appropriate substitutions for these important sources of essential nutrients. Consequently, an examination of David's diet revealed a grossly deficient intake of many essential nutrients including several "B" vitamins (e.g., thiamine and riboflavin) and minerals such as zinc, calcium, and iron. David's blood studies revealed borderline anemia. He was subsequently started on therapy with a multivitamin/mineral supplement, and

Table 24–5. FLOW CHART OF DECISION MAKING

I. Initial Intake
   A. Family health history, individual health (drugs)
   B. Nutritional history—preferences, infant feeding, allergies/sensitivities, dietary restrictions
   C. Food frequency questionnaire, 24-hour dietary recall
   D. Clinical examination—Anthropometrics (growth history), height, weight, body composition (skinfold thickness, triceps and subscapular)

If indicated by anything in the initial history, proceed to II.

II. Further Assessment
   A. 3-Day diet records
   B. Clinical examination—specifically designed to reveal early stages of specific lesion (ex: visual acuity, presence of skin lesions, immunocompetence, neurologic examination). Biochemistry tests to be chosen are based on dietary information that may reveal potential deficiencies in specific nutrients.

If specific nutritional problems are revealed, proceed to III.

III. Intervention
   A. Supplementation with specific nutrient to be followed by:
   B. Clinical biochemical examination using same protocols as in II
   C. Continuous periodic follow-up, including effective education and counseling program and random urinalysis to document compliance

his parents were counseled about menu planning and appropriate food substitutions. He eventually returned to his previous level of performance and health.

This case is similar to the previously presented case study in several respects. Most important, the clinical diagnosis, in this instance food allergy, and the appropriate treatment were not followed. The point is that nutrition is an essential component of total health care and all too often it is ignored or dismissed as being inconsequential. In both of these cases the nutritional problem was unmasked as a result of a casual observation by someone without a vested interest in any particular treatment modality. A representation of a flow chart for the assessment of nutritional status is presented in Table 24–5.

Sweeteners

The approach to the examination of the sugar–behavior connection has many parallels to the investigation of the Feingold diet. Table 24–6 is a list of selected studies of the effects of sugar on behavior. Like the studies of the food additive question, there has been an overreliance on behavioral observation and other global measures of change. More importantly, other than the popular belief that sugar affects behavior, studies of its effects on behavior have lacked a theoretical foundation. There has heretofore been no hypothesis offered to explain either the possibility of an adverse effect of sugar or the absence of any functional changes that would be expected to occur during these metabolic manipulations. There is experimental evidence to suggest that sucrose can have either a direct effect via an interaction with catecholaminergic structures (Smith 1947) or an indirect effect mediated by the influence of glucose/insulin concentrations and large neutral amino acid ratios on neurotransmitter precursor availability as described by Wurtman and colleagues (1981). Moreover, there is a large body of evidence that supports the contention that attention deficit hyperactivity

Table 24–6. SELECTED STUDIES OF THE EFFECTS OF SUGAR ON BEHAVIOR

Chronic Consumption Studies
1. Prinz et al. (1980): observed intake of "sugary" foods and observable classroom behaviors in hyperactive children.
2. Wolraich et al. (1986): observed correlations between percent of the dietary carbohydrate as sugar and actometer readings, grid-crossing, on-task (negative) and attention shifts.
3. Kruesi et al. (1987a): observed no differences in intakes of sugar between presumed sugar "responders" and matched peers.
4. Raiten et al. (in press): found no difference in dietary intakes between ADHD and normal children. A significant difference was found in fasted blood levels of glucose. It was possible to discriminate between groups based on dietary and blood parameters.

Challenge Studies
1. Behar et al. (1984): no significant group effect of sugars were found on behavior rating scales.
2. Kruesi et al. (1987b): 18 "responders" and 12 control preschool children found lack of significant group increase in activity following sugars.
3. Milich and Pelham (1986): 16 boys challenged with sucrose or aspartame showed no significant group effects.
4. Conners et al. (1987): 36 ADHD and 26 control children were challenged with either sucrose or aspartame, with the index group demonstrating a differential response to the sugar challenge under different meal conditions.

disorder (ADHD) is associated with an anomaly in the regulation of catecholaminergic transmission (Oades 1987). It is logical to suppose that a dietary manipulation that might influence those systems associated with these types of behavioral problems might serve as a useful probe into the pathology of ADHD.

Conners and associates (1987) suggested that this may be the case in children with ADHD. In this study under specific dietary conditions (i.e., protein, carbohydrate, or fasted breakfast condition), children with ADHD were found to respond differently and paradoxically to a sugar challenge. The responses were seen as changes in performance on a continuous performance task, changes in visual evoked potential, and differential metabolic responses as reflected by paradoxical shifts in hormone levels. The paradoxical nature of this last effect (e.g., an apparent lack of suppression of cortisol and growth hormone during a carbohydrate load) and the well-known interaction between the release of these hormones and the putative neurotransmitters, serotonin and the catecholamines, could be extrapolated to be indicative of the potential use of nutrients, either sugar or amino acid precursors, as probes of an underlying neurochemical anomaly in children with ADHD. Additional evidence for this hypothesis comes from preliminary data by the same group (Raiten et al., 1988) that revealed baseline differences in blood levels of glucose that could not be accounted for by diet and an ability to discriminate between diagnostic groups based on blood parameters. As in Prinz and co-workers' (1980) study there were also significant correlations between behavior and dietary intake, but unlike this study these relationships were based on behavioral rating scales (i.e., factor scores on both the Conners Parent and Teacher Questionnaires), reflective of long-term diet–behavior interaction across situational settings rather than just during a classroom observation. The findings of differential physiological responses to metabolic challenges need to be replicated. If true, the results may have revealed a functional assessment probe for the study of ADHD. Another benefit to this approach is that it provides an opportunity to evaluate the functional significance of dietary alterations of the amino acid precursors, a test of the precursor hypothesis.

As opposed to the situations with sugar and food additives there is a well-established theory to explain the proposed neurologic effects of aspartame. Aspartame is a dipeptide composed of two amino acids, aspartic acid and phenylalanine. The cornerstone of the concern about this substance is the precursor model of Wurtman and co-workers (1981), outlined earlier. There are several other related and independent lines of evidence that have raised suspicion about aspartame:

1. Aspartic acid is an excitotoxic amino acid that has been found to produce lesions in susceptible areas of the brain (Olney 1984).

2. Methanol, one of the metabolic by-products of aspartame, has been shown to be behaviorally toxic in prenatally exposed animals (Infurna and Weiss 1986).

3. Animal studies have demonstrated decreases in neurologic responses in young animals prenatally exposed to aspartame (Mahalik and Gautieri 1984).

4. Increases in blood concentrations of phenylalanine following aspartame ingestion result in changes in brain neurochemistry (Coulombe and Sharma 1986; Yokogoshi et al. 1984).

5. Aspartame ingestion may be associated with an increased risk for seizures (Maher 1986).

Once again, the questions about aspartame revolve around our ability to convert theory into function. Of additional concern is whether exposure to this substance during gestation will lead to subsequent problems in infants and children. We do not know how developmentally sensitive the young nervous system is to aspartame and its metabolites. We also do not know what the effects of chronic intakes of this substance may be in children during the most important periods in the growth and development of the nervous system.

The evidence about its safety is suggestive enough to generate serious concerns about the unquestioned and rampant use of this substance by the entire population. Aspartame is a sugar substitute developed for persons who need it, such as diabetics. Ironically, the use of aspartame as a weight reduction aid has come into question by Blundell and Hill (1986), who suggest that the combination of its potential for raising the levels of neurotransmitters and peptides associated with appetite stimulation and the ingestion of sweets without calories (thus bypassing many metabolic regulatory signals) may work paradoxically to increase appetite.

Even though aspartame is derived from two naturally occurring compounds, we should not be deceived into thinking that it is an innocuous substance. As demonstrated repeatedly, amino acids, especially phenylalanine, when taken in an unbalanced manner can cause changes in brain chemistry. Because studies have not yet made a definitive link between acute challenges of aspartame and observable changes in global measures of behavior does not mean that the potential for such changes does not exist. The consuming public should not lose sight of the fact that this is not an essential nutrient; it is a sugar substitute and, as such, does not and should not be an integral part of a child's food supply.

Environmental Toxins: Lead

One final area that should be covered in any discussion of exogenous influences on behavior is the effects of environmental toxicants. Graef (1983), in his review of environmental toxins, discussed the mechanisms of exposure and metabolism of many of the known pollutants. While the list of these substances is long and growing, the substance that has received the most attention has been lead. The clinical sequelae of lead poisoning have been known since antiquity and have been described extensively (Silbergeld 1982). Chronic severe lead exposure is most often associated with encephalopathy, an acute condition that has a 25% mortality rate (Greenhouse 1982). Early signs of this condition may include nonspecific symptoms such as irritability, insomnia, restlessness, memory loss, and confusion. Even after treatment, the child may still have convulsions, paralysis, mental retardation, and cognitive or behavioral problems. Lead encephalopathy is distinguished pathologically by edema or swelling and by hemorrhage (Goldstein et al. 1974).

With the passage of the Lead Based Paint Poisoning Prevention Act in 1971 and the Clean Air Act, and the subsequent phasing out of lead as a gasoline additive, the incidence of severe lead poisoning, which had reached epidemic proportions, has begun to decline (Lin-Fu 1982). Despite these attempts at legislation, the problem of low-level lead exposure still exists because of the omnipresent nature of lead in the human environment. Hammond (1982) pointed out that lead is a natural constituent of rocks and soil and that as a consequence of hundreds of years of industrialization there is probably a "generalized pollution" of our environment.

Despite the vast areas of controversy regarding lead there is a professional consensus that children, especially during the growth spurt of the first 6 years, are most susceptible to the effects of lead. Otto and co-workers (1982) identified four factors that predispose young children to the effects of lead: (1) the vulnerability of the immature growing brain, (2) a five times greater absorption of lead than adults, (3) the tendency of young children to eat inorganic material (a condition referred to as pica), and (4) the prevalence of dietary iron and calcium deficiencies, both related to increased lead absorption. The developmental effects of lead on cognitive functioning and neural plasticity, as well as its neurotoxicology, have been reviewed extensively (Petit 1986; Audesirk 1985).

Byers and Lord (1943) first raised the possibility of an idiopathic neuropsychological effect of lead in children. Since then numerous studies have linked low-level lead exposure to reduced electrical activity, decreased intelligence, behavioral problems, and learning disabilities (Otto et al. 1982; Needleman 1982; Rutter 1980). None of the work to date has been able to definitively ascertain the mechanism for lead neurotoxicity or the minimum amount of exposure before the appearance of functional changes. Another factor that has received minimal attention is the interaction between nutrition and lead exposure. As mentioned earlier, calcium and iron deficiencies enhance lead absorption. Additional nutritional factors include deficiencies in total calories, zinc, and phosphorus (Mahaffey 1983) and "B" complex vitamins (Tandon et al. 1984). An excellent review of the interaction of nutrition and lead has been provided by DeMichele (1984).

CONCLUSIONS

The essentiality of nutrition in the ontogeny of the nervous system is incontrovertible.

The challenge of researchers and clinicians is to define those situations when and where the organism is most vulnerable. We must begin to refine our ability to identify changes or aberrations from normal development before the damage becomes irreversible. The identification of the functional consequences of insults such as dietary inadequacy, food additives, sweeteners and other nutritional insults and environmental toxins depends on the function assessed, the sensitivity of the measurement, the nature of the interaction with other environmental factors, and the developmental stage during which the exposure occurred.

References

Albright, F., Butler, A.M., and Bloomberg, E. 1937. Rickets resistant to vitamin D therapy. *Am. J. Dis. Child.* 54:529–547.

Anderson, J.A. 1986. The establishment of common language concerning adverse reactions to foods and food additives. *J. Allergy Clin. Immunol.* 78:140–144.

Anderson, G.H. 1981. Diet, neurotransmitters, and brain function. *Br. Med. Bull.* 37:95–100.

Audesirk, G. 1985. Effects of lead exposure on the physiology of neurons. *Prog. Neurobiol.* 24:199–231.

Barnes, R.H., Levitsky, D.A., Pond, W.G., and Moore, U. 1975. Effects of postnatal dietary protein and energy restriction on exploratory behavior in young pigs. *Dev. Psychobiol.* 9:425–435.

Barnet, A.A., Weiss, I.P., Sotillo, M.V., et al. 1978. Abnormal auditory evoked potentials in early human malnutrition. *Science* 201:450–452.

Bartel, P.R., Robinson, E., Conradie, J.M., and Prinsloo, J.G. 1986. Brainstem auditory evoked potentials in severely malnourished children with kwashiorkor. *Neuropediatrics* 17:178–182.

Behar, D., Rapoport, J.L., Adams, A.J., et al. 1984. Sugar challenge testing with children considered behaviorally "sugar reactive." *Nutr. Behav.* 1:277–288.

Blundell, J.E., and Hill, A.J. 1986. Paradoxical effects of an intense sweetener (aspartame) on appetite. *Lancet* 1:1092–1093.

Byers, R.K., and Lord, E.E. 1943. Late effects of lead poisoning on mental development. *Am. J. Dis. Child.* 66:471–494.

Calame, A., Fawer, C.L., Claeys, V., et al. 1986. Neurodevelopmental outcome and school performance of very low birth weight infants at 8 years of age. *Eur. J. Pediatrics* 145:461–466.

Capel, D., Pinnock, M.H., Darrell, H.M., et al. 1981. Comparison of concentrations of some trace, bulk, and toxic metals in the hair of normal dyslexic children. *Clin. Chem.* 27:875–881.

Cohen, E.L., and Wurtman, R.J. 1976. Brain acetylcholine: Control by dietary choline. *Science* 191:561–562.

Conners, C.K. 1980. *Food Additives and Hyperactive Children.* New York: Plenum Press.

Conners, C.K., Glascow, A., Raiten, D.J., et al. 1987. *Hyperactives Differ from Normals in Blood Sugar and Hormonal Response to Sucrose* (abstr). New York: American Psychological Association.

Conners, C.K., Goyette, C., Southwick, D., et al. 1976. Food additives and hyperkinesis: A controlled double-blind experiment. *Pediatrics* 58:154–166.

Conners, C.K., and Blouin, A.G. 1982. Nutritional effects on behavior of children. *J. Psychiatr. Res.* 17:193–201.

Coulombe, R.A., and Sharma, R.P. 1986. Neurobiochemical alterations induced by the artificial sweetener aspartame (Nutrasweet). *Toxicol. Appl. Pharmacol.* 83:79–85.

Crane, J.P., and Kopta, M.M. 1979. Prediction of intra-uterine growth retardation via ultrasonically measured head/abdominal circumference ratios. *Obstet. Gynecol.* 54:597–601.

Cravioto, J., and Arrieta, R. 1986. Nutrition, mental development and learning. In Falkner, F., and Tanner, J.M. (eds.): *Human Growth.* New York: Plenum Publishing Corp.

Cravioto, J., and DeLicardie, E.R. 1970. The long-term consequence of protein-calorie malnutrition. *Nutr. Rev.* 29:107–111.

Crnic, L.S. 1983. Effects of nutrition and environment on brain biochemistry and behavior. *Dev. Psychobiol.* 16:129–145.

Crook, W.G. 1975. Food allergy—The great masquerader. *Pediatr. Clin. North Am.* 22:227–238.

David, T.J., Waddington, E., and Stanton, R.H.J. 1984. Nutritional hazards of elimination diets in children with atopic eczema. *Arch. Dis. Child.* 59:323–325.

Delaney, A.J., Samorajski, T., Fuller, G.N., and Wiggins, R.C. 1981. A morphometric comparison of central and peripheral hypomyclination induced by postnatal undernourishment of rats. *J. Nutr.* 111:746–754.

DeMichele, S.J. 1984. Nutrition of lead. *Comp. Biochem. Physiol.* 78:401–408.

Dobbing, J. 1984. Infant nutrition and later achievement. *Nutr. Rev.* 42:1–7.

Dobbing, J., and Sands, J. 1973. Quantitative growth and development of the human brain. *Arch. Dis. Child* 48:757–767.

Dockhorn, R.J. 1984. Diagnostic tests for allergic disease. In: *Allergy: Theory and Practice.* New York: Grune & Stratton, Inc.

Evans, C.D.H., and Lacey, J.H. 1986. Toxicity of vitamins: Complications of a health movement. *Br. Med. J.* 292:509–510.

Feingold, B.F. 1975. Hyperkinesis and learning disabilities linked to artificial food flavors and colors. *Am. J. Nursing* 75:797–803.

Fernhoff, P.M., Danner, D.J., and Elsas, L.J. 1982. Vitamin responsive disorders. In Garry, P.J., and Marcum, V.S. (eds.): *Human Nutrition—Clinical and Biochemical Aspects.* Washington, D.C.: American Association of Clinical Chemistry.

Fernstrom, J.D. 1981. Dietary precursors and brain neurotransmitter formation. *Ann. Rev. Med.* 32:413–425.

Fernstrom, J.D., and Wurtman, R.J., 1971. Brain serotonin content: Physiological dependence on plasma tryptophan levels. *Science* 173:149–152.

Floeter, M.K., and Greenough, W.T. 1979. Cerebellar plasticity: Modification of Purkinje cell structure by differential rearing in monkeys. *Science* 206:227–229.

Frankova, S., and Barnes, R.H. 1968. Influence of malnutrition in early life on exploratory behavior of rats. *J. Nutr.* 96:477–484.

Freed, W.J., DeMedinacelli, L., and Wyatt, R.J. 1985. Promoting functional plasticity in the damaged nervous system. *Science* 227:1544–1552.

Fuller, P.W., Guthrie, R.D., and Alvord, E.C. 1983. A proposed neuropathological basis for learning disabilities in children born prematurely. *Dev. Med. Child Neurol.* 25:214–231.

Galler, J.R., Ramsey, F., and Forde, V. 1986. A follow-up study of the influence of early malnutrition on subsequent development: Intellectual performance during adolescence. *Nutr. Behav.* 3:211–222.

Galler, J.R., Ramsey, F., and Solimano, G. 1984. The influence of early malnutrition on subsequent behavioral development: III. Learning disabilities as a sequel to malnutrition. *Pediatr. Res.* 18:309–313.

Gallo, P.V. 1982. Physiological and behavioral consequences of maternal and post-weaning posterior restriction. *Physiol. Behav.* 26:77–84.

Goldstein, G., Asbury, A., and Diamond, I. 1974. Pathogenesis of lead encephalopathy: Uptake of lead and reaction of brain capillaries. *Arch. Neurol.* 31:382–389.

Graef, J.W. 1983. Environmental toxins. In Levine, M.D., Carey, W.B., Crocker, A.C., and Gross, R.T. (eds.): *Developmental-Behavioral Pediatrics*. Philadelphia: WB Saunders Co.

Grantham-McGregor, S., Schofield, W., and Harris, L. 1983. Effect of psychosocial stimulation on mental development of severely malnourished children: An interim report. *Pediatrics* 72:239–243.

Greenhouse, A.H. 1982. Heavy metals and the nervous system. *Clin. Neuropharmacol.* 5:45–92.

Guthrie, H.A. 1986. *Introductory Nutrition*, 6th. ed. St. Louis: Times Mirror/Mosby College Publishers.

Hammond, P.B. 1982. Exposure to lead. In Chisolm, J.J., and O'Hara, D.M. (eds.): *Lead Absorption in Children*. Baltimore: Urban & Schwarzenberg.

Harley, J.P., Ray, R.S., Tomasi, L., et al. 1978. Hyperkinesis and food additives: Testing the Feingold hypothesis. *Pediatrics* 61:818–828.

Harper, P.H., Goyette, C.H., and Conners, C.K. 1978. Nutrient intakes of children on the hyperkinesis diet. *J. Am. Diet. Assoc.* 73:515–519.

Hathcock, J.N. 1982. Nutritional toxicology: A definition and scope. *Nutr. Toxicol.* 1:1–15.

Hay, W.W. 1986. Justification for total parenteral nutrition in the premature and compromised newborn. In: Lebenthal, E. (ed.): *Total Parenteral Nutrition: Indications, Utilization, Complications and Pathophysiological Considerations*. New York: Raven Press.

Heath, R.G. 1972. Electroencephalographic studies in isolation raised monkeys with behavioral impairment. *Dis. Nerv. Syst.* 33:157–163.

Houscham, K.C., DeVilliers, J.F.K. 1987. Computed tomography in severe protein energy malnutrition. *Arch. Dis. Child.* 62:589–592.

Hunt, A.D., Stokes, J., McCrory, W.W., and Stroud, H.H. 1954. Pyridoxine dependency: Report of a case of intractable convulsions in an infant controlled by pyridoxine. *Pediatrics* 13:140–145.

Hutchings, D.E. 1983. Behavioral teratology: A new frontier in neurobehavioral research. In Johnson, E.M., and Kochhar, D.M. (eds.): *Handbook of Experimental Pharmacology*. Berlin: Springer-Verlag.

Infurna, R., and Weiss, B. 1986. Neonatal behavioral toxicity in rats following prenatal exposure to methanol. *Teratology* 33:259–265.

Jones, D.G., and Dyson, S.E. 1981. The influence of protein restriction, rehabilitation and changing nutritional status on synaptic development: A quantitative study in rat brain. *Brain Res.* 208:97–11.

Kaplita, P.V., and Triggle, D.J. 1982. Food dyes: Behavioral and neurochemical actions. *Trends Pharmacol. Sci.* 3:70–71.

Kruesi, M.J.P., Rapoport, J.L., Berg, C.J., et al. 1987a. Seven-day carbohydrate and other nutrient intakes of preschool boys alleged to be behavioral responsive to sugar intake and their peers. In Essman, W.B. (ed.): *Nutrition and Brain Function*. Basel: Karger.

Kruesi, M.J.P., Rapoport, J.L., Cummings, E.M., et al. 1987b. Effects of sugar and aspartame on aggression and activity in children. *Am. J. Psychiatry* 144:1487–1490.

Lehnert, H., Reinstein, D.K., Strowbridge, B.W., and Wurtman, R.J. 1984. Neurochemical and behavioral consequences of acute, uncontrollable stress: Effects of dietary tyrosine. *Brain Res.* 303:215–223.

Levitsky, D.A., Goldberger, L., and Massaro, T.F. 1979. Malnutrition, learning and animal models. In Winick, M. (ed.): *Human Nutrition*, Vol. 1: *Nutrition: Pre- and Postnatal Development*. New York: Plenum Press.

Levy, F., Dumbrell, S., Hobbes, G., et al. 1978. Hyperkinesis and diet: A double-blind crossover trial with a tartrazine challenge. *Med. J. Aust.* 1:61–64.

Lin-Fu, J.S. 1982. The evolution of childhood lead poisoning as a public health problem. In Chisolm, J.J., and O'Hare, D.M. (eds.): *Lead Absorption in Children*. Baltimore: Urban & Schwarzenberg.

Lucas, A., and Bates, C. 1984. Transient riboflavin depletion in preterm infants. *Arch. Dis. Child.* 59:837–841.

Mahaffey, K.B. 1983. Biotoxicity of lead: Influence of various factors. *Fed. Proc.* 42:1730–1734.

Mahalik, M.P., and Gautieri, R.F. 1984. Reflex responsiveness of cf-1 mouse neonates following maternal aspartame exposure. *Res. Commun. Psychol. Psychiatr. Behav.* 9:385–403.

Maher, T.J. 1986. Neurotoxicology of food additives. *Neurotoxicology* 7:183–196.

Massaro, T.F., Levitsky, D.A., and Barnes, R.H. 1977a. Early protein malnutrition in the rat: Behavioral changes during rehabilitation. *Dev. Psychobiol.* 10:105–111.

Massaro, T.F., Levitsky, D.A., and Barnes, R.H. 1977b. Protein malnutrition induced during gestation: Its effects on pup development and maternal behavior. *Dev. Psychobiol.* 10:339–345.

Massaro, T.F., Levitsky, D.A., and Barnes, R.H. 1974. Protein malnutrition in the rat: Its effects on maternal behavior and pup development. *Dev. Psychobiol.* 7:551–561.

Massaro, T.F., Raiten, D.J., and Zuckerman, C.H. 1983. Trace mineral concentrations and behavior: Clinical utility in the assessment of developmental disabilities. *Top. Early Child. Special Educ.* 3:55–61.

Mattes, J.A., and Gittleman-Klein, R. 1978. A crossover study of artificial food colorings in a hyperkinetic child. *Am. J. Psychiatry* 135:987–988.

Metcalfe, D.D. 1984. Diagnostic procedures for immunologically mediated food sensitivity. *Nutr. Rev.* 42:92–97.

Milich, R., and Pelham, W.E. 1986. Effects of sugar ingestion on the classroom and playgroup behavior of attention deficit disordered boys. *J. Consult. Clin. Psychol.* 54:714–718.

Miller, D.R., and Hayes, R.C. 1982. Vitamin excess and toxicity. *Nutr. Toxicol.* 1:81–133.

National Advisory Committee on Hyperkinesis and Food Additives. June, 1975. *Report to the Nutrition Foundation*. New York: Nutrition Foundation.

National Advisory Committee on Hyperkinesis and Food Additives. 1980. *Final Report to the Nutrition Foundation*. New York: Nutrition Foundation.

Needleman, H.L. 1982. The neurobehavioral consequences of low lead exposure in childhood. *Neurobehav. Toxicol. Teratol.* 4:729–732.

Oades, R.D. 1987. Attention deficit disorder with hyperactivity (ADD/H): The contribution of catecholaminergic activity. *Prog. Neurobiol.* 29:365–391.

Olney, J.W. 1984. Excitotoxic food additives: Relevance of animal studies to human safety. *Neurobehav. Toxicol. Teratol.* 6:455–462.

Otto, D., Benignus, V., Muller, K., et al. 1982. Effects of low to moderate lead exposure on slow cortical potentials in young children: Two year follow-up study. *Neurobehav. Toxicol. Teratol.* 4:733–737.

Pauling, L. 1969. Orthomolecular psychiatry. *Science* 160:265–271.

Peters, J.C., and Harper, A.E. 1984. Influence of dietary protein level on protein self-selection and plasma and brain amino acid concentrations. *Physiol. Behav.* 33:783–790.

Petit, T.L. 1986. Developmental effects of lead: Its mechanism in intellectual functioning and neural plasticity. *Neurotoxicology* 7:483–496.

Piaget, J. 1971. *Biology and Knowledge.* B. Walsh, trans. Chicago: University of Chicago Press.

Pines, M. 1981. The civilizing of Genie. *Psychol. Today* September, pp. 28–34.

Prinz, R.J., Roberts, W.A., and Hantman, E. 1980. Dietary correlates of hyperactive behavior in children. *J. Consult. Clin. Psychol.* 48:760–769.

Raiten, D.J. 1987. Nutrition and developmental disabilities: Issues in chronic care. In Schopler, E. and Mesibov, G.B. (eds.): *Neurobiological Issues in Autism.* New York: Plenum Press.

Raiten, D.J. 1988. Nutrition and developmental disabilities: Clinical assessment. In Schopler, E. and Mesibov, G.B. (eds.): *Diagnosis and Assessment in Autism.* New York: Plenum Press.

Raiten, D.J., Andon, M., Robbins, S., et al. 1987. Low serum pyridoxal phosphate in VLBW premature infants (abstr). American Society of Parenteral and Enteral Nutrition—National Meeting, New Orleans, Louisiana, February.

Raiten, D.J., and Massaro, T.F. 1987. Nutrition and developmental disabilities: An examination of the orthomolecular hypothesis. In Cohen, D.J., Donnellan, A.M., and Paul, R. (eds.): *Handbook of Autism and Pervasive Developmental Disorders.* New York: John Wiley & Sons.

Raiten, D.J., Massaro, T.F., and Zuckerman, C. 1984. Vitamin and trace element assessment of autistic and learning disabled children. *Nutr. Behav.* 2:9–17.

Read, M.S. 1982. *Malnutrition and Behavior.* Occasional Paper Series No. 9. Chapel Hill, N.C.: Institute of Nutrition.

Reinstein, D.K., Lehnert, H., and Wurtman, R.J. 1985. Dietary tyrosine suppresses the rise in plasma corticosterone following acute stress in rats. *Life Sci.* 37:2157–2163.

Rutter, M. 1980. Raised lead levels and impaired cognitive/behavioral functioning: A review of the evidence. *Dev. Med. Child. Neurol.* 22(Suppl):1–7.

Salamy, J., Shucard, D., Alexander, H., et al. 1982. Physiological changes in hyperactive children following the ingestion of food additives. *Int. J. Neurosci.* 16:241–246.

Sampson, H.A. 1986. Differential diagnosis in adverse reactions to foods. *J. Allerg. Clin. Immunol.* 78:212–219.

Sann, L., Darre, E., Lasne, Y., et al. 1986. Effects of prematurity and dysmaturity on growth at age 5 years. *J. Pediatr.* 109:681–686.

Shaywitz, B.A., Goldenring, J.R., and Wool, R.S. 1979. Effects of chronic administration of food colorings on activity levels and cognitive performance in develop-

ing rat pups treated with 6-hydroxydopamine. *Neurobehav. Toxicol.* 1:41–47.

Silbergeld, E.K. 1982. Neurochemical and ionic mechanisms of lead toxicity. In Prasad, K.N. and Vernadakis, A. (eds.): *Mechanisms of Actions of Neurotoxic Substances.* New York: Raven Press.

Smith, C.A. 1947. The effect of wartime starvation in Holland upon pregnancy and its product. *Am. J. Obstet. Gynecol.* 53:599–605.

Spector, R. 1977. Vitamin homeostasis in the central nervous system. *N. Engl. J. Med.* 296:1393–1398.

Stoch, M.B., Smythe, P.M., Moodie, A.D. and Bradshaw, D. 1982. Psychosocial outcome and CT findings after gross undernourishment during infancy: A 20-year developmental study. *Dev. Med. Child. Neurol.* 24:419–436.

Swanson, J.M., and Kinsbourne, M. 1980. Food dyes impair performance of hyperactive children on a laboratory learning test. *Science* 207:1485–1486.

Tandon, S.K., Flora, S.J.S., and Singh, S. 1984. Influence of vitamin B complex on lead intoxication in young rats. *Ind. J. Med. Res.* 80:444–448.

Thatcher, R.W., and Lester, M.L. 1985. Nutrition, environmental toxins and computerized EEG: A minimax approach to learning disabilities. *J. Learn. Disabil.* 18:287–296.

Thatcher, R.W., Walker, R.A., and Guidice, S. 1986. Human cerebral hemisphere development at different rates and ages. *Science* 236:1110–1113.

Trulson, M.E. 1985. Dietary tryptophan does not alter the function of brain serotonin neurons. *Life Sci.* 37:1067–1072.

Weiss, B. 1986. Food additives as a source of behavioral disturbances in children. *Neurotoxicology* 7:197–208.

Weiss, B., Williams, J.H., Margen, S., et al. 1980. Behavioral responses to artificial food colors. *Science* 207:1487–1489.

Williams, J.I., Cram, D.M., Tausig, F.T., and Webster, E. 1978. Relative effects of drugs and diet on hyperactive behaviors: An experimental study. *Pediatrics* 61:811–817.

Winick, M. 1975. Nutrition and brain development. In: Serban, G. (ed.): *Nutrition and Mental Functions.* New York: Plenum Press.

Winick, M. 1976. *Malnutrition and Brain Development.* New York: Oxford University Press.

Winick, M. 1979. Malnutrition and mental development. In Alfin-Slater, R.B. and Kritchevsky, D. (eds.): *Human Nutrition.* New York: Plenum Press.

Winick, M., Meyer, K., and Harris, R. 1975. Malnutrition and environmental enrichment by early adoption. *Science* 190:1173–1175.

Wolraich, M.L., Stumbo, P.J., Milch, R., and Schultz, F. 1986. Dietary characteristics of hyperactive and control boys. *J. Am. Diet. Assoc.* 86:500–504.

Wurtman, R.J., Hefti, F., and Melamed, E. 1981. Precursor control of neurotransmitter synthesis. *Pharmacol. Rev.* 32:315–335.

Wurtman, R.J., Larin, F., Mostafapour, S., and Fernstrom, J.D. 1974. Brain catechol synthesis: Control by brain tyrosine concentrations. *Science* 185:183–184.

Yokogoshi, H., Roberts, C.H., Caballero, B., and Wurtman, R.J. 1984. Effects of aspartame and glucose administration on brain and plasma levels of large neutral amino acids and brain 5-hydroxyindoles. *Am. J. Clin. Nutr.* 40:1–7.

Zimmerman, R.R., Stroebel, D.A., and Maguire, D. 1975. Neophobic reactions in protein malnourished infant monkeys. American Dietetic Association, Proceedings of the 78th Annual Convention 6:187–188.

25

Adoption

PAUL D. STEINHAUER, M.D.

HISTORY OF ADOPTION

Adoption has been used since ancient times as one way of dealing with orphaned and homeless children. Until relatively recently, however, those who adopted generally did so to further their own interests, rather than out of concern for the welfare of the child. Reasons for such adoptions would include attempts to ensure the continuity of the male line, to secure a family's fortune in future generations, or to forge a political alliance. Following World War II, adoption changed from a service obtaining children for families who wanted them to one providing suitable families for children who needed them. Increased knowledge of genetics, a decreased emphasis on meticulous attempts to match the physical characteristics of the child to the adoptive family, and an increased awareness of the importance of attachment and bonding favored placing adoptees in their adoptive families as soon as possible after birth. At the same time, however, a marked decrease in the number of normal, healthy infants available for adoption led to the placement of many "special need" children who, at an earlier time, would have been considered "unadoptable" because of significant physical, mental, and/or emotional handicaps or because of race. One other previously avoided trend was the adoption of older children, which had caused problems because of the persistence of strong residual attachments to members of their birth families and long-term foster families.

In marked contrast to foster care, adoption is essentially a middle-class phenomenon. Foster care, which has always been less prestigious, relies primarily on obtaining working-class parents. It was only in the 1960s that foster parents began to be seen as the candidates of choice to adopt eligible children already in their care. Previously, any expressed wish to change from fostering to become adopting parents would have been considered evidence of inappropriate involvement and, therefore, of unsuitability for fostering.

One other major change in recent years has been the shift from *extrafamilial* to *intrafamilial* adoptions. An extrafamilial adoption is one in which the adoptee has no preexisting blood tie with either adoptive parent. In an intrafamilial adoption, a blood tie with one of the adoptive parents is present. Many intrafamilial adoptions result when step-parents adopt their spouses' children from a previous marriage. The marked increase in divorce and remarriage since the 1960s has led to intrafamilial adoptions of this sort constituting up to 70% of all adoptions in Great Britain (Office of Population Censuses and Surveys 1976) and over 55% of those in Canada (Hepworth 1980). A much less common and more problematic form of intrafamiliial adoption occurs when the parents or relatives of an unmarried mother adopt her child and raise it as their own. This chapter will, from this point, use the word adoption to describe extrafamilial adoptions, unless otherwise indicated.

THE USE OF ADOPTION STUDIES IN PSYCHIATRIC RESEARCH

Adoption studies can help identify the relative contributions of heredity, environment, or their combination in transmitting a psychiatric syndrome to the next generation. Typically, one selects a sample of psychiatrically disordered biological parents whose children were adopted at an early age. These children and their adoptive and biological parents are then studied. The frequency of the disorder in the children is compared with its occurrence in a matched group of adoptees whose biological parents lack the disorder but some of whose adoptive parents have it. Genetic transmission is suggested by the disorder's presence in a significant number of the adoptees. Environmental transmission is suggested by an occurrence in the children resembling that in the affected adoptive parents more than that in their nonaffected biological parents. Most adoptive studies suggest that more adoptees show the biological parents' disorder than resemble the adoptive parents (Tarter 1983). Hutchings and Mednick (1975), for example, studied the transmission of antisocial behavior from parents to child. The authors matched 143 adoptees with a criminal record with a control group. The incidence of criminal and psychiatric histories in the biological and adoptive families was determined. The results are summarized in Table 25–1 and show the percentage of each group with a criminal record.

In analyzing these data the authors reached the following conclusions:

1. Genetic factors favor criminality despite the absence of criminality in the home environment (compare squares A and B).

Table 25–1. FREQUENCY OF CRIMINAL BEHAVIOR IN ADOPTEES

	Biological Father			
	No Criminal Record		Criminal Record	
Adoptive Father:				
No Criminal Record	11%	(A)	24%	(B)
Criminal Record	12%	(C)	36%	(D)

(Data from Hutchings, B., and Mednick, S. 1975. Registered criminality in the adoptive and biological parents of registered male criminal adoptees. In Fieve, R., Rosenthal, D., and Brill, H. [eds.]: *Genetic Research in Psychiatry.* Baltimore: Johns Hopkins University Press.)

Table 25–2. PSYCHIATRIC DISORDERS TRANSMITTED

Parental Disorder	Adoption Studies Useful in Studying Transmission
Alcoholism	Goodwin et al. 1974
	Bohman 1978
Bipolar affective disorder	Mendlewicz and Rainer 1977
	Cadoret 1978a, 1978b
Schizophrenia	Heston 1966
	Kety et al. 1976
Antisocial personality	Crowe 1974
Criminality	Hutchings and Mednick, 1975
Hyperactivity	Cantwell 1975
	Morrison 1973
	Morrison and Stewart 1971

(Compiled from McGuffin, P., and Gottesman, I. I. 1985. Genetic influences in normal and abnormal development. In Rutter, M., and Hersov, L. [eds.]: *Child and Adolescent Psychiatry: Modern Approaches,* 2nd. ed. Oxford: Blackwell Scientific Publications; and Tarter, R. E. [ed.]. 1983. *The Child at Psychiatric Risk.* New York: Oxford University Press.)

2. A home environment without genetic predisposition does not favor the development of criminality (compare squares A and C).

3. Where both biological and adoptive fathers were criminal, the rate of criminality was highest of all (36%), which suggests a transactional effect between genetic and environmental precursors (see square D) (McGuffin and Gottesman 1985).

Cloninger and co-workers (1981) demonstrated that placing children in unfavorable homes increased the risk of petty criminality only for those whose fathers had a criminal record. Bohman (1981) also has shown that favorable homes can protect adoptive children from conduct disorders to which they would have been liable if raised by their criminal or alcoholic biological fathers or their unwed biological mothers. But, in another study, Bohman (1978) found that alcoholism but not criminality was genetically transmitted. In earlier studies (1971, 1972), the same author found that the daughters but not the sons of criminal fathers were more likely to be less well adjusted than those whose fathers were not criminal.

Table 25–2 lists a number of psychiatric disorders whose transmission has been clarified by adoptive studies.

CHANGING PATTERNS OF ADOPTION

Most infant adoptees are born of illegitimate pregnancies, especially those of unmarried mothers younger than 20 years of age (Guyatt 1980; Hepworth 1980; Hersov 1983). Although the incidence of illegitimate children remains significantly above that of the early 1960s, the number of healthy infants available for adoption has sharply decreased. Reasons for this include the increased availability of birth control information and contraceptive materials, the legalization of abortion, and the increased number of unmarried teenage mothers now electing to keep and raise their infants (Guyatt 1980; Hepworth 1980; Hersov 1983). Since there has been no corresponding decrease in the popularity of adoption, the result has been many more adoptive applicants than infants. This, in turn, has led to the increasingly aggressive promotion of adoption of "special needs" children, who, until recently would have been considered unadoptable. Such "special needs" children currently constitute up to two thirds of all adoption placements, compared with only about one third in 1961–1962 (Hepworth 1980; Rowe and Lambert 1973). Many of these are older children with long histories of neglect and abuse, multiple placements, problems relating to others, and preexisting conduct disorders; all of these factors would, at one time, have been considered barriers to successful adoption.

It is generally agreed that success or failure in adoption depends on three factors: (1) the characteristics of the adoptive parents, (2) those of the adopted child, and (3) the ability of each to meet the other's needs and to accept the other's limitations.

CHARACTERISTICS OF ADOPTED PARENTS

Generally accepted qualities sought in prospective adoptive parents are summarized in Table 25–3. Other qualities crucial to success in the adoption of older "special needs" children are summarized in Table 25–4. Since adoptive applicants may lack many of these qualities, a thorough psychological and psychiatric assessment of potential adopting parents should precede any adoption placement. The older the child, the more complicated the potential adoption and the more rigorous this preadoption assessment should be. In practice, however, agencies are increasingly willing to accept, as adoptive parents, applicants only marginally qualified because of

Table 25–3. QUALITIES GENERALLY SOUGHT IN PROSPECTIVE ADOPTIVE PARENTS

1. Good physical health
2. Solid emotional and social adjustment
3. Emotional maturity
4. A stable marital relationship
5. Positive feelings regarding children
6. Lack of continuing distress regarding their own childlessness
7. Appropriate motivation for adoption
8. Genuine recognition that no predictions can be made as to whether or how a child will change
9. Ability to accept a child as is, *even if the child does not improve*
10. Ability to remain committed to a child who does not seem to be benefitting from their care
11. Ability to seek and accept outside help when the need arises
12. Honest recognition of the fact that there but for the grace of God might they be in the shoes of either the birth parents or the adoptee
13. Certainty that they have faced all areas of their own sexual vulnerability

their age, state of health, psychological adjustment, or marital relationship, provided they agree to adopt what would once have been considered an "unadoptable" child. In practice, adoptive parents are generally older and, despite qualifying medical examinations, less healthy than biological parents (Bohman 1970; Grey and Blunden 1971). Humphrey (1969) has noted that adoptive parents whose relationships with their own parents were strained, whose self-esteem is low, and who had trouble separating from their own families are likely to have more difficulty raising another's child. Others at risk include those remaining ashamed or tor-

Table 25–4. QUALITIES CRUCIAL TO THE SUCCESSFUL ADOPTION OF OLDER AND HANDICAPPED CHILDREN

1. Ability to honor their parenting commitment to any natural children in the face of ongoing stress
2. Truly nonjudgmental acceptance of the rights of the birth family and the child to maintain or reestablish contact with each other
3. Honest recognition of the need to communicate openly with the spouse, with both natural and adopted children, and with helping resources
4. Ability to live comfortably with the prospect of being called on at any time to deal with the unexpected or the unknown
5. The stubbornness or determination required to "hang in" even in the face of chronic and at times agonizing adversity, and to see the adoption as something that they believed in and took responsibility for, as something that they will, therefore, see through

mented by their own childlessness and those who deny any difference between the situation of the adopted child and that of the child raised by biological parents. Adoptive parents who need a child who can rapidly learn to return their affection and/or one who will quickly give up established patterns of undesirable behavior are likely to be disappointed, especially if given an older adoptee. Those adoptive parents requiring a child whose sense of identity remains sufficiently open to allow him or her to totally surrender the past and to merge completely within their family can be very reluctant to meet the needs of the problematic older children placed for adoption. For adoption to be the least detrimental alternative for an older child, the prospective adoptive parents must have found meaning to their lives that does not depend on the child's ability to provide fulfillment.

CHARACTERISTICS OF ADOPTIVE CHILDREN

Despite considerable controversy on methodologic grounds, it is generally concluded that adopted children are moderately overrepresented in mental health clinical populations. Critically reviewing the British, Canadian, American, and Swedish literature, Hersov (1983) suggested that boys are more likely to be disturbed than girls and that conduct and character disorders are more common than emotional and anxiety disorders. Steinhauer's (1983) review of possible reasons for the increased incidence of disturbance in adopted children is summarized in Table 25–5. A number of clearly identified characteristics that are correlated with success in adoption are summarized in Table 25–6.

FACTORS AFFECTING THE "FIT" BETWEEN ADOPTEE/ADOPTIVE FAMILY

Assessment, Matching, and Placement

How can a knowledge of the foregoing factors be applied to "match" successfully children to adoptive parents? One begins by ensuring that a carefully considered decision in favor of adoption of this child by this

Table 25–5. POSSIBLE REASONS FOR THE INCREASED INCIDENCE OF DISTURBANCE IN ADOPTED CHILDREN

Factor	Supporting References
Biological inheritance	Cadoret 1978a Clarke 1981 Cunningham et al. 1975
Poor prenatal/perinatal care of unmarried teenage mothers; widespread abuse of alcohol and other drugs deleteriously affecting fetal development	Baldwin and Cain 1980 Crellin et al. 1971 Hepworth 1980 Hausknecht 1972 Vaitenas 1981
Neglect, abuse, lack of continuity of placements and/or attachment figures prior to adoption	Clarke 1981 Rutter 1972 Tizard 1977
Problems of adoptees consolidating their psychological identity due to the continuing presence (in reality or fantasy) of at least two sets of parents	Schechter 1960 Sorosky et al. 1975 Triseliotis 1970
Experiences in the adoptive family	Steinhauer 1983 Ward 1978

family has been agreed on by the adoptive parents, placement personnel, and the adoptee (as much as is consistent with age and potential for understanding). One should ex-

Table 25–6. FACTORS NEGATIVELY CORRELATED WITH SUCCESS IN ADOPTION

Factor	Supporting Reference
Previous severe deprivation, especially within first 2 years of life	Kadushin 1970 Rutter 1979
Multiple placements	Kadushin 1970 Rutter 1979 Steinhauer 1980
Diagnosable conduct disorder prior to placement	Kadushin 1970
Sudden removal from successful long-term placement (e.g., foster family) in which child has bonded and is developing well	Steinhauer 1980 Goldstein et al. 1973
Adoptions involving severing a strong emotional bond to a birth parent, foster parent or natural sibling (unless access is granted and supported)	Goldstein et al. 1973 Kadushin 1970 Steinhauer 1983
Adoptions in which the child, as a result of prior experience, has developed an established personality, set ways of behaving, and/or exaggerated needs likely to decrease acceptability to adoptive parents	Eldred et al. 1976

plore and carefully consider how much each member of the prospective adoptive family is likely to meet the needs and accept the limitations of the others. This must begin with a thorough and realistic assessment, involving all those who know the child best, to pinpoint carefully the specific and complex needs of the child. Prospective adoptive families should be chosen for their ability to meet these identified needs, giving due consideration to the abilities of all family members, including all children natural and adopted, to give and take. Movement toward placement should be deliberate, since it is during the placement process that the foundation for a successful adoption is either laid or undermined. This is the stage at which the process of integrating a new child into an established family begins. Considering natural anxieties and the stakes involved, this is necessarily a difficult time. No stone should be left unturned to resolve any danger signals; the stress of placement is likely to ignite unresolved and deep-seated issues, which must then be addressed. Children, adoptive families, and placement personnel are often tempted to hurry this process along, with the result that other children may begin to feel negatively; adoptive parents may be upset by behavior incompatible with their values; normal family routines may break down, causing unexpected anxiety; or one parent may be hurt by the other's excessive attention to the child. All such issues must be discussed and fully worked through at that time since the communication and problem-solving patterns established at this stage will be required again and again over the years. Issues avoided at one stage become even harder to discuss and resolve at a later stage. Placement should not occur until everyone involved is satisfied that an adequate problem-solving mechanism has been established. The older the child involved, the more complex the placement process becomes; but if the adoptive parents are comfortable with the child's heritage and the child (age permitting) has an honest desire to be adopted, the subsequent handling of the child's adoptive status within the family should not constitute a major problem.

Age of Adoption

The definition of "older child" for adoption purposes is very vague and often involves a number of personality and emotional factors requiring careful consideration. In general, most children between 8 months and 4 years are likely to find any separation hard to tolerate and resolve successfully. Any child younger than 6 years is almost totally at the mercy of adults to decide for or against placement during adoption; most legislation expects children to speak for themselves at age 12. While wholeheartedly supporting the total involvement of all children in their own life decisions, it should be noted that these are very complex and delicate issues involving different levels of awareness, understanding, and insight. Despite repeated exploratory and supportive discussions of what the contemplated change is likely to mean, everyone involved must be prepared to take a chance. A prerequisite to success is that the child wants the adoption to succeed and is prepared to work hard to make it succeed. Frequently children say that they want to be adopted but without awareness and understanding of their own feelings and motivations, some of which may work to undermine the adoptive process. This idea will be discussed further in the section on factors correlated with lack of success in adoption.

Interaction Between Child and Parents

Adoptive parents are frequently reluctant to discuss information about their child's biological parentage and preadoption history (Jaffee and Fanshel 1970; Sorosky et al. 1975; Triseliotis 1970). The greater the empathy of the adoptive family for the birth family, the more easily and naturally the adoption will be achieved. The more secure the adoptive parents are as individuals and in their marriage, the more easily they will handle difficult and potentially threatening questions. All this appears eminently straightforward on paper. In practice, however, the different participants have widely differing needs from the situation. Often unstated and unrecognized needs of the adoptive parents, such as their drive to prove their adequacy in the face of infertility, or of children deeply traumatized by separation to bring repeated rejections upon themselves are, at the time, more obvious to others than to the participants themselves. It is crucial that, as these needs surface, they be honestly confronted and addressed. If this is not done these issues will serve to fester and undermine the adoption and, in some cases, even the solidarity of the new adoptive family. Adoption, especially of older children, is not a natural process: it is experienced differently by each individual involved. This issue must be recognized and dealt with candidly in order for the process to succeed.

Psychological Problems Related to Adoption

Little controversy exists about the psychological conflicts almost universally experienced by adopted children that are specific to their adopted status. First, is the adopted children's need to resolve those complex problems arising from having two sets of parents in their lives (Schechter et al. 1964; Sorosky et al. 1975). Identity confusion during adolescence is exaggerated for many adoptees (American Academy of Pediatrics 1971; Sorosky et al. 1975) because of the frequency of attachment problems that undermine the child's sense of belonging within the adoptive family and continuing presence (in fantasy or in real life) of the birth parents. This latter reason favors excessive reliance on the use of the mental mechanism of splitting, that is, imagining that some people (sets of parents) are all good and others all bad, as a psychological defense. This, in turn, makes it harder for the child to see anyone, including himself or herself, as partly good and partly bad, thus undermining his or her ability to develop a clear and realistic sense of self that remains constant over time (Schechter 1960; Schechter et al. 1964; Sorosky et al. 1975).

Adoptive parents, too, face special difficulties. They are vulnerable to stresses unique to their status, which include the competition (real or imagined) from the memory of biological and/or much loved foster parents, the child's prior history and biological inheritance, and unresolved issues related to their own fertility (Kirk 1964; Sorosky et al. 1975).

Adoptive boys are significantly more likely to be disturbed than girls (Bohman 1970; Tizard 1977). Adoptive children are more hostile, insecure, and attention-seeking than nonadoptive children, although less so than illegitimate children raised by their own

mothers or those restored to natural families after a period of care (Tizard 1977; Tizard and Rees 1975). Although there is controversy about how much the child's age at placement affects adoption success, difficulties occurring following adoption are more likely to present as social, behavioral, or emotional problems rather than as an overt resistance to reattachment or integration within the adoptive family (Eldred et al. 1976; Jaffee and Fanshel 1970; Kadushin and Seidl 1971; Tizard 1977). Bohman and Sigvardsson (1979) reported on 624 infant candidates for adoption who were investigated at 11 and 15 years of age. At 11 years, they showed more nervous disturbances and maladjustment than their classmates, whether living in adoptive homes, in foster homes, or with their biological mothers. At 15 years, the adoptees did almost as well as their classmates, while those reared in foster homes or by biological mothers showed increased social maladjustment and/or school underachievement. By age 18, they were average medically, psychiatrically, and socially, although a number of authors have found increased rates of alcoholism and antisocial personality in adoptees.

This study emphasizes the importance of good placement procedures for children on adoption and their adoptive parents. It stresses the need to make decisions about children's futures as quickly as possible, in order to minimize the time they remain in limbo (Goldstein et al. 1973). The value of ongoing preventive work with mothers who having considered placing their children in adoption decide instead to rear them on their own despite social and psychological adversity is also stressed (Hersov 1985).

Ways in Which Special Status is Managed in Adoptive Families

Both adoptees and their adoptive parents know that the adopted child's biological inheritance differs from that of other family members. This establishes the child as "special," and any child with special status is particularly vulnerable to scapegoating and/or rejection, especially at points of increased stress for the adoptive parents or in their marriage. Inherited temperamental factors, especially when aggravated by the long-term sequelae of deprivation and discontinuity, leave many older adoptees difficult to live with, let alone love. If natural (previously unable to be conceived) children are born subsequent to an adoption undertaken because of supposed infertility, many adoptive parents ascribe all difficulties encountered with the adopted child solely to genetics and/or prior experience. By doing so, they distance the child, absolving themselves of any need to examine the role their own attitudes and interactions contributed to the problem (Tooley 1978).

Two particular problems are related to the special status of the adopted child. The first involves how the child's status as an adoptee is managed, a process closely related to the development of the adopted child's identity. A second problem is the reluctance of some adoptive parents to discuss their adopted child's biological heritage. This is manifested in the controversy as to the best age to discuss a child's adoption. Although there are exceptions (Schechter 1960), most authorities encourage adoptive parents to be as frank as possible with adopted children from day one. At some point, all such children will learn of their adopted (i.e., different) status. Failure to discuss adoption and the child's origins openly can be related to general parenting style (i.e., lack of open communication and/or marked overprotection) or to the parents' need to deny that which is special about their adoptive status (Jaffee and Fanshel 1970; Sorosky et al. 1975; Triseliotis 1973). Such attempts at distorting reality usually reflect significant discomfort with their status as adoptive parents. Unless this problem is resolved early and effectively, it places the parent–child relationship and the child's subsequent development at considerable risk. Parental shame related to infertility, however, may be less of a problem today than 20 years ago because of societal factors. The tone and attitude in which discussions of adoptive status are carried out may be as or more important than the actual information communicated. The greater the comfort of the adoptive parents with their special status, the more easily and naturally such discussions proceed.

Second, since at some point all adopted children are likely to learn about their special status, it is better that they first do so in a supportive and natural way from trusted parents than to have the facts withheld from them (Triseliotis 1973). What, when, and how the child is told about the adoption is an important issue. Although there is no single right way (all parents must say and do what is natural for them), a number of guidelines are suggested.

Parents should begin with a simple and concrete statement as soon as children begin to show an interest in the origin of babies. If this is done, the toddlers will at least have been introduced to the word "adoption," even though they will not at first fully understand it. Beyond that, children should generally be told what they want to know, no more and no less. If they sense that the topic is an open one, they will return for more information when they are ready for it.

A second general problem faced by adoptive families is the normal ambivalence parents and children have toward each other throughout the course of development. In some families, by confronting their parents with their adoptive status (e.g., "You're not my real parents") adoptees learn that their adoption can be an ideal weapon, one that natural children do not have at their disposal. Secure adoptive parents are not overwhelmed by this tactic and deal with the child's behavior appropriately. Many adoptive parents, however, are less secure, and the greater the insecurity aroused by the child's attack on their status, the more complex the feelings and interactional problems that may result. Depending on the balance of stresses and supports available to the parents, this can lead to a real crisis in the parent–child relationship. Some adoptive children handle much of their normal hostility toward their parents through claims they feel unloved or hints they prefer their birth parents. They may follow this up by making excessive demands on vulnerable parents or by blackmailing them into colluding with outrageous behavior. In response, already insecure parents become increasingly anxious, then resentful and finally guilty. In some such psychologically susceptible parents, extreme guilt in response to mounting anger is defended against by reaction formation. In this way, the hostile component of the parents' ambivalence is replaced by its opposite—extreme overindulgence, overinvolvement, and permissiveness—which leave them unable to limit or discipline the child, thus causing future problems.

Other adoptees experience different difficulties dealing with the hostile component of their ambivalence toward their parents. Some children, especially those who have been told how their adoptive family saved them from a life of poverty and degradation, feel they have no right to express or feel anger against the family that has done so much for them. Others handle the same situation by feeling that just as they were "chosen" so may they be "unchosen." Both of these defensive patterns complicate the open expression and normal resolution of hostility, a resolution necessary to the ongoing maturation of child, family, and the parent–child relationship.

The most problems usually occur when adoptive children reach adolescence. The mother may be struggling with the menopause; the father may be burned out by career pressures and the need to raise many thousands of dollars for his children's education. The children may be at a variety of stages, all with their own developmental tasks and hazards. Simultaneously, the family may be dealing with the demands of elderly, ill, or dying grandparents. These are but a few of the more common stresses commonly affecting families at this stage in their life cycle. This is often a stage when some families, not just those faced with the additional stresses resulting from adoption, are in need of outside support of a personal or professional nature. This recalls the earlier discussion on assessment for adoption, where the importance of the desire to communicate, the development of techniques for problem-solving, and the need to establish support systems at the start of the adoptive process were stressed. Support is more likely to be accepted from others who have been in a similar situation. Hence, there is value of post-adoption groups, even though the need for them is not often appreciated at the time of the adoption, which might have to be included as a component of the normal adoption process. The frequent tendency of adoptive parents to deny or minimize what others report as major problems until after rejection of the adopted child has been commented on (Bohman 1970; Westhues and Cohen 1988; Jaffee and Fanshel 1970; Schechter 1960; Tizard 1977). All adoptive families should have such supports in place and know how to activate them, for a time of need will almost inevitably come.

Issues Related to the Adopted Child's Having Two Sets of Parents: The Movement Toward More Open Adoption

There are two sets of parents involved in any adoption. One may exist only psychologically or be actively involved in the child's ongoing reality, but, in either case, the birth parents are present in the child. However constructive the adoptive environment, one can only hope that it serves to balance inherited tendencies that have an above average tendency to produce a psychosocially vulnerable child (Cadoret 1978a; Cunningham et al. 1975). Clarke (1981) has demonstrated that children adopted early resemble their biological parents more than their adoptive relatives. Vaitenas (1981) stresses the importance of perinatal risk factors such as those resulting from low birth weight, prematurity, and fetal alcohol syndrome, all of which can contribute to the nature of the child who is placed within the adoptive home. Children may have no control over the various sets of parental figures that have contributed to making them what they are, but most, at some point or other, will fantasize about birth parents and compare them with adoptive parents. This must be expected and is one of the issues that adoptive parents need to accept with equanimity. Ideally, adoptive parents will be confident enough to support the child's search for his or her own sense of identity without suffering an intolerable loss in their own self-esteem or sense-of-connectedness with the child. There is no question that, at some point, the child will need to consolidate his or her own identity. The potential problem lies in the comfort, commitment, and honesty of the adoptive parents, all of which may affect their response to this attempt. Attempts to block the child's understanding and coming to grips with his or her origins may temporarily succeed, but they succeed at the cost of building up even more internalized tension that is only detrimental to the child. In contrast, if the adoptive parents are prepared for and recognize this striving as natural or minimally threatening, they can deal with it gradually, at a pace that everyone can tolerate without unbearable distress.

Adoption is not the natural way to have a family. Successful adoption depends on the ability of adoptive families, including children, to balance the rights and needs of the adoptee against those of other members of the adoptive family. Adoption does not automatically lend itself to the fulfillment of the usual needs aroused in parents by the process of child-raising.

Much has been written since 1975 on the concept of open adoption, which involves the disclosure of information, the unsealing of adoption records, and reunions with birth parents. It is not surprising that in the present social climate, where individual rights and the concept of "roots" are highly valued, adoptees are beginning to demand these long buried claims. Because of the somewhat conflicting needs of the various parties involved, open adoption is far from straightforward. The literature reflects this controversy. There is much support for the opening of sealed adoption records (Baran et al. 1976, 1977; Dukette 1984; Pannor and Baran 1984; Semancik 1979). Those supporting open adoption submit that while adoption of older children has been open for many years, all adoptions should be similarly open in order to minimize psychological problems. Dukette (1984) suggests that the maintenance of biological ties may actually facilitate the establishment and maintenance of attachment and bonding within the adoptive family for older adoptees without disrupting significant current ties. Although Sorosky and co-workers (1975) showed that 80% of adult adoptees studied reported reunion with their birth parents satisfying, only 10% of the birth parents, and considerably more adoptive parents, reacted negatively. How does one meet the needs of adoptive children without inflicting undue damage to any of the other parties in this complex triangular relationship (Andrews 1971)? Aymend and Barrett (1984) found that adoptees who did not seek out their birth parents had more positive self-concepts and more constructive attitudes toward their adoptive parents, whom they considered emotionally more involved. Triseliotis (1973) also found that adoptees who demanded reunion with their biological parents differed from those who sought only nonidentifying information about them. The reunion-seekers were characterized by long-standing dissatisfaction with the adoptive family, low self-esteem, chronic problematic adjustment in many aspects of life, and non-disclosure or disclosure only of disparaging information by the adoptive parents. In an unpublished 1978 pilot study of 79 adoptees over the age of majority seeking either non-identifying information and/or reunion with their biological parents, D'Iorio and Steinhauer basically replicated Triseliotis's results with one additional finding. They found that those seeking reunion divided naturally into two groups, a group of urgent seekers who demanded immediate access to their biological parents as a matter of right regardless of how either the biological or the adoptive parents felt, and a group of nonurgent seekers who, while sympathetic to both their biological and adoptive parents' feelings about their search, had an interest in meeting their biological parents. They looked to reunion more to help them clarify their own identities than as the definitive answer to a life of misery. D'Iorio and Steinhauer found the nonurgent seekers emotionally and socially well adjusted, in contrast to the urgent seekers, who were severely, chronically, and pervasively disturbed. The urgent seekers' response to reunion was often mixed, but even when the reunion itself involved bitter disappointment they claimed the reunions were helpful in coming to grips with their situation, whether or not this was accompanied by evidence of objective behavioral change. The disappointment experienced by some urgent seekers following reunion with their birth parents was not, in itself, an argument against reunion but rather a necessary stage in that adoptee's finally coming to terms with reality.

These data, along with those of Jaffe and Fanshel (1970) found an association between long-standing dissatisfaction, problematic adjustment, complaints of insufficient disclosures and/or hostile disclosures about the birth parents and suggest the importance of adoption agencies' routinely supplying background information to all adoptive parents, stressing that it be shared as freely and naturally as possible well before the child enters adolescence.

These data also suggest that the adoptee's requests for either nonidentifying information or reunion be viewed not as isolated events but as important stages in the consolidation of their sense of personal identity. Sensitive casework at this point from a worker familiar with identity formation in adoptees can be extremely helpful to the adoptees themselves, to their adoptive families, and to the birth parents. Obviously, workers who are seen as part of an ongoing support network (i.e., the adoptive agency) rather than someone newly introduced have a greater chance of proving helpful.

In 1977, Minnesota passed legislation allowing the release of a sealed birth certificate to adult adoptees on the consent of their birth parents. Stephenson (1975) discussed the controversy surrounding the Canadian (Manitoba, New Brunswick, Ontario, Saskatchewan) adoption reunion registry that enables reunion after the adoptee has reached legal age, given three-party consent. Amendments to the Child and Family Services Act (Bill 77) (1987) have brought into law some progressive changes in Ontario. As a result, the government will conduct an active search for parents, grandparents, or adult siblings on the request of an adult adoptee without consent of adoptive parents.

In evaluating these changes, it is clear that a single solution that can protect all parties from damage is unattainable. However, if one considers children as being "on loan" to parents whose job it is to nurture them in the direction of independence, how can one justify parents denying children the comfort derived from consolidation of their personal identity? We know that some children require more information and contact. The situation is further confused since earlier adoptions took place under conditions in which anonymity was guaranteed to both biological and adoptive parents. In contrast, contemporary adoptees and their prospective families are being prepared for a variety of possibilities that may address identity-related issues in the future.

The current perspective is that an adoptee of legal age should have the right to contact birth parents if the latter are in agreement and strongly questions the right of adoptive parents to veto such reunions by withholding their consent. For them to try to do so seems analogous to the attempts of some natural parents to control their child's career, marriage choices, and so on, other than by supplying their input within the dynamics of a mutually respectful and constructive relationship. Still, there is no question that this position is somewhat unfair, especially to earlier adoptive parents who were told that they could rely on guarantees of anonymity that are no longer being honored. We can only suggest, however, that we are living in a time in which societal attitudes have shifted so that the rights of some are being given priority over those of others. This attitudinal shift, added to the fact that the modern world is now dealing with the choices of an adult, is sufficient to merit giving the choice to the adult adoptee even in the face of adoptive parents' disapproval. Until the adoptee reaches the legal age, however, the adoptive parents' agreement should be a necessary condition for reunion. These proposals are not without some risk during a crisis point in the life of adoptee and adoptive family, one during which the availability of external support for those involved is highly indicated. Mandatory professional counseling should be given to all parties if an actual or proposed reunion is strongly indicated in order to ensure empathic and objective help in resolving issues reactivated by the search process.

FACTORS CORRELATED WITH LACK OF SUCCESS IN ADOPTION

History of Deprivation and Multiple Placements

Children with a history of severe deprivation and multiple placements, especially within the first 2 years of life, are at higher risk of adoption breakdown (Kadushin 1970; Rutter 1979). Such children are likely to have more frequent problems in school, in their social behavior outside the home, and in their social relationships. Taken together, these will inevitably place additional strain on their relationships with their adoptive parents, however accepting the latter may be.

Children With a Diagnosable Conduct Disorder

Children with a diagnosable conduct disorder are at higher risk of adoption breakdown (Kadushin 1970).

Children Who Are Removed From a Successful Long-Term Placement

Children whose foster parents have become their psychological parents also face an increased risk of adoption breakdown. Currently, in North America, there is strong pressure toward adopting or restoring to their birth families all children in long-term foster care in order to ensure permanence. Many of the sources of this pressure seem political and economic (i.e., to eliminate the cost of maintaining children in foster care) rather than psychologically or humanely motivated. The arguments that foster homes are inherently unstable, that the permanence of even planned permanent foster placements cannot be guaranteed from breakdown during the child's adolescence, and that foster parents seeking them must be only minimally committed or they would be proceeding toward adoption are all used to demand permanent (i.e., adoptive) placement. But one cannot, by legal means, ensure the permanence of a given placement, however good the intentions (Emlen et al. 1978). A number of authors have suggested that foster placements in which children have formed a stable attachment and are developing satisfactorily deserve to be supported and stabilized (Cooper 1978; Derdeyn 1977; Goldstein et al. 1973, 1979; Steinhauer 1980, 1983; Wiltse 1976).

To accommodate such situations, a variety of intermediate alternatives such as "planned permanent" foster care, foster care with tenure, and "subsidized adoption" are being used increasingly for children developing well in stable foster placements with families disinclined towards adoption (Derdeyn 1977; Cooper 1978; Berridge and Cleaver 1988). In the absence of reliable experimental evidence for the least detrimental alternative for this group of children, we recommend Cooper's (1978) suggestion of careful planning on an individualized basis, using the full participation of all involved in order to find the currently available solution most likely to provide maximal continuity for that child.

Adoptions Involving a Child Who Continues to Retain a Strong Emotional Tie

When this situation occurs with members of the birth family or foster family, the adoption is vulnerable unless the existing attachment is not merely tolerated but actively protected, with continuing access guaranteed. In such cases, forced separation is likely to favor retention and idealization in fantasy of the lost attachment figure, thus interfering with the child's ability to attach successfully to adoptive parents (Goldstein et al. 1973; Kadushin 1970; Steinhauer 1980, 1983).

Adoptions in Which One or Both Adoptive Parents Have Excessive Expectations

In some cases the child is so badly needed to meet the needs of the adoptive couple (e.g., to replace a dead child, to be the ideal companion for an only child, to fill an empty nest, or to give the adoptive parents' lives meaning) that the parents are unable to accept the child for himself or herself (Schechter 1960).

Adoption in Which the Child Has Developed a Well-Established Personality

Children with set ways of behaving and/ or exaggerated needs that interfere with acceptability and integration within the adoptive family are at higher risk of adoption breakdown (Eldred et al. 1976).

The Age at Adoption

Controversy remains about how much the age at adoption affects the likelihood of adoption success (Eldred et al. 1976; Jaffee and Fanshel 1970; Kadushin and Seidl 1971; Rae-Grant 1978; Tizard 1977). Humphrey and Ounsted (1963) found a higher rate of disturbance, especially in boys placed prior to 6 months of age, but Offord and co-workers (1969) and Kadushin and Seidl (1971) found that frequency and severity of antisocial behavior varied directly with the age of adoption.

However, other studies (Eldred et al. 1976; Menlove 1965) suggested that the age at adoption did not significantly affect adoptive outcome. Jaffee and Fanshel (1970) agreed, while Kadushin (1970) in a follow-up of children placed on adoption between the ages of 5 and 12, found that only 14% of adoptive parents expressed dissatisfaction. This figure has been widely used to support the claim that older child adoptions are as likely to be successful as infant adoptions, and, in fact, most adoption studies report a parent satisfaction rate of 78% to 85% regardless of the age at adoption (Tizard 1977). However, since these studies rate adoptive success according to parent satisfaction only, since adoptive parents typically deny what others report as fairly major problems (Bohman 1970; Jaffee and Fanshel, 1970; Schechter 1960; Tizard 1977; Westhues and Cohen, 1988), these findings may be unduly optimistic. These rates are further altered since some studies include only adoptions that have successfully survived the probation period (Jaffee and Fanshel, 1970) and others (Eldred et al. 1976) lack precise criteria to define success and failure. Nevertheless, although available data certainly suggest that the risk in adoption of older children is considerably less than previously believed, it is generally accepted that, to minimize the risks, adoption should occur at the earliest possible age.

References

American Academy of Pediatrics. 1971. Identity development in adopted children. *Pediatrics* 47:948–949.

Andrews, R.G. 1971. When is subsidized adoption preferable to long-term foster care? *Child Welfare* 50:194–200.

Aymend, S.A., and Barrett, M.C. 1984. Self-concept and attitudes toward adoption: A comparison of searching and non-searching adult adoptees. *Child Welfare* 63:251–259.

Baldwin, W., and Cain, V. 1980. The children of teenage parents. *Fam Plann Perspect* 12:34–43.

Baran, A., Pannor, R., and Sorosky, A.D. 1976. Open adoption. *Social Work* 21:97–100.

Baran A., Pannor, R., and Sorosky, A.D. 1977. Adoptive parents and the sealed record controversy. *Social Casework* 55:531–536.

Berridge, D., and Cleaver, H. 1988. Long-term fostering. In: *Foster Home Breakdown*. New York: Basil Blackwell.

Bohman, M. 1970. *Adopted Children and their Families*. Stockholm: Proprius.

Bohman, M. 1971. A comparative study of adopted children, foster children and children in their biological environment born after undesired pregnancies. *Acta Paediatr. Scand. Suppl.* 221:1.

Bohman, M. 1972. A study of adopted children, their background, environment, and adjustment. *Acta Paediatr. Scand.* 61:90–97.

Bohman, M. 1978. Some genetic aspects of alcoholism and criminality: A population of adoptions. *Arch. Gen. Psychiatry* 35:269–276.

Bohman, M. 1981. The interaction of heredity and childhood environment: Some adoption studies. *J. Child Psychol. Psychiatry* 22:195–200.

Bohman, M., and Sigvardsson, S. 1979. Long-term effects of early institutional care: A prospective longitudinal study. *J. Child Psychol. Psychiatry* 20:111–117.

Cadoret, R.J. 1978a. Evidence for genetic inheritance of primary affective disorder in adoptees. *Am. J. Psychiatry* 135:463–466.

Cadoret, R.J. 1978b. Psychopathology in adopted-away offspring of biologic parents with antisocial behaviour. *Arch. Gen. Psychiatry* 35:176–184.

Cantwell, D. 1975. Genetic studies of hyperactive children. In Fieve, R., Rosenthal, D., and Brill, H. (eds.): *Genetic Research in Psychiatry*. Baltimore: Johns Hopkins Press.

Clarke, A.M. 1981. Adoption studies and human development. *Adoption Fostering* 104:17–29.

Cloninger, C.R., Bohman, M., and Sigvardsson, S. 1981. Inheritance of alcohol abuse: Cross-fostering analysis of adopted men. *Arch. Gen. Psychiatry* 38:861–868.

Cooper, J.D. 1978. *Pattern of Family Placement: Current Issues in Fostering and Adoption*. London: National Children's Bureau.

Crellin, E., Pringle, M.L., Kellmer, D., and West, P. 1971. *Born Illegitimate, Social and Educational Implications*. Windsor: National Foundation for Educational Research.

Crowe, R.R. 1974. An adoption study of antisocial personality. *Arch. Gen. Psychiatry* 31:785–791.

Cunningham, L., Cadoret, R.J., Loftus, R., and Edwards, J. 1975. Studies of adoptees from psychiatrically disturbed biological parents: Psychiatric conditions in childhood and adolescence. *Br. J. Psychiatry* 126:534–549.

Derdeyn, A.P. 1977. A case for permanent foster placement of dependent, neglected and abused children. *Am. J. Orthopsychiatry* 47:604–614.

D'Iorio, M., and Steinhauer, P. 1978. Seeking out one's birth parents: Acting out a fantasy of reattachment. Presentation at Conference on Current Issues in Child Psychiatry. Geneva Park, Ontario.

Dukette, R. 1984. Value issues in present-day adoption. *Child Welfare* 63:233–243.

Eldred, C., et al. 1976. Some aspects of adoption in selected samples of adult adoptees. *Am. J. Orthopsychiatry* 46:279–290.

Emlen, A., et al. 1978. *Overcoming Barriers to Planning for Children in Foster Care*. Washington, D.C.: Department of Health, Education and Welfare, Publication No. (OHDS) 78–30138.

Goldstein, J., Freud, A., and Solnit, A. 1973. *Beyond the Best Interests of the Child*. New York: Free Press.

Goldstein J., Freud, A., and Solnit, A. 1979. *Before the Best Interests of the Child*. New York: Free Press.

Goodwin, D., Schulsinger, F., Moller, N., et al. 1974. Drinking problems in adopted and nonadopted sons of alcoholics. *Arch. Gen. Psychiatry* 31:164–169.

Grey, E., and Blunden, R. M. 1971. *A Survey of Adoption in Great Britain*. Home Office Research Studies. London: Her Majesty's Stationery Office.

Guyatt, D.E. 1980. Panel on adolescent pregnancy and motherhood. Presented at St. John's, Newfoundland June 18, 1980. Toronto: Ontario Ministry of Community and Social Services.

Hausknecht, R.D. 1972. The termination of pregnancy in adolescent women. *Paediatr. Clin. North Am.* 19:803–810.

Hepworth, H.P. 1980. *Foster Care and Adoption in Canada*. Ottawa: Canadian Council on Social Development.

Hersov, L. 1983. Adoption and fostering. In Rutter, M., and Hersov, L. (eds.): *Child and Adolescent Psychiatry*. Oxford: Blackwell Scientific Publications.

Hersov, L. 1985. Adoption and fostering. In Rutter, M., and Hersov, L. (eds): *Child and Adolescent Psychiatry:*

Modern Approaches, 2nd. ed. Oxford: Blackwell Scientific Publications.

Heston, L.L. 1966. Psychiatric disorder in foster home reared children of schizophrenic mothers. *Br. J. Psychiatry* 112:819–825.

Humphrey, M. 1969. *The Hostage Seekers.* The National Bureau for Cooperation in Child Care. London: Longmans.

Humphrey, M., and Ounsted, D. 1963. Adoptive families referred for psychiatric advice: I. The children. *Br. J. Psychiatry* 109:599–608.

Hutchings, B., and Mednick, S. 1975. Registered criminality in the adoptive and biological parents of registered male criminal adoptees. In Fieve, R., Rosenthal, D., and Brill, H. (eds.): *Genetic Research in Psychiatry.* Baltimore: John Hopkins University Press.

Jaffee, B., and Fanshell, D. 1970. *How They Fared in Adoption: A Follow-up Study.* New York: Columbia University Press.

Kadushin, A. 1970. *Adopting Older Children.* New York: Columbia University Press.

Kadushin, A., and Seidl, F.W. 1971. Adoption failure: A social work postmortem. *Social Work* 16:32–38.

Kety, S.S., Rosenthal, D., Wender, P.H., and Schulsinger, F. 1976. Studies based on a total sample of adopted individuals and their relatives: Why they were necessary, what they demonstrated and failed to demonstrate. *Schizophr Bull.* 2:413–428.

Kirk, H.D. 1964. *Shared Fate: A Theory of Adoption and Mental Health.* London: The Free Press of Glencoe.

McGuffin, P., and Gottesman, I.I. 1985. Genetic influences on normal and abnormal development. In Rutter, M., and Hersov, L. (eds.): *Child and Adolescent Psychiatry: Modern Approaches,* 2nd. ed. Oxford: Blackwell Scientific Publications.

Mendlewicz, J., and Rainer, J. 1977. Adoption study supporting genetic transmission in manic depressive illness. *Nature* 268:327–329.

Menlove, F. 1965. Aggressive symptoms in emotionally disturbed adopted children. *Child Dev.* 46:519–532.

Morrison, J. 1973. The psychiatric status of the legal families of adopted hyperactive children. *Arch. Gen. Psychiatry* 28:888–891.

Morrison, J., and Stewart, M. 1971. A family study of the hyperactive child syndrome. *Biol. Psychiatry* 3:189–195.

Office of Population Censuses and Surveys. 1976. *Adoption.* London: Her Majesty's Stationery Office.

Offord, D.R., Aponte, J.F., and Cross, L.A. 1969. Presenting symptomatology of adopted children. *Arch. Gen. Psychiatry* 20:110–116.

Pannor, R., and Baran, A. 1984. Open adoption as standard practice. *Child Welfare* 63:245–250.

Rae-Grant, N. 1978. But they didn't live happily ever after. . . . *J. Ontario Assn. Child. Aid Societies* 21:3–8.

Rowe, J., and Lambert, L. 1973. *Children Who Wait.* London: Association of British Adoption Agencies.

Rutter, M. 1972. *Maternal Deprivation Reassessed.* Hamondsworth, England: Penguin Books.

Rutter, M. 1979. *Changing Youth in a Changing Society: Patterns of Adolescent Development and Disorder.* London: Nuffield Provincial Hospitals Trust. (Cambridge, Mass.: Harvard University Press, 1980).

Schechter, M.D. 1960. Observations of adopted children. *Arch. Gen. Psychiatry* 3:21–32.

Schechter, M.D., Carlson, P.V., Simmons, J.Q., et al. 1964. Emotional problems in the adoptee. *Arch. Gen. Psychiatry* 10:109–118.

Semancik, J. 1979. Adoption: The changing scene. *Social Thought* 5(4):3–61.

Sorosky, A.D., Baran, A., and Pannor, R. 1975. Identity conflicts in adoptees. *Am. J. Orthopsychiatry* 45:18–27.

Steinhauer, P.D. 1980. *How to Succeed in the Business of Creating Psychopaths Without Even Trying.* Vols. 2 and 4, *Training Resources in Understanding, Supporting and Treating Abused Children. Foster Parents Training Program for Children's Aid Societies.* Toronto: Ministry of Community and Social Services.

Steinhauer, P.D. 1983. Issues of attachment and separation: Foster care and adoption. In Steinhauer, P.D., and Rae-Grant, Q. (eds.): *Psychological Problems of the Child in the Family.* New York: Basic Books.

Stephenson, P.D. 1975. The emotional implications of adoption policy. *Comp. Psychiatry* 16:363–367.

Tarter, R.E. (ed.) 1983. *The Child at Psychiatric Risk.* New York: Oxford University Press.

Tizard, B. 1977. *Adoption: A Second Chance.* London: Open Books.

Tizard, B., and Rees, J. 1975. The effect of early institutional rearing on the behaviour problems and affectional relationships of four-year-old children. *J. Child Psychol. Psychiatry* 16:61–73.

Tooley, K.M. 1978. Irreconcilable differences between parent and child: A case report of interactional pathology. *Am. J. Orthopsychiatry* 48:703–716.

Triseliotis, J. 1970. *Evaluation of Adoption Policy and Practice.* Edinburgh: University of Edinburgh.

Triseliotis, J. 1973. *In Search of Origins: The Experiences of Adopted People.* London: Routledge and Kegan Paul.

Vaitenas, R.E. 1981. Children with special needs: Perinatal education for adoption workers. *Child Welfare* 60:405–411.

Ward, M. 1978. Full house: Adoption of a large sibling group. *Child Welfare* 57:233–241.

Westhues, A., and Cohen, J. 1988. *How to Reduce the Risk: Healthy Functioning Families for Adoptive and Foster Children.* Toronto: University of Toronto Press.

Wiltse, K.T. 1976. Decision-making needs in foster care. *Child. Today* 5:2–5.

Weidell, R.C. 1980. Unsealing sealed birth certificates in Minnesota. *Child Welfare* 59:113–119.

Five

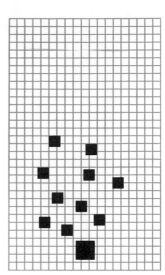

TECHNIQUES IN CHILD
AND ADOLESCENT
PSYCHIATRY

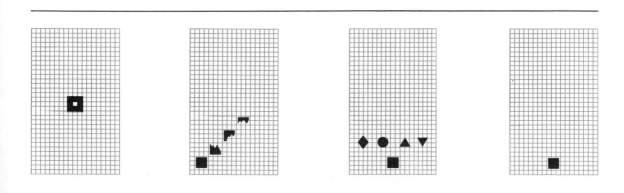

26

Interviewing Children and Adolescents*

J. GERALD YOUNG, M.D.
LEN LEVEN, M.D.
WENDY LUDMAN, PSY.D.
HITEN KISNADWALA, M.D.
JOHN D. O'BRIEN, M.D.

THE INTERVIEW AS A MEDICAL PROCEDURE

Patients view medical procedures differently than physicians. Novel technology catapulted genetic and imaging methods to new levels of sophistication and clinical use, and physicians turn to it for answers to patient care problems. Physicians view their capacity to apply state-of-the-art technology in their research and clinical practice as an indication of the high quality of care they provide. Patients, on the other hand, judge clinical competence on the basis of their interview with the physician. Comments such as "She's easy to talk to," "He seemed to understand my problem," or "I get along with him" are very common when a patient recommends his or her doctor to someone else. Such comments are often less valued by physicians as of secondary importance when compared with other indicators of clinical competence, such as technically complex instrumental procedures.

Physicians will be wise to consider the patient's perspective. The clinical interview is the primary source of information used to determine diagnosis and guide treatment. The ability of the physician to establish satisfactory rapport with a patient is essential to obtaining full information from the patient, which will be the basis for subsequent diagnostic studies. Moreover, many studies have pointed out that even the best planned treatment protocol is subject to a remarkably high rate of patient noncompliance. A good relationship with the patient, established through the clinical interview, is the single most important procedure that can be used to improve treatment compliance.

Psychiatrists have studied the clinical interview and refined techniques considerably, leading to their identification among their medical colleagues as experts in this procedure. In many respects, the requirement for these refined methods is most obvious in the care of children. Children and adolescents often find interviews confusing and difficult. The child and adolescent psychiatrist must be especially skillful in understanding the developmental capacities and individual concerns of children if one is to enlist the necessary cooperation. In addition, the clinician must be able to competently interview others in the child's world, such as parents, brothers and sisters, teachers, friends, and others.

Recognition of its central role has stimu-

*This work was supported by a grant from the Medical Fellows Program of the Office of Mental Retardation and Developmental Disabilities, State of New York.

lated substantial study of the clinical interview. On the one hand, this attention has enhanced the understanding of factors influencing the success of interviews. On the other hand, however, the attempt to study "the clinical interview" has the potential for detrimental effects. This results in attempts by clinical investigators to improve "the clinical interview" or to train young physicians in better ways to conduct "a clinical interview." This is not unlike asking a physician to obtain a blood sample but failing to indicate whether it is for a complete blood cell count or for blood chemistries, or recommending that a patient take a medication for an illness without specifying which one. There is no single clinical interview. Undertaking a clinical interview with a patient requires prior preparation so that the proper interview format can be selected ahead of time and specific procedures be used during the time with the patient. This approach, however, may have to be adapted to the changing needs of the patient at a given time.

TYPES OF INTERVIEWS

The illusion that the clinical interview is a single entity has arisen, in part, because of the uniform goals for diagnostic interviews when applied by most physicians, and, in other settings, because of the power of clinical interview techniques developed by psychoanalysts. For example, all physicians have an interest in defining the patient's problem, considering its anatomical location, describing its qualities, and determining what aggravates the problem and what relieves it. In contrast to this unanimous agreement on necessary diagnostic information is the demonstration by psychoanalysts of the many types of information that can be derived from an interview and the effects of using different interview techniques to influence the nature of the information produced. Experienced interviewers can elicit previously unknown facts by giving meticulous attention to the conflicts, affects, defenses, and symptoms of the patient. The results of psychoanalytical interview techniques are so powerful that clinicians made the cultivation of these skills the primary pursuit of psychiatrists in training. Eliciting and clarifying unconscious thoughts and feelings can sometimes lead to

rapid understanding of the patient's problems.

Regrettably, overemphasis on single interview techniques eventually led to a loss of confidence in the status of the interview as a scientific source of significant data. However, the central scientific role of the interview for child and adolescent psychiatrists is evident when the clinical interview is considered to consist of many "types," and attention is given to the requirements and components for each type of interview.

Determinants of Interview Structure and Technique

INTERVIEW OBJECTIVES

Several features of the interview determine the type of interview selected. Whatever the age of the patient, a first requirement for an optimally productive interview is to decide what type of information is sought and select among the numerous categories of interviews available (Table 26–1). This choice among alternative objectives for the interview has profound effects on the techniques used. This is evident in examples such as the diagnostic interview, the psychodynamic interview, or formal psychological testing.

Table 26–1. TYPES OF PSYCHIATRIC INTERVIEWS

1. Diagnostic (psychiatric)
   a. Symptom history (history of the present illness)
   b. Past psychiatric history
2. Diagnostic (medical)
   a. Medical review of organ systems
   b. Past medical history
3. Psychoanalytical/psychodynamic
4. Family dynamics and interactions
5. Developmental history
6. Mental status examination
7. Play interview
8. Genetic history
9. Review of referral records (medical, educational, community)
10. Infant developmental history and examination
11. Toddler/preschool history and examination
12. Physical examination
13. Neurologic and special neurologic examinations
14. Psychological testing
15. Behavior rating
16. Summary of diagnoses and treatment recommendations
17. Therapeutic (many subtypes)
18. Psychopharmacologic
19. Follow-up/outcome

INTERVIEWER TRAINING AND SKILLS

The native skills and training of the interviewer must be carefully considered. Interviewer educational background can range from partial college education to psychoanalytical training. For example, large epidemiologic research projects employ lay interviewers who use completely structured interview formats that include preworded "probes" (questions) to identify symptoms. College students might be assigned as interviewers. At the other pole, it requires years of training to carefully elicit indicators of unconscious conflicts in order to help the patient recognize habitual defense mechanisms and the phenomena that evoke them. However, the personal skills of the interviewer sometimes override his or her training. For example, some interviewers are not proficient in psychodynamic interview techniques in spite of full training, while expert psychodynamic interviewers might perform poorly when attempting to obtain sufficient diagnostic information in the space of a single hour.

SOURCE OF INFORMATION: INFORMANT CAPACITIES AND CHARACTERISTICS

The source of information places constraints on an interview. Most teachers will not cooperate with a 2-hour interview about a student unless they initiated the evaluation request. A preschool child's assessment of his or her abilities would not be reliable when completing an assessment of daily living skills through an instrument such as the Vineland Adaptive Behavior Scale. This influence is related to the obvious effects of the developmental and intellectual levels of the patient. Infants and toddlers require special approaches because of their immaturity, while developmental and past psychiatric histories cannot be obtained from a severely retarded adult. Similarly, some highly intelligent adults may lack certain components of general education, making it difficult to obtain a satisfactory medical review of systems or a past medical history.

INTERVIEW CONDITIONS

Finally, clinicians are often unrealistically neglectful of the effects of concrete interview conditions. The time available may be insufficient, but the clinician attempts a full interview anyway, risking an erroneous diagnostic formulation. The site and resources are often not tailored to the requirements of the interview. The room might be small, and the cramped conditions become a distorting influence on a family therapy interview. A lack of toys and materials for drawing may cause a preschooler to appear unresponsive and unimaginative. This inattention to interview conditions is derived from a common attitude that a good clinician should be able to carry out a clinical interview rapidly under any circumstances. This neglects the inherent complexity of interviews.

Categories of Interview Structure and Technique

"UNSTRUCTURED," PSYCHODYNAMIC INTERVIEWS

"Nondirective" or "unstructured" psychoanalytical interviews are actually highly structured interviews that use a less visible framework. This requires that the psychiatrist give "evenly hovering attention" to the comments of the patient and that the topics are chosen by the patient for long periods of the interview. This allows the psychiatrist to be attentive to patterns that may emerge: topics about which the child is conflicted, habitual defenses, or an emotional valence surrounding certain circumstances that was not initially visible. The conscious and unconscious components emerging in the interview can then be used to aid the patient by clarification of patterns of response or emotion, confrontation of the patient in relation to specific behaviors or their possible meanings, or suggestion of potential links that may foster insight in the patient. This procedure is far from unstructured, and one major locus of clinical skill is the psychiatrist's capacity to adhere to carefully organized psychodynamic interview techniques while maintaining an empathic, humane attitude and relationship with the patient.

The psychodynamic assessment seeks to determine whether unconscious conflicts have contributed to the child's symptom formation. If so, the treatment process can use interpretations, and the child's transference to the psychiatrist of unconscious thoughts and feelings, as a basis for therapy.

A problem for child psychiatrists has been to integrate this model with the assessment and therapeutic challenges posed by the immature capacities of the child, which make the discrimination of normal developmental ebb and flow from symptoms treacherous. Minimal differentiation of somatic and psychic functions is recognized in a greater reliance on dimensional analysis, looking for progress but respecting the inevitability of normal periods of regression for each child. Further descriptions of psychoanalytical methods applied in interviews of the pre-school- and school-age child are available (Goldblatt 1972).

DIRECTED INTERVIEWS

Directed interviews, on the other hand, have other goals that require a different strategy. This method requires that the clinician determine the selection of topics and the pace of the interview. He or she will frequently, but tactfully, cut short discussion by the patient. This is necessary in order to ensure that the full set of topics assigned to the interview are covered. This persistent, but necessary redirection of the discussion will be understood by some patients, but can be irritating to others. The interviewer must manage this skillfully, recalling that the patient might be experiencing considerable relief when describing his or her problems to a psychiatrist. The clinician must gradually gain the alliance of the patient in setting an additional goal for the interview. The most common example of the directed interview is the interview to obtain historical information about the current problem. Failure to direct the topics and pace of the interview can give a truncated information base, possibly missing essential data.

STRUCTURED AND SEMISTRUCTURED INTERVIEWS

Structured interviews are a further extension that stand at the opposite pole from nondirective interviews. The format, topics, and sequence are prearranged. The probes are specifically worded to avoid subtle influences from the interviewer. Answers are limited to a choice from a group of specific responses, each of which is coded. Semistructured interviews are an intermediate species between directed and fully structured interview formats. They have the advantages of each. The format of the interview consists of a preset sequence of topics, as well as many sections that are fully structured with

specific wording of probes. These sections provide essential information, such as inclusion and exclusion criteria for diagnosis. However, in other sections only the topics and symptoms that are to be the subject of inquiry are indicated, while the clinician is to use his or her judgment about the best approach for eliciting the data. Examples are given as anchor points.

FORMAL TESTING

Formal testing situations are often not considered to be interviews, but clinicians who give formal tests are well aware that the patient will gradually respond as if it were an interview and he or she is warming up to the interviewer. For some children, the highly structured conditions of formal testing ease their anxiety and make it possible for them to be more relaxed and forthcoming. An open-ended, nondirective interview can sometimes be experienced as so stressful that the patient withdraws from the interview. Similarly, while behavior rating sessions are not usually designed as interviews, the subject being rated will sometimes want to talk to a rater, so that a relationship is gradually established. In other settings, such as a private office, the psychiatrist may expect this to occur because the behavior rating interview is directed to effects of a drug in the context of an ongoing therapeutic relationship. In these instances there can be contradictory purposes for the interview behavior of the psychiatrist: an unbiased elicitation of beneficial or side effects and a fostering of the therapeutic alliance.

ALTERNATIVE INTERVIEW STRUCTURES AND TECHNIQUES

Categorizing a few types of interview structures and techniques should not restrict clinicians to these types, but open their awareness to the diverse needs of children and families as a basis for alternative interview structures and techniques. For example, some children will require a wholly or largely nonverbal interview format because of their age, developmental status (e.g., moderate or severe mental retardation), or their diagnosis (e.g., elective mutism). Such factors lead to the requirement that special formats be designed to solve particular interview challenges. For example, estimation of the intellectual and developmental status of young autistic or retarded children who are nonverbal can be facilitated by the use of the Leiter test battery, which requires no language. Similarly, skillful application of nonverbal techniques in the play interview will sometimes open a window into the inner life of a child previously hidden from all observers.

THE CONTEXT OF THE CLINICAL INTERVIEW: THE NATURE AND ROLE OF ASSESSMENT IN CHILD AND ADOLESCENT PSYCHIATRY

The Need for Improved Assessment

The need to fine-tune evaluation procedures is derived from the primary objective of our professional activities: to provide optimal care for the children and families who turn to us for help. This objective is achieved as we develop assessment procedures that more accurately determine diagnoses and etiologies. Sophisticated, accurate initial evaluation is a cornerstone for establishing preferred types of treatment, rational determination of treatment progress, and adequate treatment outcome measures. Excellent descriptions of methods for evaluating children map our continuing efforts to achieve an all-inclusive, but practical assessment procedure (Simmons 1987; Lewis 1989).

The Nature of Assessment

SEQUENCE

Initial Assessment. Assessments in child and adolescent psychiatry are sequential and ongoing. The form of an evaluation is determined by its position in the overall assessment sequence: initial evaluation, periodic assessment, or outcome assessment. Assessments differ principally in relation to the scope of the methods applied. In theory, the initial evaluation should be comprehensive and detailed, using all available current methods and instrumentation. In practice, the clinician is limited by the financial and time cost to the family; the need for rapid initiation of treatment measures because of acute, disturbing symptoms; the requirement that the length of the evaluation not exceed the reasonable patience of the family; and

the repertoire of skills and instrumentation available to individual practitioners or groups of clinicians. The child and family will suffer if an abbreviated evaluation fails to detect existing disabilities requiring treatment. Nevertheless, parents are prone to rushing the evaluation process, reflecting their lack of understanding of the purposes and components of the evaluation. The clinician must carefully explain, in language understandable to laymen, the reasons why it is necessary to complete the assessment. He or she must then decide on the components to be included in the child's evaluation. The child psychiatrist must be aware of the components of the most comprehensive evaluation and indicate in writing the reasons why one or more are determined to be unnecessary or impractical for an individual patient. This emphasizes the use of a standard assessment instrument battery that is consulted at the time of this selection process. It guards against unintentionally neglecting any significant component of the evaluation.

Periodic Assessments. Periodic assessments can be carried out by using one of several methods. The most common is for the child psychiatrist to meet with the family at a mutually chosen frequency, typically every 6 months or year, in order to review the child's progress. This procedure has several associated risks: disagreement concerning which symptoms are to be assessed, lack of clarity about who is to assess progress, and confusion because a method for evaluating progress was never decided on. Clinicians sometimes observe gradual improvement in a child's symptoms, corroborated by independent observers, only to confront angry parents who are dissatisfied with the child's current behavior. Symptom changes are typically gradual, so that those grappling with the child's problems on a continuous basis (usually the family and teachers) may lose sight of the original symptom severity and obvious progress; he or she is overwhelmed by current problems and the disruption they continue to cause. These problems in the implementation of periodic assessments are the basis for a recommendation that the family and clinician discuss what can be anticipated at the beginning of treatment. If one component of the treatment is psychotherapy and it is expected that there will be a temporary symptom exacerbation, the parents should be informed that there will be ups and downs in progress, and a method of evaluation that accounts for this agreed on. The foundation for practical periodic assessments is that clinician and family select a few target symptoms and a specific assessment method for each. The assessment technique might be a rating scale, an anticipated report from school, or some other method. This decision also incorporates the choice of the persons performing the rating of the target symptoms.

Outcome Assessments. Outcome assessments following a child's treatment are crucial to the further care and development of the child. They are also fundamental to our understanding of treatment methods and our ability to improve them. The scope of outcome assessments varies, ranging from the original target symptoms followed at periodic assessments to a readministration of all components of the original evaluation in order to determine a profile of change along all major functional dimensions. Examining outcome assessments across multiple dimensions gives a broad view of treatment effects but can be confusing because it detracts from a hypothesis-based experimental design. In an experimental design the clinician systematically alters specific components of the therapy until their effects and utility are well understood. Habitual integration of outcome assessment into clinical practice is an important protection against pessimism, illusions, and simple sloppy practice; it increases the likelihood that a clinician will select treatments for individual patients in a knowledgeable and less biased manner. It also avoids abrupt termination of treatment because of sudden frustration with treatment progress; the clinician can point out the advantage of waiting until the end of the mutually agreed on time period marked by the outcome assessment.

SPECIAL CONSIDERATIONS

When working with individual patients the nature of the population sample is not considered; yet it is applicable in the sense that the choice of clinical instruments should include an awareness of the population samples in which the instruments were employed previously. It is especially important to know if these instruments were specifically designed for limited samples, which may make them inapplicable to certain types of

patients. Control groups are similarly not a formal concern when using assessment instruments with individual patients; yet the experienced clinician has accumulated a patient group for comparison to which he or she can refer each time he or she interviews or tests a new patient. It is important for the clinician to examine the literature for the control and patient groups to which an instrument has been applied and to assess how closely his or her experience with the instrument coincides with the experiences of others.

Finally, assessment of treatment can be imperiled by the wish of both physician and patient to see progress. This raises the possibility that the clinician, even though not conducting a formal research protocol, might want to keep the patient blind to the nature of a pharmacologic treatment. In this situation, the physician will consider giving a placebo to evaluate the nature of the patient's response to the active agent more fully. This can be done most successfully if the patient goes through one or more "crossovers" from one agent to the other while the physician is assessing any alteration in treatment response. While all of these measures are drawn from traditional clinical research techniques, they can be used to make routine treatment follow-up interviews more accurate and useful.

COMPONENTS OF THE CLINICAL NEUROPSYCHIATRIC EVALUATION IN CHILDHOOD AND ADOLESCENCE

Psychiatric Evaluation of the Child or Adolescent

The assessment of a child differs in several essentials from that of an adult. The informant is almost always the patient in the evaluation of an adult. This is seldom true in the assessment of children, for whom much information is gathered from the parents, teacher, guidance counselor, pediatrician, and other persons or agencies concerned with the child. During the evaluation of a child the school is consulted as soon as the parents have signed a consent form; yet a psychiatrist rarely contacts the employer or co-workers of the adult patient.

The symptoms for which a child is brought to treatment are most often troublesome to others rather than to the child. The child sees the problem as caused by others, outside himself or herself and beyond his or her control. The child sometimes does not come to an appointment with a psychiatrist with a view of him or her as an expert, but often sees the clinician as an agent of the parents, a frightening figure, or a teacher-like individual. These unique features of the initial interview with the child influence the technique to be employed in the interview. The initial phase of evaluation and treatment of an adult usually is accompanied by a positive therapeutic alliance, even if minimal. This will typically be absent in the initial interview with a child so that a major objective in this phase is to put the child at ease, help him or her understand the purpose of the assessment, and form a positive therapeutic alliance.

For the adolescent, the interview procedures adopted are intermediate to those described above for adults and children. During early adolescence the procedures resemble more those used with children, while the increasing independence, intellectual capacity, and judgment acquired during middle and late adolescence suggest that interview techniques quite similar to those for adults be used.

COMPONENTS OF THE INITIAL DIAGNOSTIC INTERVIEWS

Three types of initial diagnostic interviews for children and adolescents are employed: the child (adolescent) interview, the parent interview, and the family interview. All three are commonly used in the diagnostic evaluation, but only one or two of these interviews may be completed in some circumstances. The sequence of the interviews is the subject of unending debate. A traditional model has been that a child psychiatrist see the child in the first interview while a social worker concurrently interviews the parents. Another common model is for the child psychiatrist to interview the parents first, without the child present. The benefit of this approach is that the parents can rapidly provide a history of the child's current problem without concern that discussion of certain topics will be disturbing or harmful to a child who is listening. It is for this reason that beginning the evaluation with a family interview has been less common, in spite of its one great advan-

tage. This is the only opportunity for the child psychiatrist to observe pure family interactions, untainted by the biases that can result from beginning alliances with family members from prior interviews. It provides the conditions for the psychiatrist to observe the presenting complaints unfolding before him or her and the resulting anguish that makes the family want help and may give an initial understanding of unconscious motivations and defenses that maintain the symptom structure within the family.

Specific categories of information must be obtained during the diagnostic evaluation. Circumstances often limit the time available for the initial diagnostic assessment to only one or two sessions (e.g., inadequate funding for a longer evaluation, inability of parents to reliably return for multiple sessions before treatment begins). Paradoxically, in these circumstances the child psychiatrist is often most likely to keep all diagnostic interview components in mind and devote at least a modicum of attention to each. The major components of the interview are each composed of specific items (Table 26–2) that the child psychiatrist uses to direct the questions to various informants. The principal categories in a diagnostic interview are (1) the history of the current problem and other types of historical information; (2) the mental status examination; (3) examination of family interactions and dynamics, (4) determination of further information to be obtained from outside sources and additional examination procedures required; (5) formulation of the principal elements of the child's disorder and their interactions; (6) the differential diagnosis; (7) the diagnoses (using the *Diagnostic and Statistical Manual of Mental Disorders*, third edition, revised [DSM-III-R], with all five axes, or the *International Classification of Diseases*, ninth edition [ICD-9]) and a phrase describing prognoses; and (8) a treatment plan.

THE PARENT INTERVIEW: HISTORICAL INFORMATION AND THE PARENTS' VIEW

The clinical interview of the parents (or guardians of the child) has several purposes, the most important of which is to obtain facts about the current problem, treatments already attempted, and the child's development. A second, closely associated purpose is to understand the parents' ideas about the

Table 26–2. COMPONENTS OF THE DIAGNOSTIC INTERVIEW FOR CHILDREN AND ADOLESCENTS

A. History
　　1. Chief complaint
　　2. History of the present illness
　　3. Medical history and medications
　　4. Past psychiatric history and treatment
　　5. Genetic and family history
　　6. Pregnancy and birth history
　　7. Developmental and school history
　　8. Social history and friends
　　9. Sexual history and acquired immunodeficiency syndrome
　　10. Aggression history
　　11. Drug abuse history
　　12. Future plans
B. Mental Status
　　1. Appearance
　　2. Attitude, demeanor, relation to examiner
　　3. Motor behavior
　　4. Speech and language
　　5. Reading and writing
　　6. Orientation
　　7. Information
　　8. Memory
　　9. Cognition and attention
　　10. Abstraction
　　11. Intelligence estimate
　　12. Thought content (delusions)
　　13. Thought form (loose associations)
　　14. Perceptual (hallucinations, illusions)
　　15. Mood/affect
　　16. Symptoms (depression, mania, anxiety, phobias, obsessions, compulsions, impulsivity)
　　17. Suicidal thoughts or behaviors
　　18. Homicidal thoughts or behaviors
　　19. Drives (aggressive, sexual)
　　20. Conscience
　　21. Defenses and conflicts
　　22. Object relations
　　23. Self-esteem

　　24. Insight and judgment
　　25. Adaptive capacities, strengths, and assets
C. Examination of Family Interactions and Dynamics
D. Further Information to be Considered
　　1. Family interview
　　2. Interviews with parents individually
　　3. Previous medical reports
　　4. School reports
　　5. Psychological tests and academic achievement tests
　　6. Neuropsychological tests
　　7. Adaptive behavior scale
　　8. Clinical blood and urine tests
　　9. Electrocardiogram
　　10. Neuroimaging
　　11. Electroencephalogram
　　12. Medical specialty consultations
E. Formulation
　　1. Genetic/biological/medication influences
　　2. Developmental
　　3. Family
　　4. Psychodynamic
　　5. School
　　6. Social/religious
　　7. Friends
F. Differential Diagnosis
G. Diagnoses and Prognoses (five axes)
　　1. Diagnostic criteria
　　2. *DSM-III-R* and *ICD-9*
　　3. Global assessment scale
H. Treatment Plan
　　1. Genetic/physical/medication
　　2. Development
　　3. Psychological/intellectual
　　4. Family
　　5. Educational
　　6. Social/religious
　　7. Friends

problem and their expectations of the evaluation. A third goal is to begin to know the parents as individuals and as parents, gaining a perspective on how they might have affected (aggravated or mitigated) symptom development and the influences that they are likely to have on whatever treatment recommendations are eventually made. In addition, this interview provides an opportunity to determine what preparation the parents have given their child for the evaluation and to recommend any additional approaches that may facilitate the child's ease and participation. Finally, the interview serves to gather information that may facilitate the psychiatrist's assessment of the child, such as favorite toys, interests, and hobbies.

THE INTERVIEW WITH THE CHILD

Play and Verbal Interviews. Two types of interviews are available for children, a verbal interview and a play interview. Chronologic age, mental age, verbal facility, and the co-operation of the child guide the selection of interview format. During the conversation with a child, the psychiatrist attempts to reduce the child's anxiety (by beginning with either a neutral or positive topic or by encouraging the child to talk about his or her feelings concerning the interview), to ascertain the child's ideas about the reason for the interview, to tell the child the psychiatrist's view about why they are talking, and to assess both the strengths and psychopathology of the child. This last objective is often compromised by a focus on what is wrong; in order to accurately evaluate the child, his or her strengths and coping abilities must be taken into account. Finally, it is sometimes difficult to recall that the purpose of the interview is evaluation, not the initiation of treatment. For some children, the process of initiating an assessment begins treatment. In order to offset this, the psychiatrist should observe the child and keep interventions to a minimum, other than to test the strength of defenses or his or her capacity for change. In this regard, dreams and fantasies, character of play, and the psychiatrist's response to the child will be assessment elements additional to those formally included in an evaluation outline (see Table 26–2).

A play interview is essential when working with a child younger than age 7, but it should be carried out with all prepubertal children (with modifications for the preadolescent period) as a technique for delving below surface responses that are commonly uninformative in children. Play is the natural discourse for children. Many phenomena can be observed in play that would not be elicited verbally from a child. The manner in which a child plays is as important as the content of the play. The mode of initiation of play, appropriateness to age and gender, creativity, structure, flow, and intensity (especially in relation to aggressive and sexual themes) should all be recounted. It is not enough to simply watch the play during the interview; attempts should be made to elicit the accompanying fantasies and affects.

The Mental Status Examination. The foundation of the interview with the child is a survey of the child's intellect and emotions. The mental status examination is a formal list of specific items to be included in this inventory. It ensures that all significant components are examined and the clinician obtains an accurate estimate of the child's mental capacities and symptoms (see Table 26–2). Detailed descriptions of the meaning of each item and techniques for eliciting relevant information are available (e.g., Simmons 1987; Lewis 1982; Lewis 1989) and are too extensive to be included in this chapter.

THE FAMILY INTERVIEW

Interactions between the child and others in the family provide an invaluable glimpse of the origins and meanings of a child's symptoms. The manner in which characteristic interaction sequences are initiated and sustained, the child's role in the process, the emotions evoked, the defenses employed, and the level of judgment and insight are significant features to be examined. The psychiatrist can begin to determine the child's

role within the family, and biological, cultural, and habitual interactional determinants of family functioning can be observed. Finally, the interviewer has the opportunity to consider the sensitivity of the family as a whole to its individual members and their capacity for change.

THE GROUP DIAGNOSTIC INTERVIEW

The nature of a child's relationships and interactions with his or her peers can be very revealing. While adults fond of a child can unconsciously moderate many comments about his problems, other children respond viscerally in ways that give their impression of the patient. This information is almost always received second hand from parent or school reports. Of course, children will usually mention their friends during the play interview, giving this essential perspective. In some diagnostic centers, children are seen in a group diagnostic interview with other children in order to assess their interactions directly. This is similar to the common practice of group interviews in private schools, enabling teachers to estimate the child's ability to get along with others in a regular classroom.

VIEWS FROM OTHERS IN THE CHILD'S COMMUNITY

The child psychiatrist is dependent on the quality of the information given him or her during the interview. It is useful, reassuring, and necessary to obtain information from others in the child's world. Bringing it back to the interview with parents or family sometimes stimulates further information or discussion that is essential to diagnosis and treatment.

The school report is the most important, because of the teacher's long periods of time with the child, the opportunity to observe the child's response to work demands, and the natural setting for continual interactions with other children. Many referrals to child psychiatrists and clinics are directly from the school or because a teacher has prompted the child's parents. The school is a unique situation for the child in which the child's behavior and symptomatology can be quite different than anywhere else. For example, a child may be hyperactive in the classroom while only intermittently so at home and not at all in the one-to-one interview. This emphasizes the natural situational sculpting of childhood symptomatology, too often considered an indicator of erroneous information rather than an informative indicator of environmental determinants of symptoms. Formal teacher rating scales provide a format that is easy and efficient for the school and maximally informative and reliable for the psychiatrist. They give structure to information gained when the clinician meets with staff at the school or speaks to the teacher on the phone.

The pediatrician is often neglected during the interview process. Yet, he or she sometimes illuminates symptom patterns in surprising ways by informing the psychiatrist of a chronic illness in the child or a family member or by describing a persistent pattern of refusing medication and/or refusing psychiatric consultation over the years for what the family now describes as an acute illness. These examples emphasize that a pediatrician contributes both a medical perspective and a longitudinal view of the child's and family's development not commonly available from other sources.

Significant facts are occasionally accessible through community agencies, although the physician rarely contacts them until specific comments or hints in the interview suggest this step. The results of the inquiry can then be presented at the next interview. Neglect of religious influences on a child's behavior can be perilous when religion is the focal point of the family's life. Data from social agencies, such as the Bureau of Child Welfare, foster care agencies, or a visiting nurse service can sometimes explain confusing elements of the assessment. Family courts, probation officers, and the police may be the primary social forces motivating the child's behavior, yet they may not be mentioned in the interview with the child.

The continuing theme of these considerations is the attempt to discover in the interview how the child organizes his or her behavior, the feelings and thoughts that motivate this behavior, and which social forces the child and family use to guide participation in his or her culture. Hobbies, group activities, and athletics can be a gauge of how the child organizes his or her life. They measure coping mechanisms by suggesting how the child follows rules, competitive strategies, capacity to function as a member of a team, and view of himself or herself and relations with other children. The child's willingness to accept delay, capacity to persevere, ability to organize a project, and creativity can be estimated in these activities. The physician can ease the child's anxiety by asking parents about the child's pleasures and preferences beforehand and using them as a basis for the interview. This also can be a means for engaging the child in further interviews and enhancing his or her self-esteem.

THE SUMMARY DIAGNOSTIC AND TREATMENT RECOMMENDATION INTERVIEW

The summary interview should be conducted without the child present, unless he or she is a middle adolescent or older. This makes it possible to discuss material with the parents that would be unintelligible, confusing, or provocative for the child. However, the child should then have the opportunity to discuss the findings with the physician and his or her parents, in order to understand the outcome and treatment plans. Discussion with the parents and/or child must be conducted in language that is clear and understandable to those involved. It can be anticipated that the family will approach this interview with considerable anxiety. This anxiety, intermixed with personality traits, will partly determine their attention or inattention to the topics discussed. This suggests that the psychiatrist should repeat diagnoses and treatment plans several times in different ways. Symptomatology in childhood is multidetermined, so explanations of various factors influencing the child's symptoms, and their relation to treatment, should be attempted. However, the parents commonly have one or two explanations in mind and will often find it difficult to consider other views. For example, parental guilt and anxiety may reinforce pathologic patterns in the family, leading to rigid formulations explaining the symptoms. These matters should be discussed openly with the parents so that they are able to move on to discuss other possible causes. It is helpful to ask the parents and the child what they understand about the information given them and how they feel about it. The psychiatrist should explicitly state that he or she is available for questions after the final interview (by telephone or in person) because it is common for parents to forget certain questions during the interview or to have new questions generated by the interview. A follow-up interview might be scheduled in order to determine how the parents are reacting to the interview information and whether they are implementing the recommendations.

STANDARDIZED ASSESSMENT PROCEDURES

There were earlier doubts about the clinical application of formally structured rating instruments on the grounds that they lacked subtlety, interfered with the therapeutic alliance and distanced the interviewer from the patient, and were so easily misinterpreted as to be unreliable. However, their use has been demonstrated and they are now broadly used as a routine part of child psychiatric practice. For the practitioner who does not have a team of research assistants available to administer such scales this means that he or she must adapt routine interview procedures to include the use of selected instruments with the family. These instruments include structured clinical interviews, questionnaires, behavior checklists, general symptom rating scales, syndrome-specific rating scales, medication side-effects scales, developmental and family history forms, demographic data forms, and so on. Enhanced reliability and thoroughness are primary advantages of these clinical tools. In addition, most can be administered by less highly trained professionals, paraprofessionals, and lay personnel, reducing expense and extending their applicability. They are especially useful for screening and routine, sequential follow-up ratings. An extension of this concept has been the use of computer programs. These programs have been used in a variety of ways, including direct entry by parents or patients sitting at the keyboard or later entry of salient facts and parent responses by the clinician.

Behavior checklists are designed for use by clinicians, teachers, parents, and lay personnel and provide an inventory of the most common childhood and adolescent symptoms (Achenbach and Edelbrock 1978). Self-rating checklists are similar forms filled out by the child. The inventory items typically inquire about the presence or absence of a symptom, with a yes/no, true/false, or similar response structure. Clinical rating scales are nearly identical in format but additionally ask the respondent to specify the severity and frequency of the symptom. This is achieved through the selection of a graded response (a 0 to 4 scale is most common) given a clinical base through related descriptor phrases (e.g., "never, occasionally, sometimes"). These descriptors, however, are not specific anchor points, and the respondent necessarily sets his or her own criteria for the relative meaning of each of these scoring levels. An alternative arrangement for these descriptors is a preprinted line representing a continuum of severity or frequency, onto which the respondent places a mark representing a response along the continuum; this is known as a Likert type of scale. The names "behavior checklist" and "behavior rating scale" are commonly used interchangeably, so the format of the scale cannot be judged by the name.

Behavior rating scales designed for specific syndromes and symptoms (e.g., depression, tics) improve clinical assessment in syndrome-specific research. They are similar to general symptom rating scales and have gained broad use among clinicians.

Global assessment scales are quite useful in preparation for the summary diagnostic and treatment recommendation interview. A number or a range is assigned to portray the overall level of the patient's symptom severity, functioning, and adaptation. The scales use specific anchor points: scores on the scale are accompanied by descriptive clinical examples intended to give the rater a clear concept of the relative functional level intended. Parents often ask how serious their child's illness is, so that a score recorded prior to this interview gives a sound basis for the psychiatrist's response.

Rating scales and structured clinical interviews must be used thoughtfully. Just as a strong case can be made that reliability and thoroughness demand the use of standardized forms, the subtleties and gestalt of certain aspects of the interview are better obtained in the traditional unstructured clinical format or clinician rating. In addition, the clinician must determine the purpose of a particular rating scale, which might differ from the use that he or she intends for it (e.g., screening, severity rating, diagnosis). Another consideration is that observers can "see" differently, meaning that parents, teachers, psychiatrists, and pediatricians can all rate the same symptoms on videotape somewhat differently and ascribe different meanings to the same behavior (observation variance). Finally, the reports of respondents should be anticipated to differ in certain circumstances. For example, children and parents will not report identical ratings on items concerning depression, suicide, anxiety, and other symptoms that involve private information or less concrete behavioral phenomena.

Finally, systematic assessment of family interactions and family psychodynamics is a fundamental task when interviewing children and adolescents. Nevertheless, adequate methods for standardized ratings of these phenomena have lagged behind because of their complexity, and existing measures tend to be controversial.

General Medical and Neuropsychiatric Evaluations

PURPOSES

It might seem unnecessary to comment that it is mandatory for the child and adolescent psychiatrist to conduct a careful inventory of medical history and symptoms and carry out a meticulous physical examination, but it is common practice to leave these activities to the child's pediatrician. The active role of the pediatrician is essential, but the child psychiatrist should keep his or her own medical role broad and active in order to avoid missing significant historical facts or physical signs. Unrecognized physical illnesses are the prime cause of psychiatric symptomatology in 5% to 18% of adult psychiatric patients, despite a prior diagnosis of "functional" illness by other physicians. Similar studies are not available for child psychiatric patients, but avoidance of similar misdiagnosis in children and adolescents is more likely when the physician systematically considers physical illnesses known to cause specific psychiatric symptoms and inquires about these and other symptoms of the illnesses. Second, physical illnesses with psychological sequelae are common in childhood and disproportionately present in child psychiatric practice. Third, somatic treatments frequently alter physical parameters, so routine assessment of baseline values at the time of initial evaluation is recommended if somatic treatment is a possibility at any point. Fourth, comprehensive assessment of the child facilitates an alliance with the family and reduces splitting of different professional caregivers by the family. This reassures the family, suggests a practical and efficient approach to treatment, and indicates that responsibility is being taken for the child's well-being.

COMPONENTS OF THE GENERAL MEDICAL AND NEUROPSYCHIATRIC ASSESSMENT

Review of Organ Systems, Past Medical History, and General Physical Examination. These medical evaluation components are required for children for whom the diagnosis and etiology are not obvious; the only special features are an emphasis on the central nervous system (CNS), an awareness of the symptoms of special importance in the interview (as described previously), and careful attention to physical signs likely to indicate a covert medical illness.

Neurologic and Special Neurologic Examinations. These examinations are essential to the comprehensive psychiatric evaluation of a child and adolescent. Parents will often respond quite differently to the psychiatrist in subsequent interviews, sensing that he or she is thorough and knows their child in detail; most importantly, the neurologic examination will sometimes direct a significant new avenue of questions in the interviews, such as the history of previously unmentioned motor clumsiness or a minor physical anomaly. Surprisingly, however, the neurologic examination of a child who has been followed regularly by a pediatrician will usually add no new information. It has two main purposes other than the salutary effects on the interviews: (1) assurance that a major physical factor has not been overlooked in the past or suddenly appeared and (2) the research purpose (for the individual physician) of enhancing his or her skill and experience with the special neurologic examination with the hope that the meaning of various "soft" neurologic signs will gradually be clarified.

The differentiation of "hard" and "soft" neurologic signs has been a pivotal concept in pediatric neuropsychiatry in the past 3 decades, particularly in the evaluation of attention-deficit hyperactivity disorder. Hard neurologic signs are those elicited on the classic neurologic examination, distinguished by the clear presence of an abnormality and a frequent localizing value. They are often indicative of underlying anatomical and/or pathophysiological lesions, and examples are hyperreflexia, muscle weakness, or a particular type of nystagmus. Soft signs, however, have an undetermined significance that underlies the term "soft," since they are not localizing nor invariably associated with specific structural, anatomical damage nor currently detectable pathophysiological factors. Examples are clumsiness in the performance of rapid alternating movements (presumably cerebellar in origin) or mirror movements. Their clinical significance has been variably interpreted by different clinicians; arbitrary hierarchical attributions have been assigned, such as a pathologic significance occurring when three soft signs are present. They are closely related to the child's developmental status, because many are normal at an early age and are often referred to as evidence of developmental immaturity or lag as they persist in older children (rather than aberrant CNS function). In addition, their subtlety means that they can be difficult to elicit in an unruly and uncooperative child, which is common among younger normal children and very common among children referred to psychiatrists for inattention, hyperactivity and impulsivity. Experience with the special neurologic examination therefore becomes essential if the clinician is to sensibly interpret the significance of various findings, and standardization is imperative. Useful "neurologic play examinations" are an important means for making the procedure more enjoyable for children and informative to psychiatrists (Goodman and Sours 1967). Thus, the inherent meaning of soft neurologic signs, already difficult to interpret, is complicated by both developmental and clinical examination factors. Soft signs are slightly more common in children with several different types of psychiatric disorder (e.g., autism or Tourette's disorder), but they vary in type and frequency in these disorders, are nonspecific, and can also be found in normal children. This means that it is currently impossible to attach well-defined clinical significance to soft signs. Nevertheless, some investigative work has suggested that, within a specific diagnostic group selected by other clinical means, they might have predictive value. The use of better selected, more efficient, and increasingly standardized and age-normed special neurologic examination procedures (especially the Neurological Examination for Subtle Signs [NESS] or the Yale Neuromaturational Examination) should improve the use of these measures (Denckla 1985; Shaywitz et al. 1984).

The detection of minor congenital anomalies during the physical and neurologic examinations may be more clinically pertinent. These stigmata are correlated with a variety of behavioral and intellectual deviations, even in children with no major physical pathology who do not fall into conventional diagnostic categories. They also may have value in suggesting a chromosomal abnormality or an insult to the fetus during the first trimester of pregnancy. An example of a systematic instrument useful for documenting such congenital anomalies is the Yale Stigmata Schedule.

Family and Genetic Evaluations. This component of the evaluation interview comprises two sectors that are widely differing in their purposes, yet inherently linked. Clearly, the essential clinical approach to obtaining genetic information about a child's disorder is to obtain a family history of related phenomena in the nuclear and, if possible, the extended family. This seems far removed from eliciting information about family dynamics and interactions. However, when done in relation to one another, the characteristics of individual family members, or the pattern of interactions among the family, can take on a new meaning; an example is when symptoms of affective disorders are found in several relatives of an impulsive child of a moody father. Similarly, the hint of tics in cousins and an uncle can illuminate the understanding of obsessive-compulsive symptoms of a child and her mother.

A straightforward family medical history should always be undertaken in order to discern any of the multiple inherited conditions ranging from diabetes to acute intermittent porphyria to Huntington's chorea. It is more common for psychiatrists to consider subtle genetic factors that contribute to such illnesses as conduct disorders, alcoholism, and schizotypal disorder. Two major interviewing methods have been applied to this challenge. First is the family history method, in which the psychiatrist interviews one or a few family members about symptoms among "all" members of the extended family. While this is usually the only practical method available to the practitioner, it is important to be aware of the obvious superiority of the alternative direct family interview method. In this procedure, the nuclear family or extended family members are each interviewed directly to determine the presence of symptoms and disorders. The family history method typically underestimates the prevalence of disorders in the family. These methods are the principal procedures for recognizing single gene and multifactorial, polygenic disorders.

Chromosomal analysis is an expensive procedure that is now becoming a necessity in specific disorders. The prime example is autism, since approximately 10% of autistic patients may have the fragile X syndrome; other infrequent chromosomal aberrations can also cause autism. This raises the point of another purpose of clinical interviews with children, which is to recognize those children for whom chromosomal analyses (karyotyping) should be carried out. Genetic studies have shown differences in the expression and penetrance of various syndromes (again, autism is a prime example), so that an awareness of the varieties of phenotypic expression can guide the clinician to karyotyping and a diagnosis that would otherwise be missed.

Endocrine, Metabolic, and Nutritional Parameters. These factors are too extensive to review in this context, but several examples are sufficient to demonstrate the importance of considering them. When alert to hints in interview responses, the psychiatrist can ask questions that guide the selection of laboratory tests capable of uncovering a covert metabolic disorder. Psychiatric disturbance can be the earliest manifestation of an endocrine disturbance. Thyroid dysfunction is known to play this role, and thyroxine (T_4), triiodothyronine (T_3), and thyroid stimulating hormone (TSH) levels are useful measures. Thyroxine binding by a specific protein (thyroid binding globulin) is commonly measured as a component of the T_4 assay in order to determine the serum free T_4 level, and the TSH level indicates pituitary activation of the thyroid. This battery of thyroid tests is occasionally insufficient to detect, for example, early hypothyroidism in a subgroup of depressed patients, so that measurement of TSH change after stimulation with the thyrotropin-releasing hormone (TRH, its hypothalamic releasing factor) may be necessary. Finally, measurement of antimicrosomal antibodies and antithyroglobulin titers may unmask an autoimmune thyroiditis (Prange et al. 1987). Clinical application of this battery of thyroid function tests is a useful example of the interaction between directed interviewing and the selection of specific laboratory tests. These tests assess different components of the endocrine system involved, and the tests vary from well-established clinical indices to research measures. It is essential for the psychiatrist to discuss the purposes and relative clinical use of all laboratory tests with the parents during the interviews.

The complexity of endocrine function can confound well-organized attempts to define a specific laboratory index of psychiatric dysfunction. An example is the elusive set of measures of adrenocortical function. Psychiatric symptoms accompany adrenocortical excess in Cushing's syndrome (e.g., depression, anhedonia, suicide, hypomania, confusion, delusions) or adrenal insufficiency in Addison's disease (e.g., lethargy, weakness, inability to concentrate, irritability, intermittent depression). Plasma cortisol and adrenocorticotropic hormone (ACTH), saliva cortisol, and urinary glucocorticoid and free cortisol levels have been found to be useful basal measures in the detection of dysregulation of the hypothalamic-pituitary-adrenocortical axis in adult mood disorders. However, no laboratory method has been entirely satisfactory, so that attempts to challenge this axis by various dynamic stimulation/suppression tests (corticotropin releasing hormone, ACTH, metyrapone, insulin, vasopressin) have enhanced our understanding of the physiology of this axis and have some clinical use (Stokes and Sikes 1987). The dexamethasone suppression test (DST) has been examined as a clinical laboratory marker for a subgroup of depressed patients. The history of the DST illustrates the judgment required of the interviewer when describing research laboratory diagnostic tests to parents in two respects. First, determination of the clinical use of the DST is dependent on reliable interview techniques for eliciting accompanying symptoms of depression, as well as factors that can confound interpretation of the DST (such as weight loss). Second, the DST is sometimes presented to parents as a specific and reliable test of depression, but this has not been substantiated by the extensive research data available. Careful, honest explanation of each research test is basic to proper clinical interviews.

Both hypoparathyroidism and hyperparathyroidism can first present with psychiatric symptoms (e.g., depression, confusion, intellectual impairment); cogent questions may lead to the recognition of possible parathyroid dysfunction and screening of calcium and phosphorus levels. Juvenile diabetes and hypoglycemia occasionally are accompanied by changes in affect or level of consciousness that appear prior to other symptoms. Fasting glucose levels and a later glucose tolerance test may be obtained because of information derived from careful questions in the interview.

Inborn errors of metabolism can cause neuropsychiatric symptomatology in childhood and can go undetected in spite of nearly universal neonatal screening programs. For example, children with autism or other pervasive developmental disorders in rare cases have phenylketonuria or other metabolic disorders. Urinary screening for aminoacidurias is simple, noninvasive, and inexpensive and should be arranged when interviews of the parents and child suggest symptoms of these disorders.

One of the most predictable questions to be raised in interviews with parents is their request for a discussion about the role of diet in the genesis of their child's symptoms. They also ask that laboratory tests be performed to detect the dietary problem. The manner in which the psychiatrist responds to this question can often have a significant effect on the success of the remainder of the interview, since opinions about the etiologic role of dietary factors are often strongly held. It provides an excellent example of how interview skills can alter the course of an evaluation. As usual, the parents are not being foolish when they ask this question. Diet is known to have a direct effect on specific neurotransmitter levels in discrete locations in the brain, altering the activity of postsynaptic cells. This knowledge can be used to manipulate behavior, as in the recommendation that foods high in serotonin precursor levels be ingested to aid in sleep induction.

The common concern of parents is that specific dietary substances are the undetected cause of their child's symptoms. In fact, no substances have been determined to have this effect. Nevertheless, it has been shown that on rare occasions a dietary substance can be toxic to an individual child. In sum, a lack of adequate laboratory tests and the apparently rare frequency of toxic effects make it difficult to pursue this avenue of inquiry for parents. Explanation of this situation, plus testing for a few dietary factors, can reassure them that the physician takes these matters seriously.

Some vitamins have been linked to neuropsychiatric disorders, making them primary candidates for screening. Deficiencies of vitamin B_{12} and folic acid are associated with mental status changes in adults. Examination of blood levels of these vitamins in children with psychiatric disorders who might be at risk for such deficiencies failed to demonstrate abnormalities. The basis for continued research on the clinical relevance of folic acid to pediatric neuropsychiatric disorders is the occasional report of its beneficial effects in individual children with specific inborn errors of metabolism. An example is the improvement of behavior in a child with homocystinuria following folate therapy.

Pyridoxine (vitamin B_6) deficiency has been classically associated with seizure disorders of infancy. Some investigators have also reported it to accompany disorders of mood in adults, although this remains controversial. Systematic screening in children with neuropsychiatric disorders has not been attempted.

A new concern about vitamins has emerged in the past 2 decades. This is the problem of excessive ingestion in persons preoccupied with health and nutrition. Well-documented instances of excessive vitamin intake (e.g., vitamins A and D) indicate the necessity of considering this factor in children with unexplained neuropsychiatric symptoms. However, little research with children on this topic is available for guidance.

Effects of Renal and Hepatic Function on Metabolism. Consideration of renal function in the interview is necessary for several reasons. Uremia is associated with mental status changes, and possible toxic effects of lithium on the kidney during a long course of therapy require a baseline value and regular monitoring. Finally, reduced clearance of any psychotropic medications due to compromised renal function for any reason can have dramatic deleterious effects. A routine baseline screening battery can be obtained, particularly if suggested by data from the interview, and might include determination of blood urea nitrogen and creatinine values and routine urinalysis; a 24-hour urine volume measurement can be obtained as suggested by results from this initial screening.

Mental processes are also affected by impaired hepatic function. This is a rare cause of neuropsychiatric symptoms in children, so the interviewer must be particularly alert. First, Wilson's disease (hepatolenticular degeneration) may initially present itself solely through psychiatric symptoms. Second, most psychotropic medications are metabolized in the liver, so intact function is necessary. Impairment will alter blood levels of these drugs, and the drugs themselves can cause hepatic dysfunction, such as a drug-induced hepatitis. A baseline screening battery of serum glutamic oxaloacetic transaminase, serum glutamic pyruvic transaminase, lactate dehydrogenase, alkaline phosphatase, and bilirubin can be suggested to parents in the interview, reassuring them that possible side effects of a drug taken by their child will be closely monitored. Albumin and globulin levels are also sometimes obtained, with the purpose of giving a broad view of nutritional status, since these indices can be disturbed by clinical conditions in which decreased food intake occurs.

Cardiac, Hematologic, and Other Organ System Examinations. Each system should be reviewed carefully in the interview, and the resulting information becomes the basis for organizing the other components of the evaluation, whether it is laboratory testing for an infectious disease or further evaluation of the child's sensory functions. The examples given above describe the approach of the physician, emphasizing the powerful role of the interview as a triage point for initiating other evaluation components, facilitating the participation of the family in the sometimes long process of assessment, and expanding their understanding of the assessment and possible cause of their child's difficulties.

Review of Medications. Careful review of all drugs administered to a child can sometimes be very time consuming but is essential. This component of the interview can, when methodically pursued, give a clear outline of the child's responses to specific medications, both beneficial effects and side effects, which can save months of medication trials in some instances. It is useful to ask the parents to write down drugs, dosages, time periods administered, and effects before the next interview, allowing the parent to gather the information without taking too much of the available interview time.

Assessment of Environmental Toxins. The interviewer must be cognizant of the possibility that the child might have ingested a toxin. Lead is the prototype of common environmental toxins possibly having a detrimental effect on a large number of children. Common, nonspecific symptoms can be ascribed to the effects of toxins, making reliable determination of the effects of the toxin very difficult and yet simultaneously the subject of public attention. For example, lead ingestion has been described to be a cause of hyperactivity; this nonspecific symptom with many causes is very difficult to investigate because so many etiologies have to be considered. In addition, the nature and strength of the association is controversial, because the arbitrary definition of neurotoxicity has been revised to lower blood lead concentrations several times; tying neurotoxicity levels to levels having toxic effects on other organ systems has been an unsuccessful method for resolving this problem. Nevertheless, plasma and urinary lead measurements detect this potentially reversible condition at minimal cost and discomfort to the patient and remain useful.

Interview Recommendations for Further Diagnostic Medical Assessment. The education of parents concerning the role of imaging, electrophysiology, sleep architecture, genetics, and neurochemistry is an essential step in comprehensive interviews for families of a child with a neuropsychiatric disorder. Technology that today is applied to these disorders in only a few research centers will be standard, mandatory components of tomorrow's assessment batteries. During the transitional period the psychiatrist should understand the difficulties of the parents' position and devote time to an explanation of these medical procedures and their research and clinical status. On the one hand, parents may have heard or read about an exciting new technical breakthrough and want it to be immediately applied to the diagnostic evaluation of their child's chronic illness. The psychiatrist must help them understand the capacities, limitations, and any dangers of the new method, as well as its relation to other established diagnostic tests. On the other hand, the parents may not be aware of a new technical approach to diagnosis that is available in a clinical research protocol. In this circumstance, the psychiatrist must carefully weigh its usefulness for the child and explain the advantages and risks to the parents. Many novel diagnostic medical techniques are emerging at this time, and child psychiatrists must gain a general understanding of them in order to be optimally informative to families.

Psychological and Educational Testing

The standardized assessment of intelligence, visuomotor integration, sensory function, fine and gross motor coordination, academic achievement, and the motivating effects of mood, emotions, and conflicts (through projective testing) have been included in various standard testing batteries administered by psychologists, special educators, psychiatrists, and other clinicians. The realm of formal testing continues to expand and become more specific as neuropsychological, memory, learning, attentional, and other tests are developed. These assessments tend to examine functions close to the basic activities and capacities of children that are most affected by symptoms. The child psychiatrist should periodically update himself or herself on emerging tests in order to provide optimal preparation and explanation to parents during the interviews prior to formal testing. A failure of thoughtful discussion and interactive planning among the various professionals conducting the evaluation is highly detrimental to the diagnosis and treatment plan, and these ill effects will be visible in the summary interview to both parents and clinicians.

Evaluation of Infants, Toddlers, and Preschoolers

If the observer imagines a setting in which clinician and preschooler sit across from each other, in adult-sized chairs, with the child dangling his or her feet in mid-air and the clinician poised for the question and answer format involved in the interviewing process for older persons, one quickly realizes that this interview will most likely be doomed to failure. Imposing an adult clinical model on the young child soon demonstrates that the limitations far outweigh the benefits. The child, for example, probably will not sit still for very long, he or she may or may not talk,

and if the child does speak, conversation may instead be directed toward "Mom," the often necessary but unintended intruder into the process.

Instead, picture adult interviewer and child sitting side by side in the sandbox or as partners in play exploring the inner sanctuary of a dollhouse. This is where play—the serious work of a child—takes place: a time when a child begins to master his or her environment and learn skills that provide the necessary building blocks of the future.

To interview the preschool-aged child one must attempt to understand the youngster from his or her perspective. The interviewer discovers early on that the clinical interview of a child of this age is both a simple yet highly complex process. To explore the nature of the child, one must rely on both the child's creativity and the clinician's ability to engage that child in sustained play. This may involve interpretation of nonverbal cues and the skill of meeting a child at his or her level both literally and figuratively. Imagination and creativity can be assessed as soon as the child walks into the play environment. Assuming that there is a wide variety of toys, which are easily accessible to the child, one can see how he or she explores these new surroundings and imposes structure on the world. Does the child slowly and cautiously examine one toy at a time, gradually making his or her way across the room, or does the child simply flit from item to item with little sustained attention? Is there an attempt to explore and manipulate objects or does he or she become easily frustrated? Are the toys chosen age appropriate? Does the child attempt to engage the clinician in play with or without the objects? Is there fantasy play while still maintaining the boundaries of reality, and how is a balance achieved between the two? These are just a few of the questions that can be explored in a structured and unstructured play setting.

While no single instrument is sufficient in itself for "interviewing" the preschool child, toddler, or infant, the clinician's task can be greatly facilitated by using standardized developmental assessments (Table 26–3). Whether the Bayley Scales of Infant Development are used for the child of 2 years or younger to obtain a better understanding of their mental and psychomotor competencies or the Merrill-Palmer, Stanford-Binet, or Wechsler Preschool and Primary Scale of In-

Table 26–3. DEVELOPMENTAL TESTS AVAILABLE FOR CLINICAL ASSESSMENT IN EARLY CHILDHOOD

Age Range	Test
Birth–30 days	Brazelton Neonatal Behavioral Assessment Scale (NBAS)
	Content: Behavior and neonatal reflexes
1–30* months	Bayley Scales of Infant Development
	Content: Mental, motor, behavior
1 month–6 years	Yale Revised Developmental Schedule
	Content: Gross motor, fine motor, adaptive, personal-social, language
Birth–72 months	Denver Developmental Screening Test
	Content: Gross motor, fine motor, receptive and expressive language, personal-social
Birth–19 years	Vineland Adaptive Behavior Scales
	Content: Adaptive functioning (daily living, socialization, communication, motor skills, leisure time)
18–71 months	Merrill-Palmer Scale of Mental Tests
	Content: General intelligence*
2 years–adult	Stanford-Binet Intelligence Test
	Content: General intelligence*
2.5–8.5 years	McCarthy Scales of Children's Abilities
	Content: Verbal, perceptual performance, quantitative, memory, motor, general cognitive
4–6.5 years	Wechsler Preschool and Primary Scale of Intelligence (WPPSI)
	Content: Verbal, performance, full scale IQ

*These tests do not give specific subscores, but an experienced examiner can estimate expressive and receptive language, gross and fine motor development, and personal-social behavior.

telligence is used for a slightly older child, these tests will complement a structured play interview and provide valuable insight into the child's cognitive, social, emotional, language, motor, and behavioral repertoire. One can get a developmental or cognitive index, a mental age, or an intelligence quotient in an endeavor to more fully understand a child's level of functioning. The developmental and play evaluation are integral components in the overall clinical interview of the preschool-aged child and, when done properly, provide an enormous wealth of information.

SKEPTICISM CONCERNING THE VALUE OF DATA OBTAINED FROM CLINICAL INTERVIEWS

Problems of Credibility

If the clinical interview is the primary tool used to determine diagnoses and guide treatment, then the nature of interview-generated data and how they are obtained logically should receive intensive study. It did not for many years (Rutter and Graham 1968).

Clinicians neglected to thoroughly examine the nature of the information obtained in a clinical interview—whether it was accurate data, included all important facts about a disorder, and was consistent among different respondents—and the interview receded further from scientific scrutiny.

Sources of Error

The paucity of research led to criticism that clinical interviews were quasi-scientific, biased procedures. Their ability to achieve clinical objectives was not verified. Simultaneously, innovative methods in psychiatric practice (neurobiological, genetic, epidemiologic, therapeutic) made development of improved diagnostic classification methods mandatory in order to take advantage of the advances. All clinical research was compromised by the inability to achieve reliable diagnoses. Clinicians seeking reasons for diagnostic disagreement among interviewers identified two principal sources: the use of varying rules for assigning a diagnosis (criterion variance) and the choice of different interview methods to obtain facts (information variance). Specific, standard, operationalized criteria for diagnoses (i.e., at least minimal operating instructions to guide the clinician in the decision whether a symptom or diagnosis is present) are now in common use among clinicians. Nevertheless, standardization of the form of interviews has been a more difficult and controversial undertaking.

Two principles underlie attempts to reduce

erroneous interview data in clinical practice. The behavioral feature must be observable, permitting agreement among expert observers (i.e., it can be observed reliably when present), and verifiable, indicating that it occurs as hypothesized in the construct (i.e., it is valid). Rigorous investigation of sources of error in interview techniques with children was uncommon until 10 years ago. This deficiency was harmful to efforts to define childhood disorders and determine optimal therapies.

THE CLINICAL LABORATORY: CONCEPTS AND MEASURES

The Diagnostic Interview

DEFINING VARIANCE

Criterion Variance. Clinicians assigning diagnoses to the same patient too often failed to agree, leading to an effort to build a new classification system for psychiatric diagnoses. An essential requirement of the new system was the use of operationally defined criteria for the presence of a disorder, replacing where appropriate the subjective and varying judgments of clinicians. This substantially improved diagnostic procedures, but psychiatrists understood the limitations of operational definitions. The clinician must decide whether a patient fulfills these criteria, a decision requiring subjective evaluation of sometimes incomplete and inconsistent reports and evidence. For example, by what ultimate, practical means does a clinician determine that a child is inattentive rather than impulsive?

An operational definition provides a repeatable sequence of rules or steps to obtain a measurement, in this case a diagnosis. Operational definitions can be unsatisfactory because each set of measurement (diagnostic) rules contains both an element of error and some unintended, random factors. Therefore, reliance on a single operational definition confines our understanding of a concept (or diagnosis) to those features monitored by the specific set of rules, and limits opportunities to improve the operational steps. Research methodologists caution against the use of single operational definitions in measurement systems. Operational definitions are inherently imperfect; if they are not, the construct measured is self-evident and does

not require the development of any definitions. The use of several measures avoids the pitfall of an assumed "final, perfect" operational definition and generates productive comparisons among measures. Different measures (e.g., rating scales and structured interviews) are a check on one another, as the errors and biases in each are open to scrutiny. This is similar to improving reliability and validity by the use of multiple probes (derived from operational definitions) in a structured interview (Young et al. 1987).

Information Variance. There are so many sources of erroneous information in the clinical interview that it is difficult to control all of them simultaneously (see Table 26–4 for examples). Surprisingly, questions about apparently straightforward, simple facts can elicit erroneous answers. For example, when answers by adult respondents were com-

Table 26–4. COMMON SOURCES OF INTERVIEW MISINFORMATION

A. Structure of the Interview
 1. Lack of specificity in the question
 2. Concepts of question are complex and multidimensional
 3. Sequence of questions
 4. Number of questions
 5. Question structure
 6. Unwarranted assumptions in the question
 7. More than one question embedded in a single probe
 8. Sensitive or threatening element in the questions
 9. Wording of the question
  a. Inexact terms
  b. Ambiguous or vague terms
  c. Complex terms and sentences
  d. Biased words
 10. Halo effects
B. Respondent
 1. Need to give socially desirable answers
 2. Lack of understanding of the questions
 3. Memory lapses
 4. Experience of questioning as stressful
 5. No true opinion
 6. Differing emotional intensity among respondents
 7. Variable perceptions of the situation and purpose
 8. Timing of interview
C. Interviewer
 1. Interviewer characteristics
 2. Preferences and biases
 3. Variable emotional intensity
 4. Variable verbal facility
 5. Variable understanding of the questions
 6. Recording errors

Adapted from Young, JG et al. 1987. *J. Am. Acad. Child Adolesc. Psychiatry* 26:613–620, with permission.

pared with official records it was found that a large number inaccurately reported whether they had contributed to the United Fund (40%) or registered and voted in a recent election (25%); 17% even gave their age incorrectly (Parry and Crossley 1950). Alternative structures and styles of clinical interviews can be employed to obtain the diverse, complex information required to fulfill differing purposes, just as many types of measures are applied to the comprehensive evaluation of children (Rutter et al. 1981; Young et al. 1982).

QUALITY CONTROL: MEASURING THE ACCURACY AND PRECISION OF THE CLINICAL DIAGNOSTIC INTERVIEW

Clinical assessment procedures are subject to the same quality control requirements that hold for laboratory assay procedures. However, the delayed development of clinical assessment quality control was related to two problems. First, the constructs and phenomena encountered in the clinical setting appeared vague in comparison with laboratory measures. In fact, this reflects a lack of understanding by clinicians of the frustrating problems encountered in the laboratory every day in relation to many difficulties. These include recovery of a substance following sample preparation and cleanup (comparable to a specification of losses of clinical material occurring by selecting one specific clinical scale rather than another); "proof" of the actual biochemical identity of the substance measured (comparable to clinical validation studies); establishment of the coefficient of variation of an assay within the same day (comparable to internal consistency reliability research); examination of assay variation across laboratories (comparable to interrater reliability investigations); and determination of the stability of a compound in clinical specimens unfrozen or frozen at different temperatures for different time periods (comparable to test–retest reliability research) (Young et al. 1985).

Second, investigators had to decide what to measure for quality control in clinical research. This question arose because many clinical constructs and phenomena contribute to the disorders of interest, creating controversy about the selection of methods and instruments. In addition, clinical quality control procedures are time consuming and ex-

pensive for personnel, discouraging rigorous research in an area lacking glamour. Finally, the relative lack of quality control procedures meant that there was no agreement about how to decide which research results were correct. These difficulties have been overcome for the most part.

The accuracy, precision, and efficiency with which the clinical interview accomplishes its goals—in this instance, assigning "correct" diagnoses—are conceptualized in terms of validity and reliability. These clinical concepts are parallel to the two major sources of variance considered in quality control measures in a clinical chemistry laboratory, accuracy and precision. "Accuracy is concerned with the relationship of a set of results to the true value" (Whitehead 1977). Validity describes how well a test or instrument measures what it is supposed to measure. "Precision measurements are concerned with the agreement between replicate analyses" (Whitehead 1977). Reliability indicates the replicability, consistency, and stability of a test or instrument when it is applied by multiple individuals in several circumstances, yielding an estimation of the "error variance" of the instrument. Meticulous attention to measures of validity and reliability is as much the responsibility of the clinician as measures of accuracy and precision are for the biochemist.

The inherent relationship of validity and reliability to one another clarifies the meaning of the individual terms. Conceptually, reliability is subordinate to validity: it describes the degree to which the error variance of a measurement instrument limits its validity. When reliability measures are described as "attenuation statistics," the description indicates that reliability measures are an estimate of how much specific rating errors restrict or attenuate validity (Carey and Gottesman 1978).

Reliability and validity can also be thought of as poles of a continuum. At one end, reliability indicates correlations associated with tests that are almost identical; an example is two interviewers using the same rating scale with a single patient. At the other end, validity refers to correlations among measures that are dissimilar (measuring constructs that are related but different), tending to avoid shared sources of error. The association between a patient's self-rating and nurses' symptom descriptions in the patient's medical chart is an example of an index of validity.

When we use two or more measurement instruments we can examine correlations between them and determine the common variance; this gives an estimate of the validity and error variance. As instruments become more dissimilar, it is less likely that irrelevant components will be identical and remain undetected. When the instruments are maximally dissimilar, any shared variance is significant because it is likely to reflect the variable or construct intended, rather than irrelevant components or error (Kidder and Judd 1986). If two disparate procedures (like the self-rating and the chart review in the example above) indicate the presence of a thought disorder, then it is highly probable that there has been a psychotic episode.

The gradation of agreement and disagreement among different informants concerning clinical phenomena further exemplifies this point. Diagnostic agreement in the range of 0.8 (Pearson correlation coefficient) is typically achieved for structured interview diagnoses by clinicians training and working together. Parents, or other pairs playing a generally similar role in relation to the child (e.g., a pair of teachers), reach a range of agreement around 0.6 when rating behavioral and emotional items. However, different types of informants (e.g., parent and teacher) commonly demonstrate an agreement level no better than approximately 0.3 (Achenbach et al. 1987). The gradient of agreement associated with these informant relationships runs from a reliability measure (high agreement) to indices related to validity (low agreement). Clinicians with similar training are likely to agree about behaviors they simultaneously observe. In contrast, different types of informants in different situations will agree less, yet provide valuable information that enhances their understanding of the behaviors. This conceptualization of agreement and disagreement can be very informative for clinical assessment, as clinicians come to recognize that "poor agreement" between different informants can be generative instead of disappointing. This represents a shift from an exclusive emphasis on reliable observations to a concurrent focus on valid observations that fill in a full and accurate picture of the behaviors (Young et al. 1987).

If validity refers to the capacity of measures to reflect a construct, then the understanding of construct validity is enhanced when informant- and/or situation-specific elements of the construct are differentiated. This might be described as differential validity; it is related but not equivalent to discriminant validity, because the objective is not to distinguish divergent constructs. Instead, the measure identifies differential characteristics of behavior or emotion according to the informant and situation. For example, the ratings of a child's impulsivity by teachers and parents help establish the validity of the construct, but they also reflect the separate situational influences on a child's impulsive behavior and ratings of the behaviors by different adults.

DEVELOPMENT AND APPLICATION OF STRUCTURED DIAGNOSTIC INTERVIEWS

Structured Diagnostic Interviews for Adults. The development of structured interviews for adults in the 1960s and 1970s was a response to the poor reliability of data derived from the clinical interview. There were many sources of variability: differences in topics discussed; variable phrasing of questions; alternative interview procedures by the same interviewer at different times; the interaction of variable interview styles and patient characteristics; the contributions of clinical judgment in unspecified ways; and informal methods for recording information. Awareness that nonstandardization caused many of these problems guided a move toward greater methodologic rigor. Questionnaires or rating scales and other observational methods were substituted in some instances, but most clinicians felt that interviews had certain unique advantages in the evaluation of psychopathology. Standardized interview schedules were developed to specify interview content, techniques, and recording format. They were shown to have greater reliability and to differentiate patient groups.

Examination of the reliability of structured diagnostic interviews in adult psychiatric patients has generally produced satisfactory results. They typically achieve moderate to high rates of agreement that are superior to traditional interview methods (Helzer et al. 1977; 1981; 1985; Hyler et al. 1982; Robins 1985; Pulver and Carpenter 1983; Burnam et al. 1983; Hendricks et al. 1983; Hesselbrock et al. 1982; Wittchen et al. 1985). In addition, structured interviews with adults are useful for epidemiologic purposes according to the results of the initial Epidemiologic Catchment Area (ECA) surveys. However, structured interviews are not without problems at this stage of their development. When disagreement was observed, it appeared that it was related to several potential sources: insufficient or inadequate information; incomplete criterion coverage by the interviewer; overinclusive questions in the structured interview; recency of disorder; and the degree of reliance of lay interviewer-administered structured interviews on subject symptom reports (Anthony et al. 1985).

The use of clinical diagnoses in psychiatry reflects the categorical approach required for many aspects of medical evaluation and treatment. On the other hand, clinicians recognize that this can be somewhat artificial with certain disorders for which a clearly validated status as a single etiology disease is lacking. The absence of biological markers to designate discontinuities among such diagnoses sometimes leads the clinician to use a pragmatic approach in which the patient's status on functional and symptom dimensions is rated. In this dimensional approach, symptom grouping and enumeration become a guide for clinical diagnosis and treatment, ultimately reliant on the choice of a "cutting point" for inclusion or exclusion from a diagnostic category among a population in which nonpatients will have some symptoms. Obviously, where the cutting point is placed will have an important effect on the percentage of correctly identified cases (sensitivity) and noncases (specificity). This is an essential consideration when estimating agreement obtained through the use of structured interviews (Young et al. 1987).

Best Estimate Diagnosis. The search for a "gold standard" or final criterion of validity for comparisons of clinical instruments is never fully successful, other than through the discovery of specific etiologies of subgroups within a disorder. This led to the ironic use of the terms *LEAD* standard (an acronym indicating *l*ongitudinal, *e*xpert, and *a*ll *d*ata) and *PLASTIC* standard (*p*rospective, *l*ongitudinal, *a*ll *s*ource, *t*reatment, *i*mpairment, and *c*linical presentation). The current reference standard for validity measures is the "best estimate diagnosis." It is derived

from all data and the optimal clinical diagnostic process, anchored in the clinical interview. Increasing correspondence among different measures of a clinical construct, particularly in relation to the best estimate diagnosis, encourages confidence that they are achieving greater validity. The best estimate diagnosis method is a complex and time-consuming undertaking, because it employs multiple types of measures. No single best estimate diagnosis procedure has been agreed on beyond reliance on expert clinician interviews and multiple data sources. The preferred procedure for generating a best estimate diagnosis for children has not been determined, but assessments of children might employ a broad range of measures, including ratings by parents, teachers, peers, and the child; structured interviews of the child and parents; physical and neurologic examinations; and standardized tests of the child (Young et al. 1987).

Training in the Use of Structured Interviews. There are several sources of observation variance. Common examples are the level of professional experience (more experienced clinicians rating symptoms less severely), the theoretical background of the interviewer, the professional training of the observer, and the prevailing clinical practices of the interviewer's institution. When these factors are combined with personality characteristics of the interviewer, consistent biases in individual ratings occur; they are identified as the "response style" of the interviewer, a habitual tendency that is independent of the phenomena observed. Efforts to reduce rater biases were gradually formally consolidated into joint training, testing, and calibration of interviewers using standard procedures. The associated financial and time expense has caused controversy concerning the use and necessity of specialized training in procedures for structured interviews; nevertheless, some investigators believe that failure to undertake such a training program compromises the reliability of the diagnoses (Gibbon et al. 1981). A standard training sequence is used for each of the major structured interviews. A typical training program includes four phases related to the format for presenting the diagnostic interview material: case histories, videotaped (or audiotaped) interviews, live interviews by trainees, and continued monitoring to maintain reliability (Young et al. 1987).

Are Structured Interviews Beneficial and

Table 26–5. CONSIDERATIONS FOR SELECTION OF STRUCTURED DIAGNOSTIC INTERVIEWS FOR CHILDREN AND ADOLESCENTS

	CAS	DICA	DISC	K-SADS-P[x]	ISC
Primary Application	Clinical research	Epidemiologic/clinical research	Epidemiologic	Clinical research	Clinical research
Time to Administer†	C 60 P 60	C 40 P 45	C 45–60 P 60–90	C 60–90 P 60–90	C 45–90 P 90–150
Age Range	7–17	6–17	8–17	6–18	8–17
Format‡					
Introduction	Structured	Structured	Structured	Unstructured	Unstructured
Diagnostic Assessment	Structured	Structured	Structured	Semistructured	Semistructured
Organization	Functional Domains	Functional Domains	Functional Domains	Diagnostic Complexes	Diagnostic Complexes
Time Frame for Inquiry	Present	Lifetime: past, present	Present: past year/6 months	Present: symptoms most severe this episode; past week	Present: 2 weeks/6 months
Severity Ratings	N	N	N	Y	Y
Interviewer Observations	Y	Y	N	Y	Y
Informants	Parent/child parallel forms	Parent/child parallel forms	Parent/child parallel forms	Parent/child single form	Parent/child single form
Level of Clinical Skills Advised	Clinicians	Clinicians	Lay interview	Clinicians	Clinicians
Computer Algorithm	Y	Y	Y	Y	N

CAS, Child Assessment Schedule; DICA, Diagnostic Interview for Children and Adolescents; DISC, NIMH Diagnostic Interview Schedule for Children; K-SADS-P, Schedule for Affective Disorders and Schizophrenia for School-Age Children (present episode version); ISC, Interview Schedule for Children; Y, yes; N, no.

*The K-SADS-E (epidemiologic version) differs from the K-SADS-P in the following respects: its primary application is both epidemiologic and clinical. The time frame for inquiries includes the current episode and the most severe past episode of any symptom. Severity of symptoms is not recorded.

†Estimated time in minutes to administer to child (C) and parent (P).

‡Level of structure of introductory section and queries to assess diagnostic criteria (diagnostic assessment).

Reprinted from Gutterman EM, O'Brien JD, and Young JG 1987. *J. Am. Acad. Child Adolesc. Psychiatry* 26:621–630, with permission.

Practical for Routine Clinical Use? If structured interviews have been used primarily for research purposes, can it be assumed that they are beneficial for patients in routine clinical use? Research indicates that they increase the number of clinical observations and the amount of relevant patient information that is recorded. A substantial amount of significant information is omitted in "unstructured" interviews, including phenomena such as suicidal thoughts, delusions, and weight loss. When using structured interviews, clinicians tend not to restrict themselves to the presenting symptoms in their diagnostic formulations and have higher reliability (Helzer 1982; Cox et al. 1981). But, is the use of structured interviews in ordinary clinical circumstances feasible? Some clinicians fear that they will interfere with rapport with the patient or the flow of the interview.

However, interviewers who use both methods consider themselves to be equally empathic when using interview schedules. Structured interviews may require somewhat more time to complete, although experience leads to increasing efficiency and little time difference. For example, psychiatric residents on a busy consultation service, having no prior experience with structured interviews, were willing to use them. Among the subset of patients for whom they were not used, the largest group was patients with organic brain syndrome; this suggested that they were used when patients were examinable. Some diagnoses that were fulfilled according to the coding were not assigned by the interviewer, while some diagnoses not present according to coded answers were listed. These discrepancies appear because of oversight or complexities of coding (Helzer 1982).

Table 26–6. DSM-III CATEGORIES INCLUDED IN STRUCTURED DIAGNOSTIC INTERVIEWS

| | Interview | | | | | |
Category	CAS	DICA	DISC	K-SADS-P	K-SADS-E	ISC
AXIS I						
Adjustment disorder	N	Y*	N	N	N	N
Affective disorder						
Bipolar	SC	Y	Y	Y	Y	Y
Major depression	Y	Y	Y	Y	Y	Y
Cyclothymic disorder	SC	N	Y	Y	Y	Y
Dysthymic disorder	Y	N	Y	Y	Y	Y
Anxiety disorder						
Avoidant	Y	N	Y	N	N	Y
Overanxious	Y	Y	Y	N	Y	Y
Separation	Y	Y	Y	Y	Y	Y
Generalized anxiety	SC	N	N	Y	N	Y
Obsessive-compulsive	Y	Y	Y	Y	Y	Y
Panic	SC	N	Y	Y	Y	Y
Phobia	Y	Y	Y	Y	Y	Y
Attention-deficit disorder	Y	Y	Y	N	Y	Y
Conduct disorder	Y	Y	Y	Y	Y	Y
Eating disorder						
Anorexia nervosa	SC	Y	Y	Y	Y	N
Bulimia	SC	Y	Y	Y	N	N
Gender identity	N	Y	Y	N	N	N
Movement disorders						
Tic disorder	SC	N	Y	N	N	N
Tourette's syndrome	SC	N	Y	N	N	N
Oppositional disorder	Y	Y	Y	N	N	Y
Pervasive developmental disorder	N	N	Y	N	Y	N
Physical function disorder						
Encopresis	Y	Y	Y	N	N	Y
Enuresis	Y	Y	Y	N	N	Y
Sleep disorder	SC	N	N	N	N	N
Psychotic disorders	SC†	SC†				
Schizophrenia	N	N	Y	Y	Y	Y
Schizoaffective	N	N	N	Y	Y	N
Schizoid disorder	Y	N	N	N	N	Y
Substance use						
Alcohol	SC	Y	Y	N	Y	Y
Drug	SC	Y	Y	N	Y	Y
AXIS II						
Personality disorders	N	N	N	N	N	Y‡

Y, yes; N, no; SC, screening item only.
*Adjustment disorder with depressed mood.
†Screening item for psychoses.
‡Includes assessment of the following: borderline, compulsive, histrionic, and schizotypal personality disorders.
Reprinted from Gutterman EM, O'Brien JD, and Young JG 1987. *J. Am. Acad. Child Adolesc. Psychiatry* 26:621–630, with permission.

Structured Diagnostic Interviews for Children and Adolescents. Several structured interviews for children and adolescents are now available. Each is undergoing continuous revision in response to research and changes in the major diagnostic systems. Choice of a diagnostic interview depends on the goals for the interview, and the characteristics of each should be studied carefully before selecting one (Gutterman et al. 1987, and Tables 26–5 and 26–6).

The Psychoanalytical Interview

The success of structured interviews for diagnostic purposes encourages the use of the structured format for other types of interviews. For example, this would be an essential step toward improved validity and reliability of psychoanalytical and psychodynamic interviews. First phase work might describe the principal phenomena observed and responded to in a psychoanalytical interview and specify the types of variance to be monitored. This requires a subsequent stage in which procedures for the application of validity and reliability measures are agreed on, making it possible to estimate the accuracy and precision of psychodynamic data monitored by these methods. Comparison of results obtained with different psychoanalytical interviewers for several disorders would estimate the use of this approach.

CONCLUSIONS

The Achilles heel of the clinical interview for investigators is its complexity; the successful grasp of one component in our research is so often at the cost of another slipping away. Yet, this is also the source of its immense power as a clinical tool to help families. Advances in technical investigative methods encourage the view that the interview is now becoming a refined, valid, and reliable research instrument.

References

Achenbach, T.M., McConaughy, S.H., and Howell, C.T. 1987. Child/adolescent behavioral and emotional problems: Implications of cross-informant correlations for situational specificity. *Am. Psychol.* 101:213–232.

Achenbach, T.M., and Edelbrock, C.S. 1978. The classification of child psychopathology: A review and analysis of empirical efforts. *Psychol. Bull.* 85:1275–1301.

Anthony, J.C., Folstein, M., Romanoski, A.J., et al. 1985. Comparison of the lay diagnostic interview schedules and a standardized psychiatric diagnosis. *Arch. Gen. Psychiatry* 42:667–675.

Burnam, M.A., Karno, M., Hough R.L., et al. 1983. The Spanish Diagnostic Interview Schedule: Reliability and comparison with clinical diagnosis. *Arch. Gen. Psychiatry* 40:1143–1155.

Carey, G., and Gottesman, I. 1978. Reliability and validity in binary ratings. *Arch. Gen. Psychiatry* 35:1454–1459.

Cox, A., Hopkinson, K., and Rutter, M. 1981. Psychiatric interviewing techniques: II. Naturalistic study: Eliciting factual information. *Br. J. Psychiatry* 138:283–291.

Denckla, M.B. 1985. Revised neurological examination for subtle signs. *Psychopharmacol. Bull.* 21:773–789.

Gibbon, M., McDonald-Scott, P., and Endicott, J. 1981. Mastering the art of research interviewing: A model training procedure for diagnostic evaluation. *Arch. Gen. Psychiatry* 38:1259–1262.

Goldblatt, M. 1972. Psychoanalysis of the schoolchild. In Wolman, B.B. (ed.): *Handbook of Child Psychoanalysis.* New York: Van Nostrand Reinhold Co.

Goodman, J., and Sours, J. 1967. *The Child Mental Status Examination.* New York: Basic Books.

Gutterman, E.M., O'Brien, J.D., and Young, J.G. 1987. Structured diagnostic interviews for children and adolescents: Current status and future directions. *J. Am. Acad. Child Adolesc. Psychiatry* 26:621–630.

Helzer, J.E. 1982. The use of a structured diagnostic interview for routine psychiatric evaluations. *J. Nerv. Ment. Dis.* 169:45–49.

Helzer, J.E., Clayton, J., Pambakian R., et al. 1977. Reliability of psychiatric diagnosis: II The test/retest reliability of diagnostic classifications. *Arch. Gen. Psychiatry* 34:129–133.

Helzer, J.E., McEvoy, L.T., Spitznagel, E.L., et al. 1985. A comparison of clinical and diagnostic interview schedule diagnoses. *Arch. Gen. Psychiatry* 42:657–666.

Helzer, J.E., Robins, L.N., Crughan, J. L., and Welner, A. 1981. Renard Diagnostic Interview: Its reliability and procedural validity with physicians and lay interviewers. *Arch. Gen. Psychiatry* 38:393–398.

Hendricks, L., Bayton, J.A., Collins, J.L., et al. 1983. The NIMH Diagnostic Interview Schedule: A test of its validity in a population of black adults. *J. Natl. Med. Assoc.* 75:667–671.

Hesselbrock, V., Stabenau, J., Hesselbrock, M., et al. 1982. A comparison of two interview schedules: The Schedule for Affective Disorders and Schizophrenia—Lifetime and the National Institutes of Mental Health Diagnostic Interview Schedule. *Arch. Gen. Psychiatry* 39:674–677.

Hyler, S.E., Williams, J.B.W., and Spitzer, R.K. 1982. Reliability in the *DSM-III* field trials: Interview versus case summary. *Arch. Gen. Psychiatry* 39:1275–1278.

Kidder, L.H., and Judd, C.M. 1986. *Research Methods in Social Relations.* New York: Holt, Rinehart and Winston.

Lewis, M. 1982. *Clinical Aspects of Child Development,* 2nd. ed. Philadelphia: Lea & Febiger.

Lewis, M. 1989. Psychiatric examination of the infant, child, and adolescent. In Kaplan, H., and Sadock, B. (eds.): *Comprehensive Textbook of Psychiatry,* V. Baltimore: Williams & Wilkins.

Parry, H.J., and Crossley, H.M. 1950. Validity of responses to survey questions. *Publ. Opin. Q.* 14:61–80.

Prange, A.J., Jr., Garbutt, J.C., and Loosen, P.T. 1987. The hypothalamic-pituitary-thyroid axis in affective disorders. In Meltzer, H.Y. (ed.): *Psychopharmacology: The Third Generation of Progress.* New York: Raven Press.

Pulver, A.E., and Carpenter, W.T. 1983. Lifetime psychotic symptoms assessed with the DIS. *Schizophr. Bull.* 9:377–382.

Robins, L.N., Helzer, J.E., Croughan, J., and Ratcliff, K.S. 1981. National Institute of Mental Health Diagnostic Interview schedule: Its history, characteristics and validity. *Arch. Gen. Psychiatry* 38:393–398.

Robins, L.N. 1985. Epidemiology: Reflections on testing the validity of psychiatric interviews. *Arch. Gen. Psychiatry* 42:918–924.

Rutter, M., and Graham, P. 1968. The reliability and validity of the psychiatric assessment of the child: I. Interview with the child. *Br. J. Psychiatry* 114:563–579.

Rutter, M., Cox, A., Egert, S., et al. 1981. Psychiatric interviewing techniques: IV. Experimental study: Four contrasting styles. *Br. J. Psychiatry* 138:456–465.

Shaywitz, S.E. 1982. The Yale Neuropsychoeducational Assessment Scales. *Schizophr. Bull.* 8:372–424.

Shaywitz, S.E., Shaywitz, B.A., McGraw, B.S., et al. 1984. Current status of the Neuromaturational Examination as an index of learning disability. *J. Pediatr.* 104:819–825.

Simmons, J.E. 1987. *Psychiatric Examination of Children,* 4th. ed. Philadelphia: Lea & Febiger.

Stokes, P.E., and Sikes, C.R. 1987. Hypothalamic-pituitary-adrenal axis in affective disorders. In Meltzer, H.Y. (ed.): *Psychopharmacology: The Third Generation of Progress*. New York: Raven Press.

Whitehead, T.P. 1977. *Quality Control in Clinical Chemistry*. New York: John Wiley & Sons.

Wittchen, H., Semler, G., and von Zerssen, D. 1985. A comparison of two diagnostic methods. *Arch. Gen. Psychiatry* 42:677–684.

Young, J.G., Cohen, D.J., Shaywitz, S.E., et al. 1982.

Assessment of brain function in clinical pediatric research: Behavioral and biological strategies. *Schizophr. Bull.* 8:205–235.

Young, J.G., Leven, L.I., and Cohen, D.J. 1985. Clinical neurochemical strategies in child psychiatry. In Michels, R., and Cavenar, J.O. (eds.): *Psychiatry*. Philadelphia: J.B. Lippincott Co.

Young, J.G., O'Brien, J.D., Gutterman, E.M., and Cohen, P. 1987. Research on the Clinical Interview. *J. Am. Acad. Child Adolesc. Psychiatry* 26:613–620.

27

Functional Neuropsychological Assessment in Child Psychiatry

GERALD J. AUGUST, Ph.D.

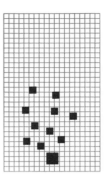

The psychological examination of the child referred for evaluation of behavioral or emotional problems has traditionally consisted of intelligence testing, personality and projective techniques, and specific tests for sensorimotor delays, perceptual deficits, and learning disabilities. The pattern of test results was frequently used by clinicians to support claims for the differential diagnosis of organic versus functional psychiatric disturbance. In recent years it has become apparent that the often-made distinction between organic and functional mental disorders is not as clear as once assumed. The assumption had been that functional disorders were related to psychosocial influences while organic disorders were caused by brain injuries. Recent technologic advances (computed axial tomography, positron emission tomography, magnetic resonance imaging) have produced a data base that questions the narrow view of structural and neurochemical normality in the brains of patients with psychiatric disorders previously presumed to be functional. These advances have led to an increased awareness of neuropsychological aspects of mental disorders with the subsequent development of assessment techniques designed to assess a diverse range of brain functions.

Specific brain–behavior relationships have been identified for a number of adult central nervous system (CNS) disorders, leading to a more accurate understanding of the relationship between brain structure and function. Abnormalities can now be identified in the brain structure and function of adult patients with both affective disorders and schizophrenia. Both patient groups have shown specific patterns on neuropsychological measures. Despite the significant amount of information that has been learned from the study of adults with specific brain lesions and those with psychiatric disorders, the adult models have provided little guidance for understanding the neuropsychological functioning of the disturbed child. There are a number of obstacles confronting researchers who conduct neuropsychological research with children that preclude the generalization of neuropsychological findings from adults to children. First, the type of brain damage seen in adults is seldom observed in children. Research in adult human neuropsychology has been largely dependent on the evaluation of behavior in persons with documented lesions of the brain. These brain lesions are most often produced by catastrophic events such as cerebrovascular accidents, traumatic (penetrating) head injuries, and intracerebral tumors that result in localized damage. In contrast, research in child neuropsychology has relied on the study of children who suffer from developmental disorders, such as those produced by genetic abnormalities, birth trauma, and postnatal infection. In these disorders brain damage is inferred from delays or deviations in development and believed to be more diffuse. Second, because the child's brain is in a process of development compared with the static adult brain, brain injuries in children produce qualitatively different effects than brain injuries sustained by adults. Children, for example, experience much greater generalized rather than specific functional impairment, the opposite being true for adults, and very different neuropsychological assessment profiles emerge in the two types. Third, the identification of brain–behavior relationships in children is inherently more difficult because of the progressive anatomical organization of the child's brain. It is a popular notion, for example, that when young children sustain head trauma, the mechanisms of neural plasticity allow for the recovery of function to occur. Thus, damage to the left cerebral hemisphere occurring at an early age may lead to a transfer of linguistic function to the right cerebral hemisphere (Alajouanine and Lhermitte 1965). With advancing age the apparent plasticity of the brain diminishes, cerebral lateralization becomes more fully established, and damage to the left cerebral hemisphere produces more persistent language deficits. A fourth obstacle to the assessment of brain–behavior relationships in children is the consideration of confounding variables more unique to children with behavior and emotional disorders. Individual differences in attitude, motivation, effort, and compliance may affect a child's test performance, making it difficult to make inferences concerning the primacy of skill deficits. Even in cases in which evidence of neurologic insult exists, it often becomes difficult to separate out the effects of brain injury from stress reactions associated with perceived changes in functioning.

Ultimately, the extrapolation of neuropsychological findings from adult to child patients may not be fruitful for an understanding of childhood psychopathology. It is very unlikely that children's psychiatric disorders will be traced to focal lesions in brain structure, and the discovery of a one-to-one correspondence between a psychiatric symptom and a specific skill deficit would be unexpected. A more plausible connection would be mediated in several stages. Attention-deficit hyperactivity disorder, for example, would be visualized as resulting, under certain environmental and contextual circumstances, from disturbances in one or more basic psychological processes. These processes would be related to anatomical pathways and neurotransmitter systems that are

themselves undergoing progressive change as a consequence of development and maturation. Assessment approaches that include tests of "brain damage" and seek only to make inferences regarding CNS disorders are likely to lead to vague and ambiguous concepts such as minimal brain dysfunction and organic brain syndrome, which have little value for treatment implications. What is needed is an assessment approach that emphasizes the behavioral and cognitive capacities of the child rather than the neurologic workings of the child's brain. This approach would make allowances for developmental factors, would incorporate environmental influences, and would seek to uncover weaknesses in general psychological abilities and component skills underlying the disorder.

Taylor and his colleagues (Fletcher and Taylor 1983; Taylor et al. 1984) have proposed a "functional" approach to the neuropsychological assessment of children that has specific relevance for the evaluation of childhood psychopathology. The primary goal of a functional approach is neither to make clinical diagnoses nor to draw CNS inferences but rather to evaluate developing behavioral, cognitive, and adaptive skills associated with the disability in question. In this respect the functional model is compatible with the multiaxial scheme adopted by the *Diagnostic and Statistical Manual of Mental Disorders*, third edition, revised *(DSM-III-R)*, which allows for consideration of physical, adaptive, and environmental factors associated with the patient's primary diagnosis. Children referred for evaluation of psychiatric disturbance are often found to display multiple clinical problems (co-morbidity), including deficits in social adaptation and academic achievement. These associated problems are often more critical to the child's mental health and adjustment than are the primary psychiatric symptoms. By drawing attention to the matrix of developmental, cognitive, and adaptive variables that are associated with the psychiatric disorder, the functional assessment process assumes a descriptive-prescriptive role rather than simply a diagnostic role. This results in a situation in which the clinician is concerned not only with making a psychiatric diagnosis but, more importantly, using the diagnostic information to develop a plan of education and treatment that will promote the most positive outcome for the patient.

The functional model outlined by Taylor and co-workers (1984) provides a structure that ensures that all important aspects of the child's functioning are considered in the assessment process. Four assessment variables are defined:

1. Analysis of the child's manifest disability

2. Measurement of behavioral and cognitive correlates of the disability (basic competencies)

3. Consideration of psychosocial and environmental factors that influence how the child copes with basic skill weaknesses (moderator variables)

4. A review of biological factors that predispose the child toward a given disability

These four variables do not act independently but instead interact with each other to produce diverse variations of clinical symptomatology. By extending the range of clinical inquiry to include aspects of basic competence, adjustment, and adaptability, the functional approach yields data that are useful in the planning of educational and management strategies. In this respect, the functional approach is compatible with Public Law 94-142, which mandates a free and appropriate education be provided to all handicapped persons from birth to 21 years of age. The provisions of this law require that an individualized program of instruction be developed and recorded for each child identified as having a handicapping condition. The identification of a handicapping condition and the formulation of the individualized education program require that a comprehensive evaluation of the child's pattern of function and dysfunction be conducted, and it is at this point that a functional-based neuropsychological assessment becomes useful.

At the University of Minnesota Medical School the basic framework of the Taylor et al. (1984) functional model has been adopted in conducting psychological examinations of psychiatrically disturbed children. Modifications have been made to each of the assessment variables to address the specific needs of a psychiatric population. A description of each of the assessment variables is provided below followed by examples of specific measurement techniques applicable for each characteristic.

ASSESSMENT VARIABLES

Manifest Disability

Functional assessment begins with a comprehensive description of the clinical phenomenology (i.e., manifest disability). A thorough review of the referral complaints and all associated problems manifested by the child is conducted. Examples might include short attention span, failure to complete tasks, social aloofness, ritualistic behavior, physical aggressiveness, school refusal, negative affect, or academic failure. In addition to the identification of symptomatic behaviors it is important to document the severity of the symptoms. Severity is determined by assessing how much adaptive functioning is impaired. This would include measurement of communication, socialization, and daily living skills. Identification of specific situations and events that elicit symptoms will also help distinguish primary, idiopathic symptoms from those that are reactive. This comprehensive review of the manifest disability should allow the clinician to identify associations that may exist between behavioral symptoms and also guide decisions about possible skill deficits that underlie the symptoms.

Basic Competencies

The next step in the assessment process is to evaluate basic competencies of the child with special attention to the identification of weaknesses in general abilities and deficits in component skills. This begins with assessment of general intellectual functions, academic achievement, language abilities, and attentional resources. It expands to a more precise analysis of neuropsychological component skills in selected areas such as sensorimotor functions, perception, visuospatial and constructional skills, and memory. Depending on the child's manifest disability one or several of these competencies may be selected for assessment. It is important to bear in mind that a skill deficit found in association with a specific manifest disability does not imply, ipso facto, that the deficient skill is a primary cause of the behavior problem. As is the case with so many other areas of assessment, there may be significant covariation of basic skills, making it difficult to isolate one specific deficit underlying the clinical problem. Of additional interest are the possible dissociations that may exist between general abilities and/or component skills. The child who excels on tasks of visual sequential memory but is weak on tasks of auditory sequential memory may have a generalized deficiency in auditory processing and not a memory impairment per se.

Moderator Variables

A third type of variable to be considered in the assessment process covers the full range of psychosocial, personality, and motivational factors that influence how the child compensates for, or copes with, his or her basic skill weaknesses (i.e., moderator variables). Children with learning disabilities frequently become frustrated with and demoralized by academic failure and, as a consequence, lack self-confidence, develop low self-esteem, and may become clinically depressed. Such maladaptive reactions may further complicate the basic competencies and result in a more severe expression of the manifest disability. On the other hand, support from both the home and school can lead to high achievement motivation that enables the child to compensate for and overcome the adverse effects of the specific skill deficiencies.

Biological Indices

A fourth variable included in the functional neuropsychological assessment model considers biological factors that may predispose a child toward a given disability and its associated behavioral and cognitive correlates. While actual brain lesions are seldom identifiable in children, knowledge of an early history of seizure activity may alert one to the biological basis of the child's problems. Other biological markers such as physical anomalies, prenatal, perinatal, and neonatal complications, serious medical illnesses, accidents resulting in head trauma, and family history of nervous and mental disorders help to establish certain biological vulnerabilities or predisposition in a particular child. This knowledge is useful in terms of understanding the limits imposed on basic competencies and also helpful in determining how to treat a patient and plan for effective remediation and management.

MEASUREMENT TECHNIQUES FOR FUNCTIONAL ASSESSMENT VARIABLES

Manifest Disability

The measurement of the manifest disability involves the collection of relevant clinical information from multiple informed sources. While the initial complaints may highlight noncompliance, academic underachievement, and attitude problems, such clinical symptoms are vague and often situation specific. A careful and comprehensive review of the reason for the child's referral and all possible behavioral changes manifested by the child is an essential step in the assessment process. There are a number of procedures for obtaining this information.

BEHAVIORAL RATING SCALES

Behavior rating scales provide objective information about the observable behavioral problems of children. Typically completed by the child's parent and/or teacher, these instruments can be used for a number of purposes, including clarifying the presence or absence of a significant behavioral problem and its severity, targeting specific behaviors that require direct intervention, and assessing the efficacy of an intervention strategy. Two behavioral rating scales that have proved useful in identifying behavioral problems are the Conners Symptom Questionnaire (Conners 1973) and the Child Behavior Checklist (Achenbach 1978; Achenbach and Edelbrock 1979). Both instruments include separate parent and teacher versions and have been shown to have satisfactory psychometric properties. The primary asset of these scales is that they provide a comprehensive sampling of various behavior problems and permit a quantitative measurement of the relative severity of specific problem areas.

The Conners Symptom Questionnaire (parent version) originally consisted of 93 items, but the version in more frequent use is a 48-item scale that includes five factor-analyzed groupings: (1) conduct problems, (2) impulsivity-hyperactivity, (3) psychosomatic, (4) learning problems, and (5) anxiety.

Ten of the items are also used to compose a hyperactivity index. Each item is rated on a 4-point continuum from "not at all" (scored 0) to "very much" (scored 3). Norms are available for males and females aged 3 to 17 years of age. The various factor scores have been shown to be highly related to children's age and sex. The Conners Symptom Questionnaire is often used to identify hyperactivity and/or inattention, with a mean score of 1.5 on the hyperactivity index serving as a lower limit for establishing the problem. The Child Behavior Checklist, which is also based on a dimensional or factorial approach to diagnostic classification, yields two "broad band" factors (internalizing versus externalizing) and nine "narrow band" factors. This scale takes about 20 minutes for parents to complete and consists of 118 items. The parents are asked to rate the child's behavior during the previous 6 months. Raw scores are converted into percentiles and normalized "T" scores, and profiles may be plotted as a function of the converted scores.

INTERVIEW OF PARENT

A second method of assessing the manifest disability is the parental interview. The parent interview should be organized to obtain detailed information about the target behaviors, variables that modify their expression, as well as data concerning pertinent developmental antecedents. In addition, symptoms can be further specified by asking for recent examples of behavior, the frequency of behavior, and the context of its occurrence. Circumstances that appear to precipitate certain aspects of behavior and those that ameliorate certain symptomatic problems can be specified. Also the age at onset and the chronicity of the disorder can be discussed during the interview. If the interview is conducted in a semi-structured manner, this will allow the interviewer to observe first-hand verbal and nonverbal information and communication regarding the child and family in reaction to a variety of topics. One extremely important issue that should be addressed in the parental interview is the clinical significance and impact of the child's presenting problems. Frequently, child referrals are based on unrealistic expectations by parents or teachers, rather than genuine problems. In such cases, the child's behavior may not necessarily be deviant in comparison with that of peers. To determine clinical significance, the child's behavior must be compared against existing information on normal children of a similar age. Those behaviors that deviate from the average for normal children may be viewed as clinically significant. In addition to normative comparisons of behavior, it is advisable to evaluate other functional areas of development, including socialization, daily living skills, language and communication, and motor skills. The Vineland Adaptive Behavior Scales (Sparrow et al. 1984) is a structured interview administered to parents (a teacher version is also available) that provides age-normed scales that assess primary areas of the child's functioning in the context of the environmental demands.

STRUCTURED PSYCHIATRIC INTERVIEWS

Clinicians may desire more precision and quantification of symptom data than that afforded by the semi-structured parent interview procedure. The use of structured psychiatric interviews has been shown to reduce information variance in the diagnostic process and to boost diagnostic reliability. A structured psychiatric interview is a list of target behaviors and symptoms with rather explicit rules for conducting interviews and recording the data. By specifying a standard sequence and wording of questions and using well-defined rules for rating and recording informant responses, the variance found in clinical judgment has been narrowed. In the past few years, several diagnostic interview schedules for children and adolescents have been developed, some of which are tied directly to a diagnostic system such as that embodied in the *DSM-III-R*. These include the Kiddie–Schedule of Affective Disorders and Schizophrenia (Puig-Antich and Chambers 1978), the Diagnostic Interview Schedule for Children (Costello et al. 1982), and the Diagnostic Interview for Children and Adolescents (Herjanic and Reich 1982). Many structured interviews also include separate versions administered to the child that elicit information regarding the child's own feelings, behavior, and social relationships. Despite the obvious advantages of the structured interview schedule in producing objective and quantifiable data, there are a number of shortcomings that minimize its use in the assessment of the child's manifest disability. For example, although the structured interview reliably detects the presence or absence of a specific symptom or disorder, it is less likely to assess frequency and severity of specific behaviors. Structured interviews also provide little clarity of the contexts and precipitants of behavior that could be used to determine whether reported problems are of endogenous or secondary significance. Lastly, it has been shown that poor agreement exists between parent and child as informants.

Several criteria for assessing the manifest disability can be drawn from behavior questionnaires, parent interview techniques, and structured psychiatric interviews. These establish the presence of clinical symptoms, their frequency, age at onset, duration and pervasiveness, as well as their statistical deviance in relation to the behavior of normal children of the same age. Furthermore, they can be used to assess the child's adaptive and developmental status and to obtain information of the family context in which the problem behaviors occur and the perceptions that various family members have concerning the origin of the problems. The methods and instruments described above do not constitute an exhaustive list of measurement possibilities. Self-reports of the child's attitudes, feelings, and other behaviors may be extremely valuable when evaluating internalizing behavior problems such as depression and anxiety. Direct behavioral observation, either in natural or simulated environments, may be of equal value in validating the occurrence and severity of externalizing behaviors such as hyperactivity and conduct disturbance.

A comprehensive evaluation of the child's manifest disability reveals a variety of behavioral problems that are perceived by different persons in the child's environment as being clinically deviant. Although this information is necessary for making clinical diagnoses, it is not sufficient for understanding more fundamental deficits associated with the symptoms and thus is of limited value in the formulation of comprehensive treatment programs. This is best illustrated by children who exhibit attentional problems. Inattention is a very common reason for referral among young children with diverse clinical diagnoses. Inattention, however, is a very complex symptom that may apply to one or several defective processes, including activation, selection, vigilance, search, organi-

zation, and regulation. To further complicate matters, in some cases inattention may reflect a nonspecific, transitory state, with situational and contextual factors determining the degree to which the child complies with external demands. In other instances inattention may be expressed as uniform deficiency made in response to specific information processing demands. It is in accordance with this latter usage that we may speak of the excessive narrowing of attention in infantile autism. It is difficult and often impossible to make a functional distinction of inattentive behavior on the sole basis of ratings, parent interviews, or observation. It is at this point that the assessment of the basic skill competencies is essential in qualifying the origins of the behavioral symptom.

Basic Skill Competencies

The assessment of the child's basic competencies includes the use of standardized psychometric instruments that evaluate general psychological abilities plus specialized tests and measures that provide a more qualitative analysis of component skill deficits. The clinician, guided by a careful and comprehensive analysis of the manifest disability, will formulate hypotheses about underlying and associated skill deficits and will select assessment methods that reliably measure these deficits with greater precision. The assessment of basic skill competencies should address the child's strengths and weaknesses. It should also identify the pattern and relative discrepancy observed among skill areas that can act as a guide in suggesting areas for further evaluation.

GENERAL PSYCHOLOGICAL ABILITIES

Intellectual Abilities. Tests of intelligence have an important role in assessing children referred because of developmental, behavioral, or academic problems. They allow for a relatively unbiased estimate of the child's current level of functioning over a wide range of abilities. Among tests of children's intelligence, the most widely used are the Wechsler Intelligence Scale for Children—Revised (WISC-R); the McCarthy Scales of Children's Abilities (MSCA), and the Kaufman Assessment Battery for Children (K-ABC). Of greatest importance to the present discussion is that these intelligence tests yield data on most or all of the neuropsychological functions subserving the acquisition of more complex abilities. The WISC-R, for example, provides scores for verbal-linguistic skills, visuospatial-constructive skills, and sequential-analytical skills. The verbal and performance format is an important characteristic, making the scale of particular value in assessing children who may show specific strengths or weaknesses in various skill areas. It has been shown, for example, that children who show verbal performance discrepancies of greater than 15 points are likely to experience difficulty in the acquisition of fundamental achievement skills such as reading, spelling, and arithmetic. This is suggestive of a specific learning disorder. The MSCA includes 18 subtests that are grouped into six scales: verbal, perceptual-performance, quantitative, general cognitive, memory, and motor. This instrument is appropriate for children 2½ through 8½ years of age and may be particularly useful for assessing cognitive abilities in children suspected of developmental delays and or disabilities. The K-ABC, which is a relatively new test of intelligence (Kaufman and Kaufman 1983) is based on a model of cognitive processing that distinguishes sequential from simultaneous processing. Sequential processing involves the integration of stimuli into tempo rally organized series, whereas simultaneous processing pertains to a more holistic integration of stimuli. It has been demonstrated that sequential-simultaneous discrepancies are more accurate in identifying children with focal lesions (localized to a hemisphere or lobe) than are verbal performance discrepancies on the WISC-R (Shapiro and Dotan 1986).

Academic Achievement. A significant number of children with psychiatric disorders are likely to have specific learning disabilities. What this means is that despite adequate intelligence or opportunity, certain children may show significant deficits in reading, writing, spelling, or mathematical calculations. It is therefore necessary that the evaluation of the psychiatrically disturbed child include well-standardized measures of academic achievement skills. There are a number of standardized tests of academic achievement in current use. The Wide Range Achievement Tests—Revised (WRAT-R) can be used with children at any grade level and

provide scores in reading recognition, spelling, and arithmetic calculation. In addition to yielding standard scores and grade norms that can compare a child's current functioning relative to expectations, the format of the WRAT-R permits an analysis of the quality of errors made in spelling and calculation. Subtests of the Peabody Individual Achievement Tests–Revised (PIAT-R) may be used to supplement the WRAT-R. One unique advantage of the PIAT-R is the use of a multiple-choice response format that requires neither an oral explanation of the answer nor a written response, only an indication of the answer. A child who performs substantially poorer on the WRAT-R spelling subtest than on the PIAT-R spelling subtest may have difficulty in written expression. Both the WRAT-R and the PIAT-R can be administered in a short period of time, and both adequately survey the fundamental areas of academic achievement. As such they provide for a very good screening of the child's achievement skills. When significant problems, however, are revealed on individual subtests, more thorough evaluation is recommended.

Comprehensive achievement batteries are available that provide more detailed coverage of reading, spelling, and arithmetic skills that may be deficient in the low achiever. For example, the Woodcock Reading Mastery Test and the Stanford Diagnostic Reading Test include subtests designed to measure the major components of the reading process that can be used to facilitate the development of appropriate teaching strategies and materials. Some achievement tests provide more precise differentiation of achievement skill deficits. The Boder Diagnostic Reading-Spelling Test (Boder and Jerrico 1982), for example, evaluates the child's ability to perform reading and spelling of phonetic and nonphonetic words, both known (sight) and unknown. On the basis of reading–spelling patterns, each subject is then classified as a normal, nonspecific, or dyslexic (dysphonetic or dyseidetic) reader. Dysphonetic readers lack word analysis skills and are inclined to read entirely by recognition of visual gestalts. They often guess from minimal clues and read more efficiently from text. They can spell words stored in visual memory but are unable to use basic phonetic rules to spell unknown words. Conversely, dyseidetic readers have difficulty with visual decoding, often misperceiving and reversing visual symbols. They read by phonetic analysis, decoding new words and demonstrating good phonetic misspellings. They spell by sound and demonstrate a weakness in visual recall of whole nonphonetic words.

Language Abilities. Language is a general ability that has a profound effect on intellectual development, academic achievement, and emotional expression. Because language and speech play such a central role in the child's functional development, language and speech functions should be assessed as part of the comprehensive psychological evaluation even when specific language problems are not overt. Language problems present as a spectrum of disturbance ranging from the mute toddler to the preschooler with behavioral problems to the older child in a special class because of a learning disability. The functional assessment of language abilities involves a determination of (1) whether a language problem exists and (2) the relationship between language and the manifest disability if a language impairment is identified. The latter task, which is critical for a functional analysis, involves a determination of the extent to which a behavioral, emotional, or cognitive disorder is secondary or associated with a language disorder.

The assessment of the child's language functions requires an integration of quantitative and qualitative information. Quantitative data are derived from a child's performance on standardized tests of language competence. Qualitative information is obtained by recording a sample of the child's speech or by accessing information from different sources (e.g., parents, teachers). I have found the Comprehensive Evaluation of Language Functions Battery (CELF) (Semel and Wiig 1980) to be particularly useful in evaluating aspects of language disorder that underlie learning disabilities and learning delays. The CELF features 11 subtests that probe selected aspects of language functioning in the areas of word meanings (semantics), sentence structure (syntax), and recall and retrieval (memory) and two supplementary subtests designed to probe aspects of processing and production at the level of speech sounds.

Attentional Resources. Children with behavioral or emotional disturbance rarely display specific sensorimotor, perceptual, or memory deficits when these constructs are isolated for objective assessment. On the other hand, direct observation often reveals questions concerning the child's impulsivity, concentration skills, attention span, organization and planning strategies, and the ability to follow directions. It is difficult to determine whether such symptoms implicate defective attentional mechanisms that are enduring or whether these symptoms are transient reactions caused by frustration and stress. Formal assessment of the child's ability to attend to tasks and to allocate attentional resources effectively, therefore, should be included in the assessment of basic competencies. While there exists a plethora of experimental tasks to measure vigilance, selective attention, and impulsivity, such tasks often require sophisticated equipment and most lack appropriate norms to allow meaningful interpretation. One standardized instrument that I have found to be useful in the measurement of attention is the Detroit Tests of Learning Aptitude (DTLA-2) (Hammill 1985). Although this instrument purports to measure a number of specific intellectual abilities, six of the 11 subtests clearly place an emphasis on concentration and attentional capacity (i.e., Sentence Imitation, Oral Directions, Word Sequences, Object Sequences, Letter Sequences, and Design Reproduction). Low scores on these attention-enhanced subtests of the DTLA-2 are often found in association with behavioral symptoms of inattention, poor concentration, and distractibility.

COMPONENT SKILLS

The child's performance on tests of intelligence, academic achievement, language, and attention may be instructive as a point of departure for parsing the young child's functional deficits. *Parsing* means resolving something into its component parts and describing how these parts contribute, individually or collectively, to the child's manifest disability. Parsing the brain through analysis of a specific functional system (e.g., memory) involves selecting features according to how they sustain or disrupt the memory performance of children or adolescents. The contribution of neuropsychological assessment, from this perspective, should not be seen solely as a means to identify those patients with and without brain damage, but rather to fractionalize the child's general ability weaknesses into primary component skill deficits.

A review of Luria's concept of a functional system may be helpful for understanding the assessment of component skills. According to Luria (1980), every function involves an interactive system of many areas of the brain. The system constitutes the function, and the different areas make separate contributions to the overall system. When brain damage involves part of the system, the entire system is affected. Logically, this would imply that individual components of the system cannot be isolated. Rather, brain damage changes the entire system. Therefore, a test may only be useful in bringing out a particular way in which an entire system is qualitatively changed. Luria does admit, however, that damage in one area of the brain affects the system differentially from damage in another area, since different components are involved. The problem for psychometric theory is to determine how individual tests can be used to parse different components of the system. The solution is that a particular task required by a test places different stress on different components of the system. By changing the nature of the task, the stress on different components may be varied. Therefore, individual components can be isolated for assessment by placing stress on a particular component skill of the system and testing to determine that the other components of the system are functioning normally.

The traditional method for assessing component skills has been the use of the neuropsychological test battery. There are two different approaches as to how to use the test battery. One approach employs a rather rigid format where tests are decided a priori and many different components of brain function are evaluated. The rigid approach is illustrated by the Halstead-Reitan Neuropsychological Battery for Children (Reitan and Davidson 1974). The battery consists of nine standardized and quantitative subtests: Category, Rhythm, Speech Sounds Perception, Finger-Tapping, Tactual Performance, Trailing Making (A and B), Sensory-Perceptual Examination, and Aphasia Exam, plus the WISC-R and WRAT-R. The battery represents a relatively comprehensive evaluation of brain function and has proved successful in differentiating normal from brain-damaged and learning-disabled children (Selz

and Reitan 1979). While the Halstead-Reitan Battery is highly accurate in identifying brain-damaged patients, it lacks a unifying theory of brain function that permits an understanding of how performance deficits on individual tests are related to each other and to the child's manifest disability.

The Luria-Nebraska Neuropsychological Battery—Children's Revision (Golden 1987) is a rigid battery that is based on Luria's functional systems theory of brain organization. This battery claims to analyze the individual components of a functional system by varying specific aspects of tasks believed to be related to the system. It includes 149 items grouped into 11 scales. Test items were selected that identify and localize brain dysfunction, including motor functions, acoustic-motor organization, tactile functions, visual functions, receptive and expressive language, writing, reading, and arithmetic skills, memory functions, and intellectual processes. Three additional clinical summary scales have been developed that provide further information regarding the discrimination between brain-injured and normal children: (1) Pathognomonic, (2) Left Sensory Motor, and (3) Right Sensory Motor scales. The clinical interpretation of the Luria-Nebraska battery is based on both quantitative and qualitative scores, the pattern of individual items responses, configural analysis, comparison of obtained scores with the scale patterns for children with known localized brain dysfunction, and integration of test data with information from clinical observations.

An alternative or supplement to the fixed battery approach is provided by the flexible battery. The flexible battery maximizes information accrual for clinical diagnosis, because whatever tests need to be administered are administered. On a case-by-case basis, no boundaries on the assessment process are imposed. On the basis of the child's manifest disability and guided by weaknesses revealed by testing of general abilities, specific tests are selected that evaluate particular functional systems. In other words, rather than relying only on those tests that individually identify a general brain-damaged sample with a high level of accuracy, tests that discriminate component skill deficits are included. For example, if the clinician has been led by evaluation results to consider the possibility of a memory deficit, then the use of a memory battery is warranted. The selection of tests to be included in the memory battery should be guided by an existing theory of memory. An attempt should be made to obtain complete coverage of all the general types of memory that have been identified. For example, tests should be selected to assess both verbal and nonverbal memory systems. Within each system, recent (short-term) and remote (long-term) aspects of memory should be examined, with particular stress placed on component skills such as storage, retention, and retrieval. There are a number of tests that purport to measure memory; many lack a theoretical foundation, and most confound component memory skills. The selective reminding procedure developed by Buschke (1974) and Buschke and Fuld (1974) has become a popular assessment method of verbal memory in neuropsychological batteries. The selective reminding procedure is based on contemporary information-processing theory, and this allows for discriminations between different stages of memory, including storage, retention, and retrieval. The selective reminding procedure employs a multi-trial free recall verbal learning task. The difficulty of the procedure can be varied systematically by altering the number of test items (e.g., words), the difficulty of each item (as assessed by frequency of usage, imagery rating, content), list composition (unrelated vs. related items), and trials to criterion. Subjects are orally presented with a list on the first trial. The subject then attempts to recall, in any order, as many items as possible. On subsequent trials, only those items not recalled by the child on the preceding trials are repeated. By reminding the child of words not recalled, selective reminding indices permit an evaluation of when words are acquired and how well words are retrieved after recall.

Assessment of Moderator Variables

As noted earlier, the functional approach to assessment acknowledges the adverse effect that weaknesses in basic competencies have on the child's ability to adapt to the environment. Weaknesses in basic skill competencies invariably contribute to the child's manifest disability. Behavioral problems and associated skill deficits affect, and are affected by, the child's psychosocial experi-ences. A family environment, for example, where roles and responsibilities of individual members are well defined, where realistic limits and expectations are imposed, and where nurturance and support are readily available will have a mitigating effect on the expression of a particular disability. Conversely, a chaotic and disorganized home environment typically exacerbates the behavior or emotional problems. The psychologist employing the functional model is not simply interested in identifying primary skill deficits but is equally concerned with those environmental factors that modify the expression of the disability. The assessment of family functioning is one moderating variable that may yield important data pertinent to a functional understanding of the child's manifest disability. While information about family systems can be collected as part of the parent interview procedure, it may be more parsimonious to use an objective measurement instrument. One such instrument is the Family Assessment Measure (FAM) (Skinner et al. 1983). This is a self-report instrument that provides quantitative indices of family strengths and weaknesses. The basic tasks assessed by the FAM include task accomplishment, role performance, communication, affective expression, involvement, control, values, and norms. The FAM consists of three components: (1) a General Scale, which focuses on the family as a system; (2) a Dyadic Relationships Scale, which examines relationships between specific pairs; and (3) a Self-Rating Scale, which assesses the person's perception of his or her functioning in the family. The application of instruments such as the FAM provides an important contribution to the functional assessment by providing an objective and independent verification of family functioning, by identifying an external factor that may be contributing to the child's psychopathology, and by evaluating the therapeutic potential of the child's primary support system.

It is not possible in the space provided to cover all the possible moderator variables that interact with child psychopathology. Suffice it to say that psychological factors such as a child's attitude, motivation, and self-esteem will have important functional effects on the child's manifest disability, and these factors should be covered in the assessment process.

Assessment of Biological Factors

Few cases referred for child psychiatric assessment involve actual brain disease. Nevertheless, it is clinically apparent that there is a large group of children who show evidence, either from direct observation or from historical accounts, that is indicative of biological vulnerability of the CNS. Indicators of biological vulnerability include prenatal, perinatal and neonatal complications; minor physical anomalies; neurologic "soft" signs; early-onset seizures; closed-head injuries; and family histories of nervous, mental, or cognitive disorders. Any of these factors may be conceptualized as one part of a multifactorial etiology that predisposes the child toward a given disability and its behavioral and cognitive correlates. Because of this possibility, indices of possible biological vulnerability should be gathered as part of the comprehensive assessment process.

Pathognomonic signs of neurologic disease, such as seizure activity, hemiplegia, or abnormal reflexes, may be observed in children with developmental psychopathology such as infantile autism but are rare in a general child psychiatric population. Similarly, reports of acute regression of behavior or mentation, headaches, dizziness, or severe auditory or visual field deficits following a medical illness or head injury qualify as signs of probable CNS impairment and should be evaluated by a neurologist or neuropsychologist experienced with such CNS symptoms.

An index of biological liability more common among child psychiatric populations is the detection of neurologic "soft" signs, which includes delay in the acquisition of developmental milestones. The psychological examination should make provisions for assessment of possible neurologic soft signs.

ASSESSMENT OF NEUROLOGIC SOFT SIGNS

The term *neurologic soft sign* was conceived by Bender (1947) in her description of 100 schizophrenic children whom she tested on neurologic examination. It was later elevated to prominence in the description of children with the minimal brain dysfunction syndrome by Strauss and Lehtinen (1947). Although this term has been the source of considerable controversy over the years, it still has some clinical utility. Currently, it is popular to make a distinction between de-velopmental soft signs and soft signs of abnormality (Tupper 1986). Developmental soft signs are those that would be considered normal in a younger child and that, because they persist, are abnormal in the older child. This type of sign may also be expressed as the delayed acquisition of a developmental milestone such as speech. Soft signs of abnormality are those whose appearance at any age would be considered abnormal, although they may not appear particularly severe in expression. Examples included reflex asymmetries, nystagmus, and hyperkinesis, as well as specific neuropsychological deficits such as dysnomia or dysgraphesthesia. The measurement of either type of soft sign is replete with methodologic problems, including interrater reliability, construct validity, lack of normative data, as well as the confounding effects of low intelligence, cultural difference, and socioeconomic status. Many clinicians chose to develop their own items and examinations for soft sign screening. Nevertheless, there are standard examinations available such as the PANESS (Guy 1976) that are widely used in the assessment of neurologic soft signs. The PANESS consists of two parts: the first part includes 15 items that cover physical characteristics such as the child's height, pulse, and head circumference. The second part consists of 43 items, scored from 1 (performed correctly) to 4 (unsuccessful), that assess finger nose touching, identifying figures traced in the hand, finger tapping, motor persistence, and others.

DEVELOPMENTAL SCREENING

Screening for general developmental delays is particularly useful in the assessment of the young child with psychiatric disturbance. By identifying developmental delays and deviations, developmental screening tests alert clinicians to biological aspects underlying the behavioral disorder. More importantly, the results of developmental screening tests can be used to teach parents what to expect from their children and to guide appropriate educational placement and remedial programming. Developmental screening tests tend to be multidimensional instruments that assess many aspects of the child's development. These tests usually provide extensive normative information that permit interpretation relative to an expected age standard. I frequently use the Minnesota

Child Developmental Inventory (MCDI) (Ireton and Thwing 1974). The MCDI is designed for the identification of developmental deviations in children from 1 to 6 years of age. The inventory, which is completed by the mother on the basis of her personal observations of the child, provides a concise picture of the child's current development on a profile of eight developmental scales: General Development, Gross Motor, Fine Motor, Expressive Language, Comprehension-Conceptual, Situation Comprehension, Self-Help, and Personal-Social. A profile analysis of the MCDI allows the examiner to compare rates of development in selected areas and sequences of developmental strengths and weaknesses.

Case Illustration

A 10-year old boy was referred to the child psychiatry outpatient service because of scholastic difficulties involving both learning problems and behavioral disturbance. According to the referral information he exhibits fine and gross motor delays, low self-esteem, low frustration tolerance, inattention, distractibility, impulsivity, and poor socialization skills. He is presently receiving special education service in language arts and mathematics and attends an adaptive physical education class to promote development of his motor skills. Both school personnel and parents are concerned with his lack of progress in learning and feel that behavior and emotional problems are interfering with instructional efforts.

ASSESSMENT OF THE MANIFEST DISABILITY

The Conners Symptom Questionnaire was completed by both parents and teacher as a means of identifying primary problem behaviors. The parent form revealed significant factor scores for impulsivity-hyperactivity and learning problems, but not for conduct problems, psychosomatic problems, or anxiety. The teacher form identified only inattention-passivity as a significant problem area. These data help establish the saliency of inattention, impulsivity, and hyperactivity as primary behavior problems and raise the possibility that this youth may have a specific learning disability. The parent interview corroborated and further amplified problems

reported by the behavior rating scales. The mother described her son's difficulty attending to and completing daily class work and went on to attribute this to his distractibility and poor concentration. She stated that her son was not hyperactive but rather excessively energetic and restless. She also expressed concern with her son's difficulty making and sustaining friendships and his low self-esteem. A review of developmental history uncovered several events of possible etiologic significance. It was reported that the boy was delivered full term, but with the umbilical cord wrapped around his neck. Apparently, the attending physician had a very difficult time inducing the boy to breathe. Within a few hours following birth, the boy had a seizure. He remained in the hospital for 16 days for observation and evaluation and was placed on an anticonvulsant medication for 1 year. Since that time three additional seizures were observed; in all cases they followed an illness with high fever. The boy was also very slow to reach most developmental milestones, including walking and speaking, and by age 2 he was identified by a developmental screening process in his community to be in need of special services.

At this point in the assessment process identification of the child's manifest disability was established. Symptoms of attentional deficit were brought to light, but the clinical picture was complicated by motor delays, learning problems, and socialization difficulties. The possibility of a pervasive developmental disorder could not be ruled out, although there was no evidence to indicate intellectual retardation or adaptive behavior deficits. In accordance with the functional assessment model, the next step was to evaluate the boy's basic skill competencies.

BASIC COMPETENCIES

The results from the assessment of general psychological abilities of this boy are shown in Table 27–1. On the WISC-R the boy obtained a verbal IQ of 88 and a performance IQ of 98. Although the discrepancy (10 points) is not large enough to indicate clinical significance, it does raise the possibility that this youngster is experiencing difficulty with the processing of verbal-linguistic information. There was significant intersubtest variability noted, particularly on the performance

Table 27–1. ASSESSMENT OF GENERAL PSYCHOLOGICAL ABILITIES OF A 10-YEAR-OLD BOY

Weschler Intelligence Scale for Children—Revised (WISC-R)	*Verbal Scale*		*Performance Scale*	
	SUBTESTS	SCALE SCORES	SUBTESTS	SCALE SCORES
	Information	6	Picture Completion	11
	Similarities	9	Picture Arrangement	14
	Arithmetic	6	Block Design	9
	Vocabulary	9	Object Assembly	8
	Comprehension	11	Coding	7
	(Digit Span)	6		

Verbal IQ = 88   Performance IQ = 98   Full Scale IQ = 92

Wide-Range Achievement Test—Revised (WRAT-R)			
	SUBTESTS	STANDARD SCORES	PERCENTILE RANK
	Reading	65	1
	Spelling	71	3
	Arithmetic	91	27

Gray Oral Reading Test—Revised (GORT-R)			
		STANDARD SCORES	PERCENTILE RANK
	Comprehension	6	9
	Passage Score	4	2

Overall Reading Quotient = 70

Detroit Tests of Learning Aptitude (DTLA-2)			
	SUBTESTS	STANDARD SCORES	PERCENTILE RANK
	Word Opposites	7	16
	Symbolic Relations	6	9
	Conceptual Matching	9	37
	Word Fragments	7	16
	Sentence Imitation	8	25
	Oral Directions	9	37
	Word Sequences	7	16
	Design Reproduction	6	9
	Object Sequences	5	5
	Letter Sequences	2	1

scale. A superior score on the picture arrangement subtest suggests excellent planning ability and understanding of the sequences and patterns of social situations. It should also be noted that the child's highest score on the verbal scale was on the comprehension subtest, a measure of social judgment. These scores are puzzling in light of the reported socialization difficulties but reduce the likelihood that this boy has a deficit in social cognition. A comparison of individual performance subtests indicated good visual organization on motor-reduced tasks but rather poor abilities on visual tasks that required motor coordination, speed, and spatial relations. Scores on the ACID subtests (arithmetic, coding, information, and digit span) were noticeably inferior to other scores. This profile is often observed in children with attention and learning problems.

A survey of academic achievement skills was conducted with the WRAT-R. Results revealed significant underachievement in reading and spelling while calculation ability (arithmetic) was in the low average range. The boy's reading impairment was further evidenced by a reading quotient of 70 on the Gray Oral Reading Test. The Boder Reading–Spelling Test was administered to further clarify the type of reading disability. The pattern observed was indicative of a dysphonetic reader, with the implication that language functions may also be deficient. Evaluation of language ability was assessed with the Peabody Picture Ability Test (PPVT) and the Clinical Evaluation of Language Functions (CELF) test. A PPVT IQ of 98 indicated average receptive language ability, but results of the CELF indicated linguistic weaknesses in the productive or expressive skills as well as auditory short-term memory.

The DTLA-2 was administered to evaluate

the child's performance on tests that stress attention and concentration abilities. The child's overall performance on the battery was poor (including measures of abstract-conceptual reasoning), and he displayed particular weakness on those subtests most sensitive to attention and concentration impairment. Thus, he obtained standard scores of 7, 6, 5, and 2 on the word sequences, design reproduction, object sequences, and letter sequences, respectively. Thus, irrespective of modality of presentation (oral vs. visual) or nature of stimuli (words, designs, pictured objects, random letters), impaired performance was observed. It is important to note that each of these subtests assess rather complex functions that tap both attention and memory resources, and it is not possible to specify whether one or both components are impaired.

The Luria-Nebraska Children's Battery was administered to separate the general ability weaknesses into more specific component skill deficits. As noted in Table 27–2, motor functions (motor speed, coordination and construction skills) and tactile functions (movement detection, shape discrimination, finger localization and stereognostic skills) were within the normal range. Neither the Left Sensory Motor nor the Right Sensory Motor Clinical Scales showed elevated scores. Acoustic-motor organization (e.g., perception of tones, discrimination of audi-tory stimuli) and visual functions were marginally elevated but did not reach the critical level. These results indicated that lower-level sensorimotor functions involving both the right and left hemispheres were relatively intact. In contrast, critical elevations were found on scales measuring higher level left-hemisphere functions, including expressive speech, writing, reading, and arithmetic. The child's most significant impairment was found on the memory scale, which evaluates verbal and nonverbal memory with and without interference. The pattern of relative strengths and weaknesses on this boy's profile suggests neurologic dysfunction involving secondary and/or tertiary areas of Luria's sensory input functional unit. The secondary areas of this unit process information sequentially. This allows the brain to be aware of stimulus changes and to link events temporally. This is quite important in the case of speech, in which phonemes may be sequentially linked to form words and sentences. Tertiary areas are responsible for cross-modality integration. Auditory-visual integration is necessary for reading, while auditory-tactile integration is necessary for writing. Arithmetic, as well as body location in space and visuospatial skills, depends on visuotactile integration. Injuries or maturational delays in the tertiary areas, depending on location and severity, can lead to loss of, or impairment of, learning skills, usually through the loss of the ability to integrate effectively across two or three sensory modalities. This can lead to specific developmental learning disorders such as dyslexia, dsgraphia, dysnomia, or dyspraxia.

A memory deficiency was consistently observed across the various testing procedures. As is the case of so many areas of assessment, a child's difficulty on a memory task may be difficult to ascribe to a memory impairment per se. Tests of memory are frequently confounded with motor, visuoconstructional skill as well as attentional abilities and learning skill deficits. A more comprehensive evaluation of memory functions was conducted with the selective reminding procedure in order to isolate individual memory components. This measure includes the provision of separate measures of storage, retention, retrieval, and consistency of retrieval that may be helpful in specifying the source of the performance deficit. The boy was asked to learn a list of 12 words by verbal recall in

Table 27–2. ASSESSMENT OF NEUROPSYCHOLOGICAL FUNCTIONS OF A 10-YEAR-OLD BOY WITH THE LURIA-NEBRASKA NEUROPSYCHOLOGICAL BATTERY— CHILDREN'S REVISION

Subtests	T-Score	Significance
Motor Functions	53	No
Rhythm	60	No
Tactile Functions	50	No
Visual Functions	62	No
Receptive Speech	62	No
Expressive Speech	65	Yes
Writing Scale	83	Yes
Reading Scale	70	Yes
Arithmetic	68	Yes
Memory Scale	70	Yes
Intellectual Processes Scale	53	No
Summary Scales:		
Pathognomonic	75	Yes
Left Sensory Motor	53	No
Right Sensory Motor	53	No

any order. The words were high-frequency nouns that did not exceed five letters in length. In accordance with the selective reminding format, the entire list was read aloud (reading was not required by the boy) at a 2-second rate before his first recall attempt. Thereafter, he was selectively reminded only of those items that he had not recalled on the immediately preceding trial. Comparison of this boy's learning with that of a normal child of the same age indicated that verbal memory was impaired. He continued to need reminders for many trials and never was able to consistently recall the entire list without further presentation. Of the 12 words, only 5 ever reached long-term storage, and this was not accomplished until the 12th trial. Even when words were entered into storage, they could not be consistently retrieved without further reminders. Analysis of this boy's learning performance seemed to indicate that he had definite impairment in encoding operations necessary for initial storage into long-term memory and also retrieval difficulty likely resulting from attention and distractibility problems.

MODERATOR VARIABLES

The Family Assessment Measure (FAM) was administered to the boy, his older brother, and both parents and revealed congruence and discrepancies among family members in their perception of family strengths and weaknesses. The results may be summarized as follows. In general, all four family members rated certain aspects of family functioning as problematic. The mother and her older son reported problems with task accomplishment, role performance, affective expression, and affective involvement. The father highlighted communication and affective expression as major problem areas in the family. The youngest son (patient) acknowledged only affective expression as a problem area. All family members agreed that there is inadequate affective communication expressed in the home. This suggested that family members may not openly or honestly express their emotions or feelings about ongoing events. The FAM General Scale also indicated that the father was quite defensive in his endorsement of areas of family dysfunction, while the mother and the older son readily admitted to family problems. The results from the FAM suggest that

there was concern among several family members concerning role assignment and decision-making strategies. The major issue, however, appears to be how to increase understanding of each other's feelings and how to feel comfortable expressing emotions.

The Children's Depression Rating Scale (CDRS) was administered to the boy in light of the parents' concern with his very low self-esteem. He obtained a score slightly below the usual cutoff score for clinical depression but nevertheless indicative of a high level of depressive symptomatology. His responses to the CDRS indicated no vegetative symptoms of depression, but he did endorse symptoms pertaining to low self-esteem, daily crying spells, and general dysphoria.

BIOLOGICAL INDICES

No pathognomonic signs of demonstrable neurologic disorder were observed or reported from history. The youth did experience three seizures early in life, and several developmental soft signs (e.g., motor and speech delays) were documented. Because of the seizure episodes a comprehensive pediatric neurologic examination was requested. Little new information was provided by this examination, although it was noted that the boy showed signs of proximal motor weakness. A review of family history was negative for major psychiatric disorders. The boy's biological father indicated that he might be learning disabled but offered no documentation to support his suspicion.

SUMMARY AND INTEGRATION OF ASSESSMENT RESULTS

This 10-year old boy satisfied the *DSM-III-R* criteria for an Axis I diagnosis of attention-deficit hyperactivity disorder. This diagnostic label alone fails to convey critical information about other behavioral and cognitive correlates of the disorder, as well as etiologic and psychosocial factors that may be contributing to the presenting symptomatology. A functional neuropsychological assessment revealed a more complicated clinical picture and uncovered weaknesses in general psychological abilities and deficits in component skills that are of considerable importance for understanding the nature of this child's disability and for planning appropriate intervention strategies. Intelligence and academic achievement testing indicated the presence of an Axis II developmental reading disorder. Analysis of the reading disability revealed a rather severe problem in phoneme analysis and phoneme-to-grapheme translation. This means that the boy relies primarily on whole-word (sight) recognition when decoding words. Whole-word recognition requires that words be stored in a letter-by-letter sequence in some internal lexicon. This visual-based strategy may be successful in the reading and spelling of common or overlearned words that are stored in his internal lexicon. However, when new or rare words are encountered the visuolexical route will prove insufficient and he will have to rely on phonemic analysis. For certain reading-disabled children, such as this child, it appears that when there is a failure of the lexical route, the phonologic route cannot be used successfully as a back-up strategy. The expression of this type of deficiency is likely to include impairment in other language-based processing skills. On tests of language competence, the boy showed relative strength on measures of receptive language but was deficient on tasks involving productive or expressive language. While the diagnosis of a specific reading disability is appropriate for this child, it is obvious that this is a complex type of learning deficiency. It was evident from the assessment of general abilities that this boy had serious difficulty on tasks of auditory and visual sequential memory and attention. Assessment of individual components of his memory system revealed deficits in both the encoding (storage) and retrieval of verbal information. This cognitive deficit is likely to further complicate the expression of his reading disability. As stated previously, this boy relies on whole-word recognition in reading and spelling. Reading via the whole-word recognition route requires an intact lexical memory system, a system that appears to be seriously impaired in this child. As a consequence, it is unlikely that he will be adequately compensated for his severe phonetic processing deficits.

This boy's clinical condition is further complicated by his low self-esteem and poor social relationships. Such problems are commonly observed in children with serious learning deficits and appear to be maladaptive reactions to perceived inadequacy and failure. His family does not appear to be a source of immediate support for him, and this may be contributing to his general dysphoria.

Finally, there is indication that this child's primary psychopathology has biological origins. Although maturational factors and intensive remediation and treatment may result in noticeable improvement of his condition, residual deficits will likely remain. The results of this functional neuropsychological assessment suggest that a multimodality treatment program would have to be implemented. Different aspects of this boy's condition will require qualitatively distinct treatment approaches. Medication therapy may be beneficial for treating the inattention, distractibility, and impulse control problems and in doing so may increase this child's receptiveness to instruction. On the other hand, medication will not act to remediate basic cognitive deficiencies. An intensive educational program that includes both compensatory and remedial approaches will be most beneficial. Finally, this boy's emotional and social well-being are targets for immediate therapeutic intervention. Social skills training using a small group format can focus on the improvement of peer interactions and self-esteem, while family therapy may be helpful for promoting effective communication and affective expression among family members.

References

Achenbach, T.M. 1978. The child behavior profile: I. Boys aged 6–11. *J. Consult. Clin. Psychol.* 46:478–488.

Achenbach, T.M., and Edelbrock, C.S. 1979. The child behavioral profile: II. Boys aged 12–16 and girls aged 6–11 and 12–16. *J. Consult. Clin. Psychol.* 47:223–233.

Alajouanine, T., and Lhermitte, F. 1965. Acquired aphasis in children. *Brain* 88:853–862.

Bender, L. 1947. Childhood schizophrenia: Clinical study of one hundred schizophrenic children. *Am. J. Orthopsychiatry* 17:40–56.

Boder, E., and Jerrico, S. 1982. *The Boder Test of Reading-Spelling Patterns.* New York: Grune & Stratton.

Buschke, H. 1974. Components of verbal learning in children: Analysis by selective reminding. *J. Exp. Child Psychol.* 18:488–496.

Buschke, H., and Fuld, A.P. 1974. Evaluating storage, retention, and retrieval in disordered memory and learning. *Neurology* 24:1019–1025.

Conners, C.K. 1973. Rating scales for use in drug studies with children. *Psychopharmacol. Bull.* Special issue: 24–84.

Costello, A.J., Edelbrock, C., Kalas, R., et al. 1982. *The NIMH Diagnostic Interview Schedule for Children (DISC).* Pittsburgh: Authors.

Fletcher, J.M., and Taylor, H.G. 1983. Neuropsychological approaches to children: Towards a developmental neuropsychology. *J. Clin. Neuropsychol.* 6:39–56.

Golden, C.J. 1987. *Manual for the Luria-Nebraska Neuropsychological Battery: Children's Revision.* Los Angeles: Western Psychological Services.

Guy, W. 1976. Physical and Neurological Examination for Soft Signs (PANESS), In Guy, W. (ed.): *ECDEU Assessment Manual for Psychopharmacology.* Rockville, Md.: National Institute of Mental Health.

Hammill, D.D. 1985. *Detroit Tests of Learning Aptitude.* Austin, Tex.: Pro-Ed.

Herjanic, B., and Reich, W. 1982. Development of a structured psychiatric interview for children: Agreement between child and parent on individual symptoms. *J. Abnorm. Child Psychol.* 10:307–324.

Ireton, H., and Thwing, E. 1974. *Minnesota Child Development Inventory.* Minneapolis, Minn.: Behavioral Science Systems.

Kaufman, A.S., and Kaufman, H. 1983. *The Kaufman Assessment Battery for Children.* Circle Pines, Minn.: American Guidance Service.

Luria, A.R. 1980. *Higher Cortical Functions in Man.* New York: Basic Books.

Puig-Antich, J., and Chambers, W. 1978. *The Schedule for Affective Disorders and Schizophrenia for School-aged Children.* New York: New York State Psychiatric Institute.

Reitan, R.M., and Davidson, L.A. (eds.). 1974. *Clinical Neuropsychology: Current Status and Applications.* Washington, D.C.: VH Winston & Sons.

Selz, M., and Reitan, R.M. 1979. Rules for neuropsychological diagnosis: Classification of brain function in older children. *J. Consult. Clin. Psychol.* 47:258–264.

Semel, E.M., and Wiig, E.H. 1980. *CELF: Clinical Evaluation of Language Functions: Diagnostic Battery Examiner's Manual.* Columbus, Ohio: Merrill.

Shapiro, E.G., and Dotan, N. 1986. Neurological findings for the Kaufman Assessment Battery for Children. *Dev. Neuropsychol.* 2:51–64.

Skinner, H.A., Steinhauer, P.D., and Santa-Barbara, J. 1983. The Family Assessment Measure. *Can. J. Comm. Ment. Health* 2:91–105.

Sparrow, S.S., Balla, D.A., and Ciccetti, D.V. 1984. *Vineland Adaptive Behavior Scales.* Circle Pines, Minn.: American Guidance Service.

Strauss, A.A., and Lehtinen, L.E. 1947. *Psychopathology and Education of the Brain-Injured Child.* New York: Grune & Stratton.

Taylor, H.G., Fletcher, J.M., and Satz, P. 1984. Neuropsychological assessment of children. In Goldstein, G. and Hersen, M. (eds.): *Handbook of Psychological Assessment.* New York: Pergamon Press.

Tupper, D.E. 1986. Neuropsychological Screening and Soft Signs. In Obrzut, J.E., and Hynd, G.W. (eds.): *Child Neuropsychology,* vol. 2. Orlando, Fla.: Academic Press.

Principles of Psychiatric Care of Children and Adolescents With Medical Illnesses

28

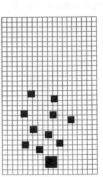

ABBY L. WASSERMAN, M.D.

Most children become ill at some point in their lives with inevitable consequences for both themselves and their families. In this chapter the psychological responses to illness manifested by children and their families are examined. Although acute illness is discussed briefly, the major emphasis is on chronic illness. The developmental level of the child has a major affect on the psychological response to illness and is explored in detail; problem areas of treatment are discussed, and recommendations for successful management are given. Health care professionals taking care of children and adolescents need to know how to manage the psychological ramifications of illness when caring for the total person.

How children react to an illness is a reflection of their age; stage of development; discomfort from the illness; the type of treatment and its side effects; the limitations placed on them; their understanding of the illness; the reactions of other persons (especially family members); and their emotional makeup and personality. The parents, on the other hand, are responsive not only to the illness, its treatment, and the reaction of their child but also to their own feelings and personal problems, which might predate the diagnosis. The reactions of children and the parents, both positive and negative, are interdependent. During the course of an illness there are predictable periods of increased stress for these children and their families (Table 28–1); it is at these times that families

require extra support from the medical establishment.

The diagnosis of a serious illness, whether it be life threatening or one that is chronic, is extremely difficult for parents, older children, and adolescents. They typically experience certain stages of emotional release until they are able to accept the diagnosis (Table 28–2). During the course of the illness, as complications are diagnosed or as the growing child recognizes certain limitations, these stages may be repeated. It is hoped that the parents and the adolescents reach the stage of acceptance of the disease; however, if either or both get overwhelmed at any particular stage and cannot progress, psychiatric intervention is indicated to help them come to accept the disease.

ACUTE ILLNESS

Acute illnesses can be minor, such as common upper respiratory tract infections and gastrointestinal upsets, or major, such as meningitis and severe pneumonia. One of the aspects that differentiates acute illness from chronic illness is the self-limiting nature with minimal residua.

Yet even acute illnesses have an impact on the life of the child and the family. The child is usually irritable and/or drowsy and perhaps has painful episodes. Treatment may not be pleasant. The child is kept out of school, which means no social contacts and

---

Table 28–1. TIME PERIODS OF INCREASED STRESS FOR CHILDREN/ADOLESCENTS WITH CHRONIC AND ACUTE ILLNESSES AND THEIR FAMILIES

1. Onset and diagnosis
2. Hospitalization
3. Appearance of major complications
4. Changing from an acute to a chronic condition
5. Failure of a given therapy
6. Exacerbation or recurrences of the disease
7. Major therapeutic choices especially if a research protocol
8. Terminal care

---

school work to be made up. The parents may have to miss work or other activities to stay home and care for the child. In some cases, the child might even have to be hospitalized.

Usually the acute illness passes and the family returns to its normal routine. However, sometimes school refusal starts after an illness. The child is so anxious about missed school work and tests that he or she starts having psychosomatic complaints on school days. Sometimes, the child liked being at home alone with the mother (and the mother liked devoting herself to the child) so that after the child has recovered, other physical complaints become manifest requiring the child to stay home from school.

Acute illnesses can be life threatening. Sometimes after the child has recovered from a life-threatening illness or even an illness that the parents perceived as life threatening, the parents see the child as "vulnerable" (Green and Solnit 1964). These parents treat their children as "special"; they may fear developmental delay or future fatal disease without any medical basis. These children then grow up seeing themselves as sickly, and hypochondriasis may be the end result. If these parents cannot be helped to understand that they have a normal child and should treat him or her as such, psychiatric referral should be made.

Table 28–2. STAGES PARENTS AND ADOLESCENTS GO THROUGH AFTER THE DIAGNOSIS OF A SERIOUS ILLNESS

1. Shock and disbelief (denial)
2. Anger and resentment
3. Blame
4. Sadness (may develop into depression)
5. Acceptance

CHRONIC ILLNESS

Chronic illness is a disorder with a protracted course. The illness may be progressive and eventually fatal or may result in impaired physical or mental functioning with a normal life span. Usually, chronic illnesses require extended or sequential services.

As can be seen in Table 28–3, chronic diseases and conditions affect approximately 13% of the children in the United States. Although the majority of disabilities are considered minor (e.g., mild asthma, hearing and visual impairment), all of these problems do affect the child burdened with the disability.

Psychological maladjustment does not al-

Table 28–3. ESTIMATED PREVALENCE OF CHRONIC DISEASES AND CONDITIONS IN CHILDREN: AGES BIRTH TO 20 IN THE UNITED STATES—1980

Disorder	Prevalence Estimates Per 1,000	Range of Prevalence Estimates per 1,000
Arthritis	2.2	1.0–3.0
Asthma	38.0	20.0–53.0
Moderate to severe	10.0	8.0–15.0
Autism	0.44	0.40–0.48
Central nervous system injury		
Traumatic brain injury	0.05	
Paralysis	2.1	2.0–2.3
Cerebral palsy	2.5	1.4–5.1
Chronic renal failure	0.080	
Terminal	0.010	
Nonterminal	0.070	
Cleft lip/palate*	1.5	1.3–2.0
Congenital heart disease	7.0	2.0–7.0
Severe congenital heart disease*	0.50	
Cystic fibrosis*	0.20	
Diabetes mellitus	1.8	1.2–2.0
Down's syndrome*	1.1	
Hearing impairment	16.0	
Deafness	0.1	0.06–0.15
Hemophilia*	0.15	
Leukemia		
Acute lymphocytic leukemia†	0.11	
Mental retardation	25.0	20.0–30.0
Muscular dystrophy*	0.06	
Neural tube defect*	0.45	
Spina bifida*	0.40	
Encephalocele*	0.05	
Phenylketonuria*	0.10	
Sickle cell disease*	0.46	
Sickle cell anemia*	0.28	
Seizure disorder	3.5	2.6–4.6
Visual impairment	30.0	20.0–35.0
Impaired visual acuity	20.0	
Blind	0.6	0.5–1.0

*Estimated using prevalence at birth and survival data.
†Estimated using incidence and duration data.
(From Gortmaker, S. L., and Sappenfield, W. 1984. Chronic childhood disorders: Prevalence and impact. *Pediatr. Clin. North Am.* 31:3–18.)

ways accompany chronic illness. Although the proportion of children negatively affected emotionally and socially is two and one-half times greater than that expected among healthy children, fewer than a third of those with chronic illnesses are affected. The specific nature of the disability does not appear to be an important determinant of the psychological and social consequences, except that children with central nervous system involvement are more likely to have emotional disturbances. Moreover, age at onset of the chronic condition as a predictive measure of emotional disturbance has not been born out in recent research (Nolan and Pless 1986). However, if the disease begins at a time of a developmental milestone (e.g., learning to walk, school entry, time for independence), there is a greater risk of psychological problems. A large number of variables relating to the child, the illness, the family, the social environment, and the medical situation may strengthen or weaken the association between illness and adjustment (Nolan and Pless 1986).

The disability and limitations caused by the illness are two of the greatest factors influencing emotional maladjustment. There is a greater frequency of psychosocial problems among children with sensory disorders and central nervous system involvement (including mental retardation) compared with children with other chronic diseases (including those causing physical deformity). Those with mild disabilities may suffer as much or even more so than those whose condition is more severe (Pless 1984). Those with mild diseases or those with no outward manifestations may be at risk for emotional problems because the very nature of the condition allows denial of the illness to grow until there is an exacerbation, at which time their method of coping can no longer sustain them and they are thrown into emotional turmoil. In addition, when denial is present, either in the child and/or in the parents, there is less compliance with medical regimens, thus worsening the physical disease.

Teddy was diagnosed with cystic fibrosis because of a chronic cough at four years of age. He was chunky, active, and looked completely healthy. During his second hospitalization for pneumonia in a four-month period, a psychiatric referral was requested because he refused to take his medicines or to allow his respiratory therapy treatments. During the evaluation, it became obvious that the parents were still denying his diagnosis since he looked so normal. After his parents were able to work through their feelings and accept that he had cystic fibrosis, Teddy started complying with the medical treatment. By the time of the first follow-up visit after discharge, Teddy was reminding his parents if they forgot any of his medications.

Episodic disease states appear to be more stressful than persistent conditions even if the persistent condition is more severe (Pless 1984). For the child and the family the constant tension of not knowing what will happen from one day to the next is stressful. Having to cancel previously made plans because of a flare up of the illness causes anger in every member of the family, including the ill child.

The personality of the child plays a role in emotional problems. A carefree child who does not let things get him down will be less likely to have psychological disturbances than the very introverted, self-absorbed, narcissistic youngster. Any attributes and skills that may be regarded as "assets" diminish the likelihood of psychosocial problems, whereas clear-cut liabilities such as unattractiveness tend to increase the probability of problems (Pless 1984).

The most critical factor in the risk of developing psychosocial maladjustment in the chronically ill is probably the way the family functions and is able to adapt to the child's illness (Pless 1984).

Jay was 16 years old when his right arm was amputated for osteogenic sarcoma. Eric was 15½ when his left arm was amputated for the same cancer. Both adolescents knew each other since their amputations were a week apart and they were hospitalized for their treatments on the same schedule. However, their acceptance of the disease, their disabilities, and their support from their families were completely opposite. Jay's parents were professionals and supported all their children's endeavors. Jay was close to his older brother, who was away at college but who kept in touch, visiting him whenever possible. He was able to work through his anger and accept his disability. He quickly learned to write with his left hand, to drive a car with one arm, and to participate in all his former activities, including trick-skateboarding. The family made plans to start visiting colleges during their coming summer vacation. Eric, on the other hand, came from a family of discord in which the father favored the brother, the mother favored Eric, and the older sister had run away from home to get married. Eric's parents separated when he was in the hospital during one of his treatments. Eric went into periodic depressions necessitating medication and would refuse to take responsibility for simple chores. His school work deteriorated even further, and he contemplated dropping out of school. He refused to recognize how his anger (at his disease as well as at his family circumstances) was affecting him.

How well the family accepts the illness and reacts to the child is very important in the way the child sees himself or herself and how the child develops his or her self-concept. Most of the time the illness in the child will magnify preexisting strengths and weaknesses in the family. In addition, other persons take their cues on how to treat the child from the family. Relatives, schoolteachers, peers, and others are more likely to treat the child normally if the family handles the ill child as normally as possible.

Practically all children with chronic disabilities will occasionally try to take advantage of their disease in order to avoid an unpleasant situation. However, prolonged poor psychosocial adaptation is different. According to Mattsson (1972), children and adolescents with prolonged poor adjustment to their chronic disorder tend to show one of the following three behavior patterns. The first is characterized by the patients' fearfulness, inactivity, lack of outside interests, and a marked dependency on their parents, frequently their mothers. These children present the psychiatric picture of early passive dependent states, and their parents are usually constantly worried and overprotective of them.

The second group contains the overly independent, often daring young patients who may engage in prohibited, risk-taking activities. Such youngsters make a strong use of denial of realistic dangers and fears. At times their reality sense is impaired and they seem to seek out certain feared situations, challenging the risk of trauma. Since early childhood, many of these rebellious patients have been raised by oversolicitous, guilt-ridden mothers. Usually at puberty they rebel against the maternal interference and turn into overly active, defiant adolescents.

A third, less common pattern of maladjustment is seen in older children and adolescents with congenital deformities and handicaps. They appear as shy, lonely persons harboring resentful, hostile attitudes toward normal persons, whom they see as owing them compensation for their life-long sufferings. Usually these patients were raised by parents who emphasized their defectiveness and tended to isolate or "hide" them in an embarrassed fashion. They have come to identify with their parents' view of them and developed a self-image of a defective outsider.

Other parents and children show their strengths and well-developed sense of self-esteem through the way they cope with the illnesses and disabilities. These parents join together for mutual support. They consider the ill child's feelings, but do not let the child take advantage of the situation.

> Denise was 13 years old when she became progressively unable to do her cheerleading stunts and dermatomyositis was diagnosed. Six months later her intestines ruptured, which is usually a fatal complication of the disease; this complication necessitated more than 15 surgical procedures. Denise was maintained on parenteral hyperalimentation. During her 9 months in the intensive care unit she was frequently in pain. Since movement brought on bouts of pain, she refused to be moved in any way. Her mother, who stayed with her the entire time, except for some short periods when the maternal grandmother stayed, insisted that Denise do what was prescribed for her. Her mother became an integral part of the medical team and did a lot of her care. Her stepfather visited each weekend, and her younger sister came once a month. She had episodes of depression that were seen as medical emergencies, since everyone felt it was her determination to live that kept her alive. Ten months after the first surgery she was discharged on hyperalimentation, with an ostomy bag, and in a wheelchair. She insisted on going back to school as soon as she was able. A year after her discharge, after her last operation to reanastomose her intestinal tract, she asked if she would always have the indentations, skin puckerings, and large scars over her abdomen. She was told that they would become a little less conspicuous but would always be there; however, plastic surgery might be able to smooth out her skin. Her response was, "Oh no, no more surgery! If someone doesn't like me because of my scars, they are not worth liking anyway."

One way the parents and physicians can help the chronically ill child reduce the risk of maladaptation is to talk to the child about the disease, their own feelings, and the child's feelings. Knowledge helps reduce the uncertainty and allows the child to feel some control over the situation; it provides the basis for making decisions and for coming to terms with the illness. Without accurate information, children are left at the mercy of their imagination and fantasies; the resultant misconstrued ideas are often far more disturbing and damaging than the truth itself (Weitzman 1984). Also, chronically ill children need guidance in how to talk about their disease (Weitzman 1984). Talking about the physical problems serves as an opportunity to discuss the range of likely reactions of peers and others so that neither the child nor the parents are caught totally unprepared by embarrassing or hostile remarks or questions. This exchange also tends to build rapport between the child and parents and opens up the lines of communication not only about the illness itself but about issues in general.

Age, Developmental Stage

INFANTS

Infants directly reflect the feelings of the caregivers. A tense, anxious mother who has trouble holding and cuddling her infant will have a more irritable child than the mother who can sooth her upset child. Infants do not have an awareness of self and therefore do not realize that they may have an illness or disability. They may be irritable or cry out because of discomfort generated by the illness itself (e.g., milk intolerance), or they may derive no satisfaction from sucking, which is a normal way infants use to calm themselves down and to learn about the environment, since there is no knowledge of the relationship of the infirmity and displeasure.

The birth of a defective child confirms the worst fears of the pregnant woman. The parents have to work through their feelings, including mourning the loss of the normal child they had hoped for but did not have. Guilt, resentfulness, and anger are felt; the more visible the defect the more revulsion the parents may feel. The parents, especially the mother, may feel defective, with a drop in their self-esteem. Guilt and blame are especially felt if the illness is found to be genetic or because of indiscretions (e.g., use

of drugs, alcohol) during pregnancy. An infant who is physically deformed or socially unresponsive because of a sensory or neurologic deficit provides less social feedback (smiling, loving) to parents and thus may decrease the parents' nurturing and even attachment to the infant (Perrin and Gerrity 1984).

In some families, these negative feelings are never worked through, resulting in poor parent-child relations (either rejection or overprotection). The child, in turn, has a hard time accepting himself or herself. Low self-esteem then follows, making it difficult for the child at each subsequent stage of development. Adjustment reactions, depression, anxiety, and other psychiatric illness often follow.

However, in most cases, the parents gradually accept their child and set realistic goals and expectations. The child can then grow and develop as normally as possible, in spite of the limitations caused by the illness; development includes feelings of accomplishment and positive self-worth as the child succeeds in meeting these realistic expectations. The strengths and coping abilities of these children outweigh their disease-induced weaknesses.

TODDLERS

Children between the ages of 18 months and 3 years are exploring, manipulating, and trying to do everything by themselves. This period is called the "terrible two's" because the children are into everything, must be constantly watched, and are constantly saying "no." This is a time for parents to start setting limits on the child.

Chronic illness may put restrictions on the normal development of autonomy during toddlerhood. The needed adherence to schedules for medication, physical therapy, and special diets interferes with the child's desire for control, which in turn causes problems in the development of a sense of self. They may become apathetic, passive, and clinging. The parents, in turn, may be reluctant to set appropriate limits on ill children's behavior, which interferes with the normal development of impulse control (Perrin and Gerrity 1984).

Toddlers are egocentric and feel that illness and hospitalization are things that they caused to happen. Toddlers see their illness only in concrete terms as it actually affects their day-to-day life—something that hurts or interferes with their exploring. This age child tends to suffer the most from hospitalizations, especially if he or she has to be separated from the mother. The recent policy of allowing a parent to stay with a hospitalized child has helped eliminate many of the repercussions of forced separations.

Although having parents stay with a hospitalized child is encouraged, it must be kept in mind that this policy puts other stresses on the family. Caretakers for the other children must be found; expenses mount as the mother or father may be missing work; the cost of eating hospital food is high; and the absent parent is missed at home by the rest of the family. Yet, even with these disadvantages, most parents welcome the opportunity to stay with their hospitalized child.

EARLY CHILDHOOD

Ages 3 to 6 years are generally considered early childhood. Physical illness during this period may limit the child's ability to achieve motor control and social competence; the child may have fewer opportunities for peer interaction and social approval. Parents may limit the child's activities as a means to try to prevent recurrences or exacerbations of illness. This further limits the child's sense of mastery and may result in a child who is fearful, passive, and excessively dependent on adults (Perrin and Gerrity 1984). Since children at this age are very concrete thinkers as well as egocentric, they interpret their pain and other symptoms as punishment for "being bad." School entrance may be delayed, which might contribute to increased dependency on the parents or anger and resentment at not being able to be like other children. During early childhood, the child needs to be constantly reminded that he or she did not do anything to bring on the illness. However, if noncompliance is an issue, it must be stressed that the child can help control the illness by partaking of the recommended treatment. Positive reinforcement (e.g., a chart on which the child receives stickers or stars for compliance) works exceedingly well in this age group (and even in somewhat older children).

SCHOOL-AGE CHILDREN

School-age children, ages 6 to 12 years, whether or not they have a chronic illness, become more and more influenced by their peer group and experiences in school. The following are the major developmental tasks of this age group (Weitzman 1984):

1. Separating from the family and a sense of belonging and identification with the peer group and society

2. Acquiring social skills

3. Developing a sense of accomplishment

4. Learning how to cope with stress, anxiety, impulses, and frustrations and to discharge emotions in a socially acceptable fashion

5. Adjusting to a school setting and acquiring the skills and attitudes that will eventually result in self-sufficiency

The presence of a chronic illness may interfere in a number of ways with these normal developmental processes. These children may worry about how they are different from their normal peers and how their illness interferes with development of peer relations. Children of this age can be very cruel toward each other. The normal child may avoid or make fun of the disabled child in his or her own struggle toward conformity and acceptance.

School is a very important aspect in the lives of children of this age. Besides being the place to learn academic skills, it is also the place where socialization takes place. The successes, failures, and social relationships that children experience in school have a very strong influence on their evolving sense of self, their relatedness to others, and their perceptions of their ability to perform and cope effectively (Weitzman 1984).

The majority of children with chronic illness or physical disability are of normal intelligence. Despite this fact, there is evidence from a number of studies that suggests chronically ill children as a whole underachieve and do worse academically than do their healthy peers (Weitzman 1984). The reasons for this include limited alertness or stamina, side effects of medication, altered expectations, preferential and prejudicial treatment, psychosocial maladjustment, and excessive days missed because of illness (Weitzman 1984). Chronically ill children are thus at risk to become underachievers and failures in their eyes and the eyes of their peers (Perrin and Gerrity 1984). When a child repeatedly does poorly in school, he or she tends to become discouraged and develops concomitant emotional problems.

Frequently, chronically ill children miss school because of acute exacerbations, doctor's visits, or hospitalizations. Whether the child has a prolonged absence or multiple brief absences does not matter since both affect academic achievement and peer relationships. Absences may contribute to some chronically ill children's sense of futility and faltering maturation. Depression may ensue and may contribute to physical complaints, which in turn cause more school absenteeism, thus creating a recurring cycle. For others, the anticipation of missing school, falling behind, and having to make up missed school work can result in significant anxiety, which in turn may interfere with cognitive skills and the child's ability to concentrate (Weitzman 1984). This additional anxiety may also cause exacerbations of the medical illness itself (e.g., asthma, Crohn's disease).

When children miss a significant amount of school, home-bound teaching is necessary. If the absences are intermittent such that the child does not meet the criteria for home-bound teaching, then extra tutoring to help the child keep up is needed. The parents, with the encouragement of the physician, need to keep in touch with the school to make sure that the child is receiving assignments and doing the appropriate work. The parents should know how well their child is doing before the end of the term, so if extra help is necessary, the child can receive it. It is much harder to reverse the damage a failing grade does to a child's self-esteem and how he or she is perceived by teachers and peers than to encourage the use of tutors to prevent failure.

ADOLESCENTS

With the advances in medical science over the past several decades, more children with once-fatal diseases are now surviving into adolescence and adulthood. Adolescence itself poses many tasks of development: sexuality, body image, independence, vocational prospects, and self-identity. Chronic illness, whether first diagnosed in adolescence or maintained through adolescence, makes the mastery of these developmental issues much more difficult.

Many chronic illnesses change the adolescent's physical appearance either through the pathology of the illness itself (e.g., rheumatoid arthritis) or the medication necessary to treat the disease (e.g., corticosteroids). These physical changes make it even more difficult for the emergence of a secure physical and sexual identity. Growth failure and delayed puberty, associated with some chronic illnesses, cause the adolescent to appear younger, and therefore others treat him or her as being younger. The adolescent can acquiesce to this expectation and remain immature or may rebel and become angry at being perceived as being younger.

The possibility of infertility is raised with some diseases and must be discussed. There is some evidence that adolescent girls with a serious chronic illness may be at greater risk of pregnancy than those with less serious illnesses (Coupey and Cohen 1984). Both male and female adolescents with visible deformities (e.g., amputations, ostomies) need counseling about how their deformities relate to their expressions of sexuality. They need to know that they can be sexually desirable regardless of their disfigurement.

The illness itself can become the battleground in the adolescent's struggle for independence. Diets, medications, therapies, and doctor's visits are all forced on the adolescent; some patients become overly compliant, even compulsive about their medical care, whereas others become rebellious, risk-taking, and noncompliant in the need to express independence.

> David was 14 years old when he was diagnosed as having Hodgkin's disease. Soon after the diagnosis he started to smoke marijuana and to use street drugs. When he obtained his driver's license, he bought a motorcycle, which he rode to his clinic appointments. With a group of boys he would get drunk and would break into houses to steal. He was put into jail but did not go to reform school with the rest of the group because of his cancer. He admitted to taking risks because he did not care about anything. He felt cheated; why did he have to get sick? He felt like the world owed him something because he "didn't get his fair share of the good life."

Allowing the adolescent to have some say in his or her treatment increases feelings of independence and thus increases the likelihood of compliance. In addition, by having the adolescent take part in the decision-making process regarding treatment, he or she sees that his or her ideas and feelings are important, which contributes to self-worth.

Matt was diagnosed with osteogenic sarcoma of the right leg when he was 11 years old. Five years later after having battled three pulmonary relapses, a fourth pulmonary metastasis was found. After his thoracotomy and three doses of an experimental drug, he said he did not want any more treatment, that he would rather be dead. After talking it over with him and his mother, it was decided to go along with his wishes since he was fully cognizant of all the ramifications. After this decision to stop therapy, he went back to school (he had quit as soon as he was able), his alcohol abuse ceased, and he became much more responsible. A year later, he was still disease free.

The possibility of increased complications and/or a shortened life span is understood by the adolescent. As the adolescent thinks about these prognoses, depression may ensue, along with the contemplation of suicide. Sometimes noncompliance with medical care is the adolescent's way of expressing suicidal ideation.

Antidepressants and anxiolytic medications are sometimes used in the treatment of the adolescent with chronic illness. What medications the child has been prescribed and the interactions of the various drugs must be kept in mind. If psychiatric drugs are to be used, a lower dose than usual is used initially, the dose is increased more slowly, and the adolescent is monitored very closely.

Adolescents are especially prone to two dangers in assessing their life plans and goals in light of their illness: (1) overstressing the limitations and potential interferences of the illness and succumbing to a sense of futility and despair or (2) denying their realistic limitations, often setting themselves up for great disappointments when their unrealistic goals cannot be achieved (Perrin and Gerrity 1984). In both cases the stage is set for a depressive episode. Counseling can sometimes help the adolescent make more realistic plans so that psychiatric disability can be avoided. However, psychiatric therapy may be the first chance the adolescent has to come to terms with the disease and to mourn the loss of the healthy person he or she would have liked to have been. Some adolescents resort to fantasy and denial as they try to cope with the very real problems of rejection, scorn, and embarrassment. Depending on the intensity and frequency of these defense mechanisms, they need not be pathologic

(Blum 1984) and in fact may be a healthy way of dealing with the illness.

Family Reactions to Illness in a Child

Having a child with a chronic illness does affect the family unit, but how is not really known. Most studies assessing the effect of chronic illness on families have actually studied the effect on the mother; a few have studied the siblings.

Parents, most notably mothers, pass through predictable stages after a diagnosis of a serious illness in one of their children is made, as indicated earlier (Sabbeth 1984; Mattsson 1972) (see Table 28–2). The initial reaction is shock coupled with acute fear and anxiety of the possible fatal outcome of the disease. Disbelief or even denial is associated with the shock, especially if the child does not or no longer appears ill; anger and resentment follow, coupled with blame (of spouse, of self). Sadness and even clinical depression come next. In the majority of cases, acceptance of the situation is the end result. During the child's course, the parents may fluctuate from one stage to the next and back again; there is no problem with this unless they get stuck in a stage to the detriment of their mental well-being as well as the child's health. Many studies have found a high rate of depression in mothers of children with chronic illness (Sabbeth 1984). A depressed mother not only has a difficult time managing her sick child but also her other children. Although divorce in parents of chronically ill children does not appear to be increased over the normal population, parents of the chronically ill do experience more marital distress (Sabbeth 1984). Parents who have successfully adapted to the challenge of raising a chronically ill child will enforce necessary and realistic restrictions on him or her, encourage self-care and regular school attendance, and promote reasonable physical activities with the child's peers (Mattsson 1972).

In Drotar and Crawford's (1985) review article, they found that studies of the psychological adjustment of physically healthy siblings to a sibling's chronic illness indicate that there is not a one-to-one correspondence between the presence of a chronic illness and the risk for psychological disturbances in unafflicted children. Although the presence of a chronic illness may increase siblings' subjective distress, effects of a chronic illness on the psychological adjustment of siblings are selective and vary with age, sex, and type of illness. Sibling adjustment depends not only on child variables but also on the family environment. The quality of the family functioning and communication is probably a major mediator of the effects of the chronic illness on the siblings.

Some of the factors that have been found to be stressors for the siblings are increased isolation from the parents, lack of information about their sibling's condition, readjustment of family routines, and witnessing sibling's pain (Drotar and Crawford 1985). Specific fears of the siblings include catching the disease and caring for the sick sibling when the parents are no longer able (Sabbeth 1984). Most siblings feel embarrassed at times by their sick sibling and then may feel guilty about the embarrassment. They may also be jealous of the extra attention their sick sibling needs. In the case of genetic diseases, many siblings, especially females, insist that they will not have children for fear that they will be in the same position as their parents with a sick child. These siblings should be told about genetic counseling and the possibility of prenatal diagnosis for many genetic diseases.

How Treatment Affects the Psychological Response of Ill Children

Various aspects of treatment for chronic diseases cause problems for children and adolescents (Table 28–4). They wish that they did not have to bother with the treatment regimen and at times do not. Their feelings

Table 28–4. SPHERES OF TREATMENT THAT CAN CAUSE DISTRESS FOR CHILDREN AND ADOLESCENTS WITH CHRONIC DISEASES

1. Medications
2. Diet
3. Limits on activities
4. Therapies (e.g., physical, occupational, respiratory)
5. Environmental limitations (e.g., no pets, no carpets)
6. Blood and urine testing
7. Appliances (e.g., eyeglasses, hearing aids, wheelchairs, prostheses)
8. Special schooling
9. Hospitalization
10. Clinic visits

about the disease and its treatment, in addition to how the parents cope with these aspects, will determine if the noncompliance becomes a long-term problem or a passing phase in their lives.

One of the most important, although often overlooked, causes of emotional and behavioral problems is the medication that the patient is taking. The drugs themselves can make the child drowsy, irritable, nauseated, anxious, or even depressed. Some drugs, by changing one's appearance (notably corticosteroids) cause many types of problems for the patient, especially the adolescent.

Children who are cognitively unable to understand the reason why they must take certain medicines, especially many times a day when they are feeling fine, have a hard time complying. Having to take medication during school time is a problem for many children. They do not want other children to see that they have to take medication; they may have to go to the nurse's office for it; or if rules forbid school personnel from dispensing medication, a parent may have to come to school daily. All of these alternatives make the children feel different at a time in their lives when they want to be like everyone else. In addition, if the medication causes diuresis or diarrhea and the child needs to go to the bathroom frequently, he or she may get embarrassed, the other children may tease him or her about it, and/or the teacher may not allow frequent absences from the classroom.

The child who is falling asleep in school because of antihistamine or seizure medication is missing educational material, which may result in poor grades. The teacher may feel that the child is just lazy, and the other children may laugh at the sleepy child. In order to cope with the school situation, the child may refuse to take the medication or hold the medication in the mouth for disposal at a later time. He or she may even find excuses for not attending school. The school administrators and especially the teachers need to be informed of the consequences of the medication so that they will not burden the child with negative responses to the side effects.

The cushingoid appearance caused by corticosteroids is difficult for most patients to accept. An obese face, pendulous abdomen, thin hair, and acne are the very features all adolescents dislike. In addition, muscle weakness, particularly involving the proximal muscles, may occur, thus limiting participation in athletics. Appetite is increased, often markedly; growth may be permanently retarded. Mood changes, either elevation or depression, may occur, especially with the institution of or tapering off of corticosteroid dosage. To know that a medication is responsible for these body changes is reason to consider not taking the drug. Many adolescents prefer to tolerate the signs and symptoms of their disease rather than the changes in appearance that occur with drug therapy. Others refuse to go to school or be seen in public when they are taking their course of high-dose corticosteroids.

> Terry was in her senior year of high school when lymphoblastic leukemia was diagnosed. Her appearance was very important to her, and even before she lost any hair she had bought three wigs. Her treatment protocol required 6 weeks of high-dose prednisone every 24 weeks. She would get anxious and depressed just thinking about her course of corticosteroids. She was finally able to accept the therapy without the emotional turmoil when she was allowed to stay home from school when the cushingoid features were present.

When possible, most physicians will try to get their patients on lower dosages of corticosteroids, given every other day, to minimize the changes in appearance.

Probably the most frightening side effect for the family is a corticosteroid-induced psychosis. The family has to understand that the child is not "crazy," that he or she is just having a reaction to the medication. The family's reaction will affect how the child reacts. Many adolescents have been able to relate very scary hallucinations calmly because their parents have been calm and supportive during the episode of psychosis. Usually the psychosis responds well to lowering the dose of corticosteroids coupled with the use of antipsychotic medication.

Children with chronic illnesses must take medication at one time or another. For an outline of the side effects of some of the more commonly used pediatric medications, see Appendix 28–1.

Having to stay on a specific diet results in great dissatisfaction in children and adolescents. Eating is a social activity; by not being able to eat what the others are eating the child feels like an outsider. When the participants of a diabetes camp were asked what they thought was the worst thing about having diabetes, they answered "the diet" regardless of their age (a few of the very young campers mentioned "the shots").

Staying on a specific diet becomes more and more the responsibility of the child as he or she gets older and spends more time away from the parents. In order to fit in, the child may eat indiscriminately. Afterward, he or she may feel ill, have abnormal blood or urine tests, or just feel guilty about the indiscretion. When the parents find out about the eating of the forbidden food, they may limit the child's being away from home at mealtime or going to social events where food will be served. These limitations may make the child angry and rebellious in ways that may cause further noncompliance. A vicious circle may ensue, damaging the parent-child relationship and interfering with the treatment of the disease.

Children and adolescents must be told that it is acceptable behavior to bring their own food to parties. By bringing enough of their special foods to share with the other party goers, their limitations seem less onerous. Also, if the host or hostess knows ahead of time about a guest's dietary restrictions, he or she usually makes allowances so that some appropriate food is available.

No child regardless of age likes to be told that he or she cannot do something. Since most children are physically active, to be told that they should not run, play contact sports, or exert themselves causes anguish in children battling a chronic illness. Boys have a harder time with the restriction on their activities than do girls because sports and physical activity constitute more of their peer interaction.

From the time of diagnosis, children who will be limited in physical activities should be encouraged to excel in quieter activities (e.g., chess, painting, music, collecting objects, building models). There are some sports that are less physically taxing that the child or adolescent can be encouraged to play (e.g., bowling, billiards, marksmanship, archery). Competitive activities are even available for those confined to a wheelchair. If the child or adolescent dwells on the activities he or she cannot do, underlying depression and anger at the illness itself may be present and must be dealt with.

Any regimentation, especially one that

APPENDIX 28–1. COMMONLY USED MEDICATIONS AND THEIR PRINCIPAL SIDE EFFECTS (ESPECIALLY EMOTIONAL AND BEHAVIORAL)

General Class of Drug	Generic Name	Trade Name	Common Indications	Principal Side Effects (Rare Psychiatric Side Effects Included*)
Alkylating agent	Cyclophosphamide	Cytoxan	Corticosteroid-resistant, nephrotic syndrome, lupus, transplants, cancer	Alopecia, hemorrhagic cystitis, leukopenia
Analgesics	Acetaminophen	Tylenol, Panadol, Anacin-3	Pain, fever	Overdosage, causes hepatic toxicity
	Aspirin (acetylsalicylic acid)	Bayer, Bufferin, Ecotrin	Pain, inflammation, fever	Gastrointestinal symptoms (pain, heartburn, nausea, vomiting) and bleeding; clotting problems, dizziness, tinnitus, impaired hearing
	Ibuprofen	Advil, Medipren, Midol 200	Pain, fever	Heartburn, upset stomach, stomach pain
Narcotics	Codeine, morphine and opium derivatives and combinations	Demerol, Dilaudid	Pain	Psychic dependence, physical dependence, tolerance, respiratory depression, nausea, vomiting, sedation, drowsiness, mental clouding, lethargy, impairment of mental and physical performance, anxiety, fear, dysphoria, dizziness, mood changes, constipation, orthostatic hypotension, depression of cough reflex, smooth muscle spasm, sweating, weakness, agitation, tremor, transient hallucinations and disorientation, visual disturbance, dry mouth, palpitations, syncope, facial flushing, rashes
Anticholinergics	Atropine sulfate, ipratropium bromide	Atropine, Atrovent	Asthma	Palpitations, dizziness, headache, flushing, tachycardia, nervousness, dry mouth, blurred vision, rash, nausea, vomiting, tremor
Antihistamines	Diphenhydramine	Benadryl	Allergic reaction, parkinsonism, motion sickness, insomnia	Sedation, dizziness, disturbed coordination, confusion, restlessness, irritability, epigastric pain, anorexia, nausea, vomiting, urinary retention, hypotension, tachycardia, dryness of mouth and nose, rash, headache, palpitations, vertigo, tinnitus, fatigue, excitation, nervousness, insomnia, euphoria, paresthesias, blurred vision
	Hydroxyzine	Atarax, Visteril	Anxiety, tension, pruritus, sedation, allergic reaction	Drowsiness, dry mouth, involuntary motor activity
Antihypertensives Peripheral vasodilator	Minoxidil	Loniten	Hypertension	Hirsutism, salt and water retention, tachycardia, rash, breast tenderness

APPENDIX 28–1. COMMONLY USED MEDICATIONS AND THEIR PRINCIPAL SIDE EFFECTS (ESPECIALLY EMOTIONAL AND BEHAVIORAL) Continued

General Class of Drug	Generic Name	Trade Name	Common Indications	Principal Side Effects (Rare Psychiatric Side Effects Included*)
Antihypertensives (*Continued*)	Prazosin	Minipress	Hypertension	Syncopal episodes, dizziness, drowsiness, headache, lack of energy, weakness, palpitations, nausea, vomiting, diarrhea, vertigo, depression, nervousness, rash, paresthesias,* hallucinations*
Calcium channel blocker	Nifedipine	Procardia	Hypertension	Constipation, weakness, dizziness, nausea, hypotension, flushing, edema, headache, fatigue, muscle cramps, tremor, nervousness, mood changes, confusion,* insomnia,* paresthesias,* psychosis,* somnolence,* depression*
	Verapamil	Colan, Isoptin	Arrhythmias, hypertension	
Anti-inflammatory agents (nonsteroidal)	Naproxen	Naprosyn	Arthritis	Gastrointestinal irritation, nausea, vomiting, diarrhea, constipation, pruritus, tinnitus, drowsiness, headache, vertigo, epigastric discomfort, depression, somnolence, fatigue, anxiety,* insomnia,* psychosis,* mental confusion*
	Indomethacin	Indocin		
	Sulfasalazine	Azulfidine	Inflammatory bowel disease	Anorexia, headache, rash, pruritus, nausea, vomiting, fever, anemias, depression,* hallucinations,* drowsiness*
β-Adrenoreceptor blocker	Propranolol	Inderal	Hypertension, migraine headaches, essential tremor, hypertrophic subaortic stenosis	Weakness, fatigue, bradycardia, depression, insomnia, hallucinations, vivid dreams, acute reversible organic brain syndrome
Cardiac medications Digitalis glycoside	Digoxin	Lanoxin	Heart failure, arrhythmias	Toxicity may present as visual disturbances, headache, weakness, apathy, psychosis, anorexia, nausea, vomiting
Antiarrhythmic	Procainamide	Procan Pronestyl	Arrhythmias	Lupus-like syndrome, anorexia, nausea, vomiting, psychosis,* confusion,* depression*
Corticosteroids	Prednisone Methylprednisolone Beclomethasone diproprionate Hydrocortisone	Deltasone Medrol, Solu-Medrol Beconase, Vanceril Hydrocortone	Endocrine disorders (adrenocortical insufficiency, nonsuppurative thyroiditis), rheumatic disorders, collagen diseases, dermatologic diseases, allergic conditions, ophthalmologic diseases, respiratory diseases, hematologic disorders, cancer, gastrointestinal disorders, nephrotic syndrome, transplant recipients	Cushingoid habitus, acne, hirsutism, hypertension, ecchymoses, osteoporosis, salt retention, striae, euphoria, insomnia, malaise, psychoses, disturbances in growth, retardation of sexual maturation, weakness, mood swings, personality changes, increased appetite, nausea, thin fragile skin

Table continued on following page

APPENDIX 28–1. COMMONLY USED MEDICATIONS AND THEIR PRINCIPAL SIDE EFFECTS
(ESPECIALLY EMOTIONAL AND BEHAVIORAL) Continued

General Class of Drug	Generic Name	Trade Name	Common Indications	Principal Side Effects (Rare Psychiatric Side Effects Included*)
Diuretics	Furosemide Chlorothiazide	Lasix Diuril	Edema, hypertension, cardiac failure	Polyuria (may be bedwetting), dizziness, vertigo, paresthesias, headache, blurred vision, tinnitus, anorexia, nausea, vomiting, diarrhea, constipation, rash, muscle spasms, weakness
Aldosterone antagonist	Spironolactone	Aldactone	Hyperaldosteronism, edema	Drowsiness, lethargy, headache, gastrointestinal symptoms, mental confusion, ataxia, gynecomastia, problems with erections, problems with menses, hirsutism
Carbonic anhydrase inhibitor	Acetazolamide	Diamox	Epilepsy, cardiac edema	Drowsiness, paresthesias
Endocrine preparations	Insulin L-thyroxine	Humulin, Novolin Synthroid, Levothyroid	Diabetes mellitus Hypothyrodism	Hypoglycemia, rashes, pruritus, bruises Too little: sluggish Too much: nervousness, weight loss, palpitations, tremors, headache, insomnia, heat intolerance
	Vasopressin	Pitressin, DDAVP		Too little: polyuria, polydipsia, anxiety Too much: seizures, weakness
	Propylthiouracil Methimazol	PTU Tapazole	Hyperthyroidism	Rash, pain, stiffness in the joints, agranulocytosis
Histamine H_2 receptor antagonist	Cimetidine	Tagamet	Peptic ulcers, esophagitis, gastritis	Confusional states, behavior disturbance, headache, diarrhea, dizziness, psychosis*
Immunosuppressant	Cyclosporine	Sandimmune	Transplants, nephrotic syndrome	Hirsutism, hypertension, tremors, renal toxicity, hyperkalemia
Neurologic medications	Phenobarbital	Phenobarbital	Seizures (tonic-clonic, psychomotor)	Drowsiness, irritability, hyperactivity, nausea, vomiting, rash, learning problems
	Phenytoin	Dilantin	Seizures (tonic-clonic, psychomotor), migraine headaches	Coarsening of the facial features, enlargement of the lips, gingival hypertrophy, nausea, vomiting, constipation, ataxia, malaise, rash, slurred speech, mental confusion, transient nervousness, insomnia, hirsutism
	Diazepam	Valium	Seizures (tonic-clonic)	Drowsiness, fatigue, ataxia, confusion, depression, nausea, headache, tremor, paradoxic reactions, hyperexcited state, anxiety, hallucinations, insomnia, rage, sleep disturbance
	Primidone	Mysoline	Seizures (tonic-clonic, psychomotor)	Ataxia, vertigo, nausea, vomiting, anorexia, fatigue, hyperirritability, emotional disturbance, drowsiness, rash, learning problems

APPENDIX 28–1. COMMONLY USED MEDICATIONS AND THEIR PRINCIPAL SIDE EFFECTS (ESPECIALLY EMOTIONAL AND BEHAVIORAL) Continued

General Class of Drug	Generic Name	Trade Name	Common Indications	Principal Side Effects (Rare Psychiatric Side Effects Included*)
Neurologic medications *(Continued)*	Carbamazepine	Tegretol	Seizures (tonic-clonic, psychomotor)	Aplastic anemia, rash, nausea, vomiting, fever, liver damage, urinary frequency or retention, dizziness, drowsiness, confusion, headache, fatigue, visual hallucinations, peripheral neuritis and paresthesias, depression with agitation, talkativeness, tinnitus, hyperacusis
	Ethosuximide	Zarontin	Seizures (absence)	Nausea, vomiting, anorexia, blood dyscrasias, liver damage, lupus, drowsiness, headache, dizziness, euphoria, hiccups, irritability, hyperactivity, lethargy, fatigue, ataxia, disturbance of sleep, night terrors, inability to concentrate, aggressiveness, depression,* paranoid psychosis*
	Valproic acid	Depakene	Seizures (absence)	Drowsiness, weight loss or gain, hair loss, nausea, vomiting, liver dysfunction, coagulation dysfunction, tremor, ataxia, headache, dizziness, emotional upset, depression, psychosis, aggression, hyperactivity, behavioral deterioration, weakness, edema
	Methsuximide	Celontin	Seizures (absence)	Nausea, vomiting, anorexia, diarrhea, weight loss, epigastric and abdominal pain, constipation, rash, drowsiness, ataxia, dizziness, irritability, nervousness, headache, hiccups, insomnia, confusion, instability, mental slowness, depression, hypochondriacal behavior, aggressiveness, psychosis,* suicidal behavior,* auditory hallucinations*
	Haloperidol	Haldol	Tourette's syndrome, psychosis, combative, explosive hyperexcitability	Extrapyramidal reactions, autonomic reaction, tardive dyskinesia, insomnia, restlessness, anxiety, euphoria, agitation, drowsiness, depression, lethargy, headache, confusion, tachycardia, hypotension, nausea, vomiting, anorexia, constipation, diarrhea
Promotility agent	Metoclopramide		Slow gastrointestinal tract	Lethargy
Sympathomimetics	Metaproterenol Albuterol Isoetharine Epinephrine	Alupent, Metaprel Ventolin, Proventil Bronkosol Epinephrine Sus-Phrine	Asthma, cystic fibrosis	Nausea, tachycardia, hypertension, palpitations, anxiety, headache, arrhythmias, tremors, hyperactivity, dizziness, insomnia, restlessness, weakness, nervousness

Table continued on following page

APPENDIX 28–1. *COMMONLY USED MEDICATIONS AND THEIR PRINCIPAL SIDE EFFECTS (ESPECIALLY EMOTIONAL AND BEHAVIORAL)* Continued

General Class of Drug	Generic Name	Trade Name	Common Indications	Principal Side Effects (Rare Psychiatric Side Effects Included*)
Xanthines	Theophylline	Slo-bid; Slo-Phyllin, Theo-Dur	Asthma	Headaches, irritability, restlessness, insomnia, seizures, nausea, vomiting, epigastric pain, diarrhea, palpitations, tachycardia, ventricular arrhythmias, tachypnea, alopecia, rash
	Aminophylline	Somophyllin		
Miscellaneous	Gold sodium thiomalate	Myochrysine	Rheumatoid disease	Blood dyscrasias, rashes, stomatitis, conjunctivitis, nephrotic syndrome, glomerulitis, flushing, fainting, dizziness, sweating, nausea, vomiting, malaise, weakness, anorexia, abdominal cramps, diarrhea, confusion, hallucinations, seizures, peripheral hemopathy
	Potassium chloride	K-Lor, K-lyte Kaochlor	Potassium supplement	Nausea, vomiting, abdominal discomfort, diarrhea, rashes, hyperkalemia
	Vitamin A		Vitamin A supplement	Pseudotumor cerebri, hypervitaminosis A syndrome
	Pancrealipase	Pancrease	Cystic fibrosis, chronic pancreatitis	Constipation, uric acid stones
	Cromolyn sodium	Intal, Nasalcron, Opticrom 4% solution	Asthma	Rash, cough, nasal congestion

may be uncomfortable and in which the child or adolescent has no say, will cause problems. Physical therapy, occupational therapy, speech therapy, and respiratory therapy all fall into this category. As the patient struggles to string the beads or to say the "r" sound, he or she is reminded again and again of his or her major limitations. As the physical therapist, or even the patient's mother, stretches the tight muscles, the child may wonder if this therapy will go on forever. The need for the therapies, what can be expected from them, and the expected duration all need to be discussed with the child. Also, by allowing the child or adolescent to have some say as to when the therapies are to be done engenders cooperation.

Most children desire a pet, but for children with allergies to animals, pets are contraindicated. It is very difficult for a family to get rid of its beloved animal even if all know that one of their members is allergic to it. Even well-meaning parents who confine the pet to the out-of-doors make exceptions and reintroduce the animal into the home at certain times. Not only does the child with

allergies feel terrible, but the other children in the family often blame the allergic child and make him or her feel more miserable. Working with the family as a whole and discussing the problem of the pet openly usually helps. Sometimes the siblings come up with a solution (letting the pet live with the grandparents or with a neighbor). If the family decides as a whole, then there is less resentment toward the child whose illness necessitated the removal of the animal, or any other environmental change.

Explaining that it is necessary to check urine and stool samples to see how their bodies are functioning tells children that their feelings of disgust for their body's waste are normal but that the tests must be done. As far as blood tests are concerned, most children and adolescents do not like the needle prick. Here again, by giving them permission not to like it makes it easier on all concerned. Many of the children then decide that they are stronger than other children; that they do not mind the blood test, and the lancet or needle does not bother them a bit!

Although eyeglasses are fashionable, most

children dislike them because they make them appear different than their peers. Other classmates may even tease them. As children get older, one or more of their peers start wearing glasses, so there is less differentiation. Also, contact lens are available and are a welcomed relief to the child or adolescent who hates wearing glasses.

Things are not so easy for the child with a hearing aid, wheelchair, or prosthesis. There are small hearing aids that can fit into the ear and can be covered by one's hair, but these are not always the type indicated for the hearing-impaired child. Children and adolescents with appliances that are of low incidence in the general population have to be introduced to others of their age who utilize the same device. Most areas have ostomy groups where persons of all ages get together to discuss problems associated with their ostomy. Adolescent groups can usually be found in more densely populated areas. When no group is available locally, it is up to the physician or parent to get children or adolescents together who wear the same type of appliance. Together they can share coping strategies not known by those unfamiliar with the problems encountered by them.

Sometimes children meet each other in school, especially if their limitations force them to go to a special school. Special school is looked on as both a blessing and a detriment. Although children like to be with other children like themselves, most special schools group children with various disabilities together. Those less involved feel misplaced, especially if their neighborhood friends all go to another school. If possible, children should be mainstreamed as much as possible. With the willingness and some accommodation on the part of the school, most children can be taught in their local school. There have been cases of children in wheelchairs having all their classes on the first floor after some teachers exchanged classrooms to accomplish this.

Hospitalizations and clinic visits are disliked because they force the child or adolescent to miss school and activities with friends. Hospitalization also keeps the child away from familiar surroundings and his or her family. Moreover, visits to the physician usually mean tests that the patient views as unpleasant. If the clinic visit or hospitalization is elective, the child will be more willing to go if he or she has some input into sched-

uling it. Most of the time, if the patient is acutely ill, he or she realizes the necessity of the visit and cooperates.

In all of the treatment regimens required by chronically ill children or adolescents, it is necessary to tell them the reasons for the treatment and get them involved as much as possible. Their input is very important, not only to ensure cooperation but also to show them that someone cares and respects their opinion.

TERMINAL ILLNESS

At some point in the course of their illness, all children and adolescents and their families wonder about the future. In some cases the projected outcome is a shortened life span. The understanding of the concept of death is dependent on the child's developmental stage.

The young child sees death as a transient, reversible phenomenon. By age 6 or 7 the permanence of death is understood but may not be seen as the consequence of the ceasing of biological activity. Adolescents comprehend death like adults.

As far as their own impending death is concerned, children know when they are seriously ill. Not only do they feel sick, are in pain, and/or have difficulty breathing, but they also sense the distress in those around them. For some children, as for some adults, death is a welcomed relief from the pain and suffering of their disease.

> Brenda was a healthy active child until age 5 when she developed Stevens-Johnson syndrome believed to be a reaction to an antibiotic. Her mucous membrane lesions healed during her hospitalization, but her pulmonary function progressively worsened. As her oxygen requirements increased, she was able to do fewer of the activities she enjoyed due to fatigue. Being very intelligent, she was able to talk about her worsening condition and eventual death. One morning before her mother returned to the hospital with her laundry, she sent her father to the cafeteria for some soda. When he returned to her room he found her lying on her bed with the nasal cannula for the oxygen at her side. Brenda could not be resuscitated. Her mother summed up her death by saying, "She was tired of suffering."

Parents should be encouraged to talk about the impending death with the child or adolescent. It allows the patient and parents to express their love and to say good-bye; the parents usually regret not doing this after the child has died. As far as the death itself, the child or adolescent most fears being alone, in pain, and forgotten. The physician can assure the child that enough medication will be available so that the child need not be in much pain (and this should then be followed through). The parents need to tell the child that they will be with him or her when he or she dies and that they will always remember the child. Some children like to put their photos and other memorabilia in an album for the family during their terminal illness in order to ensure that they are not forgotten.

POSITIVE ASPECTS

Having a chronic illness is not necessarily all negative. For some families, the contact with the medical community and the additional services available through the clinics for these illnesses can provide services that patients and their families may not have had otherwise available.

Mark was 19 years old when his left leg was amputated for osteogenic sarcoma. Although he attended his rural school, he had the equivalent of about 1 year of education. He was mentally retarded and was believed to be unteachable, so he was left to play with the younger children or daydream. In the hospital it became evident that he did understand what was going on and was probably in the mild range of retardation. He accepted some tutoring by the teacher assigned to the hospital, and he started to read. The hospital experience improved his self-esteem and his family's expectations of him. After he no longer had to take treatment for his cancer, he was enrolled in a vocational training program. He is now on the waiting list to go to a permanent supervised adult-living situation

where having a job or going to school is mandatory for acceptance.

Physical illness has a profound effect on children and their families. How they manage it depends on the various aspects discussed in this chapter. One of the major ways the medical community can help these children and families is to anticipate the various problem areas, discuss these areas, and help them resolve the problems before they become unmanageable. It is hoped that these children will be psychologically healthy even if they do suffer from a debilitating chronic illness.

References

Blum, R.W. 1984. *Chronic Illness and Disabilities in Childhood and Adolescence.* New York: Grune & Stratton.

Coupey, S.M., and Cohen, M.I. 1984. Special considerations for the health care of adolescents with chronic illnesses. *Pediatr. Clin. North. Am.* 31:211–219.

Drotar, D., and Crawford, P. 1985. Psychological adaptation of siblings of chronically ill children: Research and practice implications. *J. Dev. Behav. Pediatr.* 6:355–362.

Gortmaker, S.L., and Sappenfield, W. 1984. Chronic childhood disorders: Prevalence and impact. *Pediatr. Clin. North Am.* 31:3–18.

Green, M., and Solnit, A.J. 1964. Reactions to the threatened loss of a child: A vulnerable child syndrome. *Pediatrics* 34:58–66.

Mattsson, A. 1972. Long-term physical illness in childhood: A challenge to psychosocial adaptation. *Pediatrics* 50:801–811.

Nolan, T., Pless, I.B. 1986. Emotional correlates and consequences of birth defects. *J. Pediatr.* 109(suppl.): 201–216.

Perrin, E.C., and Gerrity, P.S. 1984. Development of children with a chronic illness. *Pediatr. Clin. North Am.* 31:19–31.

Pless, I.B. 1984. Clinical assessment: Physical and psychological functioning. *Pediatr. Clin. North Am.* 31:33–45.

Sabbeth, B. 1984. Understanding the impact of chronic childhood illness on families. *Pediatr. Clin. North Am.* 31:47–57.

Weitzman, M. 1984. School and peer relations. *Pediatr. Clin. North Am.* 31:59–69.

Multidimensional Psychotherapy for Children and Adolescents

29

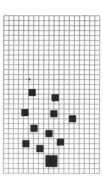

HARRY M. HOBERMAN, PH.D.
CAROL B. PETERSON

Psychosocial interventions for the treatment of psychiatric disorders in children and adolescents are of relatively recent origin. Compared with the field of adult psychotherapy, child psychotherapy has failed to receive the scientific scrutiny that the increasing numbers of children and adolescents who receive psychotherapy for their psychiatric disorders would justify. While multiple models of psychosocial treatment have proliferated for dysfunctional adults, the majority of children with psychiatric disorders continue to be treated according to the "same" model of psychotherapy in vogue 30 or even 50 years ago. A relative lack of innovation has characterized both theorists and researchers in the field of child psychotherapy. There has been insufficient progress achieved in empirically delineating the specific psychosocial factors that might ameliorate the psychiatric disorders of youth. Furthermore, the actual practice of psychotherapy with young persons has lagged even farther behind the meager theoretical advances, with most child clinicians continuing to deliver a "traditional" form of psychotherapy to children with psychiatric disorders. As recently as 1978, reviews of the then available studies of traditional psychotherapy with children (e.g., Barrett, et al. 1978) indicated that little difference in outcome appeared to exist between treated and untreated children. Current psychotherapeutic practices with children, therefore, may reflect an anachronistic model of intervention with little empiric demonstration of its efficacy.

Fortunately, the most recent reviews of the psychotherapy literature offer more assurance that psychosocial interventions are effective with children and adolescents. Both Casey and Berman (1985) and Weisz and co-workers (1987) conducted meta-analyses of the existing well-designed outcome studies in this area. In both reviews, the results demonstrated that psychotherapy with youth is similar in effectiveness to that with adult populations with 70% to 80% of those treated improved. The majority of these studies fell into the category of behavioral or cognitive-behavioral interventions. Weisz and co-workers found that such interventions proved more effective than nonbehavioral treatments regardless of the type of treated problem. As a caveat, it is worth noting that many of the studies available for these reviews focused on relatively specific dimensions of problematic child behavior (e.g., noncompliance, social withdrawal) as opposed to the treatment of children with single or multiple diagnoses. Thus, it is unclear as to the actual efficacy of psychosocial interventions with children presenting with one or more specific psychiatric disorders. The results of these reviews are instructive, however, in setting the direction for psychosocial interventions in order to more effectively remediate the psychiatric problems of children and adolescents.

The purpose of this chapter is twofold.

First, an attempt is made to articulate a model of a multidimensional approach to child and adolescent psychiatric disorders. Such a model represents an integration of the advances made in the development of cognitive-behavioral strategies for addressing psychopathology with certain psychodynamic principles that characterize the more traditional psychotherapeutic model with children. The multidimensional approach to treatment is one informed by theoretical advances in the understanding of children's psychiatric disorders, the empiric evidence for the efficacy of certain strategies for establishing a therapeutic alliance and effecting behavior change, and the evolving demands and constraints of the mental health care system. A second goal of this chapter is to offer recommendations for the treatment of particular types of psychiatric disorders—to attempt to match psychotherapeutic strategies to particular etiologic factors and symptomatic behaviors that characterize specific psychiatric disorders.

Traditional psychotherapies for children and adolescents are still the most commonly applied method of treatment for the variety of problems that determine referral to mental health providers (Kovacs and Paulaskas 1987). Two characteristics appear central to such approaches:

1. They emphasize developmentally based, intrapsychic conflicts rooted in early experiences predominantly of an interpersonal nature.

2. The central therapeutic mechanism is the nature of the relationship between the therapist and the child or adolescent. Particular interpersonal experiences are employed to promote self-awareness on the part of the youths; self-awareness or insight into the internalized determinants of behavior is presumed to lead to changes in the patient's behavior.

Traditional psychotherapies for youth generally share a number of features. Few limitations are set on the direction of therapy; it is child directed. The use of educative measures or direct attempts to change the child's environment are restricted as much as possible. The therapist behaves in a relatively passive and neutral manner in order to not limit the patient's varying perceptions of him or her; these perceptions are assumed to provide the most significant means of facilitating the patient's self-awareness. Frequent contacts (e.g., four to five sessions per week) are recommended in order to increase opportunities for observation and interaction and to heighten the intensity of the interpersonal alliance. For younger and less verbal children, the use of play is used as a means to enable the patient to reveal intrapsychic conflicts. The length of traditional psychotherapy is almost always long term, typically lasting several years; the goal of treatment has been to reshape the child's personality and, thus, fulfill the person's development to the greatest degree possible.

In recent years, however, numerous forces have converged to produce an impetus among mental health practitioners toward delivering different types of treatment to children and adolescents. In contrast to traditional approaches, such treatments are characterized predominantly by time limits imposed on the length of treatment, a much more active role on the part of the therapist, more directiveness in the content of therapy, and more limited and specific treatment goals. At least six forces have resulted in a shift toward more active and direct treatment of youth:

1. The empiric evidence that traditional psychotherapy for children and adolescents is efficacious is, at best, very meager.

2. As a result of progress in the delineating and study of psychiatric disorders, a greater understanding of the etiologic factors and the natural course of these disorders has been obtained. This, in turn, allows for more specified interventions and those that take into account the often episodic or chronic nature of childhood psychiatric disorders.

3. The goals and model for delivery of treatment have changed. Rather than aiming to produce a cure or complete mental health, practitioners increasingly accept that psychotherapy provides more limited possibilities in what it can accomplish, such as the improvement or containment of a particular problem, as opposed to its elimination. There has been a recognition that treatment may be most useful and accepted by patients when it is intermittent or discontinuous over a period of time and conducted on an ''as needed'' basis.

4. Perhaps the most obvious force in the movement toward a different model of treatment has been the dramatically increased cost of mental health care and the reluctance of both the public and third-party providers

to pay for indefinite length of care. Moreover, there is a clear trend toward imposing such limitations in the authorization of psychotherapy.

5. Still another factor central to the shift toward more active, time-limited psychotherapy is the tremendous need for the treatment of disturbed youth. Epidemiologic studies indicate that at least 12% to 20% of children and adolescents require mental health services. A very limited number of professionals are available to provide such care for youth; furthermore, studies indicate that often it is the least symptomatic children who are the most likely to receive treatment. The demand of large numbers of persons needing treatment argues for an increased emphasis on providing more focal and time-limited interventions in order to serve as many youth as possible.

6. A last factor in the movement away from traditional treatment is consumerism. Many patients' preferences and behavior in treatment demonstrate that they desire briefer and more focused therapy. Most often, the typical child patient stays in treatment for only five to ten sessions. Thus, the reality of clinical practice is that most treatment is time limited, something that many clinicians fail to appreciate. Rather than simply attribute this fact to resistance on the part of patients, therapists must reconsider how to provide the types of treatment that patients desire and to match their treatment goals and practices to the circumstances of their patients.

Rutter (1986) has described the changes that have taken place regarding the goals of psychotherapy for children and adolescents. Symptom reduction, and in particular, the alleviation of distress, is a necessary and primary goal. In addition, treatment should promote normal development. To whatever degree possible, maladaptive behavior must be diminished so that a child can be reintegrated into the mainstream of normal socializing experiences; such experiences are the means by which the average youth acquires and refines those skills and beliefs that mediate successful adjustment. Psychotherapy must also attempt to foster a child's autonomy and self-reliance, both to reduce the likelihood of relapse and to increase their ability to deal with future problems. Relatedly, intervention must consider the generalization of improvement across environ-

ments and its persistence over time. Finally, clinicians must adopt an ecologic perspective on the nature of psychiatric disorders among the young, with attention directed toward changing both the environment and the person in order to most effectively meet these goals.

A MULTIDIMENSIONAL PERSPECTIVE ON ETIOLOGY

Psychiatric disorders are clearly overdetermined phenomena; available research points to the likelihood of multiple influences (e.g., stress-diathesis-competencies) contributing to the development of most such disorders, as opposed to any single factor being necessary and sufficient for causation. In the great majority of cases, risk factors for psychiatric disorders converge and aggregate in eliciting an episode of psychopathology. Moreover, these risk factors impinge on multiple levels of the child's psychological functioning: overt behavior as well as less-observable affects and cognitions. The effect of a given risk factor will also depend on the developmental level of the child when he or she encounters that factor, as well as on the developmental tasks that the child's family is confronting.

These notions are illustrated in Figure 29–1. Both parenting behavior and biogenetic vulnerabilities are significant determinants in children's psychiatric disorders. Parenting behavior can be impaired by a parent's own psychiatric or, more broadly, psychological dysfunction or by life stresses. Impaired parenting behavior can affect a child on a number of different levels. Dysfunctional parenting can interfere with child management skills leading to noncompliance and antisocial behavior; it can also lead to overcontrol of a child. The consequences of overcontrol are typically inhibition or repression of a variety of experiences and heightened anxiety and self-consciousness. An impaired parent may have difficulty displaying affection and encouragement to a child; the parent may also promote premature independence or, conversely, age-inappropriate dependency. Parents who are themselves psychiatrically impaired are less likely to teach or model competent behavior across a range of areas for their children. Furthermore, to the extent that risk factors do aggregate, dysfunctional parenting behavior is likely to in-

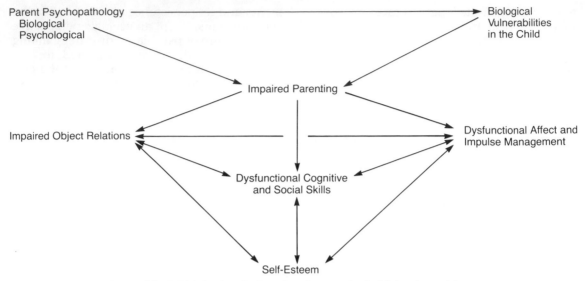

***Figure 29–1.** Risk factors in the development of children's problems.*

teract with a child's biogenetic vulnerabilities; thus, a moody or inattentive-impulsive child is likely to exacerbate a parent's deficits in child-rearing, which, in turn, affects the child's development. Too often, parenting weaknesses are inversely "matched" to a great degree by a child's special needs for parenting.

Both extreme and subtle impairments in parenting have significant implications for a child's developing psychological and behavioral competencies. To begin with, early parent–child interactions have a profound impact on the child's acquisition of ideas about persons, both self and others, and consequently, on the child's basic orientation toward the world (e.g., safe or threatening, responsive or indifferent). The cognitive structures or mental representations that incorporate knowledge about self and others constitute what has been referred to as object relations. Being rooted initially in pleasurable and unpleasurable experiences of gratification and frustration of needs, object relations reflect the internalization of the adequacy of caretaking behavior. They then provide intrapsychic, psychological mechanisms for the modulation of affects and impulses and, thus, for the capacity to transcend the immediate environment. Based on early social learning of core beliefs about self and others, they determine and direct the nature of current and future relationships. In particular, because early relationships involve some

combination of frustration and gratification, and thus conflict, the nature of later relationships is likely to include elements of conflict and ambivalence.

Later parent–child interactions are important determinants of the degree to which a child acquires a wide range of specific skills or competencies. Behaviorally, children should progressively learn more refined and efficacious behaviors necessary for interacting with other children and adults in order to minimize conflict and maximize a variety of social gains (e.g., belonging, intimacy, self-appraisal, assistance, and self-esteem). Dysfunctional parenting can retard the development of these processes in a variety of ways. Similarly, less than adequate parenting can have a number of consequences for a child's cognitive development and skills. On the process level, children can (1) fail to learn effective problem solving, reflective thinking, or perspective taking; (2) be taught to pay too little or too much attention to their affective or somatic experiences; or (3) be too lax or stringent in their self-evaluation or self-rewards. On a content level, impaired parenting can lead children to develop negative, pathogenic beliefs about themselves and their world and, subsequently, a greater number of cognitive distortions in terms of their expectations, perceptions, and attributions. Both the process and content of children's cognitive style have important roles in the child's development of self-esteem. Finally, children of dysfunctional parents are likely to demonstrate serious problems in their ability to manage both impulses and affective experiences because they lack basic cognitive skills.

As seen in Figure 29–1, the potential for interactions among these various potential etiologic factors is great. "Vulnerabilities" may be counteracted by the "immunizing" effect of competencies. In contrast, multiple vulnerabilities for psychopathology may act in additive or transactional manners to magnify their individual effects. Thus, constitutional tendencies to mood dysregulation or impulsivity, for example, will have implications for the development of object relations as well as the need for, and acquisition of, cognitive and behavioral skills. Intrapsychic issues may interact with behavioral and cognitive ones; impaired object relations will be exacerbated in children who lack the social skills to realize their needs for social relations as well as in children who lack cognitive-behavioral skills in the management of distress. Similarly, cognitive and behavioral deficits can interact with one another, such as when impulsive, nonreflective children do not understand or practice social skills that will include them in peer interactions.

Rather than subscribing to a single factor, linear theory of the etiology of psychiatric disorders (e.g., "X" causes "Y"), it makes more sense to appreciate the complexity of etiology and take this into account in formulating an intervention. Given the complex determinants of a specific child or adolescent's psychiatric disorders, it follows that interventions that are multidimensional in their assessment and treatment and targeted at the particular child in question are most likely to be maximally effective. Given the multiple possible characteristics and influences in children's psychiatric problems, it stands to reason that two patients assigned the same diagnoses based on criteria of the *Diagnostic and Statistical Manual of Mental Disorders,* third edition, revised *(DSM-III-R),* may require very different intervention approaches (Looney 1984). To this end, a multidimensional assessment is one that (1) considers the range of potential critical determinants of a child's problems; (2) considers their relative significance in the context of one another; and (3) assigns them clinical priorities based on their centrality to the presenting problem as well as their amena-

bility to treatment. A good example of the use of clinical goal setting in a multidimensional treatment is provided by Gries (1986). Relatedly, a multidimensional intervention is one that considers the range of potential intervention strategies and selects and orders those approaches in a manner to have the greatest impact on a particular child's problems. As McDermott and Char (1984) have stated, "Today, the mainstream of child psychotherapy goes beyond a single theory or individual approach. It is eclectic, often involving a more complicated multidimensional model with varying strategic combinations of cognitive mastery, emotional experience, and behavioral change in differing sequences according to the needs of the patient and family."

PSYCHODYNAMIC ELEMENTS IN TREATING CHILDREN'S PSYCHIATRIC DISORDERS

From a psychodynamic perspective, children and adolescents suffer from both the ill effects of past interpersonal experiences, which have been internalized and continue to influence their behavior, and from the distress of adapting to an environment that is intrinsically imperfect and frustrating. Contemporary psychodynamic viewpoints emphasize the effect of developmental factors on the experience and regulation of affects and impulses, self-esteem, and interpersonal relationships. As noted earlier, certain interpersonal experiences, predominantly with caretakers, influence the child's development of internal psychological processes important in the child's modulation of affect and impulses. These and other experiences may result in children internalizing conflicts based on learning that some feeling, impulse, behavior, or wish is unacceptable for cultural (e.g., aggression) or idiographic reasons (e.g., a parent believes the expression of affection is inappropriate). Subsequently, the child experiences tension, typically as a result of perceived fear of rejection or abandonment by their caretaker when they experience unacceptable feelings, impulses, or wishes. Consequently, children use a variety of psychological defenses (e.g., denial, displacement) to shield themselves from this tension, which, in turn, interferes with their accurate perception of and inter-action with the environment.

There are a number of common areas of psychological vulnerability that have their roots in psychodynamic processes; these are listed in Table 29–1. Difficulties with affect management are common to a number of psychiatric disorders. Some persons have problems tolerating affects such as anxiety, dysphoria, anger, or guilt because they are unable to modulate the intensity of those states. Other persons are overly sensitive to those states as a means of controlling their experiences. Similarly, some children or ad-olescents are intolerant of frustration of their needs or impulses and press for immediate gratification; often this impulsivity has its roots in early deprivation experiences. In contrast, other children fear their needs and impulses and avoid awareness of those states. Children may have difficulty seeking or accepting comfort in relationships, often secondary to the negative consequences of early separation, loss, abuse, or intrusive caretaking; they are often intolerant of rejec-tion or disappointment by significant others. All persons, depending on their develop-mental stage, experience conflicts finding a healthy balance between dependence and independence. Children referred for treat-ment are often conflicted in this area and respond by taking an extreme position on this dimension. Conflicts are common as youth attempt to separate from caretakers and persons in terms of their values and identity; in particular, difficulties modulating aggressive impulses and subsequent guilt often interfere with the process of separation. Self-esteem issues also characterize children and adolescents with psychiatric disorders; while some children display a heightened degree of omnipotence and entitlement, oth-ers are characterized by a striking sensitivity to their perceived inadequacies. Such issues are often a function of the child's self-per-ceived mastery or competence in meeting their needs. The variety of conflicts and other difficulties a person possesses are usually expressed in the major areas of their lives, particularly in their goal-directed behavior and social relations, including their partici-pation in psychotherapy.

Clues to the psychodynamic determinants of a child's problems are usually apparent in the type of recurrent interpersonal problems found in his or her personal history. Several basic mechanisms characterize psychody-namic approaches to intervention. The first is the provision of a so-called *holding environ-ment* for the patient in the structure and process of the treatment. In general, the therapist strives to provide the elements of *good enough parenting* in interactions with the patient, typically along the dimensions of appropriate warmth, control, and socializa-tion. The therapist is characterized by em-pathic availability, reliability and consistency, tolerance of regressive behavior, and support of individuation. By creating *conditions of safety* based on a specific person's needs, the therapist allows the child to more openly engage in self-examination. Moreover, the therapist pays special attention to acting in such a way as to reverse a current or earlier pattern of maladaptive caretaking on the part of parents. The degree to which therapy succeeds in providing a corrective holding environment for the child or adolescent is the degree to which the patient is enabled to understand and experience his or her true feelings, needs, impulses, and wishes and the conflicts between them and to attempt a resolution of those conflicts.

The second vehicle for psychodynamic in-tervention is centered more on the patient's behavior both in and out of the session. The actions and experiences of the child are clar-ified and interpreted to varying degrees in order to facilitate awareness of the determi-nants of experience; support and encourage-ment are offered to assist youth in dealing with previously hidden dimensions of expe-rience. In particular, the patient is helped to become aware of the relationships between past experiences (typically with caretakers) and current experiences, and the degree to which those past experiences have a distort-ing or maladaptive effect on one's current behavior. Such distortions often include those involving the therapist, such as trans-ference, which is the degree to which the child responds to the therapist based not on

---

Table 29–1. PSYCHODYNAMIC ISSUES IN CHILDREN'S PSYCHIATRIC PROBLEMS

Affect management
Impulse control
Attachments and losses
Independence and dependence
Self-esteem and competence
Recurrent interpersonal difficulties

his or her actual behavior but rather on overlearned patterns that are derived from earlier experiences with parents. Transference phenomena are important because they are actual experiences shared by both patient and therapist; thus, they are particularly vivid and salient learning experiences for patients.

Several weaknesses characterize the psychodynamic approach to treatment. First, it tends to view a patient's intrapsychic conflicts as the primary force in determining a child's psychiatric disorder; this is clearly an overestimation of their significance. Additionally, it places too much reliance on the therapeutic relationship as a nondirective influence in effecting change in a child's presenting problems. Psychodynamic approaches overvalue the effect of insight to actually change problematic conditions in a child's life. Knowledge without direction in actually implementing the behavioral change necessary typically leaves the child without the means of knowing how to act in a more adaptive manner.

COGNITIVE-BEHAVIORAL APPROACH TO TREATING CHILDREN'S PSYCHIATRIC DISORDERS

Cognitive-behavioral therapy (CBT) is rooted in social learning theory, which emphasizes that adaptive and maladaptive behavior is learned through both active and passive interactions with the environment, particularly social interactions. CBT postulates a reciprocal interaction among environmental events, thoughts and feelings, and behavior. Each of these domains is assumed to impact on the others. Thus, intervention can be effectively targeted at any of the three areas. CBT is a particularly empowering clinical orientation in its assertion that persons can gain greater control over their lives by changing some aspect of themselves or their environment.

CBT is based on a number of assumptions. First, CBT distinguishes between past determinants (e.g., initiating or causal factors) and current determinants (e.g., maintaining or perpetuating factors) of a presenting problem; in contrast to psychodynamic perspectives, CBT emphasizes the latter factors. Consequently, cognitive-behavioral strategies are concerned with a focus on directly changing

maladaptive behavior. Additionally, CBT advocates ongoing assessment of a disorder or problem to determine the effectiveness of treatment and thus to allow modification of treatment strategies and tactics. *Collaborative empiricism* is a term often applied to characterize CBT; the notion is that therapist and patient work together to evaluate the problem, select potential solutions, and test the value of these behavioral and cognitive solutions in the patient's natural environment. The emphasis of CBT is inherently a rational, problem-solving one, as well as a psychoeducational one, in which patients are typically taught a number of specific cognitive and behavioral skills.

A number of characteristics are common to most CBT interventions; these features are presented in Table 29–2. Presenting problems are defined in terms that can be understood by both child and therapist. These provide the child with hope and a sense of control and suggest specific cognitive-behavioral interventions. Patients are taught self-change skills: to identify and decide on a particular behavior to change, to assess their current level of functioning in that area (e.g., baseline performance), and to identify potential triggers and consequences of their behavior. More specifically, children are taught to break down global concerns into smaller, graduated subgoals in order to direct the course of treatment and to guarantee successful mastery; thus subgoals are defined that are both specific and attainable. CBT relies heavily on the use of verbal and written contracts by which patients agree to try certain courses of action between treatment sessions. CBT is predicated on the belief that the child's activities outside the treatment session are at least as important as in-session interactions. Thus, changes in thoughts, feelings, and behavior are viewed as occurring primarily as the child is able to experiment with new ways of being and behaving in real life situations and not simply in the therapy session.

Consequently, CBT involves extensive re-

Table 29–2. CHARACTERISTICS OF COGNITIVE-BEHAVIOR THERAPY WITH CHILDREN

Shared rationale	Contracting
Self-change skills	Homework
Goal definition	Directive therapist
Graduated mastery experiences	

liance on homework or home-practice where patients can test clinical hypotheses. These practice opportunities allow them to gather information about their beliefs and behavior and to experiment with different ways of behaving and interpreting events. Material and social rewards and, gradually, self-praise, are used to motivate patients and provide reinforcement for accomplishment of homework assignments and more general treatment goals. The role of the therapist in CBT is an active, directive one, providing "here and now" explanations of problem behaviors as well as prescriptions for modifying thoughts, behaviors, or situations. Treatment sessions are predominantly devoted to problem-solving specific areas of difficulty for the patient, teaching him or her specific skills to remediate problems, and reviewing previous efforts at cognitive or behavioral change.

There are limitations in the cognitive-behavioral perspective on treatment. Generally, CBT therapists have not viewed the relationship between the therapist and the patient as a primary means of understanding or influencing the patient's problems. However, given that the relationship between patient and therapist has been demonstrated to be important, particularly for children, this orientation unnecessarily minimizes this particular means of reaching treatment goals. Moreover, by adopting an exclusively rational approach to psychotherapy, CBT assumes that patients will simply enact the skills taught in treatment. Clinical experience regarding the lack of compliance with homework demonstrates that factors such as intrapsychic conflicts interfere with a patient's willingness or ability to begin thinking or behaving in a different manner.

MULTIDIMENSIONAL PSYCHOTHERAPY: INTEGRATING PSYCHODYNAMIC AND COGNITIVE-BEHAVIORAL APPROACHES

A multidimensional intervention for children and adolescents takes advantage of the strengths of both psychodynamic and CBT strategies. Interpretations and explanations of current problems and psychiatric disorders based on psychodynamic principles are employed in helping children and their parents in understanding the source of dysfunctional behavior and directing the remainder of the

intervention. Additionally, the provision of a holding environment and interpretations of psychological issues outside the awareness of the child and of transference phenomena can play an important role in the treatment process. At the same time, child patients usually need specific and direct remediation in a number of areas of behavioral and cognitive life skills. They need to learn and practice these adaptive skills to compensate for the fact that their maladaptive behavior is typically overlearned and overused. However, children benefit from the conditions of safety demonstrated in a holding environment in order to overcome their anxieties about behaving in new ways. An understanding of intrapsychic conflicts better enables a therapist to appreciate the complex difficulties, including resistance, a child may evidence in enacting new cognitive and behavioral skills. Insight into the intrapsychic conflicts can motivate children to comply with assignments and take risks in making behavioral changes, in part, by providing a rationale for the basis of maladaptive behavior.

Multidimensional treatment thus involves an appreciation of the importance of past-based internalized conflicts and the significance of the relationship between the child patient and clinician. However, the primary focus of such treatment is in facilitating awareness of the primary factors involved in maintaining and exacerbating a child's problems in present, everyday life and then working with the child to change those factors. Thus, the central work of treatment is to identify and modify environmental factors, cognitions, and behaviors that are critical to the causation and maintenance of the child's disorder. Specific cognitive-behavioral interventions for a particular child's presenting problems are identified through assessment of the interaction of environmental events, the child's thoughts and feelings, and his or her behavior. The emphasis of this assessment is on identifying the *function* of these factors in the child's experience.

In determining the relative value of an insight-oriented approach to psychotherapy, Weiner (1986) has distinguished between two levels of psychotherapeutic intervention based on the psychological maturity of the patient. Repressive psychotherapy is used with persons who have little capacity or motivation for self-awareness or when exploration of unconscious materials is potentially disequilibrating. Treatment goals include enhancing reality-testing, reducing involvement in magical thinking, and teaching impulse-control and affect regulation. The focus of intervention is on current behavior, the development of the patient's strengths, active cultivation of a positive therapeutic relationship, and promotion of identification with the therapist. While the therapist's understanding of the child's disorder is informed by psychodynamic principles, treatment strategies are primarily present oriented and cognitive behavioral. Repressive psychotherapy is often the level of intervention appropriate for children with conduct disorders, substance abuse, and borderline personality disorder.

For patients with greater psychological resources, a more traditional ego-supportive approach can be employed. The clinician encourages patients to be aware of, and responsible for, their feelings and behavior. Maladaptive psychological defenses (e.g., denial, projection, rationalization) are confronted and interpreted. Direct feedback regarding interpersonal behavior, both in and out of the session, is used, particularly regarding distorted perceptions of the therapist. The therapist models self-acceptance and responsibility for his or her own behavior. Overall, the goal is to facilitate the development of insight into patterns of interpersonal relationships as a means of directing and motivating cognitive and behavioral change.

Behavioral Interventions

A variety of behavioral procedures are employed with children to change the quality of their interactions with their environment. It is worth noting that most behavioral, as well as cognitive, techniques are simply more structured, "purified" approaches found in the everyday repertoire of effective parents. Much of what cognitive-behavioral approaches accomplish, in effect, is the socialization or resocialization of children whose actions or thinking is maladaptive. Detailed descriptions of many cognitive and behavioral tactics are presented by Barth (1986), Bornstein and Kazdin (1985), Hersen and Van Hasselt (1985), and Meyers and Craig-

head (1984). A list of behavioral interventions is found in Table 29–3.

A primary means of determining what aspects of the child's life are in need of changing is through self-monitoring. This process involves having the child or a parent monitor events, usually on a daily basis. They also track or rate the nature and degree of specific emotions such as anger, sadness, anxiety, or guilt and the content of their thoughts. An example of a self-monitoring form is presented in Figure 29–2; any combination of events, thoughts, and feelings can be used. Younger children are asked to rate their feelings on a one- to five-point scale, while adolescents rate their affects on a nine-point scale. Self-monitoring accomplishes a number of goals. First, it helps children to identify specific emotional determinants of their cognitions and behavior and to appreciate the degree of emotional response to environmental events and thoughts. Second, it helps the child pinpoint which characteristics of themselves and their environment are related to their problems; these conditions then become the targets of specific skills remediation or environmental modification. Third, heightened self-awareness can, in and of itself, be sufficient for patients to begin to change and control their behavior; that is, self-awareness is a reactive procedure. Thus, monitoring one's mood and daily events can often lead to an improvement in mood. Finally, self-monitoring provides an ongoing assessment of the effect of treatment; in this way, if specific interventions are not having the desired effect, the therapist can change or modify clinical strategies to improve the eventual outcome of treatment.

Several different types of relaxation training can be used to teach children and adoles-

Table 29–3. BEHAVIORAL INTERVENTIONS WITH CHILDREN
Self-monitoring
Relaxation training
Systematic desensitization
In vivo desensitization
Modeling
Positive practice
Changing contingencies
Shaping
Reinforcing alternative responses
Social skills
Assertiveness training
Negotiation skills

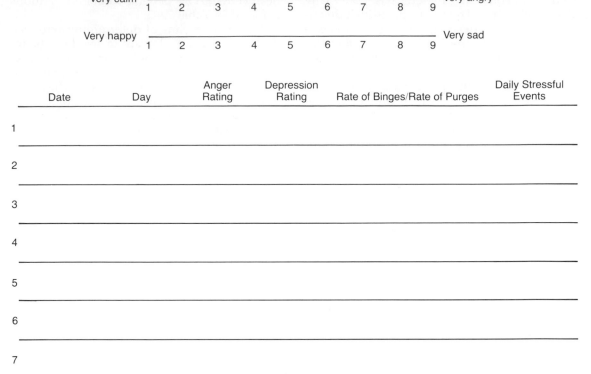

Figure 29–2. Sample self-monitoring form (for a patient with bulimia nervosa).

cents to self-regulate anxiety, anger, or tension. They can be encouraged to take advantage of natural relaxers such as hot baths, exercise, or music. Youth can be taught to be more calm in actual tension-producing situations by identifying these conditions and their triggers and relaxing before-hand, using either deep-breathing or positive mental imagery. Desensitization procedures are those that use gradual, hierarchical exposure to feared or disturbing experiences either in imagination (systematic desensitization) or in reality (in vivo desensitization) paired with relaxation. In fact, this is a more focused procedure for what has typically been the content of traditional psychotherapy (e.g., repeated graduated discussions of what a child fears).

A variety of modeling experiences can be used to instruct a child in more adaptive approaches to his or her areas of difficulty. Symbolic modeling involves the presentation of a model through film or videotape, while covert modeling has a person imagine a model performing some relevant behaviors. In live modeling, a child actually observes a person engage in the desired actions. Finally,

participant modeling consists of having the child first observe a model (e.g., therapist or peer) demonstrate adaptive behavior and then imitate and practice the observed action. Structured, graduated competent behaviors are learned and practiced, initially in session and then out of session in real-life situations. Positive practice involves having a child repeat the physical movements of a desired behavioral sequence a number of times and is useful in breaking well-ingrained habits.

The use of contingencies is a well-known feature of behavioral approaches. Arranging positive contingencies (commonly referred to as rewards) can encourage children and adolescents to change maladaptive behaviors and try novel, more competent approaches to problem situations. Initially, material rewards are used in conjunction with social praise with the hope that, over time, social rewards, and eventually self-rewards, will be sufficient to maintain new behavior. Shaping is a technique that involves rewarding or praising behaviors that gradually approach competent or desired responses. Reinforcing alternative responses, which are incompatible with a previously preferred response, is the least restrictive means of reducing undesirable behavior. Administering rewards in the context of a point program is one of the most systematic approaches to changing a child's behavior. Points are assigned for the child's performing some desired behaviors and are redeemed at the end of the day and/or week for successfully behaving in more adaptive ways. Withdrawing desired consequences is an initial approach to changing negative or maladaptive behavior. Total or selective ignoring of mild, negative behavior can be effective, although usually not without some temporary intensification of the target behavior on the child's part. Imposing prearranged response costs following undesirable behavior, such as withdrawal of a pleasure, privilege, or earned points, or the performance of additional chores, is a particularly effective means of changing problem behavior. The application of a well-designed time-out procedure removes the child from a reinforcing environment or removes rewarding experiences from the child and has been proven effective at reducing and eliminating many negative behaviors. Unfortunately, many parents have attempted misinformed, half-hearted versions of time-out without success and need to be persuaded and coached to apply it in a comprehensive manner.

Social skills represent a particularly important focus of behavioral approaches to treatment. The interpersonal realm is a central area of human behavior, and many children and adolescents with psychiatric disorders have distinct problems interacting with peers and adults. Social skills training involves teaching children more adaptive ways of behaving with others and operates at various levels of social dysfunction. Typically, social skills involve instruction and modeling on the part of the therapist and behavioral rehearsal on the part of the patient, followed by feedback and practice both in and out of the session. Seriously disturbed children often need attention directed toward nonverbal and paralinguistic aspects of social interaction, such as making eye contact and voice tone or coaching in skills to initiate and maintain conversation. Communication skills in effectively sending and receiving informational and emotional messages are appropriate for many youth. In particular, many psychiatrically disturbed adolescents benefit from some variant of assertiveness training

to enhance their ability to communicate their needs and desires directly and openly. Many children and adolescents have difficulty with circumscribed areas of social interaction (e.g., heterosocial interaction, peer pressure), and treatment can be directed at remediating these particular social problems.

Finally, a great number of adolescents and their families are troubled by an inability to resolve the often inevitable conflicts of social interaction. Teaching these families negotiation and conflict-management skills can be one of the most important accomplishments of any treatment of adolescent disorders, particularly since conflict tends to magnify the effect of many psychiatric symptoms. Detailed descriptions of negotiation procedures are presented in Barth (1986) and Robin (1979). Most conflict-management procedures involve (1) teaching participants more effective communication skills; (2) encouraging attention to each participant's perspective; (3) generating multiple possible solutions; (4) evaluating short- and long-term consequences of possible solutions; and (5) emphasizing the importance of compromises and contracting.

Cognitive Interventions

To a certain extent, cognitive therapies can be viewed as derivative of the psychodynamic perspective. Both approaches call attention to the powerful effect of certain beliefs that distort a person's interactions with the world. However, cognitive therapy downplays the significance of the historical roots of those beliefs. Rather, this approach emphasizes the current effect of those beliefs and the use of modifying thoughts as they are expressed in daily behavior. The premise of most cognitive therapies is that a patient's reaction or response to some trigger event (as an environmental change) is a function of how the experience is expected, perceived, evaluated, and attributed. These different types of cognitive processes provide events with their particular meaning and are themselves influenced by underlying core beliefs that patients have about themselves and the world. When children's and adolescent's responses to the environment appear nonnormative or irrational, it suggests that their cognitive processes are disturbed, typically as a result of such maladaptive core beliefs.

Patients may be aware or unaware of these underlying pathogenic beliefs or of their effect on their cognitive processes. Cognitive therapy is the process of facilitating a patient's awareness of dysfunctional cognitive processes and underlying pathogenic beliefs and then changing both processes and beliefs to be more accurate and/or adaptive. Specific cognitive interventions are listed in Table 29–4.

The basic strategy for cognitive therapy begins with having children and adolescents monitor their own negative thoughts in addition to affects and daily events. Initially, with the therapist's assistance and later on their own, patients are taught to articulate their expectations, perceptions, evaluations, and attributions. Next, they are trained to examine the evidence for the validity of their negative thoughts, both intellectually and through behavioral testing. Through a "socratic dialogue" and prompting, a child is assisted in correcting cognitive distortions and in developing more realistic and appropriate thought patterns. This process is termed cognitive modification. Principles of rational-emotive therapy (RET) can be employed to more systematically address more central or underlying pathogenic beliefs (e.g., "I'm a no good child"). Bernard and Joyce (1984) provide an overview of the application of RET to the psychiatric problems of children. In employing RET, the child can be taught to complete an A-B-C-D exercise, an example of which is presented in Figure 29–3. First, they identify an upsetting, "activating" event (A) and an emotional consequence (C). Second, they consider what negative belief or interpretation (B) would lead from the event to the particular feeling they experienced. Last, the child is assisted in disputing (D) irrational decisions or beliefs—those that involve catastrophizing, overgeneralization, and dichotomous think-

ing. A variety of cognitive therapy techniques, many of which can be adapted to children and adolescents, are described by McMullin (1986).

In addition to correcting cognitive distortions, therapy can aim to remediate so-called cognitive absences or deficiencies when a youth appears unable to engage in some cognitive process. Kendall and Braswell (1985) describe a well-researched program designed to teach impulsive children to become more reflective and gain self-control. Treatment components of self-control therapy include repeated sessions where children are taught to define the problem, select an approach to its solution, focus their attention on problem-solving, and self-evaluate their performance. Therapists act like coaches, verbally and behaviorally modeling task performance skills. Self-instruction has been used in other ways. To assist youth in developing cognitive processes to mediate disturbing emotional reactions such as anxiety or anger, they can be taught coping self-statements to help them prepare for and confront a stressor and to cope with being emotionally overwhelmed. Examples of coping self-statements used in anxiety or anger-inoculation are found in Meichenbaum (1985) and Novaco (1975, 1979). Research has indicated that many children with so-called externalizing disorders show deficits in their ability to be empathic and, more generally, in demonstrating interpersonal understanding. To counter these deficiencies, Selman (1980) has developed and studied a program to teach children to develop their ability in perspective taking.

Many children with psychiatric disorders evidence impairment in general problem-solving skills. Consequently, when they encounter stress and conflict, their maladaptive response tends to be inappropriate and ineffective. Thus, these children can be taught steps to more successful problem solving. These include problem definition and formulation and the generation of multiple possible solutions. Next, children are taught decision making: to estimate the probable consequences of different alternative solutions and choose the consequence with the best combination of desirability and probability. Finally, the patient is encouraged to enact the solution, to test its outcome, and, if necessary, to select another solution. Spivack and Shure (1974) have developed and

---

Table 29–4. COGNITIVE INTERVENTIONS WITH CHILDREN

Self-monitoring
Cognitive modification
Rational-emotive therapy
Self-control therapy
Perspective-taking skills
Anxiety/anger inoculation (coping self-statements)
Problem-solving skills
Interpersonal cognitive problem-solving
Self-esteem exercises

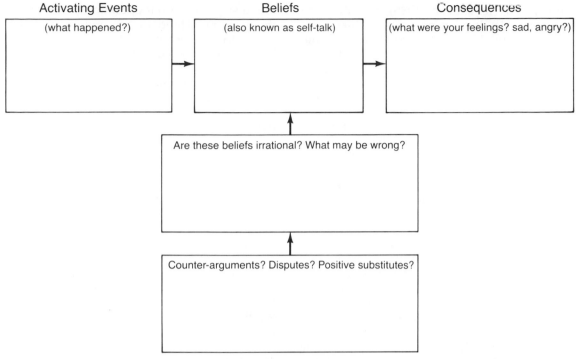

***Figure 29–3.** The A-B-C-D method.*

tested a program to teach children interpersonal cognitive problem solving (ICPS). ICPS emphasizes the acquisition of five cognitive skills: (1) the analysis of social behavior in terms of cause and effect; (2) the ability to generate multiple solutions to social problems; (3) the ability to consider both short- and long-term social consequences in decision making; (4) the ability to view a problem situation from the perspective of others; and (5) the ability to develop a step-by-step plan to reach a given social end and to cope with obstacles that might occur.

For many children referred to mental health professionals, low self-esteem is a common and critical factor. McKay and Fanning (1987) describe a number of strategies for identifying and remediating self-esteem issues in adults that are easily modified for use with children and adolescents. Initially, exercises can be used to help youth identify and monitor their pathogenic "critical voice," to identify the kind of cognitive distortions involved, and to dispute those distortions. A self-concept inventory is employed to assess a variety of areas central to self-image; these are then grouped according to strengths and weaknesses. Weaknesses are then reworded to be less perjorative and self-demeaning.

Finally, another self-concept inventory is developed that is both more positive and more realistic; the child is encouraged to practice using this new self-script. A variety of other approaches are presented that can be very useful in helping to build the self-esteem of children and adolescents with a variety of presenting problems.

DEVELOPMENTAL CONSIDERATIONS IN THE TREATMENT OF CHILDREN AND ADOLESCENTS

Psychotherapy with children and adolescents is necessarily different from that conducted with adults. In general, these differences are based on the fact that younger persons are in the process of developing basic life skills and beliefs to a much greater extent than adults; not only must developmental tasks be taken into account but the very existence or evolution of basic cognitive and affective skills must be carefully considered. Many failures in the treatment of children and adolescents are based on an ignorance of the principles of child development and of current advances in the knowledge of developmental psychology. Both Harter

(1983) and Achenbach (1986) provide good reviews of developmental considerations necessary in the effective treatment of children with psychiatric problems. Interventions with children and adolescents must be developmentally informed, particularly with regard to cognitive, affective, and social development.

To begin with, most youth are not self-referred. Often they do not acknowledge or even conceive of themselves as having a problem. Relatedly, they do not always look to a therapist as an ally; in fact, more often than not a therapist is initially perceived as an agent of a social institution such as parents, schools, or the court system. Children and early adolescents, in particular, do not possess much capacity for abstract thinking. Consequently, they may have difficulty in using interpretations of defense mechanisms or of hidden motivations. Interpretations should be specific, concrete, and practical. Similarly, younger persons demonstrate limitations in causal inference, in differentiating between situational and dispositional determinants of behavior, in appreciating emotional complexity, and in perspective-taking. Children only begin to acquire the ability to self-observe and become self-conscious in middle childhood.

Thus, psychotherapy of this population must attend to these developmental issues. Treatment does not have to be greatly reconstructive; rather, it should be developmentally expansive and growth oriented. Interventions should focus more on the consequences of behavior than on its motivation. The impact of immediate experiences can be so great for a child that the actual relationship with a therapist can, at times, be more important and effective than any specific intervention. Given the tendency of children to be rooted in the present, themes and accomplishments may not carry over from session to session; therefore, considerable refocusing and reiteration of therapeutic themes and achievements is necessary and should be accompanied by encouragements for out-of-session practice.

Adolescents present their own unique features, which are best acknowledged in order to provide effective psychotherapy. Adolescents will often remain silent for relatively long periods of time or refuse to discuss certain topics. Again, adolescents (as well as many adults) will not have attained the cognitive stage of formal operations; thus, their thoughts may tend to be concrete and oriented to the present. They may be more likely to discuss current events or interests in their lives, as opposed to targeting more "clinically substantial" phenomena (e.g., feelings and fantasies). Adolescents are often sensitive to probing questions and may experience interpretations as criticism. They may be fearful of self-exposure, are often easily overwhelmed by increased awareness of affects and impulses, and may resort to more primitive defenses such as denial or avoidance of therapy. Adolescents are often disturbed by heightened, albeit temporary, dependence on a therapist. In general, adolescents may have difficulty establishing a trusting relationship with a therapist.

A number of suggestions can be made in working with adolescents (Awad 1981; Rossman 1982). First, one must attempt to reduce the threat posed by being in psychotherapy. Establishing oneself as independent of the referral source (e.g., court or parents) is an important beginning. It is useful to predict and validate the adolescent's initial mistrust and suspicions. The potential benefits of psychotherapy should be discussed to clarify any magical or devaluing fantasies the adolescent may possess. A therapeutic alliance is most often developed by empathically addressing the emotional distress that underlies the presenting problem. As Meeks (1986) has argued, "the key to establishing a therapeutic alliance resides in the careful and systematic interpretation of affective states as they present early in the treatment process." In addition, the clinician must establish clear boundaries with parents regarding the confidentiality of sessions. The therapist should cultivate an active clinical posture, assisting the adolescent out of long silences with "open-ended" or "multiple-choice" questions. Greater tolerance of noncompliance and other testing behavior, at least initially, opens the door to pursuing the potential meaning of or solving such behavior. A collaborative atmosphere can be created by being attuned to the patient's interests and concerns and by developing a rationale for intervention procedures. By alternating between problem-oriented discussion and more informal conversations, one communicates that the patient is seen as a whole person and not simply as a problem. In turn, this sets the stage for exploration of more emotionally laden or complex issues. More effective psychotherapy typically results from focusing on one or two themes per session and assigning specific and concrete homework assignments.

THE RELATIONSHIP BETWEEN PSYCHOSOCIAL AND PHARMACOLOGIC INTERVENTIONS

It is worth commenting on the relationship of psychotherapy and psychopharmacologic interventions. The latter are playing an increasingly important role in the treatment of children and adolescents. *However, it should be a rare circumstance in which medicines are employed in the absence of an ongoing therapeutic relationship.* Moreover, psychotherapies offer a number of advantages either when applied on their own or in conjunction with pharmacologic agents. First, psychological interventions typically offer patients and their families new behavioral skills and new ways of thinking about themselves. Often, this can empower patients and their families by providing evidence that they can confront and change problematic situations. Second, the combination of psychotherapy with medication can significantly decrease the dropout rate from outpatient treatment. It can facilitate compliance with medical regimens. In addition, in its application to a child's social system, psychotherapy can modify predisposing or etiologically critical interactions by restructuring the content of these problematic interactions. Finally, children or adolescents who either refuse or cannot take medication, or who do not respond to adequate trials of medicine, may respond to psychotherapy.

TIME-LIMITED PSYCHOTHERAPY WITH CHILDREN AND ADOLESCENTS

With recent changes in the mental health system, increasing constraints have been imposed on the length of treatment. Growing pressure exists to provide treatment for patients in briefer periods of time than has been traditional. Most treatment experiences are actually short-term; a variety of studies have indicated that the majority of patients, including children, remain in treatment for approximately 6 months or less. In part, this

is due to a number of patients and families who elect to discontinue treatment prematurely, at least from the clinician's perspective. Nonetheless, it becomes incumbent on the practitioner to anticipate and plan for a briefer duration of treatment, to organize interventions so that they will be maximally effective in a specified length of time. Moreover, the available evidence regarding planned, time-limited psychotherapy actually indicates that it has certain advantages over time-unlimited, longer-term psychotherapy. Studies have demonstrated that when patients know that treatment is time limited, they display more motivation and take more risks during psychotherapy and are less likely to drop out of treatment. Termination becomes less problematic because it has been anticipated and scheduled from the onset of treatment.

Relatively little attention has been directed toward the practice of time-limited psychotherapy with children and adolescents. Butcher and Koss (1978) have described the common elements of brief treatment. They include specific and limited goals; focused interventions to reach those goals; activity and directedness on the part of the therapist; rapid assessment and clinical formulation; and special attention toward developing a therapeutic relationship with the patient. Given this description, it is apparent that a multidimensional approach to psychotherapy is well suited for conducting treatment for children within a time-limited framework.

Time-limited treatment begins with an attempt to delimit the presenting problem and, thus, the scope of treatment. Treatment goals are determined by weighing the most central issues for the child or family against the time available for treatment and the types of clinical strategies applicable within the time framework. Both skill deficits and psychodynamic issues are appropriate choices for target goals. Peterlin and Sloves (1985) discuss the formulation of treatment goals in time-limited treatment of children. In particular, they advocate the development of a central *theme* as the focus of therapy in order to orient both therapist and patient to the purpose of psychotherapy. A central theme attempts to make the child's presenting problem understandable by identifying it as a developmentally based maladaptive self-solution to past and current difficulties. This sets the stage for defining a treatment contract centered on working with the child to acquire more competent ways of functioning in the world. Peterlin and Sloves also suggest that the length of treatment be specified in advance to the child. The patient is encouraged to "count down" the remaining number of sessions, which heightens the child's attention to, and involvement in, psychotherapy. They recommend that the central theme be restated at the beginning of each session with the child to serve as a bridge between the current and previous sessions and thus to refocus the child to the goals of treatment. In general, time-limited psychotherapy with children and adolescents cultivates the existing competencies of a child or his or her family; it attempts to extend those strengths to new arenas or to teach new ways of coping with past or current problems.

In conducting time-limited treatments, a number of modifications in the treatment process can be made to maximize the effectiveness of the actual contact time. Patients and their families can be asked to complete a variety of self-report assessments prior to and following appointment times to facilitate the definition of treatment goals and the selection of strategies. Prior to treatment, children and their parents can benefit from an orientation as to what the psychotherapy process involves; by creating shared, realistic expectations of psychotherapy, resistances can be reduced and treatment can be made more effective. Similarly, treatment contracts can reduce later resistance by including agreements to set aside time for homework assignments on a daily basis. The length and frequency of sessions can be modified in several ways. Half-hour sessions can be appropriate for children or resistant adolescents; such sessions can be used more frequently (e.g., twice a week) in the beginning of psychotherapy. Later, longer sessions can be chosen or sessions can be scheduled for every 2 weeks. During these times, homework assignments are especially important in extending the impact of treatment. In a different vein, skills are often best taught in groups; agencies or treatment centers can often be well-served by employing paraprofessionals to conduct skills training groups.

In both time-limited as well as time-unlimited psychotherapy, attention must be paid to the maintenance of treatment gains. In order to minimize the recurrence of symptomatic behavior, several strategies can be applied. First, patients can be taught to expect slips or recurrences of problematic behavior or situations. On this basis, before the end of treatment, they can be taught to identify early signs of difficulty and be helped to develop a relapse plan of strategies to cope with future challenges. Clinicians should schedule "booster sessions" after the end of treatment, typically after 1, 3, and 6 month periods; such sessions can be used to consolidate treatment gains and to intervene if relapse seems possible. Similarly, evidence suggests that former patients, especially those with chronic or recurrent disorders, should be encouraged to schedule biannual "mental health check-ups" in order to solve new or ongoing difficulties, as well as to reinforce previously successful coping efforts; again, a small dose of prevention can go a long way. Often, it can be useful to help patients connect to diagnosis-based support groups in the community or to various activities that will provide more general social integration and support, all of which can enhance the momentum of improvement and decrease the likelihood of relapse.

TREATMENT PLANNING

Selecting intervention strategies that best match the particular needs of the child patient is a task of singular importance. Yet as Looney (1984) has noted, the clinician's expertise in treatment planning often lags behind skills in diagnosis and treatment procedures. To some degree, this issue is a function of the multidetermined, developmentally influenced nature of children's psychiatric disorders. However, it also reflects the lack of systematic study, and thus the clinician's understanding, of the mechanism and outcome of treatment plans. According to Looney (1984), two basic tasks are central to treatment planning. First, the clinician must clearly formulate the problem(s) so that the aims of intervention are apparent and understandable. Second, based on the goals of treatment, appropriate therapeutic strategies must be selected. The choice of treatment modalities is based on those that would be "most powerful, most rapid, least restrictive, and most cost-effective."

As simple as this process might be considered to be, the reality of treatment planning is quite difficult. On a descriptive level, most children who present to clinicians are characterized by psychiatric co-morbidity (the presence of more than one disorder). Following from the multidetermined nature of psychiatric disorders, biological, familial, and psychological factors must be delineated and evaluated. Complicating matters is that children and adolescents often have difficulty in describing their experience or history, while many parents are poor judges of their children's inner experiences or have incomplete knowledge of their children's actual life experiences (e.g., abuse).

Significant elements of the treatment planning process are represented in Figure 29–4. Three components of assessment seem minimally necessary for an adequate formulation of a child's presenting problem. A relatively thorough *diagnostic assessment* must occur, in which the child and parents are interviewed separately regarding the past and present occurrence of the range of possible psychiatric disorders. In this way, more subtle and perhaps less easily reported disorders (e.g., depressions) can be discovered and considered alongside more obvious ones (e.g., conduct disorders). The onset and duration of all current disorders must be determined to establish a chronology of disorders, including the primary/secondary distinction. In addition, the likely chronicity and recurrence of disorders must be considered. A *functional assessment* must also take place to identify the unique factors in a child's psychiatric disorders, particularly the everyday events that impinge on and exacerbate the disorders. Such an assessment is typically best accomplished by assigning parents to monitor their own behavior and that of their child and by assigning children to self-monitor their own thoughts, feelings, and behaviors. As a result

of the functional assessment, a clinician should be able to identify specific environmental factors and cognitive and behavioral skill deficits, as well as to clarify potential pathogenic belief structures. Last, a careful *psychosocial history* should be collected. In particular, three areas should be considered. First, the structure and continuity of important relationships (e.g., deaths, separations, or absences of caretakers) should be explored. Second, the quality of early relations with caretakers should be evaluated; to what degree were caretakers able to provide appropriate control, warmth, empathy, encouragement of individuality, and adequate socialization experiences? Third, recurrent patterns of interpersonal difficulty should be identified and the contribution of thematic influences and skills deficits be determined. Finally, a careful family history of psychopathology can also be helpful in identifying the child's psychosocial and genetic vulnerabilities.

Most children with psychiatric disorders present a number of potential targets of intervention. Given the multidetermined nature of these disorders, it is possible to conceptualize intervention from several different theoretical perspectives. In attempting to decide which psychotherapeutic strategies will work best with a particular child's presenting problems, it is useful to systematically articulate the range of potential clinical concerns. For example, a clinician might evaluate the degree to which the psychodynamic issues raised in Table 29–1 and the behavioral and cognitive skills listed in Tables 29–3 and 29–4 apply to a given child (a similar listing of potential family issues should also be considered). Each issue or skill that applies to a child should be rated in terms of its relative

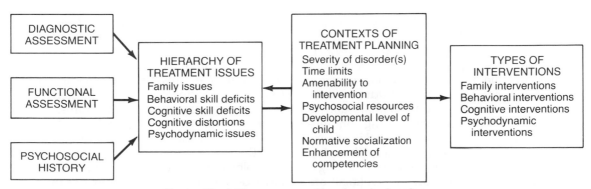

Figure 29–4. The process of treatment planning.

importance to the child's well-being (e.g., on a 5-point scale). In this way, one obtains an initial hierarchy of treatment goals.

Once treatment goals have been identified, the selection of treatment strategies must be considered within several contexts. First, the availability of a child (or family) for psychotherapy may be limited by health insurance, agency policy, or the child (or family's) own preferences; thus, time limits may play a role in determining the type and sequence of psychotherapeutic interventions. The amenability of the child (or family) to treatment, including the ego-syntonicity of symptoms, or simply resistance, will influence the nature and range of treatment goals. For children (and families) who resist the entry into psychotherapy, more limited goals can be set or the length of treatment extended. Another consideration in treatment planning must be the available resources, both social and psychological, to which the child and the parents have access. Typically, the more resources the clients possess, the less likely a clinician will need to devote considerable time to skills training. The developmental level of the child may also be an important factor to consider. In general, the younger the child, the more likely a clinician is to emphasize work with the parents and to train them to become more effective in interacting with their child. In this manner, the parents become the mediators of the clinician's expertise, which constitutes a more naturalistic intervention than individual psychotherapy with the child. With older children, one is more likely to work either exclusively with the child or iteratively with the child and the parents.

Two other related factors need to be considered in developing a treatment plan. First, a primary consideration must always be to either maintain or reconnect a child to mainstream socialization experiences. Normative social interaction is critical to establishing a platform for learning age-appropriate skills and magnifying the impact of psychotherapy. Thus, keeping a child in school or out of the juvenile justice system is usually a significant goal in treating children. Similarly, psychotherapy should usually aim to be explicitly competency-creating or -enhancing. Particular psychologic skills (e.g., self-soothing, problem-solving, delaying gratification, identifying different feelings, understanding determinants of feelings) are essential for adequate functioning. Conse-

quently, regardless of what other treatment goals are selected, psychotherapy should strive to leave children more competent as a result of intervention. A similar argument is offered by Strayhorn (1988), who has described a competence-based intervention/prevention model for work with children.

The selection of particular intervention strategies is a function of evaluating the hierarchy of potential treatment issues within the contextual factors just described. More discrete treatment goals will generally be defined by the following "constraining factors": time limits on the length of psychotherapy, resistant patients, limited resources, and younger children. In a similar manner, the contexts of the treatment process also play a significant role in determining the selection of specific psychotherapy approaches or strategies. In the presence of one or more constraining factors, interventions will tend to be more direct and symptom focused. Thus, the psychotherapy will be more likely to emphasize behavioral and cognitive skills for either the child or parents. In extreme cases of high constraints, treatment may consist primarily of crisis intervention and immediate problem solving. With fewer constraining factors present, treatment is more likely to include and emphasize more psychodynamic elements contributing to the disorders. In addition, resistance on the part of the child may preclude behavioral or cognitive interventions. In this case, regardless of constraining factors, a psychodynamic approach to clarifying and reducing the resistance may often remain the only means of establishing an alliance with the defensive patient. With such an alliance in place, a platform exists for more directive interventions.

DEPRESSIVE DISORDERS AND SUICIDAL BEHAVIOR

Relatively little has been written about the treatment of depressed and suicidal youth. Clarke and Lewinsohn (1985) modified a CBT program developed for adult depressives to apply to adolescents; Lewinsohn and his associates (1987) showed that this program was effective in improving depressive disorders in adolescents. Bedrosian and Epstein (1984) have described the application of cognitive therapy to depressed and suicidal youth, while Ross and Motto (1984) have reported on a competency-promoting group for suicidal adolescents. Bemporad (1978) and Pfeffer (1986) have written on psychodynamic principles in treating depressed and suicidal youth, respectively.

Treatment may begin with attempts to help the child understand determinants of his or her distress. Self-monitoring of negative affect (e.g., sadness, anger, or guilt) and everyday events, behavior, or thoughts helps the person to learn to label his or her affects and to realize that daily moods are a function of current events and how he or she interprets the meaning of those events. In particular, sources of frustration or conflict can be distinguished. From a psychodynamic perspective, goals include identifying the emotional effects of recent disappointments, social losses, or conflicts. Historical events that might have led a child to develop a sensitivity to such events could be highlighted. Conflicts over experiencing or verbalizing anger, often based in a fear of rejection, are explored as a source of emotional numbness or anhedonia.

Any of a number of behavioral tactics can be used to mobilize the depressed youth, with the particular order matched to the needs or situation of each patient. Typically, relaxation exercises are useful in the early part of treatment and, in addition, help to build a therapeutic alliance. Across a number of areas of activity, graduated efforts can be initiated to build a sense of mastery or competence. Scheduling activities to reduce time spent passively or engaging in ruminations is usually important; after school time, weekends, and sometimes evenings can be planned in advance. In particular, working with the child or adolescent to first identify potential pleasant activities and then to systematically increase the number of such activities on a daily basis can be a turning point in the lifting of the depression. As the youth's activity level increases, including social interactions, interpersonal problems will become more apparent. Evaluating and remediating basic communication skills is an initial step. Training and practice in assertiveness are often central components in treatment of depressives; learning to appropriately express anger and frustration helps such children to overcome their fears that such behavior will "destroy" relationships. Many depressed children benefit from focusing on coping with a variety of specific social situations (e.g., dating, handling criticism).

Heightened self-criticism and low self-esteem are targets of the cognitive interventions. Again, self-monitoring helps to clarify the role that a person's perceptions and interpretations play in mediating affect and life events. The self-esteem exercises described earlier become an essential component of intervention. Identifying the often unrealistic wishes or expectations a youth possesses can reveal the basis for their sense of personal inadequacy. For many children, working through impossible wishes and perfectionistic standards is a slow process akin to grieving. They must learn to establish their self-worth as independent of "perfect performance." Moreover, they need help in learning to accept their mistakes as educational instead of viewing them as signs of personal failure. Additionally, psychotherapy can identify the extent to which youthful depressives rely on others for approval and the degree of guilt and shame that perceived disapproval elicits. The clinician can help the patient to challenge the core belief that universal approval is "necessary" through hypothesis-testing in the child's daily environment.

A number of transference issues are common in treating depressed and suicidal youth. Such patients are often characterized by their perception of the therapist as critical or hostile or as cold and indifferent. They may alternate between an idealizing and dependent posture and one of devaluation and distance. Depressed and suicidal children are typically highly sensitive to concerns of abandonment and loss. Consequently, breaks in treatment or termination require focused attention in the psychotherapy.

ATTENTION-DEFICIT HYPERACTIVITY DISORDER AND LEARNING DISORDERS

Stimulant medication is the most frequently used treatment for attention-deficit hyperactivity disorder (ADHD), typically impacting on concentration and sustained attention, which, in turn, improve compliance and social interaction; academic achievement does not usually change with pharmacologic interventions (Barkley 1985). Some evidence suggests that cognitive training to improve attention or cognitive style may not add substantially to the effects of medication (e.g., Abikoff and Gittleman 1985; Brown et al.

1985). These results should not be construed to suggest that all children or adolescents with ADHD do not benefit from cognitive training or, more broadly, psychotherapy. Several studies have demonstrated that as many as half of all children treated for ADHD later develop serious emotional and behavioral disorders. Moreover, studies of both suicide attempters and suicide completers indicate that a diagnosis of ADHD is a risk factor for such events. Results of investigations of individualized, multimodal treatment for children with ADHD (e.g., Satterfield et al. 1987) have demonstrated the positive consequences of interventions that affect the child's life as a whole.

A number of cognitive-behavioral programs that use self-instructional procedures to teach children to "stop and think" have been developed. The most studied of these interventions is that described by Kendall and Braswell (1985). Characterized by a problem-solving orientation, this approach was discussed earlier. As summarized by Barkley (1985), self-control training of this sort involves teaching the child to (1) recognize problem situations; (2) delay responding in the problem setting; (3) use self-directed speech to clarify the problem, generate possible solutions, and evaluate short- and long-term consequences of these possibilities; (4) choose and implement the best solution; and (5) evaluate the outcome and the process of self-control. It is worth noting that the major difficulty with such therapy is the effort that must be devoted to generalization, both across problems and across situations. To be successful, treatment requires substantial practice of these skills in different settings (e.g., home, school) with supportive supervision by parents and teachers.

The presence of ADHD can have a major effect on the quality of relationships with parents, siblings, teachers, and peers. The cognitive deficits of these children tend to lead to developmental lags, particularly in social skills. Noncompliance or poor rule-governed behavior is a central feature of children with ADHD; as a result, they are often disliked and, consequently, rejected. Furthermore, noncompliance is the steppingstone to antisocial behavior that often co-occurs with ADHD. Barkley (1981, 1985) has presented a parent-training program designed especially for youth with ADHD. This program uses education and training in contingency management (rewards and response-costs) to help parents control their children's behavior both at home and at school.

Within an individual psychotherapy, several things can be done to facilitate remediating the child's deficits. Santostefano (1984) has described cognitive control therapy that involves teaching children who have difficulties "learning how to learn" how to regulate affects and aggression. Communication and other social skills can be taught. In particular, children can be taught to "de-escalate" potentially negative encounters with parents and teachers (Barkley 1985). Youth with ADHD can often benefit from training in perspective-taking and applying problem-solving skills to social situations. Finding a peer model can also be used to help these children refine their social interaction. Given the history of failure experiences and social conflict, it is the odd child with ADHD who does not suffer from diminished self-esteem. Graduated competence experiences can help to build a sense of mastery, while the self-esteem exercises described earlier can be helpful in identifying an accurate self-concept for the youngster. Traditional cognitive therapy can help children with ADHD (and their families) to modify their expectations of academic and social achievement to better match their abilities. Furthermore, such tactics can be used to increase a child's tolerance for appreciating the necessity of working hard in order to be more successful.

CONDUCT DISORDERS

Disorders characterized by noncompliance, aggression, and other antisocial behaviors constitute the largest source of referrals to juvenile mental health practitioners. Moreover, they are also the most difficult to treat. Recent conceptualizations of conduct disorders suggest that they are multiply-determined phenomena and may best be regarded in terms of a chronic disease model (e.g., Kazdin 1987). As such, they may be thought of as conditions that require continued intervention over the period of childhood and adolescence directed at home, school, and other situations.

Patterson (1982) has identified several critical characteristics of antisocial children that have implications for treatment. First, he notes that such youth are egocentric and tend to act on the basis of short-term gains versus long-term consequences. In addition, they are distinguished by a generally low level of competent and adaptive behaviors. Finally, antisocial youth tend to be hyporesponsive to social approval or disapproval. The early familial experiences of these children are often of the type in which adults reward antisocial behavior with attention and/or are unable or unwilling to set limits on inappropriate behaviors. Consequently, these children often learn to be coercive in their social interactions. They fail to learn more prosocial ways of resolving conflict and how to tolerate frustration and negative affects. With a limited repertoire of socially adaptive behaviors, relative to their peers, these children experience increasing social conflict with both adults and peers, followed by rejection. Excluded from further opportunities to acquire more refined prosocial behavior, they demonstrate a developmental drift toward increased maladaptive and deviant behavior.

A primary goal of treatment with antisocial youth is to create or re-create parental control over their behavior. With younger children (aged 13 and under), parent management training (PMT) is the intervention of choice. Kazdin (1987) succinctly describes it as follows:

PMT is designed to alter the pattern of interchanges between parent and child so that prosocial rather than coercive behavior is directly reinforced and supported within the family. This requires developing several parenting behaviors, such as establishing the rules for the child to follow, providing positive reinforcement for appropriate behavior, delivering mild forms of punishment to suppress behavior, and negotiating compromises.

More detailed descriptions of PMT are found in Barth (1986) and Chamberlain and Patterson (1985).

Regarding antisocial adolescents, functional family therapy (FFT) (Barton and Alexander 1981) is clearly the most effective intervention to date. FFT incorporates both systems and behavioral perspectives in its treatment strategies. Family members are assisted in identifying the functions that antisocial behavior serves and in considering alternate ways of construing the maladaptive behavior of the patient. Intervention strategies emphasize the development of communication and problem-solving skills. In partic-

ular, negotiation and contracting skills are taught and practiced to facilitate the resolution of conflicts and the identification of interpersonal solutions. Privileges are exchanged for increases in adaptive behavior and attempts are made to build the relationship between parents and the antisocial child.

Interventions directed primarily at the parents or the family as a whole are the starting point for the treatment of antisocial youth. They provide the framework for containing and reversing the drift toward maladaptive behavior. While in some cases this may constitute a sufficient intervention, additional psychotherapy for the youth will often be required. The lack of appropriate parenting behaviors early on can have a host of implications for intrapsychic problems, prosocial behavior, and cognitive deficits and distortions. In addition, some parents or families, as a result of their degree of dysfunction, may not be viable candidates for PMT or FFT.

Antisocial youth are typically lacking in a variety of behavioral and cognitive skills. A prominent area of deficiency is in modulating affect, especially anger or rage. Early in the psychotherapy, emphasis on affect labeling can be employed to differentiate the range and intensity of negative affects. Feindler and Ecton (1986) describe a comprehensive program for teaching adolescents anger control in both group and individual therapy modalities. Relaxation training can be used to induce a calmer stance toward negotiating with frustrating situations. Self-monitoring arousing situations (e.g., conflict, teasing) can help to pinpoint the environmental and cognitive determinants of anger. Self-instructional approaches, involving the teaching and practice of positive coping self-statements, are used to assist the child or adolescent in containing distress at provocation or frustration. Standard RET can also be applied to reduce the degree of upset antisocial youth experience. Key irrational ideas for such children include "it's awful not to get what you want" and "I can't stand it; it's not fair." Learning to identify and dispute such beliefs can help to improve the ability to tolerate frustration. General problem-solving skills are useful in providing antisocial youths the tools to identify and evaluate problems and potential solutions as well as to develop a plan for self-change.

Aggressive children have a tendency to

attribute hostile intent to others; this type of attribution is particularly true if social cues are ambiguous. Reattribution training consists of working with the youngster to make accurate assessments of the motivation of others and to refrain from attributing their own self-interested or aggressive intent to other persons. Since aggressive youth tend to be less empathic, teaching them perspective-taking can increase their empathy and reduce antisocial behavior. Shure and Spivack's (1982) interpersonal cognitive problem-solving skills (ICPS) can be useful with antisocial youth. The generation of multiple possible solutions to problems, anticipation of short- and long-term consequences, and the development of a realistic plan to reach particular ends, which includes some thought to possible obstacles, can all provide youth with effective means to meet their needs.

Finally, given the antisocial youth's increasing reliance on coercive or aggressive strategies in social interaction, most will benefit from social skills training. Learning prosocial behavior can break the vicious spiral of maladaptive behavior that increasingly haunts these children. Communication skills are often a good place to begin, followed by role-playing and practice of appropriate social behaviors.

PERVASIVE DEVELOPMENTAL DISORDERS

Pervasive developmental disorders, including autistic disorder, are characterized by severe impairment in skills required for reciprocal communication and social interaction. Because of the behavioral manifestations of this type of psychopathology, clinical interventions emphasize operant management of maladaptive behavior. The development of self-care, language, and interpersonal skills is emphasized, while attempts are made to decrease self-stimulatory, self-injurious, and other behaviors interfering with more adaptive functioning. Detailed accounts of these procedures are provided by Dunlap and co-workers (1985); Egel and associates (1980); and Lovaas (1981). Cognitive approaches or insight-oriented treatments are not typically employed with autistic children, although they may be useful for family members in helping them to cope with the difficulties involved in raising an autistic

child. Research on pervasive developmental disorders indicates that early diagnosis can facilitate better treatment outcome since interventions initiated at younger ages are more likely to have lasting effects on behavior. Careful assessment is especially important in targeting specific behavioral excesses and deficits for intervention.

In implementing an intervention program, the clinician must enlist the help of persons from all of the child's environmental settings. Teachers, parents, and babysitters must all be familiar with specific reinforcement procedures; techniques for this type of training are described elsewhere (Harris 1983; Koegel et al. 1982). If interventions are administered in the clinic only, behavioral changes are not likely to generalize across different settings or be maintained on a long-term basis. Generalization across settings can be facilitated by employing a consistent set of cues and rewards.

When behavioral management is initiated, the clinician must first identify effective reinforcers. Although praise and other forms of social reinforcement are the most appropriate incentives to use in a long-term program, food, music, toys, or other tangible rewards may be necessary in the beginning of instruction. After the selection of reinforcers, the clinician can begin by teaching the child instructional skills necessary to participate in the behavioral management procedures. These skills include maintaining eye contact, listening, sitting still, and imitating the instructor. Successive approximations of these behaviors should be rewarded as the clinician slowly shapes the child's actions to enable continued training in these and other skills.

Self-stimulation, self-injury, and tantrums pose significant obstacles to the acquisition of adaptive behaviors. Thus, intervention programs often require an early focus on decreasing these types of actions. Since the child's acting out often reflects an inability to communicate his or her needs in more healthy forms of expression, communication skills training should be initiated early in treatment; acquisition of communication strategies can lead to a reduction in destructive actions.

Maladaptive behaviors can be targeted more directly by identifying and altering circumstances that reinforce them. Many self-stimulatory behaviors are rewarding to the child because of their intrinsic sensory consequences. If these reinforcing elements are reduced, the accompanying behavior often decreases. If a child enjoys repetitive banging of objects on a table, for example, carpeting the table can reduce the reinforcement derived from the auditory stimulation.

Self-stimulation and self-injurious behaviors can also be reinforcing for the attention, concern, and affection they elicit from others. In these cases, social reinforcement should be eliminated and the behavior ignored. Because of the severity of some forms of self-injurious behaviors, however, this technique may be dangerous in some cases. Also, social reinforcement may not be the primary rewarding aspect of the behavior. If so, other procedures can be implemented. For instance, the child can be rewarded every time he or she engages in nonstimulatory actions. The clinician can also teach the child competing or distracting behaviors. With a child who engages in object-banging, for example, learning to play a simple musical instrument can provide a healthier form of auditory stimulation. Overcorrection procedures in which the child is taught to substitute behaviors incompatible with his or her self-stimulation patterns have also proven successful in suppressing maladaptive actions (Foxx and Azrin 1973). For instance, a child who repetitively claps his or her hands can be led through a series of arm movements incompatible with clapping. After the behavior has been successfully eliminated, verbal warnings can be substituted for the competing motor sequence. Physical exercise can also be beneficial in reducing self-stimulation.

Time-out or seclusion can be effective in decreasing the frequency of tantrums since these strategies remove the reinforcing elements of the tantrum behavior (e.g., attention). Time-out will not be successful, however, if it either allows the child to engage in a pleasurable self-stimulatory behavior or enables the child to escape from a demanding task. In these cases, time-out may actually increase tantrums. If a certain task or situation elicits tantrums, the clinician should first determine whether the demands on the child exceed his or her present capabilities; expectations should be modified if necessary. The tantrum can be extinguished by presenting the task requirement and allowing the child to have a tantrum without removing him or her from the situation or the demand for compliance. After initial increases in frequency and intensity, tantrum behaviors will usually decrease.

As disruptive behaviors decline, the child can begin to acquire self-care and social skills. These behaviors are usually taught using nonverbal imitation of the instructor paired with positive reinforcement. Rewarding successive approximations can be helpful in eliciting behaviors more difficult for the child. Chaining, in which longer sequences of behavior are broken down into components, also facilitates skill acquisition. In dressing one's self, for example, the child first learns the simplest procedures involved in putting on and removing articles of clothing. These skills are practiced and reinforced until the child is quite comfortable with them. Button and zipper manipulations and other more complicated tasks are introduced independently at a later time. Ultimately, the child is taught how to combine all previously learned behaviors.

Like skills training, language instruction involves breaking down tasks into manageable components (Lovaas 1977). Usually, the child is first taught to imitate the therapist's vocalizations. This procedure often involves shaping with successive approximations. If the child is mute, for example, he or she is first rewarded for any audible vocalization; later, the child is reinforced for how similar his or her vocalization is to the instructor's. In vocabulary acquisition, which follows, the child is taught how to label objects and associate them with specific words. Concrete nouns should be emphasized first, followed by verbs and adjectives that can be easily demonstrated. Eventually, instruction proceeds to more abstract vocabulary and conversational speech. For children with severe verbal deficits, sign language can be used as an alternative means of communication. Given the likelihood of multiple settings, it is often most useful to use the therapist for language training while parents and teachers help the child practice new skills.

TREATMENT OF MEDICAL ILLNESSES AND SOMATOFORM DISORDERS

Although conventional medical procedures are usually the primary forms of intervention, children with chronic physical conditions including asthma, arthritis, seizures, recurrent abdominal pain, and headaches often respond to adjunct psychological treatment. Psychological techniques can be used to help the child cope with and prevent the onset of symptoms; in some cases, behavioral interventions may even reduce the frequency of symptom episodes.

Cognitive and behavioral interventions typically aim both to alter perception of pain and to regulate its intensity. Cognitive procedures focus primarily on altering the child's subjective experience of painful episodes. A number of techniques have been used to reduce the discomfort of symptoms, including relaxation training, meditation, and self-hypnosis (e.g., Jay et al. 1987). These procedures are believed to be beneficial in their reduction of anxiety and muscle tension, both of which are thought to exacerbate the pain experience.

Mental imagery is another useful technique and serves the dual purpose of inducing relaxation and providing vivid distraction material. At first, the clinician may wish to conduct guided mental imagery in which the child imagines himself or herself experiencing a pleasurable event, visiting an exciting place, or having a conversation with a favorite hero or celebrity. The clinician should encourage the child to experience the imagery in as many sensory domains as possible (visual, auditory, kinesthetic). After children learn to visualize without the clinician's descriptions, they can use imagery techniques by themselves outside sessions.

Children can also be taught coping self-statements to say to themselves at the onset of symptoms. These self-scripts can be distracting (e.g., "I remember the time when I went to the zoo"), self-efficacious (e.g., "I know I can handle this"), or self-soothing (e.g., "The pain will pass soon; I just have to wait it out a little longer") in content. It is helpful to have the child write and practice these statements during symptom-free periods in order to have them well rehearsed.

Biofeedback techniques can also help children with somatic complaints. Thermal or electromyographic feedback paired with autogenic training has been found to allow for some regulation of symptoms (Williamson et al. 1985). After learning these procedures and recognizing symptom cues, the child may also be able to prevent or modulate the onset of pain.

Stress management training can also contribute to prevention of symptoms. The child

is taught to use relaxation strategies on sensing idiosyncratic cues of symptom onset. Since stress often precipitates these physical complications, anxiety reduction may result in a decrease in their frequency. Self-monitoring and problem-solving procedures can be used to identify and alter environmental stressors. Assertiveness training may also be helpful in modifying stressful circumstances.

Behavioral contingency strategies have also been used to manage physical symptoms. Assuming physical conditions can be maintained by psychological factors, clinicians can teach parents to provide positive reinforcement for both symptom-free periods and adaptive behaviors, while minimizing secondary gains (e.g., attention or escape from unpleasant environments) the child might receive for being symptomatic. While the clinician should certainly sympathize with the child, excessive empathy and responsiveness to symptoms may inadvertently interfere with recovery. According to proponents of this approach, these techniques are suitable for truly organic as well as psychologically based symptoms (Devaney and Nelson 1986). For example, seizure-free periods are appropriately rewarded since pseudoseizures frequently coexist with real seizures; such reinforcement can reduce pseudoseizure activity.

Psychodynamic issues should be explored in conjunction with other types of interventions. Such issues include those underlying symptomatology and those arising in response to physical symptoms. In considering underlying issues, the clinician should evaluate the degree to which physical pain may reflect the internalization of affect. From a psychodynamic perspective, symptoms most often signify the redirection and internalization of anger felt toward others and/or distress in response to environmental circumstances. The child should be encouraged to openly discuss fears, concerns, and feelings. In order to learn about the functional role that physical symptoms may play in their life, children can be instructed to evaluate their affective states immediately prior to the onset of pain. Efforts should also be made to help the child seek nurturance directly from others instead of indirectly through sympathy received from their symptomatology.

Psychodynamic issues arising in response to chronic pain conditions include a sense of one's self as "flawed," anger about enduring uncomfortable symptoms, and feelings of being victimized or betrayed by one's own body. Experiencing a profound sense of being "out of control" of one's health, some children attempt to create an illusion of control through manipulation of other factors: social approval, food intake, exercise, or superstitious behaviors. Other children may externalize their anger in the form of aggression. Treatment should focus on encouraging the children to express emotions in more adaptive ways, while gaining insight into the current and historical determinants of their behaviors.

Somatoform Disorders

Although many of the techniques described above are relevant to the treatment of somatoform disorders (e.g., minimizing secondary gain, identifying and reducing environmental stress, training in biofeedback and relaxation techniques), the etiologic significance of psychological factors often necessitates more intensive psychotherapeutic interventions. Detailed descriptions of treatment strategies are presented by Shapiro and Rosenfeld (1987).

Childhood somatoform disorders often arise in family systems that deny the necessity and value of emotional experiences and that encourage the channeling of emotional needs into physical symptoms. Thus, parent training in the management of their child's symptoms is crucial. Explicit instructions in ways of minimizing secondary gains must be provided for parents (for instance, that the child must make up all work missed at school). Within this context, collaboration with school staff can also be helpful. Often, family therapy is necessary since parents tend to focus on dealing with their child's symptoms instead of confronting more difficult issues in their own lives. Therapy should direct the family system to become more adept at problem solving and expressing emotional issues directly instead of covertly through the child's physical symptoms.

One of the most critical aspects of interventions with somatoform children and their parents involves how feedback about a diagnostic evaluation is presented. If a somatoform disorder is even a remote possibility, parents should be told at the outset that psychological factors can produce and exacerbate symptoms believed to be organic. If no physical etiology is detected, it should be emphasized to the parents that the child's pain and symptoms are very real; the psychological origin of symptoms need not imply that they are "all in the head" of the child. If the clinician seems to invalidate the child's symptoms in any way, the parents are likely to seek medical evaluation from another clinician and thus delay appropriate treatment for the child.

Individual treatment with the child should take the function of the physical symptom into account. Instead of viewing the physical complaints as "fake," the clinician must attempt to emphatically understand what purpose(s) they serve for the child. The eradication of symptoms without consideration of their importance to the child, and without providing alternative coping strategies, may leave the youngster without a way of dealing with emotional stress.

Interventions should assist the child in identifying and coping with anxiety and other affects more directly. They can be helped to cope with distress through more adaptive avenues rather than somatizing by learning problem-solving skills, discussing feelings with others, and using coping self-statements. The child should be instructed to view the onset of his or her symptoms as a cue to deal with psychological issues that may have gone unrecognized; instead of focusing on the physical pain, the child should ask himself or herself, "Is something upsetting me? How can I handle it directly?"

The clinician should explore the possible occurrence and meaning of a psychological trauma (e.g., an incident of physical or sexual abuse) as a precipitant to the onset of symptoms. Transference issues with somatoform cases include excessive approval seeking, conflict avoidance, and denial of negative affect. The child should be encouraged to experiment with anger and other "unacceptable" feelings in his or her relationship with the clinician; for example, the child can learn that direct expression of anger toward the therapist does not result in rejection or abandonment.

In addition to relaxation and biofeedback training, patients with somatoform disorders often respond to physical therapy. Direct suggestion has also been extremely useful in managing somatoform symptoms. For example, the child should be told that his or her symptoms will show gradual reduction in frequency and severity. Future-tense statements should imply that the child will be symptom free. Direct suggestion can also be made using hypnosis or self-hypnosis techniques.

Medical Procedures

Since surgery and other medical procedures are confusing and upsetting to children, psychological techniques can help to minimize the child's discomfort and to increase compliance during the treatment process (Kendall and Braswell 1986). Behavioral contingency strategies can be used to reinforce cooperation during examinations and more painful procedures. The clinician can employ brief time intervals for which the child is rewarded (e.g., a sticker every 5 minutes) instead of delaying reinforcement until the end of the session. The child can also be provided with positive reinforcement for behaviors incompatible with distress (e.g., deep breathing exercises, muscle relaxation, story telling).

Modeling procedures are quite useful in a medical context. If a child is to undergo surgery, for example, he or she can watch a videotape of a child coping successfully with their fears of the same medical procedures. In order to answer questions, allay fears, and provide the child with a stronger sense of control, the clinician might familiarize the child with aspects of the procedure a few days ahead of time. Allowing the child to try on a surgical mask, use a stethoscope, and identify the location of the operating room can increase his or her sense of mastery and subsequent ability to cope with the distress. Similarly, behavioral rehearsal with dolls, stuffed animals, or even drawings can facilitate a better psychological recovery. For instance, the child can view a demonstration of the preoperative process on a doll. By using such "play techniques" prior to the procedure, the clinician can help the child to understand the experience more clearly. Children frequently have highly inaccurate or irrational conceptions about medical procedures (e.g., that they are having surgery because they have "done something wrong"); if the child is encouraged to articulate these beliefs, the clinician can help to correct them. Both prior to and following

medical procedures, encouraging the child to play with dolls and medical instruments allows him or her to work through feelings of anger, fear, and helplessness.

Relaxation and imagery techniques are useful in distracting the child during painful procedures. The clinician can also employ self-instructional training in which the child learns to recite distracting scripts (describing a favorite birthday party, for example) or self-efficacious statements (telling one's self "you are being brave, this will be over soon") out loud or silently.

If treatment requires compliance on the part of the child (such as taking regular medication), the clinician can work collaboratively with the child and parents to set up a plan ahead of time to facilitate adherence. For instance, the clinician and child might agree to a systematic reward system of compliant behavior. Involving the child in this process can increase subsequent levels of behavioral compliance.

CHILD ABUSE

The definition of child physical and sexual abuse varies depending on the sociocultural, psychological, and legal context. When working with abuse cases, the clinician often takes on additional roles, including legal evaluator, expert witness, and family mediator. For instance, the clinician might be involved in deciding whether the child should be removed from the household (if the perpetrator is a family member) and placed into foster care. Each clinician must familiarize himself or herself with relevant laws of the state and maintain an awareness of legal responsibilities involved in both assessment and treatment of child abuse.

In assessing abuse issues, the clinician should convey an open-minded, nonjudgmental attitude to the parent(s). The stance of parents of abused children is often highly defensive and suspicious. If the perpetrator is not a parent, the child's mother and father may still exhibit defensiveness for having failed to prevent the abuse. In providing an accepting environment, the clinician enables the parents to express their frustrations and present their own perspective(s). It can be helpful for the clinician to describe abuse in terms of a behavioral perspective, explaining that abusive practices are an acquired behavior that can be changed with appropriate learning opportunities.

Motivation and compliance are two common obstacles to treatment since the parent often is not in the clinical setting by choice. In order to facilitate treatment success, the clinician and parents can collaborate in developing a treatment contract. By allowing parents to help establish intervention goals and set time limits, the clinician encourages a more active involvement of family members in treatment.

Abusive Parents

Structured programs for changing parents' abusive behavior have emphasized psychoeducational and cognitive-behavioral approaches to treatment (Kelly 1983; Wolfe et al. 1981). The goals of parent training include (1) creating personal and social controls that inhibit violence toward family members; (2) facilitating social support; and (3) reducing environmental stress that interferes with parenting.

Central components of interventions directed toward the abusive parent are educational. In order to correct inaccurate beliefs regarding a child's cognitive and behavioral capabilities, parents are provided with information about both child development and optimal parenting practices. Perspective-taking from the child's point of view is also encouraged. Parents should be instructed in appropriate and effective child management techniques, similar to those described earlier for conduct disorders. For instance, they are encouraged to provide positive reinforcement in response to desirable behaviors while ignoring or punishing inappropriate actions on the child's part. Nonviolent punishment techniques, including time-out procedures, are discussed and practiced. Interventions can also include information about how to improve the more subtle quality of parental interactions with the child. In providing written and verbal instruction, the clinician must keep the educational level of the parents in mind. Modeling can be used as an instructional tool (e.g., having parents view videotapes of adults coping effectively with a difficult child). Once information and examples have been provided, intervention procedures should focus on implementing new behaviors. Parents can participate in

behavioral rehearsal through role-playing exercises with direct feedback from the clinician during or following real-life interactions. Due to the artificiality of the clinical setting, however, conducting these feedback sessions in the home is important in generalizing behavioral changes to critical environments.

Parent training can also involve skills instruction in anger management, including problem-solving and relaxation strategies (e.g., DeNicola and Sandler, 1980). Once these techniques are acquired, parents can self-monitor their progress. Specific problem situations should be identified in order to make necessary modifications. Another significant component of parental interventions involves the facilitation of social support. This element is most often encouraged by conducting group treatment programs; group members can both support and learn from each other. In general, parents should be encouraged to seek supportive relationships with other adults. Social skills instruction may be useful in furthering this goal.

Since the family system is strained by a person's own problems, a number of adjunct interventions relevant to the abusive parent should be considered. Often, the parent's family of origin was abusive itself. Referring a parent for individual psychotherapy can be helpful and necessary in many cases. Similarly, the clinician should consider the possibility of adding more extensive family therapy to the intervention program. Marital counseling is often appropriate. Finally, attention should be directed toward the family's financial situation. Referrals to community resources and training in financial management can be helpful in reducing the domestic stress that often serves as the context for child abuse.

Abused Children

Regarding the abused child, the clinician's first responsibility is to evaluate the safety of the child's home environment. Ensuring the child is no longer subjected to abuse often requires the involvement of the local child protection agency. In collaboration with legal advisors, the clinician may also need to restrict the child's contact with the abuser or alleged perpetrator. Early intervention procedures often involve making direct changes in the child's life circumstances. Initially, the clinician must conduct a careful assessment to determine the presence of specific psychiatric disorders; mood and anxiety disorders and substance abuse, for example, are highly prevalent in abused populations.

One of the most critical elements of treatment with abused children is the establishment of a therapeutic alliance. Although the clinician is often pressured to collect assessment data for legal proceedings, the child needs to gain a sense of trust in the clinician before he or she will accurately disclose information. This process may involve a number of introductory sessions before the abuse issue is even raised with the child. Development of a trusting relationship requires consistency, patience, warmth, and empathy on the part of the clinician.

Intervention procedures with abused children often involve substantial educational components. In addition to its emotional impact, abusive behavior often confuses a child. An abuser sometimes tells the youngster falsehoods in order to engender a sense of fear. Such false beliefs should be assessed, identified as false, and corrected. The clinician must explain that, in spite of the shame he or she might feel, the child is not at fault for the abusive act. Sexually abused children need clarification about the appropriateness of sexual behavior.

Sustained abuse usually results in low self-esteem. The cognitive techniques described earlier can be used to challenge and modify a child's sense of worthlessness. Initially, the clinician must identify the child's cognitive distortions through discussion and self-monitoring; opportunities for the child to develop more accurate and adaptive beliefs can then be designed. In particular, reframing, decentering, and reattributional techniques can be used to reduce a child's self-blame.

Although the abuse should in no way be considered the fault of the child, the clinician may find it helpful to identify actions that frequently precipitated abuse; adjustments in these types of interactions are especially important if the child is to remain in the abuser's household. Behavioral contingency programs can be used to alter acting-out patterns.

The abusive act is significant both in itself and within the interpersonal context in which it occurs since the abuser is often a family member, friend, or someone close to the child. Because of the power differential inherent in the abusive relationship, the child will often experience a sense of having been betrayed along with a profound feeling of helplessness.

The abuse victim often experiences conflicted feelings toward an abuser, including both anger and idealization of the perpetrator. Even as their cognitive development allows children to see the abuse incident(s) as a result of the perpetrator's unhealthiness, the abused child may maintain a sense that he or she did something "wrong" or is "flawed" in some way that rendered him or her deserving of the abuse. Instead of minimizing contact with the perpetrator, the child often pursues interactions in which an attempt is made to "prove" himself or herself "worthy" of the adult's affections. Psychodynamic interventions involve identifying and working with these themes. The child should be encouraged to express and work out conflicted feelings of anger, disappointment, betrayal, and the sense of wanting to elicit respect from the perpetrator. As anger toward the perpetrator often intensifies with treatment, the child should be instructed to strike a balance between healthy expressions of rage and self-soothing strategies to modulate the intensity of the affective experience.

Sexual abuse involves a number of specific issues. This type of abuse experience can lead to precocious sexuality, a preoccupation with sexual material, and a sense that one's body can be used to gain affection from others. Due to the child's traumatic sexualization, sexual issues may need to be addressed at an earlier age than the developmental norm. The child should be provided with information and an opportunity to express sexually related concerns and emotions. Approaches to treatment of sexually abused children have been elaborated on by a number of authors, including Jones (1986) and Finkelhor (1984).

In treatment of abused children, transference issues involving trust are most frequent. The clinician must ensure that the therapeutic alliance serves as a healthy example of a trusting relationship. The child's sense of suspiciousness may persist. This issue can be addressed directly. The clinician can also facilitate trust through consistency in behavior; it can also be helpful to set strict guidelines regarding confidentiality of treatment sessions, especially if the abuser was a parent. Because of the nature of the abusive relationship, the child may also display alternating feelings of anger toward and idealization of the clinician. Fears of abandonment are also common. In working with sexually abused children, the clinician may encounter sexual acting-out behavior on the part of the child; in these cases, treatment can focus on more appropriate and healthy ways of asserting interpersonal needs.

ANXIETY DISORDERS

Anxiety disorders involve the experience of anxiety in response to situations of varying specificity: real or imagined separation from a caretaker (separation anxiety disorder); excessive withdrawal from unfamiliar figures (avoidance disorder); and excessive worrying and self-consciousness regarding a range of circumstances (overanxious disorder). In other cases, both focal and more generalized concerns may be associated with obsessive preoccupations and repetitive, stereotypical behavior (obsessive-compulsive disorder). Beck and Emery (1985) have suggested a conceptual framework that speaks to a common mechanism of action across anxiety disorders. Their model views fear, the cognitive appraisal of a potentially threatening stimulus as "dangerous," as the critical core of anxiety disorders. The degree of fear experienced is influenced by one's evaluation of the nature and likelihood of the threat (primary appraisal) and one's evaluation of the resources available for dealing with it (secondary appraisal). Fears are elicited by exposure or potential exposure to the dangerous conditions; anxiety is viewed as the emotional response to the appraised threat. Typically, the experienced anxiety results in some form of maladaptive coping (e.g., clinging behavior, social withdrawal, compulsions, or avoidance). It is likely that younger patients tend to overestimate the probability and relative danger of undesirable circumstances; they may underestimate their ability or resources to cope with the perceived threat. Moreover, anxiety disorders are best characterized as a vicious circle of self-perpetuation: fears arouse anxiety; anxiety results in hypervigilance, which impairs performance efforts at coping and mastery; and unsuccessful behavior leads to more established attributions that the initial fears were valid. Typically, a child realizes secondary

gains through the avoidance of feared situations (e.g., a child who, by staying home from school, is allowed contact with a parent or watches television).

Clinical as well as epidemiologic reports indicate a commonality among children's pathologic fears. Foremost among these fears is that related to possible rejection or abandonment by caretakers. Subsidiary fears include the fear of disapproval or failure and the fear of a loss of safety or security, including fears of personal injury. It is important to note that fears may be rooted in real experiences of potential loss or threat and, thus, may have a rational basis. Conversely, they may result from a child's developmentally immature perception and evaluation of events and have a more irrational basis. Children are often not aware of, or actively repress, the original circumstances that initiated their fears. In addition, a factor in a child's anxiety disorder may involve fears over the expression of affect, particularly anger, toward a parent or other adult.

Almost all of the available empirical literature on anxiety disorders in children focuses on the treatment of especially discrete fears such as phobias, typically through behavior therapy. Such approaches are reviewed by Carlson and colleagues (1986), Siegel and Ridley-Johnson (1985), and Wells and Vitulano (1985). Unfortunately, little has been written regarding the treatment of more general or diffuse anxiety disorders in children.

Treatment of the anxious child begins with attempts to identify the current conditions that elicit the fear–anxiety response. Self-monitoring of daily events, the degree of anxiety associated with those events, and the thoughts that mediate the anxiety response can begin to help the child understand the determinants of his or her fears. In this way, a child can begin to articulate the nature of what he or she fears. Historical events or circumstances can be referred to as possible sources of fears, thus providing a rationale and meaning for anxious responses in the present. To the extent that current environmental conditions induce fear, such factors need to be addressed. Thus, parents who threaten loss of love or approval or whose continued presence in the home may be questioned because of discord or their own psychiatric impairment may be an appropriate subject for intervention.

Relaxation training can provide a child with a means of regulating a heightened sensitivity to those events. In particular, systematic desensitization or in vivo desensitization is often the best means of addressing discrete irrational fears or the components of those fears. Desensitization can be accomplished simply through repeated discussions of the nature of the child's fears in the therapy session. The thrust of these approaches is to effect a counter-conditioning of the patient's anxiety. In general, exposure to the feared stimulus in real life has been identified as the crucial dimension in the treatment process for anxiety disorders. Consequently, efforts directed at encouraging the child to confront the feared event or social interaction are often an essential part of the psychotherapy. Shaping the child's initial responses to feared stimuli with material rewards and praise (e.g., reinforced practice) can lay the groundwork for graduated mastery of the fear. A variety of modeling approaches (symbolic, imaginary, or participant modeling) can also be employed to assist the patient. Instructing the child in the use of coping self-statements and problem-solving as means of modulating their anxiety can be helpful in their attempts to master their fears. Social skills training, including assertiveness, can prepare the child for more satisfying relationships with both feared adults and peers.

Given the strong cognitive component involved in anxiety disorders, approaches aimed at modifying a child's thinking about undesirable events may be particularly effective. Scheduling "worrying time" can be an effective means of creating some control by the child of obsessive fears; in so doing, one accepts the need to worry but confines the worrying to a particular time and place. Again, self-monitoring thoughts in anxiety-arousing situations can facilitate the identification of maladaptive perceptions, evaluations, attributions, and beliefs. The child can be encouraged to "analyze" the evidence for the fear, to collect additional information, and to test his or her own as well as more adaptive hypotheses. Alternative ways of conceptualizing past and present circumstances can be explored; the child can be asked to "decenter" and examine the situation from a peer or adult's perspective and different attributions can be entertained. In certain cases in which feared stimuli may be invariant or unmodifiable, the patient can be asked to consider the actual consequences of an event's occurrence: how probable is the event? how awful will it be? can one accept or deal with the worst outcome? The RET approach can be applied to teach the child to dispute certain irrational ideas. Common ideas for anxious children and adolescents include "I must do well and be lovable in all respects or I will be rejected"; "I must succeed at all times; to fall short of my standards would prove I'm a failure"; "I can't tolerate any sort of public embarrassment or attention"; "The world is a dangerous place and I must worry constantly to protect myself against future uncertainties"; "I can't stand pain or discomfort; I must be on constant watch to avoid potential anxiety." Finally, anxious children, as a result of their avoidance or their impaired performance, are often characterized by low self-esteem; consequently, exercises directed at remediating a damaged self-concept are an important component of treatment.

In working with anxious children, the therapist must be especially sensitive to providing the patient with a safe environment that is consistent, predictable, and nonjudgmental. Such children are often hypervigilant with regard to the possibility of disapproval, rejection, or separation; they may evidence a tendency to become dependent on the therapist. All of these issues are likely to emerge as transference and may be accompanied by various expressions of hostility at the dependency or perceived threats. With anxious patients, particular attention is often necessary around breaks in the psychotherapy or termination.

ANOREXIA AND BULIMIA NERVOSA

Both anorexia and bulimia nervosa are complex disorders whose etiology reflects multiple pathogenic sources. A vulnerable personality results from the combined, synergistic interaction of particular dysfunctional parenting practices and sociocultural values about the role of females. This vulnerable personality is characterized by a number of psychological deficits: alexithymia, a difficulty in perception and tolerance of affective and visceral states; difficulties in the self-regulation of affect and impulses; perfectionism and an accompanying sense of ineffectiveness; self-esteem that is predominantly contingent on the approval of others; and difficulties in establishing trusting, intimate relationships. For persons with anorexia nervosa, there are also strong fears of maturity and adult status, while for persons with bulimia nervosa, there are difficulties with impulse control across a range of behavioral domains. In the face of the developmental tasks of adolescence, especially separation and individuation, and within a social context that overvalues relative thinness, certain of these vulnerable youth acquire a drive for thinness and/or a fear of being overweight. Subsequently, they adopt rigid dieting practices or a combination of dieting, binges, and purging. These patients' eating disorder behaviors typically evolve to serve a number of secondary functions both intrapsychically (e.g., affect regulation) and intrafamilially (e.g., forced dependence). A significant characteristic of patients with eating disorders is that their symptomatology becomes egosyntonic and, thus, they tend to deny their psychopathology. Moreover, since many patients with both anorexia and bulimia nervosa are in a biological state of starvation, the symptoms of starvation tend to interact with, and exacerbate, their more psychological symptoms.

Given the multiple etiologic factors involved, the psychological treatment of persons with eating disorders must necessarily be multidimensional. In particular, efforts must be directed at remediating the psychological vulnerabilities as well as reversing inappropriate eating behavior. An initial decision must be made as to the necessity of hospitalization; guidelines in this regard are found in Garner and Garfinkel (1984) and Strober and Yager (1984). Currently, the consensus is that many patients with eating disorders can, and should, be treated on an outpatient basis. While recognizing that certain psychological, biological, and familial factors differentiate persons with anorexia nervosa from those with bulimia nervosa, in general, intervention follows the same principle for both disorders.

Psychotherapy begins with an education of both the patient and family as to the multiple origins of eating disorders and the biology of weight regulation and starvation. A primary goal is to redirect the patient and family's attention from a preoccupation with weight to issues concerning emotional disturbance and self-esteem. Given the ego-

syntonicity and denial that characterize the eating disordered patient, early attempts to change the eating behavior will be met with resistance and thus be unsuccessful. Rather, efforts should be directed toward developing a trusting alliance with the patient. This can be accomplished through careful attention toward creating a "holding environment" for the patient where the patient's emotional distress can be clarified and validated. By addressing the patient's pain and sense of inadequacy, the clinician can establish a sense of nonjudgmental care and rapport that, in turn, provides the foundation for the development of trust. The initial phase of psychotherapy involves a collaborative attempt with the patient to develop an understanding of the historical, developmental, and sociocultural roots of the psychological dimensions that underlie the eating disorder. The current manifestations of these factors are highlighted. Toward this end, patients are asked to self-monitor their moods, daily events, and the rates or severity of their eating-disordered behavior; through this means, eating disorder symptoms become connected to (1) affective and self-esteem issues, (2) family interactions, and (3) life events.

Over the course of the psychotherapy, general goals are to help the patient recognize, accept, and act on his or her needs and feelings, to encourage greater introspection as well as a more realistic personal appraisal, to identify intrapsychic conflicts and facilitate their resolution, and to increase understanding of and support efforts at separation and individuation. Transference issues that typically arise include those of trust and intimacy, fear of the clinician's disapproval, particularly for anger or self-perceived mistakes, and fear of both independent functioning as well as dependence.

Once an initial alliance is in place, efforts can be directed toward behavioral treatment tactics and family therapy. The patient can be encouraged to take an "empiric" approach to changing the eating-disordered behavior. Through self-monitoring, he or she typically identifies antecedents of his or her dieting or binges; these cue situations can then be modified or avoided. In addition, the knowledge that a number of the distressing symptoms (e.g., preoccupation with food and weight, dysphoria, and irritability) are a function of the degree of starvation can motivate patients to begin to change their eating patterns. Patients are asked to experiment with eating three regular meals with nutritional balance and increasing caloric content. Adjunct nutritional counseling is often appropriate. Fears of becoming substantially overweight are heightened during attempts at more regulated eating, but their validity can be tested over time. For persons with bulimia nervosa, several tactics can be employed to decrease the binges and vomiting. Self-control of impulsive bulimic behavior can gradually be developed by increased periods of response delay (e.g., delay the behavior for 2 minutes, then 5 minutes, and so forth). The structure of bulimic behavior can be varied by planning binges for atypical times of the day and having the patient choose limited quantities of binge food or less caloric food. In some cases, exposure and response prevention can be employed in which the patient consumes a normal meal but is prevented from purging and then is assisted in dealing with the accompanying distress. Persons with bulimia can be directed to schedule competing behaviors during peak times for binges; in particular, they can select social and enjoyable activities during these times to counteract feelings of isolation and dysphoria.

Other behavioral tactics can be employed to facilitate the eating-disordered patient's recovery. Relaxation training and stress-management (e.g., the development of coping self-statements) can be taught to mediate affect and impulse regulation. Assertiveness and other social skills can be taught to enable the patients to meet their needs and reduce their emotional distress through direct social interaction as opposed to dysfunctional eating behaviors.

Cognitive therapy plays a very important role in the treatment of patients with eating disorders; such tactics can be introduced earlier or later in psychotherapy depending on the particular patient. In general, behavioral changes and cognitive therapy interact, with progress in one area providing opportunity for more success in the other. Initially, patients are asked to articulate the various maladaptive beliefs and assumptions linking beliefs about eating and weight to their eating-disordered behavior. Through a combination of behavioral hypothesis testing, collaborative empiricism, and cognitive disputation, including the A-B-C-D method, patients can develop more accurate and adaptive beliefs about themselves in general as well as more specifically with regard to weight and body shape. In particular, beliefs regarding the sociocultural expectations for females in the areas of weight, shape, appearance, and achievement should be challenged. Patients need to be encouraged to evaluate whether stereotypical images of the ideal female, often conveyed by the popular media, are realistic, healthy, or attainable. For patients who obsess about eating and weight issues, thought interruption or scheduling worrying time can be effective. Self-esteem exercises are especially useful tools to build a healthier self-esteem. Problem-solving approaches, particularly in the social realm, can also be helpful. Body-image distortions are a significant factor in more long-standing cases of eating disorders and can be relatively resistant to treatment; Wooley and Wooley (1984) present a number of strategies for addressing this issue.

At the same time that the individual psychotherapy begins to address behavioral issues with the patient, family therapy can be initiated in earnest. Early sessions with the family can be used to discuss and validate family characteristics and developmental events that may be related to the patient's psychological vulnerabilities. Typically, families of eating-disordered patients need assistance in learning to accept and tolerate emotionality and to resolve conflicts through negotiation as opposed to avoiding or denying them. In addition, family sessions can be directed at identifying and reducing such maladaptive characteristics as enmeshment, intrusiveness, overprotectiveness, and perfectionism. Families are encouraged to demonstrate their acceptance of the patient despite self-perceived inadequacies or differences in values or beliefs. To this end, families are helped to allow the patient to make his or her own choices and, thus, to individuate and separate from the family.

CONCLUSIONS

Psychotherapy can provide effective treatment for most psychiatric disorders of children and adolescents. Clinicians need to develop a sophisticated and integrative perspective regarding the variety of biological, environmental, and psychological processes that interact in the development, maintenance, and recurrence of psychiatric disorders. Similarly, psychotherapists must understand and be able to implement a variety of psychosocial interventions. The most effective psychotherapy will be one that is individualized to the specific needs and circumstances of the specific child or family. However, certain principles of treatment are common among particular populations of children and types of disorders. Development of a core group of personal competencies, such as affect and impulse regulation, problem solving, self-esteem maintenance, and social skills, in most, if not all, dysfunctional children is critical. The challenge for the clinician is to create a competency-enhancing intervention that recognizes and takes account of the specific experiences and meanings that characterize their youthful patients.

References

Abikoff, H., and Gittleman, R. 1985. Hyperactive children treated with stimulants: Is cognitive training a useful adjunct? *Arch. Gen. Psychiatry* 42:953–961.

Achenbach, T.M. 1986. The developmental study of psychopathology: Implications for psychotherapy and behavior change. In Garfield, S.L. and Bergin, A.E. (eds.): *Handbook of Psychotherapy and Behavior Change.* New York: John Wiley & Sons.

Awad, G.A. 1981. The early phase of psychotherapy with antisocial early adolescents. *Can. J. Psychiatry* 26:38–42.

Barkley, R.A. 1985. Attention-deficit disorders. In Bornstein, P.H., and Kazdin, A.E. (eds.): *Handbook of Clinical Behavior Therapy with Children.* Homewood, Ill: Dorsey.

Barkley, R.A. 1981. *Hyperactive Children: A Handbook for Diagnosis and Treatment.* New York: Guilford Press.

Barrett, C.L., Hampe, I.E., and Miller, L.C. 1978. Research on child psychotherapy. In Garfield, S.L., and Bergin, A.E. (eds.): *Handbook of Psychotherapy and Behavior Change: An Empirical Analysis.* New York: Wiley.

Barth, R.P. 1986. *Social and Cognitive Treatment of Children and Adolescents.* San Francisco: Jossey-Bass.

Barton, C., and Alexander, J.F. 1981. Functional family therapy. In Gurman, A.S., and Kniskern, D.P. (eds.): *Handbook of Family Therapy.* New York: Brunner/Mazel.

Beck, A., and Emery, G. 1985. *Cognitive Therapy for Anxiety Disorders.* New York: Basic Books.

Bedrosian, R.C., and Epstein, N. 1984. Cognitive therapy of depressed and suicidal adolescents. In Sudak, H.S., Ford, A.B., and Rushforth, N.B. (eds.): *Suicide in the Young.* Boston: John Wright.

Bemporad, J.R. 1978. Psychotherapy of depression in children and adolescents. In Arieti, S., and Bemporad, J.R. (eds.): *Severe and Mild Depression: The Psychotherapeutic Approach.* New York: Basic Books.

Bernard, M.E., and Joyce, M.R. 1984. *Rational Emotive Therapy with Children and Adolescents.* New York: John Wiley & Sons.

Bornstein, P.H., and Kazdin, A.E. 1985. *Handbook of Clinical Behavior Therapy with Children.* Homewood, Ill.: Dorsey.

Brown, R.T., Wynne, M.E., and Medenis, R. 1985. Methylphenidate and cognitive therapy: A comparison of treatment approaches with hyperactive boys. *J. Abnorm. Child Psychol.* 13.

Butcher, J.N., and Koss, M.P. 1978. Research on brief and crisis-oriented psychotherapies. In Garfield, S.L., and Bergin, A.E. (eds.): *Handbook of Psychotherapy and Behavior Change.* New York: Wiley.

Carlson, C.L., Figueroa, R.G., and Lahey, B.B. 1986. Behavior therapy for childhood anxiety disorders. In Gittleman, R.(ed.): *Anxiety Disorders of Childhood.* New York: Guilford Press.

Casey, R.J., and Berman, J.S. 1985. The outcome of psychotherapy with children. *Psychol. Bull.* 98:388–400.

Chamberlain, P., and Patterson, G.R. 1985. Aggressive behavior in middle childhood. In Shaffer, D., Ehrhardt, A.A., and Greenhill, L.L. (eds.): *The Clinical Guide to Child Psychiatry.* New York: Free Press.

Clarke, G.N., and Lewinsohn, P.M. 1985. *The Coping with Depression Course for Adolescents and Parents.* Unpublished manuscript, University of Oregon, Eugene, Oregon.

DeNicola J., and Sandler J. 1980. Training abusive parents in cognitive-behavioral techniques. *Behav. Ther.* 11:263–270.

Devaney, J.M., and Nelson, R.O. 1986. Behavioral approaches to treatment. In Quay, H.C., and Werry, J.S. (eds.): *Psychopathological Disorders of Childhood.* New York: John Wiley & Sons.

Dunlap, G., Koegel, R.L., and O'Neill, R. 1985. Pervasive developmental disorders. In Bornstein, P.M., and Kazdin, A.E. (eds.): *Handbook of Clinical Behavior Therapy with Children.* Homewood, Ill.: Dorsey.

Egel, A.L., Koegel, R.L., and Schreibman, L. 1980. A review of educational treatment procedures for autistic children. In Mann, L., and Sabitino, D. (eds.): *Fourth Review of Special Education.* New York: Grune & Stratton.

Feindler, E.L., and Ecton, R.B. 1986. *Adolescent Anger Control: Cognitive Behavioral Techniques.* New York: Pergamon.

Finkelhor, D. 1984. *Child Sexual Abuse.* New York: Free Press.

Foxx, R., and Azrin, N. 1973. The elimination of autistic self-stimulatory behavior by overcorrection. *J. Appl. Behav. Anal.* 6:1–14.

Garner, D.M., and Garfinkel, P.E. 1984. *Handbook of Psychotherapy for Anorexia Nervosa and Bulimia.* New York: Guilford Press.

Garfinkel, P.E., and Garner, D.M. 1982. *Anorexia Nervosa: A Multidimensional Perspective.* New York: Brunner/Mazel.

Gries, L.T. 1986. The use of multiple goals in the treatment of foster children with emotional disorders. *Profess. Psychol. Res. Pract.* 17:381–390.

Harris, S.L. 1983. *Families of the Developmentally Disabled: A Guide to Behavioral Intervention.* Elmsford, N.Y.: Pergamon.

Harter, S. 1983. Cognitive-developmental considerations in the conduct of play therapy. In Schaefer, C.E., and O'Conner, K.J. (eds.): *Handbook of Play Therapy.* New York: John Wiley & Sons.

Hersen, M., and Van Hasselt, V.B. 1985. *Behavior Therapy with Children and Adolescents: A Clinical Approach.* New York: John Wiley & Sons.

Jay, S.M., Elliott, C.M., Katz, E., and Siegel S. 1987. Cognitive-behavioral and pharmacologic interventions for children's distress during painful medical procedures. *J. Consult. Clin. Psychol.* 55:860–865.

Jones, D. 1986. Individual psychotherapy for the sexually abused child. *Child Abuse Negl.* 10:377–385.

Kazdin, A.E. 1987. Treatment of antisocial behavior in children: Current status and the future directions. *Psychol. Bull.* 102:187–203.

Kelly, J.A. 1983. *Treating Abusive Families: Intervention Based on Skills Training Principles*. New York: Plenum Press.

Kendall, P.C., and Braswell, L. 1985. *Cognitive Behavioral Therapy for Impulsive Children*. New York: Guilford Press.

Kendall, P.C., and Braswell, L. 1986. Medical applications of cognitive-behavioral interventions with children. *J. Dev. Behav. Pediatr.* 7:257–264.

Koegel, R.L., Schreibman, L., Britten, R., et al. 1982. A comparison of parent training to direct child treatment. In Koegel, R.L., Rinconer, A., and Egel, A.L. (eds.): *Educating and Understanding Autistic Children*. San Diego, Calif.: College-Hill.

Kovacs, M., and Paulauskas, S. 1987. The traditional psychotherapies. In Quay, H.C., and Werry, J.S. (eds.): *Psychopathological Disorders of Childhood*. New York: John Wiley & Sons.

Lewinsohn, P.M., Hopps, H., Williams, J.A., et al. 1987. Cognitive behavioral treatment for depressed adolescents. Paper presented at the annual meeting of the American Academy of Child and Adolescent Psychiatry, Washington, D.C.

Looney, J.G. 1984. Treatment planning and child psychiatry. *J. Am. Acad. Child Psychiatry* 23:529–536.

Lovaas, O.I. 1977. *The Autistic Child: Language Development Through Behavior Modification*. New York: Irvington.

Lovaas, O.I. 1981. *Teaching Developmentally Disabled Children: The Me Book*. Baltimore: University Park Press.

McDermott, J.F., and Char, W.F. 1984. Stage-related models of psychotherapy with children. *J. Am. Acad. Child Psychiatry.* 23:537–543.

McKay, M., and Fanning, P. 1987. *Self-esteem*. Oakland, Calif.: New Harbinger.

McMullin, R.E. 1986. *Handbook of Cognitive Therapy Techniques*. New York: W.W. Norton & Co.

Meeks, J.E. 1986. *The Fragile Alliance*. Malabar, Fla.: R.E. Krieger.

Meichenbaum, D. 1985. *Stress Inoculation Training*. New York: Pergamon.

Meyers, A.W., and Craighead, W.E. 1984. *Cognitive Behavioral Therapy with Children*. New York: Plenum Press.

Novaco, R.W. 1975. *Anger Control: The Development and Evaluation of an Experimental Treatment*. Lexington, Mass.: D.C. Heath & Co.

Novaco, R.W. 1979. The cognitive regulation of anger and stress. In Kendall, P., and Hollon, S. (eds.): *Cognitive-Behavioral Interventions: Research and Procedures*. New York: Academic Press.

Patterson, G.R. 1982. *Coercive Family Process*. Eugene, Ore.: Castalia.

Peterlin, K., and Sloves, R. 1985. Time-limited psychotherapy with children: Central theme and time as major tools. *J. Am. Acad. Child Psychiatry.* 24:788–792.

Pfeffer, C.R. 1986. *The Suicidal Child*. New York: Guilford Press.

Robin, A.L. 1979. Problem-solving communication training: A behavioral approach to the treatment of parent-adolescent conflict. *Am. J. Fam. Ther.* 7:69–82.

Ross, C.P., and Motto, J.A. 1984. Group counseling for suicidal adolescents. In Sudak, H.S., Ford, A.B., and Rushforth, N.B. (eds.): *Suicide in the Young*. Boston: John Wright.

Rossman, P.G. 1982. Psychotherapeutic approaches with depressed, acting out adolescents: Interpretative tactics and their rationale. *Adolesc. Psychiatry.* 455–468.

Rutter, M. 1986. Psychological therapies in child psychiatry: Issues and prospects. In Hersov, L., and Rutter, M., (eds.): *Modern Child Psychiatry*. London: Blackwell Scientific Publications.

Santostefano, S. 1984. Cognitive control therapy with children: Rationale and technique. *Psychotherapy*, 21:76–91.

Satterfield, J.H., Satterfield, B.T., and Schell, A.M. 1987. Therapeutic interventions to prevent delinquency in hyperactive boys. *J. Am. Acad. Child Adolesc. Psychiatry.* 26:56–64.

Selman, R. 1980. *The Development of Interpersonal Understanding*. New York: Academic Press.

Shapiro, E.G., and Rosenfeld, A.A. 1987. *The Somaticizing Child: Diagnosis and Treatment of Conversion and Somaticization Disorders*. New York: Springer-Verlag.

Shure, M.B., and Spivack, G. 1982. Interpersonal Problem Solving in Young Children: A Cognitive Approach to Prevention. *Am. J. Community Psychol.* 10:341–356.

Siegel, L.J., and Ridley-Johnson, R. 1985. Anxiety Disorders of Childhood and Adolescence. In Bornstein, P.M., and Kazdin, A.E. (eds.): *Handbook of Clinical Behavior Therapy with Children*. Homewood, Ill.: Dorsey.

Spivack, G., and Shure, M.B. 1974. *Social Adjustment of Young Children*. San Francisco: Jossey-Bass.

Steinhauer, P.D., and Rae-Grant, Q. (eds.). 1983. *Psychological Problems of the Child and the Family*. New York: Basic Books, Inc.

Strayhorn, J.N. 1988. *The Competent Child: An Approach to Psychotherapy and Preventive Mental Health*. New York: Guilford Press.

Strober, M., and Yager, J. 1984. A developmental perspective on the treatment of anorexia nervosa in adolescents. In Garner, D.N., and Garfinkel, P.E., (eds.): *Handbook of Psychotherapy for Anorexia Nervosa and Bulimia*. New York: Guilford Press.

Weiner, M.F. 1986. *Practical Psychotherapy*. New York: Brunner/Mazel.

Weisz, J.R., Weiss, B., Alicke, M.D., and Klotz, M.L. 1987. Affectiveness of psychotherapy with children and adolescents: A meta-analysis for clinicians. *J. Consult. Clin. Psychol.* 55:542–549.

Wells, K.C., and Vitulano, L.A. 1985. Anxiety disorders in childhood. In Turner, S.M. (ed.): *Behavioral Theories and Treatment of Anxiety*. New York: Plenum Press.

Williamson, D.A., McKenzie, S.J., Goreczny, A.J., and Faulstich, M. 1985. Psychophysiological disorders. In Hersen, M., and Van Hasselt, V.B. (eds.): *Behavior Therapy with Children and Adolescents: A Clinical Approach*. New York: John Wiley & Sons.

Wolfe, G.A., Kaufman, K., Aragoni, J., and Sander, J. 1981. *The Child Management Program for Abusive Parents: Procedures for Developing a Child Abuse Intervention Program*. Winter Park, Fla.: Anna.

Wooley, S.C., and Wooley, O.W. 1984. Intensive Outpatient and Residential Treatment for Bulimia. In Garner, D.N., and Garfinkel, P.E. (eds.): *Handbook of Psychotherapy for Anorexia Nervosa and Bulimia*. New York: Guilford Press.

30

Families and Family Therapy

PAUL D. STEINHAUER, M.D.

There are several important differences between child psychiatry and other areas of medicine. In most medical practice, the patient is obviously suffering from an illness and brings it to the attention of a physician. However, within child psychiatry this is often not the case. Consider the following example:

Dale, age 11, was admitted to a medical ward of a large pediatric hospital because of repeated episodes of monarticular arthritis, which had occurred for 4 years. For 2½ years despite repeated normal physical, laboratory, and radiologic examinations, he had been treated empirically with corticosteroids in sufficient dosage that the risk of growth retardation caused serious concern. When, despite his medication, unrelieved pain in his left hip limited his mobility and threatened to interfere with Dale's attending school, his family doctor requested a consultation from a major diagnostic center over 100 miles from his home for help in diagnosis and future management.

On admission, Dale was a pleasant, slightly shy boy who appeared his stated age. He complained of persistent pain in his left hip and walked with a limp. Following a thorough investigation by ward staff and a consultation by rheumatology, the history (including a brief psychosocial history that was part of the functional inquiry) and results of a physical examination and thorough battery of laboratory and radiologic tests proved noncontributory. The attending pediatrician requested a psychiatric consultation, "not because we see any evidence of a psychiatric problem, but because we're completely in the dark."

On psychiatric examination, Dale appeared pleasant and cooperative. He had no idea why he was seeing a psychiatrist, since he denied having any psychiatric or emotional problems. Once again, a routine functional inquiry related to psychosocial functioning appeared negative: he got along well enough with his mother and two sisters (his father had died 6 years before); he presented no behavior problems at home, at school, or in the community; and he was an average student in school with many friends. The consulting psychiatrist had no idea at this point whether Dale's life was really going as well as he implied or whether there were areas of dissatisfaction and conflict that were being glossed over or denied. In an attempt to clarify this, the child psychiatrist began to probe a bit deeper. As he did so, a remarkably different picture began to emerge.

The child psychiatrist began by asking Dale what his interests were. He listed a number of hobbies and activities that he had been involved in. Further inquiry, however, made it clear that over the past 3 years he had virtually abandoned these interests because of lack of energy. In school, Dale's performance had gradually slipped by 15% over the previous 3 years, although he was still passing all subjects. Outside of school, all Dale did was watch television, but he had no favorite programs; he watched whatever was on, usually by himself. The doctors commented that Dale seemed to spend a great deal of time on his own and wondered if he was ever lonely. Dale did not reply, but the first of a steady stream of tears began to run down his cheek. Over the next 10 minutes he cried silently, but when asked to describe how he was feeling or whether he was sad, he could only say that he was "all right."

Shortly after Dale began to cry, the psychiatrist invited his mother to join the interview. On entering the room, she appeared not to notice that Dale was crying. She denied that he had been sad or depressed, stating she had not seen him cry in years. More significantly, she showed absolutely no response to Dale's uninterrupted flow of tears. She did not ask what was upsetting him, acknowledge his distress, or attempt in any way to comfort him. Instead, she talked continuously (in a monotone) as if she had not noticed he was upset, though, of course, she had.

A second interview with Dale's mother revealed more information. Crying continuously, she told of Dale's father's death in an industrial accident. The marriage had been a stormy one, and the accident had occurred after a particularly violent battle during which the wife had screamed that she never wanted to see her husband again. His subsequent death, understandably, was a source of enormous guilt. She was overwhelmed at the prospect of having to raise Dale, then age 6, and his two younger sisters on her own. She was unable to deal with her own reaction to Dale's father's death, let alone help Dale. In an attempt to diminish the responsibility, she rushed into a loveless marriage with a rigid widower over 15 years her senior, intending him to take care of herself and her children. Instead, he refused to adopt or to have anything to do with her children and held her responsible for keeping them quiet and out of his way. Dale's mother became so distressed that she was unable to cope with her own frustration or help Dale deal with his feelings regarding his father's death, his mother's inaccessibility, or her subsequent remarriage; she became increasingly withdrawn and emotionally unavailable. Almost the only times that she and Dale were involved with each other were focused around her caring for him when he was ill.

The above case, in which Dale's somatic symptoms, loss of interests and energy, increasing withdrawal, and deteriorating school performance were characteristics of depression, illustrates the following points:

1. Any attempt to diagnose and treat the problem in Dale's musculoskeletal system was doomed to failure.

2. When one expanded the field of inquiry (i.e., the definition of the patient) to include not just Dale's hip but also Dale's mind, a careful psychiatric examination revealed evidence of depression. It did not, however, explain why Dale had become depressed nor did it offer any leads from which to plan an appropriate intervention.

3. It was only when one pushed the field of inquiry even further to obtain a picture of the total family situation that the reasons for Dale's symptoms became clear; only then could Dale's hip pain be understood as symptomatic of a malaise or dysfunction that was not confined to him but involved his entire family. Dale served as the "symptom-bearer" or the "identified patient" within a family that, as a unit, was in serious and chronic distress. As the "ticket of admission," it was his symptoms that brought the family to seek medical attention, but they could only be successfully understood and treated when in their family context.

4. Children frequently present with physical, emotional, behavioral, and/or academic difficulties that occur in response to psychosocial problems involving their families. Chronic marital tensions; children's responses to marital separation, divorce, and/or remarriage; and parent–child problems all predispose children to a wide range of emotional and conduct disorders.

5. Not only do children respond to family tensions, but the reverse is also true. Any serious chronic or congenital deformity or emotional, behavioral, and/or academic disorder in a child will increase pressure on the family as a unit. Being born with a difficult temperament will have a similar effect (Thomas and Chess 1977).

The more one child misbehaves or refuses to attend school, the more pressure will be experienced by the parents to "do something" to remedy the situation. Particularly in families where the parents are unable to agree on and implement appropriate reactions, their ineffectiveness, excessive and/or inappropriate responses to the stress aroused by their symptomatic child(ren) may aggravate the child's symptomatic feelings and behavior. What one sees is a vicious circle; the child's disturbance is aggravated by the parents' responses but, at the same time, the nature of the parental responses is in part shaped by the child's behavior. This situation, termed *circular causality*, is illustrated schematically by Figure 30–1, which portrays how family members are continuously influencing and being influenced by feedback to and from other family members.

Family members often understand and try to explain their functioning in straight "A causes B" terms (i.e., linear causality). But all family therapists consider attempts to ex-

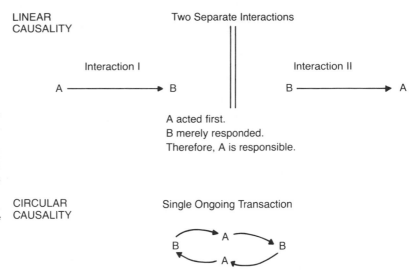

LINEAR
CAUSALITY

Two Separate Interactions

Interaction I

Interaction II

A ⟶ B

B ⟶ A

A acted first.
B merely responded.
Therefore, A is responsible.

Figure 30–1. Linear and circular causality. (From Steinhauer, P. D., and Rae-Grant, Q., eds. 1983. Psychological Problems of the Child and the Family. *New York: Basic Books, p. 56. Copyright © 1983 by Basic Books, Inc. Reprinted by permission of Basic Books, Inc., Publishers.)*

CIRCULAR
CAUSALITY

Single Ongoing Transaction

Neither came first.
Neither is solely responsible for any part of the transaction isolated from the context.
Both share responsibility for the ongoing transactional patterns.

plain family functioning via linear causality a serious oversimplification. They agree circular causality is more accurate, since if family transactions are viewed as a never-ending cycle of "A" ↔ "B," then neither "A" nor "B" is responsible for beginning the transaction and, therefore, solely to blame.

THE FAMILY AS A SYSTEM IN EQUILIBRIUM

The family can be best understood as a system in equilibrium on three interrelated levels (Fig. 30–2). At an intrapsychic level, each person must establish and maintain a balance between conflicting biological, psychological, and social demands. The tension existing between these powerful, yet often incompatible, sets of drives and the ways each member develops to defend against the anxiety this tension generates constitute the intrapsychic (psychological) level of equilibrium. At an interpersonal level, all members are affecting and being affected by each other, since they are constantly responding to each others' behavior whether they choose to or not. At the social level, all family members (and the family as a unit) are constantly influencing and being influenced by the extrafamilial (social) environment.

Since these three levels of equilibrium are interrelated, what occurs at one level will inevitably affect responses at other levels of the family system. For example, a child's school failure (social level) is likely to profoundly influence his or her relationship with parents and probably with siblings (interpersonal level). It may also undermine the interpersonal relationship between the parents, that is, should they have trouble agreeing on how to remedy the problem or slip into blaming each other for its existence. The subsequent effects on the self-esteem and self-confidence of the child along with the guilt and sense of personal inadequacy aroused in either or both parents by the child's failure may also contribute to feelings of loss and sadness (intrapsychic level).

Similarly, severe marital conflict (interpersonal level) may result from long-standing attitudes and behaviors that were established long before the parents met and married (intrapsychic level). Both the parents' personal psychopathology (intrapsychic level) and their ability to agree on what to expect of their children and how to respond if they do not get it (interpersonal level) contribute to their child's development. Poor development may lead to problems in peer relationships, in following the rules at school, and with neighbors (social level), all of which

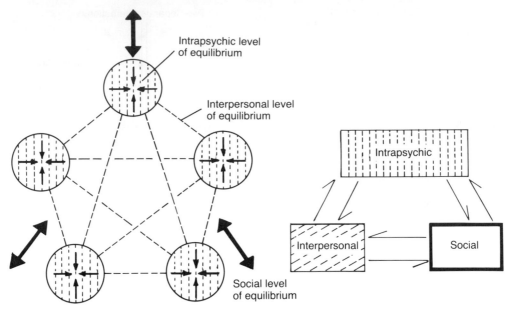

Figure 30–2. *The family as a system in equilibrium. (From Steinhauer, P. D., and Rae-Grant, Q., eds. 1983. Psychological Problems of the Child and the Family. New York: Basic Books, p. 58. Copyright © 1983 by Basic Books, Inc. Reprinted by permission of Basic Books, Inc., Publishers.)*

might in turn aggravate conflict between the child and parents and, possibly, between husband and wife (interpersonal level).

BASIC PRINCIPLES OF FAMILY EQUILIBRIUM

Six basic principles govern family structure and equilibrium.

1. Within any family, all members are assigned and assume roles that cause them to behave in repetitive and highly characteristic ways. As part of the family system, members also play a part in defining the roles of other family members.

2. Each family's structure is defined by a set of rules all are expected to obey that allow members to relate to one another. Some of these are explicit, while others are merely implied. At times, there may be conflict between explicit and implicit rules. In families, it is usually the implicit rules that are the more compelling; the conflict between the two sets of rules is often a source of considerable confusion and anxiety.

For example, nobody may come right out and say, "In this family, we never mention that Aunt Minnie gets drunk; instead, we talk about her headaches, her 'feeling poorly,' her having had a bad day, etc." Any child rash enough (or young enough) to openly state that Aunt Minnie had had too much to drink would have this denied and would be scolded or even punished for mentioning the unmentionable. After some confusion, the child in such a family would learn the unspoken rule and either not refer to the drunkenness at all or do so via a euphemism acceptable to the family.

3. The roles and rules that govern a family's behavior define the structure characteristic of that family. Within a given family, one often finds that the family approaches all problems in much the same way: the same members make the decisions, while there are those who opt out, openly challenge, or covertly defy the decision-making process. This occurs whether the task at hand involves interpreting a proverb, deciding what movie to go to, or dealing with a major family crisis such as a serious illness or loss of job.

4. The family equilibrium is constantly being challenged and redefined in the course of day-to-day interaction; this redefinition causes much of the normal and inevitable tension of family life.

5. The family equilibrium is a homeostatic or self-perpetuating equilibrium, so that attempts to change it from within (e.g., change in a member) or from without (e.g., input from a therapist or counselor) can be expected to evoke opposition. The strength of

this inherent resistance to change varies from family to family; in general, the more satisfactory the prevailing level of family functioning, the more likely the family is to adapt to appropriate demands for change; it should be noted that this tendency to resist change may operate largely unwittingly. Parents who are distressed and seeking help for their child's behavioral problems may sabotage all their therapist's suggestions. They may forget to try the suggestions or come up with reasons why they were not worth trying, but those same parents would be likely to react with disbelief were the therapist to suggest they were being uncooperative.

6. The family equilibrium is a communal coping mechanism that the family adopts to deal with the twin threats of disruption and/or pain (anxiety, depression, rage, intolerable sexual feelings).

FAMILY STRUCTURE

During the course of evolution, families develop a characteristic structure—a well-defined, repetitive, and self-perpetuating pattern of roles and rules within which members are expected to function. There is general agreement on the major common elements of universal family functioning. These have been organized into a number of models of family functioning in attempts to provide a unifying structure around which to organize both research and clinical findings about families, to provide a guide for a comprehensive assessment of family functioning, to develop goals for ongoing treatment, and to generate hypotheses for further research into family functioning and responses to treatment (Epstein et al. 1978; Olson et al. 1979; Fleck 1980; Walsh 1982). One such model is the Process Model of Family Functioning (Steinhauer et al. 1984).

All families have certain tasks they must accomplish. The nature of these will vary over the family's life cycle, but their accomplishment will use the same basic skills and processes at any point in the cycle (Carter and McGoldrick 1980; Walsh 1982; Glick 1955). Thus, the ultimate goal of family functioning is *task accomplishment*. Some of a family's tasks are dictated by the culture (Minuchin 1975; Rutter 1976), while others are unique, but all are influenced by each family's values and norms. These values and

norms, in turn, are derived largely from the parents' experiences growing up within their own families, their internalized (psychological) derivatives of these experiences, the ongoing influence of the society in which they are living, and their common history and influences since coming together to create a new nuclear family. For task accomplishment to be effective, the family must first define and perform a number of roles (role performance). Families use communication to send and receive the information needed to define these roles and accomplish the essential tasks (Epstein et al. 1968; Ruesch and Bateson 1951). Information exchanged will include messages essential for the accomplishment of the tasks of everyday life (instrumental communication), as well as expressions of feeling (affective communication), which may either assist or hinder the necessary task accomplishment and role performance. In addition, the quality and the intensity of family members' emotional involvement with each other (affective involvement) and how members influence each others' behavior (control) will either facilitate or impede task accomplishment. The structure of a family is determined by the interrelationship among these universal dimensions of family functioning. Figure 30–3 contains a diagrammatic view of these dimensions and their relationships.

EVOLUTION OF A FAMILY STRUCTURE

Task Accomplishment

As soon as a couple chooses to live together and to share a common existence, they are immediately faced with a number of tasks. This is the first major dimension of family functioning. The essential tasks can be divided into three major groups (Epstein and Bishop 1981):

1. Basic tasks—those tasks essential to physical survival, such as the provision of food, shelter, health care, and clothing.

2. Developmental tasks—those tasks that provide for the continuing development of all family members (Lidz 1979; Schertz 1971).

3. Crisis tasks—those tasks related to the family's mobilizing to cope with stresses so numerous and/or severe that they threaten to temporarily overwhelm the family's ability

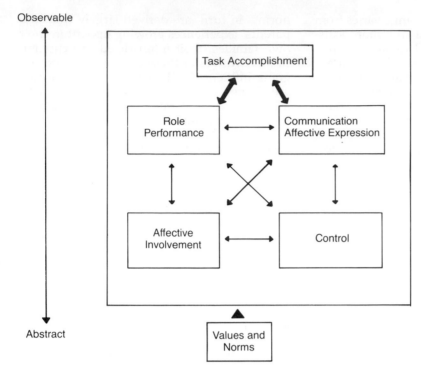

Figure 30–3. *Diagrammatic representation of family structure. (From Steinhauer, P.D., Santa-Barbara, J., and Skinner, H.A. 1984. The process model of family functioning. Can. J. Psychiatry 29:77–87.)*

to deal with them, thus disrupting the family's level of equilibrium (Steinhauer 1985).

The decision to live as a couple immediately confronts the partners with a number of developmental tasks that call for major adjustments on both their parts (Jacobson 1981). Behaviors and habits that were quite acceptable while each lived separately may require modification and/or renunciation if unacceptable to the partner. Alternatively, the partner might be persuaded to develop new tolerances, in which case the behaviors might be retained. Thus, one of the first major developmental tasks faced by the new couple involves defining the rules by which they will live together. The accomplishment of this task is partly conscious, through direct negotiation of each partner's preferences, demands, expectations, and dislikes, and partly an unwitting accommodation to the perceived needs and preferences of the other. If this task is successfully accomplished, both members of the couple will feel satisfied that their needs are being met. If, however, either partner is left feeling dissatisfied, abused, cheated, or unfulfilled, both the bond and their ability to function successfully as a couple will be compromised. To be successful in accomplishing these tasks, the new family will simultaneously have to develop along a number of universal dimensions.

Role Performance

The second major dimension of universal family functioning that is essential for successful task accomplishment is role performance. To achieve their task of mutual accommodation, the new couple will first have to define their respective roles. This process of role definition, along with the willingness of each partner to accept and perform roles assigned by the other, will be influenced by various factors.

Both partners usually come into a marriage or relationship with fairly definite ideas about how a husband and wife should behave and relate to each other. These basic expectations may be a carbon copy of how, when they were growing up, they saw their own parents deal with each other (i.e., role modeling) (Meissner 1978). Alternatively, either or both partners may react against their parents' definitions of marital roles by deliberately attempting to define their role differently from their original family (i.e., negative identification). The partner may or may not be fully aware of the redefinition.

Cultural and subcultural influences, as well as those of the family of origin, may exert a major influence on role expectations (Pearce 1980). For example, before World War II very few married women worked outside the home or had their own careers, and for them to do so at that time would have generally been taken as evidence that their husbands were not good providers. A need for women in industry during World War II, economic pressures, and the redefinition of sex roles by the feminist movement encouraged more married women to join the work force. At the same time, a shift in social attitudes began to define the inadequate husband not as the man whose wife needed to work but as the one who could not tolerate his wife's working. The husband who facilitated his wife's career began to be seen as "liberated."

The greater the parity in role expectations with which the members of a couple enter their marriage/relationship, the less they will need to modify, negotiate, and/or learn to tolerate the process of accommodating successfully to the needs of the other. Fears and expectations resulting from past experiences may contaminate and distort how either partner perceives the other's role performance. Such distorted perceptions, especially in the absence of adequate communication, can seriously threaten marital harmony, effective functioning, and the future of the relationship.

Successful role performance must satisfy two essential criteria. First, it must be comprehensive (that is, all required activities must be assigned and accepted) and it must also be complementary, meaning that the various roles must mesh with each other in a way that is both efficient and acceptable to all (Berman and Lief 1975; Tharp 1963; Levinger 1965). If role performance is both comprehensive and complementary, there will be little dissatisfaction or arguing about who should do what since each member will have adequate role satisfaction.

There is no single "ideal" or "best" way to define the traditional roles of various family members. Much more important than how any person's role is defined is that there be internal role consistency, that is, that all members define their roles as others do, so that there is general acceptance of what is expected of each family member. There

should also be sufficient complementarity of roles to allow for successful role integration. At times, role definitions may not be consistent with actual role performance; should these differ significantly, confusion, disharmony, disequilibrium, and even family breakdown may result.

Ideally, role definitions will take into account the needs of each family member. Frustration and growing dissatisfaction will ultimately result if any members continually sacrifice their own needs to meet those of others. What matters, in the long run, is that the family find some definition of roles that works for it; one that provides enough cohesion to hold the family together while remaining flexible enough to allow the family to adapt to change.

Communication

The successful exchange of information is needed for the mutual understanding required to define and readjust roles. For such an exchange, both partners must be able to identify and express their thoughts, feelings, and needs clearly, directly, and with sufficient force. At the same time, each must be physically available and psychologically open to considering the other's point of view.

Any communication (message) contains elements from two levels: (1) the content level, the subject matter of the message, and (2) the metacommunicative level, the manner in which the message is communicated. This latter includes those messages conveyed by tone of voice, facial expression, body language, or choice of words. The metacommunication reflects the relationship and the feelings between sender and receiver when the message was sent. The receiver's reaction will depend not just on the content of the message and on its metacommunication but also on how the message was received and interpreted. This may be incomplete or distorted depending on the clarity and directness of the sender and on the receiver's freedom to hear and interpret correctly. One cannot avoid responding to a message that has been received. Silence or "ignoring it" communicates that one is avoiding a direct response and also, at a metacommunicative level, sends a powerful message likely to increase tension between sender and receiver. Although one cannot choose the messages that one receives, one can learn to control the nature of one's responses.

Epstein and co-workers (1968, 1981) have classified communications as belonging to three main categories:

1. *Affective communications* are those in which the message is primarily emotional (e.g., ''I hate your guts.'').

2. *Instrumental communications* are those whose message is necessary to accomplish the ongoing tasks of everyday life (e.g., ''What time will you be home for supper?'' or ''Pass the zucchini, please.'').

3. *Neutral communications* transmit messages that are neither instrumental nor related to affect (e.g., ''What a gorgeous day it is today.'' or ''What do you think of the Rolling Stones?'').

Within each of these categories two other sets of variables merit consideration:

1. Is the message clear or unclear (i.e., masked, disguised, ambiguous)? Lack of clarity is associated with greater ambiguity and increased confusion, anxiety, and possibility of distortion by its receiver.

2. Is the message direct or displaced, that is, is it addressed to the person for whom it was intended or was it deflected to someone else?

Consider the following scenario:

Clear Direct Communication	''For Pete's sake, Mary, will you get off the phone and wipe Johnny's nose!''
Direct Masked Communication	''Hey, Mary, how many hours are you planning to stay on that damn phone?''
Displaced/Masked Communication	''What the hell's going on around here?'' or ''Suzy, will you turn down that damn radio! I can't hear myself think!''

The more dysfunctional a family, the more that family's affective communications are likely to be disturbed. What we commonly call a ''breakdown in communication'' is usually a sign of a deeper relationship problem among those who are not communicating. The greater the disturbance in affective communication, the more likely the disturbance in instrumental and neutral communications.

The first to be contaminated is instrumental communication. When this occurs, a sim-

ple request is interpreted, and responded to, as an attack or an attempt to manipulate or control (i.e., a masked, hostile communication). In such families, any requests or orders are responded to as an attack; the refusal to obey is the routine response (i.e., counterattack). Power struggles are frequent, and members are so preoccupied with who will dominate and control whom that disagreements are rarely resolved. Instead of solving them on the basis of what is appropriate, one person imposes his or her will on someone else on the basis of power.

In even more disturbed families, neutral communication is contaminated by the displaced feelings, so that comments on, for example, tastes in music or even the weather are attacked.

Some families send many ambiguous or paradoxic communications. A paradoxic communication (mixed message) contains two simultaneous messages (often verbal and subverbal) that are mutually incompatible: for example, the statement, ''Of course I love you. Give me a kiss,'' if said when the speaker is disinterested, upset, and turning away when the demanded kiss is delivered. Mixed messages invite confusion in the receiver. To which level should the person respond? This dilemma is most marked in what Bateson and colleagues (1956) have termed the double bind, in which (1) any attempted response to the mixed message is unacceptable and is attacked; (2) the receiver cannot resolve the confusion because the sender will not allow clarification of the conflicting messages; and (3) the receiver cannot afford to antagonize or be rejected by the sender, on whom he is dependent.

Several authors have noted the frequency of double binds in the families of schizophrenics (Bateson et al. 1956; Lidz et al. 1957; Lidz 1979). At one time, the ''double bind hypothesis of schizophrenia'' held that schizophrenia resulted from a defensive withdrawal by the psychotic family member from the extreme anxiety generated by unrelieved exposure to massive and continuous double binding. More recently, it is agreed that the double bind hypothesis was originally oversold (Berger 1978; Watzlawick 1963; Grunebaum and Chasin 1980; Wynne 1976). The double bind is neither confined to the families of schizophrenics nor specific to any single disorder. However, frequent double binding interferes with successful communication, undermines relationships and problem-solving, and contributes to chronic illness, tension, and confusion.

The more disturbed a family, the more inadequate and distorted will be the communication. Communication (family) therapists assume that if a family can learn to communicate successfully it will need no further therapy. This implies that their improved communication will promptly allow them to identify and resolve problems inevitably generated in the course of living. Once this has been achieved, the family as a system will be functioning at a level that will use the improved communication both to solve existing problems and to keep pressures from building up again.

Affective Involvement

Affective involvement concerns the degree and quality of each partner's emotional investment and concern for the other (Epstein and Bishop 1981). Partners who are meeting each other's need for affective involvement will contribute to each other's emotional security while at the same time tolerating the other's independence of thought, feeling, and action. The autonomy of both partners is thus assured. They are close enough to meet the other's need for affection, thus strengthening the bond between them.

Control

The process by which family members influence each other's behavior is called control (Epstein and Bishop 1981). The reciprocal nature of role performance in families implies that members will constantly influence and be influenced by others, according to the rules of "circular causality" (Jackson et al. 1967). The more passive one marital partner is, the more the other will be encouraged to be dominant. Simultaneously, the more dominant the second partner, the more the dominance will reinforce the passivity of the original partner.

There are two major aspects of control:

1. Maintenance control—how members influence each other to ensure that day-to-day tasks are accomplished.

2. Adaptational control—the family's ability to alter its functioning, when necessary, in response to changing developmental or environmental demands.

Example of One Family Structure

Consider, for example, one couple's reaction to the birth of their first child (LaPerriere 1980). If the child were temperamentally difficult (e.g., predominantly unpleasant mood, marked biological irregularity, low threshold for and high persistence of responses to stress, tending to withdraw from new situations), the new mother would likely feel overwhelmed and inadequate. This, in turn, would undermine her meeting the baby's needs in a relaxed manner, leaving her feeling fatigued, discouraged, and much in need of both practical help and psychological support from her husband. He, too, would find the addition of the new baby unsettling. His sleep would be frequently disrupted, which might interfere with his job performance. His wife, upset and preoccupied with the baby, would probably have less time and might be less receptive to him. Also, she would likely make increased demands on his time (to help her with night feedings, caring for the baby, sharing household chores and shopping) and on his emotional resources (through her need for emotional support and encouragement), which he might have difficulty understanding and meeting. In short, the birth of such a child would require some readjustment in all major dimensions of the new family's functioning as follows:

Task Accomplishment. Many new tasks will need to be accomplished following the birth of the new baby:

1. The baby will need to be fed, bathed, changed, held, taken to the doctor periodically, and so on.

2. Multiple additional costs will result from the birth of the baby, possibly along with the loss of one source of income if the mother previously worked.

3. For the baby's emotional development to proceed, at least one or preferably both parents will have to bond to the baby, who will then be able to form an attachment to them. This process would be facilitated by the parents' meeting the infant's needs in a relaxed, competent manner, while providing adequate physical contact and stimulation. The more difficult the baby temperamentally,

the more stressful and the more difficult it will be for them to meet these needs.

Role Performance. The arrival of the new baby confronts the parents with a variety of new tasks and demands. These require new role definitions in order to divide the new responsibilities. This, in turn, will be governed by how both husband and wife define their new roles of mother and father. Should their definitions coincide, there should be little role conflict, but if the wife expects and demands more or different help than her husband feels he should or can give, the potential for serious role conflict will exist.

Communication. The process of dividing these new tasks now that they are parents as well as husband and wife will require that both parents articulate their needs, expectations, and dissatisfactions, in order to explore what the other might do to meet them. This may severely test the adequacy of the communication between husband and wife. Any existing block in adequate, clear, direct communication could lead to a damming up and displacement of frustration and resentment in one partner and a corresponding lack of understanding with subsequent anxiety, frustration, and resentment in the other. A tendency of either partner to withdraw, thus being less available to receive and understand the other's attempts to communicate, would have a similar effect.

Affective Involvement. If the couple were able to communicate all the essential information and, as a result, to perceive correctly and respond adequately to the other's needs, each would feel understood and supported by the other. If so, the bond of closeness between them would be strengthened. If, however, either felt let down and unsupported by the other, the resulting disappointment and frustration could lead to resentment, anxiety, or guilt, which, unless promptly and effectively resolved through adequate communication, might seriously undermine the closeness between them and the ability of either to respond effectively to the baby.

Control. The addition of the new baby has demanded from the couple a major adaptation in order to accommodate a variety of new tasks. The ways in which each influences the other to accept his or her desired role in the accomplishment of these tasks is a function of the control dimension. Furthermore, each major event in the development

of the child or the life of the family (e.g., when the baby first becomes mobile, when the child first starts school, when a second child is born, as older children demand increasing independence) will similarly require new adaptations, thus affecting all aspects of the family's functioning.

SYMPTOMS AS AN EXPRESSION OF FAMILY DYSFUNCTION

The symptoms of an identified patient may play a key role in attempts by family members to influence each other and to maintain a dysfunctional family's equilibrium. Freud acknowledged that symptoms can at times prove useful in a person's relationships with others. This he called secondary gain, emphasizing that while such symptoms at times offer apparent advantages, the primary gain is the defense against feeling disturbed. The family therapist, however, considers that symptoms, regardless of their origin, are largely maintained by environmental responses. As long as the symptoms are understood for both the person and for the family, both will continue to perpetuate symptomatic behavior, even though consciously all may express a desire for change. When symptomatic behavior no longer works for the individual and for the family, both are forced to reappraise the situation. This is part of what causes a family to seek treatment; the symptom is no longer working well enough or has become too frightening. Therapists are not manipulated by symptomatic behavior. Instead, they focus on how the patient uses the symptom to control others, including the therapist. When the usual distortions, threats, attacks, hysterical outbursts, attempts at emotional blackmail, bursts of charm, and so on do not succeed in manipulating the therapist, the patient and family are left more aware of the maneuvers and of the fact that they are not working. The therapist can then help the patient recognize how much similar behaviors are relied on in attempts to manipulate and control others.

In some families, for example, any attempt to discuss the identified patient's behavior results in outbursts of tears or accusations of being picked on. One soon learns that this is not unique to therapy; it happens at home whenever anyone tries to deal with the undesirable behavior. The result, typically, is that family members either learn to put up with the symptoms to avoid a scene or are forced to justify their interventions in the face of accusations that they are being unfair or the discussion gets sidetracked by the ways in which the member is defending himself or herself (i.e., the unreasonableness of the scene). In any case, the original issue has been successfully deflected, and therefore, defended against, by the maneuvers of the person whose behavior was under discussion. But if this member is placed in an interpersonal situation where the typical defense will no longer work—for example in therapy, provided the therapist avoids intimidation, deflection, or diversion—the patient and family can learn to recognize their reliance on response to such defensive maneuvers. This will then allow them to achieve more direct, rational, effective methods of dealing with problems. Here are some common uses and meanings of symptoms.

1. Symptoms may have considerable communication value. For example, a statement of how miserable, lonely, hurt, or helpless one is, may be
   a. A plea for support and/or pity
   b. An implied reproach (e.g., "How unfair to expect me to change when you know how miserable I feel!")
   c. An attempt to control
2. Other symptoms may constitute a more direct attack. The child who vomits when angry not only demands attention but also punishes the parents by making them clean up. Similarly, the rituals of the obsessive-compulsive person may enable the psychologically crippled spouse to dominate totally a rigid and authoritarian partner.
3. Symptomatic behavior may mask a demand that the environment relax expectations since the patient, being symptomatic, is not up to them. It is as if the patient said, "How can you expect me to be pleasant or to carry my weight in the family when I'm so nervous, depressed, or crazy?"
4. Finally, some symptoms take the place of sudden, intense feeling outbursts. Examples include the increased stuttering at times of emotional tension or anger or the exacerbation of psychosomatic symptoms (asthma, migraine, peptic ulcer) in moments of repressed rage or grief.

THE FAMILY AS A UNIT OF TREATMENT

The viewpoints in this chapter have definite implications both for diagnosis and for treatment. A proper diagnosis needs to consider all levels of the family equilibrium, (intrapsychic, interpersonal, and social) as well as the interactions between them.

1. The unit of pathology is no one person but the family system.
2. The member originally referred is seen as the symptom-bearer for the family, meaning that his or her symptoms are merely the obvious part of a pathologic process involving the family system.
3. The aim of treatment becomes not merely to remove the symptoms of the identified patient but to modify the pathologic structure and equilibrium of the family unit (Bowen 1971; Minuchin 1974).

DIFFERENT APPROACHES TO FAMILY THERAPY

Over the 30 years since the origin of family therapy, the rapid expansion of the field has led to the development of a number of distinct approaches or schools. These are not mutually exclusive, and most experienced family therapists combine elements of a number of them in their work. Attempts to relate the form of therapy or the type of family involved to success in family therapy have shown no important correlations, although therapists' relationship skills have been shown to relate to therapeutic outcome.

These will not be described in detail, since highly condensed descriptions tend to blur the distinctions between them. For the reader interested in finding out more about any of these approaches, Table 30–1 includes a listing of a number of the major schools, along with one or two references describing each.

GUIDELINES FOR FAMILY ASSESSMENT AND TREATMENT

1. *Join the family.* To do this, the potential family therapist must make himself or herself known to the family members and gain their acceptance enough to establish a personal alliance (which in time can develop into an alliance for therapy) with them.

Table 30–1. MAJOR SCHOOLS OF FAMILY THERAPY	
School	**References**
Communications theory	Satir 1967
Behavioral family therapy	Patterson 1976a and b
	Birchler and Spinks 1980
Family group therapy	Bell 1971; Skynner 1981
Psychodynamic	Ackerman 1958
(including	Boszormenyi-Nagy and
intergenerational)	Spark 1984
family therapies	Bowen 1980
Structural family therapy	Minuchin 1974; Nichols
	1987; Aponte 1981
Strategic family therapy	Selvini-Palazzoli 1978;
	Madanes 1981;
	Hoffman 1981
Integrated family/	Steinhauer 1985; Nichols
individual therapy	and Everett 1986

2. *Conduct the assessment.* The therapist must assess the family system. This can be done in a single, often extended, session or over an initial two or three diagnostic sessions. One excellent model for conducting a family assessment is detailed by Weber and associates (1985). In the course of the assessment, it is important that the therapist:

a. Obtain an understanding of the problems that brought the family into therapy and a knowledge of how these are seen and understood by other family members.

b. Develop a clear picture of the roles that family members take in relating to each other; the roles (explicit and implicit) that govern family interaction; the nature of the family's problem solving; the nature and extent of how emotionally involved members are with each other, who is allied with whom and against whom; and the state of the boundaries existing among the members as individuals, between the parents and their own parents, and between generations.

c. Augment the assessment process through available standardized self-report tests of family functioning by drawing the examiner's and the family's attention to the problem areas missed in the clinical assessment, by highlighting differences in perception of various family members, by pinpointing and presenting in a concrete form major areas of difficulty that some

members would like to minimize, and by allowing some nonverbal members a more acceptable way of expressing themselves (Skinner et al. 1983; Olson et al. 1982; Moos and Moos 1981). These should, if used, be seen as an adjunct to, not a substitute for, a thorough clinical assessment.

3. *Shift the tone from blaming to problem-solving.* During the assessment, the examiner must establish and maintain the tone for each assessment interview as exploratory and problem solving, not critical, accusatory, or blaming. If left to their own devices, many families will become hostile and attacking, so that the atmosphere can become destructive. The therapist needs to have control over the assessment process to prevent this occurring. This does not mean that difficult areas should be avoided but that they be explored with tact and control, with respect for the feelings of all involved, and for the purpose of understanding the problem at hand, not blaming or ridiculing any family member.

4. *Structure the interview.* In order to obtain and maintain sufficient control over the session, the examiner should slow down the family's interaction to the point where one understands each point from every member's perspective. If left to their own devices, families will often replicate in the examiner's office the pathologic structure they live with at home. It is for the therapist, by imposing a structure on each interview, not to let this happen, for if it does, it will leave the members feeling that it is not safe to participate openly in the assessment. The hope is that through the assessment the family may begin to pinpoint and resolve its problems. Also, unless the therapist slows down the interaction, one can be flooded with partial, confusing, and contradictory impressions and will be unsure of what it means. This is no time for a therapist to be passive. The therapist must be clear on the agenda (i.e., what one needs to know) and move steadily forward, using spontaneous family interaction to achieve goals, but restructuring the interview to keep the process in control and to avoid an avalanche of negative feeling that will frighten the family away; this is particularly important in families that handle stress via scape-

goating. The anxiety generated by the assessment risks aggravating the scapegoating process, leaving the family feeling distraught, guilty, and furious at the examiner whom, not entirely without reason, they blame for making things worse.

The therapist can structure and slow down an interview in a number of ways:

a. By reframing the statement, restating it in a positive rather than a negative manner:

Parent:	"He's so lazy, it's impossible. It's like pulling teeth to get him to do his homework."
Examiner:	"So you'd like him to take responsibility for seeing that his homework gets done."
Parent:	"Yes."
Examiner:	"And if he did take responsibility on his own, would that help you get along better?"
Parent:	"Of course it would."

b. By diffusing the attack:

"You've told me what upsets you about Jeremy. Now what other sources of tension are there in the family?"
"We've heard what mom and dad think about this. How do the rest of you see it?"

c. By including a change of tone (inviting a move from attack to problem solving/empathy/understanding).

"So Jeremy's soiling makes you all furious at him, so much so that you don't want to have anything to do with him. How do you think Jeremy feels when he knows how all of you feel about him?"
"Why do you think he persists in soiling when it so obviously alienates all of you—what's the pay-off for him?"

d. By encouraging the family to take a more dyadic/triadic view:

"And when Jeremy does that, how do you react? And how does he respond to your reaction?"
"Do you and your husband respond to this the same way? If not, what's different about your two responses? How do you deal with these differences?"

e. By exploring to elicit potential sources of support:

"Mother seems pretty fed up with Jeremy. Are there any of you who feel she's too down on him?"

f. By shifting the family's focus onto another item on the agenda:

"All right. I think I understand about Jeremy's soiling. Now I need to know something about how you deal with disagreements in the family."

g. By using the topic to explore the differences between all family members' perceptions, feelings, and reactions:

"Dad has made it clear how he feels about Steven's behavior. I wonder if I could ask all of you in turn how this compares with how you respond to Steven's behavior."

5. *Maintain objectivity.* The examiner's position and attitude must be objective. While, later in therapy, a therapist may temporarily side with one coalition in order to shift the family process and structure, this can be done safely only when the therapist has developed a therapeutic alliance with the family and achieved a measure of trust. The inexperienced therapist should be careful to avoid being set up to fight anyone's battle for him or her. If he sides with a teenager against the parents or with the parents against that adolescent, he will quickly lose his credibility, his effectiveness, and, often, the family. Instead, he should encourage the person who is setting him up to express his or her feelings directly, rather than relying on the therapist to do it for him or her. The distance between therapist and family is of crucial importance; if the therapist remains too aloof, he or she risks being seen as disinterested and uncaring, but if the therapist becomes too involved, he or she may be seen as intrusive and manipulative.

6. *Avoid manipulation, premature closure.* The examiner should never believe what "A" tells him or her about "B" without first having listened to "B's" version of the situation. As obvious as this seems, it is surprising how frequently doctors will accept as fact, without any corroboration, whatever someone tells them about someone else. Consciously or not, family members often prevaricate to get an examiner or therapist on their side. How they tell their story, how they sense and play on

the examiner's sympathy and biases, and how they attempt to forge secret alliances by telephone contacts between the sessions, run the risk of seducing the examiner into premature and inappropriate alliances. The examiner must avoid such seductions to maintain his or her position and credibility.

7. *Help them recognize/transcend "uproar."* The examiner will soon recognize that families that are upset about, but unable to discuss, major problems will often displace their feelings onto minor issues to which they overreact. This is common in families that are constantly fighting about trivial incidents while their real concerns are never discussed. An examiner can often help them move beyond this by making them aware of the pattern formulated above and by asking them to look for major concerns currently bothering the family that should be discussed but have not been put on the table.

8. *Negotiate a contract.* At the end of the assessment period, the examiner negotiates a contract with the family. After reflecting back over the family's major problems, one discusses with the family their alternatives, ranging from doing nothing to various forms of therapy. In recommending a course of family therapy, it is important to tie down such details as time and duration of appointments, which family members will attend, the importance of regular attendance, what the family could expect of the therapist, and what the therapist would expect of the family. It should be made clear, as often as necessary, that effective therapy requires active participation by the family, not just for the weekly hour in the therapist's office but throughout the week. What is expected of the family in therapy should be spelled out. The therapist must take an active role in structuring early therapy sessions since many families approach treatment with naive and unrealistic expectations, as if to say, "There! I've told you the problem. Now it's up to you to solve it." This is commonly how patients relate to other physicians. Far too often the need for the patient to retain the responsibility for doing the work, so often discouraged in other areas of medicine, is expected but never clearly articulated in contracting for psychotherapy. As a re-

sult, a failure to understand what was never made clear is misread as resistance to involvement in therapy.

9. *Structure the therapy.* Throughout therapy, a prime responsibility of the therapist is to maintain control of the interaction to structure the sessions, especially the early ones, to ensure that the ongoing process is directed toward achieving the goals agreed on. It is important, particularly in the early stages, to avoid confronting tenuous defenses that elicit more anxiety than families can bear. A high level of activity, the provision of adequate structure especially toward the beginning of treatment, and sensitivity combined with good judgment as to which defenses to respect and which to confront are among the qualities in therapists known to ensure successful outcome (Gurman and Kniskern 1981).

OUTCOME STUDIES IN FAMILY THERAPY

The types of outcome studies in the family therapy literature fall into two main categories.

1. In-depth studies provide much knowledge about family pathology, its relationship to individual psychopathology, and family therapy. This type of research is problematic, however, since one must somehow establish that the population being studied is typical of the group as a whole and because of the risk of overgeneralization because of the lack of a model or control group's normal functioning.

2. Prospective studies are well controlled and based on good sampling. These studies also have their problems, among which are the fuzziness of inclusion criteria and the lack of pure technique because what therapists from different schools actually do is far less distinct than they claim. Another difficulty in prospective studies is the problem of establishing the relative contributions of the technique and the personal qualities of the therapist to the result. Finally, studies differ in how they define and attempt to measure change occurring during therapy. Some measure changes in the presenting symptoms, others attempt to demonstrate changes in family structure; some report change as measured by an objective observer, while others rely on self-report measures of change (Russell et al. 1983). Finally, families in ther-

Table 30-2. TREATMENT OF MARITAL PROBLEMS	
By Individual Therapy	**Family Approaches**
48% success	61% success
11.6% worse	5.6% worse

apy over time do not change in a uniform manner; some individuals and dyads may improve, while others may remain the same or even deteriorate. With all these problems, it is not surprising that even the better prospective studies are hard to compare.

Nevertheless, in their comprehensive review of the literature, Gurman and Kniskern were able to establish that:

1. Family and marital therapies are effective beyond chance (Gurman and Kniskern 1977, 1978a).

2. Less disturbed families and couples respond best to these therapies.

3. For marital problems, family approaches are more successful than individual approaches (Gurman and Kniskern 1978a and 1978b) (Table 30-2).

4. Increased communication skills are the only factors consistently empirically related to success in marital therapy (Birchler and Spinks 1980; Gurman and Kniskern 1978a; Jacobson 1978).

5. Conjoint behaviorally oriented therapy is the treatment of choice for sexual dysfunction (Gurman and Kniskern 1981).

6. Family therapy is often more effective than individual psychotherapy, even for those problems that appear to be individual (i.e., intraapsychic) (Gurman and Kniskern 1981).

7. Family approaches matched to a specific diagnosis are listed in Table 30-3.

In the future, outcome research in family therapy would be assisted if a consensus were reached about how to define client populations and how to define and measure improvement. The agreement on a common terminology, coding systems, and so on would greatly favor the replication of promising studies. Each study should routinely include a listing of the proportion of families that improved and deteriorated and a description of the dimensions of family functioning on which this judgment is based. Above all, there is a need for a consensus on indices of improvement and/or deterioration that are both clinically relevant and psychometrically sound.

INDICATIONS FOR AND CONTRAINDICATIONS TO FAMILY THERAPY

To understand the behavioral, emotional, and, at times, physical symptoms of a child, one must first understand the structure and functioning of that child's family system. That done, there remains the question of when family therapy is the treatment of choice to relieve the symptoms and modify the family pressures contributing to the problem. This chapter will conclude by providing guidelines for the selective use of family therapy, either alone or combined with individual psychotherapy of the child presenting with the problem. (These guidelines will, of course, be influenced by the differing assessment, formulation, and treatment skills of those applying them.)

The more that disturbed family interaction seems central to the problem, the more one will require a treatment that will affect not just the identified patient but also the family system. This can be done in two ways: one may see the family members together in *conjoint family therapy* or may see parents and child separately in what is traditionally called *collaborative therapy*. If family members seem to be reacting primarily to each other or to common stresses affecting them all (e.g., a

Table 30-3. MATCHING OF SPECIFIC APPROACH TO DIAGNOSIS		
Diagnosis	**School**	**Reference**
Intrafamilial child aggression	Behavioral family therapy	Patterson 1976a and b
Psychosomatic disorders in children	Structural family therapy	Minuchin et al. 1978
Drug addiction (adults)	Structural family therapy	Stanton 1979
Soft juvenile delinquency	Behavioral family therapy	Gordon and Davidson 1981

death, a lost job, a marital separation), conjoint family therapy is suggested, especially if the total family can tolerate and support change in its members. There are two exceptions, however. One is when the parents cannot tolerate letting all members speak freely in the treatment. The second is when there is scapegoating of one family member that stubbornly persists despite any attempts to have the family deal with other problems or relationships. Faced with such fixed scapegoating, a therapist has only two alternatives: he or she can repeatedly defend the scapegoat against the rest of the family, in which case, he or she alienates the more powerful family members and is soon fired, or he or she can let them continue their scapegoating. This is no better, since the scapegoat will become increasingly distressed, losing trust in the therapist, who is seen as unable to stop the family's scapegoating. Meanwhile the family, increasingly upset and guilty at the scapegoat's mounting distress, blames the therapist for making things worse. For these reasons, fixed scapegoating of a single member is best treated by a collaborative approach, where the scapegoat is seen alone while another therapist sees the parents "for the sake of the child," initially accepting their definition of the child as the problem but using the contacts with them to reframe their perception and to increase their empathy with the scapegoated child and their awareness of their role in the total problem (Steinhauer 1968).

When severe individual psychopathology exists in one or more family members who cannot recognize their part in the problem even when it is pointed out to them, family therapy can be extremely helpful, especially in the opening phase of treatment. Members of such families, even if they agree that treatment is needed, see clearly everyone else's problems but not their own. Family therapy can help clarify what part each is playing in their common problems. As members begin to see and accept their roles, one of two things happens: either they can modify their behavior as they become more aware of its consequences—in which case, the family therapy alone proves sufficient—or they cannot. In the case of the latter, one would consider combining individual and family therapy, but only when the persons themselves see the need for it, since a premature referral of someone who still does not see

himself or herself as having a problem is unlikely to succeed. The stronger the family's opposition to improved family functioning, the more likely a combination of family and individual therapy will be required.

Family therapy, alone or in combination with individual therapy, is contraindicated if the therapist is unable to control increasing acting out or decompensation of the family system in response to the attempted treatment. It is not impossible for a single therapist to provide both components of collaborative treatment, but this should not be attempted by a therapist who is not experienced and skilled in both forms of therapy. These issues are discussed in greater detail by Malone (1983), Pinsoff (1983), Nichols (1984), and Steinhauer (1985).

References

Ackerman, N.W. 1958. *The Psychodynamics of Family Life.* New York: Basic Books.

Aponte, H.J., and vanDeusen, J.M. 1981. Structural family therapy. In Gurman, A.S., and Kniskern, D.P. (eds.): *Handbook of Family Therapy.* New York: Brunner/Mazel.

Bateson, G., Jackson, D.D., Haley, J., and Weakland, J. 1956. Toward a theory of schizophrenia. *Behav. Sci.* 1:251–264.

Bell, J.E. 1971. Family group therapy: A method for psychological treatment of older children, adolescents and their parents. Public Health Monograph No. 64. Washington, D.C.: U.S. Department of Health, Education and Welfare.

Berger, M.M. (ed.). 1978. *Beyond the Double Bind.* New York: Brunner/Mazel.

Berman, E.M., and Lief, H.I. 1975. Marital therapy from a psychiatric perspective: An overview. *Am. J. Psychiatry* 132:583–592.

Birchler, G.R., and Spinks, S.H. 1980. Behavioral-systems marital and family therapy, integration and clinical applications. *Am. J. Fam. Ther.* 8(2):6–28.

Boszormenyi-Nagy, I., and Spark, G.M. 1984. *Invisible Loyalties.* New York: Brunner/Mazel.

Bowen, M. 1971. The use of family theory in clinical practice. In Haley, J. (ed.): *Changing Families.* New York: Grune & Stratton.

Bowen, M. 1980. Family systems theory. In Harrison, S., McDermott, J. (eds.): *New Directions in Childhood Psychopathology,* Vol. I, *Developmental Considerations.* New York: International Universities Press.

Carter, E.A., and McGoldrick, M. (eds.). 1980. *The Family Life Cycle: A Framework for Family Therapy.* New York: Gardner Press.

Epstein N.G., and Bishop, D.S. 1981. Problem-centered systems therapy of the family. In Gurman, A.S., and Kniskern, D.P. (eds.): *Handbook of Family Therapy.* New York: Brunner/Mazel.

Epstein, N.G., Bishop, D., and Levin, S. 1978. The McMaster model of family functioning. *J. Marriage Fam. Counsel.* 4:19–31.

Epstein, N.B., Rakoff, V., and Sigal, J.J. 1968. Family categories schema. Monograph prepared in the Family Research Group of the Department of Psychiatry, Jewish General Hospital, Montreal, Quebec, in collaboration with the McGill University Human Development Study.

Fleck, S. 1980. Family functioning and family pathology. *Psychiatr. Ann.* 10:46–57.

Glick, I.D. 1955. Life cycle of the family. *J. Marriage and Fam. Living* 18:3–9.

Gordon, S.B., and Davidson, N. 1981. Behavioural parent training. In Gurman, A.S., and Kniskern, D.P. (eds.): *Handbook of Family Therapy*. New York: Brunner/Mazel.

Grunebaum, H., and Chasin, R. 1980. Thinking like a family therapist. In Flomenhaft, K., Christ, A.E. (eds.): *The Challenge of Family Therapy: A Dialogue for Child Psychiatric Educators*. New York: Plenum Press.

Gurman, A.S., and Kniskern, D.P. 1977. Enriching research on marital enrichment programs. *J. Marr. Fam. Counsel.* 3:3–11.

Gurman, A.S., and Kniskern, D.P. 1978a. Research on marital and family therapy: Progress, perspective and prospect. In Garfield, A.E., and Bergin, A.E. (eds.): *Handbook of Psychotherapy and Behaviour Change: An Empirical Analysis*, 2nd. ed. New York: Wiley.

Gurman, A.S., and Kniskern, D.P. 1978b. Deterioration in marital and family therapy: Empirical, clinical and conceptual issues. *Fam. Process* 17:30–40.

Gurman, A.S., and Kniskern, D.P. (eds.). 1981. *Handbook of Family Therapy*. New York: Brunner/Mazel.

Hill, R. 1965. Generic features of families under stress. In Parad, H.J. (ed.): *Crisis Intervention: Selected Readings*. New York: Family Assessments of America.

Hoffman, L. 1981. *Foundations of Family Therapy*. New York: Basic Books.

Jackson, D.D., Beavin, J.H. and Watzlawick, P. 1967. *Pragmatics of Human Communication*. New York: W.W. Norton.

Jacobson, N.S. 1978. A review of the research on the effectiveness of marital therapy. In Paolino, T.L., and McCrady, B.S. (eds.): *Marriage and Marital Therapy*. New York: Brunner/Mazel.

Jacobson, N.S. 1981. Behavioural marital therapy. In Gurman, A.S., and Kniskern D.P. (eds.): *Handbook of Family Therapy*. New York: Brunner/Mazel.

LaPerriere, K. 1980. On children, adults and families: The critical transition from couple to parents. In Pearce, J.K., and Friedman, L.J. (eds.): *Family Therapy: Combining Psychodynamic and Family Systems Approaches*. New York: Grune & Stratton.

Levinger, G. 1965. Marital cohesiveness and dissolution: An integrative review. *J. Marriage Fam.* 27: 19–28.

Lidz, T. 1979. Family studies and changing concepts of personality development. *Can. Psychiatr. Assoc. J.* 24:621–632.

Lidz, T., Cornelison, A.R., Fleck, S., and Terry, D. 1957. The intrafamilial environment of schizophrenic patients: Marital schism and marital skew. *Am. J. Psychiatry.* 114:241–248.

Madanes, C. 1981. *Strategic Family Therapy*. San Francisco: Jossey-Bass.

Malone, C.A. 1983. The problem of integrating child and family therapy. Presented at the Annual Meeting of the American Academy of Child Psychiatry.

Meissner, W.W. 1978. The conceptualization of marriage and family dynamics from a psychoanalytic perspective. In Paolino, T.J., and McCrady, B.S. (eds.): *Marriage and Marital Therapy*. New York: Brunner/Mazel.

Minuchin, S. 1974. *Families and Family Therapy*. Cambridge, Mass.: Harvard University Press.

Minuchin, S. 1975. *Families of the Slums*. New York: Basic Books.

Minuchin, S., Rosman, B.O., and Baker, L. 1978. *Psychosomatic Families*. Cambridge, Mass. Harvard University Press.

Moos, R.H., and Moos, B.C. 1981. *Family Environmental Scale Manual*. Palo Alto, Calif.: Consulting Psychologists Press.

Nichols, M. 1984. The theoretical context of family therapy. In *Family Therapy, Concepts, Methods*. New York: Gardner Press.

Nichols, W.C., and Everett, C.A. 1986. *Systemic Family Therapy*. New York: Guilford Press.

Olson, D.H., Sprenkel, D.H., and Russel, C.S. 1979. Circumplex model of marital and family systems: I: Cohesion and adaptability, dimensions, family types, and clinical applications. *Fam. Process* 18:3–28.

Olson, D.H., Portner, J., and Bell, R. 1982. Faces: II. Family adaptability and cohesion evaluation scales. St. Paul, Minn.: Family Social Science, University of Minnesota.

Patterson, G. 1976a. *Living with Children*. Champaign, Ill.: Research Press.

Patterson, G. 1976b. The aggressive child: Victim and architect of a coercive system. In Mash, E.H., Hamerlynck, L.A., and Handy, L.C. (eds.): *Behaviour Modification and Families*. New York: Brunner/Mazel.

Pearce, J.K. 1980. Ethnicity and family therapy. In Pearce, J.K., and Freidman, L.J. (eds.): *Family Therapy: Combining Psychodynamic and Family Systems Approaches*. New York: Grune & Stratton.

Pinsoff, W. 1983. Integrated problem-centered therapy: Towards the synthesis of family and individual psychotherapy. *J. Marital Fam. Ther.* 9:19–35.

Ruesch, J., and Bateson, G. 1951. *Communication: the Social Matrix of Psychiatry*. New York: W.W. Norton.

Russell, C., Olson, D.H., Sprenkle, D.H., and Atilano, R.B. 1983. From family symptom to family system: Review of family therapy research. *Am. J. Fam. Ther.* 11(3):3–14.

Rutter, M. 1976. Sociocultural influences. In Rutter, M., and Hersov, L. (eds.): *Child Psychiatry Modern Approaches*. Oxford: Blackwell Scientific.

Satir, V. 1967. *Conjoint Family Therapy*. Palo Alto, Calif.: Science and Behaviour Books.

Scherz, F.H. 1971. Maturational crises and parent–child interaction. *Social Casework* 52:362–369.

Selvini-Palazzoli, M. 1978. *Paradox and Counterparadox*. New York: Jason Aronson.

Skinner, H., Steinhauer, P.D., and Santa-Barbara, J. 1983. The Family Assessment Measure. *Can. J. Commun. Ment. Health* 2(2).

Skynner, A.C.R. 1981. An open-systems, group-analytic approach to family therapy. In Gurman, A.S., and Kniskern, D.P. (eds.): *Handbook of Family Therapy*. New York: Brunner/Mazel.

Stanton, M.D. 1979. Family treatment approaches to drug abuse problems: A review. *Fam. Process* 18:251–280.

Steinhauer, P.D. 1985. Beyond family therapy—towards a systemic and integrated view. *Psychiatry Clin. North Amer.* 8:923–945.

Steinhauer, P.D. 1968. Reflections on criteria for selection and prognosis in family therapy. *Can. J. Psychiatry.* 13:317–321.

Steinhauer, P.D., Santa-Barbara, J., and Skinner, H.A. 1984. The process model of family functioning. *Can. J. Psychiatry* 29:77–87.

Tharp, R.G. 1963. Psychological patterning in marriage. *Psychol. Bull.* 60:97–117.

Thomas, A., and Chess, S. 1977. *Temperament and Development.* New York: Brunner/Mazel.

Walsh, F. 1982. *Normal Family Processes.* New York: Guilford Press.

Watzlawick, P. 1963. A review of the double bind theory. *Fam. Process* 2:132–153.

Weber, T., McKeever, J., and McDaniel, S.H. 1985. The beginner's guide to the problem-oriented first family interview. *Fam. Process* 24:357–364.

Wynne, L.C. 1976. On the anguish and creative passions of not escaping double-bind: A reformulation. In Sluzki, C.E., and Ransom, D.S. (eds.): *The Double-Bind: Foundations of the Communication Approaches to the Family.* New York: Grune & Stratton.

Index

Note: Page numbers in *italics* refer to illustrations; page numbers followed by *t* refer to tables.